THE
CONSTITUTIONAL REFORM
SERIES

BOOK SERIES EDITOR

ROBERT BLACKBURN

Professor of Constitutional Law
King's College, University of London

Other titles in this series

Institute for Public Policy Research
A Written Constitution for the United Kingdom

Dawn Oliver and Gavin Drewry
Public Service Reforms: Issues of Accountability and Public Law

Towards a Constitutional Bill of Rights for the United Kingdom

COMMENTARY AND DOCUMENTS

Robert Blackburn

PINTER

London and New York

First published 1999 by
Pinter, *A Cassell Imprint*
Wellington House, 125 Strand, London WC2R 0BB
370 Lexington Avenue, New York, NY 10017–6550

British Library Cataloguing in Publication Data
A catalogue record for this book is available from the British Library.
ISBN 1 85567 529 3 (Hardback)

Library of Congress Cataloging-in-Publication Data
Blackburn, Robert, 1952-
    Towards a constitutional Bill of Rights for the United Kingdom : commentary and
documents/Robert Blackburn.
        p. cm. – (The constitutional reform series)
    Includes bibliographical references and index.
    ISBN 1-85567-529-3 (hardback)
    1. Civil rights – Great Britain. I. Title. II. Series.
KD4080.B58 1999
342.41'085–dc21   97–44743
                                                                                                          CIP

Typeset by York House Typographic Ltd
Printed and bound in Great Britain by Cromwell Press, Trowbridge, Wiltshire

CONTENTS

OUTLINE OF COMMENTARY

TOWARDS A CONSTITUTIONAL BILL OF RIGHTS

I   The History of the Bill of Rights Debate
The present Labour government's commitment

II   The Case for a UK Bill of Rights
The existing protection of human rights in the UK
The UK's commitment to the international community
A legal remedy for human rights grievances
A Bill of Rights as part of a new constitution
The social and political value of a Bill of Rights

III   The Contents of a UK Bill of Rights
The fundamental rights and freedoms to be protected
The legal and judicial process under a Bill of Rights
Methods of entrenching a UK Bill of Rights
Procedures for amendment and derogation
The role and powers of a Human Rights Commission
Parliamentary scrutiny reforms under a Bill of Rights

IV   Preparing and Implementing the Reform

OUTLINE OF DOCUMENTS

Chapter 1
CIVIL RIGHTS AND FREEDOMS IN THE UK

(A) Historical Documents of Political and Civil Liberty

(B) The British Constitution and the Protection of Freedom, 1885–98

Chapter 2
INTERNATIONAL BILLS OF RIGHTS

(A) International Human Rights Treaties

(B) The Influence of the European Convention on Human Rights, 1966–98

Within the UK

Chapter 3
STATUTORY INCORPORATION OF THE EUROPEAN CONVENTION ON HUMAN RIGHTS IN THE UK

Chapter 4

COMPARATIVE BILLS OF RIGHTS (EUROPE, THE COMMONWEALTH AND AMERICA)

Chapter 5

PROPOSALS FOR A UK BILL OF RIGHTS

(A) Detailed Blueprints for a Constitutional Bill of Rights

(B) The Entrenchment of a Constitutional Bill of Rights in the UK

Chapter 7
POLITICAL OPINION ON A BILL OF RIGHTS

(A) The House of Lords

(B) The House of Commons

(C) The Policies of the Political Parties

The Liberal Democrats

The Conservative Party

Chapter 8

WRITINGS AND SPEECHES ON A BILL OF RIGHTS

Chapter 9

IMPLEMENTATION OF A UK BILL OF RIGHTS

CITATION AND STRUCTURE OF DOCUMENTS

CITATION OF DOCUMENTS IN PART I: COMMENTARY

The documents included in Part II of this book are numbered and described in the Outline of Documents. References to a document made in the Commentary (Part I of the book) and elsewhere in my writing is by way of citation of the respective document number, appearing in bold within square brackets (eg. [40]). Where an explanatory note accompanies a document in Part II, it describes itself as an author's note ('*RB NOTE*') and appears in italics.

CHAPTER STRUCTURE IN PART II: DOCUMENTS

I have structured the documents in Part II of the book according to particular aspects of relevance to a Bill of Rights. First, Chapter 1 sets out the background by dealing with Britain's traditional approach to protecting individual rights and freedoms in its constitutional law and theory. Chapter 2 then documents the international human rights treaties to which Britain is a party, chief among them being the International Covenant on Civil and Political Rights (ICCPR) and the European Convention on Human Rights (ECHR). The Human Rights Act 1998 incorporating the ECHR into UK law is set out in Chapter 3, along with the original text of the government Bill and explanatory memorandum, the white paper accompanying introduction of the Bill, and extracts from parliamentary debates in which not only expressions of political opinion can be found but also ministerial statements of use in future interpretation of the Act, following the House of Lords decision in *Pepper* v. *Hart* [1993] AC 593 to admit such materials in legal argument before the courts.

Providing detailed precedents and ideas for future British reform, overseas Bills of Rights operating in Europe, the Commonwealth and America are set out at length in Chapter 4; and the major proposals put forward for enacting a British Bill of Rights, researched and prepared by leading public policy institutes and legal writers, are to be found in Chapter 5.

In Chapter 6, matters relating to the judiciary in their application and enforcement of a Bill of Rights are addressed, and leading documents and writings on the question of entrenchment in British law are given. Expressions of parliamentary opinion on a Bill of Rights in recent decades are to be found in Chapter 7. Debates on this subject in the chamber of either House have been relatively rare, and have usually arisen in the context of incorporation of the European Convention on Human Rights. Indeed among politicians over the past 25 years, the proposal for a Bill of Rights and proposal for incorporating the ECHR have regularly been described and argued about in similar terms (and my commentary on the case for a Bill of Rights tries to fuse the way in which the advantages of both incorporation of the ECHR and enactment by a Bill of Rights have been presented). The documents included in Chapter 7, therefore, contain extracts from debates on early attempts to incorporate the ECHR. The development of policy on a Bill of Rights by the respective three main political parties is also documented in Chapter 7, culminating in both Labour and Liberal Democrat objectives being couched in terms of a two-stage approach to a Bill of Rights, incorporation of the ECHR being a preliminary stage towards a British Bill of Rights.

The suggestion that Britain should adopt a code of citizens' rights and freedoms in a new Bill of Rights – being one of a quite different nature to the 1689 document of the same name that asserted the supremacy of Parliament over the Crown – has been deeply controversial. It raises fundamental issues about the constitutional structure and the balance of power operating within it, and presents a challenge to Britain's common law heritage of which it has rightly been proud in the past. A selection and flavour of the many speeches and writings on the subject, presenting all sides of the argument, are extracted in two chapters, 6 and 8. Chapter 6 concentrates particularly on questions of sovereignty, and also includes some reform materials on the position of the judiciary. Finally, Chapter 9 gathers together some materials on practical issues affecting the preparation and enactment of the reform. A comprehensive bibliography of books, reports and Hansard debates is laid out, immediately prior to a full index of all the subject-matter covered in this work.

ABBREVIATIONS

Common abbreviations to be found in this work include the following:

All ER	All England Law Reports
Cmd	Command Paper 1919–56
Cmnd	Command Paper 1956–86
Cm	Command Paper 1986 onwards
ECHR	European Convention on Human Rights
EHRR	European Human Rights Reports
EU	European Union
HC	House of Commons Paper
HC Deb	House of Commons Debates
HL	House of Lords Paper
HL Deb	House of Lords Debate
ICCPR	International Covenant on Civil and Political Rights
IPPR	Institute for Public Policy Research
SACHR	Standing Advisory Committee on Human Rights for Northern Ireland
UN	United Nations
WLR	Weekly Law Reports

The term 'Britain' is used informally throughout this work to mean the United Kingdom of Great Britain (comprising Scotland, England and Wales) and Northern Ireland except where the context indicates otherwise.

ACKNOWLEDGEMENTS

The author and publishers are indebted to all who have given permission to reproduce copyright material in this book, including those mentioned below. The source from which extracts are drawn is generally given beneath each document and/or referred to in the document title.

British Broadcasting Corporation (Lord Hailsham, *Elective Dictatorship*; Lord McCluskey, *Law, Justice and Democracy*); Butterworths (Halsbury's Laws; All England Law Reports); Chatto & Windus (R. Dworkin, *A Bill of Rights for Britain*; O. Hood Phillips, *Reform of the Constitution*); Heinemann (Ferdinand Mount, *The Constitution Now*); Incorporated Council of Law Reporting for England and Wales (Law Reports); Macmillan Press (A. V. Dicey, *Law of the Constitution*, 10th edn; S. Bailey (ed.), *Human Rights and Responsibilities*); Open University Press (D. Oliver, *Government in the United Kingdom*, 1991); Penguin Books (S. de Smith and R. Brazier, *Constitutional and Administrative Law*; Lord Gifford, *Where's the Justice?*; G. Robertson, *Freedom, the Individual and the Law*); Sweet and Maxwell (C. Palley, *The United Kingdom and Human Rights*; H. W. R. Wade, *Constitutional Fundamentals*; Sir Leslie Scarman, *English Law – New Dimensions*; N. Grief, 'Domestic Impact of the ECHR as Mediated through Community Law', *Public Law*, 1991; Sir John Laws, 'Law and Democracy', *Public Law*, 1995; Lord Irvine, 'The Development of Human Rights in Britain', *Public Law*, 1998; F. Klug, 'The Human Rights Act: Pepper v. Hart and All That', *Public Law*, 1999).

Reproduced by permission of Oxford University Press are extracts from J. Jaconelli, *Enacting a Bill of Rights*, 1980; D. Feldman, *Civil Liberties and Human Rights*, 1993; R. Gordon and R. Wilmot-Smith (eds), *Human Rights in the United Kingdom*, 1997; R. Brazier, *Constitutional Reform*, 1991). Reprinted by permission of Addison Wesley Longman Ltd is an extract from A. Bradley and K. Ewing, *Constitutional and Administrative Law*, 12th edn.

Crown and parliamentary copyright (government publications, Hansard and parliamentary papers) is reproduced with the permission of the Controller of Her Majesty's Stationery Office. Acknowledgement is made to the following for permission to reproduce extracts from international and constitutional materials in respect of which they are the publisher or hold copyright: Council of Europe; the European Commission, Parliament and Council; United Nations; Commonwealth of Australia; Queen's Printer for Canada; the Governments of the Federal Republic of Germany, France, New Zealand, South Africa and United States of America; and the Government Printers of Antigua and Barbuda, Jamaica, Trinidad and Tobago. The author and publishers are indebted to the Labour Party, the Liberal Democrats, the Society of Conservative Lawyers, MORI, the Institute for Public Policy Research, the National Council for Civil Liberties, the Constitution Unit and British Institute of Human Rights for permission to reproduce copyright material; and to persons for permission to reproduce extracts from their writing or speeches, including (in addition to those mentioned above) Anthony Lester, J. A. G. Griffith, Nicolas Bratza, Peter Wallington, Jeremy McBride, John Major MP, Brian Mawhinney MP and Lord Mackay of Clashfern.

There are some passages in the commentary and documents which are reproduced from earlier writings of mine, including 'Legal and Political Arguments for a UK Bill of Rights', in Robert Blackburn and John Taylor (eds), *Human Rights for the 1990s* (Mansell, 1991); 'A Bill of Rights for the 21st Century', in Robert Blackburn and James Busuttil (eds), *Human Rights for the 21st Century* (Pinter, 1997); and 'A Parliamentary Committee on Human Rights', in Robert Blackburn amd Raymond Plant (eds), *Constitutional Reform: The Labour Government's Constitutional Reform Agenda* (Longman, 1999).

I express my thanks to the many people who have commented and offered advice on my work for this book, particularly John McEldowney, Francesca Klug and Sarah Spencer.

R.B.

INTRODUCTION

This book gives a history of the background and pressures that led to the Human Rights Act 1998, and sets out the arguments and options for the future preparation and enactment of a home-grown constitutional Bill of Rights for the United Kingdom. It does so by collecting together a wide range of documentation and source-material preceded by a Commentary. It is hoped that the book will prove useful to political scientists, constitutional lawyers and historians; to government officials, parliamentarians and policy researchers; and to all who are concerned with the protection of human rights and civil liberties today and the development of a Bill of Rights appropriate to society in the twenty-first century.

My decision to embark on this project came as a response to the comprehensive policy review on the constitution conducted by the Labour Party in 1992–3, resulting in its report entitled *A New Agenda for Democracy: Labour's Proposals for Constitutional Reform* [**112**].[1] That review proved to be a significant turning point in Labour Party thinking, not only on constitutional reform generally but on human rights reform in particular. John Smith, then leader of the Party, and Tony Blair, then home and constitutional affairs spokesman, firmly placed individual rights at the forefront of Labour's policy programme for future government office. John Smith's rhetoric at that time was unequivocal concerning the need for radical reform:

> Are we going to limp into the 21st century on a constitution built for the 19th? ... We need a new constitution for a new century ... We must modernise our system of government so that it is underpinned by the specific recognition of individual rights. The time has come when we should commit ourselves to a Bill of Rights. [**110**]

Tony Blair since his succession to the Labour leadership has powerfully supported Smith's legacy to the party in the field of

---

1 (1993). On the parties' policies on this issue, see Commentary and Chapter 7(c).

constitutional affairs. In his leadership election statement in 1994, Tony Blair personally endorsed the commitment 'to entrenching clear rights for every citizen in a Bill of Rights for Britain' [**114**]. Later the same year, at his first party conference as party leader, he promised that Labour in government would put forward 'the biggest programme of change to democracy ever proposed by a political party', involving as one of its primary tasks, 'every citizen to be protected by fundamental rights that cannot be taken away by the state or their fellow citizens enshrined in a Bill of Rights'.

Labour's reform programme in 1992–3 proposed a two-stage approach to a Bill of Rights. First, the European Convention on Human Rights should be incorporated into UK domestic law, a task now accomplished by the Human Rights Act 1998. Then, second, after a period of time in which that initial reform is allowed to be fully and successfully implemented into our judicial and parliamentary systems, work should begin on developing a constitutional Bill of Rights indigenous to the UK. As Labour's 1992–3 review concluded, while 'the incorporation of the European Convention on Human Rights is a necessary first step … it is not a substitute for our own written Bill of Rights … There is a good case for drafting our own Bill of Rights'. The second stage of reform towards a Bill of Rights, Labour's report recommended, would involve 'the establishment of an all-party commission that will be charged with drafting the Bill of Rights and considering a suitable method of entrenchment. This should report to Parliament within a specified and limited period of time' [**112**].

Statutory incorporation of the European Convention on Human Rights in itself is not the same thing as a constitutional Bill of Rights: they are essentially separate and distinct concepts both legally and politically.[2] The incorporation of principles contained in international treaties to which a state has become a signatory is common elsewhere, and is automatic on the ratification of a treaty under the constitutional law of most other European states. Treaties, as incorporated, allow for explicit judicial recognition of international obligations in domestic law, and disputes as to the meaning of those

---

2 Generally see J. P. Gardner (ed.), *Aspects of Incorporation of the European Convention on Human Rights into Domestic Law* (1993); and Robert Blackburn and Jorg Polakiewicz (eds), *The European Convention on Human Rights: The Impact of the ECHR on the Legal and Political Systems of Member States, 1950–2000* (Cassell, forthcoming).

obligations may be subject to a right to appeal to an international court, such as the Court of Human Rights at Strasbourg under the terms of the ECHR. A national Bill of Rights, by contrast, is drafted specifically and exclusively for internal application within a country's constitutional system, usually forming a body of fundamental law within the state, and there is no external judicial appeal on the meaning of its provisions.

Since the ECHR's ratification by its founding member states in the early 1950s, particularly so for European states with their own constitutional Bills of Rights, the principal logic behind incorporation of the ECHR has been international in nature, rather than being concerned with a country's constitutional structure and system of checks and balances. One of the strongest practical factors persuading the British legal establishment of the need for incorporation of the ECHR has been that only by internalizing our human rights law treaty obligations will the British legal system be able to redress the growing number of glaring inconsistencies that have emerged in the administration of justice with respect to European law generally (see Commentary, pages 29–32). It is likely to substantially improve the UK government's standing before the European Court of Human Rights at Strasbourg, where its record of defeats and human rights violations has been relatively high [**33**]; and it will serve to reduce the number of UK cases needing to be taken to Strasbourg at all, since it is widely recognized that most legal questions that have arisen concerning the principles of the ECHR could have been dealt with and resolved satisfactorily by our own domestic courts [**38**].

It is impossible, as yet, to predict accurately when the stage two objective of a Bill of Rights might be approved and acted upon by the Labour leadership in government. Labour's pre-election literature of 1996–7 made no mention of a home-grown Bill of Rights, concentrating instead on what was desirable and achievable in its first term of office [**115–117, 150**]. But whatever the Labour Cabinet's current views on the matter may be (or be presented as being), there is already substantial existing support for a home-grown Bill of Rights [**149**], and this will almost certainly grow as the successful implementation of the Human Rights Act acclimatises our traditions and processes of government to the notion of a positive legal statement of

---

3 For example in Germany, where under its Basic Law a treaty ranks as a federal statute. See F. G. Jacobs and S. Roberts (eds), *The Effect of Treaties in Domestic Law* (1987).

human rights. Some influential think-tanks on the centre-Left such as the Institute for Public Policy Research and pressure groups such as Liberty have published policy analyses on the subject, giving their full support to a British Bill of Rights and even offering their own legislative blueprints on the subject [**49, 50**]. On the centre-Right, the Conservative leadership in its present early phase of opposition may oppose a Bill of Rights for the time being, but we should recall that it was members of the Conservative frontbench team in the years prior to taking office in 1979 who were among the leading early advocates of a Bill of Rights [**124**].[4] Indeed, the 1979 Conservative election manifesto contained a specific promise to hold all-party talks on a Bill of Rights (a pledge which was subsequently dropped once the party was in office) [**95**].

Also of significance is the fact that the Liberal Democrats have endorsed as official party policy a comprehensive programme of reform which includes a written constitution and entrenched Bill of Rights [**93**]. As a source of influence on government policy in the future, the Liberal Democrats are already actively co-operating with Labour in the field of constitutional reform, as evidenced by the two parties' Joint Consultative Committee Report on Constitutional Reform in March 1997 [**150**] and by Tony Blair's creation of a special Cabinet Committee with Liberal Democrat membership, whose terms of reference are 'to consider policy issues of joint interest to the Government and Liberal Democrats' [**151**]. Liberal Democrat objectives may become even more significant if a change in the electoral system is forthcoming, in line with the Report of the Independent Commission on the Voting System, which would have the result of their electoral support being translated into a greater number of Liberal Democrat MPs being elected to the Commons.[5]

The detailed construction of a constitutional Bill of Rights for the UK will require some form of special advisory body being created to prepare the ground for a government-sponsored parliamentary Bill, which will collect expert evidence and consult widely before presenting a report with recommendations on the detail of the proposed legislation [**147**]. As already mentioned, Labour in 1993 proposed the establishment of an all-party commission charged with drafting the

---

4 See Commentary below, pp. 8–9; and the views expressed during parliamentary debates at Doc. 88.

5 Cm 4090, 1998; and see the projected outcomes under different electoral systems at p. 59 of the Report.

document and recommending a method of entrenchment. The Liberal Democrats have suggested a Constitutional Assembly for the purpose [93]. Many important questions will require close attention in the enactment of a UK Bill of Rights, such as whether a constitutional court should be created, what role a Human Rights Commission might play in the enforcement of its provisions, whether liability for human rights violations should extend to other private individuals and companies as well as public authorities, and in what emergency circumstances (if any) might the government suspend the Bill of Rights and its human rights obligations to its citizens.[6]

The two key elements to be settled, however, will be the selection and wording of the exact individual rights and freedoms to be protected, and the legal status and priority the document is to possess in relation to other laws and legislative enactments. The nature and content of the individual rights and freedoms to go into the Bill of Rights are likely to be expressed in broad and general terms, in common with other comparative and international Bills of Rights, allowing for reinterpretation over a period of time so as to adapt to changing political and social developments. Constitutional rights are usually limited to those of a civil and political nature, the classic examples being the right to life, personal liberty, freedom from inhuman or degrading treatment, non-discrimination, freedom from arbitrary detention, freedom of expression, association and peaceful assembly, and privacy [41–48]. By contrast, rights of an economic or welfare nature, for example to housing, employment or social security, are generally thought less amenable to the judicial process intrinsic to a Bill of Rights. The architects of a UK Bill of Rights can be expected to draw heavily upon the articles of freedom contained in the principal international human rights law instruments, notably the United Nations International Covenanant on Civil and Political Rights (ICCPR) [20] and the ECHR [22], and also upon a number of comparative well drafted and highly regarded existing Bills of Rights, including for example the Charter of Rights and Freedoms adopted

---

6 These and other issues relating to the content and application of a Bill of Rights are discussed in the Commentary and the documents in Chapter 5: Proposals for a UK Bill of Rights. Methods of entrenchment are dealt with separately in the Commentary and in Chapter 6: Sovereignty, the Judiciary and a Bill of Rights. Foreign Bills of Rights, as possible precedents, are documented in Chapter 4: Comparative Bills of Rights.

by Canada in 1982 and most recently the Bill of Rights drafted as part of the new constitution in South Africa in 1996 [**45**, **48**].

Questions of entrenchment – in other words, establishing the fundamental status and legal priority of the Bill of Rights in relation to ordinary Acts of Parliament, and creating a special legislative process for amending or derogating from its articles – will go to the heart of its constitutional nature. As Francesca Klug has put it, 'any Bill of Rights worthy of its name ... must be a superior act to which all other legislation must conform'.[7] The aims and advantages of enacting a Bill of Rights are numerous, but perhaps the most important among them is that human rights should form part of the 'rules of the game' under which the system of politics and government is conducted. It is a primary feature of most Bills of Rights so-called, though not all [**46**][8], that they possess some elevated moral and legal authority in the country to which they belong. Indeed, in the great majority of countries the Bill of Rights forms part of a written constitution, being the fundamental law of the state [**42**, **43**, **44**, **48**]. A constitutional Bill of Rights drafted for the UK, therefore, can be expected to give some measure of power to the judicial or other body which is vested with responsibility for examining alleged human rights violations, to declare incompatible laws and governmental acts or decisions invalid.

This book originally went to press in 1997, shortly after Labour's electoral victory on 1 May that year. However, the incoming government moved swiftly to act upon its human rights reform programme, and a Bill to incorporate the European Convention on Human Rights was included in the first Queen's Speech of the new Parliament. Subsequently, production of the book was suspended at proof stage pending the presentation and passage of the Human Rights Bill in the 1997–8 session, so that its final legislative text and accompanying documentation could be included in this work [**40**]. This has allowed me to complete the picture of the historical process by which the Convention, originally signed in 1950, came to form part of the law of the UK 48 years later. A short commentary on the Human Rights Act 1998, and its significance in the movement towards a

---

7 F. Klug, 'The Role of a Bill of Rights in a Democratic Constitution', in A. Barnett, C. Ellis and P. Hirst (eds), *Debating the Constitution* (1993), p. 45.

8 Some countries have enacted interpretative legal measures calling themselves 'Bill of Rights', notably the New Zealand Bill of Rights Act 1990, but these are not constitutional Bills of Rights in the generally accepted sense.

constitutional Bill of Rights for the UK, has been added as a separate note appearing below, and some up-dating and references to the Act have been added to the Commentary.

November 1998

THE HUMAN RIGHTS ACT

The first step towards a constitutional Bill of Rights for the United Kingdom

The successful passage through Parliament of the Human Rights Act 1998 [**40**], which received the royal assent on 9 November 1998, represents a major landmark in Britain's constitutional history. This statute of great practical and symbolic importance provides for the express legal recognition[1] within our judicial, parliamentary and governmental systems of the fundamental rights and freedoms laid down in the European Convention on Human Rights, an international treaty of the Council of Europe to which the UK was a founding member in 1950 [**22**].[2]

The Human Rights Act is thereby ushering into our legal system a whole new field of jurisprudence to which previously our courts could only allude without taking direct notice [**29, 32**]. Under section 3 of the Human Rights Act, the human rights principles of the ECHR will become mandatory relevant considerations in the exercise of public discretionary power affecting the individual, enforceable by way of judicial review proceedings. Section 6 makes it unlawful for a public authority to act in any way which is incompatible with a Convention right. The full range of existing forms of relief or remedies will be available to the courts at their discretion to enforce these

---

1 This book regards the Human Rights Act 1998 as having 'incorporated' the ECHR into UK law, being the general view shared by most parliamentarians and lawyers. However, it should be noted that Lord Irvine, the Lord Chancellor and minister responsible for introducing the Bill to Parliament, believes this is an inappropriate term with which to describe the effect of the Act: see Doc. 40D, p. 388.
2 See the Commentary and documents in Chapter 2(b) on the ECHR and its role in UK affairs since 1950.

new positive rights of the individual, including damages under section 8. And, what is unique and unprecedented in our constitutional law, the superior courts are to be empowered to pass judgment on the legitimacy of provisions in primary parliamentary legislation itself. Under section 4, the court may make a formal 'declaration of incompatibility' between the legislation in dispute and the human rights articles of the ECHR. Whilst these declarations will not affect the continuing validity of the relevant sections in the offending legislation, yet this process of judicial scrutiny of primary parliamentary Acts is of great significance for the future potential and development of a homegrown constitutional Bill of Rights.

Within Whitehall it is now a mandatory requirement for government ministers and their civil servants to examine and draw up a written report on the human rights implications of all legislation that is being prepared. Section 19 provides that the minister in charge of a Bill in either House of Parliament must either make and publish a written statement to the effect that in his view the provisions of the Bill are compatible with the Convention rights or, if he or she is unable to make such a statement, the minister must certify that the government nevertheless wishes the House to proceed with the Bill. In the latter case MPs and peers will be on express notice of the implications of the legislation that is being proposed. This internal audit procedure is just part of the Labour government's declared intention to create a new awareness – or 'culture' – of human rights within and across official bureaucracies generally.

The net effect of the Human Rights Act will also be to considerably extend the role of parliamentary scrutiny in the field of human rights affairs. Not only are the human rights articles of the ECHR bound to figure much larger in the minds of MPs and peers as a result of incorporation into the judicial system and by being specially referred to in human rights impact statements accompanying each Bill, but under section 10 a new legislative process is created whereby fast-track Remedial Orders may be enacted to respond swiftly to human rights violations in our existing body of primary parliamentary legislation, as determined either by a decision of the European Court of Human Rights at Strasbourg or by a declaration of incompatibility by the High Court or appellate bodies. These Remedial Orders will be affirmative statutory instruments (subject to a single stage of approval in each House) yet they will be authorized under the terms of the Human Rights Act to amend measures of primary legislation where considered appropriate. The introduction of the Remedial Order procedure under the Act therefore, being an extraordinary process in itself coupled with this 'Henry VIII' clause, has served to galvanize pressures at Westminister towards the establishment of a parliamentary committee on human rights [59]. Furthermore, of particular poignance at this point in time when the long-term functions of a reformed Second Chamber are being focused upon as a Royal Commission considers a permanent basis of reform following removal of the hereditary peerage, a more distinctive role for the House of Lords in the context of human rights is becoming ever-more probable [82].[3]

As explained earlier in the introduction, constitutional Bills of Rights have a number of distinguishing characteristics. One relates to the source and nature of the individual rights and freedoms which are included within the document. A second is the degree of special legal status and priority which is afforded to the document. In both these respects the Human Rights Act is not equivalent to a Bill of Rights in a proper constitutional sense, though it is an important step in that direction. The purpose of the Human Rights Act is to give legal recognition in UK law to an international treaty negotiated between member states of the Council of Europe in 1950. As stated in the explanatory memorandum accompanying the Bill when presented to Parliament, the legislation seeks 'to give further effect in domestic law' to the ECHR. Whereas a constitutional Bill of Rights would be a UK-drafted code of basic rights and freedoms operating as the basis for a self-contained judicial and legal process within this country, the international court at Strasbourg, the European Court of Human Rights, will continue to give the final ruling on the application of the articles of the ECHR as set out in Schedule 1 of the Human Rights Act.

As time goes on, the flaws in the drafting of the ECHR as a charter of rights for the individual citizen in the UK will become increasingly apparent. It is unsurprising that an international Convention drafted in 1950 is not an entirely accurate reflection of prevailing perceptions of individual or minority rights and freedoms in the more advanced state of British society today. Most obviously, over the past 50 years major social and moral developments have been taking place in the field of equality and non-discrimination. The revolution in information technology has thrown up major new difficulties affecting the

---

3 See Commentary below; and Robert Blackburn, 'The House of Lords', in Robert Blackburn and Raymond Plant (eds), *Constitutional Reform* (1999).

protection of privacy. John Wadham, Director of the National Council for Civil Liberties (Liberty), has identified a range of key 'missing rights' in the Convention – and therefore the Human Rights Act itself [143].[4] These include provisions covering the right to information; the rights of immigrants, asylum seekers and those being extradited; anti-discrimination measures; the absence of any specific rights for children; gaps in standards guaranteed for the criminal justice system and procedures for detention; and a weak provision on personal privacy not even extending to basic procedural matters covering intrusion into homes and surveillance of individuals. Once we have accommodated the idea of positive human rights in our legal and parliamentary systems, a growing need will be perceived for a more soundly drafted and up-to-date legal statement of citizens' fundamental rights and freedoms. This is so not simply because of the credibility of the law and the judicial process which seeks to apply those positive human rights in cases brought before the courts, but because whatever document we regard as laying down our basic rights – and currently the Human Rights Act is the nearest document we possess – will acquire an immense authority as an official point of reference and set of principles permeating the work of Parliament in all its business both in chamber and committee. No doubt in the drafting of a home-grown Bill of Rights, the articles of the ECHR (and of the International Covenant on Civil and Political Rights) will form a starting point for whatever elaboration is thought appropriate and necessary, for our national Bill of Rights will need to be consistent with our wider international obligations. Clear political acceptance of the need to develop the ECHR further, for indigenous purposes, has been expressly acknowledged by the government in the context of Northern Ireland. The agreement reached at the multiparty talks in April 1998 has led to the creation of a Northern Ireland Human Rights Commission, one of whose functions is to consult and advise on legislation for additional rights attuned to the particular requirements and needs of the area [152].[5]

The second distinguishing characteristic of Bills of Rights mentioned above – that of their entrenched status and priority over other

---

4 See also John Wadham, 'A Bill of Rights', in Robert Blackburn and Raymond Plant (eds), *Constitutional Reform* (1999).
5 The same agreement stated that these rights, together with the ECHR, were 'to constitute a Bill of Rights for Northern Ireland': see Cm 3883, p. 17, and further discussion below, pp. 94–5.

forms of law – means that they serve as a higher body of moral and legal principle to which ordinary administrative and legislative measures must conform, and some special legislative process is necessary for amending or derogating from its provisions. The development of a home-grown Bill of Rights, therefore, will entail a legal and parliamentary distinction being drawn between human rights law (perhaps encompassed within a wider notion of constitutional law) and ordinary legislative enactments. By reference to parliamentary practice elsewhere, for example, it would be normal for amendments to require the consent of both Houses and/or special voting majorities. The Human Rights Act 1998, by contrast, is not a formally entrenched document in this way. Instead, its legal effect is interpretative. Under the terms of the Act the role of the courts, whenever it is alleged in legal proceedings that a citizen's rights and freedoms have been unlawfully infringed, is to interpret the law or administrative power in question by reference to the articles of the ECHR and jurisprudence on the subject. The Convention's principles will themselves become grounds for challenging the exercise of statutory discretionary powers and administrative decisions. But if the power or regulation in question is clearly incompatible, then the offending legislative measure prevails. As expressed in section 3, 'So far as it is possible to do so, primary legislation and subordinate legislation must be read and given effect in a way which is compatible with the Convention rights'. While this approach adopted by the Labour administration – the 'British model of incorporation' as its spokesmen termed it [40c] – is appropriate to a legal measure seeking to give further effect in UK domestic law to an international treaty, it does not meet the normal criteria for a Bill of Rights.

Nonetheless, there is no doubt that the Human Rights Act contains the seeds of a major, growing distinction emerging in our judicial and parliamentary systems between human rights law and ordinary legislation. In at least three interconnected respects the Act requires human rights matters to be dealt with by the courts and by Parliament in a manner that is distinct and constitutionally different from ordinary law. First, section 3's new rule of judicial interpretation makes the status of the Convention's principles substantially stronger than any normal interpretation Act would do. The white paper accompanying the Human Rights Bill made it clear that the intention behind the Act was for the judiciary to go

far beyond the present rule which enables the courts to take the

Convention into account in resolving any ambiguity in a legislative provision. The courts will be required to interpret
legislation so as to uphold the Convention rights unless the
legislation itself is *so clearly incompatible with the Convention
that it is impossible to do so* [**40c**].[6]

This is the most powerful rule of interpretation possible, requiring a
very clear and emphatic contradiction to the articles and jurisprudence of the ECHR before they can be overriden.

Secondly, wherever the High Court, Court of Appeal or House of
Lords finds itself unable to reconcile a provision of primary legislation with our obligations under the ECHR, the courts may issue a
declaration of incompatibility. The net effect of such a declaration of
incompatibility under section 4 of the Human Rights Act will be to
require the government to remedy the violation and present legislative proposals to Parliament to bring the law into conformity with
the judicial ruling. This is analagous to the international obligation
already owed by the UK (and member states of the Council of
Europe) whereby it must take positive action in response to adverse
rulings before the European Court of Human Rights. What is so
interesting about this power under section 4, in the context of the
development of a constitutional Bill of Rights, is that its practice will
serve to familiarise our legal and parliamentary traditions with the
concept of a domestic court adjudiating upon the validity of an Act of
Parliament upon expressly stated human rights principles. In other
words, it will help smooth the transition towards a constitutional Bill
of Rights by facilitating general acceptance of its practice and
desirability.

Thirdly, the Human Rights Act lays down a special legislative
process for dealing with human rights legislation. Under section 10,
as mentioned above, a fast-track procedure has been approved by
Parliament, whereby the government may respond promptly to
declarations of incompatibility in our domestic courts or an adverse
ruling in Strasbourg. In suitable situations where swift action is
necessary to redress a human rights injustice and a Bill procedure
would be politically impracticable that session, the government may
present a draft Order to Parliament with a one-stop method of
approval in each House similar to an affirmative statutory instrument. Since such Orders fall outside the scope of the Parliament Acts

6 Author's italics.

1911–49, the House of Lords retains its original power of legislative veto.[7] Therefore its approval to such Remedial Orders will always be necessary before they can take permanent legal effect. The wider parliamentary significance of this is considerable. It is in effect serving to elevate the role of the House of Lords as a parliamentary mechanism to safeguard against any possible future misuse of the Remedial Order procedure – an end-result which is soundly based on good constitutional logic. Its significance as to the future role and power of the House of Lords, however, was a fact largely unnoticed during the parliamentary debates on the Human Rights Bill [**40d**].

The election of the Labour government in 1997, supported by a clear mandate and a 179-seat majority in the House of Commons, has heralded a new attitude to human rights in the UK. The Human Rights Act 1998, drafted and enacted within the first annual session of the new Parliament, represents the beginning of a process of human rights legislation reform that has further to go and will have far-reaching effects on the political and legal structure, as well as on social outlook. A major first step has been taken towards a constitutional Bill of Rights for the UK.

ROBERT BLACKBURN
King's College London

---

7 On the legislative effect of the Parliament Acts, see J. A. G. Griffith and M. Ryle, *Parliament: Functions, Practice and Procedures* (1989), pp. 503ff.

There must be a constitutional restraint placed upon the legislative power which is designed to protect the individual from instant legislation, conceived in fear or prejudice and enacted in breach of human rights . . . This calls for entrenched or fundamental laws protected by a Bill of Rights – a constitutional law which it is the duty of the courts to protect even against the power of Parliament.

SIR LESLIE SCARMAN, 1974

There is a strong case for a code of citizens' rights which guarantee the rights of individuals to basic freedoms and opportunities . . . I support Labour's commitment to entrenching clear rights for every citizen in a Bill of Rights for Britain.

TONY BLAIR MP, 1994-6

Incorporation of the European Convention on Human Rights is a necessary first step, but it is not a substitute for our own written Bill of Rights . . . We therefore propose the establishment of an all-party commission that will be charged with drafting the Bill of Rights and considering a suitable method of entrenchment.

LABOUR PARTY, 1993

There is a real value in Bills of Rights which it is both easy, and mistaken, to underestimate. Granted that the people are educated to the appreciation of their purpose, they serve to draw attention, as attention needs to be drawn, to the fact that vigilance is essential in the realm of what Cromwell called fundamentals. Bills of Rights are, quite undoubtedly, a check upon possible excess in the government of the day.

HAROLD LASKI, 1937

PART I

Commentary

Towards a Constitutional Bill of Rights

1
The History of the Bill of Rights Debate

Pressure for a modern constitutional settlement for the UK which gives
a new emphasis to citizens' rights and freedoms, entrenching them in
our legal system and declaring them to be an important practical and
symbolic part of British society, has developed slowly over the four
decades since the suggestion for a Bill of Rights was first put forward in
the House of Commons.[1] The history of the postwar movement
towards adoption of a Bill of Rights has been a reflection of changing
political and popular attitudes generally towards the British constitution. Although the present British political system contains no written
constitution with entrenched rules, its ancient evolutionary structure
contains an immense inertia against fundamental change of any sort,
especially if the subject matter in question has anything to do with the
prerogatives of the Executive or the jurisdiction of Parliament. Modernizing measures in Britain's constitutional affairs, even when of a
technically straightforward nature, have rarely taken place with any
great rapidity; and so far as a Bill of Rights is concerned, several
aspects of its implementation, particularly the compatibility of fundamental, positive rights with the British traditions of its common law
and theory of parliamentary sovereignty, raise questions that go to the
very heart of the country's ancient constitutional system. As in the
past, for example over female emancipation and the right to vote in
1918 or the UK's membership of the Europe Community in 1972, both
of which were only achieved after many years of controversy and
national discussion, so today the case for a Bill of Rights and other
modernizing measures such as a Freedom of Information Act and a
recomposed parliamentary Second Chamber, have had to be campaigned for over a long period of time. Britain's political culture, it
seems, demands a tremendous amount of sustained effort to be
expended by campaigners before general acceptance of the need for
constitutional change is achieved.

1 Generally see M. Zander, *A Bill of Rights?* (4th edn, 1996). On the historical
   background of the European Convention on Human Rights, see A. Lester, 'Fundamental Rights: the United Kingdom Isolated?', *Public Law* (1984), p. 46.

It took two decades from the establishment of the Council of Europe in 1949 and enactment of the European Convention of Human Rights [22] following World War II, for the idea of a Bill of Rights for the UK to be taken seriously in political and legal circles. In the 1950s and early 1960s, it was ridiculed by virtually all respectable lawyers and politicians as being eccentric, un-British and unnecessary. But by the end of the 1960s, it was gaining currency as a constitutional proposal that merited serious debate. Pamphlets calling for a Bill of Rights were written by Anthony Lester in 1968 and by John Macdonald in 1969, both practising barristers (now QCs), which served to draw attention to the idea [120, 51]. Motions for debate on the constitutional protec-tion of human rights were raised in Parliament, in the House of Lords by Lord Wade in 1969, and in the House of Commons by Emlyn Hooson in 1969 and by Sam Silkin and Peter Archer in 1971.[2] A milestone in the Bill of Rights debate came in 1974 when Sir Leslie (later Lord) Scarman delivered his Hamlyn Lectures on *English Law – The New Dimension* [122]. Prominently reported and discussed in the media, Lord Scarman argued that the common law was no longer capable of protecting individual liberties from the growing mass of government legislation each year, particularly so in times of social tension or economic crisis when prejudice and fear were most likely to produce illiberal, intolerant and oppressive administrative powers or laws. Furthermore, Britain's membership of the European Commu-nity, he argued, meant that the whole context of British law now required a basic common structure that was consistent with human rights standards throughout the rest of the Community. 'This calls for entrenched or fundamental laws protected by a Bill of Rights – a constitutional law which it is the duty of the courts to protect even against the power of Parliament.'

The following five years of the Labour government, under prime ministers Harold Wilson 1974–6 and James Callaghan 1976–9, wit-nessed a surge of interest in the subject. In 1975, a general debate on a UK Bill of Rights took place in the House of Commons [88]. In 1976, Lord Wade presented a Bill of Rights Bill, prompting a debate in the House of Lords on the subject, with contributions from Lords Gardi-ner, Harris, Hailsham, Denning and Lloyd. A Labour Party discussion document was produced the same year on *A Charter of Human Rights*, which backed incorporation of the ECHR in the form of an ordinary Act of Parliament [106]. The Home Office released a discussion

2 Respectively on 18 June 1969, 22 July 1969, 2 April 1971.

document on *Legislation on Human Rights* in 1976, which while offering no recommendation provided valuable civil service-orientated advice on the existing and alternative methods, including a Bill of Rights, by which human rights could be protected in UK law [**16**]. In 1977 the Standing Advisory Committee on Human Rights for Northern Ireland (SACHR) published a report favouring a charter of human rights, founded on the principles of the ECHR, extending preferably to the whole of the UK but otherwise to Northern Ireland alone. Then in 1978, a House of Lords Select Committee published a Report on 'the question whether a Bill of Rights is desirable and, if so, what form it should take'. Its Report, together with the Minutes of Evidence taken from a wide number of experts, was published in 1978 and remains today one of the clearest analyses of the legal and political issues involved [**83**]. By a majority of its members, the Committee recommended that a Bill of Rights should be adopted into UK law, initially with its contents being based on the principles of the ECHR.

A feature of the political debate on a Bill of Rights for much of the past 30 years has been its cross-party nature. Ministerial members of the Labour governments in the 1970s were reluctant to express individual opinions for breach of the convention of collective respon-sibility, at a time when official cabinet policy remained either unpersuaded of the case for a Bill of Rights or else was still considering the matter before making up its mind. Nonetheless, in June 1976 Labour's Roy Jenkins (subsequently a founder member of the Social Democratic Party (SDP), and now a Liberal Democrat peer) declared his own personal conversion in favour of adopting the ECHR into British law in an article published on 29 September, two weeks after he relinquished the post of Home Secretary in order to become a European Commissioner at Brussels.[3] Labour backbench MPs, and former ministers or front-bench spokespersons when in opposition, could feel freer to express personal opinions. Some of the best-known early Labour supporters of a Bill of Rights joined the SDP in the early 1980s (including the former Labour Foreign Secretary Dr David Owen, the former Education Secretary Shirley Williams, and former Labour minister William Rodgers and Robert Maclennan), but a substantial body of Labour opinion supporting a British Bill of Rights remained within the party and continued to develop throughout the 1980s and 1990s. Other Labour ministers from the 1970s, including

3 See *Law Society Gazette*, 29 September 1976, p. 774.

the attorney-general Sam Silkin and the cabinet member Roy Mason, publicly expressed their personal opinions favouring incorporation of the ECHR. Patricia Hewitt, press secretary to Neil Kinnock in the 1980s and now a Labour MP, argued for a Bill of Rights in her book on *The Abuse of Power* (1982) and was later co-author of one of the major detailed proposals on the subject, *A British Bill of Rights* (1991) produced by the Institute for Public Policy (IPPR) [49]. Meanwhile, Liberal Democrats (and their predecessors, the Liberal Party and the SDP) have consistently backed the establishment of a Bill of Rights in their policy documents and election manifestos. Indeed the Liberal Party's 1979 general election pledge on the subject, prepared under David Steel's leadership, contained a not dissimilar wording to that adopted by the Labour Party for its policy commitment today. The 1979 Liberal manifesto read, 'We need a Bill of Rights – as a first step, Britain should incorporate the European Convention on Human Rights into United Kingdom law'.

While in the 1980s both Margaret Thatcher's Conservative government and the Labour opposition under the leadership of Michael Foot and Neil Kinnock remained formally opposed to any form of Bill of Rights and/or incorporation of the ECHR, yet there were many parliamentary attempts by backbench MPs of all political parties to incorporate the ECHR into domestic law. The most prominent of these was the Human Rights Bill 1986, introduced for debate in the House of Commons by the Conservative Sir Edward Gardner [39c], after he won a place in the annual ballot of MPs for the limited number of days reserved for private members' business. Sir Edward Gardner's Bill was presented to the Commons with the formal support of Labour MPs John Gilbert, Greville Janner, Maurice Miller and Austin Mitchell; the Liberal–SDPs Robert Maclennan and Alex Carlisle; Plaid Cymru's Dafydd Wigley; and the Conservatives' Terence Higgins, Norman St John Stevas and Geoffrey Ripon. In the House of Lords, Bills to incorporate the ECHR into British law were approved on several occasions with cross-party support. Lord Wade's Bill of Rights Bill was passed in both 1979 and 1981 [39b]. Lords Scarman and Broxbourne's Human Rights and Fundamental Freedoms Bill 1985 also passed through all its legislative stages in the Lords [39c], but as with earlier attempts was not proceeded with in the House of Commons. While these parliamentary events were unsuccessful in terms of reaching the statute book, given the resistance of the government and opposition front benches, they succeeded in keeping the measure on the political agenda and serving as a forum for updating the arguments supporting a British Bill of Rights in the changing social and political environment leading up to the 1990s.[4]

Between 1974 and 1979, the Conservative Party in opposition contained many members who were vocal in their support of a Bill of Rights. A major advocate was Sir Keith Joseph, a cabinet minister in Edward Heath's 1970–4 government and later in Margaret Thatcher's cabinet, was a leading advocate. In 'Freedom Under Law' (1975), a speech delivered to a Conservative Political Centre conference, he argued that a Bill of Rights was now necessary to control 'the unbridled supremacy of Parliament' and a flood of interventionist legislation which he saw as eroding the rule of law and our traditional liberties. 'If we are to save the law from Parliament and Parliament from itself, we need a new safeguard', he wrote. The Bill of Rights would 'outline the division of powers, as far as possible restoring to the courts their function of the protection of the individual'. Among other declared Conservative supporters of a Bill of Rights were the future attorney-general and lord chancellor Sir Michael Havers, former minister Lord Lambton, Norman (later Lord) St John Stevas (later a cabinet minister in Margaret Thatcher's first cabinet), and Jonathan Aitken (later a cabinet member in John Major's government). The Society of Conservative Lawyers published a pamphlet on the subject in 1976 recommending 'the ECHR be statutorily incorporated in English law and given overriding effect' [123]. But the most powerful case for constitutional reform and a Bill of Rights was delivered by Lord Hailsham, lord chancellor 1970–4 and later under Margaret Thatcher 1979–87. In a televised Dimbleby lecture, he memorably described the existing state of British democracy as one of 'elective dictatorship' [124]. 'The time has come to take stock', he said, 'and to recognize how far this nation, supposedly dedicated to freedom under law, has moved towards a totalitarianism which can only be altered by a systematic and radical overhaul of our constitution'. Calling for 'nothing less than a written constitution for the United Kingdom', Lord Hailsham backed 'a Bill of Rights, equally entrenched, containing as a minimum the rights defined by the European Convention'.

The Conservative leadership went into the 1979 general election campaign with a published manifesto commitment to hold all-party talks on a Bill of Rights [95]. However, after winning the election and

---

4 See Robert Blackburn, 'Parliamentary Opinion on a New Bill of Rights', *Political Quarterly* (1989), p. 469.

subsequently in office, the Conservative cabinet started back-pedalling on the undertaking they had given. When asked about the matter in parliamentary questions, Conservative ministers at first began replying that the question of a Bill of Rights raised important constitutional questions and in their view the time was not 'ripe' for such talks [96]. At the 1983 general election, and in subsequent party manifestos, any suggestion of a Bill of Rights or inter-party discussions on the subject were simply abandoned. Soon, the then prime minister Margaret Thatcher was expressing in Parliament her outright opposi-tion to incorporation of the ECHR and/or a Bill of Rights [97], and her successor in 1990, John Major, proceeded to adopt a similar line [98]. During the final term of John Major's government, 1992–7, Con-servative ministers routinely rehearsed the arguments against a Bill of Rights whenever the matter was raised in Parliament [99–102] or elsewhere in debate or speeches on constitutional affairs [103–4]. Throughout the entire eighteen years in which the Conservative Party was in office, no government initiative along the lines promised in their 1979 election manifesto was ever forthcoming. However, now that the Conservatives have returned to opposition, it remains to be seen whether the previous enthusiasm many of its members displayed towards the proposal for a British Bill of Rights might once more resurface.

THE PRESENT LABOUR GOVERNMENT'S COMMITMENT

Despite the fact that in the 1970s many Labour members including senior ministers in the Wilson and Callaghan governments had moved towards support for a human rights charter for the UK, throughout the 1980s the formal position of the Labour Party remained opposed to a British Bill of Rights and/or incorporation of the ECHR. Even following Neil Kinnock's decision to launch a major review of party policy following the party's 1987 election defeat, Labour's concluding report in 1989, *Meet the Challenge Make the Change*, decided that, 'A Bill of Rights ... would not provide the protection which we regard as necessary ... A Bill of Rights would need constant and detailed interpretation by the courts, with no certainty that its general provi-sions would protect the most vulnerable members of the community' [107]. Instead, a 1991 Charter of Rights policy document, describing itself as a draft white paper on the subject, promised a series of individual and specific Acts of Parliament dealing with areas covered by the Charter – children's rights, legal rights, employees' rights and the right of assembly.

But then in the twelve months immediately preceding the 1992 general election, the party leadership underwent a shift of opinion on the matter, deciding that some general statement of human rights should indeed be placed on the statute book. Senior spokesmen started openly backing a general statement of individual rights that should be placed on the statute book and have the force of law. This important development in the Bill of Rights debate first became apparent when Roy Hattersley, who was then deputy leader and home affairs spokesman of the party with responsibility for constitutional policy, circulated to the press a speech he delivered at South Bank Polytechnic, in which he said, 'We should set out a statement of principles. They should be more than declaratory. Indeed, though inevitably general, they should possess the full force of law. Whether or not they are called a Bill of Rights is of no real consequence ... The principles would perform the Bill of Rights' basic task of establishing in law the framework of a free society.' This conversion of Labour front-bench policy was confirmed by later developments that year. At the party conference in October, Neil Kinnock, during his keynote speech as party leader, declared that, 'We will enact our Charter of Rights, backed up by a complementary Bill of Rights'. Labour's 1992 election manifesto, prepared the following spring, was eventually to read that, 'Our Charter of Rights, backed up by a complementary and democratically enforced Bill of Rights, will establish in law the specific rights of every citizen' [**108**]. Precisely what a 'democratically enforced Bill of Rights' meant was not entirely clear, but during an election campaign press conference on 2 April 1992, Roy Hattersley indicated that it involved a reformed parliamentary second chamber possessing 'the power to delay, for the life of a full Parliament, any new legislation which is adjudged to reduce civil liberties or human rights' and that in this way Labour's 'rights legislation will be entrenched'. Nor was it clear during Labour's 1992 election campaign whether incorporation of the ECHR was party policy or not, since it had not been specifically included in published policy documents or the election manifesto, yet some party officials in their public speeches were now stating that incorporation was Labour policy, including Lord Cledwyn, the party's chief spokesman in the House of Lords [**109**].

Clarity over Labour Party policy came with the selection of John Smith as leader in 1992, following the party's general election defeat. John Smith was never quite perceived in the public eye as the genuinely radical constitutional reformer he actually was. Almost immediately upon his selection as leader, he galvanized Labour's constitutional reform programme by appointing new front-bench spokespersons on constitutional issues, establishing policy reviews on constitutional problems, and giving a personal lead by publicly declaring his own strong personal backing for a comprehensive modernization of the constitution including a Bill of Rights. In a landmark speech at Church House, Westminster, on 1 March 1993, widely distributed to and prominently reported in the media, John Smith powerfully argued the case for constitutional reform and a Bill of Rights for Britain, 'a new deal between the people and the state that puts the citizen centre stage' [**110**]. The party's comprehensive review of its constitutional programme for government was undertaken in 1992–3, with Tony Blair taking the lead as the then shadow home affairs spokesman with responsibility for constitutional reform. The final recommendations of the review, approved in 1993 by the National Executive Committee, were published under the title *A New Agenda for Democracy: Labour's Proposals for Constitutional Reform* [**112**]. Its opening section was devoted to a Bill of Rights. It advocated, as a first step, the statutory incorporation of the European Convention on Human Rights and the creation of a Human Rights Commission. The second stage it promised was to be the development of a home-grown Bill of Rights. This would involve a public process of inquiry and consultation designed to achieve an as wide as possible consensus of support for the measure. As mentioned in the Introduction and considered further below (page 92), it proposed that there should be an all-party commission established to bring forward recommendations on the drafting of the articles of Bill of Rights and on a suitable method of entrenchment for the document.

In 1995–7, in advance of the general election which it was confidently predicted Labour would win, further planning took place on precisely how and when its policy objectives concerning human rights legislation generally might be achieved. For reasons discussed in the Introduction above, it was recognized that a Labour government was unlikely to be able to implement a homegrown Bill of Rights in its first term of office, and that immediate planning should concentrate on incorporation of the ECHR and a possible Human Rights Commission. Reflecting this view in November 1995, Jack Straw (then shadow home affairs spokesman) said, 'If this project [a Bill of Rights] is to have real meaning, it is essential that the public feels some sense of ownership of it and commitment towards it. This will mean that the project will take some time – beyond a single Parliament'.[5] Tony Blair's electoral strategy in 1995–7 depended heavily on making firm public pledges on a limited number of achievable objects for his first term of office, while at the same time publicly emphasizing that his longer-term objectives (such as a Bill of Rights) would be worked for through a step-by-step approach rather than by dramatic changes.[6] Consequently, the 1996 draft election manifesto (which was endorsed by a vote of all party members) [**115**] and the final manifesto commitments produced for the 1997 election [**117**], focused more on 'the first step' mentioned in the 1993 policy document, namely incorporation of the ECHR. As an indication of the Labour leadership's seriousness that incorporation would indeed be carried out early in the new Parliament, in December 1996, Labour issued a consultation paper on the detailed form which the legislation should take, with responses to be returned to Jack Straw by the end of February 1997 [**116**]. An important component of Labour's advance planning for government was the establishment of the Labour–Liberal Democrat Joint Consultative Committee on Constitutional Reform, whose aim was to help smooth passage of future constitutional legislation by negotiating between the two parties areas of clear common agreement on what was attainable in a first-term Labour government. Its agreed report, published in March 1997 [**150**], included incorporation of the ECHR, the creation of a Human Rights Commission, and recognition of the need for a homegrown Bill of Rights to be drafted subsequent to incorporation.

Historically, this progression in Labour Party policy over the period 1991–7 will be regarded by later generations as a turning-point in the postwar movement towards a UK Bill of Rights. As a constitutional proposal, acceptance for the measure had been worked for and had steadily gathered support over the preceding three decades. But only with the Labour Party leadership's espousal of the case for a Bill of Rights, and its adoption in the party's official policy objectives for government leading up to the 1997 general election, was the matter

5 "From Dependence to Mutual Responsibility', Annual Ambassador's Lecture for Community Links, 7 November 1995.
6 See for example the interview with Tony Blair in *The Times*, 25 April 1997.

finally brought into the realm of practical politics. This was then consecrated by Labour's overwhelming victory at the polls, endorsing its programme for government, and installing Tony Blair as the party's fifth leader to take office as prime minister.

The Case for a UK Bill of Rights

Domestic arrangements

Currently, the UK enjoys a favourable international reputation for the quality of the rights and freedoms enjoyed by its citizens. This is not to say that the state of human rights in the UK is without its critics, which are in fact numerous,[7] nor that there have been no blatant violations of international standards of human rights, of which there have been many in recent years including some which have been addressed by the European Court of Human Rights.[8] Indeed, it would be fair to say that over the past 25 years there has been a growing concern that 'liberty is ill in Britain', in Ronald Dworkin's phrase [**135**], and that a real decline in Britain's traditional concern for the civil liberties of its citizens has taken place, combined with a steady accretion of new regulatory and intrusive powers by the state and its officials which may be open to misuse. However, the case for reform and a Bill of Rights is not so much that the existing situation in the UK is intolerable or even, in comparative terms, bad; it is that our constitutional and legal system can be improved and made much better.

Britain's constitutional arrangements and method of protecting civil liberties are the product of its history rather than any modern rational design.[9] The primary characteristic of UK public law is that there is no written constitution or codified body of fundamental legal principles governing the government of the country. This is unlike the USA, all

---

7 See eg K. Ewing and C. Gearty, *Freedom under Thatcher* (1990).
8 See further below, p. 26 and Doc. 24.
9 For general works on the subject, see S. A. de Smith and R. Brazier, *Constitutional and Administrative Law* (7th edn, 1994); Wade and Bradley, *Constitutional and Administrative Law* (8th edn by A. Bradley and K. Ewing, 1997); J. McEldowney, *Public Law* (2nd edn, 1997); D. Feldman, *Civil Liberties and Human Rights in England and Wales* (1993).

other member states of the European Union, and every other independent Commonwealth country.[10] Indeed, the only liberal democracies in the world not to possess a written constitution are the UK and Israel. A second, related characteristic is the omnicompetence of Parliament. An Act of the UK Parliament is in legal theory absolute and unlimited in its jurisdiction. This legal doctrine, consecrated in the constitutional settlement of 1688 and known as 'parliamentary sovereignty', dictates that a parliamentary statute possesses an inherent right to make or unmake any law whatsover [**5**].[11] British parliamentary sovereignty means that there is no legal distinction to be drawn between constitutional and ordinary law in the sense that the former has a higher status and priority over the latter.[12] Third, there is no technical classification of constitutional law in the eyes of the courts and Parliament. In the UK no domestic principles of law are held out as possessing a fundamental moral claim, on human rights or any other ground, which might have the effect of challenging or overriding the application of some other legal rule, restriction or executive power.

An important part of this inherited legal syndrome is the fact that there is no modern Bill of Rights, whether entrenched as higher law or otherwise, which declares the fundamental rights and freedoms of the people of the UK. There is the Bill of Rights 1688, it is true. Its long title described itself, 'An Act for declaring the Rights and Liberties of the Subject' [**4**]. The Petition of Right 1628 had earlier similarly provided for 'divers Rights and Liberties of the Subjects' [**2**]. And before them both, there was Magna Carta, enacted in successive versions in 1215, 1216, 1217 and 1225, known as the 'Great Charter of the Liberties of England' [**1**]. But these documents, hugely important as they were in the past for establishing the idea of limited government that would influence the rest of the western world, are not Bills of Rights in the sense of the contemporary constitutional reform which makes up the subject of this book. Their contents, while fascinating historical

10 See S. E. Finer, V. Bogdanor and B. Rudden, *Comparing Constitutions* (1995).

11 See further, pp. 57–9. This power would include, since 1974, withdrawal from the European Union and revocation of any existing Community laws and restrictions.

12 Though in Scotland, it is believed theoretically possible for an ordinary Act of Parliament to be declared void under a fundamental term of the Treaty of Union 1707. Generally see S. A. de Smith and R. Brazier, *Constitutional and Administrative Law*, 6th edn, 1989, pp. 73–4.

reading, are archaic and belong to a different social order. The significance of Magna Carta for later centuries lay in its implications. It provided a powerful symbol for the concept of government under law, and what is now called the rule of law [6]. The Bill of Rights 1688 (most of which is now obsolete or repealed), though it dealt with some matters carrying civil liberties implications (notably concerning conditions of detention), was a description of the settlement between Parliament and the Crown following the enforced abdication of King James II and acceptance of William and Mary on the throne. The Bill's purpose was to curtail the actual and pretended prerogatives of the monarchy, and to safeguard the constitutional rights of Parliament, rather than the people. Henceforth it was Parliament that was sovereign, and Parliament as the nation's representative assembly was to be regarded as the constitutional mechanism for safeguarding our liberties, rather than any basic law of human rights enforceable directly by individuals through the legal process. By contrast, the written constitutions that later emerged elsewhere in the western world have usually provided that it is the people who are to be regarded as legitimizing government, and that government therefore is to be limited in law by the people's inherent and inalienable rights.

The common law principles on which the protection of individual liberty were developed in England were, first, that individuals were free to do whatever they pleased so long as they did not infringe any general law or the enforceable rights of others; and second, that public authorities could only infringe the freedom of the individual if so empowered by some specific common law or statutory authority [9]. 'The starting point in our domestic law is that every citizen has a right to do what he likes, unless restrained by the common law or by statute', as Lord Donaldson, then Master of the Rolls, said in the *Spycatcher* case.[13] The safeguards for the individual have consisted of an ad hoc development of specific remedies to meet particular problems. The most famous English remedy in our history has been *habeas corpus*,[14] securing the right of personal liberty from unlawful or arbitary detention [3]. In the postwar era, newer non-judicial remedies emerged to deal with complaints about abuse of bureaucratic power, such as the Parliamentary Commissioner for Administration established in 1967. In the courts, the growth of judicial review of

---

13 *Attorney-General* v *Guardian* (No. 2) [1988] 3 All ER 594 at 596–7.
14 R. G. Sharpe, *The Law of Habeas Corpus* (2nd edn, 1989).

administrative action, and the elaboration of its principles, has proved the most rapid development in the common law.[15] Detailed equality legislation has been enacted to combat specific forms of discrimination, notably the Sex Discrimination Act and Race Relations Act under the Labour government in the 1970s, and the Disability Discrimination Act under the Conservative administration in the 1990s [13].

The government's report to the United Nations Human Rights Committee in 1989 explained that the reason for the absence of a written constitution or a comprehensive Bill of Rights in the UK is that 'the rights and freedoms recognized in other countries' constitutions are inherent in the British legal system and are protected by it and by Parliament unless they are removed or restricted by statute' [18]. This general scheme of arrangement is commonly described as protecting human rights 'negatively'. As discussed further below (page 25), and with the exception of the existing anti-discrimination legislation referred to in the last paragraph, human rights cannot be asserted positively in any court of law as actionable rights. In Britain, as Sir Ivor Jennings put it, we must 'be careful in using the word 'rights'. If it is meant that they are natural rights, or if they are accepted as part of the logic of free or democratic government, the word is used in a sense different from its meaning in the phrases 'contractual right', 'right to damages'. It is a distinction between essential constitutional principles and rights actually conferred by statute law or common law' [7]. Civil and political liberties, therefore, are treated as a purely residual property, being what remains over after all the growing number of legal controls and infringements on human activities by public and private bodies are taken into account.

This British way of dealing with human rights in the late twentieth century stands starkly in contrast to the constitutional provisions of most other countries which, as discussed below, have now developed some form of Bill of Rights for the modern era. In the UK, there still remains no official general statement, legal or non-legal, of what the fundamental rights and freedoms of the citizen are. As a point of reference or definition, the British people must turn either to the dubious rhetoric of party politicians or abstract works of moral philosophy, or else abroad to the British government's international human rights obligations as members of the United Nations and the Council of Europe.

15 P. P. Craig, *Administrative Law* (3rd edn, 1994).

International arrangements

The UK is a contracting party to two major international human rights treaties, being the International Covenant on Civil and Political Rights (ICCPR) [20] which entered into force in 1976, and the European Convention on Human Rights (ECHR) [22] which was adopted in 1950. Both these human rights instruments contain a range of civil rights and freedoms provisions which are analogous to many of the principles which could be included in a UK Bill of Rights. To be read along with the ICCPR, as part of what is known as the United Nations International Bill of Rights, is the earlier Universal Declaration of Human Rights in 1948 [19] (which was not in itself a treaty but a declaration of the UN General Assembly) and the International Covenant on Economic, Social and Cultural Rights effective since 1976 dealing with rights of a kind less suitable for enforcement through courts of law [21].[16] The Council of Europe enacted a Social Charter in 1965, prescribing policies with respect to labour standards, but this is not part of the work of the ECHR or subject to a system of judicial enforcement [23].[17]

At the international level, both the ICCPR and the ECHR have their own enforcement machinery, the principal agencies of which are respectively the UN Human Rights Committee and the European Court of Human Rights. The Human Rights Committee operating at Geneva receives periodic reports from each member state on the quality and protection of human rights in their country and the measures they have adopted to give effect to the rights under the Covenant. The Committee responds to these reports and may require further information or investigations. Complaints by one member state that another is not fulfilling its human rights obligations will go to the Committee. Under an Optional Protocol member countries can permit their individual citizens to bring human rights complaints before the Committee. In the case of the UK, the government has declined to ratify the Protocol.[18]

---

16 On the enforcement of social and economic principles in a Bill of Rights, see below pp. 49–50.

17 See P. O'Higgins, 'The European Social Charter', in R. Blackburn and J. Taylor (eds), *Human Rights for the 1990s* (1991).

18 See P. Sieghart, *The International Law of Human Rights* (1981); A. H. Robertson and J. G. Merrills, *Human Rights in the World* (1992).

The European Court of Human Rights at Strasbourg receives inter-state complaints for resolution and judgment, but the bulk of its work lies in dealing with applications from individuals claiming their rights under the Convention have been violated. The UK government granted to its citizens the right of individual petition to the Strasbourg enforcement machinery in 1966 (a decision which is renewable every five years, most recently in January 1996).[19] Under article 35 of the ECHR, individual applicants must have exhausted all domestic legal remedies in their own country before their complaint will be heard under the Strasbourg enforcement machinery. Under Protocol No. 11 of the Convention, shortly to be put into effect, the previous two-tier arrangements of a part-time Commission (receiving petitions in the first instance) and a part-time Court is replaced by a full-time Court. The Court alone will now take all decisions on the merits of cases, and the Committee of Ministers, representing member states, now has a reduced role in this respect. Whereas previously the Committee of Ministers had jurisdiction to determine a case which had not been referred to the Court within three months of the Commission's report, it will now concentrate on matters relating to the execution of the Court's judgments. The Court of Human Rights is henceforth to be structured into Committees of three judges, Chambers of seven judges, and a Grand Chamber of seventeen judges. Applications in the first instance go to a Committee with the power to declare cases inadmissible, where such a decision can be reached unanimously without further examination. Remaining applications are then forwarded to a Chamber which will try the merits of the case, and, where appropriate, attempt to promote a friendly settlement between the parties. Only cases involving a serious question of interpretation of the Convention will be referred to the Grand Chamber.

A reading of some selected illustrative UK cases that have been taken to the Commission and Court of Human Rights since 1966 displays a wide range of legitimate human rights grievances that have arisen in this country recently [24]. It also gives a flavour of the types of cases and kind of issues that would be dealt with by UK courts following the enactment of a UK Bill of Rights. As at 3 November 1998, the total number of cases in which the European Court of Human Rights had found at least one breach of the ECHR by member states of the Council of Europe were Austria 44, Belgium 25, Cyprus 2,

---

19 F. G. Jacobs and R. C. White, *The European Convention on Human Rights* (2nd edn, 1996); R. Beddard, *Human Rights and Europe* (3rd edn, 1993).

Denmark 3, Finland 4, France 63, Germany 15, Greece 27, Iceland 2, Ireland 6, Italy 101, Malta 1, Netherlands 30, Norway 3, Portugal 11, Spain 9, Sweden 21, Switzerland 14, and the United Kingdom 56 [**33**]. The existence of the Strasbourg Commission and Court has undoubtedly helped promote some greater measure of awareness and emphasis on human rights considerations within the UK official bureaucracy, and how these are to be weighed against official decisions and actions which are based upon administrative convenience alone. In 1987, for example, the Cabinet Office produced an administrative circular for civil servants on how to adopt good practices with respect to human rights considerations and so reduce the risk of legal challenge under the ECHR [**26**]. Frivolous or poorly founded actions taken to Strasbourg have been easily dismissed, but cases of injustice, maladministration or oppressive government action have been corrected by reference to the humanitarian considerations contained in the ECHR. Few dispute that the great majority of the numerous changes in public regulations and statutory provisions in the UK brought about as a direct result of human rights cases heard in Strasbourg have been just and correct. Violations are frequently settled by mutual agreement between the parties without needing to proceed to the expense of court proceedings, following a coherently presented case from a human rights lawyer on behalf of the complainant being received by the public body or official concerned. After the enactment of a UK Bill of Rights, the resolution of such cases would become an everyday part of the UK's own system of justice, avoiding the need for many present grievances to be taken abroad to the international tribunal at Strasbourg.

THE UK's COMMITMENT TO THE INTERNATIONAL COMMUNITY

The case for a UK Bill of Rights rests upon five distinct but associated grounds of reasoning. These concern (1) the level of the UK's commitment to the international community and its human rights treaties, (2) the need for new legal remedies in UK law where individual rights and freedoms are inadequately protected, (3) the need to stem the rising tide of inconsistencies between national and European human rights law, (4) the need for a new constitution for the UK, with a new legal settlement that emphasizes the rights and freedoms of its citizens; and

(5) the social and political advantages to be gained from a national statement of fundamental values with respect to citizenship. Since the 1960s, a similar line of reasoning has applied to both incorporation of the ECHR and a constitutional Bill of Rights in respect of some of the grounds referred to above, particularly the first three. Indeed, the public debate on both measures has often been conducted interchangeably, by referring to incorporation of the ECHR as a 'Bill of Rights' – this has often been apparent in Parliament's own deliberations on the question of a Bill of Rights [83–92] – though for reasons already given (see Introduction, pages xxviiif. and xxxvf.) this can be misleading. The case for a homegrown constitutional Bill of Rights, then, as distinct from incorporation of the ECHR treaty, rests on similar arguments as have been applied to incorporation, but also in addition on the need for a more fundamental modernization of UK's legal and political system.

The most immediate advantage of a UK Bill of Rights will be to establish a national legal framework for the protection of human rights which conforms more closely with our treaty obligations and is more consonant with the legal methods for the protection of human rights operating generally throughout the western world. This consideration applies with particular force in the context of Europe – both the European Union and the wider body of Council of Europe states. It also applies with respect to the Commonwealth and the UK's treaty obligations and commitments under the Universal Declaration of Human Rights. The UK is the only member of the twelve European Union states without a written constitution or enforceable Bill of Rights. The majority of the 40 Council of Europe member states not only have their own constitutional Bill of Rights but have in addition incorporated the human rights provisions of the ECHR directly into their own national system of law. At the time of writing, and until the Human Rights Act 1998 incorporating the ECHR is finally implemented into UK law, the courts remain unable to apply any code of human rights principles directly, and there is no rule of law which empowers them to take the Convention and the jurisprudence of the Court of Human Rights into account in judicial review proceedings – even in those cases where there are clear human rights implications [25]. For half a century after the initiatives taken following the cessation of World War II to build a closer relationship within Europe and construct a universal framework for the protection of human rights, the British system of justice has remained in a state of growing isolation from the progressive developments in human rights law that have taken place elsewhere. Beyond Europe, our arrangements are now different from those of the USA, with its written constitution embodying an entrenched Bill of Rights, and they are increasingly out-of-step with the growing number of Commonwealth countries since the 1950s who have enacted Bills of Rights of their own for the better protection of human rights including in the West Indies [44], in Canada [45], in New Zealand [46], and (most recently) South Africa [48]. The human rights provisions within all these national Bills of Rights are broadly similar, following the general pattern of the ECHR and Universal Declaration, with differences of emphasis or detail in reflection of national or regional matters of importance and more modern social developments.

As discussed elsewhere, progress towards a constitutional Bill of Rights will now considerably benefit from, as a first stage, the Human Rights Act 1998 incorporating the principles of the ECHR by statute into the legal system of the UK. This will have the advantage of laying the foundations for the recognition of fundamental rights and freedoms in our courts and Parliament, and serve to harmonize those human rights principles directly with those operating across Europe. Until a homegrown Bill of Rights for the UK is developed and enacted, many will regard the Human Rights Act as an interim Bill of Rights. Furthermore, as is elaborated upon below (see page 47 and Docs 49 and 50), the architects of the UK Bill of Rights will naturally draw extensively upon the United Nations and Council of Europe treaties, in order to settle the principles and wording of the individual rights and freedoms to go into the document, not least for reasons of ensuring domestic conformity.

Meanwhile, in the absence of any domestically recognized human rights charter, the work of the Council of Europe has itself suffered from the UK's ostensible lack of a full commitment. For the past twenty years, senior Council of Europe officials, among them the Secretary-General and the President of the Court of Human Rights, have urged the UK to adopt the Convention in its national law [27, 30]. New members of the Council of Europe, particularly those from the former eastern European bloc of nations now struggling to develop a framework for democratic political and legal methods themselves, have been understandably bemused by the UK's ostensibly ambivalent commitment to European human rights, evidenced not only in its past refusal to incorporate the ECHR but in some regrettable episodes of public criticism by UK ministers on the judgments of the Human Rights Court when the UK government was found to be in breach of the ECHR. Furthermore, the UK government has so far refused to appoint a senior judicial figure as its nominee to the bench of the Human Rights Court, preferring instead its former civil service legal advisers. By contrast, the commitment of the EU as an international body has been unequivocal. The EU has openly embraced the human rights principles of the Convention, referring to them in the preamble to the Maastricht Treaty [37], encompassing them in a joint declaration issued by the European Parliament, Council and Commission [34], and being adopted as principles of legal construction in the work of the European Court of Justice [36]. The Commission is now pursuing the proposal that the EU as a legal body formally applies to the Council of Europe to accede to the ECHR, thereby making the human rights principles of the Convention directly enforceable by all citizens of EU member states through the medium of European Community law [38]. The European Parliament has issued its own Declaration of Fundamental Rights and Freedoms, which goes further than the more traditional rights listed in the ECHR, and has called on all member states to recognize and associate themselves with its provisions [35].

An unfortunate result of the UK's isolation from the international community with respect to human rights law has been the inability of the British legal system to contribute and help forge new judicial principles and procedures on the basis of its own practical experience in interpreting and applying human rights principles. There is an organic relationship between international and national legal systems, with the application and enforcement mechanisms of the ECHR and other treaties drawing heavily upon the jurisprudence of the national legal systems of member states. The UK in centuries past had good reason to be proud of its successful invention and development of judicial concepts and procedures that promoted equality and freedom. Indeed, after World War II many English inventions were codified in the declarations or phrases of the ECHR and Universal Declaration, as well as in the domestic Bills of Rights of Commonwealth and other countries. But then over the past five decades, the UK effectively excluded its judiciary from making a direct contribution on how these basic general rights and freedoms enumerated in the treaties should be developed to meet changing contemporary circumstances. The integrity and intellectual calibre of the UK judiciary is unquestionably as high as ever it was in the past, and today it has a good claim to be regarded as second-to-none in the world. The potential for our judicial system to respond to the new challenge of human rights law cannot seriously be doubted, and, as is further described below (see page 28), many senior judicial figures them-selves have been openly expressing their willingness to interpret and apply positive general statements of human rights law, if Parliament enacts that they may do so [142]. The effect of a UK Bill of Rights will be, in Ronald Dworkin's words, that, 'British judges began to create as well as follow constitutional jurisprudence ... their decisions would be bound to influence the Commission and Court in Strasbourg, as well as the courts of the other nations ... Britain could become once again a leader in defining and protecting individual freedom' [135]. For too long the lack of direct participation by the UK judiciary in the newly developing human rights jurisprudence of the western world has deprived the international community of an important contribu-tion that the UK and its legal culture could make. For too long also, the UK has chosen to remove itself from yet another important sphere of influence it might have upon the supranational government and law of the world community.

A LEGAL REMEDY FOR HUMAN RIGHTS GRIEVANCES

The ground supporting a Bill of Rights most specific to the individual citizen, or minority protection, is that a comprehensive statement of basic rights and freedoms is more likely to offer a direct legal remedy for an alleged human rights violation, where no such remedy might currently be found to exist.

A Bill of Rights would vest individual citizens with enforceable rights and freedoms expressed as general principles of law. Under existing British law, as stated above (page 17), civil liberties are protected 'negatively', meaning that the basic individual rights to be found in a Bill of Rights and the ECHR (such as the right to liberty and security of the person, freedom of association and assembly, equality and freedom from discrimination, and privacy or respect for one's private life) may not be used by citizens in the UK to found a legal action in the courts in the same way that legal actions may be founded upon rights derived from breach of contract, trespass or negligence claims. Specific remedies are widely available for specific circum-stances, such as monetary or reinstatement orders by an industrial tribunal for sex discrimination at work, but the absence of a national framework for the protection of human rights means that gaps in the UK system for protecting human rights will inevitably at some point arise, and indeed do now exist. The UK method of protecting human rights, relying as it does upon case-by-case progression of common-law principle and piecemeal development of statutory reform, has meant whole fields of civil rights jurisprudence, which are now recognized internationally and in other states' legal system, have yet still to be conceived in UK law.

The most glaring gap in the UK's protection of basic rights has been the protection of personal privacy. As Lord Williams for the Labour Party stated in a 1995 parliamentary debate, 'It is notorious that our law recognizes no right to privacy as such. The common law is dumb. It is not effective ... The individual, however mean, lowly and insignificant, has no shield from the common law when his privacy is grossly interfered with and abused'.[20] The absence of any common-law tort or general statutory right of privacy has caused the UK government to be held to be in violation of human rights several times before the European Court of Human Rights. In the *Golder* case (1975),[21] a prisoner had his complaint concerning interference with his correspondence with his solicitor upheld. In the *Malone* case (1979),[22] an antiques dealer had his complaint upheld about clandes-tine tapping of his private telephone conversations (which subsequently obliged the British government to introduce the Inter-ception of Communications Act 1985) [**24**]. Numerous other specific gaps in the common law and statute for protection of basic rights are identifiable. In his strongly argued critique of the 'rule of law' in Britain today, Geoffrey Robertson QC in his book *Freedom, the Individual and the Law* catalogued a wide range of characteristics of government in Britain where a Bill of Rights would substantially help buttress the legal protection of civil liberties, which included: in the review of wide discretionary powers which are vested in the state, over such matters including surveillance and data collection on individuals and the treatment of immigrants; in the review of nominal ministerial controls, including the granting of asylum and decisions on the release date of life-sentence prisoners; in extending rights of access to official information in a system of administration endemic with secrecy, including for the discovery of details of decisions affecting civil liberties; in replacing 'sham protections' for citizens, such as the Press

20 HL Deb., 25 January 1995, col. 1161.
21 *Golder* v *UK* (1979–80) 1 EHRR 524.
22 *Malone* v *UK* (1985) 7 EHRR 14.

Complaints commission; and in strengthening the constitutional scrutiny of emergency legislation, where Parliament is vulnerable [**138**].

From the viewpoint of the individual citizen, an entrenched Bill of Rights would offer distinct practical advantages over the existing state of affairs. Apart from the extension of legal rights available to the citizen, complaints of alleged human rights violation would rarely need to be taken to the European Court of Human Rights. The need for UK citizens to petition the Strasbourg court should recede following the UK's incorporation of the ECHR, promised shortly by the Labour government; under a newly drafted constitutional Bill of Rights, with directly actionable rights more closely attuned to contemporary British society, the scope and jurisdiction for the Strasbourg court will diminish even further. By comparison, in the past whenever the fundamental rights included in the ECHR have been prima facie breached, the citizen has been obliged to exhaust all possible domestic legal remedies before presenting his petition at Strasbourg. If applicable, this commonly consists of an application for judicial review in the High Court with appeals up to the House of Lords in which the judiciary will inquire into the alleged injustice without reference to any UK code of basic civil rights and freedoms. Currently, citizens are regularly advised by their lawyers that they have been the victims of human rights violations, but before embarking on a petition to Strasbourg they must pursue legal actions against the relevant public authority in the UK courts where their chances of winning on the basis of domestic legal principles are hopeless. There has often been an element of futility about such domestic legal proceedings, as well as that of 'justice delayed being justice denied'. The time and expense in bringing human rights cases since 1965 has been very great indeed, not to mention the personal stress involved and user-unfriendliness of the entire process. The great majority of successful litigants before the Court of Human Rights have been exceptionally determined individuals or ones who are supported morally and financially by a human rights campaigning body or pressure group. Even after all the relevant hearings in the domestic UK courts have been completed, the laborious procedures for bringing a case before the Court of Human Rights will take three years at quickest (and some cases have dragged on for as long as nine). Even after a victory at Strasbourg court, 'no doubt that is a triumph morally', to quote Lord Scarman, 'but it is not very useful to the citizen after so much delay' [**84**].

It should be made plain that the argument for a Bill of Rights as a framework for human rights law is that the document will supplement rather than displace existing and future detailed statutory legislation providing for and regulating specific rights. Similarly, judicial procedures for the protection of individuals under the Bill of Rights will work with other statutory remedial procedures and institutions where these are provided, such as the central and local government ombudsmen. As the British Institute of Human Rights put it, when presenting its evidence to the House of Lords Select Committee on a Bill of Rights, 'The enactment of a Bill of Rights and piece-meal reform should not be regarded as mutually exclusive alternatives; they are inter-dependent' [127]. Few would dispute the desirability that Parliament should legislate in detail to protect particular basic rights, and where Parliament has chosen to do so, the courts will continue as at present to apply the relevant statutory provisions (save only exceptionally where the statutory regulations themselves are found to be in violation of fundamental human rights). But the political reality is that legislatures, particularly ones that tend to be dominated by the executive as in the UK, rarely make the statutory protection of human rights an ongoing major priority in their programme of business.

RESTORING INTEGRITY TO UK CIVIL LIBERTIES LAW

Significantly, judicial opinion is now clearly receptive to the idea of a human rights charter for the UK. Many present and former senior judges since the mid-1970s have been calling for incorporation of the ECHR into UK law, saying that they would have no problem with interpreting and applying a human rights document. The most vocal judge in this respect has been Lord Bingham, the lord chief justice [142]. In a widely publicized lecture in 1993, he complained that, 'The ability of English judges to protect human rights in this country and reconcile conflicting rights ... is inhibited by the failure of successive governments over many years to incorporate into United Kingdom law the European Convention on Human Rights'. In a public lecture at King's College London in 1996, Lord Bingham vigorously supported the Labour Party's proposals for a Human Rights Act, rejecting criticisms that it would represent any fundamental change in the functions of the judiciary or of the judiciary's relations with the legislature or executive. He commented that, 'Constitutional arrangements, like motor cars, require periodic inspection and overhaul, so that worn-out parts may be renewed and ill-fitting parts adjusted. The fact that a constitution such as ours has been on the road for a very long time makes this attention more necessary, not less.' Among the other senior judicial figures who have publicly declared their support for statutory adoption of the human rights principles contained in the ECHR are the Master of the Rolls, Lord Woolf, Lord Browne-Wilkinson, Lord Slynn, and Lord Bingham's predecessor as lord chief justice, Lord Taylor.[23]

An important factor contributing towards the judiciary's receptiveness to reform is their far greater appreciation than most other people of the importance of European law today, both Community law as directly recognized and enforced in our domestic courts, and human rights law under the ECHR as has now permeated the jurisprudence of the EU and most of its member states. The work of the Strasbourg Court of Human Rights has developed enormously in terms of its caseload and public profile. The number of member states has rapidly grown from 22 in 1989 to 40 by July 1998. The number of applications registered with the Commission rose from 404 in 1981 to 2,037 in 1993 to 44,035 by 31 October 1998. Prior to 1988 there were never more than 25 cases each year referred to the Court of Human Rights, but in recent years there have been between 50 and 100 and this number now looks set to increase even further. As mentioned above, the operation and achievements of the Commission and Court of Human Rights, now being restructured into a single court system under Protocol 11 which entered into force on 1 November 1998, have been widely praised within the legal establishment. The care with which the reports and decisions of the Human Rights Commission and Court have been expressed, taken in a manner to avoid unnecessary confrontation with member states, has impressed international lawyers and diplomats, with the 'friendly settlement' procedure designed to resolve human rights problems without recourse to official rulings being identified as having been particularly successful. The growing reputation of the Convention for its work and the success of its enforcement machinery has served to project a positive image of European human rights law to the minds of many lawyers and judges in the UK. This, in turn, has greatly facilitated

---

23 See the opinions expressed in the debates on the Human Rights Bills 1994–6, Doc. 87; also Lord Taylor's view broadcast in a televised Dimbleby lecture, *The Judiciary in the Nineties* (1992), pp. 13–14.

arguments for the Convention's human rights principles to be adopted directly into UK law.

Many judges and jurists pointed to the inconsistent, even absurd, position of the Thatcher and Major governments continuing to oppose incorporation of the ECHR yet formally accepting the very explicit recognition of human rights within the constitutional law of the EU and in the jurisprudence of the European Court of Justice [34–8]. The Maastricht Treaty in 1992 declared that, 'the Union shall respect fundamental rights, as guaranteed by the European Convention for the Protection of Human Rights and Fundamental Freedoms ... and as they result from the constitutional traditions common to member states, as general principles of Community law.' This means, as Lord Slynn, formerly a judicial member of the European Court of Justice and today a law lord who supports a Human Rights Act, has pointed out, 'Every time the European Court recognises a principle set out in the Convention as being part of Community law, it must be enforced in the UK courts in relation to Community law matters, but not in domestic law. So the Convention becomes in part a part of our law through the back door because we have to apply the Convention in respect of Community law matters as a part of Community law' [38]. The illogicality since the 1960s of the UK government being a party to the ECHR and granting our citizens the right to petition the Commission and Court of Human Rights but not actually incorporating its human rights principles into our domestic legislation until 1998 was compounded further by the fact that the Convention's human rights principles had in any event entered into judicial recognition through the mediation of the rulings of the European Court of Justice [36].

For many people in this country it has been a matter of profound regret that the UK government and its system of law has so often and regularly been held to be in violation of basic human rights and freedoms by the European Court of Human Rights. This is particularly so as it was likely that the same result would have been reached in many cases by a UK court had it been empowered by statute to apply the Convention's human rights principles and/or those of a domestic Bill of Rights. As one Labour MP argued in a Commons debate in 1987, 'It would help the image of Britain if those rights were brought into our law, because fewer cases would be ruled admissible by the court [at Strasbourg], to the humiliation of this country. We have been ruled against in twice as many cases as any other country in Europe. That is a national humiliation. We would not face that if we could pursue rights in our own courts in our own way. That is a major practical argument' [**91**]. The numerous defeats suffered by the UK before the European Court of Human Rights is regularly referred to by our senior judges with deep disapproval. In the law lord Nicolas Browne-Wilkinson's view, 'That this country with its history should be found so repeatedly in breach of its international obligations to provide freedoms is very shocking' [**87**].

What undoubtedly fuelled the growing sense of degradation in human rights cases among the UK judiciary in the 1980s and 1990s was the self-evident awkwardness many displayed in being duty-bound to decide a particular case in a manner which is clearly contrary to European human rights law. In these circumstances, the judge and court faced the probability that the case decided would be challenged in Strasbourg under the ECHR where the UK judge's ruling will be held to be in violation of human rights. This represented both a moral and professional embarrassment to the minds of many judges. Such situations up to 1998 arose many times. The *Malone* case in 1979 (mentioned above, page 26) proved a landmark in this respect, and it represented a turning-point in the opinion of many judges towards the desirability of a domestic UK human rights charter. For in *Malone*, a UK court for the first time expressly recognized and publicly stated that its own decision was in breach of the human rights principles of the ECHR. But, the court acknowledged, in the existing state of UK law there was nothing it could do to apply the Convention so as to avoid eventual defeat in Strasbourg [**25**]. Referring to Article 8 of the Convention, which guarantees the right to respect for private life and correspondence, and the interpretation of that article (together with the requirement for an effective remedy under article 13) adopted by the Court of Human Rights in the leading case of *Klass*[24] the previous year, Sir Robert Megarry, then vice-chancellor, said in his judgment, 'It is impossible to read the judgment in the *Klass* case without it becoming abundantly clear that a system which has no legal safeguards whatever has small chance of satisfying the requirements of that court, whatever administrative provisions there may be [and that it is] impossible to see how English law could be said to satisfy the requirements of the Convention, as interpreted in the *Klass* case.' As the number of human rights cases being taken to Strasbourg has increased, so too have the number of cases where our judges at home have felt impotent when faced with an inconsistency between UK law and the ECHR. The irrationality and injustice of this situation was

24 *Klass and others* v *Germany* (1979–80) 2 EHRR 214.

referred to in the course of a parliamentary debate in 1995, in which the law lord Nicolas Browne-Wilkinson complained, 'I have on occasion had to reach conclusions in cases which I knew to be contrary to the Convention because I was not able to do otherwise. Why cannot we enable our courts to administer what the European Court of Human Rights does many months, many years, many hundreds of thousands of pounds later?' [**87**].

To a large extent, the deficiencies in UK civil liberties law which are the subject of this growing chorus of complaint among the senior judiciary and others will now be redressed by incorporation of the ECHR through the Human Rights Act. A more secure arrangement, however, will only be set in place when the long-term programme envisaged by the Labour Party and Liberal Democrats in their policy documents [**112, 93**] is completed through the adoption of an entrenched home-grown Bill of Rights. As is discussed further below, the human rights articles of the Bill of Rights will then both encompass the UK's existing international obligations under the ECHR and ICCPR and elaborate upon them further to suit contemporary UK domestic conditions and the perceived future challenges ahead in the twenty-first century.

A BILL OF RIGHTS AS PART OF A NEW CONSTITUTION

The most famous of the late John Smith's public lectures on the constitution was delivered at Church House, Westminster, on 1 March 1993. When he asked his audience to question seriously whether we should 'limp into the 21st century on a constitution built for the 19th' (see above page xxvii), he was not overstating the case. His argument that 'we need a new constitution for a new century' is widely accepted and shared across the three major political parties, though currently only the Labour government and the Liberal Democrats have developed policies for a comprehensive modernization of the constitution.

Perhaps the most fundamental ground for a UK Bill of Rights, therefore, is that the basic structure of the constitution as inherited from our Victorian past needs to be updated to meet contemporary conditions as we enter the new century. Moulded and designed for social and political conditions far removed from today, it fails to provide effective political and legal safeguards against the abuse of power. Major changes that have occurred over the course of the twentieth century have brought about new threats to the individual, while the substance of Britain's traditional checks and balances in the nineteenth century, particularly in the House of Commons and in the House of Lords, have fallen into decline. What has emerged is a highly centralized structure of government with inadequate guarantees for the individual – an elective dictatorship, as the UK's political system is now commonly described – requiring a major programme of modernization and reform. An entrenched Bill of Rights has been regarded as a central component in this wider process of constitutional renewal now required. It would perform a key role in underpinning the constitution with respect for individual rights and freedoms in a modern British democracy.

The scale of the Labour Party's overall reform objectives can justifiably claim, in the words of its 1993 policy document *A New Agenda for Democracy*, to be 'the most radical package of democratic reform ever presented to the British people by a major political party ... Though these reforms do not mean a formal written constitution, in which each aspect of government and citizens' rights is set out, they are nonetheless a significant step in that direction' [**112**]. Though a new or modernized constitution does not necessarily involve the adoption of a written constitution, yet there are now many individual Labour members who support the principle of a written constitution as a long-term goal, including for example the present government whip Graham Allen MP who, as constitutional spokesman for the party in Tony Blair's shadow home affairs team under John Smith's leadership, presented a Written Constitution Bill to the House of Commons in 1992 [**78**]. The Institute for Public Policy Research, the left-of-centre think-tank influential in Labour's development of its policies generally, in 1991 pioneered the serious consideration of a written UK constitution when it produced a detailed blueprint of what such a document might look like and how it could be drafted.[25]

Many others, across the political spectrum, have felt equally strongly that the UK's constitutional system now requires some comprehensive measure of reform tantamount to a new constitution. On the Conservative side, it was Lord Hailsham, the former party chairman and lord chancellor, who first successfully committed the

25 Institute for Public Policy Research, *A Written Constitution for the United Kingdom* (Cassell, The Constitutional Reform Series, rev. edn 1993). The work was first published under the title *The Constitution of the United Kingdom.* (IPPR, 1991).

language of 'elective dictatorship' into contemporary political debate [**124**]. Giving the televised Dimbleby Lecture in 1976, he delivered a stinging critique of the state of the UK's failing political institutions as a means of protecting freedom. 'Our constitution is wearing out', he said. 'We live under an elective dictatorship . . . [This] is a fact and not just a lawyer's theory'. Calling for 'nothing less than a written constitution for the United Kingdom', Lord Hailsham backed 'a Bill of Rights, equally entrenched, containing as a minimum the rights defined by the European Convention to which we are already a party'. Lord Hailsham's basic proposition, that there has arisen in the course of the twentieth century an excessive concentration of power in the hands of government leaders requiring new measures of constitutional reform, has been a view shared by others within his party, despite the fact that the Conservative administrations of Margaret Thatcher and John Major continued to resist any significant measures of constitutional change between 1979–97. Since the merger of the Liberal and SDP parties in 1988, the Liberal Democrats have consistently endorsed the principle of an entrenched Bill of Rights and a written constitution in their official policy documents [**93–4**]. On Labour's left wing, Tony Benn MP has been no less scathing than Lord Hailsham in his diagnosis of Britain's failing constitutional structure, both in his book *Arguments for Democracy* published in 1981 and in his recent speeches and publications supporting his own proposal for a written constitution, the Commonwealth of Britain Bill 1991 [**54**]. Among the senior judiciary, Lord Scarman has been perhaps the best-known advocate of a written constitution embodying an entrenched Bill of Rights, in a series of speeches following his 1974 Hamlyn Lectures.[26] Lobby groups have emerged over the past ten years to champion the cause of a new constitution, the most high profile of which has been Charter 88. Within the public at large, a MORI opinion poll for the Joseph Rowntree Reform Trust in 1996 indicated that 74 per cent of the electorate now believe that Britain needs a written constitution.

The principal elements which have led to Britain's constitutional decline this century, requiring wide-ranging reform today, are the huge enlargement in the scale and range of government and public administration, the eclipse of earlier forms of checks and balances within the parliamentary process, and the growing anachronism of parliamentary sovereignty as the basis for constitutionalism in the

---

26 See eg Lord Scarman, 'Why Britain needs a Written Constitution', The Fourth Sovereignty Lecture, Charter 88, 1992.

modern state. It needs to be recalled that government activity in previous centuries was principally confined to maintaining civil order, defending the realm and conducting international relations: as such, it interfered very little in the ordinary lives of people. By the early decades of this century, in contrast, the western world had undergone revolutionary social and economic changes, expanding massively in size to operate welfare, utility and economic management of society. The modern state had become an interventionist enterprise, engaged in administrative provision, regulation and supervision of most aspects of our personal lives and social and economic well-being [**15**]. In the UK, these universal tendencies were accompanied by a steady accretion of centralized power in Whitehall and Westminster, with a slow decline in regional and local control over communities' own social and administrative affairs. By the 1960s, the executive had become a huge permanent centralized bureaucracy, generating an ever-growing mass of legislation, now leaving hardly any part of an individual's working or private life unregulated. These social changes and the technological developments which have driven them have brought great rewards for the individual, not only in terms of his physical well-being and relative prosperity, but also in his or her freedom of choice, opportunity and movement. But they have also created conditions which have led to an imbalance in the constitutional relationship between the power of the state and the safeguards necessary to protect the rights and freedoms of the individual. The modern state has brought with it greater dangers to civil liberty from potential abuse of official power, some threats already evident and others no doubt being shored up for the future. As the former Liberal leader Sir David Steel argued in the House of Commons, backing the case for a Bill of Rights, 'The increase in the executive arm of government and in the number of areas of government activity, under governments of all parties, and in the increasing complexity and speed of modern life have meant that the individual is in need of greater protection, but is afforded less ... The sheer scope of government activity and the bureaucracy and technology that support it have increased exponentially ... The individual is at an increasing disadvantage in the massive system of social management and ultimately of control, which is inherent in the world of computer files, satellite surveillance and telephone tapping' [**91**].

Fundamental to a new constitution, and of special importance to the enactment of a Bill of Rights, will be replacement or redefinition of the doctrine of parliamentary sovereignty. This is one of the most radical aspects of instituting a Bill of Rights, and one which has troubled most of those opposed to the reform [**61, 63, 128, 133**]. It is also an aspect which raises as an ancillary matter the issue of possible reforms in judicial appointments, to ensure public confidence in the social representativeness of those entering the judicial profession, since a Bill of Rights would involve a more elevated constitutional role for the courts [**65–72**]. The case for a Bill of Rights rests heavily on the view that the notion of the unlimited and unfettered power of a parliamentary statute over any subject-matter whatsover, however fundamental in nature, has become an anachronism in the modern world. As a constitutional principle, it belongs to a completely differ-ent political and social era. It originated from the constitutional settlement of 1688, when James II was forced to abdicate and William III accepted the throne on terms which secured the supremacy of Parliament over the Crown. Over the course of the next three cen-turies, the transcendance of Parliament's authority over all other moral claims was upheld by the courts and became transformed into a rigid legal dogma [**12**]. Lawyers such as A. V. Dicey continued to expound that Parliament 'had the right to make or unmake any law whatever' [**5**], but even in the nineteenth century there were numerous political theorists who despaired of this suggestion. The philospher Herbert Spencer disparagingly wrote about the doctrine as a 'great political superstition',[27] and J. S. Mill warned that without new constitutional limitations on the power of democratic legislatures there would be a 'tyranny of the majority' [**118**]. Twentieth century developments with respect to the growth of government, the proliferation of new forms and methods of legislation of an interventionist nature, and the arrival of social democracy have revolutionized the previous equilibrium of the constitution and made it necessary that formal distinctions are drawn in the law of the modern state. The mass of legislation gen-erated each year since the early part of the century (annually now comprising around 50 parliamentary statutes and 1500 statutory instruments) is dominated by administrative orders and the conferring of regulatory powers to be exercised at the discretion of state officials. Such laws are of an obviously quite different nature to constitutional principles affecting the political structure of the state and the human rights of its citizens, yet are afforded the same status in the eyes of the

27 *Contemporary Review* 1884, republished in *The Man versus the State* (1914), p. 66.

courts and in the process by which Parliament may revoke or impliedly repeal them.

Equally, the theory that the common law, being subject to parliamentary sovereignty and its statutes, can still protect our human rights through its presumptions in favour of individual liberty is barely credible today. The common law may have operated successfully to protect basic freedoms in centuries past in the era before parliamentary statutes had become instruments of social and administrative regulation, but in the different framework of the modern state legal rights are now necessary in order to challenge oppressive state action when it occurs. As Nicolas Browne-Wilkinson, a law lord, has recently said in a House of Lords debate, 'Our traditional English freedoms are freedoms, not rights; and like any other common law freedoms they are subject to abridgement and curtailment by Act of Parliament … We have been found wanting by accident. It is an essential feature of any legislation in the modern state that it is bound to confer discretionary powers on the Exercise to operate the powers that are conferred by Parliament. Ministers are given power to make such regulations as they may think fit to achieve this result or others. It is the operation of those powers that has given rise to most of our infringements [of human rights at the European Court]' [**87**].

If a Bill of Rights is to provide a legal guarantee for the rights and freedoms it confers, the new constitution of which it forms part will need to distinguish between constitutional and ordinary law, with the former being deemed superior as a form of law to the latter. The same distinction will be necessary in our parliamentary procedures, with respect to the revocation or creation of constitutional matters. The constitution would thereby be entrenched as a body of fundamental or higher order law, committing certain fundamental 'rules of the game' of which human rights form an important part into the UK's political and legal system [**139**]. Such an arrangement is commonplace in the constitutional affairs of other countries. Its logic, as recently expressed by Sir John Laws, is that, 'The fundamental sinews of the constitution, the cornerstones of democracy and of inalienable rights, ought not by law to be in the keeping of the government, because the only means by which these principles may be enshrined in the state is by their possessing a status which no government has the right to destroy' [**141**].

But a new constitution will involve more than a redefinition of the power of Parliament; it must reform the internal workings of both Houses themselves. Since its Victorian heyday, at the height of the

British empire, Parliament has undergone a remorseless decline in its authority with respect to government and public affairs. The relationship between the House of Commons and the government was fundamentally altered early this century by the emergence of tightly organized party systems. A rigid party discipline emerged, such that parliamentary parties today have become instruments for managing and controlling the legislature, allowing party leaders in office to legislate at their discretion. The first-past-the-post electoral system has magnified the government's party majorities, made worse by the phasing-out of earlier double or multimember constituencies shortly after the 1945 election. The UK now operates the most distorted system of political representation of any country in Europe.[28] The UK electoral system produces a result that a party which fails by a wide margin to gain a majority of the popular vote can still command an overall majority of MPs and thus total control of the legislature and its law-making for the following five years. Margaret Thatcher's greatest electoral triumph in 1983 secured her 61 per cent of seats in the Commons from just 42 per cent of the popular vote. Tony Blair's even more historic electoral triumph in 1997, with a huge overall majority of 179 Labour MPs, was founded on 44 per cent of all votes cast at the general election. Meanwhile, the House of Lords, in previous centuries the most potent political check upon the executive, possessing a legislative veto over government measures of which it disapproved, has been allowed to become an indefensible anachronism for want of reform. First the executive neutralized its powers (culminating in the Parliament Act 1949),[29] and then successive governments have failed to modernize its hereditary-dominated membership so as to restore the chamber's authority.

Radical measures of parliamentary reform will therefore be necessary as part of a new constitutional settlement of which a Bill of Rights should form part. Although early days, the newly elected Labour government has clearly indicated that its programme of constitutional reform will embrace most of the most important issues. Labour's 1993 policy document *A New Agenda for Democracy* accepted that, 'Parliament itself is hopelessly out of date in the way it works'.[30] The Blair government's key reform proposals for action within its first term were laid out in the 1997 report of the Joint Consultative Committee on

28 See Robert Blackburn, *The Electoral System in Britain* (1995), Ch. 8.
29 See P. A. Bromhead, *The House of Lords and Contemporary Politics* (1958).
30 p. 35.

Constitutional Reform agreed with the Liberal Democrats, and extended to the workings of the Commons, the electoral system, and the future of the House of Lords. A Select Committee on modernizing the procedures of the House of Commons has now already been formed in order to examine parliamentary procedures and working methods generally. The Jenkins commission on the voting system for the House of Commons has recommended a proportional alternative to the first-past-the-post system, which is to be put to a referendum. Reform of the second chamber, the House of Lords, was perhaps the most prominently featured of all Labour's constitutional commitments leading up to the 1997 election campaign. 'There is an urgent need for radical reform of the Lords', both Labour and the Liberal Democrats have agreed.[31] Most immediately, the right of hereditary peers to sit and vote in the House is shortly to be abolished. A Royal Commission is being established to bring forward detailed proposals on the structure and functions for a new second chamber. In its deliberations, this Commission will be able to consider the wider implications of Lords' reform for other constitutional changes being considered, and examine any special role the Lords should play with respect to human rights generally, including legislative scrutiny for compliance with the ECHR and the approval of amendments or derogations to the provisions of any future UK Bill of Rights.[32]

THE SOCIAL AND POLITICAL VALUE OF A BILL OF RIGHTS

The fifth general ground for a Bill of Rights is that the measure would draw attention to fundamental values and serve as a point of reference in discussions on moral or political issues and in the scrutiny of public affairs. The educative and moral force of a Bill of Rights is an aspect of its implementation which has received little attention from lawyers, who continue to dominate the public and parliamentary debates on incorporation of the ECHR and a Bill of Rights in this country. Lawyers by virtue of their profession are riveted by the justifiability of a Bill of Rights and their arguments tend to revolve around how such a document might be interpreted and applied by the judiciary and what

31 Report of the Joint Committee on Constitutional Reform (1997), p. 17.
32 See below, p. 67ff.; and Robert Blackburn, 'The House of Lords', in Robert Blackburn and Raymond Plant (eds), *Constitutional Reform* (1999).

its impact would be upon the legal reasoning laid before the courts. But of course only a small proportion of the population will ever desire or need to commence litigation under the Bill of Rights. For the great mass of people, the chief significance of a Bill of Rights is less as a tool of legal litigation than as a symbolic political declaration of what their civil rights and freedoms are or should be. As the once Labour chairman and politics professor Harold J. Laski powerfully argued in his classic work *Liberty in the Modern State,* 'There is a real value in Bills of Rights which it is both easy, and mistaken, to under-estimate. Granted that the people are educated to the appreciation of their purpose, they serve to draw attention, as attention needs to be drawn, to the fact that vigilance is essential in the realm of what Cromwell called fundamentals' [**119**].

The quality of freedom in a country rests principally on its political and social culture – 'the spirit of a free people', as Sir Ivor Jennings put it [**10**] – together with widely diffused habits of toleration and a respect for minorities [**8**]. Even if the existence of a Bill of Rights is not in itself a pre-prerequisite of liberty, yet such a document can significantly help promote and mould the political and social conditions which are essential. Any society, particularly in a period of rapid change, requires the constant instilling of ethical concepts about human rights if they are to be widely respected and shared [**121**]. In the UK, there is no official statement of precisely what the constitutional rights and freedoms of the individual are, apart from the rather vague notion of a 'right to be let alone' – defined judicially by Lord Donaldson in the *Spycatcher* case as being 'every citizen has the right to do what he likes, unless restrained by the common law or by statute'. Guiding principles or values in more specific matters concerning individual rights and freedoms, dealing for example with sexual equality, free-dom of information, or personal privacy, are lacking. A Bill of Rights, then, could facilitate greater public awareness of human rights and civil liberties, as well as stressing the importance to be attached to them. In questions and discussions raising moral issues affecting them, whether conducted in political discourse, educational classes or people's everyday discussions, the principles and values expressed in our national Bill of Rights would be invoked and provide a point of reference. As the Institute for Public Policy Research has remarked, 'The Bill of Rights would provide us with a statement of principles, a set of basic values on which there would be a general consensus of support across the political spectrum (even though there would be disagreements about their implementation in practice). Learning about these principles would become part of the school curriculum and adult education, encouraging pupils and students to debate the importance of protecting human rights and the difficulties which arise when they conflict. Such a development would encourage a more informed public, more sensitive to the implications of restricting civil liberties and of extending them' [**139**].

The need for a UK Bill of Rights to perform this role in fostering and re-emphasizing respect for individual rights and freedoms has become stronger with a growing concern that whereas Britain was once a 'fortress for freedom', our contemporary history has in fact become one of steady erosion in our civil liberties, with individual rights and freedoms now widely regarded as being under threat from public and private power. Numerous instances of statutory provisions and administrative practices unjustified in human rights terms have arisen in recent decades, some of the most blatant being struck down by the European Court of Human Rights and others being the subject of critical commentary in legal expositions of civil liberties law in the UK.[33] These developments are as much a symptom as a cause of Britain's worrying decline in the international human rights community. Anthony Lester has described the UK's existing condition as one of 'ethical aimlessness and excessive bureaucratic discretionary powers' [**87**]. Observing that 'liberty is ill' in Britain, the American legal philosopher Ronald Dworkin has suggested that the UK is 'under threat by a decline in the *culture* of liberty – the community's shared sense that individual privacy and dignity and freedom of speech and conscience are crucially important and that they are worth considerable sacrifices or official inconvenience or public expense to protect' [**135**].

Within government and officialdom, a Bill of Rights will act as a point of reference to which public officeholders at all levels may refer and be referred. Until the Human Rights Act 1998, within our administrative and legislative process, there was no express recognition of human rights and nothing to encourage public officeholders systematically to take human rights factors into account when reaching their decisions. So far as Parliament itself is concerned, in Professor David Feldman's words, 'In order to protect rights, politicians must think them important' [**140**]. Parliament is traditionally the protector of our

---

33 See eg G. Robertson, *Freedom, the Individual and the Law* (7th edn, 1993); K. Ewing and C. Gearty, *Freedom under Thatcher* (1990); R. Dworkin, *A Bill of Rights for Britain* (1990).

civil liberties, yet formerly there was no rule or practice of parliamentary proceedings which explicitly drew the attention of MPs and peers to any domestic or international statements of basic individual rights. Government ministers routinely assured MPs that 'Strasbourg-proofing' arrangements existed within their departments so that those responsible for the preparation of legislation took the principles of the ECHR into account [26], though the UK's poor record before the Court of Human Rights [33] suggested considerably greater measures of internal audit were required.

A major advance in this important process of promoting internal government auditing of its own legislative preparation has now come through section 19 of the Human Rights Act 1998 [40a]. This provision requires the minister in charge of a Bill in either House to make a public statement to the effect that in his view the provisions of the Bill are compatible with the ECHR (a 'statement of compatibility'). In practice, such ministerial statements of compatibility are now published on the front of all government Bills presented to Parliament. Wherever in the future a minister is unable to make such a statement, under section 19(1)(b) he must instead publicly state that he is unable to make a statement of compatibility but the government nevertheless wishes Parliament to proceed with the Bill. The role of the forthcoming parliamentary committee on human rights, as promised by the Labour government, will be an important part of this new development, with an express remit for scrutinizing legislative measures against the principles of the ECHR and Strasbourg jurisprudence (see further below page 77).

A home-grown constitutional Bill of Rights, then, would take this whole process further, by sharpening politicians' attitudes towards civil liberties and human rights questions. It would elevate the quality of parliamentary scrutiny over particular items of proposed legislation for compliance with human rights by providing MPs and peers with a written framework of fundamental guiding principles to which all legislation should conform. Indeed, the terms of the Bill of Rights would very likely be adopted by at least one Standing and/or Select Committee in the House of Commons as part of its terms of reference for carrying out its legislative or administrative scrutiny. If the method of entrenching the Bill of Rights followed the proposal to give a reformed House of Lords a special function with respect to human rights [82], peers would already have the Bill of Rights built into its operational terms of reference. The government itself, both ministers and civil servants, would be subject to a far stronger discipline than that which exists at present to have regard to human rights principles in the preparation of legislation, and would be under an incentive to avoid judicial review proceedings being based upon the articles of the Bill of Rights.

Within the administration of justice, a Bill of Rights would raise the consciousness of lawyers and judges of the existence and importance of human rights. The system of justice would be driven to internalize the notion of human rights, with the courts permitting direct reference to them whether as expressed in the ECHR and/or a domestic Bill of Rights. At present there is an air of unreality about the legal arguments and judgments in cases carrying obvious implications for the freedom of the individual, such as those involving official secrecy, telephone-tapping or discrimination against gays in the armed forces, which must be argued in court in terms of private or normal administrative law principles. Furthermore, whereas many human rights complaints of individuals and minorities are effectively suppressed altogether because no legal basis exists upon which to challenge the decision of a public authority or official, too many grievances are simply allowed to fester. This is an unhealthy state of affairs, breeding alienation from the institutions of our democracy. Under a Bill of Rights by contrast, such prima facie grievances could be properly ventilated in court, with public authorities being required to justify their actions. In this way, a human rights culture would develop in the administration and use of the courts, one that was indigenous to the UK while consonant with our international human rights treaties. The process of familiarizing and educating UK judges at all levels, down to circuit judges, recorders and stipendiary magistrates will take a period of time, possibly up to two generations to achieve, similar to the process by which European Community law was slowly integrated into the legal culture of the UK following the 1972 European Communities Act over the course of the 1970s and 1980s. Against a fruitful background of the existing jurisprudence of the European Court of Human Rights and the body of comparative case law already developed in other Commonwealth common-law jurisdictions with human rights instruments, such as Canada and New Zealand, the administration of justice in the UK would adapt and accommodate the changes, supported by legal education and professional interests. As Ferdinand Mount has commented, 'The familiar argument that incorporation [of the ECHR] would diminish the relative importance of English common law seems to me precisely the reverse of the truth . . . Only by incorporating the European Convention do we rescue and revitalise the common law tradition – in much the same way as it has been rescued and revitalised in earlier centuries by the incorporation of other great charters into our law' [136]. Or as Lord Scarman has put it, the adoption of a Bill of Rights would 'freshen up the principles of the common law'.

That a UK Bill of Rights could serve as a valuable ethical and moral influence in modern society has been stressed many times by religious leaders in recent years. In 1988, a report on *Human Rights and Responsibilities in Britain and Ireland* produced by the Commission of the Churches of Britain and Ireland regarded the matter as being 'one of the first importance for all the inhabitants of these islands, especially for those who are members of minority communities', and urged the governments of the UK and Ireland to incorporate the human rights principles of the ECHR into their national legal systems [134]. The present Archbishop of Canterbury, George Carey, has indicated his support for incorporation of the ECHR in a speech he gave to the Council of Europe in 1993. The Bishop of Oxford in 1985 explained his support for a UK Bill of Rights upon the basis of his belief that there was a widespread fear among ordinary people in the UK that their human rights and fundamental freedoms were 'gradually being eroded' [84]. More recently when the subject was been raised in the House of Lords during debate on Lord Lester's Human Rights Bill in 1995, the Bishop of Southwark remarked that, 'The rights of the individual and the responsibility of nation states to maintain those rights are matters to which the Christian community is deeply committed ... What we should be supporting here is the opportunity to make the citizens of this nation more aware of their rights ... I believe that fundamentally we have nothing to fear from the proposal but much to gain' [87].

It is significant that a Bill of Rights has overwhelming public backing in the UK. There is a clear, self-evident popular appetite for the idea of individual rights being committed into writing, which in the case of constitutional and human rights will to some extent be fed by the low threshold of public awareness and understanding of what they are. Professional opinion polling confirms this mood backing a Bill of Rights [149]. In 1991, Market and Opinion Research International (MORI) undertook an extensive polling programme on constitutional issues for the Joseph Rowntree Trust, published as 'State of the Nation'. In response to the proposition, 'Rights and liberties can be most effectively protected if they are written down in a single law, a Bill of Rights', 79 per cent of respondents agreed, with only 5 per cent disagreeing (10 per cent undecided). To the more direct proposition,

'Britain needs a Bill of Rights to protect the liberty of the individual', again 79 per cent agreed. In 1995, a second MORI 'State of the Nation' survey again showed a strong majority supporting a Bill of Rights, extending further into widespread support for the associated, if more radical, proposal for a written Constitution. To the proposition, 'Britain needs a written Constitution providing clear legal rules within which Government ministers and civil servants are forced to operate', over 75 per cent of respondents agreed. Within British public opinion there is now a widespread, popular gut-feeling that the time for a new, modern constitutional framework has arrived, and one which will give central emphasis to the human rights and civil liberties of the individual.

As was pointed out during a parliamentary debate on a Bill of Rights in 1985, 'It is high time the voice of the citizen be heard in this discussion, not of course in contribution to the legal disputes but in definition of the social ends which the legal techniques are required to achieve' [84]. The symbolic and defining role of a Bill of Rights within society and our politics more generally may prove one of its most valuable constitutional functions.

III

The Contents of a UK Bill of Rights

THE FUNDAMENTAL RIGHTS AND FREEDOMS
TO BE PROTECTED

The initial major piece of work to confront a future commission charged with drafting a UK Bill of Rights will lie in the selection and wording of the individual rights and freedoms to be included in the document. Three considerations are likely to be of particular influence in its broad approach to this task. First, the commission will almost certainly define the nature of the articles to go into the Bill of Rights in terms of their political and civil nature (freedom of speech, personal liberty, equality and the like), as distinct from rights of a more social or economic nature (health, housing, social security and the like). This would certainly follow the pattern of virtually all comparative Bills of Rights abroad and the general view that social and economic rights tend not to be appropriate for interpretation and enforcement by courts of law. Second, the detail of the Bill of Rights should be compatible with the UK's international human rights law obligations, notably under the International Covenant on Civil and Political Rights and the European Convention on Human Rights. Third, the articles should be drafted in such a way as to command the widest possible consensus of support in parliamentary, legal and popular opinion. This last consideration is perhaps the most problematic. It is clearly desirable that the Bill of Rights commission presents its drafting of the human rights articles to go into the Bill which stands a good prospect of being acceptable as a whole across the political spectrum. If events prove otherwise, there is a danger – the level of its gravity depending upon the political situation and the precise relations between the political parties at any particular moment in time – of the political parties or factional sections within the House of Commons arguing interminably over which are the most basic human rights to be included in a Bill of Rights, and where the greater emphasis should lie in drafting the balance between the rights of the individual and collective interests of the community.

These considerations will lead the future Bill of Rights commission to draw heavily upon existing international and comparative Bill of Rights (the most important and relevant of which are documented in Chapters 2 and 4). The provisions of the ECHR and ICCPR will be specially influential and are likely to provide the starting point for the Bill of Rights commission, particularly so if, as now seems certain, the ECHR will by then have been incorporated by Act of Parliament into the UK legal system as an interpretative instrument. Within the UK, there have already been a number of valuable blueprints for reform, giving detailed drafts and explanations of what a UK Bill of Rights might consist, the most important of which have indeed chosen to adopt or adapt the articles and wording of the ICCPR and/or the ECHR.

The most important of these blueprints was produced in 1991 as part of the comprehensive constitutional reform project undertaken by the Institute for Public Policy Research (IPPR) led by James Cornford, published as *A Written Constitution for the United Kingdom.*[34] IPPR's large-scale work has had a significant impact on the reform debate across the political left-of-centre, described by the New Statesman as 'a genuinely pioneering exercise ... one of the most valuable initiatives in modern British politics',[35] and prompting the Labour Party's constitutional spokesman at that time to present a Written Constitution Bill to the House of Commons [**78**]. An important component of IPPR's written constitution was its draft Bill of Rights, a free-standing version of which was published earlier in 1990, under the title *A British Bill of Rights* [**49**]. It is the model for reform which currently commands the widest consensus of support across the Labour and Liberal Democrat parties, the latter of whom have expressed their support for it in their own policy documents [**93**]. IPPR's drafting of the human rights articles was drawn exclusively from the ECHR and ICCPR, with only one exception (on rights to asylum, where neither international treaty contains any provision), forming an amalgam of the best wording from each or that which is most appropriate for UK conditions. A second valuable blueprint for reform drawing on the international human rights treaties came from the National Council for Civil Liberties (Liberty) in 1991, published as *A People's Charter* [**50**]. Its recommended drafting of individual rights and freedoms was largely based on the ECHR, but included additional or alternative

34 *Supra*, note 25.
35 *New Statesman*, 20 August 1993.

elements from a wide range of other international and comparative documents, and occasionally including some of its own principles or those of other civil liberties organizations of which it approved, for example in relation to the extent of prohibited grounds for discrimination, the right to public information, and freedom from medical experimentation without informed consent. Earlier significant models for a Bill of Rights, including those of John Macdonald QC in 1969 [**51**] and Joseph Jaconelli in 1980 [**53**], are largely of historical interest today. John Macdonald has recently lent his support to the IPPR draft Bill of Rights.

Abroad, most Bills of Rights among the liberal democracies, particularly members of the Commonwealth, have been strongly influenced by the ECHR and ICCPR. In Hong Kong, shortly before the British government's transfer of authority for its government to China, the UK supervised the legal construction of a Bill of Rights based on articles of the ICCPR to which China is a party [**47**]. Most recently, the South African Bill of Rights, drafted as part of the new constitution of the country, contains several interesting and new developments which might be of influence in the UK, such as in relation to rights concerning disability discrimination and the environment [**48**].

In the past, some have suggested that the articles of the ECHR should be adopted, exactly as they stand, for a UK Bill of Rights. The House of Lords Select Committee on a Bill of Rights recommended this in 1977, expressing the view that in the circumstances then prevailing 'the only feasible way of proceeding was to rest on the European Convention on Human Rights' [**83**]. Most of the legislative proposals on the subject coming from MPs and Peers inside Parliament have chosen to take this approach, including Alan Beith's Bill of Rights Bill 1975 and Lord Wade's Bill of Rights Bill 1981 [**39**]. So did Peter Wallington and Jeremy McBride (both now law professors) in their draft Bill of Rights for their 1976 booklet *Civil Liberties and a Bill of Rights* [**52**]. Even if these proposals are viewed as a form of Bill of Rights, most people would still see adoption of the ECHR principles in a Bill of Rights as a transitional stage towards a charter of rights being drafted specifically for our own indigenous social and political purposes. The great majority of those today who wish to see a constitutional Bill of Rights constructed for the UK view the proposal for legal recognition as of the ECHR as a quite separate matter concerning its 'incorporation' as a code of European obligations directly applicable in our domestic legal system. Certainly, the human rights principles of the ECHR should, and shortly will, be incorporated and made available to the UK courts for general interpretative purposes, in the review of administrative discretionary powers, and to achieve consistency between the principles of European law with our own.[36] But, for reasons emphasized throughout this book, this is something additional and separate to a constitutional Bill of Rights, not a substitute.

Elsewhere among the 40 present members of the Council of Europe, all other member states except Ireland have incorporated the ECHR and in addition the great majority of these countries possess their own constitutional Bill of Rights. Within the European Union, all other countries except Ireland have incorporated the ECHR and every member state including Ireland has its own indigenous Bill of Rights. While, as stated, the ECHR together with the ICCPR represents a good starting point for a UK code on human rights, having been tried and tested as a broad common denominator in the international law of the Council of Europe for the past 40 years, as a constitutional statement of the rights and freedoms to which the British people aspire in the twenty-first century, the principles of the Convention need extending and their focus sharpening. Labour's own 1993 policy document expressly recognized this [**112**], and writers including John Wadham and Joseph Jaconelli have presented detailed reasons why the principles of the ECHR are insufficient as articles for a domestic Bill of Rights [**143, 130**]. Some of the ECHR's restrictions on the freedoms, which were recognized as necessary in the aftermath of World War II, are not appropriate in the UK today. Most obviously, ideological developments have taken place in our social and moral values (for example in the field of discrimination and sexuality) and technological developments have thrown up new difficulties (affecting for example the right to information and the protection of privacy).

It has been suggested that the architects of a UK Bill of Rights are unlikely to include rights of a social and economic nature in the document. However, even if human rights relating to the workplace,

---

36 In so far as some of these blueprints for reform seek to give the articles of the ECHR a measure of superiority in UK law, so that they will prevail over earlier legislation and in certain circumstances later enactments, these documents do bear some of the hallmarks of a constitutional measure and a Bill of Rights. Thus each of Wallington and McBride's proposal [**52**], Graham Allen's Human Rights Bill 1994 [**39d**] and Lord Lester's Human Rights Bill 1994 [**39e**] contained semi entrenchment clauses (see pages 62–4) which would be similar in their legal effect to Canada's Charter of Rights and Freedoms and have a higher status in law than the New Zealand Bill of Rights.

housing, social security, health and the like are accepted as not being amenable to the legal process of judicial enforcement under a constitutional Bill of Rights, consideration could be given to the drafting of a statement of social and economic rights to serve as an authoritative declaration of principles upon which existing and future government policy should be conducted.[37] This declaration could appear in a separate part of the Bill, making reference also to the relevant international covenants and charters to which the UK is a treaty signatory, notably the Council of Europe Social Charter (1961) [23], the UN Covenant on Economic, Social and Cultural Rights (1966) [21] and the Community Charter of Fundamental Social Rights for Workers (1990). The value of this declaration, if deemed suitable for inclusion in the Bill, would therefore not lie in the realm of legal remedies but as a point of public and parliamentary reference. It might also form part of the responsibilities of the future Human Rights Commission to prepare advisory reports on the compatibility of legislative and administrative developments with the social and economic principles expressed in the Bill.

37 The Institute for Public Policy Research prepared a non-legal declaration of social and economic rights, not as part of its Bill of Rights proposal [49] but in its later report on *A Written Constitution for the United Kingdom* (1993). Under Article 27, it provided:

> In making provision for the social and economic welfare of the people of the United Kingdom, Parliament . . . shall be guided by the principles contained in the International Covenants and Charters to which the United Kingdom is signatory, and in particular by –
>
> (1)   the right of workers to earn their living in an occupation freely entered upon;
>
> (2)   the right of everyone to an adequate standard of living, including adequate food, clothing and housing;
>
> (3)   the right of everyone to social security;
>
> (4)   the right of everyone to the enjoyment of the highest attainable standard of physical and mental health;
>
> (5)   the right of everyone to education;
>
> (6)   the right of workers to resort to collective action in the event of a conflict of interest, including the right to strike;
>
> (7)   the right of every worker to enjoy satisfactory health and safety conditions in their working environment.

THE LEGAL AND JUDICIAL PROCESS UNDER A BILL OF
RIGHTS

Most draft proposals for a Bill of Rights would permit the individual
rights conferred to be enforceable through the ordinary courts. British
citizens would be able to institute legal proceedings upon the basis
that their human rights and freedoms, as conferred by the Bill of
Rights, had been infringed, seeking from the court restraining orders as
appropriate and/or damages. The majority view, therefore, including
the IPPR and Liberty draft Bills, does not recommend that a special
court be established for hearing complaints of human rights violations.
Thus the human rights principles of both the incorporated Convention
and a new, home-grown Bill of Rights would become a full part of the
legal and judicial process as a whole, not confined to some special
tribunal with exclusive jurisidiction. The only exception to this might
be that whenever the validity of any provision of an Act of Parliament
was challenged under the Bill of Rights, the question should be
referred to the High Court or, as the case may be, the Court of Session
in Scotland or the Northern Ireland High Court. This would be similar
to the procedure under the Human Rights Act 1998, section 4, where
only specified superior courts may make 'a declaration of incompatibility' between domestic legislation and the principles of the ECHR.
Applications founded upon an alleged breach of one of the articles in
a home-grown Bill of Rights would therefore be made to the High
Court, with the Rule Committee of the Royal Courts of Justice determining details of procedure. If the originating process was by way of
judicial review proceedings, as envisaged in the IPPR proposal, it
would be natural for human rights cases to go to the Divisional Court
of the Queen's Bench Division. A right of appeal would lie to the
Court of Appeal and thereafter on a point of law of public general
importance to the House of Lords.

There have been two sources of suggestions for some special form
of human rights court, however. First, the Labour Party's 1993 policy
document [112], and an article in similar terms written in 1996 by
Lord Irvine,[38] now lord chancellor, for the Society of Labour Lawyers
on incorporation of the ECHR, envisaged the addition to the final
appellate court (the House of Lords) of three non-lawyer members

---

38 Lord Irvine, 'The Legal System and Law Reform under Labour', in D. Bean (ed.),
Law Reform for All (1996), p. 20.

when deciding a case involving human rights law. This is an interesting proposal, and poses some difficult questions. For example, would the lay members give reasoned judgments along with the law lords, and assuming that they must do so, what would the legal authority (both in theory and practice) of their published judgments be for future cases? The qualification of these three lay persons, the Labour document says, would be that they were drawn from a panel of persons 'with knowledge and understanding of society and of human rights in the broad sense'. This too poses some practical problems, particularly as to a clear understanding and general acceptance as to precisely who or what discipline is able to claim such expert understanding and knowledge of society and individual liberty. Second, and bearing some similarity, in 1977 Peter Wallington and Jeremy McBride proposed a Constitutional Court to which all questions of law concerning the interpretation, application or effect of the Bill of Rights would be referred when they arose in any court or tribunal proceedings [52]. This Court would consist of nine judges, six of whom were qualified to hold high judicial office, and three of whom to be persons 'not necessarily legally qualified, who have knowledge and experience in the field of human rights'. Wallington and McBride also recommended that the appointment of all nine judges should be subject to the approval of the House of Commons, expressed in a resolution passed by a two-thirds majority of those present and voting.

Unless otherwise provided for, corporations would be able to bring legal proceedings under the terms of the Bill of Rights as well as individuals. In other words, it would be possible for commercial companies to challenge the validity of administrative regulations and statutory provisions on grounds of their incompatibility with fundamental freedoms. Other foreign Bills of Rights allow this form of litigation, though it is rare, including the Canadian Charter (where for example legislation prohibiting Sunday trading has been held to be in violation of freedom of religion and conscience).[39] The ECHR, too, grants corporations certain fundamental rights, notably protection of property (guaranteed under article 1 of the first Protocol to every 'natural or legal person') and freedom of expression, empowering UK newspapers to bring several well-known cases before the Strasbourg Court of Human Rights (for example, the *Thalidomide* and *Spycatcher* cases brought by *The Sunday Times* and *Guardian* newspapers

---

39 P. W. Hogg, *Constitutional Law of Canada* (3rd edn, 1992).

respectively). However, the Labour Party has expressed serious concern about the prospect of commercially associated human rights
litigation, leading both John Smith in his 1993 speech on constitutional reform [**110**] and Lord Irvine in his 1996 article (referred to
above) to say that a Human Rights Act incorporating the ECHR should
be drafted in such a manner that corporations were not to be protected
in UK courts by its terms. 'The rights we seek to protect are those of the
individual against the state', they both stated, with John Smith explaining that, 'We do not want to repeat here the confusion and injustice
that has occurred in some other countries, where companies and
commercial organisations have tried to resist social legislation controlling their activities by claiming that it infringes their 'human rights'
'. If this view prevails, then the Bill of Rights for the sake of clarity
should state its application to be limited to 'natural persons', as
recommended in the Liberty proposal [**50**].

The framers of a UK Bill of Rights will then need to address the
problem of whether liability for human rights violations should be
confined to government and public bodies alone, or whether liability
should apply generally and extend to private bodies and individuals.
The question of liability has both symbolic and practical importance
in the protection of basic rights. Within the Labour Party, there has
been a long-standing suspicion of private power, combined with the
view that restrictions to safeguard individuals from oppressive actions
by powerful private sector bodies are equally as important as controls
over the public sector. Clearly there are many private bodies, particularly large corporate employers and media organizations, which
possess great power over individuals open to the possibility of abuse
in human rights terms. Factors conducive to leaving liability open to
both private and public sector alike include the fact that in recent
years state functions which affect fundamental rights in the UK have
increasingly been transferred to the private sector. Furthermore, under
the ECHR, member states are obliged to take measures to protect
individuals from violations of their rights by private bodies and
individuals.

The formula likely to emerge under a home-grown Bill of Rights,
however, is likely to restrict liability for human rights violations to
persons or bodies who can be said to be performing some kind of
'public' function or business. The provisions framed by the government for the purposes of the Human Rights Act 1998, at sections 6 and
7, limited liability for breaches of the ECHR to a 'public authority'.
This term is further defined in section 6(3)(b) to include 'any person

certain of whose functions are functions of a public nature'. Thus, whilst the precise extent of liability under the Act awaits elaboration in future cases brought over the next few years, it clearly extends beyond obviously public bodies (such as government departments, local authorities, the police and immigration officials) to other bodies carrying on services or undertakings of a public nature. Such quasi-public bodies will be liable for breaches of the ECHR only whilst acting in the performance of their public functions. During parliamentary debate on the Human Rights Bill, Lord Irvine (the Lord Chancellor) gave Railtrack as an example. The company would be liable in its business as a safety regulator, he said, but not in its capacity as a property developer [**40d**].

Most of the draft Bill of Rights that has so far been produced, including those of IPPR and Liberty, have similarly taken a middle course of stating that their human rights articles are to apply to any person or body 'in the performance of any public function' [**49, 50**]. Graham Allen's Human Rights Bill 1994 [**39d**] presents a more elaborate model, providing for the liability of 'a) a Minister of the Crown or any person or body acting on behalf of, or for the purposes of, the Crown, and b) any statutory body, public body, or any person holding statutory office or exercising any public function'. 'Public body' is then defined to extend to any 'body of persons, whether corporate or unincorporate, carrying on a service or undertaking of a public nature and includes public authorities of all descriptions and any individual or body that exercises any public function.'

On the remedies that might be sought by a person for civil rights violations, the IPPR blueprint provides a right to damages, the relevant clause on legal proceedings stating that, 'Without prejudice to any right to apply for judicial review, any person whose rights or freedoms protected by the Bill of Rights have been infringed or are threatened with infringement may bring civil proceedings for damages, an injunction or any other relief authorised by rules of court'. Lord Lester's Human Rights Bill 1994 in its original drafting might prove a useful legislative precedent on this point [**39e**], containing a clause that would have treated a violation of its principles by any person in the performance of any public function as being actionable as a breach of statutory duty, thereby conferring a right to damages, 'creating what is in essence a constitutional tort', as Lord Lester put it.

By contrast, under the Human Rights Act 1998, the courts will be left to develop their own discretionary remedies in such cases. Under section 8, the court 'may grant such relief or remedy, or make such order, within its powers as it considers just and appropriate'. However, while discretionary remedies may be acceptable for incorporation of the ECHR, particularly as the courts in any event would be bound by Article 13 of the Convention which directs them to provide an 'effective remedy' against public authorities, under a new Bill of Rights the aggrieved citizen should have a stronger claim. Liberty's Bill of Rights, at Article 24, went furthest in expressing the remedies that might be available to petitioners, expressly providing for financial compensation, injunctions, orders quashing the decision of any public body held to be in breach of the Bill of Rights, and enforcement orders [50].

Virtually all existing Bill of Rights proposals agree that the courts, in interpreting the precise meaning and application of the principles and wording of the Bill of Rights in any case before them, should view their meaning within the context of international perceptions of them. 'Judicial notice', in other words legal argument by advocates before the court and the reasoned judgments of the court, should take into account the reports of the European Commission of Human Rights and the judgments and advisory opinions of the European Court of Human Rights. For the purposes of the Human Rights Act, any court or tribunal determining a question relating to the ECHR must 'take into account' (but, it should be noted, is not bound by) the jurisprudence and decisions of the European Court and Commission of Human Rights. The Liberty and IPPR Bills of Rights would further direct the courts to take judicial notice of the UN International Covenant on Civil and Political Rights, which would include the reports and expressions of views by the UN Human Rights Committee. The British courts, when interpreting a new Bill of Rights, can be expected of their own volition to be prepared to admit arguments founded upon analogous legal cases decided abroad, especially in the USA and Commonwealth countries. So too, should they be expected to pay attention to the rulings of international human rights tribunals. A widely shared sentiment among those who favour a British Bill of Rights is that it should operate firmly within the context of international human rights law.

METHODS OF ENTRENCHING A UK BILL OF RIGHTS

One of the most controversial issues to be settled in the construction of a UK Bill of Rights concerns the legal and constitutional status of the document. A Bill of Rights will need to be entrenched in some way, according to most supporters of the reform, as is most commonly the case with Bills of Rights in other countries. Entrenchment will involve some superior legal status and priority over ordinary legislation being conferred upon the Bill of Rights, as well as some special legislative process being laid down governing future amendments or measures to suspend the operation of the Bill of Rights (see below, page 67). There are, effectively, three broad types of model which will need to be considered by the framers of a Bill of Rights in considering the status of the document. These might usefully be categorized as:

1. constitutional entrenchment;
2. qualified entrenchment, creating a quasi-constitutional instrument;
3. judicial interpretative status, or some hybrid variant distinguishing between earlier and later laws.

As will be seen, the first option challenges traditional dogmas about the possibility of ever being able to establish a body of higher law or a written constitution in the UK. The second option has proved the most widely recommended formula by those who have presented blueprints on what the form of a UK Bill of Rights might be. The third option deserves consideration because this is the status given to the principles of the ECHR in the Human Rights Act, and also because of recent experiments abroad (notably in New Zealand and Hong Kong) which have given interpretative status to legal documents termed a 'Bill of Rights'. An interpretative code of citizens' rights, however, is not an entrenched document. While suitable as a form of incorporating judicial recognition of international human rights obligations such as the ECHR or ICCPR directly into domestic law, it is is ill-suited to the constitutional requirements expected of a true Bill of Rights.

Constitutional entrenchment

In order to appreciate the problems and realistic alternatives with which the framers of a UK Bill of Rights will be faced, it is important first to be clear about the legal and constitutional context within which the Bill of Rights would be enacted. If a UK Bill of Rights was to be enacted as a normal Act of Parliament, its provisions would be overriden by later legislative developments, including ones which clearly infringed the articles of the Bill of Rights, either deliberately or inadvertently. This is because the traditional guiding principle of the common law is that where two statutes conflict, provisions in the later one should always be held to prevail. However, although Bills of Rights do exist in other countries as either merely interpretative devices in judicial review (such as New Zealand) or even possessing a non-legal status altogether (such as in Holland), most supporters of a constitutional Bill of Rights for the UK do intend the document to possess some special legal and parliamentary significance, such that it will indeed exert some measure of control over offending provisions in later legislation which are held to be in violation of human rights principles. Labour's 1993 policy document specifically mentioned that the commission established on a Bill of Rights will inquire into a 'suitable method of entrenchment' [**112**].

The difficulty confronting full entrenchment of a Bill of Rights in the UK is that under its unwritten constitution there is no technical distinction between constitutional law and ordinary legislation. Thus, a taxation statute has a similar legal standing as the Habeas Corpus or the Sex Discrimination Acts. Under orthodox UK legal doctrine, there is no such thing as a 'higher order law'. The classic exposition of this view, well-known to all lawyers, was propounded in 1885 by the Oxford jurist A. V. Dicey, writing in his influential book *The Law of the Constitution*. Referring to the doctrine as that of 'parliamentary sovereignty', Dicey described its three traits as being, 'First, the power of the legislature to alter any law, fundamental or otherwise, as freely and in the same manner as other laws; secondly, the absence of any legal distinction between constitutional and other laws; thirdly, the non-existence of any judicial or other authority having the right to nullify an Act of Parliament, or to treat it as void or unconstitutional' [**5**].

The traditional view of entrenchment in the UK, therefore, whereby a legal document might seek primacy for itself over future parliamentary legislation, is that it is a legal impossibility. Regretfully, this source of technical obstruction was given greater credibility by the Report of the House of Lords Select Committee on a Bill of Rights in 1978. Although the Committee backed a UK Bill of Rights, it was a disappointment to many advocates of a Bill of Rights (and indeed despite some authoritative advice favourable to the possibility of entrenchment, including from the former lord chancellor, Lord Hailsham) that its Report accepted that 'there is no way in which a Bill of Rights could be made immune altogether from amendment or repeal by a subsequent Act' [**83**]. Their specialist adviser, Mr G. Rippengal, adopted a restrictive legal approach to the issue, relying heavily on some judicial precedents, notably *Vauxhall Estates* v *Liverpool Corporation* (1932)[40] and *Re Ellen Street* (1934),[41] which were clearly distinguishable on grounds of their subject-matter and relative constitutional importance, to evince a conclusion that clauses in a Bill of Rights purporting to apply to future legislation would be inoperable and a conflicting later statute would always prevail. In his memorandum to the Committee, he wrote that 'under our existing constitution there is no way in which the provisions of a Bill of Rights could effectively be entrenched' [74]. According to Mr Rippengal's analysis, all offensive statutes passed after a UK purportedly entrenched Bill of Rights would be upheld, and the Bill of Rights as a statement of fundamental human rights law would thereby be progressively eroded.[42]

Such legal arguments when applied to the prospect of a fully entrenched UK Bill of Rights are misplaced. They fail to recognize the political significance of the constitutional change that is being considered. A fully entrenched Bill of Rights would be equivalent in status to that of a written constitution. Exactly the same technical legal objections on grounds of parliamentary sovereignty could be addressed at the prospect of a comprehensive written constitution for the UK, as proposed in recent years by the IPPR, by the Liberal Democrat party, by Tony Benn MP, and by Labour's former constitutional spokesman Graham Allen MP. If a new, written constitution for the UK was introduced, it would itself become the fundamental source of legal authority in the state, as in the USA, Germany or France, and it would politically supercede earlier common-law notions about the sovereignty of the Crown-in-Parliament. Any suggestions from lawyers about the impossibility of entrenching the provisions of a written constitution, because of the doctrine of parliamentary sovereignty, would clearly be misconceived. That line of argument would become as politically relevant as any view held since 1688 that parliamentary sovereignty was itself unlawful by reference to earlier concepts of the Divine Right of Kings.

The implementation of a fully entrenched Bill of Rights, as with the implementation of a written constitution, would be a political act,

---

40 [1932] 1 KB 733.
41 [1934] 1 KB 590.
42 For a critique of Mr. Rippengal's analysis, see A. W. Bradley, 'The Sovereignty of Parliament – in Perpetuity?', in J. Jowell and D. Oliver (eds), *The Changing Constitution* (3rd edn, 1994), p. 104.

introducing a new legal settlement within the structure of government. The determining factor in the enactment of any constitutional reform touching on the fundamentals of government is the political will of the nation, not questions of legal technicality. All constitutions are in essence political. They are born of political purpose, they describe political facts, and they depend upon political acceptance. If Parliament convenes a new constitutional and legal settlement, as would be the case in the implementation of a fully entrenched Bill of Rights, it is most unlikely the judges will refuse to accept it. The question is not what judges *can* do, but what they *will* do. If they accept the purpose of the Bill of Rights, they will find means of judicial principle to follow. The implementation of full entrenchment might present formidable obstacles but these are by no means insuperable. Clearly, some special legal and political devices would be necessary to help legitimize the new state of affairs, and a simple declaration of legal entrenchment in the enactment of a Bill of Rights would be inadequate. If the measure were railroaded through the House of Commons and House of Lords in the teeth of opposition, it might prove difficult for judges wholly to accept its purpose. However, so long as care is taken in the political and legal implementation of entrenchment, judges would not assert a superior political right to reject it founded upon legal precedent; they would embrace its purpose. Means of facilitating acceptance of a fully entrenched Bill of Rights in legal doctrine might include a number of devices. First, it would be politically desirable for an express constitutional statement to be agreed by Parliament and published along with the Bill of Rights, proclaiming the primacy of the Bill of Rights over the common-law rule known as 'parliamentary sovereignty'. Second, the Bill of Rights, and the establishment of this revised legal basis of the constitution, would significantly benefit from a clear expression of political and popular endorsement. In practice, this would require the moral backing of a referendum in its favour, and preferably a clear consensus of all-party support. Third, as Sir William Wade has suggested [76], the terms of the judicial oath of office might be altered by general agreement to include a reference to the Bill of Rights and its supremacy in the legal system. And fourth, the lord chancellor might submit a Practice Statement for approval by the House of Lords referring to the special position of the Bill of Rights, in the same way that in 1966 the House of Lords by Practice Statement made the important change in legal doctrine that it was no longer bound by its own earlier decisions.

The first option, therefore, for entrenching a UK Bill of Rights is to constitute the Bill of Rights' provisions as a fundamental corpus of law having priority over all earlier and later ordinary legislation. The Bill of Rights' status would be that of a higher order than that of a normal Act of Parliament, similar to the civil liberties and human rights articles to be found within written constitutions around the world.

Qualified entrenchment

The commission established to inquire into a UK Bill of Rights may conclude that a fully entrenched Bill of Rights is too revolutionary to existing British traditions, and that such direct confrontation with legal and constitutional dogma is best sidestepped if at all possible, assuming some other effective form of entrenchment can be found. A number of alternatives exist for establishing a system of qualified judicial entrenchment, endowing the Bill of Rights with a quasi-constitutional status. These possibilities all involve (a) some suitable form of wording being inserted into a section of the Bill of Rights dealing with its effect on earlier and later enactments, which creates an elevated status in law for the document and its human rights principles, but (b) envisage either expressly or impliedly that Parliament fully retains the power to legislate in direct contradiction to the Bill of Rights if it expressly chooses so to do. There are various drafting models to be considered in the legal systems of other Commonwealth or European countries and in the detailed proposals formulated by some parliamentarians and research bodies, which fall within this category of limited entrenchment (generally, see Chapters 4 and 5 in Part Two of the book). Each of these models presents some difference of emphasis in terms of its instruction to the courts or the precise status of the Bill of Rights, and some of the suggestions combine different mechanisms in the parliamentary process for overriding the Bill of Rights.

A widely favoured scheme is for the Bill of Rights to contain a declaration of primacy over all other law (either directly, or using a form of words incontrovertably having this effect), but provide for later Acts of Parliament to prevail if they contain a section expressing an intention to take effect notwithstanding the Bill of Rights. Such a legislative model was envisaged in Labour's 1993 policy document as to the legal status sought for a Human Rights Act incorporating the ECHR (which, in the event, seems unlikely to be carried out). This is in effect the method of entrenchment adopted by Canada in its Charter of Rights and Freedoms [**45**]. Section 33 of the Canadian Charter states that the federal Parliament or the legislature of a province 'may expressly declare in an Act of Parliament or of the legislature, as the case may be, that the Act or a provision thereof shall operate notwithstanding' the fundamental rights and freedoms contained in the Charter. This formula for conferring upon a UK Bill of Rights a superior status in the legal system might appear to be much more firmly qualified than one which was drafted simply to assert that all existing law and later legislation should be construed and applied subject to its human rights principles, by virtue of the fact that the limitations upon its primacy are actually envisaged within the document and expressly provided for. However, this formula is likely to achieve a form of entrenchment that is in fact more deeply rooted. This is because, first, a simple statement of legal primacy would not serve to effect full entrenchment. As stated above, full entrenchment would require some further act of constitutional resettlement. Its effect, at best, would be to emulate the judicial interpretation of the entrenchment section contained within the European Communities Act 1972 [**77**]. Second, a judicial implication which might clearly be drawn from this method of entrenchment providing for later 'notwithstanding' legislation is that in the construction of all ordinary legislation, Parliament must have intended that any possible future conflict of its provisions with the Bill of Rights should be resolved in favour of basic human rights and freedoms. For if Parliament had intended otherwise, it would have included a 'notwithstanding' clause in the legislation.

The effect of this particular method of entrenchment, therefore, is to provide the judiciary with a stronger legal argument whereby they may attribute primacy to principles contained within the Bill of Rights in the process of interpreting any legislation which does not contain a 'notwithstanding' clause. This has certainly proved the case in Canada where its Supreme Court has invalidated provisions in an Act of Parliament for being inconsistent with the Bill of Rights.[43] Along even stronger lines, the UK courts could alternatively take the view that the effect of a Canadian-style notwithstanding clause scheme is that it falls within the scope of the 'manner and form' doctrine,[44] well-known to

---

43 *R. v. Drybones* [1970] SCR 282. Generally see P. W. Hogg, *Constitutional Law of Canada* (3rd edn, 1992), Ch. 32.
44 See also Wade and Bradley, *Constitutional and Administrative Law* (7th edn by A. Bradley and K. Ewing, 1993), Ch. 5, part C.

all UK and Commonwealth constitutional lawyers when addressing legal problems of parliamentary sovereignty [**81**]. If this proved to be the analysis of the courts, Parliament would be regarded as having bound itself as to the future manner and form of any of its Acts which may be held inconsistent with the Bill of Rights: such legislation must be enacted complete with a notwithstanding clause. Third, the actual limitation on entrenchment represented by the proviso for notwith-standing clause legislation is likely in practice to prove politically very restrictive. To include such a clause in government legislation would advertise the fact that ministers knew they were debasing human rights. The House of Commons and House of Lords are most unlikely to agree to such a clause in any legislation, in the absence of real emergency or crisis conditions where there exists strong overriding reasons of national interest.

Most of the proposals for a UK Bill of Rights have sought some form of qualified entrenchment of the kind under discussion. The commission on a Bill of Rights will find useful precedents in the IPPR and Liberty proposals, and also in a few of the blueprints for incorporation of the ECHR where a form of qualified entrenchment was included, notably Lord Lester's Human Rights Bill 1994 in its original form. Of interest also in this respect is Labour's 1993 policy document on incorporation of the ECHR, where it advocates a Canadian form of qualified superiority for the ECHR in UK law. 'It is often argued', the policy document reads, 'that in technical terms a British Act of Parliament cannot be "entrenched". We propose to protect the Human Rights Act from being undermined by either Parliament or the courts by a clause that requires that any other Act that is intended to introduce laws inconsistent with the Convention must do so specifically and in express terms' [**112**].

A comparison between the recommendations of IPPR, Lord Lester and Liberty on matters relating to the compatibility between human rights and ordinary legislation is instructive. IPPR's Bill of Rights, as worded in clause C, would ostensibly permit the High Court to nullify *any* Act of Parliament, or subordinate legislation, that conflicted with the terms of the Bill of Rights. The relevant part of their Bill provides that, 'Any provision of an Act of Parliament or subordinate legislation shall be void if and to the extent that (a) it requires or authorises anything to be done or omitted in contravention of any provision of the Bill of Rights; or (b) it prohibits the exercise of any right or freedom protected by the Bill of Rights; or (c) it restricts the exercise of any such right or freedom in a manner not authorised by the Bill of Rights.'

Similarly, on the face of its wording, Lord Lester's Human Rights Bill 1994 provided that the incorporated principles of the ECHR 'shall have effect notwithstanding any rule of law to the contrary' and that, 'An Act of Parliament or any instrument made by or under an Act of Parliament or an Order in Council (whether passed or made before or after the passing of this Act) shall not be enforced and may not be relied upon in any legal proceedings . . . if and to the extent that to do so would deprive a person of any of the rights and freedoms defined [in the Convention].'

However, the net effect of these two clauses of IPPR and Lord Lester, as their authors were aware, would fail to achieve full legal superiority over later Acts of Parliament that expressly sought to take effect in breach of the Bill of Rights. The legal consequence of both provisions could be no more than that they were treated by the judiciary in the same way as the courts have interpreted the application of section 2(4) of the European Communities Act 1972, which specifies that any domestic Act of Parliament 'shall be construed and have effect subject to' the laws of the European Community. As graphically seen in the *Ex parte Factortame* case (1991), where a House of Lords ruling suspended the operation of the Merchant Shipping Act 1988, the entrenching words in the 1972 Act has succeeded in directing our courts to interpret all legislative provisions and the common law so as to comply with European legal obligations [**77**]. It has thereby succeeded in conferring superiority upon European law, subject to a proviso, as put by Lord Denning in *Macarthys* v *Smith* (1979), that, 'If the time should come when our Parliament deliberately passes an Act with the intention of repudiating the Treaty or any provision in it or intentionally of acting inconsistently with it and says so in express terms then I should have thought it would be the duty of our courts to follow the statute of our Parliament'.[45] In other words, under IPPR's and Lord Lester's proposals, the Bill of Rights would be given primacy over all later conflicting legislation except for Acts of Parliament which contained an express provision that it would take effect notwithstanding anything to the contrary contained within the Bill of Rights.

The legal status which Liberty's proposals would confer upon the Bill of Rights is broadly similar in its effect to IPPR's and Lord Lester's, being one of primacy over all later legislation except for statutes containing a 'notwithstanding clause'. However, Liberty specifically

45 [1979] 3 All ER 325, [1981] QB 180.

drafts into its entrenchment mechanism the exception about Acts of Parliament containing 'notwithstanding clauses', in contrast to IPPR's and Lord Lester's schemes where the same exception operates through the process of the common law. In this respect, therefore, the Liberty proposal is similar to the Canadian Charter of Rights and Freedoms.

Judicial interpretation status

A third option would be to make the Bill of Rights an interpretative document only. This would have the effect that, where the meaning or application of any statutory wording or rule of the common law was unclear or capable for more than one interpretation, the courts should give preference to whatever interpretion of the law was most consistent with the principles of the Bill of Rights. Or stated from a slightly different perspective, the clause dictating the effect of the Bill of Rights would create a judicial presumption that Parliament intends that all its statutes to operate within the limits of the Bill of Rights and not to have any meaning or effect in contradiction of its principles. However, where the meaning of any statutory wording or rule of the common law was quite clear, it would still operate and be enforced by the courts regardless of whether it conflicted with human rights. An interpretative Bill of Rights would not be an entrenched document as such, and would not possess any legal priority over later ordinary Acts of Parliament.

This is the type of legal status which the articles of the ECHR possess under the Human Rights Act 1998. The wording of section 3(1) reads: 'So far as it is possible to do so, primary legislation and subordinate legislation must be read and given effect in a way which is compatible with the Convention rights.'[46] Interpretation clauses were also drafted for most of the legislative proposals to incorporate the ECHR prior to the Human Rights Act [39]. The main variations were in the precise wording employed and the consequential weight of presumption in favour of the ECHR's principles and jurisprudence, where uncertainties and ambiguities exist in UK law. Sir Edward Gardner's Human Rights Bill, for example, which was debated in the House of Commons in 1987 [91] developed a form of wording used earlier by Lords

---

46 For further comment on this new rule of statutory interpretation, see Introduction above; also G, Marshall, 'Interpreting Interpretation in the Human Rights Bill', *Public Law* (1998), p. 167.

Broxbourne and Scarman [**39c**], to propose that, 'No provision of an Act passed after the passing of this Act shall be constructed as authorising or requiring the doing of an act that infringes any of the fundamental rights and freedoms, or as conferring power to make any subordinate instrument authorising or requiring the doing of any such act, unless such a construction is unavoidable if effect is to be given that provision and to the other provisions of the Act'.

The comparative Bill of Rights which fits this model most closely is the New Zealand Bill of Rights 1990 [**46**]. The interpretative status of the Bill of Rights is laid down in section 6, which reads that, 'Wherever an enactment can be given a meaning that is consistent with the rights and freedoms contained in this Bill of Rights, that meaning shall be preferred to any other meaning'. A particularly interesting aspect of the New Zealand approach is that it expressly excludes the possibility of legislation being overridden by the Bill of Rights. This is provided for in section 4, which states that, 'No court shall, in relation to any enactment (whether passed or made before or after the commence-ment of this Bill of Rights) – (a) hold any provision of the enactment to be impliedly repealed or invoked, or to be in any way invalid or ineffective; or (b) decline to apply any provision of the enactment – by reason only that the provision is inconsistent with any provision of this Bill of Rights.' The courts are thus prohibited from treating the Bill of Rights in any way which might develop into a theory or jurisprudence of higher order law. Furthermore, there is nothing in the New Zealand Bill of Rights to restrict its own provisions from being amended by ordinary legislative process.[47]

There are some variants of this interpretative approach which would be less restrictive to the Bill of Rights serving as a form of higher law. In particular, while still providing an interpretative role for later statues, the Bill of Rights might be declared to possess an elevated legal status with respect to all pre-existing laws. In 1978, the report of the House of Lords Select Committee on a Bill of Rights recommended distinguishing between previous and subsequent enactments, propos-ing that the Bill of Rights should have a supreme status over all pre-existing Acts of Parliament and principles of the common law where cases of conflict arose. With regard to future enactments, however, an interpretative approach was preferred so that, in cases of conflict, statutory provisions should be construed subject to the Bill of Rights 'unless such subsequent enactment provides otherwise or does

47 See P. Joseph, *Constitutional and Administrative Law in New Zealand* (1993).

not admit of any construction compatible' with its provisions. How-ever, it must be remembered that the Committee believed that it should recommend only what it felt to be practically possible, and it was acting on misconceived advice that the implementation of any form of entrenchment designed to control future legislation was impossible under the doctrine of parliamentary sovereignty (see ear-lier comments on pages 57–9). Accepting this view from its specialist adviser, the Report said that 'Parliament cannot bind itself as to the future and a later Act must always prevail over an earlier one if it is inconsistent with it, whether the inconsistency is express or implied ... [The Committee's] view is that there is no way in which a Bill of Rights could protect itself from encroachment ... The most that such a Bill could do would be to include an interpretation provision which ensured that the Bill of Rights was always taken into account in the construction of later Acts and that, so far as a later Act could be construed in a way that was compatible with a Bill of Rights, such a construction would be preferable to one that was not' [**83**].

Two recent forms of legislative drafting, distinguished between past and future law, are to be found within the Hong Kong Bill of Rights 1991 [**47**] and Lord Lester's Human Rights Bill 1996 [**39f**]. The Hong Kong document, which was drafted by British government officials in preparation for the colony's handover to China, distinguishes between earlier and later Acts of Parliament, by declaring pre-existing legisla-tion that conflicts with the Bill of Rights to be 'repealed', and all subsequent legislation 'to be construed so as to be consistent with [the human rights principles] ... to the extent that it admits of such a construction'. Lord Lester's 1996 Bill, which was different in this respect to his earlier 1994 legislative proposal, would displace any earlier rule of law which was regarded by the courts as incompatible with its human rights provisions. Clause 1(2) reads that, 'this Act shall have effect notwithstanding any rule of law to the contrary'. His interpretation clause for future legislation was drafted to read, 'When-ever an enactment can be given a meaning that is consistent with the provisions set out in Schedule 1 to this Act [the human rights articles], that meaning shall be preferred to any other meaning.'

Few supporters of a constitutional Bill of Rights for the UK today would advocate a merely interpretative basis for the document. As such, it would not perform any major role in the legal and political control of government or one that could not be easily overridden. Its value would be limited to extending the grounds upon which admin-istrative discretions might be reviewed by the courts, and to serve as a point of reference in parliamentary and public affairs. But if unsatisfactory as a legal foundation for a national UK Bill of Rights serving as a constitutional instrument, such a scheme of arrangement will be suitable as the legal basis for the forthcoming legislation incorporating the ECHR into UK law. Though in the event the Labour government's chosen method of incorporating the ECHR has indeed been to adopt this interpretive approach [**40**], many would have preferred the 'hybrid' model of distinguishing between earlier and later legislation, along the lines of the Hong Kong Bill of Rights 1991 [**47**] and Lord Lester's Human Rights Bill 1996 [**39f**].

Finally, the great significance of the procedure for 'declarations of compatibility' under section 4 of the Human Rights Act 1998 should again be remarked upon in this context [**40a**] (see earlier comments in Introduction). The invention of this procedure for the Act was masterly in many respects. Since the declarations lack legal effect, parliamentary sovereignty can be claimed to remain intact. The procedure possesses a neat symmetry with the work of the European Court of Human Rights, whose judgments at Strasbourg also lack direct legal effect. In both cases, the government is simply relied upon to honour a political obligation to introduce legislation to change the law of the country so as to bring it into conformity with the ruling of the Court. But, in terms of the establishment and public gaining familiarity and experience of the judiciary going about the business of adjudicating upon the legitimacy of primary Acts of Parliaments (even if, under the Act, these declarations of compatibility lack legal force), this procedure will considerably smooth the pathway towards a constitutional Bill of Rights. For such adjudication and pronouncements upon primary statutes, but with full legal effect, is precisely what would be involved under an entrenched or semi-entrenched Bill of Rights.

PROCEDURES FOR FUTURE AMENDMENTS AND EMERGENCY DEROGATIONS

The architects of a UK Bill of Rights will need to consider matters of constitutional procedure in prescribing the circumstances in which the Bill of Rights or any of its articles might be made subject to some permanent amendment (whether being some modification, subtraction or addition) or might be temporarily suspended ('derogated from').

Amendments to the Bill of Rights

Amendments to the Bill of Rights will become desirable from time to time in order to modernize and refine its human rights articles to meet changing social circumstances. If the British government had adopted the self-same human rights articles for itself in a domestic UK Bill of Rights in the 1950s and 1960s such as those which it helped draft for the rest of the Council of Europe in 1950 and for other members of the Commonwealth such as Jamaica in 1962, serious consideration would be being given today to amendments, for example, to its non-discrimination articles so as to include grounds of sexual orientation, age and disability, and to its freedom of the person articles so as to add a prohibition on medical or scientific experimentation on individuals without their informed consent. The facility with which permanent amendments might be made under the terms of the Bill of Rights, however, needs to bear in mind the negative possibility of a misguided or less-than-benevolent political leader or party taking office which sets about increasing the number of restrictions and qualifications of human rights and freedoms, for the bureaucratic convenience of its own administrative powers or for authoritarian doctrinal reasons.

Particularly if, as is likely, the Bill of Rights is to be entrenched in some way as a form of higher law, the framers of a UK Bill of Rights will need to consider some special legislative process for amending its articles. Precise methods for amending constitutional documents such as a Bill of Rights vary widely, but there are three broad types of procedure which are commonly adopted. First, there is virtually always a requirement for both legislative chambers to agree to the proposed change. Second, there is often a requirement for special voting majorities in either or both chambers. For example, in the USA a two-thirds majority is required in both the House of Representatives and the Senate; and in Germany, amendments affecting its Basic Law require a two-thirds majority in both the Bundestag and the Bundes-rag. Third, a referendum of the electorate is sometimes required.

Under UK constitutional affairs as they stand, by far the most important of these procedures will be to establish a requirement that the second chamber (the House of Lords) must give its approval to all proposed amendments to the Bill of Rights. This will in effect be conferring an elevated constitutional authority upon the House of Lords, which otherwise at present under the terms of the Parliament Acts 1911–49 only possesses a power of one year's delay over legislation of any kind (with the exception of Bills to suspend general elections and the approval of statutory instruments).[48] The implementation of this amendment procedure would need to form part of a wider programme of parliamentary reform involving abolition of the hereditary peerage and a satisfactory basis being worked out for the future composition of the second chamber, a matter which the Labour Party and Liberal Democrats have pledged themselves to address in their pre-1997 election policy documents. This wider reform needs also to involve some modernizing redefinition of the functions and powers of the UK second chamber generally. These might include, among others, the scrutiny and approval of emergency derogating measures from the Bill of Rights (see below), and the consideration of administrative and legislative compliance with human rights generally, which is the subject of further consideration in the context of parliamentary scrutiny procedures (see page 77). Drafting the provision in the Bill of Rights that future amendments will require the consent of both Houses of Parliament will be straightforward. All that is necessary is a reference to the 1911 Parliament Act, excepting amendments to the Bill of Rights from the terms of its provisions [**82**].

Both special majority voting and a referendum are more problematic, principally because neither is an established part of existing UK constitutional and political practice, and also to some extent because of legal dilemmas concerning what the doctrine of parliamentary sovereignty might allow. There is no existing precedent for special majority voting in Parliament, although standing orders regulate voting practice in various ways, for example in laying down that for closure of debate motions in the House of Commons to be decided in the affirmative, not fewer than 100 MPs must vote in support.[49] The British government has included special majority voting in the amendment process of many of the Commonwealth constitutions it has drafted, or helped draft, for its former colonies and dominions, including Australia and South Africa. The precise requirement for amending a UK Bill of Rights might be that the votes in favour must exceed one-half of the total membership of the House concerned, or it might be for a two-thirds majority among those present and voting. Different or similar voting requirements might apply in each House. A two-thirds

48 See Erskine May, *Parliamentary Practice* (22nd edn, 1997), Ch. 22; J. A. G. Griffith and M. Ryle, *Parliament* (1989), Part IV; S. A. de Smith and R. Brazier, ibid., Ch. 16.
49 Standing Orders of the House of Commons, Public Business, 1997, No. 37.

majority in both legislative chambers is comparatively most usual abroad, and has been supported by both IPPR and Liberty in their draft Bills of Rights [**49–50**].[50] A few theorists might seek to maintain that such entrenchment procedures would be inoperative because a sovereign Parliament cannot bind its own future actions, and consequently a later Act passed under ordinary legislative procedures (for simple majority voting) amending or repealing the Bill of Rights would be enforced by the courts. Apart from the fact that such logic would be misplaced in the political context of enacting a constitutional Bill of Rights (on which see further above, pages 57–9), the better jurisprudential view is that Parliament can bind itself as to the 'manner and form' of future legislation. As Professors Stanley de Smith and Rodney Brazier have commented, 'There is no logical reason why the United Kingdom Parliament should be incompetent so to redefine itself (or redefine the procedure for enacting legislation on any given matter) ... If Parliament can make it easier to legislate, as by passing the Parliament Acts or abolishing the House of Lords, it can also make it harder to legislate' [**81**].

There is currently little support behind a referendum being made part of the amendment process.[51] None of the leading Bill of Rights blueprints drawn up in the UK have proposed it. A permanent referendum machinery would represent a far more novel development in the UK legislative process from the aspect of parliamentary sovereignty. In effect, it would be introducing a fourth estate into the definition of Parliament along with the House of Commons, the House of Lords and the Head of State. Only four referendums have ever taken place in the UK, being the Northern Ireland border poll in 1973, the referendum on UK membership of the European Community in 1975, and the two devolution referendums in Scotland and Wales in 1979.[52] Each was held upon an ad hoc basis and was essentially advisory in effect, as opposed to the mandatory requirement that would need to be laid down in any Bill of Rights entrenchment procedure. British opinion on the desirability of referendums is hard to gauge. Histor-

---

50 IPPR's preferred amendment procedures were published in its written constitution proposal, *A Written Constitution for the United Kingdom* (1993), in which see Article 69.

51 On referendums abroad, see H. Suksi, *Bringing in the People: A Comparison of Constitutional Forms and Practices of the Referendum* (1993); D. Butler and Austin Ranney (eds), *Referendums around the World* (1994).

52 For a history of these referendums in the UK, see V. Bogdanor, *Devolution* (1979) and *The People and the Party System* (1981).

ically, when British politicians have advocated a referendum they have often done so less out of a genuine conviction in its virtue as a sound constitutional mechanism, than for reasons of subjective political advantage (for example, because what they propose is otherwise unlikely to be accepted through the normal parliamentary process, or else to reach a decision on some controversial subject upon which the party in government is divided). Although a referendum is ostensibly laudible in terms of majoritarian democratic principle, some maintain that it is the politicians who are elected to Westminster to govern the country who should be firmly responsible for deciding on major issues of state, particularly if they are of a complex nature. However even if, under present circumstances, a UK Bill of Rights is unlikely to include a mandatory referendum as part of its amendment process, this does not rule out the possibility of a range of consultancy referendums to support the establishment of some new constitutional reforms affecting the fundamentals of the state. For this reason, there are good grounds for the Labour government holding the referendums it has promised on a Scottish Parliament, a Welsh Assembly, reform of the electoral system to the House of Commons, and a London regional authority. There will also be good reason to give moral sanction to the entrenchment of a constitutional Bill of Rights in the UK by calling a special referendum to endorse its implementation (see further below, page 97).

Emergency derogating measures

Most Bills of Rights, including international human rights treaties, confer powers upon the executive to suspend certain human rights obligations in times of national crisis or emergency. Such provisions represent a potential loophole in the judicial guarantee of human rights against oppressive executive or legislative acts of government, particularly since crisis or emergency situations are precisely the time when civil liberties are most at risk. However, the legal construction of any Bill of Rights has to accept that there may be extraordinary occasions when the executive, as a matter of overriding practical necessity, must subordinate normal human rights principles to the abnormal exigencies of what the national interest requires in order to combat some profound crisis or emergency.

The UK Bill of Rights should therefore seek to define the conditions in which a derogation is permissible, it should address matters relating to the duration of any derogation, it should control the range of human rights and freedoms that may be suspended (making it clear which, if any, principles may never be overridden), and it should lay down a parliamentary mechanism for approving or rejecting proposed derogations and extensions thereof. A drafting precedent exists in the ECHR at Article 15 (which is likely to be adopted as it stands for the forthcoming legislation incorporating the ECHR into UK law), providing that member states may take measures suspending its human rights obligations 'in time of war or other public emergency threatening the life of the nation . . . to the extent strictly required by the exigencies of the situation'. As applied for international purposes by the European Court of Human Rights, this has been interpreted rather broadly and no derogating measures of a member state have ever been held to be unjustified. The UK currently has one derogation lodged at the Council of Europe, dating from 1988, with respect to temporary police powers of detention designed to combat terrorism connected with the affairs of Northern Ireland [22]. The derogation came about as a result of the case of *Brogan and Others* in which the European Court of Human Rights held section 12 of the Prevention of Terrorism (Temporary Provisions) Act 1984 to be in violation of Article 5(3) of the ECHR.[53] The ECHR provides that there can be no derogation at all from the right to life, except in respect of deaths resulting from lawful acts of war, and from its prohibitions on retrospective criminal liability, torture and slavery.

For a UK Bill of Rights, the statutory wording that derogations are only permissible 'in time of war or other public emergency threatening the life of the nation . . . to the extent strictly required by the exigencies of the situation' might be adopted from the ECHR, but otherwise substantial modifications and additional provision will be necessary. Most people believe there are further human rights which should never be derogated from, and these might include freedom of thought and the right to recognition as a person before the law, as suggested by IPPR [49]. Acts of derogation by the UK government from its obligations under the ECHR can be effected without any form of parliamentary control, consistent with the conduct of international affairs and treaty-making generally, which takes place under royal prerogative powers (which are now widely viewed as an anachronism

---

53 *Brogan* v *UK* (1988) 11 EHRR 117.

and in need of reform[54]). For the constitutional purposes of the UK, however, it would be essential for the Bill of Rights to lay down democratic procedures under which Parliament is vested with the power to approve or reject government proposals with respect to the suspension of human rights. It would be natural for any such derogation normally to take place by way of a draft Order in Council, being prepared and presented to Parliament for its prior scrutiny and debate. If the second chamber (the House of Lords) is reconstructed in its membership and given a watchdog role over constitutional affairs and civil liberties, as suggested above, then it would make sense to stipulate a similar parliamentary voting procedure to that laid down for amendments. This might be, then, a two-thirds majority in both Houses of Parliament, as recommended by IPPR. The derogation clause in the Bill of Rights might provide that in the event that the urgency of the situation made it impracticable for Parliament to convene (because, for example, there was a special need for speed of action to combat the emergency, or it was physically impossible for MPs to hold a meeting), the Order might come into effect immediately but it would lapse as soon as it was possible for Parliament to meet and vote on the matter. It would be desirable for the Bill of Rights to state that the precise duration for each derogation should be specified by the Order in Council, up to a maximum of one year, with any extension of time requiring the agreement of both Houses. Finally, there should be express clarification about the possibility of judicial review proceedings, to deal with any questions or challenges concerning the validity of the Order or the procedures under which it had come into effect.

THE ROLE AND POWERS OF A UK HUMAN RIGHTS COMMISSION

A Human Rights Commission or Commissioner will need to be created as part of any legislation enacting a UK Bill of Rights. If one is already established beforehand, possibly shortly after implementation of the Human Rights Act incorporating the ECHR,[55] then its terms of

54 See Robert Blackburn and Raymond Plant, 'Monarchy and the Royal Prerogative', in Robert Blackburn and Raymond Plant (eds), *Constitutional Reform* (1999).

55 There was substantial parliamentary support for creating a Human Rights Commission expressed during the debates on the Human Rights Bill [**40d**].

reference will need to be enlarged or modified. The general purpose of such a Commission will be to promote and facilitate the influence and effect of the Bill of Rights throughout British society and in its system of law and government. Both the Labour Party and the Liberal Democrats have made it clear in their policy documents that they wish to set up such a Human Rights Commission [**112, 93, 150**], and in recent years various proposals and suggestions for a Commission have come from numerous sources including Liberty [**50**], Graham Allen MP [**56**], the Constitution Unit [**57**] and the Institute for Public Policy Research [**58**].

Important decisions of principle will need to be made in shaping the precise nature and operation of the Commission. Chief among these will be the delineation of its working functions, for the name Human Rights Commission could conceivably cover several very different sorts of agency. This reflects the fact that there are a wide range of valuable initiatives and tasks that might be usefully undertaken in the interests of promoting human rights in the UK. Some, including the Labour Party [**112**], have suggested that the Commission could simply be broadly modelled on the functions and powers of the Equal Opportunities Commission (EOC) and the Commission for Racial Equality (CRE), which involve investigation and enforcement functions. If this is to be so, then the Commission would possess powers to institute legal proceedings in its own name, assist individuals with the presentation of their legal complaints before the courts, investigate unlawful practices, and issue notices ordering individuals or bodies to desist from continuing or repeating some specified activity [**13**]. However, it is by no means clear that such an analogy is in fact appropriate. The Human Rights Commission's span of concern will be far wider that those of the EOC and CRE, covering all the human rights articles in the Bill of Rights and subsuming those in the ECHR and ICCPR. The question would also arise of the precise working relationship between the Human Rights Commission and the EOC and CRE (and other similar bodies which might emerge) and whether the new Commission would take over the functions of the others, or else how they would operate in combination so as to avoid duplication of function and work.

A markedly different type of Commission would be if it was to serve as some form of adjudicatory body, dealing with complaints of human rights violations, inquiring into them, and rendering reports and recommendations, either being presented to the Secretary of State for him to act upon or not as he or she thought fit, or else being directly binding in law and enforceable by the courts. In 1971 Samuel Silkin QC, the late former cabinet minister, presented a Bill to Parliament along these lines [55], which would have created a UK body carrying out prior analogous work to that of the European Commission on Human Rights. Under this proposal, any person entitled to petition the Strasbourg machinery would be entitled to present their human rights complaint first to the UK Human Rights Commission, which would investigate the matter possessing powers to examine persons and documents, and present its findings to Parliament indicating, in the event of a human rights violation, the steps or compensation required to remedy such violation.

The Home Office, or other body entrusted with bringing forward recommendations on a Human Rights Commission, might well conclude that the role of the Commission should be narrowly, rather than widely, drawn, and that its principal function should be advisory rather than investigative, adjudicatory or concerned with matters of enforcement. This advisory role could embrace many different subjects and forms of work, and might be taken to include matters of law and administrative reform. It could keep under review and produce annual reports to be laid before Parliament on developments in the field of human rights, both social and public developments, and matters relating to the jurisprudence of the Bill of Rights and the UK's international human rights obligations under the ECHR and ICCPR. The Commission might, at the request of the Home Secretary or other relevant minister (the Northern Ireland and Scottish Secretaries, or the lord chancellor) examine special problems and present detailed authoritative reports. Legal experts on the Commission might be empowered to appear as *amicus curiae*, offering legal analysis and advice in court proceedings where an important or difficult principle of human rights law was involved. Particularly on human rights subjects largely devoid of political controversy, the Commission might assist or produce recommendations for draft primary and secondary legislation in the manner of the Law Commission. It could produce suggested codes of practice for administrative and other bodies, where such advice was sought. It could also act as a focal point for ordinary people who wished to seek general information about human rights and citizenship in the UK.

Two further considerations will be of importance in shaping the Commission. First, the construction of a Human Rights Commission will need to bear in mind the potential incompatibility of carrying out different functions. For example, an investigative role does not sit well alongside a prosecution or enforcement role, because, as is universally recognized, it may lead to overzealous and subjectively influenced prosecutions leading to miscarriages of justice. Neither do investigative and enforcement roles combine well with functions relating to law reform and advisory work, not simply because it may impinge on necessary objectivity of the Commission, but because they are likely to dominate the preoccupations and resources of the Commission.

Second, a resolution of the complexities surrounding how best to proceed with the form and powers of Human Rights Commission will depend largely upon an accurate appreciation of the extent to which other institutions or bodies can be expected to develop in response to the establishment of a Bill of Rights. In the absence of other enforcement arrangements being made, the Director of Public Prosecutions is likely to assume responsibility for enforcing the general law against those perpetrating human rights violations, particularly if liability extends to the private sector. The central and local government ombudsmen will interpret their roles in investigating allegations of maladministration causing injustice to include official conduct amounting to a violation of human rights. Such developments in response to the enactment of a Bill of Rights will also be true with respect to the working of Parliament and its general functions of scrutinizing legislation and government, which is considered further below. It can confidently be expected that both Houses of Parliament will adopt the Bill of Rights as a moral yardstick in many of its deliberations, both in the chamber and in committee. At least one new select committee devoted to human rights law is likely to be created in response to incorporation of the ECHR and a new Bill of Rights. It is highly doubtful, therefore, that any formal functions of legislative scrutiny by the Human Rights Commission, as suggested by Liberty [50] and Graham Allen's Human Rights Bill 1994 [56] would be necessary, even if considered constitutionally appropriate by parliamentarians themselves.

PARLIAMENTARY SCRUTINY REFORMS UNDER A BILL OF RIGHTS

The Labour government has indicated its firm commitment to establishing a parliamentary committee on human rights [**40c** and **d, 116,**

150]. Prior to the 1997 general election, human rights formed no part of the terms of reference of any parliamentary procedure or committee, including the House of Commons Standing Committees which examine legislative proposals in detail, the Commons Select Committees which are concerned with the expenditure, administration and policy of government, and the Joint Select Committee on Statutory Instruments. Formerly, it was felt that Parliament conducted its scrutiny arrangements with respect to human rights as adequately as could be expected, and no special reforms in this respect were necessary. This rested upon the traditional theory that civil rights and freedom are part of the moral principles already applied by parliamentarians in the conduct of all their business. Largely for this reason, the House of Lords Select Committee on a Bill of Rights in 1977 reported that it was sceptical of the usefulness of a human rights scrutiny committee, believing that it was unlikely that such a body would succeed in detecting a violation of such rights in proposed legislation which had escaped the notice of the various stages of preparation through which it had already passed [**83**].

Over the past two decades, however, there have been some important developments, both within the process of parliamentary scrutiny arrangements generally, and within parliamentary opinion on the desirability of human rights scrutiny arrangements in particular. These recent developments in parliamentary procedure have come about because of a growing concern that Parliament's control over the executive has become steadily weaker, and a more specialized, detailed form of examination is now required by committees of MPs and peers, who can take oral and written evidence in their inquiries and, where necessary, take outside expert advice. In 1979, a new system of departmentally related Select Committees was established in the House of Commons, to consider the administration, expenditure and policy of government departments, with powers to send for persons, papers and records.[56] Since 1980, a new procedure for Special Standing Committees has been established in the Commons, empowering legislative committees to adopt powers equivalent to a Select Committee in taking oral and written evidence to assist their examination of Bills.[57] The Select Committees in both Houses of

---

56 See. J. A. G. Griffith and M. Ryle, *Parliament* (1989), Ch. 11; G. Drewry (ed), *The New Select Committees* (1985).

57 HC, Standing Order No. 91 (1997); J. A. G. Griffith and M. Ryle, ibid., pp. 276, 318; Erskine May, ibid., 594.

Parliament on European secondary legislation, established in 1974, have been substantially extended over the past two decades, particularly in the House of Lords where there are now six separate sub-committees inquiring into different spheres of European affairs.[58] In 1992, a Select Committee on the Scrutiny of Delegated Powers was set up in the House of Lords, to examine the appropriateness or otherwise of government proposals in Bills to delegate legislative powers to itself.[59] Against this background of parliamentary reform, a new scrutiny committee procedure devoted to the cause of human rights has become perfectly feasible.

Pre-Bill of Rights Scrutiny for Compliance with the European Convention on Human Rights

One measure of proposed reform which now seems certain to be implemented in 1999 or 2000, and will therefore precede the enactment of a Bill of Rights, will be to set up a system of parliamentary scrutiny whereby one or more committees were given responsibility for examining legislative proposals for their conformity with the law of the ECHR. Particularly following the Human Rights Act 1998, there is widespread support for such an initiative, to improve the quality of the UK's pre-legislative compliance with its international human rights obligations, and to help reduce the number of cases going before the European Court of Human Rights in which UK legislation has been found to be in violation of human rights. Between 1985 and 1991 alone, there were 15 findings of statutory violations by the UK. The work involved in this scrutiny process will be relatively technical, in terms of requiring an understanding of international human rights law and an expertise in, or access to expert advice on, up-to-date developments in the jurisprudence of the European Court of Human Rights.

Several suggestions have been made as to the committee or committees which might be entrusted with this function [59].[60] A

---

58 See A. Cygan, *The United Kingdom Parliament and European Union Legislation* (1998).

59 C. M. G. Himsworth, 'The Delegated Powers Scrutiny Committee', *Public Law* (1995) 343.

60 Doc. 59 considers the options for pre-Bill of Rights scrutiny, and for a further account see Robert Blackburn, 'A Parliamentay Committee on Human Rights', in Robert Blackburn and Raymond Plant (eds), *Constitutional Reform* (1999).

committee might be established in either or both of the Houses of Parliament or be constituted jointly between the two Houses. The Liaison Committee in the House of Lords has been considering a proposal by Lord Lester to establish a new Select Committee 'to scrutinize legislation for consistency with the European Convention on Human Rights'.[61] Keith Ewing and Conor Gearty have suggested a Constitutional Committee in the House of Commons for a similar purpose.[62]

A useful distinction is to be drawn between the examination of primary legislation (Bills) and subordinate legislation (Statutory Instruments). If these were to become separate scrutiny processes, the scrutiny of subordinate legislation could conveniently be entrusted to the present Joint Select Committee on Statutory Instruments, with its terms of reference being amended to cover scrutiny for compliance with the ECHR. Then, operating similarly as joint process between the two Houses, the scrutiny of primary legislation might be entrusted to a new Joint Committee established specially for the purpose. Such a procedure is analogous to parliamentary scrutiny arrangements in Australia, and was advocated by David Kinley in a book published in 1993.[63] The Labour Party, in its 1996 consultation paper on incorporation of the ECHR, has similarly proposed a Joint Committee on Human Rights, with continuing responsibility to monitor the operation of the Act incorporating the ECHR and other aspects of the UK's human rights obligations. It suggested the Committee might possess powers to compel the attendance of witnesses and call upon other bodies to assist its work, though adding that 'more detailed work would need to be undertaken on how the Joint Committee would work in practice'[**116**].

It is important that the construction of any new parliamentary scrutiny procedures to accompany incorporation of the ECHR should carefully take into account how these procedures can be expected to evolve and fit into a long-term scheme of arrangements taking place as part of the implementation of a Bill of Rights. In other words, the scrutiny procedures relating to the ECHR will necessarily be interim

---

61 1st Report of the Liaison Committee, HL [1993–4] 88, agreed at HL Deb., 2 November 1994, cols 843–8. See also Lord Lester's maiden speech on the subject, HL Deb., 23 November 1993, col. 169.
62 *Democracy or a Bill of Rights* (1991).
63 *The European Convention on Human Rights. Compliance without Incorporation* (1993).

arrangements, to be superseded in due course by a more fundamental parliamentary reform. Bearing this in mind, one way forward might be to allocate responsibility for examining primary legislation (Bills) for their consistency with the ECHR to some pre-existing committee (with widened terms of reference). Furthermore, as Michael Ryle, former Clerk to the Committees in the House of Commons, has said, 'parliamentary reform is usually most successful when it builds on established procedures'.[64]

There are two suitable existing bodies which might perform this scrutiny function of Bills, being the Select Committee on the Scrutiny of Delegated Powers and the Select Committee on the European Communities, both in the House of Lords. The Select Committee on the Scrutiny of Delegated Powers currently considers every parliamentary Bill to establish if there is a delegation of legislative power in it. If there is, the Committee will inquire into the appropriateness or otherwise of its provisions, and prepare a report on the matter. The work of the Committee since 1992 has been impressive and widely praised.[65] Its recommendations have proved very influential, with virtually all matters of concern raised by the Committee being accepted by ministers and reflected in amendments made to the Bill under scrutiny. That the Committee might in due course take on additional functions including the examination of Bills for conformity with the ECHR and European law generally has been proposed and widely supported, including by the Hansard Society Committee on the Legislative Process.[66]

The European Committee considers European legislative proposals before they are presented to the Council of Ministers, and makes reports on those which raise important questions of policy or principle and on other matters which the Committee considers that the special attention of the House should be drawn. Although the European Committee was established to scrutinize the affairs of the European Union rather than the Council of Europe (the parent organization of the ECHR), yet the ECHR has become an important component in the work of the Union. All European Union states are members of the Council of Europe and therefore share a common

64 'Pre-legislative scrutiny: a prophylactic approach to protection of human rights', *Public Law* (1994), p. 195.
65 See C. M. G. Himsworth, ibid.
66 Hansard Society, *Making the Law: The Report of the Hansard Society Commission on the Legislative Process* (1993).

human rights law framework. In 1977, the European Parliament, Council and Commission issued a declaration expressly recognizing the ECHR as being of 'prime importance' in the exercise of their powers [**34**]. The European Court of Justice has expressly adopted the ECHR as a set of legal interpretative principles for its judicial work [**36**]. The preamble to the Maastricht Treaty in 1992 commits the European Union to promote democracy on the basis of the principles and objectives of the ECHR [**37**]. There are currently six subcommittees of the Select Committee on the European Communities, and it would be possible either for the Select Committee to establish an additional subcommittee specifically for the purpose of examining UK legislative proposals for compliance with the ECHR, or else simply for the terms of the existing subcommittee on Law and Institutions ('E') to be modified to take on this new function. If either of these two House of Lords committees was to be responsible for scrutiny under the terms of the ECHR, this would accommodate the immediate requirement, while not pre-empting or complicating later consideration by Parliament and the architects of a UK Bill of Rights as to the most appropriate permanent parliamentary machinery for scrutiny on human rights and civil liberties matters.

However, if the Labour government proceeds to initiate procedural reform involving a new Joint Committee on Human Rights as it has proposed, then in its detailed construction certain factors should be borne in mind. The two Houses contributing equal members to the Committee will bring markedly differing working habits and traditions with them, the Lords more deliberative and detailed, the Commons more politicized. Joint committees are unusual parliamentary institutions, the only precedents being ones dealing with statutory instruments, consolidation bills and ecclesiastical measures – all of which have a narrow remit, concentrating on technical and specified matters. A Joint Committee on Human Rights with wide-ranging powers of scrutiny would be unique, particularly given the often highly controversial nature of the subject matter it would often have to examine and report on. Several important points of procedure would need to be settled, which might necessitate legislation or provision in the Bill of Rights itself, rather than being left to a change in Standing Orders. For example, the powers of a Joint Committee would need to be clearly agreed in advance between the two Houses, because a joint committee's powers cannot be enlarged on the authority of one House acting alone (which might become significant if one House was deliberately obstructing the work of the Committee). Whereas the Committee on Statutory Instruments meets informally and in private, a Committee on Human Rights, as a far more high-profile parliamentary body, should clearly conduct its proceedings in public, and with scrupulous attention to procedural detail. A rule should be clearly agreed that, on matters into which the Joint Committee is inquiring, there should be no final debate leading to a resolution or passage of a legislative measure until the Committee's findings have been completed and their report received by members of both Houses. Currently, the Commons regards itself as bound by no such obligation in the case of the Joint Committee on Statutory Instruments Committee, for example.

Scrutiny procedures under the Bill of Rights

The implementation of the UK Bill of Rights will have more profound ramifications on parliamentary functions and general scrutiny procedures. Chief among these will be the process for amending the Bill of Rights and considering derogations from its terms in times of national crisis, as considered above (page 67). If the parliamentary second chamber, the House of Lords, is modernized in its composition, as Labour and the Liberal Democrats have promised, and it is entrusted with extended powers with respect to amendment and derogation of the Bill of Rights, then it is virtually inevitable that a general redefinition of its general functions and purpose will take place concomitantly. Such redefinition will retain its long-standing traditional functions, including the revision of legislation, scrutiny of public affairs, and the judicial work of its appellate committee. But as part of its process of modernization, special emphasis is likely to be given to its international and constitutional roles. Its universally praised work in the scrutiny of European legislation is likely to be given new emphasis. Its broader focus of scrutiny would cover the government's human rights reporting obligations under the United Nations International Covenant.[67] If and when Labour carries out its 1993 policy objectives to reform the prerogative powers in respect of treaty-making and declarations of war in order to make them more

---

67 For a criticism of present arrangements, see A. Lester, 'Taking Human Rights Seriously', Ch. 4 in Robert Blackburn and James Busuttil (eds), *Human Rights for the 21st Century*, 1997.

accountable to Parliament,[68] some new role with respect to the scrutiny and ratification of these major acts of state (including amendments to the constitution of the European Union and new protocols being added to the European Convention on Human Rights) can be expected. All these developments described above have implications for the future role of the House of Lords, and point to a likely scenario that it will be perceived as an assembly with a particular role to play with respect to human rights generally.

This impinges on the question whether it will be necessary for the House of Commons to establish its own new human rights committee (or one that would operate permanently as a joint committee with the House of Lords). Liberty has proposed a powerful Human Rights Scrutiny Committee in the House of Commons, with extensive functions and powers including those of reversing judicial decisions made in cases brought under the Bill of Rights [**50**]. The Labour Party and others who are now suggesting a Joint Committee on Human Rights as part of the process whereby the ECHR is incorporated into UK law might expect its powers to be enlarged after the enactment of a Bill of Rights, to extend not only to additional and more elaborate human rights and civil liberties criteria in a domestically drafted Bill of Rights, but to a far wider range of functions than legislative scrutiny alone (including the scrutiny of public administration and international affairs, for example, and other matters referred to below). If intended and set up as being complementary to the new constitutional role of the House of Lords, as suggested in the paragraph above, then either of these committees might be feasible in terms of their parliamentary efficiency and worthwhile. But if they were to be conceived as a general scheme of scrutiny that was to serve as an alternative to a reconstituted and reformed House of Lords, they would prove poor substitutes. There are serious doubts as to whether a committee of MPs, reflecting the composition of a government-dominated House of Commons, can realistically be expected to act with sufficient independence and detachment from party politics to serve as a principal form of constitutional control over government abuse of power. This would be particularly so where the outcome of a case on which MPs were being asked to rule would involve political loss-of-face and electoral embarrassment to their party leaders. Legislative measures

---

68 *A New Agenda for Democracy* (1993), p. 33; and see Robert Blackburn and Raymond Plant, 'Monarchy and the Royal Prerogative', in Robert Blackburn and Raymond Plant (eds), *Constitutional Reform* (1999).

with human rights implications have regularly served as political footballs in the House of Commons, the Official Secrets Act and the Prevention of Terrorism (Temporary Provisions) Act to name but two well-known recent instances. MPs depend upon their front-bench leaders and the party whips for promotion to ministerial office, or shadow ministerial office, and other forms of patronage and advancement within the party hierarchy.

If the parliamentary second chamber, the House of Lords, becomes the principal constitutional mechanism for protecting and promoting the Bill of Rights, any further major developments in the House of Commons in the form of new committee work additional to the functions and procedures established in 1999 or 2000 (pre-Bill of Rights) may not be strictly necessary, and could lead to duplication of work. In the proceedings of the House of Commons, the Bill of Rights would become a powerful de facto set of principles for official reference, both in the chamber and in all its committees. Greater use could be made of existing procedures for Special Standing Committees, where the Commons wish to examine provisions affecting human rights principles in greater depth than usual. These Special Standing Committees, now established under Standing Orders since 1986, have greater powers than normal legislative Standing Committees, and permit them to carry out inquiries and take oral and written evidence. In the scrutiny of public administration and issue-based inquiries, it might be useful (though not essential) for the terms of reference of certain departmentally related Committees concerned with human rights matters to be amended so as expressly to include matters affecting the Bill of Rights, such as the Home Affairs Committee, the Northern Ireland and Scottish Committees, and any future Select Committee on Justice and Legal Affairs (covering the lord chancellor's office) as promised by Labour in its pre-1997 election policy statements. There would thus be ample parliamentary opportunities for MPs undertaking issue-based inquiries into human rights problems, including, where necessary, the examination of government and official practices. More effective administrative accountability to Parliament will be facilitated by greater freedom of access to official information, to which the Labour government is committed. More efficient parliamentary scrutiny of legislation would be helped by new procedures extending the newly strengthened Strasbourg-proofing arrangements and system of ministerial statements of compatibility with the ECHR under section 19 of the Human Rights Act 1998 [**40a**] (see above page 41). Such procedures might require government departments to certify their internal checking of the measure for compliance with the Bill of Rights, drawing the attention of Parliament to any special matters in the Explanatory Memorandum attached to the Bill.

In the reconstructed second chamber, the primary constitutional role will be the scrutiny and approval of special legislative measures affecting the Bill of Rights, namely amendments and derogations, as considered above, and possibly also Bills designed to take effect notwithstanding the Bill of Rights. For if, as seems probable, the status and priority of the Bill of Rights is to be one of qualified entrenchment, with Acts of Parliament prevailing over the Bill of Rights only if it contains a 'notwithstanding clause', then it would be logical for the Bill of Rights to provide the House of Lords with a legislative power equivalent to that which it possesses over amending and derogating provisions. In addition to its normal legislative role, Bills raising issues of importance to the human rights articles in the Bill of Rights or international treaties might be referred to a new specialist committee. Depending on the pre-Bill of Rights scrutiny arrangements with respect to ensuring legislative compliance with the ECHR (but especially if they had been given to the Select Committee on the Scrutiny of Delegated Powers or the Select Committee on the European Communities, as suggested above), this new Select Committee on Human Rights might take over the function of legislative examination for compliance with human rights articles at home and under international law. Scrutiny of the conduct of government, or inquiries into matters of public concern on human rights grounds, could be effected by the creation of ad hoc Select Committees. The precise nature of any further functions and scrutiny arrangements will depend upon other associated reforms, but might well involve the Select Committee in the auditing of government policy on selected areas such as nondiscrimination, the initiation research into specific human rights problems, the consideration of government reports on human rights subjects including under the terms of the International Covenant, and the scrutiny of and reporting on proposed amendments or protocols to the international human rights treaties.

Central to the consideration of all scrutiny arrangements, both inside and outside Parliament, which are designed to support the UK Bill of Rights, will be the overriding objective of establishing the most efficient interrelated system whereby human rights violations, or potential violations, can be identified and corrected pre-emptively, without the disadvantages and costs involved in needing to resort to legal litigation concerning the validity of administrative conduct or legislative provisions in the national or European courts. All agree that the prevention of conduct and legislation likely to infringe basic civil liberties and human rights is far preferable, wherever possible, than awaiting the need for a judicial ruling on the matter.

Preparing and Implementing the Reform

Although the present Labour government is committed to the general principle of developing a constitutional Bill of Rights, there are many administrative and political problems ahead to be resolved in the eventual emergence of the legislation necessary to effect the change.[69] A commission of some kind, or other officially appointed body, will need to be established to consider the range of options relating to the contents of the document, and to prepare a report with recommendations for the government and Parliament. A timetable will need to be considered, to fit in with the implementation of Labour's other constitutional reform objectives, particularly those of relevance to the Bill of Rights itself (both those now in the course of being prepared, such as incorporation of the ECHR, and longer-term aspirations such as agreement on the future role and composition of the House of Lords). A process of consensus-building behind the need for a homegrown Bill of Rights will be necessary, for the efficiency of all our constitutional arrangements depends heavily upon their degree of political support and acceptance. All these factors mean that the enactment of a constitutional Bill of Rights is to be regarded as a medium-term objective, substantial progress towards which cannot realistically be expected before a renewed, second term of office for the present Labour administration. However, while it may be impracticable for the necessary processes involved to be completed within the lifetime of the present Parliament, yet it is important that the Labour government initiates the preparatory thinking behind the development of the Bill of Rights at the earliest opportunity if the eventual implementation of the reform is to be completed within the first decade of the twenty-first century.

The Labour–Liberal Democrat shared policy objectives on human rights legislation comprises the mutually supportive components of first, incorporation of the ECHR into UK law; second, the creation of a

---

69 Generally see Katy Donnelly and Nicole Smith, 'Implementing Constitutional Reform', in Robert Blackburn and Raymond Plant (eds), *Constitutional Reform* (1999), and Constitution Unit, *Delivering Constitutional Reform* (1996).

Human Rights Commission; and third, a home-grown, constitutional Bill of Rights. These three measures, which will be implemented incrementally, will each significantly facilitate the operation of the others. In particular, the decision to incorporate the European Convention on Human Rights is a necessary and preliminary act to a constitutional Bill of Rights. It will prepare the way towards the implementation of a domestic Bill of Rights by implanting the general idea of positive rights in our law for the first time. It will provide experience and practical lessons for the future, including matters to be taken account of in determining the precise form of the later UK Bill of Rights. Those people who are suspicious of any rights-based charter will be able to see that it can be successfully accommodated into the legal systems of the UK, and operates in practice to the public benefit generally in the UK. The creation of a UK Human Rights Commission, discussed above, will perform a valuable role in its advisory and other public work in promoting a greater awareness and understanding of civil and political rights and how they interrelate with people's ordinary lives. Incorporation of the ECHR and the Human Rights Commission therefore will help smooth the passage towards a UK Bill of Rights, by acclimatizing the country towards human rights reform legislation generally, and by convincing a wider body of persons of the relevance and usefulness of a Bill of Rights.

The present prospects for a broad cross-party political consensus in support of a UK Bill of Rights are good. It is of great significance that the Labour Party and Liberal Democrats were willing to form a Joint Consultative Committee on Constitutional Reform in 1996, agreeing on a wide range of issues two months prior to the 1997 general election [**150**]; and that subsequently, at the invitation of Tony Blair as prime minister, the two parties now continue to collaborate on constitutional policy matters in a special Cabinet Committee [**151**]. It signals that these two parties, which between them account for 456 (419 and 46 respectively) out of the total of 659 MPs – 71 per cent of the composition of the House of Commons – have already signalled their commitment to a cooperative approach to modernizing the constitution, and agreed a general framework against which the details of any individual legislative reform can be worked out in a positive manner. The refusal of the Conservative leadership under John Major between 1990–7 to enter into discussions on any new constitutional measure that signified a limitation or dilution of their political and administrative power at Westminster and in Whitehall, may well mutate now the party is in opposition. As described earlier (page 9), Conservatives were in the vanguard of the Bill of Rights movement while in opposition in the 1970s, with prominent figures such as Lord Hailsham and Sir Keith Joseph decrying the 'elective dictatorship' of the present system and arguing that a Bill of Rights had become a vital component in buttressing the rule of law and protecting basic freedoms in the UK, leading to the 1979 Conservative manifesto expressly including a proposal for all-party talks on a Bill of Rights [**95**]. Such sentiments are likely to re-emerge from the Conservative opposition, particularly now that the 100 or so MPs who were formerly ministers (or their parliamentary private secretaries) are released from the convention of ministerial responsibility requiring a public display of unanimous support for official government policy, and will be freer to contribute their own personal views on the subject.

A key element in the implementation of such a fundamental measure of law reform will be the extent to which the judiciary are receptive to the idea of a code of human rights law. Here too, the present position and prospects are highly favourable to reform. As described above (page 28), in addition to long-standing judicial supporters of an entrenched Bill of Rights, such as the former law lord Leslie Scarman, since 1989 many present and former judges have been publicly urging the government immediately to make the human rights articles of the European Convention directly enforceable in UK law, emphasizing their willingness and capacity to construe and apply general principles of individual rights and freedoms. Indeed this now appears to have become the majority view among the senior judiciary, with the present lord chief justice, Lord Bingham, the present Master of the Rolls, Lord Woolf, and several law lords such as Lord Browne-Wilkinson and Lord Slynn vigorously advocating incorporation of the ECHR. This development in UK judicial opinion has become more transparent as a result of the lord chancellor's decision to relax the rule that formerly restricted members of the judiciary from expressing in public their own personal opinions on matters of political debate.[70] Clearly, if the courts are competent to apply the human rights principles of the ECHR, they are competent to apply the human rights principles of a UK Bill of Rights, which, as commented upon earlier, will in any event draw heavily upon the drafting of the ECHR and International Covenant. Any remaining doubts in this respect will fade

---

70 The guidelines are laid out in a letter dated 16 October 1989 from the lord chancellor, then Lord Mackay, to the lord chief justice, then Lord Lane.

as the courts gain experience, post-incorporation of the ECHR, of applying human rights principles directly in their legal reasoning and judgments. Meanwhile, a powerful strand of judicial opinion shares the view of the former lord chief justice, Lord Taylor, speaking in a parliamentary debate in 1995, that, 'It is not the proposed change but the present situation which is worrying from a constitutional viewpoint' [87].

Politically, a very great deal will depend upon the resolve, determination and leadership of members of the Labour cabinet, especially the prime minister Tony Blair and his senior colleagues with a special interest in constitutional reform, including Robin Cook (the chairman of the Joint Labour–Liberal Democrat Consultative Committee on Constitutional Reform 1996–7), Jack Straw (the present home secretary, with responsibility for constitutional affairs) and Lord Irvine (the present lord chancellor, with responsibility for the administration of justice). Few reforms of major constitutional importance have ever been carried out without the strong personal commitment and initiative of the prime minister, or that of a senior cabinet colleague taking ministerial responsibility with the prime minister's active backing. As historical examples, the leadership of prime minister Herbert Asquith was crucial to the reform of the House of Lords in 1911, as was prime minister Edward Heath's personal commitment to the UK's accession to the European Community in 1972. As the Constitution Unit has written, in observation of international experience in the implementation of Bills of Rights elsewhere, 'The development of a Bill of Rights will not come to fruition without (ideally) government sponsorship at the outset and (certainly) government support for a specific course of action. Most important is the personal commitment and authoritative leadership of a senior government figure both during the development process and in 'selling' the outcome to Parliament' [148].

An important question affecting the degree of political resolve behind a Bill of Rights is which department of state and minister will be responsible for the implementation and legislative process involved. Ostensibly, ministerial responsibility would fall upon the home secretary, currently Jack Straw. Under existing arrangements the Home Office has administrative jurisdiction for constitutional law and civil rights generally throughout the UK, although particular aspects sometimes straddle or cross over into other departments of state, particularly the Northern Ireland Office, the Scottish Office, and the lord chancellor's department. A problem arises with the Home Office in respect of human rights law, in that the size of that department is very large and it is already seized of more immediate and more politically high-profile policy fields, including law and order, prisons, immigration control, and national security. The principal nature of its work is that of social control. The protection of human rights and individual liberties, therefore, does not naturally fall very high on its administrative and ministerial agenda, and in practice its interests regularly conflict with other policy objectives which are seemingly always more pressing, both managerially and politically. This may explain, for example, the curious reference of Jack Straw to a future UK 'Bill of Rights and Responsibilities', which was inserted in the final paragraph of Labour's 1996 human rights consultation document [**116**], thereby confusing the constitutional character of a Bill of Rights with the quite different concept of a charter of social and community obligations. This is not to say that the Home Office is unsuited to the task of developing a Bill of Rights (its anti-discrimination Acts in the 1970s [**13**] are clear evidence of its competence in preparing human rights legislation), but it does strengthen the case for some rationalization of ministerial responsibility for legal affairs generally. Labour's 1993 document, *A New Agenda for Democracy*, said that 'Labour is committed to establishing a proper Ministry of Justice' [**71**], which would involve a significant rationalization of law and justice affairs between the Home Office and the present lord chancellor's department. In the short term, even prior to a Ministry of Justice being created, there is a good case to be made for transferring human rights law (both European and domestic) and the development of a UK Bill of Rights to the lord chancellor's department, whose central field of ministerial responsibility is more sympathetic and compatible, being concerned with the legal system and the administration of justice.

Prior to the 1997 general election, there was a view among many supporters of Labour's constitutional programme that it would facilitate matters if there was to be established a senior new ministerial post, based in the Cabinet Office with a special constitution unit of civil servants and political advisers attached, to which strategic authority might be given for the overall harmonization of all or a specified range of constitutional measures being carried out, the development of a UK Bill of Rights being included. Given the very wide range of constitutional measures forming part of the in-coming Labour administration's plans – devolution to Scotland and Wales, reform of the House of Lords, a referendum on electoral reform, incorporation of the ECHR, the creation of a London strategic authority, a Freedom of Information Act, implementation of the EU Inter-Governmental Conference, and more – the work of the minister would have been to coordinate, where necessary, the individual efforts of individual departments concerned with individual reforms, as well as providing an overall leadership and momentum behind Labour's constitutional proposals. Alternatively, it was thought that some traditional ministerial office might take on this role, for example the leader of the House of Commons and lord president of the Privy Council (the posts Richard Crossman held when implementing the experimental Select Committees and the Parliamentary Commissioner for Administration during 1966–8) or possibly even the deputy prime minister [**148**]. In the event, Tony Blair on being appointed prime minister has (at least for the time being) stopped short of appointing a minister with special responsibility for constitutional reform, and instead has put into effect two significant organizational changes within the Cabinet Office, the net effect of which may prove to be of equal value. First, Tony Blair has recognized the value of appointing a minister of this kind more generally, by appointing an additional minister of state (who was initially Peter Mandelson) at the Cabinet Office, with a role to oversee the implementation of Labour's 'contract with the people' published in its 1997 election manifesto, one of whose ten pledges concerned the constitution.[71] Second, a powerful new secretariat has been created within the Cabinet Office specifically devoted to constitutional reform. Currently the secretariat is structured into three divisions, two of which are concerned with devolution to Scotland and Wales, as the most difficult and immediate matter of reform, and the third of which will work on other constitutional matters.

Apart from the political leadership necessary from the prime minister and cabinet, the most pivotal work in implementing a UK Bill of Rights will come from the commission or other similar body set up by the government to bring forward recommendations on the detail of the reform Bill. As related earlier (pages xxviii and 12), the Labour Party has proposed 'the establishment of an all-party commission that will be charged with drafting the Bill of Rights and considering a suitable method of entrenchment. This should report to Parliament within a specified and limited period of time'. There are several different kinds of commission which might be considered for this task. It could take the form of a Royal Commission, being a traditional forum for independent experts (in this case legal and constitutional affairs) together with a cross-section of people from relevant professions and dis-

71 *New Labour Because Britain Deserves Better* (1997), p. 5.

ciplines. The last such form of inquiry into a question of constitutional reform was the Royal Commission on the Constitution, appointed under the chairmanship of Lord Kilbrandon. It was created in 1968 (reporting in 1973) by the then prime minister, Harold Wilson, in response to Scottish and Welsh nationalist pressures, and its terms of reference were 'to examine the present functions of the central legislature and government in relation to the several countries, nations and regions in the United Kingdom'. Some, notably Professor Rodney Brazier, have advocated the establishment of a permanent royal commission on the constitution – a Constitutional Commission – which would keep the state of UK constitutional law under constant review, and consider and report on any matter of reform referred to it by the government [**146**].

Another possible form of commission for the task of drafting a Bill of Rights would be an ad hoc government or departmental committee of inquiry, which is largely similar in composition and operation to a royal commission. There is no real significance in the title of a 'Royal' Commission, apart from the prestige and status ostensibly being afforded to it. A government committee would similarly be appointed by the Crown at the formal instigation of the prime minister. If the prime minister deemed that responsibility for the reform should rest solely with a single ministry such as the Home Office, lord chancellor's department or a future Ministry of Justice, then the commission could be appointed as a departmental committee. All these forms of commissions mentioned may be appointed under the prerogative, though government and departmental committees can also be created by Act of Parliament – the UK Bill of Rights Commission proposed as part of the Human Rights Bill 1994 would be a statutory committee of this sort [**147**]. Statutory commissions require parliamentary discussion and approval of their terms of reference, composition and manner of operation, whereas prerogative bodies are established and constructed by the government without recourse to Parliament.

Distinct from the above models as a form of Bill of Rights commission would be a parliamentary select committee established for the purpose. This would mean that the membership of the commission was composed entirely of politicians. It might be a committee of one House alone, either in the Commons or in the Lords (similar to the Lords' Select Committee on a Bill of Rights 1976–7). A Speaker's Conference in the House of Commons is another possibility and would have the advantage of possessing the authority of the Speaker in the chair, presiding over the work of party representatives. A more ambitious suggestion, more appropriate to full-scale reform of the constitution and beyond the parameters of the current Labour–Liberal Democrat joint agreement applicable for the present Parliament [**150**], is the Constituent Assembly proposed by the Liberal Democrats in their policy documents [**93**]. This would involve the House of Commons convening itself in a special capacity to consider and legislate a written constitution into existence of which an entrenched Bill of Rights would form part.

If the Bill of Rights commission took the form of a joint committee of both Houses of Parliament, it would be able to combine the political representativeness of members of the Commons with the more detatched political qualities and source of legal expertise to be found in the Lords. In the preparation of the 1982 Canadian Charter of Rights and Freedoms, a Special Joint Committee of the Senate and the House of Commons on the Constitution of Canada was created, with resources provided by the federal government. It was not strictly speaking a body set up to initiate a draft Bill, since it was formally acting as a special committee to consider a draft Charter of Rights drawn up by Pierre Trudeau's Liberal government. However, in practice the Joint Committee served a largely similar purpose to that which will be required of a preparatory UK Bill of Rights commission, in that its role was to take expert evidence, undertake a wide public consultation exercise required, and serve as the broker between the differing political viewpoints on the draft (which eventually led to 70 changes being made to the original proposal presented to it). A joint parliamentary committee of this kind, acting as an ad hoc instrument of inquiry, could well prove effective. Furthermore, the Labour government has already indicated its approval of the principle of a joint committee of both Houses as a form of inquiry into constitutional change, expressed in its proposals for reform of the House of Lords.[72]

A final option would depend upon whether a UK Human Rights Commission, as considered above (page 74), is established in the near future, prior to the development of a Bill of Rights. As an expert source for producing an authoritative draft document, or offering key advice on the Bill's contents, the Commission would be widely regarded as being well qualified. It is of some significance that the agreement

---

72 See *Reforming the House of Lords,* Cm 4183 (1999); and Report of the Labour–
Liberal Democrat Joint Committee on Constitutional Reform (1997), p. 17.

reached at the multi-party talks on Northern Ireland in April 1998[73] backed the creation of a new Northern Ireland Human Rights Commission,[74] one of whose tasks is currently to consult and advise the British government on the content of Westminster legislation for rights additional to those contained in the ECHR, which would 'constitute a Bill of Rights for Northern Ireland' [**152**].

The most appropriate form of commission selected from these possible options will be determined by the prime minister's own views concerning the commission's most important purposes, at the time it is created. Two factors will be of particular relevance. First, the commission will need to comprise a body of interdisciplinary expertise, particularly in constitutional and legal affairs. Although members will in any event take extensive evidence from others who are expert or interested in a Bill of Rights and its various aspects, the commission itself must clearly possess a level of expertise of its own, so as not only to be in a position to assess the range of options presented to it, but in order to be approaching the various problems and asking the most pertinent questions in the first place. Such expertise need not necessarily be drawn upon from political outsiders, and there is a pool of MPs and other politicians who are knowledgeable in the relevant subject matter. Second, apart from serving as an authoritative source from which recommendations are forthcoming, the commission will need to approach its task in such a manner as to maximize the opportunity for reaching public consensus and the highest level of political support behind the measure. This will involve not simply public consultation, but (to a greater or lesser extent depending on the prevailing state of parliamentary opinion on the reform) negotiation between the political parties or factions within and across them. This function will almost certainly require political representation that a body exclusively comprising independent experts would lack.

These factors point to the desirability of senior politicians being directly involved on the Bill of Rights commission which prepares the draft Bill of Rights. It is membership of the commission, rather than any particular title or form given to whatever type of body is appointed, that will be most crucial to its success. Some officially appointed committee of around twelve to eighteen persons comprising a majority of senior politicians from all parties joined by selected persons with special expertise in the subject would seem most appropriate to the

73 Cm 3883, see pp. 16–17.
74 Now provided for in the Northern Ireland Act 1998, ss.68–9.

task. The type of membership which composed the non-official Labour–Liberal Democrat Joint Consultative Committee on Constitutional Reform, with party representatives (led by MPs Robin Cook for Labour and Robert Maclennan for the Liberal Democrats) joined by constitutional experts nominated by each side (such as Professor Lord Plant for Labour and Lord Lester for the Liberal Democrats) could serve as a model for the composition of such a body, to which invited representatives from the Conservative Party (and possibly also regional parties) would be added. The non-official 1989–93 Scottish Constitutional Convention on devolution to a Scottish Parliament, comprising Scottish Labour and Liberal Democrat politicians and representatives of other professional and social groups in Scotland, might be regarded as providing another precedent of this kind (though with a larger body of persons than would be necessary for a Bill of Rights commission). Though unusual for a government committee to contain party politicians, there is no practical or constitutional objection to an advisory commission bearing this flexible membership for the inquiry on a Bill of Rights. A final determinant in the precise nature of the commission, however, is likely to be whether the cabinet believes it tactically most appropriate for it to be a government or parliamentary body. The differing consequences between the two are less marked than one might suppose. For while formally a commission that is a government committee reports to the prime minister (or departmental minister) and one that is a parliamentary committee reports to Parliament, yet the response that matters in the enactment of the commission's recommendations for a draft Bill of Rights would in both cases lie with the cabinet which possesses the initiation and control of legislative business. Furthermore, while a government committee would certainly allow the mixed political–expert membership suggested above as being desirable, yet a joint parliamentary committee might also be constituted along virtually identical lines, with party representatives being drawn from the Commons and legal and other experts being drawn from the Lords.

Following the report of the Bill of Rights commission, with its accompanying detailed draft legislation, the final stage in the implementation of the reform will be the government's sponsorship of the measure in Parliament. If the commission has successfully negotiated an acceptable consensus around it recommendations, it will be unlikely that the government will wish to make modifications in the form of the Bill which is presented to Parliament. Parliamentarians, however, particularly backbenchers and minority opponents of parts or all of the legislation will wish to scrutinize the proposed Bill of Rights closely. As a constitutional Bill, the normal parliamentary procedures for its passage would be the usual debates and approval at three Readings, with the committee stage examining the measure clause by clause being taken in the chamber of each House, rather than being remitted in the Commons to a standing committee. To avoid filibustering tactics by opponents in the Commons, partial referral of suitable clauses to a committee might be the subject of a government resolution for approval by the Commons, together with a schedule or timetable of the various parliamentary stages being agreed upon in advance between the parties.[75]

The implementation of a Bill of Rights, as with any major item of constitutional change, will be substantially strengthened by clear evidence of popular support. It will provide a powerful endorsement for the Labour government when preparing and enacting the legislation for a Bill of Rights, and it will render minority dissent of an obstructive nature easier to overcome, particularly in the parliamentary passage of the measure. Public attitudes towards reform of the constitution and political system of the UK generally have undergone a marked shift over the past two decades, and a prevalent view undoubtedly now exists which is highly supportive of modernizing measures including a Bill of Rights. Numerous indicators, including the high level of interest shown in the work reform lobby groups such as Charter 88, the growing number of publications on the subject by national figures such as Andrew Marr and Will Hutton,[76] and the results of professional market research regularly commissioned by Joseph Rowntree Trust and others, all clearly point to this state of affairs. Opinion polls throughout the 1990s have disclosed an unequivocal, consistent and overwhelming level of popular opinion in favour of a UK Bill of Rights. Thus opinion polls undertaken by MORI in 1991, 1995 and 1997 put the level of support for a Bill of Rights at over 70 per cent [**149**].

A referendum on this issue remains a possibility, depending on future circumstances particularly concerning the precise content of the Bill of Rights. As a prior consultation of popular opinion on the

---

75 On this aspect of implementation, see Katy Donnelly, 'Parliamentary Reform: Paving the Way for Constitutional Reform', *Parliamentary Affairs* (1997), p. 246, and more generally The Constitution Unit, *Delivering Constitutional Reform* (1996), Ch. 4.

76 Andrew Marr, *Ruling Britannia* (1995); Will Hutton, *The State We're In* (1995).

principle of the matter, it is unlikely to be necessary. The idea of a charter of human rights will already have been implanted in our legal and political system through incorporation of the ECHR – a Labour manifesto commitment voted on at the 1997 election, and one which contained no suggestion of the need for a referendum. Although referendums are a common mechanism under written constitutions abroad for effecting fundamental changes, they have not been a conventional procedure in the UK. Neither have they ever been used in the adoption or approval of any Bill of Rights enacted abroad.[77] Opinion and attitudes towards referendums generally may change, however, as a result of ones taking place on some other matters of major constitutional importance under the new Labour government, including devolution for Scotland and Wales and electoral reform. A common denominator of those particular policies, however, as with the referendums held in mainland Britain in the 1970s over devolution and continued membership of the European Community, is that they are controversial within the governing Labour party itself. In these cases, Labour has effectively agreed to unite around the verdict of the people. Currently, the proposal for a Bill of Rights has acquired a strong level of support within the Labour Party (and an even stronger level within the Liberal Democrats), and the policy is not of a similarly deep controversial nature. However, in the unlikely event that the party became seriously disunited on the policy objective of a Bill of Rights, then rather than withdraw from the commitment as a whole, it would be preferable for a commission on a Bill of Rights to complete its work, and two options (for the recommended reform or the status quo) to be put to the electorate at a referendum, similar to the process currently promised by Tony Blair and the Labour government over the issue of electoral reform.

The strongest argument for a referendum on a Bill of Rights is limited to the more narrow issue of entrenchment. If it proved to be the recommendation of the Bill of Rights commission or that of the government that the Bill of Rights required a method of entrenchment in law that clearly moved in the direction of a written constitution and would effect a substantial amendment or qualification to the principle of parliamentary sovereignty (see above, page 57), then it might well be desirable to secure the moral backing of a democratic vote of the

---

77 See The Constitution Unit, *Human Rights Legislation* (1996), p. 122. See also more generally The Constitution Unit/Electoral Reform Society, *The Conduct of Referendums* (1996).

electorate. This would serve to bind the government and Parliament politically as to their future courses of action, and it would also be recognized in the reality of the constitutional framework of the country by the UK judiciary. The details of the referendum should be tailored towards its purpose. Since, as said, acceptance of the principle of a Bill of Rights could be assumed, it would be the specific form of legislation enacting the Bill of Rights for which electoral approval would need to be sought. In other words, the referendum should be post-legislative. The statute creating the Bill of Rights should contain a section stating that its commencement was subject to a positive vote being carried in a referendum. A simple majority in favour would be adequate, although higher requirements commonly operate in other countries' referendum arrangements (stipulating, for example, that a certain proportion of registered electors must vote in support). Clearly, the higher the actual vote in favour, the greater the moral endorsement of the Bill of Rights there would be. The government should declare in advance that the effect of the referendum is to be regarded as mandatory. So, for example, if the Bill of Rights is approved, a Commencement Order will be laid before Parliament for an affirmative vote; if it fails to pass the necessary threshold of required support, an Order for the repeal of the Bill of Rights would be put before Parliament.[78] The holding of a referendum would entail a prior campaign in which politicians and interested lobby organizations could participate, and the government would need to make arrangements for explanatory information to be published and made available to the public. In its constitutional policy document in 1993, the Labour Party promised the creation of a permanent Electoral Commission,[79] and if such a body was in existence by the time of enactment of a Bill of Rights, it could perform the central function in regulating the conduct of the referendum. The simple question for electors, with Yes and No boxes following, could then be: 'Do you want the provisions of the Bill of Rights Act to be put into effect?'

78 On such procedures, see The Constitution Unit/Electoral Reform Society, ibid., pp. 37–8.
79 *A New Agenda for Democracy* (1993) p. 39. See Constitutional Unit Briefing Paper, *Establishing an Electoral Commission* (1997), and Robert Blackburn and Raymond Plant (eds), *Constitutional Reform* (1999).

PART II

Documents

CHAPTER 1

CIVIL RIGHTS AND FREEDOMS IN THE UK

Historical Documents of Political and Civil Liberty

1 MAGNA CARTA, 1215

John, by the grace of God King of England, Lord of Ireland, Duke of Normandy and Aquitaine, and Count of Anjou, to his archbishops, bishops, abbots, earls, barons, justices, foresters, sheriffs, stewards, servants, and to all his officials and loyal subjects, Greeting.

Know that before God, for the health of our soul and those of our ancestors and heirs, to the honour of God, the exaltation of the holy Church, and the better ordering of our kingdom, at the advice of ... loyal subjects:

(1) First, that we have granted to God, and by this present charter have confirmed for us and our heirs in perpetuity, that the English Church shall be free, and shall have its rights undiminished, and its liberties unimpaired.

To all free men of our kingdom we have also granted, for us and our heirs for ever, all the liberties written out below, to have and to keep for them and their heirs, of us and our heirs:

(2) If any earl, baron, or other person that holds lands directly of the Crown, for military service, shall die, and at his death his heir shall be of full age and owe a 'relief', the heir shall have his inheritance on payment of the ancient scale of 'relief'. That is to say, the heir or heirs of an earl shall pay £100 for the entire earl's barony, the heir or heirs of a knight 100*s*. at most for the entire knight's 'fee', and any man that owes less shall pay less, in accordance with the ancient usage of 'fees' ...

(9) Neither we nor our officials will seize any land or rent in payment of a debt, so long as the debtor has movable goods sufficient to discharge the debt. A debtor's sureties shall not be distrained upon so long as the debtor himself can discharge his debt. If, for lack of means, the debtor is unable to discharge his debt, his sureties shall be answerable for it. If they so desire, they may have the debtor's lands and rents until they have received satisfaction for the debt that they paid for him, unless the debtor can show that he has settled his obligations to them ...

(12) No 'scutage' or 'aid' may be levied in our kingdom without general consent, unless it is for the ransom of our person, to make our eldest son a knight, and (once) to marry our eldest daughter. For these purposes only a reasonable 'aid' may be levied. 'Aids' from the city of London are to be treated similarly.

(13) The city of London shall enjoy all its ancient liberties and free customs, both by land and by water. We also will and grant that all other

cities, boroughs, towns, and ports shall enjoy all their liberties and free customs.

(14) To obtain the general consent for the assessment of an 'aid' – except in the three cases specified above – or a 'scutage', we will cause the archbishops, bishops, abbots, earls, and greater barons to be summoned individually by letter. To those who hold lands directly of us we will cause a general summons to be issued, through the sheriffs and other officials, to come together on a fixed day (of which at least forty days notice shall be given) and at a fixed place. In all letters of summons, the cause of the summons will be stated. When a summons has been issued, the business appointed for the day shall go forward in accordance with the resolution of those present, even if not all those who were summoned have appeared.

(15) In future we will allow no one to levy an 'aid' from his free men, except to ransom his person, to make his eldest son a knight, and (once) to marry his eldest daughter. For these purposes only a reasonable 'aid' may be levied.

(16) No man shall be forced to perform more service for a knight's 'fee', or other free holding of land, than is due from it.

(17) Ordinary lawsuits shall not follow the royal court around, but shall be held in a fixed place.

(18) Inquests of *novel disseisin, mort d'ancestor*, and *darrein presentment* shall be taken only in their proper county court. We ourselves, or in our absence abroad our chief justice, will send two justices to each county four times a year, and these justices, with four knights of the county elected by the county itself, shall hold the assizes in the county court, on the day and in the place where the court meets.

(19) If any assizes cannot be taken on the day of the county court, as many knights and freeholders shall afterwards remain behind, of those who have attended the court, as will suffice for the administration of justice, having regard to the volume of business to be done.

(20) For a trivial offence, a free man shall be fined only in proportion to the degree of his offence, and for a serious offence correspondingly, but not so heavily as to deprive him of his livelihood. In the same way, a merchant shall be spared his merchandise, and a husbandman the implements of his husbandry, if they fall upon the mercy of a royal court. None of these fines shall be imposed except by the assessment of reputable men of the neighbourhood.

(21) Earls and barons shall be fined only by their equals, and in proportion to the gravity of their offence ...

(24) No sheriff, constable, coroners, or other royal officials are to hold lawsuits that should be held by the royal justices ...

(27) If a free man dies intestate, his movable goods are to be distributed by his next-of-kin and friends, under the supervision of the Church. The rights of his debtors are to be preserved.

(28) No constable or other royal official shall take corn or other movable goods from any man without immediate payment, unless the seller voluntarily offers postponement of this ...

(30) No sheriff, royal official, or other person shall take horses or carts for transport from any free man, without his consent.

(31) Neither we nor any royal official will take wood for our castle, or for any other purpose, without the consent of the owner.

(32) We will not keep the lands of people convicted of felony in our hand for longer than a year and a day, after which they shall be returned to the lords of the 'fees' concerned.

(34) The writ called *precipe* shall not in future be issued to anyone in respect of any holding of land, if a free man could thereby be deprived of the right of trial in his own lord's court.

(35) There shall be standard measures of wine, ale, and corn (the London quarter), throughout the kingdom. There shall also be a standard width of dyed cloth, russett, and haberject, namely two ells within the selvedges. Weights are to be standardised similarly. . . .

(38) In future no official shall place a man on trial upon his own unsupported statement, without producing credible witnesses to the truth of it.

(39) No free man shall be seized or imprisoned, or stripped of his rights or possessions, or outlawed or exiled, or deprived of his standing in any other way, nor will we proceed with force against him, or send others to do so, except by the lawful judgement of his equals or by the law of the land.

(40) To no one will we sell, to no one deny or delay right or justice.

(41) All merchants may enter or leave England unharmed and without fear, and may stay or travel within it, by land or water, for purposes of trade, free from all illegal exactions, in accordance with ancient and lawful customs. This, however, does not apply in time of war to merchants from a country that is at war with us. Any such merchants found in our country at the outbreak of war shall be detained without injury to their persons or property, until we or our chief justice have discovered how our own merchants are being treated in the country at war with us. If our own merchants are safe they shall be safe too . . .

(45) We will appoint as justices, constables, sheriffs, or other officials, only men that know the law of the realm and are minded to keep it well. . . .

(52) To any man whom we have deprived or dispossessed of lands, castles, liberties, or rights, without the lawful judgement of his equals, we will at once restore these. In cases of dispute the matter shall be resolved by the judgement of the twenty-five barons referred to below in the clause for securing the peace (§ 61). In cases, however, where a man was deprived or dispossessed of something without the lawful judgement of his equals by our father King Henry or our brother King Richard, and it remains in our hands or is held by others under our warranty, we shall have respite for the period commonly allowed to Crusaders, unless a lawsuit had been begun, or an enquiry had been made at our order, before we took the Cross as a Crusader. On our return from the Crusade, or if we abandon it, we will at once render justice in full. . . .

(56) If we have deprived or dispossessed any Welshmen of lands, liberties,

or anything else in England or in Wales, without the lawful judgement of their equals, these are at once to be returned to them. A dispute on this point shall be determined in the Marches by the judgement of equals. English law shall apply to holdings of land in England, Welsh law to those in Wales, and the law of the Marches to those in the Marches. The Welsh shall treat us and ours in the same way. . . .

(60) All these customs and liberties that we have granted shall be observed in our kingdom in so far as concerns our own relations with our subjects. Let all men of our kingdom, whether clergy or laymen, observe them similarly in their relations with their own men.

(61) Since we have granted all these things for God, for the better ordering of our kingdom, and to allay the discord that has arisen between us and our barons, and since we desire that they shall be enjoyed in their entirety, with lasting strength, for ever, we give and grant to the barons the following security:

The barons shall elect twenty-five of their number to keep, and cause to be observed with all their might, the peace and liberties granted and confirmed to them by this charter.

If we, our chief justice, our officials, or any of our servants offend in any respect against any man, or transgress any of the articles of the peace or of this security, and the offence is made known to four of the said twenty-five barons, they shall come to us – or in our absence from the kingdom to the chief justice – to declare it and claim immediate redress. If we, or in our absence abroad the chief justice, make no redress within forty days, reckoning from the day on which the offence was declared to us or to him, the four barons shall refer the matter to the rest of the twenty-five barons, who may distrain upon and assail us in every way possible, with the support of the whole community of the land, by seizing our castles, lands, possessions, or anything else saving only our own person and those of the queen and our children, until they have secured such redress as they have determined upon. Having secured the redress, they may then resume their normal obedience to us. . . .

In the event of disagreement among the twenty-five barons on any matter referred to them for decision, the verdict of the majority present shall have the same validity as a unanimous verdict of the whole twenty-five, whether these were all present or some of those summoned were unwilling or unable to appear.

The twenty-five barons shall swear to obey all the above articles faithfully, and shall cause them to be obeyed by others to the best of their power. . . .

(63) It is accordingly our wish and command that the English Church shall be free, and that men in our kingdom shall have and keep all these liberties, rights, and concessions, well and peaceably in their fulness and entirety for them and their heirs, of us and our heirs, in all things and all places for ever.

Given by our hand in the meadow that is called Runnymede, between Windsor and Staines, on the fifteenth day of June in the seventeenth year of our reign.

2   THE PETITION OF RIGHT, 1628

The Petition exhibited to His Majesty by the Lords Spiritual and Temporal, and Commons in this present Parliament assembled, concerning divers Rights and Liberties of the Subjects, with the King's Majesty's Royal Answer thereunto in full Parliament.

To the King's Most Excellent Majesty.

Humbly show unto our Sovereign Lord the King, the Lords Spiritual and Temporal, and Commons in Parliament assembled, that whereas it is declared and enacted by a statute made in the time of the reign of King Edward the First, commonly called *Statutum de Tallagio non concedendo*, that no tallage or aid shall be laid or levied by the King or his heirs in this realm, without the goodwill and assent of the Archbishops, Bishops, Earls, Barons, Knights, Burgesses, and other the freemen of the commonalty of this realm: and by authority of Parliament holden in the five and twentieth year of the reign of King Edward the Third, it is declared and enacted, that from thenceforth no person shall be compelled to make any loans to the King against his will, because such loans were against reason and the franchise of the land; and by other laws of this realm it is provided, that none should be charged by any charge or imposition, called a Benevolence, or by such like charge, by which the statutes before-mentioned, and other the good laws and statutes of this realm, your subjects have inherited this freedom, that they should not be compelled to contribute to any tax, tallage, aid, or other like charge, not set by common consent in Parliament:

Yet nevertheless, of late divers commissions directed to sundry Commissioners in several counties with instructions have issued, by means whereof your people have been in divers places assembled, and required to lend certain sums of money unto your Majesty, and many of them upon their refusal so to do, have had an oath administered unto them, not warrantable by the laws or statutes of this realm, and have been constrained to become bound to make appearance and give attendance before your Privy Council, and in other places, and others of them have been therefore imprisoned, confined, and sundry other ways molested and disquieted: and divers other charges have been laid and levied upon your people in several counties, by Lords Lieutenants, Deputy Lieutenants, Commissioners for Musters, Justices of Peace and others, by command or direction from your Majesty or your Privy Council, against the laws and free customs of this realm:

And where also by the statute called, 'The Great Charter of the Liberties of England' [Magna Carta], it is declared and enacted, that no freeman may be taken or imprisoned or be disseised of his freeholds or liberties, or his free customs, or be outlawed or exiled; or in any manner destroyed, but by the lawful judgment of his peers, or by the law of the land:

And in the eight and twentieth year of the reign of King Edward the Third, it was declared and enacted by authority of Parliament, that no man of what estate or condition that he be, should be put out of his lands or tenements, nor taken, nor imprisoned, nor disherited, nor put to death, without being brought to answer by due process of law:

Nevertheless, against the tenor of the said statutes, and other the good laws and statutes of your realm, to that end provided, divers of your subjects have of late been imprisoned without any cause showed, and when for their deliverance they were brought before your Justices, by your Majesty's writs of Habeas Corpus, there to undergo and receive as the Court should order, and their keepers commanded to certify the causes of their detainer; no cause was certified, but that they were detained by your Majesty's special command, signified by the Lords of your Privy Council, and yet were returned back to several prisons, without being charged with anything to which they might make answer according to the law:

And whereas of late great companies of soldiers and mariners have been dispersed into divers counties of the realm, and the inhabitants against their wills have been compelled to receive them into their houses, and there to suffer them to sojourn, against the laws and customs of this realm, and to the great grievance and vexation of the people:

And whereas also by authority of Parliament, in the 25th year of the reign of King Edward the Third, it is declared and enacted, that no man shall be forejudged of life or limb against the form of the Great Charter, and the law of the land: and by the said Great Charter and other the laws and statutes of this your realm, no man ought to be adjudged to death; but by the laws established in this your realm, either by the customs of the same realm or by Acts of Parliament: and whereas no offender of what kind soever is exempted from the proceedings to be used, and punishments to be inflicted by the laws and statutes of this your realm: nevertheless of late divers commissions under your Majesty's Great Seal have issued forth, by which certain persons have been assigned and appointed Commissioners with power and authority to proceed within the land, according to the justice of martial law against such soldiers and mariners, or other dissolute persons joining with them, as should commit any murder, robbery, felony, mutiny, or other outrage or misdemeanour whatsoever, and by such summary course and order, as is agreeable to martial law, and is used in armies in time of war, to proceed to the trial and condemnation of such offenders, and them to cause to be executed and put to death, according to the law martial:

By pretext whereof, some of your Majesty's subjects have been by some of the said Commissioners put to death, when and where, if by the laws and statutes of the land they had deserved death, by the same laws and statutes also they might, and by no other ought to have been, adjudged and executed:

And also sundry grievous offenders by colour thereof, claiming an exemption, have escaped the punishments due to them by the laws and statutes of this your realm, by reason that divers of your officers and ministers of justice have unjustly refused, or forborne to proceed against such offenders according to the same laws and statutes, upon pretence that the said offenders were punishable only by martial law, and by authority of such commissions as aforesaid, which commissions, and all other of like nature, are wholly and directly contrary to the said laws and statutes of this your realm:

They do therefore humbly pray your Most Excellent Majesty, that no man hereafter be compelled to make or yield any gift, loan, benevolence, tax, or such like charge, without common consent by Act of Parliament; and that none be called to make answer, or take such oath, or to give attendance, or be confined, or otherwise molested or disquieted concerning the same, or for refusal thereof; and that no freeman, in any such manner as is before-mentioned, be imprisoned or detained; and that your Majesty will be pleased to remove the said soldiers and mariners, and that your people may not be so burdened in time to come; and that the foresaid commissions for proceeding by martial law, may be revoked and annulled; and that hereafter no commissions of like nature may issue forth to any person or persons whatsoever, to be executed as aforesaid, lest by colour of them any of your Majesty's subjects be destroyed or put to death, contrary to the laws and franchise of the land.

All which they most humbly pray of your Most Excellent Majesty, as their rights and liberties according to the laws and statutes of this realm: and that your Majesty would also vouchsafe to declare, that the awards, doings, and proceedings to the prejudice of your people, in any of the premises, shall not be drawn hereafter into consequence or example: and that your Majesty would be also graciously pleased, for the further comfort and safety of your people, to declare your royal will and pleasure, that in the things aforesaid all your officers and ministers shall serve you, according to the laws and statutes of this realm, as they tender the honour of your Majesty, and the prosperity of this kingdom.

[Which Petition being read the 2nd of June 1628, the King's answer was thus delivered unto it.

The King willeth that right be done according to the laws and customs of the realm; and that the statutes be put in due execution, that his subjects may have no cause to complain of any wrong or oppressions, contrary to their just rights and liberties, to the preservation whereof he holds himself as well obliged as of his prerogative.

On June 7 the answer was given in the accustomed form, *Soit droit fait comme il est désiré.*]

3   HABEAS CORPUS ACT, 1679

An Act for the better securing the liberty of the subject

[I.] Whensoever any person or persons shall bring any Habeas Corpus directed unto any sheriff or sheriffs, gaoler, minister, or other person whatsoever, for any person in his or their custody, and the said writ shall be served upon the said officer, or left at the gaol or prison with any of the under officers, under keepers or deputy of the said officers or keepers, that the said officer or officers etc. shall, within three days after the service thereof as aforesaid, (unless the commitment aforesaid were for treason or felony, plainly or specially expressed in the warrant of commitment), upon payment or tender of the charges of bringing the said prisoner, to be ascertained by the judge or court that awarded the same, and indorsed upon the same writ, not exceeding twelvepence per mile, and upon security given by his own bond to pay the charges of carrying back the prisoner, if he shall be remanded by the court or judge to which he shall be brought according to the true intent of this present Act, and that he will not make any escape by the way, make return of such writ; and bring, or cause to be brought, the body of the party so committed or restrained, unto or before the Lord Chancellor, or Lord Keeper of the Great Seal of England for the time being, or the judges or barons of the said court from whence the said writ shall issue, or unto or before such other person or persons before whom the said writ is made returnable, according to the command thereof; and shall then likewise certify the true causes of his detainer or imprisonment, unless the commitment of the said party be in any place beyond the distance of twenty miles, from the place or places where such court or person is or shall be residing; and if beyond the distance of twenty miles, and not above one hundred miles, then within the space of ten days, and if beyond the distance of one hundred miles, then within the space of twenty days, after such delivery aforesaid, and not longer.

[II.] And to the intent that no sheriff, gaoler, or other officer may pretend ignorance of the import of any such writ; be it enacted . . . that all such writs shall be marked in this manner, *per statutum tricesimo primo Caroli secundi regis*, and shall be signed by the person that awards the same; and if any person or persons shall be or stand committed or detained as aforesaid, for any crime, unless for felony or treason plainly expressed in the warrant of commitment, in the vacation time, and out of term, it shall and may be lawful to and for the person or persons so committed or detained (other than persons convict or in execution by legal process) or any one on his or their behalf, to appeal or complain to the Lord Chancellor or Lord Keeper, or any one of his Majesty's Justices, either of the one bench or of the other, or the barons of the exchequer of the degree of the coif; and the said Lord Chancellor etc. or any of them, upon view of the copy or copies of the warrant or warrants of commitment or detainer, or otherwise upon oath made that such copy or copies were denied to be given by such person or persons in whose custody the prisoner or prisoners is or are detained, are hereby authorised and required, upon request made in writing by such person or persons, or any on his, her or their behalf, attested and subscribed by two witnesses who were present at the delivery of the same, to award and grant a Habeas Corpus under the seal of such court whereof he shall then be one of the judges, to be directed to the officer or officers in whose custody the party so committed or detained shall be; returnable immediate before the said Lord Chancellor, or Lord Keeper, or such justice, baron, or any other justice or baron of the degree of the coif of any of the said courts; and upon service thereof as aforesaid, the officer or officers etc. in whose custody the party is so committed or detained, shall, within the times respectively before limited, bring such prisoner or prisoners before the said Lord Chancellor or Lord Keeper, or such justices, barons or one of them, before whom the said writ is made returnable, and in case of his absence, before any other of them, with the return of such writ, and the true causes of the commitment and detainer; and thereupon within two days after the party shall be brought before them, the said Lord Chancellor or Lord Keeper etc. shall discharge the said prisoner from his imprisonment, taking his or their recognizance, with one or more surety or sureties, in any sum according to their discretions, having regard to the quality of the prisoner and nature of the offence, for his or their appearance in the Court of King's Bench the term following, or at the next assizes, sessions or general gaol-delivery of and for such county, city or place where the commitment was, or where the offence was committed, or in such other court where the said offence is properly cognizable, as the case shall require, and then shall certify the said writ with the return thereof, and the said recognizance or recognizances into the said court where such appearance is to be made; unless it shall appear unto the said Lord Chancellor or Lord Keeper etc. that the party so committed is detained upon a legal process, order or warrant, out of some court that hath jurisdiction of criminal matters, or by some warrant signed and sealed with the hand and seal of any of the said justices or barons, or some justice or justices of the peace, for such matters or offences for the which by the law the prisoner is not bailable. ...

[IV.] And be it further enacted by the authority aforesaid, that if any officer or officers etc. shall neglect or refuse to make the returns aforesaid, or to bring the body or bodies of the prisoner or prisoners according to the command of the said writ, within the respective times aforesaid, or upon demand made by the prisoner or person in his behalf, shall refuse to deliver, or within the space of six hours after demand shall not deliver, to the person so demanding, a true copy of the warrant or warrants of commitment and detainer of such prisoner, which he and they are hereby required to deliver accordingly; all and every the head gaolers and keepers of such prisons, and such other persons in whose custody the prisoner shall be detained, shall for the first offence forfeit to the prisoner or party grieved the sum of one hundred pounds; and for the second offence the sum of two hundred pounds; and shall and is hereby made incapable to hold or execute his said office.

4 THE BILL OF RIGHTS, 1688

An Act for declaring the rights and liberties of the subject and settling the succession of the crown

Whereas the lords spiritual and temporal, and commons, assembled at Westminster, lawfully, fully, and freely representing all the estates of the people of this realm, did upon the thirteenth day of February, in the year of our Lord one thousand six hundred eighty eight, present unto their Majesties, then called and known by the names and stile of William and Mary, prince and princess of Orange, being present in their proper persons, a certain declaration in writing, made by the said lords and commons, in the words following: viz.

Whereas the late King James the Second, by the assistance of divers evil counsellors, judges, and ministers employed by him, did endeavour to subvert and extirpate the protestant religion, and the laws and liberties of this kingdom.

1. By assuming and exercising a power of dispensing with and suspending of laws, and the execution of laws, without consent of parliament.

2. By committing and prosecuting divers worthy prelates, for humbly petitioning to be excused concurring to the said assumed power.

3. By issuing and causing to be executed a commission under the great seal for erecting a court called the court of commissioners for ecclesiastical causes.

4. By levying money for and to the use of the crown, by pretence of prerogative, for other time, and in other manner, than the same was granted by parliament.

5. By raising and keeping a standing army within this kingdom in time of peace, without consent of parliament, and quartering soldiers contrary to law.

6. By causing several good subjects, being protestants, to be disarmed, at the same time when papists were both armed and employed, contrary to law.

7. By violating the freedom of election of members to serve in parliament.

8. By prosecutions in the court of King's bench, for matters and causes cognizable only in parliament; and by divers other arbitrary and illegal courses.

9. And whereas of late years, partial, corrupt, and unqualified persons have been returned and served on juries in trials and particularly divers jurors in trials for high treason, which were not freeholders.

10. And excessive bail hath been required of persons committed in criminal cases, to elude the benefit of the laws made for the liberty of the subjects.

11. And excessive fines have been imposed; and illegal and cruel punishments inflicted.

12. And several grants and promises made of fines and forfeitures, before any conviction or judgment against the persons, upon whom the same were to be levied.

All which are utterly and directly contrary to the known laws and statutes, and freedom of this realm.

And whereas the said late King James the Second having abdicated the government, and the throne being thereby vacant, his highness the Prince of Orange (whom it hath pleased Almighty God to make the glorious instrument of delivering this kingdom from popery and arbitrary power) did (by the advice of the lords spiritual and temporal, and divers principal persons of the commons) cause letters to be written to the lords spiritual and temporal, being protestants; and other letters to the several counties, cities, universities, boroughs, and cinque-ports, for the choosing of such persons to represent them, as were of right to be sent to parliament, to meet and sit at Westminster upon the two and twentieth day of January, in this year one thousand six hundred eighty eight, in order to such an establishment, as that their religion, laws, and liberties might not again be in danger of being subverted: upon which letters, elections have been accordingly made.

And thereupon the said lords spiritual and temporal, and commons, pursuant to their respective letters and elections, being now assembled in a full and free representative of this nation, taking into their most serious consideration the best means for attaining the ends aforesaid; do in the first place (as their ancestors in like case have usually done) for the vindicating and asserting their ancient rights and liberties, declare:

1. That the pretended power of suspending of laws, or the execution of laws, by regal authority, without consent of parliament, is illegal.

2. That the pretended power of dispensing with laws, or the execution of laws, by regal authority, as it hath been assumed and exercised of late, is illegal.

3. That the commission for erecting the late court of commissioners for ecclesiastical causes, and all other commissions and courts of like nature are illegal and pernicious.

4. That levying money for or to the use of the crown, by pretence of prerogative, without grant of parliament, for longer time, or in other manner than the same is or shall be granted, is illegal.

5. That it is the right of the subjects to petition the King, and all commitments and prosecutions for such petitioning are illegal.

6. That the raising or keeping a standing army within the kingdom in time of peace, unless it be with consent of parliament, is against law.

7. That the subjects which are protestants, may have arms for their defence suitable to their conditions, and as allowed by law.

8. That election of members of parliament ought to be free.

9. That the freedom of speech, and debates or proceedings in parliament, ought not to be impeached or questioned in any court or place out of parliament.

10. That excessive bail ought not to be required, nor excessive fines imposed; nor cruel and unusual punishments inflicted.

11. That jurors ought to be duly impanelled and returned, and jurors which pass upon men in trials for high treason ought to be freeholders.

12. That all grants and promises of fines and forfeitures of particular persons before conviction, are illegal and void.

13. And that for redress of all grievances, and for the amending, strengthening and preserving of the laws, parliaments ought to be held frequently.

And they do claim, demand, and insist upon all and singular the premisses, as their undoubted rights and liberties; and that no declarations, judgments, doings or proceedings, to the prejudice of the people in any of the said premisses, ought in any wise to be drawn hereafter into consequence or example. . . .

(B)

The British Constitution and the Protection Of Freedom, 1885–98

---

5 THE LAW PROFESSOR A. V. DICEY ON THE SOVEREIGNTY OF PARLIAMENT IN NINETEENTH-CENTURY BRITAIN, 1885

The sovereignty of Parliament is (from a legal point of view) the dominant characteristic of our political institutions . . . Parliament is, under the British constitution, an absolutely sovereign legislature.

Parliament means, in the mouth of a lawyer (though the word has often a different sense in ordinary conversation), the Queen, the House of Lords, and the House of Commons; these three bodies acting together may be aptly described as the 'Queen in Parliament,' and constitute Parliament.

The principle of Parliamentary sovereignty means neither more nor less than this, namely, that Parliament thus defined has, under the English constitution, the right to make or unmake any law whatever; and, further, that no person or body is recognised by the law of England as having a right to override or set aside the legislation of Parliament.

A law may, for our present purpose, be defined as 'any rule which will be enforced by the courts.' The principle then of Parliamentary sovereignty may, looked at from its positive side, be thus described: Any Act of Parliament, or any part of an Act of Parliament, which makes a new law, or repeals or modifies an existing law, will be obeyed by the courts. The same principle, looked at from its negative side, may be thus stated: There is no person or body of persons who can, under the English constitution, make rules which override or derogate from an Act of Parliament, or which (to express the same thing in other words) will be enforced by the courts in contravention of an Act of Parliament. . . .

The characteristics of Parliamentary sovereignty may be deduced from the term itself. But these traits are apt to escape the attention of Englishmen, who have been so accustomed to live under the rule of a supreme legislature, that they almost, without knowing it, assume that all legislative bodies are supreme, and hardly therefore keep clear before their minds the properties of a supreme as contrasted with a non-sovereign law-making body. In this matter foreign observers are, as is natural, clearer-sighted than Englishmen. De Lolme, Gneist, and de Tocqueville seize at once upon the sovereignty of Parliament as a salient feature of the English constitution, and recognise the far-reaching effects of this marked peculiarity in our institutions.

'In England,' writes de Tocqueville, 'the Parliament has an acknowledged right to modify the constitution; as, therefore, the constitution may undergo perpetual changes, it does not in reality exist; the Parliament is at once a legislative and a constituent assembly.'

His expressions are wanting in accuracy, and might provoke some criticism, but the description of the English Parliament as at once 'a legislative and a constituent assembly' supplies a convenient formula for summing up the fact that Parliament can change any law whatever. Being a 'legislative' assembly it can make ordinary laws, being a 'constituent' assembly it can make laws which shift the basis of the constitution. The results which ensue from this fact may be brought under three heads.

First, There is no law which Parliament cannot change, or (to put the same thing somewhat differently), fundamental or so-called constitutional laws are under our constitution changed by the same body and in the same manner as other laws, namely, by Parliament acting in its ordinary legislative character.

A Bill for reforming the House of Commons, a Bill for abolishing the House of Lords, a Bill to give London a municipality, a Bill to make valid marriages celebrated by a pretended clergyman, who is found after their celebration not to be in orders, are each equally within the competence of Parliament, they each may be passed in substantially the same manner, they none of them when passed will be, legally speaking, a whit more sacred or immutable than the others, for they each will be neither more nor less than an Act of Parliament, which can be repealed as it has been passed by Parliament, and cannot be annulled by any other power.

Secondly, There is under the English constitution no marked or clear distinction between laws which are not fundamental or constitutional and laws which are fundamental or constitutional. The very language therefore, expressing the difference between a 'legislative' assembly which can change ordinary laws and a 'constituent' assembly which can change not only ordinary but also constitutional and fundamental laws, has to be borrowed from the political phraseology of foreign countries.

This absence of any distinction between constitutional and ordinary laws has a close connection with the non-existence in England of any written or enacted constitutional statute or charter. de Tocqueville indeed, in common with other writers, apparently holds the unwritten character of the British constitution to be of its essence: 'L'Angleterre n'ayant point de constitution écrite, qui peut dire qu'on change sa constitution?' But here de Tocqueville falls into an error, characteristic both of his nation and of the weaker side of his own rare genius. He has treated the form of the constitution as the cause of its substantial qualities, and has inverted the relation of cause and effect. The constitution, he seems to have thought, was changeable because it was not reduced to a written or statutory form. It is far nearer the truth to assert that the constitution has never been reduced to a written or statutory form because each and every part of it is changeable at the will of Parliament.

When a country is governed under a constitution which is intended either to be unchangeable or at any rate to be changeable only with special difficulty, the constitution, which is nothing else than the laws which are intended to have a character of permanence or immutability, is necessarily expressed in writing, or, to use English phraseology, is enacted as a statute. Where, on the other hand, every law can be legally changed with equal ease or with equal difficulty, there arises no absolute need for reducing the constitution to a written form, or even for looking upon a definite set of laws as specially making up the constitution. One main reason then why constitutional laws have not in England been recognised under that name, and in many cases have not been reduced to the form of a statutory enactment, is that one law, whatever its importance, can be passed and changed by exactly the same method as every other law. But it is a mistake to think that the whole law of the English constitution might not be reduced to writing and be enacted in the form of a constitutional code. The Belgian constitution indeed comes very near to a written reproduction of the English constitution, and the constitution of England might easily be turned into an Act of Parliament without suffering any material transformation of character, provided only that the English Parliament retained—what the Belgian Parliament, by the way, does not possess—the unrestricted power of repealing or amending the constitutional code.

Thirdly, There does not exist in any part of the British Empire any person or body of persons, executive, legislative or judicial, which can pronounce void any enactment passed by the British Parliament on the ground of such enactment being opposed to the constitution, or on any ground whatever, except, of course, its being repealed by Parliament.

These then are the three traits of Parliamentary sovereignty as it exists in England: first, the power of the legislature to alter any law, fundamental or otherwise, as freely and in the same manner as other laws; secondly, the absence of any legal distinction between constitutional and other laws; thirdly, the non-existence of any judicial or other authority having the right to nullify an Act of Parliament, or to treat it as void or unconstitutional.

These traits are all exemplifications of the quality which [are] happily denominated the 'flexibility' of the British constitution. Every part of it can be expanded, curtailed, amended, or abolished, with equal ease. It is the most flexible polity in existence.

The Law of the Constitution, 10th edn 1985, pp. 39–41, 87–91.

---

6 A. V. DICEY'S THEORY OF THE RULE OF LAW PROTECTING INDIVIDUAL FREEDOM IN BRITAIN, 1885

Whenever we talk of Englishmen as loving the government of law, or of the supremacy of law as being a characteristic of the English constitution, [we] are using words which, though they possess a real significance, are nevertheless to most persons who employ them full of vagueness and ambiguity. If therefore we are ever to appreciate the full import of the idea denoted by the term 'rule, supremacy, or predominance of law,' we must first determine precisely what we mean by such expressions when we apply them to the British constitution.

When we say that the supremacy or the rule of law is a characteristic of the English constitution, we generally include under one expression at least three distinct though kindred conceptions. . . .

That 'rule of law' . . . which forms a fundamental principle of the constitution, has three meanings, or may be regarded from three different points of view.

It means, in the first place, the absolute supremacy or predominance of regular law as opposed to the influence of arbitrary power, and excludes the existence of arbitrariness, of prerogative, or even of wide discretionary authority on the part of the government. Englishmen are ruled by the law, and by the law alone; a man may with us be punished for a breach of law, but he can be punished for nothing else.

It means, again, equality before the law, or the equal subjection of all classes to the ordinary law of the land administered by the ordinary law courts; the 'rule of law' in this sense excludes the idea of any exemption of officials or others from the duty of obedience to the law which governs other citizens or from the jurisdiction of the ordinary tribunals. . . .

The 'rule of law,' lastly, may be used as a formula for expressing the fact that with us the law of the constitution, the rules which in foreign countries naturally form part of a constitutional code, are not the source but the consequence of the rights of individuals, as defined and enforced by the courts; that, in short, the principles of private law have with us been by the action of the courts and Parliament so extended as to determine the position of the Crown and of its servants; thus the constitution is the result of the ordinary law of the land. . . .

There is in the English constitution an absence of those declarations or definitions of rights so dear to foreign constitutionalists. Such principles, moreover, as you can discover in the English constitution are, like all maxims established by judicial legislation, mere generalisations drawn either from the decisions or dicta of judges, or from statutes which, being passed to meet special grievances, bear a close resemblance to judicial decisions, and are in effect judgments pronounced by the High Court of Parliament. To put what is really the same thing in a somewhat different shape, the relation of the rights of individuals to the principles of the constitution is not quite the same in countries like Belgium, where the constitution is the result of a legislative act, as it is in England, where the constitution itself is based upon legal decisions. In Belgium, which may be taken as a type of countries possessing a constitution formed by a deliberate act of legislation, you may say with truth that the rights of individuals to personal liberty flow from or are secured by the constitution. In England the right to individual liberty is part of the constitution, because it is secured by the decisions of the courts, extended or confirmed as they are by the Habeas Corpus Acts. If it be allowable to apply the formulas of logic to questions of law, the difference in this matter between the constitution of Belgium and the English constitution may be described by the statement that in Belgium individual rights are deductions drawn from the principles of the constitution, whilst in England the so-called principles of the constitution are inductions or generalisations based upon particular decisions pronounced by the courts as to the rights of given individuals.

This is of course a merely formal difference. Liberty is as well secured in Belgium as in England, and as long as this is so it matters nothing whether we say that individuals are free from all risk of arbitrary arrest, because liberty of person is guaranteed by the constitution, or that the right to personal freedom, or in other words to protection from arbitrary arrest, forms part of the constitution because it is secured by the ordinary law of the land. But though this merely formal distinction is in itself of no moment, provided always that the rights of individuals are really secure, the question whether the right to personal freedom or the right to freedom of worship is likely to be secure does depend a good deal upon the answer to the inquiry whether the persons who consciously or unconsciously build up the constitution of their country begin with definitions or declarations of rights, or with the contrivance of remedies by which rights may be enforced or secured.

Now, most foreign constitution-makers have begun with declarations of rights. For this they have often been in nowise to blame. Their course of action has more often than not been forced upon them by the stress of circumstances, and by the consideration that to lay down general principles of law is the proper and natural function of legislators. ...

On the other hand, there runs through the English constitution that inseparable connection between the means of enforcing a right and the right to be enforced which is the strength of judicial legislation. The saw, *ubi jus ibi remedium*, becomes from this point of view something much more important than a mere tautologous proposition. In its bearing upon constitutional law, it means that the Englishmen whose labours gradually framed the complicated set of laws and institutions which we call the Constitution, fixed their minds far more intently on providing remedies for the enforcement of particular rights or (what is merely the same thing looked at from the other side) for averting definite wrongs, than upon any declaration of the Rights of Man or of Englishmen. The Habeas Corpus Acts declare no principle and define no rights, but they are for practical purposes worth a hundred constitutional articles guaranteeing individual liberty. Nor let it be supposed that this connection between rights and remedies which depends upon the spirit of law pervading English institutions is inconsistent with the existence of a written constitution, or even with the existence of constitutional declarations of rights. The Constitution of the United States and the constitutions of the separate States are embodied in written or printed documents, and contain declarations of rights. But the statesmen of America have shown unrivalled skill in providing means for giving legal security to the rights declared by American constitutions. The rule of law is as marked a feature of the United States as of England.

The Law of the Constitution, 10th edn 1985, pp. 186–8, 197–200, 202–3.

---

7 SIR IVOR JENNINGS QC ON FUNDAMENTAL LIBERTIES, 1933

The protection of minorities

The fundamental principle of democracy is that government shall be carried on for the benefit of the governed, and, since it is considered that only the governed themselves can determine what is for their benefit, under their control. The object of most constitutions is to set up machinery by which the wishes of the governed may determine the nature of the government. It is never entirely successful. But even if it were it would leave unsolved one most important problem. The wishes of the governed mean at best the wishes of a majority of them. Yet the minority, too, is composed of excellent persons, perhaps more intelligent and certainly less orthodox. The problem of government, therefore, is not only to provide for government by the majority, but also to protect the minority.

It is not possible to prevent the Government, supported by a majority, from interfering in accordance with law with the liberty and property of a minority. It is not desirable that the attempt should be made. But there are certain rights which are commonly recognised as essential for effective social life and which, being considered to be inherent in the idea of justice, should be protected even against the majority. Exactly what they are depends upon the state of opinion and the organisation of society. If religion is militant, protection may be needed by those who profess a religious belief not accepted by the majority. If education is the passport to a full life, free education may be made compulsory. If the means of production are not equally distributed, the right to sustenance may be the most insistent of the demands made.

Government by opinion

There are some rights, however, which are inherent in a system of government by opinion. This system implies the right to create opinion and to organise it with a view to influencing the conduct of government. There can be no such system if minority opinions cannot be expressed, or if people cannot meet together to discuss their opinions and their actions, or if those who think alike on any subject cannot associate for mutual support and for the propagation of their common ideas. Yet these rights are those most likely to be attacked. For those in power can, *ex hypothesi*, continue in power only so long as they command the support of the majority. If a sufficient section of the majority is converted to the views of a large section of the minority, their right to govern is gone, and at the next general election they lose the attractions of office.

Fundamental rights

The problem is not merely one of limiting the powers of the administration. Its solution involves limiting the powers of the legislature as well; for it is normally the majority of the legislature which claims to represent most closely the opinions of the majority of the population. It is therefore usually regarded as desirable not only that the ordinary law shall protect the right of free speech, the right of association, and the right of public meeting, but also that the powers of changing the law, whether by legislation or administrative regulation, shall be so restricted that these rights may not be interfered with.

With a written constitution, this is an end which in principle is fairly easy to accomplish. Certain 'fundamental rights' are inserted in the constitution, and every institution of government is forbidden to change them. A fundamental right can then be limited or taken away only by constitutional amendment, and if the process is in any way difficult or formal, such a limitation becomes plain for all to see. Nearly all written constitutions contain such provisions, though with varying definiteness of expression. Nearly all of them, too, provide for freedom of speech, freedom of association, and freedom of assembly.

Difficulties: (1) need for special machinery

Three difficulties at once suggest themselves. The first is that the protection may be very ineffective if there is no machinery for determining when a fundamental right is being infringed. In the United States of America this function was assumed by the Supreme Court. In countries which follow the French tradition this is regarded as a usurpation by the judicial authorities of a function which does not rightly belong to them. The question is one between the legislature and the electorate which the courts are considered incapable of settling. But where the American precedent is followed, as it is in many countries, the consequence is to place upon the courts the duty of acting as guardians of fundamental rights.

Difficulties: (2) changing ideas of what is fundamental

The second difficulty is that what are regarded as fundamental rights by one generation may be considered to be inconvenient limitations upon legislative power by another generation. For example, the fifth and fourteenth Amendments to the Constitution of the United States prevented the United States Congress and the legislatures of the States from depriving any person of life, liberty, or property, 'without due process of law.' This has been used by the Supreme Court to limit very seriously the enactment of social legislation dealing with such matters as hours of labour, minimum wages, and workmen's compensation. This is due, perhaps, as much to the beliefs of some of the judges of the Supreme Court as to the framers of the Constitution. It is nevertheless clear that the provisions of a constitution drawn up before the development of modern industrial society are likely to lead to such complications.

Difficulties: (3) the right cannot be absolute

The third difficulty is that even the rights of free speech, of association, and of assembly cannot be regarded as being without limitation. They may be used not for creating opinion in order to turn out the Government by lawful means, but to persuade a small minority to use force to coerce the rest of the population. In their extreme meanings, the rights conflict with the fundamental requirements of public order. National emergencies, too, may demand a limitation upon the rights of individuals which would not be permissible in ordinary times. Two consequences follow. The first is that limitations must commonly be placed upon the rights expressed in the constitution, thereby making them much less effective in practice. The second is that some special provision must be inserted or implied for times of emergency, thereby depriving a minority of its rights just when the majority is least capable of rational appreciation of the contentious nature of its own ideas and when, therefore, the minority stands most in need of protection.

Fundamental rights in England

Since the United Kingdom has no such written constitution, there are no fundamental rights in this sense. If it is attempted to talk about such 'rights' in England, it becomes at once apparent that the word is ambiguous. Certain 'rights' were inserted in the American Declaration of Independence because they were regarded as natural rights of man. 'We hold these truths to be self-evident, that all men are created equal, that they are endowed by their Creator with certain inalienable rights; that among these are life, liberty, and the pursuit of happiness; that, to secure these rights, governments are instituted among men deriving their just powers from the consent of the governed, that, whenever any form of government becomes destructive of these ends, it is the right of the people to alter or to abolish it, and to institute new government, laying its foundations on such principles, and organising its powers in such form, as to them shall seem most likely to effect their safety and happiness. ...' Fundamental rights were therefore inserted in the constitutions of the States, and the First Congress of the United States proposed amendments to the Constitution of the United States, of which ten were accepted and became known as the American 'Bill of Rights.' Thus the 'natural rights' became rights given or recognised by positive law. They are binding upon the Congress and are applied by the Supreme Court to determine the validity of legislation.

These rights were founded essentially upon English traditions, and, indeed upon the apologia of the Revolution settlement made by John Locke. The American Bill of Rights goes further than the British practice of the eighteenth century, for the American Revolution was a protest against the tyranny of George III and his ministers. In large part, however, it repeats the substance of English experience. The other famous set of political principles, or fundamental or natural rights, the French Declaration of the Rights of Man, promulgated by the Assembly of 1791, was also founded upon British traditions and experience, though moulded by the political philosophy of the era that preceded the French Revolution. The Constitution of 1791, to which it was the preface, has long since rolled into the dust, yet French constitutional lawyers continue to recognise the validity of its principles, either as principles of natural law, or as essential principles of political action in a free and democratic country. In Great Britain, too, the validity of the essential principles of the American Bill of Rights or the Declaration of the Rights of Man remains almost uncontested. ... The principles themselves, however, are accepted by all democrats as being not only necessary to but also implied in free or democratic government. A State is free only because its citizens are free.

We must nevertheless be careful in using the word 'rights.' If it is meant that they are natural rights, or if they are accepted as part of the logic of free or democratic government, the word is used in a sense different from its meaning in the phrases 'contractual right,' 'right to damages.' It is a distinction between essential constitutional principles and rights actually conferred by statute law or common law. Some writers use the word 'right' only as correlative to a duty imposed upon some other person by positive law. If I contract with B to pay him £600 for a motor car, I have a right to the car and I owe a duty to pay the price, while B has a right to the price and owes a duty to deliver the car. Either of us can go to a court to enforce his right. On the other hand, I may enter into a contract with B or any other person, but no person is bound to enter into a contract with me. I may enter into the contract simply because there are no legal restrictions on my doing so. Similarly, I may invite my friends to tea in my house and they may assemble on my invitation not because there is any 'right of assembly' (though, possibly, each may have a contractual right against me), but because there is no law which prevents them from doing so. In this sense, the right of assembly is a liberty, a freedom from restriction. It arises from the tautologous principle that anything is lawful which is not unlawful. There is no more a 'right of free speech' than there is a 'right to tie up my shoe-lace'; or, if there is a right of free speech, there is also a right to tie up my shoe-lace. The question to be discussed in each case is the nature of the legal restrictions. The 'right' is the obverse of the rules of civil, criminal, and administrative law. A man may say what he pleases provided that he does not offend against the laws relating to treason, sedition, libel, obscenity, blasphemy, perjury, official secrets, etc. He may form associations provided that he does not offend against the laws relating to trade unions, friendly societies, religion, public order, and unlawful oaths. He may hold a meeting where and how he pleases so long as he does not offend against the laws relating to riot, unlawful assemblies, nuisance, highways, property, etc.

This principle of the illegality of illegal acts (for it is nothing else) is, too, the simple way of asserting what is called 'the right to personal freedom.' The right to personal freedom is a liberty to so much personal freedom as is not taken away by law. It asserts the principle of legality, that everything is legal that is not illegal. It includes, therefore, the 'rights' of free speech, of association, and of assembly. For they assert only that a man may not be deprived of his personal freedom for doing certain kinds of acts – expressing opinions, associating, and meeting together – unless in so doing he offends against the law. The 'right of personal freedom' asserts that a man may not be deprived of his freedom for doing *any* act unless in so doing he offends against the law. The last is the genus of which the others are species.

Essential characteristics

The position is different where the 'rights' are set out in a written constitution, for then they govern the restrictions, and restrictions which infringe the rights are not law. With us, the nature of the liberties can be found only by examining the restrictions imposed by the law. We shall proceed presently to examine the restrictions; but for the moment it is essential that three characteristics of the British system should be borne in mind. In the first place, the law can always be altered by Parliament, and it is likely to be altered in time of emergency, such as a war. A Government with a majority in both Houses of Parliament can restrict liberty as it pleases. It must be remembered, however, that in normal times the free tradition is extremely strong in Great Britain, and that it is as noticeable in the House of Commons as elsewhere. There have been many examples in which the House, without distinction of party, has shown itself extremely critical of police action which had a suspicion of unfair tactics. There is nothing that the House does better than to protest against individual acts of oppression, whether legal or illegal. ... It must be emphasised that this is in normal times. In wartime and other times of national hysteria, the dissident minority can expect no more mercy or toleration from the House of Commons than from the Government itself. ... In such exceptional times the supremacy of Parliament is a very great danger, especially to minorities.

The Law and the Constitution, 5th edn, 1959, pp. 255–65.

---

8   THE POLITICS PROFESSOR HAROLD LASKI ON THE PREREQUISITES OF SUCCESSFUL REPRESENTATIVE GOVERNMENT, 1938

The 'prerequisites,' as Bagehot called them, of successful representative government are, indeed, both manifold and complex. It requires something more than intelligence and virtue. It presupposes a body of citizens who are fundamentally at one upon all the major objects of governmental activity; so fundamentally at one, it may be added, that the thought of conflict as a way of change is incapable of entering the minds of more than an insignificant portion of the nation. It requires, in the second place, a sense in the nation that no single class of any importance in the community is permanently excluded from power.

A third condition of successful representative government is that it should be built upon widely diffused habits of tolerance throughout the nation. Men who are to live together peacefully must be able to argue together peacefully. They must not run to suppress criticism of things as they are; rather they must be willing, if pressed, to invite its examination. They must refrain from pressing upon a significant minority principles of legislation by which the latter is outraged. Without this tolerance there is no prospect in the society of compromise; and every subject of division then becomes a high-road to disruption.

It is, I think, historically obvious that the habits of tolerance are born of a sense of security. By that I mean that the members of the society are confident, above all in matters of economic constitution, that their established expectations will be fulfilled. For tolerance depends on the existence of a mood in which men are susceptible to rational argument; and nothing is so destructive of this temper as the fear that is born of the disturbance of a wonted routine.

Parliamentary Government in England, 1938, pp. 14–15.

---

9 A SCOTTISH CONSTITUTIONAL LAWYER ANNOTATES THE LEGAL BASIS OF THE RIGHTS OF THE SUBJECT, 1939

The liberties of the subject rest on the two principles: (1) that the subject may say or do what he pleases so long as he does not infringe the substantive law or the rights of others; and (2) that public authorities can do only what is permitted by common law or statute. Hence, apart from the principles of the four great statutes [Magna Carta 1215, The Petition of Right 1628, the Bill of Rights 1688 and the Act of Settlement 1701] regulating the relations of the Crown and people, there is no special code of fundamental rights. But the lack of such definition is made good by the strong popular opinion in favour of the rights of the subject, which allows only in war invasion of these rights. ...

The protection of the liberties is due to (1) the high development of the action of trespass; (2) the use of the prerogative writs, now orders, including that of *habeas corpus*; (3) the right to have jury trial in serious crimes or common law actions, especially those involving false imprisonment or malicious arrest; (4) the rule of equal liability to the jurisdiction of the Courts of all persons save the Crown, with limited exceptions; and (5) the rule of construction that statutes are so to be interpreted as not to interfere with the vested rights of the subject. Of not less importance is the activity of the Press and of public opinion which will take up eagerly any perversion of justice.

A. Berriedale Keith, *Constitutional Law*, 1939, p. 28.

---

10   THE SOURCE OF LIBERTY IN BRITAIN LIES NOT IN LAWS OR INSTITUTIONS BUT IN THE SPIRIT OF A FREE PEOPLE, 1941

Emphasis is rightly placed on the laws and institutions which protect liberty in this country. What is less often realised is that liberty is a consequence not of laws and institutions but of an attitude of mind. Laws can be broken and institutions subverted. A people can be forcibly enslaved but it cannot be 'forced to be free'. It becomes free because it desires to be free, and it remains free because it so intends. Civil and religious liberty came to Great Britain as a lesson drawn from bitter experience. The lesson was first learned in the sphere of religious liberty, though religious and political liberty could not then be clearly distinguished. Those who believe that they have found truth and that those who spurn it have souls in danger of eternal damnation may reasonably think it their duty to stamp out heresy. Roman Catholics, the Reformed Church of England, the Scottish Covenanters, the English 'Saints', had their own brands of truth and their own standards of heresy. Oliver Cromwell, the statesman who had to govern a multitude of sects, might make fine speeches on toleration. His secretary, John Milton, might in *Areopagitica* write the finest defence of liberty in the English language. They were, however, in advance of their time. Not until the 'age of reason' in the eighteenth century was it recognised that truth, if there was such a thing, was many-sided and that any Protestant might have learned a portion of it. Not until after Culloden, when Romanism ceased to be sedition, could Roman Catholics begin to worship in peace, and not until 1829 were their main legal disabilities swept away. Even the age of reason could not accept agnosticism or atheism as arguable propositions, and the political disabilities of Jews and dissenters were not all abolished until late in the nineteenth century. ...

It is true that long before the eighteenth century civil liberty in the narrow sense had been established. A host of foreign commentators, among them Montesquieu, Voltaire and de Lolme, bore testimony to the freedom that prevailed in England. A conflict against the King and the King's religion was a conflict for the liberty and the property of the individual. The Court of Star Chamber went the way of the Court of High Commission. The abolition of newspaper licensing was almost an accident. The Parliament that tried to exclude James II from the throne passed the Habeas Corpus Act. The Bill of Rights which declared the abdication of James II dealt with jurors and excessive bail. The Act of Settlement which transferred the Crown to a more remote Protestant line provided for the independence of judges. Toleration was being erected into a principle, but it is not too much to say that civil liberty was gradually established as a series of empirical solutions of problems raised by the general and religious opinions of the Stuarts.

The result was, however, clear. The great Whig improvisations became the great Whig principles. All were in danger when the French Revolution of 1789 sent the Old Corps into the arms of the Tories. Charles James Fox and the second Earl Grey fought a gallant rearguard action, and countless almost unknown heroes resisted in the battle which culminated in the failure of the Six Acts. Earl Grey was carried along on the rising tide of the new middle class, and the Whig principles of 1689 became the principles of both political parties.

To explain what these principles are is no easy matter because their precise connotation varies with the functions of the State. For much of the nineteenth century they meant *laissez-faire*, and they are frequently asserted in that extreme form even to-day, when all parties are more or less collectivist. Even the most concrete application can rarely be stated without qualification. To say that 'no man can be kept imprisoned except on the orders of a court', for instance, is false, because lunatics, mental deficients, persons suffering from infectious disease, and so on, may be detained without their consent. It must again be emphasised that liberty is the consequence of an attitude of mind rather than of precise rules. It involves insistence on the idea that the action of the State must be directed to achieve the happiness and prosperity of all sections of the community, without regard to wealth, social prestige, 'race' or religion. It recognises that the advantage of the many ought not to be purchased at the expense of the suffering of the few. It stresses the autonomy of the individual without asserting that a substantial degree of regulation may not be desirable. It forbids anti-social activity without making the individual a slave tied to a machine.

These are generalities which give infinite scope for differences of opinion as to their application. If they are applied too widely they tend to the creation of a social and economic anarchy because they make the individual free to be enslaved. If the qualifications are interpreted too widely, they make the individual a slave to a machine. Between the extremes is an area in which true friends of liberty may hold different opinions without denying the essential idea. Within that area British political parties formulate their programmes.

Certain institutions are, however, clearly necessary. The first is an honest and impartial administration of justice. That has certainly been attained. No suggestion of corruption is ever made against our judges. They may often be mistaken; their remedies may sometimes be unavailable to poor men because they are too costly; but they enjoy a reputation for probity which many nations have cause to envy. Moreover, they are independent of political control and political influence. They take orders from nobody except Parliament and superior courts. Though sometimes they have been appointed (more often in the remoter past than in the past generation) because of their political success, they do their best to be impartial, and they would openly and forcibly spurn any attempt at political pressure.

It is necessary, however, that there should be not only impartiality in the judges but also impartiality in the laws. This does not mean, as some have assumed, that all laws must apply equally to everyone. There must be special laws for bankers, and not everyone is a banker. What it does mean is that the laws must not make irrelevant distinctions. The law of banking must apply equally to all bankers, whether they are Jews or Gentiles, Conservatives or Socialists, Roman Catholics or Quakers, moderate drinkers or total abstainers. The more general the evil to be avoided or the advantage to be gained, the more general the law. The law of murder or of theft can make no distinctions between peers and poets, rich men and poor, public servants and private employees. On the other hand, generality and impartiality do not mean that special classes of persons like publicans or public officials may not have special obligations imposed upon them. Nor does it mean that individual owners may not be deprived of their property or have special restrictions imposed upon it in the general interest. In such a case, one property owner is distinguished from another for relevant and not irrelevant considerations like 'race', religion or political opinion. Since there is a differentiation, however, it is recognised that compensation must be paid. In other words, what this application of the general idea means is that deprivation of liberty or property must be by 'due process of law'. In particular, 'race', religion and political opinion are irrelevant except in so far as they tend to promote disorder or subvert our democratic Constitution.

The impartiality of laws is not maintained except by the impartiality of their application. The impartiality of the judges is one means by which this is secured. So far as judges are competent and judicial procedure is appropriate, therefore, the application should be left to the Courts. Frequently, however, judges are incompetent because expert knowledge is required and judicial procedure is inappropriate because its cost and formality hinder proper investigation and prevent poor persons from protecting their interests. Judges cannot administer the law of education; judicial procedure is not an appropriate instrument for determining whether it is reasonable to refuse to allow a house to be built by the side of a main road; the judicial procedure is too dilatory and costly to determine whether John Smith is genuinely in search of work. The greater the activity of the State, therefore, the greater the need for honest and impartial administration. Here, too, the British Constitution teaches more lessons than it can learn. Its success is in part due to the civil service which has already been described; in part it is due to the system of local government. It is, however, also due to the control which the courts exercise over public authorities. This system cannot be praised without qualification, because the methods have been dilatory and expensive, and they have not always been applied with proper understanding of the problems involved. Nevertheless, the courts have set their faces sternly against partiality and corruption, and they have insisted that 'justice must not only be done but must be seen to be done'.

Of the technical methods by which these functions have been exercised ... every Englishman has heard of *habeas corpus*, because it has sometimes lain near the centre of political controversy. He ought also to know about *mandamus*, prohibition and *certiorari*. Nor is this all. Justice and liberty are not maintained only through remedies with Latin names. It is the ordinary administration of civil and criminal law and the interpretation of administrative statutes which matters most. There are defects with which every lawyer is familiar. There are some methods adopted elsewhere, notably by the French, which might be adopted here. The law is in many parts still the 'ungodly jumble' of which Carlyle spoke. Yet this certainly English (and Scottish) law does provide, that no man is penalised because he is a Jew, or poor, or without political or social influence, or because he belongs to a party, or because he has unusual notions about a future life.

Nevertheless, we must return to our main point. All this is not so because of technical devices and peculiar rules of law. The law is what Parliament provides, and it is in Parliament that the focus of our liberties must be found. Civil liberty is a consequence of political liberty, and political liberty is the result of a long evolution. The freedom of debate in Parliament asserted by the Bill of Rights is one of the most important political principles. The symbol of liberty is Her Majesty's Opposition. This too requires a background of liberty. Without free elections there can be no true parliamentary freedom – though it was only in 1872 that Parliament was convinced that in order to be free voting must be secret. Without freedom of speech, freedom of public meeting, and freedom of association there cannot be free elections. These liberties are not absolute, for freedom to work the Constitution cannot imply freedom to subvert the Constitution, and there is not always agreement on the extent of the qualifications. Nevertheless, the principles are accepted. Moreover, it is because they are accepted that they remain. A Government with a majority in both Houses would find no technical difficulty in sweeping them away.

It is clear, therefore, that the source of our liberty is not in laws or institutions, but in the spirit of a free people. It is the more firmly founded because it expanded so slowly. The liberty for which our forefathers took up arms was a very limited liberty – freedom for a reformed Church, freedom from royal absolutism, parliamentary freedom. For the rest, liberty has 'broadened down from precedent to precedent'.

Sir Ivor Jennings, *The British Constitution*, 5th edn 1966, pp. 203–9.

---

11   AN OXFORD COMPARATIVE CONSTITUTIONALIST SAYS THE IDEAL CONSTITUTION CONTAINS FEW OR NO DECLARATIONS OF RIGHTS, 1951

The United States illustrates very well the dilemma in which Constitution makers are placed when they consider this question of a declaration of rights. If they are framing a Constitution for people who are likely to respect rights, then a hard and fast declaration of rights in a Constitution is hardly necessary – their recognition in the ordinary law would be more flexible and just as effective. If on the other hand they are framing a Constitution for people who are not likely to respect rights, will the enunciation of certain rights in the Constitution go far towards ensuring their effective exercise? Would it not be better to proceed slowly by the process of ordinary law and by persuasion? ... Declarations of rights may prove to be in practice little more than words in communities where the Executive is held in greater awe than the Constitution, where people are not free to organize themselves or where they lack knowledge and capacity to form a public opinion.

The ideal Constitution, then, would contain few or no declarations of rights, though the ideal system of law would define and guarantee many rights. Rights cannot be declared in a Constitution except in absolute and unqualified terms, unless indeed they are so qualified as to be meaningless – and we have seen many examples of this. It is in the ordinary law itself that the careful definition of rights can be best undertaken, with the added guarantee that the law, since it has been passed by a legislature, may in most cases be in line with dominant public opinion.

To confine a Constitution to the bare statement of the rules which establish the principal political institutions of the state may seem unduly austere. Let it be said at once that a preamble to a Constitution, which is not itself part of the Constitution and therefore not part of the law, is not only permissible but even desirable. In this respect the framers of the American Constitution set an admirable example when, in 1787, they prefaced their document with this one compact and eloquent sentence: 'We, the people of the United States, in order to form a more perfect Union, establish justice, insure domestic tranquillity, provide for the common defence, promote the general welfare, and secure the blessings of liberty to ourselves and our posterity, do ordain and establish this Constitution for the United States of America.' The framers of the Constitution of the Fifth French Republic dealt with the problem of a declaration of rights – an historic and traditional part of French Constitution making – by placing it in the Preamble to the Constitution and contenting themselves with proclaiming 'their attachment to the Rights of Man and the principles of National Sovereignty' ....

But while a preamble is right and proper, it is worth remarking that a Constitution is, first of all, a legal document. It is intended to state supreme rules of law. It should confine itself, therefore, as completely as possible to stating rules of law, not opinions, aspirations, directives, and policies. Moreover, if it is to state rules of law and if, in particular, those rules are to constitute supreme law, binding the legislature equally with the executive and judiciary – and this is the avowed intention of most Constitutions, as we have seen – then these rules should be few, they should be general, and they should be fundamental. They should relate to subjects which it is fitting and proper to attempt to describe and regulate in terms of a rule of law. Finally, the language employed, though inevitably general and wide in some matters, should at the same time avoid so far as possible the ambiguous, the emotional and the tendentious.

If it is desired that a Constitution should evoke not only the respect due to law but also the added reverence due to a supreme law, then surely it is wise to exclude from its confines, as completely as possible, anything that is not intended to be regarded as a rule of law. This, at any rate, is the way in which a Constitution is viewed by those brought up and trained in what may be called the English view of constitutional law.

Sir Kenneth Wheare, *Modern Constitutions*, 1951, pp. 70–3.

---

12   CLAIRE PALLEY LECTURES ON THE CHARACTERISTICS OF UK HUMAN RIGHTS LAW, 1991

I must now explain the relationship between our constitutional and legal system and how human legal rights have been established in the United Kingdom. It is a commonplace that the United Kingdom does not have a comprehensively stated and constitutionally guaranteed set of human legal rights and that human rights are legal rights only to the extent that they can be found to exist in ordinary law. If the body of United Kingdom law were to be computerised and the file for human legal rights retrieved, nearly all the international human rights standards, civil, political, economic, social and cultural, would, subject to varying degrees of restriction, appear on the printout. Furthermore, if statutes and judicial decisions over the centuries were consolidated into a single constitutional instrument, not only would all those rights appear, but so would the structure and details of the constitution. The computer operator could easily shift around the legal rights, choosing the basic ones as a preface to any document. They would in effect make a Bill of Rights. Any such Bill would, as United Kingdom law now stands, have to set out variations and provisos as to the applicability of the rights in England, Scotland and Northern Ireland, because of their different legal traditions and systems. The Scots system would prove the most libertarian, because of its better criminal justice provisions and safeguards against police misconduct, only recently in part adopted in England. That of Northern Ireland, despite the reforms of the 1970s, would, so far as concerns public order laws and criminal procedures, because of the continuing emergency situation, be the least liberal, yet it would best exemplify institutional mechanisms devised to protect human legal rights, such as a Fair Employment Commission, a Standing Advisory Commission for Human Rights and legal prohibitions against discrimination on the ground of religious belief or political opinion and against occasioning religious hatred. The latter prohibitions sadly but graphically illustrate the limits of law in restraining passionate beliefs and consequent misconduct.

The explanation for the United Kingdom having neither a written constitution, whether with a preliminary Bill enumerating basic rights or with specific articles in its main body comprehensively delineating basic human legal rights, lies in its history. The Constitution has evolved over centuries through judicial decisions, statutes, subordinate legislation and customary parliamentary and governmental practices. There are numerous major Acts of Parliament, particularly the Petition of Right 1628, the Bill of Rights and the Scottish Claim of Right of 1689, the Habeas Corpus Acts 1679 and 1816, the Representation of the People Act 1949, the Race Relations Acts 1968 and 1976 and the Sex Discrimination Act 1975, all of which set out rights, impose prohibitions on conduct which would effectively infringe these rights and lay down remedial procedures for enforcing claims following their unjustified invasion. (Early Bills of Rights in the British American colonies drew on and built upon the 17th century measures.) The various Acts listed reflect values, for example, personal liberty, freedom of speech, democracy, equality and absence of discrimination, while the Race Relations and the Sex Discrimination Acts go further by prohibiting conduct in conflict with such values and seeking in the long run to alter attitudes, that is beliefs and ultimately notions about values.

Two technical characteristics of United Kingdom human legal rights law, sometimes misunderstood as criticism, must now be mentioned. These characteristics are, firstly, that liberty, that is, freedom to act, is merely residual, and, secondly, that only if the courts or another governmental institution will afford a remedy, is there a right. In fact, these are characteristics of legal rights in *all* legal systems, but are more remarked upon in the United Kingdom, because of the absence of a written constitution setting out the major legal human rights and the untheoretical, ungeneralised historic pattern of English legal development. Common Law, as judicially developed, is pragmatic, dealing with problems only when they arise. Judges do not normally enunciate broad generalisations or principles in advance of conduct putting them in issue. Seldom, until it recently became more fashionable, did they opine about 'liberty of the person,' 'individual liberties' and 'constitutional liberties,' let alone 'human rights' and 'fundamental rights.' Those judges who do, do so intermittently, while statutory draftsmen sheer away from such unorthodox imagery. With the odd striking exception, British judges currently perceive their judicial task as being confined to determining whether conduct involves breach of contract or other specific obligation, commission of a tort, or breach of a statutory duty or of the criminal law. If the nature of the conduct is such as to invade a specific right of another person, or if it breaches a criminal law prohibition, then and only then will a remedy be awarded. Such specificity has the result that persons are free to conduct themselves, so long as they do not invade the persons or property of others or transgress any specific restraining provisions. Since freedom to act is restricted by the rights of others and by specific legal provisions, it is obvious that freedom is of necessity 'residual.' The word 'liberty' aptly expresses these connotations.

The residual character of human legal rights also arises from the fact that until recently there was no higher law in the United Kingdom, a point to which I will revert. This was because English 17th century thinkers imported the doctrine of sovereignty, a concept first formulated in the 16th century by the French political theorist, Bodin (1529–1596) who was concerned about the conditions under which order could be secured. Sovereignty referred to the absolute, unlimited and illimitable power of rulers. Stuart monarchs claimed to have sovereignty, but it was eventually regarded as being definitively vested in the English Parliament as a whole (Monarch, Lords, and Commons) from the time of the 1688 Revolution. From 1707 that Parliament was merged by the Act of Union with the Scottish Parliament. On an Anglocentric view, which had become prevalent by 1717, the new Parliament has continued to enjoy sovereignty, despite the earlier and later medieval view about limits on the power of rulers and supremacy of the law and arguments about fundamental law with the early Stuarts. English judges and writers have declared that Acts of Parliament can make or unmake any law whatever, with later Acts prevailing over earlier Acts and the common law. For those who accept such a view the law includes the doctrine of sovereignty of Parliament. The result is that parliamentary power is legally unbounded, so that a new Act or authorised subordinate legislative measure can diminish any human legal right, however basic that right may be, by imposing limitations or conditions on its exercise, or by cutting down its scope, and may even extinguish it.

The United Kingdom and Human Rights, Hamlyn Lectures, 1991, pp. 109–13.

---

13 CIVIL RIGHTS LEGISLATION: SEX, RACE AND DISABILITY DISCRIMINATION, 1975–95

(A) Sex Discrimination Act 1975

An Act to render unlawful certain kinds of sex discrimination and discrimination on the ground of marriage, and establish a Commission with the function of working towards the elimination of such discrimination and promoting equality of opportunity between men and women generally.

Be it enacted by the Queen's most Excellent Majesty, by and with the advice and consent of the Lords Spiritual and Temporal, and Commons, in this present Parliament assembled, and by the authority of the same, as follows:—

PART I

DISCRIMINATION TO WHICH ACT APPLIES

1.—(1) A person discriminates against a woman in any circumstances relevant for the purposes of any provision of this Act if—

   (*a*) on the ground of her sex he treats her less favourably than he treats or would treat a man, or

(*b*) he applies to her a requirement or condition which he applies or
would apply equally to a man but—
  (i)   which is such that the proportion of women who can comply
        with it is considerably smaller than the proportion of men
        who can comply with it, and
  (ii) which he cannot show to be justifiable irrespective of the sex
        of the person to whom it is applied, and
  (iii) which is to her detriment because she cannot comply with
        it.

(2) If a person treats or would treat a man differently according to the
man's marital status, his treatment of a woman is for the purposes of
subsection (1)(*a*) to be compared to his treatment of a man having the like
marital status.

2.—(1) Section 1, and the provisions of Parts II and III relating to sex
discrimination against women, are to be read as applying equally to the
treatment of men, and for that purpose shall have effect with such modifications as are requisite.

(2) In the application of subsection (1) no account shall be taken of
special treatment afforded to women in connection with pregnancy or
childbirth.

3.—(1) A person discriminates against a married person of either sex in
any circumstances relevant for the purposes of any provision of Part II if—
  (*a*) on the ground of his or her marital status he treats that person less
       favourably than he treats or would treat an unmarried person of
       the same sex, or
  (*b*) he applies to that person a requirement or condition which he
       applies or would apply equally to an unmarried person but—
    (i)   which is such that the proportion of married persons who
          can comply with it is considerably smaller than the propor-
          tion of unmarried persons of the same sex who can comply
          with it, and
    (ii) which he cannot show to be justifiable irrespective of the
          marital status of the person to whom it is applied, and
    (iii) which is to that person's detriment because he cannot com-
          ply with it.

(2) For the purposes of subsection (1), a provision of Part II framed with
reference to discrimination against women shall be treated as applying
equally to the treatment of men, and for that purpose shall have effect with
such modifications as are requisite.

4.—(1) A person ('the discriminator') discriminates against another person ('the person victimised') in any circumstances relevant for the purposes
of any provision of this Act if he treats the person victimised less favourably
than in those circumstances he treats or would treat other persons, and does
so by reason that the person victimised has—

(*a*) brought proceedings against the discriminator or any other person under this Act or the Equal Pay Act 1970, or

(*b*) given evidence or information in connection with proceedings brought by any person against the discriminator or any other person under this Act or the Equal Pay Act 1970, or

(*c*) otherwise done anything under or by reference to this Act or the Equal Pay Act 1970 in relation to the discriminator or any other person, or

(*d*) alleged that the discriminator or any other person has committed an act which (whether or not the allegation so states) would amount to a contravention of this Act or give rise to a claim under the Equal Pay Act 1970,

or by reason that the discriminator knows the person victimised intends to do any of those things, or suspects the person victimised has done, or intends to do, any of them.

(2) Subsection (1) does not apply to treatment of a person by reason of any allegation made by him if the allegation was false and not made in good faith.

(3) For the purposes of subsection (1), a provision of Part II or III framed with reference to discrimination against women shall be treated as applying equally to the treatment of men and for that purpose shall have effect with such modifications as are requisite. . . .

Part II
Discrimination in the Employment Field

Discrimination by employers

6.—(1) It is unlawful for a person, in relation to employment by him at an establishment in Great Britain, to discriminate against a woman—

(*a*) in the arrangements he makes for the purpose of determining who should be offered that employment, or

(*b*) in the terms on which he offers her that employment, or

(*c*) by refusing or deliberately omitting to offer her that employment.

(2) It is unlawful for a person, in the case of a woman employed by him at an establishment in Great Britain, to discriminate against her—

(*a*) in the way he affords her access to opportunities for promotion, transfer or training, or to any other benefits, facilities or services, or by refusing or deliberately omitting to afford her access to them, or

(*b*) by dismissing her, or subjecting her to any other detriment. . . .

7.—(1) In relation to sex discrimination—

(*a*) section 6(1)(a) or (c) does not apply to any employment where being a man is a genuine occupational qualification for the job, and (*b*) section 6(2)(a) does not apply to opportunities for promotion or transfer to, or training for, such employment.

PART III
DISCRIMINATION IN OTHER FIELDS

Education

22.—It is unlawful in relation to an educational establishment ... for a person ... to discriminate against a woman—

   (*a*) in the terms on which it offers to admit her to the establishment as a pupil, or

   (*b*) by refusing or deliberately omitting to accept an application for her admission to the establishment as a pupil, or

   (*c*) where she is a pupil of the establishment—

   (i)   in the way it affords her access to any benefits, facilities or services, or by refusing or deliberately omitting to afford her access to them, or

   (ii) by excluding her from the establishment or subjecting her to any other detriment.

29.—(1) It is unlawful for any person concerned with the provision (for payment or not) of goods, facilities or services to the public or a section of the public to discriminate against a woman who seeks to obtain or use those goods, facilities or services—

   (*a*) by refusing or deliberately omitting to provide her with any of them, or

   (*b*) by refusing or deliberately omitting to provide her with goods, facilities or services of the like quality, in the like manner and on the like terms as are normal in his case in relation to male members of the public or (where she belongs to a section of the public) to male members of that section.

(2) The following are examples of the facilities and services mentioned in subsection (1)—

   (*a*) access to and use of any place which members of the public or a section of the public are permitted to enter;

   (*b*) accommodation in a hotel, boarding house or other similar establishment;

   (*c*) facilities by way of banking or insurance or for grants, loans, credit or finance;

   (*d*) facilities for education;

   (*e*) facilities for entertainment, recreation or refreshment;

   (*f*) facilities for transport or travel;

   (*g*) the services of any profession or trade, or any local or other public authority.

30.—(1) It is unlawful for a person, in relation to premises in Great Britain of which he has power to dispose, to discriminate against a woman—

(*a*) in the terms on which he offers her those premises, or

(*b*) by refusing her application for those premises, or

(*c*) in his treatment of her in relation to any list of persons in need of premises of that description.

(2) It is unlawful for a person, in relation to premises managed by him, to discriminate against a woman occupying the premises—

(*a*) in the way he affords her access to any benefits or facilities, or by refusing or deliberately omitting to afford her access to them, or

(*b*) by evicting her, or subjecting her to any other detriment.

PART VI
EQUAL OPPORTUNITIES COMMISSION

53.—(1) There shall be a body of Commissioners named the Equal Opportunities Commission, consisting of at least eight but not more than fifteen individuals each appointed by the Secretary of State on a full-time or part-time basis, which shall have the following duties—

(*a*) to work towards the elimination of discrimination,

(*b*) to promote equality of opportunity between men and women generally, and

(*c*) to keep under review the working of this Act and the Equal Pay Act 1970 and, when they are so required by the Secretary of State or otherwise think it necessary, draw up and submit to the Secretary of State proposals for amending them.

54.—(1) The Commission may undertake or assist (financially or otherwise) the undertaking by other persons of any research, and any educational activities, which appear to the Commission necessary or expedient for the purposes of section 53(1).

(2) The Commission may make charges for educational or other facilities or services made available by them. . . .

56.—(1) As soon as practicable after the end of each calendar year the Commission shall make to the Secretary of State a report on their activities during the year (an 'annual report').

(2) Each annual report shall include a general survey of developments, during the period to which it relates, in respect of matters falling within the scope of the Commission's duties.

(3) The Secretary of State shall lay a copy of every annual report before each House of Parliament, and shall cause the report to be published.

57.—(1) Without prejudice to their general power to do anything requisite for the performance of their duties under section 53(1), the Commission may if they think fit, and shall if required by the Secretary of State, conduct a formal investigation for any purpose connected with the carrying out of those duties. . . .

67.—(2) If in the course of a formal investigation the Commission become satisfied that a person is committing, or has committed, any such acts, the Commission may in the prescribed manner serve on him a notice in the prescribed form ('a non-discrimination notice') requiring him—

    (*a*) not to commit any such acts, and

    (*b*) where compliance with paragraph (a) involves changes in any of his practices or other arrangements—

        (i)   to inform the Commission that he has effected those changes and what those changes are, and

        (ii) to take such steps as may be reasonably required by the notice for the purpose of affording that information to other persons concerned. . . .

75.—(1) Where, in relation to proceedings or prospective proceedings either under this Act or in respect of an equality clause, an individual who is an actual or prospective complainant or claimant applies to the Commission for assistance under this section, the Commission shall consider the application and may grant it if they think fit to do so on the ground that—

    (*a*) the case raises a question of principle, or

    (*b*) it is unreasonable, having regard to the complexity of the case or the applicant's position in relation to the respondent or another person involved or any other matter, to expect the applicant to deal with the case unaided,

or by reason of any other special consideration.

(2) Assistance by the Commission under this section may include—

    (*a*) giving advice;

    (*b*) procuring or attempting to procure the settlement of any matter in dispute;

    (*c*) arranging for the giving of advice or assistance by a solicitor or counsel;

    (*d*) arranging for representation by any person including all such assistance as is usually given by a solicitor or counsel in the steps preliminary or incidental to any proceedings, or in arriving at or giving effect to a compromise to avoid or bring to an end any proceedings.

(B) Race Relations Act 1976

An Act to make fresh provision with respect to discrimination on racial grounds and relations between people of different racial groups.

Be it enacted by the Queen's most Excellent Majesty, by and with the advice and consent of the Lords Spiritual and Temporal, and Commons, in this present Parliament assembled, and by the authority of the same, as follows:—

Part I
Discrimination to Which Act Applies

1.—(1) A person discriminates against another in any circumstances relevant for the purposes of any provision of this Act if—

    (*a*) on racial grounds he treats that other less favourably than he treats or would treat other persons; or

    (*b*) he applies to that other a requirement or condition which he applies or would apply equally to persons not of the same racial group as that other but—

        (i)   which is such that the proportion of persons of the same racial groups as that other who can comply with it is considerably smaller than the proportion of persons not of that racial group who can comply with it; and

        (ii) which he cannot show to be justifiable irrespective of the colour race, nationality or ethnic or national origins of the person to whom it is applied; and

        (iii) which is to the detriment of that other because he cannot comply with it.

(2) It is hereby declared that, for the purposes of this Act, segregating a person from other persons on racial grounds is treating him less favourably than they are treated.

2.—(1) A person ('the discriminator') discriminates against another person ('the person victimised') in any circumstances relevant for the purposes of any provision of this Act if he treats the person victimised less favourably than in those circumstances he treats or would treat other persons, and does so by reason that the person victimised has—

    (*a*) brought proceedings against the discriminator or any other person under this Act; or

    (*b*) given evidence or information in connection with proceedings brought by any person against the discriminator or any other person under this Act; or

    (*c*) otherwise done anything under or by reference to this Act in relation to the discriminator or any other person; or

    (*d*) alleged that the discriminator or any other person has committed an act which (whether or not the allegation so states) would amount to a contravention of this Act,

or by reason that the discriminator knows that the person victimised intends to do any of those things, or suspects that the person victimised has done, or intends to do, any of them.

(2) Subsection (1) does not apply to treatment of a person by reason of any allegation made by him if the allegation was false and not made in good faith.

3.—(1) In this Act, unless the context otherwise requires—

    'racial grounds' means any of the following grounds, namely colour, race, nationality or ethnic or national origins;

'racial group' means a group of persons defined by reference to colour, race, nationality or ethnic or national origins, and references to a person's racial group refer to any racial group into which he falls.

(2) The fact that a racial group comprises two or more distinct racial groups does not prevent it from constituting a particular racial group for the purposes of this Act.

RB NOTE: *The Race Relations Act then contains provisions governing discrimination in the employment field (Part II), and with respect to education, goods, services and premises (Part III), the wording of which is similar to equivalent provisions in the Sex Discrimination Act (see above).*

PART VII
THE COMMISSION FOR RACIAL EQUALITY

General

43.—(1) There shall be a body of Commissioners named the Commission for Racial Equality consisting of at least eight but not more than fifteen individuals each appointed by the Secretary of State on a full-time or part-time basis, which shall have the following duties—
   (*a*) to work towards the elimination of discrimination;
   (*b*) to promote equality of opportunity, and good relations, between persons of different racial groups generally; and
   (*c*) to keep under review the working of this Act and, when they are so required by the Secretary of State or otherwise think it necessary, draw up and submit to the Secretary of State proposals for amending it.

44.—(1) The Commission may give financial or other assistance to any organisation appearing to the Commission to be concerned with the promotion of equality of opportunity, and good relations, between persons of different racial groups,

45.—(1) The Commission may undertake or assist (financially or otherwise) the undertaking by other persons of any research, and any educational activities, which appear to the Commission necessary or expedient for the purposes of section 43(1).

46.—(1) As soon as practicable after the end of each calendar year the Commission shall make to the Secretary of State a report on their activities during the year (an 'annual report').

(2) Each annual report shall include a general survey of developments, during the period to which it relates, in respect of matters falling within the scope of the Commission's functions.

(3) The Secretary of State shall lay a copy of every annual report before each House of Parliament, and shall cause the report to be published.

Codes of practice

47.—(1) The Commission may issue codes of practice containing such practical guidance as the Commission think fit for either or both of the following purposes, namely—
  (*a*) the elimination of discrimination in the field of employment;
  (*b*) the promotion of equality of opportunity in that field between persons of different racial groups.

(2) When the Commission propose to issue a code of practice, they shall prepare and publish a draft of that code, shall consider any representations made to them about the draft and may modify the draft accordingly.

RB NOTE: The Race Relations Act then provides powers for the Commission for Racial Equality to conduct formal investigations, issue nondiscrimination notices, and give assistance to individuals, the wording of which is similar to equivalent powers of the Equal Opportunities Commission in the Sex Discrimination Act (see above).

(C) Disability Discrimination Act 1995

An Act to make it unlawful to discriminate against disabled persons in connection with employment, the provision of goods, facilities and services or the disposal or management of premises; to make provision about the employment of disabled persons; and to establish a National Disability Council.

Be it enacted by the Queen's most Excellent Majesty, by and with the advice and consent of the Lords Spiritual and Temporal, and Commons, in this present Parliament assembled, and by the authority of the same, as follows:—

PART I
DISABILITY

1.—(1) Subject to the provisions of Schedule 1, a person has a disability for the purposes of this Act if he has a physical or mental impairment which has a substantial and long-term adverse effect on his ability to carry out normal day-to-day activities. . . .

3.—(1) The Secretary of State may issue guidance about the matters to be taken into account in determining—
  (a) whether an impairment has a substantial adverse effect on a person's ability to carry out normal day-to-day activities; or

(b) whether such an impairment has a long-term effect.

(2) The guidance may, among other things, give examples of—
  (a) effects which it would be reasonable, in relation to particular activities, to regard for such purposes of this Act as substantial adverse effects;
  (b) effects which it would not be reasonable, in relation to particular activities, to regard for such purposes as substantial adverse effects;
  (c) substantial adverse effects which it would be reasonable to regard, for such purposes, as long-term;
  (d) substantial adverse effects which it would not be reasonable to regard, for such purposes, as long-term.

PART II
EMPLOYMENT

Discrimination by employers

4.—(1) It is unlawful for an employer to discriminate against a disabled person—
  (a) in the arrangements which he makes for the purpose of determining to whom he should offer employment;
  (b) in the terms on which he offers that person employment; or
  (c) by refusing to offer, or deliberately not offering, him employment.

(2) It is unlawful for an employer to discriminate against a disabled person whom he employs—
  (a) in the terms of employment which he affords him;
  (b) in the opportunities which he affords him for promotion, a transfer, training or receiving any other benefit;
  (c) by refusing to afford him, or deliberately not affording him, any such opportunity; or
  (d) by dismissing him, or subjecting him to any other detriment.

5.—(1) For the purposes of this Part, an employer discriminates against a disabled person if—
  (a) for a reason which relates to the disabled person's disability, he treats him less favourably than he treats or would treat others to whom that reason does not or would not apply; and
  (b) he cannot show that the treatment in question is justified.

6.—(1) Where—
  (a) any arrangements made by or on behalf of an employer, or
  (b) any physical feature of premises occupied by the employer,

place the disabled person concerned at a substantial disadvantage in comparison with persons who are not disabled, it is the duty of the employer to take such steps as it is reasonable, in all the circumstances of the case, for him to have to take in order to prevent the arrangements or feature having that effect.

(2) Subsection (1)(a) applies only in relation to—
   (a) arrangements for determining to whom employment should be offered;
   (b) any term, condition or arrangements on which employment, promotion, a transfer, training or any other benefit is offered or afforded.

(3) The following are examples of steps which an employer may have to take in relation to a disabled person in order to comply with subsection (1)—
   (a) making adjustments to premises;
   (b) allocating some of the disabled person's duties to another person;
   (c) transferring him to fill an existing vacancy;
   (d) altering his working hours;
   (e) assigning him to a different place of work;
   (f) allowing him to be absent during working hours for rehabilitation, assessment or treatment;
   (g) giving him, or arranging for him to be given, training;
   (h) acquiring or modifying equipment;
   (i) modifying instructions or reference manuals;
   (j) modifying procedures for testing or assessment;
   (k) providing a reader or interpreter;
   (l) providing supervision.

(4) In determining whether it is reasonable for an employer to have to take a particular step in order to comply with subsection (1), regard shall be had, in particular, to—
   (a) the extent to which taking the step would prevent the effect in question;
   (b) the extent to which it is practicable for the employer to take the step;
   (c) the financial and other costs which would be incurred by the employer in taking the step and the extent to which taking it would disrupt any of his activities;
   (d) the extent of the employer's financial and other resources;
   (e) the availability to the employer of financial or other assistance with respect to taking the step.

7.—(1) Nothing in this Part applies in relation to an employer who has fewer than 20 employees.

PART III

DISCRIMINATION IN OTHER AREAS

Goods, facilities and services

19.—(1) It is unlawful for a provider of services to discriminate against a disabled person—

(a) in refusing to provide, or deliberately not providing, to the disabled person any service which he provides, or is prepared to provide, to members of the public;

(b) in failing to comply with any duty imposed on him by section 21 in circumstances in which the effect of that failure is to make it impossible or unreasonably difficult for the disabled person to make use of any such service;

(c) in the standard of service which he provides to the disabled person or the manner in which he provides it to him; or

(d) in the terms on which he provides a service to the disabled person. . . .

(3) The following are examples of services to which this section and section 20 and 21 apply—

(a) access to and use of any place which members of the public are permitted to enter;

(b) access to and use of means of communication;

(c) access to and use of information services;

(d) accommodation in a hotel, boarding house or other similar establishment;

(e) facilities by way of banking or insurance or for grants, loans, credit or finance;

(f) facilities for entertainment, recreation or refreshment;

(g) facilities provided by employment agencies or under section 2 of the Employment and Training Act 1973;

(h) the services of any profession or trade, or any local or other public authority.

20.—(1) For the purposes of section 19, a provider of services discriminates against a disabled person if—

(a) for a reason which relates to the disabled person's disability, he treats him less favourably than he treats or would treat others to whom that reason does not or would not apply; and

(b) he cannot show that the treatment in question is justified.

(2) For the purposes of section 19, a provider of services also discriminates against a disabled person if—

(a) he fails to comply with a section 21 duty imposed on him in relation to the disabled person; and

(b) he cannot show that his failure to comply with that duty is justified.

(3) For the purposes of this section, treatment is justified only if—

(a) in the opinion of the provider of services, one or more of the conditions mentioned in subsection (4) are satisfied; and

(b) it is reasonable, in all the circumstances of the case, for him to hold that opinion.

(4) The conditions are that—

(a) in any case, the treatment is necessary in order not to endanger the health or safety of any person (which may include that of the disabled person);

(b) in any case, the disabled person is incapable of entering into an enforceable agreement, or of giving an informed consent, and for that reason the treatment is reasonable in that case;

(c) in a case falling within section 19(1)(a), the treatment is necessary because the provider of services would otherwise be unable to provide the service to members of the public;

(d) in a case falling within section 19(1)(c) or (d), the treatment is necessary in order for the provider of services to be able to provide the service to the disabled person or to other members of the public;

(e) in a case falling within section 19(1)(d), the difference in the terms on which the service is provided to the disabled person and those on which it is provided to other members of the public reflects the greater cost to the provider of services in providing the service to the disabled person.

(5) Any increase in the cost of providing a service to a disabled person which results from compliance by a provider of services with a section 21 duty shall be disregarded for the purposes of subsection (4)(e). . . .

21.—(1) Where a provider of services has a practice, policy or procedure which makes it impossible or unreasonably difficult for disabled persons to make use of a service which he provides, or is prepared to provide, to other members of the public, it is his duty to take such steps as it is reasonable, in all the circumstances of the case, for him to have to take in order to change that practice, policy or procedure so that it no longer has that effect.

(2) Where a physical feature (for example, one arising from the design or construction of a building or the approach or access to premises) makes it impossible or unreasonably difficult for disabled persons to make use of such a service, it is the duty of the provider of that service to take such steps as it is reasonable, in all the circumstances of the case, for him to have to take in order to—

(a) remove the feature;

(b) alter it so that it no longer has that effect;

(c) provide a reasonable means of avoiding the feature; or

(d) provide a reasonable alternative method of making the service in question available to disabled persons.

Premises

22.—(1) It is unlawful for a person with power to dispose of any premises to discriminate against a disabled person—

    (a) in the terms on which he offers to dispose of those premises to the disabled person;

    (b) by refusing to dispose of those premises to the disabled person; or

    (c) in his treatment of the disabled person in relation to any list of persons in need of premises of that description. . . .

(3) It is unlawful for a person managing any premises to discriminate against a disabled person occupying those premises—

    (a) in the way he permits the disabled person to make use of any benefits or facilities;

    (b) by refusing or deliberately omitting to permit the disabled person to make use of any benefits or facilities; or

    (c) by evicting the disabled person, or subjecting him to any other detriment.

(4) It is unlawful for any person whose licence or consent is required for the disposal of any premises comprised in, or (in Scotland) the subject of, a tenancy to discriminate against a disabled person by withholding his licence or consent for the disposal of the premises to the disabled person.

24.—(1) For the purposes of section 22, a person ('A') discriminates against a disabled person if—

    (a) for a reason which relates to the disabled person's disability, he treats him less favourably than he treats or would treat others to whom that reason does not or would not apply; and

    (b) he cannot show that the treatment in question is justified.

(2) For the purposes of this section, treatment is justified only if—

    (a) in A's opinion, one or more of the conditions mentioned in subsection (3) are satisfied; and

    (b) it is reasonable, in all the circumstances of the case, for him to hold that opinion.

(3) The conditions are that—

    (a) in any case, the treatment is necessary in order not to endanger the health or safety of any person (which may include that of the disabled person);

    (b) in any case, the disabled person is incapable of entering into an enforceable agreement, or of giving an informed consent, and for that reason the treatment is reasonable in that case;

    (c) in a case falling within section 22(3)(a), the treatment is necessary in order for the disabled person or the occupiers of other premises forming part of the building to make use of the benefit or facility;

    (d) in a case falling within section 22(3)(b), the treatment is necessary in order for the occupiers of other premises forming part of the building to make use of the benefit or facility.

Public service vehicles

40.—(1) The Secretary of State may make regulations ('PSV accessibility regulations') for the purpose of securing that it is possible for disabled persons—

(a) to get on to and off regulated public service vehicles in safety and without unreasonable difficulty (and, in the case of disabled persons in wheelchairs, to do so while remaining in their wheelchairs); and

(b) to be carried in such vehicles in safety and in reasonable comfort.

(2) PSV accessibility regulations may, in particular, make provision as to the construction, use and maintenance of regulated public service vehicles including provision as to—

(a) the fitting of equipment to vehicles;

(b) equipment to be carried by vehicles;

(c) the design of equipment to be fitted to, or carried by, vehicles;

(d) the fitting and use of restraining devices designed to ensure the stability of wheelchairs while vehicles are moving;

(e) the position in which wheelchairs are to be secured while vehicles are moving.

(3) Any person who—

(a) contravenes or fails to comply with any provision of the PSV accessibility regulations,

(b) uses on a road a regulated public service vehicle which does not conform with any provision of the regulations with which it is required to conform, or

(c) causes or permits to be used on a road such a regulated public service vehicle,

is guilty of an offence.

RB NOTE: Analogous provisions empowering regulations governing taxi accessibility and rail vehicles are also included in the Act.

PART VI
THE NATIONAL DISABILITY COUNCIL

50.—(1) There shall be a body to be known as the National Disability Council (but in this Act referred to as 'the Council').

(2) It shall be the duty of the Council to advise the Secretary of State, either on its own initiative or when asked to do so by the Secretary of State—

(a) on matters relevant to the elimination of discrimination against disabled persons and persons who have had a disability;

    (b) on measures which are likely to reduce or eliminate such discrimination; and

    (c) on matters related to the operation of this Act or of provisions made under this Act.

(3) The Secretary of State may be order confer additional functions on the Council.

(4) The power conferred by subsection (3) does not include power to confer on the Council any functions with respect to the investigation of any complaint which may be the subject of proceedings under this Act.

(5) In discharging its duties under this section, the Council shall in particular have regard to—

    (a) the extent and nature of the benefits which would be likely to result from the implementation of any recommendation which it makes; and

    (b) the likely cost of implementing any such recommendation.

(6) Where the Council makes any recommendation in the discharge of any of its functions under this section it shall, if it is reasonably practicable to do so, make an assessment of—

    (a) the likely cost of implementing the recommendation; and

    (b) the likely financial benefits which would result from implementing it.

(7) Where the Council proposes to give the Secretary of State advice on a matter, it shall before doing so—

    (a) consult any body—

        (i) established by any enactment or by a Minister of the Crown for the purpose of giving advice in relation to disability, or any aspect of disability; and

        (ii) having functions in relation to the matter to which the advice relates;

    (b) consult such other persons as it considers appropriate; and

    (c) have regard to any representations made to it as a result of any such consultations.

51.—(1) It shall be the duty of the Council, when asked to do so by the Secretary of State—

    (a) to prepare proposals for a code of practice dealing with the matters to which the Secretary of State's request relates; or

    (b) to review a code and, if it considers it appropriate, propose alterations.

SCHEDULE 1: PROVISIONS SUPPLEMENTING SECTION 1
[Meaning of 'disability']

Impairment

1.—(1) 'Mental impairment' includes an impairment resulting from or consisting of a mental illness only if the illness is a clinically well-recognised illness.

(2) Regulations may make provision, for the purposes of this Act—
  (a) for conditions of a prescribed description to be treated as amounting to impairments;
  (b) for conditions of a prescribed description to be treated as not amounting to impairments.

(3) Regulations made under sub-paragraph (2) may make provision as to the meaning of 'condition' for the purposes of those regulations.

Long-term effects

2.—(1) The effect of an impairment is a long-term effect if—
  (a) it has lasted at least 12 months;
  (b) the period for which it lasts is likely to be at least 12 months; or
  (c) it is likely to last for the rest of the life of the person affected.

(2) Where an impairment ceases to have a substantial adverse effect on a person's ability to carry out normal day-to-day activities, it is to be treated as continuing to have that effect if that effect is likely to recur.

(3) For the purposes of sub-paragraph (2), the likelihood of an effect recurring shall be disregarded in prescribed circumstances.

(4) Regulations may prescribe circumstances in which, for the purposes of this Act—
  (a) an effect which would not otherwise be a long-term effect is to be treated as such an effect; or
  (b) an effect which would otherwise be a long-term effect is to be treated as not being such an effect.

Severe disfigurement

3.—(1) An impairment which consists of a severe disfigurement is to be treated as having a substantial adverse effect on the ability of the person concerned to carry out normal day-to-day activities.

(2) Regulations may provide that in prescribed circumstances a severe disfigurement is not to be treated as having that effect.

(3) Regulations under sub-paragraph (2) may, in particular, make provision with respect to deliberately acquired disfigurements.

Normal day-to-day activities

4.—(1) An impairment is to be taken to affect the ability of the person concerned to carry out normal day-to-day activities only if it affects one of the following—

(a) mobility;
(b) manual dexterity;
(c) physical co-ordination;
(d) continence;
(e) ability to lift, carry or otherwise move everyday objects;
(f) speech, hearing or eyesight;
(g) memory or ability to concentrate, learn or understand; or
(h) perception of the risk of physical danger.

(2) Regulations may prescribe—
   (a) circumstances in which an impairment which does not have an effect falling within sub-paragraph (1) is to be taken to affect the ability of the person concerned to carry out normal day-to-day activities;
   (b) circumstances in which an impairment which has an effect falling within sub-paragraph (1) is to be taken not to affect the ability of the person concerned to carry out normal day-to-day activities.

Substantial adverse effects

5. Regulations may make provision for the purposes of this Act—
   (a) for an effect of a prescribed kind on the ability of a person to carry out normal day-to-day activities to be treated as a substantial adverse effect;
   (b) for an effect of a prescribed kind on the ability of a person to carry out normal day-to-day activities to be treated as not being a substantial adverse effect.

Effect of medical treatment

6.—(1) An impairment which would be likely to have a substantial adverse effect on the ability of the person concerned to carry out normal day-to-day activities, but for the fact that measures are being taken to treat or correct it, is to be treated as having that effect.

(2) In sub-paragraph (1) 'measures' includes, in particular, medical treatment and the use of a prosthesis or other aid.

(3) Sub-paragraph (1) does not apply—
   (a) in relation to the impairment of a person's sight, to the extent that the impairment is, in his case, correctable by spectacles or contact lenses or in such other ways as may be prescribed; or
   (b) in relation to such other impairments as may be prescribed, in such circumstances as may be prescribed.

Persons deemed to be disabled

7.—(1) Sub-paragraph (2) applies to any person whose name is, both on 12th January 1995 and on the date when this paragraph comes into force, in the register of disabled persons maintained under section 6 of the Disabled Persons (Employment) Act 1944.

(2) That person is to be deemed—
  (a) during the initial period, to have a disability, and hence to be a disabled person; and
  (b) afterwards, to have had a disability and hence to have been a disabled person during that period.

(3) A certificate of registration shall be conclusive evidence, in relation to the person with respect to whom it was issued, of the matters certified.

(4) Unless the contrary is shown, any document purporting to be a certificate of registration shall be taken to be such a certificate and to have been validly issued.

(5) Regulations may provide for prescribed descriptions of person to be deemed to have disabilities, and hence to be disabled persons, for the purposes of this Act.

(6) Regulations may prescribe circumstances in which a person who has been deemed to be a disabled person by the provisions of sub-paragraph (1) or regulations made under sub-paragraph (5) is to be treated as no longer being deemed to be such a person.

(7) In this paragraph—
  'certificate of registration' means a certificate issued under regulations made under section 6 of the Act of 1944; and
  'initial period' means the period of three years beginning with the date on which this paragraph comes into force.

Progressive conditions

8.—(1) Where—
  (a) a person has a progressive condition (such as cancer, multiple sclerosis or muscular dystrophy or infection by the human immunodeficiency virus),
  (b) as a result of that condition, he has an impairment which has (or had) an effect on his ability to carry out normal day-to-day activities, but
  (c) that effect is not (or was not) a substantial adverse effect,
he shall be taken to have an impairment which has such a substantial adverse effect if the condition is likely to result in his having such an impairment.

(2) Regulations may make provision, for the purposes of this paragraph—
  (a) for conditions of a prescribed description to be treated as being progressive;
  (b) for conditions of a prescribed description to be treated as not being progressive.

14 CONTEMPORARY CONSTITUTIONAL LAW TEXTBOOKS ON THE BRITISH APPROACH TO THE PROTECTION OF CIVIL LIBERTIES, 1993–97

A. De Smith and Brazier

The traditional legal approach to civil liberties in Britain can be summed up in three propositions. First, freedoms are not to be guaranteed by statements of general principle. Secondly, they are residual. Freedom of public assembly, for example, means the liberty to gather wherever one chooses except in so far as others are legally entitled to prevent the assembly from being held or in so far as the holding or conduct of the assembly is a civil wrong or a criminal offence. To define the content of liberty one has merely to subtract from its totality the sum of the legal restraints to which it is subject. Thirdly, for every wrongful encroachment upon one's liberty there is a legal remedy awarded by an independent court of justice. *Ubi jus, ibi remedium.*

The origins of the fundamental rights and liberties of the citizens of this country, like the origins of constitutional government, are matters of continuing historical controversy, reflecting different strands of English political philosophy and Whig and Tory interpretations of the Revolution of 1688. They may be said to derive both from the concept of popular rights and popular sovereignty, reflected in the reference in the Act of Settlement to the laws of England as being the 'birthright of the people, as well as from the concept of parliamentary sovereignty and of a compact between monarch and Parliament, whereby the rights and liberties of the subject were declared in the Bill of Rights, and further secured in the Act of Settlement.

In traditional English legal terms, the concept of popular rights and popular sovereignty has been eclipsed by the concept of parliamentary sovereignty, according to which, since Parliament is sovereign (in place of the monarch), the subject cannot possess fundamental rights such as are guaranteed to the citizen by many foreign and Commonwealth constitutions, as well as by international and European law. According to this traditional view of the doctrine of parliamentary sovereignty, the liberties of the subject are merely implications drawn from two principles, namely: (1) that individuals may say or do what they please, provided they do not transgress the substantive law, or infringe the legal rights of others; and (2) that public authorities (including the Crown) may do nothing but what they are authorised to do by some rule of common law (including the royal prerogative) or statute, and in particular may not interfere with the liberties of individuals without statutory authority. Where public authorities are not authorised to interfere with the individual, the individual has liberties. It is in this sense that such liberties are residual, rather than fundamental and positive, in their nature.

Apart from the general provisions ensuring the peaceful enjoyment of rights of property, and the freedom of the individual from illegal detention, duress, punishment or taxation, contained in the four great charters or statutes which regulate the relations between the Crown and people [Magna Carta, The Petition of Right, the Bill of Rights and the Act of Settlement: see docs 1, 2 and 4], and apart from specific legislation conferring particular rights [see doc. 14], the fundamental rights and liberties of the individual are not expressly defined in any United Kingdom law or code. However, the provisions of the Convention for the Protection of Human Rights and Fundamental Freedoms are commonly taken into account by English courts when cases involving human rights issues arise [*RB NOTE: now incorporated into UK law: see Doc. 40*]. Furthermore, an alleged victim of a violation of that Convention may have recourse to the European Commission and Court of Human Rights for redress, after exhausting any effective domestic remedies.

S.A. de Smith and Rodney Brazier, Constitutional and Administrative Law
(7th edn. 1994), p. 457.

B. *Halsbury's Laws of England*

In the absence of an entrenched Bill of Rights for the United Kingdom, the fundamental rights and liberties of the individual owe their main legal protection to:

(1) the provisions of the Convention for the Protection of Human Rights and Fundamental Freedoms as applied both in English courts and through the machinery for their enforcement in the European Commission and Court of Human Rights at Strasbourg,

(2) those provisions of European Community law which protect the rights of individuals,

(3) the development of the action of trespass in its various forms,

(4) the prerogative orders, including the writ of habeas corpus, as reinforced by the Habeas Corpus Acts,

(5) the fact that the individual can insist upon having common law actions affecting some of his most treasured rights, as well as all accusations of serious crime, tried by a random collection of ordinary persons, that is by a jury,

(6) the fact that, except in the case of the monarch, who can do no wrong in the eyes of the law, and whose person is inviolable, and, excepting too the protection afforded to the judiciary whilst acting in their official capacity, and the limited protection afforded to magistrates and justices of the peace, all persons are subject to the jurisdiction of the courts, and may be made liable for any infringement of the rights and liberties of others unless some statutory authorisation for the infringement is found, and

(7) the rule of construction that statutes and other legislative acts are so far as possible to be interpreted so as not to cause any interference with the vested rights of the individual.

The traditional British approach to the protection of civil liberties has been greatly influenced by Dicey [*RB NOTE: see Doc. 6*]. For him there was no need for any statement of fundamental principles operating as a kind of higher law because political freedom was adequately protected by the common law and by an independent Parliament acting as a watchdog against any excess of zeal by the executive. Under the common law, a wide measure of individual liberty was guaranteed by the principle that citizens are free to do as they like unless expressly prohibited by law. So people already enjoy the freedom of religion, the freedom of expression, and the freedom of assembly, and may be restrained from exercising these freedoms only if there are clear common law or statutory restrictions. This approach is illustrated by a number of classical decisions, the first of which is *Entick v Carrington* (1765) 19 St Tr 1030 where the Secretary of State issued a warrant to search the premises of John Entick and to seize any seditious literature. When the legality of the conduct was challenged, the minister claimed that the existence and exercise of such a power were necessary in the interests of the state. But the court upheld the challenge on the ground that there was no authority in the common law or in statute for warrants to be issued in this way. A second example is *Beatty v Gillbanks* (1882) 9 QBD 308 where members of the Salvation Army in Weston-super-Mare were forbidden to march on Sundays because their presence attracted a large hostile crowd of people, thereby causing a breach of the peace. When the Salvationists ignored the order not to assemble, they were bound over to keep the peace for having committed the crime of unlawful assembly. The order binding them over was set aside on appeal because they had done nothing wrong. In the view of the court, they could not be prohibited from assembling merely because their lawful conduct might induce others to act unlawfully.

Although there are thus important illustrations of the principle, it is open to question whether this approach is an adequate basis for the protection of liberty. In the first place, the common law rule that people are free to do anything which is not prohibited by law applies (it would seem) equally to the government. As a result, the government may violate individual freedom even though it is not formally empowered to do so, on the ground that it is doing nothing which is prohibited by law. So in *Malone v Metropolitan Police Commissioner* [1979] Ch. 344 [*RB NOTE: see Doc. 25*] the practice of telephone tapping was exposed as being done by the executive without any clear lawful authority. But when Mr Malone sought a declaration that the tapping of his telephone was unlawful, he failed because he could not point to any legal right of his which it was the duty of the government not to invade. There was no violation of his property rights, no breach of confidence, and no invasion of any right to privacy recognised by the law. A second difficulty with the British approach is that liberty is particularly vulnerable to erosion. The common law merely recognises that people are free to do anything which is not unlawful, but is powerless to prevent new restrictions from being enacted by the legislature. . . .

Halsbury's Laws of England (4th ed.), Vol. 8(2): *Constitutional Law and Human Rights* by Lord Lester and Dawn Oliver (1996).

C. Bradley and Ewing

Another weakness of the traditional British approach relates to the decline in the power of Parliament. The late 19th century, when Dicey was writing, was in many ways the high-water mark of an independent Parliament acting as a watchdog of the executive. This was the time when Parliament was 'a body which chose the government, maintained it and could reject it' and which 'operated as an intermediary between the electorate and the executive'. Since then, however, the inexorable growth of the party system and its attendant discipline has seen the executive increasingly gain control of the House of Commons. As a result, the government in the 1990s, unlike the position in the 1890s, can now expect its Bills to be passed by a largely quiescent House of Commons.

A.W. Bradley and K.D. Ewing, *Constitutional and Administrative Law* (12th ed. 1997), pp. 460–1.

(C)

Official Views on the State and the Individual in the Late Twentieth Century

> 15 A ROYAL COMMISSION ON THE CONSTITUTION CONSIDERS THE GROWTH AND CHANGE IN GOVERNMENT, 1973

The Scope of Government

The subject matter of government

227. Throughout most of the nineteenth century government was concerned mainly with law and order, external affairs and defence, the regulation of overseas trade and the raising of revenue; it exercised a narrow range of regulatory functions, but its attitude in domestic affairs was mostly passive and non-interventionist. There was little or no involvement in many matters – such as the performance of industry and the economy, the quality of the environment and standards of health and welfare – which are major preoccupations of modern government. The situation today is quite different; there are now very few areas of public and even personal life with which government can be said to have no concern at all.

228. This expansion of government, while a constant feature of modern history, has markedly quickened its pace at certain times. In this century two periods stand out, both associated with the world wars.

229. The first period extended from 1908 to 1919. It began with the extensive social reforms which were embodied in the Old Age Pensions Act 1908, the Labour Exchanges Act 1909 and the National Insurance Act 1911.

There followed in war-time the imposition of a widening range of administrative and economic controls. After the war those controls were quickly wound up, but many of the new government departments, including those established for Pensions, Labour, Air and Scientific and Industrial Research, remained in being, and two additional departments, for Transport and Health, were set up. Each of these new departments represented an enlarged area of government intervention.

230. The second period of rapid expansion was the decade from 1940. Apart again from the complex apparatus of war-time controls, finally dismantled in the 1950's, there were major developments in the social services and in the economic and environmental fields. Legislation was passed to bring about major changes in the arrangements for education, social security, health, agriculture, and town and country planning, and the Government's direct involvement in industry and the economy was increased through a series of Acts providing for the nationalisation of basic industries. Changes in the character of economic intervention were also implicit in the acceptance by the war-time Government of responsibility for maintaining full employment.

231. In these and other ways government responsibilities have, within the lifetime of many people now living, widened immensely. The range of subjects that may now be raised in Parliament provides some illustration of this. We have examined a recent series of Parliamentary Questions to see how far it would have been appropriate to put them at the beginning of the century. Our analysis covered Questions receiving both oral and written reply in the House of Commons in one week in June 1971. There were 718 Questions in all, and we estimate that between 80 and 90 per cent. of them could not have been tabled in 1900 since they related to matters which were not then of government concern. There has been no comparable increase over the same period in the total number of Questions tabled, no doubt because of the limited opportunities for receiving oral reply and the procedural restrictions which have been imposed; the growth of government responsibilities, and possibly of public anxieties, has been reflected instead in a vast increase in correspondence between Members of Parliament and Ministers.

Effect on the lives of the people

232. The cumulative effect of government expansion on people's lives and activities has been considerable. The individual a hundred years ago hardly needed to know that the central government existed. His birth, marriage and death would be registered, and he might be conscious of the safeguards for his security provided by the forces of law and order and of imperial defence; but, except for the very limited provisions of the poor law and factory legislation, his welfare and progress were matters for which he alone bore the responsibility. By the turn of the century the position was not much changed. Today, however, the individual citizen submits himself to the guidance of the state at all times. His schooling is enforced; his physical well-being can be looked after in a comprehensive health service; he may be helped by government agencies to find and train for a job; he is obliged

while in employment to insure against sickness, accident and unemployment; his house may be let to him by a public authority or he may be assisted in its purchase or improvement; he can avail himself of a wide range of government welfare allowances and services; and he draws a state pension on his retirement. In these and many other ways unknown to his counterpart of a century ago, he is brought into close and regular contact with government and its agencies.

233. Industrialists, too, are much more involved with government. An industrialist in the nineteenth century, if he wished to build a factory, could do so by entirely private arrangement, and government hardly needed to know about the project. In these days, however, a prospective factory developer is faced with a host of Acts and regulations – to do, for instance, with environmental planning, industrial development certificates, government grants, allowances and inducements, the welfare and training of employees, employee insurance and taxation, industrial relations, licences, waste disposal, air pollution and the collection of trade statistics – any aspect of which his nineteenth century forebear might well have regarded as an unwarranted interference.

THE SCALE OF GOVERNMENT

The number of ministers

234. As the scope of government has increased, so naturally has its size. This increase is well illustrated by the changes in the numbers of Ministers and civil servants and in the cost of government. For most of the nineteenth century the Cabinet consisted of twelve to fifteen members and Ministerial appointments outside the Cabinet were few. In this century, there has been no great increase in the Cabinet, which usually includes about twenty Ministers, but the total number of Ministerial appointments of all kinds has risen to over one hundred, about three times as many as in the days of Disraeli and Gladstone.

The size of the public service

235. The corresponding increase in government organisation has ultimately been reflected in the size rather than in the number of separate government departments. While new departments have been created from time to time to deal with expanding government functions, the pattern of organisation has undergone many changes and the tendency in recent years to merge ministries with similar or associated functions has led to a structure of fewer, but much larger, main departments. The Ministry of Defence, the Department of the Environment, the Department of Health and Social Security and the Department of Trade and Industry together cover the tasks formerly carried out by a dozen or so separate ministries.

236. Increases in manpower give a clearer idea of the great growth that has taken place in the departments. Up to the end of the nineteenth century, the strength of the non-industrial civil service (excluding the Post Office)

did not exceed 50,000. In this century there has been a tenfold increase in that number, to around 500,000, while the population of the country has risen only by half. Employment in the public service generally has also greatly expanded. In October 1972, the total was about 6,400,000, including 691,000 industrial and non-industrial civil servants, 408,000 in the Post Office, 1,900,00 in the other nationalised industries, 2,600,000 in local government and 775,000 in the National Health Service. Thus just over a quarter of the total employed population is now engaged in the various public services and industries, a proportion some six times as great as at the beginning of this century.

The cost of government

237. The rise in government expenditure has been even more dramatic, largely because transfer payments in the form of social security and other benefits to persons have risen at a much faster rate than direct purchases by government of materials and labour services. In 1870, total government expenditure was about £3 per head of population, whereas in 1970 it had reached some £400 per head; expressed as a percentage of national income (gross national product at factor cost), expenditure rose from 9 per cent. to 43 per cent. The rise in transfer payments alone was from about 0.2 per cent. of national income in 1870 to 12.5 per cent. in 1970, when the Government was claiming over 25 per cent. of the annual output of resources for its own direct use.

238. The centralisation of government is reflected in the changing financial responsibilities of central and local government. More than half of total government expenditure in 1870 was undertaken by local authorities; but, despite the large increase in their functions, this proportion had fallen to less than one-third by 1970. Equally striking is the fall in the proportion of local authorities' expenditure financed by themselves. In 1870 probably about 80 per cent. of local expenditure was financed by local rates, fees and charges, but this percentage had fallen to around 45 per cent. a century later. Thus the changing size and structure of government viewed alongside the growth in population and incomes indicates its increasing domination over the management of the nation's economic affairs.

THE COMPLEXITY OF GOVERNMENT

The processes of government

239. Other changes that have taken place in the nature of government are less easy to quantify. The tasks of government have become not only vaster but also more complex and burdensome, more difficult for Ministers and Parliament to control and for people to follow. Whereas in the last century it was entirely feasible for Ministers to keep a close watch on the activities of their departments and to take all policy decisions themselves, often without the advice of civil servants or experts, today a Minister cannot be expected to know about more than a small proportion of the decisions that are made

in his name, and policies have to be submitted to a complex network of internal and perhaps external consultation, specialist examination and often research before they reach Ministers for consideration. Many of these processes are conducted anonymously and without publicity. In these circumstances, the degree of control exercised by Ministers is bound to be lessened, and the citizen can hardly be expected to have any deep understanding of government operations.

240. Not only does government effectively fall more and more into the hands of the expert; it also increasingly requires an expert to appreciate its processes. The closing of a coal mine or the demolition of houses to make way for a new road may seem to those directly affected to be fairly simple issues of right and wrong, but such operations are likely to have derived from calculations of great complexity which demonstrate, to specialists at least, that they are the best options in the interests of the public at large. It is increasingly probable that the answers will have been obtained with the help of a computer, which facilitates far more refinement in decision making than was possible for governments of an earlier age.

Legislation

241. As government has penetrated more widely and deeply into the life of the nation, the scope and often the complexity of legislation has increased. Long before this century began Parliament found itself obliged to delegate to Ministers the power to make instruments which would carry the force of law. For many reasons – the much greater range of legislative activity, the limitations on Parliamentary time, the need to consult experts and outside interests on questions of detail and the importance of adjusting quickly to new conditions – reliance on delegated legislation has greatly increased. In the twenty years from 1951 to 1970, over 43,000 statutory instruments were made, an average of over 2,000 a year or nearly double the number at the beginning of the century. The volume of the instruments made each year is now about three times that of the Acts of Parliament passed. Many of these instruments are complex and technical, not easily comprehended even by the people they directly affect; and many provide penalties for contravention. It might be observed that in these circumstances ignorance of the law may sometimes be not only excusable but inevitable.

FUTURE PROSPECTS

Attempts to check the growth of government

242. What we have said suffices to indicate how government has grown in scope, in scale and in complexity. It might well seem to the ordinary citizen that such a vast and spreading organism is beyond his powers to understand, let alone influence. It is natural in these circumstances to enquire whether the expansion is likely to continue or whether it can be halted or even reversed.

243. It is a concern of all governments to keep the public service and

public expenditure within appropriate limits. With an eye to the need for economy, and to the general desire for a reduction in the tax burden, special attempts are made from time to time to curtail expenditure in one sector or another, or in the public sector as a whole. In the early 1950s, for instance, as after the First World War, it became public policy to make a 'bonfire' of war-time controls. Between 1950 and 1958 there was in fact a steady decline in the number of non-industrial civil servants and some check in the rise in public expenditure, though both trends were later reversed. A White Paper (*The Reorganisation of Central Government*, Cmnd. 4506) published in October 1970 stated the Government's belief that 'government has been attempting to do too much. This has placed an excessive burden on industry, and on the people of this country as a whole, and has also overloaded the government machine itself'. Every activity of government was to be examined with a view to deciding whether it was still relevant and whether it had necessarily to be undertaken by central government.

The pressures on government

244. But while attempts to curb the growth of government may meet with some successes, the inexorable pressures continue. People now look to government, not only as in the last century for protection against attack from without and against disorder and crime, disease and extreme distress, but also for greater equality of opportunity, more and constantly improving public services and the enhancement of living standards. To a very great extent it is under these pressures that government has grown and continues to grow. There is no little degree of resistance to change, and especially to rapid change, in our governmental arrangements, but it is almost a natural assumption when social, economic or industrial problems arise that it is primarily for the Government to solve them. The roots of most government measures, even those described as unpopular, are to be found in the known or assumed requirements of the population. To some extent the political parties anticipate and interpret the wishes of the electorate in presenting their manifestos for approval; but for the most part the expansion of government is a reaction to the continuous pressures and problems of the community.

245. New policies usually involve higher government expenditure and more civil servants. While government may be urgently called upon to act, there may be less disposition on the part of the public to recognise the implications of that action. Having willed the end, they may resent the financial cost. But voices raised in favour of economy in government are now, perhaps, weaker than they used to be. The social and personal services which the government administer are by their nature expensive in money and manpower; they are little amenable to savings through greater productivity, and there are both practical and political limits to the curtailments which can be made. Even the growing complexities of government largely derive from the general desire that an ever-widening range of interests, national, sectional and individual, should be brought into account in the taking of decisions.

246. In recent years, with the development of broadcasting, the pressures on government have built up more quickly and intensively. Radio and television have fostered a wider and more immediate appreciation of current issues and a swifter response to them. Very soon after new problems have broken through to the surface—they may concern pollution, fire hazards, cruelty to animals, the collapse of an insurance company, the adoption of children, bad housing, reservoir schemes, pornography, the needs of developing countries, conflict or disaster abroad, or any one of an interminable list of subjects—they are widely discussed on radio and television, and in the press. Public protests and pressure groups mount, usually focusing their demands for action on government, and dissatisfaction increases if action is not taken or is not immediately effective. Thus government, however reluctant it may be at the outset, may be compelled to extend its sphere of activity.

247. It is clear that these pressures will continue and that what the 1970 White Paper described as 'the increasingly complex and technical character of the processes of government and administration in modern society' will persist. While machinery reforms and occasional excursions with the pruning knife may do something to make government more manageable, there is no prospect of halting, still less of reversing, the long-term trend of growth in its scope, scale and complexity.

CHANGES IN OUR POLITICAL INSTITUTIONS

Parliament

248. We now consider the ways in which the institutions of government have been modified to deal with the greater volume of business. We start with Parliament. The first point to note is that the growth in the resources at its disposal has in no way matched the increase in the demands made upon it. Indeed in one respect these resources have been diminished, since about a hundred of its Members are now Ministers and so part of the executive which Parliament has to control, compared with only just over forty in 1900. Representation in the European Parliament has placed a large additional burden on the remaining Members. There has been no great increase in the staff at their disposal. In 1966 the number of House of Commons Clerks was thirty-six, one fewer than in 1900; by 1972 the number had risen to forty-eight. And the number of sitting days has not substantially changed; since 1945 it has averaged 163 days a year, compared with 149 days between the wars and 129 days before the First World War.

249. Parliament has, however, shown consciousness of the need to reform its own procedures to match the changed situation. It has been recognised that the traditional processes of Parliament—set debates on Bills and motions, formal proceedings in Committee, questions and statements on the floor of the House—are not now adequate for probing in depth the actions of government departments. Accordingly, within the last twenty years in particular, experiments have been made and procedures brought in to enable the legislature to scrutinise more closely the policies and acts of the

executive and generally to bring government more into the open. Some of the experiments have not been pursued; others have proved to be workable and seem likely to become established as permanent features of the Parliamentary arrangements.

250. Changes have been made mainly through development of the work of Parliamentary Select Committees. . . .

252. Parliament has recently appointed a Joint Select Committee of both Houses to improve its control over the great volume of regulations, orders and statutory instruments of all kinds. It is the task of the Committee to consider such instruments and to report to Parliament any unusual or unexpected use in the instruments of the powers granted by Act of Parliament and any technical or other flaws they might contain. More recently, a Select Committee of the House of Commons has been established to examine also the merits of statutory instruments.

253. Despite these modifications, there is an evident contrast between the enormous increase in the scope, scale and complexity of government and the extent and pace of change in the Parliamentary institutions. Fundamentally, except in the curtailment of the powers of the House of Lords ... Parliament has changed hardly at all in this century. A Member who had sat in the House of Commons in 1901 would find little in its mode of operation (though much in its subject matter) to surprise him today.

The executive

254. During the same period, the organisation of the executive has undergone more profound changes, possibly reflecting the fact that Parliament, as a legislative, deliberative and critical body, matured much earlier than did the machinery of government. We have already noted the great increase in the number of Ministers, the development of the Scottish and Welsh Offices, the creation of many other new departments to take over the new functions of government, and the more recent tendency to group related subjects in a smaller number of departments with the aim of securing greater cohesion in strategy and policy. . . .

255. The civil service has also undergone profound change. It has, as we have seen, increased enormously in numbers and in the range of skills it provides. Instead of being housed almost wholly in headquarters offices in London, the staffs of most departments are now to a considerable extent deployed in a network of regional and local offices so that fewer than one-third of the total are at headquarters. Some of the headquarters staffs have themselves been dispersed to the provinces to relieve the pressure on accommodation in London. . . .

Appointed bodies

257. Another feature of modern government is the rapid growth in the number of bodies operating between central and local government. There are now several hundred bodies of one kind or another which have been appointed by the Government to carry out specialised functions. This is by no means a new development. Government boards were set up after the

industrial revolution to deal with poor law, health and education. But today the number and range of these bodies are very much greater. Many are purely advisory, having no powers of executive action, though they bring influence to bear, as they were intended to do, on the actions of government. Others may act as appeal tribunals to adjudicate on the interests of individuals, or they may, like the boards of nationalised industries, have considerable executive and spending powers and loom large in the commercial life of the nation. In some cases the powers which they have been given, for instance in relation to hospitals and gas and electricity, may previously have been exercised by elected local authorities. We examine the constitution and functions of these bodies more fully in Chapter 18. For the most part they are appointed by Ministers rather than elected, and they are able to carry out their functions, whether executive, appellate, advisory or of some other character, with a considerable degree of independent discretion. They are now an integral part of our changing pattern of government. Many of them operate on a regional basis.

Local government

258. Local government has itself experienced many changes during the course of the twentieth century. As the scope of government has increased it has acquired many new functions, while it has lost to the new appointed bodies some of its older traditional functions. ...

SAFEGUARDS FOR THE INDIVIDUAL

Avenues of complaint

259. With government touching the lives of people at so many points, occasions for individual complaint have inevitably increased. People with grievances against government departments or public bodies usually have a choice of courses open to them. If the complaint is that an executive body has exceeded or misused its powers, the ordinary courts may give redress. In certain circumstances administrative tribunals are available to consider appeals. If the complaint lies against a public corporation, there may be a body, as in the case of the nationalised industries, specifically established to examine and report on representations by the public. Many people prefer to put their grievances to their Members of Parliament, who may pursue them through letters to Ministers or through Questions in Parliament. The press and broadcasting are also quick to take up complaints of maladministration or injustice, and in this way too the Government may be induced to institute enquiries leading to remedial action.

The Parliamentary Commissioner for Administration

260. Since 1967 a further means of redress has been established with the appointment of the Parliamentary Commissioner for Administration. The Commissioner may receive and investigate complaints about public admin-

istration which are submitted to him by a Member of Parliament. Broadly speaking his jurisdiction extends only to maladministration by government departments, and he is not able to deal with complaints against other public bodies. The Commissioner reports on his enquiries into a particular case to the department concerned, and it is for the department to decide whether action should be taken. He also makes an annual report to Parliament.

261. There has been pressure for this procedure to be applied to a wider field. In legislation for the reorganisation of the National Health Services powers are being taken for the appointment of Health Service Commissioners. In the case of local authorities, the Government has indicated its acceptance of the need for improved complaints machinery and is considering in the light of comments by local authorities the form that this should take.

262. There has therefore been in recent years some elaboration of the arrangements for examining complaints about public administration and they are expected to be further developed. These procedures, which are broadly derived from experience in other European countries, may still be regarded as somewhat experimental in this country, but there seems little reason to doubt that they will become, in their present or some other form, an accepted and permanent part of our constitutional arrangements.

Summary

263. In this chapter we have very briefly reviewed the changes that have taken place in the scope and scale of government activity and in the institutions of government over the last hundred years. The most notable feature has been the immense increase in the range and complexity of government business and in the manpower and other resources devoted to it.

Report of the Royal Commission on the Constitution, Cmnd. 5460, pp. 75–84.

---

16   THE HOME OFFICE ON THE BRITISH CONSTITUTIONAL TRADITION ON HUMAN RIGHTS, 1976

Why No Bill of Rights Already?

2.01—Our arrangements for the protection of human rights are different from those of most other countries. The differences are related to differences in our constitutional traditions. Although our present constitution may be regarded as deriving in part from the revolution settlement of 1688–89, consolidated by the Union of 1707, we, unlike our European neighbours and many Commonwealth countries, do not owe our present system of government either to a revolution or to a struggle for independence. The United Kingdom—

a. has an omnicompetent Parliament, with absolute power to enact any law and change any previous law; the courts in England and Wales have not, since the seventeenth century, recognised even in theory any higher legal order by reference to which Acts of Parliament could be held void; in Scotland the courts, while reserving the right to treat an Act as void for breaching a fundamental term of the Treaty of Union, have made it clear that they foresee no likely circumstances in which they would do so;

b. unlike other modern democracies, has no written constitution;

c. unlike countries in the civil law tradition, makes no fundamental distinction, as regards rights or remedies, between 'public law' governing the actions of the State and its agents, and 'private law' regulating the relationships of private citizens with one another; nor have we a coherent system of administrative law applied by specialised tribunals or courts and with its own appropriate remedies;

d. has not generally codified its law, and our courts adopt a relatively narrow and literal approach to the interpretation of statutes;

e. unlike the majority of EEC countries and the United States, does not, by ratifying a treaty or convention, make it automatically part of the domestic law (nor do we normally give effect to such an international agreement by incorporating the agreement itself into our law).

2.02—In other countries the rights of the citizen are usually (though not universally) to be found enunciated in general terms in a Bill of Rights or other constitutional document. The effectiveness of such instruments varies greatly. A Bill of Rights is not an automatic guarantee of liberty; its efficacy depends on the integrity of the institutions which apply it, and ultimately on the determination of the people that it should be maintained.

2.03—The United Kingdom as such has no Bill of Rights of this kind. The Bill of Rights of 1688, though more concerned with the relationship between the English Parliament and the Crown, did contain some important safeguards for personal liberty – as did the Claim of Right of 1689, its Scottish equivalent. Among the provisions common to both the Bill of Rights and the Claim of Right are declarations that excessive bail is illegal and that it is the right of subjects to petition the Crown without incurring penalties. But the protection given by these instruments to the rights and liberties of the citizen is much narrower than the constitutional guarantees now afforded in many other democratic countries.

2.04—The effect of the United Kingdom system of law is to provide, through the development of the common law and by express statutory enactment, a diversity of specific rights with their accompanying remedies. Thus, to secure the individual's right to freedom from unlawful or arbitrary detention, our law provides specific and detailed remedies such as habeas corpus and the action for false imprisonment. The rights which have been afforded in this way are for the most part negative rights to be protected from interference from others, rather than positive rights to behave in a particular way. Those rights which have emerged in the common law can always be modified by Parliament. Parliament's role is all-pervasive – potentially, at least. It continually adapts existing rights and remedies and provides new ones, and no doubt this process would continue even if a comprehensive Bill of Rights were enacted.

2.05—The legal remedies provided for interference with the citizen's rights have in recent times been overlaid by procedures which are designed to afford not so much remedies in the strict sense of the term as facilities for obtaining independent and impartial scrutiny of action by public bodies about which an individual believes he has cause for complaint, even though the action may have been within the body's legal powers. For example, the actions of central Government Departments are open to scrutiny by the Parliamentary Commissioner for Administration; those of local authorities by the Local Commissioners for Administration; and complaints about the administration of the National Health Service are investigated by the Health Service Commissioners.

2.06—Thus, Parliament – omnicompetent and representative of the people – has been at the centre of our arrangements for redressing grievances, by making specific changes in the law and calling the responsible authorities to account.

Home Office discussion document, *Legislation on Human Rights*, 1976.

---

17 THE CENTRAL OFFICE OF INFORMATION PUBLICIZES HOW HUMAN RIGHTS ARE SAFEGUARDED IN THE UK, 1978

Respect for individual freedom and for the citizen's rights against the State is embedded in the constitutional traditions of the United Kingdom. British people attach great importance to the exercise of human rights and the way in which they are preserved and enlarged through political and legal institutions. ...

The British system of law provides, through the development of the common law and by legislation, a diversity of specific rights and their accompanying remedies. Thus, for example, to secure the individual's right to freedom from unlawful or arbitrary detention, there are specific and detailed remedies such as 'habeas corpus' and the action for false imprisonment. The preservation of these rights is guaranteed by the judicial system which is strictly independent of the executive.

Legal remedies provided for interference with citizens' rights are supplemented by procedures designed to obtain independent and impartial scrutiny of action by public bodies about which an individual believes he has cause for complaint, even though the action may have been within the body's legal powers. The actions of central government departments, for example, are open to investigation by the Parliamentary Commissioners for Administration and those of local authorities by the Local Commissioners for Administration and the Northern Ireland Commissioner for Complaints. Complaints about the National Health Service are investigated by the Health Service Commissioner and the Northern Ireland Commissioner for Complaints. Complaints against the police in England and Wales may involve the independent Police Complaints Board. There is a similar board in Northern Ireland.

As well as the legal safeguards provided by Parliament and courts whose judges are strictly independent of the executive, there are vital non-legal safeguards against the abuse of governmental power; these include unwritten parliamentary conventions, the sense of 'fair play' of legislators and administrators, the vigilance of the parliamentary opposition parties and of individual Members of Parliament, the influence of a free Press and public opinion, and the right to change the Government through free elections with a secret ballot.

Several features of British government need to be borne in mind when considering the questions of the preservation and extension of human rights in the United Kingdom:

(1) Parliament has absolute theoretical power to enact any law and change any previous law. The courts in England and Wales have not, since the seventeenth century, recognised even in theory any higher legal order by reference to which parliamentary legislation could be held void; however, because of British membership of the European Community, Community law prevails over domestic law in certain circumstances. In Scotland the courts reserve the right to treat legislation as void for breaching a fundamental term of the 1707 Treaty of Union, although there is as yet no case in which they have done so.

(2) The constitution of the United Kingdom is to be found partly in conventions and customs and partly in statute; there is no written constitution or bill of rights.

(3) Unlike some countries, British law makes no fundamental distinction, as regards rights or remedies, between 'public law' governing the actions of the State and its agents, and 'private law' regulating the relationships of private citizens with one another; nor is there a separate system of administrative law (and remedies) applied by specialised tribunals or courts. Any person may take proceedings against the Government or local government authorities to protect his (or her) legal rights and to obtain a remedy for any injury he has suffered, in the same way as he can against an individual.

(4) The United Kingdom has not generally codified its law, and courts adopt a relatively strict and literal approach to the interpretation of statutes.

(5) The United Kingdom does not, by ratifying a treaty or convention, make it automatically part of the domestic law. Where necessary,

domestic law is amended to conform to the terms of the convention so that it may be ratified.

In the United Kingdom and other countries there is concern about violations of human rights throughout the world. There is also a growing recognition world-wide that the abuse of human rights is the legitimate subject of international concern and that the enforcement of human rights can no longer be left to national governments alone.

Human Rights in the United Kingdom, 1978, pp. 1–2; see also 1992 edn.

---

18 THE BRITISH GOVERNMENT REPORTS TO THE UNITED NATIONS HUMAN RIGHTS COMMITTEE ON HOW HUMAN RIGHTS ARE PROTECTED IN THE UK, 1989–94

THIRD PERIODIC REPORT, 1989

1. The United Kingdom has a long history of concern for human rights and some important achievements to its credit. *Magna Carta* in 1215, the *Habeas Corpus* Acts, the Bill of Rights in 1688 and the Scottish Claim of Right in 1689, the progressive development of parliamentary democracy, the establishment of religious freedom, the extension of the franchise and the beginnings of the trade union movement are all landmarks in British history; and in more recent years the United Kingdom has made important contributions to the drafting and adoption of the European Convention on Human Rights and to the International Covenant on Civil and Political Rights itself.

2. The country has not during this period felt the need for a written constitution or a comprehensive bill of rights: the principle has been that the rights and freedoms recognized in other countries' constitutions are inherent in the British legal system and are protected by it and by Parliament unless they are removed or restricted by statute. The position has been summed up by the late Stanley de Smith, an eminent constitutional lawyer, in his statement that freedoms are not to be guaranteed by statements of general principle, that they are residual, and that for every wrongful encroachment on these liberties there is a legal remedy.

3. The rights and freedom protected in this way have at various times been reinforced by legislation to deal with specific problems as they have arisen. Examples include the abolition of slavery and the prohibitions on the exploitation of children in the 19th century; measures to protect freedom of expression while prohibiting extremist incitement to public disorder in the 1930s; and the Equal Opportunities legislation of the 1970s which dealt with discrimination on grounds of race or sex. Other measures from that period included legislation on industrial relations and trades unions, and on immigration from the Commonwealth, for example the Industrial Relations Act

1971, the Trade Unions and Labour Relations Act 1974, the Immigration Appeals Act 1969, and the Fair Employment (Northern Ireland) Act 1989, each of which incorporated statutory safeguards to protect individual rights and freedoms. Such measures typically provided for the formation of statutory bodies or tribunals with specific responsibilities for promoting good practice – for example, the Commission on Racial Equality and the Equal Opportunities Commission – or for hearing appeals (industrial tribunals, immigration appeals).

4. Some legislation is introduced with the intention or the effect of enabling the United Kingdom to subscribe to international agreements or to incorporate their provisions on a statutory basis. For example, the Criminal Justice Act 1988 contained provisions on compensation for wrongful conviction, which secures the United Kingdom's compliance with article 14, paragraph 6, of the Covenant, and on the proscription of torture, following which the United Kingdom ratified the United Nations Convention against Torture and Other Cruel, Inhuman or Degrading Treatment or Punishment.

5. A further development during the last 12 years or so has been the increasing influence of the European Commission and Court of Human Rights and of judicial review in the domestic courts. The United Kingdom must abide by judgements of the European Court in cases to which it is party. The rulings of the Court have had a considerable impact on United Kingdom law and practice, often giving increased priority or urgency to changes which were already under consideration. Sometimes the judgement of the Court has required the insertion of judicial procedures into what had previously been regarded as an administrative process where accountability was to Parliament through Ministers. Examples of Court decisions which have led to changes in United Kingdom law are those of *Dudgeon* on homosexuality in Northern Ireland and *Abdulaziz, Balkandali and Cabales* on sex discrimination in immigration rules. The Government routinely scrutinizes draft legislation and proposals for administrative change to see whether they are compatible with international human rights instruments to which the United Kingdom is party.

6. The case for more comprehensive human rights legislation has been argued at various times during the past 15 years. The incorporation of the European Convention on Human Rights in United Kingdom domestic law has been the solution most often favoured; but neither of the two largest political parties has adopted it as its policy, and a series of bills introduced by private Members in both Houses of Parliament has failed to attract sufficient support to make progress.

7. Reasons against legislation of this kind have been that the broad propositions in the Convention are often unsuited to the close textual analysis of statutes undertaken to determine the will of Parliament; the risk of damaging conflict between the courts on the one hand and the Government and Parliament on the other, with courts being used as a means of challenging unpopular action by the government of the day which has

received the support of Parliament; and the view that injustice or unfairness of the kind which such a bill would be designed to correct could in the United Kingdom context be more suitably and more effectively challenged in Parliament.

8. As the Attorney-General, Sir Patrick Mayhew, QC, then Solicitor-General, said on 6 February 1987 in opposing Sir Edward Gardner's Human Rights Bill, which would have incorporated the European Convention on Human Rights:

> 'The judiciary must be seen to be impartial. More especially, as far as practicable it must be kept free from political controversy. We must take great care not to propel judges into the political arena. However, that is what we would do if we asked them to take policy decisions of a nature that we [Parliament] ought properly to take ourselves and which under our present constitution we do take. We would increase that danger if we required or permitted them to alter or even reverse decisions taken by Parliament .... Our constitutional history rather strongly shows that over the centuries the British people have preferred that these matters should be decided by people whom they can elect and sack rather than people immune from either process – wiser, less opportunist or even less venal though such people might well be considered to be.'

9. Areas where issues of human rights and personal freedom are at present a matter of particular concern include:

(a) The need for firm and effective action to prevent terrorism, including procedures for the detention, questioning and trial of suspects in which the rights of the individual have to be balanced by the protection and safety of the public;

(b) Immigration and claims to asylum, where the continuing pressure of immigration from certain parts of the world makes it necessary to operate tight controls and apply rigorous investigative procedures which may involve inconvenience or distress for the individuals concerned;

(c) The extent to which direct and indirect discrimination on grounds of race and sex is still practised by individuals and institutions, not only in ways which are prohibited by law but often in subtle and even unconscious ways which are difficult to identify and even more difficult to correct;

(d) The difficulty of conducting fair and impartial investigations, the results of which will command general acceptance and public confidence, into complaints of misconduct by public officials, members of the security forces or others, or into alleged miscarriages of justice in the three areas indicated in (a)–(c) above.

Fourth Periodic Report, 1994

2. In the past five years, the question of the best means of providing for the human rights recognised in the Covenant and those other international instruments to which the United Kingdom is party has been a subject of debate. This reflects, in part, the way in which interest in human rights issues has been stimulated by the United Kingdom's extensive participation in work in this area.

3. The United Kingdom has given close attention to meeting the reporting requirements under those international instruments and to assisting and responding to the work of any visiting committee. The United Kingdom has also played a leading role in recent work to reform the institutions and procedures established under the European Convention on Human Rights. The revised arrangements are contained in the 11th Protocol to the Convention, which also makes mandatory and permanent the right of individual petition to the European Court of Human Rights. The United Kingdom signed the 11th Protocol in May 1994 and hopes to ratify it by the end of the year.

4. In the debates on human rights issues that have occurred in Parliament and elsewhere in recent years, the Government has maintained the long-established principle that the rights and freedoms recognised in international instruments and in the constitutions of those countries that have enacted a comprehensive Bill of Rights are inherent in the United Kingdom's legal system and are protected by it and by Parliament unless they are removed or restricted by statute. The Government does not consider that it is properly the role of the legislature to confer rights and freedoms which are naturally possessed by all members of society. It also believes that Parliament should retain the supreme responsibility for enacting or changing the law, including that affecting individual rights and freedoms, while it is properly the role of the judiciary to interpret specific legislation.

5. The incorporation of an international human rights instrument into domestic law is not necessary to ensure that the United Kingdom's obligations under such instruments are reflected in the deliberations of government and of the courts. The United Kingdom's human rights obligations are routinely considered by Ministers and their officials in the formulation and application of Government policy, while judgments of the House of Lords have made clear that such obligations are part of the legal context in which the judges consider themselves to operate:

> There is a *prima facie* presumption that Parliament does not intend to act in breach of international law, including therein specific treaty obligations; and if one of the meanings which can reasonably be ascribed to the legislation is consonant with the treaty obligations and another or others are not, the meaning which is consonant is to be preferred. (*Salomon v the Commissioners of Customs and Excise* [1967] 2 QB 116)

The application of this principle (extended to the common law) in relation to the European Convention on Human Rights may be seen in *Derbyshire County Council v Times Newspapers Limited* [1992] 3 WLR 28. (The decision was upheld on different grounds in the House of Lords, where their Lordships found no ambiguity in the common law, [1993] AC 534).

6. Nor is the ratification of the Optional Protocol to the Covenant allowing the right of individual petition to the Human Rights Committee necessary to ensure the protection of individual rights in this country. Whether in civil or criminal proceedings or in the developing field of judicial review of executive decision-making, the domestic courts continue to play an effective role as protectors of individual rights, while since 1966 individuals in the United Kingdom have had access to an additional means of redress through the procedures and institutions established under the European Convention on Human Rights. That machinery provides protection which is now familiar and well used and the Government does not believe that ratification of the Optional Protocol to the Covenant would significantly enhance the protection of individuals under the United Kingdom's jurisdiction.

CHAPTER 2

INTERNATIONAL BILLS OF RIGHTS

(A)

International Human Rights Treaties

19   THE UNITED NATIONS: THE UNIVERSAL DECLARATION OF HUMAN RIGHTS, 1948

Preamble

Whereas recognition of the inherent dignity and of the equal and inalienable rights of all members of the human family is the foundation of freedom, justice and peace in the world,

Whereas disregard and contempt for human rights have resulted in barbarous acts which have outraged the conscience of mankind, and the advent of a world in which human beings shall enjoy freedom of speech and belief and freedom from fear and want has been proclaimed as the highest aspiration of the common people,

Whereas it is essential, if man is not to be compelled to have recourse, as a last resort, to rebellion against tyranny and oppression, that human rights should be protected by the rule of law,

Whereas it is essential to promote the development of friendly relations between nations,

Whereas the peoples of the United Nations have in the Charter reaffirmed their faith in fundamental human rights, in the dignity and worth of the human person and in the equal rights of men and women and have determined to promote social progress and better standards of life in larger freedom,

Whereas Member States have pledged themselves to achieve, in co-operation with the United Nations, the promotion of universal respect for and observance of human rights and fundamental freedoms,

Whereas a common understanding of these rights and freedoms is of the greatest importance for the full realization of this pledge,

Now, therefore, THE GENERAL ASSEMBLY *proclaims*

This Universal Declaration of Human Rights as a common standard of achievement for all peoples and all nations, to the end that every individual and every organ of society, keeping this Declaration constantly in mind, shall strive by teaching and education to promote respect for these rights and freedoms and by progressive measures, national and international, to secure their universal and effective recognition and observance, both among the peoples of Member States themselves and among the peoples of territories under their jurisdiction.

Article 1

All human beings are born free and equal in dignity and rights. They are endowed with reason and conscience and should act towards one another in a spirit of brotherhood.

Article 2

Everyone is entitled to all the rights and freedoms set forth in this Declaration, without distinction of any kind, such as race, colour, sex, language, religion, political or other opinion, national or social origin, property, birth or other status.

Furthermore, no distinction shall be made on the basis of the political, jurisdictional or international status of the country or territory to which a person belongs, whether it be independent, trust, non-self-governing or under any other limitation of sovereignty.

Article 3

Everyone has the right to life, liberty and security of person.

Article 4

No one shall be held in slavery or servitude; slavery and the slave trade shall be prohibited in all their forms.

Article 5

No one shall be subjected to torture or to cruel, inhuman or degrading treatment or punishment.

Article 6

Everyone has the right to recognition everywhere as a person before the law.

Article 7

All are equal before the law and are entitled without any discrimination to equal protection of the law. All are entitled to equal protection against any discrimination in violation of this Declaration and against any incitement to such discrimination.

Article 8

Everyone has the right to an effective remedy by the competent national tribunals for acts violating the fundamental rights granted him by the constitution or by law.

Article 9

No one shall be subjected to arbitrary arrest, detention or exile.

Article 10

Everyone is entitled in full equality to a fair and public hearing by an independent and impartial tribunal, in the determination of his rights and obligations and of any criminal charge against him.

Article 11

1. Everyone charged with a penal offence has the right to be presumed innocent until proved guilty according to law in a public trial at which he has had all the guarantees necessary for his defence.
2. No one shall be held guilty of any penal offence on account of any act or omission which did not constitute a penal offence, under national or international law, at the time when it was committed. Nor shall a heavier penalty be imposed than the one that was applicable at the time the penal offence was committed.

Article 12

No one shall be subjected to arbitrary interference with his privacy, family, home or correspondence, nor to attacks upon his honour and reputation. Everyone has the right to the protection of the law against such interference or attacks.

Article 13

1. Everyone has the right to freedom of movement and residence within the borders of each state.
2. Everyone has the right to leave any country, including his own, and to return to his country.

Article 14

1. Everyone has the right to seek and to enjoy in other countries asylum from persecution.
2. This right may not be invoked in the case of prosecutions genuinely arising from non-political crimes or from acts contrary to the purposes and principles of the United Nations.

Article 15

1. Everyone has the right to a nationality.
2. No one shall be arbitrarily deprived of his nationality nor denied the right to change his nationality.

Article 16

1. Men and women of full age, without any limitation due to race, nationality or religion, have the right to marry and to found a family. They are entitled to equal rights as to marriage, during marriage and at its dissolution.
2. Marriage shall be entered into only with the free and full consent of the intending spouses.
3. The family is the natural and fundamental group unit of society and is entitled to protection by society and the State.

Article 17

1. Everyone has the right to own property alone as well as in association with others.
2. No one shall be arbitrarily deprived of his property.

Article 18

Everyone has the right to freedom of thought, conscience and religion; this right includes freedom to change his religion or belief, and freedom, either alone or in community with others and in public or private, to manifest his religion or belief in teaching, practice, worship and observance.

Article 19

Everyone has the right to freedom of opinion and expression; this right includes freedom to hold opinions without interference and to seek, receive and impart information and ideas through any media and regardless of frontiers.

Article 20

1. Everyone has the right to freedom of peaceful assembly and association.
2. No one may be compelled to belong to an association.

Article 21

1. Everyone has the right to take part in the government of his country, directly or through freely chosen representatives.
2. Everyone has the right of equal access to public service in his country.
3. The will of the people shall be the basis of the authority of government; this will shall be expressed in periodic and genuine elections which shall be

by universal and equal suffrage and shall be held by secret vote or by
equivalent free voting procedures.

Article 22

Everyone, as a member of society, has the right to social security and is
entitled to realization, through national effort and international co-
operation and in accordance with the organization and resources of each
State, of the economic, social and cultural rights indispensable for his
dignity and the free development of his personality.

Article 23

1. Everyone has the right to work, to free choice of employment, to just and
favourable conditions of work and to protection against unemployment.
2. Everyone, without any discrimination, has the right to equal pay for equal
work.
3. Everyone who works has the right to just and favourable remuneration
ensuring for himself and his family an existence worthy of human dignity,
and supplemented, if necessary, by other means of social protection.
4. Everyone has the right to form and to join trade unions for the protection
of his interests.

Article 24

Everyone has the right to rest and leisure, including reasonable limitation of
working hours and periodic holidays with pay.

Article 25

1. Everyone has the right to a standard of living adequate for the health and
well-being of himself and of his family, including food, clothing, housing
and medical care and necessary social services, and the right to security in
the event of unemployment, sickness, disability, widowhood, old age or
other lack of livelihood in circumstances beyond his control.
2. Motherhood and childhood are entitled to special care and assistance. All
children, whether born in or out of wedlock, shall enjoy the same social
protection.

Article 26

1. Everyone has the right to education. Education shall be free, at least in
the elementary and fundamental stages. Elementary education shall be
compulsory. Technical and professional education shall be made generally
available and higher education shall be equally accessible to all on the basis
of merit.
2. Education shall be directed to the full development of the human
personality and to the strengthening of respect for human rights and
fundamental freedoms. It shall promote understanding, tolerance

and friendship among all nations, racial or religious groups, and shall further the activities of the United Nations for the maintenance of peace.

3. Parents have a prior right to choose the kind of education that shall be given to their children.

Article 27

1. Everyone has the right freely to participate in the cultural life of the community, to enjoy the arts and to share in scientific advancement and its benefits.

2. Everyone has the right to the protection of the moral and material interests resulting from any scientific, literary or artistic production of which he is the author.

Article 28

Everyone is entitled to a social and international order in which the rights and freedoms set forth in this Declaration can be fully realized.

Article 29

1. Everyone has duties to the community in which alone the free and full development of his personality is possible.

2. In the exercise of his rights and freedoms, everyone shall be subject only to such limitations as are determined by law solely for the purpose of securing due recognition and respect for the rights and freedoms of others and of meeting the just requirements of morality, public order and the general welfare in a democratic society.

3. These rights and freedoms may in no case be exercised contrary to the purposes and principles of the United Nations.

Article 30

Nothing in this Declaration may be interpreted as implying for any State, group or person any right to engage in any activity or to perform any act aimed at the destruction of any of the rights and freedoms set forth herein.

---

20 THE UNITED NATIONS: INTERNATIONAL COVENANT ON CIVIL AND POLITICAL RIGHTS, 1976

THE STATES PARTIES TO THE PRESENT COVENANT,

Considering that, in accordance with the principles proclaimed in the Charter of the United Nations, recognition of the inherent dignity and of the equal and inalienable rights of all members of the human family is the foundation of freedom, justice and peace in the world,

Recognizing that these rights derive from the inherent dignity of the human person,

Recognizing that, in accordance with the Universal Declaration of Human Rights, the ideal of free human beings enjoying civil and political freedom and freedom from fear and want can only be achieved if conditions are created whereby everyone may enjoy his civil and political rights, as well as his economic, social and cultural rights,

Considering the obligation of States under the Charter of the United Nations to promote universal respect for, and observance of, human rights and freedoms,

Realizing that the individual, having duties to other individuals and to the community to which he belongs, is under a responsibility to strive for the promotion and observance of the rights recognized in the present Covenant,

Agree upon the following articles:

PART I

Article 1

1. All peoples have the right of self-determination. By virtue of that right they freely determine their political status and freely pursue their economic, social and cultural development.

2. All peoples may, for their own ends, freely dispose of their natural wealth and resources without prejudice to any obligations arising out of international economic co-operation, based upon the principle of mutual benefit, and international law. In no case may a people be deprived of its own means of subsistence.

3. The States Parties to the present Covenant, including those having responsibility for the administration of Non-Self-Governing and Trust Territories, shall promote the realization of the right of self-determination, and shall respect that right, in conformity with the provisions of the Charter of the United Nations.

PART II

Article 2

1. Each State Party to the present Covenant undertakes to respect and to ensure to all individuals within its territory and subject to its jurisdiction the rights recognized in the present Covenant, without distinction of any kind, such as race, colour, sex, language, religion, political or other opinion, national or social origin, property, birth or other status.

2. Where not already provided for by existing legislative or other measures, each State Party to the present Covenant undertakes to take the necessary

steps, in accordance with its constitutional processes and with the provisions of the present Covenant, to adopt such legislative or other measures as may be necessary to give effect to the rights recognized in the present Covenant.

3. Each State Party to the present Covenant undertakes:

   (a) To ensure that any person whose rights or freedoms as herein recognized are violated shall have an effective remedy, notwithstanding that the violation has been committed by persons acting in an official capacity;

   (b) To ensure that any person claiming such a remedy shall have his right thereto determined by competent judicial, administrative or legislative authorities, or by any other competent authority provided for by the legal system of the State, and to develop the possibilities of judicial remedy;

   (c) To ensure that the competent authorities shall enforce such remedies when granted.

Article 3

The States Parties to the present Covenant undertake to ensure the equal right of men and women to the enjoyment of all civil and political rights set forth in the present Covenant.

Article 4

1. In time of public emergency which threatens the life of the nation and the existence of which is officially proclaimed, the States Parties to the present Covenant may take measures derogating from their obligations under the present Covenant to the extent strictly required by the exigencies of the situation, provided that such measures are not inconsistent with their other obligations under international law and do not involve discrimination solely on the ground of race, colour, sex, language, religion or social origin.

2. No derogation from articles 6, 7, 8 (paragraphs 1 and 2), 11, 15, 16 and 18 may be made under this provision.

3. Any State Party to the present Covenant availing itself of the right of derogation shall immediately inform the other States Parties to the present Covenant, through the intermediary of the Secretary-General of the United Nations, of the provisions from which it has derogated and of the reasons by which it was actuated. A further communication shall be made, through the same intermediary, on the date on which it terminates such derogation.

Article 5

1. Nothing in the present Covenant may be interpreted as implying for any State, group or person any right to engage in any activity or perform any act aimed at the destruction of any of the rights and freedoms recognized herein or at their limitation to a greater extent than is provided for in the present Covenant.

2. There shall be no restriction upon or derogation from any of the

fundamental human rights recognized or existing in any State Party to the present Covenant pursuant to law, conventions, regulations or custom on the pretext that the present Covenant does not recognize such rights or that it recognizes them to a lesser extent.

PART III

Article 6

1. Every human being has the inherent right to life. This right shall be protected by law. No one shall be arbitrarily deprived of his life.
2. In countries which have not abolished the death penalty, sentence of death may be imposed only for the most serious crimes in accordance with the law in force at the time of the commission of the crime and not contrary to the provisions of the present Covenant and to the Convention on the Prevention and Punishment of the Crime of Genocide. This penalty can only be carried out pursuant to a final judgement rendered by a competent court.
3. When deprivation of life constitutes the crime of genocide, it is understood that nothing in this article shall authorize any State Party to the present Covenant to derogate in any way from any obligation assumed under the provisions of the Convention on the Prevention and Punishment of the Crime of Genocide.
4. Anyone sentenced to death shall have the right to seek pardon or commutation of the sentence. Amnesty, pardon or commutation of the sentence of death may be granted in all cases.
5. Sentence of death shall not be imposed for crimes committed by persons below eighteen years of age and shall not be carried out on pregnant women.
6. Nothing in this article shall be invoked to delay or to prevent the abolition of capital punishment by any State Party to the present Covenant.

Article 7

No one shall be subjected to torture or to cruel, inhuman or degrading treatment or punishment. In particular, no one shall be subjected without his free consent to medical or scientific experimentation.

Article 8

1. No one shall be held in slavery; slavery and the slave-trade in all their forms shall be prohibited.
2. No one shall be held in servitude.
3. (*a*) No one shall be required to perform forced or compulsory labour;
   (*b*) Paragraph 3 (*a*) shall not be held to preclude, in countries where imprisonment with hard labour may be imposed as a punishment for

a crime, the performance of hard labour in pursuance of a sentence to such punishment by a competent court;

(c) For the purpose of this paragraph the term 'forced or compulsory labour' shall not include:

  (i) Any work or service, not referred to in sub-paragraph *(b)*, normally required of a person who is under detention in consequence of a lawful order of a court, or of a person during conditional release from such detention;

  (ii) Any service of a military character and, in countries where conscientious objection is recognized, any national service required by law of conscientious objectors;

  (iii) Any service exacted in cases of emergency or calamity threatening the life or well-being of the community;

  (iv) Any work or service which forms part of normal civil obligations.

Article 9

1. Everyone has the right to liberty and security of person. No one shall be subjected to arbitrary arrest or detention. No one shall be deprived of his liberty except on such grounds and in accordance with such procedure as are established by law.

2. Anyone who is arrested shall be informed, at the time of arrest, of the reasons for his arrest and shall be promptly informed of any charges against him.

3. Anyone arrested or detained on a criminal charge shall be brought promptly before a judge or other officer authorized by law to exercise judicial power and shall be entitled to trial within a reasonable time or to release. It shall not be the general rule that persons awaiting trial shall be detained in custody, but release may be subject to guarantees to appear for trial, at any other stage of the judicial proceedings, and, should occasion arise, for execution of the judgement.

4. Anyone who is deprived of his liberty by arrest or detention shall be entitled to take proceedings before a court, in order that that court may decide without delay on the lawfulness of his detention and order his release if the detention is not lawful.

5. Anyone who has been the victim of unlawful arrest or detention shall have an enforceable right to compensation.

Article 10

1. All persons deprived of their liberty shall be treated with humanity and with respect for the inherent dignity of the human person.

2. (*a*) Accused persons shall, save in exceptional circumstances, be segregated from convicted persons and shall be subject to separate treatment appropriate to their status as unconvicted persons;

  (*b*) Accused juvenile persons shall be separated from adults and brought as speedily as possible for adjudication.

3. The penitentiary system shall comprise treatment of prisoners the essential aim of which shall be their reformation and social rehabilitation. Juvenile offenders shall be segregated from adults and be accorded treatment appropriate to their age and legal status.

Article 11

No one shall be imprisoned merely on the ground of inability to fulfil a contractual obligation.

Article 12

1. Everyone lawfully within the territory of a State shall, within that territory, have the right to liberty of movement and freedom to choose his residence.
2. Everyone shall be free to leave any country, including his own.
3. The above-mentioned rights shall not be subject to any restrictions except those which are provided by law, are necessary to protect national security, public order (*ordre public*), public health or morals or the rights and freedoms of others, and are consistent with the other rights recognized in the present Covenant.
4. No one shall be arbitrarily deprived of the right to enter his own country.

Article 13

An alien lawfully in the territory of a State Party to the present Covenant may be expelled therefrom only in pursuance of a decision reached in accordance with law and shall, except where compelling reasons of national security otherwise require, be allowed to submit the reasons against his expulsion and to have his case reviewed by, and be represented for the purpose before, the competent authority or a person or persons especially designated by the competent authority.

Article 14

1. All persons shall be equal before the courts and tribunals. In the determination of any criminal charge against him, or of his rights and obligations in a suit at law, everyone shall be entitled to a fair and public hearing by a competent, independent and impartial tribunal established by law. The Press and the public may be excluded from all or part of a trial for reasons of morals, public order (*ordre public*) or national security in a democratic society, or when the interest of the private lives of the parties so requires, or to the extent strictly necessary in the opinion of the court in special circumstances where publicity would prejudice the interests of justice; but any judgement rendered in a criminal case or in a suit at law shall be made public except where the interest of juvenile persons otherwise

requires or the proceedings concern matrimonial disputes or the guardian-ship of children.

2. Everyone charged with a criminal offence shall have the right to be presumed innocent until proved guilty according to law.

3. In the determination of any criminal charge against him, everyone shall be entitled to the following minimum guarantees, in full equality:

    (*a*) To be informed promptly and in detail in a language which he understands of the nature and cause of the charge against him;

    (*b*) To have adequate time and facilities for the preparation of his defence and to communicate with counsel of his own choosing;

    (*c*) To be tried without undue delay;

    (*d*) To be tried in his presence, and to defend himself in person or through legal assistance of his own choosing; to be informed, if he does not have legal assistance, of this right; and to have legal assistance assigned to him, in any case where the interests of justice so require, and without payment by him in any such case if he does not have sufficient means to pay for it;

    (*e*) To examine, or have examined, the witnesses against him and to obtain the attendance and examination of witnesses on his behalf under the same conditions as witnesses against him;

    (*f*) To have the free assistance of an interpreter if he cannot understand or speak the language used in court;

    (*g*) Not to be compelled to testify against himself or to confess guilt.

4. In the case of juvenile persons, the procedure shall be such as will take account of their age and the desirability of promoting their rehabilitation.

5. Everyone convicted of a crime shall have the right to his conviction and sentence being reviewed by a higher tribunal according to law.

6. When a person has by a final decision been convicted of a criminal offence and when subsequently his conviction has been reversed or he has been pardoned on the ground that a new or newly discovered fact shows con-clusively that there has been a miscarriage of justice, the person who has suffered punishment as a result of such conviction shall be compensated according to law, unless it is proved that the non-disclosure of the unknown fact in time is wholly or partly attributable to him.

7. No one shall be liable to be tried or punished again for an offence for which he has already been finally convicted or acquitted in accordance with the law and penal procedure of each country.

Article 15

1. No one shall be held guilty of any criminal offence on account of any act or omission which did not constitute a criminal offence, under national or international law, at the time when it was committed. Nor shall a heavier penalty be imposed than the one that was applicable at the time when the criminal offence was committed. If, subsequent to the commission of the offence, provision is made by law for the imposition of a lighter penalty, the offender shall benefit thereby.

2. Nothing in this article shall prejudice the trial and punishment of any

person for any act or omission which, at the time when it was committed, was criminal according to the general principles of law recognized by the community of nations.

Article 16

Everyone shall have the right to recognition everywhere as a person before the law.

Article 17

1. No one shall be subjected to arbitrary or unlawful interference with his privacy, family, home or correspondence, nor to unlawful attacks on his honour and reputation.
2. Everyone has the right to the protection of the law against such interference or attacks.

Article 18

1. Everyone shall have the right to freedom of thought, conscience and religion. This right shall include freedom to have or to adopt a religion or belief of his choice, and freedom, either individually or in community with others and in public or private, to manifest his religion or belief in worship, observance, practice and teaching.
2. No one shall be subject to coercion which would impair his freedom to have or to adopt a religion or belief of his choice.
3. Freedom to manifest one's religion or beliefs may be subject only to such limitations as are prescribed by law and are necessary to protect public safety, order, health, or morals or the fundamental rights and freedoms of others.
4. The States Parties to the present Covenant undertake to have respect for the liberty of parents and, when applicable, legal guardians to ensure the religious and moral education of their children in conformity with their own convictions.

Article 19

1. Everyone shall have the right to hold opinions without interference.
2. Everyone shall have the right to freedom of expression; this right shall include freedom to seek, receive and impart information and ideas of all kinds, regardless of frontiers, either orally, in writing or in print, in the form of art, or through any other media of his choice.
3. The exercise of the rights provided for in paragraph 2 of this article carries with it special duties and responsibilities. It may therefore be subject to certain restrictions, but these shall only be such as are provided by law and are necessary:

   (*a*) For respect of the rights or reputations of others;

(*b*) For the protection of national security or of public order (*ordre public*), or of public health or morals.

Article 20

1. Any propaganda for war shall be prohibited by law.
2. Any advocacy of national, racial or religious hatred that constitutes incitement to discrimination, hostility or violence shall be prohibited by law.

Article 21

The right of peaceful assembly shall be recognized. No restrictions may be placed on the exercise of this right other than those imposed in conformity with the law and which are necessary in a democratic society in the interests of national security or public safety, public order (*ordre public*), the protection of public health or morals or the protection of the rights and freedoms of others.

Article 22

1. Everyone shall have the right to freedom of association with others, including the right to form and join trade unions for the protection of his interests.
2. No restrictions may be placed on the exercise of this right other than those which are prescribed by law and which are necessary in a democratic society in the interests of national security or public safety, public order (*ordre public*), the protection of public health or morals or the protection of the rights and freedoms of others. This article shall not prevent the imposition of lawful restrictions on members of the armed forces and of the police in their exercise of this right.
3. Nothing in this article shall authorize States Parties to the International Labour Organisation Convention of 1948 concerning Freedom of Association and Protection of the Right to Organize to take legislative measures which would prejudice, or to apply the law in such a manner as to prejudice, the guarantees provided for in that Convention.

Article 23

1. The family is the natural and fundamental group unit of society and is entitled to protection by society and the State.
2. The right of men and women of marriageable age to marry and to found a family shall be recognized.
3. No marriage shall be entered into without the free and full consent of the intending spouses.
4. States Parties to the present Covenant shall take appropriate steps to ensure equality of rights and responsibilities of spouses as to marriage, during marriage and at its dissolution. In the case of dissolution, provision shall be made for the necessary protection of any children.

Article 24

1. Every child shall have, without any discrimination as to race, colour, sex, language, religion, national or social origin, property or birth, the right to such measures of protection as are required by his status as a minor, on the part of his family, society and the State.
2. Every child shall be registered immediately after birth and shall have a name.
3. Every child has the right to acquire a nationality.

Article 25

Every citizen shall have the right and the opportunity, without any of the distinctions mentioned in article 2 and without unreasonable restrictions:
 (*a*) To take part in the conduct of public affairs, directly or through freely chosen representatives;
 (*b*) To vote and to be elected at genuine periodic elections which shall be by universal and equal suffrage and shall be held by secret ballot, guaranteeing the free expression of the will of the electors;
 (*c*) To have access, on general terms of equality, to public service in his country;

Article 26

All persons are equal before the law and are entitled without any discrimination to the equal protection of the law. In this respect, the law shall prohibit any discrimination and guarantee to all persons equal and effective protection against discrimination on any ground such as race, colour, sex, language, religion, political or other opinion, national or social origin, property, birth or other status.

Article 27

In those States in which ethnic, religious or linguistic minorities exist, persons belonging to such minorities shall not be denied the right, in community with the other members of their group, to enjoy their own culture, to profess and practise their own religion, or to use their own language.

PART IV

Article 28

1. There shall be established a Human Rights Committee (hereafter referred to in the present Covenant as the Committee). It shall consist of eighteen members and shall carry out the functions hereinafter provided.
2. The Committee shall be composed of nationals of the States Parties to the present Covenant who shall be persons of high moral character and recognized competence in the field of human rights, consideration being given to

the usefulness of the participation of some persons having legal experience.

3. The members of the Committee shall be elected and shall serve in their personal capacity.

Article 29

1. The members of the Committee shall be elected by secret ballot from a list of persons possessing the qualifications prescribed in article 28 and nominated for the purpose by the States Parties to the present Covenant.

2. Each State Party to the present Covenant may nominate not more than two persons. These persons shall be nationals of the nominating State.

3. A person shall be eligible for renomination.

Article 30

1. The initial election shall be held no later than six months after the date of the entry into force of the present Covenant.

2. At least four months before the date of each election to the Committee, other than an election to fill a vacancy declared in accordance with article 34, the Secretary-General of the United Nations shall address a written invitation to the States Parties to the present Covenant to submit their nominations for membership of the Committee within three months.

3. The Secretary-General of the United Nations shall prepare a list in alphabetical order of all the persons thus nominated, with an indication of the States Parties which have nominated them, and shall submit it to the States Parties to the present Covenant no later than one month before the date of each election.

4. Elections of the members of the Committee shall be held at a meeting of the States Parties to the present Covenant convened by the Secretary-General of the United Nations at the Headquarters of the United Nations. At that meeting, for which two thirds of the States Parties to the present Covenant shall constitute a quorum, the persons elected to the Committee shall be those nominees who obtain the largest number of votes and an absolute majority of the votes of the representatives of States Parties present and voting.

Article 31

1. The Committee may not include more than one national of the same State.

2. In the election of the Committee, consideration shall be given to equitable geographical distribution of membership and to the representation of the different forms of civilization and of the principal legal systems.

Article 32

1. The members of the Committee shall be elected for a term of four years. They shall be eligible for re-election if renominated. However, the terms of

nine of the members elected at the first election shall expire at the end of two years; immediately after the first election, the names of these nine members shall be chosen by lot by the Chairman of the meeting referred to in article 30, paragraph 4.

2. Elections at the expiry of office shall be held in accordance with the preceding articles of this part of the present Covenant.

Article 38

Every member of the Committee shall, before taking up his duties, make a solemn declaration in open committee that he will perform his functions impartially and conscientiously.

Article 39

1. The Committee shall elect its officers for a term of two years. They may be re-elected.

2. The Committee shall establish its own rules of procedure, but these rules shall provide, *inter alia*, that:
   (*a*) Twelve members shall constitute a quorum;
   (*b*) Decisions of the Committee shall be made by a majority vote of the members present.

Article 40

1. The States Parties to the present Covenant undertake to submit reports on the measures they have adopted which give effect to the rights recognized herein and on the progress made in the enjoyment of those rights:
   (*a*) Within one year of the entry into force of the present Covenant for the States Parties concerned;
   (*b*) Thereafter whenever the Committee so requests.

2. All reports shall be submitted to the Secretary-General of the United Nations, who shall transmit them to the Committee for consideration. Reports shall indicate the factors and difficulties, if any, affecting the implementation of the present Covenant.

3. The Secretary-General of the United Nations may, after consultation with the Committee, transmit to the specialized agencies concerned copies of such parts of the reports as may fall within their field of competence.

4. The Committee shall study the reports submitted by the States Parties to the present Covenant. It shall transmit its reports, and such general comments as it may consider appropriate, to the States Parties. The Committee may also transmit to the Economic and Social Council these comments along with the copies of the reports it has received from States Parties to the present Covenant.

5. The States Parties to the present Covenant may submit to the Committee observations on any comments that may be made in accordance with paragraph 4 of this article.

Article 41

1. A State Party to the present Covenant may at any time declare under this article that it recognizes the competence of the Committee to receive and consider communications to the effect that a State Party claims that another State Party is not fulfilling its obligations under the present Covenant. Communications under this article may be received and considered only if submitted by a State Party which has made a declaration recognizing in regard to itself the competence of the Committee. No communication shall be received by the Committee if it concerns a State Party which has not made such a declaration. Communications received under this article shall be dealt with in accordance with the following procedure:

(*a*) If a State Party to the present Covenant considers that another State Party is not giving effect to the provisions of the present Covenant, it may, by written communication, bring the matter to the attention of that State Party. Within three months after the receipt of the communication, the receiving State shall afford the State which sent the communication an explanation or any other statement in writing clarifying the matter, which should include, to the extent possible and pertinent, reference to domestic procedures and remedies taken, pending, or available in the matter.

(*b*) If the matter is not adjusted to the satisfaction of both States Parties concerned within six months after the receipt by the receiving State of the initial communication, either State shall have the right to refer the matter to the Committee, by notice given to the Committee and to the other State.

(*c*) The Committee shall deal with the matter referred to it only after it has ascertained that all available domestic remedies have been invoked and exhausted in the matter, in conformity with the generally recognized principles of international law. This shall not be the rule where the application of the remedies is unreasonably prolonged.

(*d*) The Committee shall hold closed meetings when examining communications under this article.

(*e*) Subject to the provisions of sub-paragraph (*c*), the Committee shall make available its good offices to the States Parties concerned with a view to a friendly solution of the matter on the basis of respect for human rights and fundamental freedoms as recognized in the present Covenant.

(*f*) In any matter referred to it, the Committee may call upon the States Parties concerned, referred to in sub-paragraph (*b*), to supply any relevant information.

(*g*) The States Parties concerned, referred to in sub-paragraph (*b*), shall have the right to be represented when the matter is being considered in the Committee and to make submissions orally and/or in writing.

(*h*) The Committee shall, within twelve months after the date of receipt of notice under sub-paragraph (*b*), submit a report:

(i)   If a solution within the terms of sub-paragraph (*e*) is reached, the Committee shall confine its report to a brief statement of the facts and of the solution reached;

(ii) If a solution within the terms of sub-paragraph (*e*) is not reached, the Committee shall confine its report to a brief statement of the facts; the written submissions and record of the oral submissions made by the States parties concerned shall be attached to the report.

In every matter, the report shall be communicated to the States Parties concerned.

2. The provisions of this article shall come into force when ten States Parties to the present Covenant have made declarations under paragraph 1 of this article. Such declarations shall be deposited by the States Parties with the Secretary-General of the United Nations, who shall transmit copies thereof to the other States Parties. A declaration may be withdrawn at any time by notification to the Secretary-General. Such a withdrawal shall not prejudice the consideration of any matter which is the subject of a communication already transmitted under this article; no further communication by any State Party shall be received after the notification of withdrawal of the declaration has been received by the Secretary-General, unless the State Party concerned had made a new declaration.

Article 42

1. (*a*) If a matter referred to the Committee in accordance with article 41 is not resolved to the satisfaction of the States Parties concerned, the Committee may, with the prior consent of the States Parties concerned, appoint an *ad hoc* Conciliation Commission (hereinafter referred to as the Commission). The good offices of the Commission shall be made available to the States Parties concerned with a view to an amicable solution of the matter on the basis of respect for the present Covenant;

(*b*) The Commission shall consist of five persons acceptable to the States Parties concerned. If the States Parties concerned fail to reach agreement within three months on all or part of the composition of the Commission, the members of the Commission concerning whom no agreement has been reached shall be elected by secret ballot by a two-thirds majority vote of the Committee from among its members.

OPTIONAL PROTOCOL TO THE INTERNATIONAL COVENANT ON CIVIL AND POLITICAL RIGHTS

The states parties to the present protocol,

Considering that in order further to achieve the purposes of the Covenant on Civil and Political Rights (hereinafter referred to as the Covenant) and the implementation of its provisions it would be appropriate to enable the

Human Rights Committee set up in part IV of the Covenant (hereinafter referred to as the Committee) to receive and consider, as provided in the present Protocol, communications from individuals claiming to be victims of violations of any of the rights set forth in the Covenant,

Have agreed as follows:

Article 1

A State Party to the Covenant that becomes a party to the present Protocol recognizes the competence of the Committee to receive and consider communications from individuals subject to its jurisdiction who claim to be victims of a violation by that State Party of any of the rights set forth in the Covenant. No communication shall be received by the Committee if it concerns a State Party to the Covenant which is not a party to the present Protocol.

Article 2

Subject to the provisions of article 1, individuals who claim that any of their rights enumerated in the Covenant have been violated and who have exhausted all available domestic remedies may submit a written communication to the Committee for consideration.

Article 3

The Committee shall consider inadmissible any communication under the present Protocol which is anonymous, or which it considers to be an abuse of the rights of submission of such communications or to be incompatible with the provisions of the Covenant.

Article 4

1. Subject to the provisions of article 3, the Committee shall bring any communications submitted to it under the present Protocol to the attention of the State Party to the present Protocol alleged to be violating any provisions of the Covenant.

2. Within six months, the receiving State shall submit to the Committee written explanations or statements clarifying the matter and the remedy, if any, that may have been taken by that State.

Article 5

1. The Committee shall consider communications received under the present Protocol in the light of all written information made available to it by the individual and by the State Party concerned.

2. The Committee shall not consider any communication from an individual unless it has ascertained that:

(*a*) The same matter is not being examined under another procedure of international investigation or settlement;

(*b*) The individual has exhausted all available domestic remedies. This shall not be the rule where the application of the remedies is unreasonably prolonged.

3. The Committee shall hold closed meetings when examining communications under the present Protocol.

4. The Committee shall forward its views to the State Party concerned and to the individual.

---

21   THE UNITED NATIONS: INTERNATIONAL COVENANT ON ECONOMIC, SOCIAL AND CULTURAL RIGHTS, 1976

Article 2

1. Each State Party to the present Covenant undertakes to take steps, individually and through international assistance and co-operation, especially economic and technical, to the maximum of its available resources, with a view to achieving progressively the full realization of the rights recognized in the present Covenant by all appropriate means, including particularly the adoption of legislative measures.

2. The States Parties to the present Covenant undertake to guarantee that the rights enunciated in the present Covenant will be exercised without discrimination of any kind as to race, colour, sex, language, religion, political or other opinion, national or social origin, property, birth or other status.

3. Developing countries, with due regard to human rights and their national economy, may determine to what extent they would guarantee the economic rights recognized in the present Covenant to non-nationals.

Article 3

The States Parties to the present Covenant undertake to ensure the equal right of men and women to the enjoyment of all economic, social and cultural rights set forth in the present Covenant.

Article 4

The State Parties to the present Covenant recognize that, in the enjoyment of those rights provided by the State in conformity with the present Covenant, the State may subject such rights only to such limitations as are determined by law only in so far as this may be compatible with the nature of these rights and solely for the purpose of promoting the general welfare in a democratic society.

Article 5

1. Nothing in the present Covenant may be interpreted as implying for any State, group or person any right to engage in any activity or to perform any act aimed at the destruction of any of the rights or freedoms recognized herein, or at their limitation to a greater extent than is provided for in the present Covenant.

2. No restriction upon or derogation from any of the fundamental human rights recognized or existing in any country in virtue of law, conventions, regulations or custom shall be admitted on the pretext that the present Covenant does not recognize such rights or that it recognizes them to a lesser extent.

Article 6

1. The States Parties to the present Covenant recognize the right to work, which includes the right of everyone to the opportunity to gain his living by work which he freely chooses or accepts, and will take appropriate steps to safeguard this right.

2. The steps to be taken by a State Party to the present Covenant to achieve the full realization of this right shall include technical and vocational guidance and training programmes, policies and techniques to achieve steady economic, social and cultural development and full and productive employment under conditions safeguarding fundamental political and economic freedoms to the individual.

Article 7

The States Parties to the present Covenant recognize the right of everyone to the enjoyment of just and favourable conditions of work which ensure, in particular:

    (a) Remuneration which provides all workers, as a minimum, with:
        (i)   Fair wages and equal remuneration for work of equal value without distinction of any kind, in particular women being guaranteed conditions of work not inferior to those enjoyed by men, with equal pay for equal work;
        (ii) A decent living for themselves and their families in accordance with the provisions of the present Covenant;
    (b) Safe and healthy working conditions;
    (c) Equal opportunity for everyone to be promoted in his employment to an appropriate higher level, subject to no considerations other than those of seniority and competence;
    (d) Rest, leisure and reasonable limitation of working hours and periodic holidays with pay, as well as remuneration for public holidays.

Article 8

1. The States Parties to the present Covenant undertake to ensure:
    (a) The right of everyone to form trade unions and join the trade union

of his choice, subject only to the rules of the organization concerned, for the promotion and protection of his economic and social interests. No restrictions may be placed on the exercise of this right other than those prescribed by law and which are necessary in a democratic society in the interests of national security or public order or for the protection of the rights and freedoms of others;

(*b*) The right of trade unions to establish national federations or confederations and the right of the latter to form or join international trade-union organizations;

(*c*) The right of trade unions to function freely subject to no limitations other than those prescribed by law and which are necessary in a democratic society in the interests of national security or public order or for the protection of the rights and freedoms of others;

(*d*) The right to strike, provided that it is exercised in conformity with the laws of the particular country.

2. This article shall not prevent the imposition of lawful restrictions on the exercise of these rights by members of the armed forces or of the police or of the administration of the State.

3. Nothing in this article shall authorize States Parties to the International Labour Organisation Convention of 1948 concerning Freedom of Association and Protection of the Right to Organize to take legislative measures which would prejudice, or apply the law in such a manner as would prejudice, the guarantees provided for in that Convention.

Article 9

The States Parties to the present Covenant recognize the right of everyone to social security, including social insurance.

Article 10

The States Parties to the present Covenant recognize that:

1. The widest possible protection and assistance should be accorded to the family, which is the natural and fundamental group unit of society, particularly for its establishment and while it is responsible for the care and education of dependent children. Marriage must be entered into with the free consent of the intending spouses.

2. Special protection should be accorded to mothers during a reasonable period before and after childbirth. During such period working mothers should be accorded paid leave or leave with adequate social security benefits.

3. Special measures of protection and assistance should be taken on behalf of all children and young persons without any discrimination for reasons of parentage or other conditions. Children and young persons should be protected from economic and social exploitation. Their employment in work harmful to their morals or health or dangerous to life or likely to hamper their normal development should be punishable by law. States should also set age limits below which the paid employment of child labour should be prohibited and punishable by law.

Article 11

1. The States Parties to the present Covenant recognize the right of everyone to an adequate standard of living for himself and his family, including adequate food, clothing and housing, and to the continuous improvement of living conditions. The States Parties will take appropriate steps to ensure the realization of this right, recognizing to this effect the essential importance of international co-operation based on free consent.

2. The States Parties to the present Covenant, recognizing the fundamental right of everyone to be free from hunger, shall take, individually and through international co-operation, the measures, including specific programmes, which are needed:

(*a*) To improve methods of production, conservation and distribution of food by making full use of technical and scientific knowledge, by disseminating knowledge of the principles of nutrition and by developing or reforming agrarian systems in such a way as to achieve the most efficient development and utilization of natural resources;

(*b*) Taking into account the problems of both food-importing and food-exporting countries, to ensure an equitable distribution of world food supplies in relation to need.

Article 12

1. The States parties to the present Covenant recognize the right of everyone to the enjoyment of the highest attainable standard of physical and mental health.

2. The steps to be taken by the States Parties to the present Covenant to achieve the full realization of this right shall include those necessary for:

(*a*) The provision for the reduction of the stillbirth-rate and of infant mortality and for the healthy development of the child;

(*b*) The improvement of all aspects of environmental and industrial hygiene;

(*c*) The prevention, treatment and control of epidemic, endemic, occupational and other diseases;

(*d*) The creation of conditions which would assure to all medical service and medical attention in the event of sickness.

Article 13

1. The States Parties to the present Covenant recognize the right of everyone to education. They agree that education shall be directed to the full development of the human personality and the sense of its dignity, and shall strengthen the respect for human rights and fundamental freedoms. They further agree that education shall enable all persons to participate effectively in a free society, promote understanding, tolerance and friendship among all nations and all racial, ethnic or religious groups, and further the activities of the United Nations for the maintenance of peace.

2. The States Parties to the present Covenant recognize that, with a view to achieving the full realization of this right:

(*a*) Primary education shall be compulsory and available free to all;

(*b*) Secondary education in its different forms, including technical and vocational secondary education, shall be made generally available and accessible to all by every appropriate means, and in particular by the progressive introduction of free education;

(*c*) Higher education shall be made equally accessible to all, on the basis of capacity, by every appropriate means, and in particular by the progressive introduction of free education;

(*d*) Fundamental education shall be encouraged or intensified as far as possible for those persons who have not received or completed the whole period of their primary education;

(*e*) The development of a system of schools at all levels shall be actively pursued, an adequate fellowship system shall be established, and the material conditions of teaching staff shall be continuously improved.

3. The States Parties to the present Covenant undertake to have respect for the liberty of parents and, when applicable, legal guardians to choose for their children schools, other than those established by the public authorities, which conform to such minimum educational standards as may be laid down or approved by the State and to ensure the religious and moral education of their children in conformity with their own convictions.

4. No part of this article shall be construed so as to interfere with the liberty of individuals and bodies to establish and direct educational institutions, subject always to the observance of the principles set forth in paragraph 1 of this article and to the requirement that the education given in such institutions shall conform to such minimum standards as may be laid down by the State.

Article 14

Each State Party to the present Covenant which, at the time of becoming a Party, has not been able to secure in its metropolitan territory or other territories under its jurisdiction compulsory primary education, free of charge, undertakes, within two years, to work out and adopt a detailed plan of action for the progressive implementation, within a reasonable number of years, to be fixed in the plan, of the principle of compulsory education free of charge for all.

Article 15

1. The States Parties to the present Covenant recognize the right of everyone:

(*a*) To take part in cultural life;

(*b*) To enjoy the benefits of scientific progress and its applications;

(*c*) To benefit from the protection of the moral and material interests resulting from any scientific, literary or artistic production of which he is the author.

2. The steps to be taken by the States Parties to the present Covenant to

achieve the full realization of this right shall include those necessary for the conservation, the development and the diffusion of science and culture.

3. The States Parties to the present Covenant undertake to respect the freedom indispensable for scientific research and creative activity.

4. The States Parties to the present Covenant recognize the benefits to be derived from the encouragement and development of international contacts and co-operation in the scientific and cultural fields.

Article 16

1. The States Parties to the present Covenant undertake to submit in conformity with this part of the Covenant reports on the measures which they have adopted and the progress made in achieving the observance of the rights recognized herein.

2. (*a*) All reports shall be submitted to the Secretary-General of the United Nations, who shall transmit copies to the Economic and Social Council for consideration in accordance with the provisions of the present Covenant.

   (*b*) The Secretary-General of the United Nations shall also transmit to the specialized agencies copies of the reports, or any relevant parts therefrom, from States Parties to the present Covenant which are also members of these specialized agencies in so far as these reports, or parts therefrom, relate to any matters which fall within the responsibilities of the said agencies in accordance with their constitutional instruments.

Article 17

1. The States Parties to the present Covenant shall furnish their reports in stages, in accordance with a programme to be established by the Economic and Social Council within one year of the entry into force of the present Covenant after consultation with the States Parties and the specialized agencies concerned.

2. Reports may indicate factors and difficulties affecting the degree of fulfilment of obligations under the present Covenant.

3. Where relevant information has previously been furnished to the United Nations or to any specialized agency by any State Party to the present Covenant, it will not be necessary to reproduce that information, but a precise reference to the information so furnished will suffice.

Article 18

Pursuant to its responsibilities under the Charter of the United Nations in the field of human rights and fundamental freedoms, the Economic and Social Council may make arrangements with the specialized agencies in respect of their reporting to it on the progress made in achieving the observance of the provisions of the present Covenant falling within the scope of their activities. These reports may include particulars of decisions and recommendations on such implementation adopted by their competent organs.

Article 19

The Economic and Social Council may transmit to the Commission on Human Rights for study and general recommendations or, as appropriate, for information the reports concerning human rights submitted by States in accordance with articles 16 and 17, and those concerning human rights submitted by the specialized agencies in accordance with article 18.

---

22   THE COUNCIL OF EUROPE: THE EUROPEAN CONVENTION ON HUMAN RIGHTS, 1950

RB NOTE: The text of the Convention as shown below is the one currently in force, as amended by Protocol 11 whose date of entry into force was 1 November 1998. The provisions of the original text of the Convention signed on 4 November 1950 at Rome, and subsequent amending protocols, are replaced or repeated by Protocol 11.

Convention for the Protection of Human Rights and Fundamental Freedoms

The Governments signatory hereto, being Members of the Council of Europe,

Considering the Universal Declaration of Human Rights proclaimed by the General Assembly of the United Nations on 10th December 1948;

Considering that this Declaration aims at securing the universal and effective recognition and observance of the rights therein declared;

Considering that the aim of the Council of Europe is the achievement of greater unity between its Members and that one of the methods by which that aim is to be pursued is the maintenance and further realisation of Human Rights and Fundamental Freedoms;

Reaffirming their profound belief in those Fundamental Freedoms which are the foundation of justice and peace in the world and are best maintained on the one hand by an effective political democracy and on the other by a common understanding and observance of the Human Rights upon which they depend;

Being resolved, as the Governments of European countries which are like-minded and have a common heritage of political traditions, ideals, freedom and the rule of law, to take the first steps for the collective enforcement of certain of the rights stated in the Universal Declaration;

Have agreed as follows:

Article 1 – Obligation to respect human rights

The High Contracting Parties shall secure to everyone within their jurisdiction the rights and freedoms defined in Section 1 of this Convention.

SECTION I – RIGHTS AND FREEDOMS

Article 2 – Right to life

1. Everyone's right to life shall be protected by law. No one shall be deprived of his life intentionally save in the execution of a sentence of a court following his conviction of a crime for which this penalty is provided by law.
2. Deprivation of life shall not be regarded as inflicted in contravention of this Article when it results from the use of force which is no more than absolutely necessary:
    (a) in defence of any person from unlawful violence;
    (b) in order to effect a lawful arrest or to prevent the escape of a person lawfully detained;
    (c) in action lawfully taken for the purpose of quelling a riot or insurrection.

Article 3 – Prohibition of torture

No one shall be subjected to torture or to inhuman or degrading treatment or punishment.

Article 4 – Prohibition of slavery and forced labour

1. No one shall be held in slavery or servitude.
2. No one shall be required to perform forced or compulsory labour.
3. For the purpose of this Article the term 'forced or compulsory labour' shall not include:
    (a) any work required to be done in the ordinary course of detention imposed according to the provisions of Article 5 of this Convention or during conditional release from such detention;
    (b) any service of a military character or, in case of conscientious objectors in countries where they are recognised, service exacted instead of compulsory military service;
    (c) any service exacted in case of an emergency or calamity threatening the life or well-being of the community;
    (d) any work or service which forms part of normal civic obligations.

Article 5 – Right to liberty and security

1. Everyone has the right to liberty and security of person. No one shall be deprived of his liberty save in the following cases and in accordance with a procedure prescribed by law:

(*a*) the lawful detention of a person after conviction by a competent court;

(*b*) the lawful arrest or detention of a person for non-compliance with the lawful order of a court or in order to secure the fulfilment of any obligation prescribed by law;

(*c*) the lawful arrest or detention of a person effected for the purpose of bringing him before the competent legal authority on reasonable suspicion of having committed an offence or when it is reasonably considered necessary to prevent his committing an offence or fleeing after having done so;

(*d*) the detention of a minor by lawful order for the purpose of educational supervision or his lawful detention for the purpose of bringing him before the competent legal authority;

(*e*) the lawful detention of persons for the prevention of the spreading of infectious diseases, of persons of unsound mind, alcoholics or drug addicts or vagrants;

(*f*) the lawful arrest or detention of a person to prevent his effecting an unauthorised entry into the country or of a person against whom action is being taken with a view to deportation or extradition.

2. Everyone who is arrested shall be informed promptly, in a language which he understands, of the reasons for his arrest and of any charge against him.

3. Everyone arrested or detained in accordance with the provisions of paragraph 1.*c* of this Article shall be brought promptly before a judge or other officer authorised by law to exercise judicial power and shall be entitled to trial within a reasonable time or to release pending trial. Release may be conditioned by guarantees to appear for trial.

4. Everyone who is deprived of his liberty by arrest or detention shall be entitled to take proceedings by which the lawfulness of his detention shall be decided speedily by a court and his release ordered if the detention is not lawful.

5. Everyone who has been the victim of arrest or detention in contravention of the provisions of this Article shall have an enforceable right to compensation.

Article 6 – Right to a fair trial

1. In the determination of his civil rights and obligations or of any criminal charge against him, everyone is entitled to a fair and public hearing within a reasonable time by an independent and impartial tribunal established by law. Judgment shall be pronounced publicly but the press and public may be excluded from all or part of the trial in the interest of morals, public order or national security in a democratic society, where the interests of juveniles or the protection of the private life of the parties so require, or to the extent strictly necessary in the opinion of the court in special circumstances where publicity would prejudice the interests of justice.

2. Everyone charged with a criminal offence shall be presumed innocent until proved guilty according to law.

3. Everyone charged with a criminal offence has the following minimum rights:

(*a*) to be informed promptly, in a language which he understands and in detail, of the nature and cause of the accusation against him;

(*b*) to have adequate time and facilities for the preparation of his defence;

(*c*) to defend himself in person or through legal assistance of his own choosing or, if he has not sufficient means to pay for legal assistance, to be given it free when the interests of justice so require;

(*d*) to examine or have examined witnesses against him and to obtain the attendance and examination of witnesses on his behalf under the same conditions as witnesses against him;

(*e*) to have the free assistance of an interpreter if he cannot understand or speak the language used in court.

Article 7 – No punishment without law

1. No one shall be held guilty of any criminal offence on account of any act or omission which did not constitute a criminal offence under national or international law at the time when it was committed. Nor shall a heavier penalty be imposed than the one that was applicable at the time the criminal offence was committed.

2. This Article shall not prejudice the trial and punishment of any person for any act or omission which, at the time when it was committed, was criminal according to the general principles of law recognised by civilised nations.

Article 8 – Right to respect for private and family life

1. Everyone has the right to respect for his private and family life, his home and his correspondence.

2. There shall be no interference by a public authority with the exercise of this right except such as is in accordance with the law and is necessary in a democratic society in the interests of national security, public safety or the economic well-being of the country, for the prevention of disorder or crime, for the protection of health or morals, or for the protection of the rights and freedoms of others.

Article 9 – Freedom of thought, conscience and religion

1. Everyone has the right to freedom of thought, conscience and religion; this right includes freedom to change his religion or belief and freedom, either alone or in community with others and in public or in private, to manifest his religion or belief, in worship, teaching, practice and observance.

2. Freedom to manifest one's religion or beliefs shall be subject only to such limitations as are prescribed by law and are necessary in a democratic society in the interests of public safety, for the protection of public order,

health or morals, or for the protection of the rights and freedoms of others.

Article 10 – Freedom of expression

1. Everyone has the right to freedom of expression. This right shall include freedom to hold opinions and to receive and impart information and ideas without interference by public authority and regardless of frontiers. This Article shall not prevent States from requiring the licensing of broadcasting, television or cinema enterprises.
2. The exercise of these freedoms, since it carries with it duties and responsibilities, may be subject to such formalities, conditions, restrictions or penalties as are prescribed by law and are necessary in a democratic society, in the interests of national security, territorial integrity or public safety, for the prevention of disorder or crime, for the protection of health or morals, for the protection of the reputation or rights of others, for preventing the disclosure of information received in confidence, or for maintaining the authority and impartiality of the judiciary.

Article 11 – Freedom of assembly and association

1. Everyone has the right to freedom of peaceful assembly and to freedom of association with others, including the right to form and to join trade unions for the protection of his interests.
2. No restrictions shall be placed on the exercise of these rights other than such as are prescribed by law and are necessary in a democratic society in the interests of national security or public safety, for the prevention of disorder or crime, for the protection of health or morals or for the protection of the rights and freedoms of others. This Article shall not prevent the imposition of lawful restrictions on the exercise of these rights by members of the armed forces, of the police or of the administration of the State.

Article 12 – Right to marry

Men and women of marriageable age have the right to marry and to found a family, according to the national laws governing the exercise of this right.

Article 13 – Right to an effective remedy

Everyone whose rights and freedoms as set forth in this Convention are violated shall have an effective remedy before a national authority notwithstanding that the violation has been committed by persons acting in an official capacity.

Article 14 – Prohibition of discrimination

The enjoyment of the rights and freedoms set forth in this Convention shall be secured without discrimination on any ground such as sex, race, colour, language, religion, political or other opinion, national or social origin, association with a national minority, property, birth or other status.

Article 15 – Derogation in time of emergency

1. In time of war or other public emergency threatening the life of the nation any High Contracting Party may take measures derogating from its obligations under this Convention to the extent strictly required by the exigencies of the situation, provided that such measures are not inconsistent with its other obligations under international law.
2. No derogation from Article 2, except in respect of deaths resulting from lawful acts of war, or from Articles 3, 4 (paragraph 1) and 7 shall be made under this provision.
3. Any High Contracting Party availing itself of this right of derogation shall keep the Secretary General of the Council of Europe fully informed of the measures which it has taken and the reasons therefor. It shall also inform the Secretary General of the Council of Europe when such measures have ceased to operate and the provisions of the Convention are again being fully executed.

Article 16 – Restrictions on political activity of aliens

Nothing in Articles 10, 11, and 14 shall be regarded as preventing the High Contracting Parties from imposing restrictions on the political activity of aliens.

Article 17 – Prohibition of abuse of rights

Nothing in this Convention may be interpreted as implying for any State, group or person any right to engage in any activity or perform any act aimed at the destruction of any of the rights and freedoms set forth herein or at their limitation to a greater extent than is provided for in the Convention.

Article 18 – Limitation on use of restrictions on rights

The restrictions permitted under this Convention to the said rights and freedoms shall not be applied for any purpose other than those for which they have been prescribed.

SECTION II – EUROPEAN COURT OF HUMAN RIGHTS

Article 19 – Establishment of the Court

To ensure the observance of the engagements undertaken by the High Contracting Parties in the Convention and the protocols thereto, there shall be set up a European Court of Human Rights, hereinafter referred to as 'the Court'. It shall function on a permanent basis.

Article 20 – Number of judges

The Court shall consist of a number of judges equal to that of the High Contracting Parties.

Article 21 – Criteria for office

1. The judges shall be of high moral character and must either possess the qualifications required for appointment to high judicial office or be jurisconsults of recognised competence.
2. The judges shall sit on the Court in their individual capacity.
3. During their term of office the judges shall not engage in any activity which is incompatible with their independence, impartiality or with the demands of a full-time office; all questions arising from the application of this paragraph shall be decided by the Court.

Article 22 – Election of judges

1. The judges shall be elected by the Parliamentary Assembly with respect to each High Contracting Party by a majority of votes cast from a list of three candidates nominated by the High Contracting Party.
2. The same procedure shall be followed to complete the Court in the event of the accession of new High Contracting Parties and in filling casual vacancies.

Article 23 – Terms of office

1. The judges shall be elected for a period of six years. They may be re-elected. However, the terms of office of one-half of the judges elected at the first election shall expire at the end of three years.
2. The judges whose terms of office are to expire at the end of the initial period of three years shall be chosen by lot by the Secretary General of the Council of Europe immediately after their election.
3. In order to ensure that, as far as possible, the terms of office of one-half of the judges are renewed every three years, the Parliamentary Assembly may decide, before proceeding to any subsequent election, that the term or terms of office of one or more judges to be elected shall be for a period other than six years but not more than nine and not less than three years.
4. In cases where more than one term of office is involved and where the Parliamentary Assembly applies the preceding paragraph, the allocation of the terms of office shall be effected by a drawing of lots by the Secretary General of the Council of Europe immediately after the election.
5. A judge elected to replace a judge whose term of office has not expired shall hold office for the remainder of his predecessor's term.
6. The terms of office of judges shall expire when they reach the age of 70.
7. The judges shall hold office until replaced. They shall, however, continue to deal with such cases as they already have under consideration.

Article 24 – Dismissal

No judge may be dismissed from his office unless the other judges decide by a majority of two-thirds that he has ceased to fulfil the required conditions.

Article 25 – Registry and legal secretaries

The Court shall have a registry, the functions and organisation of which shall be laid down in the rules of the Court. The Court shall be assisted by legal secretaries.

Article 26 – Plenary Court

The plenary Court shall
    a.   elect its President and one or two Vice-Presidents for a period of three years; they may be re-elected;
    b.   set up Chambers, constituted for a fixed period of time;
    c.   elect the Presidents of the Chambers of the Court; they may be re-elected;
    d.   adopt the rules of the Court; and
    e.   elect the Registrar and one or more Deputy Registrars.

Article 27 – Committees, Chambers and Grand Chamber

1. To consider cases brought before it, the Court shall sit in committees of three judges, in Chambers of seven judges and in a Grand Chamber of seventeen judges. The Court's Chambers shall set up committees for a fixed period of time.
2. There shall sit as an *ex officio* member of the Chamber and the Grand Chamber the judge elected in respect of the State Party concerned or, if there is none or if he is unable to sit, a person of its choice who shall sit in the capacity of judge.
3. The Grand Chamber shall also include the President of the Court, the Vice-Presidents, the Presidents of the Chambers and other judges chosen in accordance with the rules of the Court. When a case is referred to the Grand Chamber under Article 43, no judge from the Chamber which rendered the judgment shall sit in the Grand Chamber, with the exception of the President of the Chamber and the judge who sat in respect of the State Party concerned.

Article 28 – Declarations of inadmissibility by committees

A committee may, by a unanimous vote, declare inadmissible or strike out of its list of cases an individual application submitted under Article 34 where such a decision can be taken without further examination. The decision shall be final.

Article 29 – Decisions by Chambers on admissibility and merits

1. If no decision is taken under Article 28, a Chamber shall decide on the admissibility and merits of individual applications submitted under Article 34.
2. A Chamber shall decide on the admissibility and merits of inter-State applications submitted under Article 33.
3. The decision on admissibility shall be taken separately unless the Court, in exceptional cases, decides otherwise.

Article 30 – Relinquishment of jurisdiction to the Grand Chamber

Where a case pending before a Chamber raises a serious question affecting the interpretation of the Convention or the protocols thereto or where the resolution of a question before it might have a result inconsistent with a judgment previously delivered by the Court, the Chamber may, at any time before it has rendered its judgment, relinquish jurisdiction in favour of the Grand Chamber, unless one of the parties to the case objects.

Article 31 – Powers of the Grand Chamber

The Grand Chamber shall
   a. determine applications submitted either under Article 33 or Article 34 when a Chamber has relinquished jurisdiction under Article 30 or when the case has been referred to it under Article 43; and
   b. consider requests for advisory opinions submitted under Article 47.

Article 32 – Jurisdiction of the Court

1. The jurisdiction of the Court shall extend to all matters concerning the interpretation and application of the Convention and the protocols thereto which are referred to it as provided in Articles 33, 34 and 47.
2. In the event of dispute as to whether the Court has jurisdiction, the Court shall decide.

Article 33 – Inter-State cases

Any High Contracting Party may refer to the Court any alleged breach of the provisions of the Convention and the protocols thereto by another High Contracting Party.

Article 34 – Individual applications

The Court may receive applications from any person, non-governmental organisation or group of individuals claiming to be the victim of a violation by one of the High Contracting Parties of the rights set forth in the

Convention or the protocols thereto. The High Contracting Parties undertake not to hinder in any way the effective exercise of this right.

Article 35 – Admissibility criteria

1. The Court may only deal with the matter after all domestic remedies have been exhausted, according to the generally recognised rules of international law, and within a period of six months from the date on which the final decision was taken.
2. The Court shall not deal with any individual application submitted under Article 34 that
   a. is anonymous; or
   b. is substantially the same as a matter that has already been examined by the Court or has already been submitted to another procedure of international investigation or settlement and contains no relevant new information.
3. The Court shall declare inadmissible any individual application submitted under Article 34 which it considers incompatible with the provisions of the Convention or the protocols thereto, manifestly ill-founded, or an abuse of the right of application.
4. The Court shall reject any application which it considers inadmissible under this Article. It may do so at any stage of the proceedings.

Article 36 – Third-party intervention

1. In all cases before a Chamber or the Grand Chamber, a High Contracting Party one of whose nationals is an applicant shall have the right to submit written comments and to take part in hearings.
2. The President of the Court may, in the interest of the proper administration of justice, invite any High Contracting Party which is not a party to the proceedings or any person concerned who is not the applicant to submit written comments or take part in hearings.

Article 37 – Striking out applications

1. The Court may at any stage of the proceedings decide to strike an application out of its list of cases where the circumstances lead to the conclusion that
   a. the applicant does not intend to pursue his application; or
   b. the matter has been resolved; or
   c. for any other reason established by the Court, it is no longer justified to continue the examination of the application.
   However, the Court shall continue the examination of the application if respect for human rights as defined in the Convention and the protocols thereto so requires.
2. The Court may decide to restore an application to its list of cases if it considers that the circumstances justify such a course.

Article 38 – Examination of the case and friendly settlement proceedings

1. If the Court declares the application admissible, it shall
   a. pursue the examination of the case, together with the representatives of the parties, and if need be, undertake an investigation, for the effective conduct of which the States concerned shall furnish all necessary facilities;
   b. place itself at the disposal of the parties concerned with a view to securing a friendly settlement of the matter on the basis of respect for human rights as defined in the Convention and the protocols thereto.
2. Proceedings conducted under paragraph 1.b shall be confidential.

Article 39 – Finding of a friendly settlement

If a friendly settlement is effected, the Court shall strike the case out of its list by means of a decision which shall be confined to a brief statement of the facts and of the solution reached.

Article 40 – Public hearings and access to documents

1. Hearings shall be public unless the Court in exceptional circumstances decides otherwise.
2. Documents deposited with the Registrar shall be accessible to the public unless the President of the Court decides otherwise.

Article 41 – Just satisfaction

If the Court finds that there has been a violation of the Convention or the protocols thereto, and if the internal law of the High Contracting Party concerned allows only partial reparation to be made, the Court shall, if necessary, afford just satisfaction to the injured party.

Article 42 – Judgments of Chambers

Judgments of Chambers shall become final in accordance with the provisions of Article 44, paragraph 2.

Article 43 – Referral to the Grand Chamber

1. Within a period of three months from the date of the judgment of the Chamber, any party to the case may, in exceptional cases, request that the case be referred to the Grand Chamber.
2. A panel of five judges of the Grand Chamber shall accept the request if the case raises a serious question affecting the interpretation or application of the Convention or the protocols thereto, or a serious issue of general importance.
3. If the panel accepts the request, the Grand Chamber shall decide the case by means of a judgment.

Article 44 – Final judgments

1. The judgment of the Grand Chamber shall be final.
2. The judgment of a Chamber shall become final
    a. when the parties declare that they will not request that the case be referred to the Grand Chamber; or
    b. three months after the date of the judgment, if reference of the case to the Grand Chamber has not been requested; or
    c. when the panel of the Grand Chamber rejects the request to refer under Article 43.
3. The final judgment shall be published.

Article 45 – Reasons for judgments and decisions

1. Reasons shall be given for judgments as well as for decisions declaring applications admissible or inadmissible.
2. If a judgment does not represent, in whole or in part, the unanimous opinion of the judges, any judge shall be entitled to deliver a separate opinion.

Article 46 – Binding force and execution of judgments

1. The High Contracting Parties undertake to abide by the final judgment of the Court in any case to which they are parties.
2. The final judgment of the Court shall be transmitted to the Committee of Ministers, which shall supervise its execution.

Article 47 – Advisory opinions

1. The Court may, at the request of the Committee of Ministers, give advisory opinions on legal questions concerning the interpretation of the Convention and the protocols thereto.
2. Such opinions shall not deal with any question relating to the content or scope of the rights or freedoms defined in Section I of the Convention and the protocols thereto, or with any other question which the Court or the Committee of Ministers might have to consider in consequence of any such proceedings as could be instituted in accordance with the Convention.
3. Decisions of the Committee of Ministers to request an advisory opinion of the Court shall require a majority vote of the representatives entitled to sit on the Committee.

Article 48 – Advisory jurisdiction of the Court

The Court shall decide whether a request for an advisory opinion submitted by the Committee of Ministers is within its competence as defined in Article 47.

Article 49 – Reasons for advisory opinions

1. Reasons shall be given for advisory opinions of the Court.
2. If the advisory opinion does not represent, in whole or in part, the

unanimous opinion of the judges, any judge shall be entitled to deliver a separate opinion.

3. Advisory opinions of the Court shall be communicated to the Committee of Ministers.

Section III: Miscellaneous Provisions

Article 52

On receipt of a request from the Secretary General of the Council of Europe any High Contracting Party shall furnish an explanation of the manner in which its internal law ensures the effective implementation of any of the provisions of this Convention.

Article 53

Nothing in this Convention shall be construed as limiting or derogating from any of the human rights and fundamental freedoms which may be ensured under the laws of any High Contracting Party or under any other agreement to which it is a party.

Article 54

Nothing in this Convention shall prejudice the powers conferred on the Committee of Ministers by the Statute of the Council of Europe.

Article 55

The High Contracting Parties agree that, except by special agreement, they will not avail themselves of treaties, conventions or declarations in force between them for the purpose of submitting, by way of petition, a dispute arising out of the interpretation or application of this Convention to a means of settlement other than those provided for in this Convention.

Article 56

1. Any State may at the time of its ratification or at any time thereafter declare by notification addressed to the Secretary General of the Council of Europe that the present Convention shall subject to paragraph 4 of this Article extend to all or any of the territories for whose international relations it is responsible.

2. The Convention shall extend to the territory or territories named in the notification as from the thirtieth day after the receipt of this notification by the Secretary General of the Council of Europe.

3. The provisions of this Convention shall be applied in such territories with due regard, however, to local requirements.

4. Any State which has made a declaration in accordance with paragraph 1 of this Article may at any time thereafter declare on behalf of one or

more of the territories to which the declaration relates that it accepts the competence of the Court to receive applications from individuals, non-governmental organisations or groups of individuals as provided by Article 34 of the Convention.

Article 57

1. Any State may, when signing this Convention or when depositing its instrument of ratification, make a reservation in respect of any particular provision of the Convention to the extent that any law then in force in its territory is not in conformity with the provision. Reservations of a general character shall not be permitted under this Article.
2. Any reservation made under this Article shall contain a brief statement of the law concerned.

Article 58

1. A High Contracting Party may denounce the present Convention only after the expiry of five years from the date on which it became a Party to it and after six months' notice contained in a notification addressed to the Secretary General of the Council of Europe, who shall inform the other High Contracting Parties.
2. Such a denunciation shall not have the effect of releasing the High Contracting Party concerned from its obligations under this Convention in respect of any act which, being capable of constituting a violation of such obligations, may have been performed by it before the date at which the denunciation became effective.
3. Any High Contracting Party which shall cease to be a Member of the Council of Europe shall cease to be a Party to this Convention under the same conditions.
4. The Convention may be denounced in accordance with the provisions of the preceding paragraphs in respect of any territory to which it has been declared to extend under the terms of Article 56.

Article 59

1. This Convention shall be open to the signature of the Members of the Council of Europe. It shall be ratified. Ratifications shall be deposited with the Secretary General of the Council of Europe.
2. The present Convention shall come into force after the deposit of ten instruments of ratification.
3. As regards any signatory ratifying subsequently, the Convention shall come into force at the date of the deposit of its instrument of ratification.
4. The Secretary General of the Council of Europe shall notify all the Members of the Council of Europe of the entry into force of the Convention, the names of the High Contracting Parties who have ratified it, and the deposit of all instruments of ratification which may be effected subsequently.

Protocol (1952)

Article 1 – Protection of property

Every natural or legal person is entitled to the peaceful enjoyment of his possessions. No one shall be deprived of his possessions except in the public interest and subject to the conditions provided for by law and by the general principles of international law.

The preceding provisions shall not, however, in any way impair the right of a State to enforce such laws as it deems necessary to control the use of property in accordance with the general interest or to secure the payment of taxes or other contributions or penalties.

Article 2 – Right to education

No person shall be denied the right to education. In the exercise of any functions which it assumes in relation to education and to teaching, the State shall respect the right of parents to ensure such education and teaching in conformity with their own religious and philosophical convictions.

Article 3 – Right to free elections

The High Contracting Parties undertake to hold free elections at reasonable intervals by secret ballot, under conditions which will ensure the free expression of the opinion of the people in the choice of the legislature.

Protocol No. 4 (1963)

Article 1 – Prohibition of imprisonment for debt

No one shall be deprived of his liberty merely on the ground of inability to fulfil a contractual obligation.

Article 2 – Freedom of movement

1. Everyone lawfully within the territory of a State shall, within that territory, have the right to liberty of movement and freedom to choose his residence.
2. Everyone shall be free to leave any country, including his own.
3. No restrictions shall be placed on the exercise of these rights other than such as are in accordance with law and are necessary in a democratic society in the interests of national security or public safety, for the maintenance of *ordre public*, for the prevention of crime, for the protection of health or morals, or for the protection of the rights and freedoms of others.
4. The rights set forth in paragraph 1 may also be subject, in particular areas,

to restrictions imposed in accordance with law and justified by the public interest in a democratic society.

Article 3 – Prohibition of expulsion of nationals

1. No one shall be expelled, by means either of an individual or of a collective measure, from the territory of the State of which he is a national.
2. No one shall be deprived of the right to enter the territory of the State of which he is a national.

Article 4 – Prohibition of collective expulsion of aliens

Collective expulsion of aliens is prohibited.

Protocol No. 6 (1983)

Article 1 – Abolition of death penalty

The death penalty shall be abolished. No one shall be condemned to such penalty or executed.

Article 2 – Death penalty in time of war

A State may make provision in its law for the death penalty in respect of acts committed in time of war or if imminent threat of war; such penalty shall be applied only in the instances laid down in the law and in accordance with its provisions. The State shall communicate to the Secretary General of the Council of Europe the relevant provisions of that law.

Article 3 – Prohibition of derogations

No derogation from the provisions of this Protocol shall be made under Article 15 of the Convention.

Article 4 – Prohibition of reservations

No reservation may be made under Article 57 of the Convention in respect of the provisions of this Protocol.

Protocol No. 7 (1984)

Article 1 – Procedural safeguards relating to the expulsion of aliens

1. An alien lawfully resident in the territory of a State shall not be expelled therefrom except in pursuance of a decision reached in accordance with law and shall be allowed:

a. to submit reasons against his expulsion,

b. to have his case reviewed, and

c. to be represented for these purposes before the competent authority or a person or persons designated by that authority.

2. An alien may be expelled before the exercise of his rights under paragraph 1. a, b and c of this Article, when such expulsion is necessary in the interests of public order or is grounded on reasons of national security.

Article 2 – Right of appeal in criminal matters

1. Everyone convicted of a criminal offence by a tribunal shall have the right to have his conviction or sentence reviewed by a higher tribunal. The exercise of this right, including the grounds on which it may be exercised, shall be governed by law.

2. This right may be subject to exceptions in regard to offences of a minor character, as prescribed by law, or in cases in which the person concerned was tried in the first instance by the highest tribunal or was convicted following an appeal against acquittal.

Article 3 – Compensation for wrongful conviction

When a person has by a final decision been convicted of a criminal offence and when subsequently his conviction has been reversed, or he has been pardoned, on the ground that a new or newly discovered fact shows conclusively that there has been a miscarriage of justice, the person who has suffered punishment as a result of such conviction shall be compensated according to the law or the practice of the State concerned, unless it is proved that the non-disclosure of the unknown fact in time is wholly or partly attributable to him.

Article 4 – Right not to be tried or punished twice

1. No one shall be liable to be tried or punished again in criminal proceedings under the jurisdiction of the same State for an offence for which he has already been finally acquitted or convicted in accordance with the law and penal procedure of that State.

2. The provisions of the preceding paragraph shall not prevent the reopening of the case in accordance with the law and penal procedure of the State concerned, if there is evidence of new or newly discovered facts, or if there has been a fundamental defect in the previous proceedings, which could affect the outcome of the case.

3. No derogation from this Article shall be made under Article 15 of the Convention.

Article 5 – Equality between spouses

Spouses shall enjoy equality of rights and responsibilities of a private law character between them, and in their relations with their children, as to marriage, during marriage and in the event of its dissolution. This Article shall not prevent States from taking such measures as are necessary in the interests of the children.

Derogation and reservation made by the UK government

DEROGATION

The 1988 Notification

The United Kingdom Permanent Representative to the Council of Europe presents his compliments to the Secretary General of the Council, and has the honour to convey the following information in order to ensure compliance with the obligations of Her Majesty's Government in the United Kingdom under Article 15(3) of the Convention for the Protection of Human Rights and Fundamental Freedoms signed at Rome on 5 November 1950.

There have been in the United Kingdom in recent years campaigns of organised terrorism connected with the affairs of Northern Ireland which have manifested themselves in activities which have included repeated murder, attempted murder, maiming, intimidation and violent civil disturbance and in bombing and fire raising which have resulted in death, injury and widespread destruction of property. As a result, a public emergency within the meaning of Article 15(1) of the Convention exists in the United Kingdom.

The Government found it necessary in 1974 to introduce and since then, in cases concerning persons reasonably suspected of involvement in terrorism connected with the affairs of Northern Ireland, or of certain offences under the legislation, who have been detained for 48 hours, to exercise powers enabling further detention without charge, for periods of up to five days, on the authority of the Secretary of State. These powers are at present to be found in Section 12 of the Prevention of Terrorism (Temporary Provisions) Act 1984, Article 9 of the Prevention of Terrorism (Supplemental Temporary Provisions) Order 1984 and Article 10 of the Prevention of Terrorism (Supplemental Temporary Provisions) (Northern Ireland) Order 1984.

Section 12 of the Prevention of Terrorism (Temporary Provisions) Act 1984 provides for a person whom a constable has arrested on reasonable grounds of suspecting him to be guilty of an offence under Section 1,9 or 10 of the Act, or to be or to have been involved in terrorism connected with the affairs of Northern Ireland, to be detained in right of the arrest for up to 48 hours and thereafter, where the Secretary of State extends the detention period, for up to a further five days. Section 12 substantially re-enacted Section 12 of the Prevention of Terrorism (Temporary Provisions) Act 1976 which, in turn, substantially re-enacted Section 7 of the Prevention of Terrorism (Temporary Provisions) Act 1974.

Article 10 of the Prevention of Terrorism (Supplemental Temporary Provisions) (Northern Ireland) Order 1984 (SI 1984/417) and Article 9 of the Prevention of Terrorism (Supplemental Temporary Provisions) Order 1984 (SI 1984/418) were both made under Sections 13 and 14 of and Schedule 3 to the 1984 Act and substantially re-enacted powers of detention in Orders made under the 1974 and 1976 Acts. A person who is being examined under Article 4 of either Order on his arrival in, or on seeking to leave, Northern Ireland or Great Britain for the purpose of determining whether he is or has been involved in terrorism connected with the affairs of Northern Ireland, or whether there are grounds for suspecting that he has committed an offence under Section 9 of the 1984 Act, may be detained under Article 4 or 10, as appropriate, pending the conclusion of his examination. The period of this examination may exceed 12 hours if an examining officer has reasonable grounds for suspecting him to be or to have been involved in acts of terrorism connected with the affairs of Northern Ireland.

Where such a person is detained under the said Article 9 or 10 he may be detained for up to 48 hours on the authority of an examining officer and thereafter, where the Secretary of State extends the detention period, for up to a further five days.

In its judgment of 29 November 1988 in the Case of *Brogan and Others*, the European Court of Human Rights held that there had been a violation of Article 5(3) in respect of each of the applicants, all of whom had been detained under Section 12 of the 1984 Act. The Court held that even the shortest of the four periods of detention concerned, namely four days and six hours, fell outside the constraints as to time permitted by the first part of Article 5(3). In addition, the Court held that there had been a violation of Article 5(3) in the case of each applicant. Following this judgment, the Secretary of State for the Home Department informed Parliament on 6 December 1988 that, against the background of the terrorist campaign, and the over-riding need to bring terrorists to justice, the Government did not believe that the maximum period of detention should be reduced. He informed Parliament that the Government were examining the matter with a view to responding to the judgment. On 22 December 1988, the Secretary of State further informed Parliament that it remained the Government's wish, if it could be achieved, to find a judicial process under which extended detention might be reviewed and where appropriate authorised by a judge or other judicial officer. But a further period of reflection and consultation was necessary before the Government could bring forward a firm and final view.

Since the judgment of 29 November as well as previously, the Government have found it necessary to continue to exercise, in relation to terrorism connected with the affairs of Northern Ireland, the powers described above enabling further detention without charge for periods of up to 5 days, on the authority of the Secretary of State, to the extent strictly required by the exigencies of the situation to enable necessary enquiries and investigations properly to be completed in order to decide whether criminal proceedings should be instituted. To the extent that the exercise of these powers may be inconsistent with the obligations imposed by the Convention the Government has availed itself of the right of derogation conferred by Article 15(1) of the Convention and will continue to do so until further notice.

Dated 23 December 1988.

The 1989 Notification

The United Kingdom Permanent Representative to the Council of Europe presents his compliments to the Secretary General of the Council, and has the honour to convey the following information.

In his communication to the Secretary General of 23 December 1988, reference was made to the introduction and exercise of certain powers under section 12 of the Prevention of Terrorism (Temporary Provisions) Act 1984, Article 9 of the Prevention of Terrorism (Supplemental Temporary Provisions) Order 1984 and Article 10 of the Prevention of Terrorism (Supplemental Temporary Provisions) (Northern Ireland) Order 1984.

These provisions have been replaced by section 14 of and paragraph 6 of Schedule 5 to the Prevention of Terrorism (Temporary Provisions) Act 1989, which make comparable provision. They came into force on 22 March 1989. A copy of these provisions is enclosed.

The United Kingdom Permanent Representative avails himself of this opportunity to renew to the Secretary General the assurance of his highest consideration.

23 March 1989.

RESERVATION

At the time of signing the present (First) Protocol, I declare that, in view of certain provisions of the Education Acts in the United Kingdom, the principle affirmed in the second sentence of Article 2 is accepted by the United Kingdom only so far as it is compatible with the provision of efficient instruction and training, and the avoidance of unreasonable public expenditure.

Dated 20 March 1952. Made by the United Kingdom Permanent Representative to the Council of Europe.

---

23   THE COUNCIL OF EUROPE: THE EUROPEAN SOCIAL CHARTER, 1965

The governments signatory hereto, being Members of the Council of Europe,

Considering that the aim of the Council of Europe is the achievement of greater unity between its Members for the purpose of safeguarding and realising the ideals and principles which are their common heritage and of facilitating their economic and social progress, in particular by the maintenance and further realisation of human rights and fundamental freedoms;

Considering that in the European Convention for the Protection of Human Rights and Fundamental Freedoms signed at Rome on 4th November 1950, and the Protocol thereto signed at Paris on 20th March 1952, the member states of the Council of Europe agreed to secure to their populations the civil and political rights and freedoms therein specified;

Considering that the enjoyment of social rights should be secured without discrimination on grounds of race, colour, sex, religion, political opinion, national extraction or social origin;

Being resolved to make every effort in common to improve the standard of living and to promote the social well-being of both their urban and rural populations by means of appropriate institutions and action,

Have agreed as follows:

Part I

The Contracting Parties accept as the aim of their policy, to be pursued by all appropriate means, both national and international in character, the attainment of conditions in which the following rights and principles may be effectively realised:

1. Everyone shall have the opportunity to earn his living in an occupation freely entered upon.

2. All workers have the right to just conditions of work.

3. All workers have the right to safe and healthy working conditions.

4. All workers have the right to a fair remuneration sufficient for a decent standard of living for themselves and their families.

5. All workers and employers have the right to freedom of association in national or international organisations for the protection of their economic and social interests.

6. All workers and employers have the right to bargain collectively.

7. Children and young persons have the right to a special protection against the physical and moral hazards to which they are exposed.

8. Employed women, in case of maternity, and other employed women as appropriate, have the right to a special protection in their work.

9. Everyone has the right to appropriate facilities for vocational guidance with a view to helping him choose an occupation suited to his personal aptitude and interests.

10. Everyone has the right to appropriate facilities for vocational training.

11. Everyone has the right to benefit from any measures enabling him to enjoy the highest possible standard of health attainable.

12. All workers and their dependents have the right to social security.

13. Anyone without adequate resources has the right to social and medical assistance.

14. Everyone has the right to benefit from social welfare services.

15. Disabled persons have the right to vocational training, rehabilitation and resettlement, whatever the origin and nature of their disability.

16. The family as a fundamental unit of society has the right to appropriate social, legal and economic protection to ensure its full development.

17. Mothers and children, irrespective of marital status and family relations, have the right to appropriate social and economic protection.

18. The nationals of any one of the Contracting Parties have the right to engage in any gainful occupation in the territory of any one of the others on a footing of equality with the nationals of the latter, subject to restrictions based on cogent economic or social reasons.

19. Migrant workers who are nationals of a Contracting Party and their families have the right to protection and assistance in the territory of any other Contracting Party.

PART II

The Contracting Parties undertake, as provided for in Part III, to consider themselves bound by the obligations laid down in the following Articles and paragraphs.

Article 1 – The right to work

With a view to ensuring the effective exercise of the right to work, the Contracting Parties undertake:

1. to accept as one of their primary aims and responsibilities the achievement and maintenance of as high and stable a level of employment as possible, with a view to the attainment of full employment;

2. to protect effectively the right of the worker to earn his living in an occupation freely entered upon;

3. to establish or maintain free employment services for all workers;

4. to provide or promote appropriate vocational guidance, training and rehabilitation.

Article 2 – The right to just conditions of work

With a view to ensuring the effective exercise of the right to just conditions of work, the Contracting Parties undertake:

1. to provide for reasonable daily and weekly working hours, the working week to be progressively reduced to the extent that the increase of productivity and other relevant factors permit;

2. to provide for public holidays with pay;

3. to provide for a minimum of two weeks' annual holiday with pay;

4. to provide for additional paid holidays or reduced working hours for workers engaged in dangerous or unhealthy occupations as prescribed;

5. to ensure a weekly rest period which shall, as far as possible, coincide with the day recognised by tradition or custom in the country or region concerned as a day of rest.

Article 3 – The right to safe and healthy working conditions

With a view to ensuring the effective exercise of the right to safe and healthy working conditions, the Contracting Parties undertake:
1. to issue safety and health regulations;
2. to provide for the enforcement of such regulations by measures of supervision;
3. to consult, as appropriate, employers' and workers' organisations on measures intended to improve industrial safety and health.

Article 4 – The right to a fair remuneration

With a view to ensuring the effective exercise of the right to a fair remuneration, the Contracting Parties undertake:
1. to recognise the right of workers to a remuneration such as will give them and their families a decent standard of living;
2. to recognise the right of workers to an increased rate of remuneration for overtime work, subject to exceptions in particular cases;
3. to recognise the right of men and women workers to equal pay for work of equal value;
4. to recognise the right of all workers to a reasonable period of notice for termination of employment;
5. to permit deductions from wages only under conditions and to the extent prescribed by national laws or regulations or fixed by collective agreements or arbitration awards.

The exercise of these rights shall be achieved by freely concluded collective agreements, by statutory wage-fixing machinery, or by other means appropriate to national conditions.

Article 5 – The right to organise

With a view to ensuring or promoting the freedom of workers and employers to form local, national or international organisations for the protection of their economic and social interests and to join those organisations, the Contracting Parties undertake that national law shall not be such as to impair, nor shall it be so applied as to impair, this freedom. The extent to which the guarantees provided for in this Article shall apply to the police shall be determined by national laws or regulations. The principle governing the application to the members of the armed forces of these guarantees and the extent to which they shall apply to persons in this category shall equally be determined by national laws or regulations.

Article 6 – The right to bargain collectively

With a view to ensuring the effective exercise of the right to bargain collectively, the Contracting Parties undertake:
1. to promote joint consultation between workers and employers;
2. to promote, where necessary and appropriate, machinery for voluntary negotiations between employers or employers' organisations and workers'

organisations, with a view to the regulation of terms and conditions of employment by means of collective agreements;

3. to promote the establishment and use of appropriate machinery for conciliation and voluntary arbitration for the settlement of labour disputes;

and recognise:

4. the right of workers and employers to collective action in cases of conflicts of interest, including the right to strike, subject to obligations that might arise out of collective agreements previously entered into.

Article 7 – The right of children and young persons to protection

With a view to ensuring the effective exercise of the right of children and young persons to protection, the Contracting Parties undertake:

1. to provide that the minimum age of admission to employment shall be 15 years, subject to exceptions for children employed in prescribed light work without harm to their health, morals or education;

2. to provide that a higher minimum age of admission to employment shall be fixed with respect to prescribed occupations regarded as dangerous or unhealthy;

3. to provide that persons who are still subject to compulsory education shall not be employed in such work as would deprive them of the full benefit of their education;

4. to provide that the working hours of persons under 16 years of age shall be limited in accordance with the needs of their development, and particularly with their need for vocational training;

5. to recognise the right of young workers and apprentices to a fair wage or other appropriate allowances;

6. to provide that the time spent by young persons in vocational training during the normal working hours with the consent of the employer shall be treated as forming part of the working day;

7. to provide that employed persons of under 18 years of age shall be entitled to not less than three weeks' annual holiday with pay;

8. to provide that persons under 18 years of age shall not be employed in night work with the exception of certain occupations provided for by national laws or regulations;

9. to provide that persons under 18 years of age employed in occupations prescribed by national laws or regulations shall be subject to regular medical control;

10. to ensure special protection against physical and moral dangers to which children and young persons are exposed, and particularly against those resulting directly or indirectly from their work.

Article 8 – The right of employed women to protection

With a view to ensuring the effective exercise of the right of employed women to protection, the Contracting Parties undertake:

1. to provide either by paid leave, by adequate social security benefits or by

benefits from public funds for women to take leave before and after childbirth up to a total of at least 12 weeks;

2. to consider it as unlawful for an employer to give a woman notice of dismissal during her absence on maternity leave or to give her notice of dismissal at such a time that the notice would expire during such absence;

3. to provide that mothers who are nursing their infants shall be entitled to sufficient time off for this purpose;

4. a. to regulate the employment of women workers on night work in industrial employment;

   b. to prohibit the employment of women workers in underground mining, and, as appropriate, on all other work which is unsuitable for them by reason of its dangerous, unhealthy, or arduous nature.

Article 9 – The right to vocational guidance

With a view to ensuring the effective exercise of the right to vocational guidance, the Contracting Parties undertake to provide or promote, as necessary, a service which will assist all persons, including the handicapped, to solve problems related to occupational choice and progress, with due regard to the individual's characteristics and their relation to occupational opportunity: this assistance should be available free of charge, both to young persons, including school children, and to adults.

Article 10 – The right to vocational training

With a view to ensuring the effective exercise of the right to vocational training, the Contracting Parties undertake:

1. to provide or promote, as necessary, the technical and vocational training of all persons, including the handicapped, in consultation with employers' and workers' organisations, and to grant facilities for access to higher technical and university education, based solely on individual aptitude;

2. to provide or promote a system of apprenticeship and other systematic arrangements for training young boys and girls in their various employments;

3. to provide or promote, as necessary:

   a. adequate and readily available training facilities for adult workers;

   b. special facilities for the re-training of adult workers needed as a result of technological development or new trends in employment;

4. to encourage the full utilisation of the facilities provided by appropriate measures such as:

   a. reducing or abolishing any fees or charges;

   b. granting financial assistance in appropriate cases;

   c. including in the normal working hours time spent on supplementary training taken by the worker, at the request of his employer, during employment;

   d. ensuring, through adequate supervision, in consultation with the employers' and workers' organisations, the efficiency of apprenticeship and other training arrangements for young workers, and the adequate protection of young workers generally.

Article 11 – The right to protection of health

With a view to ensuring the effective exercise of the right to protection of health, the Contracting Parties undertake, either directly or in co-operation with public or private organisations, to take appropriate measures designed inter alia:
1. to remove as far as possible the causes of ill-health;
2. to provide advisory and educational facilities for the promotion of health and the encouragement of individual responsibility in matters of health;
3. to prevent as far as possible epidemic, endemic and other diseases.

Article 12 – The right to social security

With a view to ensuring the effective exercise of the right to social security, the Contracting Parties undertake:
1. to establish or maintain a system of social security;
2. to maintain the social security system at a satisfactory level at least equal to that required for ratification of International Labour Convention (No. 102) Concerning Minimum Standards of Social Security;
3. to endeavour to raise progressively the system of social security to a higher level;
4. to take steps, by the conclusion of appropriate bilateral and multilateral agreements, or by other means, and subject to the conditions laid down in such agreements, in order to ensure:
   a. equal treatment with their own nationals of the nationals of other Contracting Parties in respect of social security rights, including the retention of benefits arising out of social security legislation, whatever movements the persons protected may undertake between the territories of the Contracting Parties;
   b. the granting, maintenance and resumption of social security rights by such means as the accumulation of insurance or employment periods completed under the legislation of each of the Contracting Parties.

Article 13 – The right to social and medical assistance

With a view to ensuring the effective exercise of the right to social and medical assistance, the Contracting Parties undertake:
1. to ensure that any person who is without adequate resources and who is unable to secure such resources either by his own efforts or from other sources, in particular by benefits under a social security scheme, be granted adequate assistance, and, in case of sickness, the care necessitated by this condition;
2. to ensure that persons receiving such assistance shall not, for that reason, suffer from a diminution of their political or social rights;
3. to provide that everyone may receive by appropriate public or private services such advice and personal help as may be required to prevent, to remove, or to alleviate personal or family want;
4. to apply the provisions referred to in paragraphs 1, 2 and 3 of this Article on an equal footing with their nationals to nationals of other Contracting

Parties lawfully within their territories, in accordance with their obligations under the European Convention on Social and Medical Assistance, signed at Paris on 11th December 1953.

Article 14 – The right to benefit from social welfare services

With a view to ensuring the effective exercise of the right to benefit from social welfare services, the Contracting Parties undertake:
1. to promote or provide services which, by using methods of social work, would contribute to the welfare and development of both individuals and groups in the community, and to their adjustment to the social environment;
2. to encourage the participation of individuals and voluntary or other organisations in the establishment and maintenance of such services.

Article 15 – The right of physically or mentally disabled persons to vocational training, rehabilitation and social resettlement

With a view to ensuring the effective exercise of the right of the physically or mentally disabled to vocational training, rehabilitation and resettlement, the Contracting Parties undertake:
1. to take adequate measures for the provision of training facilities, including, where necessary, specialised institutions, public or private;
2. to take adequate measures for the placing of disabled persons in employment, such as specialised placing services, facilities for sheltered employment and measures to encourage employers to admit disabled persons to employment.

Article 16 – The right of the family to social, legal and economic protection

With a view to ensuring the necessary conditions for the full development of the family, which is a fundamental unit of society, the Contracting Parties undertake to promote the economic, legal and social protection of family life by such means as social and family benefits, fiscal arrangements, provision of family housing, benefits for the newly married, and other appropriate means.

Article 17 – The right of mothers and children to social and economic protection

With a view to ensuring the effective exercise of the right of mothers and children to social and economic protection, the Contracting Parties will take all appropriate and necessary measures to that end, including the establishment or maintenance of appropriate institutions or services.

Article 18 – The right to engage in a gainful occupation in the territory of other Contracting Parties

With a view to ensuring the effective exercise of the right to engage in a gainful occupation in the territory of any other Contracting Party, the Contracting Parties undertake:
1. to apply existing regulations in a spirit of liberality;
2. to simplify existing formalities and to reduce or abolish chancery dues and other charges payable by foreign workers or their employers;
3. to liberalise, individually or collectively, regulations governing the employment of foreign workers;
and recognise:
4. the right of their nationals to leave the country to engage in a gainful occupation in the territories of the other Contracting Parties.

Article 19 – The right of migrant workers and their families to protection and assistance

With a view to ensuring the effective exercise of the right of migrant workers and their families to protection and assistance in the territory of any other Contracting Party, the Contracting Parties undertake:
1. to maintain or to satisfy themselves that there are maintained adequate and free services to assist such workers, particularly in obtaining accurate information, and to take all appropriate steps, so far as national laws and regulations permit, against misleading propaganda relating to emigration and immigration;
2. to adopt appropriate measures within their own jurisdiction to facilitate the departure, journey and reception of such workers and their families, and to provide, within their own jurisdiction, appropriate services for health, medical attention and good hygienic conditions during the journey;
3. to promote co-operation, as appropriate, between social services, public and private, in emigration and immigration countries;
4. to secure for such workers lawfully within their territories, in so far as such matters are regulated by law or regulations or are subject to the control of administrative authorities, treatment not less favourable than that of their own nationals in respect of the following matters:
   a.   remuneration and other employment and working conditions;
   b.   membership of trade unions and enjoyment of the benefits of collective bargaining;
   c.   accommodation;
5. to secure for such workers lawfully within their territories treatment not less favourable than that of their own nationals with regard to employment taxes, dues or contributions payable in respect of employed persons;
6. to facilitate as far as possible the reunion of the family of a foreign worker permitted to establish himself in the territory;

7. to secure for such workers lawfully within their territories treatment not less favourable than that of their own nationals in respect of legal proceedings relating to matters referred to in this Article;

8. to secure that such workers lawfully residing within their territories are not expelled unless they endanger national security or offend against public interest or morality;

9. to permit, within legal limits, the transfer of such parts of the earnings and savings of such workers as they may desire;

10. to extend the protection and assistance provided for in this Article to self-employed migrants in so far as such measures apply.

Part III

Article 20 – Undertakings

1. Each of the Contracting Parties undertakes:
   - *a.* to consider Part I of this Charter as a declaration of the aims which it will pursue by all appropriate means, as stated in the introductory paragraph of that Part;
   - *b.* to consider itself bound by at least five of the following Articles of Part II of this Charter: Articles 1,5,6,12,13,16 and 19.
   - *c.* in addition to the Articles selected by it in accordance with the preceding sub-paragraph, to consider itself bound by such a number of Articles or numbered paragraphs of Part II of the Charter as it may select, provided that the total number of Articles or numbered paragraphs by which it is bound is not less than 10 Articles or 45 numbered paragraphs.

2. The Articles or paragraphs selected in accordance with sub-paragraphs *b* and *c* of paragraph 1 of this Article shall be notified to the Secretary General of the Council of Europe at the time when the instrument of ratification or approval of the Contracting Party concerned is deposited.

3. Any Contracting Party may, at a later date, declare by notification to the Secretary General that it considers itself bound by any Articles or any numbered paragraphs of Part II of the Charter which it has not already accepted under the terms of paragraph 1 of this Article. Such undertakings subsequently given shall be deemed to be an integral part of the ratification or approval, and shall have the same effect as from the thirtieth day after the date of the notification.

4. The Secretary General shall communicate to all the signatory governments and to the Director General of the International Labour Office any notification which he shall have received pursuant to this Part of the Charter.

5. Each Contracting Party shall maintain a system of labour inspection appropriate to national conditions.

Part IV

Article 21 – Reports concerning accepted provisions

The Contracting Parties shall send to the Secretary General of the Council of Europe a report at two-yearly intervals, in a form to be determined by the Committee of Ministers, concerning the application of such provisions of Part II of the Charter as they have accepted.

Article 22 – Reports concerning provisions which are not accepted

The Contracting Parties shall send to the Secretary General, at appropriate intervals as requested by the Committee of Ministers, reports relating to the provisions of Part II of the Charter which they did not accept at the time of their ratification or approval or in a subsequent notification. The Committee of Ministers shall determine from time to time in respect of which provisions such reports shall be requested and the form of the reports to be provided.

Article 23 – Communication of copies

1. Each Contracting Party shall communicate copies of its reports referred to in Articles 21 and 22 to such of its national organisations as are members of the international organisations of employers and trade unions to be invited under Article 27, paragraph 2, to be represented at meetings of the Sub-Committee of the Governmental Social Committee.
2. The Contracting Parties shall forward to the Secretary General any comments on the said reports received from these national organisations, if so requested by them.

Article 24 – Examination of the reports

The reports sent to the Secretary General in accordance with Articles 21 and 22 shall be examined by a committee of experts, who shall have also before them any comments forwarded to the Secretary General in accordance with paragraph 2 of Article 23.

Article 25 – Committee of experts

1. The committee of experts shall consist of not more than seven members appointed by the Committee of Ministers from a list of independent experts of the highest integrity and of recognised competence in international social questions, nominated by the Contracting Parties.
2. The members of the committee shall be appointed for a period of six years. They may be reappointed. However, of the members first appointed, the terms of office of two members shall expire at the end of four years.
3. The members whose terms of office are to expire at the end of the initial period of four years shall be chosen by lot by the Committee of Ministers immediately after the first appointment has been made.

4. A member of the committee of experts appointed to replace a member whose term of office has not expired shall hold office for the remainder of his predecessor's term.

Article 26 – Participation of the International Labour Organisation

The International Labour Organisation shall be invited to nominate a representative to participate in a consultative capacity in the deliberations of the committee of experts.

Article 27 – Sub-Committee of the Governmental Social Committee

1. The reports of the Contracting Parties and the conclusions of the committee of experts shall be submitted for examination to a Sub-Committee of the Governmental Social Committee of the Council of Europe.
2. The sub-committee shall be composed of one representative of each of the Contracting Parties. It shall invite no more than two international organisations of employers and no more than two international trade union organisations as it may designate to be represented as observers in a consultative capacity at its meetings. Moreover, it may consult no more than two representatives of international non-governmental organisations having consultative status with the Council of Europe, in respect of questions with which the organisations are particularly qualified to deal, such as social welfare, and the economic and social protection of the family.
3. The sub-committee shall present to the Committee of Ministers a report containing its conclusions and append the report of the committee of experts.

Article 28 – Consultative Assembly

The Secretary General of the Council of Europe shall transmit to the Consultative Assembly the conclusions of the committee of experts. The Consultative Assembly shall communicate its views on these conclusions to the Committee of Ministers.

Article 29 – Committee of Ministers

By a majority of two thirds of the members entitled to sit on the Committee, the Committee of Ministers may, on the basis of the report of the sub-committee, and after consultation with the Consultative Assembly, make to each Contracting Party any necessary recommendations.

PART V

Article 30 – Derogations in time of war or public emergency

1. In time of war or other public emergency threatening the life of the nation any Contracting Party may take measures derogating from its obligations

under this Charter to the extent strictly required by the exigencies of the situation, provided that such measures are not inconsistent with its other obligations under international law.

2. Any Contracting Party which has availed itself of this right of derogation shall, within a reasonable lapse of time, keep the Secretary General of the Council of Europe fully informed of the measures taken and of the reasons therefor. It shall likewise inform the Secretary General when such measures have ceased to operate and the provisions of the Charter which it has accepted are again being fully executed.

3. The Secretary General shall in turn inform other Contracting Parties and the Director General of the International Labour Office of all communications received in accordance with paragraph 2 of this Article.

Article 31 – Restrictions

1. The rights and principles set forth in Part I when effectively realised, and their effective exercise as provided for in Part II, shall not be subject to any restrictions or limitations not specified in those Parts, except such as are prescribed by law and are necessary in a democratic society for the protection of the rights and freedoms of others or for the protection of public interest, national security, public health, or morals.

2. The restrictions permitted under this Charter to the rights and obligations set forth herein shall not be applied for any purpose other than that for which they have been prescribed.

Article 32 – Relations between the Charter and domestic law or international agreements

The provisions of this Charter shall not prejudice the provisions of domestic law or of any bilateral or multilateral treaties, conventions or agreements which are already in force, or may come into force, under which more favourable treatment would be accorded to the persons protected.

Article 33 – Implementation by collective agreements

1. In member states where the provisions of paragraphs 1, 2, 3, 4 and 5 of Article 2, paragraphs 4, 6, and 7 of Article 7 and paragraphs 1, 2, 3 and 4 of Article 10 of Part II of this Charter are matters normally left to agreements between employers or employers' organisations and workers' organisations, or are normally carried out otherwise than by law, the undertakings of those paragraphs may be given and compliance with them shall be treated as effective if their provisions are applied through such agreements of other means to the great majority of the workers concerned.

2. In member states where these provisions are normally the subject of legislation, the undertakings concerned may likewise be given, and compliance with them shall be regarded as effective if the provisions are applied by law to the great majority of the workers concerned.

(B)

The Influence of the European Convention on Human Rights, 1966–98

(I) Within the UK

---

24 BRITISH CITIZENS ARE GRANTED THE RIGHT OF
INDIVIDUAL PETITION UNDER THE EUROPEAN
CONVENTION ON HUMAN RIGHTS, 1966

RB NOTE: The following are selected illustrative cases against the UK since 1965 resulting in various forms of positive action by the government.

PRISONS

Golder and others

In 1970, an applicant (*Golder v U.K.*: No. 4451/70) detained in Parkhurst Prison was not allowed by the Home Secretary to correspond with a solicitor in order to bring a civil action against a prison officer for damages for defamation. He alleged violations of his rights to respect for correspondence (Art. 8) and to judicial determination of a civil right (Art. 6 (1)). The Commission, in its Report (Art. 31) of June 1973, found violations of Art. 8 and also of Art. 6 (1) on the ground that the right to have a civil right determined by a court included the right to have *access* to a court in order to bring a civil action and to consult solicitors for that purpose. The Court in its judgment in February 1975 also found violations of Art. 6 (1) and 8. The Committee of Ministers (Art. 54) in June 1976 decided to take no further action after noting information from H.M.G. that the immediate introduction of new procedures would abolish the procedure complained of and would substitute a simple application which would always be granted provided that the prisoner had first ventilated his complaint through the normal internal channels. However, in a later case in 1973 (*Kiss v U.K.*: No. 6224/73) the Commission found the same violations, and the Committee of Ministers in April 1978 (Resolution DH (78) 3) took the same decision (Art. 32). Between about 1975 and 1981, the Commission received some 50 applications from prisoners concerning control of their correspondence by censorship. In May 1976 the Commission selected as test cases seven of these cases (*Silver and Other v U.K.* · Nos. 5947/72, 6205/73, 7052/75, 7061/75, 7107/75, 7113/75, 7136/75) and adjourned the others. The letters which had been stopped were addressed to various people (e.g. solicitors, Members of Parliament, persons in public administration, members of their families, friends and acquaintances) and dealt with different subjects (e.g. prison conditions, various civil or criminal proceedings, business affairs, family problems). In October 1980, the Commission adopted its Report (Art. 31) finding violations of the applicants' right of correspondence which was in 58 out of 64 letters not justified under Art. 8 (2). In anticipation of the Court's judgment, the Standing Orders relating to prisoners' correspondence were revised as from December 1981 and, in particular, the 'prior ventilation' rule was replaced by the 'simultaneous ventilation' rule. The Court in its judgment in March 1983, confirming the Commission's Report, found that Silver had been denied access to the civil courts in 1972 contrary to Art. 6 (1) and that censorship of 57 of his letters violated Art. 8. The Court also found a breach of Art. 13 in connection with Art. 8, as a petition to the Home Secretary was not an effective remedy regarding a complaint as to the validity of administrative directives.

Ireland v. U.K. cases

Two interstate cases (Art. 24) were brought by the *Irish Government against the U.K. Government* in 1971 and 1972. In the *first* case (5310/71), the Irish Government referred to the Civil Authorities (Special Powers) Act, Northern Ireland 1922 and the connected Statutory Rules, Regulations and Orders and alleged that this legislation was itself a failure by the U.K. Government to secure to everybody within its jurisdiction the rights and freedoms in the Convention (Art. 1), and that the methods employed in the implementation of this legislation constituted an administrative practice in violation of Art. 1. The Irish Government also submitted that certain deaths in Northern Ireland in August and October 1971 showed a violation of the right to life (Art. 2).

The Irish Government then referred to the taking into custody of persons on or after 9th May 1971 under the Special Powers Act and alleged that in about 90 cases they were subjected to torture and inhuman and degrading treatment (Art. 3). They also alleged that internment without trial as carried out after 9th August 1971 violated the right to liberty and security (Art. 5) and the right to a fair hearing by an independent and impartial tribunal (Art. 6). Finally, the Irish Government alleged that the exercise by the U.K. Government and the security forces of their powers to detain and intern, as well as to search houses, were carried out with discrimination on the grounds of political opinion (Art. 14). As to the notification in 1957 and 1971 by the U.K. Government of measures of derogation (Art. 15), the Irish Government submitted that there could be no derogation under Art. 2 and that the measures concerned were more extensive than allowed under Art. 15.

In the *second* case (5451/72), the Irish Government alleged that the 'Northern Ireland Act 1972', concerning the powers of Parliament in Northern Ireland with regard to H.M. Forces, constituted a failure by the U.K. Government (Art. 1) to protect residents in Northern Ireland from retrospective legislation (Art. 7) and was itself a violation of Art. 7.

In October 1972, the Commission struck the *second* case off its list of cases following an undertaking by the U.K. Government that there would be no retrospective prosecutions of offences under the Northern Ireland Act 1972, and a withdrawal by the Irish Government of an alleged violation of Art. 7.

The Commission found the *first* case inadmissible under Art. 2, but admissible under Arts. 3, 5 and 6 and under Art. 14 in conjunction with Arts. 5 and 6. Other issues were reserved. After the Commission had heard 113 witnesses in various localities and had also heard the parties' final conclusions in March 1975, it adopted its Report (Art. 31) in January 1976. The Commission found in particular under Art. 3 that the combined use of the 'five techniques' in aid of interrogation constituted a practice of torture and inhuman treatment, that there had been inhuman treatment by the security forces in 11 cases, that at Palace Barracks, Hollywood, in autumn 1971 there had been a practice in connection with interrogation of prisoners by the R.U.C. which was inhuman treatment, but that there had been no violation of Art. 3 as regards other allegations.

The Irish Government referred the case to the Court in March 1976 and during subsequent hearings the U.K. Government undertook that the 'five techniques', which had been abandoned in 1972, would never be reintroduced. In its judgment in January 1978, the Court held that under Art. 3 that the 'five techniques' amounted to a practice of inhuman treatment but not of torture; that similarly at Palace Barracks there had been a practice of inhuman treatment but not of torture. They confirmed the Commission's finding that other treatment of detainees had not violated Art. 3. The Court then held that extra-judicial deprivation of liberty violated Art. 5, but was covered by the Government's derogation (Art. 15), and it also held that no discrimination (Art. 14) in the use of special powers of detention and internment had been established. Finally, the Court held that it could not direct, as the Irish Government had requested, the U.K. Government to institute criminal or disciplinary proceedings against those who had committed, condoned or tolerated the above breaches of Art. 3. In fact, many complainants later obtained damages in civil proceedings.

MENTAL HEALTH

A

In a 1974 case (*A. v U.K.* 6840/74) the applicant had been held in Broadmoor special hospital since February 1973 on the basis of orders made under Section 60 and 65 of the Mental Health Act 1959. He was later transferred to Lincoln Hospital and then released. In May 1974, after being suspected of having started a fire, he was transferred to an intensive care unit where for about five weeks he was held in a secure single room with only limited opportunities for exercise and association with other persons. He alleged that the length of this solitary confinement and the insanitary conditions were inhuman or degrading treatment (Art. 3). Five delegates of the Commission visited Broadmoor in July 1977 and also visited the applicant at Lincoln. In a settlement reached in July 1980, the U.K. Government first informed the Commission of substantial refurbishment in the intensive care unit, including new single room accommodation, as well as a long term project for developing Broadmoor. Detailed information as to new guidelines adopted for the regime of patients in seclusion were also given. Finally, the Government undertook to make an ex gratia payment of £500 to the applicant and to keep these new guidelines under review. The applicant's solicitor withdrew his case.

X

Several cases concerned convicted persons ordered to be detained in mental hospitals under the Mental Health Act 1959, and their complaints about the lack of judicial proceedings under the Act or otherwise to decide the lawfulness of their detention. The leading case was that of *X. v U.K.* (No. 6998/75). The applicant had been convicted in 1968 and ordered to be detained indefinitely in Broadmoor hospital, pursuant to Section 60 and 65 of the Mental Health Act 1959. His condition improved and he was conditionally discharged by the Home Secretary in May 1971, but, following his wife's denunciation, the Home Secretary ordered his recall. He was arrested in April 1974 and was returned to Broadmoor. He there unsuccessfully applied for a writ of habeas corpus. In his application to the Commission he alleged that he was detained although not of unsound mind (Art. 5(i)(e)), that he was not promptly given reasons for his arrest (Art. 5(ii)), that there was no procedure to test speedily before a court the lawfulness of his detention (Art. 5(iv)), and that his recall to Broadmoor was inhuman and degrading treatment (Art. 3).

The Commission did not admit the Art. 3 complaint and, in its report (Art. 31) of 16th July 1980, found no violation of Art. 5(i), but found a violation of Art. 5(ii) as there was no reason to withhold reasons for the applicant's arrest from his solicitors even if he could not understand the details, and a violation of Art. 5 (iv) as the right to judicial determination of the lawfulness of detention applied to his recall, and the remedies of the Mental Health Tribunal or habeas corpus did not satisfy this requirement.

In November 1981 the Court similarly found no violation of Art. 5(i), as his recall and subsequent detention until 1976 had been justified on the basis of the medical evidence. The Court then found violation of Art. 5(iv) as regards his recall and subsequent detention. It noted that a person confined in a mental institution for an indefinite period was entitled, at any rate where there is no automatic periodic review of a judicial nature, to take proceedings at reasonable intervals before a court to test the lawfulness of his detention. Habeas corpus and Mental Health Tribunal proceedings were inadequate. The Court did not find it necessary also to decide on his complaint under Art. 5(ii).

In October 1982, the Court noted the parties' agreement on costs (£7000 less about £2000 received in legal aid) of Strasbourg proceedings. It also held that H.M.G. should pay the applicant's estate (he had died in 1979) £324 in respect-of certain legal costs in the U.K. The Court also noted new draft legislation (which became the Mental Health Act 1983) specifically introduced by H.M.G. to allow a restricted patient to apply to, and in appropriate cases to be discharged by, a Mental Health Tribunal.

CORPORAL PUNISHMENT

The Tyrer case

An applicant in 1972 (*Tyrer v U.K.* No. 5856/72) was an 18-year-old youth from the Isle of Man who complained of his punishment of birching ordered by a Juvenile Court, confirmed on appeal by the Manx Court of Criminal Appeal under the Summary Jurisdiction Act 1960 (Isle of Man) which allows such punishment for young males.

His main allegations were under Art. 3 (forbidding torture, inhuman or degrading treatment) and under Art. 14 (discrimination) on the ground that such punishment was primarily pronounced on persons from financially and socially deprived homes. In January 1976 the Commission was notified that the applicant wished to withdraw his case, but it did not accept his request 'since the case raised questions of a general character affecting the observance of the Convention which necessitated a further examination of the issues involved'. In its Report (Art. 31) in December 1976, the Commission found that his punishment by birching was degrading (Art. 3), but it did not pursue the Art. 14 issue. The Court in its judgment of 25th April 1978 agreed that the punishment was degrading, and it also found it unnecessary to examine the Art. 14 issue. The Court had particularly noted the absence of such penalty in the system of the great majority of Member States.

The Committee of Ministers raised the general issue with the U.K. Government which communicated the Court's judgment to the Isle of Man Government, with the opinion that such punishment must now be held to violate the Convention. The Isle of Man Chief Justice passed this on to all judicial instances concerned. No instances of birching have occurred since, and, indeed, in a later case in the Isle of Man, where the Trial Court passed a birching sentence, the Court of Appeal, considering that the U.K. Government had undertaken to implement the Convention, set aside the sentence which was not mandatory and ordered the lower court to fix an alternative sentence. In 1981, when H.M.G. renewed its recognition of the Art. 25 competence, the Isle of Man was omitted from the list of territories (Art. 63) to which the Convention applied.

Campbell and Cosans

Complaints were brought in 1976 by *Mrs. Campbell* and *Mrs. Cosans* (Nos. 7511/76 and 7743/76 v U.K.) as to the existence of corporal punishment as a disciplinary measure in Scottish schools. Mrs. Campbell's nine-year-old son had never been so punished, but the authorities refused to guarantee that he would not be. Mrs. Cosans fifteen-year-old son had been reported for corporal punishment, but had refused to accept it and had been suspended from school. The applicants submitted that the refusal to exempt their children from corporal punishment violated their right as parents to ensure that the education and teaching received by their children was in conformity with their religious and philosophical convictions. (Prot. No. 1, Art. 2).

The Commission in its Report in May 1980 found that the use of corporal punishment in schools was a function assumed by the State in relation to education, and that the failure to respect the applicants' philosophical convictions in this respect violated Art. 2 of Prot. No. 1. The Court in its judgment in February 1982 first dealt with the question under Art. 3 which protects a person from inhuman or degrading treatment. In this respect the Court found a) that the threat of conduct in violation of Art. 3 might, if sufficiently real and immediate, itself violate Art. 3, but there was here no such violation as pupils were not humilated or debased; b) that Prot. No. 1 Art. 2 had been violated as discipline was an integral part of an education system. The Court ordered H.M.G. to pay contributions to both complainants' legal fees (£850 to A; £8,500 to B; and damages to B and B's son £3000).

In October 1984 it was announced in the press that a law would be passed in the next parliamentary session having regard to the Court's judgment in this case, and that this law would allow parents to exempt their children from all forms of corporal punishment at school as already was allowed in religious education. In January 1985 the Bill was published which became law in 1985 under which provision is made for parents who favour corporal punishment for their children to have their names placed on a special school register. At the same time the Government announced that this Bill would enable the U.K. to comply with the ruling from the European Court in this case.

Private Life

Dudgeon

In 1976, an applicant, *Mr. Dudgeon* (No. 7625/76 v U.K.), living in Belfast, claimed that being a homosexual, the Northern Ireland laws prohibiting homosexual activities between consenting male adults were an unjustified interference with his right to respect for his private life (Art. 8). He also made the same complaint in that there had been a police investigation under the Misuse of Drugs Act 1971 in January 1976 at his address. Papers had been seized and he had been questioned for several hours at the police station on his sexual life. In February 1977 he was informed that he would not be prosecuted for gross indecency and his papers were returned to him. He also claimed unjustifiable discrimination (Art. 14) in that he was subject to greater restrictions than (a) female homosexuals, (b) male homosexuals in England and Wales, where such acts between males over 21 were not criminal.

The Commission in its Report (Art. 31) of 13th March 1980 found that the applicant's private life (Art. 8) had been violated even though he had not been prosecuted. It then found that a legal prohibition of such acts involving (a) males under 21 did not violate Art. 8(2), as it was for the 'protection of rights of others', (b) males over 21 did violate Art. 8. The Commission did not find it necessary to consider the question of discrimination (Art. 14). The Court, in a long judgment of 22nd October 1981, found that maintenance of this legislation which had the effect of criminalising homosexual relations in private between consenting adult males was a continued interference with Mr. Dudgeon's private life (Art. 8) and, considering the permitted limitations (Art. 8, para (2)), it decided that such interference was not 'necessary in a democratic society' as there was no 'pressing social need' in Northern Ireland. In particular, there was no evidence of injury to moral standards in Northern Ireland or of public demand for stricter enforcement of the laws concerned. The Court also noted that in the majority of Member States it was not considered appropriate or necessary to apply to homosexual practices the sanctions of criminal law. The Court, like the Commission, found it unnecessary to consider the question of discrimination (Art. 14). The Court in a later judgment of 24th February 1983 awarded the applicant £3,315 costs, but no damages. In 1982, an Order in Council brought Northern Ireland laws into line with U.K. laws in this respect, as had also in the meanwhile been done for Scotland.

Mark Rees

Mark Rees v U.K. (No. 9532/81), a transsexual, complained before the Commission in April 1974 that the refusal of the U.K. authorities to change his birth register and thereby to recognise his change of sex from female to male violates his right to respect for his private life (Art. 8); he also alleged a violation of his right to marry (Art. 12) as it was impossible under U.K. law for him to enter into a valid contract of marriage with a woman. The Commission declared the application admissible in March 1984, and in its Report of December 1984 it expressed the unanimous opinion that there had been a violation of Art. 8 but not of Art. 12. The case was referred to the Court in March 1985.

The Court in its judgment of 17th October 1986 found that there had been no violation of the Convention. As regards Art. 8, the Court considered the obligations inherent in an effective respect for private life. It noted that there was little common ground between the legal situations in the different Contracting States, and that these obligations depended on the 'fair balance' between the general interest of the community and the interests of the individual. In this case the Government had tried to meet the applicant's demands as far as possible under its existing system, in which the birth certificate is a record of historical fact and there is no provision for legally valid civil status certificates. The striking of a 'fair balance' could not therefore require the introduction of a new type of documentation showing proof of current civil status. This had not hitherto been considered necessary in the U.K.; it would have important administrative consequences and would impose new duties on the rest of the population. For example, it would complicate factual issues arising in family and succession law which would necessitate detailed legislation. However, the Court added that 'for the time being it must be left to the respondent State to determine to what extent it can meet the remaining demands of transsexuals ... The Convention has always to be interpreted and applied in the light of current circumstances ... The need for appropriate legal measures should therefore be kept under review having regard particularly to scientific and societal developments.'

As regards Art. 12, the right to marry refers to traditional marriage between persons of opposite biological sex. The legal impediments in the U.K. on marriage of persons who are not of the opposite sex cannot be said to restrict or reduce the right to marry to an extent that its very existence is impaired.

Malone

An applicant, *Mr. Malone* (No. 8691/79 v U.K.), had been charged in 1977 with offences concerning the alleged dishonest handling of stolen goods. In May 1979 he was acquitted after two trials in each of which the jury failed to agree. The applicant believed that since 1971 he had been kept under police surveillance and alleged that his correspondence was intercepted and his telephone lines tapped. During the first trial it was accepted by the Crown that one telephone conversation had been intercepted. At the second trial the Government confirmed this, but did not disclose whether other telephone conversations or the applicant's correspondence were intercepted. Nor did they disclose whether the applicant's own telephone number had at any time been tapped.

After his first trial, the applicant instituted proceedings against the Metropolitan Police Commissioner seeking to challenge the legality of telephone tapping. He sought declarations to the effect that the interception, monitoring or recording of conversations on his telephone line was unlawful, even if done pursuant to a warrant issued by the Home Secretary, and contrary to the Convention (Art. 8). His action was dismissed by the Vice-Chancellor on 28th February 1979. He held that telephone tapping effected from wires which are not on the telephone subscriber's premises was not unlawful and that he had no jurisdiction to make a declaration that it infringed the Convention, since the Convention did not have force of law in England. [*RB NOTE: For an extract from the judgment, see Doc. 25.*]

Before the Commission, the applicant complained of the interception of his own communications and of the relevant law and practice which exposed him to a risk of secret surveillance. He maintained that as a result of these matters he was the victim of interference with his right to private life and correspondence (Art. 8). Although Art. 8(2) permitted interference with these rights under certain conditions, the applicant maintained that they were not 'in accordance with the law' or 'necessary in a democratic society' since the restrictions on telephone tapping and mail interception were purely administrative and there were no adequate legal safeguards or effective remedies (Art. 13) to protect the individual against abuse.

In December 1982, the Commission adopted its Report finding:

> (a) violations of Art. 8 by the admitted interception of his telephone conversation and by the law and practice governing the inter-

ception of postal and telephone communications on behalf of police;

(b) it was unnecessary to decide if 'metering' was a violation;

(c) violation of Art. 13 as U.K. law gave no effective remedy.

In a long judgment of 2nd August 1984 the Court first agreed with the Commission that the existence of laws and practices which permit a system for effecting secret surveillance of communications amounted in itself to an 'interference with the exercise' of the applicant's rights under Art. 8. The Court then considered whether the interferences were justified under para (2) or Art. 8. As to the question whether they were 'in accordance with the law' the Court first considered whether the 'essential elements of this power to intercept were laid down with reasonable precision in accessible legal rules'. It found that there was no reasonable clarity or scope of relevant discretion of public authorities and the interceptions were therefore not 'in accordance with the law'. As to the question whether the interceptions were 'necessary in a democratic society', the Court considered that there was a danger of abuse but found it unnecessary to decide.

It was announced at the opening of Parliament on 6th November 1984 that a Bill would establish 'a new and comprehensive statutory framework governing the interception of communications'. A White Paper giving details of the Bill was published in February 1985.

FAMILY LIFE

O, H, W, B and R

Five cases (*O (9276/81), H (9580/81), W (9749/82), B (9840/82) and R (10496/83) v U.K.*) were brought by applicants complaining that the procedures followed by a local authority in reaching certain decisions regarding the applicants' children who were in its care had failed to respect the applicants' family life (Art. 8); secondly; that they were unable, while their children were in public care, to have the question of their access to them determined by a tribunal in accordance with Art. 6(1); thirdly, that the length of the proceedings dealing with access to the children in care and with the adoption of certain children had exceeded a 'reasonable time' (Art. 6(1)) and given rise to a failure to respect the applicants' family life (Art. 8).

The cases had been lodged with the Commission on various dates between 1980 and 1983 and declared admissible on various dates in 1983 and 1984. The Commission, having declared the cases admissible, found in its reports adopted in October or December 1985 that there had been breaches of Art. 6(1) in all five cases, and of Art. 8 in the cases of H, W, B, and R, but not in the case of O. The Commission referred the cases to the Court in January 1986.

The Court in its judgment of 8th July 1987 first stated that it was not, in the circumstances, competent to examine or comment on the justification for such matters as the taking into public care or the adoption of the children concerned or the restriction or termination of the applicants' access to them.

This issue had either not been raised before the Commission or had been declared inadmissible by it.

The Court then considered the issues under Art. 8 and first dealt with the cases *of W, B and R.* It held that the process had to be such as to secure that the views and interests of the natural parents were made known to, and duly taken into account by, the authority and that they were able to exercise in due time any remedies available to them. Having regard to the particular circumstances of the case, had the parents been involved in the decision-making process to a degree sufficient to provide them with the requisite protection of their interests? If not, there would have been a failure of respect for their family life, and the interference resulting from the decision would not be capable of being regarded as 'necessary' within the meaning of Art. 8.

The Court held in each case a violation of Art. 8, since the applicant had been insufficiently involved in the local authority's decision-making process, for example, by being consulted in advance about the decision or by being informed of it promptly. The Court also took account, in the W and R cases, of the length of certain related court proceedings and, in the B case, of the interruption of the applicant's access to her child resulting from the social workers' strike. In the case of 0, the applicant also alleged a breach of Art. 8 on account of the procedures followed by the local authorities in reaching its decision to terminate his access to his five children. The Court did not consider that the material before it was sufficient to find a violation and it rejected this claim. In the case of H, the Court, having found a breach of Art. 6(1) because of the delays in the proceedings complained of, also found a breach of Art. 8: the question of her future relations with the child should be determined solely in the light of all relevant circumstances and not by the 'mere effluxion of time' but this had not been the case.

The Court then dealt with these applicants' complaints under Art. 6(1) as regards the determination of the proceedings relating to their right of access to their children.

The Court first considered the cases of *O, W, B and R.* It did not accept the Government's argument that no 'right' was in issue as, even after the making of the care orders, it could be said that the applicants could claim a right in regard to their access to the children. The Court also did not accept the Government's alternative plea that the applicants would have had a protection of that right to satisfy Art. 6(1). Their challenge before a court of the care orders or parental rights resolutions would not have been directed towards the isolated theme of access. The Court found a violation of Art. 6(1) in these four cases.

As regards the *case of H*, the Court reviewed the various phases of the proceedings, including the degree of complexity of the case, the conduct of the parties and of the courts concerned. In particular, it considered the length of the proceedings which was partly due to the fact that the local authority filed its evidence more than five months after the time-limit. The Court placed special emphasis 'on the importance of what was at stake for the applicant in these proceedings, being decisive for her future relations with her child.' The authorities were under a duty to exercise 'exceptional diligence' and the Court concluded that the proceedings had not been concluded with a 'reasonable time' and there had therefore been a violation of Art. 6 (1).

Applicants *O, W, B and R* alleged violations of Art 13 as no effective remedy before a national authority was available to them as regards access to their children. The Court held that it was not necessary to examine this issue.

On 9th June 1988 the Court awarded O £5000, H £12,000, W £12,000, B £12,000 and £10,500 costs, and R £8000.

Earlier, on 19th July 1982 the Government announced in the House of Lords that the *Children and Young Persons Act 1969* would be amended by the Criminal Justice Bill in order to change regulations on placing children in care so as to avoid a risk of violation of the decision of the Strasbourg Court. Further modifications were also later effected by the Children Act 1989.

IMMIGRATION

Mohamed Khan

The first case (No. 2991/66 v U.K.) was that in 1966 of a Pakistani, Mohamed Alam, who in July 1966 was returning to the U.K. with his 13-year-old son, Mohamed Khan. The father was allowed to enter but the son was refused entry by the immigration authorities at London Airport under the 1962 Commonwealth Immigrants Act. They alleged right of family life (Art. 8) and to a fair hearing by an independent tribunal to determine their civil rights (Art. 6(1)).

In 1967 the case was declared admissible by the Commission and in December 1969 it was settled. H.M.G. agreed to make an ex gratia payment of the cost of an air ticket for Khan from Pakistan to London as they had agreed in March 1969 to grant him an entry certificate, and the applicants withdrew their case. The Commission also noted Government information that the 'Immigrants Appeals Bill 1968' and the draft 'Aliens (Appeal) Order', which would give aliens the right of appeal, had been introduced into Parliament in November 1968. These provisions were re-enacted in the Immigration Act 1971.

Abdulaziz

Three cases in 1980/81 concern three women from Malawi, Philippines and Egypt who are now lawfully settled in the U.K., and the last is a citizen of the U.K. (*Abdulaziz, Cabales and Balkandali v U.K.* Nos. 9214/83, 9473/81, 9474/81). Their husbands, respectively Portuguese, Philippine and Turkish, were refused permission to enter or remain in the U.K. following the immigration rules then in force. The applicants complain that they were victims of sex and race discrimination (Art. 14) in connection with their right to family life (Art. 8) because men lawfully resident in the U.K., whether or not of British nationality with the territorial birth link, would be entitled to be joined by their foreign wives.

The Commission in its Report of May 1983 found sexual, but not racial, discrimination affecting their right to family life (Art. 8), and also, in the last case, a discrimination on the ground of birth; in all cases there was a violation of the right to an effective domestic remedy (Art. 13) but in no case a discrimination amounting to degrading treatment. The Commission referred the case to the Court on 14th October 1983.

The Court, having heard the parties on 25th September 1984, held in its judgment of 28th May 1985 that the authorities' refusal, under the immigration rules, to permit the three husbands to remain with, or to join, the applicants in the U.K. did not violate Art. 8 (family life) or Art. 3 (degrading treatment). However, the Court held a breach of Art. 14 (discrimination) together with Art. 8 on the ground of sex, as under the rules wives could be accepted for settlement in the U.K. more easily than husbands. The Court held no other breach of Art. 14 together with Art. 8 on the ground either of race or (in the case of Mrs. Balkandali) of birth. The Court also found a violation of Art. 13 (right to effective remedy before national authorities) as regards the complaints of discrimination on the ground of sex.

Under Art. 50 (claim to just satisfaction) the Court did not accept the applicants' claim for 'substantial' compensation for non-pecuniary damage, although they had suffered 'distress and anxiety'. The Court considered that its findings of violation themselves constituted 'sufficient just satisfaction'. The Court, however, ordered the Government to pay the applicants the amounts claimed by them for their expenses in relation to the proceedings before the Commission and Court.

The Immigration Rules have been changed to the effect that, as from 1st January 1983 and regardless of their place of birth, husbands married to U.K. citizens would be eligible for entry into the U.K. Similarly, a foreign wife, wishing to join or remain with her husband living lawfully in the U.K., will obtain leave to do so whether or not he is a British citizen.

FREEDOM OF EXPRESSION

Evans

In January 1974, *Mr. Harold Evans* (No. 6538/74 v U.K.), acting both personally and as editor of the *Sunday Times* and the *Times* newspapers, brought complaints as to the violation of their right to impart information (Art. 10). Between 1959 and 1969 a number of children were born who were deformed, allegedly by their mothers having taken thalidomide as a tranquilliser during pregnancy.

In September 1972 the *Sunday Times* published an article 'Our Thalidomide Children: a Cause for National Shame', and announced that it would publish a long article tracing the history of the tragedy. In October 1972 Distillers Company (Biochemicals) Ltd. (the maker and seller of thalidomide in the U.K.) made representations to the Attorney General claiming that this article constituted contempt of court in view of the outstanding litigation between parents of affected children and the company. An injunction was granted by the High Court restraining publication in November

1972. On appeal by Times Newspapers Ltd. the Court's order was reversed by the Court of Appeal, but, on the Attorney General's further appeal to the House of Lords, the Law Lords in July 1973 unanimously confirmed the order finding that the proposed article sought to interfere with pending court proceedings including settlement negotiations, and therefore constituted contempt of court.

The Commission in its Report (Art. 31) found that the restriction on the applicants' freedom of expression violated Art. 10 as regards the applicants' right 'to impart information' and 'to impart ideas'. As regards the question of the justification of this restriction (Art. 10(2), the Commission all found that the restriction was 'prescribed by law' but the majority found that it was not 'necessary in a democratic society' as only the most pressing grounds could be sufficient to justify the authorities stopping information on such matters whose clarification seemed to be in the public interest. In April 1979 the Court found violation of Art. 10 and, in great detail, found no justification (para 2) as the restriction was not necessary in a democratic society for maintaining the authority of the judiciary.

In November 1980, the Court delivered judgment on the award of 'just satisfaction' (Art. 50) and ruled that the Government should pay the applicants, £22,626.78 for their Strasbourg costs. The Contempt of Court Act 1981 was subsequently enacted to bring UK has into line with the Strasbourg ruling.

Harman

In *Harman v U.K.* (No. 10038/82), the applicant, Ms. H. Harman M.P, when legal officer of the National Council of Civil Liberties, was representing a prisoner in a civil action against the Home Office for false imprisonment in a special control unit. During the proceedings, discovery of certain documents had been granted under court order on condition that they would only be used for N.C.C.L. purposes.

At the beginning of the 22-day hearing in February 1980, the applicant read out the material part of 800 pages of the documents disclosed by the Home Office, and afterwards allowed Mr. David Leigh, a journalist working with the *Guardian* newspaper, to see in her office documents already read out in court. Mr. Leigh then wrote an article in the *Guardian* in April 1980, commenting on the control units concerned. In November 1980, following an application by the Home Office, the Divisional Court ruled that she had acted in contempt of court, although in good faith. Her appeal to the Court of Appeal was dismissed with costs in February 1981 and a further appeal to the House of Lords was dismissed with costs in February 1982 when a majority held that the good administration of justice required that the implied obligation of confidentiality continued, notwithstanding the use of the documents in the course of a trial open to the public.

Ms. Harman complained to the Commission of a breach of her freedom of expression and her freedom to report information (Art. 10). The case was admitted in May 1984 and the Commission then put itself at the disposal of the parties with a view to securing a friendly settlement (Art. 28(b)). After an exchange of written proposals, the Secretary met each of the parties separately in June 1985, and in November 1985, the Agent of the U.K. Government informed the Commission that the Government 'were prepared to undertake to seek to change the law so that it will no longer be a contempt of court to make public material contained in documents compulsorily disclosed in civil proceedings, once those documents have been read out in open court'. The implied undertaking given by the person to whom such disclosure has been made not to use the document except in the proper conduct of his case should not prevent him making that document known to any person. This change would not apply where the court had ordered prevention of disclosure otherwise than to the parties in the case.

The applicant's lawyer indicated in a letter in April 1986 that the applicant accepted this offer subject to an agreement on costs. In May 1986, the Government's Agent stated that the Government had agreed to pay the applicant £36,320 in respect of legal costs and expenses. This offer was accepted by the applicant and the Commission approved the settlement and adopted its Report (Art. 26(4)) in May 1986.

Freedom of Association

Young, James and Webster

Three British Rail employees, Messrs. *Young, James and Webster v U.K.* (Nos. 7611/76, 7806/77) were dismissed in 1976 for refusing to join one of the three trade unions specified in a 'closed shop' agreement concluded in 1975 between British Rail and those unions. Membership of one of those unions thereby became a condition of employment. The applicants alleged violations of their rights to freedom of thought (Art. 9), freedom of expression (Art. 10) and, more importantly, freedom to form and to join trade unions (Art. 11). They also alleged violations of their right to an effective domestic remedy (Art. 13). Their respective claims for reinstatement were rejected by various appeal bodies acting under the Trade Union and Labour Relations Act 1974.

The Commission in its Report (Art. 31) of December 1979 found violations of Art. 11 only. The Court, to whom the cases had been referred in May 1980, heard the parties, including T.U.C. intervention, in March 1981 and gave its judgment on 13th August 1981. The Court first stated that it did not have to review the closed shop system as such, but only its effects on the applicants. The Court then found under Art. 11 that, even if there was in the Convention no general rule against compulsory membership of a trades union, it did not follow that every such compulsion was compatible with Art. 11. The threat of dismissal was a most serious form of compulsion and had been directed against employees engaged *before* the introduction of any obligation to join a particular union. This was interference with the freedom under Art. 11. Since the applicants would anyway have been dismissed, the fact that they might have formed or joined an additional union of their choice did not alter the compulsion. The rights under Art. 9 and Art. 10 were also one purpose of freedom of association and thus were further violations of Art. 11. As regards the permitted limitations under para 2 of Art. 11 (not argued by Government), the Court considered what was 'necessary in a democratic society ... for the protection of the rights and freedom of others'. In fact, many closed shop systems did not require existing non-union members to join a specified union and statistics showed that the majority of union members were against such compulsion. In 1975 more than 95% of B.R. employees belonged to one of the specified unions. The Court found that the unions would therefore not have been prevented from striving for the protection of their members' interests even if legislation had not permitted such compulsory membership. The detriment so suffered by the applicants went further than was required to achieve a proper balance between the conflicting interests of those involved, and could not be regarded as proportionate to the aims pursued.

The Court announced on 18th October 1982 that the Government would pay the applicants £146,000 of which £65,000 was for legal costs and the rest for compensation of different sums to each applicant. The Committee of Ministers in March 1983 (Art. 54) noted that H.M.G. had complied with the judgment of the Court of October 1982 and also noted the subsequent information by H.M.G. that the Employment Act 1982, re-enacting and strengthening the provisions of the 1980 Employment Act, provided that dismissal from employment in such circumstances was to be regarded as unfair dismissal and any employees so dismissed would be entitled to a legal remedy. The Act also set up a £2 million compensation fund.

Conroy

In *Conroy v U.K.* (No. 10061/82), the applicant was an Irish citizen, born in 1922, and lived in Manchester. In 1979 he was dismissed from his post as a printer's assistant by his employees, Cunliffe Engravers at Walkden, a firm which since 1970 had operated a 'closed shop' agreement with SOGAT (Society of Graphical and Allied Trades). His dismissal was the consequence of the applicant's expulsion from his trade union. He had been an active member of SOGAT for 35 years and was, in 1976, chairman of the SOGAT Chapel in Cunliffe's. He subsequently became involved in a dispute with SOGAT and distributed pamphlets alleging financial irregularities and breaches of union rules by branch officers of the union.

He was then summoned to appear before the union's National Executive Council. The hearing of the Council took place in the applicant's absence on 14th March 1979. He was charged and found guilty of breaching union rules by distributing pamphlets and thus acting to the detriment of the union. He was then expelled from the union. An appeal to the Independent Review Committee of the T.U.C. against this decision was unsuccessful.

As a consequence of his expulsion from the union he was dismissed by his employees on 20th April 1979. The applicant then brought an action for unfair dismissal before an Industrial Tribunal in Manchester. However, the Tribunal found that the applicant was in fundamental breach of his contract of employment which required union membership, and his dismissal had to be regarded as fair under the applicable legal provisions. In July 1980 he was refused legal aid by the Law Society for the purpose of an appeal to the Employment Appeal Tribunal.

The applicant was subsequently granted legal aid to bring proceedings against SOGAT before the High Court. In his action, initiated on 22nd May 1981, the applicant claimed that the procedure leading to his expulsion was in breach of the rules of natural justice. He sought his reinstatement as a member of the union, damages, interest and costs. Legal aid was subsequently withdrawn by the Law Society on 31st January 1984 after receipt of counsel's opinion that the applicant's action was unlikely to succeed.

The applicant decided to continue with the action and to represent himself in the proceedings. The action was dismissed by the Manchester High Court following a hearing from 21st–25th January 1985. An appeal against this decision to the Court of Appeal was dismissed sometime in November 1985.

In his application to the Commission in March 1981, the applicant complained that as a consequence of his dismissal from SOGAT he had been deprived of his job and livelihood. In December 1983 the Commission decided to communicate the application to the Government for observations on its admissibility and merits insofar as it raised issues under inter alia Arts. 10 (freedom of expression) and 11 (freedom of association) of the Convention. The Commission subsequently declared the application admissible in a decision in July 1985.

The Commission then placed itself at the disposal of the parties with a view to securing a friendly settlement (Art. 28(b)). In a letter dated 3rd March 1986, the Government offered compensation of £37,600 for loss of earnings and £550 for non-pecuniary losses (anxiety and stress). A full narrative of legal costs was requested from the applicant's legal representative. The applicant's legal representative accepted the offer in respect of loss of earnings and non-pecuniary loss in a letter dated 11th April 1986 and provided the information requested as regards legal costs. In a letter dated 9th May 1986 the Agent of the Government stated that, as regards legal costs, the sum of £1,518 (including V.A.T.) had been agreed with the applicant's solicitor as the amount to be paid for all the legal costs incurred by the applicant. The applicant's representative stated in a letter of 12th May 1986 that agreement had thereby been reached. On 15th May 1986 the Commission found that a friendly settlement had been reached and adopted its Report (Art. 28(b)).

PROPERTY

Gillow

The complainants *Mr. and Mrs. Gillow* (No. 9063/80) are U.K. citizens who moved to Guernsey in 1956 where they built a house. They originally had the necessary residence qualifications which they lost under the new 1970 law. In 1960 they had left Guernsey to work abroad and did not know of the 1970 law until they returned in 1978. Their requests for residence licences were refused by Guernsey Housing Authority in 1979. They alleged violations of the right to respect for their home (Art. 8) and their property (Prot. No. 1, Art. 1).

The Commission's Report (Art. 31) of 11th October 1984 found violations of both articles, and was referred to the Court. The Court, in its judgment of 24th November 1986, unanimously held that there had been a breach of Art. 8 as far as the application of the contested legislation was concerned, but not as regards the legislation itself; also that there had been no breach of Arts. 6 and 14, and finally that Protocol No. 1 was not applicable in this case. The Court on 14th September 1987 unanimously held that the respondent Government was to pay Mr. Gillow £10,735 as damages and £2,134 for costs and expenses.

Baggs

In *Baggs v. U.K.* (9310/81), the applicant and his family lived about $\frac{1}{4}$ mile from Heathrow's southern runway at the western side of the airport. He owned the freehold of the property which was used as the family residence and for his business of market gardening and poultry keeping. The applicant first leased the property in 1943. He purchased the freehold in 1945 and built a bungalow on it in 1950. The property is overflown by aircraft half of the day and also at night. The applicant claimed that the aircraft noise levels varied from 83 to 127 decibels, and that certain measures e.g. double glazing insulation had not resolved the problem described in various expert reports as 'appalling' and 'intolerable'. Heathrow Airport had been vastly expanded since the applicant's family moved to the district. He was refused planning permission to sell his property for commercial uses and thus obtain a reasonable price to enable him to buy a similar property elsewhere.

The applicant complained to the Commission of noise and vibration nuisances amounting to a violation of his right to respect for his family life and home (Art. 8) and of his property rights (Prot. No. 1, Art. 1). He also complained of a denial of access to court in the determination of his civil rights (Art. 6) and of an absence of effective domestic remedies (Art. 13). The application was introduced on 31st December 1980, registered on 23rd March 1981, and after a hearing of the parties in October 1985, declared admissible.

The Commission then placed itself at the disposal of the parties with a view to securing a friendly settlement (Art. 28(b)). The Government informed the Commission in September 1986 of relevant legislation and administrative changes in the Airports Act 1986 providing for the dissolution of the British Airports Authority and the transfer of its property, rights and liabilities to a public limited company, Heathrow Airport Limited, with sufficient powers to buy 'noise-blighted' property like that of the applicant. A Scheme was drawn up providing for the purchase of certain properties, including the applicant's, and for the settlement of the price by independent arbitration failing agreement between the parties. This Scheme came into force on 1st July 1987.

The applicant also claimed compensation and costs. In June 1987 the Government wrote to the Commission recalling the above Scheme and stating that a formal offer had been made by Heathrow Airport Ltd. to the applicant. The Government then said they were prepared to make an ex gratia payment to the applicant of £24,000 to include costs in order to achieve a settlement. The applicant then informed the Commission that he accepted this payment in 'full and final satisfaction of his claim.' The Commission approved this settlement on 8th July 1987.

Extract from report prepared by A.B. McNulty and Robert Blackburn, 1986. (For an account of movement cases, see Sue Farran, *The UK Before the European Court of Human Rights*, 1996.)

---

25   THE HIGH COURT REFUSES TO APPLY THE EUROPEAN CONVENTION WHILE RECOGNIZING THAT BRITISH LAW IS IN BREACH OF ITS HUMAN RIGHTS STANDARDS: THE MALONE CASE, 1979

MALONE V. METROPOLITAN POLICE COMMISSIONER [1979] 1 Ch 344

Fifth, there is Mr. Ross-Munro's second main head, based on the European Convention for the Protection of Human Rights and Fundamental Freedoms and the *Klass* case. The first limb of this relates to the direct rights conferred by the Convention. Any such right is, as I have said, a direct right in relation to the European Commission of Human Rights and the European Court of Human Rights, and not in relation to the courts of this country; for the Convention is not law here. Article 1 of the Convention provides that the High Contracting Parties 'shall secure to everyone within their jurisdiction the rights and freedoms defined in Section I of this Convention'; and those rights and freedoms are those which are set out in articles 1 to 18 inclusive. The United Kingdom, as a High Contracting Party which ratified the Convention on March 8, 1951, has thus long been under an obligation to secure these rights and freedoms to everyone. That obligation, however, is an obligation under a treaty which is not justiciable in the courts of this country. Whether that obligation has been carried out is not for me to say. It is, I suppose, possible to contend that the de facto practice in this country sufficiently secures these rights and freedoms, without legislation for the purpose being needed. It is also plainly possible to contend that, among other things, the existing safeguards against unbridled telephone tapping, being merely administrative in nature and not imposed by law, fall far short of making any rights and freedoms 'secure' to anyone. However, as I have said, that is not for me to decide. All that I do is to hold that the Convention does not, as a matter of English law, confer any direct rights on the plaintiff that he can enforce in the English courts.

Sixth, there is the second limb of Mr. Ross-Munro's contentions, based on the Convention and the *Klass* case as assisting the court to determine what English law is on a point on which authority is lacking or uncertain. Can it be said that in this case two courses are reasonably open to the court, one of which is inconsistent with the Convention and the other consonant with it? I refer, of course, to the words of Scarman L.J. in the *Pan-American* case [1976] 1 Lloyd's Rep. 257 that I have already quoted. I readily accept that if the question before me were one of construing a statute enacted with the purpose of giving effect to obligations imposed by the Convention, the court would readily seek to construe the legislation in a way that would effectuate the Convention rather than frustrate it. However, no relevant legislation of that sort is in existence. It seems to me that where Parliament has abstained from legislating on a point that is plainly suitable for legislation, it is indeed difficult for the court to lay down new rules of common law or equity that will carry out the Crown's treaty obligations, or to discover for the first time that such rules have always existed.

Now the West German system that came under scrutiny in the *Klass* case was laid down by statute, and it contained a number of statutory safeguards. There must be imminent danger: other methods of surveillance must be at least considerably more difficult; both the person making the request for surveillance and the method of making it are limited; the period of surveillance is limited in time, and in any case must cease when the need has passed; the person subjected to surveillance must be notified as soon as this will not jeopardise the purpose of surveillance; no information is made available to the police unless an official qualified for judicial office is satisfied that it is within the safeguards; all other information obtained must be destroyed; the process is supervised by a Parliamentary board on which the opposition is represented; and there is also a supervising commission which may order that surveillance is to cease, or that notification of it is to be given to the person who has been subjected to it. Not a single one of these safeguards is to be found as a matter of established law in England, and only a few corresponding provisions exist as a matter of administrative procedure.

It does not, of course, follow that a system with fewer or different safeguards will fail to satisfy article 8 in the eyes of the European Court of Human Rights. At the same time, it is impossible to read the judgment in the *Klass* case without its becoming abundantly clear that a system which has no legal safeguards whatever has small chance of satisfying the requirements of that court, whatever administrative provisions there may be. Broadly, the court was concerned to see whether the German legislation provided 'adequate and effective safeguards against abuse.' Though in principle it was desirable that there should be judicial control of tapping, the court was satisfied that the German system provided an adequate substitute in the independence of the board and Commission from the authorities carrying out the surveillance. Further, the provisions for the subsequent notification of the surveillance when this would not frustrate its purpose were also considered to be adequate. In England, on the other hand, the system in operation provides no such independence, and contains no provision what- ever for subsequent notification. Even if the system were to be considered adequate in its conditions, it is laid down merely as a matter of admin- istrative procedure, so that it is unenforceable in law, and as a matter of law could at any time be altered without warning or subsequent notification. Certainly in law any 'adequate and effective safeguards against abuse' are wanting. In this respect English law compares most unfavourably with West German law: this is not a subject on which it is possible to feel any pride in English law.

I therefore find it impossible to see how English law could be said to satisfy the requirements of the Convention, as interpreted in the *Klass* case, unless that law not only prohibited all telephone tapping save in suitably limited classes of case, but also laid down detailed restrictions on the exercise of the power in those limited classes. It may perhaps be that the common law is sufficiently fertile to achieve what is required by the first limb of this; possible ways of expressing such a rule may be seen in what I have already said. But I see the greatest difficulty in the common law framing the safeguards required by the second limb. Various institutions or offices would have to be brought into being to exercise various defined functions. The more complex and indefinite the subject matter, the greater the difficulty in the court doing what it is really appropriate, and only appropriate, for the legislature to do. Furthermore, I find it hard to see what there is in the present case to require the English courts to struggle with such a problem. Give full rein to the Convention, and it is clear that when the object of the surveillance is the detection of crime, the question is not whether there ought to be a general prohibition of all surveillance, but in what circumstances, and subject to what conditions and restrictions, it ought to be permitted. It is those circumstances, conditions and restrictions which are at the centre of this case; and yet it is they which are the least suitable for determination by judicial decision.

It appears to me that to decide this case in the way that Mr. Ross-Munro seeks would carry me far beyond any possible function of the Convention as influencing English law that has ever been suggested; and it would be most undesirable. Any regulation of so complex a matter as telephone tapping is essentially a matter for Parliament, not the courts; and neither the Convention nor the *Klass* case can, I think, play any proper part in deciding the issue before me. Accordingly, the second limb of Mr. Ross-Munro's second main contention also fails.

I would only add that, even if it was not clear before, this case seems to me to make it plain that telephone tapping is a subject which cries out for legislation. Privacy and confidentiality are, of course, subjects of considerable complexity. Yet however desirable it may be that they should at least to some extent be defined and regulated by statute, rather than being left for slow and expensive evolution in individual cases brought at the expense of litigants and the legal aid fund, the difficulty of the subject matter is liable to discourage legislative zeal. Telephone tapping lies in a much narrower compass; the difficulties in legislating on the subject ought not to prove insuperable; and the requirements of the Convention should provide a spur to action, even if belated. This, however, is not for me to decide. I can do no more than express a hope, and offer a proleptic welcome to any statute on the subject. However much the protection of the public against crime demands that in proper cases the police should have the assistance of telephone tapping, I would have thought that in any civilised system of law the claims of liberty and justice would require that telephone users should have effective and independent safeguards against possible abuses. The fact that a telephone user is suspected of crime increases rather than diminishes this requirement: suspicions, however reasonably held, may sometimes prove to be wholly unfounded. If there were effective and independent safeguards, these would not only exclude some cases of excessive zeal but also, by their mere existence, provide some degree of reassurance for those who are resentful of the police or believe themselves to be persecuted. I may perhaps add that it would be wrong to allow my decision in this case to be influenced by the consideration that if the courts were to hold that all telephone tapping was illegal, this might well offer a strong and prompt inducement to the government to persuade Parliament to legislate on the subject.

Per Sir Robert Megarry V.-C., pp. 378–81.

> ## 26   THE BRITISH GOVERNMENT'S STRASBOURG-PROOFING ARRANGEMENTS IN ITS PREPARATION OF LEGISLATION, 1987

REDUCING THE RISK OF LEGAL CHALLENGE

Decisions by the Government have increasingly come under challenge in the domestic courts, mostly by way of application for judicial review. Similar challenges have also frequently been brought before the European Commission and Court of Human Rights. In order to minimise the risk of successful challenge the following guidance has been issued by the Cabinet Office.

(I) CHALLENGES IN THE UK COURTS

Consultation

1. A ground for judicial review to which the judges appear to be paying particular attention is the lack, or alleged inadequacy, of consultation with those affected by the decision. The risk of challenge on this ground therefore needs to be carefully borne in mind when formulating policy. This does not mean that consultation should always precede a controversial decision; there are bound to be circumstances where consultation is not possible or desirable if a decision is to be implemented quickly and effectively. In deciding whether to consult, departments should consider whether consultation is required by legislation and, if it is not, whether it has been undertaken in the past or whether there is a legitimate expectation of it. In deciding to proceed without full consultation, Ministers need to have had

drawn to their attention any heightened risk of legal challenge that may result.

Preparation of legislation

2. The risk of challenge to administrative action can be reduced if the legislation governing that action is expressed in the clearest possible language, even at the cost of drafting in terms that are presentationally or politically unattractive. The courts are reluctant to go against something which is clearly the express wish of Parliament, and making decisions subject to Parliamentary procedure may therefore be an important safeguard. They will also be influenced in their decisions by such factors as the provision in legislation of avenues of appeal for those affected. Again, there are no hard and fast rules in these areas; but the possibility of reducing the risks of challenge in these ways is a factor which Ministers will need to weigh when making decisions on the shape of legislation, and departments should ensure that it is drawn to their attention.

3. Proposals for legislation should be scrutinised for likely subjects of challenge. Since the source of challenge to legislative provisions often lies in opposition to the provision on policy grounds, prompting a minute examination of the drafting of the legislation, the lead in departmental scrutiny of draft Bills must come from Ministers and their policy advisers. It is for them to alert their legal advisers and Parliamentary Counsel to those aspects of the policy which are liable to be principally opposed, so that the draftsman can focus on the likely areas of technical challenge. In case of difficulty legal advisers should (following the usual principles concerning the reference of questions to the Law Officers) seek the Law Officers' advice, and should do so as early as possible in the drafting process.

Vetting of draft legislation by outside Counsel

4. Where there is a history of legal challenges being mounted in a particular area, there may be advantage in having draft legislation seen by an outside Counsel expert in that field. A department wishing to follow that course should consult the draftsman and the Law Officers' Department or, in respect of Scotland, the Lord Advocate's Department.

Cabinet documents

5. Memoranda submitted to a Cabinet Committee seeking policy decisions should draw attention to any perceived risks of legal challenge. Memoranda accompanying Bills submitted to Legislation Committee should draw attention to any steps taken to reduce the risk of legal challenge.

(II) THE EUROPEAN CONVENTION ON HUMAN RIGHTS

Introduction

6. The UK has been a party to the European Convention on Human Rights (TS No 71 of 1953, Cmnd. 8969) since 1951, and is also a party to several of

the Protocols to it. Since 1966 the UK has accepted the right of individuals claiming to be victims of a violation of the Convention by the UK to make direct application to the European Commission of Human Rights. The Government is obliged to give effect to judgments of the European Court of Human Rights and decisions of the Committee of Ministers concerning violations by the United Kingdom. Important changes in law and practice have been required as a result. The main rights and freedoms protected concern, briefly: life; torture and inhuman and degrading treatment or punishment; liberty and security (ie freedom from wrongful arrest and detention); fair trial; private and family life; home and correspondence; religion; expression and information; peaceful assembly and association; marriage; property; education; and free elections. Most of the rights permit certain exceptions. There is much case-law of the Commission and Court interpreting the Convention – often on the basis of its purposes rather than literally – and a consistently high level of applications and decisions concern the UK. The Convention has been held to apply in areas where it might not have been initially considered e.g. school corporal punishment and aircraft noise. Questions on it can sometimes arise in most of the areas of law administered by departments.

Preparation of legislation and administrative measures

7. It should be standard practice when preparing a policy initiative for officials in individual departments, in consultation with their legal advisers, to consider the effect of existing (or expected) ECHR jurisprudence on any proposed legislative or administrative measure. Wherever possible, officials should at this stage alert any other departments likely to be affected by the initiative in a similar way. If departments are in any doubt about the likely implications of the Convention in connection with any particular measure, they should seek ad hoc guidance from the Foreign and Commonwealth Office. This request for advice should always be copied to the Law Officers' Department, the Lord Advocate's Department, the Home Office, the Scottish Home and Health Department and the Northern Ireland Office.

Cabinet documents

8. Any memoranda submitted to a Cabinet committee, or accompanying a Bill submitted to Legislation Committee, should include an assessment of the impact, if any, of the European Convention on Human Rights on the action proposed (much as Departments already do for European Community implications).

Settlement of cases

9. Where applications to the ECHR have been referred to the Government and there is a serious risk of an adverse finding by the Commission or Court, departments should give early consideration to the possibility of friendly settlement if this seems likely to offer a less damaging outcome. The Convention expressly provides for settlement to be considered after the

Commissions decision on admissibility, but it is possible at any stage, including during proceedings before the Court. (in the nature of things, however, friendly settlement will not in practice be available where an application has been brought as a test case in order to get a ruling from the Court.) Before a friendly settlement is offered in Strasbourg, the responsible department must ensure that other departments which will be affected by the outcome of the case are given sufficient opportunity to comment.

Existing measures

10. Although it is not intended that departments should conduct a systematic retrospective look at all existing measures, they should nevertheless consider whether action is needed on existing measures where it is clear that there is a serious risk of an adverse finding at Strasbourg which will affect them.

Cabinet Office circular, 1987.

---

27 THE PRESIDENT OF THE EUROPEAN COURT OF HUMAN RIGHTS ON THE ADVANTAGES OF INCORPORATION OF THE EUROPEAN CONVENTION ON HUMAN RIGHTS INTO THE DOMESTIC LAW OF MEMBER STATES, 1990

The aim and purpose of our European system for the protection of human rights can only be to supplement, when necessary, the protection provided in the domestic legal system of each of our States. As the Court has repeatedly observed, ... the machinery set up by the Convention is of a subsidiary nature; in other words it falls in the first place to the national authorities and in particular the national courts to ensure that the rights and freedoms of the individual are protected. It is thus essential that the domestic legal system makes provision for appeals and remedies appropriate to prevent, and if necessary, to redress and compensate the violation of the rights and freedoms guaranteed. Experience has shown that the incorporation of the Convention into domestic law constitutes one of the most effective manners of avoiding being brought before the Strasbourg organs. It has in fact two advantages: it provides the national court with the possibility of taking account of the Convention and the Strasbourg case-law to resolve the dispute before it, and at the same time it gives the European organs an opportunity to discover the views of the national courts regarding the interpretation of the Convention and its application to a specific set of circumstances. The dialogue which thus develops between those who are called upon to apply the Convention on the domestic level and those who must do so on the European level is crucial for an effective protection of the rights guaranteed under the Convention.

For the Convention to be deeply anchored in the domestic legal system of our States is therefore an essential aspect of any reform of the European protection machinery itself. No European system, I am convinced of this, can operate without 'co-operation', if I may put it that way, between the national courts and the European organs.

Judge Rolv Ryssdal, Cour (90) 318.

---

28   A MAJOR MISSED OPPORTUNITY FOR THE LAW LORDS TO GIVE JUDICIAL RECOGNITION TO FUNDAMENTAL RIGHTS: THE *BRIND* CASE, 1991

REGINA V. SECRETARY OF STATE FOR THE HOME DEPARTMENT, EX PARTE BRIND AND OTHERS [1991] 1 A.C. 696

Court of Appeal

There have been a number of cases in which the European Convention for the Protection of Human Rights and Fundamental Freedoms has been introduced into the argument and has accordingly featured in the judgments. In most of them the reference has been fleeting and usually consisted of an assertion, in which I would concur, that you have to look long and hard before you can detect any difference between the English common law and the principles set out in the Convention, at least if the Convention is viewed through English judicial eyes. However, in this case we are invited to grapple with the fundamental question of the effect of the Convention as distinct from any common law to the like effect. Indeed, this was in the forefront of the argument of Mr. Lester appearing for the applicants, and of the counter-argument of Mr. Laws, appearing for the Secretary of State.

The Convention is contained in an international treaty to which the United Kingdom is a party and, by article 1, binds its signatories to 'secure to everyone within their jurisdiction the rights and freedoms defined in Section 1 of this Convention.' The United Kingdom Government can give effect to this treaty obligation in more than one way. It could, for example, 'domesticate' or 'patriate' the Convention itself, as has been done in the case of the treaties mentioned in the European Communities Act 1972, and there are many well-informed supporters of this course. Their view has not, as yet, prevailed. If it had done so, the Convention would have been part of English domestic law. Alternatively, it can review English common and statute law with a view to amending it, if and in so far as it is inconsistent with the Convention, at the same time seeking to ensure that all new statute law is consistent with it. This is the course which has in fact been adopted. Whether it has been wholly successful is a matter for the European Court of Human Rights in Strasbourg and not for the English courts. By contrast, the duty of the English courts is to decide disputes in accordance with English domestic law as it is, and not as it would be if full effect were given to this country's obligations under the Treaty, assuming that there is any difference between the two.

It follows from this that in most cases the English courts will be wholly unconcerned with the terms of the Convention. The sole exception is when the terms of primary legislation are fairly capable of bearing two or more meanings and the court, in pursuance of its duty to apply domestic law, is concerned to divine and define its true and only meaning. In that situation various prima facie rules of construction have to be applied, such as that, in the absence of very clear words indicating the contrary, legislation is not retrospective or penal in effect. To these can be added, in appropriate cases, a presumption that Parliament has legislated in a manner consistent, rather than inconsistent, with the United Kingdom's treaty obligations. ...

Thus far I have referred only to primary legislation, but it is also necessary to consider subordinate legislation and executive action, whether it be under the authority of primary or secondary legislation. Mr. Lester submits that, where there is an ambiguity in primary legislation and it may accordingly be appropriate to consider the terms of the Convention, the ambiguity may sometimes be resolved by imputing an intention to Parliament that the delegated power to legislate or, as the case may be, the authority to take executive action, shall be subject to the limitation that it be consistent with the terms of the Convention. This I unhesitatingly and unreservedly reject, because it involves imputing to Parliament an intention to import the Convention into domestic law by the back door, when it has quite clearly refrained from doing so by the front door. ...

Per Lord Donaldson M.R., pp. 717–18.

House of Lords

It is submitted, when a statute confers upon an administrative authority a discretion capable of being exercised in a way which infringes any basic human right protected by the Convention, it may similarly be presumed that the legislative intention was that the discretion should be exercised within the limitations which the Convention imposes. I confess that I found considerable persuasive force in this submission. But in the end I have been convinced that the logic of it is flawed. When confronted with a simple choice between two possible interpretations of some specific statutory provision, the presumption whereby the courts prefer that which avoids conflict between our domestic legislation and our international treaty obligations is a mere canon of construction which involves no importation of international law into the domestic field. But where Parliament has conferred on the executive an administrative discretion without indicating the precise limits within which it must be exercised, to presume that it must be exercised within Convention limits would be to go far beyond the resolution of an ambiguity. It would be to impute to Parliament an intention not only that the executive should exercise the discretion in conformity with the Convention, but also that the domestic courts should enforce that conformity by the importation into domestic administrative law of the text of the Convention and the jurisprudence of the European Court of Human Rights in the interpretation and application of it. If such a presumption is to apply to the statutory discretion exercised by the Secretary of State under section 29(3) of the Act of 1981 in the instant case, it must also apply to any other statutory discretion exercised by the executive which is capable of involving an infringement of Convention rights. When Parliament has been content for so long to leave those who complain that their Convention rights have been infringed to seek their remedy in Strasbourg, it would be surprising suddenly to find that the judiciary had, without Parliament's aid, the means to incorporate the Convention into such an important area of domestic law and I cannot escape the conclusion that this would be a judicial usurpation of the legislative function.

Per Lord Bridge, p. 748.

> ## 29   NICOLAS BRATZA QC, THE UK JUDGE AT THE EUROPEAN COURT OF HUMAN RIGHTS, ON THE TREATMENT AND INTERPRETATION OF THE CONVENTION'S PRINCIPLES BY THE BRITISH COURTS, 1991

In a case decided in 1982 and called *Taylor v. Co-operative Retails Services Ltd* [1982] I.C.R. 600 the Court of Appeal was required to consider a claim by a milk-roundsman who had been dismissed by his employers, the defendants, on the grounds of his refusal to leave one union and join another in accordance with a closed shop agreement. The Court of Appeal rejected his appeal on the grounds that by the terms of the Trade Union and Labour Relations Act 1974 and the Amendment Act of 1976 his dismissal was to be treated as fair. However, in typically trenchant terms, Lord Denning expressed his view that the appellant had been subjected to a degree of compulsion which was contrary to the freedom guaranteed by Article 11 of the Convention and that the Acts of 1974 and 1976 were themselves inconsistent with the rights guaranteed by that Article. Since however the Convention was not part of our law the appellant could not recover compensation in the domestic courts. This prompted Lord Denning to add the following somewhat bleak footnote:

> If he applies to the European Court of Human Rights, he may in the long run – and I am afraid it may be a long run – obtain compensation there. So in the end justice may be done. But not here.

On the facts of that case it is perhaps difficult to argue with Lord Denning's view. What is much more debatable is the broader question whether the failure of the United Kingdom to incorporate the Convention means that the national courts are in general unable to provide a remedy where fundamental human rights have been violated or whether the incorporation of the Convention as part of domestic law would in practice add little to the protection already afforded to the individual by statute and by the common law. This paper provides a very brief overview of the way in which the Convention has been treated by the domestic courts, even though not forming part of our domestic law. This is done by looking at the three main areas in which regard has been had to the Convention by the courts; as an aid to statutory interpretation; as guidance in the development of the common law; and in the field of judicial review.

So far as the author can discover, the Convention was first referred to in a judgment of the courts of this country in 1974 in *R. v. Miah* [1974] 1 W.L.R. 683 a case in which the House of Lords rejected an argument that the Immigration Act 1971 had created retroactive criminal offences. In delivering the only speech, Lord Reid stated that it was important to bear in mind Article 7 of the Convention and noted that in the light of that Article it was hardly credible that any Government department would promote, or that Parliament would pass, retroactive criminal legislation.

Since that date the trickle of cases in which reference has been made to the Convention by domestic courts has turned, if not into a flood, at least into a steady stream. A recent Lexis search reveals that the Convention has been referred to in the judgments of domestic courts and tribunals well over 200 times. It is true that in the majority of cases the reference has been a passing one. But what an analysis of the authorities does show is an increasing readiness on the part of the courts to consider the Convention even in cases which do not at first sight appear to raise Convention issues. One finds less commonly in the more recent judgments statements such as are to be found in *R. v. Chief Immigration Officer, Heathrow Airport, ex p. Salamat Bibi* [1976] 1 W.L.R. 979 to the effect that Article 8 of the Convention is 'too wide to be of practical application' and that the Convention is 'not the sort of thing which we can easily digest'.

This greater readiness to look at the Convention itself has gone hand in hand with a willingness on the part of the courts to examine the jurisprudence of the European Court and Commission and to draw on concepts developed by the Convention organs. In particular, in a number of decisions relating in the main to freedom of expression, the concept of a 'pressing social need' has been invoked and applied by the domestic courts.

Having said this, it is right to add that, in the vast majority of the 200 plus cases where the Convention has been referred to, the Convention appears to have made little or no difference to the result at which the court has arrived. More often than not, the Convention has been invoked by the court to reinforce the view which has already plainly been formed by the court as to the proper outcome of the case. This is not necessarily intended as a criticism. It is true that the Convention – and more particularly the restrictions contained in paragraph 2 of Articles 8–11 – have been prayed in aid as justifying the court in taking a restrictive view of the right or freedom in issue. But this has not always been the case. Particularly in the case of freedom of expression – and the judgments in and following the substantive hearing of the *Spycatcher* litigation are a good example – the Convention and Convention jurisprudence have been invoked by the courts as providing an important justification for their refusal to continue in force any form of injunctive relief.

The following sections consider the treatment of the Convention by the domestic courts in the three main areas indicated above.

Statutory interpretation

The extent to which the Convention could be invoked where the provisions of an Act of Parliament were in issue was first considered by the courts in a succession of cases arising under the Immigration Act 1971. The first of these – *Birdi v. Secretary of State for Home Affairs*, 11 February 1975, Bar Library Transcript No. 67B of 1975 – contained the most radical statement of principle, Lord Denning going as far as to suggest, albeit obiter, that if an Act of Parliament did not conform to the Convention he might be inclined to hold it invalid. Lord Denning very quickly recanted, holding in the case of *R. v. Home Secretary, ex p. Bhajan Singh* [1976] 1 Q.B. 198 that his earlier statement had been 'very tentative' and had gone too far. Instead, he restated the orthodox rule which has since been consistently adhered to that 'if an Act of Parliament contained any provisions contrary to the Convention, the Act of Parliament must prevail'.

In the subsequent case of *R. v. Secretary of State for the Home Department ex p. Phansopkar* [1976] 1 Q.B. 606, Scarman LJ expressed the view, in reliance on the decision in *Bhajan Singh*, that it was:

> the duty of our public authorities in administering the law, including the Immigration Act 1971, and of our courts in interpreting and applying the law, including the Act, to have regard [to the Convention].

He added that it was the duty of the courts, so long as they did not defy or disregard clear unequivocal provisions, to construe statutes in a manner which promoted, and did not endanger those rights.

Even that relatively modest formulation was held in the subsequent case of *Bibi* to have been too widely expressed. In that case Roskill LJ took issue both with the suggestion that public authorities should be required to have regard to the Convention in administering the law and with the suggestion that the courts should consider the Convention even in a case where the statute did not expressly or impliedly incorporate it into English law.

In subsequent authorities the courts have had regard to the Convention as an aid to statutory construction even in cases where the statute could not sensibly be said either expressly or impliedly to incorporate the Convention. However, in passing note the recent decision of the Court of Appeal in *R. v. General Medical Council, ex p. Colman* [1990] 1 All ER 489 where there is at least a suggestion that regard should be had to the Convention as an aid to statutory construction only where the subject matter of the statutory provision in question may properly be regarded as the subject matter of an international obligation under the Convention – a test which I suggest is going to be very difficult to apply in practice.

Where the courts have been consistent is in their requirement that recourse may be had to the Convention only for the purpose of resolving ambiguities: where the statute is clear and unambiguous there is no room for introducing the Convention. The point is perhaps most succinctly made by Lord Bridge in *R v. Secretary of State for the Home Department ex p. Brind* [1991] 1 A.C. 696 where he noted that:

> it is ... well settled that, in construing any provision in domestic legislation which is ambiguous in the sense that it is capable of a meaning which either conforms to or conflicts with the Convention, the courts will presume that Parliament intended to legislate in conformity with the Convention, not in conflict with it.

This principle has been invoked by the courts in several cases concerned with statutory interpretation. However, an analysis of the cases shows that this potentially fruitful area for the application of the Convention has in practice proved of little value. The usefulness of the principle has been undermined by the courts' insistence that the statutory provision should be ambiguous before recourse may be had to the Convention and, it is ventured, an over-readiness on the part of the courts to hold that the words of a statute are plain and unambiguous.

A recent example is in the case of *R. v. Secretary of State for the Home Department, ex parte* K. [1990] 1 W.L.R. 168 in which the Court of Appeal was faced with the question whether the Secretary of State could issue a warrant to recall a patient who had been conditionally discharged from a mental hospital in a case where there was no evidence that the patient was at the time of recall suffering from mental disorder. The power of recall was contained in section 42(3) of the Mental Health Act 1983 which was admittedly cast in wide terms. It was argued on behalf of the appellant with some justification that the section should be construed in accordance with Article 5 of the Convention and with various decisions of the European Court of Human Rights to which the 1983 Act was, at least in part, intended to give effect. The argument was rejected by the Court of Appeal on the short ground that the section was plain and unambiguous in its terms and that it was accordingly not open to the court to look for assistance to the Convention. This was so even if, as the appellant argued, the section as so interpreted was clearly inconsistent with the United Kingdom's Convention obligations.

Even in those relatively few cases where the courts have invoked the Convention as an aid to statutory interpretation, the discussion of the Convention does not appear to have affected the disputed point of interpretation. Thus, for example in *Ahmad v. I.L.E.A.* [1978] Q.B. 36, a majority of the Court of Appeal held that I.L.E.A. was not in breach of section 30 of the 1944 Education Act by requiring the appellant, a Muslim, to become a part-time teacher, if he wanted time off work each Friday for prayer. The section provided, *inter alia*, that no teacher should receive any less emolument by reason of his attending religious worship. It was Scarman

LJ who drew attention to Article 9 of the Convention in the course of argument and who, in a dissenting judgment, held that section 30 should be broadly construed against the background of Article 9. While the majority of the Court also made reference to Article 9, they did so only after they had already expressed the view that section 30 could not be read literally and without qualification so as to entitle the appellant to take time off for his prayers without loss of pay. Article 9 was then somewhat perfunctorily dealt with on the grounds that it could not be construed as entitling an employee to absent himself from his place of work for the purpose of religious worship.

I should mention, however, one area in which the Convention has perhaps proved of some value as an aid to statutory interpretation, namely as to what constitutes inhuman or degrading treatment or punishment or, as it is expressed in the Bill of Rights of 1688, cruel and unusual punishment. In this context the Privy Council has on several occasions had recourse to the Convention in determining issues arising under the Constitutions of Commonwealth countries. But it has also been used by the domestic courts. In three cases involving prison treatment or condition – *Williams* [1981] 1 All ER 1211, *Herbage* [1987] Q.B. 872 and *Weldon* [1992] A.C. 58 – Article 3 of the Convention was invoked by the Court in conjunction with the Bill of Rights in relation to complaints by the applicant that he had been subjected to unacceptable conditions of detention. It is right to say that in each of these cases the court's treatment of the Convention was cautious and that the courts were at pains to stress that the Convention standards were not part of our domestic law. Nevertheless the cases reveal at least a readiness on the part of the courts to have regard to those standards as a guide to what constitutes lawful conditions of detention.

In the same context one Northern Ireland decision is of interest, the case of *R. v. McCormick* [1977] N.I. 105, in which a bolder line was adopted by McConigal LJ. The issue concerned the admissibility of statements made by the accused and the provisions of section 6 of the Northern Ireland (Emergency Provision) Act 1973 which provided that statements were to be admissible unless '*prima facie* evidence is adduced that the accused was subjected to torture or inhuman or degrading treatment'. McConigal LJ considered that, in using those words, Parliament was plainly adopting the standards laid down in Article 3 and incorporating them into domestic legislation. He consequently felt free to treat the meaning ascribed to the words by the Convention organs as being at the very least of persuasive value, even if not decisive, and he proceeded to carry out a careful analysis of the Commission's case-law under Article 3.

Development of the common law

Here again the courts have shown a perhaps understandable reticence in using the Convention to develop the common law, particularly in a novel or complex field of law. The point was well expressed in *Malone v. Metropolitan Police Commission* [1979] Ch. 344 – the telephone tapping case – in which Sir Robert Megarry noted that, where Parliament had abstained from legislating on a point that was plainly suitable for legislation, it was:

> indeed difficult for the court to lay down new rules of common law or equity that will carry out the Crown's treaty obligations or discover for the first time that such rules have always existed.

What is more, as in the case of statutes, when the law is clearly and unambiguously defined in established case law, it is apparent that invocation of the Convention will prove fruitless. This is clear from the case of *In re M. & H. (Minors)* [1990] 1 A.C. 686 in which the House of Lords rejected an attempt by the appellant to invoke the Convention as the basis for persuading the House of Lords to depart from two previous decisions of its own.

The Convention has nevertheless proved of some limited value in resolving uncertainties in the common law and in pointing the way in which the common law should develop. Two examples in particular are worth mentioning.

First, in the area of contempt of court. With the proliferation of administrative and quasi-judicial tribunals, one of the difficult questions with which the domestic courts have on occasions been faced is whether a particular tribunal is to be treated as a 'court' for the purposes of the law of contempt. In resolving this question recourse has been had to the Convention. Article 10 of the Convention was invoked by two members of the House of Lords in *A.G. v. B.B.C.* [1981] A.C. 303 as providing strong support for their view that an extension of the law of contempt to include proceedings in a local valuation court would not be justified: to countenance such an extension so that comment on proceedings pending in a valuation court could be restrained as a contempt would in their view have given rise to an unjustifiable interference with freedom of expression. By contrast in *P. v. Liverpool Post plc* [1990] 2 W.L.R. 494 the Court of Appeal relied on Article 5 of the Convention in support of its conclusion that a Mental Health Appeal Tribunal was a court for the purposes of contempt, the argument being that if such a tribunal was not a 'court' for all purposes, Article 5(4) of the Convention, which requires that the lawfulness of a person's detention should be decided speedily 'by a court,' would not be complied with.

Again, Article 6 of the Convention as interpreted by the European Court of Human Rights in the *Golder* case was relied on by the House of Lords in *Raymond v. Honey* [1983] 1 A.C. 1. as affirming the principle that the denial of access to court by a prisoner was a contempt of court, as being an interference with the due administration of justice. The same principle also played an important part in the reasoning of the Divisional Court in *R. v. Secretary of State for the Home Department ex p. Anderson* [1984] Q.B. 778, the case in which a challenge was made to the so-called 'simultaneous ventilation' rule whereby prisoners wishing to make a complaint in correspondence about prison treatment were obliged simultaneously to ventilate the complaint internally through a prescribed procedure. The Court held, applying the principle in the *Golder* case, that the rule served as an impediment to a prisoner's right of access to a legal adviser and thereby his right of access to a court and on this ground held the rule to be *ultra vires*.

The second area of the common law which is worthy of mention is the law of blasphemy.

In the case of *R. v. Lemon* [1979] A.C. 617 the House of Lords held, *inter alia*, that a blasphemous libel was a publication which was calculated to outrage the feelings of Christians. In a case decided by the Divisional Court called *R. v. Chief Metropolitan Stipendiary Magistrate ex p. Choudhury* [1991] 1 Q.B. 429 an attempt was made to persuade the Court that the common law offence was not restricted to the Christian religion but should extend to other religions. The case involved an attempt to prosecute Salman Rushdie and his publishers for blasphemy for the publication of 'The Satanic Verses'.

In support of his argument the applicant sought to rely on the provisions of Article 9 of the Convention – the right to freedom of religion – and Article 14 – freedom from discriminatory treatment. A substantial part of the Court's interesting judgment was devoted to a careful analysis of the Convention under the expert guidance of Anthony Lester, who appeared for the respondents. The judgment contained not only a convincing explanation as to why Articles 9 and 14 did not require the extension of a law of blasphemy to include other religions but an equally convincing explanation as to why any such extension would run the risk of violating Articles 7 and 10 of the Convention.

Judicial review of administrative decisions

It is perhaps here that the scope for invoking the Convention might be thought to be greatest. Certainly there was a promising start: in *Bhajan Singh* Lord Denning held that not only were the courts bound to take the Convention into account whenever interpreting a statute affecting the rights and liberties of the individual, but that immigration officers and the Secretary of State were also required to bear in mind the principles stated in the Convention when exercising their decision-making functions.

This view was short-lived. In the following year in the *Bibi* case Lord Denning again recanted, stating that it would be too much to expect immigration officers to know or to apply the Convention.

The same approach was adopted by the Court of Appeal in *Fernandes v. Secretary of State for the Home Department*, [1981] Imm. A.R.1 in which the Court held that there was no legal obligation on the Secretary of State to consider whether or not a particular course of action would contravene the Convention.

In the 10-year period between the *Fernandes* case and the cases of *Brind* and *Colman* the authorities contain very little discussion of the Convention in the context of challenges to administrative decisions. However, two decisions may be of some interest.

The first is the case of *R. v. Secretary of State for the Home Department, ex p. McAvoy* [1984] 1 W.L.R. 1408 in which the Court held that, in deciding to transfer a prisoner from one prison to another, the Secretary of State was obliged to have regard to two rights enjoyed by an unconvicted prisoner: the right to visits from his family and the right to visits from his solicitor and, thereby, the right of access to a court and the right to a fair trial. The Court accepted that these were not what were described in the judgment as 'traditional common law rights' and that they were not rights which were conferred in terms by the Prison Act or the Prison Rules. They were to be found, if anywhere, in Articles 8 and 6 of the Convention. Without deciding whether these Convention rights were in themselves justiciable, the Court felt able to say that these rights were reflected in the provisions of the Prison Rules and thus were matters to which the Secretary of State was bound to have regard.

The other case is the House of Lords case of *R. v. Board of Visitors of H.M. Prison, The Maze, ex p. Hone and McCartan* [1988] A.C 379 decided in 1988. The only issue raised in the appeal to the House of Lords was whether a prisoner appearing before a Board of Visitors was entitled as of right to legal representation at the hearing. The House answered the question in the negative, approving the decision of the Divisional Court in *R. v. Secretary of State for the Home Department ex p. Tarrant* [1985] Q.B. 251 to the effect that the question whether legal representation should be allowed was a matter of discretion. In so doing the House examined the jurisprudence of the European Court of Human Rights in the *Engel* case and in the case of *Campbell and Fell* for the purpose of determining whether any such absolute right to representation existed under the Convention. The House concluded that it did not. More importantly perhaps, it concluded that the factors which the Convention organs took into account in determining whether particular disciplinary proceedings fell within Article 6 at all (namely, the seriousness of the offence and the severity of the possible penalty) were precisely the same factors to which the Board of Visitors would be required to have regard in the exercise of their discretion.

I turn finally to the case of *Brind*. There would seem to be three principle strands in the reasoning of the House.

First, it is clearly established that the presumption, which applies in a case of ambiguity or uncertainty, that Parliament intended to legislate in conformity with the Convention cannot be applied by analogy to the exercise of a statutory discretion. To apply such a presumption would be, to use the words of Lord Bridge:

> to go far beyond the resolution of an ambiguity. It would be to impute to Parliament an intention not only that the executive should exercise the discretion in conformity with the Convention, but also that the domestic courts should enforce that conformity by the importation into domestic administrative law of the text of the Convention and the jurisprudence of the European Court of Human Rights in the interpretation and application of it.

In the view of the Lords this would in effect be to incorporate the Convention into an important area of domestic law and would be a judicial usurpation of the legislative functions.

Secondly, however, this did not mean that the courts were powerless to prevent the exercise by the executive of administrative discretion, even a discretion conferred in unlimited terms, in a way which infringed fundamental human rights. The courts were entitled to start from the premise that any restriction of the right to freedom of expression (or presumably any other Convention right) required to be justified and that nothing less than an important competing public interest would be sufficient to justify it. The primary judgment fell to be made by the Secretary of State. But the courts were entitled to exercise a secondary judgment in accordance with *Wednesbury* principles by asking whether a reasonable Secretary of State, on the material before him, could reasonably make that primary judgment.

Thirdly, the principle of 'proportionality', which is recognised in the administrative law of several member states of the EEC and to which reference was made by Lord Diplock in the *G.C.H.Q.* case, did not yet form part of our administrative law and could not be applied in the present case, since to do so would be for the court to substitute its own judgment for that of the Secretary of State.

It is the second strand which appears to me to be the most important for present purposes. The Lords held that, on the particular facts of the *Brind* case, the interference complained of was minimal and the reasons given by the Secretary of State for imposing the broadcasting ban were compelling. For this reason the Lords had no hesitation in holding that the Secretary of State had not exceeded the limits of his discretion and that his decision to impose the ban was not 'irrational' according to *Wednesbury* principles.

But the significance of the decision is the apparent recognition in the judgments of three of their Lordships – Lord Bridge, Lord Roskill and Lord Templeman – that an executive decision which restricts or interferes with fundamental rights and freedoms may be treated by the domestic courts as 'irrational' unless the decision maker could reasonably conclude on the material before him that the particular restriction was justified by a competing public interest or, to use the words of Lord Templeman, that the interference was 'necessary and proportionate to the damage which the restriction is designed to prevent'.

If this is the correct interpretation of the judgments, which the author does not find altogether easy, it is clearly a decision of some considerable potential importance: even if this interpretation is correct, the precise limits of the principle would have to be worked out. In particular, what would an applicant have to show in order to satisfy the court that a decision was irrational? Presumably he would have to do more than show that the decision would or was likely to involve a breach of the Convention, otherwise this would be tantamount to the judicial incorporation of the Convention which the House of Lords regarded as unacceptable. On the other hand, if the applicant were required to show that no reasonable Minister could ever have concluded, on the basis of the material before him, that the restriction or interference was justified in terms of the Convention, the burden is likely to prove difficult if not impossible to discharge.

The record of the domestic courts in addressing the Convention and in their treatment of Convention issues has been patchy. This is perhaps inevitable in view of the concern of the courts not to usurp the function of Parliament and not to be seen to be admitting the Convention by the back door, where the legislature has refused it admission by the front. Nevertheless, even within these obvious limitations, there have been positive and welcome developments in which imaginative use has been made by the courts of the Convention, particularly in the area of prisons and prisoners' rights. There still remains ample scope in my view for a bolder use of the Convention both in the development of the common law and in the review of administrative decisions. Although in the result the *Brind* case is hardly promising, it may provide at least a basis for a more imaginative judicial approach in the future. This would be a welcome development.

'The Treatment and Interpretation of the European Convention on Human Rights by the English Courts', in J.P. Gardner (ed.), *Aspects of Incorporation of the European Convention on Human Rights into Domestic Law*, 1991. (*RB NOTE: Nicolas Bratza wrote this article in a personal capacity prior to becoming a member of the European Commission of Human Rights in 1994 and Judge of the Court of Human Rights in 1998.*)

---

30 DANIEL TARSCHYS, SECRETARY-GENERAL OF THE COUNCIL OF EUROPE, URGES THE UK TO INCORPORATE THE CONVENTION, 1995

Before concluding I would like to say something about the United Kingdom and the Council of Europe. I referred earlier to Winston Churchill, who provided the inspiration for the establishment of the Council of Europe. Our statute [establishing the Council of Europe] was signed here in London in May 1949. British statesmen and British lawyers subsequently played a pre-eminent role in shaping our organization and in drafting the European Human Rights Convention.

I realize that over the years British involvement in Europe has often been keenly debated and I do not wish to fuel that particular discussion now. However, allow me to say that seen from a Council of Europe perspective Britain's commitment to Europe is an essential prerequisite both for the effectiveness of the European Union and for the stability of that wider Europe which we are trying to build.

Second, as regards the current debate about the status of the European Human Rights Convention in domestic law, this is obviously a matter for the British Parliament to resolve. However, it does strike me as sensible to allow British judges to enforce the Convention in British courts. Incorporation of the Convention into domestic law ... would not only reduce the number of cases from the United Kingdom reaching Strasbourg (approximately 200 registered each year) but it would also be in keeping with the principle of subsidiarity which you are keen to apply here and which we should seek to encourage in our new member countries.

'The Council of Europe: the Challenge of Enlargement', Speech to the Royal Institute of International Affairs, 15 February 1995.

---
31   THE BRITISH GOVERNMENT ON ITS PUBLIC
OFFICIALS' DUTY OF COMPLIANCE WITH THE
EUROPEAN CONVENTION ON HUMAN RIGHTS, 1995

PARLIAMENTARY QUESTION

Human rights treaties: duty of compliance

Lord Lester of Herne Hill asked Her Majesty's Government:

Whether they consider that Ministers and civil servants, in discharging
their public functions, have a duty to comply with the European
Convention on Human Rights and the International Covenant on
Civil and Political Rights.

Baroness Chalker of Wallasey: International treaties are binding on
states and not on individuals. the United Kingdom is party to both treaties
and it must comply with its obligations under them. In so far as acts of
Ministers and civil servants in the discharge of their public functions
constitute acts which engage the responsibility of the United Kingdom, they
must comply with the terms of the treaties.

HL Deb, 7 December 1994, col. WA84.

Human rights: duty of compliance

Lord Lester of Herne Hill asked Her Majesty's Government:

Further to their Answer of 7th December 1994 (HL *WA 84*), whether
they consider that local authorities, in discharging their public func-
tions, have a duty to comply with the terms of the European
Convention on Human Rights and the International Covenant on
Civil and Political Rights; and
Further to their Answer of 7th December 1994 (HL *WA 84*), how, in
the absence of legislation to incorporate the European Convention on
Human Rights and the International Covenant on Civil and Political
Rights into the law of the United Kingdom, victims of failure by
Ministers and civil servants to comply with the terms of the treaties, in
the discharge of their public functions, are able to obtain effective
domestic remedies against the Crown; and
Further to their Answer of 7th December 1994 (HL *WA 84*),
whether they consider that Her Majesty's judges, in discharging their
public functions, have a duty to comply with the European Covenant
of Human Rights and International Covenant on Civil and Political
Rights.

**The Minister of State, Foreign and Commonwealth Office (Baroness
Chalker of Wallasey):** As I stated in my Answer of 7th December, the

treaties referred to, in common with treaties in general, are binding on States party to them and not individuals. The acts or omissions of public officers or authorities may engage the international responsibility of the United Kingdom in so far as they raise issues in respect of the fulfilment of the United Kingdom's obligations under the treaty. The position in international law in this regard is no different for the treaties referred to by the noble Lord than for other treaties. In the cases of the European Convention on Human Rights and the International Covenant on Civil and Political Rights, the determination whether a particular act or omission does engage the responsibility of the United Kingdom is specially entrusted (subject to the rules and procedures laid down in the treaties) to the supervisory bodies established by those treaties.

The obligation to provide an effective domestic remedy is an obligation of the State under the treaties in question. Whether the United Kingdom has complied with that obligation falls to be determined in the same way as whether it has complied with any of the other obligations under those treaties. In so far as the European Convention of Human Rights is concerned, the European Court of Human Rights has consistently held that the Convention does not lay down for the Contracting States any given manner for ensuring within their internal law the effective implementation of any of its provisions.

HL Deb, 9 January 1995, col. WA1.

---

32 LORD BINGHAM, LORD CHIEF JUSTICE, ON THE LEGAL PRINCIPLES WHEREBY THE EUROPEAN CONVENTION ON HUMAN RIGHTS MAY INFLUENCE DOMESTIC LEGAL PROCEEDINGS IN THE UK, 1996

The noble Lords who have already spoken have touched on matters of fundamental importance to our nation and people. These are deep and turbulent waters into which only powerful and experienced swimmers are wise to venture. Your Lordships will, I hope, understand if I myself linger in a modest and maidenly manner in the shallow end.

There is just one issue upon which, with your Lordships' leave, I wish to touch; that is, the constitutional relationship between the British courts, the European Court of Human Rights in Strasbourg and the current status of the European convention in our courts. I raise that topic not to argue any case, but to record where, as I understand, we now are on the principle that it is desirable to know where one is before deciding where, if anywhere, one wishes to go.

The starting point is, of course, that we are a state that ratified the convention; we are bound in international law to honour the obligations which we have undertaken. When any breach of the convention has been established on the part of any public authority, we are bound to amend our laws and procedures to make good the breach and prevent a recurrence. That is an obligation which has, I believe, been scrupulously observed by successive governments of both political colours.

But the convention is not part of our domestic law. The courts have no powers to enforce convention rights directly. If domestic legislation plainly conflicts with the enforcement of the convention, then the courts apply the domestic legislation. That is a principle which your Lordships' House, sitting judicially, has unambiguously laid down and it is a rule which the courts have loyally observed, despite ingenious and persistent invitations by counsel to depart from it.

In some countries treaties, once ratified, have the force of law. That is not so here and it is that fact which gives continuing vitality to the debate on incorporation. It might be thought to follow form that that the convention is a matter for Parliament and the Government, with which the courts have nothing whatever to do. But that, I suggest, would not be entirely right and I hope that your Lordships will permit me to touch briefly on six respects in which I suggest the convention can, and in practice does, have an influence in our domestic proceedings.

First, as the noble and learned Lord the Lord Chancellor observed, where a United Kingdom statute is capable of two interpretations, one consistent with the convention and one inconsistent, then the courts will presume that Parliament intended to legislate in conformity with the convention and not in conflict with it. In other words, the courts will presume that Parliament did not intend to legislate in violation of international law. That may be thought by your Lordships to be a modest presumption.

Secondly, if the common law is uncertain, unclear or incomplete, the courts have to make a choice; they cannot abdicate their power of decision. In declaring what the law is, they will rule, wherever possible, in a manner which conforms with the convention and does not conflict with it. Any other course would be futile since a rule laid down in defiance of the convention would be likely to prove short-lived.

There is, of course, one field – freedom of expression – in which respected Members of this House have declared that they see no inconsistency between the common law and the convention. That is reassuring; it is also wholly unsurprising since we have a long record as a pioneer in the field of freedom of expression. But it means that the courts are encouraged to look to the convention and the jurisprudence of the European Court of Human Rights when resolving problems on the common law.

Thirdly, when the courts are called upon to construe a domestic statute enacted to fulfil a convention obligation, the courts will ordinarily assume that the statute was intended to be effective to that end. That is mere common sense, but common sense is the stock-in-trade of much judicial decision-making.

Fourthly, where the courts have a discretion to exercise that is, they can act in one way or another – one or more of which violates the convention and another of which does not, they seek to act in a way which does not violate the convention. That again is usually common sense and requires no elaboration. However, it is not an invariable rule and your Lordships' House, sitting judicially, gave an important judgment only yesterday in which the convention right to privacy was held to be obliged to give way to the greater interests of justice.

Fifthly, when, as sometimes happens, the courts are called upon to decide what, in a given situation, public policy demands, it has been held to be legitimate that we shall have regard to our international obligations enshrined in the convention as a source of guidance on what British public policy requires.

Sixthly and lastly, matters covered by the law of the European Community – that is, the law administered by the European Court of Justice in Luxembourg and not Strasbourg – on occasion give effect to matters covered by convention law. The Court of Justice takes the view that on matters subject to Community law, the law common to the member states is part of the law which applies. All member states are parties to the convention and it so happens from time to time that laws derived from the convention are incorporated as part of the law of the Community. That of course is a law which the courts in this country must apply since we are bound by Act of Parliament to do so, and that is a means by which, indirectly, convention rights find their way into domestic law.

HL Deb., 1996, cols. 1465–7.

33 EUROPEAN CONVENTION ON HUMAN RIGHTS CASES AND VIOLATIONS: COMPARABLE TABLES OF THE UNITED KINGDOM AND OTHER MEMBER STATES, 1997

European Commission of Human Rights (statistics up to 31 October 1998)

	Date of ratification of art. 25 (right to individual petition)	*Applications registered*	*Applications declared admissible*
Albania	02/10/1996	3	0
Andorra	22/01/1996	3	0
Austria	03/09/1958	3277	274
Belgium	05/07/1955	1901	107
Bulgaria	07/09/1992	213	16
Croatia	05/11/1997	24	0
Cyprus	01/01/1989	89	14
Czech Rep.	01/01/1993	327	2
Czechoslovakia	31/12/1992	6	0
Denmark	13/04/1953	469	18
Estonia	16/04/1996	24	0
Finland	10/05/1990	582	19
France	02/10/1981	4872	653
Germany	05/07/1955	6967	81
Greece	20/11/1985	546	178
Hungary	05/11/1992	468	9
Iceland	29/03/1955	59	5
Ireland	25/02/1953	256	12
Italy	01/08/1973	4792	2366
Latvia	27/06/1997	6	0
Liechtenstein	08/09/1982	15	1
Lithuania	20/06/1995	66	1
Luxembourg	28/04/1958	149	4
Malta	01/05/1987	35	4
Moldova	12/09/1997	10	0
Netherlands	28/06/1960	1761	167
Norway	10/12/1955	241	9
Poland	01/05/1993	1765	32
Portugal	09/11/1978	529	174
Romania	20/06/1994	457	10
Russia (Fed)	05/05/1998	63	0
San Marino	22/03/1989	23	7
Slovakia	01/01/1993	318	10
Slovenia	28/06/1994	91	2
Spain	01/07/1981	1234	29
Sweden	04/02/1952	1783	94
Switzerland	28/11/1974	1862	91
Fyro Macedonia	10/04/1997	7	0
Turkey	28/01/1987	2453	187
Ukraine	11/09/1997	171	2
United Kingdom	14/01/1996	6118	447
Total		44035	5025

European Court of Human Rights: Referrals to and judgments and decisions of the Court 1960–98 (statistics up to 3 November 1998)

State concerned	References (including Protocol 9 cases)	Cases which gave rise to a finding of		Cases which gave rise to no finding on the merits				Cases pending			Total
		At least one violation	Non-violation	Cases struck out of the list	Cases not examined on the merits	Protocol 9 cases not accepted for consideration	Protocol 9 screening panel cases	On the merits	Just satisfaction Article 50	Revision Interpretation	
Austria	96[1](30)*	44	18	6	–	27	–	–	–	–	–
Belgium	42(4)*	25	8	4	1	4	–	1	–	–	1
Bulgaria	3	2	1	–	–	1	–	1	–	–	1
Cyprus	5(1)	2	1	–	–	1	–	1	–	–	1
Denmark	7	3	4	–	–	–	–	–	–	–	–
Finland	9(3)*	4	2	–	–	3	–	–	–	–	–
France	118[2,6,9]	63[2,6,9]	32	11	3	1	–	8	–	–	8
Germany	35(1)*	15	17	1	5	–	–	2	–	–	2
Greece	41[8]	27	3	1	–	–	–	3	–	–	3
Hungary	1	1	–	–	–	–	–	1	–	–	1
Iceland	3	2	–	1	–	–	–	–	–	–	–
Ireland	8(1)*	6	1[3]	1	–	1	–	1	–	–	1
Italy	295(139)*	101[3]	31	18[4]	3	136	–	7(1)*	1	–	7
Liechtenstein	1	1	–	–	–	–	–	1	–	–	1
Luxembourg	–	–	–	–	–	–	–	–	–	–	–
Malta	3	3	–	–	–	–	–	2	–	–	2
Netherlands	51[5](7)*	30	13	1	–	4	–	1(1)	–	–	1
Norway	5	3	1	–	–	1	–	–	–	–	–
Poland	8(1)	3	1	–	–	1	–	–	–	–	–
Portugal	19(3)*	11	3	2	–	3	–	3	–	–	3
Romania	3	2	–	–	–	–	–	1	–	–	1
San Marino	1(1)	–	–	–	–	1	–	1	–	–	1
Slovakia	3(1)	3	–	–	–	1	–	1	–	–	1
Spain	21[9]	9	9	1	1	–	–	1	–	–	1
Sweden	44(6)*	22	14	4	–	4	–	–	–	–	–
Switzerland	40(2)*	21	14	3	–	2	–	–	–	–	–
Turkey	48	24	3	1	2	–	–	18	–	–	18
United Kingdom	135[7]	56[6]	35	4	–	–	–	38	–	–	38
Total	1045(198)*	481	210	56	15	188	–	91(2)*	1	–	92

[1] Including the Mauer cases (nos 1 and 2), which were joined by the Court and are here counted as two.

[2] Including the Kemmache cases (nos 1 and 2) and Reinhardt and Slimane-Kaïd, which were joined by the Court but are here counted as two.

[3] The Colozza and Rubinat case, after being severed, gave rise to two judgments, one finding a violation (Colozza) and the other striking the case out of the list (Rubinat). Only Colozza has been taken into account.

[4] Not including Rubinat.

[5] Including the Schouten and Meldrum cases, which were joined by the Court but are here counted as two.

[6] Including the Soering, Beldjoudi and Nasri cases: finding of a potential violation (which in the event did not occur).

[7] Including the Stubbings and Others and I.D.S. v. the United Kingdom and Sheffield and Horsham which were joined by the Court but are here counted as two.

[8] Including the cases of Gitonas, Kavaratzis and Giakoumatos, which were joined by the Court but are here counted as three.

[9] Certain totals do not tally as the Drozd and Janousek case is entered under each of the two respondent States (France and Spain) and the judgments in Pardo, Allenet de Ribemont and Hentrich have given rise to applications respectively for revision and interpretation.

* The figures in brackets indicate cases referred under Protocol No. 9.

(II) Within the European Union

---

34   JOINT DECLARATION ON FUNDAMENTAL RIGHTS BY THE EUROPEAN PARLIAMENT, COUNCIL AND COMMISSION, 1977

'The European Parliament, the Council and the Commission

Whereas the Treaties establishing the European Communities are based on the principle of respect for the law;

Whereas, as the Court of Justice has recognized, that law comprises, over and above the rules embodied in the Treaties and secondary Community legislation, the general principles of law and in particular the fundamental rights, principles and rights on which the constitutional law of the Member States is based;

Whereas, in particular, all the Member States are Contracting Parties to the European Convention for the Protection of Human Rights and Fundamental Freedoms signed in Rome on 4 November 1950.

Have adopted the following declaration:

1. The European Parliament, the Council and the Commission stress the prime importance they attach to the protection of fundamental rights, as derived in particular from the constitutions of the Member States and the European Convention for the Protection of Human Rights and Fundamental Freedoms.

2. In the exercise of their powers and in pursuance of the aims of the European Communities they respect and will continue to respect these rights.'

5 April 1977

---

35   THE EUROPEAN PARLIAMENT ISSUES A DECLARATION OF FUNDAMENTAL RIGHTS AND FREEDOMS, 1989

RESOLUTION ADOPTING THE DECLARATION OF FUNDAMENTAL RIGHTS AND FREEDOMS

The European Parliament

— having regard to the motion for a resolution tabled by Mr Luster and Mr Pfennig to supplement the draft Treaty establishing the European Union (Doc. 2-363/84),

— having regard to the Treaties establishing the European Communities,
— having regard to its draft Treaty establishing the European Union adopted on 14 February 1984, in particular Articles 4(3) and 7,
— having regard to its resolution of 29 October 1982 on the Memorandum from the Commission on the accession of the European Community to the Convention for the Protection of Human Rights and Fundamental Freedoms,
— having regard to the Joint Declaration on Fundamental Rights,
— having regard to the preamble to the Single Act,
— having regard to the shared general principles of the law of the Member States,
— having regard to the case law of the Court of Justice of the European Communities,
— having regard to the Universal Declaration of Human Rights,
— having regard to the United Nations Covenants on Civil and Political Rights and on Economic, Social and Cultural Rights,
— having regard to the European Convention for the Protection of Human Rights and Fundamental Freedoms and its Protocols,
— having regard to the European Social Charter and its Protocol,
— having regard to the report of the Committee on Institutional Affairs and the opinion of the Committee on Social Affairs and Employment (Doc. A2-3/89),

    A. whereas, as pointed out in the preamble to the Single Act, it is essential to promote democracy on the basis of fundamental rights,

    B. whereas respect for fundamental rights is indispensable for the legitimacy of the Community,

    C. whereas it is up to the European Parliament to contribute to the development of a model of society which is based on respect for fundamental rights and freedoms and tolerance,

    D. whereas the identity of the Community makes it essential to give expression to the shared values of the citizens of Europe,

    E. whereas there can be no European citizenship unless every citizen enjoys equal protection of his rights and freedoms in the field of application of Community law,

    F. whereas it is determined to sustain its efforts to promote the achievement of European Union,

    G. whereas it is determined to achieve a basic Community instrument with a binding legal character guaranteeing fundamental rights,

    H. whereas in the meantime, pending ratification of such an instrument, Parliament restates the legal principles already accepted by the Community,

    I. whereas completion of the single market scheduled for 1993 lends greater urgency to the need to adopt a Declaration of rights and freedoms guaranteed in and by Community law,

J.   whereas it is the responsibility of the European Parliament directly elected by the citizens of Europe to draw up such a Declaration,

1.   Hereby adopts the following Declaration and invites the other Community institutions and the Member States to associate themselves normally with this Declaration;

2.   Instructs its President to forward this resolution and the Declaration to the other Community institutions and the Governments of the Member States.

DECLARATION OF FUNDAMENTAL RIGHTS AND FREEDOMS

Preamble

In the name of the Peoples of Europe

Whereas with a view to continuing and reviving the democratic unification of Europe, having regard to the creation of an internal area without frontiers and mindful of the particular responsibility of the European Parliament with regard to the well-being of men and women, it is essential that Europe reaffirm the existence of a common legal tradition based on respect for human dignity and fundamental rights,

Whereas measures incompatible with fundamental rights are inadmissible and recalling that these rights derive from the Treaties establishing the European Communities, the constitutional traditions common to the Member States, the European Convention for the Protection of Human Rights and Fundamental Freedoms and the institutional instruments in force and have been developed in the case law of the Court of Justice of the European Communities,

The European Parliament, lending expression to these rights, hereby adopts the following Declaration, calls on all citizens actively to uphold it and present it to the Parliament which is to be elected in June 1989.

Article 1 – (Dignity)

Human dignity shall be inviolable.

Article 2 – (Right to life)

Everyone shall have the right to life, liberty and security of person.

No one shall be subjected to torture or to inhuman or degrading treatment or punishment.

Article 3 – (Equality before the law)

1. In the field of application of Community law, everyone shall be equal before the law.

2. Any discrimination on grounds such as race, colour, sex, language, religion, political or other opinion, national or social origin, association with a national minority, property, birth or other status shall be prohibited.

3. Any discrimination between European citizens on the grounds of nationality shall be prohibited.

4. Equality must be secured between men and women before the law, particularly in the areas of work, education, the family, social welfare and training.

Article 4 – (Freedom of thought)

Everyone shall have the right to freedom of thought, conscience and religion.

Article 5 – (Freedom of opinion and information)

1. Everyone shall have the right to freedom of expression. This right shall include freedom of opinion and the freedom to receive and impart information and ideas, particularly philosophical, political and religious.

2. Art, science and research shall be free of constraint. Academic freedom shall be respected.

Article 6 – (Privacy)

1. Everyone shall have the right to respect and protection for their identity.

2. Respect for privacy and family life, reputation, the home and private correspondence shall be guaranteed.

Article 7 – (Protection of family)

The family shall enjoy legal, economic and social protection.

Article 8 – (Freedom of movement)

1. Community citizens shall have the right to move freely and choose their residence within Community territory. They may pursue the occupation of their choice within that territory.

2. Community citizens shall be free to leave and return to Community territory.

3. The above rights shall not be subject to any restrictions except those that are in conformity with the Treaties establishing the European Communities.

Article 9 – (Right of ownership)

The right of ownership shall be guaranteed. No one shall be deprived of their possessions except where deemed necessary in the public interest and in the cases and subject to the conditions provided for by law and subject to fair compensation.

Article 10 – (Freedom of assembly)

Everyone shall have the right to take part in peaceful meetings and demonstrations.

Article 11 – (Freedom of association)

1. Everyone shall have the right to freedom of association including the right to form and join political parties and trade unions.
2. No one shall in their private life be required to disclose their membership of any association which is not illegal.

Article 12 – (Freedom to choose an occupation)

1. Everyone shall have the right to choose freely an occupation and a place of work and to pursue freely that occupation.
2. Everyone shall have the right to appropriate vocational training in accordance with their abilities and fitting them for work.
3. No one shall be arbitrarily deprived of their work and no one shall be forced to take up specific work.

Article 13 – (Working conditions)

1. Everyone shall have the right to just working conditions.
2. The necessary measures shall be taken with a view to guaranteeing health and safety in the workplace and a level of remuneration which makes it possible to lead a decent life.

Article 14 – (Collective social rights)

1. The right of negotiation between employers and employees shall be guaranteed.
2. The right to take collective action, including the right to strike, shall be guaranteed subject to obligations that might arise from existing laws and collective agreements.
3. Workers shall have the right to be informed regularly of the economic and financial situation of their undertaking and to be consulted on decisions likely to affect their interests.

Article 15 – (Social welfare)

1. Everyone shall have the right to benefit from all measures enabling them to enjoy the best possible state of health.
2. Workers, self-employed persons and their dependants shall have the right to social security or an equivalent system.
3. Anyone lacking sufficient resources shall have the right to social and medical assistance.
4. Those who, through no fault of their own, are unable to house themselves adequately, shall have the right to assistance in this respect from the appropriate public authorities.

Article 16 – (Right to education)

Everyone shall have the right to education and vocational training appropriate to their abilities.

There shall be freedom in education.

Parents shall have the right to make provision for such education in accordance with their religious and philosophical convictions.

Article 17 – (Principle of democracy)

1. All public authority emanates from the people and must be exercised in accordance with the principles of the rule of law.
2. Every public authority must be directly elected or answerable to a directly elected parliament.
3. European citizens shall have the right to take part in the election of Members of the European Parliament by free, direct and secret universal suffrage.
4. European citizens shall have an equal right to vote and stand for election.
5. The above rights shall not be subject to restrictions except where such restrictions are in conformity with the Treaties establishing the European Communities.

Article 18 – (Right of access to information)

Everyone shall be guaranteed the right of access and the right to corrections to administrative documents and data concerning them.

Article 19 – (Access to the courts)

1. Anyone whose rights and freedoms have been infringed shall have the right to bring an action in a court or tribunal specified by law.
2. Everyone shall be entitled to have their case heard fairly, publicly and within a reasonable time limit by an independent and impartial court or tribunal established by law.
3. Access to justice shall be effective and shall involve the provision of legal aid to those who lack sufficient resources otherwise to afford legal representation.

Article 20 – (Non bis in idem)

No one shall be tried or convicted for offences for which they have already been acquitted or convicted.

Article 21 – (Non-retroactivity)

No liability shall be incurred for any act or omission to which no liability applied under the law at the time when it was committed.

Article 22 – (Death penalty)

The death penalty shall be abolished.

Article 23 – (Right of petition)

Everyone shall have the right to address written requests or complaints to the European Parliament.

The detailed provisions governing the exercise of this right shall be laid down by the European Parliament.

Article 24 – (Environment and consumer protection)

1. The following shall form an integral part of Community policy:
— the preservation, protection and improvement of the quality of the environment,
— the protection of consumers and users against the risks of damage to their health and safety and against unfair commercial transactions.
2. The Community institutions shall be required to adopt all the measures necessary for the attainment of these objectives.

Article 25 – (Field of application)

1. This Declaration shall afford protection for every citizen in the field of application of Community law.

2. Where certain rights are set aside for Community citizens, its may be decided to extend all or part of the benefit of these rights to other persons.

3. A Community citizen within the meaning of this Declaration shall be any person possessing the nationality of one of the Member States.

Article 26 – (Limits)

The rights and freedoms set out in this Declaration may be restricted within reasonable limits necessary in a democratic society only by a law which must at all events respect the substance of such rights and freedoms.

Article 27 – (Degree of protection)

No provision in this Declaration shall be interpreted as restricting the protection afforded by Community law, the law of the Member States, international law and international conventions and accord on fundamental rights and freedoms or as standing in the way of its development.

Article 28 – (Abuse of rights)

No provision in this Declaration shall be interpreted as implying any right to engage in any activity or perform any act aimed at restricting or destroying the rights and freedoms set out therein.

INDEX

Article 2: Right to life
Article 3: Equality before the law
Article 4: Freedom of thought
Article 5: Freedom of opinion and information
Article 6: Privacy
Article 7: Protection of family
Article 8: Freedom of movement
Article 9: Right of ownership
Article 10: Freedom of assembly
Article 11: Freedom of association
Article 12: Freedom to choose an occupation
Article 13: Working conditions
Article 14: Collective social rights
Article 15: Social welfare
Article 16: Right to education
Article 17: Principle of democracy
Article 18: Right of access to information
Article 19: Access to the courts
Article 20: Non bis in idem
Article 21: Non-retroactivity
Article 22: Death penalty
Article 23: Right of petition
Article 24: Environment and consumer protection

FINAL PROVISIONS

Article 25: Field of application
Article 26: Limits
Article 27: Degree of protection
Article 28: Abuse of rights

(12 April 1989, A2–3/89)

---

36   THE DOMESTIC IMPACT OF THE EUROPEAN CONVENTION ON HUMAN RIGHTS AS MEDIATED THROUGH COMMUNITY LAW, 1991

The House of Lords' ruling in *Brind* v. *Secretary of State for the Home Department* (1991) [RB NOTE: *see Doc. 29*] has renewed discussion of the legal status of the European Convention on Human Rights in the United Kingdom and its influence upon British courts. This article examines one aspect of that issue, namely the domestic impact of the Convention arising from its relationship with European Community law, as reflected in the case law of the European Court of Justice (E.C.J.). It will be argued that in certain circumstances the Court of Justice would be competent to determine the compatibility of a national statutory provision with the Convention, and that the President of the Court could even order the suspension of a statute in so far as it was inconsistent with principles in the Convention, even though the Convention itself has not been incorporated into domestic law. Moreover, the E.C.J.'s decisions concerning the Convention restrict the scope and effect of the *Brind* judgment.

THE EUROPEAN COURT OF JUSTICE AND THE EUROPEAN CONVENTION ON HUMAN RIGHTS

The Court of Justice has long made it clear that it will ensure respect for fundamental human rights in the context of the legal order of the European Community. Whereas the main source of such rights is the 'constitutional traditions common to the Member States,' in *Nold v. Commission* Case 4/73 [1974] E.C.R. 491 or 507 the Court added that

> 'international treaties for the protection of human rights on which the Member States have collaborated, or of which they are signatories, can supply guidelines which should be followed within the framework of Community law.'

All 12 member states of the Community are parties to the E.C.H.R., not merely signatories of it, and the preamble to the Single European Act expresses their determination 'to work together to promote democracy on the basis of the fundamental rights recognised in the Convention'. Prior to the Single European Act, the Court of Justice was accustomed to holding that the principles on which the Convention is based must be taken into consideration in Community law. Since the Act's entry into force, there has been evidence of the Court's willingness to emphasise the Convention as a direct source of Community law.

In assessing the impact of the Convention within the Community legal order, a distinction can be drawn between those cases where the Convention has been employed by the E.C.J. as an aid to the construction of Community provisions or as a yardstick for determining the validity of Community acts, and others in which the Court has used it in considering the legality of the actions of member states themselves. As will be seen, both bodies of case law have important domestic implications.

(i) The European Convention as a constraint upon Community legislative and administrative action

On April 5, 1977, three of the Community's political institutions – the Commission, the Council of Ministers and the European Parliament – issued a Joint Declaration on Fundamental Rights [RB NOTE: see Doc. 23]. Although the Declaration is not considered to be legally binding, it is a factor in the interpretation of Community acts and at least justifies the presumption that they are not intended to violate fundamental rights. Indeed, the question of its legal effects is largely academic in view of the policy of the Court of Justice concerning the protection of fundamental rights and freedoms.

There have been several cases in which the Court has indicated that it regards the Convention as a constraint upon Community legislative and administrative action. In *Prais* v. *Council* Case 130/75, [1976] E.C.R. 1589 the plaintiff invoked article 9 E.C.H.R., claiming that her fundamental right to freedom of religion had been infringed because the Council had failed to take account of her religious convictions when setting the date for the written test in a Community entrance competition to recruit a translator. Although the E.C.J. dismissed the claim on the facts, it accepted the principle that the Convention had to be taken into consideration by the Council. The Court held that

> 'in so far as the defendant, if informed of the difficulty in good time, would have been obliged to take reasonable steps to avoid fixing for a test a date which would make it impossible for a person of a particular religious persuasion to undergo the test, it can be said that the defendant was not informed of the unsuitability of certain days until the date for the test had been fixed, and the defendant was ... entitled to refuse to fix a different date when other candidates had already been convoked.'

In *National Panasonic (U.K.) Ltd.* v. *Commission* Case 136/79, [1980] E.C.R. 2033 in the context of the enforcement of the Community's competition rules, the applicant claimed that by failing to communicate to it beforehand a decision ordering an investigation into its alleged anti-competitive practices, the Commission had infringed fundamental rights guaranteed by article 8 E.C.H.R., which the applicant considered applicable *mutatis mutandis* to legal persons. The E.C.J. observed that 'in so far as it applies to legal persons,' article 8(2) permits interference by a public authority with the exercise of the right to respect for private and family life, home and correspondence to the extent that such interference is in accordance with the law and necessary in a democratic society in the interests of certain stated purposes, including the economic well-being of the country and the protection of the rights and freedoms of others.

The Court then considered whether Council Regulation No. 17 (article 14 of which empowers the Commission to carry out investigations without previously notifying the company concerned) infringed article 8 E.C.H.R. It concluded that there was no infringement because the aim of the search and seizure powers is to enable the Commission to ensure the application of the Community's competition rules, the function of the latter being to prevent competition from being distorted to the detriment of the public interest, individual undertakings and consumers. Consequently, the exercise of those powers contributes to the maintenance of the system of competition intended by the Treaty. In other words, the Court considered that the interference complained of was in accordance with article 8(2) of the Convention.

Similarly, in *Orkem* v. *Commission* Case 374/87, [1989] E.C.R. 3283 the applicant company sought the annulment of a Commission decision requiring it to reply to certain questions relating to the Commission's investigation of its alleged anti-competitive practices. The company argued, *inter alia*, that there had been a breach of the rights of the defence in so far as the Commission sought to compel it to incriminate itself by confessing to an infringement of the Community's competition rules. The E.C.J. accepted that article 6 E.C.H.R. (which lays down procedural guarantees intended to ensure a fair trial) can be relied upon by an undertaking in the context of a Commission investigation relating to competition law, but observed that 'neither the wording of that article nor the decisions of the European Court of Human Rights indicate that it upholds the right not to give evidence against oneself.'

In *Hauer* v. *Land Rheinland-Pfalz*, Case 44/79, [1979] E.C.R. 3727, the applicant challenged a decision of the German authorities refusing her permission to plant vines on her land. The questions referred by the German court to the European Court of Justice led the latter to consider whether a Council regulation which prohibited the new planting of vines for a period of three years infringed the right to property guaranteed by article 1 of the First Protocol to the Convention. The validity of the Regulation was thus at issue. The E.C.J. observed that although the Protocol declares that every person is entitled to the peaceful enjoyment of their possessions, it allows restrictions upon the use of property provided that they are deemed necessary for the protection of the general interest. After considering the constitutional rules and practices of the member states, the Court held that the applicant's right to property had not been infringed since the planting restrictions in question were justified by objectives of general interest pursued by the Community – the immediate reduction of production surpluses and the long-term restructuring of the European wine industry.

More recently, in *R.* v. *Ministry of Agriculture, Fisheries and Food ex parte Fédération Européenne de la Santé Animale* Case C-331/88, [1991] 1 C.M.L.R. 507 (hereafter *ex parte* FEDESA) which concerned the validity of Council Directive 88/146/EEC prohibiting the use in livestock farming of certain substances having a hormonal action, one of the issues was the Council's alleged infringement of the principle that legislation should not be retroactive. The directive, which had been adopted on March 7, 1988, stipulated that it was to be implemented by January 1, 1988. Drawing a distinction between penal and non-penal provisions, the E.C.J. declared that 'the principle that penal provisions may not have retroactive effect is ... enshrined in Article 7 of the European Convention ... as a fundamental mental right which takes its place among the general principles of law whose observance is ensured by the Court of Justice.' Thus the directive could not be interpreted as requiring member states to adopt measures which violated that principle. Neither could it sanction criminal proceedings instituted under national provisions adopted in implementation, and solely on the basis, of the annulled directive.

As regards the retroactive effect of the directive outside the criminal sphere, the Court held that although the principle of legal certainty generally precludes a Community measure from taking effect before its publication, retroactivity is exceptionally permitted where the purpose so demands and the legitimate expectations of those concerned are respected.

From the above cases, it is apparent that the principles enshrined in the European Convention and its related Protocols will be taken into consideration by the E.C.J. when reviewing Community acts under article 173 EEC (the action for annulment) and article 184 EEC (the plea of illegality), and in interpreting such acts, or determining their validity, in references from national courts and tribunals under article 177 EEC. The Convention's principles are also relevant in the context of actions for damages against the Community under articles 178 and 215(2) EEC, when the Court of Justice must decide whether the Community's non-contractual liability is engaged. In so far as national courts are called upon to interpret the acts of Community institutions, moreover, they must use the Convention and its Protocols in the same way as the E.C.J.

(ii) The European Convention as a constraint upon the member states

Even more important from the point of view of the member states is the E.C.J.'s use of the European Convention to restrict the activities of national authorities. In *Rutili* v. *Minister of the Interior* Case 36/75, [1975] E.C.R. 1219, where the French authorities prohibited an Italian national involved in political activities from residing in certain *départements*, the Court of Justice held that limitations cannot be imposed on the right of a national of any member state to enter the territory of another member state, to stay there and to move freely within it unless his presence or conduct constitutes a genuine and sufficiently serious threat to public policy. It concluded that

> 'these limitations on the powers of Member States ... are a specific manifestation of the more general principle, enshrined in Articles 8, 9, 10 and 11 of the [E.C.H.R.] and in Article 2 of Protocol No. 4 to the same Convention ... which provide ... that no restrictions in the interests of national security or public safety shall be placed on the rights secured by the above-quoted articles other than such as are necessary for the protection of those interests 'in a democratic society.''

Besides highlighting the Convention as a source of general principles to which it will have recourse, the E.C.J.'s ruling suggested that provisions of Community law must be construed and applied by member states with reference to those principles.

In *R.* v. *Kirk* Case 63/83, [1984] E.C.R. 2689, the Court of Justice applied the principle that penal provisions may not be retroactive, which is enshrined in article 7 E.C.H.R., in the context of a dispute concerning the validity of British regulations prohibiting Danish vessels from fishing within the United Kingdom's 12-mile fishery zone. Article 100 of the 1972 Act of Accession had authorised the United Kingdom to restrict fishing by other member states' nationals until December 31, 1982. Following the Council's failure to adopt Community provisions for the conservation and management of fishery resources after that date, the Commission declared that member states could adopt national conservation measures, subject to its approval. The United Kingdom's Sea Fish Order 1982 was approved by the Commission on January 5, 1983, and the following day Captain Kirk was arrested for unlawful fishing. He was subsequently fined £30,000 by a magistrates' court.

The retroactivity point arose after the Court of Justice ruled that member states had not been entitled to adopt measures which prohibited access to national waters and were not intended to achieve an objective of conservation. The United Kingdom and the Commission argued that the Sea Fish Order was nevertheless sanctioned by article 6(1) of Council Regulation No. 170/83 of January 25, 1983, which authorised retroactively (as from January 1, 1983) the retention of national measures derogating from the Community principle of non-discrimination on grounds of nationality. Acknowledging that the prohibition of retroactive penal provisions constitutes a fundamental human right, the E.C.J. held that the retroactivity of the regulation 'may not ... have the effect of validating *ex post facto* national measures of a penal nature which impose penalties for an act which, in fact, was not punishable at the time at which it was committed.' Indirectly, therefore, the principle enshrined in article 7 of the Convention was used by the Court as a constraint upon the United Kingdom.

In *Johnston* v. *Chief Constable of the R.U.C.* [1986] E.C.R. 1651, concerning the legality of the policy of not issuing firearms to female members of the Royal Ulster Constabulary, one of the questions involved the applicant's right to an effective judicial remedy. The Court of Justice ruled that article 6 of the Equal Treatment Directive had to be interpreted in the light of the principle of judicial control, which reflects a general principle of law underlying the constitutional traditions common to the member states and is laid down in articles 6 and 13 E.C.H.R.:

> 'By virtue of Article 6 of [the Directive], interpreted in the light of the general principle stated above, all persons have the right to obtain an effective remedy in a competent court against measures which they consider to be contrary to the principle of equal treatment for men and women ...'

It followed that article 53(2) of the Sex Discrimination (Northern Ireland) Order 1976, according to which a certificate issued by the Secretary of State was conclusive evidence that derogation from the equality principle was justified, was contrary to the principle of effective judicial control.

A similar issue arose in *U.N.E.C.T.E.F.* v. *Heylens* Case 222/86, [1987] E.C.R. 4097, following the French Football Association's refusal to recognise a Belgian trainer's Belgian diploma. The E.C.J. reiterated its view that the requirement of judicial review reflects a general principle of law underlying the member states' constitutional traditions and enshrined in articles 6 and 13 of the Convention, and concluded:

> 'Consequently ... the principle of free movement of workers laid down in Article 48 E.E.C. requires that it must be possible for a decision refusing to recognise the equivalence of a diploma ... to be

made the subject of judicial proceedings in which its legality under Community law can be reviewed, and for the person concerned to ascertain the reasons for the decision.'

In *E.C. Commission* v. *Germany* Case 249/86, [1987] E.C.R. 1263, the E.C.J. held that the provisions in Council Regulation No. 1612/68 on equal treatment for the families of migrant workers must be interpreted, *inter alia*,

'in the light of the requirement of respect for family life set out in Article 8 of the Convention ... That requirement is one of the fundamental rights which, according to the Court's settled case law, restated in the preamble to the Single European Act, are recognised by Community law.'

It followed that article 10(3) of the regulation, according to which the immigration rights of a migrant worker's family are dependent upon the worker's having available for them housing of a standard considered normal for national workers in the region concerned, applies solely as a condition under which each member of the family is permitted to come to live with the migrant worker. If, after the family has been brought together, the accommodation deteriorates below an acceptable standard as a result of a new event, such as a child's birth or arrival at adulthood, the migrant worker cannot be treated differently from national workers with regard to housing requirements. By adopting national provisions which made renewal of the residence permit of members of the family of Community migrant workers conditional upon their living in appropriate housing, not only at the time when they came to live with the worker but for the entire duration of their residence, Germany had failed to fulfil its obligations under the regulation.

The above decisions illustrate the E.C.J.'s long-standing commitment to the use of the European Convention to restrict member states' freedom of action in the implementation of Community law. Significantly, however, in other cases the Court of Justice has indicated that, in certain circumstances, it is actually prepared to consider whether national law is compatible with the Convention, in much the same way that the European Court of Human Rights would do. This was apparent in *Cinéthèque* v. *Fédération Nationale des Cinémas Français* Joined Cases 60–61/84, [1985] E.C.R. 2505, where the plaintiff alleged that a French statute concerning the distribution of cinematographic works violated article 10 of the Convention (the right to freedom of expression) and was thus incompatible with Community law. The Court of Justice held:

'Although ... it is the duty of this Court to ensure observance of fundamental rights in the field of Community law, it has no power to examine the compatibility with the European Convention of national legislation which concerns, as in this case, an area which falls within the jurisdiction of the national legislator.'

That decision was followed in *Demirel* Case 12/86, [1987] E.C.R. 3719, a case which helps to clarify the circumstances in which the E.C.J. would consider whether national law was consistent with the European Convention. There, a Turkish wife who had been refused leave to stay in Germany with her Turkish husband (who had himself acquired residence in Germany under German laws on family reunification), invoked article 8 of the Convention (the right to respect for family life). The E.C.J. ruled that article 8 had no bearing on the case, but only because the national rules under which the plaintiff had been refused leave to stay fell outside the scope of Community law, there being no provision of Community law defining the conditions in which member states must permit the family reunification of Turkish workers lawfully settled in the Community:

> 'It follows that the national rules at issue ... did not have to implement a provision of Community law. In these circumstances the Court does not have jurisdiction to determine whether (the) national rules ... are compatible with the principles enshrined in Article 8 of the European Convention ...'

If the national rules concerned had been within the scope of Community law, it seems that the Court would have been prepared to consider their compatibility with the Convention.

The E.C.J. clearly has no power to examine the compatibility with the European Convention of national legislation lying outside the scope of Community law. As regards national rules which are within the framework of Community law, however, the Court implies both that it has such power and that it will ensure observance of the principles enshrined in the Convention. Whilst there will undoubtedly be critics of such a claim, it reflects the importance attributed to the Convention in the preamble to the Single European Act and may be seen as a logical development of the Court's earlier case law. As *Demirel* indicates, national rules will be regarded as 'within the scope of Community law' if the issue in question is governed by Community provisions. In that case, however, there was no Community law requiring member states to permit the family reunification of Turkish workers and thus no Community obligation requiring national implementation.

If the necessary Community connection exists, the failure of a member state to respect the principles of the Convention could lead the E.C.J. to declare a violation of Community law. This would normally occur in the context of an enforcement action brought by the Commission under article 169 EEC. Incompatibility with the Convention could also come to light following a request for a preliminary ruling under article 177 EEC, although the E.C.J. is not competent to consider the validity of national provisions in such proceedings. In appropriate circumstances, moreover, the President of the Court could conceivably order the suspension of the offending national provision, as in *Re Nationality of Fishermen: E.C. Commission* v. *United Kingdom* Case 246/89R, [1989] 3 C.M.L.R. 601. There, pending the Court's judgment in article 169 proceedings concerning the validity of the nationality requirements of the Merchant Shipping Act 1988, the President of the E.C.J. ordered the suspension of the Act's nationality provisions as regards the nationals of other member states and in respect of fishing vessels which, until March 31, 1989, had operated under the British flag and under a British fishing licence.

THE IMPLICATIONS FOR BRITISH COURTS

Since the European Convention on Human Rights is used by the European Court of Justice as an aid to the construction of the Community Treaties and the legislative and administrative acts of the Community institutions, section 3(1) of the European Communities Act 1972 requires British courts (if they do not seek a preliminary ruling under article 177) to determine the meaning and effect of Community provisions in the light of the Convention. To this end they must have regard to any relevant decisions of the E.C.J. and the European Court of Human Rights. The possibility of inconsistent interpretations of the Convention by the two European Courts cannot be ruled out, especially since there is no mechanism whereby the E.C.J. can refer a question concerning the Convention's construction to the Court of Human Rights. However, the *Hoechst* and *Orkem* cases suggest that the Luxembourg Court will defer to the Strasbourg Court's jurisprudence – rightly, since the Court of Human Rights is the supreme interpreter of the Convention – and national courts should do likewise.

In the event of the E.C.J. declaring a statutory provision to be incompatible with the principles enshrined in the Convention (and thus with Community law), national courts would have to refuse to apply the offending provision if it would undermine the effectiveness of Community rules, whether or not the Convention had been incorporated into domestic law. As the Court of Justice held in *Factortame (No. 2)* Case C-213/89, [1991] 1 All E.R. 70, it is for national courts, in application of the principle of co-operation laid down in article 5 EEC, to ensure the legal protection derived from the direct effect of Community law. Further,

> 'any provision of a national legal system and any legislative, administrative or judicial practice which might impair the effectiveness of Community law by withholding from the national court . . . the power to . . . set aside national legislative provisions which might prevent . . . Community rules from having full force and effect are incompatible with those requirements, which are the very essence of Community law.'

Potentially more important is the European Convention's impact upon domestic executive action in the context of the implementation of Community obligations. Although the House of Lords in *Brind* rejected the appellants' submission that administrative discretion must be exercised in conformity with the Convention, the E.C.J.'s case law makes it clear that the Convention is at least relevant with regard to the domestic implementation of Community law. Despite Lord Bridge's concern that the judiciary should not 'without Parliament's aid . . . incorporate the Convention into such an important area of domestic law,' therefore, executive action in pursuance of Community obligations (whether through delegated legislation or the exercise of administrative discretion) *is* subject to the Convention's constraints, and national courts must bear this in mind when reviewing the legality of such action and when construing implementing legislation.

Nicholas Grief, 'The Domestic Impact of the European Convention on Human Rights as Mediated through Community Law', *Public Law*, 1991, pp. 555–67.

---

37   THE HEADS OF STATE OF THE EUROPEAN UNION COUNTRIES CONFIRM THEIR ESPOUSAL OF FUNDAMENTAL RIGHTS AND FREEDOMS, 1986–92

Single European Act, 1986

HIS MAJESTY THE KING OF THE BELGIANS,
HER MAJESTY THE QUEEN OF DENMARK.
THE PRESIDENT OF THE FEDERAL REPUBLIC OF GERMANY,
THE PRESIDENT OF THE HELLENIC REPUBLIC,
HIS MAJESTY THE KING OF SPAIN,
THE PRESIDENT OF THE FRENCH REPUBLIC,
THE PRESIDENT OF IRELAND,
THE PRESIDENT OF THE ITALIAN REPUBLIC,
HIS ROYAL HIGHNESS THE GRAND DUKE OF LUXEMBOURG,
HER MAJESTY THE QUEEN OF THE NETHERLANDS,
THE PRESIDENT OF THE PORTUGUESE REPUBLIC,
HER MAJESTY THE QUEEN OF THE UNITED KINGDOM OF GREAT BRITAIN AND NORTHERN IRELAND,

Moved by the will to continue the work undertaken on the basis of the Treaties establishing the European Communities and to transform relations as a whole among their States into a European Union, in accordance with the Solemn Declaration of Stuttgart of 19 June 1983,

Resolved to implement this European Union on the basis, firstly, of the Communities operating in accordance with their own rules and, secondly, of European Cooperation among the Signatory States in the sphere of foreign policy and to invest this union with the necessary means of action,

Determined to work together to promote democracy on the basis of the fundamental rights recognized in the constitutions and laws of the Member States, in the Convention for the Protection of Human Rights and Fundamental Freedoms and the European Social Charter, notably freedom, equality and social justice,

Convinced that the European idea, the results achieved in the fields of economic integration and political cooperation, and the need for new developments correspond to the wishes of the democratic peoples of

Europe, for whom the European Parliament, elected by universal suffrage, is an indispensable means of expression,

Aware of the responsibility incumbent upon Europe to aim at speaking ever increasingly with one voice and to act with consistency and solidarity in order more effectively to protect its common interests and independence, in particular to display the principles of democracy and compliance with the law and with human rights to which they are attached, so that together they may make their own contribution to the preservation of international peace and security in accordance with the undertaking entered into by them within the framework of the United Nations Charter,

Determined to improve the economic and social situation by extending common policies and pursuing new objectives, and to ensure a smoother functioning of the Communities by enabling the institutions to exercise their powers under conditions most in keeping with Community interests

Treaty on European Union, 1992
(The 'Maastricht Treaty')

HIS MAJESTY THE KING OF THE BELGIANS,
HER MAJESTY THE QUEEN OF DENMARK,
THE PRESIDENT OF THE FEDERAL REPUBLIC OF GERMANY,
THE PRESIDENT OF THE HELLENIC REPUBLIC,
HIS MAJESTY THE KING OF SPAIN,
THE PRESIDENT OF THE FRENCH REPUBLIC,
THE PRESIDENT OF IRELAND,
THE PRESIDENT OF THE ITALIAN REPUBLIC,
HIS ROYAL HIGHNESS THE GRAND DUKE OF LUXEMBOURG,
HER MAJESTY THE QUEEN OF THE NETHERLANDS,
THE PRESIDENT OF THE PORTUGUESE REPUBLIC,
HER MAJESTY THE QUEEN OF THE UNITED KINGDOM OF GREAT BRITAIN AND NORTHERN IRELAND,

Resolved to mark a new stage in the process of European integration undertaken with the establishment of the European Communities,

Recalling the historic importance of the ending of the division of the European continent and the need to create firm bases for the construction of the future Europe,

Confirming their attachment to the principles of liberty, democracy and respect for human rights and fundamental freedoms and of the rule of law,

Desiring to deepen the solidarity between their peoples while respecting their history, their culture and their traditions,

Desiring to enhance further the democratic and efficient functioning of the institutions so as to enable them better to carry out, within a single institutional framework, the tasks entrusted to them,

Resolved to achieve the strengthening and the convergence of their economies and to establish an economic and monetary union including, in accordance with the provisions of this Treaty, a single and stable currency,

Determined to promote economic and social progress for their peoples, within the context of the accomplishment of the internal market and of reinforced cohesion and environmental protection, and to implement policies ensuring that advances in economic integration are accompanied by parallel progress in other fields,

Resolved to establish a citizenship common to nationals of their countries,

Resolved to implement a common foreign and security policy including the eventual framing of a common defence policy, which might in time lead to a common defence, thereby reinforcing the European identity and its independence in order to promote peace, security and progress in Europe and in the world,

Reaffirming their objective to facilitate the free movement of persons, while ensuring the safety and security of their peoples, by including provisions on justice and home affairs in this Treaty,

Resolved to continue the process of creating an ever closer union among the peoples of Europe, in which decisions are taken as closely as possible to the citizen in accordance with the principle of subsidiarity,

In view of further steps to be taken in order to advance European integration,

Have decided to establish a European Union ...

COMMON PROVISIONS

Article B

The Union shall set itself the following objectives:

— to promote economic and social progress which is balanced and sustainable, in particular through the creation of an area without internal frontiers, through the strengthening of economic and social cohesion and through the establishment of economic and monetary union, ultimately including a single currency in accordance with the provisions of this Treaty;

— to assert its identity on the international scene, in particular through the implementation of a common foreign and security policy including the eventual framing of a common defence policy, which might in time lead to a common defence;

— to strengthen the protection of the rights and interests of the nationals of its Member States through the introduction of a citizenship of the Union;

— to develop close cooperation on justice and home affairs;

— to maintain in full the *acquis communautaire* and build on it with a view to considering, through the procedure referred to in Article N (2), to what extent the policies and forms of cooperation introduced by this Treaty may need to be revised with the aim of ensuring the effectiveness of the mechanisms and the institutions of the Community.

The objectives of the Union shall be achieved as provided in this Treaty and in accordance with the conditions and the timetable set out therein while respecting the principle of subsidiarity as defined in Article 3b of the Treaty establishing the European Community. ...

Article F

1. The Union shall respect the national identities of its Member States, whose systems of government are founded on the principles of democracy.

2. The Union shall respect fundamental rights, as guaranteed by the European Convention for the Protection of Human Rights and Fundamental Freedoms signed in Rome on 4 November 1950 and as they result from the constitutional traditions common to the Member States, as general principles of Community law.

3. The Union shall provide itself with the means necessary to attain its objectives and carry through its policies.

CITIZENSHIP OF THE UNION

Article 8

1. Citizenship of the Union is hereby established.

Every person holding the nationality of a Member State shall be a citizen of the Union.

2. Citizens of the Union shall enjoy the rights conferred by this Treaty and shall be subject to the duties imposed thereby.

Article 8a

1. Every citizen of the Union shall have the right to move and reside freely within the territory of the Member States, subject to the limitations and conditions laid down in this Treaty and by the measures adopted to give it effect.

2. The Council may adopt provisions with a view to facilitating the exercise of the rights referred to in paragraph 1; save as otherwise provided in this Treaty, the Council shall act unanimously on a proposal from the Commission and after obtaining the assent of the European Parliament.

Article 8b

1. Every citizen of the Union residing in a Member State of which he is not a national shall have the right to vote and to stand as a candidate at municipal elections in the Member State in which he resides, under the same conditions as nationals of that State. This right shall be exercised subject to detailed arrangements to be adopted before 31 December 1994 by the Council, acting unanimously on a proposal from the Commission and after consulting the European Parliament; these arrangements may provide for derogations where warranted by problems specific to a Member State.

2. Without prejudice to Article 138(3) and to the provisions adopted for its

implementation, every citizen of the Union residing in a Member State of which he is not a national shall have the right to vote and to stand as a candidate in elections to the European Parliament in the Member State in which he resides, under the same conditions as nationals of that State. This right shall be exercised subject to detailed arrangements to be adopted before 31 December 1993 by the Council, acting unanimously on a proposal from the Commission and after consulting the European Parliament; these arrangements may provide for derogations where warranted by problems specific to a Member State.

Article 8c

Every citizen of the Union shall, in the territory of a third country in which the Member State of which he is a national is not represented, be entitled to protection by the diplomatic or consular authorities of any Member State, on the same conditions as the nationals of that State. Before 31 December 1993, Member States shall establish the necessary rules among themselves and start the international negotiations required to secure this protection.

Article 8d

Every citizen of the Union shall have the right to petition the European Parliament in accordance with Article 138d.

Every citizen of the Union may apply to the Ombudsman established in accordance with Article 138e.

Article 8e

The Commission shall report to the European Parliament, to the Council and to the Economic and Social Committee before 31 December 1993 and then every three years on the application of the provisions of this Part. This report shall take account of the development of the Union.

On this basis, and without prejudice to the other provisions of this Treaty, the Council, acting unanimously on a proposal from the Commission and after consulting the European Parliament, may adopt provisions to strengthen or to add to the rights laid down in this Part, which it shall recommend to the Member States for adoption in accordance with their respective constitutional requirements.

---

38   LORD SLYNN, LAW LORD AND FORMER JUDGE AT THE EUROPEAN COURT OF JUSTICE, ON THE PROPOSAL THAT THE EUROPEAN UNION ACCEDE TO THE CONVENTION ON HUMAN RIGHTS, 1992

My Lords, the protection of human rights is a subject which can generate strong feelings, so on the first occasion when I have the privilege of speaking in your Lordships' House I must steer between the Scylla of being controversial or at any rate too controversial and the Charybdis of being so anodyne that at the end it may be thought that I have said nothing. Whether or not I steer between those dangers in the course of my speech, for which I ask the indulgence of the House, I thank the noble Baroness, Lady Elles, for the gracious words with which she began her speech and for the kind remarks made by the noble and learned Lord, Lord Archer of Sandwell.

The proposal that it should be made possible for the European Community to accede to the Convention on Human Rights, and that the Community should do so, has had a somewhat checkered history. When I was asked by the noble and learned Lord, Lord Hailsham of Saint Marylebone, as Lord Chancellor, to go to the European Court of Justice 12 years ago, I found that senior lawyers in the Commission seemed very enthusiastic about the idea. Then, perhaps partly because of the report of the Select Committee of this House on human rights, but also for other reasons, the enthusiasm seemed to cool and the idea was put aside.

Now, the proposal has been revived and, as I understand it, with more vigour. There is plainly nothing wrong in the Commission reviving a proposal after leaving it on one side. On the contrary, it seems to me that the proposal needs to looked at from time to time, if it is not adopted.

The question, however, as I see it at the moment, is whether it is now right to adopt the proposal that the Community and indeed perhaps the three communities should accede to the Convention on Human Rights. There are clearly arguments in favour of doing so, as has been shown in the speech of the noble and learned Lord, Lord Archer of Sandwell.

It is a natural progression, when all the member states have ratified and granted rights of individual petition. It looks right, since nationals of all member states would have a right of access to an independent commission of inquiry and a Court of Human Rights in Strasbourg, if breaches of the convention by the Community or by the institutions are alleged. Accession would avoid the peculiarity of the European Court of Justice being both defendant and judge in cases brought by officials of the Court alleging breaches of human rights.

Yet, on the other hand, it is quite clear that accession by the Community would only open up such a right to go to the Court in areas concerned with Community activity. It would not affect, it would not enlarge, the citizen's rights against his own member state and it seems to me that the number of cases at the moment which are likely to be involved will be few.

In that regard, it is a critical factor, as the noble Baroness has already indicated, that from the early days the European Court of Justice has established that fundamental principles of law exist beyond those spelt out in the treaty. The Court recognised that certain rules of fairness, reasonableness and legal certainty are observed by all the member states, which member states must have intended to apply to action in the Community. Those principles, I venture to suggest, have had a very beneficial effect in protecting the citizen against arbitrary and unreasonable conduct.

The Court of Justice slowly recognised that fundamental or human rights were included among those general principles. After France had ratified the convention, she finally accepted that the principles set out in the convention should be reflected in Community law.

I suggest that that was a major step and the Court of Justice now asserts categorically that these fundamental human rights are part of the law of the Community which it is the Court's duty to secure and enforce. It has thus recognised such fundamental rights as the right not to be discriminated against on the basis of religious faith; the right to develop property as set out in the protocol to the European convention, subject to acceptable restrictions in the general interest by way of planning controls and otherwise. The Court has recognised rights of the defence such as the right to a fair hearing. It has recognised that retroactive legislation making acts criminal which were not criminal at the time is wholly illegal and unacceptable.

It is important, I think, to bear in mind that in all this the European Court in Luxembourg has followed the interpretation of the convention adopted by the Court and the Commission in Strasbourg and has refrained from laying down wide-ranging decisions in uncharted areas. So there is considerable consistency between what has been done by the Court of Justice and what is done by the Court and Commission in Strasbourg. I doubt very much whether it can really be said, as I think was suggested by some of the witnesses to the committee, that the court in Luxembourg is not in a position to be informed of what is going on in the Strasbourg institutions.

It is clear, on the other hand, that if these cases have been few – and they have been very few where both the principle and a breach of the principle have been established – in the definition of the rights, the Court has done much and is capable of doing much in the limited area of Community activity. It has done so – and I think this is important – to such an extent that even the German Supreme Constitutional Court – which has a basic law of human rights which at one time it was disposed to insist upon against Community legislation – now accepts that it will not test the validity of Community directives against that basic law, but will leave it to the Court of Justice to apply the necessary rules of fundamental rights.

A special point has been raised in the discussion before the committee, as appears from the report, about officials and other employees of the Community. Is it necessary that the Community should accede to the Convention on Human Rights in order to protect the interests of those officials? I doubt very much whether that is necessary. It seems to me that the detailed rules governing the conditions of employment of employees of the Community are dealt with by the new court of first instance and by the Court of Justice in a way which sufficiently protects their interests. I doubt very much whether allegations of breach of the convention are likely to be raised by officials in many cases.

So for my own part I do not feel concern that in practice – whatever the theoretical or cosmetic objections may be – officials of the Court or of the other institutions are likely to be prejudiced.

The Commission has suggested that there may be gaps. There is undoubtedly a risk that some cases will not get to the Court of Justice. The Court can only deal with situations falling within the area of Community law which come before it. But I observe that Mr. Anthony Lester (who has been referred to and who has great experience in this area and who 10 years ago was against the Community acceding to the convention) now feels on balance – I repeat on balance – that the Community should accede.

If I were satisfied that there were serious gaps, I should agree with that. But on balance I do not consider that in practice it has been shown that there is any need for the Community to accede.

Finally, it would be perhaps somewhat strange for the United Kingdom to be supporting accession when we have not made the convention part of our domestic law. This is something which I suggest needs now to be thought about again in the light of the subjects raised in the report of this committee.

On the one hand, some people are perturbed by the block which seems to have occurred in the Supreme Court of Canada by the number of cases flowing from the adoption of the charter of human rights. On the other hand, I commend to the House two considerations which arise out of this report. The first is that every time the European Court recognises a principle set out in the convention as being part of Community law, it must be enforced in the United Kingdom courts in relation to Community law matters, but not in domestic law. So the convention becomes in part a part of our law through the back door because we have to apply the convention in respect of Community law matters as a part of Community law.

Secondly, when I was counsel for the United Kingdom on many occasions in the court of the commission on human rights at Strasbourg it was quite plain that many, although perhaps not all, of the cases could be dealt with just as well and more expeditiously by our own judges here.

I have for many years felt it would be right that the convention should now become part of our domestic law. Having read the report of the committee I feel fortified in that view. I mention this briefly because it seems to me to put in perspective the proposal that the Community should accede to the convention. The committee is right to conclude that the Community for the moment has more urgent and more immediate things to do, yet the topic is an important one and the situation must be monitored. I am grateful to the noble Baroness, Lady Elles, for having introduced this debate.

HL Deb., 26 November 1992, cols. 1095–8.

CHAPTER 3

STATUTORY INCORPORATION OF THE EUROPEAN CONVENTION ON HUMAN RIGHTS IN THE UK

39 DRAFT LEGISLATION TO INCORPORATE THE EUROPEAN CONVENTION ON HUMAN RIGHTS INTO THE DOMESTIC LAW OF THE UK, 1975–96

(A) BILL OF RIGHTS BILL 1975 (Alan Beith)

A Bill to declare the inalienable rights and liberties of the subject.

Be it enacted by the Queen's most Excellent Majesty, by and with the advice and consent of the Lords Spiritual and Temporal, and Commons, in this present Parliament assembled, and by the authority of the same, as follows:—

1. The Convention for the Protection of Human Rights and Fundamental Freedoms signed by Governments being Members of the Council of Europe at Rome on 4th November 1950, together with the five Protocols thereto, shall without any reservation immediately upon the passing of this Act have the force of law, and shall be enforceable by action in the Courts of the United Kingdom. For the purposes of this Act the texts of the said Convention and Protocols shall be those set out in Schedules 1 to 6 hereto.

2. In case of conflict between any enactment prior to the passing of this Act and the provisions of the said Convention and Protocols, the said Convention and Protocols shall prevail.

3. In case of conflict between any enactment subsequent to the passing of this Act and the provisions of the said Convention and Protocols, the said Convention and Protocols shall prevail unless subsequent enactment shall explicitly state otherwise.

4.—(1) This Act may be cited as the Bill of Rights Act 1975.

(2) This Act extends to Northern Ireland.

RB NOTE: The Schedules then laid out the provisions of the European Convention on Human Rights and its Protocols, for which see Doc. 20 above.

HC [1974–5] 59.

(B) BILL OF RIGHTS BILL 1981 (Lord Wade)

RB NOTE: Earlier in 1976, Lord Wade introduced a Bill of Rights Bill [1976–7] 11, identical in form to Alan Beith's Bill (see above), which led to the appointment of the Select Committee on a Bill of Rights which reported in 1977 (see Doc. 83). Lord Wade's 1981 Bill, shown below, significantly amended the terms of the earlier legislation.

An Act to render the provisions of the European Convention for the Protection of Human Rights enforceable in the courts of the United Kingdom.

Be it enacted by the Queen's most Excellent Majesty, by and with the advice and consent of the Lords Spiritual and Temporal, and Commons, in this present Parliament assembled, and by the authority of the same, as follows:—

1. The Convention for the Protection of Human Rights and Fundamental Freedoms signed by Governments being Members of the Council of Europe at Rome on 4th November 1950, together with such Protocols thereto as shall have been ratified by the Government of the United Kingdom, shall subject to any reservations thereto by the Government of the United Kingdom immediately upon the passing of this Act have the force of law, and shall be enforceable by action in the Courts of the United Kingdom.

2. In case of conflict between any laws or enactments prior to the passing of this Act and the provisions of the said Convention and such Protocols as shall have been ratified by the Government of the United Kingdom and subject to any reservations thereto, the said Convention and Protocols shall prevail.

3. In case of conflict between any enactment subsequent to the passing of this Act and the provisions of the said Convention and such Protocols as shall have been ratified by the Government of the United Kingdom and subject to any reservations thereto, such enactment passed after the passing of this Act shall be deemed to be subject to the provisions of the said Convention and Protocols and shall be so construed unless such subsequent enactment provides otherwise or does not admit of any construction compatible with the provisions of this Act.

4.—(1) Notwithstanding anything contained in section 1 of this Act and subject to subsections (2) and (3) of this section, in time of war or other public emergency threatening the life of the nation Her Majesty by Order in Council may take measures derogating from the obligations of the Government of the United Kingdom under the said Convention and Protocols ('derogating measures').

(2) No measures derogating from Articles 2 (except in respect of deaths resulting from lawful acts of war), 3, 4 (paragraph 1) and 7 of the said Convention shall be made under the provisions of this section.

(3) No derogating measures shall have any effect on the obligations of the Government of the United Kingdom under international law.

(4) For the purposes of this Act, a declaration by Her Majesty by Order in Council that there exists for the purposes of any derogating measure a time of war or other emergency threatening the life of the nation shall be conclusive.

5. For the purposes of this Act—
  'Convention' means Articles 1 to 18 inclusive and Article 60 of the said
    Convention;
  'Protocols' means Articles 1 to 3 inclusive of the (First) Protocol to the
    said Convention;
  'reservations' means the Reservation made to the (First) Protocol (Arti-
    cle 2) by the United Kingdom under Article 64 of the said
    Convention.

6.—(1) This Act may be cited as the Bill of Rights Act 1981.

(2) This Act extends to Northern Ireland.

*RB NOTE: The Schedules then laid out the provisions of the European
Convention on Human Rights and Protocol, for which see Doc. 20 above.*

(HL), HC [1980–1] 60.

(C) HUMAN RIGHTS AND FUNDAMENTAL FREEDOMS BILL 1985
(Lords Broxbourne and Scarman)

*RB NOTE: The Human Rights and Fundamental Freedoms Bill 1985 was
similar in content to the earlier European Human Rights Bill 1984 presented
by Robert Maclennan (HC, 1983–4, 73) and the later Human Rights Bill 1986
presented by Sir Edward Gardner (HC, 1986–7, 19).*

*The only slight variation between these three Bills was that the wording in
clause 4(2) dealing with the effect on later enactments in Sir Edward
Gardner's Human Rights Bill 1986 read as follows:*

*'No provision of an Act passed after the passing of this Act shall be
construed as authorising or requiring the doing of an act that infringes any of
the fundamental rights and freedoms, or as conferring power to make any
subordinate instrument authorising or requiring the doing of any such act,
unless such a construction is unavoidable if effect is to be given to that
provision and to the other provisions of the Act.'*

Explanatory memorandum

The Bill provides for protection to be afforded in the courts of the United
Kingdom for the rights and freedoms specified in the European Convention
for the Protection of Human Rights and Fundamental Freedoms to which
the United Kingdom is a party.

Specifically, the purposes of the Bill are:
  (*a*) to ensure that a remedy exists within the United Kingdom for all
    within its jurisdiction who are able to establish infringement by
    public authority of a right or freedom specified in the Conven-
    tion;
  (*b*) to provide judicial remedies within the United Kingdom in respect
    of such infringements;

(c) to clarify the law of the United Kingdom in relation to the rights specified in the Convention.

Clause 1 *and Schedules* 1 *and* 2 introduce the principal definitions and in particular those of the 'fundamental rights and freedoms'. These mean the rights and freedoms guaranteed by the Convention and by Protocol No. 1 to the Convention as set out in Schedule 1.

Clause 2 gives to the fundamental rights and freedoms the force of law in the United Kingdom.

Clause 3 provides that no person shall do any act to which it applies which infringes any of the fundamental rights and freedoms of any other person within the jurisdiction of the United Kingdom.

It applies to acts done by or for the purposes of the Crown or of a Minister of the Crown or of various public authorities. The duty created by Clause 3 is actionable in the United Kingdom.

Clause 4 makes provision for the effect on existing and future enactments. Existing enactments which authorise or require any act to be done are to be taken to require any such act to be done only in a manner or to an extent that does not infringe the fundamental rights and freedoms. Future enactments are to be taken to have the same effect save in so far as they expressly otherwise provide.

Clause 5 requires proceedings under Clause 3 to be brought within six months from the doing of the act complained of unless the Court considers that it is just and equitable to consider the proceedings out of time.

Clause 6 deals with the treatment and proof of the Convention, the Protocols and the jurisprudence of the European Court and Commission of Human Rights in legal proceedings in the United Kingdom.

Clause 7 *and Schedule* 3 ensure that where questions arise in proceedings under the Bill, notice is given to the appropriate Law Officer who is thereby enabled to take part as a party in the proceedings.

Clause 8 provides that proceedings against the Crown are to be treated as civil proceedings.

Clause 9 enables Her Majesty by Order in Council to take derogating measures under the Convention which may abridge or abrogate certain of the fundamental rights and freedoms. An Order in Council under Clause 9 may not be questioned in any proceedings.

Manpower implications

The Bill is not expected to have any significant implications on public service manpower.

A Bill intituled

An Act to provide protection in the courts of the United Kingdom for the rights and freedoms specified in the European Convention for the Protection of Human Rights and Fundamental Freedoms to which the United Kingdom is a party.

Be it enacted by the Queen's most Excellent Majesty, by and with the advice and consent of the Lords Spiritual and Temporal, and Commons, in this present Parliament assembled, and by the authority of the same, as follows:—

1.—(1) This Act may be cited as the Human Rights and Fundamental Freedoms Act 1985.

(2) In this Act, except in so far as the context otherwise requires—

'the Convention' means the European Convention for the Protection of Human Rights and Fundamental Freedoms signed at Rome on 4th November 1950;

'the Protocol' means Protocol No. 1 to the Convention signed at Paris on 20th March 1952;

'fundamental rights and freedoms' means the rights and freedoms guaranteed by the Convention and the Protocol as set out in Schedule 1 to this Act, subject to the restrictions thereto permitted by the Convention and the Protocol, and subject also to the reservations thereto made by the Government of the United Kingdom as set out in Schedule 2 to this Act;

'act' includes a deliberate omission;

'enactment' includes any Order in Council or instrument made under any enactment;

'statutory body' means a body established by or in pursuance of any enactment, and 'statutory office' means an office so established;

'public body' means a body of persons, whether corporate or unincorporate, carrying on a service or undertaking of a public nature and includes public authorities of all descriptions, and 'public office' shall be construed accordingly;

'the Crown' does not include Her Majesty in Her private capacity, or in the right of her Duchy of Lancaster, or the Duchy of Cornwall.

2.—Subject to the provisions of this Act, the fundamental rights and freedoms shall have the force of law in the United Kingdom.

3.—(1) Subject to the provisions of this Act, no person shall do any act to which this section applies and which infringes any of the fundamental rights and freedoms of any other person within the jurisdiction of the United Kingdom.

(2) This section applies—

(*a*) to an act done by or for the purposes of the Crown or of a Minister of the Crown,

(*b*) to an act done by or for the purposes of a statutory body, a person holding a statutory office, a public body, or a person holding public office.

(3) The obligation to comply with subsection (1) above is a duty owed to any person within the jurisdiction of the United Kingdom who may be adversely affected by a contravention of that subsection, and any breach of that duty is actionable in the United Kingdom accordingly.

4.—(1) Any enactment made or passed before the passing of this Act which authorises or requires any act to be done shall be taken to authorise or require that act to be done only in a manner and to the extent that it does not infringe any of the fundamental rights and freedoms of any person within the jurisdiction of the United Kingdom.

(2) Any enactment made or passed after the passing of this Act which authorises or requires any act to be done shall be taken to authorise or require that act to be done only in a manner and to the extent that it does not infringe any of the fundamental rights and freedoms of any person within the jurisdiction of the United Kingdom, save in so far as such enactment is an Act which expressly directs that this subsection shall not apply to the doing of the act in question or is made pursuant to a power conferred by an Act which expressly so directs.

5.—(1) No proceedings shall be brought under section 3 of this Act after the end of a period of six months from the doing of the act complained of.

(2) A court may nevertheless consider any such proceedings which are out of time if, in all the circumstances, the court considers that it is just and equitable to do so.

6. For the purpose of this Act judicial notice shall be taken of the Convention and the Protocols and of all published judgments of the European Court of Human Rights and of all published reports and decisions of the European Commission of Human Rights established by the Convention.

7. Schedule 3 to this Act shall have effect with respect to the legal proceedings and questions mentioned therein.

8.—(1) The provisions of Parts II to IV of the Crown Proceedings Act 1947 shall apply to proceedings against the Crown under this Act as they apply to proceedings in England and Wales and in Northern Ireland which by virtue of section 23 of that Act are treated for the purposes of Part II of that Act as civil proceedings by or against the Crown.

(2) The provisions of Part V of the Crown Proceedings Act 1947 shall apply to proceedings against the Crown under this Act as they apply to proceedings in Scotland which by virtue of the said Part are treated as civil proceedings by or against the Crown.

9.—(1) If at any time Her Majesty declares by Order in Council that there exists a state of war or other public emergency threatening the life of the nation, and for so long as that Order remains in force, Her Majesty may by Order in Council take such measures as may appear to her to be strictly required by the exigencies of the situation, notwithstanding that such measures may abridge or abrogate one or more of the fundamental rights and freedoms, provided that no such measure shall abridge or abrogate any of the fundamental rights or freedoms guaranteed by Article 2 (except in respect of death resulting from lawful acts of war), Article 3, Article 4 (paragraph 1) or Article 7 of the Convention.

(2) No Order in Council made under this section may be questioned in any proceedings whatsoever.

SCHEDULES

RB NOTE: Schedule 1 then gives the provisions of the European Convention on Human Rights and Protocol and Schedule 2 gives the Reservation made by the UK, for which see doc. 22 above.

Schedule 3: Legal proceedings involving human rights issues

1. In this Schedule:
   'human rights issue' means a question arising under sections 2 to 4 of this Act;
   'the appropriate Law Officer' means—
   (*a*) in proceedings in England and Wales, the Attorney General;
   (*b*) in proceedings in Scotland, the Lord Advocate;
   (*c*) in proceedings in Northern Ireland, the Attorney General for Northern Ireland.

2. A human rights issue shall not be taken to arise in any legal proceedings by reason only of any contention of a party to the proceedings which appears to the court or tribunal before which the proceedings take place to be frivolous or vexatious.

3. Where a human rights issue arises in any proceedings before any court or tribunal, the court or tribunal shall, unless the Crown is already a party to the proceedings, order notice or intimation of the human rights issue to be given to the appropriate Law Officer, who may thereupon take part as a party in the proceedings so far as they relate to a human rights issue.

4. Where it appears to the court or tribunal before which any proceedings take place that the participation of the appropriate Law Officer in pursuance of paragraph 3 above has occasioned any party to the proceedings additional expense, the court or tribunal may take account of it in deciding any question as to costs or expenses and may, whatever the decision on the human rights issue, award the whole or part of the additional expense as costs or, as the case may be, expenses, to that party.

HL [1985–6] 21.

(D) HUMAN RIGHTS BILL 1994 (Graham Allen)

A Bill to

Provide protection to individuals and in the courts of the United Kingdom for the rights and freedoms specified in the European Convention of

Human Rights and Fundamental Freedoms; to entrench those rights and freedoms; to establish a Human Rights Commission; to make further provision with regard to the protection of civil, political, economic and social rights; and for connected purposes.

Be it enacted by the Queen's most Excellent Majesty, by and with the advice and consent of the Lords Spiritual and Temporal, and Commons, in this present Parliament assembled, and by the authority of the same, as follows:—

Part I: The European Convention of Human Rights and Fundamental Freedoms

1.—(1) The fundamental rights and freedoms set out in Section I of the Convention and the Protocols thereto, set out in Schedule 1 to this Act, shall, subject to the provisions of this Act and the restrictions permitted by the Convention and its Protocols and the reservations contained in Schedule 2 to this Act, have the force of law.

(2) The obligation on the part of any person to whom this Act applies to comply with the provisions of the Convention is owed to any natural person and any such person who may be adversely affected by a breach of that obligation shall, without prejudice to any other claim, have a cause of action in like manner as in any other such claim, being a claim in tort or delict under any system of law in the United Kingdom.

2.—(1) It shall be unlawful for any person or body defined in subsection (3) below to do any act which infringes any of the fundamental rights and freedoms of any natural person.

(2) It shall be the duty of any person or body defined in subsection (3) below to promote the fundamental rights and freedoms referred to in section 1 above.

(3) This section applies to—
    (a) a Minister of the Crown or any person or body acting on behalf of, or for the purposes of, the Crown, and
    (b) any statutory body, public body, or any person holding statutory office, any other public office or exercising any public function, or any body or person acting on behalf of, or for the purposes of, any such body or person.

3. Any natural person whose fundamental rights and freedoms are being, have been or are about to be infringed shall have an effective remedy before a tribunal or court and in the absence of, and without prejudice to, any other established remedy shall have a cause of action in the High Court or, in Scotland, the Court of Session and in any case shall be entitled to such of the following remedies as are appropriate in all the circumstances—
    (a) a declaration of the effect of those fundamental rights and freedoms in the particular circumstances;

(b) damages for such infringements including where appropriate exemplary and aggravated damages;

(c) an order restraining future infringements;

(d) an order to enforce fundamental rights and freedoms; or

(e) an order quashing the act of any person or body defined in subsection (3) of section 2 above.

4.—(1) Any provision in any enactment or in any statutory instrument made before the passing of this Act or any provision or construction of the common law taking effect before or after the passing of this Act which authorises or requires any act to be done—

(a) shall be taken to authorise or require that act to be done only in a manner and to the extent that it does not infringe any of the fundamental rights and freedoms of any natural person; and

(b) to the extent that it purports to authorise or to require any act to be done which infringes any of the fundamental rights and freedoms of any natural person, shall cease to have effect.

(2) No provision of any Act passed or statutory instrument made after the passing of this Act shall be construed or applied as if it authorised or required the doing of an act that infringes any of the fundamental rights and freedoms, or as if it conferred power to make any statutory instrument authorising or requiring the doing of any such act unless the Act contains a provision specifying that the relevant powers apply notwithstanding the fact that they are, or may be, contrary to any of the rights and freedoms referred to in subsection (1) of section 1 above.

5.—(1) A court or tribunal may by virtue of section 4 of this Act rule as to whether an Act of Parliament or part thereof or Statutory Instrument or part thereof has ceased to have effect.

(2) Schedule 3 to this Act shall have effect in respect of proceedings where a ruling under subsection (1) above is sought.

6. All courts and tribunals shall have regard to the whole of the Convention and all of its Protocols and of all judgments of the European Court of Human Rights and of all published reports and decisions of the European Commission of Human Rights established by the Convention.

RB NOTE: Section 7 then provides for the establishment and functions of a Human Rights Commission, separately shown in Doc. 56 below.

8.—(1) The provisions of Parts II to IV of the Crown Proceedings Act 1947 shall apply to any proceedings taken against the Crown under this Part of this Act in England and Wales and in Northern Ireland which by virtue of section 23 of that Act are treated for the purposes of Part II of that Act as civil proceedings by or against the Crown.

(2) The provisions of Part V of the Crown Proceedings Act 1947 shall

apply to any proceedings taken against the Crown under this Part of this Act in Scotland which by virtue of the said Part are treated as civil proceedings by or against the Crown. . . .

RB NOTE: Part II, Section 9, then provides for the establishment and functions of a Bill of Rights Commission, separately shown in Doc. 147 below.

PART III: MISCELLANEOUS, GENERAL AND SUPPLEMENTAL PROVISIONS

10.—(1) There shall be paid out of money provided by Parliament—

    (a) payments made by any Minister of the Crown by way of grant in aid to the Commission and the Bill of Rights Commission of such sums and subject to such terms and conditions as he may with the consent of the Treasury determine;

    (b) any expenses of any Minister of the Crown under this Act; and

    (c) any increase attributable to this Act in the sums payable out of such moneys under any other Act.

(2) There shall be paid into the Consolidated Fund any sums received by the Commission under paragraph 15 of Schedule 4 below.

11. In this Act, except in so far as the context otherwise requires—

    'the Convention' means the European Convention for the Protection of Human Rights and Fundamental Freedoms signed at Rome on 4th November 1950;

    'the Protocols' means Protocol No. 1 to the Convention signed at Paris on 20th March 1952 and any other Protocols to that Convention that are ratified by the United Kingdom Government after the commencement of this Act;

    'fundamental rights and freedoms' means the rights and freedoms set out in Section I of the Convention and Articles 1, 2 and 3 of Protocol No. 1 as set out in Schedule 1 to this Act; and any other Protocols that are ratified by the United Kingdom Government after the commencement of this Act; subject to the restrictions thereto permitted by the Convention and the Protocols;

    'act' includes deliberate omission;

    'effective remedy' has the same meaning as in Article 13 of the Convention and as interpreted by the judgments of the European Court of Human Rights and the published reports of the European Commission of Human Rights established by the Convention;

    'enactment' includes any Order in Council or instrument made under any enactment;

    'natural person' means any natural person from the moment of their birth and does not include bodies of persons whether incorporated or unincorporated and whether or not such bodies are referred to by implication or specifically in the Convention or the Protocols;

    'statutory body' means a body established by or in pursuance of any

enactment, and 'statutory office' means an office so established;

'public body' means a body of persons, whether corporate or unincorporate, carrying on a service or undertaking of a public
nature and includes public authorities of all descriptions and any
individual or body that exercises any public function, and

'public office' shall be construed accordingly; and

'the Crown' does not include Her Majesty in Her private capacity, in the
right of Her Duchy of Lancaster, or the Duchy of Cornwall.

12.—(1) This Act may be cited as the Human Rights Act 1994.

(2) Part I of this Act shall come into force on such date as the Secretary of
State may by statutory instrument appoint; and different dates may be
appointed for different provisions, except that sections 1, 2, 3, 4, 5 and 6 shall
come into force at the same time.

(3) This Act shall not have effect in relation to anything done before it
comes into force unless any such infringement of the fundamental rights and
freedoms referred to in section 1 above continues after section 1 of this Act
has come into force.

*RB NOTE: Schedule 1 gives the provisions of the European Convention on
Human Rights and Protocol, and Schedule 2 gives the Reservation made by
the UK, for which see Doc. 22 above.*

Schedule 3: Legal proceedings involving a challenge to the validity of an Act of Parliament

1. If in the course of any proceedings in an inferior court or tribunal the
court is asked to rule on whether by virtue of sections 4 and 5 of this Act an
Act of Parliament or part thereof or Statutory Instrument or part thereof
has ceased to have effect, that court or tribunal shall first consider whether
there is an arguable point on which a ruling should be given and if so shall
then either rule on that question or refer the question to the High Court or
the Court of Session for decision.

2. In exercising its discretion in paragraph 1 above as to whether to refer the
matter, the court or tribunal shall take into account the importance of the
question, the convenience and wishes of the parties and the interests of
justice.

3. Where such a question is referred to the High Court or the Court of
Session or where such a question arises in any other proceedings in the High
Court, the Court of Session, the Court of Appeal or the House of Lords—

   (a) unless the Crown is already a party to those proceedings, the party
   making that challenge shall give reasonable notice to the Attorney
   General or the Lord Advocate, who may then participate in the
   proceedings so far as they relate to that challenge; and

   (b) the party making that challenge shall give reasonable notice to the

Human Rights Commission of that challenge, which may then participate in the proceedings so far as they relate to that challenge.

4. Where it appears to the court before which any proceedings take place that participation of the Attorney General, the Lord Advocate or the Human Rights Commission, following the giving of notice required by paragraph 2 above, has occasioned any party to the proceedings additional expense, the court may take account of it in deciding any question as to costs and expenses and may, whatever decision was reached on the challenge to the validity of the Act of Parliament, award the whole or part of the additional expense as costs or, as the case may be, expenses, to that party.

RB NOTE: Schedule 4 makes further provision in relation to section 7 on the composition and working of the Human Rights Commission, separately shown in Doc. 56 below, Schedule 5 makes further provision in relation to section 9 on the composition and working of the Bill of Rights Commission, separately shown in Doc. 147 below.

HC [1993–4] 30.

(E) HUMAN RIGHTS BILL 1994 (Lord Lester)

Explanatory memorandum

The Bill incorporates into the law of the United Kingdom those provisions of the Convention for the Protection of Human Rights and Fundamental Freedoms agreed by the Council of Europe at Rome on 4th November 1950 ('the Convention') which establish certain human rights and fundamental freedoms.

Clause 1 and Schedule 1 provide for the incorporation of the Convention into United Kingdom law.

Clause 1(1) makes Section 1 of the Convention ('Section 1') and the First Protocol to the Convention ('the Protocol') set out in Schedule 1 to the Bill part of the law of the United Kingdom and ensures that the provisions of Section 1 and the Protocol will be given full legal effect in accordance with the Bill.

Clause 1(2) has the effect of abrogating any existing rule of law in so far as it is inconsistent with any provision of Section 1 or the Protocol, and *Clause 1(3)* prevents any Act of Parliament or statutory instrument from being enforced or from being relied upon in any way in any legal proceedings to the extent that it is inconsistent with any such provision.

Clause 1(4) ensures that the meaning of any provision of Section 1 or the Protocol is treated as a question of law and not as a question of fact, and *Clause 1(5)* provides that judicial notice is to be taken of the decisions of the European Court and the published decisions of the European Commission.

Clause 1(6) defines the Convention, the European Court of Human Rights and the European Commission of Human Rights for the purposes of the Bill as the European Convention for the Protection of Human Rights and Fundamental Freedoms, the Court established under that Convention and the Commission established under that Convention respectively.

Clause 2 ensures that the courts in the United Kingdom take account of the derogation and reservation entered by the United Kingdom (as set out in *Schedule 2* to the Bill), in the same way as the European Court and the European Commission have to take account of them now.

Clause 3 enables the Secretary of State, by order made by statutory instrument subject to the approval of both Houses of Parliament, to amend Schedule 1 to include the provisions of any other Protocol to the Convention which may come into force for the United Kingdom; and to amend Schedule 2 to give effect to any derogation or reservation duly made by the Government after the Bill is enacted, or to remove any derogation or reservation which subsequently ceases to have effect.

Clause 4 creates a right of action, as breach of statutory duty, for any violation of any provision of Schedule 1 to the Bill by any person in the performance of any public function, but allows for a petition to the Commission to be brought in such a case.

Clause 5 provides that the Bill binds the Crown and *Clause 6* makes provision for the short title, commencement and extent.

Financial and public service manpower effects of the bill

The Bill will have no effect on public expenditure or on public service manpower.

An Act to incorporate Section 1 of the Convention for the Protection of Human Rights and Fundamental Freedoms agreed by the Council of Europe at Rome on 4th November 1950 and the First Protocol to that Convention into the law of the United Kingdom.

Be it enacted by the Queen's most Excellent Majesty, by and with the advice and consent of the Lords Spiritual and Temporal, and Commons, in this present Parliament assembled, and by the authority of the same, as follows:—

1.—(1) The provisions set out in Schedule 1 to this Act, being—
    (a) Section I of the Convention for the Protection of Human Rights and Fundamental Freedoms agreed by the Council of Europe at Rome on 4th November 1950 (as amended by the Third, Fifth and Eighth Protocols to that Convention), and
    (b) the First Protocol to that Convention,
are hereby incorporated in the law of the United Kingdom, and shall be given full legal effect in accordance with this Act.

(2) The provisions set out in Schedule 1 shall have effect notwithstanding any rule of law to the contrary.

(3) An Act of Parliament or any instrument made by or under an Act of Parliament or an Order in Council (whether passed or made before or after the passing of this Act) shall not be enforced and may not be relied upon in

any legal proceedings (including those commenced before this Act comes into force) if and to the extent that to do so would deprive a person of any of the rights and freedoms defined in Schedule 1.

(4) For the purposes of all legal proceedings (including those commenced before this Act comes into force) any question as to the meaning or effect of any provision set out in Schedule 1 shall be treated as a question of law and shall be determined in accordance with the principles enunciated by the European Court of Human Rights.

(5) Judicial notice shall be taken of the Convention, the decisions of the European Court of Human Rights and the published decisions of the European Commission of Human Rights.

(6) In this Act—
'the Convention' means the Convention referred to in subsection (1) above;
'the European Commission of Human Rights' means the Commission established under the Convention; and
'the European Court of Human Rights' means the Court established under the Convention.

2.—(1) The derogations and reservations set out in Schedule 2 to this Act shall have effect in accordance with the Convention and the Protocols to the Convention, but no other derogation or reservation shall have effect.

(2) Section 17(2) of the Interpretation Act 1978 (construction of references to repealed enactments) applies for the interpretation of Schedule 2.

3.—(1) The Secretary of State may by order made by statutory instrument amend Schedule 1 to this Act but an order shall not be made under this subsection except in so far as such amendment may be necessary to give effect to any Protocol to the Convention.

(2) The Secretary of State may by order made by statutory instrument amend Schedule 2 to this Act but an order shall not be made under this subsection except in so far as such amendment may be necessary to give effect to any derogation or reservation duly made in accordance with the Convention or any Protocol to the Convention or to remove any derogation or reservation.

(3) An order shall not be made under this section unless a draft of the order has been approved by resolution of each House of Parliament.

4.—(1) A violation of any provision of Schedule 1 by any person in the performance of any public function shall be actionable as breach of statutory duty.

(2) For the avoidance of doubt it is hereby declared that nothing in this Act shall be taken to prejudice the right of any person to petition the

European Commission of Human Rights claiming to be a victim of a violation of the rights set out in the Convention.

5. This Act binds the Crown.

6.—(1) This Act may be cited as the Human Rights Act 1995.

(2) This Act extends to Scotland and Northern Ireland.

(3) This Act shall come into force on 1st January 1996.

RB NOTE: Schedule 1 then gives the provisions of the European Convention on Human Rights and Protocol, and Schedule 2 sets out the Derogation and Reservation made by the UK, for which see Doc. 22 above.

The Bill was significantly amended in its Committee and Report stages in relation to the effect the measure would have on other legislation. As amended in Committee, section 1 then read:

'(2) The provisions set out in Schedule 1 shall have effect notwithstanding any rule of law to the contrary.

(3) So far as the context permits, enactments (whenever passed or made) shall be construed consistently with the rights and freedoms defined in Schedule 1.

(4) For the purposes of all legal proceedings (including those commenced before this Act comes into force) any question as to the meaning or effect of any provision set out in Schedule 1 shall be treated as a question of law and shall be determined in accordance with the principles enunciated by the European Court of Human Rights.'

As further amended at Report stage, section 1 read:

'(2) The provisions set out in Schedule 1 shall –
(a) be an aid to the interpretation of any enactment; and
(b) be taken into account in equity and at common law, so that effect may be given to them in legal proceedings in accordance with the principles established by the jurisprudence of the European Court of Human Rights.
(3) For the purposes of this section the procedure at first instance and on appeal shall be governed by such Rules of Court or Practice Directions as may be made.'

HL [1994–95] 5.

(F) HUMAN RIGHTS BILL 1996 (Lord Lester)

Explanatory memorandum

The Bill incorporates into the law of the United Kingdom those provisions of the Convention for the Protection of Human Rights and Fundamental Freedoms agreed by the Council of Europe at Rome on 4th November 1950 ('the Convention') which establish certain human rights and fundamental freedoms.

Clause 1 and Schedule 1 provide for the incorporation of the Convention and the Protocol into United Kingdom law.

Clause 1(1) makes Section 1 of the Convention and the First Protocol to the Convention, set out in *Schedule 1* to the Bill, part of the law of the United Kingdom and ensures that the rights and freedoms contained in Schedule 1 are given full legal effect in accordance with the Bill.

Clause 1(2) has the effect of displacing any existing rule of law in so far as it is inconsistent with any right or freedom contained in Schedule 1.

Clause 1(3) ensures that the Bill applies only to acts done by or on behalf of a Minister of the Crown or by any person or body in the performance of a public function.

Clause 1(4) provides that wherever an enactment can be given a meaning consistent with the Bill, that meaning is to be preferred.

Clause 1(5) provides that judicial notice is to be taken of the decisions of the European Court and the published decisions of the European Commission.

Clause 2 provides that a court or tribunal may grant any remedy or relief or make other appropriate order to give effect to the provisions of Schedule 1.

Clause 3 requires Ministers, when introducing Bills into Parliament, to explain why any provision is, or appears to be, inconsistent with the provisions of Schedule 1.

Clause 4 ensures that the courts in the United Kingdom take account of the derogation and reservation entered by the United Kingdom (as set out in *Schedule* 2 to the Bill), in the same way as the European Court and the European Commission have to take account of them now.

Clause 5 enables the Secretary of State to amend Schedule 1 to include the provisions of any other Protocol to the Convention which may come into force for the United Kingdom; and to amend Schedule 2 to give effect to any derogation or reservation duly made by the Government after the Bill is enacted, or to remove any derogation or reservation which subsequently ceases to have effect.

Clause 6 provides that the Bill binds the Crown and *Clause 7* makes provision for the short title, commencement and extent.

Financial and public service manpower effects of the Bill

The Bill will have no effect on public expenditure or on public service manpower.

An Act to incorporate Section 1 of the Convention for the Protection of Human Rights and Fundamental Freedoms agreed by the Council of Europe at Rome on 4th November 1950 and the First Protocol to that Convention into the law of the United Kingdom; and for connected purposes.

Be it enacted by the Queen's most Excellent Majesty, by and with the advice and consent of the Lords Spiritual and Temporal, and Commons, in this present Parliament assembled, and by the authority of the same, as follows:-

1.—(1) The rights and freedoms contained in provisions set out in Schedule 1 to this Act, being—
   (a) Section 1 of the Convention for the Protection of Human Rights and Fundamental Freedoms, agreed by the Council of Europe at Rome on 4th November 1950, and
   (b) the First Protocol to that Convention,
are hereby affirmed and incorporated into the law of the United Kingdom and shall be given full legal effect in accordance with this Act.

(2) The provisions set out in Schedule 1 to this Act shall have effect notwithstanding any rule of law to the contrary.

(3) This Act applies to acts done—
   (a) by or on behalf of a Minister of the Crown; or
   (b) by any person or body performing or executing, or purporting to perform or execute, any public function, power or duty.

(4) Whenever an enactment can be given a meaning that is consistent with the provisions set out in Schedule 1 to this Act, that meaning shall be preferred to any other meaning.

(5) Judicial notice shall be taken of the Convention, the decisions of the European Court of Human Rights and the published decisions of the European Commission of Human Rights.

(6) In this Act—
'act' includes a deliberate omission;
'the Convention' means the Convention referred to in subsection (1) above;
'the European Commission of Human Rights' means the Commission established under the Convention;
'the European Court of Human Rights' means the Court established under the Convention; and
'enactment' includes an Order in Council, any Northern Ireland legislation and any instrument made under an Act or any Northern Ireland legislation.

2.—A court or tribunal may in proceeding within its jurisdiction grant such remedy or relief or make such order as it considers appropriate and just in the circumstances to give effect in accordance with this Act to the provisions set out in Schedule 1.

3.—Where a Bill introduced into either House of Parliament by a Minister of the Crown contains any provision which is or appears to be inconsistent with the provisions set out in Schedule 1 to this Act, notification shall forthwith be sent by that Minister to the Lord Chancellor and to the Speaker of the House of Commons drawing attention to the inconsistency or apparent inconsistency and explaining the reasons for that inconsistency or apparent inconsistency.

4.—(1) The derogation and reservation set out in Schedule 2 to this Act shall have effect in accordance with the Convention and the Protocols to the Convention, but no other derogation or reservation shall have effect.

(2) Section 17(2) of the Interpretation Act 1978 (construction of references to repealed enactments) applies for the interpretation of Schedule 2.

5.—(1) The Secretary of State may by order made by statutory instrument amend Schedule 1 to this Act but no such order may be made save as is necessary to give effect to any Protocol to the Convention.

(2) The Secretary of State may be order made by statutory instrument amend Schedule 2 to this Act but no such order may be made save as is necessary to give effect to—
    (a) any derogation or reservation duly made in accordance with the Convention or any Protocol to the Convention, or
    (b) the withdrawal of any such derogation or reservation.

(3) An order shall not be made under this section unless a draft of it has been laid before and approved by resolution of each House of Parliament.

6.—This Act binds the Crown.

7.—(1) This Act may be cited as the Human Rights Act 1997.

(2) This Act shall come into force on 1st January 1998.

(3) This Act extends to Scotland and Northern Ireland.

RB NOTE: The Schedules then laid out were similar to those in Lord Lester's Bill in 1994–95 (see above, E).

HL [1996–7] 11

---

40   THE HUMAN RIGHTS ACT 1998

RB NOTE: The Human Rights Act was presented for its first reading as a Bill in the House of Lords by the Lord Chancellor, Lord Irvine, on 23 October 1997. It received the royal assent over a year later, on 9 November 1998, after having gone through several important detailed changes, affecting inter alia press freedom, its application to religious bodies, parliamentary scrutiny arrangments for remedial orders, and the addition of Protocol 6 (abolishing the death penalty). The materials below include (A) the final legislative text, and (B) the original form of the bill showing where the pressures led to successful amendments being made. The original bill also contains the government's explanatory memorandum on the legislation, which is useful as an indication of the purpose of the various statutory provisions, as is the government's white paper, set out in section (C) below, which was published simultaneously with the first reading of the Bill. Extracts from parliamentary debates and ministerial statements on the Bill's provisions are set out in section (D).

(A) LEGISLATIVE TEXT

Human Rights Act 1998

ARRANGEMENT OF SECTIONS

Introduction

Section

Legislation

Public authorities

Remedial action

Other rights and proceedings

Derogations and reservations

16. Period for which designated derogations have effect.
17. Periodic review of designated reservations.

Judges of the European Court of Human Rights

18. Appointment to European Court of Human Rights.

Parliamentary procedure

19. Statements of compatibility.

Supplemental

20. Orders etc. under this Act.
21. Interpretation, etc.
22. Short title, commencement, application and extent.

SCHEDULES:

Schedule I—The Articles.
　　Part I—The Convention.
　　Part II—The First Protocol.
　　Part III—The Sixth Protocol.
Schedule 2—Remedial Orders.
Schedule 3—Derogation and Reservation.
　　Part I—Derogation.
　　Part II—Reservation.
Schedule 4—Judicial Pensions.

Human Rights Act 1998

An Act to give further effect to rights and freedoms guaranteed under the European Convention on Human Rights; to make provision with respect to holders of certain judicial offices who become judges of the European Court of Human Rights; and for connected purposes.　　　　[9th November 1998]

BE IT ENACTED by the Queen's most Excellent Majesty, by and with the advice and consent of the Lords Spiritual and Temporal, and Commons, in this present Parliament assembled, and by the authority of the same, as follows:—

Introduction

1. The Convention rights

(1) In this Act 'the Convention rights' means the rights and fundamental freedoms set out in—

    (a) Articles 2 to 12 and 14 of the Convention,
    (b) Articles 1 to 3 of the First Protocol, and
    (c) Articles 1 and 2 of the Sixth Protocol,
as read with Articles 16 to 18 of the Convention.

(2) Those Articles are to have effect for the purposes of this Act subject to any designated derogation or reservation (as to which see sections 14 and 15).

(3) The Articles are set out in Schedule 1.

(4) The Secretary of State may by order make such amendments to this Act as he considers appropriate to reflect the effect, in relation to the United Kingdom, of a protocol.

(5) In subsection (4) 'protocol' means a protocol to the Convention—
    (a) which the United Kingdom has ratified; or
    (b) which the United Kingdom has signed with a view to ratifica-
        tion.

(6) No amendment may be made by an order under subsection (4) so as to come into force before the protocol concerned is in force in relation to the United Kingdom.

2. Interpretation of Convention rights

(1) A court or tribunal determining a question which has arisen in connection with a Convention right must take into account any—
    (a) judgment, decision, declaration or advisory opinion of the Euro-
        pean Court of Human Rights,
    (b) opinion of the Commission given in a report adopted under
        Article 31 of the Convention,
    (c) decision of the Commission in connection with Article 26 or 27(2)
        of the Convention, or
    (d) decision of the Committee of Ministers taken under Article 46 of
        the Convention,
whenever made or given, so far as, in the opinion of the court or tribunal, it is relevant to the proceedings in which that question has arisen.

(2) Evidence of any judgment, decision, declaration or opinion of which account may have to be taken under this section is to be given in proceedings before any court or tribunal in such manner as may be provided by rules.

(3) In this section 'rules' means rules of court or, in the case of proceedings before a tribunal, rules made for the purposes of this section—
    (a) by the Lord Chancellor or the Secretary of State, in relation to any
        proceedings outside Scotland;
    (b) by the Secretary of State, in relation to proceedings in Scotland;
        or
    (c) by a Northern Ireland department, in relation to proceedings
        before a tribunal in Northern Ireland—

    (i)   which deals with transferred matters; and

    (ii) for which no rules made under paragraph (a) are in force.

Legislation

3. Interpretation of legislation

(1) So far as it is possible to do so, primary legislation and subordinate legislation must be read and given effect in a way which is compatible with the Convention rights.

(2) This section—

    (a) applies to primary legislation and subordinate legislation when-ever enacted;

    (b) does not affect the validity, continuing operation or enforcement of any incompatible primary legislation; and

    (c) does not affect the validity, continuing operation or enforcement of any incompatible subordinate legislation if (disregarding any possibility of revocation) primary legislation prevents removal of the incompatibility.

4. Declaration of incompatibility

(1) Subsection (2) applies in any proceedings in which a court determines whether a provision of primary legislation is compatible with a Convention right.

(2) If the court is satisfied that the provision is incompatible with a Convention right, it may make a declaration of that incompatibility.

(3) Subsection (4) applies in any proceedings in which a court determines whether a provision of subordinate legislation, made in the exercise of a power conferred by primary legislation, is compatible with a Convention right.

(4) If the court is satisfied—

    (a) that the provision is incompatible with a Convention right, and

    (b) that (disregarding any possibility of revocation) the primary legis-lation concerned prevents removal of the incompatibility,

it may make a declaration of that incompatibility.

(5) In this section 'court' means—

    (a) the House of Lords;

    (b) the Judicial Committee of the Privy Council;

    (c) the Courts-Martial Appeal Court;

    (d) in Scotland, the High Court of Justiciary sitting otherwise than as a trial court or the Court of Session;

    (e) in England and Wales or Northern Ireland, the High Court or the Court of Appeal.

(6) A declaration under this section ('a declaration of incompatibility')—

    (a) does not affect the validity, continuing operation or enforcement of the provision in respect of which it is given; and

(b) is not binding on the parties to the proceedings in which it is made.

5. Right of Crown to intervene

(1) Where a court is considering whether to make a declaration of incompatibility, the Crown is entitled to notice in accordance with rules of court.

(2) In any case to which subsection (1) applies—
    (a) a Minister of the Crown (or a person nominated by him),
    (b) a member of the Scottish Executive,
    (c) a Northern Ireland Minister,
    (d) a Northern Ireland department,
is entitled, on giving notice in accordance with rules of court, to be joined as a party to the proceedings.

(3) Notice under subsection (2) may be given at any time during the proceedings.

(4) A person who has been made a party to criminal proceedings (other than in Scotland) as the result of a notice under subsection (2) may, with leave, appeal to the House of Lords against any declaration of incompatibility made in the proceedings.

(5) In subsection (4)—
'criminal proceedings' includes all proceedings before the Courts-Martial Appeal Court; and
'leave' means leave granted by the court making the declaration of incompatibility or by the House of Lords.

Public authorities

6. Acts of public authorities

(1) It is unlawful for a public authority to act in a way which is incompatible with a Convention right.

(2) Subsection (1) does not apply to an act if—
    (a) as the result of one or more provisions of primary legislation, the authority could not have acted differently; or
    (b) in the case of one or more provisions of, or made under, primary legislation which cannot be read or given effect in a way which is compatible with the Convention rights, the authority was acting so as to give effect to or enforce those provisions.

(3) In this section 'public authority' includes—
    (a) a court or tribunal, and
    (b) any person certain of whose functions are functions of a public nature,
but does not include either House of Parliament or a person exercising functions in connection with proceedings in Parliament.

(4) In subsection (3) 'Parliament' does not include the House of Lords in its judicial capacity.

(5) In relation to a particular act, a person is not a public authority by virtue only of subsection (3)(b) if the nature of the act is private.

(6) 'An act' includes a failure to act but does not include a failure to—
    (a) introduce in, or lay before, Parliament a proposal for legislation; or
    (b) make any primary legislation or remedial order.

7. Proceedings

(1) A person who claims that a public authority has acted (or proposes to act) in a way which is made unlawful by section 6(1) may—
    (a) bring proceedings against the authority under this Act in the appropriate court or tribunal, or
    (b) rely on the Convention right or rights concerned in any legal proceedings,
but only if he is (or would be) a victim of the unlawful act.

(2) In subsection (1)(a) 'appropriate court or tribunal' means such court or tribunal as may be determined in accordance with rules; and proceedings against an authority include a counterclaim or similar proceeding.

(3) If the proceedings are brought on an application for judicial review, the applicant is to be taken to have a sufficient interest in relation to the unlawful act only if he is, or would be, a victim of that act.

(4) If the proceedings are made by way of a petition for judicial review in Scotland, the applicant shall be taken to have title and interest to sue in relation to the unlawful act only if he is, or would be, a victim of that act.

(5) Proceedings under subsection (1)(a) must be brought before the end of—
    (a) the period of one year beginning with the date on which the act complained of took place; or
    (b) such longer period as the court or tribunal considers equitable having regard to all the circumstances,
but that is subject to any rule imposing a stricter time limit in relation to the procedure in question.

(6) In subsection (1)(b) 'legal proceedings' includes—
    (a) proceedings brought by or at the instigation of a public authority; and
    (b) an appeal against the decision of a court or tribunal.

(7) For the purposes of this section, a person is a victim of an unlawful act only if he would be a victim for the purposes of Article 34 of the Convention if proceedings were brought in the European Court of Human Rights in respect of that act.

(8) Nothing in this Act creates a criminal offence.

(9) In this section 'rules' means—
    (a) in relation to proceedings before a court or tribunal outside

Scotland, rules made by the Lord Chancellor or the Secretary of State for the purposes of this section or rules of court,

(b) in relation to proceedings before a court or tribunal in Scotland, rules made by the Secretary of State for those purposes,

(c) in relation to proceedings before a tribunal in Northern Ireland—
   (i)   which deals with transferred matters; and
   (ii) for which no rules made under paragraph (a) are in force.
   rules made by a Northern Ireland department for those purposes,

and includes provision made by order under section 1 of the Courts and Legal Services Act 1990.

(10) In making rules, regard must be had to section 9.

(11) The Minister who has power to make rules in relation to a particular tribunal may, to the extent he considers it necessary to ensure that the tribunal can provide an appropriate remedy in relation to an act (or proposed act) of a public authority which is (or would be) unlawful as a result of section 6(1), by order add to—

(a) the relief or remedies which the tribunal may grant; or

(b) the grounds on which it may grant any of them.

(12) An order made under subsection (11) may contain such incidental, supplemental, consequential or transitional provision as the Minister making it considers appropriate.

(13) 'The Minister' includes the Northern Ireland department concerned.

8. Judicial remedies

(1) In relation to any act (or proposed act) of a public authority which the court finds is (or would be) unlawful, it may grant such relief or remedy, or make such order, within its powers as it considers just and appropriate.

(2) But damages may be awarded only by a court which has power to award damages; or to order the payment of compensation, in civil proceedings.

(3) No award of damages is to be made unless, taking account of all the circumstances of the case, including—

(a) any other relief or remedy granted, or order made, in relation to the act in question (by that or any other court), and

(b) the consequences of any decision (of that or any other court) in respect of that act,

the court is satisfied that the award is necessary to afford just satisfaction to the person in whose favour it is made.

(4) In determining—

(a) whether to award damages, or

(b) the amount of an award,

the court must take into account the principles applied by the European

Court of Human Rights in relation to the award of compensation under Article 41 of the Convention.

(5) A public authority against which damages are awarded is to be treated—

    (a) in Scotland, for the purposes of section 3 of the Law Reform (Miscellaneous Provisions) (Scotland) Act 1940 as if the award were made in an action of damages in which the authority has been found liable in respect of loss or damage to the person to whom the award is made;

    (b) for the purposes of the Civil Liability (Contribution) Act 1978 as liable in respect of damage suffered by the person to whom the award is made.

(6) In this section—

'court' includes a tribunal;

'damages' means damages for an unlawful act of a public authority; and

'unlawful' means unlawful under section 6(1).

9. Judicial acts

(1) Proceedings under section 7(1)(a) in respect of a judicial act may be brought only—

    (a) by exercising a right of appeal;

    (b) on an application (in Scotland a petition) for judicial review; or

    (c) in such other forum as may be prescribed by rules.

(2) That does not affect any rule of law which prevents a court from being the subject of judicial review.

(3) In proceedings under this Act in respect of a judicial act done in good faith, damages may not be awarded otherwise than to compensate a person to the extent required by Article 5(5) of the Convention.

(4) An award of damages permitted by subsection (3) is to be made against the Crown; but no award may be made unless the appropriate person, if not a party to the proceedings, is joined.

(5) In this section—

'appropriate person' means the Minister responsible for the court concerned, or a person or government department nominated by him;

'court' includes a tribunal;

'judge' includes a member of a tribunal, a justice of the peace and a clerk or other officer entitled to exercise the jurisdiction of a court;

'judicial act' means a judicial act of a court and includes an act done on the instructions, or on behalf, of a judge; and

'rules' has the same meaning as in section 7(9).

Remedial action

10. Power to take remedial action

(1) This section applies if—

    (a) a provision of legislation has been declared under section 4 to be incompatible with a Convention right and, if an appeal lies—

        (i)   all persons who may appeal have stated in writing that they do not intend to do so;

        (ii) the time for bringing an appeal has expired and no appeal has been brought within that time; or

        (iii) an appeal brought within that time has been determined or abandoned; or

    (b) it appears to a Minister of the Crown or Her Majesty in Council that, having regard to a finding of the European Court of Human Rights made after the coming into force of this section in proceedings against the United Kingdom, a provision of legislation is incompatible with an obligation of the United Kingdom arising from the Convention.

(2) If a Minister of the Crown considers that there are compelling reasons for proceeding under this section, he may by order make such amendments to the legislation as he considers necessary to remove the incompatibility.

(3) If, in the case of subordinate legislation, a Minister of the Crown considers—

    (a) that it is necessary to amend the primary legislation under which the subordinate legislation in question was made, in order to enable the incompatibility to be removed, and

    (b) that there are compelling reasons for proceeding under this section,

he may by order make such amendments to the primary legislation as he considers necessary.

(4) This section also applies where the provision in question is in subordinate legislation and has been quashed, or declared invalid, by reason of incompatibility with a Convention right and the Minister proposes to proceed under paragraph 2(b) of Schedule 2.

(5) If the legislation is an Order in Council, the power conferred by subsection (2) or (3) is exercisable by Her Majesty in Council.

(6) In this section 'legislation' does not include a Measure of the Church Assembly or of the General Synod of the Church of England.

(7) Schedule 2 makes further provision about remedial orders.

Other rights and proceedings

11. Safeguard for existing human rights

A person's reliance on a Convention right does not restrict—

    (a) any other right or freedom conferred on him by or under any law having effect in any part of the United Kingdom; or

(b) his right to make any claim or bring any proceedings which he could make or bring apart from sections 7 to 9.

12. Freedom of expression

(1) This section applies if a court is considering whether to grant any relief which, if granted, might affect the exercise of the Convention right to freedom of expression.

(2) If the person against whom the application for relief is made ('the respondent') is neither present nor represented, no such relief is to be granted unless the court is satisfied—

    (a) that the applicant has taken all practicable steps to notify the respondent; or

    (b) that there are compelling reasons why the respondent should not be notified.

(3) No such relief is to be granted so as to restrain publication before trial unless the court is satisfied that the applicant is likely to establish that publication should not be allowed.

(4) The court must have particular regard to the importance of the Convention right to freedom of expression and, where the proceedings relate to material which the respondent claims, or which appears to the court, to be journalistic, literary or artistic material (or to conduct connected with such material), to—

    (a) the extent to which—

        (i) the material has, or is about to, become available to the public; or

        (ii) it is, or would be, in the public interest for the material to be published;

    (b) any relevant privacy code.

(5) In this section—

'court' includes a tribunal; and

'relief' includes any remedy or order (other than in criminal proceedings).

13. Freedom of thought, conscience and religion

(1) If a court's determination of any question arising under this Act might affect the exercise by a religious organisation (itself or its members collectively) of the Convention right to freedom of thought, conscience and religion, it must have particular regard to the importance of that right.

(2) In this section 'court' includes a tribunal.

Derogations and reservations

14. Derogations

(1) In this Act 'designated derogation' means—

    (a) the United Kingdom's derogation from Article 5(3) of the Convention; and

(b) any derogation by the United Kingdom from an Article of the Convention, or of any protocol to the Convention, which is designated for the purposes of this Act in an order made by the Secretary of State.

(2) The derogation referred to in subsection (1)(a) is set out in Part I of Schedule 3.

(3) If a designated derogation is amended or replaced it ceases to be a designated derogation.

(4) But subsection (3) does not prevent the Secretary of State from exercising his power under subsection (1)(b) to make a fresh designation order in respect of the Article concerned.

(5) The Secretary of State must by order make such amendments to Schedule 3 as he considers appropriate to reflect—
   (a) any designation order; or
   (b) the effect of subsection (3).

(6) A designation order may be made in anticipation of the making by the United Kingdom of a proposed derogation.

15. Reservations

(1) In this Act 'designated reservation' means—
   (a) the United Kingdom's reservation to Article 2 of the First Protocol to the Convention; and
   (b) any other reservation by the United Kingdom to an Article of the Convention, or of any protocol to the Convention, which is designated for the purposes of this Act in an order made by the Secretary of State.

(2) The text of the reservation referred to in subsection (1)(a) is set out in Part II of Schedule 3.

(3) If a designated reservation is withdrawn wholly or in part it ceases to be a designated reservation.

(4) But subsection (3) does not prevent the Secretary of State from exercising his power under subsection (1)(b) to make a fresh designation order in respect of the Article concerned.

(5) The Secretary of State must by order make such amendments to this Act as he considers appropriate to reflect—
   (a) any designation order; or
   (b) the effect of subsection (3).

16. Period for which designated derogations have effect

(1) If it has not already been withdrawn by the United Kingdom, a designated derogation ceases to have effect for the purposes of this Act—
   (a) in the case of the derogation referred to in section 14(1)(a), at the end of the period of five years beginning with the date on which section 1(2) came into force;

(b) in the case of any other derogation, at the end of the period of five years beginning with the date on which the order designating it was made.

(2) At any time before the period—
    (a) fixed by subsection (1)(a) or (b), or
    (b) extended by an order under this subsection,
comes to an end, the Secretary of State may by order extend it by a further period of five years.

(3) An order under section 14(1)(b) ceases to have effect at the end of the period for consideration, unless a resolution has been passed by each House approving the order.

(4) Subsection (3) does not affect—
    (a) anything done in reliance on the order; or
    (b) the power to make a fresh order under section 14(1)(b).

(5) In subsection (3) 'period for consideration' means the period of forty days beginning with the day on which the order was made.

(6) In calculating the period for consideration, no account is to be taken of any time during which—
    (a) Parliament is dissolved or prorogued; or
    (b) both Houses are adjourned for more than four days.

(7) If a designated derogation is withdrawn by the United Kingdom, the Secretary of State must by order make such amendments to this Act as he considers are required to reflect that withdrawal.

17. Periodic review of designated reservations

(1) The appropriate Minister must review the designated reservation referred to in section 15(1)(a)—
    (a) before the end of the period of five years beginning with the date on which section 1(2) came into force; and
    (b) if that designation is still in force, before the end of the period of five years beginning with the date on which the last report relating to it was laid under subsection (3).

(2) The appropriate Minister must review each of the other designated reservations (if any)—
    (a) before the end of the period of five years beginning with the date on which the order designating the reservation first came into force; and
    (b) if the designation is still in force, before the end of the period of five years beginning with the date on which the last report relating to it was laid under subsection (3).

(3) The Minister conducting a review under this section must prepare a report on the result of the review and lay a copy of it before each House of Parliament.

Judges of the European Court of Human Rights

18. Appointment to European Court of Human Rights

(1) In this section 'judicial office' means the office of—

   (a) Lord Justice of Appeal, Justice of the High Court or Circuit judge, in England and Wales;

   (b) judge of the Court of Session or sheriff, in Scotland;

   (c) Lord Justice of Appeal, judge of the High Court or county court judge, in Northern Ireland.

(2) The holder of a judicial office may become a judge of the European Court of Human Rights ('the Court') without being required to relinquish his office.

(3) But he is not required to perform the duties of his judicial office while he is a judge of the Court.

(4) In respect of any period during which he is a judge of the Court—

   (a) a Lord Justice of Appeal or Justice of the High Court is not to count as a judge of the relevant court for the purposes of section 2(1) or 4(1) of the Supreme Court Act 1981 (maximum number of judges) nor as a judge of the Supreme Court for the purposes of section 12(1) to (6) of that Act (salaries etc.);

   (b) a judge of the Court of Session is not to count as a judge of that court for the purposes of section 1(1) of the Court of Session Act 1988 (maximum number of judges) or of section 9(1)(c) of the Administration of Justice Act 1973 ('the 1973 Act') (salaries etc.);

   (c) a Lord Justice of Appeal or judge of the High Court in Northern Ireland is not to count as a judge of the relevant court for the purposes of section 2(1) or 3(1) of the Judicature (Northern Ireland) Act 1978 (maximum number of judges) nor as a judge of the Supreme Court of Northern Ireland for the purposes of section 9(1)(d) of the 1973 Act (salaries etc.);

   (d) a Circuit judge is not to count as such for the purposes of section 18 of the Courts Act 1971 (salaries etc.);

   (e) a sheriff is not to count as such for the purposes of section 14 of the Sheriff Courts (Scotland) Act 1907 (salaries etc.);

   (f) a county court judge of Northern Ireland is not to count as such for the purposes of section 106 of the County Courts Act (Northern Ireland) 1959 (salaries etc.).

(5) If a sheriff principal is appointed a judge of the Court, section 11(1) of the Sheriff Courts (Scotland) Act 1971 (temporary appointment of sheriff principal) applies, while he holds that appointment, as if his office is vacant.

(6) Schedule 4 makes provision about judicial pensions in relation to the holder of a judicial office who serves as a judge of the Court.

(7) The Lord Chancellor or the Secretary of State may by order make

such transitional provision (including, in particular, provision for a temporary increase in the maximum number of judges) as he considers appropriate in relation to any holder of a judicial office who has completed his service as a judge of the Court.

Parliamentary procedure

19. Statements of compatibility

(1) A Minister of the Crown in charge of a Bill in either House of Parliament must, before Second Reading of the Bill—

    (a) make a statement to the effect that in his view the provisions of the Bill are compatible with the Convention rights ('a statement of compatibility'); or

    (b) make a statement to the effect that although he is unable to make a statement of compatibility the government nevertheless wishes the House to proceed with the Bill.

(2) The statement must be in writing and be published in such manner as the Minister making it considers appropriate.

Supplemental

20. Orders etc. under this Act

(1) Any power of a Minister of the Crown to make an order under this Act is exercisable by statutory instrument.

(2) The power of the Lord Chancellor or the Secretary of State to make rules (other than rules of court) under section 2(3) or 7(9) is exercisable by statutory instrument.

(3) Any statutory instrument made under section 14, 15 or 16(7) must be laid before Parliament.

(4) No order may be made by the Lord Chancellor or the Secretary of State under section 1(4), 7(11) or 16(2) unless a draft of the order has been laid before, and approved by, each House of Parliament.

(5) Any statutory instrument made under section 18(7) or Schedule 4, or to which subsection (2) applies, shall be subject to annulment in pursuance of a resolution of either House of Parliament.

(6) The power of a Northern Ireland department to make—

    (a) rules under section 2(3)(c) or 7(9)(c), or

    (b) an order under section 7(11),

is exercisable by statutory rule for the purposes of the Statutory Rules (Northern Ireland) Order 1979.

(7) Any rules made under section 2(3)(c) or 7(9)(c) shall be subject to negative resolution; and section 41(6) of the Interpretation Act (Northern Ireland) 1954 (meaning of 'subject to negative resolution') shall apply as if the power to make the rules were conferred by an Act of the Northern Ireland Assembly.

(8) No order may be made by a Northern Ireland department under section 7(11) unless a draft of the order has been laid before, and approved by, the Northern Ireland Assembly.

21. Interpretation, etc.

(1) In this Act—

'amend' includes repeal and apply (with or without modifications);

'the appropriate Minister' means the Minister of the Crown having charge of the appropriate authorised government department (within the meaning of the Crown Proceedings Act 1947);

'the Commission' means the European Commission of Human Rights;

'the Convention' means the Convention for the Protection of Human Rights and Fundamental Freedoms, agreed by the Council of Europe at Rome on 4th November 1950 as it has effect for the time being in relation to the United Kingdom;

'declaration of incompatibility' means a declaration under section 4;

'Minister of the Crown' has the same meaning as in the Ministers of the Crown Act 1975;

'Northern Ireland Minister' includes the First Minister and the deputy First Minister in Northern Ireland;

'primary legislation' means any—

(a) public general Act;

(b) local and personal Act;

(c) private Act;

(d) Measure of the Church Assembly;

(e) Measure of the General Synod of the Church of England:

(f) Order in Council—

(i) made in exercise of Her Majesty's Royal Prerogative;

(ii) made under section 38(1)(a) of the Northern Ireland Constitution Act 1973 or the corresponding provision of the Northern Ireland Act 1998; or

(iii) amending an Act of a kind mentioned in paragraph (a), (b) or (c);

and includes an order or other instrument made under primary legislation (otherwise than by the National Assembly for Wales, a member of the Scottish Executive, a Northern Ireland Minister or a Northern Ireland department) to the extent to which it operates to bring one or more provisions of that legislation into force or amends any primary legislation;

'the First Protocol' means the protocol to the Convention agreed at Paris on 20th March 1952;

'the Sixth Protocol' means the protocol to the Convention agreed at Strasbourg on 28th April 1983;

'the Eleventh Protocol' means the protocol to the Convention (restructuring the control machinery established by the Convention) agreed at Strasbourg on 11th May 1994;

'remedial order' means an order under section 10;

'subordinate legislation' means any—

(a) Order in Council other than one—

    (i)   made in exercise of Her Majesty's Royal Prerogative;

    (ii)   made under section 38(1)(a) of the Northern Ireland Constitution Act 1973 or the corresponding provision of the Northern Ireland Act 1998; or

    (iii)   amending an Act of a kind mentioned in the definition of primary legislation;

(b) Act of the Scottish Parliament;

(c) Act of the Parliament of Northern Ireland;

(d) Measure of the Assembly established under section 1 of the Northern Ireland Assembly Act 1973;

(e) Act of the Northern Ireland Assembly;

(f) order, rules, regulations, scheme, warrant, byelaw or other instrument made under primary legislation (except to the extent to which it operates to bring one or more provisions of that legislation into force or amends any primary legislation);

(g) order, rules, regulations, scheme, warrant, byelaw or other instrument made under legislation mentioned in paragraph (b), (c), (d) or (e) or made under an Order in Council applying only to Northern Ireland;

(h) order, rules, regulations, scheme, warrant, byelaw or other instrument made by a member of the Scottish Executive, a Northern Ireland Minister or a Northern Ireland department in exercise of prerogative or other executive functions of Her Majesty which are exercisable by such a person on behalf of Her Majesty;

'transferred matters' has the same meaning as in the Northern Ireland Act 1998; and

'tribunal' means any tribunal in which legal proceedings may be brought.

(2) The references in paragraphs (b) and (c) of section 2(1) to Articles are to Articles of the Convention as they had effect immediately before the coming into force of the Eleventh Protocol.

(3) The reference in paragraph (d) of section 2(1) to Article 46 includes a reference to Articles 32 and 54 of the Convention as they had effect immediately before the coming into force of the Eleventh Protocol.

(4) The references in section 2(1) to a report or decision of the Commission or a decision of the Committee of Ministers include references to a report or decision made as provided by paragraphs 3, 4 and 6 of Article 5 of the Eleventh Protocol (transitional provisions).

(5) Any liability under the Army Act 1955, the Air Force Act 1955 or the Naval Discipline Act 1957 to suffer death for an offence is replaced by a liability to imprisonment for life or any less punishment authorised by those Acts; and those Acts shall accordingly have effect with the necessary modifications.

22. Short title, commencement, application and extent

(1) This Act may be cited as the Human Rights Act 1998.

(2) Sections 18, 20 and 21(5) and this section come into force on the passing of this Act.

(3) The other provisions of this Act come into force on such day as the Secretary of State may by order appoint; and different days may be appointed for different purposes.

(4) Paragraph (b) of subsection (1) of section 7 applies to proceedings brought by or at the instigation of a public authority whenever the act in question took place; but otherwise that subsection does not apply to an act taking place before the coming into force of that section.

(5) This Act binds the Crown.

(6) This Act extends to Northern Ireland.

(7) Section 21(5), so far as it relates to any provision contained in the Army Act 1955, the Air Force Act 1955 or the Naval Discipline Act 1957, extends to any place to which that provision extends.

RB NOTE: The Act then contains Schedule 1 which sets out the specific ECHR articles to take effect in UK law, being Articles 2–12, 14, 16–18, First Protocol Articles 1–3, Sixth Protocol Articles 1–2. For these ECHR Articles, see Doc. 22 above.

Schedule 2: Remedial Orders

Orders

1.—(1) A remedial order may—
  (a) contain such incidental, supplemental, consequential or transitional provision as the person making it considers appropriate;
  (b) be made so as to have effect from a date earlier than that on which it is made;
  (c) make provision for the delegation of specific functions;
  (d) make different provision for different cases.

(2) The power conferred by sub-paragraph (1)(a) includes—
  (a) power to amend primary legislation (including primary legislation other than that which contains the incompatible provision); and
  (b) power to amend or revoke subordinate legislation (including subordinate legislation other than that which contains the incompatible provision).

(3) A remedial order may be made so as to have the same extent as the legislation which it affects.

(4) No person is to be guilty of an offence solely as a result of the retrospective effect of a remedial order.

Procedure

2. No remedial order may be made unless—
    (a) a draft of the order has been approved by a resolution of each House of Parliament made after the end of the period of 60 days beginning with the day on which the draft was laid; or
    (b) it is declared in the order that it appears to the person making it that, because of the urgency of the matter, it is necessary to make the order without a draft being so approved.

Orders laid in draft

3.—(1) No draft may be laid under paragraph 2(a) unless—
    (a) the person proposing to make the order has laid before Parliament a document which contains a draft of the proposed order and the required information; and
    (b) the period of 60 days, beginning with the day on which the document required by this sub-paragraph was laid, has ended.

(2) If representations have been made during that period, the draft laid under paragraph 2(a) must be accompanied by a statement containing—
    (a) a summary of the representations; and
    (b) if, as a result of the representations, the proposed order has been changed, details of the changes.

Urgent cases

4.—(1) If a remedial order ('the original order') is made without being approved in draft, the person making it must lay it before Parliament, accompanied by the required information, after it is made.

(2) If representations have been made during the period of 60 days beginning with the day on which the original order was made, the person making it must (after the end of that period) lay before Parliament a statement containing—
    (a) a summary of the representations; and
    (b) if, as a result of the representations, he considers it appropriate to make changes to the original order, details of the changes.

(3) If sub-paragraph (2)(b) applies, the person making the statement must—
    (a) make a further remedial order replacing the original order; and
    (b) lay the replacement order before Parliament.

(4) If, at the end of the period of 120 days beginning with the day on which the original order was made, a resolution has not been passed by each House approving the original or replacement order, the order ceases to have effect (but without that affecting anything previously done under either order or the power to make a fresh remedial order).

Definitions

5. In this Schedule—

'representations' means representations about a remedial order (or proposed remedial order) made to the person making (or proposing to make) it and includes any relevant Parliamentary report or resolution; and

'required information' means—

(a) an explanation of the incompatibility which the order (or proposed order) seeks to remove, including particulars of the relevant declaration, finding or order; and

(b) a statement of the reasons for proceeding under section 10 and for making an order in those terms.

Calculating periods

6. In calculating any period for the purposes of this Schedule, no account is to be taken of any time during which—

(a) Parliament is dissolved or prorogued; or

(b) both Houses are adjourned for more than four days.

RB NOTE: The Act then contains Schedule 3 which sets out the UK Derogation and Reservation from the ECHR, for which see Doc. 22 above.

SCHEDULE 4: JUDICIAL PENSIONS

Duty to make orders about pensions

1.—(1) The appropriate Minister must by order make provision with respect to pensions payable to or in respect of any holder of a judicial office who serves as an ECHR judge.

(2) A pensions order must include such provision as the Minister making it considers is necessary to secure that—

(a) an ECHR judge who was, immediately before his appointment as an ECHR judge, a member of a judicial pension scheme is entitled to remain as a member of that scheme;

(b) the terms on which he remains a member of the scheme are those which would have been applicable had he not been appointed as an ECHR judge; and

(c) entitlement to benefits payable in accordance with the scheme continues to be determined as if, while serving as an ECHR judge, his salary was that which would (but for section 18(4)) have been payable to him in respect of his continuing service as the holder of his judicial office.

Contributions

2. A pensions order may, in particular, make provision—
  (a) for any contributions which are payable by a person who remains a member of a scheme as a result of the order, and which would otherwise be payable by deduction from his salary, to be made otherwise than by deduction from his salary as an ECHR judge; and
  (b) for such contributions to be collected in such manner as may be determined by the administrators of the scheme.

Amendments of other enactments

3. A pensions order may amend any provision of, or made under, a pensions Act in such manner and to such extent as the Minister making the order considers necessary or expedient to ensure the proper administration of any scheme to which it relates.

Definitions

4. In this Schedule—
  'appropriate Minister' means—
    (a) in relation to any judicial office whose jurisdiction is exercisable exclusively in relation to Scotland, the Secretary of State; and
    (b) otherwise, the Lord Chancellor;
  'ECHR judge' means the holder of a judicial office who is serving as a judge of the Court;
  'judicial pension scheme' means a scheme established by and in accordance with a pensions Act:
  'pensions Act' means—
    (a) the County Courts Act (Northern Ireland) 1959;
    (b) the Sheriffs' Pensions (Scotland) Act 1961;
    (c) the Judicial Pensions Act 1981; or
    (d) the Judicial Pensions and Retirement Act 1993; and
  'pensions order' means an order made under paragraph 1.

(B) ORIGINAL BILL AND EXPLANATORY MEMORANDUM

Human Rights Bill [H.L.]

EXPLANATORY AND FINANCIAL MEMORANDUM

The Bill gives further effect in domestic law to rights and freedoms guaranteed under the European Convention on Human Rights, and makes provision with respect to holders of certain judicial offices who become judges of the European Court of Human Rights.

Clause 1 specifies those Articles of the Convention and the First Protocol to it ('the Convention rights') which are given further effect by the Bill (subject to any designated derogation or reservation, to which *clauses 14* and *15* refer). These Articles are set out in *Schedule 1. Clause 1* also provides that the clause and *Schedule 1* may be amended by order to reflect the effect of a protocol to the Convention which the United Kingdom has ratified, or signed with a view to ratification.

Clause 2 provides that a court or tribunal determining a question in connection with a Convention right must take account of relevant judgments, decisions, declarations and opinions made or given by the European Commission and Court of Human Rights and the Committee of Ministers of the Council of Europe.

Clause 3 provides that primary and subordinate legislation, whenever enacted, must as far as possible be read and given effect in a way which is compatible with the Convention rights. It also provides that this does not affect the validity, continuing operation or enforcement of any incompatible primary legislation, or any incompatible subordinate legislation if primary legislation prevents the removal of the incompatibility.

Clause 4 provides that specified courts may make a 'declaration of incompatibility' where they are satisfied that a provision of primary legislation is incompatible with the Convention rights, or that a provision of subordinate legislation is incompatible and the primary legislation under which it was made prevents the removal of that incompatibility. It also provides that such a declaration does not affect the validity, continuing operation or enforcement of the provision in respect of which it is given.

Clause 5 gives the Crown the right to have notice that a court is considering whether or not to make a declaration of incompatibility, and entitles the Crown to be joined as a party to the proceedings.

Clause 6 makes it unlawful for a public authority to act in a way which is incompatible with the Convention rights, unless that would be inconsistent with the effect of primary legislation. It also makes provision as to public bodies which are to be regarded as a 'public authority' for the purposes of the Bill.

Clause 7 provides that a person who claims that a public authority has acted (or proposes to act) in a way which is unlawful, because incompatible with the Convention rights, may bring proceedings against that authority under the Bill, or may rely on the Convention rights in any legal proceedings. Such a person may only bring proceedings or rely on the Convention rights if he is (or would be) a victim of the unlawful act.

Clause 8 provides that a court or tribunal may grant such relief or remedy, or make such order, within its jurisdiction as it considers appropriate where it finds an authority to have acted unlawfully. It also specifies the circumstances in which an award of damages may be made.

Clause 9 provides that proceedings against a court or tribunal under *clause 7* may be brought only by way of appeal or on an application for judicial review and that damages may not be awarded in proceedings under the Bill in relation to an act of a court or tribunal, and preserves judicial immunity.

Clause 10 enables the amendment by order of a provision of legislation which has been declared incompatible with the Convention rights or which, in view of a finding of the European Court of Human Rights, appears to a Minister of the Crown to be incompatible, so as to remove the incompatibility or possible incompatibility.

Clause 11 makes further provision with respect to such a remedial order and also provides that no person shall be guilty of an offence solely as a result of any retrospective effect of such an order.

Clause 12 provides that a remedial order is to be subject to the affirmative resolution procedure, and that, except in urgent cases, the order must be approved in draft. Where not approved in draft before it is made, it ceases to have effect if not approved by Parliament within 40 sitting days of it having been made.

Clause 13 provides that a person may rely on a Convention right without prejudice to any other right or freedom conferred on him, and that *clauses 7 to 9* do not affect the right of any person to make any claim or bring any proceedings which he could make or bring apart from those clauses.

Clause 14 makes provision in respect of a 'designated derogation', which it defines as the United Kingdom's derogation from Article 5(3) of the Convention (the text of which is set out in Part I of *Schedule 2)* and any other derogation from an Article of the Convention or of any protocol to the Convention, which is designated by order. It also provides for the amendment of *Schedule 2* to reflect the addition or removal of designated derogations.

Clause 15 makes provision in respect of a 'designated reservation', which it defines as the United Kingdom's reservation to Article 2 of the first Protocol to the Convention (the text of which is set out in Part II of *Schedule 2)*, and any other reservation to an Article which is designated by order. It also provides for the amendment of *Schedule 2* to reflect the addition or removal of designated reservations.

Clause 16 provides that a designated derogation will, if not withdrawn before then, cease to have effect for the purposes of the Bill five years after *clause 1(2)* comes into force unless extended by order for a further five years before the end of that period. *Clause 16* also provides that such an order is to be subject to the affirmative resolution procedure.

Clause 17 provides that the appropriate Minister must review the designated reservation to Article 2 of the First Protocol to the Convention within five years of *clause 1(2)* coming into force, and any other reservation within five years of its designation; requires the Minister to lay a copy of a report on the result of any such review before each House of Parliament; and provides for further periodic reviews of the designated reservation while the designation is still in force.

Clause 18 provides that a holder of one of the judicial offices to which the clause applies may become a judge of the European Court of Human Rights without being required to relinquish his office, and that he is not required to perform the duties of his judicial office while he is a judge of the Court.

Clause 19 provides that the Minister in charge of a Bill in either House of Parliament must make and publish a written statement to the effect either that in his view the provisions of the Bill are compatible with the Convention rights, or that although he is unable to make such a statement, the government nevertheless wishes the House to proceed with the Bill.

Clause 20 makes provision in respect of the making of orders under the Bill.

Clause 21 defines various terms used in the Bill, and explains how references to Articles of the Convention and the European Court of Human Rights are to be read before and after the coming into force of the 11th Protocol to the Convention.

Clause 22 makes provision about commencement and extent of the Bill. It also provides that the Bill binds the Crown.

Financial effects of the Bill

Although public authorities should already be seeking to comply with the Convention, the Bill could result in increased costs for them. The prohibition in *clause 6* on acts by public authorities which are incompatible with the Convention rights could result in their amending their procedures in response to successful challenges to those acts, or in anticipation of challenges, and this may give rise to costs.

Public authorities will be liable under *clause 8* to pay damages awarded by the courts in respect of acts which are incompatible with the Convention rights. In deciding whether to make such an award and in calculating the amount, however, the courts will be required under *clause 8* to take into account the principles applied by the European Court of Human Rights in relation to its own awards of compensation. Such awards tend to range from £5,000 to £15,000 and are not made simply because the Court finds a violation of the Convention.

Clause 6 will have the effect of applying the Bill to a wide range of public authorities of different kinds. It is impossible to calculate what the overall financial effects of the Bill will be for them, or the effect for particular public authorities, or to be sure that any amendments to their procedures would not have been made in any case regardless of the provisions of the Bill (for example, as a result of other domestic policy decisions).

Additional public expenditure on the courts and the legal aid budget is likely to arise from *clause 7* which enables Convention points to be raised in domestic proceedings involving a public authority, or to be the basis for proceedings against a public authority. Although it will be possible to raise Convention points (to the extent that they are relevant) in proceedings before any court or tribunal, the impact is likely to be greatest in relation to criminal proceedings, and on appeal, and in relation to applications for judicial review. It is also likely that the impact will be greater initially than in later years, when the courts will have become accustomed to dealing with Convention points and precedents will have been set.

International experiences of the implementation of human rights legislation provide some insights into how additional workload might accrue to the courts and what the areas of potential challenge might be, but there is no domestic precedent from which an analogy might be drawn. The Government is considering those experiences and the advice of the judiciary and practitioners from the United Kingdom and abroad in assessing how the provisions of the Bill are likely to affect the court system in practice. At present, however, there is no basis on which to estimate the additional costs to the courts and legal aid budget with any precision.

There will be an initial cost in training judges, magistrates and tribunal members to handle Convention points. This is estimated to cost up to £4.5m in England and Wales.

The other provisions of the Bill have no significant financial effects.

Any costs arising as a result of the Bill will be contained within the Government's planned overall spending totals.

Effect of the Bill on public service manpower

In so far as its provisions result in increased business for the courts, the Bill may result in an increase in posts in the courts.

Business compliance cost assessment

It is not possible to assess the impact of the Bill on businesses, charities or voluntary organisations, but since its direct application is limited to public authorities, its impact on these kinds of organisation is unlikely to be significant.

ARRANGEMENT OF CLAUSES

Introduction

Clause
1. The Convention and the First Protocol.
2. Interpretation of Convention rights.

Interpretation of legislation

3. Legislation.
4. Declaration of incompatibility.

A BILL INTITULED

An Act to give further effect to rights and freedoms guaranteed under the European Convention on Human Rights; to make provision with respect to holders of certain judicial offices who become judges of the European Court of Human Rights; and for connected purposes.

BE IT ENACTED by the Queen's most Excellent Majesty, by and with the advice and consent of the Lords Spiritual and Temporal, and Commons, in this present Parliament assembled, and by the authority of the same, as follows:—

Introduction

1. The Convention and the First Protocol

(1) In this Act, 'the Convention rights' means the rights and fundamental freedoms set out in—

    (a) Articles 2 to 12 and 14 of the Convention, and

    (b) Articles 1 to 3 of the First Protocol,

as read with Articles 16 to 18 of the Convention.

(2) Those Articles are to have effect for the purposes of this Act subject to any designated derogation or reservation (as to which see sections 14 and 15).

(3) The Articles are set out in Schedule 1.

(4) The Secretary of State may by order make such amendments to this section or Schedule 1 as he considers appropriate to reflect the effect, in relation to the United Kingdom, of a protocol.

(5) In subsection (4) 'protocol' means a protocol to the Convention—

    (a) which the United Kingdom has ratified; or

    (b) which the United Kingdom has signed with a view to ratification.

(6) No amendment may be made by an order under subsection (4) so as to come into force before the protocol concerned is in force in relation to the United Kingdom.

2. Interpretation of Convention rights

(1) A court or tribunal determining a question which has arisen under this Act in connection with a Convention right must take into account any—

    (a) judgment, decision, declaration or advisory opinion of the European Court of Human Rights,

    (b) opinion of the Commission given in a report adopted under Article 31 of the Convention,

    (c) decision of the Commission in connection with Article 26 or 27(2) of the Convention, or

    (d) decision of the Committee of Ministers taken under Article 46 of the Convention,

whenever made or given, so far as, in the opinion of the court or tribunal, it is relevant to the proceedings in which that question has arisen.

(2) Evidence of any judgment, decision, declaration or opinion of which account may have to be taken under this section is to be given in proceedings before any court or tribunal in such manner as may be provided by rules.

(3) In this section 'rules' means rules of court or, in the case of proceedings before a tribunal, rules made for the purposes of this section—
    (a) by the Lord Advocate or the Secretary of State, in relation to proceedings in Scotland; or
    (b) by the Lord Chancellor or Secretary of State, in relation to any other proceedings.

Interpretation of legislation

3. Legislation

(1) So far as it is possible to do so, primary legislation and subordinate legislation must be read and given effect in a way which is compatible with the Convention rights.

(2) This section—
    (a) applies to primary legislation and subordinate legislation whenever enacted;
    (b) does not affect the validity, continuing operation or enforcement of any incompatible primary legislation; and
    (c) does not affect the validity, continuing operation or enforcement of any incompatible subordinate legislation if (disregarding any possibility of revocation) primary legislation prevents removal of the incompatibility.

4. Declaration of incompatibility

(1) Subsection (2) applies in any proceedings in which a court determines whether a provision of primary legislation is compatible with one or more of the Convention rights.

(2) If the court is satisfied that the provision is incompatible with one or more of the Convention rights, it may make a declaration of that incompatibility.

(3) Subsection (4) applies in any proceedings in which a court determines whether a provision of subordinate legislation, made in the exercise of a power conferred by primary legislation, is compatible with one or more of the Convention rights.

(4) If the court is satisfied
    (a) that the provision is incompatible with one or more of the Convention rights, and

(b) that (disregarding any possibility of revocation) the primary legislation concerned prevents removal of the incompatibility,
it may make a declaration of that incompatibility.

(5) In this section 'court' means—
   (a) the House of Lords;
   (b) the Judicial Committee of the Privy Council;
   (c) the Courts-Martial Appeal Court;
   (d) in Scotland, the High Court of Justiciary sitting as a court of criminal appeal or the Court of Session;
   (e) in England and Wales or Northern Ireland, the High Court or the Court of Appeal.

(6) A declaration under this section ('a declaration of incompatibility')—
   (a) does not affect the validity, continuing operation or enforcement of the provision in respect of which it is given; and
   (b) is not binding on the parties to the proceedings in which it is made.

5. Right of Crown to intervene

(1) Where a court is considering whether to make a declaration of incompatibility, the Crown is entitled to notice in accordance with rules of court.

(2) In any case to which subsection (1) applies—
   (a) a Minister of the Crown, or
   (b) a person nominated by a Minister of the Crown,
is entitled, on an application made to the court in accordance with rules of court, to be joined as a party to the proceedings.

(3) An application under subsection (2) may be made at any time during the proceedings.

(4) A person who has been made a party to criminal proceedings (other than in Scotland) as the result of an application under this section may, with leave, appeal to the House of Lords against any declaration of incompatibility made in the proceedings.

(5) In subsection (4)—
'leave' means leave granted by the court making the declaration of incompatibility or by the House of Lords; and
'criminal proceedings' includes all proceedings before the Courts-Martial Appeal Court.

Public authorities

6. Acts of public authorities

(1) It is unlawful for a public authority to act in a way which is incompatible with one or more of the Convention rights.

(2) Subsection (1) does not apply to an act if—

(a) as the result of one or more provisions of primary legislation, the authority could not have acted differently; or

(b) in the case of one or more provisions of, or made under, primary legislation which cannot be read or given effect in a way which is compatible with the Convention rights, the authority was acting so as to give effect to or enforce those provisions.

(3) In this section, 'public authority' includes—

(a) a court,

(b) a tribunal which exercises functions in relation to legal proceedings, and

(c) any person certain of whose functions are functions of a public nature,

but does not include either House of Parliament or a person exercising functions in connection with proceedings in Parliament.

(4) In subsection (3) 'Parliament' does not include the House of Lords in its judicial capacity.

(5) In relation to a particular act, a person is not a public authority by virtue only of subsection (3)(c) if the nature of the act is private.

(6) 'An act' includes a failure to act but does not include a failure to—

(a) introduce in, or lay before, Parliament a proposal for legislation; or

(b) make any primary legislation or remedial order.

7. Proceedings

(1) A person who claims that a public authority has acted (or proposes to act) in a way which is made unlawful by section 6(1) may—

(a) bring proceedings against the authority under this Act in the appropriate court or tribunal, or

(b) rely on the Convention right or rights concerned in any legal proceedings,

but only if he is (or would be) a victim of the unlawful act.

(2) In subsection (1)(a) 'appropriate court or tribunal' means such court or tribunal as may be determined in accordance with rules; and proceedings against an authority includes a counterclaim or similar proceeding.

(3) If the proceedings are brought on an application for judicial review, the applicant is to be taken to have a sufficient interest in relation to the unlawful act only if he is, or would be, a victim of that act.

(4) If the proceedings are made by way of a petition for judicial review in Scotland, the applicant shall be taken to have title and interest to sue in relation to the unlawful act only if he is, or would be, a victim of the unlawful act.

(5) In subsection (1)(b) 'legal proceedings' includes—

(a) proceedings brought by or at the instigation of a public authority; and

(b) an appeal against the decision of a court or tribunal.

(6) For the purposes of this section, a person is a victim of an unlawful act only if he would be a victim for the purposes of Article 34 of the Convention if proceedings were brought in the European Court of Human Rights in respect of that act.

(7) Nothing in this Act creates a criminal offence.

(8) In this section 'rules' means—
   (a) in relation to proceedings before a court in Scotland, rules made by the Secretary of State for the purposes of this section.
   (b) in relation to proceedings before a tribunal in Scotland, rules made by the Lord Advocate or the Secretary of State for those purposes,
   (c) in relation to proceedings before any other court or tribunal, rules made by the Secretary of State or the Lord Chancellor for those purposes or rules of court,

and includes provision made by order under section 1 of the Courts and Legal Services Act 1990.

(9) In making rules regard must be had to section 9.

8. Judicial remedies

(1) In relation to any act (or proposed act) of a public authority which the court finds is (or would be) unlawful, it may grant such relief or remedy, or make such order, within its jurisdiction as it considers just and appropriate.

(2) But damages may be awarded only by a court which has power to award damages, or to order the payment of compensation, in civil proceedings.

(3) No award of damages is to be made unless, taking account of all the circumstances of the case, including—
   (a) any other relief or remedy granted, or order made, in relation to the act in question (by that or any other court), and
   (b) the consequences of any decision (of that or any other court) in respect of that act,

the court is satisfied that the award is necessary to afford just satisfaction to the person in whose favour it is made.

(4) In determining—
   (a) whether to award damages, or
   (b) the amount of an award,

the court must take into account the principles applied by the European Court of Human Rights in relation to the award of compensation under Article 41 of the Convention.

(5) In this section—

'court' includes a tribunal;

'damages' means damages for an unlawful act of a public authority; and

'unlawful' means unlawful under section 6(1).

9. Acts of courts and tribunals

(1) Proceedings under section 7(1)(a) in respect of any act of a court may be brought only by way of an appeal against the decision, or on an application (in Scotland a petition) for judicial review.

(2) That does not affect any rule of law which prevents a court from being the subject of judicial review.

(3) Damages may not be awarded in proceedings under this Act in respect of any act of a court.

(4) Nothing in this Act makes a person personally liable in relation to—

    (a) the exercise (or purported exercise) of the jurisdiction of a court, or

    (b) the administration of a court.

(5) In this section—

'act' includes a failure to act; and

'court' includes a tribunal, a justice of the peace, a justice's clerk and (in Northern Ireland) a clerk of petty session.

Remedial action

10. Power to take remedial action

(1) This section applies if—

    (a) a provision of legislation has been declared under section 4 to be incompatible with one or more of the Convention rights; or

    (b) it appears to a Minister of the Crown or Her Majesty in Council that, having regard to a finding of the European Court of Human Rights, a provision of legislation is incompatible with one or more of the obligations of the United Kingdom arising from the Convention.

(2) If a Minister of the Crown considers that, in order to remove the incompatibility, it is appropriate to amend the legislation using the power conferred by this subsection, he may by order make such amendments to it as he considers appropriate.

(3) If the legislation is an Order in Council, the power conferred by subsection (2) is exercisable by Her Majesty in Council.

(4) If, in the case of subordinate legislation, a Minister of the Crown considers—

    (a) that it is necessary to amend the primary legislation under which the subordinate legislation in question was made, in order to enable the incompatibility to be removed, and

    (b) that it is appropriate to do so using the power conferred by this subsection,

he may by order make such amendments to the primary legislation as he considers appropriate.

    (5) In this section 'amendments' includes repeals and the application of provisions subject to modifications.

11. Remedial orders

    (1) An order made under section 10 (a 'remedial order') may—

      (a) contain such incidental, supplemental, consequential and transitional provision as the person making it considers appropriate;

      (b) be made so as to have effect from a date earlier than that on which it is made;

      (c) make provision for the delegation of specific functions; and

      (d) make different provision for different cases.

    (2) The power conferred by subsection (1)(a) includes—

      (a) power to amend or repeal primary legislation (including primary legislation other than that which contains the incompatible provision); and

      (b) power to amend or revoke subordinate legislation (including subordinate legislation other than that which contains the incompatible provision).

    (3) No person is to be guilty of an offence solely as a result of the retrospective effect of a remedial order.

12. Procedure

    (1) No remedial order may be made unless—

      (a) a draft of the order has been approved by resolution of each House of Parliament; or

      (b) it is declared in the order that it appears to the Minister making it, or Her Majesty in Council, that because of the urgency of the matter it is necessary to make the order without a draft being so approved.

    (2) If a remedial order is made without being approved in draft—

      (a) the order must be laid before Parliament after it is made; and

      (b) if at the end of the period for consideration a resolution has not been passed by each House approving the order, the order ceases to have effect (but without that affecting anything previously done under the order or the power to make a fresh remedial order).

    (3) In subsection (2) 'period for consideration' means the period of forty days beginning with the day on which the order was made.

    (4) In calculating the period for consideration, no account is to be taken of any time during which—

      (a) Parliament is dissolved or prorogued; or

(b) both Houses are adjourned for more than four days.

Other rights and proceedings

13. Other rights and proceedings

(1) A person may rely on a Convention right without prejudice to any other right or freedom conferred on him by or under any law having effect in any part of the United Kingdom.

(2) Sections 7 to 9 do not affect the right of any person to make any claim or bring any proceedings which he could make or bring apart from those sections.

Derogations and reservations

14. Derogations

(1) In this Act, 'designated derogation' means—
- (a) the United Kingdom's derogation from Article 5(3) of the Convention; and
- (b) any derogation by the United Kingdom from an Article of the Convention, or of any protocol to the Convention, which is designated for the purposes of this Act in an order made by the Secretary of State.

(2) The derogation referred to in subsection (1)(a) is set out in Part I of Schedule 2.

(3) If a designated derogation is amended or replaced it ceases to be a designated derogation.

(4) But subsection (3) does not prevent the Secretary of State from exercising his power under subsection (1)(b) to make a fresh designation order in respect of the Article concerned.

(5) The Secretary of State must by order make such amendments to Schedule 2 as he considers appropriate to reflect—
- (a) any order made under subsection (1)(b); or
- (b) the effect of subsection (3).

(6) A designation order may be made in anticipation of the making by the United Kingdom of a proposed derogation.

15. Reservations

(1) In this Act, 'designated reservation' means—
- (a) the United Kingdom's reservation to Article 2 of the First Protocol to the Convention; and
- (b) any other reservation by the United Kingdom to an Article of the Convention, or of any protocol to the Convention, which is designated for the purposes of this Act in an order made by the Secretary of State.

(2) The text of the reservation referred to in subsection (1)(a) is set out in Part II of Schedule 2.

(3) If a designated reservation is withdrawn wholly or in part it ceases to be a designated reservation.

(4) But subsection (3) does not prevent the Secretary of State from exercising his power under subsection (1)(b) to make a fresh designation order in respect of the Article concerned.

(5) The Secretary of State must by order make such amendments to Schedule 2 as he considers appropriate to reflect—
    (a) any order made under subsection (1)(b); or
    (b) the effect of subsection (3).

16. Period for which designated derogations have effect

(1) If it has not already been withdrawn by the United Kingdom, a designated derogation ceases to have effect for the purposes of this Act—
    (a) in the case of the derogation referred to in section 14(1)(a), at the end of the period of five years beginning with the date on which section 1(2) came into force;
    (b) in the case of any other derogation, at the end of the period of five years beginning with the date on which the order designating it was made.

(2) At any time before the period—
    (a) fixed by subsection (1)(a) or (b), or
    (b) extended by an order under this subsection,
comes to an end, the Secretary of State may by order extend it by a further period of five years.

(3) An order under section 14(1)(b) ceases to have effect at the end of the period for consideration, unless a resolution has been passed by each House approving the order.

(4) Subsection (3) does not affect—
    (a) anything done in reliance on the order; or
    (b) the power to make a fresh order under section 14(1)(b).

(5) In subsection (3) 'period for consideration' means the period of forty days beginning with the day on which the order was made.

(6) In calculating the period for consideration, no account is to be taken of any time during which—
    (a) Parliament is dissolved or prorogued; or
    (b) both Houses are adjourned for more than four days.

(7) If a designated derogation is withdrawn by the United Kingdom, the Secretary of State must by order make such amendments to this Act as he considers are required to reflect that withdrawal.

17. Periodic review of designated reservations

(1) The appropriate Minister must review the designated reservation referred to in section 15(1)(a)—

(a) before the end of the period of five years beginning with the date on which section 1(2) came into force; and

(b) if that designation is still in force, before the end of the period of five years beginning with the date on which the last report relating to it was laid under subsection (3).

(2) The appropriate Minister must review each of the other designated reservations (if any)—

(a) before the end of the period of five years beginning with the date on which the order designating the reservation first came into force; and

(b) if the designation is still in force, before the end of the period of five years beginning with the date on which the last report relating to it was laid under subsection (3).

(3) The Minister conducting a review under this section must prepare a report on the result of the review and lay a copy of it before each House of Parliament.

Judges of the European Court of Human Rights

18. Appointment to European Court of Human Rights

(1) In this section 'judicial office' means the office of—

(a) Lord Justice of Appeal, Justice of the High Court or Circuit judge, in England and Wales;

(b) judge of the Court of Session or sheriff, in Scotland;

(c) Lord Justice of Appeal, judge of the High Court or county court judge, in Northern Ireland.

(2) The holder of a judicial office may become a judge of the European Court of Human Rights ('the Court') without being required to relinquish his office.

(3) But he is not required to perform the duties of his judicial office while he is a judge of the Court.

(4) In respect of any period during which he is a judge of the Court—

(a) a Lord Justice of Appeal or Justice of the High Court is not to count as a judge of the relevant court for the purposes of section 2(1) or 4(1) of the Supreme Court Act 1981 (maximum number of judges) nor as a judge of the Supreme Court for the purposes of section 12 of that Act (salaries etc.);

(b) a judge of the Court of Session is not to count as a judge of that court for the purposes of section 1(1) of the Court of Session Act 1988 (maximum number of judges) or of section 9(1)(c) of the Administration of Justice Act 1973 ('the 1973 Act') (salaries etc.);

(c) a Lord Justice of Appeal or a judge of the High Court in Northern Ireland is not to count as a judge of the relevant court for the purposes of section 2(1) or 3(1) of the Judicature (Northern Ireland) Act 1978 (maximum number of judges) nor as a judge of

the Supreme Court of Northern Ireland for the purposes of
section 9(1)(d) of the 1973 Act (salaries etc.);

(d) a Circuit judge is not to count as such for the purposes of section
18 of the Courts Act 1971 (salaries etc.);

(e) a sheriff is not to count as such for the purposes of section 14 of the
Sheriff Courts (Scotland) Act 1907 (salaries etc.);

(f) a county court judge of Northern Ireland is not to count as such for
the purposes of section 106 of the County Courts Act (Northern
Ireland) 1959 (salaries etc.).

(5) If a sheriff principal is appointed a judge of the Court, section 11(1) of
the Sheriff Courts (Scotland) Act 1971 (temporary appointment of sheriff
principal) applies, while he holds that appointment, as if his office is
vacant.

(6) The Lord Chancellor or the Secretary of State may by order—

(a) make such provision with respect to pensions payable to or in
respect of any holder of a judicial office who serves as a judge of
the Court as he considers appropriate;

(b) make such transitional provision (including, in particular, provision for a temporary increase in the maximum number of judges)
as he considers appropriate in relation to any holder of a judicial
office who has completed his service as a judge of the Court.

Parliamentary procedure

19. Statements of compatibility

(1) A Minister of the Crown in charge of a Bill in either House of
Parliament must, before Second Reading of the Bill—

(a) make a statement to the effect that in his view the provisions of the
Bill are compatible with the Convention rights ('a statement of
compatibility'); or

(b) make a statement to the effect that although he is unable to make
a statement of compatibility the government nevertheless wishes
the House to proceed with the Bill.

(2) The statement must be in writing and be published in such manner as
the Minister making it considers appropriate.

Supplemental

20. Orders under this Act

(1) Any power to make an order under this Act is exercisable by statutory
instrument.

(2) Any such instrument made under section 14, 15 or 16 must be laid
before Parliament.

(3) No order may be made under section 1(4) or 16(2) unless a draft of the
order has been laid before, and approved by, each House of Parliament.

(4) Any statutory instrument made under section 18(5) shall be subject to annulment in pursuance of a resolution of either House of Parliament.

21. Interpretation, etc

(1) In this Act—

'the appropriate Minister' means the Minister of the Crown having charge of the appropriate authorised government department (within the meaning of the Crown Proceedings Act 1947);

'the Convention' means the Convention for the Protection of Human Rights and Fundamental Freedoms, agreed by the Council of Europe at Rome on 4th November 1950 as it has effect for the time being in relation to the United Kingdom;

'the Commission' means the European Commission of Human Rights;

'declaration of incompatibility' means a declaration under section 4;

'Minister of the Crown' has the same meaning as in the Ministers of the Crown Act 1975;

'primary legislation' means any—

(a) public general Act;

(b) local and personal Act;

(c) private Act;

(d) Measure of the Church Assembly;

(e) Measure of the General Synod of the Church of England;

(f) Order in Council made under section 38(1)(a) of the Northern Ireland Constitution Act 1973;

(g) Order in Council made in exercise of Her Majesty's Royal Prerogative;

and includes an order or other instrument made under primary legislation to the extent to which it operates to bring one or more provisions of that legislation into force or amends any primary legislation.

'the First Protocol' means the protocol to the Convention agreed at Paris on 20th March 1952;

'11th Protocol' means the protocol to the Convention (restructuring the control machinery established by the Convention) agreed at Strasbourg on 11th May 1994;

'remedial order' means an order under section 10:

'subordinate legislation' means any—

(a) Order in Council other than one made in exercise of Her Majesty's Royal Prerogative or under section 38(1)(a) of the Northern Ireland Constitution Act 1973;

(b) Act of the Parliament of Northern Ireland;

(c) Measure of the Northern Ireland Assembly;

(d) order, rules, regulations, scheme, warrant, byelaw or other instrument made under primary legislation (except to the extent to which it operates to bring one or more provisions of that legislation into force or amends any primary legislation);

(e) order, rules, regulations, scheme, warrant, byelaw or other instrument made under legislation mentioned in paragraphs (b) or (c)

or made under an Order in Council applying only to Northern
Ireland;
'tribunal' means any tribunal in which legal proceedings may be brought.

(2) The references in paragraphs (b) and (c) of section 2(1) to Articles are
to Articles of the Convention as they had effect immediately before the
coming into force of the 11th Protocol.

(3) The reference in paragraph (d) of section 2(1) to Article 46 includes a
reference to Articles 32 and 54 of the Convention as they had effect
immediately before the coming into force of the 11th Protocol.

(4) The references in section 2(1) to a report or decision of the Commission or a decision of the Committee of Ministers include references to a
report or decision made as provided by paragraphs 3, 4 and 6 of Article 5 of
the 11th Protocol (transitional provisions).

(5) In section 4(3) of the Northern Ireland Constitution Act 1973 (status
of Measures of Northern Ireland Assembly), after 'below' insert—
'and to section 21(1) of the Human Rights Act 1998'.

22. Short title, commencement, application and extent
(1) This Act may be cited as the Human Rights Act 1998.

(2) Sections 18 and 20 and this section come into force on the passing of
this Act.

(3) The other provisions of this Act come into force on such day as the
Secretary of State may by order appoint; and different days may be
appointed for different purposes.

(4) Paragraph (b) of subsection (1) of section 7 applies to proceedings
brought by or at the instigation of a public authority whenever the act in
question took place; but otherwise that subsection does not apply to an act
committed before the coming into force of that section.

(5) This Act binds the Crown.

(6) This Act extends to Northern Ireland.

*RB NOTE: The Bill then contained two Schedules. Schedule 1 contained
Articles 2–12, 14, 16–18 and First Protocol Articles 1–3 of the ECHR, for
which see Doc. 22 above; and Schedule 2 contained the UK reservation and
derogation from the ECHR, for which also see Doc. 22.*

(C) ACCOMPANYING GOVERNMENT WHITE PAPER

RB NOTE: For the articles and Protocols of the ECHR as referred to in the White Paper below, see Doc. 22.

Preface by the Prime Minister

The Government is pledged to modernise British politics. We are committed to a comprehensive programme of constitutional reform. We believe it is right to increase individual rights, to decentralise power, to open up government and to reform Parliament. . . .

This White Paper explains the proposals contained in the Human Rights Bill which we are introducing into Parliament. The Bill marks a major step forward in the achievement of our programme of reform. It will give people in the United Kingdom opportunities to enforce their rights under the European Convention in British courts rather than having to incur the cost and delay of taking a case to the European Human Rights Commission and Court in Strasbourg. It will enhance the awareness of human rights in our society. And it stands alongside our decision to put the promotion of human rights at the forefront of our foreign policy.

I warmly commend these proposals to Parliament and to the people of this country.

Relationship to current law in the United Kingdom

1.11 When the United Kingdom ratified the Convention the view was taken that the rights and freedoms which the Convention guarantees were already, in substance, fully protected in British law. It was not considered necessary to write the Convention itself into British law, or to introduce any new laws in the United Kingdom in order to be sure of being able to comply with the Convention.

1.12 From the point of view of the *international* obligation which the United Kingdom was undertaking when it signed and ratified the Convention, this was understandable. Moreover, the European Court of Human Rights explicitly confirmed that it was not a necessary part of proper observance of the Convention that it should be incorporated into the laws of the States concerned.

1.13 However, since its drafting nearly 50 years ago, almost all the States which are party to the European Convention on Human Rights have gradually incorporated it into their domestic law in one way or another. Ireland and Norway have not done so, but Ireland has a Bill of Rights which guarantees rights similar to those guaranteed by the Convention and Norway is also in the process of incorporating the Convention. Several other countries with which we have close links and which share the common law tradition, such as Canada and New Zealand, have provided similar protection for human rights in their own legal systems.

The case for incorporation

1.14 The effect of non-incorporation on the British people is a very practical one. The rights, originally developed with major help from the United Kingdom Government, are no longer actually seen as British rights. And enforcing them takes too long and costs too much. It takes on average five years to get an action into the European Court of Human Rights once all domestic remedies have been exhausted; and it costs an average of £30,000. Bringing these rights home will mean that the British people will be able to argue for their rights in the British courts – without this inordinate delay and cost. It will also mean that the rights will be brought much more fully into the jurisprudence of the courts throughout the United Kingdom, and their interpretation will thus be far more subtly and powerfully woven into our law. And there will be another distinct benefit. British judges will be enabled to make a distinctively British contribution to the development of the jurisprudence of human rights in Europe.

1.15 Moreover, in the Government's view, the approach which the United Kingdom has so far adopted towards the Convention does not sufficiently reflect its importance and has not stood the test of time.

1.16 The most obvious proof of this lies in the number of cases in which the European Commission and Court have found that there have been violations of the Convention rights in the United Kingdom. The causes vary. The Government recognises that interpretations of the rights guaranteed under the Convention have developed over the years, reflecting changes in society and attitudes. Sometimes United Kingdom laws have proved to be inherently at odds with the Convention rights. On other occasions, although the law has been satisfactory, something has been done which our courts have held to be lawful by United Kingdom standards but which breaches the Convention. In other cases again, there has simply been no framework within which the compatibility with the Convention rights of an executive act or decision can be tested in the British courts: these courts can of course review the exercise of executive discretion, but they can do so only on the basis of what is lawful or unlawful according to the law in the United Kingdom as it stands. It is plainly unsatisfactory that someone should be the victim of a breach of the Convention standards by the State yet cannot bring any case at all in the British courts, simply because British law does not recognise the right in the same terms as one contained in the Convention.

1.17 For individuals, and for those advising them, the road to Strasbourg is long and hard. Even when they get there, the Convention enforcement machinery is subject to long delays. This might be convenient for a government which was half-hearted about the Convention and the right of individuals to apply under it, since it postpones the moment at which changes in domestic law or practice must be made. But it is not in keeping with the importance which this Government attaches to the observance of basic human rights.

Bringing Rights Home

1.18 We therefore believe that the time has come to enable people to enforce their Convention rights against the State in the British courts, rather than having to incur the delays and expense which are involved in taking a case to the European Human Rights Commission and Court in Strasbourg and which may altogether deter some people from pursuing their rights. Enabling courts in the United Kingdom to rule on the application of the Convention will also help to influence the development of case law on the Convention by the European Court of Human Rights on the basis of familiarity with our laws and customs and of sensitivity to practices and procedures in the United Kingdom. Our courts' decisions will provide the European Court with a useful source of information and reasoning for its own decisions. United Kingdom judges have a very high reputation internationally, but the fact that they do not deal in the same concepts as the European Court of Human Rights limits the extent to which their judgments can be drawn upon and followed. Enabling the Convention rights to be judged by British courts will also lead to closer scrutiny of the human rights implications of new legislation and new policies. If legislation is enacted which is incompatible with the Convention, a ruling by the domestic courts to that effect will be much more direct and immediate than a ruling from the European Court of Human Rights. The Government of the day, and Parliament, will want to minimise the risk of that happening.

1.19 Our aim is a straightforward one. It is to make more directly accessible the rights which the British people already enjoy under the Convention. In other words, to bring those rights home.

CHAPTER 2   THE GOVERNMENT'S PROPOSALS FOR ENFORCING THE
CONVENTION RIGHTS

2.1 The essential feature of the Human Rights Bill is that the United Kingdom will not be bound to give effect to the Convention rights merely as a matter of international law, but will also give them further effect directly in our domestic law. But there is more than one way of achieving this. This Chapter explains the choices which the Government has made for the Bill.

A new requirement on public authorities

2.2 Although the United Kingdom has an international obligation to comply with the Convention, there at present is no requirement in our domestic law on central and local government, or others exercising similar executive powers, to exercise those powers in a way which is compatible with the Convention. This Bill will change that by making it unlawful for public authorities to act in a way which is incompatible with the Convention rights. The definition of what constitutes a public authority is in wide terms. Examples of persons or organisations whose acts or omissions it is intended should be able to be challenged include central government (including executive agencies); local government; the police; immigration officers; prisons; courts and tribunals themselves; and, to the extent that they are exercising public functions, companies responsible for areas of activity which were previously within the public sector, such as the privatised utilities. The actions of Parliament, however, are excluded.

2.3 A person who is aggrieved by an act or omission on the part of a public authority which is incompatible with the Convention rights will be able to challenge the act or omission in the courts. The effects will be wide-ranging. They will extend both to legal actions which a public authority pursues against individuals (for example, where a criminal prosecution is brought or where an administrative decision is being enforced through legal proceedings) and to cases which individuals pursue against a public authority (for example, for judicial review of an executive decision). Convention points will normally be taken in the context of proceedings instituted against individuals or already open to them, but, if none is available, it will be possible for people to bring cases on Convention grounds alone. Individuals or organisations seeking judicial review of decisions by public authorities on Convention grounds will need to show that they have been directly affected, as they must if they take a case to Strasbourg.

2.4 It is our intention that people or organisations should be able to argue that their Convention rights have been infringed by a public authority in our courts at any level. This will enable the Convention rights to be applied from the outset against the facts and background of a particular case, and the people concerned to obtain their remedy at the earliest possible moment. We think this is preferable to allowing cases to run their ordinary course but then referring them to some kind of separate constitutional court which, like the European Court of Human Rights, would simply review cases which had already passed through the regular legal machinery. In considering Convention points, our courts will be required to take account of relevant decisions of the European Commission and Court of Human Rights (although these will not be binding).

2.5 The Convention is often described as a 'living instrument' because it is interpreted by the European Court in the light of present day conditions and therefore reflects changing social attitudes and the changes in the circumstances of society. In future our judges will be able to contribute to this dynamic and evolving interpretation of the Convention. In particular, our courts will be required to balance the protection of individuals' fundamental rights against the demands of the general interest of the community, particularly in relation to Articles 8–11 where a State may restrict the protected right to the extent that this is 'necessary in a democratic society'.

Remedies for a failure to comply with the Convention

2.6 A public authority which is found to have acted unlawfully by failing to comply with the Convention will not be exposed to criminal penalties. But the court or tribunal will be able to grant the injured person any remedy which is within its normal powers to grant and which it considers appropriate and just in the circumstances. What remedy is appropriate will of course depend both on the facts of the case and on a proper balance between the rights of the individual and the public interest. In some cases, the right course may be for the decision of the public authority in the particular case to be quashed. In other cases, the only appropriate remedy may be an award of damages. The Bill provides that, in considering an award of damages on Convention grounds, the courts are to take into account the principles applied by the European Court of Human Rights in awarding compensation, so that people will be able to receive compensation from a domestic court equivalent to what they would have received in Strasbourg.

Interpretation of legislation

2.7 The Bill provides for legislation – both Acts of Parliament and secondary legislation – to be interpreted so far as possible so as to be compatible with the Convention. This goes far beyond the present rule which enables the courts to take the Convention into account in resolving any ambiguity in a legislative provision. The courts will be required to interpret legislation so as to uphold the Convention rights unless the legislation itself is so clearly incompatible with the Convention that it is impossible to do so.

2.8 This 'rule of construction' is to apply to past as well as to future legislation. To the extent that it affects the meaning of a legislative provision, the courts will not be bound by previous interpretations. They will be able to build a new body of case law, taking into account the Convention rights.

A declaration of incompatibility with the Convention rights

2.9 If the courts decide in any case that it is impossible to interpret an Act of Parliament in a way which is compatible with the Convention, the Bill enables a formal declaration to be made that its provisions are incompatible with the Convention. A declaration of incompatibility will be an important statement to make, and the power to make it will be reserved to the higher courts. They will be able to make a declaration in any proceedings before them, whether the case originated with them (as, in the High Court, on judicial review of an executive act) or in considering an appeal from a lower court or tribunal. The Government will have the right to intervene in any proceedings where such a declaration is a possible outcome. A decision by the High Court or Court of Appeal, determining whether or not such a declaration should be made, will itself be appealable.

Effect of court decisions on legislation

2.10 A declaration that legislation is incompatible with the Convention rights will not of itself have the effect of changing the law, which will continue to apply. But it will almost certainly prompt the Government and Parliament to change the law.

2.11 The Government has considered very carefully whether it would be right for the Bill to go further, and give to courts in the United Kingdom the power to set aside an Act of Parliament which they believe is incompatible with the Convention rights. In considering this question, we have looked at a number of models. The Canadian Charter of Rights and Freedoms 1982 enables the courts to strike down any legislation which is inconsistent with the Charter, unless the legislation contains an explicit statement that it is to apply 'notwithstanding' the provisions of the Charter. But legislation which has been struck down may be re-enacted with a 'notwithstanding' clause. In New Zealand, on the other hand, although there was an earlier proposal for legislation on lines similar to the Canadian Charter, the human rights legislation which was eventually enacted after wide consultation took a different form. The New Zealand Bill of Rights Act 1990 is an 'interpretative' statute which requires past and future legislation to be interpreted consistently with the rights contained in the Act as far as possible but provides that legislation stands if that is impossible. In Hong Kong, a middle course was adopted. The Hong Kong Bill of Rights Ordinance 1991 distinguishes between legislation enacted before and after the Ordinance took effect: previous legislation is subordinated to the provisions of the Ordinance, but subsequent legislation takes precedence over it.

2.12 The Government has also considered the European Communities Act 1972 which provides for European law, in cases where that law has 'direct effect', to take precedence over domestic law. There is, however, an essential difference between European Community law and the European Convention on Human Rights, because it is a *requirement* of membership of the European Union that member States give priority to directly effective EC law in their own legal systems. There is no such requirement in the Convention.

2.13 The Government has reached the conclusion that courts should not have the power to set aside primary legislation, past or future, on the ground of incompatibility with the Convention. This conclusion arises from the importance which the Government attaches to Parliamentary sovereignty. In this context, Parliamentary sovereignty means that Parliament is competent to make any law on any matter of its choosing and no court may question the validity of any Act that it passes. In enacting legislation, Parliament is making decisions about important matters of public policy. The authority to make those decisions derives from a democratic mandate. Members of Parliament in the House of Commons possess such a mandate because they are elected, accountable and representative. To make provision in the Bill for the courts to set aside Acts of Parliament would confer on the judiciary a general power over the decisions of Parliament which under our present constitutional arrangements they do not possess, and would be likely on occasions to draw the judiciary into serious conflict with Parliament. There is no evidence to suggest that they desire this power, nor that the public wish them to have it. Certainly, this Government has no mandate for any such change.

2.14 It has been suggested that the courts should be able to uphold the rights in the Human Rights Bill in preference to any provisions of earlier legislation which are incompatible with those rights. This is on the basis that a later

Act of Parliament takes precedence over an earlier Act if there is a conflict. But the Human Rights Bill is intended to provide a new basis for judicial interpretation of all legislation, not a basis for striking down any part of it. 2.15 The courts will, however, be able to strike down or set aside secondary legislation which is incompatible with the Convention, unless the terms of the parent statute make this impossible. The courts can already strike down or set aside secondary legislation when they consider it to be outside the powers conferred by the statute under which it is made, and it is right that they should be able to do so when it is incompatible with the Convention rights and could have been framed differently.

Entrenchment

2.16 On one view, human rights legislation is so important that it should be given added protection from subsequent amendment or repeal. The Constitution of the United States of America, for example, guarantees rights which can be amended or repealed only by securing qualified majorities in both the House of Representatives and the Senate, and among the States themselves. But an arrangement of this kind could not be reconciled with our own constitutional traditions, which allow any Act of Parliament to be amended or repealed by a subsequent Act of Parliament. We do not believe that it is necessary or would be desirable to attempt to devise such a special arrangement for this Bill.

Amending legislation

2.17 Although the Bill does not allow the courts to set aside Acts of Parliament, it will nevertheless have a profound impact on the way that legislation is interpreted and applied, and it will have the effect of putting the issues squarely to the Government and Parliament for further consideration. It is important to ensure that the Government and Parliament, for their part, can respond quickly. In the normal way, primary legislation can be amended only by further primary legislation, and this can take a long time. Given the volume of Government business, an early opportunity to legislate may not arise; and the process of legislating is itself protracted. Emergency legislation can be enacted very quickly indeed, but it is introduced only in the most exceptional circumstances.
2.18 The Bill provides for a fast-track procedure for changing legislation in response either to a declaration of incompatibility by our own higher courts or to a finding of a violation of the Convention in Strasbourg. The appropriate Government Minister will be able to amend the legislation by Order so as to make it compatible with the Convention. The Order will be subject to approval by both Houses of Parliament before taking effect, except where the need to amend the legislation is particularly urgent, when the Order will take effect immediately but will expire after a short period if not approved by Parliament.
2.19 There are already precedents for using secondary legislation to amend primary legislation in some circumstances, and we think the use of such a procedure is acceptable in this context and would be welcome as a means of

improving the observance of human rights. Plainly the Minister would have to exercise this power only in relation to the provisions which contravene the Convention, together with any necessary consequential amendments. In other words, Ministers would not have carte blanche to amend unrelated parts of the Act in which the breach is discovered.

Scotland

2.20 In Scotland, the position with regard to Acts of the Westminster Parliament will be the same as in England and Wales. All courts will be required to interpret the legislation in a way which is compatible with the Convention so far as possible. If a provision is found to be incompatible with the Convention, the Court of Session or the High Court will be able to make a declarator to that effect, but this will not affect the validity or continuing operation of the provision.

2.21 The position will be different, however, in relation to Acts of the Scottish Parliament when it is established. The Government has decided that the Scottish Parliament will have no power to legislate in a way which is incompatible with the Convention; and similarly that the Scottish Executive will have no power to make subordinate legislation or to take executive action which is incompatible with the Convention. It will accordingly be possible to challenge such legislation and actions in the Scottish courts on the ground that the Scottish Parliament or Executive has incorrectly applied its powers. If the challenge is successful then the legislation or action would be held to be unlawful. As with other issues concerning the powers of the Scottish Parliament, there will be a procedure for inferior courts to refer such issues to the superior Scottish courts; and those courts in turn will be able to refer the matter to the Judicial Committee of the Privy Council. If such issues are decided by the superior Scottish courts, an appeal from their decision will be to the Judicial Committee. These arrangements are in line with the Government's general approach to devolution.

Wales

2.22 Similarly, the Welsh Assembly will not have power to make subordinate legislation or take executive action which is incompatible with the Convention. It will be possible to challenge such legislation and action in the courts, and for them to be quashed, on the ground that the Assembly has exceeded its powers.

Northern Ireland

2.23 Acts of the Westminster Parliament will be treated in the same way in Northern Ireland as in the rest of the United Kingdom. But Orders in Council and other related legislation will be treated as subordinate legislation. In other words, they will be struck down by the courts if they are incompatible with the Convention. Most such legislation is a temporary means of enacting legislation which would otherwise be done by measures of a devolved Northern Ireland legislature.

CHAPTER 3   IMPROVING COMPLIANCE WITH THE CONVENTION RIGHTS

3.1 The enforcement of Convention rights will be a matter for the courts, whilst the Government and Parliament will have the different but equally important responsibility of revising legislation where necessary. But it is also highly desirable for the Government to ensure as far as possible that legislation which it places before Parliament in the normal way is compatible with the Convention rights, and for Parliament to ensure that the human rights implications of legislation are subject to proper consideration before the legislation is enacted.

Government legislation

3.2 The Human Rights Bill introduces a new procedure to make the human rights implications of proposed Government legislation more transparent. The responsible Minister will be required to provide a statement that in his or her view the proposed Bill is compatible with the Convention. The Government intends to include this statement alongside the Explanatory and Financial Memorandum which accompanies a Bill when it is introduced into each House of Parliament.

3.3 There may be occasions where such a statement cannot be provided, for example because it is essential to legislate on a particular issue but the policy in question requires a risk to be taken in relation to the Convention, or because the arguments in relation to the Convention issues raised are not clear-cut. In such cases, the Minister will indicate that he or she cannot provide a positive statement but that the Government nevertheless wishes Parliament to proceed to consider the Bill. Parliament would expect the Minister to explain his or her reasons during the normal course of the proceedings on the Bill. This will ensure that the human rights implications are debated at the earliest opportunity.

Consideration of draft legislation within Government

3.4 The new requirement to make a statement about the compliance of draft legislation with the Convention will have a significant and beneficial impact on the preparation of draft legislation within Government before its introduction into Parliament. It will ensure that all Ministers, their departments and officials are fully seized of the gravity of the Convention's obligations in respect of human rights. But we also intend to strengthen collective Government procedures so as to ensure that a proper assessment is made of the human rights implications when collective approval is sought for a new policy, as well as when any draft Bill is considered by Ministers. Revised guidance to Departments on these procedures will, like the existing guidance, be publicly available.

3.5 Some central co-ordination will also be extremely desirable in considering the approach to be taken to Convention points in criminal or civil proceedings, or in proceedings for judicial review, to which a Government department is a party. This is likely to require an inter-departmental group of lawyers and administrators meeting on a regular basis to ensure that a consistent approach is taken and to ensure that developments in case law are well understood by all those in Government who are involved in proceedings on Convention points. We do not, however, see any need to make a particular Minister responsible for promoting human rights across Government, or to set up a separate new Unit for this purpose. The responsibility for complying with human rights requirements rests on the Government as a whole.

A Parliamentary Committee on Human Rights

3.6 *Bringing Rights Home* [*RB NOTE: For the text of that earlier Labour Party document, see Doc. 116*] suggested that 'Parliament itself should play a leading role in protecting the rights which are at the heart of a parliamentary democracy'. How this is achieved is a matter for Parliament to decide, but in the Government's view the best course would be to establish a new Parliamentary Committee with functions relating to human rights. This would not require legislation or any change in Parliamentary procedure. There could be a Joint Committee of both Houses of Parliament or each House could have its own Committee; or there could be a Committee which met jointly for some purposes and separately for others.

3.7 The new Committee might conduct enquiries on a range of human rights issues relating to the Convention, and produce reports so as to assist the Government and Parliament in deciding what action to take. It might also want to range more widely, and examine issues relating to the other international obligations of the United Kingdom such as proposals to accept new rights under other human rights treaties.

Should there be a Human Rights Commission?

3.8 *Bringing Rights Home* canvassed views on the establishment of a Human Rights Commission, and this possibility has received a good deal of attention. No commitment to establish a Commission was, however, made in the Manifesto on which the Government was elected. The Government's priority is implementation of its Manifesto commitment to give further effect to the Convention rights in domestic law so that people can enforce those rights in United Kingdom courts. Establishment of a new Human Rights Commission is not central to that objective and does not need to form part of the current Bill.

3.9 Moreover, the idea of setting up a new human rights body is not universally acclaimed. Some reservations have been expressed, particularly from the point of view of the impact on existing bodies concerned with particular aspects of human rights, such as the Commission for Racial Equality and the Equal Opportunities Commission, whose primary concern is to protect the rights for which they were established. A quinquennial review is currently being conducted of the Equal Opportunities Commission, and the Government has also decided to establish a new Disability Rights Commission.

3.10 The Government's conclusion is that, before a Human Rights Commission could be established by legislation, more consideration needs to be given to how it would work in relation to such bodies, and to the new arrangements to be established for Parliamentary and Government scrutiny of human rights issues. This is necessary not only for the purposes of framing the legislation but also to justify the additional public expenditure needed to establish and run a new Commission. A range of organisational issues need more detailed consideration before the legislative and financial case for a new Commission is made, and there needs to be a greater degree of consensus on an appropriate model among existing human rights bodies.

3.11 However, the Government has not closed its mind to the idea of a new Human Rights Commission at some stage in the future in the light of practical experience of the working of the new legislation. If Parliament establishes a Committee on Human Rights, one of its main tasks might be to conduct an inquiry into whether a Human Rights Commission is needed and how it should operate. The Government would want to give full weight to the Committee's report in considering whether to create a statutory Human Rights Commission in future.

3.12 It has been suggested that a new Commission might be funded from non-Government sources. The Government would not wish to deter a move towards a non-statutory, privately-financed body if its role was limited to functions such as public education and advice to individuals.

However, a non-statutory body could not absorb any of the functions of the existing statutory bodies concerned with aspects of human rights.

CHAPTER 4   DEROGATIONS, RESERVATIONS AND OTHER PROTOCOLS

Derogations

4.1 Article 15 of the Convention permits a State to derogate from certain Articles of the Convention in time of war or other public emergency threatening the life of the nation. The United Kingdom has one derogation in place, in respect of Article 5(3) of the Convention.

4.2 The derogation arose from a case in 1988 in which the European Court of Human Rights held that the detention of the applicants in the case before it under the Prevention of Terrorism (Temporary Provisions) Act 1984 for more than four days constituted a breach of Article 5(3) of the Convention, because they had not been brought promptly before a judicial authority. The Government of the day entered a derogation following the judgment in order to preserve the Secretary of State's power under the Act to extend the period of detention of persons suspected of terrorism connected with the affairs of Northern Ireland for a total of up to seven days. The validity of the derogation was subsequently upheld by the European Court of Human Rights in another case in 1993.

4.3 We are considering what change might be made to the arrangements under the prevention of terrorism legislation. Substituting judicial for executive authority for extensions, which would mean that the derogation could be withdrawn, would require primary legislation. In the meantime, however, the derogation remains necessary. The Bill sets out the text of the derogation, and Article 5(3) will have effect in domestic law for the time being subject to its terms.

4.4 Given our commitment to promoting human rights, however, we would not want the derogation to remain in place indefinitely without good reasons. Accordingly its effect in domestic law will be time-limited. If not withdrawn earlier, it will expire five years after the Bill comes into force unless both Houses of Parliament agree that it should be renewed, and similarly thereafter. The Bill contains similar provision in respect of any new derogation which may be entered in future.

Reservations

4.5 Article 64 of the Convention allows a state to enter a reservation when a law in force is not in conformity with a Convention provision. The United Kingdom is a party to the First Protocol to the Convention, but has a reservation in place in respect of Article 2 of the Protocol. Article 2 sets out two principles. The first states that no person shall be denied the right to education. The second is that, in exercising any functions in relation to education and teaching, the State shall respect the right of parents to ensure that such education and teaching is in conformity with their own religious and philosophical convictions. The reservation makes it clear that the United Kingdom accepts this second principle only so far as it is compatible with the provision of efficient instruction and training, and the avoidance of unreasonable public expenditure.

4.6 The reservation reflects the fundamental principle originally enacted in the Education Act 1944, and now contained in section 9 of the Education Act 1996, 'that pupils are to be educated in accordance with the wishes of their parents so far as that is compatible with the provision of efficient instruction and training and the avoidance of unreasonable public expenditure'. There is similar provision in Scottish legislation. The reservation does not affect the right to education in Article 2. Nor does it deny parents the right to have account taken of their religious or philosophical convictions. Its purpose is to recognise that in the provision of State-funded education a balance must be struck in some cases between the convictions of parents and what is educationally sound and affordable.

4.7 Having carefully considered this, the Government has concluded that the reservation should be kept in place. Its text is included in the Bill, and Article 2 of the First Protocol will have effect in domestic law subject to its terms.

4.8 Whilst derogations are permitted under the Convention only in times of war or other public emergency, and so are clearly temporary, there is no such limitation in respect of reservations. We do not therefore propose to make the effect of the reservation in domestic law subject to periodic renewal by Parliament, but the Bill requires the Secretary of State (the Secretary of State for Education and Employment) to review the reservation every five years and to lay a report before Parliament.

Other Protocols

4.9 Protocols 4, 6 and 7 guarantee a number of rights additional to those in the original Convention itself and its First Protocol. These further rights have been added largely to reflect the wider range of rights subsequently included under the International Covenant on Civil and Political Rights. There is no obligation upon States who are party to the original Convention to accept these additional Protocols, but the Government has taken the opportunity to review the position of the United Kingdom on Protocols 4, 6 and 7.

4.10 Protocol 4 contains a prohibition on the deprivation of liberty on grounds of inability to fulfil contractual obligations; a right to liberty of movement; a right to non-expulsion from the home State; a right of entry to the State of which a person is a national; and a prohibition on the collective expulsion of aliens. These provisions largely reflect similar (but not identical) rights provided under the International Covenant on Civil and Political Rights. Protocol 4 was signed by the United Kingdom in 1963 but not subsequently ratified because of concerns about what is the exact extent of the obligation regarding a right of entry.

4.11 These are important rights, and we would like to see them given formal recognition in our law. But we also believe that existing laws in relation to different categories of British nationals must be maintained. It will be possible to ratify Protocol 4 only if the potential conflicts with our domestic laws can be resolved. This remains under consideration but we do not propose to ratify Protocol 4 at present.

4.12 Protocol 6 requires the complete abolition of the death penalty other than in time of war or imminent threat of war. It does not permit any derogation or reservation. The Protocol largely parallels the Second Optional Protocol to the International Covenant on Civil and Political Rights, which the United Kingdom has not accepted.

4.13 The death penalty was abolished as a sentence for murder in 1965 following a free vote in the House of Commons. It remains as a penalty for treason, piracy with violence, and certain armed forces offences. No execution for these offences has taken place since 1946, when the war-time Nazi propagandist William Joyce (known as Lord Haw-Haw) was hanged at Wandsworth prison. The last recorded execution for piracy was in 1830. Thus there might appear to be little difficulty in our ratifying Protocol 6. This would, however, make it impossible for a United Kingdom Parliament to re-introduce the death penalty for murder, short of denouncing the European Convention. The view taken so far is that the issue is not one of basic constitutional principle but is a matter of judgement and conscience to be decided by Members of Parliament as they see fit. For these reasons, we do not propose to ratify Protocol 6 at present.

4.14 Protocol 7 contains a prohibition on the expulsion of aliens without a decision in accordance with the law or opportunities for review; a right to a review of conviction or sentence after criminal conviction; a right to compensation following a miscarriage of justice; a prohibition on double jeopardy in criminal cases; and a right to equality between spouses. These rights reflect similar rights protected under the International Covenant on Civil and Political Rights.

4.15 In general, the provisions of Protocol 7 reflect principles already inherent in our law. In view of concerns in some of these areas in recent years, the Government believes that it would be particularly helpful to give these important principles the same legal status as other rights in the Convention by ratifying and incorporating Protocol 7. There is, however, a difficulty with this because a few provisions of our domestic law, for example in relation to the property rights of spouses, could not be interpreted in a way which is compatible with Protocol 7. The Government intends to legislate to remove these inconsistencies, when a suitable opportunity occurs, and then to sign and ratify the Protocol.

4.16 The Secretary of State will be able to amend the Human Rights Act by Order so as to insert into it the rights contained in any Protocols to the Convention which the United Kingdom ratifies in future. The Order will be subject to approval by both Houses of Parliament. The Bill also enables any reservation to a Protocol to be added, but as with the existing reservation it will have to be reviewed every five years if not withdrawn earlier.

1997, Cm 3782. pp. 6–18.

(D) PARLIAMENTARY DEBATES

RB NOTE: This section includes extracts from the parliamentary debates on the Human Rights Act during its passage, showing the types of argument that were employed for and against the legislation and the ministerial statements made on its provisions. The section is set out in three Parts: Part I includes extracts from debates in the House of Lords, Part II has extracts from debates in the House of Commons, and Part III contains a guide to the ministerial statements which were made throughout the parliamentary proceedings. References for all the parliamentary stages through which the Act passed before receiving the royal assent on 9 November 1998 can be found at the end of the Bibliography.

(I) In the House of Lords

Second Reading Debate

The Lord Chancellor (Lord Irvine of Lairg): I chair many Cabinet committees, but none that has given me greater satisfaction than the committee whose labours have brought this Bill forward in the first legislative Session. It occupies a central position in our integrated programme for constitutional change. It will allow British judges for the first time to make their own distinctive contribution to the development of human rights in Europe. It is today a happy reflection that British jurisprudence will shortly flow into an inspired modern building, the European Court of Human Rights in Strasbourg. . . .

This is a Government who see Britain's future as a strong and leading participant in the Council of Europe and the European Union. This Bill is further evidence of that. It was not edifying to begin Friday, 24th October by hearing the shadow Home Secretary, Sir Brian Mawhinney, on the 'Today' programme railing at judges from Albania and Bulgaria sitting with other judges in the European Court to determine human rights. I acquit the noble Lord, Lord Kingsland, of any xenophobia. He is incapable of it. I know that when he speaks in support of this Bill he speaks strongly for himself. I doubt, however, whether he speaks for his party. Tory policy before the election was clear: outright rejection of the case for incorporation. From the mouth of the then Prime Minister we had this miracle of sapience:

'We have no need of a Bill of Rights because we have freedom'.

My Lords, what enervating insularity – and what nonsense!

The traditional freedom of the individual under an unwritten constitution to do himself that which is not prohibited by law gives no protection from misuse of power by the state, nor any protection from acts or omissions of public bodies which harm individuals in a way that is incompatible with their human rights under the convention.

This Bill will bring human rights home. People will be able to argue for their rights and claim their remedies under the convention in any court or tribunal in the United Kingdom. Our courts will develop human rights throughout society. A culture of awareness of human rights will develop. Before Second Reading of any Bill the responsible Minister will make a statement that the Bill is or is not compatible with convention rights. So there will have to be close scrutiny of the human rights implications of all legislation before it goes forward. Our standing will rise internationally. The protection of human rights at home gives credibility to our foreign policy to advance the cause of human rights around the world.

Our critics say the Bill will cede powers to Europe, will politicise the judiciary and will diminish parliamentary sovereignty. We are not ceding new powers to Europe. The United Kingdom already accepts that Strasbourg rulings bind. Next, the Bill is carefully drafted and designed to respect our traditional understanding of the separation of powers. It does so intellectually convincingly and, if I may express my high regard for the parliamentary draftsman, elegantly.

The design of the Bill is to give the courts as much space as possible to protect human rights, short of a power to set aside or ignore Acts of Parliament. In the very rare cases where the higher courts will find it impossible to read and give effect to any statute in a way which is compatible with convention rights, they will be able to make a declaration of incompatibility. Then it is for Parliament to decide whether there should be remedial legislation. Parliament may, not must, and generally will, legislate. If a Minister's prior assessment of compatibility (under Clause 19) is subsequently found by declaration of incompatibility by the courts to have been mistaken, it is hard to see how a Minister could withhold remedial action. There is a fast-track route for Ministers to take remedial action by order. But the remedial action will not retrospectively make unlawful an act which was a lawful act – lawful since sanctioned by statute. This is the logic of the design of the Bill. It maximises the protection of human rights without trespassing on parliamentary sovereignty.

A declaration of incompatibility will not itself change the law. The statute will continue to apply despite its incompatibility. But the declaration is very likely to prompt the Government and Parliament to respond.

In the normal course of events, it would be necessary to await a suitable opportunity to introduce primary legislation to make an appropriate amendment. That could involve unacceptable delay when Parliamentary timetables are crowded. We have taken the view that if legislation has been declared incompatible, a prompt parliamentary remedy should be available.

We recognise that a power to amend primary legislation by means of a statutory instrument is not a power to be conferred or exercised lightly. Those clauses therefore place a number of procedural and other restrictions on its use.

The power to make a remedial order may be used only to remove an incompatibility or a possible incompatibility between legislation and the convention. It may therefore be used only to protect human rights, not to infringe them.

Lastly, the Bill does not provide for the establishment of a human rights commission. I appreciate that this will cause disappointment to some. It is suggested that a commission would have a useful role to play in promoting human rights and advising individuals how to proceed if they believe their rights have been infringed. Although we have given this proposal much thought, we have concluded that a human rights commission is not central to our main task today, which is to incorporate the convention as promised in our election manifesto. There are questions to be resolved about the relationship of a new commission with other bodies in the human rights field; for example, the Equal Opportunities Commission and the Commission for Racial Equality. Would a human rights commission take over their responsibilities, or act in partnership with them, or be an independent body independent of them? We would also want to be sure that the potential benefits of a human rights commission were sufficient to justify establishing and funding for a new non-governmental organisation. We do not rule out a human rights commission in future, but our judgment is that it would be premature to provide for one now.

We have, however, given very positive thought to the possibility of a parliamentary committee on human rights. This is not in the Bill itself because it would not require legislation to establish and because it would in any case be the responsibility of Parliament rather than the Government. But we are attracted to the idea of a parliamentary committee on human rights, whether a separate committee of each House or a joint committee of both houses. It would be a natural focus for the increased interest in human rights issues which Parliament will inevitably take when we have brought rights home. It could, for example, not only keep the protection of human rights under review, but could also be in the forefront of public education and consultation on human rights. It could receive written submissions and hold public hearings at a number of locations across the country. It could be in the van of the promotion of a human rights culture across the country.

I have tried to explain why the Government want to bring rights home and how we propose to do it. This Bill represents a major plank in our programme for constitutional change and invigoration. I have for many years been downcast by the want of protection for human rights in the United Kingdom. In a democracy it is right that the majority should govern. But that is precisely why it is also right that the human rights of individuals and minorities should be protected by law.

I am convinced that incorporation of the European convention into our domestic law will deliver a modern reconciliation of the inevitable tension between the democratic right of the majority to exercise political power and the democratic need of individuals and minorities to have their human rights secured. I commend this Bill to the House and look forward to the whole of our debate today.

Moved, That the Bill be now read a second time.—(*The Lord Chancellor.*)

Lord Kingsland: Her Majesty's loyal Opposition will not be voting against the Bill on Second Reading. Irrespective of the success or failure of our amendments thereafter, we will not vote against the Bill on Third Reading. As the Bill was foreshadowed in the manifesto, we are bound by the Salisbury Convention.

If the Bill becomes law it will be a defining moment in the life of our constitution. Perhaps the only other examples this century of such defining moments were the passage of the Parliament Acts of 1911 and 1949. As your Lordships are acutely aware, they had a dramatic effect on the balance of power between your Lordships' House and another place.

If this Bill reaches the statute book it will have an equally defining influence on the balance of power between the legislature and the judiciary. . . .

The means by which incorporation takes place is critical.

The noble and learned Lord was presented with two possible options for incorporation. For shorthand, I shall use the terms 'Canadian' and 'New Zealand' options, although the principles behind them rather than their details are what matter to me.

In some respects, I suppose, the option which conformed more closely to our constitutional traditions was the Canadian option because it fitted in perfectly with our great constitutional principle that no parliament can bind its successor. As your Lordships are aware, that means that, if the terms of a subsequent statute conflict with the terms of a previous statute, the terms of that subsequent statute prevail and the conflicting terms of the previous statute are impliedly repealed. Therefore, it would follow that if the convention were incorporated and the terms of the convention conflicted with the terms of the previous statute, the terms of that statute would be repealed.

It would fit in with our constitutional principles and it would also have two other great advantages. The first would be legal certainty. The matter would be decided there and then by the judges; and the decision would be backed by remedies for the successful litigant.

What is the difficulty? The difficulty is clear from even a cursory glance at the kind of law which the convention makes – because its terms are very general. If the terms of the convention could repeal previous statutes, what previous statute would be immune from its terms? It would create a mass of uncertainty throughout our judicial system. Almost no statute would be safe from the possibility of being struck down by a judge interpreting the convention.

And so, despite its constitutional attractiveness, perhaps I may say with due humility that I believe that the noble and learned Lord the Lord Chancellor was quite right to reject that option.

What is the other option which he had at his disposal? It is the New Zealand option, and that option reflects the opposite principle. It says that where there is a conflict between the convention and a previous statute, and if that conflict is clear, the terms of the previous statute prevail. It is then up to the legislature – in that case, the New Zealand legislature – to make up its mind whether to change the law in conformity with the New Zealand Bill of Rights. I suspect that that summary will not find favour with the noble and learned Lord, Lord Cooke, who is to speak later this afternoon but it is the best that I can do in the circumstances.

The noble and learned Lord the Lord Chancellor has also in terms rejected that solution. I suggest that he has gone for a hybrid of the two: he is not striking down the previous statute but is giving judges the power to make a declaration of incompatibility. He then gives Parliament the option to legislate not by full primary statute but by order in council.

I believe that that solution is constitutionally unacceptable for two reasons which I shall try to explain as briefly as I can. In the Bill, the courts of this country are not bound by the decisions of the court in Strasbourg. It is to have a persuasive but not obligatory effect. When a court in this country makes a declaration of incompatibility, it might be making a declaration which is not an accurate photograph of the law of the convention. Indeed, that option is expressly incorporated in the Bill. To the extent that a declaration of incompatibility does not reflect the true construction of the jurisprudence of the convention, the judges will be making a declaration about the making of new law, judge-made law. Indeed, they will be doing more than that. They will be initiating a legislative procedure in Parliament.

What is the doctrine of the separation of powers in our country? It is that judges do not interfere with the parliamentary process on the one hand and Parliament does not interfere with the judicial process on the other. That principle has stood us in enormously good stead, certainly since the Glorious Revolution more than 300 years ago. To the extent that the judges are not reflecting the jurisprudence of the convention but stating their own view about what the convention says, they are in breach of that doctrine. They are initiating new legislation.

Of course, it is true that Parliament does not have to go ahead and pass that legislation. Indeed, what I fear may flow from a judicial decision of incompatibility is a long and bitter debate in Parliament about whether the judges were right and even if they were right, whether it is right to legislate.

But more than that, we do not really know in which direction the judges will take us. Is that fair to the judges? Is it fair to the country, which elected the present Government, to introduce the law on privacy by the convention? It is not. The public are entitled to know exactly where they stand in relation to the law on privacy. If we are to sustain the relationship between judges and the legislature which has stood us in such good stead for so long, we need the Government to define much more carefully the framework within which the judges are to make the declarations of incompatibility; otherwise, we shall be faced with a whole raft of legislation as orders in council which was not properly authorised.

We must be cautious about changing our constitution which has stood us in good stead for many hundreds of years. Most other countries in the world admire it greatly. Indeed, many are very jealous of it. I do not believe that we have failed in protecting our liberties since the convention was passed, signed and ratified in 1950. I am confident that noble Lords will look at the Bill objectively, with our own constitutional principles in the forefront of their minds.

Lord Lester of Herne Hill: My Lords, it is greatly to the credit of the Prime Minister and his colleagues that they have introduced this measure setting enforceable legal limits to their huge executive powers, securing European Convention rights in the laws of the United Kingdom and providing effective domestic remedies for breaches of convention rights by public authorities. It demonstrates a welcome commitment to democratic and accountable government and to respect for human rights under the rule of law. I congratulate the Government on this well-designed and well-drafted Bill.

The rights guaranteed by the Bill are not alien; indeed, they are part of our British birthright and constitutional heritage. As we have heard, the text was drafted by British lawyers. The values that it enshrines are universal. The convention has been exported by successive British governments to become part of the written constitutions of many Commonwealth countries. The Bill does indeed bring the basic civil and political rights of everyone in this country home by allowing everyone to claim those rights against public authorities in British courts. It involves no challenge to the English dogma of absolute parliamentary sovereignty. Rather its enactment involves the much-needed exercise of parliamentary sovereignty, giving our own courts proper authority to perform their duty of interpreting and applying common law and statute law in accordance with the UK's international obligations under the convention. True to the doctrine of parliamentary sovereignty, as the noble and learned Lord the Lord Chancellor said, the courts must defer to existing and future Acts of Parliament if it is impossible to read and give effect to them in a way which is compatible with the convention.

Therefore, far from weakening Parliament's role, the Government's proposals will increase the accountability of the Executive to Parliament. The Bill does so by requiring a Minister of the Crown in charge of a Bill in either House to make a statement before Second Reading as to his view of the compatibility or otherwise of the Bill with convention rights. That would both enhance parliamentary scrutiny and also enable the courts to ascertain whether legislation enacted after incorporation was intended to comply with or to be inconsistent with the convention. In the absence of a formally expressed intention to enact inconsistent legislation, the courts will be able to act on the basis that the legislation was intended by Parliament to be compatible with convention rights.

The Bill will not empower our courts to strike down legislation which it is impossible to read in accordance with convention rights. But the command by Parliament in the Bill to the courts to read them in that way,

'so far as is possible',

represents very strong wording. The courts will no doubt strive as far as is judicially possible to save legislation from having to be declared incompatible, and hence to be amended by future further legislation. The courts will do so by construing existing and future legislation as intended to provide the necessary safeguards to ensure fairness, proportionality and legal certainty as required by the convention.

Every declaration of incompatibility will represent a systemic failure, as our statute book is already made to comply with our convention obligations. A declaration of incompatibility will also be highly inconvenient because it will mean that our courts are unable to provide an effective judicial remedy and that the inconsistency will have to be remedied by government and Parliament under the special fast-track legislative procedure; or, if not, it will have to be remedied by the overburdened European Court of Human Rights. That is why I believe that our courts will do everything within their power to ensure that there is no mismatch between legislation and convention rights, and why declarations of incompatibility will, in the words of the noble and learned Lord the Lord Chancellor, be 'very rare'.

Some have criticised the power to take remedial action by subordinate legislation as being a sinister sapping of parliamentary powers. That criticism is misconceived. At present, when a judgment of the European Court requires the amendment of primary legislation, that can only be done by new, amending primary legislation. That is a slow and cumbersome method of complying with our international obligations. It has sometimes resulted in a tardy and incomplete implementation. Similarly, where a British court decides that there is a fatal inconsistency in a statute, what is needed is a speedy means of remedying the defect and of providing a remedy for the individual victim.

Under the European Communities Act 1972 (enacted by a Conservative Government), the power to implement the UK's Community obligations may be implemented by subordinate legislation, without any requirement to obtain the affirmative approval of both Houses. But this Bill provides for stronger parliamentary control, as, except in cases of pressing urgency, the implementation of the UK's convention obligations by subordinate legislation can be done only by the affirmative procedure. To require the Government to introduce primary amending legislation to give effect to European or British judgments would be to hinder the speedy and effective implementation by Parliament of convention rights, obligations and remedies.

Lord Bingham of Cornhill: I welcome the Bill. My reasons for doing so are unsurprising and may therefore be stated briefly. First, it seems to me highly desirable that rights and freedoms which the United Kingdom has undertaken to guarantee to its citizens should be enforceable by those citizens here in the United Kingdom. It makes no sense, and, I suggest, does not make for justice that those seeking to enforce their rights have to exhaust all their domestic remedies here before embarking on the long and costly trail to Strasbourg.

Secondly, it seems to me highly desirable that we in the United Kingdom should help to mould the law by which we are governed in this area. I think – and the very distinguished president of the European Court of Human Rights has made it clear that he shares this belief – that British judges have a significant contribution to make in the development of the law of human rights. It is a contribution which so far we have not been permitted to make. But incorporation will also mean, I hope, that when cases from this country reach Strasbourg, as on occasion they will do, the court will have the benefit of a considered judgment by a British judge on the point at issue. That will mean, I hope, that some of our more idiosyncratic national procedures and practices may be better understood.

Thirdly, I consider that incorporation will strengthen the confidence of the public in our democratic and judicial institutions. At present disappointed litigants leave our courts believing that there exists elsewhere a superior form of justice which our courts are not allowed to administer. In most cases those litigants would fare no better with the benefit of the convention. But the belief that there is some superior form of justice available elsewhere is, I think, damaging and undermines confidence in our institutions. It is unhealthy; and I hope that incorporation will restore the belief of our people, once an article of faith, that human rights and fundamental freedoms flourish as luxuriantly here as anywhere else in the world. It is after all 350 years since Milton wrote in *Areopagitica*,

'Let not England forget her precedence of teaching nations how to live'.

I believe that these are solid reasons for welcoming the Bill. But I do not think that they will turn our world upside down. I do not think so badly of our institutions as to suppose that we have been routinely violating human rights and undermining fundamental freedoms all these years. I am aware, as are your Lordships, of a number of objections in principle to incorporation. The first is that it involves, so it is said, a major transfer of power from

Parliament to the judiciary. While I respect those who advance that argument, it is not one I accept. The mode of incorporation does not empower judges, as the noble and learned Lord the Lord Chancellor made clear, to overrule, set aside, disapply, or – if one wants to be even more dramatic – strike down Acts of Parliament. That is a power which throughout the recent debates the judges have made clear they do not seek. The mode of incorporation adopted is that which most fully respects the sovereignty of Parliament. Following incorporation, nothing will be decided by judges which is not already decided by judges. The difference is that British judges will in the first instance have an opportunity to provide a solution.

The Lord Bishop of Lichfield: Various speakers from the Bishops' Bench, in 1995 and 1997, assured the House that, should it pass the Bill, a substantial body of people, from other-faith communities as well as the churches, would applaud. In 1985, for instance, the Roman Catholic bishops of England and Wales strongly supported the incorporation of the European Convention on Human Rights into United Kingdom law, as did the majority of the executive committee of the then British Council of Churches. Those are not merely formal gestures of support. For some of us, there is a spiritual and religious dimension, as well as a legal and human dimension, to the Bill. It may be of more than historical interest to recall that in 1776 the American Declaration of Independence had at its heart a religious reference, declaring that:

> 'All men are created equal and are endowed by their creator with certain inalienable rights'.

I believe that there is also a moral dimension to the Bill. In a speech in your Lordships' House on 1st May 1995 my colleague, the Right Reverend Prelate the Bishop of Oxford, said:

> 'I believe that in the end [the incorporation of such articles of the convention into law] . . . is a moral matter and that the rights enshrined in the convention are not there simply because certain states decide that they will be there but because those states recognise certain fundamental moral principles which need to be enshrined in law'.— [*Official Report*, 1/5/95; col. 1279.]

I speak, therefore, as a supporter of the Bill. However, perhaps I may, for that very reason, raise two questions already aired in public discussion but on which I should be grateful to hear a further answer. I trust that noble and learned Members of this House from the legal world will bear with me if my questions are naive or confused.

First, is it the case, as some public criticism has claimed, that the convention defines the human rights which it protects in terms which are dangerously general? In particular, is it the case that the terms in which the restrictions on human rights are framed are too sweeping – broad terms such as 'national security', 'the prevention of disorder' and 'health and morals'? Some of us have read the argument that such generality is at odds with the more detailed case law-based practices of British justice. But the justification for incorporation must surely be that it will enlarge the freedoms of citizens under the law. Is there a danger that the sheer generality of some of the articles could be interpreted in such a way as to restrict those freedoms?

My second question concerns the proposed fast track for changing laws following an adverse declaration by the courts. As I understand it, the proposal is to do this under 90-minute orders. Such orders can be rejected by Parliament. Will they, with the pressure of other business, be scrutinised and amended with due care? I understand that in particularly urgent cases the order would take immediate effect, although it would expire after a short period if not approved by both Houses. A not unfriendly critic might still ask whether over a period of time, as an ongoing process, all this would not shift the balance between Parliament and the courts in ways that may not be evident for some years.

The noble Lord, Lord Habgood, and the Right Reverend Prelate the Bishop of Oxford were members of a working party on human rights and responsibilities in Britain and Ireland which reported in 1988. That report concluded that the incorporation of the European convention into domestic law could make a significant contribution to the solution of the problems of Northern Ireland by providing an additional safeguard to the rights of people. I believe that that argument still holds. Justice and the rule of law are the best basis for reconciliation in that context. I am sure that your Lordships will not take it amiss if I insist upon this point: reconciliation requires more than good law, but justice is the best foundation for peace.

In conclusion, I am convinced that many church leaders and leaders of other communities in these islands would argue, as I do, that the right of the citizen to challenge the lawfulness of any Act by the government under which they live is one of the strong foundations of democracy. The main function of this legislation is not to undermine our legal system through incorporation of foreign elements within it but genuinely to see that justice is done without unnecessary delay or exposure. The title *Bringing Human Rights Home* is well chosen.

Lord Scarman: The Bill is the beginning of a very important constitutional chapter in our history. The quality of the Bill is that it recognises that in a democracy, the democratically elected assembly – for us, that is Parliament – must be sovereign. At the same time, the Bill recognises that the European Convention on Human Rights exists and that that convention, ratified by Britain in 1951, guarantees the human rights stated in it. The Bill recognises that those rights are already in existence in the United Kingdom, although their direct enforcement is not yet possible here.

What has the Bill done? The Bill has stood up for parliamentary sovereignty. At the same time, to quote from the preamble to the Bill, it,

'gives further effect ... to rights and freedoms guaranteed under the European Convention on Human Rights'.

The Bill recognises that under our law those rights are already guaranteed and takes that as an opportunity for constitutional reform. The Bill is modest. As I have said, the legislation will be an Act to give further effect to rights and freedoms that are already guaranteed under the European convention.

The Bill has done that in a brilliant way and I congratulate the noble and learned Lord the Lord Chancellor, his colleagues in government, the civil servants and the draftsmen on the document that they have produced. We now have the protection of our primary law and the protection of the rights that are guaranteed by the European convention. That is achieved by a partnership, if I may put it like that, between Parliament and the judges. The judges do not strike down primary legislation; they merely indicate their opinion, without fuss, that certain matters are incompatible and leave it at that. When there is incompatibility between a primary statute and the European Convention on Human Rights, there will be a fast-track parliamentary procedure.

The Bill may or may not need reform or looking at again in the future, but it is the beginning of a new constitutional chapter and I see absolutely nothing in the history of English law which indicates that either the judges or Parliament will play rough. This is a new form of partnership, with the judges sticking to their judicial work and Parliament being supreme in legislation. That is absolutely right. If we are to be a democracy, the people must have the last word. Having said that, constitutionally we can ensure the protection and development of our rights, guaranteed under the convention.

A number of provisions in the Bill could well be further considered. My speech will be short, so I certainly do not propose to do that, but I should like to say this: if we go ahead, developing phase by phase along the lines suggested in the Bill, we shall work out a new constitution which will be to the infinite benefit of everyone. I have no doubt about that. It will come if the spirit of the Bill is maintained. Having heard the speeches that have been made so far, I end by saying that we need have no fears: we are on a path to constitutional reform which will preserve our democracy and our convention rights.

Lord Wilberforce: The Bill is presented as a great constitutional advance, as a great movement of freedom, in resounding phrases relating to our civil rights and fundamental freedoms. And that is right. That has been true of other considerations and other Bills of this nature. However, it is important to realise that this is the crunch date. This Bill will be passed; it will be made part of the law of the land and its carefully drafted phrases will have to be applied by judges throughout the land – from the House of Lords right down to the circuit judges; it will have to be considered by Ministers and officials in preparing legislation and must be looked at much more carefully than we have felt it necessary to look at previous draft enactments of this kind. It is surely right therefore that we should look, as several noble Lords endeavoured to do, at the problems it creates to see whether we can identify them in order, first, that we may know what we are doing and the British public understand what we are doing; and, secondly, that so far as is possible we may try to mitigate some of those problems in the course of the Committee and later stages of the Bill.

This has been said in part but noble Lords will forgive me if I say it again in slightly different words. It is essential in considering this Bill to recollect that the European Convention on Human Rights started life as an international convention at the end of the war. It was an agreement between states as to the standards of values to be observed by all countries in the future.

One only has to look at the document to know that that is so. They had their eyes firmly on what had been afflicting Europe in the previous five years – the loss of life in the concentration camps, arbitrary arrest (the Gestapo knocking at the door), torture and slavery, persecution for opinions and religion. I can pick up what was said by one of the most eminent British judges of the court about the convention. He said that it was a,

> 'collective guarantee to ensure that rules and their application are in accordance with primary principles of law as recognised by civilised nations'.

That reflects of course the language of the statute of the permanent court of international justice. It was regarded as a collective guarantee and I have no doubt that our delegates working on the text of the convention looked at it in that light. They did not regard it as laying down a charter for the UK or other states.

There is no doubt that the list [of rights] is not adequate for modern states. This is now an ageing convention. It was drawn up for limited purposes and it has now been overtaken in many respects by United Nations covenants and other covenants such as the convention on the rights of children. Many necessary rights are omitted, as indeed the White Paper agrees. However, on the other hand, it is right to say that the evidence to the House of Lords Select Committee a few years ago revealed 12 new rights not protected by the common law which were conferred by the convention. So we are getting an advantage that way – 12 new rights through the convention not protected by the common law.

On the other hand, quite a number of those recognised by the United Nations convention are not there. Some of them are dealt with in connection with Protocols 4, 6 and 7. However, I would agree respectfully with what the noble Lord, Lord Lester, said some years ago, that, in spite of that defect – in spite of the ageing character of the European convention – this represents an important first step towards a modern British Bill of Rights. I am prepared to go along with it on that basis.

Lord Donaldson of Lymington: My usual speech is, of course, in opposition to the incorporation of the convention. I have opposed it in the past on two basic grounds. First, it seemed to me, at any rate as a matter of logic, that a universal right to freedom of action or inaction unless restrained by law must be wider and should be more satisfactory than the specific rights set out in this or in the other convention. Secondly, I thought that it was for Parliament to set limits on that universal right to freedom as and when the need arose.

However, as I told my noble and learned friend, I must admit that I have changed my mind. I do not feel that in changing my mind, I am a sinner who has repented. Nor do I have any of the enthusiasm which is normally attributed to the experience by a new convert. It is simply that I have reassessed the situation as it is at present in my view.

It seems to me now that there were two conditions which had to be satisfied if a universal right to freedom was really to work properly. The first condition was there had to be a high degree of self-restraint and effective self-regulation on the part of those who were enjoying that freedom. One test, but not the only test, would be the old rubric of, 'Do as you would be done by'.

The second condition was that Parliament should be ready and willing to intervene where self-restraint and self-regulation failed and there was an acute conflict between freedoms or parts of my universal freedom. This Parliament, for one reason or another – it may be lack of time or will – has singularly failed to do that.

Most obviously that applies to the field of privacy, in respect of which the media give complete priority to freedom of expression as enshrined in Article 10 over the right to respect for private and family life as enshrined in Article 9. Their self-restraint has certainly failed and I venture to think that, while self-regulation may be making some progress, the progress is too slow and limited to be acceptable.

There it is. As I say, for those reasons I have come to welcome, or at any rate to support, the passage of this Bill. I believe it to be a very cleverly crafted Bill. I have a great professional admiration for the way in which it has been put together. I am quite satisfied that it upholds the authority of Parliament, which is one of the things that has always troubled me. It avoids any conflict between Parliament and the courts.

I know that it will not politicise the appointment of judges and I hope that it will not lead to the public perceiving judicial decisions as being political in their nature. It is true that they will involve a measure of discretion and a measure of social and judicial engineering, but it will be done under the authority of Parliament and with the guidelines, such as they may be, which can be derived from the convention and from other decisions on the convention in other jurisdictions.

I hope that one by-product of the legislation will be that the Strasbourg court will take a long hard look at decisions made in the British courts on the meaning of the convention and that it will, if necessary, extend the margin of appreciation which I am sure that that court ought to extend to most jurisdictions. I say that because what is right and proper in one country with one set of traditions and one history may be quite different from that which is right in another country with a different history, tradition and culture.

Baroness Williams of Crosby: My Lords, it is a real pleasure to be present on such an historic day as this. We are looking at what is pulsing across our constitutional Rubicon. I believe that when we look back we shall all be proud to have been here on this day. It is a remarkable day and one which many of us did not expect to see.

The balance of power, struck long ago at the time of the Glorious Revolution, has been greatly altered by the weakening of the Crown, the weakening of this House – almost all of whose amendments in a very short period of time on many pieces of critical legislation were overturned by the previous government – and in some ways the weakening of the Commons itself. Nobody should underestimate the combined power of patronage and discipline on the consciences of MPs. Finally, there is the rise in the number of cases for judicial review, which has exemplified the weakness of our confidence in the fact that human rights will always be respected by our system and which I for one regard as being a symptom of the sicknesses of our constitutional custom and practice. For all those reasons, it is right and appropriate that we are discussing this Bill today.

[A] matter of concern, again expressed by a number of noble Lords, concerns the issue of the 'fast track'. If I may pay a compliment to the noble and learned Lord the Lord Chancellor among others, it is a most ingenious solution to the problem of how to deal with both parliamentary sovereignty and the need to have a recognition of individual human rights in this country. I wonder whether we could not even further improve on the already remarkable decisions suggested by the Bill: by bringing the proposed committee on human rights to which the noble and learned Lord the Lord Chancellor referred more directly into relationship with that particular process.

For example, on the analogy of our own delegated legislation committee in this House, it should surely be possible for the new committee and its sub-committees to give an indication of their own view on proposals for affirmative resolutions to amend legislation to bring it into line with the requirements of the European convention; and perhaps also to be involved, as happens in New Zealand, with pre-legislative scrutiny of new Bills to ensure that the committee is also satisfied that they meet the requirements of the European convention. My noble friend Lord Lester referred to Australia. That is also correct; the Australian Senate has such a committee. Many of us would feel reassured by the greater involvement of Parliament without delaying the changes in the legislation that those proposals would imply.

In a speech in July the noble and learned Lord the Lord Chancellor referred to a human rights commission as a driving force for change. Earlier in this debate he said that the issue was 'not a matter of first account' in our debate today. With the greatest respect, I suggest that it is an issue of first account—and for these reasons. This country suffers from an absence of education and understanding of citizenship, which is a serious lacuna in an old democracy such as ours. Rights and their associated obligations constitute, as the right reverend Prelate indicated, a new kind of civic morality in our country – a civic morality to which, repeatedly, the new Government have referred as being at the core of their attitudes and aspirations.

I recognise the public expenditure implications of a commission, which is why I propose that it might be a very modest body at first. A commission would be charged not only with advising those seeking redress, those seeking justice, but would, I hope, become the spark for a new attempt in our education system to introduce the concept of citizenship alongside that of religion and ethics. I can think of nothing more appropriate at the beginning of a new Government than to accept the need for a culture of human rights among our children and university and college students, because that is the bedrock upon which a culture of human rights will be built in this country.

As a number of noble Lords, not least the noble and learned Lord, Lord Wilberforce, have indicated, the European convention is itself a rather old document. For example, it makes no reference to the right to information from government agencies; it makes no reference to some of the most troubling ethical issues of our times, those associated with scientific advance – genetic engineering, cloning and electronic surveillance. It cannot make such reference because those issues did not exist when the convention was drafted. It will need to be modernised and brought up to date. But who is to do that? That is another area where I believe a human rights commission could play an important part.

That brings me to my concluding thought. I have had the honour over the past year to serve on a body called the *Comité des Sages*. It is rather nice that in French one has no sex; one is simply a 'sage', and I like that. As a sage, I have been involved with conferences in every member state on the issue of putting fundamental human rights at the heart of the European Union treaty. The Amsterdam Treaty made small advances in that direction by amending Article F to put respect for human rights at the centre of the treaty and then, much more radically, followed that up with an amendment, Article F(a), under which a country which fails to respect human rights can have its own rights suspended under the treaty. That is an extraordinarily radical move forward.

I should like to see the UK put at the heart of its presidency of the European Union the concept of human rights in Europe for recognition and reinforcement of those rights in line with what has now happened in the United Kingdom. What we are doing for our domestic law, extended to the responsibilities that we have under the European Union treaties, could make not just Britain but the whole of Europe a continent marked by a commitment to human rights and the obligations that are part of a recognition of those rights.

HL Deb., 3 November 1997, cols. 1227f.

COMMITTEE STAGE

RB NOTE: The following passage related to the term 'public authority' (see sections 6 and 7), and includes the Lord Chancellor's examples of what might or might not fall within the meaning of the term.

The Lord Chancellor: I shall endeavour to explain.

Clause 6(1) states,

'It is unlawful for a public authority to act in a way which is incompatible with one or more of the Convention rights'.

There are some bodies which are obviously public authorities such as the police, the courts, government departments and prisons. They are obviously public authorities under Clause 6(1). However, under Clause 6(3)(c) the term 'public authority' includes,

'any person certain of whose functions are functions of a public nature'.

I ask the noble Baroness, Lady Young, to abstain from asking herself the question: is this a public authority just looking at the body in the round? That is what Clause 6(1) invites us to do. However, Clause 6(3)(c) asks whether the body in question has certain functions – not all – which are functions of a public nature. If it has any functions of a public nature, it qualifies as a public authority. However, it is certain acts by public authorities which this Bill makes unlawful. In Clause 6(5) the Bill provides:

'In relation to a particular act, a person is not a public authority by virtue only of subsection (3)(c) if the nature of the act is private'.

Therefore Railtrack, as a public utility, obviously qualifies as a public authority because some of its functions, for example its functions in relation to safety on the railway, qualify it as a public authority. However, acts carried out in its capacity as a private property developer would no doubt be held by the courts to be of a private nature and therefore not caught by the Bill.

We took a policy decision to avoid a list. The disadvantage of a list is precisely that it would be easy to regard it as exhaustive or to suggest that any non-listed body could be a public authority only if it was sufficiently analogous in its essential characteristics to a body that had qualified in the list. There are obvious public authorities – I have mentioned some – which are covered in relation to the whole of their functions by Clause 6(1). Then there are some bodies some of whose functions are public and some private. If there are some public functions the body qualifies as a public authority but not in respect of acts which are of a private nature. Those statutory principles will have to be applied case by case by the courts when issues arise. We think that it is far better to have a principle rather than a list which would be regarded as exhaustive.

HL Deb., 24 November 1997, col. 796

REPORT STAGE

RB NOTE: The following exchanges were on the extent to which the Act does, or should, incorporate the ECHR. It includes the Lord Chancellor's statement that the Act gives further effect to the ECHR, but does not incorporate it.

Lord Simon of Glasidale moved Amendment No. 75:

Line 1, leave out ('further') and insert ('domestic').

The noble and learned Lord said: My Lords, this is an amendment to the Title of the Bill. I moved it in the same form in Committee very late at night. I had hoped to move it before a full House this evening. There is nobody on the Government Back-Benches, so far as I can see. I believe that the noble Baroness, Lady Williams, has been faithful on the Liberal Democrat Benches, and there may be somebody else. I did the noble Lord, Lord Monkswell, a disservice; I did not see him enter the Chamber. As usual, the noble Lord, Lord Renton, has rightly come to invigilate on questions of statutory construction.

Tribute has rightly been paid to the draftsmanship and construction of the Bill. However, even with the best drafted measure the courts can be assisted by indications as to how it should be interpreted. There need not necessarily be an ambiguity. There is quite often matter for argument.

There are two, or possibly three, ways of indicating how a measure should be interpreted. The first is by examining the whole of the enacting provisions; but in addition (and secondly) in appropriate cases a purpose clause can be introduced. In my respectful submission, this was a very suitable measure for the inclusion of a purpose clause, and the noble Lord, Lord Mishcon, proposed one which met with general affirmation. He withdrew it in order to consider the matter further before Third Reading. It is erroneously reported in *Hansard* that the amendment was negatived. It was not, it was withdrawn.

The third method, by no means mutually exclusive with the other two, is an indication in the Long Title of a Bill. There is this to be said in favour of such an indication of construction, that unless the Long Title does that, it serves no useful purpose at all . . .

In the absence at the moment of a purpose clause, this is very much a case where the Long Title can be slightly amended in order to give an indication. At present, it reads:

'An Act to give further effect to rights and freedoms guaranteed under the European Convention'.

My noble and learned friend the Lord Chancellor said quite correctly that that was perfectly true. So it is; it is a truism. There are two directions in which the Bill gives further force to the Convention. One is that it amplifies rights already given by our common law and contributes to the European Convention. The other is that it makes the Convention rights enforceable against public authorities in our own courts. But that is clear from the contents of the Bill.

What a court of construction wants to know is whether it is intended that the Convention rights should apply in domestic law. That is precisely what the White Paper said and what my noble and learned friend has said on many occasions. So all I suggest is that in place of 'further effect', the Long Title should read 'domestic effect'. That will mean something to a court of construction, whereas the Long Title at the moment means nothing at all. I beg to move.

Lord Renton: My Lords, the noble and learned Lord, Lord Simon of Glaisdale, has put forward a case which deserves serious consideration. The word 'further' is somewhat vague anyway. Further to what? We are in effect giving our domestic courts the jurisdiction relating to the rights and freedoms guaranteed under the European Convention on Human Rights. It seems to me to be a more accurate way of describing the contents of the Bill and a more precise way to use the word 'domestic' than to use the word 'further'.

I hope that I am in order in saying that I am glad that the noble and learned Lord also raised the question of what happened to Amendment No. 1 moved by the noble Lord, Lord Mishcon, which, as he said, received a great deal of support right across the House. I was one of those who keenly supported it. I am not in a position to say whether it was actually negatived or negatived by mistake. However, when I saw in *Hansard* that it had been negatived, I was extremely surprised.

Lord Lester of Herne Hill: I am sure that the Government chose the words of the Bill carefully to enable the Bill to pass. That may explain some curious and ingenious formulae that have been used in the Bill. I suspect that the Long Title is defined as

'An Act to give further effect to rights and freedoms',

rather than,

'to give domestic effect to rights and freedoms',

not because of some doctrinal or theological objection to the notion of giving domestic effect. That is already made clear in the White Paper, as I hope the noble and learned Lord the Lord Chancellor will agree when he comes to reply. It is clear from the White Paper that this measure is designed to give domestic effect to convention rights and freedoms; it is designed to incorporate the convention into domestic law.

I cannot read the substance of the Bill in any other way. The only matter which gives me cause for concern and made me decide to put my name down in support of the amendment is that earlier in the debate the noble and learned Lord the Lord Chancellor said something which I found extremely curious. He said something along the lines, 'This Bill will not incorporate convention rights into the substance of domestic law'. That seemed to me to be an almost mystical concept which I could not understand. It seems to me that if the Bill does anything clearly, it incorporates convention rights into the substance of our domestic law and it does so in a number of ways.

One way is by commanding judges to read statutes, where possible, to comply with convention law. That is where it embodies convention rights into our statute law. Another way is that it requires judges to be a public authority bound by the convention and therefore interpreting and applying the common law and statute law to give effect to convention rights. Therefore in those ways it surely does incorporate convention rights into the substance of our domestic law. If we can agree about that, it will go a long way towards assuring me that, whatever the reasons for those curious words in the Long Title, at least it is quite plain that the central object and purpose of this Bill is to give domestic effect to convention rights and freedoms. If that is clear it may well be that this amendment is otiose.

If there were any ambiguity about it then I believe that the noble and learned Lord, Lord Simon of Glaisdale, has the better of the argument. There is a powerful case. I wish that the matter had been dealt with by a purpose clause and at an earlier stage. This is the last amendment that we shall consider today. Before we say farewell to this Bill it is important that this matter is put beyond any doubt. I therefore support the amendment.

The Lord Chancellor: The word 'further' is included in the Long Title because, in our national arrangements, the convention can, and is, already applied in a variety of different circumstances and is relied on in a range of ways by our own courts.

The Bill will greatly increase the ability of our courts to enforce convention rights, but it is not introducing a wholly new concept. The Bill as such does not incorporate convention rights into domestic law but, in accordance with the language of the Long Title, it gives further effect in the United Kingdom to convention rights by requiring the courts in Clause 3(1),

'So far as it is possible to do so'

to construe – in the language of the statute, to read and give effect to – primary legislation and subordinate legislation in a way which is compatible with the convention rights. That is an interpretative principle.

Lord Renton: My Lords, I am very reluctant to interrupt the noble and learned Lord. I believe that he said just now that it was an Act to give further effect in the United Kingdom,

'to rights and freedoms guaranteed under the European Convention on Human Rights'.

The words 'United Kingdom' do not appear in the Long Title. It merely says, 'further effect'. If we say, 'domestic effect' we make it clear that it is in the United Kingdom. The phrase that the noble and learned Lord has used would then be implemented.

The Lord Chancellor: My Lords, when I used the words 'in the United Kingdom' I was not reading from the words of the Long Title. The words in the Bill are,

'An Act to give further effect to rights and freedoms guaranteed under the European Convention on Human Rights'.

But I have not conceded that this Bill claims any extra territorial effect. I do not believe that it is a great flight of the imagination to read it as meaning in the United Kingdom.

I have to make this point absolutely plain. The European Convention on Human Rights under this Bill is not made part of our law. The Bill gives the European Convention on Human Rights a special relationship which will mean that the courts will give effect to the interpretative provisions to which I have already referred, but it does not make the convention directly justiciable as it would be if it were expressly made part of our law. I want there to be no ambiguity about that.

Lord Lester of Herne Hill: My Lords, I am extremely grateful to the Lord Chancellor; but I wonder whether he would mind explaining the difference between requiring our courts (as a public authority) to give effect to the convention; requiring our courts where possible to interpret Acts of Parliament to comply with the convention; requiring our courts in developing the common law to have regard to the convention rights, and requiring our courts to give effective remedies where there is a breach of those rights. What is the difference between all of that and incorporating the convention? What else would be needed over and above all that in order to incorporate the convention?

The Lord Chancellor: My Lords, this is fast becoming something of a theological dispute and I should like to bring it to a conclusion as quickly as I may. The short point is that if the convention rights were incorporated into our law, they would be directly justiciable and would be enforced by our courts. That is not the scheme of this Bill. If the courts find it impossible to construe primary legislation in a way which is compatible with the convention rights, the primary legislation remains in full force and effect. All that the courts may do is to make a declaration of incompatibility.

I have a feeling that in these dying moments of Report stage we are behaving in a way in which judges sometimes behave at the end of a very long case. It is almost as if they cannot bring themselves to depart from the case and to be left to consider it themselves, and question after question continues. I have given the best argument that I may.

Lord Simon of Glaisdale: My Lords, I am quite satisfied that my noble and learned friend has given the best answer that can be given. We can therefore leave this to a later stage or to the other place.

My noble and learned friend said that this Bill is not intended to incorporate the convention into our domestic law. That is at variance with various points that have been made, but so be it for the moment. The amendment to the Long Title does not suggest that it should be. All that it seeks to do is to give 'domestic' effect to the convention rights and that is incontrovertibly what it does. However, it is now nearly a quarter to ten, and I am 87 years of age, so I claim leave to withdraw the amendment.

Amendment, by leave, withdrawn.

HL Deb., Report (second day), 29 January 1998, cols.418f.

RB NOTE: The following passage related to the extent to which UK courts should take account of judgments and opinions of the European Court of Human Rights. It includes the Lord Chancellor's statements in explanation of section 2 (and rejection of a proposed amendment that the courts should be 'bound' by the Strasbourg jurisprudence).

The Lord Chancellor: As other noble Lords have said, the word 'binding' is the language of strict precedent but the convention has no rule of precedent. The amendment would therefore go further than the convention required and, for reasons that I shall give in a moment, in an undesirable direction. . . .

We take the view that the expression 'take in account' is clear enough. Should a United Kingdom court ever have a case before it which is a precise mirror of one that has been previously considered by the European Court of Human Rights, which I doubt, it may be appropriate for it to apply the European court's findings directly to that case; but in real life cases are rarely as neat and tidy as that. The courts will often be faced with cases that involve factors perhaps specific to the United Kingdom which distinguish them from cases considered by the European court. I agree with the noble and learned Lord, Lord Browne-Wilkinson, that it is important that our courts have the scope to apply that discretion so as to aid in the development of human rights law.

There may also be occasions when it would be right for the United Kingdom courts to depart from Strasbourg decisions. We must remember that the interpretation of the convention rights develops over the years. Circumstances may therefore arise in which a judgment given by the European Court of Human Rights decades ago contains pronouncements which it would not be appropriate to apply to the letter in the circumstances of today in a particular set of circumstances affecting this country. The Bill as currently drafted would allow our courts to use their common sense in applying the European court's judgment to such a case. We feel that to accept this amendment removes from the judges the flexibility and discretion that they require in developing human rights law.

HL Deb, 19 January 1998, cols 1270–71

(II) In The House of Commons

SECOND READING DEBATE

Order for Second Reading read.—[Queen's consent, on behalf of the Crown, signified.]

The Secretary of State for the Home Department (Mr. Jack Straw): I beg to move, That the Bill be now read a Second time.

Three hundred and nine years ago, Parliament enacted the 1689 Bill of Rights. That Bill delineated the relationship between Parliament, the Crown and the courts. It was a foundation stone of representative government, curbing unelected power and establishing a constitutional monarchy. One reflection of that is in the mutual respect shown by Her Majesty and the House. So I have it in command from Her Majesty the Queen to acquaint the House that Her Majesty, having been informed of the purport of the Human Rights Bill, has consented to place her prerogative and interest, so far as they are affected by the Bill, at the disposal of Parliament for the purposes of the Bill.

This is the first major Bill on human rights for more than 300 years. It will strengthen representative and democratic government. It does so by enabling citizens to challenge more easily actions of the state if they fail to match the standards set by the European convention. The Bill will thus create a new and better relationship between the Government and the people.

Nothing in the Bill will take away the freedoms that our citizens already enjoy. However, those freedoms alone are not enough: they need to be complemented by positive rights that individuals can assert when they believe that they have been treated unfairly by the state, or that the state and its institutions have failed properly to protect them. The Bill will guarantee to everyone the means to enforce a set of basic civil and political rights, establishing a floor below which standards will not be allowed to fall. The Bill will achieve that by giving further effect in our domestic law to the fundamental rights and freedoms contained in the European convention on human rights.

Since the convention's drafting nearly 50 years ago, almost all the states that are party to it have gradually incorporated it into their domestic law. Ireland and Norway have not done so, but Ireland has a Bill of Rights which guarantees rights similar to those of the convention, and Norway is in the process of incorporating the convention. Several other countries with which we share our common law tradition, such as Canada and New Zealand, have provided similar protection for human rights in their legal systems.

The effect of non-incorporation on the British people is a practical one. The rights, originally developed by Britain, are no longer seen as British, and enforcing them takes far too long and costs far too much—on average five years and £30,000 to get an action into the European Court at Strasbourg once all domestic remedies have been exhausted. Bringing these rights home will mean that the British people will be able to argue for their rights in the British courts, without inordinate delay and cost. It will also mean that the rights will be brought much more fully into the jurisprudence of the courts throughout the United Kingdom, and their interpretation will thus be far more woven into our common law.

There will be another benefit: British judges will be enabled to make a distinctively British contribution to the development of the jurisprudence of human rights across Europe. It is also now plain that the approach that the United Kingdom has so far adopted towards the convention has not stood the test of time. The most obvious proof of that lies in the number of cases in which the European Court has found that there have been violations of convention rights in the United Kingdom. It is only natural that people of all political persuasions have asked, 'Why do individuals in the United Kingdom have to go to Strasbourg to enforce their British rights? Why can they not rely on them before our domestic courts?'

Having decided that we should incorporate the convention, the most fundamental question that we faced was how to do that in a manner that strengthened, and did not undermine, the sovereignty of Parliament. Some had argued that the courts should have power to set aside primary legislation, whether past or future, on the ground of incompatibility with the convention. That is a feature of many, though by no means all, government systems with a basic law enshrined in a written constitution. It is also true that, under the European Communities Act 1972, enacted by the then Conservative Government, European law with direct effect automatically takes precedence over our domestic law and Parliament, whatever Parliament wants to do otherwise.

That is not the road that we are going down. The Bill, important though it is, has the limited function of bringing the British people's rights home. It is no part of the project to call into question constitutional arrangements that have evolved in this country to make us one of the world's most stable democracies.

The sovereignty of Parliament must be paramount. By that, I mean that Parliament must be competent to make any law on any matter of its choosing. In enacting legislation, Parliament is making decisions about important matters of public policy. The authority to make those decisions derives from a democratic mandate. Members of this place possess such a mandate because they are elected, accountable and representative.

To allow the courts to set aside Acts of Parliament would confer on the judiciary a power that it does not possess, and which could draw it into serious conflict with Parliament. As the Lord Chief Justice said on Second Reading in another place, the courts and the senior judiciary do not want such a power, and we believe that the people do not wish the judiciary to have it.

Although the Bill does not allow the courts to set aside Acts of Parliament, it will nevertheless have an impact on the way in which legislation is drafted, interpreted and applied, and it will put the issues squarely to the Government and Parliament for future consideration. It is important to ensure that, for their part, the Government and Parliament can respond quickly.

In the normal way, primary legislation can be amended only by further primary legislation. As we all know—in normal circumstances, this is entirely correct—that can take a long time. One of the consequences of not having a special procedure to remedy defects in legislation is a degree of paralysis. Until now, the remedy has been through the Strasbourg Court. The best example I can give, which should command the House's attention, is the decision almost two years ago of the European Court in Strasbourg in the Chahal case.

Chahal had been detained in prison by direction of the Secretary of State because it was considered that his presence in this country was not conducive to the public good, on national security grounds. The then Home Secretary's right to make that decision without Chahal having a right of independent appeal was challenged. The matter was fought all the way to the Court in Strasbourg, which found in favour of Chahal, who then had to be released from prison.

There was no provision, as in this Bill, for the law to continue in force unless and until it was corrected. Someone whom the previous Home Secretary had decided, on the best evidence, should be excluded from this country, on the basis that his presence here was not conducive to the public good, on national security grounds went free. Meanwhile, it was impossible for my predecessor, and it remains impossible for me, to exercise the powers under the Immigration Act 1971 to exclude anyone from this country on national security grounds.

The previous Government put in train preparations for an amending Act, and we have sought to get that legislation through both Houses as quickly as possible. That Bill commands support on both sides of the House, but it is taking many months to grind through all its stages. Consequently, the position that we are stuck with is to no one's advantage. Individual rights have not been properly brought back into line with the convention; nor, as important, is any Secretary of State for the Home Department able to exercise his duties under the 1971 Act.

Mr. Douglas Hogg: Does the right hon. Gentleman accept that hon. Members who support the principle of incorporation remain deeply concerned about the provisions of the remedial order procedure, which depend on secondary legislation Orders in Council? Can he reassure us that, in the great generality of cases, primary legislation will be amended only by primary legislation, and that the provisions in clauses 10 to 12, which deal with the affirmative resolution procedure, will be activated only in instances of real emergency? If he were able to say that, he might gain much more support in the House than would otherwise be forthcoming.

Mr. Straw: I understand the concerns expressed by the right hon. and learned Gentleman; they were raised in the other place and were the subject of extensive debate. I cannot give him the undertaking that he seeks. However, I can say, first, that occasions on which the courts declare an Act of this Parliament to be incompatible are rare; there will be very few such cases. Secondly, the purpose of remedial action is to try to resolve the current paralysis, which is to nobody's advantage. It is not to take away anyone's rights; it is to confer rights. Thirdly, hon. Members will have every opportunity to discuss this matter in great detail in Committee.

In our judgment, these fast-track provisions offer far more safeguards than were provided under the European Communities Act 1972, which the right hon. and learned Gentleman's party supported. Under the 1972 Act, Parliament cannot vote on any declaration of the European Court of Justice that our law is outwith the ECJ; the law must be changed. Furthermore, the Bill provides a better and fairer procedure for deregulation than that laid down by the previous Administration.

I shall now deal briefly with the detail of the Bill and explain exactly how it will bring rights home. Clause 1 lists the convention rights to which the Bill will give further effect in our domestic law. Clause 2 ensures that, in giving effect to those rights, our domestic courts and tribunals have regard to Strasbourg jurisprudence.

Clause 3 provides that legislation, whenever enacted, must as far as possible be read and given effect in such a way as to be compatible with convention rights. We expect that, in almost all cases, the courts will be able to interpret legislation compatibly with the convention. However, we need to provide for the rare cases where that cannot be done. Consistent with maintaining parliamentary sovereignty, clause 3 therefore provides that if a provision of primary legislation cannot be interpreted compatibly with the convention rights, that legislation will continue to have force and effect.

A declaration of incompatibility will not affect the continuing validity of the legislation in question. That would be contrary to the principle of the Bill. However, it will be a clear signal to Government and Parliament that, in the court's view, a provision of legislation does not conform to the standards of the convention. To return to a matter that I discussed earlier, it is likely that the Government and Parliament would wish to respond to such a situation and would do so rapidly. We have discussed how that would operate and no doubt there will be further detailed discussions in Committee on the Floor of the House.

Clauses 6 to 9 cover the second main way by which the Bill gives effect to the convention rights. Clause 6 makes it unlawful for public authorities to act in a way that is incompatible with a convention right, unless they are required to do so to give effect to primary legislation. I have already discussed the approach that we have taken in the Bill to defining a public authority.

Clause 7 enables individuals who believe that they have been a victim of an unlawful act of a public authority to rely on the convention rights in legal proceedings. They may do so in a number of ways: by bringing proceedings under the Bill in an appropriate court or tribunal; in seeking judicial review; as part of a defence against a criminal or civil action brought against them by a public authority; or in the course of an appeal. Clause 7 ensures that an individual will always have a means by which to raise his or her convention rights. It is intended that existing court procedures will, wherever possible, be used for that purpose. Clause 8 deals with remedies. . . . If my hon. Friend will forgive me, I need to press on. If a court or tribunal finds that a public authority has acted unlawfully, it may grant whatever remedy is available to it that it considers just and appropriate.

Clause 9 serves two main functions. It preserves the general principle of judicial immunity when a court or tribunal is found, or alleged, to have acted in a way that is made unlawful by clause 6, and it provides for the possibility of damages being awarded against the Crown in respect of a judicial act, to the extent necessary to comply with article 5(5) of the convention.

Clause 13 confirms that a person's reliance on a convention right does not restrict any other right or freedom that he enjoys under United Kingdom law. Clauses 14 to 17 cover derogations from, and reservations to, the articles of the convention and its associated protocols. Clause 18 is concerned with the appointment of judges to the Strasbourg Court.

Clause 19 is a further demonstration of our determination to improve compliance with convention rights. It places a requirement on a Minister to publish a statement in relation to any Bill that he or she introduces. The statement will either be that the provisions of the legislation are compatible with convention rights or that he or she cannot make such a statement, but that the Government nevertheless wish to proceed with the Bill.

I am sure that Ministers will want to make a positive statement whenever possible. The requirement to make a statement will have a significant impact on the scrutiny of draft legislation within Government and by

Parliament. In my judgment, it will greatly assist Parliament's consideration of Bills by highlighting the potential implications for human rights.

Finally, clauses 20 to 22 deal with various supplemental matters with which we need not detain the House.

Mr. Kaufman: I am sorry to interrupt again, but my right hon. Friend has gone through the clauses and, as is the usual practice, has not found it necessary to refer to the schedule. In schedule 1, at the top of page 18, paragraph 2 of article 10 states that 'the exercise' of 'freedoms'

'may be subject to such formalities, conditions, restrictions or penalties as are prescribed by law and are necessary in a democratic society'.

and goes on to state that such provisions include

'the protection of the reputation or rights of others',

and

'preventing the disclosure of information received in confidence'.

Will he explain the significance of the word 'and' in line 3? Does the 'and' combine 'necessary in a democratic society' with 'prescribed by law'?

Mr. Straw: Yes. That is usually how such matters are interpreted, particularly as there is no comma between 'by law' and 'and'. Although I defer, of course, to our learned friends in the Strand, I think that I can give my right hon. Friend a clear and categorical answer to that question.

The Opposition amendment seeks to block the Bill's Second Reading on three main grounds: that it will further increase the power of the Executive; that it will diminish Parliament; and that it will politicise the judiciary. As I hope I have shown, none of them has any serious foundation.

The power of the Executive will be reduced by the Bill because the state will be made far more accountable for its acts and omissions to its citizens. The Bill enhances parliamentary sovereignty in practice, and the scheme that we have chosen ensures that the judiciary will not be involved in politics.

Let me conclude by placing the Bill in a wider setting. Our manifesto commits us to a comprehensive programme of constitutional reform. It has four objectives: decentralised government; responsive government; open and honest government; and modernised government. The Bill falls squarely within that constitutional programme. It is a key component of our drive to modernise our society and refresh our democracy. It is part of a blueprint for changing the relationship between the Government and people of the United Kingdom to bring about a better balance between rights and responsibilities, between the powers of the state and the freedom of the individual. I commend the Bill to the House.

Sir Brian Mawhinney: I beg to move, To leave out from 'That' to the end of the Question, and to add instead thereof:

'this House, while confirming its strong belief in human rights, expresses its deep concern at the constitutional implications and deficiencies of the Human Rights Bill *[Lords]* because the Bill weakens one of the foundations of everyone's human rights and fundamental freedoms, which is an effective political democracy; because the Bill creates in the United Kingdom an additional, separate, and potentially incompatible, constitutional framework; because the Bill fails adequately to respect and maintain the principle of separation of powers between the executive, legislature, and judiciary fundamental in a democratic society and will therefore lead to a further increase in the power of the executive, the diminution of Parliament, and the politicisation of the judiciary; and declines to give the Bill a Second Reading.'

In a long and closely argued speech, the Home Secretary dealt in some detail with the main provisions of the Bill. As I hope to show, however, he conveniently skated over the importance of such issues as sovereignty and the fast-track approach and also the definition of a public authority. The House will have also noticed his total silence on the role of the Lord Chancellor.

I welcome the right hon. Gentleman's initial comments that, for many years, there has been broad political agreement on the issue. I should like to confirm that again. The Conservative party's commitment to human rights is just as strong as that of the right hon. Gentleman and the Government of the day. Our commitment to the European convention on human rights is as strong as his and the Government of the day. I am happy to put that on the record. In common with the right hon. Gentleman, I recognise that the convention reflects rights, freedoms and liberties that have long been embodied in the statutes and common law of the United Kingdom.

If I may offer a slightly broader interpretation of human rights, in the past 18 years our Conservative Government extended human rights as my right hon. Friend Baroness Thatcher worked with President Reagan – with the intermittent support of the Labour party – to free eastern Europe. That led to the removal of the Berlin wall and enabled human rights to be experienced in a way that had not been known previously in that part of Europe.

With the support of the Labour party, my right hon. Friend the Member for Huntingdon (Mr. Major) helped to extend human rights in Kuwait after its invasion. Without any help from the Labour party, our Government extended the human rights of trade unions by removing the closed shop.

The Bill will alter the balance of power between the legislature and the judiciary. In the United Kingdom, we have always had a separation of powers. Hon. Members are elected to the House, and hon. Members and those in another place usually pass laws following the Government's proposed legislation. Judges subsequently apply those laws in specific cases. However, all that will change.

The Bill's effect is clear: it would require courts to interpret the convention's broad and general provisions and apply them to policy spheres affecting individuals' rights and freedoms. Courts will therefore become involved in public policy matters that were previously the sole responsibility of Parliament. That consequence will be inevitable and is outwith the quality of the judiciary.

In his speech, the Home Secretary said that the Bill would not necessarily affect sovereignty; but it goes to the very heart of the sovereignty of the United Kingdom Parliament. The Government say that a declaration of incompatibility would protect Parliament's rights and will not change the law. The Home Secretary told the House that the declaration will only tell Ministers that judges think that a law should be changed, and that Ministers will decide on how to proceed. However – as the Home Secretary made clear in answer to an earlier intervention – those statements are, at best, disingenuous. If the Government do not respond to a declaration of incompatibility by judges, a litigant may go to Strasbourg. Therefore, the presumption is that when judges say that something in UK law must be changed—and, by the way, do it pretty quickly, old Parliament – Ministers will respond.

Judges will therefore consider cases in the light of UK law and against the background of the convention—which is not detailed but consists of broad principles that are entirely worthy but unexceptional. Article 2 states that everyone has a right to life. Article 4 states that

'No one shall be held in slavery or servitude.'

Article 8 says that

'Everyone has the right to respect for his private and family life, his home and his correspondence.'

Article 10 says that everyone has the right to freedom of expression.

All of those articles are hugely important to every hon. Member, in whichever corner we sit. They represent in our society – national and international – the highest moral ground. However, frequently judgments will have to be made between two or more of those articles in a particular case. How will those judgments be made?

Mr. David Lock: Does the right hon. Gentleman realise that, in his analysis of what he proposes to do, he is issuing a great insult to British judges? He is saying, 'I do not trust British judges to work out where the convention has been breached; I would prefer to trust the judges in Strasbourg,' and he trumpets the fact that the previous Government were happy to change the law if the Strasbourg judges declared it, but he is not prepared to do so when our judges make the same finding. Is not that an insult to the British judges?

Sir Brian Mawhinney: I gave way to the hon. Gentleman too soon. Had I kept going a little longer, I would have addressed that point.

I return to the question—how are judges to decide? Normally, and historically, judges decide on the basis of decisions taken in this place. We pass legislation; we say what the law should be. We give them guidance to let them know what we intended by the legislation that we passed, and judges use that to determine the outcome of specific cases. However, in this new circumstance British judges will say, 'This piece of law is outwith this convention article, in my judgment'. They will say, 'In my judgment,' because the House will have set down no Act of Parliament to enable the judges to determine how else to proceed.

Mr. Hogg: Is not the real change that the Bill is achieving, that in the past the House has always laid out statutory provisions with great particularity, stating very clearly what the House wishes to provide by way of rights or obligations? The Bill, by incorporating the convention, is stating rights in very general terms, leaving the application of the particular facts to each case and thus the enlargement of particular rights to the judges. That is a fundamental transformation in the way in which we conduct our affairs.

Sir Brian Mawhinney: I entirely agree with my right hon. and learned Friend. He put it more elegantly than I did, but in our own way we both said the same thing. He is right to point out the fundamental nature of the change which this represents, and over which the Home Secretary skated earlier.

Judges will not be obliged to abide by European Court of Human Rights judgments, so they will make their own judgments. Will they be influenced by the sense of existing United Kingdom legislation? Perhaps, but by definition, they will not be bound by it in the cases that they hear, for they will have judged the UK law to be incompatible. So they will make new judgments in the specific, as my right hon. and learned Friend the Member for Sleaford and North Hykeham (Mr. Hogg) says, and they will break new ground. On what basis will they do so? They will do so on the basis of their own views and, as these will be in the area of human rights, judges will, in effect, be producing a judicially-driven United Kingdom Bill of Rights. ...

This is not modernising the constitution. This is not modernising Britain. This is tearing up our fundamental separation of powers.

So it appears that we are heading for a UK Bill of Rights, not enacted by Parliament, and driven by judges who may take account of, but are not bound by, European Court precedent or parliamentary legislation. I stress that none of this amounts to an attack on judges. This country owes much to their fine minds and judicial experience. Our quarrel is not with the judges or the European Court: our quarrel is with the Government.

The Bill represents the most obvious example yet of the contempt in which the Government hold Parliament and – even worse – the sovereignty of Parliament. Other examples are Prime Minister's Question Time, devolution, and Parliament being the last to be informed. Now the very sovereignty of Parliament is being undermined.

This is a Home Office Bill that owes much to the Lord Chancellor. It is not about whether hon. Members support human rights for UK citizens; we do. It is not about whether we support the convention and its interpretation by the European Court of Human Rights; we support the former, and most of the time the latter. When occasionally we have not agreed with the Court, we have nevertheless amended our law as required of convention signatories.

The Bill is not even about giving human rights to our citizens – they have them already. Whether intentional or not, the Bill is about diminishing the sovereignty of Parliament; it is about weakening our democracy and changing fundamentally the balance of the separation of powers between the Executive, the legislature and the judiciary. The result will be a further increase in the power of the Executive, the diminution of Parliament and the politicisation of the judiciary.

No Act of Parliament will set out how the broad statements of the European convention should be understood in British law or to whom they should apply. Members of Parliament elected from 659 constituencies across the nation to protect the public interest will be mere bystanders as the courts interpret the meaning of the convention and, perhaps inappropriately, gag our press. The Government like to claim that they keep their promises – they say that even when they are breaking them. Before the election, the Government did not promise the British people that they would undermine the sovereignty of Parliament – but that is what they are doing in this Bill. For that reason above others, we do not support the legislation.

Mr. Kevin McNamara: We should delight in the fact that, as we are about to celebrate the 50th anniversary of the Council of Europe, the provisions to which I have referred are to be incorporated in our domestic legislation. We should all be proud of that.

We are following on in the great tradition of liberal and freedom legislation, which has its roots in our own Bill of Rights and in the American declaration of independence. The convention's rights lie also in the writings of Tom Paine and the declaration of the rights of man of the French revolution – indeed, all those great things that make for individual human liberty. Contained within the convention are all the great ideas for which people were fighting in the course of 19th century liberalism. It is sad that only at the end of the 20th century are we incorporating such rights in British law.

The main defect of the proposals that are before us is that they are concerned primarily with 19th century liberalism. Economic, cultural, ethical and other freedoms are not included in the Bill, except briefly and in a negative way in only one of the clauses.

The Bill is probably the most far-reaching and important of all the constitutional measures that have been introduced by the present Administration. It will require common law henceforth to be developed consistently with the European convention on human rights. It will require also that all primary and secondary legislation be henceforth construed as far as possible so as to be compatible with the provisions of the convention. What can possibly be wrong with that? Which of the human rights as listed do we not accept?

Mr. Douglas Hogg: The hon. Gentleman might care to focus on the problem that although the language of the convention is, of course, perfectly acceptable, rights are expressed in very general terms. For more than 40 years, the European Court has interpreted those rights to an extent quite beyond that ever contemplated by the founding fathers. It is a moving convention. It is a mistake, therefore, to talk about it as a fixed system of law. The problem is that it is a constantly changing system of law that is developed by a continuing stream of judicial interpretations outwith the contemplation of the founding fathers.

Mr. McNamara: What a splendid point. English common law developed in exactly the same way through attitudes and interpretations. Once judicial interpretations begin, we have judicial interpretations of judicial inter-pretations of judicial decisions.

I am surprised that Opposition Members, many of whom are learned in the law, find it strange that judges should be examining declarations and interpreting them, bearing in mind the generality of so many of the laws that we have introduced.

Mr. Robert Maclennan: The Bill is the centrepiece of the constitutional resettlement on which the Government embarked before the election, with the full-hearted support of my right hon. and hon. Friends. As is well known, we entered into a broad agreement on a legislative programme for constitu-tional reform that was unprecedented not only in itself, but in its scope and ambition. I have no doubt that that was right, for constitutional reform requires broad cross-party support if it is to be effective and stable.

There is much to be said for a greater separation of powers than we have known in this country. The executive arm of government is too dominant in our constitution. The present Administration deserve credit for recognising that and voluntarily taking steps in the Bill to make it more accountable. The threat to our freedoms can be found in the propensity of British Governments to use this House and this Parliament simply to ratify their will. It is fanciful to suggest that the Bill will lead to a diminution of Parliament.

Unlike earlier attempts to incorporate the convention, and unlike the European Communities Act 1972 – which, as the House was reminded, was introduced by a Conservative Government – the Bill does not give primacy to treaty rights where there is a provision in this Parliament's legislation that is incompatible with a convention right. In their endeavour to ensure the supremacy of Parliament, the Government have followed a novel course. They have provided only that the courts may make a declaration of incompatibility. They have eschewed the more normal statutory inter-pretation that there has been an implied repeal if Parliament has enacted a measure subsequently. As a result of the form in which the measure is couched, it falls to Parliament to decide whether to safeguard the conven-tion right by the means set out in clauses 10 to 12.

It might be argued that a Bill of Rights should indeed be the fundamental law of the land, impliedly repealing all incompatible legislation, but that is not the way of this Bill. Far from introducing, as the amendment suggests, an 'incompatible constitutional framework', the Bill is deferential to the sensi-tivities of the judiciary about being given an overriding constitutional power.

Looking to the future, I would favour a constitutional settlement that rebalances the powers of the Executive, the legislature and the judiciary. Such a written constitution, accepted by the people, would reflect the wider distribution of public power and secure greater accountability for its exercise. It would embody the settled view of people as to where the line should be drawn, delimiting the exercise of public power. But that is not for today.

Fiona Mactaggart: I warmly welcome the Bill because it will establish a national standard for ethical government, and for ethical relations between people and public institutions. That is especially important at a time when we are devolving power. To listen to Opposition Members, one would think that the most important feature of the British constitution is to retain every possible spot of power in this place, but that is not what the Government are committed to. They have been rearranging the constitution to devolve power closer to people; that is right and it was in the manifesto on which we were elected. It is absolutely necessary that we have a clear, unifying national ethical framework for that devolution of power and that is what the Bill provides.

Mr. Desmond Swayne: Is the hon. Lady content to have power devolved effectively to judges, who are not subject to the will of the people in the way that Members of Parliament are? The people can get rid of the rascals here if they do not like them.

Fiona Mactaggart: I do not believe that that is what is happening. We are devolving power to the people. If the judges' power conflicts with any decision of this House, there is a mechanism whereby the House is invited to look again at the legislation to ensure that all our laws contribute to and protect human rights.

It is essential that every institution and the whole of society fall within the framework of the human rights legislation that we establish.

We have no human rights education. Most Commonwealth countries place a responsibility on the Government to educate their people in human rights.

Other countries have taken that responsibility to educate people on human rights, contributing not only to better law making and to a better understanding of the law, but to people being able to exercise their rights more effectively. Those people know the difference between a human right and a gripe—which is a very important difference for people to understand. In Indian law, there is a wonderful phrase about 'combating illiteracy' in human rights. That is a powerful concept.

It is important that we do that job of educating people on human rights. I therefore hope that we might soon create a commission to take on part of that job, although I quite understand why it is difficult to establish one right now. We shall have to create a system in which bodies currently charged with human rights responsibilities, such as the Equal Opportunities Commission and the Commission for Racial Equality, can do their job and in which there is parity between those bodies, but in which there is an overarching human rights framework. I urge my hon. Friend the Minister to examine the possibility of creating a commission as soon as the Bill is well bedded in.

Until we establish a commission, I urge the Government to take urgent action on another matter that was in the White Paper: creating in the House a Committee on human rights. I have read the debate on the Bill in the other place. Those in the other place have distinguished themselves in dealing with the human rights issue and could make a substantial contribution to such a Committee. I therefore believe that there is a strong argument for such a Committee to be a joint one of both Houses. Many of those in the other place have participated in human rights cases, both in Strasbourg and internationally.

Even if we cannot immediately create a commission, we should create without delay a Joint Committee. I suggest four jobs for the Committee to do urgently. First – in performing the tasks that have been set for Ministers under clause 19 of the Bill – it should produce a statement on new legislation and its compatibility with the convention. Statements should be a powerful assessment – an audit – of the human rights impact of proposed legislation. We do not want statements to be merely a quick gesture stating that the Minister is confident that there will be no conflict; let us have an assessment of how legislation will advance and develop.

Secondly, the Committee should examine the issues – which I have already mentioned – of public education and of creating a real culture of rights.

Thirdly, the Joint Committee should examine the matter of access to rights and legal representation.

Fourthly, the Committee should examine whether there is a case for the United Kingdom to sign up to additional protocols and to other international human rights legislation. We have not signed very many of the current protocols, including some of those under the international covenant on civil and political rights, but there is a strong case for us to do so.

Those are the tasks that I think that the Joint Committee should examine. To bring rights home, we need not only a legislative framework, but action. I hope that we shall be able swiftly to rid ourselves of the barriers to creating a human rights commission, which would be able to perform those tasks even more effectively than a Joint Committee.

The Bill is a genuinely modernising Bill. People are sometimes slick and sneering about modernising government, but the Bill is what modernising government is all about. It is about creating a framework of rights, helping people realise their rights and providing them with a mechanism for exercising those rights without requiring them to have undue expertise or excessive cash.

Passing the Bill is one of the biggest ways in which we can transform the United Kingdom. It is innovatory, and it will fundamentally change the relationship between Government and the people—not in a manner that reduces our democracy, but in one that extends it. For that reason, I commend the Bill to the House.

Mr. David Ruffley: The Government have introduced the Bill under the banner – the soundbite – 'bringing rights home'. The problem is that that conceals the Bill's real thrust: to effect a massive constitutional shift from the House to unelected judges. That is a constitutional change of epic proportions.

In considering our response to the Bill, hon. Members should realise that United Kingdom judges will be making law in a way that they have never done before. Even worse, the Bill will drag judges into politics as they have never been involved before. In a very real way, they will be politicised.

What I find unsatisfactory is the idea of judges being given powers to make law on important public policy issues; I was about to list those issues. If the European convention is incorporated into domestic law by the Bill, for the first time, judges will make law on the right to an abortion, on the right to life, on the closed shop and on the right to privacy. Those are important issues, on which, in our judgment, the law should not fall to be invented by judges. The discussion of important laws, relating to the matters that I have listed, is a matter for this place, not for domestic judges.

It seems to me that something more flows from the politicisation of our judiciary – the way in which judges will be obliged to make up laws on abortion, on privacy and, conceivably, on euthanasia – namely, the prospect of a Ministry of justice tampering with the composition of the Bench. It seems to us that, in the course of his egomaniacal odyssey through White-hall, the Lord Chancellor will seek to create a Ministry of justice; and that either he or his successors will try to tamper with the composition of the Bench – introducing quotas for race, gender and so on. That is a real threat. We have already witnessed the politicisation of the USA Supreme Court under Reagan, Bush and Clinton. I foresee the same happening under a 'new Labour' Administration if the Bill is passed.

I believe that this is a bad Bill because it introduces the rule of lawyers to areas that should properly be the preserve of this House. When they finally wake up to what has happened, the British people will be appalled by what the Government are doing.

Mr. Ross Cranston: There are persuasive arguments for incorporating the European convention into our law. First, the convention has an important symbolic significance. In my view, it demonstrates clearly that this country is committed to human rights. That does not mean that we have not taken human rights seriously in the past – we obviously have: since 1951 we have adhered to the European convention at treaty level – but I agree with my right hon. Friend the Home Secretary that patriation of the convention is one way of restoring confidence in our Government.

It must seem somewhat paradoxical to ordinary people, if they know about it, that basic constitutional rights have until now been negative rights. In other words, they are enjoyed as long as Parliament does not legislate to the contrary. Incorporation of the convention will ensure that basic con-stitutional rights will become positive rights. I think that that is a great benefit.

The second persuasive argument is that it is somewhat undesirable several hon. Members have made the point – that if individuals want to pursue rights under the convention they must go to Strasbourg. They have to incur costs and are subject to the delays associated with pursuing rights before the Commission and ultimately the European Court.

My hon. Friend the Member for Birmingham, Hodge Hill (Mr. Davis) advanced a valid argument when he said that rights in practice are vital, and added that it is all very well to have rights on paper but if they are not implemented and capable of being implemented in practice, they are not worth very much. That is the effect of the current arrangements. People must be greatly disillusioned when they are told that they must exhaust their remedies in this country right up to the House of Lords, and then go further to Strasbourg. That is the second argument in favour of incorporation.

The third argument is that the United Kingdom courts, once the convention is incorporated, will be able to contribute to jurisprudence on human rights. Historically, of course, they have already done that through the development of the common law. In recent times they have referred to the convention in decision making. Under the Bill, however, they will be able to proceed directly. They will be able to take into account the decisions of the European Court—that is provided for in the Bill; it is inconceivable that that would not be open to them.

The Bill correctly provides that our courts will not be bound by European Court jurisprudence. In my view, some of the decisions of the European Court are based on faulty reasoning. In some instances, I think that it is plain wrong. The Saunders decision falls into that category. That decision did not appreciate the problems of policing corporate misbehaviour. Nor did it appreciate properly the history of insolvency and company law in this country. If our courts had handled that case under the convention, I think that a different decision would have been reached. If our courts can consider these matters, we can contribute to the development of doctrine. In an area in which legislative provisions are so open-textured, that is all important.

There are other, ancillary, advantages to incorporation, such as the benevolent effect that it will have on our attitude to statutory interpretation. The Bill provides that the convention must be interpreted in a purposive way. I hope that that approach will insinuate itself more widely into the interpretation of legislation.

A country's constitution is a living thing. The incorporation of the convention is one step in this country's constitutional development. I can see a day when we will have a human rights commission, and even a Bill of Rights in a different form. It goes without saying that the Bill, when enacted, will not be the be-all and end-all of human rights. Human rights must be put in a wider context. The Government's new deal to give dignity to young people through employment is just as important as this measure.

Sir Nicholas Lyell: The first point that I must make in opposing the Bill is to affirm the official Opposition's strong belief in human rights. It is the first point that we make in our reasoned amendment, and there will be no disagreement about it among hon. Members.

Having said that, I believe that it is essential that there is a proper balance, which is where the Bill is deeply flawed. If the European convention on human rights is ever to be satisfactorily incorporated into the United Kingdom's domestic law, the key point – which, again, we make clear in our reasoned amendment – is that there must be a proper balance between the roles of our domestic courts, the Court at Strasbourg and the United Kingdom Parliament. For that reason alone, if for no other, we would deny the Bill a Second Reading. I make it perfectly clear that the Conservative party is not convinced that the case for incorporation has been made in any event; it is certainly not made by the Bill.

Views have differed over the years on the wisdom of incorporation. I point out again that, until 1993, the Labour party – including a number of right hon. and hon. Members whom I see present – vigorously opposed incorporation; it has been on a journey to Damascus, or so it would have us believe. None the less, those who have studied this matter will realise that the convention does not fit easily into the United Kingdom's constitution or our system of common law. That is in stark distinction to the way in which it can fit into the so-called monist – it is a strange word – countries, where treaty obligations automatically have binding force in domestic law. The difference is that almost all those other countries have a detailed written constitution, as does Germany for example, or in any event place a far greater emphasis on codification and black-letter law, in which the concepts of the convention are either largely reproduced or the ability of the convention to overturn them is prevented by express words.

I have great regard for the Home Secretary, but one of the sad things about the debate is that he should have repeated the constant refrain that the United Kingdom has a bad record in relation to Strasbourg. That is not true and I am afraid that it has reflections of Henry VIII and his period– when one wants to destroy or change something, one first seeks to give it a bad name, which is what happened then with the monasteries.

The convention largely reproduces concepts that are deeply embedded in our common and statute law. Our laws and practices have been upheld by Strasbourg far more often than they have been struck down. The United Kingdom gave the right of individual petition – people can take their own case to Strasbourg from the United Kingdom – as long ago as 1966. France gave that right only many years later. As my right hon. Friend the shadow Home Secretary, the Member for North-West Cambridgeshire (Sir B. Mawhinney) made clear, a balanced analysis that takes account of the size of national populations and the length of time that a member state has given a right of individual petition, shows that far from having a bad record, the United Kingdom is among the very best. If necessary, we will ask parliamentary questions to bring that out. It is confirmed not only by past applications but by those in the pipeline. The United Kingdom has 26 current applications that are deemed admissible, which does not mean by any means that our judgments will be overturned, France has 75 – I am using only sophisticated, major western European countries as a comparison – and Italy 370. So, that puts the matter into perspective.

Our first key criticism of the Bill is that the fast-track procedure is wrong. It seriously restricts people's right to effective representation in Parliament as well as the role of Parliament itself. That is ironic in relation to the convention. I see the hon. Member for Hull, North (Mr. McNamara) in his place. He regretted the fact that the preamble to the convention had not been included in the Bill. The preamble states expressly that the fundamental freedoms that it espouses are

> 'best maintained on the one hand by an effective political democracy and on the other by a common understanding and observance of the human rights upon which they depend'.

So, the twin pillars of the fundamental freedoms in which we all believe are human rights and an effective political democracy. The two must go hand in hand. That is why our first attack is on the fast-track procedure – such procedures are wrong in principle and unnecessary in practice.

Frankly, I was disappointed by the speech of the right hon. Member for Caithness, Sutherland and Easter Ross (Mr. Maclennan), who did not seem to have bothered to read our reasoned amendment. It is not all that easy to read. Tight language is required in the drafting of such amendments, as Madam Speaker will know. However, for a lawyer like the right hon. Gentleman, it would be perfectly clear if he had taken the trouble to study it.

The first point, which was re-emphasised by the Home Secretary, is that primary legislation has always been rare and is likely to be so in future. Is that the Home Secretary's point, or is he saying that it is going to be very frequent? We believe that it will be unnecessary in practice and that it will be rare because primary legislation has been required on only 10 occasions in the 45 years of the convention's history.

I pause to tease the matter out a little. The hon. Members for Wellingborough (Mr. Stinchcombe) and for Wyre Forest (Mr. Lock) see a huge and developing role for the judiciary. It is possible. I think that there will be a flush of cases. I do not think that many will involve primary legislation being struck down.

Mr. Straw: We are trying to make predictions. I think that the best guess is that the right hon. and learned Gentleman is correct that the Judicial Committee of the House of Lords will hold only infrequently that there are incompatibilities. The speeches of many distinguished members of the senior judiciary in the other place show that the judiciary will do its best to declare Acts of Parliament consistent with the convention, as they are required to do. Although the procedure may not be used very often, which I should have thought would reassure him, I return to the practical question of whether it was satisfactory that we ended up with a two-year delay in the case of Chahal. That recognised neither individual human rights nor the needs of national security.

Sir Nicholas Lyell: I am grateful to the right hon. Gentleman for intervening because he has made what I can respectfully describe as a bad point, which I will pick up. Such declarations of incompatibility are not wrong in principle because they will be rare but because it is important that Parliament should be able to play a full part in the development of the delicate balance of rights and obligations for which the convention calls.

The Home Secretary mentioned the Chahal case. During the debate, I looked up how much time was taken by Chahal. The Home Secretary said that it took two years. My right hon. and learned Friend the Member for Folkestone and Hythe did not introduce the legislation before the general election but it took the Government only seven months to pass it. It took two hours 41 minutes of parliamentary time in the Lords and three hours 18 minutes in this House. That can hardly be regarded as excessive. More important than that – my next point will be that there must be proper parliamentary scrutiny and debate – it involved an amendment. The Minister who is to reply should remember that because he moved it. It would not have been satisfactory for the legislation to be introduced by unamendable order. The amendment provided a right of appeal from the Special Immigration Appeals Commission to the Court of Appeal. If it had been an unamendable order, the Government would have had to take it away and start again, and the measure would have taken three hours in each House.

Under the proposed structure there will be no right of appeal to Strasbourg by either the Government or a public body. In other words, once a decision has reached the House of Lords or the final courts of appeal, such as a court martial, the Appeal Court and so on under clause 4 (5), and if the Government or a public body has lost, there will be no opportunity for any further appeal to Strasbourg. No matter how serious the matter of public interest and how far our law may have strayed from what Strasbourg may find out, the case can be taken no further. Is that really what the Government intend?

It may seem far-fetched to suggest it because I have a great deal of respect for the wisdom of our judiciary, but in theory even our abortion laws could be struck down under the right to life provisions of article 1. That is not a fanciful notion because the same has happened in America and Canada under their constitutions. That action would be far more drastic than that which the Strasbourg Court would ever be likely to take.

I am not suggesting that our courts would ignore our own traditions. I am on record as acknowledging that one of the benefits that should come from a properly balanced structure is the beneficial input of the wisdom of the United Kingdom judiciary. But courts have no monopoly of wisdom. The overall balance must be right for the protection of our judiciary as well as the protection of democracy. A close reading of the Bill suggests that the Government are uncertain about how much of the convention they will entrust to the judiciary.

Why, for example, is article 13, which provides that:

'Everyone whose rights and freedoms ... are violated shall have an effective remedy before a national authority',

not incorporated? Why can cases be brought only in relation to alleged breaches by the Government or so-called public authorities? How far do the Government intend or expect the judiciary, following incorporation, to use the convention to develop the common law? Is the Press Complaints Commission a public authority? At one moment, the Government said it was not, but they took advice from David Pannick QC and then said it was.

Is that now their position and why they are now coming forward with amendments? What about ombudsmen? There are banking ombudsmen and insurance ombudsmen and all sorts of ombudsmen – are they public authorities? There must be balance.

In conclusion, it is because of the deficiencies that I have outlined that we have tabled our reasoned amendment. I am sure that it is not in the Home Secretary's character to be arrogant on such matters, but we look forward to careful answers to important questions – to an assurance that the respective roles of Executive, judiciary and legislature will be fully respected and that the substance of our reasoned amendment will be accepted. Failing that – I fear it will be failing that – I invite my right hon. and hon. Friends to join me in pressing our points firmly home in the Lobby.

The Parliamentary Under-Secretary of State for the Home Department (Mr. Mike O'Brien): My hon. Friend the Member for Slough [Fiona Mactaggart] raised the issue of a parliamentary Committee. The Government propose to strengthen Parliament's role by supporting the creation of a new parliamentary Committee on human rights. It could be a Joint Committee of both Houses or a Committee of each House; that is a matter for the House to decide. If the House so decides, the Committee's function could be to scrutinise proposed legislation, to ensure that human rights are respected, to assess UK compliance with various human rights codes and to keep the Act – as it will eventually undoubtedly become – under constant review.

The shadow Home Secretary made some points that I accept. He said that incorporation would not of itself guarantee human rights; I agree. However, incorporation might help to direct our minds to the rights of the individual against the state. I therefore think that it will help. He said also that it had been necessary for the previous Government to amend primary legislation 10 times to comply with the convention, and that they sought to comply with Strasbourg's decisions even if they did not agree with them. I accept that, in that respect, the previous Government's record was good.

I am concerned about the shadow Home Secretary's comments on politicising judges; I do not accept that that will happen. Lord Bingham's words have already been quoted in this debate. He said:

> 'judges already from time to time find themselves deciding cases which have political, sometimes even party-political implications. The judges strive to decide those cases on a firm basis of legal principle; and that is what they will continue to do when the convention is incorporated if the Bill becomes law.'—[*Official Report, House of Lords*, 3 November 1997; Vol. 582, c. 1246.]

It appears that the shadow Home Secretary trusts Strasbourg judges – but not our own judges – to change the law. In his book 'What Next in the Law?', Lord Denning said that we have to trust someone, so why not trust the judges. Does the right hon. Gentleman really say that he has no trust in our judges, and that they cannot distinguish law from their own 'socio-political theories'? He seemed to suggest that our judges would deliver 'socio-political theories'.

I almost thought – with all those socio-political theories – that I was listening to an aging Marxist decrying the establishment's conspiracy against the proletariat. However, I treat the point with seriousness because it deserves that. Judges will have to apply the law. As clause 21 makes clear, they will have to take into account judgments of the European Court of Human Rights and decisions and opinions of other bodies. They will not, of course, be bound by those decisions when our primary legislation says otherwise. They must accept primary legislation if it differs from those decisions, although judges may make a declaration of incompatibility. Our own courts – the House of Lords, the Court of Appeal and the High Court – will soon develop their own jurisprudence, and the lower courts will be bound by that.

The shadow Home Secretary mentioned having to accept decisions of the European Court of Human Rights that are based on other countries' cases and problems. Conservative Members will recall voting for the European Communities Act 1972 and for other legislation introducing European law that not only was based on case law developed across Europe, but overruled our laws. Famously, Lord Denning warned that European law would run up the rivers and estuaries of our common law. It did, and Conservatives voted for it. The convention will not overrule our primary legislation, and the Bill will preserve parliamentary sovereignty.

The purpose of the Bill is simple: it is to bring rights home. It is to reclaim, for people in this country, the rights to which they are entitled under the convention. The purpose may be simple, but the effects will be profound. The Bill will benefit individuals, Government and the whole of society.

First and most obviously, the Bill will improve people's access to their rights, as my hon. Friends the Members for Dudley, North (Mr. Cranston) and for Clwyd, West (Mr. Thomas) said. At present, those who feel that their convention rights have been infringed cannot, save in very limited circumstances, obtain redress in this country. They must take their grievances to Strasbourg. That is not a road to be taken by the faint-hearted. It takes about five years for a case to be resolved. Only those with time, patience, considerable willpower and, sometimes, considerable money are likely to stay the course. It cannot be right to ration rights so that only the dogged few can hope to benefit from them.

Enabling our courts to take account of the convention is about more than reaching quicker decisions. It will mean that the judges of a domestic court can consider all the issues relevant to the case before them. They will no longer have to put out of their mind convention arguments that might be relevant to the case, but which they are currently debarred from considering. Therefore, the Bill will change the approach that the courts adopt to convention cases.

The present situation is wholly unsatisfactory for the courts and for individuals. It is artificial to cordon off a set of rights and make them the exclusive preserve of the Court in Strasbourg. It leads to frustration and it impedes effective justice.

The right hon. Member for North-West Cambridgeshire (Sir B. Mawhinney) was worried about politicisation. I consider that our judges must be able to bring their knowledge of the United Kingdom's traditions and practices to bear on the cases that come before them. They will be able to interpret the convention rights in ways sensitive to the specific circumstances that will apply in this country. The rights under the convention will become interwoven with our laws.

The Strasbourg Court recognises that domestic courts have the primary role to play in protecting individuals' rights under the convention. The proper role of the Strasbourg Court is to act as a backstop but, at present, the Strasbourg institutions are often placed in the front line, as the first bodies to consider issues arising under the convention. That serves no one's interest.

Opponents of the Bill seem to exhibit a touch of schizophrenia. Human rights are, it seems, to be supported abroad, but ignored at home. On one hand, we have an exemplary approach to fulfilling our international obligations under the convention – I have praised the previous Government's method of doing so – but on the other, we have been almost alone in denying our people domestic access to their rights.

Half in, half out – the hokey-cokey approach will not work. It was the position of the Conservative party regarding the European Union. It had its left foot in, its right foot out – in, out, in, out and shake it all about – and that seems to be the policy that it is now adopting on the European convention. We know how ineffective the Conservatives were in their attitudes towards Brussels. Now they are wrong, too, in their attitude to the convention. We need an end to these mixed messages. Our citizens need a clear lead. The Government will give it. We are firmly committed to protecting the rights of our people, and the Bill is one demonstration of that.

Critics of the Bill seem to have adopted two main lines of attack. First, we have heard the authentic voice of empire, almost, from below the Gangway – the view that individuals in foreign countries may need the protection of rights to defend themselves from the state, but that we in the United Kingdom have no need for such protection within our country. We may have written the convention, hon. Members argue, but we did so for the other countries.

That view is flawed. We already accept the judgments of a European body in respect of the convention, and have amended our laws many times in response to its findings. Therefore, we already adapt our laws in the light of convention rights. Incorporation will mean, however, that United Kingdom courts can assist in shaping those rights in a manner sensitive to our country's ways. At present they cannot. Moreover, at a time when the United Kingdom has committed a total of 50 violations of the convention, it smacks of complacency to say that we have nothing to learn by giving effect to convention rights in our law. That does not substantiate the point made by the right hon. and learned Member for North-East Bedfordshire (Sir N. Lyell) in his closing speech. The issue is whether we have something to learn. I suspect that he, more than anyone, would agree that we can all learn something from the decisions of the Court at Strasbourg.

The other line of attack taken by opponents of the Bill is underpinned by a sort of defeatism – the view that it is almost too difficult to bring convention rights into our legal system because of this country's unique tradition. The argument goes that providing these rights is incompatible with the doctrine of parliamentary sovereignty. Judges will be drawn into unsavoury disputes with Parliament, thereby becoming politicised. I seem to recall a time – the time of Thatcher – when Conservatives prided themselves on a can-do attitude to life – where there is a will, there is a way. Not any more, it seems. Now they think that we are too inadequate for the task and say, 'Just leave us alone.' They may be inadequate to the task of governing: we are not. We can do it. It goes to show that when a Government are prepared to take control and talk to people, they can achieve far more than Governments who are not so prepared.

The Bill is part of the Government's modernisation of British politics. It is about giving people new rights in their dealings with the state. It is part of a comprehensive package of constitutional reforms which will increase individual rights, decentralise power, open up government and reform Parliament. We have moved to create a Scottish Parliament and a Welsh assembly. There is to be a Freedom of Information Act, a referendum on the voting system for the House of Commons, a long-overdue reform of the House of Lords, the abolition of the law-making powers of hereditary peers and, by means of the Bill, the introduction of the European convention on human rights into UK law. That will enable our people to access their rights in our domestic courts without having to go to Europe. The Bill empowers our people and I commend it to the House.

The House divided: Ayes 332, Noes 146.

HC Deb., 16 February 1998, cols. 769f.

COMMITTEE STAGE

RB NOTE: In the following passage the home secretary presented a government amendment to the original form of the Bill, which was enacted as section 12. It gives his statements on when restrictions on press freedom might be permissible under the Act.

Mr Straw: With these new clauses we have an opportunity to debate the potential impact of the Human Rights Bill on the freedom of the press.

As the Committee will know, there was concern in some sections of the press that the Human Rights Bill might undermine press freedom and result in a privacy law by the back door. That was not the Government's view. On the contrary, we have always believed that the Human Rights Bill would strengthen rather than weaken the freedom of the press. In practice, the European convention on human rights has been used in Strasbourg to uphold press freedom against efforts by the state to restrict it. By virtue of clause 2 of the Bill, our courts will be required to take the Strasbourg case law into account. Therefore, we are bringing home not just the rights contained in the convention but the associated jurisprudence, including the importance that the European court in Strasbourg over the years has attached to freedom of expression.

Subsection (1) provides for the new clause to apply in any case where a court is considering grating relief – for example, an injunction restraining a threatened breach of confidence; but it could be any relief apart from that relating to criminal proceedings – which might affect the exercise of the article 10 right to freedom of expression. It applies to the press, broadcasters or anyone whose right to freedom of expression might be affected. It is not limited to cases to which a public authority is a party. We have taken the opportunity to enhance press freedom in a wider way than would arise simply from the incorporation of the convention into our domestic law.

Subsection (2) provides that no relief is to be granted if the person against whom it is sought – the respondent – is not present or represented, unless the applicant has taken all practicable steps to notify the respondent or there are compelling reasons why the respondent should not be notified. The courts are well able to deal with the first limb of that exception relating to whether all practical steps have been taken to notify the respondent, and in the case of broadcasting authorities and the press, rarely would an applicant not be able to serve notice of the proceedings on the respondent.

The latter circumstance – compelling reasons – might arise in a case raising issues of national security where the mere knowledge that an injunction was being sought might cause the respondent to publish the material immediately. We do not anticipate that the limb would be sued often. In the past, such applications have been rare, but there has been at least one recent case involving the Ministry of Defence.

As I made clear on Second Reading, the provision is intended overall to ensure that ex parte injunctions are granted only in exceptional circumstances. Even where both parties are represented, we expect that injunctions will continue to be rare, as they are at present.

Subsection (3) provides that no relief is to be granted to restrain publication pending a full trial of the issues unless the court is satisfied that the applicant is likely to succeed at trial. Among concerns expressed about the Bill's possible impact on freedom of the press, there was concern that interim injunctions ... might be granted simply to preserve the status quo, with a view to a full hearing of the application later. However, by that time the story that was to be published might no longer be newsworthy. As I said earlier, time and time again the convention jurisprudence reinforces the freedom of the press against, for example, the assertion of rights under article 8. One example of that is part of the judgment of the European Court of Human Rights in the 1991 'Spycatcher' case. Dealing with the issue of interlocutory relief, the court said:

'news is a perishable commodity and to delay its publication for even a short period may well deprive it of all its value and interest.'

Given that, we believe that the courts should consider the merits of an application when it is made and should not grant an interim injunction simply to preserve the status quo ant between the parties.

We believe that the new clause would protect a respondent potential publisher from what amounts to legal or legalised intimidation. We have already discussed the difficulty of getting interlocutory relief. It will be very difficult to get it unless the applicant can satisfy the court that the applicant is likely to establish that publication should not be allowed. That is a much higher test than that there should simply be a prima facie case to get the matter into court.

Subsection (4) requires the court to have particular regard to the importance of the article 10 right to freedom of expression. Where the proceedings concern journalistic, literary or artistic material, the court must also have particular regard to the extent to which the material has or is about to become available to the public – in other words, a question of prior publication – and the extent to which publication would be in the public interest. If the court and the parties to the proceedings know that a story will shortly be published anyway, for example, in another country of on the internet, that must affect the decision whether it is appropriate to restrain publication by the print or broadcast media in this country.

Under subsection (4), the court must also have particular regard to any relevant privacy code. Depending on the circumstances, that could be the newspaper industry code of practice operated by the Press Complaints Commission, the Broadcasting Standards Commission Code, the Independent Television Commission code, or a broadcaster's internal code such as that operated by the BBC. The fact that a newspaper has complied with the terms of the code operated by the PPC – or conversely, that it has breached the code – is one of the factors that we believe the courts should take into account in considering whether to grant relief.

Mr. Dominic Grieve: I am sorry to take the right hon. Gentleman back slightly, but would he care to amplify on the definition of 'the public interest', which is a critical phrase in subsection (4)(a)(ii) of the new clause?

Mr. Straw: I was hoping not to have my brain exercised in such a challenging way. The courts are well versed in making judgments about the balance between a private interest of an applicant before them and the wider public interest. That is inherent in any case in a clash between article 10 and article 8. It is also inherent in the way in which the courts until now have dealt with many issues surrounding proceedings for defamation. the European convention and the European Court of Human Rights have devoted quite a lot of time and effort to developing the concept of the public interest. Without being too tautologous, one of the points of the public interest is, to quote the words of the Strasbourg court in Handyside v. the United Kingdom in 1976, that

'freedom of expression constitutes one of the essential foundations of a democratic society, one of the basic conditions for its progress, and for the development of every man'—

and these days, I have no doubt, every woman. That is a brief sketch of a subject on which I have every confidence in the courts' ability to make good judgments in particular cases.

Subsection (5) provides that references to a court include references to a tribunal, and that references to relief include references to any remedy or order, other than in criminal proceedings. We drafted the amendment with civil, rather than criminal, proceedings against the media in mind. Without such an exclusion, judges wanting to impose reporting restrictions in criminal trial would, for example, have to consider any relevant privacy code, although plainly it would not be appropriate in that context.

Nevertheless, as public authorities, the criminal courts will of course, in the same way as other courts, be required not to act in a way that is incompatible with articles 8 and 10 and other convention rights. The special provision that we are making in new clause 13 does not therefore exempt criminal courts from the general obligations imposed by other provisions of the Bill. However, had we included criminal proceedings under new clause 13, we would have made the running of criminal trials very complicated.

HC Deb, 2 July 1998, cols 535–40

(III) Ministerial Statements

RB NOTE: *Since the judicial ruling in the case of Pepper v. Hart [1993] AC 593 (House of Lords), ministerial statements made during the course of parliamentary proceedings may now be relied upon as evidence of the meaning and application of statutory provisions in the event of uncertainty or dispute. Given the great importance of the Human Rights Act to the operation of the legal system therefore, especially concerning questions of judicial interpretation of all other legislation and the extent of liability for human rights violations across UK society, ministerial statements made during the parliamentary passage of the Human Rights Bill will remain a significant influence on the development of the new human rights jurisprudence in the UK for many years to come.*

The following document is an extract from an article prepared by Francesca Klug as a guide to these ministerial statements on the provisions of the Human Rights Act, and also explains the major amendments made to the original form of the Bill (for which see above Doc. 40B).

The British Model of Incorporation

The Lord Chancellor summed up what ministers refer to as 'the British model' of incorporation in the following terms:

The bill is based on a number of important principles. Legislation should be construed compatibly with the convention as far as possible. The sovereignty of Parliament should not be disturbed. Where the courts cannot reconcile legislation with convention rights, Parliament should be able to do so – and more quickly, if thought appropriate, than by enacting primary legislation. Public authorities should comply

with convention rights or face the prospect of legal challenge. Remedies should be available for a breach of convention rights by a public
authority. (HL Deb, 5 February 1998, col. 839)

In other words:

The design of the Bill is to give the courts as much space as possible to
protect human rights, short of a power to set aside or ignore Acts of
Parliament. (HL Deb, 3 November 1997 col. 1228)

During its passage through parliament this basic scheme remained largely
undisturbed except that the circumstances in which a 'fast track procedure'
can be used to amend statutes which the courts declare breach the HRA
have been narrowed. There were also significant amendments to insert new
clauses relating to freedom of expression and conscience, to clarify the
powers of specialist tribunals under the Act, and to introduce time limits
under which proceedings under the Act can be brought. In addition Protocol 6, which abolishes the death penalty in peace time, was inserted into
Schedule One of the Act (part III).

I shall now cover the main statements of clarification given to explain the
purpose of all the major clauses in turn and any significant amendments
made to the bill.

The Missing Convention Rights: Articles 1 and 13

There were a number of unsuccessful attempts by the opposition benches to
have the 'missing' ECHR Articles 1 and 13 – or a variation on them –
inserted into the Bill. Article 1 provides for the state to secure to everyone
within its jurisdiction the rights and freedoms in (Articles 2–18 of) the
ECHR. Article 13 provides that everyone whose Convention rights and
freedoms are violated shall have an effective remedy. The response by the
Government was that the HRA itself covers the terrain of these missing
Articles.

The Bill gives effect to Article 1 by securing to people in the United
Kingdom the rights and freedoms of the convention. It gives effect to
Article 13 by establishing a scheme under which convention rights can
be raised before our domestic courts. To that end, remedies are
provided in Clause 8. If the concern is to ensure that the bill provides
an exhaustive code of remedies for those whose convention rights
have been violated, we believe that Clause 8 already achieves that and
that nothing further is needed. (Lord Chancellor, HL Deb, 18 November 1997, col. 475)

Countering arguments that without Article 13 the HRA may not provide
the effective remedy required by the Strasbourg Convention, the Lord
Chancellor replied:

... to incorporate expressly Article 13 may lead to the courts fashion-
ing remedies about which we know nothing other than the Clause 8

remedies which we regard as sufficient and clear. Until we are told in some specific respect how Clause 8 is, or may reasonably be antici- pated to be, deficient we maintain our present position. (Lord Chancellor, HL Deb, 18 November 1997, col. 477)

In response to a question from Lord Lester about whether the courts should nevertheless be entitled to have regard to Article 13 and its caselaw where relevant, the Lord Chancellor replied in the affirmative:

... the courts may have regard to Article 13. In particular, they may wish to do so when considering the very ample provisions of Clause 8(1) (ibid).

He threw in for good measure: 'One always has in mind *Pepper v Hart* when one is asked questions of that kind' (ibid, col. 476).

Similarly in the Commons, the Home Secretary stated on this point that:

... any tribunal will consider the bare text of any original convention by considering the way in which its application has developed – there is indeed a requirement to do so – so, in practice, the courts must take account of the large body of convention jurisprudence when consider- ing remedies. Obviously, in doing so they are bound to take judicial notice of article 13, without specifically being bound by it. (HC Deb, 20 May 1998, col. 981)

SECTION 2: CONVENTION JURISPRUDENCE

The government refused to accept an amendment moved by the Con- servative opposition in the Lords to 'bind' the domestic courts to the jurisprudence of the European Court of Human Rights. Section 2(1) requires only that the courts 'must take into account any judgment, decision, declaration or advisory opinion' of any of the Strasbourg organs. Clarifying the intention behind this wording at committee stage, the Lord Chancellor explained:

We believe that Clause 2 gets it right in requiring domestic courts to take into account judgments of the European Court but not making them binding ... The Bill would of course permit United Kingdom courts to depart from existing Strasbourg decisions and upon occasion it might well be appropriate to do so and it is possible they might give a successful lead to Strasbourg. For example, it would permit the United Kingdom courts to depart from Strasbourg decisions where there has been no precise ruling on the matter and a commission opinion which does so has not taken into account subsequent Stras- bourg court case law ... where it is relevant we would of course expect our courts to apply convention jurisprudence and its principles to the cases before them. (HL Deb, 18 November 1997, cols 514, 515)

At report stage Lord Irvine clarified this point further:

... The courts will often be faced with cases that involve factors perhaps specific to the United Kingdom which distinguish them from cases considered by the European court ... it is important that our courts have the scope to apply that discretion so as to aid in the development of human rights law ... The United Kingdom is not, of course, bound in international law to follow the court's judgments in cases to which it has not been a party and it would be strange to require courts in the United Kingdom to be bound by such decisions. (HL Deb, 19 January 1998, cols 1270, 1271)

A further Conservative amendment to clause 2 at Committee stage in the Commons would have had the contrary effect to the Lord's amendment, widening the discretion of the courts. By rejecting both amendments the Government made it clear that whilst the courts must take into account ECHR jurisprudence, they are not bound by it. This leaves the way open for jurisprudence under other international human rights treaties (or from other jurisdictions with comparable human rights legislation) to be prayed in aid where appropriate, in particular in circumstances where there is little or no steer from the Strasbourg organs (see also Sections 11 below). Conservative MP, Edward Leigh, maintained – many would say fairly – that as a result of the flexibility given the judges under clause 2:

... we are in danger of not simply incorporating the convention in our law, but going much further. What we are creating is an entirely new Bill of Rights. (HC Deb, 3 June 1998, col. 398)

Geoffrey Hoon, Parliamentary Secretary at the Lord Chancellor's Department, explained that the reason for requiring the courts to 'take into account' the opinions and decisions of the European Commission on Human Rights, as well as the Court, is that:

... many cases are settled on the basis of an opinion of the commission and do not necessarily proceed to the Court ... the commission is responsible currently for decisions on the basic admissibility of complaints ... this is an important part of the body of Strasbourg decisions and one that ... it is right for our courts to take into account. (Ibid, col. 404)

In rejecting another Conservative amendment to require the courts to have full regard to the 'margin of appreciation' accorded to states by the Strasbourg institutions, the Home Secretary explained:

The doctrine of the margin of appreciation means allowing this country a margin of appreciation when it interprets our law and the actions of our Government in an international court ... Through incorporation we are giving a profound margin of appreciation to British courts to interpret the convention in accordance with British jurisprudence as well as European jurisprudence. (Ibid)

This appears to underline the point that the 'margin of appreciation' is a principle of international law, of no necessary relevance to the domestic courts (which, of course, are free to develop their own doctrine of 'due deference', if and when appropriate, in interpreting the HRA).

SECTIONS 3 AND 4: INTERPRETATION OF LEGISLATION AND DECLARATIONS OF INCOMPATIBILITY

The heart of the 'British model' of incorporation is sketched out in Sections 3 and 4 of the HRA. Parliamentary debate reflected the package qualities of these two clauses; you cannot understand one without the other (see also Section 10 below).

The Lord Chancellor explained their twin track purpose in the Report stage in the Lords:

> The Bill sets out a scheme for giving effect to the convention rights which maximises the protection to individuals while retaining the fundamental principle of parliamentary sovereignty. Clause 3 is the central part of the scheme. Clause 3(1) requires legislation to be read and given effect to so far as it is possible to do so in a way that is compatible with the convention rights. Clause 3(2) provides that where it is not possible to ... that does not affect its validity, continuing operation or enforcement. This ensures that the courts are not empowered to strike down Acts of parliament which they find to be incompatible with the convention rights. Instead clause 4 of the bill ... introduces a new mechanism through which the courts can signal to the Government that a provision of legislation is, in their view, incompatible. It is then for government and Parliament to consider what action should be taken. (HL Deb, 19 January 1998, col. 1294)

Clarifying how the two clauses are expected to interact, the Home Secretary explained:

> We expect that, in almost all cases, the courts will be able to interpret legislation compatibly with the convention. However, we need to provide for the rare cases where that cannot be done ... A declaration of incompatibility will not affect the continuing validity of the legislation in question. That would be contrary to the principle of the Bill. However it will be a clear signal to Government and Parliament that, in the court's view, a provision of legislation does not conform to the standards of the convention. ... it is likely that the Government and Parliament would wish to respond to such a situation and would do so rapidly. (HC Deb, 16 February 1998, col. 780)

Only the higher courts can issue a 'declaration of incompatibility'. Asked whether the lower courts would be bound to follow the 'declaration' Jack Straw explained:

> No, they would not. In a judicial and political sense, the status quo ante would apply. Then, obviously, the Government would have to consider, and in most cases they would consider the position pretty rapidly. (HC Deb, 21 October 1998, col. 1306)

In both the Lords and Commons, Conservative amendments were laid to replace the requirement on the courts under clause 3(1) to interpret legislation compatibly with Convention rights where 'possible', with the requirement that they only do so when 'reasonable'. These were strongly opposed by the government as was an amendment that such an interpretation should only apply where legislation is 'ambiguous'.

Rejecting one such amendment Straw suggested that:

> The likely result – and no doubt the intention – is that the courts would not go so far down the road of interpreting legislation as they would under the terms of clause 3 as it stands. ... If we had used just the word 'reasonable' we would have created a subjective test. 'Possible' is different. It means, 'What is the possible interpretation? Let us look at this set of words and the possible interpretations. (HC Deb, 3 June 1998, cols 421, 422)

Likewise in the committee stage in the Lords, the Lord Chancellor maintained:

> ... The word possible is the plainest means that we can devise for simply asking the courts to find the construction consistent with the intentions of parliament ... All I need say in resisting this amendment is that we want the courts to construe statutes so that they bear a meaning that is consistent with the convention whenever that is possible according to the language of the statutes but not when it is impossible to achieve that. (HL Deb, 18 November 1997, col. 535)

These statements provide a riposte to Dr Geoffrey Marshall's question as to whether Section 3 is intended to change the existing rules of interpretation or not (1998 *Public Law*, 167). If the government had merely intended to codify current practice then they could have accepted the Conservative amendments (see Klug and Starmer (1997) *Public Law*, p. 223). Urged by Labour MP Paul Stinchcombe, during committee stage, to comment on this debate amongst academics the Home Secretary replied:

> I back those who have read the plain words in this clause and take the view that it moves us on from the way in which the courts currently interpret convention legislation. (HC Deb, 3 June 1998, col. 423)

This point is given greater elaboration in the *White Paper* [*RB NOTE: See Doc. 40C*] which accompanied the bill and described the 'rule of construction' created by Section 3 as one which:

> goes far beyond the present rule which enables the courts to take the Convention into account in resolving any ambiguity in a legislative provision. The courts will be required to interpret legislation so as to uphold the Convention rights unless legislation itself is so clearly incompatible with the Convention that it is impossible to do so. This 'rule of construction' is to apply to past as well as to future legislation. To the extent that it affects the meaning of a legislative provision the courts will not be bound by previous interpretations. They will be able

to build a new body of case law, taking into account the Convention rights.

Lord Irvine was similarly robust in a lecture he gave for the human rights organisation *Justice* which Lord Lester put 'on the record' by quoting from it at length during the Report stage of the bill in the House of Lords. In the lecture, Irvine insisted that clause 3

> ... goes far beyond the present rule. It will not be necessary to find an ambiguity. On the contrary the courts will be required to interpret legislation so as to uphold the convention rights unless the legislation itself is so clearly incompatible with the convention that it is impossible to do so. (Lord Lester quoting from the *Tom Sargant Memorial Lecture*, HL Deb, 19 January 1998, col. 1291)

Irvine also insisted in the same lecture that precedents involving European Community law

> show that interpretative techniques may be used to make the domestic legislation comply with community law, even when this requires straining the meaning of words or reading in words which are not there. (Ibid, col. 1292)

Subordinate legislation

Speaking in the Committee stage, the Lord Chancellor elaborated on the distinction created by clause 3(2)(c) between secondary legislation where the parent Act prevents removal of any incompatibility between it and Convention rights – which cannot be struck down by the courts – and subordinate legislation which can be struck down:

> The position simply is that at present subordinate legislation may be struck down by the courts on the same grounds as in the case of other forms of administrative action ... subordinate legislation which is incompatible with the Convention rights will thus become susceptible to challenge on *vires* grounds in the ordinary way ... The power to make a declaration of incompatibility should be, and is, reserved for those cases where it is needed because the courts have no power to do anything else. The subordinate legislation is necessarily incompatible because the parent legislation causes it to be so. The rational outcome, therefore, is that both the parent and subordinate legislation are subject to a declaration of incompatibility. (HL Deb, 18 November 1997, cols 544, 545)

For the purposes of the HRA, Acts of the new Scottish Parliament and Northern Ireland Assembly are also defined as 'subordinate legislation' under clause 21 and hence can be overturned by the courts (except for Acts made under section 38(1)(a) of the Northern Ireland Constitution Act or the corresponding provision of the Northern Ireland Act 1998).

SECTION 6: PUBLIC AUTHORITIES

Introducing the bill in the Commons the Home Secretary explained:

> Clause 6 makes it unlawful for public authorities to act in a way that is incompatible with a Convention right, unless they are required to do so to give effect to primary legislation. (HC Deb, 16 February 1998, col. 780)

The issue of which bodies should be liable for upholding Convention rights probably caused more controversy than any other, both in and out of parliament. An array of lobbies expressed support for the Human Rights Act provided it did not apply to them. The press and the church were the most vociferous of these, as a result of which the Government introduced amendments in the Commons to address their concerns, discussed below (Sections 12 and 13). There was even a failed attempt to exempt the army, to which the Lord Chancellor responded, that 'if they are not' an obvious public authority 'it is difficult to say who is' (HL Deb, 5 February 1998, col. 767). A number of other Conservative amendments aimed at narrowing the scope of bodies bound by the Act, for example by listing them or curtailing them to strict emanations of government, also failed.

The Home Secretary gave a lengthy explanation as to why the Government chose a functional approach to defining which authorities are liable under the Act rather than to list specific bodies:

> When we were drawing up the Bill, we noted that the convention had its origins in a desire to protect the individual against the abuse of power by the state, rather than to protect one individual against the actions of another ... we wanted a realistic and modern definition of the state so as to provide a correspondingly wide protection against abuse of human rights. Accordingly, liability under the Bill would go beyond the narrow category of central and local government and the police – the organisations that represent a minimalist view of what constitutes the state. The principle of bringing rights home suggested that liability in domestic proceedings should like with bodies in respect of whose actions the United Kingdom Government were answerable in Strasbourg ... As a minimum, we must accept what Strasbourg has developed and is developing ... We wanted to ensure that, when courts were already saying that a body's activities in a particular respect were a public function for the purposes of judicial review, other things being equal, that would be a basis for action under the Bill. (HC Deb, 17 June 1998, cols 406, 408)

He went on:

> ... we could not directly replicate in the Bill the definition of public authorities used by Strasbourg because, of course, the respondent to any application in the Strasbourg Court is the United Kingdom, as the state. We have therefore tried to do the best we can in terms of replication by taking into account whether a body is sufficiently public to engage the responsibility of the state ... As we are dealing with

public functions and with an evolving situation, we believe that the test must relate to the substance and nature of the act, not to the form and legal personality. (Ibid, col. 433)

The Home Secretary sought to explain the categories included in Section 6(3):

We decided that the best approach would be reference to the concept of a public function ... clause 6 accordingly provides that a public authority includes a court or tribunal and 'any person certain of whose functions are functions of a public nature'. The effect of that is to create three categories, the first of which contains organisations which might be termed 'obvious' public authorities, all of whose functions are public. The clearest examples are Government Departments, local authorities and the police ... The second category contains organisations with a mix of public and private function. One of the things with which we had to wrestle was the fact that many bodies, especially over the past 20 years, have performed public functions which are private, partly as a result of privatisation and partly as a result of contracting out ... The courts will consider the nature of a body and the activity in question. (Ibid, cols 409, 410)

Examples of these mixed or hybrid bodies quoted by Straw included railtrack monitoring the safety of train operating companies, water companies, private security firms which run prisons, the Takeover Panel, the BBC and, contrary to an earlier view expressed by the Lord Chancellor and subsequently corrected by him in the Lords, the Press Complaints Commission (PCC), but not the press (see below).

It will ultimately be a matter for the courts, but our considered view is that the Press Complaints Commission undertakes public functions but the press does not. (Ibid, col. 414)

Straw's third category covers 'organisations with no public functions – accordingly, they fall outside the scope of clause 6' (ibid, col. 410).

Under Section 6(5) the private acts of hybrid bodies are exempt from liability under the Act. Illustrations by the Lord Chancellor of what is intended by this Section included acts carried out by Railtrack as a private property developer and the guarding of commercial premises by a security firm (HL Deb, 24 November 1997, cols 796, 811) [*RB NOTE: See further above at pages 387–8*]. However there are no such exemptions for the first category of 'obvious' public authorities:

Clause 6 accordingly distinguishes between obvious public authorities, all of whose acts are subject to clause 6, and bodies with mixed functions which are caught in relation to their public acts but not their private acts. (Ibid, col. 811)

Lord Williams confirmed that the term 'a person' in Section 6(5) covers natural or legal persons both of which are liable under the Act:

... the term is well known as a term of art in our law. It is defined in the

Interpretation Act 1978 and is relied upon throughout the statute book as including any person or body of persons corporate or unincorporate. (Ibid, col. 803)

The 'horizontal effect' of the Act

A further sector explicitly included under the definition of public authority in clause 6(3) is courts and tribunals. Indeed Lord Williams affirmed that they are:

> ... in a very similar position to obvious public authorities, such as government departments, in that all their acts are to be treated as being of such a public nature as to engage the convention. (Ibid, col. 759)

The Lord Chancellor discussed the implications of this, in particular for the 'horizontal effect' of the Act, or in other words for the degree to which it is intended that the Act operates between private parties. In rejecting an amendment by Lord Wakeham, Chair of the PCC, to exempt courts and tribunals from the scope of clause 6(1) where proceedings only include private parties, Lord Irvine said:

> We also believe that it is right as a matter of principle for the courts to have the duty of acting compatibly with the convention not only in cases involving other public authorities but also in developing the common law in deciding cases between individuals. Why should they not? In preparing this Bill, we have taken the view that it is the other course, that of excluding convention considerations altogether from cases between individuals which would have to be justified ... the courts already bring convention considerations to bear and I have no doubt that they will continue to do so in developing the common law ... Clause 3 requires the courts to interpret legislation compatibly with the convention rights and to the fullest extent possible in all cases coming before them. (HL Deb, 24 November 1997, col. 783)

How will this be done? In Lord Irvine's view, the debate over whether the HRA gives the green light to the courts to develop the law of privacy provides an illustration:

> ... the courts will be able to adapt and develop the common law by relying on existing domestic principles in the laws of trespass, nuisance, copyright, confidence and the like, to fashion a common law right to privacy. (Ibid, col. 785)

However he drew a distinction between the courts developing the common law and becoming legislators:

> The scheme of the Bill is that Parliament may act to remedy a failure where the judges cannot. In my opinion, the court is not obliged to remedy the failure by legislating via the common law either where a convention right is infringed by incompatible legislation or where,

because of the absence of legislation – say privacy legislation – a convention right is left unprotected. In my view, the courts may not act as legislators and grant new remedies for infringement of convention rights unless the common law itself enables them to develop new rights or remedies. (Ibid)

Absence of legislation

In response to an amendment from the Liberal Democrat peer, Lord Meston, to omit from Section 6(6) of the Bill the failure of Parliament to legislate as a protected act, the Lord Chancellor insisted that this sub-Section must be understood purely as a safeguard of parliamentary sovereignty. He denied that it would leave potential applicants without an adequate remedy. Lord Irvine suggested that where a violation of a Convention right occurs because of an absence of legislation, the appropriate procedure should be as follows:

> If a person believes that his convention rights have been violated as a result of action by a public authority which is not governed by legislation the right course is for him to bring legal proceedings against the authority under Clause 7 of the Bill ... The fact that there is no specific legislation for the court to declare incompatible with the convention does not affect the ability of the person concerned to obtain a remedy. The absence of legislation entails that there is no legislative warrant for acts in breach of the convention by the public authority. The Minister, however ... is protected by Clause 6(6) from any claim that he is in breach by failing to bring forward legislation. That is part of the scheme of the Bill to underpin parliamentary sovereignty. (Ibid, col. 814)

What remains insufficiently clear, however, is whom a case could proceed against in the absence of legislation (or a well-established tort) when a potential breach has been committed by a private party, for example by an employer who taps employees' telephones? Under the developing Strasbourg jurisprudence, the European Court of Human Rights has established that states have 'positive obligations' to protect rights in certain circumstances even between two private parties (*X & Y v the Netherlands*, A 91, para 23 (1985); *Platform 'Arzte fur das leben v Austria'*, A 139, para 32 (1988)). In the above scenario it would clearly be open to employees to take the government to the European Court of Human Rights for failing to protect their right of privacy, but it remains to be seen whether domestic courts, as public authorities, will feel obliged to develop the common law to uphold similar 'positive obligations' under the Act. It is entirely consistent with the purpose of the Act to 'bring rights home' that they should.

Section 7: Standing and Access to Justice

Who should be entitled to take cases under the Human Rights Act, to which courts, and under what circumstances was a cause of considerable lobbying by civil rights groups and lawyers. Section 7 establishes a new cause of action for people who believe their Convention rights have been infringed:

> Under Clause 7 they will be able to rely on convention points in any legal proceedings involving a public authority; for example as part of a defence to seeking judicial review, or on appeal. They will also be able to bring proceedings against public authorities purely on convention grounds even if no other causes of action is open to them. (Lord Chancellor, HL Deb, 3 November 1997, col. 1232)

An issue of dispute centred around who has standing under the Act. The Government rejected amendments supported by both major opposition parties to allow the courts to apply the same test of 'sufficient interest' as they apply in judicial review cases, allowing interest groups to take cases on occasion. The Lord Chancellor explained:

> The purpose of the Bill is to give greater effect in our domestic law to the convention rights. It is in keeping with this approach that persons should be able to rely on the convention rights before our domestic courts in precisely the same circumstances as they can rely upon them before the Strasbourg institutions. The wording of Clause 7 therefore reflects the terms of the convention, which stipulates that petitions ... will be ruled inadmissible unless the applicant is the victim of the alleged violation. I acknowledge that a consequence of that approach is that a narrower test will be applied for bringing applications by judicial review on convention grounds than will continue to apply in applications for judicial review on other grounds. But interest groups will still be able to provide assistance to victims who bring cases under the Bill and to bring cases directly where they themselves are victims of an unlawful act. (HL Deb, 24 November 1997, cols 830, 831)

As for the issue of whether the courts in this country would accept third party interventions as they do at Strasbourg:

> The European Court of Human Rights rules of procedure allow non-parties such as national and international non-governmental organisations to make written submissions in the form of a brief. There is no reason why any change to primary legislation in this Bill is needed to allow the domestic courts to develop a similar practice in human rights cases ... So it appears to me ... our courts will be ready to permit amicus written briefs from non-governmental organisations; that is to say briefs, but not to treat them as full parties. (Ibid, col. 833)

In the Commons Mike O'Brien, under-secretary of state at the Home Office, stressed the flexibility the Strasbourg organs have shown in applying the 'victim test':

> The intention is that a victim under the Bill should be in the same position as a victim in Strasbourg. A local authority cannot be a victim under clause 7 because it cannot be a victim in Strasbourg ... In some

cases they have interpreted fairly flexibly the requirement for the applicant to be directly affected, although the jurisprudence on the issue is not always entirely consistent ... For example, children attending a school where corporal punishment was practised have been treated by the Commission as having a direct and immediate personal interest in complaining about such a punishment, even though they had not been punished. That was in the case of Campbell and Cousans v UK in 1982 ... Applications have been allowed not only by the persons immediately affected – sometimes referred to as the direct victim – but by indirect victims ... a case can be brought on behalf of a dead victim by his or her family or relatives. The best known case ... is the 'Death on the Rock' case brought on behalf of a dead IRA terrorist shot in Gibraltar. That is the sort of area that we are considering. A person may be able to claim that he or she is directly affected as a consequence of a violation of the rights of someone else. Where complaints are brought by persons threatened by deportation, that may arise. (HC Deb, 24 June 1998, cols 1084, 1085, 1086)

Access to justice and a Human Rights Commission

Turning to access to the courts for 'victims', concern was expressed by civil rights groups and some notable Liberal Democrat and Labour backbenchers that the proposed changes to legal aid, combined with the absence of a Human Rights Commission or Commissioner in the Bill, would seriously blunt its effectiveness. The Lord Chancellor replied:

> As to the questions raised about giving access to the courts ... I am giving serious consideration to Sir Peter Middleton's proposal that there should be a separate fund for public interest cases, including those involving rights under this Bill. (HL Deb, 5 February 1998, col. 810)

Rejecting amendments at Committee stage to establish a Human Rights Commission, Mike O'Brien repeated what has become the standard Government response on this issue:

> The Government do not have a closed mind on a commission – we have made our position clear. Different interest groups – the Commission for Racial Equality, the Equal Opportunities Commission and so on – have different views on whether a human rights commission would be a good thing, so the best that we can do at the moment is to ensure that the convention is accepted as part of our law. After that, the need for a human rights commission may be the subject of a future debate – we shall have to see how that develops. (HC Deb, 24 June 1998, col. 1087)

At the same time the Government resisted Conservative amendments to restrict the scope of the bill by omitting tribunals from Section 7 as a forum where Convention rights can be upheld. O'Brien explained:

> ... one of the key principles is that all courts and tribunals should take

account of convention rights whenever they are relevant to the case before them … We shall ensure that individuals can rely on their convention rights and have access to them at the earliest opportunity. We shall also make the convention rights an integral part of our legal system … In bringing rights home we want everyone in Britain to view the basic principles set out in the convention as part of their national heritage … Furthermore in a significant proportion of such cases a tribunal, not a court, will be the forum in which a case is brought. Social security, employment, housing and immigration are but a few of the many areas where tribunals handle the bulk of cases. (Ibid, 1055, 1056)

As an illustration of this commitment, the government amended Clause 7 at the Report stage in the House of Lords to enable Ministers to make an order to confer jurisdiction on tribunals to determine Convention issues and grant the appropriate remedy where necessary. This was to address a particular concern that the 1993 Asylum and Immigration Appeals Act restricts the jurisdiction of the adjudicator to considering claims under the 1951 Convention on Refugees (HL Deb, 19 January 1998, col. 1361). Clause 7 was further amended by the Government in Committee in the Commons (to become new Clause 7(11)) to avoid any doubt that the power to make such an order applies 'only where it is necessary' (HC Deb, 24 June 1998, col. 1110) to ensure that a tribunal can provide an appropriate remedy in the face of a breach of a Convention right. O'Brien emphasised that under their current powers:

The great majority of tribunals would not be debarred from having regard to the convention rights. It is an important principle of the Bill that they should do so. (Ibid)

Time limits

Attracting criticism from some civil rights campaigners and Lord Lester, a further new clause (7(5)) was inserted by the Government at Committee stage in the House of Commons to introduce time limits during which a case can be brought under the Bill. These apply only to cases brought specifically to challenge an alleged breach of Convention rights (under Section 7(1)(a)); proceedings brought under an existing cause of action which also rely on Convention rights as an additional argument in a case (Section 7(1)(b)) would operate under any existing limitation periods that apply to the case in question. Mike O'Brien explained:

The Government amendment provides that proceedings under clause 7(1)(a) must be brought within one year, beginning with the date on which the act complained of took place, or within such longer period as the court or tribunal considers equitable, having regard to all the circumstances. However that time limit is subject to any stricter time limit in relation to the procedure in question. The most obvious such case is judicial review … it is reasonable that the time limit for that procedure – which is three months – should continue to apply …

clause 7(1)(a) creates a cause of action, and the Bill would be open to criticism if it did not clearly state what limitation period was to apply to proceedings under that paragraph ... We recognise, however, that there may be circumstances where a rigid one-year cut off could lead to injustice. Our amendment does not therefore seek to provide a rigid limit, but enable a court to extend the period where it is appropriate to do so. (Ibid, cols 1094, 1096)

Rejecting a Conservative amendment to reduce time limits further, O'Brien continued:

It is not our intention to create a vast array of novel features that would allow litigants to pursue cases in courts in a way that the courts and Parliament had not intended. However someone with a genuine human rights grievance will be entitled to pursue it under clause 7(1)(a), whether or not he is within the time limit for judicial review. ... We do not want to create an artificial time limit of three months, as the Opposition seek to do ... without giving the level of flexibility that is needed ... The courts will develop their own jurisprudence on this issue ... the courts will take note of what Parliament has said and will be able to consider the points I have made ... (Ibid, col. 1099)

SECTIONS 8 AND 9: JUDICIAL ACTS AND REMEDIES

Section 8(1) allows a court or tribunal to grant 'whatever remedy is available to it and which seems just and appropriate' (HL Deb, 3 November 1997, col. 1232) where it finds that a public authority has acted incompatibly with a Convention right. According to the Lord Chancellor this might include awarding damages against a public authority, in which case the courts: 'should have regard' to the principles applied by the European Court of Human Rights.

Our aim is that people should receive damages equivalent to what they would have obtained had they taken their case to Strasbourg. (Ibid)

Emphasising the similarity between clause 8 of the HRB and Article 13 of the ECHR (see above), Lord Irvine declared:

... I cannot conceive of any state of affairs in which an English court, having held an Act to be unlawful because of its infringement of a Convention right, would under clause 8(1) be disabled from giving an effective remedy. (HL Deb, 18 November 1997, col. 479)

Under Section 8(2) a criminal court will not be able to award damages for a Convention breach unless it also has the power to award damages in civil proceedings. Lord Irvine explained:

... it is not the Bill's aim that, for example, the Crown court should be able to make awards of damages where it finds, during the course of a trial, that a violation of a person's convention rights has occurred. We believe that it is appropriate for an individual who considers that this rights have been infringed in such a case to pursue any matter of damages through the civil courts where this type of issue is normally dealt with. (HL Deb, 24 November 1997, col. 855)

The purpose of Section 9 is to 'preserve the existing principle of judicial immunity' so that proceedings against a court or tribunal on convention grounds may be brought only by an appeal or application for judicial review' (Lord Chancellor, HL Deb, 3 November 1997, col. 1232). However, after prompting from Lord Meston, the Government introduced an amendment to clause 9 in the report stage at the Lords to bring it into line with Article 5(5) of the ECHR which it was in danger of breaching. (Under this Article – the right to liberty and security – everyone who has been the victim of an arrest or detention in contravention with the provisions of that Article has an enforceable right to compensation. This is non reflected in Section 9(3) of the HRA.)

SECTION 10: FAST TRACK PROCEDURES TO AMEND LEGISLATION

The Home Secretary, on being quizzed by Sir Nicholas Lyell for the Conservative Opposition, on the likely reaction of governments once the courts have made a 'declaration of incompatibility' under Section 4, suggested two main possible responses:

> In the overwhelming majority of cases, regardless of which party was in government, I think that Ministers would examine the matter and say: 'A declaration of incompatibility has been made, and we shall have to accept it.' We shall therefore have to remedy the defects in the law spotted by the Judicial Committee of the House of Lords. Therefore ... we have included in the Bill procedures for remedial orders. (HC Deb, 21 October 1998, col. 1301)

On the other hand, Jack Straw continued, if the Judicial Committee reached the view that the abortion laws are incompatible with the Convention, for example, this could be a 'declaration of incompatibility' which:

> Ministers propose and Parliament accepts should not be accepted ... we could say we were very sorry but we disagreed ... Then, the party to the proceedings ... [could] exercise her right of appeal and go to Strasbourg. Meanwhile, we could continue to apply the existing law unless and until there was an adverse judgement in Strasbourg. (Ibid, cols 1301, 1303)

Remedial orders

The Lord Chancellor explained the function of remedial orders during the second reading in the Lords:

> A Minister of the Crown will be able to make what is to be known as a remedial order. The order will be available in response to a declaration of incompatibility by the higher courts. It will also be available if

legislation appears to a Minister to be incompatible because of a finding by the European Court of Human Rights ... the power ... may be used only to remove an incompatibility or a possible incompatibility between legislation and the convention. It may therefore be used only to protect human rights, not to infringe them. And the Bill also specifically provides that no person is to be guilty of a criminal offence solely as a result of any retrospective effect of a remedial order. (HL Deb, 3 November 1997, col. 1231)

In response to concerns from all sides that this so-called 'Henry VIIIth power' could be used for other purposes the Lord Chancellor reiterated that:

A remedial order would not be used, and in our view could not be used, for any other purpose ... [than] to remove incompatible provisions of legislation in an effective and tidy way. (HL Deb, 29 January 1998, col. 401)

Rejecting a Liberal Democrat amendment requiring Ministers to respond to a declaration of incompatibility 'within a reasonable time' Lord Williams replied:

If the Minister is dilatory he can be asked questions either by a Member of Parliament on behalf of an aggrieved victim or potential victim, or by Questions for Written Answer in either House ... One does not need to legislate for every conceivable circumstance. We believe that the legitimate pressure outside Parliament and the focused pressures within both Houses of Parliament are sufficient to direct the Minister's attention to the question if he needs any direction. (HL Deb, 27 November 1997, col. 1106)

Refusing to support a series of amendments which would have allowed an appropriate remedy to be granted to the applicant in relation to whose case a declaration of incompatibility was made, or to other affected persons, the Lord Chancellor declared:

We think it more appropriate for decisions on what remedy should be given to individuals affected by a particular act to be taken by the Government in light of the individual circumstances of every case ... should it be thought necessary for a remedial order affecting the legislation to take effect from a date earlier than that on which the order was made, this will be possible under the Bill ... this will not of itself provide a direct remedy to individuals affected by the legislation which has been retrospectively amended; but, following the order, it may be open to them to seek such a remedy. In addition to these powers in the Bill, there are prerogative powers which can be exercised and other *ex gratia* actions that could be taken to grant remedies in appropriate circumstances. (Ibid, col. 1108)

An amendment to Section 10(1) was agreed at report stage in the Lords to clarify that it is only after the appeal process is exhausted in a given case that a remedial order can be made in response to a declaration of incompatibility (HL Deb, 29 January 1998, col. 393). Further amendments were also agreed to respond to strong and repeated concerns by the opposition about the relative lack of parliamentary scrutiny inherent in remedial orders. The period for consultation on the contents of a non-urgent remedial order is now 120 days in total where representations are received; in the case of urgent orders which are made prior to consultation the period for consultation was extended from 40 to 60 days after the order is made, after which the order would fall if not approved (HL Deb, 29 October 1998, col. 2105).

A requirement that Ministers can only proceed to amend (primary or secondary) legislation through remedial orders where there are 'compelling reasons' to do so, was introduced by the Government as was a new schedule 2 which sets out the amended procedures for laying a remedial order. Mike O'Brien explained:

> The requirement for compelling reasons in clause 10(2) is itself a response to concern expressed ... about the remedial order provisions. It is there to make it absolutely clear that a remedial order is not a routine response in preference to fresh primary legislation ... 'Compelling' is a strong word. We see no need to define it by reference to particular categories ... [under] schedule 2 ... a document must be laid before Parliament containing certain information ... the document is bound to explain why the Government believe that there are compelling reasons for making a remedial order and what those are. (HC Deb, 21 October 1998, cols 1330, 1331)

O'Brien concluded:

> ... where a declaration is made, a Government who are committed to promoting human rights, as we are, will want to do something about the law in question. It is possible for primary legislation to be introduced and passed quickly, but the pressures on the timetable can make it very difficult to find a slot ... Our proposals safeguard parliamentary procedures and sovereignty, ensure proper supervision of our laws and ensure that we can begin to get the ability both to enforce human rights law and to create a human rights culture. They also ensure that we can do it in the context of not having to worry that if something is decided by the Strasbourg court or by our courts that creates an incompatibility, we do not have a mechanism to deal with it in the quick and efficient way that may be necessary. (Ibid)

SECTION 11–13: ADDITIONAL RIGHTS

The purpose of Section 11 is, in the words of the Lord Chancellor, to clarify that

> ... convention rights are, as it were, a floor of rights; and if there are different or superior rights or freedoms conferred ... by or under any law having effect in the United Kingdom, this is a Bill which only gives and does not take away. (HL Deb, 18 November 1997, col. 510)

A government amendment was introduced to clarify this point which was not immediately clear from the wording of the original clause. As such, Section 11 appears to cover similar grounds to Article 53 of the ECHR (which states 'Nothing in this Convention shall be construed as limiting or derogating from any of the human rights and fundamental freedoms which may be ensured under the laws of any High Contracting Party or under any other agreement to which it is a Party') and gives further weight to the case that the Act allows other human rights jurisprudence in addition to Strasbourg's to be 'taken into account' by the courts where appropriate (see Section 2 above).

Sections 12 and 13, however, were entirely new, added at the Committee stage in the House of Commons after a protracted, and at times heated, debate over the implications of the bill for the media and for religious bodies.

The press and free expression

New Section 12 was widely reported as a 'deal' brokered between Jack Straw and Lord Wakeham, chair of the PCC, with the aim of keeping the basic scheme of the HRB intact whilst drawing the attention of the courts to the weight given to free expression by the Strasbourg organs. Straw explained:

> We recognise the concerns expressed in the press ... we are anxious, so far as is consistent with the framework of the Bill and, above all, with our obligations under the convention, to deal constructively with the concerns expressed about the Bill. (HC Deb, 2 July 1998, col. 535)

Straw then proceeded to clarify the intention of each subsection to clause 12:

> Subsection (1) provides for the new clause to apply in any case where a court is considering granting relief ... apart from that relating to criminal proceedings ... which might affect the exercise of the article 10 right to freedom of expression. It applies to the press, broadcasters or anyone whose right to freedom of expression might be affected. It is not limited to cases to which a public authority is party ... Subsection (2) ... is intended overall to ensure that ex parte injunctions are granted only in exceptional circumstances ... Subsection (3) provides that no relief is to be granted to restrain publication pending a full trial of the issues unless the court is satisfied that the applicant is likely to succeed at trial ... we believe that the courts should consider the merits of an application when it is made and should not grant an interim injunction simply to preserve the status quo ante between the parties ... Subsection (4) requires the court to have particular regard to the importance of the article 10 right to freedom of expression ... if the court ... know that a story will shortly be published anyway ... that must affect the decision whether it is appropriate to restrain publication by the print or broadcast media in this country ... the court must

also have particular regard to any relevant privacy code ... that could be the newspaper industry code of practice operated by the Press Complaints Commission, the Broadcasting Standards Commission code, the Independent Television Commission code, or a broadcaster's internal code such as that operated by the BBC. The fact that a newspaper has complied with the terms of the code ... is one of the factors we believe the courts should take into account in considering whether to grant relief. (Ibid, cols 538, 539) [*RB NOTE: This important passage is set out at greater length at pages 414–15 above.*]

As to why subsection (4), in addition to protecting journalistic, literary or artistic material, includes 'conduct connected with such material', Straw explained:

The reference ... is intended for cases where journalistic inquiries suggest the presence of a story, but no actual material yet exists – perhaps because the story has not yet been written. (Ibid, col. 540)

Turning to the definition of 'public interest' in subsection (4) (ii), which is a further factor listed for the courts to consider in such cases, Straw continued:

The European convention and the Court of Human Rights have devoted quite a lot of time and effort to developing the concept of the public interest ... There is no direct qualification to the word 'public' in the new clause. Ultimately, it would be a matter for the courts to decide, based on common sense and proportionality. (Ibid, cols 539, 540)

Clarifying the issue further Mike O'Brien stated in winding up the debate:

... the basic question is whether the public should have particular information. For example, information might have an effect on proper political discourse, or a matter of public policy. It might also affect individual behaviour. For example, information about BSE might have affected decisions on whether to eat beef. Those are areas in which there is a proper public interest in the press revealing information. (Ibid, col. 562)

As to why Section 12 protects civil, and not criminal, proceedings:

Without such an exclusion, judges wanting to impose reporting restrictions in a criminal trial would, for example, have to consider any relevant privacy code, although plainly it would not be appropriate in that context. ... had we included criminal proceedings under the new clause 13, we would have made the running of criminal trials very complicated. (Jack Straw, ibid, col. 540)

The additional safeguards in the new clause, which are not mirrored in Article 10 of the ECHR indicate, as the Home Secretary acknowledged, that:

We have taken the opportunity to enhance press freedom in a wider way than would arise simply from the incorporation of the convention into our domestic law. (Ibid, col. 536)

At the same time the Home Secretary was at pains to emphasise that:

> In practice, the European convention on human rights has been used in Strasbourg to uphold press freedom against efforts by the state to restrict it ... time and again the convention jurisprudence reinforces the freedom of the press against, for example, the assertion of rights under article 8. (Ibid, cols 535, 536)

Rejecting an amendment which would have given precedence to Article 10 over Article 8 rights (to privacy) Jack Straw asserted that:

> The difficulty with that [amendment] is that it goes further than the terms of the convention and Strasbourg case law ... So far as we are able, in a manner consistent with the convention and its jurisprudence, we are saying to the courts that whenever there is a clash between article 8 rights and article 10 rights, they must pay particular attention to the article 10 rights. I think that that is as far as we could go ... (Ibid, cols 542, 543)

Recommending the new clause to the Lords, Lord Williams affirmed that it:

> ... relates to questions of protection of free speech and free opinion as well as maintaining a proper balance for those whose personal interests in their reputation and private life need to be properly safeguarded. (HL Deb, 29 October 1998, col. 2113)

The Church and religious freedom

New Section 13 was drafted in response to concerns that the HRA would interfere with religious practices in a number of ways. Examples cited included forcing priests to marry divorced or homosexual couples or compelling church schools and religious charities to employ or retain staff who do not share their religious beliefs or practices. A number of amendments were passed in the House of Lords reflecting the concerns of some denominations of the Christian church and their supporters (representatives of minority faiths seemed far less vexed over this issue). After meetings between the Home Secretary and leaders of the Church the Government successfully overturned most of these amendments and introduced new clause 9 (which became new Section 13) in the committee stage in the Commons. The Home Secretary explained that it would come into play:

> ... in any case in which a court's determination of any question arising out of the Bill might affect the exercise by a religious organisation of the convention right of freedom of thought, conscience and religion. In such a case it provides for the court to have particular regard – not just to have regard ... but to have particular regard – to the importance of that right. Its purpose is not to exempt Churches and other

religious organisations from the scope of the Bill ... It is to reassure them against the Bill being used to intrude upon genuinely religious beliefs or practices based on their beliefs. I emphasis the word 'practices' as well as beliefs. There is ample reassurance available on this point from convention jurisprudence ... new clause 9 is designed to bring out the point that article 9 rights attach not only to individuals but to the Churches ... There is Convention jurisprudence to the effect that a Church body or other association with religious objectives is capable of possessing and exercising the rights in Article 9 as a representative of its members. The new clause will emphasise that point to our courts. (HC Deb, 20 May 1998, cols 1020, 1021)

As with the press amendment, Straw went on to stress that the new clause did not seek to breach the balance between rights reflected in the Convention and its jurisprudence:

The Government's new clause will not provide absolute protection for churches or other religious organisations as against any claim that might possibly be made against them ... We could not possibly do that without violating the convention ... but the new clause will send a clear signal to the courts that they must pay due regard to the rights guaranteed by Article 9, including, where relevant, the right of a Church to act in accordance with religious belief. (Ibid, col. 1022)

Rejecting a Conservative amendment that would effectively have given absolute priority to Article 9, the Home Secretary insisted that this:

... would be contrary to the convention ... the right to freedom of thought, conscience and religion guaranteed by article 9.1 is not absolute ... The court must weigh the competing interests and come to a decision. It is not open to a court to give automatic priority in all cases to one convention right over another. (HC Deb, 21 October 1998, Cols 1340, 1341)

As for what is meant by 'religious organisation' in new Section 13, Straw replied:

The answer is partly that no definition is readily available, at home or in Strasbourg ... but we are confident that the term 'religious organisation' is recognisable in terms of the convention ... The key concept that we are talking about is organisations with religious objectives ... it is flexible enough to cover cases involving religious charities where Church issues form a backdrop to the case. (HC Deb, 20 May 1998, col. 1021)

Turning to when religious organisations are likely to be judged liable for upholding Convention rights under Section 6 as public bodies, Straw explained:

We do not believe that, for example, the Church of England, the Church of Scotland or the Roman Catholic Church, as bodies, would be public authorities under the Bill ... On the occasions when Churches stand in place of the state, convention rights are relevant to what they do. The two most obvious examples relate to marriages and to the provision of education in Church schools ... We think it right in principle ... that people should be able to raise convention points in respect of the actions of the Churches in those areas on the same basis as they will be able to in respect of the actions of other public authorities, however rarely such occasions may arise. (Ibid, col. 1015)

One Lords amendment relating to the church which was not overturned in the Commons was a government amendment to ensure that Measures of the Church Assembly and the General Synod could not, if declared incompatible by the courts, be amended under the remedial order procedures (Section 10(6)). A Conservative amendment which would have removed such Measures from the definition of primary legislation in Section 21 altogether, was rejected by the government (Ibid, col. 1027).

Section 19: Ministerial Statements of Compatibility

The introduction of statements of compatibility with the Human Rights Act on the face of all new bills is one of the novel features of the Act. The Lord Chancellor clarified the purpose of this measure, which is now in force, when introducing the HRB in the House of Lords:

Clause 19 imposes a new requirement on government Ministers when introducing legislation. In future, they will have to make a statement either that the provisions of the legislation are compatible with the convention or that they cannot make such a statement but nevertheless wish Parliament to proceed to consider the Bill. Ministers will obviously want to make a positive statement whenever possible. That requirement should therefore have a significant impact on the scrutiny of draft legislation within government. Where such a statement cannot be made, parliamentary scrutiny of the Bill would be intense. (HL Deb, 3 November 1997, col. 1233)

Underlining the significance of this clause at committee stage, Lord Irvine claimed that:

... Clause 19 is a demonstration of the Government's commitment to human rights ... [it] is a very large gesture, as well as being a point of substance, in favour of the development of a culture of awareness of what the convention requires in relation to domestic legislation. (HL Deb, 27 November 1997, col. 1163)

Rejecting an amendment from the Liberal Democrat peer, Baroness Williams, which would have required ministers to give reasons for their statement of compatibility, the Lord Chancellor suggested that normal parliamentary debate should achieve her desired aims:

Of course Parliament will wish to know the reasons why the Government have taken whatever view they have taken ... But the reasoning behind a statement of compatibility or the inability to make such a statement will inevitably be discussed by Parliament during the passage of the Bill. (Ibid, col. 1163)

Opposing a similar amendment in the Commons Mike O'Brien suggested:

What might be of assistance would be any report made on the Bill, for example, by a human rights committee of the House ... In due course that might certainly be a way of informing the debate, whether in Committee or elsewhere, and looking into the detail of why such a statement was made by the Government. (HC Deb, 21 October 1998, col. 1349)

Although not discussed by ministers during the passage of the bill, the interaction between Section 3 (the interpretative clause) and Section 19 was clarified by Lord Irvine in the *Tom Sargant Memorial Lecture* (see above) quoted by Lord Lester in the report stage of the bill:

Ministerial statements of compatibility will inevitably be a strong spur to the courts to find means of construing statues compatibly with the convention. (HL Deb, 19 January 1997, col. 1291)

PROTOCOL 6: ABOLITION OF THE DEATH PENALTY

Perhaps the most surprising successful amendment to the Bill was that tabled by Labour backbencher Kevin McNamara in the Committee stage in the Commons to insert articles 1 and 2 of protocol 6 of the ECHR which abolishes the death penalty in peacetime. In an extraordinary reversal of usual procedure, it was the legislature which effectively dictated to the executive that it must ratify an international treaty.

Once the Government decided to let this amendment be determined on a 'free vote' its acceptance was inevitable. Indeed the Government went further than the implications of the amendment. On 24 July 1998 the Minister for the Armed Forces announced that the Government intended to abolish the death penalty for all military offences, whether in peacetime *or war*. At report stage of the HRB in the Commons, the government introduced a series of amendments to the Armed Forces Acts which converted any liability to the death penalty under the various Acts to a liability to life imprisonment (HC Deb, 21 October 1998, col. 1353). This provision (Section 21 (5)) came into effect when the HRA received royal assent on 9 November 1998.

Mike O'Brien explained the practical effects of incorporating Protocol 6 into the Bill:

... Parliament will not be able to reintroduce the death penalty, other than for acts committed in time of war or imminent threat of war, unless the United Kingdom denounces the European convention on human rights. (Ibid, col. 1354)

On the 27th January 1999 the Home Secretary ratified Protocol 6. With remarkably little fanfare the era of regular parliamentary debates on reintroducing the death penalty was extinguished. Before coming into force, the Human Rights Act has already made its effect felt. Parliament has tied its own hands. Passing this amendment represents the first stage along the road of realisation that there are some rights which are deemed so fundamental that they are no longer in the gift of MPs or governments to easily take away.

Francesca Klug, 'The Human Rights Act 1998: Pepper v. Hart and All That', *Public Law* (1999), June issue.

CHAPTER 4

COMPARATIVE BILLS OF RIGHTS
(EUROPE, THE COMMONWEALTH AND AMERICA)

Article 1

All men are born and remain equal in their rights. Social distinctions may only be based on public utility.

Article 2

The ultimate purpose of every political institution is the preservation of the natural and imprescriptible rights of man. These rights are to liberty, property, security, and resistance to oppression.

Article 3

The source of all sovereignty lies ultimately in the nation. No body or any individual can exercise any authority that is not expressly derived from it.

Article 4

Liberty consists in the power to do anything that does not harm another. Therefore, the only limits on the exercise of the natural rights of each man shall be those that ensure the enjoyment of the same rights by other members of society. Such limits may only be established by law (*loi*).

Article 5

The law may only prohibit actions harmful to society. Anything that is not prohibited by law cannot be prevented, and no one may be forced to do anything that it does not require.

Article 6

Loi is the expression of the general will. All citizens have the right to participate in its creation, either personally or through their representatives. It must be the same for all, whether it punishes or protects. All citizens, being equal in its eyes, are equally eligible for all public dignities, positions, and employment according to their abilities, and without distinction other than that of their virtues and talents.

Article 7

No individual may be accused, arrested, or detained except where the law (*loi*) so prescribes, and in accordance with the procedures it has laid down. Those who solicit, further, execute, or arrange for the execution of arbitrary orders must be punished; but any citizen charged or detained by virtue of a *loi* must obey it immediately; resistance renders him culpable.

Article 8

The law (*loi*) may only create penalties that are strictly and evidently necessary. No one may be punished except according to a *loi* passed and promulgated prior to the offence, and lawfully applied.

Article 9

Since a man is presumed innocent until he has been declared guilty, if it is judged indispensable to arrest him, any force that is not necessary to secure his person should be severely punished by the law.

Article 10

No one may be troubled on account of his opinions or religion, provided that their expression does not infringe public policy as established by *loi*.

Article 11

The free communication of thoughts and opinions is one of the most precious rights of man; hence, every citizen may speak, write, and publish freely, save that he must answer for any abuse of such freedom in cases specified by *loi*.

Article 12

The safeguarding of the rights of man and of the citizen requires a police force; such a force is thus created for the benefit of all, and not for the private advantage of those to whom it is entrusted.

Article 13

For the upkeep of a police force and for the expenses of the administration, common taxation is indispensable. This should be shared equally among all citizens, according to their means.

Article 14

All citizens have the right to satisfy themselves, either personally or through their representatives, that a public tax is necessary, to consent to it freely, to monitor its spending, and to determine its amount, its basis of assessment, its collection, and its duration.

Article 15

Society has the right to demand an account of administration from any public official.

Article 16

Any society in which the safeguarding of rights is not assured, and the separation of powers is not established, has no constitution.

Article 17

Property, being an inviolable and sacred right, none can be deprived of it, except when public necessity, legally ascertained, evidently requires it, and on condition of a just and prior indemnity.

PREAMBLE TO THE 1946 CONSTITUTION

Paragraph 1

On the morrow of the victory won by free peoples over regimes that tried to enslave and degrade the human person, the French people proclaims anew that any human being possesses inalienable and sacred rights, without distinction as to race, religion, or beliefs. It solemnly reaffirms the rights and liberties of man and of the citizen consecrated by the Declaration of Rights of 1789, and the fundamental principles recognized by the laws of the Republic ...

Paragraph 3

The law shall guarantee to women, in all spheres, equal rights to men.

---

42   UNITED STATES OF AMERICA: THE BILL OF RIGHTS, 1791

RB NOTE: The first ten Amendments to the Constitution of the United States of America, ratified in 1791, became collectively known as the "Bill of Rights".

Later Amendments dealing with human rights and freedoms have since been added, including Amendments 13 (1865), 14 (1868), 15 (1870), 19 (1919) and 26 (1971).

Amendment 1

Congress shall make no law respecting an establishment of religion, or prohibiting the free exercise thereof; or abridging the freedom of speech, or of the press; or the right of the people peaceably to assemble, and to petition the Government for a redress of grievances.

Amendment 2

A well regulated Militia, being necessary to the security of a free State, the right of the people to keep and bear Arms, shall not be infringed.

Amendment 3

No Soldier shall in time of peace be quartered in any house without the consent of the Owner, nor in time of war, but in a manner to be prescribed by law.

Amendment 4

The right of the people to be secure in their persons, houses, papers, and effects, against unreasonable searches and seizures, shall not be violated, and no Warrants shall issue, but upon probable cause, supported by Oath or affirmation, and particularly describing the place to be searched, and the persons or things to be seized.

Amendment 5

No person shall be held to answer for a capital, or otherwise infamous crime, unless on a presentment or indictment of a Grand Jury, except in cases arising in the land or naval forces, or in the Militia, when in actual service in time of War or public danger; nor shall any person be subject for the same offence to be twice put in jeopardy of life or limb; nor shall be compelled in any criminal case to be a witness against himself, nor be deprived of life, liberty, or property, without due process of law; nor shall private property be taken for public use without just compensation.

Amendment 6

In all criminal prosecutions, the accused shall enjoy the right to a speedy and public trial, by an impartial jury of the State and district wherein the crime shall have been committed, which district shall have been previously ascertained by law, and to be informed of the nature and cause of the accusation; to be confronted with the witnesses against him; to have compulsory process for obtaining Witnesses in his favor, and to have the assistance of counsel for his defence.

Amendment 7

In Suits at common law, where the value in controversy shall exceed twenty dollars, the right of trial by jury shall be preserved, and no fact tried by a jury, shall be otherwise reexamined in any Court of the United States, than according to the rules of the common law.

Amendment 8

Excessive bail shall not be required, nor excessive fines imposed, nor cruel and unusual punishments inflicted.

Amendment 9

The enumeration in the Constitution, of certain rights, shall not be construed to deny or disparage others retained by the people.

Amendment 10

The powers not delegated to the United States by the Constitution, nor prohibited by it to the States, are reserved to the States respectively, or to the people.

Amendment 13

Section 1. Neither slavery nor involuntary servitude, except as a punishment for crime whereof the party shall have been duly convicted, shall exist within the United States, or any place subject to their jurisdiction.

   Section 2. Congress shall have power to enforce this article by appropriate legislation.

Amendment 14

Section 1. All persons born or naturalized in the United States, and subject to the jurisdiction thereof, are citizens of the United States and of the State wherein they reside. No State shall make or enforce any law which shall abridge the privileges or immunities of citizens of the United States; nor shall any State deprive any person of life, liberty, or property, without due process of law; nor deny to any person within its jurisdiction the equal protection of the laws . . .

Amendment 15

Section 1. The right of citizens of the United States to vote shall not be denied or abridged by the United States or by any State on account of race, color, or previous condition of servitude.

Section 2. The Congress shall have power to enforce this article by appropriate legislation.

Amendment 19

The right of citizens of the United States to vote shall not be denied or abridged by the United States or by any State on account of sex.

Congress shall have power to enforce this article by appropriate legislation.

Amendment 26

Section 1. The right of citizens of the United States, who are eighteen years of age or older, to vote shall not be denied or abridged by the United States or by any State on account of age.

Section 2. The Congress shall have power to enforce this article by appropriate legislation.

---

43   BASIC LAW FOR THE FEDERAL REPUBLIC OF GERMANY: BASIC RIGHTS, 1949

RB NOTE: The following text incorporates amendments made by the Unification Treaty of 31 August 1990 and the federal statutes of 19 March 1956, 24 June 1968 and 23 September 1990.

PREAMBLE

Conscious of their responsibility before God and men,

Animated by the resolve to serve world peace as an equal part in a united Europe, the German People have adopted, by virtue of their constituent power, this Basic Law.

The Germans in the Laender of Baden-Württemberg, Bavaria, Berlin, Brandenburg, Bremen, Hamburg, Hesse, Lower Saxony, Mecklenburg-Western Pomerania, North Rhine-Westphalia, Rhineland-Palatinate, Saarland, Saxony, Saxony-Anhalt, Schleswig-Holstein and Thuringia have achieved the unity and freedom of Germany in free self-determination. This Basic Law is thus valid for the entire German People.

Basic Rights

Article 1 (Protection of human dignity)

(1) The dignity of man shall be inviolable. To respect and protect it shall be the duty of all state authority.

(2) The German people therefore acknowledge inviolable and inalienable human rights as the basis of every community, of peace and of justice in the world.

(3) The following basic rights shall bind the legislature, the executive and the judiciary as directly enforceable law.

Article 2 (Rights of liberty)

(1) Everyone shall have the right to the free development of his personality insofar as he does not violate the rights of others or offend against the constitutional order or against morality.

(2) Everyone shall have the right to life and to physical integrity. The liberty of the individual shall be inviolable. Intrusion on these rights may only be made pursuant to a statute.

Article 3 (Equality before the law)

(1) All persons shall be equal before the law.

(2) Men and women shall have equal rights.

(3) No one may be disadvantaged or favoured because of his sex, his parentage, his race, his language, his homeland and origin, his faith, or his religious or political opinions.

Article 4 (Freedom of faith, of conscience and of creed)

(1) Freedom of faith, of conscience, and freedom to profess a religion or a particular philosophy (Weltanschauung) shall be inviolable.

(2) The undisturbed practice of religion shall be guaranteed.

(3) No one may be compelled against his conscience to render war service involving the use of arms. Details shall be regulated by a federal statute.

Article 5 (Freedom of expression)

(1) Everyone shall have the right freely to express and disseminate his opinion in speech, writing and pictures and freely to inform himself from generally accessible sources. Freedom of the press and freedom of reporting by means of broadcasts and films shall be guaranteed. There shall be no censorship.

(2) These rights are subject to limitations in the provisions of general statutes, in statutory provisions for the protection of youth, and in the right to respect for personal honour.

(3) Art and science, research and teaching shall be free. Freedom of teaching shall not release anybody from his allegiance to the constitution.

Article 6 (Marriage and family, illegitimate children)

(1) Marriage and family shall enjoy the special protection of the state.

(2) The care and upbringing of children shall be a natural right of and a duty primarily incumbent on the parents. The state shall watch over their endeavours in this respect.

(3) Children may not be separated from their families against the will of the persons entitled to bring them up, except, pursuant to a statute, where those so entitled fail in their duties or the children are otherwise threatened with serious neglect.

(4) Every mother shall be entitled to the protection and care of the community.

(5) Illegitimate children shall be provided by legislation with the same opportunities for their physical and mental development and for their place in society as are enjoyed by legitimate children.

Article 7 (Education)

(1) The entire schooling system shall be under the supervision of the state.

(2) The persons entitled to bring up a child shall have the right to decide whether the child shall attend religion classes.

(3) Religion classes shall form part of the ordinary curriculum in state schools, except in secular (bekenntnisfrei) schools. Without prejudice to the state's right of supervision, religious instruction shall be given in accordance with the tenets of the religious communities. No teacher may be obliged against his will to give religious instruction.

(4) The right to establish private schools shall be guaranteed. Private schools, as a substitute for state schools, shall require the approval of the state and shall be subject to the statutes of the Laender. Such approval shall be given where private schools are not inferior to the state schools in their educational aims, their facilities and the professional training of their teaching staff, and where segregation of pupils according to the means of the parents is not encouraged thereby. Approval shall be withheld where the economic and legal position of the teaching staff is not sufficiently assured.

(5) A private elementary school shall be permitted only where the education authority finds that it serves a special pedagogic interest, or where, on the application of persons entitled to bring up children, it is to be established as an interdenominational school or as a denominational school or as a school based on a particular philosophical persuasion (Weltanschauungsschule) and a state elementary school of this type does not exist in the commune (Gemeinde).

(6) Preliminary schools (Vorschulen) shall remain abolished.

Article 8 (Freedom of assembly)

(1) All Germans shall have the right to assemble peaceably and unarmed without prior notification or permission.

(2) With regard to open-air meetings, this right may be restricted by or pursuant to a statute.

Article 9 (Freedom of association)

(1) All Germans shall have the right to form associations, partnerships and corporations.

(2) Associations, the purposes or activities of which conflict with criminal statutes or which are directed against the constitutional order or the concept of international understanding, shall be prohibited.

(3) The right to form associations to safeguard and improve working and economic conditions shall be guaranteed to everyone and to all occupations. Agreements which restrict or seek to impair this right shall be null and void; measures directed to this end shall be illegal. Measures taken pursuant to Article 12a, to paragraphs (2) and (3) of Article 35, to paragraph (4) of Article 87a, or to Article 91 may not be directed against any industrial conflicts engaged in by associations within the meaning of the first sentence of this paragraph in order to safeguard and improve working and economic conditions.

Article 10 (Privacy of letters, posts and telecommunications)

(1) Privacy of letters, posts and telecommunications shall be inviolable.

(2) Restrictions may only be ordered pursuant to a statute. Where a restriction serves to protect the free democratic basic order or the existence or security of the Federation, the statute may stipulate that the person affected shall not be informed of such restriction and that recourse to the courts shall be replaced by a review of the case by bodies and auxiliary bodies appointed by Parliament.

Article 11 (Freedom of movement)

(1) All Germans shall enjoy freedom of movement throughout the federal territory.

(2) This right may be restricted only by or pursuant to a statute, and only in cases in which an adequate basis for personal existence is lacking and special burdens would result therefrom for the community, or in which such restriction is necessary to avert an imminent danger to the existence or the free democratic basic order of the Federation or a Land, to combat the danger of epidemics, to deal with natural disasters or particularly grave accidents, to protect young people from neglect or to prevent crime.

Article 12 (Right to choose an occupation, prohibition of forced labour)

(1) All Germans shall have the right freely to choose their occupation, their place of work and their place of study or training. The practice of an occupation may be regulated by or pursuant to a statute.

(2) No person may be forced to perform work of a particular kind except within the framework of a traditional compulsory community service that applies generally and equally to all.

(3) Forced labour may be imposed only on persons deprived of their liberty by court sentence.

Article 12a (Liability to military and other service)

(1) Men who have attained the age of eighteen years may be required to serve in the Armed Forces, in the Federal Border Guard, or in a civil defence organization.

(2) A person who refuses, on grounds of conscience, to render war service involving the use of arms may be required to render a substitute service. The duration of such substitute service shall not exceed the duration of military service. Details shall be regulated by a statute which shall not interfere with freedom to take a decision based on conscience and shall also provide for the possibility of a substitute service not connected with units of the Armed Forces or of the Federal Border Guard.

(3) Persons liable to military service who are not required to render service pursuant to paragraph (1) or (2) of this Article may, during a state of defence (Verteidigungsfall), be assigned by or pursuant to a statute to an employment involving civilian services for defence purposes, including the protection of the civilian population; it shall, however, not be permissible to assign persons to an employment subject to public law except for the purpose of discharging police functions or such other functions of public administration as can only be discharged by persons employed under public law. Persons may be assigned to an employment – as referred to in the first sentence of this paragraph – with the Armed Forces, including the supplying and servicing of the latter, or with public administrative authorities; assignments to employment connected with supplying and servicing the civilian population shall not be permissible except in order to meet their vital requirements or to guarantee their safety.

(4) Where, during a state of defence, civilian service requirements in the civilian health system or in the stationary military hospital organization cannot be met on a voluntary basis, women between eighteen and fifty-five years of age may be assigned to such services by or pursuant to a statute. They may on no account render service involving the use of arms.

(5) Prior to the existence of a state of defence, assignments under paragraph (3) of this Article may only be made where the requirements of paragraph (1) of Article 80a are satisfied. It shall be admissible to require persons by or pursuant to a statute to attend training courses in order to

prepare them for the performance of such services in accordance with paragraph (3) of this Article as require special knowledge or skills. To this extent, the first sentence of this paragraph shall not apply.

(6) Where, during a state of defence, staffing requirements for the purposes referred to in the second sentence of paragraph (3) of this Article cannot be met on a voluntary basis, the right of a German to quit the pursuit of his occupation or quit his place of work may be restricted by or pursuant to a statute in order to meet these requirements. The first sentence of paragraph (5) of this Article shall apply mutatis mutandis prior to the existence of a state of defence.

Article 13 (Inviolability of the home)

(1) The home shall be inviolable.

(2) Searches may be ordered only by a judge or, in the event of danger resulting in any delay in taking action, by other organs as provided by statute and may be carried out only in the form prescribed by law.

(3) Intrusions and restrictions may otherwise only be made to avert a public danger or a mortal danger to individuals, or, pursuant to a statute, to prevent substantial danger to public safety and order, in particular to relieve a housing shortage, to combat the danger of epidemics or to protect juveniles who are exposed to a moral danger.

Article 14 (Property, right of inheritance, taking of property)

(1) Property and the right of inheritance shall be guaranteed. Their content and limits shall be determined by statute.

(2) Property imposes duties. Its use should also serve the public weal.

(3) The taking of property shall only be permissible in the public weal. It may be effected only by or pursuant to a statute regulating the nature and extent of compensation. Such compensation shall be determined by establishing an equitable balance between the public interest and the interests of those affected. In case of dispute regarding the amount of compensation, recourse may be had to the courts of ordinary jurisdiction.

Article 15 (Socialization)

Land, natural resources and means of production may for the purpose of socialization be transferred to public ownership or other forms of collective enterprise for the public benefit by a statute regulating the nature and extent of compensation. In respect of such compensation the third and fourth sentences of paragraph (3) of Article 14 shall apply mutatis mutandis.

Article 16 (Deprivation of citizenship, extradition, right of asylum)

(1) No one may be deprived of his German citizenship. Citizenship may be lost only pursuant to a statute, and it may be lost against the will of the

person affected only where such person does not become stateless as a result thereof.

(2) No German may be extradited to a foreign country. Persons persecuted on political grounds shall enjoy the right of asylum.

Article 17 (Right of petition)

Everyone shall have the right individually or jointly with others to address written requests or complaints to the competent agencies and to parliaments.

Article 17a (Restriction of individual basic rights through legislation enacted for defence purposes and concerning substitute service)

(1) Statutes concerning military service and substitute service may, by provisions applying to members of the Armed Forces and of the substitute services during their period of military or substitute service, restrict the basic right freely to express and to disseminate opinions in speech, writing and pictures (first half-sentence of paragraph (1) of Article 5), the basic right of assembly (Article 8), and the right of petition (Article 17) insofar as this right permits the submission of requests or complaints jointly with others.

(2) Statutes serving defence purposes including the protection of the civilian population may provide for the restriction of the basic rights of freedom of movement (Article 11) and inviolability of the home (Article 13).

Article 18 (Forfeiture of basic rights)

Whoever abuses freedom of expression of opinion, in particular freedom of the press (paragraph (1) of Article 5), freedom of teaching (paragraph (3) of Article 5), freedom of assembly (Article 8), freedom of association (Article 9), privacy of letters, posts and telecommunications (Article 10), property (Article 14), or the right of asylum (paragraph (2) of Article 16) in order to combat the free democratic basic order shall forfeit these basic rights. Such forfeiture and the extent thereof shall be determined by the Federal Constitutional Court.

Article 19 (Restriction of basic rights)

(1) Insofar as a basic right may, under this Basic Law, be restricted by or pursuant to a statute, such statute shall apply generally and not solely to an individual case. Furthermore, such statute shall name the basic right, indicating the Article concerned.

(2) In no case may the essence of a basic right be encroached upon.

(3) The basic rights shall apply also to domestic juristic persons to the extent that the nature of such rights permits.

(4) Should any person's rights be violated by public authority, recourse to the court shall be open to him. Insofar as no other jurisdiction has been established, recourse shall be to the courts of ordinary jurisdiction. The second sentence of paragraph (2) of Article 10 shall not be affected by the provisions of this paragraph.

---

44 FUNDAMENTAL RIGHTS AND FREEDOMS IN THE WEST INDIES, 1962–81

(A) Antigua and Barbuda

PROTECTION OF FUNDAMENTAL RIGHTS AND FREEDOMS OF THE INDIVIDUAL

3. Whereas every person in Antigua and Barbuda is entitled to the fundamental rights and freedoms of the individual, that is to say, the right, regardless of race, place of origin, political opinions or affiliations, colour, creed or sex, but subject to respect for the rights and freedoms of others and for the public interest, to each and all of the following, namely—
- (*a*) life, liberty, security of the person, the enjoyment of property and the protection of the law;
- (*b*) freedom of conscience, of expression (including freedom of the press) and of peaceful assembly and association; and
- (*c*) protection for his family life, his personal privacy, the privacy of his home and other property and from deprivation of property without fair compensation,

the provisions of this Chapter shall have effect for the purpose of affording protection to the aforesaid rights and freedoms, subject to such limitations of that protection as are contained in those provisions, being limitations designed to ensure that the enjoyment of the said rights and freedoms by any individual does not prejudice the rights and freedoms of others or the public interest.

4.—(1) No person shall be deprived of his life intentionally save in execution of the sentence of a court in respect of a crime of treason or murder of which he has been convicted.

(2) A person shall not be regarded as having been deprived of his life in contravention of this section if he dies as the result of the use, to such extent

and such circumstances as are permitted by law, of such force as is reasonably justifiable—

    (*a*) for the defence of any person from violence or for the defence of property;

    (*b*) in order to effect a lawful arrest or to prevent the escape of a person lawfully detained;

    (*c*) for the purpose of suppressing a riot, insurrection or mutiny; or

    (*d*) in order lawfully to prevent the commission by that person of a criminal offence,

or if he dies as the result of a lawful act of war.

    5.—(1) No person shall be deprived of his personal liberty save as may be authorised by law in any of the following cases, that is to say—

    (*a*) in consequence of his unfitness to plead to a criminal charge;

    (*b*) in execution of the sentence or order of a court, whether established for Antigua and Barbuda or some other country, in respect of a criminal offence of which he has been convicted;

    (*c*) in execution of an order of the High Court or of the Court of Appeal or such other court as may be prescribed by Parliament on the grounds of his contempt of any such court or of another court or tribunal;

    (*d*) in execution of the order of a court made in order to secure the fulfilment of any obligation imposed on him by law;

    (*e*) for the purpose of bringing him before a court in execution of the order of a court;

    (*f*) upon reasonable suspicion of his having committed or of being about to commit a criminal offence under any law;

    (*g*) under the order of a court or with the consent of his parent or guardian, for his education or welfare during any period ending not later than the date when he attains the age of eighteen years;

    (*h*) for the purpose of preventing the spread of an infectious or contagious disease;

    (*i*) in the case of a person who is, or is reasonably suspected to be, of unsound mind, addicted to drugs or alcohol, or a vagrant, for the purpose of his care or treatment or the protection of the community;

    (*j*) for the purpose of preventing the unlawful entry of that person into Antigua and Barbuda, or for the purpose of effecting the expulsion, extradition or other lawful removal of that person from Antigua and Barbuda or for the purpose of restricting that person while he is being conveyed through Antigua and Barbuda in the course of his extradition or removal as a convicted prisoner from one country to another; or

    (*k*) to such extent as may be necessary in the execution of a lawful order requiring that person to remain within a specified area within Antigua and Barbuda or prohibiting him from being within such an area or to such extent as may be reasonably justifiable for the taking of proceedings against that person relating to the making of any such order or relating to such an order after it has been made, or to such extent as may be reasonably justifiable for restraining that person during any visit that he is permitted to make to any part of Antigua and Barbuda in which, in consequence of any such order, his presence would otherwise be unlawful.

(2) Any person who is arrested or detained shall be informed orally and in writing as soon as reasonably practicable, in language that he understands, of the reason for his arrest or detention.

(3) Any person who is arrested or detained shall have the right, at any stage and at his own expense, to retain and instruct without delay a legal practitioner of his own choice, and to hold private communications with him, and in the case of a minor he shall also be afforded a reasonable opportunity for communication with his parent or guardian.

(4) When a person is arrested, excessive bail shall not be required in those cases where bail is being granted.

(5) Any person who is arrested or detained—
   (*a*) for the purpose of bringing him before a court in execution of the order of a court; or
   (*b*) upon reasonable suspicion of his having committed or being about to commit a criminal offence under any law.
and who is not released shall be brought before the court within forty-eight hours after his detention and, in computing time for the purposes of this subsection, Sundays and public holidays shall be excluded.

(6) If any person arrested or detained as mentioned in subsection (5)(*b*) of this section is not tried within a reasonable time, then, without prejudice to any further proceedings which may be brought against him, he shall be released either unconditionally or upon reasonable conditions, including in particular such conditions as are reasonably necessary to ensure that he appears at a later date for trial or for proceedings preliminary to trial and, subject to subsection (4) of this section, such conditions may include bail.

(7) Any person who is unlawfully arrested or detained by any other person shall, subject to such defences as may be provided by law, be entitled to compensation for such unlawful arrest or detention from the person who made the arrest or effected the detention, from any person or authority on whose behalf the person making the arrest or effecting the detention was acting or from them both:
Provided that a judge, a magistrate or a justice of the peace or an officer of a court or a police officer acting in pursuance of the order of a judge, a magistrate or a justice of the peace shall not be under any personal liability to pay compensation under this subsection in consequence of any act performed by him in good faith in the discharge of the functions of his office

and any liability to pay any such compensation in consequence of any such act shall be a liability of the Crown.

(8) For the purposes of subsection (1)(*b*) of this section, a person charged with a criminal offence in respect of whom a special verdict has been returned that he was guilty of the act or omission charged but was insane when he did the act or made the omission shall be regarded as a person who has been convicted of a criminal offence and the detention of that person in consequence of such a verdict shall be regarded as detention in execution of the order of a court.

6.—(1) No person shall be held in slavery or servitude.

(2) No person shall be required to perform forced labour.

(3) For the purposes of this section, the expression 'forced labour' does not include—

    (*a*) any labour required in consequence of the sentence or order of a court;

    (*b*) any labour required of any person while he is lawfully detained that, though not required in consequence of the sentence or order of a court, is reasonably necessary in the interests of hygiene or for the maintenance of the place at which he is detained;

    (*c*) any labour required of a member of a disciplined force in pursuance of his duties as such or, in the case of a person who has conscientious objections to service as a member of a naval, military or air force, any labour that that person is required by law to perform in place of such service;

    (*d*) any labour required during any period of public emergency or, in the event of any other emergency or calamity that threatens the life and well-being of the community, to the extent that the requiring of such labour is reasonably justifiable in the circumstances of any situation arising or existing during that period or as a result of that other emergency or calamity, for the purpose of dealing with that situation.

7.—(1) No person shall be subjected to torture or to inhuman or degrading punishment or other such treatment.

(2) Nothing contained in or done under the authority of any law shall be held to be inconsistent with or in contravention of this section to the extent that the law in question authorises the infliction of any description of punishment that was lawful in Antigua on 31st October 1981.

8.—(1) A person shall not be deprived of his freedom of movement, that is to say, the right to move freely throughout Antigua and Barbuda, the right to reside in any part of Antigua and Barbuda, the right to enter Antigua and

Barbuda, the right to leave Antigua and Barbuda and immunity from expulsion from Antigua and Barbuda.

(2) Any restrictions on a person's freedom of movement that is involved in his lawful detention shall not be held to be inconsistent with or in contravention of this section.

(3) Nothing contained in or done under the authority of any law shall be held to be inconsistent with or in contravention of this section to the extent that the law in question makes provision—

- (*a*) for the imposition of restrictions on the movements or residence within Antigua and Barbuda of any person or on any person's right to leave Antigua and Barbuda that are reasonably required in the interests of defence, public safety or public order;
- (*b*) for the imposition of restrictions on the movements or residence within Antigua and Barbuda or on the right to leave Antigua and Barbuda of persons generally or any class of persons in the interests of defence, public safety, public order, public morality, or public health or, in respect of the right to leave Antigua and Barbuda, of securing compliance with any international obligation of Antigua and Barbuda particulars of which have been laid before the House and except so far as that provision or, as the case may be, the thing done under the authority thereof is shown not to be reasonably justifiable in a democratic society;
- (*c*) for the imposition of restrictions, by order of a court, on the movement or residence within Antigua and Barbuda of any person or on any person's right to leave Antigua and Barbuda either in consequence of his having been found guilty of a criminal offence under a law or for the purpose of ensuring that he appears before a court at a later date for trial of such a criminal offence or for proceedings relating to his extradition or lawful removal from Antigua and Barbuda;
- (*d*) for the imposition of restrictions on the freedom of movement of any person who is not a citizen;
- (*e*) for the imposition of restrictions on the acquisition or use by any person of land or other property in Antigua and Barbuda;
- (*f*) for the imposition of restrictions upon the movement or residence within Antigua and Barbuda or on the right to leave Antigua and Barbuda of any public officer that are reasonably required for the proper performance of his functions;
- (*g*) for the removal of a person from Antigua and Barbuda to be tried or punished in some other country for a criminal offence under the law of that other country or to undergo imprisonment in some other country in execution of the sentence of a court in respect of a criminal offence under a law of which he has been convicted; or
- (*h*) for the imposition of restrictions on the right of any person to leave Antigua and Barbuda that are reasonably required in order to secure the fulfilment of any obligations imposed on that person

by law and except so far as that provision or, as the case may be, the thing done under the authority thereof is shown not to be reasonably justifiable in a democratic society.

(4) If any person whose freedom of movement has been restricted by virtue of such a provision as is referred to in subsection (3)(*a*) of this section so requests at any time during the period of that restriction not earlier than two months after the restriction was imposed or two months after he last made such a request, as the case may be, his case shall be reviewed by an independent and impartial tribunal consisting of a president who shall be a legal practitioner of not less than seven years standing appointed by the Chief Justice and two other members appointed by the Governor-General acting in his discretion.

(5) On any review by a tribunal in pursuance of subsection (4) of this section of the case of any person whose freedom of movement has been restricted, the tribunal may make recommendations concerning the necessity for or expediency of the continuation of that restriction to the authority by whom it was ordered and, unless it is otherwise provided by law, that authority shall be obliged to act in accordance with any such recommendations.

9.—(1) No property of any description shall be compulsorily taken possession of, and no interest in or right to or over property of any description shall be compulsorily acquired, except for public use and except in accordance with the provisions of a law applicable to that taking of possession or acquisition and for the payment of fair compensation within a reasonable time.

(2) Every person having an interest in or right to or over property which is compulsorily taken possession of or whose interest in or right to or over any property is compulsorily acquired shall have the right of access to the High Court for—

(*a*) the determination of his interest or right, the legality of the taking of possession or acquisition of the property, interest or right and the amount of any compensation to which he is entitled; and

(*b*) the purpose of obtaining payment of that compensation:

Provided that if Parliament so provides in relation to any matter referred to in paragraph (*a*) of this subsection the right of access shall be by way of appeal (exercisable as of right at the instance of the person having the interest in or right to or over the property) from a tribunal or authority, other than the High Court, having jurisdiction under any law to determine that matter.

(3) The Chief Justice may make rules with respect to the practice and procedure of the High Court or any other tribunal or authority in relation to the jurisdiction conferred on the High Court by subsection (2) of this section or exercisable by the other tribunal or authority for the purposes of that subsection (including rules with respect to the time within which application or appeals to the High Court or applications to the other tribunals or authority may be brought).

(4) Nothing contained in or done under the authority of any law shall be held to be inconsistent with or in contravention of subsection (1) of this section—

(*a*) to the extent that the law in question makes provision for the taking of possession or acquisition of any property, interest or right—

(i)   in satisfaction of any tax, rate or due;

(ii)   by way of penalty for breach of the law or forfeiture in consequence of breach of the law;

(iii)   as an incident of a lease, tenancy, mortgage, charge, bill of sale, pledge or contract;

(iv)   in the execution of judgments or orders of a court in proceedings for the determination of civil rights or obligations;

(v)   in circumstances where it is reasonably necessary so to do because the property is in a dangerous state or likely to be injurious to the health of human beings, animals or plants;

(vi)   in consequence of any law with respect to the limitation of actions;

(vii)   for so long as may be necessary for the purposes of any examination, investigation, trial or enquiry or, in the case of land, for the purposes of the carrying out thereon of work of soil conservation or the conservation of other natural resources or work relating to agricultural development or improvement (being work relating to such development or improvement that the owner or occupier of the land has been required, and has without reasonable excuse refused or failed, to carry out),

and except so far as the provision or, as the case may be, the thing done under the authority thereof is shown not to be reasonably justifiable in a democratic society;

(*b*) to the extent that the law in question makes provision for the taking of possession or acquisition of any of the following property (including an interest in or right to or over property), that is to say—

(i)   enemy property;

(ii)   property of a deceased person, a person of unsound mind or a person who had not attained the age of eighteen years, for the purpose of its administration for the benefit of the persons entitled to the beneficial interest therein;

(iii)   the property of a person adjudged bankrupt or a body corporate in liquidation, for the purpose of its administration for the benefit of the creditors of the bankrupt or body corporate and, subject thereto, for the benefit of other persons entitled to the beneficial interest in the property; or

(iv)   property subject to a trust, for the purpose of vesting the property in persons appointed as trustees under the instrument creating the trust or by a court or by order of a court for the purposes of giving effect to the trust.

(5) Nothing contained in or done under the authority of any law enacted by Parliament shall be held to be inconsistent with or in contravention of this section to the extent that the law in question makes provision for the compulsory taking of possession of any property, or the compulsory acquisition of any interest in or right to or over property, where that property, interest or right is held by a body corporate established by law for public purposes in which no monies have been invested other than monies provided by Parliament or any legislature established for the former colony or Associated State of Antigua.

(6) For the purposes of this section, 'use' is 'public' if it is intended to result or results in a benefit or advantage to the public and, without prejudice to its generality, includes any use affecting the physical, economic, social or aesthetic well-being of the public.

10.—(1) Except with his own consent, no person shall be subjected to the search of his person or his property or the entry by others on his premises.

(2) Nothing contained in or done under the authority of any law shall be held to be inconsistent with or in contravention of this section to the extent that the law in question makes provision—

    (*a*) that is reasonably required in the interests of defence, public safety, public order, public morality, public health, public revenue, town and country planning or the development and utilization of property in such a manner as to promote the public benefit;

    (*b*) that authorises an office or agent of the Government, a local government authority or a body corporate established by law for public purposes to enter on the premises of any person in order to inspect those premises or anything thereon for the purpose of any tax, rate or due in order to carry out work connected with any property that is lawfully on those premises and that belongs to the Government, or to that authority or body corporate, as the case may be;

    (*c*) that is reasonably required for the purpose of preventing or detecting crime;

    (*d*) that is reasonably required for the purpose of protecting the rights or freedoms of other persons; or

    (*e*) that authorises, for the purpose of enforcing the judgment or order of a court in any proceedings, the search of any person or property by order of a court or entry upon any premises by such order.

and except so far as that provision or, as the case may be, anything done under the authority thereof is shown not to be reasonably justifiable in a democratic society.

11.—(1) Except with his own consent, no person shall be hindered in the enjoyment of his freedom of conscience, and for the purposes of this section the said freedom includes freedom of thought and of religion, freedom to change his religion or belief, and freedom, either alone or in community with others, and both in public and in private, to manifest and propagate his religion or belief in worship, teaching, practice and observance.

(2) Except with his own consent (or, if he is under the age of eighteen years, the consent of his parent or guardian) no person attending any place of education shall be required to receive religious instruction or to take part in or attend any religious ceremony or observance if that instruction, ceremony or observance relates to a religion other than his own.

(3) No person shall be compelled to take any oath which is contrary to his religion or belief or to take any oath in a manner which is contrary to his religion or belief.

(4) Nothing contained in or done under the authority of any law shall be held to be inconsistent with or in contravention of this section to the extent that the law in question makes provision that is reasonably required—

    (*a*) in the interests of defence, public safety, public order, public morality or public health; or

    (*b*) for the purpose of protecting the rights and freedoms of other persons, including the right to observe and practise any religion without the unsolicited intervention of members of any other religion,

and except so far as that provision or, as the case may be, the thing done under the authority thereof is shown not to be reasonably justifiable in a democratic society.

(5) Reference in this section to a religion shall be construed as including references to a religious denomination, and cognate expressions shall be construed accordingly.

12.—(1) Except with his own consent, no person shall be hindered in the enjoyment of his freedom of expression.

(2) For the purposes of this section the said freedom includes the freedom to hold opinions without interference, freedom to receive information and ideas without interference, freedom to disseminate information and ideas without interference (whether the dissemination be to the public generally or to any person or class of persons) and freedom from interference with his correspondence or other means of communication.

(3) For the purposes of this section expression may be oral or written or by codes, signals, signs or symbols and includes recordings, broadcasts (whether on radio or television), printed publications, photographs (whether still or moving), drawings, carvings and sculptures or any other means of artistic expression.

(4) Nothing contained in or done under the authority of any law shall be

held to be inconsistent with or in contravention of this section to the extent that the law in question makes provision—

(*a*) that is reasonably required—

    (i)   in the interests of defence, public safety, public order, public morality or public health; or

    (ii) for the purpose of protecting the reputations, rights and freedoms of other persons, or the private lives of persons concerned in legal proceedings and proceedings before statutory tribunals, preventing the disclosure of information received in confidence, maintaining the authority and independence of Parliament and the courts, or regulating telephony, posts, broadcasting or other means of communication, public entertainments, public shows; or

(*b*) that imposes restrictions upon public officers that are reasonably required for the proper performance of their functions.

and except so far as that provision or, as the case may be, the thing done under the authority thereof is shown not to be reasonably justifiable in a democratic society.

13.—(1) Except with his own consent, no person shall be hindered in the enjoyment of his freedom of peaceful assembly and association, that is to say, his right peacefully to assemble freely and associate with other persons and in particular to form or belong to trade unions or other associations for the promotion and protection of his interests.

(2) Nothing contained in or done under the authority of any law shall be held to be inconsistent with or in contravention of this section to the extent that the law in question makes provision—

(*a*) that is reasonably required—

    (i)   in the interests of defence, public order, public morality or public health; or

    (ii) for the purpose of protecting the rights or freedoms of other persons; or

(*b*) that imposes restrictions upon public officers that are reasonably required for the proper performance of their functions,

and except so far as that provision or, as the case may be, the thing done under the authority thereof is shown not to be reasonably justifiable in a democratic society.

14.—(1) Subject to the provisions of subsections (4), (5) and (7) of this section, no law shall make any provision that is discriminatory either of itself or in its effect.

(2) Subject to the provisions of subsections (6), (7) and (8) of this section, no person shall be treated in a discriminatory manner by any person acting by virtue of any law or in the performance of the functions of any public office or any public authority.

(3) In this section, the expression 'discriminatory' means affording differ-

ent treatment to different persons attributable wholly or mainly to their respective descriptions by race, place of origin, political opinions or affiliations, colour, creed, or sex whereby persons of one such description are subjected to disabilities or restrictions to which persons of another such description are not made subject or are accorded privileges or advantages that are not accorded to persons of another such description.

(4) Subsection (1) of this section shall not apply to any law so far as the law makes provision—

(*a*) for the appropriation of public revenues or other public funds;

(*b*) with respect to persons who are not citizens; or

(*c*) whereby persons of any such description as is mentioned in subsection (3) of this section may be subjected to any disability or restriction or may be accorded any privilege or advantage that, having regard to its nature and to special circumstances pertaining to those persons or to persons of any other such description, is reasonably justifiable in a democratic society.

(5) Nothing contained in any law shall be held to be inconsistent with or in contravention of subsection (1) of this section to the extent that it makes provision with respect to qualifications (not being qualifications specifically relating to race, place of origin, political opinions or affiliations, colour, creed or sex) for service as a public officer or as a member of a disciplined force or for the service of a local government authority or a body corporate established by any law for public purposes.

(6) Subsection (2) of this section shall not apply to anything that is expressly or by necessary implication authorised to be done by any such provision of law as is referred to in subsection (4) or (5) of this section.

(7) Nothing contained in or done under the authority of any law shall be held to be inconsistent with or in contravention of this section to the extent that the law in question makes provision whereby persons of any such description as is mentioned in subsection (3) of this section may be subjected to any restriction on the rights and freedoms guaranteed by sections 8, 10, 11, 12 and 13 of this Constitution, being such a restriction as is authorised by paragraph (*a*) or (*b*) of subsection (3) of section 8, subsection (2) of section 10, subsection (4) of section 11, subsection (4) of section 12 or subsection (2) of section 13, as the case may be.

(8) Nothing in subsection (2) of this section shall affect any discretion relating to the institution, conduct or discontinuance of civil or criminal proceedings in any court that is vested in any person by or under this Constitution or any other law.

15.—(1) If any person is charged with a criminal offence then, unless the charge is withdrawn, he shall be afforded a fair hearing within a reasonable time by an independent and impartial court established by law.

(2) Every person who is charged with a criminal offence —

(*a*) shall be presumed to be innocent until he is proved or has pleaded guilty;

(*b*) shall be informed orally and in writing as soon as reasonably practicable, in language that he understands, of the nature of the offence with which he is charged;

(*c*) shall be given adequate time and facilities for the preparation of his defence;

(*d*) shall be permitted to defend himself before the court in person or by a legal practitioner of his own choice;

(*e*) shall be afforded facilities to examine in person or by his legal representative the witnesses called by the prosecution before the court and to obtain the attendance and carry out the examination of witnesses to testify on his behalf before the court on the same conditions as those applying to witnesses called by the prosecution; and

(*f*) shall be permitted to have without payment the assistance of an interpreter if he cannot understand the language used at the trial of the charge,

and except with his own consent the trial shall not take place in his absence—

(i) except where, under the provisions of any law entitling him thereto, he is given adequate notice of the charge, the date, time and place of the trial or continuance thereof and afforded a reasonable opportunity of appearing before the court;

Provided that where the foregoing conditions have been complied with, and the court is satisfied that owing to circumstances beyond his control he cannot appear, the trial shall not take place or continue in his absence; or

(ii) unless he so conducts himself as to render the continuance of the proceedings in his presence impracticable and the court has ordered him to be removed and the trial to proceed in his absence.

(3) When a person is tried for any criminal offence the accused person or any person authorised by him in that behalf shall, if he so requires and subject to payment of such reasonable fees as may be prescribed by law, be given within a reasonable time after judgment a copy of any record of the proceedings made by or on behalf of the court.

(4) No person shall be held to be guilty of a criminal offence on account of any act or omission that did not, at the time it took place, constitute such an offence, and no penalty shall be imposed for any criminal offence that is more severe in degree or description than the maximum penalty that might have been imposed for that offence at the time when it was committed.

(5) No person who shows that he has been tried by a competent court for a criminal offence and either convicted or acquitted shall again be tried for that offence or for any criminal offence of which he could have been convicted at the trial for the offence, save upon the order of a superior court in the course of appeal or review proceedings relating to the conviction or acquittal.

(6) No person shall be tried for a criminal offence if he shows that he has been pardoned for that offence.

(7) No person who is tried for a criminal offence shall be compelled to give evidence at the trial.

(8) Any court or other authority prescribed by law for the determination of the existence or extent of any civil right or obligation shall be established by law and shall be independent and impartial; and where proceedings for such a determination are instituted by any persons before such a court or other authority, the case shall be given a fair hearing within a reasonable time.

(9) Except with the agreement of all the parties thereto, all proceedings of every court and proceedings for the determination of the existence or extent of any civil right or obligation before any other authority, including the announcement of the decision of the court or other authority, shall be held in public.

(10) Nothing in subsection (9) of this section shall prevent the court or other authority from excluding from the proceedings persons other than the parties thereto and the legal practitioners representing them to such an extent as the court or other authority—

(a) may by law be empowered to do and may consider necessary or expedient in circumstances where publicity would prejudice the interests of justice or in interlocutory proceedings or in the interests of public morality, the welfare of persons under the age of eighteen years or the protection of the private lives of persons concerned in the proceedings; or

(b) may by law be empowered or required to do in the interests of defence, public safety, public order or public morality.

(11) Nothing contained in or done under the authority of any law shall be held to be inconsistent with or in contravention of—

(a) subsection (2)(a) of this section, to the extent that the law in question imposes upon any person charged with a criminal offence the burden of proving particular facts;

(b) subsection (2)(e) of this section, to the extent that the law in question imposes reasonable conditions that must be satisfied if witnesses called to testify on behalf of an accused person are to be paid their expenses out of public funds; or

(c) subsection (5) of this section, to the extent that the law in question authorises a court to try a member of a disciplined force for a criminal offence notwithstanding any trial and conviction or acquittal of that member under the disciplinary law of that force so however, that any court so trying such a member and convicting him shall in sentencing him to any punishment take into account any punishment awarded him under that disciplinary law.

(12) In the case of any person who is held in lawful detention, the provisions of subsection (1), paragraphs (d) and (e) of subsection (2), and

subsection (3) of this section shall not apply in relation to his trial for a criminal offence under the law regulating the discipline of persons held in such detention.

(13) Nothing contained in or done under the authority of any law shall be held to be inconsistent with or in contravention of subsection (2) of this section to the extent that it authorises the trial of a defendant by a magistrate for a summary offence to take place in the defendant's absence.

(14) In this section 'criminal offence' means a criminal offence under any law.

16. Nothing contained in or done under the authority of a law enacted by Parliament shall be held to be inconsistent with or in contravention of section 5 or section 14 of this Constitution to the extent that the law authorises the taking during any period of public emergency of measures that are reasonably justifiable, for dealing with the situation that exists in Antigua and Barbuda during that period.

17.—(1) When a person is detained by virtue of any such law as is referred to in section 16 of this Constitution the following provisions shall apply, that is to say—

(*a*) he shall, with reasonable promptitude and in any case not more than seven days after the commencement of his detention, be informed in a language that he understands and in detail of the grounds upon which he is detained and furnished with a written statement in English specifying those grounds in detail;

(*b*) not more than fourteen days after the commencement of his detention a notification shall be published in the Official Gazette stating that he has been detained and giving particulars of the provision of law under which his detention is authorised;

(*c*) not more than one month after the commencement of his detention and thereafter during the detention at intervals of not more than six months, his case shall be reviewed by an independent and impartial tribunal established by law and presided over by a suitably qualified legal practitioner of at least seven years standing appointed by the Chief Justice;

(*d*) he shall be afforded reasonable facilities to consult a legal representative of his own choice who shall be permitted to make representations to the tribunal appointed for the review of the case of the detained person; and

(*e*) at the hearing of his case by the tribunal appointed for the review of his case he shall be permitted to appear in person or by a legal practitioner of his own choice.

(2) On any review by a tribunal in pursuance of this section of the case of a detained person, the tribunal may make recommendations concerning the necessity or expediency of continuing his detention to the authority by

which it was ordered but, unless it is otherwise provided by law, that authority shall not be obliged to act in accordance with any such recommendations.

(3) Nothing contained in subsection (1)(*d*) or subsection (1)(*e*) of this section shall be construed as entitling a person to legal representation at public expense.

18.—(1) If any person alleges that any of the provisions of sections 3 to 17 (inclusive) of this Constitution has been, is being or is likely to be contravened in relation to him (or, in the case of a person who is detained, if any other person alleges such a contravention in relation to the detained person), then, without prejudice to any other action with respect to the same matter that is lawfully available, that person (or that other person) may apply to the High Court for redress.

(2) The High Court shall have original jurisdiction—
  (*a*) to hear and determine any application made by any person in pursuance of subsection (1) of this section; and
  (*b*) to determine any question arising in the case of any person that is referred to it in pursuance of subsection (3) of this section,
and may make such declaration and orders, issue such writs and give such directions as it may consider appropriate for the purpose of enforcing or securing the enforcement of any of the provisions of sections 3 to 17 (inclusive) of this Constitution:
Provided that the High Court may decline to exercise its powers under this subsection if it is satisfied that adequate means of redress for the contravention alleged are or have been available to the person concerned under any other law.

(3) If in any proceedings in any court (other than the Court of Appeal, the High Court or a court-martial) any question arises as to the contravention of any of the provisions of section 3 to 17 (inclusive) of this Constitution, the person presiding in that court may, and shall if any party to the proceedings so requests, refer the question to the High Court unless, in his opinion, the raising of the question is merely frivolous or vexatious.

(4) Where any question is referred to the High Court in pursuance of subsection (3) of this section, the High Court shall give its decision upon the question and the court in which the question arose shall dispose of the case in accordance with that decision or, if that decision is the subject of an appeal to the Court of Appeal or to Her Majesty in Council, in accordance with the decision of the Court of Appeal or, as the case may be, of Her Majesty in Council.

(5) There shall be such provision as may be made by Parliament for conferring upon the High Court such powers in addition to those conferred by this section as may appear to be necessary or desirable for the purpose of enabling that court more effectively to exercise the jurisdiction conferred upon it by this section.

(6) The Chief Justice may make rules with respect to the practice and procedure of the High Court in relation to the jurisdiction and powers conferred on it by or under this section (including rules with respect to the time within which applications may be brought and references shall be made to the High Court).

19. Except as is otherwise expressly provided in this Constitution, no law may abrogate, abridge or infringe or authorise the abrogation, abridgement or infringement of any of the fundamental rights and freedoms of the individual hereinbefore recognised and declared.

20.—(1) The Governor-General may, by Proclamation which shall be published in the Official Gazette, declare that a state of public emergency exists for the purposes of this Chapter.

(2) Every declaration shall lapse—
    (*a*) in the case of a declaration made when Parliament is sitting, at the expiration of a period of seven days beginning with the date of publication of the declaration; and
    (*b*) in any other case, at the expiration of a period of twenty-one days beginning with the date of publication of the declaration, unless it has in the meantime been approved by resolutions of both Houses of Parliament.

(3) A declaration of public emergency may at any time be revoked by the Governor-General by Proclamation which shall be published in the Official Gazette.

(4) A declaration of public emergency that has been approved of by resolutions of the Houses of Parliament in pursuance of subsection (2) of this section shall, subject to the provisions of subsection (3) of this section, remain in force so long as the resolutions of those Houses remain in force and no longer.

(5) A resolution of a House of Parliament passed for the purposes of this section shall remain in force for three months or such shorter period as may be specified therein:
Provided that any such resolution may be extended from time to time by a further such resolution each extension not exceeding three months from the date of the resolution effecting the extension and any such resolution may be revoked at any time by a resolution of that House.

(6) Any provision of this section that a declaration of emergency shall lapse or cease to be in force at any particular time is without prejudice to the making of a further such declaration whether before or after that time.

(7) A resolution of a House of Parliament for the purposes of subsection (2) of this section and a resolution extending any such resolution shall not be passed unless it is supported by the votes of a majority of all members of that House.

(8) The Governor-General may summon the Houses of Parliament to

meet for the purpose of subsection (2) of this section notwithstanding that Parliament stands dissolved, and the persons who were members of the Senate and the House immediately before the dissolution shall be deemed, for those purposes, still to be members of those Houses, but, subject to the provisions of sections 33 and 42 of this Constitution (which relate to the election of the President, Vice-President, the Speaker, and the Deputy Speaker) a House of Parliament shall not, when summoned by virtue of this subsection, transact any business other than debating and voting upon a resolution for the purposes of subsection (2) of this section.

21.—(1) In this Chapter, unless the context otherwise requires—

'contravention', in relation to any requirement, includes a failure to comply with that requirement, and cognate expressions shall be construed accordingly;

'court' means any court of law having jurisdiction in Antigua and Barbuda other than a court established by a disciplinary law, and includes Her Majesty in Council and, in section 4 of this Constitution, a court established by a disciplinary law;

'disciplinary law' means a law regulating the discipline of any disciplined force;

'disciplined force' means—

(*a*) a naval, military or air force;

(*b*) the Police Force; or

(*c*) a prison service;

'member', in relation to a disciplined force, includes any person who, under the law regulating the discipline of that force, is subject to that discipline;

'legal practitioner' means a person entitled to practise as a barrister in Antigua and Barbuda or, except in relation to proceedings before a court in which a solicitor has no right of audience, entitled to practise as a solicitor in Antigua and Barbuda.

(2) In relation to any person who is a member of a disciplined force raised under any law, nothing contained in or done under the authority of the disciplinary law of that force shall be held to be inconsistent with or in contravention of any of the provisions of this Chapter other than sections 4, 6 and 7 of this Constitution.

(3) In relation to any person who is a member of a disciplined force raised otherwise than as aforesaid and lawfully present in Antigua and Barbuda, nothing contained in or done under the authority of the disciplinary law of that force shall be held to be inconsistent with or in contravention of any of the provisions of this Chapter.

(4) In this Chapter 'public emergency' means any period during which—

(*a*) Her Majesty is at war; or

(*b*) there is in force a declaration of emergency under section 20 of this Constitution, or there are in force resolution of both Houses of Parliament supported by the votes of not less than two-thirds of all the members of each House declaring that democratic institutions in Antigua and Barbuda are threatened by subversion.

(5) A Proclamation made by the Governor-General shall not be effective for the purposes of section 20 of this Constitution unless it contains a declaration that the Governor-General is satisfied—

    (*a*) that a public emergency has arisen as a result of the imminence of a state of war between Her Majesty and a foreign State or as a result of the occurrence of any earthquake, hurricane, flood, fire, outbreak of pestilence, outbreak of infectious disease or other calamity whether similar to the foregoing or not; or

    (*b*) that action has been taken or is immediately threatened by any person or body of persons of such a nature and on so extensive a scale as to be likely to endanger the public safety or to deprive the community, or any substantial portion of the community, of supplies or services essential to life.

Antigua and Barbuda Constitution Order 1981 (SI 1981 No. 1106).

(B) Jamaica

FUNDAMENTAL RIGHTS AND FREEDOMS

13. Whereas every person in Jamaica is entitled to the fundamental rights and freedoms of the individual, that is to say, has the right, whatever his race, place of origin, political opinions, colour, creed or sex, but subject to respect for the rights and freedoms of others and for the public interest, to each and all of the following, namely:

    (a) life, liberty, security of the person, the enjoyment of property and the protection of the law;

    (b) freedom of conscience, of expression and of peaceful assembly and association; and

    (c) respect for his private and family life,

the subsequent provisions of this Chapter shall have effect for the purpose of affording protection to the aforesaid rights and freedoms, subject to such limitations of that protection as are contained in those provisions being limitations designed to ensure that the enjoyment of the said rights and freedoms by any individual does not prejudice the rights and freedoms of others or the public interest.

14. (1) No person shall intentionally be deprived of his life save in execution of the sentence of a court in respect of a criminal offence of which he has been convicted.

(2) Without prejudice to any liability for a contravention of any other law

with respect to the use of force in such cases as are hereinafter mentioned, a person shall not be regarded as having been deprived of his life in contravention of this section if he dies as the result of the use of force to such extent as is reasonably justifiable in the circumstances of the case:

(a) for the defence of any person from violence or for the defence of property;

(b) in order to effect a lawful arrest or to prevent the escape of a person lawfully detained;

(c) for the purpose of suppressing a riot, insurrection or mutiny; or

(d) in order lawfully to prevent the commission by that person of a criminal offence,

or if he dies as the result of a lawful act of war.

15. (1) No person shall be deprived of his personal liberty save as may in any of the following cases be authorised by law:

(a) in consequence of his unfitness to plead to a criminal charge; or

(b) in execution of the sentence or order of a court, whether in Jamaica or elsewhere, in respect of a criminal offence of which he has been convicted; or

(c) in execution of an order of the Supreme Court or of the Court of Appeal or such other court as may be prescribed by Parliament on the grounds of his contempt of any such court or of another court or tribunal; or

(d) in execution of the order of a court made in order to secure the fulfilment of any obligation imposed on him by law; or

(e) for the purpose of bringing him before a court in execution of the order of a court; or

(f) upon reasonable suspicion of his having committed or of being about to commit a criminal offence; or

(g) in the case of a person who has not attained the age of twenty-one years, for the purpose of his education or welfare; or

(h) for the purpose of preventing the spread of an infectious or contagious disease; or

(i) in the case of a person who is, or is reasonably suspected to be, of unsound mind, addicted to drugs or alcohol, or a vagrant, for the purpose of his care or treatment or the protection of the community; or

(j) for the purpose of preventing the unlawful entry of that person into Jamaica, or for the purpose of effecting the expulsion, extradition or other lawful removal of that person from Jamaica or the taking of proceedings relating thereto; or

(k) to such extent as may be necessary in the execution of a lawful order requiring that person to remain within a specified area within Jamaica or prohibiting him from being within such an area, or to such extent as may be reasonably justifiable for the taking of proceedings against that person relating to the making of any such order, or to such extent as may be reasonably justifiable for restraining that person during any visit that he is permitted to make to any part of Jamaica in which, in consequence of any such order, his presence would otherwise be unlawful.

(2) Any person who is arrested or detained shall be informed as soon as reasonably practicable, in a language which he understands, of the reasons for his arrest or detention.

(3) Any person who is arrested or detained:
  (a) for the purpose of bringing him before a court in execution of the order of a court; or
  (b) upon reasonable suspicion of his having committed or being about to commit a criminal offence,
and who is not released, shall be brought without delay before a court; and if any person arrested or detained upon reasonable suspicion of his having committed or being about to commit a criminal offence is not tried within a reasonable time, then, without prejudice to any further proceedings which may be brought against him, he shall be released either unconditionally or upon reasonable conditions, including in particular such conditions as are reasonably necessary to ensure that he appears at a later date for trial or for proceedings preliminary to trial.

(4) Any person who is unlawfully arrested or detained by any other person shall be entitled to compensation therefor from that person.

(5) Nothing contained in or done under the authority of any law shall be held to be inconsistent with or in contravention of this section to the extent that the law in question authorises the taking during a period of public emergency of measures that are reasonably justifiable for the purpose of dealing with the situation that exists during that period of public emergency.

(6) If any person who is lawfully detained by virtue only of such a law as is referred to in subsection (5) of this section so requests at any time during the period of that detention not earlier than six months after he last made such a request during that period, his case shall be reviewed by an independent and impartial tribunal established by law and presided over by a person appointed by the Chief Justice of Jamaica from among the persons entitled to practise or to be admitted to practise in Jamaica as barristers or solicitors.

(7) On any review by a tribunal in pursuance of subsection (6) of this section of the case of any detained person, the tribunal may make recommendations concerning the necessity or expediency of continuing his detention to the authority by whom it was ordered but, unless it is otherwise provided by law, that authority shall not be obliged to act in accordance with any such recommendations.

16. (1) No person shall be deprived of his freedom of movement, and for the purposes of this section the said freedom means the right to move freely throughout Jamaica, the right to reside in any part of Jamaica, the right to enter Jamaica and immunity from expulsion from Jamaica.

(2) Any restriction on a person's freedom of movement which is involved in his lawful detention shall not be held to be inconsistent with or in contravention of this section.

(3) Nothing contained in or done under the authority of any law shall be held to be inconsistent with or in contravention of this section to the extent that the law in question makes provision:
>   (a) which is reasonably required in the interests of defence, public safety, public order, public morality or public health; or
>   (b) for the imposition of restrictions on the movement or residence within Jamaica of any person who is not citizen thereof or the exclusion or expulsion from Jamaica of any such person; or
>   (c) for the imposition of restrictions on the acquisition or use by any person of land or other property in Jamaica; or
>   (d) for the imposition of restrictions upon the movement or residence within Jamaica of public officers, police officers or members of a defence force; or
>   (e) for the removal of a person from Jamaica to be tried outside Jamaica for a criminal offence or to undergo imprisonment outside Jamaica in execution of the sentence of a court in respect of a criminal offence of which he has been convicted.

(4) If any person whose freedom of movement has been restricted by virtue only of such a provision as is referred to in paragraph (a) of subsection (3) of this section so requests at any time during the period of that restriction not earlier than six months after he last made such a request during that period, his case shall be reviewed by an independent and impartial tribunal established by law and presided over by a person appointed by the Chief Justice of Jamaica from among the persons entitled to practise or to be admitted to practise in Jamaica as barristers or solicitors.

(5) On any review by a tribunal in pursuance of subsection (4) of this section of the case of any person whose freedom of movement has been restricted, the tribunal may make recommendations concerning the necessity or expediency of continuing that restriction to the authority by whom it was ordered but, unless it is otherwise provided by law, that authority shall not be obliged to act in accordance with any such recommendations.

17. (1) No person shall be subjected to torture or to inhuman or degrading punishment or other treatment.

(2) Nothing contained in or done under the authority of any law shall be held to be inconsistent with or in contravention of this section to the extent that the law in question authorises the infliction of any description of punishment which was lawful in Jamaica immediately before the appointed day.

18. (1) No property of any description shall be compulsorily taken possession of and no interest in or right over property of any description shall be compulsorily acquired except by or under the provisions of a law that:

(a) prescribes the principles on which and the manner in which compensation therefor is to be determined and given; and

(b) secures to any person claiming an interest in or right over such property a right of access to a court for the purpose of:
  (i) establishing such interest or right (if any);
  (ii) determining the amount of such compensation (if any) to which he is entitled; and
  (iii) enforcing his right to any such compensation.

(2) Nothing in this section shall be construed as affecting the making or operation of any law so far as it provides for the taking of possession or acquisition of property:

(a) in satisfaction of any tax, rate or due;

(b) by way of penalty for breach of the law, whether under civil process or after conviction of a criminal offence;

(c) upon the attempted removal of the property in question out of or into Jamaica in contravention of any law;

(d) by way of the taking of a sample for the purposes of any law;

(e) where the property consists of an animal upon its being found trespassing or straying;

(f) as an incident of a lease, tenancy, licence, mortgage, charge, bill of sale, pledge or contract;

(g) by way of the vesting or administration of trust property, enemy property, or the property of persons adjudged or otherwise declared bankrupt or insolvent, persons of unsound mind, deceased persons, or bodies corporate or unincorporate in the course of being wound up;

(h) in the execution of judgments or orders of courts;

(i) by reason of its being in a dangerous state or injurious to the health of human beings, animals or plants;

(j) in consequence of any law with respect to the limitation of actions;

(k) for so long only as may be necessary for the purposes of any examination, investigation, trial or inquiry or, in the case of land, the carrying out thereon:
  (i) of work of soil conservation or the conservation of other natural resources; or
  (ii) of agricultural development or improvement which the owner or occupier of the land has been required, and has without reasonable and lawful excuse refused or failed, to carry out.

(3) Nothing in this section shall be construed as affecting the making or operation of any law so far as it provides for the orderly marketing or production or growth or extraction of any agricultural product or mineral or any article or thing prepared for market or manufactured therefor or for the reasonable restriction of the use of any property in the interests of safeguarding the interests of others or the protection of tenants, licensees or others having rights in or over such property.

(4) Nothing in this section shall be construed as affecting the making or operation of any law for the compulsory taking of possession in the public interest of any property, or the compulsory acquisition in the public interest of any interest in or right over property, where that property, interest or right is held by a body corporate which is established for public purposes by any law and in which no monies have been invested other than monies provided by Parliament or by the Legislature of the former Colony of Jamaica.

(5) In this section 'compensation' means the consideration to be given to a person for any interest or right which he may have in or over property which has been compulsorily taken possession of or compulsorily acquired as prescribed and determined in accordance with the provisions of the law by or under which the property has been compulsorily taken possession of or compulsorily acquired.

19. (1) Except with his own consent, no person shall be subjected to the search of his person or his property or the entry by others on his premises.

(2) Nothing contained in or done under the authority of any law shall be held to be inconsistent with or in contravention of this section to the extent that the law in question makes provision which is reasonably required:

   (a) in the interests of defence, public safety, public order, public morality, public health, public revenue, town and country planning or the development and utilisation of any property in such a manner as to promote the public benefit; or
   (b) to enable any body corporate established by any law for public purposes or any department of the Government of Jamaica or any local government authority to enter on the premises of any person in order to carry out work connected with any property or installation which is lawfully on such premises and which belongs to that body corporate or that Government or that authority, as the case may be; or
   (c) for the purpose of preventing or detecting crime; or
   (d) for the purpose of protecting the rights or freedoms of other persons.

20. (1) Whenever any person is charged with a criminal offence he shall, unless the charge is withdrawn, be afforded a fair hearing within a reasonable time by an independent and impartial court established by law.

(2) Any court or other authority prescribed by law for the determination of the existence or the extent of civil rights or obligations shall be independent and impartial; and where proceedings for such a determination are instituted by any person before such a court or other authority, the case shall be given a fair hearing within a reasonable time.

(3) All proceedings of every court and proceedings relating to the determination of the existence or the extent of a person's civil rights or

obligations before any court or other authority, including the announcement of the decision of the court or other authority, shall be held in
public.

(4) Nothing in subsection (8) of this section shall prevent any court or any
authority such as is mentioned in that subsection from excluding from the
proceedings persons other than the parties thereto and their legal representatives:

(a) in interlocutory civil proceedings; or

(b) in appeal proceedings under any law relating to income tax; or

(c) to such extent as the court or other authority:

    (i)   may consider necessary or expedient in circumstances where
publicity would prejudice the interests of justice; or

    (ii) may be empowered or required by law to do so in the
interests of defence, public safety, public order, public
morality, the welfare of persons under the age of twenty-one
years or the protection of the private lives of persons concerned in the proceedings.

(5) Every person who is charged with a criminal offence shall be presumed to be innocent until he is proved or has pleaded guilty:

Provided that nothing contained in or done under the authority of any law
shall be held to be inconsistent with or in contravention of this subsection to
the extent that the law in question imposes upon any person charged as
aforesaid the burden of proving particular facts.

(6) Every person who is charged with a criminal offence:

(a) shall be informed as soon as reasonably practicable, in a language
which he understands, of the nature of the offence charged;

(b) shall be given adequate time and facilities for the preparation of
his defence;

(c) shall be permitted to defend himself in person or by a legal
representative of his own choice;

(d) shall be afforded facilities to examine in person or by his legal
representative the witnesses called by the prosecution before any
court and to obtain the attendance of witnesses, subject to the
payment of their reasonable expenses, and carry out the examination of such witnesses to testify on his behalf before the court on
the same conditions as those applying to witnesses called by the
prosecution; and

(e) shall be permitted to have without payment the assistance of an
interpreter if he cannot understand the English language.

(7) No person shall be held to be guilty of a criminal offence on account
of any act or omission which did not, at the time it took place, constitute
such an offence, and no penalty shall be imposed for any criminal offence
which is severer in degree or description than the maximum penalty which
might have been imposed for that offence at the time when it was committed.

(8) No person who shows that he has been tried by any competent court

for a criminal offence and either convicted or acquitted shall again be tried for that offence or for any other criminal offence of which he could have been convicted at the trial for that offence save upon the order of a superior court made in the course of appeal proceedings relating to the conviction or acquittal; and no person shall be tried for a criminal offence if he shows that he has been pardoned for that offence:

Provided that nothing in any law shall be held to be inconsistent with or in contravention of this subsection by reason only that it authorises any court to try a member of a defence force for a criminal offence notwithstanding any trial and conviction or acquittal of that member under service law; but any court so trying such a member and convicting him shall in sentencing him to any punishment take into account any punishment awarded him under service law.

(9) Nothing contained in or done under the authority of any law shall be held to be inconsistent with or in contravention of any provision of this section other than subsection (7) thereof to the extent that the law in question authorises the taking during a period of public emergency of measures that are reasonably justifiable for the purpose of dealing with the situation that exists during that period of public emergency.

(10) In paragraph (c) and (d) of subsection (6) of this section 'legal representative' means a barrister entitled to practise as such in Jamaica or, except in relation to proceedings before a court in which a solicitor has no right of audience, a solicitor who is so entitled.

21. (1) Except with his own consent, no person shall be hindered in the enjoyment of his freedom of conscience, and for the purposes of this section the said freedom includes freedom of thought and of religion, freedom to change his religion or belief, and freedom, either alone or in community with others, and both in public and in private, to manifest and propagate his religion or belief in worship, teaching, practice and observance.

(2) Except with his own consent (or, if he is a minor, the consent of his parent or guardian), no person attending any place of education shall be required to receive religious instruction or to take part in or attend any religious ceremony or observance if that instruction, ceremony or observance relates to a religion or a religious body or denomination other than his own.

(3) The constitution of a religious body or denomination shall not be altered except with the consent of the governing authority of that body or denomination.

(4) No religious body or denomination shall be prevented from providing religious instruction for persons of that body or denomination in the course of any education provided by that body or denomination whether or not that body or denomination is in receipt of any government subsidy, grant or other form of financial assistance designed to meet, in whole or in part, the cost of such course of education.

(5) No person shall be compelled to take any oath which is contrary to his religion or belief or to take any oath in a manner which is contrary to his religion or belief.

(6) Nothing contained in or done under the authority of any law shall be held to be inconsistent with or in contravention of this section to the extent that the law in question makes provision which is reasonably required:

    (a) in the interests of defence, public safety, public order, public morality or public health; or

    (b) for the purpose of protecting the rights and freedoms of other persons, including the right to observe and practise any religion without the unsolicited intervention of members of any other religion.

22. (1) Except with his own consent, no person shall be hindered in the enjoyment of his freedom of expression, and for the purposes of this section the said freedom includes the freedom to hold opinions and to receive and impart ideas and information without interference, and freedom from interference with his correspondence and other means of communication.

(2) Nothing contained in or done under the authority of any law shall be held to be inconsistent with or in contravention of this section to the extent that the law in question makes provision:

    (a) which is reasonably required:

        (i) in the interests of defence, public safety, public order, public morality or public health; or

        (ii) for the purpose of protecting the reputations, rights and freedoms of other persons, or the private lives of persons concerned in legal proceedings, preventing the disclosure of information received in confidence, maintaining the authority and independence of the courts, or regulating telephony, telegraphy, posts, wireless broadcasting, television or other means of communication, public exhibitions or public entertainments; or

    (b) which imposes restrictions upon public officers, police officers or upon members of a defence force.

23. (1) Except with his own consent, no person shall be hindered in the enjoyment of his freedom of peaceful assembly and association, that is to say, his right peacefully to assemble freely and associate with other persons and in particular to form or belong to trade unions or other associations for the protection of his interests.

(2) Nothing contained in or done under the authority of any law shall be held to be inconsistent with or in contravention of this section to the extent that the law in question makes provision:

    (a) which is reasonably required:

        (i) in the interests of defence, public safety, public order, public morality or public health; or (ii)　for the purpose of protecting the rights or freedoms of other persons; or

(b)　which imposes restrictions upon public officers, police officers or upon members of a defence force.

24. (1) Subject to the provisions of subsections (4), (5) and (7) of this section, no law shall make any provision which is discriminatory either of itself or in its effect.

(2) Subject to the provisions of subsections (6), (7) and (8) of this section, no person shall be treated in a discriminatory manner by any person acting by virtue of any written law or in the performance of the functions of any public office or any public authority.

(3) In this section, the expression 'discriminatory' means affording different treatment to different persons attributable wholly or mainly to their respective descriptions by race, place of origin, political opinions, colour or creed whereby persons of one such description are subjected to disabilities or restrictions to which persons of another such description are not made subject or are accorded privileges or advantages which are not accorded to persons of another such description.

(4) Subsection (1) of this section shall not apply to any law so far as that law makes provision:

(a)　with respect to persons who are not citizens of Jamaica; or

(b)　with respect to adoption, marriage, divorce, burial, devolution of property on death or other matters of personal law; or

(c)　for authorising the taking during a period of public emergency of measures that are reasonably justifiable for the purpose of dealing with the situation that exists during that period of public emergency; or

(d)　for the imposition of taxation or appropriation of revenue by the Government of Jamaica or any local authority or body for local purposes.

(5) Nothing contained in any law shall be held to be inconsistent with or in contravention of subsection (1) of this section to the extent that it makes provision with respect to qualifications for service as a public officer, police officer or as a member of a defence force or for the service of a local government authority or a body corporate established by any law for public purposes.

(6) Subsection (2) of this section shall not apply to anything which is expressly or by necessary implication authorised to be done by any such provision of law as is referred to in subsection (4) or (5) of this section.

(7) Nothing contained in or done under the authority of any law shall be held to be inconsistent with or in contravention of this section to the extent that the law in question makes provision whereby persons of any such description as is mentioned in subsection (8) of this section may be subjected to any restriction on the rights and freedoms guaranteed by sections

16, 19, 21, 22 and 23 of this Constitution, being such a restriction as is authorised by paragraph (a) of subsection (3) of section 16, subsection (2) of section 19, subsection (6) of section 21, subsection (2) of section 22 or subsection (2) of section 23, as the case may be.

(8) Nothing in subsection (2) of this section shall affect any discretion relating to the institution, conduct or discontinuance of civil or criminal proceedings in any court that is vested in any person by or under this Constitution or any other law.

25. (1) Subject to the provisions of subsection (4) of this section, if any person alleges that any of the provisions of sections 14 to 24 (inclusive) of this Constitution has been, is being or is likely to be contravened in relation to him, then, without prejudice to any other action with respect to the same matter which is lawfully available, that person may apply to the Supreme Court for redress.

(2) The Supreme Court shall have original jurisdiction to hear and determine any application made by any person in pursuance of subsection (1) of this section and may make such orders, issue such writs and give such directions as it may consider appropriate for the purpose of enforcing, or securing the enforcement of, any of the provisions of the said sections 14 to 24 (inclusive) to the protection of which the person concerned is entitled:

Provided that the Supreme Court shall not exercise its powers under this subsection if it is satisfied that adequate means of redress for the contravention alleged are or have been available to the person concerned under any other law.

(3) Any person aggrieved by any determination of the Supreme Court under this section may appeal therefrom to the Court of Appeal.

(4) Parliament may make provision, or may authorise the making of provision, with respect to the practice and procedure of any court for the purposes of this section and may confer upon that court such powers, or may authorise the conferment thereon of such powers, in addition to those conferred by this section as may appear to be necessary or desirable for the purpose of enabling that court more effectively to exercise the jurisdiction conferred upon it by this section.

26. (1) In this Chapter, save where the context otherwise requires, the following expressions have the following meanings respectively, that is to say:

'contravention', in relation to any requirement, includes a failure to comply with that requirement, and cognate expressions shall be construed accordingly;

'court' means any court of law in Jamaica other than a court constituted by or under service law and:

(i) in section 14, section 15, section 16, subsections (3), (4), (6), (8) (but not the proviso thereto) and (10) of section 20, and subsection (8) of section 24 of this Constitution includes, in relation to an offence against service law, a court so constituted; and

(ii) in section 15 and subsection (8) of section 24 of this Constitution includes, in relation to an offence against service law, an officer of a defence force, or the Police Service Commission or any person or authority to whom the disciplinary powers of that Commission have been lawfully delegated;

'member', in relation to a defence force or other armed force, includes any person who, under the law regulating the discipline of that force, is subject to that discipline;

'service law' means the law regulating the discipline of a defence force or of police officers.

(2) References in sections 14, 15, 16 and 18 of this Constitution to a 'criminal offence' shall be construed as including references to an offence against service law and such references in subsection (5) to (9) (inclusive) of section 20 of this Constitution shall, in relation to proceedings before a court constituted by or under service law, be similarly construed.

(3) Nothing done by or under the authority of the law of any country other than Jamaica to a member of an armed force raised under that law and lawfully present in Jamaica shall be held to be in contravention of this Chapter.

(4) In this Chapter 'period of public emergency' means any period during which:

(a) Jamaica is engaged in any war; or

(b) there is in force a Proclamation by the Governor-General declaring that a state of public emergency exists; or

(c) there is in force a resolution of each House supported by the votes of a majority of all the members of that House declaring that democratic institutions in Jamaica are threatened by subversion.

(5) A Proclamation made by the Governor-General shall not be effective for the purposes of subsection (4) of this section unless it is declared therein that the Governor-General is satisfied:

(a) that a public emergency has arisen as a result of the imminence of a state of war between Jamaica and a foreign State or as a result of the occurrence of any earthquake, hurricane, flood, fire, outbreak of pestilence, outbreak of infectious disease or other calamity whether similar to the foregoing or not; or

(b) that action has been taken or is immediately threatened by any person or body of persons of such a nature and on so extensive a scale as to be likely to endanger the public safety or to deprive the community, or any substantial portion of the community, of supplies or services essential to life.

(6) A Proclamation made by the Governor-General for the purposes of and in accordance with this section:

(a) shall, unless previously revoked, remain in force for one month or for such longer period, not exceeding twelve months, as the House of Representatives may determine by a resolution supported by the votes of a majority of all the members of the House;

(b) may be extended from time to time by a resolution passed in like manner as is prescribed in paragraph (a) of this subsection for further periods, not exceeding in respect of each such extension a period of twelve months; and

(c) may be revoked at any time by a resolution supported by the votes of a majority of all the members of the House of Representatives.

(7) A resolution passed by a House for the purposes of subsection (4) of this section may be revoked at any time by a resolution of that House supported by the votes of a majority of all the members thereof.

(8) Nothing contained in any law in force immediately before the appointed day shall be held to be inconsistent with any of the provisions of this Chapter; and nothing done under the authority of any such law shall be held to be done in contravention of any of these provisions.

(9) For the purposes of subsection (8) of this section a law in force immediately before the appointed day shall be deemed not to have ceased to be such a law by reason only of:

(a) any adaptations or modifications made thereto by or under section 4 of the Jamaica (Constitution) Order in Council, 1962, or

(b) its reproduction in identical form in any consolidation or revision of laws with only such adaptations or modifications as are necessary or expedient by reason of its inclusion in such consolidation or revision.

Jamaica (Constitution) Order in Council 1962.

(C) Trinidad and Tobago

THE RECOGNITION AND PROTECTION OF FUNDAMENTAL HUMAN
RIGHTS AND FREEDOMS

Part I: Rights enshrined

4. It is hereby recognised and declared that in Trinidad and Tobago there have existed and shall continue to exist without discrimination by reason of race, origin, colour, religion or sex, the following fundamental human rights and freedoms, namely:—

(*a*) the right of the individual to life, liberty, security of the person and enjoyment of property and the right not to be deprived thereof except by due process of law;

(*b*) the right of the individual to equality before the law and the protection of the law;

(*c*) the right of the individual to respect for his private and family life;

(*d*) the right of the individual to equality of treatment from any public authority in the exercise of any functions;

(*e*) the right to join political parties and to express political views;

(*f*) the right of a parent or guardian to provide a school of his own choice for the education of his child or ward;

(*g*) freedom of movement;

(*h*) freedom of conscience and religious belief and observance;

(*i*) freedom of thought and expression;

(*j*) freedom of association and assembly; and

(*k*) freedom of the press.

5. (1) Except as is otherwise expressly provided in this Chapter and in section 54, no law may abrogate, abridge or infringe or authorise the abrogation, abridgement or infringement of any of the rights and freedoms hereinbefore recognised and declared.

(2) Without prejudice to subsection (1), but subject to this Chapter and to section 54, Parliament may not—

(*a*) authorise or effect the arbitrary detention, imprisonment or exile of any person;

(*b*) impose or authorise the imposition of cruel and unusual treatment or punishment;

(*c*) deprive a person who has been arrested or detained—

    (i)   of the right to be informed promptly and with sufficient particularity of the reason for his arrest or detention;

    (ii) of the right to retain and instruct without delay a legal adviser of his own choice and to hold communication with him;

    (iii) of the right to be brought promptly before an appropriate judicial authority;

    (iv) of the remedy by way of habeas corpus for the determination of the validity of his detention and for his release if the detention is not lawful;

(*d*) authorise a court, tribunal, commission, board or other authority to compel a person to give evidence unless he is afforded protection against self-incrimination and, where necessary to ensure such protection, the right to legal representation;

(*e*) deprive a person of the right to a fair hearing in accordance with the principles of fundamental justice for the determination of his rights and obligations;

(*f*) deprive a person charged with a criminal offence of the right—

    (i)   to be presumed innocent until proved guilty according to law, but this shall not invalidate a law by reason only that the law imposes on any such person the burden of proving particular facts;

    (ii) to a fair and public hearing by an independent and impartial tribunal; or

(iii) to reasonable bail without just cause;

(*g*) deprive a person of the right to the assistance of an interpreter in any proceedings in which he is involved or in which he is a party or a witness, before a court, commission, board or other tribunal, if he does not understand or speak English; or

(*h*) deprive a person of the right to such procedural provisions as are necessary for the purpose of giving effect and protection to the aforesaid rights and freedoms.

Part II: Exceptions for existing law

6. (1) Nothing in sections 4 and 5 shall invalidate—

(*a*) an existing law;

(*b*) an enactment that repeals and re-enacts an existing law without alteration; or

(*c*) an enactment that alters an existing law but does not derogate from any fundamental right guaranteed by this Chapter in a manner in which or to an extent to which the existing law did not previously derogate from that right.

(2) Where an enactment repeals and re-enacts with modifications an existing law and is held to derogate from any fundamental right guaranteed by this Chapter in a manner in which or to an extent to which the existing law did not previously derogate from that right then, subject to sections 13 and 54, the provisions of the existing law shall be substituted for such of the provisions of the enactment as are held to derogate from the fundamental right in a manner in which or to an extent to which the existing law did not previously derogate from that right.

(3) In this section—

'alters', in relation to an existing law, includes repealing that law and re-enacting it with modifications or making different provisions in place of it or modifying it;

'existing law' means a law that had effect as part of the law of Trinidad and Tobago immediately before the commencement of this Constitution, and includes any enactment referred to in subsection (1);

'right' includes freedom.

Part III: Exceptions for emergencies

7. (1) Without prejudice to the power of Parliament to make provision in the premise, but subject to this section, where any period of public emergency exists, the President may, due regard being had to the circumstances of any situation likely to arise or exist during such period make regulations for the purpose of dealing with that situation and issue orders and instructions for the purpose of the exercise of any powers conferred on him or any other person by any Act referred to in subsection (3) or instrument made under this section or any such Act.

(2) Without prejudice to the generality of subsection (1) regulations made under that subsection may, subject to section 11, make provision for the detention of persons.

(3) An Act that is passed during a period of public emergency and is expressly declared to have effect only during that period or any regulations made under subsection (1) shall have effect even though inconsistent with sections 4 and 5 except in so far as its provisions may be shown not to be reasonably justifiable for the purpose of dealing with the situation that exists during that period.

8. (1) Subject to this section, for the purposes of this Chapter, the President may from time to time make a Proclamation declaring that a state of public emergency exists.

(2) A Proclamation made by the President under subsection (1) shall not be effective unless it contains a declaration that the President is satisfied—

    (*a*) that a public emergency has arisen as a result of the imminence of a state of war between Trinidad and Tobago and a foreign State;

    (*b*) that a public emergency has arisen as a result of the occurrence of any earthquake, hurricane, flood, fire, outbreak of pestilence or of infectious disease, or other calamity whether similar to the foregoing or not; or

    (*c*) that action has been taken, or is immediately threatened, by any person, of such a nature and on so extensive a scale, as to be likely to endanger the public safety or to deprive the community or any substantial portion of the community of supplies or services essential to life.

9. (1) Within three days of the making of the Proclamation, the President shall deliver to the Speaker for presentation to the House of Representatives a statement setting out the specific grounds on which the decision to declare the existence of a state of public emergency was based, and a date shall be fixed for a debate on this statement as soon as practicable but in any event not later that fifteen days from the date of the Proclamation.

(2) A Proclamation made by the President for the purposes of and in accordance with this section shall, unless previously revoked, remain in force for fifteen days.

10. (1) Before its expiration the Proclamation may be extended from time to time by resolution supported by a simple majority vote of the House of Representatives, so however, that no extension exceeds three months and the extensions do not in the aggregate exceed six months.

(2) The Proclamation may be further extended from time to time for not more than three months at any one time, by a resolution passed by both Houses of Parliament and supported by the votes of not less that three-fifths of all the members of each House.

(3) The Proclamation may be revoked at any time by a resolution supported by a simple majority vote of the House of Representatives.

(4) In this Chapter 'period of public emergency' means any period during which—

   (*a*) Trinidad and Tobago is engaged in any war; or

   (*b*) there is in force a Proclamation by the President declaring that a state of public emergency exists; or

   (*c*) there is in force a resolution of both Houses of Parliament supported by the votes of not less than two-thirds of all the members of each House declaring that democratic institutions in Trinidad and Tobago are threatened by subversion.

11. (1) Where any person who is lawfully detained by virtue only of such an Act or regulations as is referred to in section 7 so requests at any time during the period of that detention and thereafter not earlier than six months after he last made such a request during that period, his case shall be reviewed by an independent and impartial tribunal established by law and presided over by a person appointed by the Chief Justice from among the persons entitled to practise in Trinidad and Tobago as barristers or solicitors.

(2) On any review by a tribunal in pursuance of subsection (1) of the case of any detained person, the tribunal may make recommendations concerning the necessity or expediency of continuing his detention to the authority by whom it was ordered but, unless otherwise provided by law, that authority shall not be obliged to act in accordance with such recommendations.

12. (1) Where at any time it is impracticable or inexpedient to publish in the *Gazette* any Proclamation, Notice, Regulation or Order in pursuance of this Part, the President may cause the same to be published by notices thereof affixed to public buildings or distributed amongst the public or by oral public announcements.

(2) Upon the publication of any Proclamation under this Part all such detention orders, curfew orders or other instruments, directions or instructions as are authorised to be made, issued or given by any regulations referred to in section 7 may be made, issued or given and executed upon any person or authority, even if such regulations have not yet been published pursuant to subsection (1).

Part IV: Exceptions for certain legislation

13. (1) An Act to which this section applies may expressly declare that it shall have effect even though inconsistent with sections 4 and 5 and, if any such Act does so declare, it shall have effect accordingly unless the Act is shown not to be reasonably justifiable in a society that has a proper respect for the rights and freedoms of the individual.

(2) An Act to which this section applies is one the Bill for which has been passed by both Houses of Parliament and at the final vote thereon in each

House has been supported by the votes of not less than three-fifths of all the members of that House.

(3) For the purposes of subsection (2) the number of members of the Senate shall, notwithstanding the appointment of temporary members in accordance with section 44, be deemed to be the number of members specified in section 40(1).

Part V: General

14. (1) For the removal of doubts it is hereby declared that if any person alleges that any of the provisions of this Chapter has been, is being, or is likely to be contravened in relation to him, then without prejudice to any other action with respect to the same matter which is lawfully available, that person may apply to the High Court for redress by way of originating motion.

(2) The High Court shall have original jurisdiction—
  (*a*) to hear and determine any application made by any person in pursuance of subsection (1), and
  (*b*) to determine any question arising in the case of any person which is referred to it in pursuance of subsection (4),
and may, subject to subsection (3), make such orders, issue such writs and give such directions as it may consider appropriate for the purpose of enforcing, or securing the enforcement of, any of the provisions of this Chapter to the protection of which the person concerned is entitled.

(3) The State Liability and Proceedings Act, 1966 shall have effect for the purpose of any proceedings under this section.

(4) Where in any proceedings in any court other than the High Court or the Court of Appeal any question arises as to the contravention of any of the provisions of this Chapter the person presiding in that court may, and shall if any party to the proceedings so requests, refer the question to the High Court unless in his opinion the raising of the question is merely frivolous or vexatious.

(5) Any person aggrieved by any determination of the High Court under this section may appeal therefrom to the Court of Appeal and shall be entitled as of right to a stay of execution of the order and may in the discretion of the Court be granted bail.

(6) Nothing in this section shall limit the power of Parliament to confer on the High Court or the Court of Appeal such powers as Parliament may think fit in relation to the exercise by the High Court or the Court of Appeal, as the case may be, of its jurisdiction in respect of the matters arising under this Chapter.

The Constitution of the Republic of Trinidad and Tobago 1980.

---

45 CANADIAN CHARTER OF RIGHTS AND FREEDOMS, 1982

CANADIAN CHARTER OF RIGHTS AND FREEDOMS

Whereas Canada is founded upon principles that recognize the supremacy of God and the rule of law:

Guarantee of rights and freedoms

1. The *Canadian Charter of Rights and Freedoms* guarantees the rights and freedoms set out in it subject only to such reasonable limits prescribed by law as can be demonstrably justified in a free and democratic society.

Fundamental freedoms

2. Everyone has the following fundamental freedoms:
- (*a*) freedom of conscience and religion;
- (*b*) freedom of thought, belief, opinion and expression, including freedom of the press and other media of communication;
- (*c*) freedom of peaceful assembly; and
- (*d*) freedom of association.

Democratic rights

3. Every citizen of Canada has the right to vote in an election of members of the House of Commons or of a legislative assembly and to be qualified for membership therein.

4. (1) No House of Commons and no legislative assembly shall continue for longer than five years from the date fixed for the return of the writs of a general election of its members.(80)

(2) In time of real or apprehended war, invasion or insurrection, a House of Commons may be continued by Parliament and a legislative assembly may be continued by the legislature beyond five years if such continuation is not opposed by the votes of more than one-third of the members of the House of Commons or the legislative assembly, as the case may be.(81)

5. There shall be a sitting of Parliament and of each legislature at least once every twelve months.(82)

Mobility rights

6. (1) Every citizen of Canada has the right to enter, remain in and leave Canada.

(2) Every citizen of Canada and every person who has the status of a permanent resident of Canada has the right

    (*a*) to move to and take up residence in any province; and

    (*b*) to pursue the gaining of a livelihood in any province.

(3) The rights specified in subsection (2) are subject to

    (*a*) any laws or practices of general application in force in a province other than those that discriminate among persons primarily on the basis of province of present or previous residence; and

    (*b*) any laws providing for reasonable residency requirements as a qualification for the receipt of publicly provided social services.

(4) Subsections (2) and (3) do not preclude any law, program or activity that has as its object the amelioration in a province of conditions of individuals in that province who are socially or economically disadvantaged if the rate of employment in that province is below the rate of employment in Canada.

Legal rights

7. Everyone has the right to life, liberty and security of the person and the right not to be deprived thereof except in accordance with the principles of fundamental justice.

8. Everyone has the right to be secure against unreasonable search or seizure.

9. Everyone has the right not to be arbitrarily detained or imprisoned.

10. Everyone has the right on arrest or detention

    (*a*) to be informed promptly of the reasons therefor;

    (*b*) to retain and instruct counsel without delay and to be informed of that right; and

    (*c*) to have the validity of the detention determined by way of *habeas corpus* and to be released if the detention is not lawful.

11. Any person charged with an offence has the right

    (*a*) to be informed without unreasonable delay of the specific offence;

    (*b*) to be tried within a reasonable time;

    (*c*) not to be compelled to be a witness in proceedings against that person in respect of the offence;

    (*d*) to be presumed innocent until proven guilty according to law in a fair and public hearing by an independent and impartial tribunal;

    (*e*) not to be denied reasonable bail without just cause;

    (*f*) except in the case of an offence under military law tried before a military tribunal, to the benefit of trial by jury where the maximum punishment for the offence is imprisonment for five years or a more severe punishment;

(*g*) not to be found guilty on account of any act or omission unless, at the time of the act or omission, it constituted an offence under Canadian or international law or was criminal according to the general principles of law recognized by the community of nations;

(*h*) if finally acquitted of the offence, not to be tried for it again and, if finally found guilty and punished for the offence, not to be tried or punished for it again; and

(*i*) if found guilty of the offence and if the punishment for the offence has been varied between the time of commission and the time of sentencing, to the benefit of the lesser punishment.

12. Everyone has the right not to be subjected to any cruel and unusual treatment or punishment.

13. A witness who testifies in any proceedings has the right not to have any incriminating evidence so given used to incriminate that witness in any other proceedings, except in a prosecution for perjury or for the giving of contradictory evidence.

14. A party or witness in any proceedings who does not understand or speak the language in which the proceedings are conducted or who is deaf has the right to the assistance of an interpreter.

Equality rights

15. (1) Every individual is equal before and under the law and has the right to the equal protection and equal benefit of the law without discrimination and, in particular, without discrimination based on race, national or ethnic origin, colour, religion, sex, age or mental or physical disability.

(2) Subsection (1) does not preclude any law, program or activity that has as its object the amelioration of conditions of disadvantaged individuals or groups including those that are disadvantaged because of race, national or ethnic origin, colour, religion, sex, age or mental or physical disability. (83)

Official languages of Canada

16. (1) English and French are the official languages of Canada and have equality of status and equal rights and privileges as to their use in all institutions of the Parliament and government of Canada.

(2) English and French are the official languages of New Brunswick and have equality of status and equal rights and privileges as to their use in all institutions of the legislature and government of New Brunswick.

(3) Nothing in this Charter limits the authority of Parliament or a legislature to advance the equality of status or use of English and French.

17. (1) Everyone has the right to use English or French in any debates and other proceedings of Parliament. (84)

(2) Everyone has the right to use English or French in any debates and other proceedings of the legislature of New Brunswick. (85)

18. (1) The statutes, records and journals of Parliament shall be printed and published in English and French and both language versions are equally authoritative. (86)

(2) The statutes, records and journals of the legislature of New Brunswick shall be printed and published in English and French and both language versions are equally authoritative. (87)

19. (1) Either English or French may be used by any person in, or in any pleading in or process issuing from, any court established by Parliament. (88)

(2) Either English or French may be used by any person in, or in any pleading in or process issuing from, any court of New Brunswick.(89)

20. (1) Any member of the public in Canada has the right to communicate with, and to receive available services from, any head or central office of an institution of the Parliament or government of Canada in English or French, and has the same right with respect to any other office of any such institution where
  (*a*) there is a significant demand for communications with and services from that office in such language; or
  (*b*) due to the nature of the office, it is reasonable that communications with and services from that office be available in both English and French.

(2) Any member of the public in New Brunswick has the right to communicate with, and to receive available services from, any office of an institution of the legislature or government of New Brunswick in English or French.

21. Nothing in sections 16 to 20 abrogates or derogates from any right, privilege or obligation with respect to the English and French languages, or either of them, that exists or is continued by virtue of any other provision of the Constitution of Canada. (90)

22. Nothing in sections 16 to 20 abrogates or derogates from any legal or customary right or privilege acquired or enjoyed either before or after the coming into force of this Charter with respect to any language that is not English or French.

Minority language educational rights

23. (1) Citizens of Canada
  (*a*) whose first language learned and still understood is that of the

English or French linguistic minority population of the province in which they reside, or

(b) who have received their primary school instruction in Canada in English or French and reside in a province where the language in which they received that instruction is the language of the English or French linguistic minority population of the province,

have the right to have their children receive primary and secondary school instruction in that language in that province.(91)

(2) Citizens of Canada of whom any child has received or is receiving primary or secondary school instruction in English or French in Canada, have the right to have all their children receive primary and secondary school instruction in the same language.

(3) The right of citizens of Canada under subsections (1) and (2) to have their children receive primary and secondary school instruction in the language of the English or French linguistic minority population of a province

(a) applies wherever in the province the number of children of citizens who have such a right is sufficient to warrant the provision to them out of public funds of minority language instruction; and

(b) includes, where the number of those children so warrants, the right to have them receive that instruction in minority language educational facilities provided out of public funds.

Enforcement

24. (1) Anyone whose rights or freedoms, as guaranteed by this Charter, have been infringed or denied may apply to a court of competent jurisdiction to obtain such remedy as the court considers appropriate and just in the circumstances.

(2) Where, in proceedings under subsection (1), a court concludes that evidence was obtained in a manner that infringed or denied any rights or freedoms guaranteed by this Charter, the evidence shall be excluded if it is established that, having regard to all the circumstances, the admission of it in the proceedings would bring the administration of justice into disrepute.

General

25. The guarantee in this Charter of certain rights and freedoms shall not be construed so as to abrogate or derogate from any aboriginal, treaty or other rights or freedoms that pertain to the aboriginal peoples of Canada including

(a) any rights or freedoms that have been recognized by the Royal Proclamation of October 7, 1763; and

(b) any rights or freedoms that now exist by way of land claims agreements or may be so acquired. (92)

26. The guarantee in this Charter of certain rights and freedoms shall not be construed as denying the existence of any other rights or freedoms that exist in Canada.

27. This Charter shall be interpreted in a manner consistent with the preservation and enhancement of the multicultural heritage of Canadians.

28. Notwithstanding anything in this Charter, the rights and freedoms referred to in it are guaranteed equally to male and female persons.

29. Nothing in this Charter abrogates or derogates from any rights or privileges guaranteed by or under the Constitution of Canada in respect of denominational, separate or dissentient schools. (93)

30. A reference in this Charter to a Province or to the legislative assembly or legislature of a province shall be deemed to include a reference to the Yukon Territory and the Northwest Territories, or to the appropriate legislative authority thereof, as the case may be.

31. Nothing in this Charter extends the legislative powers of any body or authority.

Application of Charter

32. (1) This Charter applies
(a) to the Parliament and government of Canada in respect of all matters within the authority of Parliament including all matters relating to the Yukon Territory and Northwest Territories; and
(b) to the legislature and government of each province in respect of all matters within the authority of the legislature of each province.

(2) Notwithstanding subsection (1), section 15 shall not have effect until three years after this section comes into force.

33. (1) Parliament or the legislature of a province may expressly declare in an Act of Parliament or of the legislature, as the case may be, that the Act or a provision thereof shall operate notwithstanding a provision included in section 2 or sections 7 to 15 of this Charter.

(2) An Act or a provision of an Act in respect of which a declaration made under this section is in effect shall have such operation as it would have but for the provision of this Charter referred to in the declaration.

(3) A declaration made under subsection (1) shall cease to have effect five

years after it comes into force or on such earlier date as may be specified in the declaration.

(4) Parliament or the legislature of a province may re-enact a declaration made under subsection (1).

(5) Subsection (3) applies in respect of a re-enactment made under subsection (4).

Constitution Act, 1982 (79), Schedule B, Part I.

---

46   NEW ZEALAND BILL OF RIGHTS ACT, 1990

An Act—
  (a) To affirm, protect, and promote human rights and fundamental freedoms in New Zealand; and
  (b) To affirm New Zealand's commitment to the International Covenant on Civil and Political Rights

BE IT ENACTED by the Parliament of New Zealand as follows:

1. *Short title and commencement*—(1) This Act may be cited as the New Zealand Bill of Rights Act 1990.

(2) This Act shall come into force on the 28th day after the date on which it receives the Royal assent.

Part i: General provisions

2. *Rights affirmed*—The rights and freedoms contained in this Bill of Rights are affirmed.

3. *Application*—This Bill of Rights applies only to acts done—
  (a) By the legislative, executive, or judicial branches of the government of New Zealand; or
  (b) By any person or body in the performance of any public function, power, or duty conferred or imposed on that person or body by or pursuant to law.

4. *Other enactments not affected*—No court shall, in relation to any enactment (whether passed or made before or after the commencement of this Bill of Rights),—
  (a) Hold any provision of the enactment to be impliedly repealed or revoked, or to be in any way invalid or ineffective; or
  (b) Decline to apply any provision of the enactment—
by reason only that the provision is inconsistent with any provision of this Bill of Rights.

5. *Justified limitations*—Subject to section 4 of this Bill of Rights, the rights and freedoms contained in this Bill of Rights may be subject only to such reasonable limits prescribed by law as can be demonstrably justified in a free and democratic society.

6. *Interpretation consistent with Bill of Rights to be preferred*—Wherever an enactment can be given a meaning that is consistent with the rights and freedoms contained in this Bill of Rights, that meaning shall be preferred to any other meaning.

7. *Attorney-General to report to Parliament where Bill appears to be inconsistent with Bill of Rights*—Where any Bill is introduced into the House of Representatives, the Attorney-General shall,—
  (a) In the case of a Government Bill, on the introduction of that Bill; or
  (b) In any other case, as soon as practicable after the introduction of the Bill,—
bring to the attention of the House of Representatives any provision in the Bill that appears to be inconsistent with any of the rights and freedoms contained in this Bill of Rights.

PART II: CIVIL AND POLITICAL RIGHTS

Life and security of the person

8. *Right not to be deprived of life*—No one shall be deprived of life except on such grounds as are established by law and are consistent with the principles of fundamental justice.

9. *Right not to be subjected to torture or cruel treatment*—Everyone has the right not to be subjected to torture or to cruel, degrading, or disproportionately severe treatment or punishment.

10. *Right not to be subjected to medical or scientific experimentation*—Every person has the right not to be subjected to medical or scientific experimentation without that person's consent.

11. *Right to refuse to undergo medical treatment*—Everyone has the right to refuse to undergo any medical treatment.

Democratic and civil rights

12. *Electoral rights*—Every New Zealand citizen who is of or over the age of 18 years—
  (a) Has the right to vote in genuine periodic elections of members of the House of Representatives, which elections shall be by equal suffrage and by secret ballot; and

(b) Is qualified for membership of the House of Representatives.

13. *Freedom of thought, conscience, and religion*—Everyone has the right to freedom of thought, conscience, religion, and belief, including the right to adopt and to hold opinions without interference.

14. *Freedom of expression*—Everyone has the right to freedom of expression, including the freedom to seek, receive, and impart information and opinions of any kind in any form.

15. *Manifestation of religion and belief*—Every person has the right to manifest that person's religion or belief in worship, observance, practice, or teaching, either individually or in community with others, and either in public or in private.

16. *Freedom of peaceful assembly*—Everyone has the right to freedom of peaceful assembly.

17. *Freedom of association*—Everyone has the right to freedom of association.

18. *Freedom of movement*—(1) Everyone lawfully in New Zealand has the right to freedom of movement and residence in New Zealand.

(2) Every New Zealand citizen has the right to enter New Zealand.

(3) Everyone has the right to leave New Zealand.

(4) No one who is not a New Zealand citizen and who is lawfully in New Zealand shall be required to leave New Zealand except under a decision taken on grounds prescribed by law.

Non-discrimination and minority rights

19. *Freedom from discrimination*—(1) Everyone has the right to freedom from discrimination on the ground of colour, race, ethnic or national origins, sex, marital status, or religious or ethical belief.

(2) Measures taken in good faith for the purpose of assisting or advancing persons or groups of persons disadvantaged because of colour, race, ethnic or national origins, sex, marital status, or religious or ethical belief do not constitute discrimination.

20. *Rights of minorities*—A person who belongs to an ethnic, religious, or linguistic minority in New Zealand shall not be denied the right, in community with other members of that minority, to enjoy the culture, to profess and practise the religion, or to use the language, of that minority.

Search, arrest, and detention

21. *Unreasonable search and seizure*—Everyone has the right to be secure against unreasonable search or seizure, whether of the person, property, or correspondence or otherwise.

22. *Liberty of the person*—Everyone has the right not to be arbitrarily arrested or detained.

23. *Rights of persons arrested or detained*—(1) Everyone who is arrested or who is detained under any enactment—
  (a) Shall be informed at the time of the arrest or detention of the reason for it; and
  (b) Shall have the right to consult and instruct a lawyer without delay and to be informed of that right; and
  (c) Shall have the right to have the validity of the arrest or detention determined without delay by way of *habeas corpus* and to be released if the arrest or detention is not lawful.

(2) Everyone who is arrested for an offence has the right to be charged promptly or to be released.

(3) Everyone who is arrested for an offence and is not released shall be brought as soon as possible before a court or competent tribunal.

(4) Everyone who is—
  (a) Arrested; or
  (b) Detained under any enactment—
for any offence or suspected offence shall have the right to refrain from making any statement and to be informed of that right.

(5) Everyone deprived of liberty shall be treated with humanity and with respect for the inherent dignity of the person.

24. *Rights of persons charged*—Everyone who is charged with an offence—
  (a) Shall be informed promptly and in detail of the nature and cause of the charge; and
  (b) Shall be released on reasonable terms and conditions unless there is just cause for continued detention; and
  (c) Shall have the right to consult and instruct a lawyer; and
  (d) Shall have the right to adequate time and facilities to prepare a defence; and
  (e) Shall have the right, except in the case of an offence under military law tried before a military tribunal, to the benefit of a trial by jury when the penalty for the offence is or includes imprisonment for more than 3 months; and
  (f) Shall have the right to receive legal assistance without cost if the interests of justice so require and the person does not have sufficient means to provide for that assistance; and

    (g) Shall have the right to have the free assistance of an interpreter if the person cannot understand or speak the language used in court.

25. *Minimum standards of criminal procedure*—Everyone who is charged with an offence has, in relation to the determination of the charge, the following minimum rights:

    (a) The right to a fair and public hearing by an independent and impartial court;

    (b) The right to be tried without undue delay;

    (c) The right to be presumed innocent until proved guilty according to law;

    (d) The right not to be compelled to be a witness or to confess guilt;

    (e) The right to be present at the trial and to present a defence;

    (f) The right to examine the witnesses for the prosecution and to obtain the attendance and examination of witnesses for the defence under the same conditions as the prosecution;

    (g) The right, if convicted of an offence in respect of which the penalty has been varied between the commission of the offence and sentencing, to the benefit of the lesser penalty;

    (h) The right, if convicted of the offence, to appeal according to law to a higher court against the conviction or against the sentence or against both;

    (i) The right, in the case of a child, to be dealt with in a manner that takes account of the child's age.

26. *Retroactive penalties and double jeopardy*—(1) No one shall be liable to conviction of any offence on account of any act or omission which did not constitute an offence by such person under the law of New Zealand at the time it occurred.

(2) No one who has been finally acquitted or convicted of, or pardoned for, an offence shall be tried or punished for it again.

27. *Right to justice*—(1) Every person has the right to the observance of the principles of natural justice by any tribunal or other public authority which has the power to make a determination in respect of that person's rights, obligations, or interests protected or recognised by law.

(2) Every person whose rights, obligations, or interests protected or recognised by law have been affected by a determination of any tribunal or other public authority has the right to apply, in accordance with law, for judicial review of that determination.

(3) Every person has the right to bring civil proceedings against, and to defend civil proceedings brought by, the Crown, and to have those proceedings heard, according to law, in the same way as civil proceedings between individuals.

PART III: MISCELLANEOUS PROVISIONS

28. *Other rights and freedoms not affected*—An existing right or freedom shall not be held to be abrogated or restricted by reason only that the right or freedom is not included in this Bill of Rights or is included only in part.

29. *Application to legal persons*—Except where the provisions of this Bill of Rights otherwise provide, the provisions of this Bill of Rights apply, so far as practicable, for the benefit of all legal persons as well as for the benefit of all natural persons.

1990, No. 109.

47 HONG KONG BILL OF RIGHTS, 1991

An Ordinance to provide for the incorporation into the law of Hong Kong of provisions of the International Covenant on Civil and Political Rights as applied to Hong Kong; and for ancillary and connected matters.

[Cap. 383, 8 June 1991]

PART I: PRELIMINARY

1. *Short title*

This Ordinance may be cited as the Hong Kong Bill of Rights Ordinance.

2. *Interpretation*

(1) In this Ordinance, unless the context otherwise requires—
'article' means an article of the Bill of Rights;
'Bill of Rights' means the Hong Kong Bill of Rights set out in Part II;
'commencement date' means the date on which this Ordinance comes into operation;
'legislation' means legislation that can be amended by an Ordinance;
'pre-existing legislation' means legislation enacted before the commencement date.

(2) The Bill of Rights is subject to Part III.

(3) In interpreting and applying this Ordinance, regard shall be had to the fact that the purpose of this Ordinance is to provide for the incorporation into the law of Hong Kong of provisions of the International Covenant on Civil and Political Rights as applied to Hong Kong, and for ancillary and connected matters.

(4) Nothing in this Ordinance shall be interpreted as implying for the Government or any authority, group or person any right to engage in any activity or perform any act aimed at the destruction of any of the rights and freedoms recognized in the Bill of Rights or at their limitation to a greater extent than is provided for in the Bill. [*cf. ICCPR Art. 5.1*]

(5) There shall be no restriction upon or derogation from any of the fundamental human rights recognized or existing in Hong Kong pursuant to law, conventions, regulations or custom on the pretext that the Bill of Rights does not recognize such rights or that it recognizes them to a lesser extent. [*cf. ICCPR Art. 5.2*]

(6) A heading to any article does not have any legislative effect and does not in any way vary, limit or extend the meaning of the article.

3. *Effect on pre-existing legislation*

(1) All pre-existing legislation that admits of a construction consistent with this Ordinance shall be given such a construction.

(2) All pre-existing legislation that does not admit of a construction consistent with this Ordinance is, to the extent of the inconsistency, repealed.

4. *Interpretation of subsequent legislation*

All legislation enacted on or after the commencement date shall, to the extent that it admits of such a construction, be construed so as to be consistent with the International Covenant on Civil and Political Rights as applied to Hong Kong.

5. *Public emergencies*

(1) In time of public emergency which threatens the life of the nation and the existence of which is officially proclaimed, measures may be taken derogating from the Bill of Rights to the extent strictly required by the exigencies of the situation, but these measures shall be taken in accordance with law.

(2) No measure shall be taken under subsection (1) that—
    (*a*) is inconsistent with any obligation under international law that applies to Hong Kong (other than an obligation under the International Covenant on Civil and Political Rights);
    (*b*) involves discrimination solely on the ground of race, colour, sex, language, religion or social origin; or
    (*c*) derogates from articles 2, 3, 4(1) and (2), 7, 12, 13 and 15.
[*cf. ICCPR Art. 4*]

6. *Remedies for contravention of Bill of Rights*

(1) A court or tribunal—
   (*a*) in proceedings within its jurisdiction in an action for breach of this Ordinance; and
   (*b*) in other proceedings within its jurisdiction in which a violation or threatened violation of the Bill of Rights is relevant,

may grant such remedy or relief, or make such order, in respect of such a breach, violation or threatened violation as it has power to grant or make in those proceedings and as it considers appropriate and just in the circumstances.

(2) No proceedings shall be held to be outside the jurisdiction of any court or tribunal on the ground that they relate to the Bill of Rights.

7. *Binding effect of Ordinance*

(1) This Ordinance binds only—
   (a) the Government and all public authorities; and
   (b) any person acting on behalf of the Government or a public authority.

(2) In this section—
'person' includes any body of persons, corporate or unincorporate.

PART II: THE HONG KONG BILL OF RIGHTS

8. *Hong Kong Bill of Rights*

The Hong Kong Bill of Rights is as follows.

Article 1: Entitlement to rights without distinction

(1) The rights recognized in this Bill of Rights shall be enjoyed without distinction of any kind, such as race, colour, sex, language, religion, political or other opinion, national or social origin, property, birth or other status.

(2) Men and women shall have an equal right to the enjoyment of all civil and political rights set forth in this Bill of Rights.

[*cf. ICCPR Arts. 2 & 3*]

Article 2: Right to life

(1) Every human being has the inherent right to life. This right shall be protected by law. No one shall be arbitrarily deprived of his life.

(2) Sentence of death may be imposed only for the most serious crimes in

accordance with the law in force at the time of the commission of the crime and not contrary to the provisions of this Bill of Rights and to the Convention on the Prevention and Punishment of the Crime of Genocide. This penalty can only be carried out pursuant to a final judgment rendered by a competent court.

(3) When deprivation of life constitutes the crime of genocide, nothing in this article shall authorize the derogation in any way from any obligation assumed under the provisions of the Convention on the Prevention and Punishment of the Crime of Genocide.

(4) Anyone sentenced to death shall have the right to seek pardon or commutation of the sentence. Amnesty, pardon or commutation of the sentence of death may be granted in all cases.

(5) Sentence of death shall not be imposed for crimes committed by persons below 18 years of age and shall not be carried out on pregnant women.

(6) Nothing in this article shall be invoked to delay or to prevent the abolition of capital punishment in Hong Kong.

[*cf. ICCPR Art. 6*]

Article 3: No torture or inhuman treatment and no experimentation without consent

No one shall be subjected to torture or to cruel, inhuman or degrading treatment or punishment. In particular, no one shall be subjected without his free consent to medical or scientific experimentation.

[*cf. ICCPR Art. 7*]

Article 4: No slavery or servitude

(1) No one shall be held in slavery; slavery and the slave-trade in all their forms shall be prohibited.

(2) No one shall be held in servitude.

(3) (*a*)No one shall be required to perform forced or compulsory labour.

　　　(*b*) For the purpose of this paragraph the term 'forced or compulsory labour' shall not include—
　　　　　(i)　any work or service normally required of a person who is under detention in consequence of a lawful order of a court, or of a person during conditional release from such detention;
　　　　　(ii)　any service of a military character and, where conscientious objection is recognized, any national service required by law of conscientious objectors;

    (iii) any service exacted in cases of emergency or calamity threatening the life or well-being of the community;

    (iv) any work or service which forms part of normal civil obligations.

[*cf. ICCPR Art. 8*]

Article 5: Liberty and security of person

(1) Everyone has the right to liberty and security of person. No one shall be subjected to arbitrary arrest or detention. No one shall be deprived of his liberty except on such grounds and in accordance with such procedure as are established by law.

(2) Anyone who is arrested shall be informed, at the time of arrest, of the reasons for his arrest and shall be promptly informed of any charges against him.

(3) Anyone arrested or detained on a criminal charge shall be brought promptly before a judge or other officer authorized by law to exercise judicial power and shall be entitled to trial within a reasonable time or to release. It shall not be the general rule that persons awaiting trial shall be detained in custody, but release may be subject to guarantees to appear for trial, at any other stage of the judicial proceedings, and, should occasion arise, for execution of the judgment.

(4) Anyone who is deprived of his liberty by arrest or detention shall be entitled to take proceedings before a court, in order that that court may decide without delay on the lawfulness of his detention and order his release if the detention is not lawful.

(5) Anyone who has been the victim of unlawful arrest or detention shall have an enforceable right to compensation.

[*cf. ICCPR Art. 9*]

Article 6: Rights of persons deprived of their liberty

(1) All persons deprived of their liberty shall be treated with humanity and with respect for the inherent dignity of the human person.

(2)(*a*) Accused persons shall, save in exceptional circumstances, be segregated from convicted persons and shall be subject to separate treatment appropriate to their status as unconvicted persons.

   (*b*) Accused juvenile persons shall be separated from adults and brought as speedily as possible for adjudication.

(3) The penitentiary system shall comprise treatment of prisoners the essential aim of which shall be their reformation and social rehabilitation. Juvenile offenders shall be segregated from adults and be accorded treatment appropriate to their age and legal status.

[*cf. ICCPR Art. 10*]

Article 7: No imprisonment for breach of contract

No one shall be imprisoned merely on the ground of inability to fulfil a contractual obligation.

[cf. ICCPR Art. 11]

Article 8: Liberty of movement

(1) Everyone lawfully within Hong Kong shall, within Hong Kong, have the right to liberty of movement and freedom to choose his residence.

(2) Everyone shall be free to leave Hong Kong.

(3) The above-mentioned rights shall not be subject to any restrictions except those which are provided by law, are necessary to protect national security; public order (ordre public), public health or morals or the rights and freedoms of others, and are consistent with the other rights recognized in this Bill of Rights.

(4) No one who has the right of abode in Hong Kong shall be arbitrarily deprived of the right to enter Hong Kong.

[cf. ICCPR Art. 12]

Article 9: Restrictions on expulsion from Hong Kong

A person who does not have the right of abode in Hong Kong but who is lawfully in Hong Kong may be expelled therefrom only in pursuance of a decision reached in accordance with law and shall, except where compelling reasons of national security otherwise require, be allowed to submit the reasons against his expulsion and to have his case reviewed by, and be represented for the purpose before, the competent authority or a person or persons especially designated by the competent authority.

[cf. ICCPR Art. 13]

Article 10: Equality before courts and right to fair and public hearing

All persons shall be equal before the courts and tribunals. In the determination of any criminal charge against him, or of his rights and obligations in a suit at law, everyone shall be entitled to a fair and public hearing by a competent, independent and impartial tribunal established by law. The press and the public may be excluded from all or part of a trial for reasons of morals, public order (ordre public) or national security in a democratic society, or when the interest of the private lives of the parties so requires, or to the extent strictly necessary in the opinion of the court in special circumstances where publicity would prejudice the interests of justice; but any judgment rendered in a criminal case or in a suit at law shall be made public except where the interest of juvenile persons otherwise requires or the proceedings concern matrimonial disputes or the guardianship of children.

[*cf. ICCPR Art. 14.1*]

Article 11: Rights of persons charged with or convicted of criminal offence

(1) Everyone charged with a criminal offence shall have the right to be presumed innocent until proved guilty according to law.

(2) In the determination of any criminal charge against him, everyone shall be entitled to the following minimum guarantees, in full equality—

    (*a*) to be informed promptly and in detail in a language which he understands of the nature and cause of the charge against him;

    (*b*) to have adequate time and facilities for the preparation of his defence and to communicate with counsel of his own choosing;

    (*c*) to be tried without undue delay;

    (*d*) to be tried in his presence, and to defend himself in person or through legal assistance of his own choosing; to be informed, if he does not have legal assistance, of this right; and to have legal assistance assigned to him, in any case where the interests of justice so require, and without payment by him in any such case if he does not have sufficient means to pay for it;

    (*e*) to examine, or have examined, the witness against him and to obtain the attendance and examination of witnesses on his behalf under the same conditions as witnesses against him;

    (*f*) to have the free assistance of an interpreter if he cannot understand or speak the language used in court;

    (*g*) not to be compelled to testify against himself or to confess guilt.

(3) In the case of juvenile persons, the procedure shall be such as will take account of their age and the desirability of promoting their rehabilitation.

(4) Everyone convicted of a crime shall have the right to his conviction and sentence being reviewed by a higher tribunal according to law.

(5) When a person has by a final decision been convicted of a criminal offence and when subsequently his conviction has been reversed or he has been pardoned on the ground that a new or newly discovered fact shows conclusively that there has been a miscarriage of justice, the person who has suffered punishment as a result of such conviction shall be compensated according to law, unless it is proved that the non-disclosure of the unknown fact in time is wholly or partly attributable to him.

(6) No one shall be liable to be tried or punished again for an offence for which he has already been finally convicted or acquitted in accordance with the law and penal procedure of Hong Kong.

[*cf. ICCPR Art. 14.2 to 7*]

Article 12: No retrospective criminal offences or penalties

(1) No one shall be held guilty of any criminal offence on account of any act or omission which did not constitute a criminal offence, under Hong Kong or international law, at the time when it was committed. Nor shall a heavier penalty be imposed than the one that was applicable at the time when the criminal offence was committed. If, subsequent to the commission of the offence, provision is made by law for the imposition of a lighter penalty, the offender shall benefit thereby.

(2) Nothing in this article shall prejudice the trial and punishment of any person for any act or omission which, at the time when it was committed, was criminal according to the general principles of law recognized by the community of nations.

[*cf. ICCPR Art. 15*]

Article 13: Right to recognition as person before law

Everyone shall have the right to recognition everywhere as a person before the law.

[*cf. ICCPR Art. 16*]

Article 14: Protection of privacy, family, home, correspondence, honour and reputation

(1) No one shall be subjected to arbitrary or unlawful interference with his privacy, family, home or correspondence, nor to unlawful attacks on his honour and reputation.

(2) Everyone has the right to the protection of the law against such interference or attacks.

[*cf. ICCPR Art. 17*]

Article 15: Freedom of thought, conscience and religion

(1) Everyone shall have the right to freedom of thought, conscience and religion. This right shall include freedom to have or to adopt a religion or belief of his choice, and freedom, either individually or in community with others and in public or private, to manifest his religion or belief in worship, observance, practice and teaching.

(2) No one shall be subject to coercion which would impair his freedom to have or to adopt a religion or belief of his choice.

(3) Freedom to manifest one's religion or beliefs may be subject only to such limitations as are prescribed by law and are necessary to protect public

safety, order, health, or morals or the fundamental rights and freedoms of others.

(4) The liberty of parents and, when applicable, legal guardians to ensure the religious and moral education of their children in conformity with their own convictions shall be respected.

[*cf. ICCPR Art. 18*]

Article 16: Freedom of opinion and expression

(1) Everyone shall have the right to hold opinions without interference.

(2) Everyone shall have the right to freedom of expression; this right shall include freedom to seek, receive and impart information and ideas of all kinds, regardless of frontiers, either orally, in writing or in print, in the form of art, or through any other media of his choice.

(3) The exercise of the rights provided for in paragraph (2) of this article carries with it special duties and responsibilities. It may therefore be subject to certain restrictions, but these shall only be such as are provided by law and are necessary—
   (*a*) for respect of the rights or reputations of others; or
   (*b*) for the protection of national security or of public order (ordre public), or of public health or morals.

[*cf. ICCPR Art. 19*]

Article 17: Right of peaceful assembly

The right of peaceful assembly shall be recognized. No restrictions may be placed on the exercise of this right other than those imposed in conformity with the law and which are necessary in a democratic society in the interests of national security or public safety, public order (ordre public), the protection of public health or morals or the protection of the rights and freedoms of others.

[*cf. ICCPR Art. 21*]

Article 18: Freedom of association

(1) Everyone shall have the right to freedom of association with others, including the right to form and join trade unions for the protection of his interests.

(2) No restrictions may be placed on the exercise of this right other than those which are prescribed by law and which are necessary in a democratic society in the interests of national security or public safety, public order (ordre public), the protection of public health or morals or the protection of

the rights and freedoms of others. This article shall not prevent the imposition of lawful restrictions on members of the armed forces and of the police in their exercise of this right.

(3) Nothing in this article authorizes legislative measures to be taken which would prejudice, or the law to be applied in such a manner as to prejudice, the guarantees provided for in the International Labour Organization Convention of 1948 concerning Freedom of Association and Protection of the Right to Organize as it applies to Hong Kong.

[cf. ICCPR Art. 22]

Article 19: Rights in respect of marriage and family

(1) The family is the natural and fundamental group unit of society and is entitled to protection by society and the State.

(2) The right of men and women of marriageable age of marry and to found a family shall be recognized.

(3) No marriage shall be entered into without the free and full consent of the intending spouses.

(4) Spouses shall have equal rights and responsibilities as to marriage, during marriage and at its dissolution. In the case of dissolution, provision shall be made for the necessary protection of any children.

[cf. ICCPR Art. 23]

Article 20: Rights of children

(1) Every child shall have, without any discrimination as to race, colour, sex, language, religion, national or social origin, property or birth, the right to such measures of protection as are required by his status as a minor, on the part of his family, society and the State.

(2) Every child shall be registered immediately after birth and shall have a name.

[cf. ICCPR Art. 24]

Article 21: Right to participate in public life

Every permanent resident shall have the right and the opportunity, without any of the distinctions mentioned in article 1(1) and without unreasonable restrictions—

    (*a*) to take part in the conduct of public affairs, directly or through freely chosen representatives;

    (*b*) to vote and to be elected at genuine periodic elections which shall be by universal and equal suffrage and shall be held by secret ballot, guaranteeing the free expression of the will of the electors;

(c) to have access, on general terms of equality, to public service in Hong Kong.

[cf. ICCPR Art. 25]

Article 22: Equality before and equal protection of law

All persons are equal before the law and are entitled without any discrimination to the equal protection of the law. In this respect, the law shall prohibit any discrimination and guarantee to all persons equal and effective protection against discrimination on any ground such as race, colour, sex, language, religion, political or other opinion, national or social origin, property, birth or other status.

[cf. ICCPR Art. 26]

Article 23: Rights of minorities

Persons belonging to ethnic, religious or linguistic minorities shall not be denied the right, in community with the other members of their group, to enjoy their own culture, to profess and practise their own religion, or to use their own language.

[cf. ICCPR Art. 27]

PART III: EXCEPTIONS AND SAVINGS

9. Armed forces and persons detained in penal establishments

Members of and persons serving with the armed forces of the government responsible for the foreign affairs of Hong Kong and persons lawfully detained in penal establishments of whatever character are subject to such restrictions as may from time to time be authorized by law for the preservation of service and custodial discipline.

10. Juveniles under detention

Where at any time there is a lack of suitable prison facilities or where the mixing of adults and juveniles is mutually beneficial, article 6(2)(b) and (3) does not require juveniles who are detained to be accommodated separately from adults.

11. Immigration legislation

As regards person not having the right to enter and remain in Hong Kong, this Ordinance does not affect any immigration legislation governing entry into, stay in and departure from Hong Kong, or the application of any such legislation.

12. *Persons not having the right of abode*

Article 9 does not confer a right of review in respect of a decision to deport a person not having the right of abode in Hong Kong or a right to be represented for this purpose before the competent authority.

13. *Executive and Legislative Councils*

Article 21 does not require the establishment of an elected Executive or Legislative Council in Hong Kong.

14. *Temporary savings*

(1) For a period of 1 year beginning on the commencement date, this Ordinance is subject to the Ordinances listed in the Schedule.

(2) This Ordinance does not affect—
  (a) any act done (including any act done in the exercise of a discretion); or
  (b) any omission authorized or required, or occurring in the exercise of a discretion,
before the first anniversary of the commencement date, under or by any Ordinance listed in the Schedule.

(3) The Legislative Council may before the first anniversary of the commencement date by resolution amend this section for all or any of the following purposes—
  (a) to provide that, for a period of 1 year beginning on the first anniversary of the commencement date, this Ordinance is subject to such of the Ordinances listed in the Schedule as are specified in the amendment;
  (b) to provide that this Ordinance does not affect—
      (i)   any act done (including any act done in the exercise of a discretion); or
      (ii) any omission authorized or required, or occurring in the exercise of a discretion,
      before the second anniversary of the commencement date, under or by any Ordinance listed in the Schedule that is specified in the amendment; and
  (c) to repeal this subsection.

(4) In this section, a reference to an Ordinance includes a reference to any subsidiary legislation made under that Ordinance.

(5) This section operates notwithstanding section 3.

SCHEDULE

Provisions to which Section 14(1) and (2) Applies

Immigration Ordinance (Cap. 115)
Societies Ordinance (Cap. 151)
Crimes Ordinance (Cap. 200)
Prevention of Bribery Ordinance (Cap. 201)
Independent Commission Against Corruption Ordinance (Cap. 204)
Police Force Ordinance (Cap. 232)

1991, Chapter 383

48   SOUTH AFRICA, THE BILL OF RIGHTS, 1996

Constitution of Republic of South Africa 1996

CHAPTER I: FOUNDING PROVISIONS

Republic of South Africa

1. The Republic of South Africa is one sovereign democratic state founded on the following values:
   (a) Human dignity, the achievement of equality and the advancement of human rights and freedoms.
   (b) Non-racialism and non-sexism.
   (c) Supremacy of the constitution and the rule of law.
   (d) Universal adult suffrage, a national common voters roll, regular elections and a multiparty system of democratic government, to ensure accountability, responsiveness and openness.

Supremacy of Constitution

2. This Constitution is the supreme law of the Republic; law or conduct inconsistent with it is invalid, and the obligations imposed by it must be fulfilled.

Citizenship

3. (1) There is a common South African citizenship.

   (2) All citizens are—
   (a) equally entitled to the rights, privileges and benefits of citizenship, and

(b) equally subject to the duties and responsibilities of citizenship.

(3) National legislation must provide for the acquisition, loss and restoration of citizenship.

CHAPTER 2: BILL OF RIGHTS

Rights

7. (1) This Bill of Rights is a cornerstone of democracy in South Africa. It enshrines the rights of all people in our country and affirms the democratic values of human dignity, equality and freedom.

(2) The state must respect, protect, promote and fulfil the rights in the Bill of Rights.

(3) The rights in the Bill of Rights are subject to the limitations contained or referred to in section 36, or elsewhere in the Bill.

Application

8. (1) The Bill of Rights applies to all law, and binds the legislature, the executive, the judiciary and all organs of state.

(2) A provision of the Bill of Rights binds a natural or a juristic person if, and to the extent that, it is applicable, taking into account the nature of the right and the nature of any duty imposed by the right.

(3) When applying a provision of the Bill of Rights to a natural or juristic person in terms of subsection (2), a court—
    (a) in order to give effect to a right in the Bill, must apply, or if necessary develop, the common law to the extent that legislation does not give effect to that right; and
    (b) may develop rules of the common law to limit the right, provided that the limitation is in accordance with section 36(1).

(4) A juristic person is entitled to the rights in the Bill of Rights to the extent required by the nature of the rights and the nature of that juristic person.

Equality

9. (1) Everyone is equal before the law and has the right to equal protection and benefit of the law.

(2) Equality includes the full and equal enjoyment of all rights and freedoms. To promote the achievement of equality, legislative and other measures designed to protect or advance persons, or categories of persons, disadvantaged by unfair discrimination may be taken.

(3) The state may not unfairly discriminate directly or indirectly against anyone on one or more grounds, including race, gender, sex, pregnancy, marital status, ethnic or social origin, colour, sexual orientation, age, disability, religion, conscience, belief, culture, language and birth.

(4) No person may unfairly discriminate directly or indirectly against anyone on one or more grounds in terms of subsection (3). National legislation must be enacted to prevent or prohibit unfair discrimination.

(5) Discrimination on one or more of the grounds listed in subsection (3) is unfair unless it is established that the discrimination is fair.

Human dignity

10. Everyone has inherent dignity and the right to have their dignity respected and protected.

Life

11. Everyone has the right to life.

Freedom and security of the person

12. (1) Everyone has the right to freedom and security of the person, which includes the right—
    (a) not to be deprived of freedom arbitrarily or without just cause;
    (b) not to be detained without trial;
    (c) to be free from all forms of violence from either public or private sources;
    (d) not to be tortured in any way; and
    (e) not to be treated or punished in a cruel, inhuman or degrading way.

(2) Everyone has the right to bodily and psychological integrity, which includes the right—
    (a) to make decisions concerning reproduction;
    (b) to security in and control over their body; and
    (c) not to be subjected to medical or scientific experiments without their informed consent.

Slavery, servitude and forced labour

13. No one may be subjected to slavery, servitude or forced labour.

Privacy

14. Everyone has the right to privacy, which includes the right not to have—
    (a) their person or home searched;

    (b) their property searched;
    (c) their possessions seized; or
    (d) the privacy of their communications infringed.

Freedom of religion, belief and opinion

15. (1) Everyone has the right to freedom of conscience, religion, thought, belief and opinion.

(2) Religious observances may be conducted at state or state-aided institutions, provided that—
    (a) those observances follow rules made by the appropriate public authorities;
    (b) they are conducted on an equitable basis; and
    (c) attendance at them is free and voluntary.

(3) (a) This section does not prevent legislation recognising—
      (i) marriages concluded under any tradition, or a system of religious, personal or family law; or
      (ii) systems of personal and family law under any tradition, or adhered to by persons professing a particular religion.
    (b) Recognition in terms of paragraph (a) must be consistent with this section and the other provisions of the Constitution.

Freedom of expression

16. (1) Everyone has the right to freedom of expression, which includes—
    (a) freedom of the press and other media;
    (b) freedom to receive or impart information or ideas;
    (c) freedom of artistic creativity; and
    (d) academic freedom and freedom of scientific research.

(2) The right in subsection (1) does not extend to—
    (a) propaganda for war;
    (b) incitement of imminent violence; or
    (c) advocacy of hatred that is based on race, ethnicity, gender or religion, and that constitutes incitement to cause harm.

Assembly, demonstration, picket and petition

17. Everyone has the right, peacefully and unarmed, to assemble, to demonstrate, to picket and to present petitions.

Freedom of association

18. Everyone has the right to freedom of association.

Political rights

19. (1) Every citizen is free to make political choices, which includes the right—
    (a) to form a political party;
    (b) to participate in the activities of, or recruit members for, a political party; and
    (c) to campaign for a political party or cause.

(2) Every citizen has the right to free, fair and regular elections for any legislative body established in terms of the Constitution.

(3) Every adult citizen has the right—
    (a) to vote in elections for any legislative body established in terms of the Constitution, and to do so in secret; and
    (b) to stand for public office and, if elected, to hold office.

Citizenship

20. No citizen may be deprived of citizenship.

Freedom of movement and residence

21. (1) Everyone has the right to freedom of movement.

(2) Everyone has the right to leave the Republic.

(3) Every citizen has the right to enter, to remain in and to reside anywhere in, the Republic.

(4) Every citizen has the right to a passport.

Freedom of trade, occupation and profession

22. Every citizen has the right to choose their trade, occupation or profession freely. The practice of a trade, occupation or profession may be regulated by law.

Labour relations

23. (1) Everyone has the right to fair labour practices.

(2) Every worker has the right—
    (a) to form and join a trade union;
    (b) to participate in the activities and programmes of a trade union; and
    (c) to strike.

(3) Every employer has the right—

(a) to form and join an employers' organisation; and

(b) to participate in the activities and programmes of an employers' organisation.

(4) Every trade union and every employers' organisation has the right—

(a) to determine its own administration, programmes and activities;

(b) to organise; and

(c) to form and join a federation.

(5) Every trade union, employers' organisation and employer has the right to engage in collective bargaining. National legislation may be enacted to regulate collective bargaining. To the extent that the legislation may limit a right in this Chapter, the limitation must comply with section 36(1).

(6) National legislation may recognise union security arrangements contained in collective agreements. To the extent that the legislation may limit a right in this Chapter, the limitation must comply with section 36(1).

Environment

24. Everyone has the right—

(a) to an environment that is not harmful to their health or well-being; and

(b) to have the environment protected, for the benefit of present and future generations, through reasonable legislative and other measures that—

(i) prevent pollution and ecological degradation;

(ii) promote conservation; and

(iii) secure ecologically sustainable development and use of natural resources while promoting justifiable economc and social development.

Property

25. (1) No one may be deprived of property except in terms of law of general application, and no law may permit arbitrary deprivation of property.

(2) Property may be expropriated only in terms of law of general application—

(a) for a public purpose or in the public interest; and

(b) subject to compensation, the amount of which and the time and manner of payment of which have either been agreed to by those affected or decided or approved by a court.

(3) The amount of the compensation and the time and manner of payment must be just and equitable, reflecting an equitable balance between the public interest and the interests of those affected, having regard to all relevant circumstances, including—

(a) the current use of the property;

(b) the history of the acquisition and use of the property;

(c) the market value of the property;

(d) the extent of direct state investment and subsidy in the acquisition and beneficial capital improvement of the property; and

(e) the purpose of the expropriation.

(4) For the purposes of this section—

(a) the public interest includes the nation's commitment to land reform, and to reforms to bring about equitable access to all South Africa's natural resources; and

(b) property is not limited to land.

(5) The state must take reasonable legislative and other measures, within its available resources, to foster conditions which enable citizens to gain access to land on an equitable basis.

(6) A person or community whose tenure of land is legally insecure as a result of past racially discriminatory laws or practices is entitled, to the extent provided by an Act of Parliament, either to tenure which is legally secure or to comparable redress.

(7) A person or community dispossessed of property after 19 June 1913 as a result of past racially discriminatory laws or practices is entitled, to the extent provided by an Act of Parliament, either to restitution of that property or to equitable redress.

(8) No provision of this section may impede the state from taking legislative and other measures to achieve land, water and related reform, in order to redress the results of past racial discrimination, provided that any departure from the provisions of this section is in accordance with the provisions of section 36(1).

(9) Parliament must enact the legislation referred to in subsection (6).

Housing

26. (1) Everyone has the right to have access to adequate housing.

(2) The state must take reasonable legislative and other measures, within its available resources, to achieve the progressive realisation of this right.

(3) No one may be evicted from their home, or have their home demolished, without an order of court made after considering all the relevant circumstances. No legislation may permit arbitrary evictions.

Health care, food, water and social security

27. (1) Everyone has the right to have access to—

(a) health care services, including reproductive health care;

(b) sufficient food and water; and

(c) social security, including, if they are unable to support themselves and their dependants, appropriate social assistance.

(2) The state must take reasonable legislative and other measures, within its available resources, to achieve the progressive realisation of each of these rights.

(3) No one may be refused emergency medical treatment.

Children

28. (1) Every child has the right—
  (a) to a name and a nationality from birth;
  (b) to family care or parental care, or to appropriate alternative care when removed from the family environment;
  (c) to basic nutrition, shelter, basic health care services and social services;
  (d) to be protected from maltreatment, neglect, abuse or degradation;
  (e) to be protected from exploitative labour practices;
  (f) not to be required or permitted to perform work or provide services that—
    (i) are inappropriate for a person of that child's age; or
    (ii) place at risk the child's well-being, education, physical or mental health or spiritual, moral or social development;
  (g) not to be detained except as a measure of last resort, in which case, in addition to the rights a child enjoys under sections 12 and 35, the child may be detained only for the shortest appropriate period of time, and has the right to be—
    (i) kept separately from detained persons over the age of 18 years; and
    (ii) treated in a manner, and kept in conditions, that take account of the child's age;
  (h) to have a legal practitioner assigned to the child by the state, and at state expense, in civil proceedings affecting the child, if substantial injustice would otherwise result; and
    (i) not to be used directly in armed conflict, and to be protected in times of armed conflict.

(2) A child's best interests are of paramount importance in every matter concerning the child.

(3) In this section 'child' means a person under the age of 18 years.

Education

29. (1) Everyone has the right—
  (a) to a basic education, including adult basic education; and
  (b) to further education, which the state, through reasonable measures, must make progressively available and accessible.

(2) Everyone has the right to receive education in the official language or

languages of their choice in public educational institutions where that education is reasonably practicable. In order to ensure the effective access to, and implementation of, this right, the state must consider all reasonable educational alternatives, including single medium institutions, taking into account—

    (a) equity;

    (b) practicability; and

    (c) the need to redress the results of past racially discriminatory laws and practices.

(3) Everyone has the right to establish and maintain, at their own expense, independent educational institutions that—

    (a) do not discriminate on the basis of race;

    (b) are registered with the state; and

    (c) maintain standards that are not inferior to standards at comparable public educational institutions.

(4) Subsection (3) does not preclude state subsidies for independent educational institutions.

Language and culture

30. Everyone has the right to use the language and to participate in the cultural life of their choice, but no one exercising these rights may do so in a manner inconsistent with any provision of the Bill of Rights.

Cultural, religious and linguistic communities

31. (1) Persons belonging to a cultural, religious or linguistic community may not be denied the right, with other members of that community—

    (a) to enjoy their culture, practise their religion and use their language; and

    (b) to form, join and maintain cultural, religious and linguistic associations and other organs of civil society.

(2) The rights in subsection (1) may not be exercised in a manner inconsistent with any provision of the Bill of Rights.

Access to information

32. (1) Everyone has the right of access to—

    (a) any information held by the state; and

    (b) any information that is held by another person and that is required for the exercise or protection of any rights.

(2) National legislation must be enacted to give effect to this right, and may provide for reasonable measures to alleviate the administrative and financial burden on the state.

Just administrative action

33. (1) Everyone has the right to administrative action that is lawful, reasonable and procedurally fair.

(2) Everyone whose rights have been adversely affected by administrative action has the right to be given written reasons.

(3) National legislation must be enacted to give effect to these rights, and must—
- (a) provide for the review of administrative action by a court or, where appropriate, an independent and impartial tribunal;
- (b) impose a duty on the state to give effect to the rights in subsections (1) and (2); and
- (c) promote an efficient administration.

Access to courts

34. Everyone has the right to have any dispute that can be resolved by the application of law decided in a fair public hearing before a court or, where appropriate, another independent and impartial tribunal or forum.

Arrested, detained and accused persons

35. (1) Everyone who is arrested for allegedly committing an offence has the right—
- (a) to remain silent;
- (b) to be informed promptly—
  - (i) of the right to remain silent; and
  - (ii) of the consequences of not remaining silent;
- (c) not to be compelled to make any confession or admission that could be used in evidence against that person;
- (d) to be brought before a court as soon as reasonably possible, but not later than—
  - (i) 48 hours after the arrest; or
  - (ii) the end of the first court day after the expiry of the 48 hours, if the 48 hours expire outside ordinary court hours or on a day which is not an ordinary court day;
- (e) at the first court appearance after being arrested, to be charged or to be informed of the reason for the detention to continue, or to be released; and
- (f) to be released from detention if the interests of justice permit, subject to reasonable conditions.

(2) Everyone who is detained, including every sentenced prisoner, has the right—
- (a) to be informed promptly of the reason for being detained;
- (b) to choose, and to consult with, a legal practitioner, and to be informed of this right promptly;
- (c) to have a legal practitioner assigned to the detained person by the state and at state expense, if substantial injustice would otherwise result, and to be informed of this right promptly;

(d) to challenge the lawfulness of the detention in person before a court and, if the detention is unlawful, to be released;

(e) to conditions of detention that are consistent with human dignity, including at least exercise and the provision, at state expense, of adequate accommodation, nutrition, reading material and medical treatment; and

(f) to communicate with, and be visited by, that person's—
   (i) spouse or partner;
   (ii) next of kin;
   (iii) chosen religious counsellor; and
   (iv) chosen medical practitioner.

(3) Every accused person has a right to a fair trial, which includes the right—

(a) to be informed of the charge with sufficient detail to answer it;

(b) to have adequate time and facilities to prepare a defence;

(c) to a public trial before an ordinary court;

(d) to have their trial begin and conclude without unreasonable delay;

(e) to be present when being tried;

(f) to choose, and be represented by, a legal practitioner, and to be informed of this right promptly;

(g) to have a legal practitioner assigned to the accused person by the state and at state expense, if substantial injustice would otherwise result, and to be informed of this right promptly;

(h) to be presumed innocent, to remain silent, and not to testify during the proceedings;

(i) to adduce and challenge evidence;

(j) not to be compelled to give self-incriminating evidence;

(k) to be tried in a language that the accused person understands or, if that is not practicable, to have the proceedings interpreted in that language;

(l) not to be convicted for an act or omission that was not an offence under either national or international law at the time it was committed or omitted;

(m) not to be tried for an offence in respect of an act or omission for which that person has previously been either acquitted or convicted;

(n) to the benefit of the least severe of the prescribed punishments if the prescribed punishment for the offence has been changed between the time that the offence was committed and the time of sentencing; and

(o) of appeal to, or review by, a higher court.

(4) Whenever this section requires information to be given to a person, that information must be given in a language that the person understands.

(5) Evidence obtained in a manner that violates any right in the Bill of Rights must be excluded if the admission of that evidence would render the trial unfair or otherwise be detrimental to the administration of justice.

Limitation of rights

36. (1) The rights in the Bill of Rights may be limited only in terms of law of general application to the extent that the limitation is reasonable and justifiable in an open and democratic society based on human dignity, equality and freedom, taking into account all relevant factors, including—

(a) the nature of the right;

(b) the importance of the purpose of the limitation;

(c) the nature and extent of the limitation;

(d) the relation between the limitation and its purpose; and

(e) less restrictive means to achieve the purpose.

(2) Except as provided in subsection (1) or in any other provision of the Constitution, no law may limit any right entrenched in the Bill of Rights.

States of emergency

37. (1) A state of emergency may be declared only in terms of an Act of Parliament, and only when—

(a) the life of the nation is threatened by war, invasion, general insurrection, disorder, natural disaster or other public emergency; and

(b) the declaration is necessary to restore peace and order.

(2) A declaration of a state of emergency, and any legislation enacted or other action taken in consequence of that declaration, may be effective only—

(a) prospectively; and

(b) for no more than 21 days from the date of the declaration, unless the National Assembly resolves to extend the declaration. The Assembly may extend a declaration of a state of emergency for no more than three months at a time. The first extension of the state of emergency must be by a resolution adopted with a supporting vote of a majority of the members of the Assembly. Any subsequent extension must be by a resolution adopted with a supporting vote of at least 60 per cent of the members of the Assembly. A resolution in terms of this paragraph may be adopted only following a public debate in the Assembly.

(3) Any competent court may decide on the validity of—

(a) a declaration of a state of emergency;

(b) any extension of a declaration of a state of emergency; or

(c) any legislation enacted, or other action taken, in consequence of a declaration of a state of emergency.

(4) Any legislation enacted in consequence of a declaration of a state of emergency may derogate from the Bill of Rights only to the extent that—

(a) the derogation is strictly required by the emergency; and

(b) the legislation—

(i) is consistent with the Republic's obligations under international law applicable to states of emergency;

(ii)   conforms to subsection (5); and

(iii)   is published in the national Government Gazette as soon as reasonably possible after being enacted.

(5) No Act of Parliament that authorises a declaration of a state of emergency, and no legislation enacted or other action taken in consequence of a declaration, may permit or authorise—

(a)   indemnifying the state, or any person, in respect of any unlawful act;

(b)   any derogation from this section; or

(c)   any derogation from a section mentioned in column 1 of the Table of Non-Derogable Rights, to the extent indicated opposite that section in column 3 of the Table.

Table of Non-Derogable Rights

1 Section number	2 Section title	3 Extent to which the right is protected
9	Equality	With respect to unfair discrimination solely on the grounds of race, colour, ethnic or social origin, sex religion or language
10	Human dignity	Entirely
11	Life	Entirely
12	Freedom and security of the person	With respect to subsections (1)(d) and (e) and (2)(c).
13	Slavery, servitude and forced labour	With respect to slavery and servitude
28	Children	With respect to: – subsection (1)(d) and (e); – the rights in subparagraphs (i) and (ii) of subsection (1)(g); and – subsection 1(i) in respect of children of 15 years and younger
35	Arrested, detained and accused persons	With respect to: – subsections (1)(a), (b) and (c) and (2)(d); – the rights in paragraphs (a) to (o) of subsection (3), excluding paragraph (d) – subsection (4); and – subsection (5) with respect to the exclusion of evidence if the admission of that evidence would render the trial unfair.

(6) Whenever anyone is detained without trial in consequence of a derogation of rights resulting from a declaration of a state of emergency, the following conditions must be observed:

(a) An adult family member or friend of the detainee must be contacted as soon as reasonably possible, and informed that the person has been detained.

(b) A notice must be published in the national Government Gazette within five days of the person being detained, stating the detainee's name and place of detention and referring to the emergency measure in terms of which that person has been detained.

(c) The detainee must be allowed to choose, and be visited at any reasonable time by, a medical practitioner.

(d) The detainee must be allowed to choose, and be visited at any reasonable time by, a legal representative.

(e) A court must review the detention as soon as reasonably possible, but no later than 10 days after the date the person was detained, and the court must release the detainee unless it is necessary to continue the detention to restore peace and order.

(f) A detainee who is not released in terms of a review under paragraph (e), or who is not released in terms of a review under this paragraph, may apply to a court for a further review of the detention at any time after 10 days have passed since the previous review, and the court must release the detainee unless it is still necessary to continue the detention to restore peace and order.

(g) The detainee must be allowed to appear in person before any court considering the detention, to be represented by a legal practitioner at those hearings, and to make representations against continued detention.

(h) The state must present written reasons to the court to justify the continued detention of the detainee, and must give a copy of those reasons to the detainee at least two days before the court reviews the detention.

(7) If a court releases a detainee, that person may not be detained again on the same grounds unless the state first shows a court good cause for re-detaining that person.

(8) Subsections (6) and (7) do not apply to persons who are not South African citizens and who are detained in consequence of an international armed conflict. Instead, the state must comply with the standards binding on the Republic under international humanitarian law in respect of the detention of such persons.

Enforcement of rights

38. Anyone listed in this section has the right to approach a competent court, alleging that a right in the Bill of Rights has been infringed or threatened, and the court may grant appropriate relief, including a declaration of rights. The persons who may approach a court are:

(a) anyone acting in their own interest;

(b) anyone acting on behalf of another person who cannot act in their own name;

(c) anyone acting as a member of, or in the interest of, a group or class of persons;
(d) anyone acting in the public interest; and
(e) an association acting in the interest of its members.

Interpretation of Bill of Rights

39. (1) When interpreting the Bill of Rights, a court, tribunal or forum—
(a) must promote the values that underlie an open and democratic society based on human dignity, equality and freedom;
(b) must consider international law; and
(c) may consider foreign law.

(2) When interpreting any legislation, and when developing the common law or customary law, every court, tribunal or forum must promote the spirit, purport and objects of the Bill of Rights.

(3) The Bill of Rights does not deny the existence of any other rights or freedoms that are recognised or conferred by common law, customary law or legislation, to the extent that they are consistent with the Bill.

CHAPTER 8: COURTS AND ADMINISTRATION OF JUSTICE

Constitutional Court

167. (1) The Constitutional Court consists of a President, a Deputy President and nine other judges.

(2) A matter before the Constitutional Court must be heard by at least eight judges.

(3) The Constitutional Court—
(a) is the highest court in all constitutional matters;
(b) may decide only constitutional matters, and issues connected with decisions on constitutional matters; and
(c) makes the final decision whether a matter is a constitutional matter or whether an issue is connected with a decision on a constitutional matter.

(4) Only the Constitutional Court may—
(a) decide disputes between organs of state in the national or provincial sphere concerning the constitutional status, powers or functions of any of those organs of state;
(b) decide on the constitutionality of any parliamentary or provincial Bill, but may do so only in the circumstances anticipated in section 79 or 121;
(c) decide applications envisaged in section 80 or 122;

(d) decide on the constitutionality of any amendment to the Constitution;

(e) decide that Parliament or the President has failed to fulfil a constitutional obligation; or

(f) certify a provincial constitution in terms of section 144.

(5) The Constitutional Court makes the final decision whether an Act of Parliament, a provincial Act or conduct of the President is constitutional, and must confirm any order of invalidity made by the Supreme Court of Appeal, a High Court, or a court of similar status, before that order has any force.

(6) National legislation or the rules of the Constitutional Court must allow a person, when it is in the interests of justice and with leave of the Constitutional Court—

(a) to bring a matter directly to the Constitutional Court; or

(b) to appeal directly to the Constitutional Court from any other court.

(7) A constitutional matter includes any issue involving the interpretation, protection or enforcement of the Constitution.

Powers of courts in constitutional matters

172. (1) When deciding a constitutional matter within its power, a court—

(a) must declare that any law or conduct that is inconsistent with the Constitution is invalid to the extent of its inconsistency; and

(b) may make any order that is just and equitable, including—

(i)   an order limiting the retrospective effect of the declaration of invalidity; and

(ii)   an order suspending the declaration of invalidity for any period and on any conditions, to allow the competent authority to correct the defect.

(2) (a) The Supreme Court of Appeal, a High Court or a court of similar status may make an order concerning the constitutional validity of an Act of Parliament, a provincial Act or any conduct of the President, but an order of constitutional invalidity has no force unless it is confirmed by the Constitutional Court.

(b) A court which makes an order of constitutional invalidity may grant a temporary interdict or other temporary relief to a party, or may adjourn the proceedings, pending a decision of the Constitutional Court on the validity of that Act or conduct.

(c) National legislation must provide for the referral of an order of constitutional invalidity to the Constitutional Court.

(d) Any person or organ of state with a sufficient interest may appeal, or apply, directly to the Constitutional Court to confirm or vary an order of constitutional invalidity by a court in terms of this subsection.

CHAPTER 9: STATE INSTITUTIONS SUPPORTING CONSTITUTIONAL
DEMOCRACY

HUMAN RIGHTS COMMISSION

Functions of Human Rights Commission

184. (1) The Human Rights Commission must—
   (a) promote respect for human rights and a culture of human rights;
   (b) promote the protection, development and attainment of human rights; and
   (c) monitor and assess the observance of human rights in the Republic.

(2) The Human Rights Commission has the powers, as regulated by national legislation, necessary to perform its functions, including the power—
   (a) to investigate and to report on the observance of human rights;
   (b) to take steps to secure appropriate redress where human rights have been violated;
   (c) to carry out research; and
   (d) to educate.

(3) Each year, the Human Rights Commission must require relevant organs of state to provide the Commission with information on the measures that they have taken towards the realisation of the rights in the Bill of Rights concerning housing, health care, food, water, social security, education and the environment.

(4) The Human Rights Commission has the additional powers and functions prescribed by national legislation.

As adopted by the Constitutional Assembly on 8 May 1996 and as amended on 11 October 1996.

CHAPTER 5

PROPOSALS FOR A
UK BILL OF RIGHTS

DETAILED BLUEPRINTS FOR A CONSTITUTIONAL BILL OF RIGHTS

IPPR's draft Bill of Rights

> 49   A BRITISH BILL OF RIGHTS 1990 (INSTITUTE FOR
>   PUBLIC POLICY RESEARCH)

RB NOTE: This proposal has been adopted by the Liberal Democrat Party as its preferred form of drafting with minor modificaitons: see Doc. 93.

There are 18 articles which contain the substantive rights which would be protected by the Bill of Rights, and 8 clauses (lettered A–H) which define the operation and effect of the Bill. The text of each article or clause is accompanied by the Institute for Public Policy Research's explanation of the source from which its drafting is drawn. In this document, the abbreviations 'EC' refer to the European Convention on Human Rights, and 'IC' to the International Covenant on Civil and Political Rights.

Article 1 – *Right to Life*

(1) Everyone's right to life shall be protected by law. No one shall be deprived of life intentionally.
(2) Deprivation of life shall not be regarded as inflicted in contravention of this article when it results from the use of force which is no more than absolutely necessary:
    (a)   in defence of any person from unlawful violence;
    (b)   in action lawfully taken for the purpose of quelling a riot or insurrection.
(3) No one shall be condemned to death or executed.

Source
    (a)   This is EC2, with the omission of para. 2(b), which states: 'in order to effect a lawful arrest or to prevent the escape of a person lawfully dctained.' Escaping from arrest or detention cannot justify intentional killing unless it involves life-threatening violence, in which case para. 2(a) would apply.

(b) The EC allows the death penalty 'in respect of acts committed in time of war or imminent threat of war', to be applied 'only in the instances laid down in the law'. There is no restriction in respect of the type of crimes for which the death penalty can be imposed. IC allows a reservation 'which provides for the application of the death penalty in times of war pursuant to a conviction for a most serious crime of a military nature committed during war time'. This reservation is unsatisfactory as it seems to allow the death penalty for desertion but not for civilian genocide. It is our view that the death penalty is wrong in any circumstances and these provisions have therefore been omitted.

Article 2 – *Freedom from torture*

No one shall be subjected to torture or to cruel, inhuman or degrading treatment or punishment.

Source
This is EC3, with the addition of 'cruel' from IC7.

Article 3 – *Slavery*

(1) No one shall be held in slavery or servitude
(2) No one shall be required to perform forced or compulsory labour
(3) For the purpose of this Article the term 'forced or compulsory labour' does not include:
    (a) any work required to be done in the ordinary course of detention according to the provisions of Article 4 or during conditional release from such detention;
    (b) any service of a military character or, in case of conscientious objectors, service exacted instead of compulsory military service;
    (c) any service exacted in case of an emergency or calamity threatening the life or well-being of the community;
    (d) any work or service which forms part of normal civic obligations.

Source
This is EC4, omitting 'in countries where they are recognised' after 'objectors' in paras (3) (b). IC8 is very similar.

Article 4 – *Liberty and security*

(1) Everyone has the right to liberty and security of person. No one shall be deprived of their liberty except, on reasonable grounds and in accordance with fair procedures established by law, in the following cases:

(a) the lawful detention of a person after conviction by a competent court;

(b) the lawful arrest or detention of a person for non-compliance with the lawful order of a court or in order to secure the fulfilment of any obligation prescribed by law;

(c) the lawful arrest or detention of a person effected for the purpose of bringing them before the competent legal authority on reasonable suspicion of having committed an offence or when it is reasonably considered necessary to prevent their committing an offence or fleeing after having done so;

(d) the lawful detention of persons for the prevention of the spreading of infectious diseases constituting a serious threat to public health, or of persons suffering from mental disorder where necessary for the prevention of harm to themselves or others;

(e) the lawful arrest or detention of a person to prevent their effecting an unauthorised entry into the United Kingdom or of a person against whom action is being taken with a view to deportation or extradition.

(2) Anyone who is arrested shall, at the time of arrest, be informed in a language which they understand of the reasons for their arrest and shall be promptly informed of any charges against them.

(3) It shall not be the general rule that persons awaiting trial shall be detained in custody. Anyone arrested or detained on a criminal charge shall be brought promptly before a judge or other officer authorised by law to exercise judicial power and shall be entitled to trial within a reasonable time or to release pending trial. Release may be subject to guarantees to appear for trial or at any other stage of the judicial proceedings.

(4) Anyone who is deprived of liberty by arrest or detention shall be entitled to take proceedings before a court in order that the court may decide without delay on the lawfulness of the detention and may order their release if the detention is not lawful.

(5) Anyone who has been the victim of unlawful arrest or detention shall have an enforceable right to compensation.

(6) All persons deprived of their liberty shall be treated with humanity and with respect for the inherent dignity of the human person.

(7) Accused persons in detention shall, save in exceptional circumstances, be segregated from convicted persons and shall be subject to separate treatment appropriate to their status as people who have not been convicted.

(8) Accused juvenile persons in detention shall be separated from adults and brought as speedily as possible for adjudication. Juvenile convicted persons shall be separated from adults and be accorded treatment appropriate to their age and legal status.

(9) No one shall be imprisoned merely on the ground of inability to fulfil a contractual obligation.

Source

    (a) The list of exceptions to the right to liberty and security are those set out in EC5 with the deletion of references to detention of minors for educational supervision, alcoholics, drug addicts and vagrants. This does not, of course, make it unlawful to imprison drug addicts for drug offences, etc. In 1 (d), the words 'constituting a serious threat to public health' and 'where necessary for the prevention of harm to themselves or others' have been added to narrow the exception. A reference to 'persons suffering from mental disorder' is substituted for 'persons of unsound mind'.

    (b) Para (2) is IC9(2) with part of EC5(2).

    (c) Para (3) is mainly a rearranged IC9(3). The second sentence is from IC9(3), with the addition at the end of the words 'pending trial' from EC5(3). The third sentence is also from IC9(3) but omits the words at the end 'and, should occasion arise, for execution of the judgment' ...

    (d) Para (4) is IC9(4). EC5(4) is very similar.

    (e) Para (5) is IC9(5). EC5(5) is very similar.

    (f) Para (6) is IC10(1). There is no EC equivalent.

    (g) Para (7) is IC10(2)(a). There is no EC equivalent.

    (h) Para (8) is IC10(2)(b) and the second sentence of IC10(3), slightly reworded. This arrangement seems better than that in IC10. There is no EC equivalent ...

    (i) Para (9) is IC11. EC Protocol 4 is very similar.

Article 5 – *Fair and public hearing*

(1) In the determination of their civil rights and obligations or of any criminal charges against them, everyone is entitled to a fair and public hearing within a reasonable time by an independent and impartial tribunal established by law. Judgment shall be pronounced publicly but the press and public may be excluded from all or any part of the trial to the extent strictly necessary in the opinion of the court:

    (a)   in the interests of public order or national security in a democratic society;

    (b)   where the interests of juveniles or the protection of the private life of the parties so require; or

    (c)   where publicity would prejudice the interests of justice.

(2) Everyone charged with a criminal offence shall be presumed innocent until proved guilty according to law.

(3) Everyone charged with a criminal offence has the following minimum rights:

    (a)   to be informed promptly in a language which they understand and in detail of the nature and cause of the accusation against them;

    (b)   to have adequate time and facilities for the preparation of their defence;

    (c)   to defend themselves in person or through legal assistance of their own choosing or, if they have not sufficient means to pay for legal assistance, to be given it free when the interests of justice so require;

    (d)   to examine or have examined witnesses against them and to obtain the attendance and examination of witnesses on their behalf under the same conditions as witnesses against them;

    (e)   to have the free assistance of an interpreter if they cannot understand or speak the language used in court;

    (f)   not to be compelled to testify against themselves or to confess guilt.

(4) When a person has, by a final decision, been convicted of a criminal offence and has suffered punishment as a result of such conviction, and it is subsequently shown that there has been a miscarriage of justice, that person shall be compensated according to law.

(5) Everyone convicted of a crime shall have the right to their conviction and sentence being reviewed by a higher tribunal according to law.

(6) No one shall be liable to be tried or punished again for an offence for which they have already been finally convicted or acquitted in accordance with the law and penal procedure.

Source

    (a)   This is EC6 with some additions from IC14. 'Morals' has been deleted from the grounds for removing the press and public from a trial, in 5(1), as we do not consider that it could be justified to exclude the press or public on those grounds.

    (b)   Para 3(f) is IC14(3)(g) and has no equivalent in EC6.

    (c)   Para (4) is a modified version of IC14(6). There is no EC equivalent (para 5 of Article 4 above does not apply because the detention is not unlawful). IC14(6) is clumsily and too narrowly worded – it applies only if it is 'conclusively' shown by a 'newly discovered fact' that there has been a miscarriage.

    (d)   Para (5) is Para (5) of IC14. There is a similar provision in EC Protocol 7.

    (e)   Para (6) is para (7) of IC14. There is a similar provision in EC Protocol 7.

Article 6 – *Retrospective offences*

(1) No one shall be held guilty of any criminal offence on account of any act or omission which did not constitute a criminal offence under national or international law at the time when it was committed. Nor shall a heavier penalty be imposed than the one that was applicable at the time the criminal offence was committed.

(2) This Article shall not prejudice the trial and punishment of any person for any act which constitutes the crime of genocide or a crime against humanity.

Source
   (a) Para (1) is EC7(1), complete. IC15 is similar, except that it adds a sentence at the end of para 1 enabling an offender to have the benefit of any reduction in penalties made subsequent to the offence.
   (b) Para (2) is based on EC7(2). (IC15(2) is similar.) However, EC7(2) allows trial 'for any act or omission which, at the time when it was committed, was criminal according to the general principle of law recognised by civilised nations'.

Article 7 – *Private and family life*

(1) Everyone has the right to respect for their private and family life, their home and their correspondence.
(2) There shall be no interference with the exercise of this right except such as is in accordance with the law and is necessary in a democratic society:
   (a)   in the interests of national security or public safety; or
   (b)   for the prevention of disorder or crime; or
   (c)   for the protection of health or morals; or
   (d)   for the protection of the rights and freedoms of others.

Source
   (a) This is EC8, slightly reworded, with the removal of 'economic wellbeing of the country' as grounds for infringing privacy.
   (b) EC8 does not give any right to privacy as such, but only the right to respect for private and family life, home and correspondence.

Article 8 – *Freedom of thought*

(1) Everyone has the right to freedom of thought, conscience and religion. This right includes freedom to change one's religion or belief, and freedom, either alone or in community with others and in public or private, to manifest one's religion or belief in worship, teaching, practice and observance.
(2) Freedom to manifest one's religion or belief shall be subject only to such limitations as are prescribed by law and are necessary in a democratic society:
   (a)   in the interests of public safety; or
   (b)   for the preservation of public order; or
   (c)   for the protection of health or morals, or
   (d)   for the protection of the rights and freedoms of others.

Source
This is EC9, complete but slightly reworded. It is very similar to IC18(1) and (3). IC18(2) provides that 'No one shall be subject to coercion which would impair his freedom to have or to adopt a religion or belief of his choice.'

Article 9 – *Education*

(1) No person shall be denied the right to education.
(2) In the exercise of their functions in relation to education and teaching, public authorities shall respect the right of parents to ensure such education and teaching in conformity with their own religious and philosophical convictions, so far as is compatible with the provision of efficient instruction and training and the avoidance of unreasonable public expenditure.

Source
(a) This Article is based on EC Protocol 1 para 2. The opening words of (2) are altered; the original is 'In the exercise of any functions which it assumes in relation to education and to teaching, the State shall respect ...' This is not wholly appropriate to the UK, where education is mainly a local authority function.
(b) IC contains no equivalent to (1). This should clearly be included as a basic right.
(c) IC18(4) is fairly similar to (2). It contains a number of textual differences. These are:
　(a) IC18(4) speaks of the 'liberty of parents', not the 'right of parents'.
　(b) IC18(4) refers to legal guardians as well as parents.
　(c) IC18(4) refers to 'religious and moral education of their children in conformity with their own convictions'. The words 'moral' (IC) and 'philosophical' (EC) are not entirely synonymous.
(d) The words following 'convictions' follow the wording of a reservation by the UK on the ratification of the Protocol.

Article 10 – *Freedom of expression*

(1) Everyone shall have the right to hold opinions without interference.
(2) Everyone shall have the right to freedom of expression; this right shall include freedom to seek, receive and impart information and ideas of all kinds regardless of frontiers, either orally, in writing or in print, in the form of art, or through any other media of their choice.
(3) The exercise of this right carries with it special duties and responsibilities. It may therefore be subject to certain restrictions, but only such as are provided by law and are necessary in a democratic society:

    (a) for respect of the rights or reputations of others; or
    (b) for the protection of national security or of public order or of public health or morals.
(4) This Article shall not prevent the state from requiring the licensing of broadcasting, television or cinema enterprises.

Source
This is IC19 with the addition of part of EC10(1). Unlike EC10, IC19 clearly separates the right to hold opinions and does not make it subject to any restrictions. The expression of opinions can be regulated but not the right to possess them.

Article 11 – Freedom of assembly and association

(1) Everyone has the right to freedom of peaceful assembly and to freedom of association with others, including the right to form and to join trade unions.
(2) No restriction shall be placed on the exercise of these rights other than such as are prescribed by law and are necessary in a democratic society:
    (a) in the interests of national security, public safety or the preservation of public order; or
    (b) for the protection of public health or morals; or
    (c) for the protection of the rights and freedoms of others.
(3) This Article shall not prevent the imposition of restrictions prescribed by law and necessary in a democratic society on the exercise of this right by members of the armed forces or of the police or by persons charged with the administration of the state.

Source
    (a) This is EC11, with the substitution of 'the preservation of public order' in para (2) for 'for the prevention of disorder or crime'.
    (b) The IC separates freedom of assembly (IC21) from freedom of association and trade unions (IC22). Otherwise, the IC and EC versions are very similar, except that in the IC the armed forces and police exceptions do not apply to freedom of assembly.

Article 12 – Marriage

(1) Everyone of marriageable age shall have the right both to marry and to found a family.
(2) No marriage shall be entered into without the free and full consent of the intending spouses.
(3) Spouses shall have equality of rights and responsibilities as to marriage, during marriage, and at its dissolution. In the case of dissolution, provision shall be made for the necessary protection of any children.

(4) Every child shall have the right to such measures of protection as are required by their status as a minor, on the part of their family, society and public authorities.

Source

(a) Para (1) is EC12, omitting words at the end which are inappropriate in a domestic charter. IC23 (2) is similar. 'Everyone' has been substituted for the EC wording, 'men and women'.

(b) Para (2) is IC23(3). There is no EC equivalent.

(c) Para (3) is based on IC23(4), which requires States to take steps to ensure these rights. There is no EC equivalent.

(d) Para (4) is IC24(1), with the substitution of 'public authorities' for 'the State' at the end. There is no EC equivalent and we have omitted the non-discrimination provisions as being covered by Article 17 below.

(e) IC24(3) provides that every child has the right to acquire a nationality. It is our intention that another section of our draft Constitution [see IPPR, The Constitution of the United Kingdom, 1991, Articles 30–3] will provide for the basic rights to acquire British nationality and these rights will only be capable of alteration by a special parliamentary procedure. If basic citizenship rights were not entrenched in the Constitution we would include a domestic equivalent of IC24(3) and probably extend it.

Article 13 – *Possessions*

(1) Every natural or legal person is entitled to the peaceful enjoyment of their possessions. No one shall be deprived of their possessions except in the public interest and subject to the conditions provided for by law and to prompt, adequate and effective compensation.

(2) This Article shall not, however, in any way impair the right to enforce such laws as may be necessary to control the use of property in accordance with the general interest or to secure the payment of taxes or other contributions or penalties.

Source

(a) Para (1) is EC Protocol 1 Art (1), omitting at the end 'and by the general principles of international law' as being unnecessary in a domestic charter, but providing for compensation for British citizens and aliens if deprived of their possessions under the exceptions allowed. There is no IC equivalent.

(b) Para (2) is EC Protocol 1 Art 1(2), with the substitution of 'to enforce such laws as may be necessary' for 'of a State to enforce such laws as it deems necessary' ...

Article 14 – *Participation in political life and public service*

Every adult citizen shall have the right and the opportunity, without unreasonable restrictions:

(a) to take part in the conduct of public affairs directly or through freely chosen representatives;
(b) to vote and to stand for election at genuine periodic elections which shall be by universal and equal suffrage and shall be held by secret ballot, guaranteeing the free expression of the will of the people;
(c) to participate, on general terms of equality, in public service.

Source

This is essentially IC25, with the omission of a cross-reference to IC2 (on discrimination). EC Protocol I Article 3 is more limited and gives a right to vote (but not to stand for election) in terms similar to those in (b) above.

Article 15 – *Freedom of movement*

(1) Everyone lawfully within the United Kingdom shall have the right of liberty of movement and freedom to choose their residence within the United Kingdom.
(2) Everyone shall be free to leave the United Kingdom.
(3) No restrictions shall be placed on the exercise of these rights other than such as are in accordance with law and are necessary in a democratic society:
    (a) in the interests of national security, public safety or the preservation of public order; or
    (b) for the prevention of crime; or
    (c) for the protection of health; or
    (d) for the protection of the rights and freedoms of others.
(4) The rights set out in (1) may also be subject, in particular areas, to restrictions imposed in accordance with law and justified by the public interest in a democratic society.

Source

(a) This is based on EC Protocol 4 Article 2, adapted for domestic use. The UK has not ratified this Protocol because of the exclusion order powers conferred by the Prevention of Terrorism Act. IC12(1)-(3) is very similar.
(b) 'Morals' has been deleted as a grounds for restricting these rights as it is capable of wide interpretation and we do not consider it justified in this case, given the remaining exceptions for the prevention of crime and the protection of the rights and freedoms of others.

Article 16 – *Expulsion from the UK*

(1) No citizen of the United Kingdom shall be expelled from the United Kingdom or deprived of the right to enter the United Kingdom.
(2) An alien lawfully in the United Kingdom may be expelled there-

from only in pursuance of a decision reached in accordance with law and shall be allowed, prior to expulsion, to submit reasons against expulsion and to have their case reviewed by, and be represented for the purpose before, the competent authority or a person or persons especially designated by the competent authority.

(3) This Article shall not prevent the extradition of persons, through established legal procedures, for the purpose of standing trial for a criminal offence or serving a sentence lawfully imposed on them in another jurisdiction.

Source

(a) Para (1) is based on IC12 (4) and EC Protocol 4 Article 3. It is our intention that those British citizens who do not currently have a right of abode in the UK should be covered by this provision. There is currently a reservation under IC12 (4) in respect of persons not having a right of entry under current UK law.

(b) The Convention and Covenant contain no exception for extradition, which is not treated as expulsion.

(c) Para (2) is IC13, adjusted for a domestic charter. In relation to the right to submit reasons against expulsion, we have added the requirement that the right to submit reasons be 'prior to expulsion', and have omitted the exception to this right 'where compelling reasons of national security otherwise require' for which there is no justification. There is no EC equivalent to IC13.

Article 17 – *Equality*

(1) Everyone shall have the right to recognition as a person before the law.

(2) All persons are equal before the law and are entitled without any discrimination to the equal protection of the law.

(3) The equal protection of the law and the enjoyment of the rights and freedoms set forth in this Bill of Rights shall be secured without discrimination on any ground such as sex, race, colour, language, religion, political or other opinion, national or social origin, association with a national minority, property, birth, homosexuality, disability, age, or other status.

Source

(a) Para (1) is EC16.

(b) Paras (2) and (3) are an amalgam of EC14 and IC26, with the addition of three further grounds for non-discrimination, homosexuality, age and disability.

Article 18 – *Asylum*

(1) Every person has the right to seek and be granted asylum in the UK in accordance with the legislation of the UK and international conventions, if they are being pursued for political offences.

(2) In no case may an alien be deported or returned to a country, regardless of whether or not it is their country of origin, if in that country their right to life or personal freedom is in danger of being violated because of their race, nationality, religion, social status, or political opinions.

Source
Article 18 is paras (7) and (8) of the American Convention on Human Rights, with minor textual amendments. There is nothing comparable in either the EC or IC.

Clause A – *Enacting provision*

The provisions of Articles 1 to 18 shall be known as 'the Bill of Rights' and, subject to the provisions of this Constitution, shall have the force of law in the United Kingdom.

Clause B – *Applicability*

The Bill of Rights applies to any act or omission by or on behalf of any person or body (including the Crown) in the performance of any public function.

Source
This is based (rather loosely) on cl. 3 of the draft New Zealand Bill of Rights. See also s. 32 of the Canadian Charter of Rights and Freedoms. This clause does not cover Parliament, which is covered by Clause C.

Clause C – *Incompatibility of legislation with Bill of Rights*

(1) Subject to the provisions of Clause D any provision of an Act of Parliament or subordinate legislation shall be void if and to the extent that

(a) it requires or authorises anything to be done or omitted in contravention of any provision of the Bill of Rights; or

(b) it prohibits the exercise of any right or freedom protected by the Bill of Rights; or

(c) it restricts the exercise of any such right or freedom in a manner not authorised by the Bill of Rights.

(2) If the validity of any provision of an Act of Parliament is challenged in the course of proceedings in an inferior court or tribunal, the court or tribunal shall (unless it is satisfied that there is no substance in the challenge) refer the question to the High Court,

the Court of Session or the Northern Ireland High Court, as the case may be.

Clause D – *Scope of exceptions*

Where the protection of any right or freedom by the Bill of Rights is subject to any restriction or qualification, that restriction or qualification shall have no wider effect than is strictly necessary in the circumstances, and shall not be applied for any purpose other than that for which it has been prescribed.

Clause E – *Suspension of Bill of Rights*

(1) In time of war or other public emergency threatening the life of the nation Her Majesty may by Order in Council take measures suspending, to the extent strictly required by the exigencies of the situation, any provisions of the Bill of Rights other than Article 1 (except in respect of deaths resulting from lawful acts of war), Article 2, Article 3 (1), Article 6, Article 8 and Article 17 (1).

(2) Unless the urgency of the situation makes it impracticable to do so, an Order in Council under sub-clause (1) above shall not be made unless a draft of the Order has been approved by a two-thirds majority of those voting in each House of Parliament.

(3) An Order in Council which has been made without having been approved in draft by both Houses of Parliament shall cease to have effect unless, as soon as practicable, it is confirmed by a two-thirds majority of those voting in each House of Parliament.

(4) No challenge to the validity of an Order in Council under this clause shall be made except by proceedings for judicial review.

(5) An Order in Council made under this clause shall have effect only for a time specified in the Order but the duration of the Order may subsequently be extended by resolution of a two-thirds majority of those voting in each House of Parliament if, and to the extent that, the making of a new Order in Council would be justified under this clause.

Source
Sub-clause (1) is based on EC15(1) and (2), with the addition of a couple of rights (Article 8 and 17(1)) which cannot be derogated from under IC4 but can under EC15.

Clause F – *Interpretation*

(1) The Bill of Rights is intended to give effect in the United Kingdom to the International Covenant on Civil and Political Rights and the European Convention for the Protection of Human Rights and Fundamental Freedoms, and shall be interpreted and applied accordingly, but without prejudice to any rights and freedoms

protected by the Bill of Rights which are more extensive than those protected by the International Covenant or the European Convention.

(2) Judicial notice shall be taken of:

  (a) the International Covenant on Civil and Political Rights and the European Convention on Human Rights and Fundamental Freedoms;

  (b) reports and expressions of views by the United Nations Human Rights Committee;

  (c) reports of the European Commission of Human Rights; and

  (d) judgments and advisory opinions of the European Court of Human Rights.

(3) Any question as to the meaning or effect of the International Covenant or the European Convention shall be treated as a question of law and, in the case of the European Convention, shall be for determination as such in accordance with the principles laid down by, and any relevant decision of, the European Court of Human Rights.

(4) Nothing herein shall be construed as limiting or derogating from any of the human rights or fundamental freedoms which may be enjoyed under any other agreement to which the UK is a party.

Source
Paras 2 and 3 are based on the equivalent provisions of the European Communities Act 1972.

Clause G – *Damages*

(1) Without prejudice to any right to apply for judicial review, any person whose rights or freedoms protected by the Bill of Rights have been infringed or are threatened with infringement may bring civil proceedings for damages, an injunction or any other relief authorised by rules of court.

Clause H – *Abuse of freedom*

Nothing in the Bill of Rights may be interpreted as implying for any group or person any right to engage in any activity or perform any act aimed at the destruction of any of the rights and freedoms set out therein or at their limitation to a greater extent than is provided for therein.

Source
This is IC Article 5(1)

Institute for Public Policy Research, *A British Bill of Rights*, 1990.

Liberty's draft Bill of Rights

---
50   A PEOPLE'S CHARTER 1991 (NATIONAL COUNCIL
FOR CIVIL LIBERTIES)
---

*RB NOTE: The text of each article in the proposal is accompanied by Liberty's
explanation of the source from which its drafting is drawn.*

PART I – THE BILL OF RIGHTS

Article 1 – *The right to protection under a Bill of Rights*

The rights and freedoms set out below shall be known as the UK Bill of
Rights. The Bill shall have the force of law and shall apply to all individuals
within the jurisdiction of the UK without distinction of any kind. It shall be
incumbent on the state to adopt such legislative or other measures as may be
necessary to give effect to the rights and freedoms in this Bill.

Source
This is based on Article 1 of the European Convention for the Protection of
Human Rights and Fundamental Freedoms (ECHR) and Article 2(1) of the
International Covenant on Civil and Political Rights (ICCPR).

Article 2 – *The right to life*

1.   Everyone's right to life, from the moment of birth, shall be
protected by law. No one shall be deprived of life.
2.   Deprivation of life shall not contravene this Article when it results
from the use of force which is no more than absolutely necessary
in defence of any person from unlawful violence, which could
reasonably be expected to result in loss of life.
3.   No one shall be condemned to death or executed.

Sources
Clause 1 is an abridged version of ECHR, Article 2(1), omitting 'save in the
execution of a sentence of a court following conviction of a crime for which
the penalty is provided by law' and adding the phrase 'from the moment of
birth'.
Clause 2 is ECHR, Article 2 with an additional phrase concerning
reasonable expectation of loss of life and the following omissions:
'(b) in order to effect a lawful arrest or to prevent the escape of a
person lawfully detained;
(c) in action lawfully taken for the purposes of quelling a riot or
insurrection.'
Clause 3 is ECHR, Protocol 6, Article 1 (edited) which has not been signed
or ratified by the UK.

Article 3 – *The right to freedom from torture and ill-treatment*

1. No one shall be subjected to torture or to cruel, inhuman or degrading treatment or punishment.
2. No one shall be subjected without their express and informed consent to medical or scientific experimentation, testing or research.

Sources

Clause 1 is ECHR, Article 3 with the addition of the word 'cruel' from ICCPR, Article 7. This is one of the few rights defined as absolute both in the ECHR and this Bill.

Clause 2 is based on the ICCPR, Article 7 with additional phrases proposed by the AIDS charity, the Terrence Higgins Trust, which add testing and research to the areas covered by this clause and emphasise the requirement for consent.

Article 4 – *The right to freedom from slavery and forced labour*

1. No one shall be held in slavery or servitude.
2. No one shall be required to perform forced or compulsory labour other than in the ordinary course of detention imposed according to the provisions of Article 5 or during conditional release from such detention.

Sources

Clause 1 is the same as ECHR Article 4(1). This is presented as an absolute right under the ECHR and in this Bill.

Clause 2 is ECHR Article 4(2) and (3)(a) amalgamated.

(ECHR Articles 3(b) to 3(d), containing three additional exemptions to compulsory labour, have been omitted.)

The definitions of the terms used in this Article are covered in Article 23.

Article 5 – *The right to liberty and security from arbitrary arrest and detention*

1. Everyone has the right to liberty and security of person. No one shall be deprived of their liberty save on reasonable grounds in the following cases and in accordance with a fair and just procedure prescribed by law:
   (a) the lawful detention of a person after conviction of a crime by a competent court;
   (b) the lawful arrest or detention of a person for non-compliance with the lawful order of the court;
   (c) the lawful arrest or detention of a person for the purpose of bringing them before a competent legal authority on reasonable suspicion of having committed an offence or when there are reasonable grounds for suspecting either that an offence

is being attempted or that a person is fleeing after having committed an offence.

(d)   nothing in this Article shall prevent the involuntary admission into designated health facilities under strict medical supervision and on the basis of sound medical advice of:

(i)   persons where the circumstances are such that proper precautions to prevent the spread of a notifiable and serious infectious disease cannot be taken and where there is a serious risk of infection to other people if the person suffering from the said disease is not detained in hospital;

(ii) persons suffering from mental illness of a nature or degree which makes detention strictly necessary to prevent imminent and serious physical harm to themselves and others provided that the involuntary admission is initially for a short period and is subject to regular review by an independent body governed by the principles of natural justice laid down in Article 6.

2.   Everyone who is deprived of their liberty on any of the grounds in this Article shall have the following rights:

(a)   they shall be informed, at the time of their detention or involuntary admission, and in a language which they understand, of the reasons for their detention and shall be informed promptly of any charges against them.

(b)   they shall be entitled to consult a solicitor free of charge at any time.

(c)   if they are charged with a crime they shall be advised that they are not required to say anything unless they wish to do so but what they say may be given in evidence against them.

(d)   they shall be entitled to have their whereabouts notified to a person of their choice without delay.

3.   Anyone arrested or detained on a criminal charge shall be brought promptly and without delay before a judge or other officer authorised by law to exercise judicial power and shall be entitled to trial within a reasonable time or to release. It shall be the general rule that persons awaiting trial shall not be detained in custody but may be subject to guarantees to appear for trial.

4.   Anyone who is deprived of their liberty under any of the grounds in this Article shall be entitled to take proceedings before a court without delay, in order that the court may decide speedily on the lawfulness of the detention and order their release if the detention is not lawful.

5.   No one shall be deprived of their liberty solely on the grounds of inability to fulfil a contractual obligation, debt or non-payment of fine.

6.   All persons deprived of their liberty shall be treated with human-

ity and with respect for the inherent dignity of the human person.

7. (a) Accused persons in detention shall, save in exceptional circumstances, be segregated from convicted persons and shall be subject to separate treatment in accordance with their status as unconvicted persons.

    (b) Accused juveniles in detention shall be separated from adults and brought as speedily as possible for adjudication.

8. Convicted juveniles shall be segregated from adults and accorded treatment appropriate to their age and legal status.

9. The regime of custodial institutions should seek to minimise any differences between prison life and life at liberty which tend to lessen the responsibility of the prisoners or the respect due to their dignity as human beings.

Sources

Clause 1 is ECHR, Article 5(1) amended to add the phrase 'on reasonable grounds' which is in line with British statute, and the words 'fair and just' before 'procedure' as an indication that it is not sufficient for restrictions to be 'prescribed by law'; they must also be fair and just. The definition of 'security of person' is contained in Article 23.

Clauses 1(a) to (c) are an edited version of ECHR, Article 5(1)(a) to (c) except that in Clause 1(c) we have replaced 'prevent his committing an offence' with 'suspecting an offence is being attempted' which is closer to the provisions in the 1984 Police and Criminal Evidence Act (PACE) although more tightly worded.

Clause 1(d) is loosely based on ECHR, Article 5(e). The wording of 1(d)(i) comes from the Public Health (Control of Diseases) Act with the addition of 'serious' to tighten up the clause. Clause 1(d)(ii) is based on the Mental Health Act 1983 although we have substituted 'mental illness' for 'mental disorder'. We have also strengthened the wording of the Mental Health Act so that detention should only occur when 'strictly necessary' and where the potential harm is of a physical nature, 'serious' and 'imminent'.

Clause 2(a) is drawn from ECHR, Article 5(2) amended by ICCPR, Article 9(2) which slightly strengthens it. In 2(b) to (d) we have also added standard rights for detainees under British justice covering the right to silence, the right to free legal advice and the right not to be held incommunicado. None of these rights is adequately protected by either the European Convention or International Covenant. In contrast to PACE, from which the provision is drawn, we have provided an absolute right to access to legal advice for detainees. The reference to such advice being free of charge is in line with the 1988 Legal Aid Act. We have also omitted the qualifications on the right not to be held incommunicado found in PACE, on which we consult below.

Clause 3 is an abridged version of ICCPR, Article 9(3); similar to ECHR, Article 5(3) but stronger on the issue of release pending trial about which there are no obligations on the authorities under the European Convention ...

Article 6 – *The right to a fair and public trial or hearing*

1. All persons are equal before the law and are entitled without discrimination to the equal protection of the law.
2. In the determination of any civil rights and obligations or of any criminal charge everyone is entitled to:
    (a) a fair and public hearing within a reasonable time by an independent and impartial court or tribunal established by law. Judgment shall be pronounced publicly *in all circumstances* but the press and public may be excluded from, or reporting restrictions applied to, all or part of the trial in the following circumstances:
        (i)   where the interests of children and juveniles require.
        (ii)   where it is strictly necessary and to the extent that it is strictly necessary in a democratic society to protect the private lives of the parties or witnesses. In criminal proceedings the private life of the defendant shall be protected by restrictions only to the extent that any such publicity would result in the identification of a vulnerable witness or victim.
        (iii) where, in the opinion of the court, it is strictly necessary, and to the extent that it is strictly necessary in a democratic society, in exceptional circumstances, to protect public safety.
        (iv)   where, in the opinion of the court, it is strictly necessary, and to the extent that it is strictly necessary in a democratic society, in exceptional circumstances, to enable the hearing to continue. During the course of any hearing the public, or sections thereof, may be excluded from specific sessions in such circumstances but reporting restrictions may not apply.
        (v)   where it is strictly necessary, and to the extent that is strictly necessary in a democratic society, when there is a substantial risk, in the opinion of the court, that publicity would seriously prejudice the interests of justice. Reporting restrictions only, on all or part of the trial, may be applied in these specific circumstances. The risk of impediment or prejudice must in these circumstances be more than is merely incidental to publicity which is in the public interest.
    (b) be present at any hearing and to represent themselves in person or be represented through legal assistance of their own choosing; to be informed of this right and if without sufficient means to pay for legal assistance to be given it free when the interests of justice so require.
    (c) a right of appeal to a higher court from an unfavourable decision of any court or tribunal and this shall include the right of everyone convicted of a crime to appeal against

conviction and sentence. Subject to any conditions prescribed by law there shall be a final right of appeal to the
Supreme Court.

3. Everyone charged with a criminal offence shall be presumed
innocent until proved guilty according to law.

4. Everyone charged with a criminal offence has the following minimum rights:

   (a) to be informed promptly and in detail in a language which
   they understand of the nature and cause of the charge
   against them.

   (b) to have adequate time and facilities for the preparation of
   their defence, to communicate privately with counsel of
   their own choosing and to be given access to all relevant
   documents and witness statements that will assist them in
   their defence.

   (c) to be tried without undue delay.

   (d) to examine or have examined the witnesses against them,
   including expert witnesses, and to obtain the attendance and
   examination of witnesses on their behalf under the same
   conditions as witnesses against them.

   (e) to have the free assistance of an interpreter if they cannot
   understand or speak the language used in court.

   (f) not to be compelled or coerced to give evidence in their
   defence or to testify against themselves or to confess guilt.

   (g) to be tried by a jury of their peers in all cases involving
   potential loss of liberty.

5. In the case of juveniles the procedure shall be such as will take
account of their age.

6. When a person has by a final decision been convicted of a criminal
offence and has suffered punishment as a result of such a conviction, that person shall have the right to have their case reviewed
and investigated by an independent body if substantial doubt
arises about the conviction, whether as a result of new evidence or
in any other way.

7. (a) A confession of guilt by the accused shall be accepted as
   valid evidence in any criminal proceedings only if it is made
   without coercion or inducement of any kind in the presence
   of a solicitor and if it can be corroborated by independent
   evidence which implicates the defendant in the crime.

   (b) Other evidence which was obtained in breach of the law,
   including this Bill of Rights, shall not be admitted in evidence in any criminal or other proceedings.

8. No one shall be liable to be tried or punished again for an offence
for which they have already been finally convicted or acquitted in
accordance with the law and penal procedure.

Sources
Clause 1 is the first sentence of the ICCPR, Article 26.

Clause 2 is based on ECHR, Article 6(1), with some additions and omissions. The definitions of 'civil rights and obligations' and 'criminal charge' are contained in Article 23.

Clause 2(a) is ECHR, Article 6(1) but omitting exclusion of the press and public on grounds of morals, public order or national security and adding 'public safety' (in exceptional circumstances) as a ground for exclusion instead. This version also includes an option to restrict the reporting of all or part of a trial without necessarily closing the court to the press and public. An additional sentence allows courts to be partially or fully cleared during particular sessions at the discretion of the court, but only in exceptional circumstances where the disruption is such that persistent noise or other interruptions from the public threaten to prevent the case from proceeding.

Clause 2(a)(v) combines the relevant provisions of the Convention with part of the Contempt Act 1981, allowing reporting restrictions (but not closed courts) where there is a 'substantial risk' to justice through prejudicing the judge or jury without, as the ECHR seems to do in such circumstances, sanctioning secret trials. The reference to the prejudice being merely incidental to the publicity introduces a so-called 'public interest defence' in such cases.

Article 7 – *The right to justice concerning retrospective offences*

1. No one shall be held guilty of any criminal offence on account of any act or omission which did not constitute a criminal offence under national or international law at the time it was committed. Nor shall a heavier penalty be imposed than the one that was applicable at the time the criminal offence was committed. If, subsequent to the commission of the offence, provision is made by law for the imposition of a lighter penalty the offender shall benefit thereby.
2. Nothing in this Article shall prejudice the trial and punishment of any person for an act or omission which constitutes the crime of genocide or a crime against humanity.

Sources
Clause 1 is ICCPR, Article 15(1). This is the same as ECHR, Article 7(1), with the addition of a proviso regarding prisoners benefiting from a subsequent reduction in penalties for crimes for which they have been convicted and are serving sentences.

Clause 2 is an amended version of ECHR, Article 7(2) and ICCPR, Article 15(2). It is adopted from the Bill of Rights drawn up by the Institute for Public Policy Research (IPPR).

Article 8 – *The right to personal privacy*

1. Everyone has the right to respect for their private and family life, their home and their correspondence.

2. Everyone has the right to the protection of the law against interference with their privacy, family, home or correspondence and against attacks on their reputation.

3. Everyone has the right to know what public and private authorities hold information on them and for what purposes the information has been collected and will be used.

4. Everyone has the right of access to information held on them by any public or private authority and to withhold consent to personal information being disclosed to a third party.

5. Everyone has the right to be secure against unreasonable search and seizure and all searches and seizures must be prescribed by law in accordance with the following safeguards:
   (a) Unless it is strictly impractical to do so all searches must be authorised in advance by a court.
   (b) The reasons for the search and any documents or other authorisation for the search shall be given to the person searched or the occupier of the premises before the search takes place.
   (c) A written list of seized items shall be provided at the end of the search.

6. No one shall be required to obtain or carry on their person a document for the sole purpose of establishing their identity.

7. Anyone affected by inaccurate statements disseminated to the public in general by any medium of communication has the right to reply or make a correction using the same communication outlet, under such conditions as the law may establish.

8. The rights set out in Clauses 2 and 4 are subject only to such limits as are prescribed by law, strictly necessary and demonstrably justified in a democratic society for:
   (a) the protection of the rights and freedoms of others as laid down in this Bill, and
   (b) the protection of public safety to the extent that is strictly necessary in exceptional circumstances.

Sources

Clause 1 is the same as ECHR, Article 8(1), guaranteeing respect for a private life.

Clause 2 is ICCPR, Article 17(2) with the areas to be protected drawn from Article 17(1), which is stronger than ECHR, Article 8(2). It not only states that there shall be no interference with the right in Clause 1 as does the Convention, but guarantees the protection of the law against such interference, subject to the limitations in Clause 8. It also adds 'honour and reputation' to the areas given protection to safeguard against libel and slander, and refers to 'privacy' rather than 'private life'.

Clause 3 is based on Liberty policy and is also in line with the Liberal Democrat and Labour Party positions on access to personal information. Both the Convention and Covenant couch the right to privacy in broad terms and do not specifically address the issues of data access and protection. The definition of the term 'authority' is explained in Article 23 of this Bill.

Article 9 – *The right to freedom of conscience*

1. Everyone has the right to freedom of thought, conscience and religion (including the right to no religion) and to hold their own opinions. These rights include freedom to change one's religion or beliefs and freedom either alone or in community with others and in public or in private, to manifest one's religion or beliefs in worship, teaching, practice and observance.
2. Freedom to manifest one's religion or beliefs shall be subject to such limits as are prescribed by law, strictly necessary and demonstrably justified in a democratic society for the protection of individuals from imminent physical harm and for the protection of the rights and freedoms of others as laid down in this Bill.

Sources

Clause 1 is ECHR, Article 9(1) amended in two ways. First, to include the right to hold opinions which is taken from ICCPR Article 19(1). Secondly, to include the right to have no religion at all, which is from the draft Bill of Rights for Northern Ireland produced by the Committee on the Administration of Justice.

Clause 2 is ECHR, Article 9(2) with the limiting clause amended along the same lines as in Article 8(8) except that we have introduced a new ground for limitations under this Article; 'protection of individuals from imminent physical harm' and have omitted 'public safety'.

Article 10 – *The right to freedom of information and expression*

1. Everyone shall have the right to freedom of expression. This right shall include freedom to seek, receive and impart information and ideas of all kinds regardless of frontiers either orally, in writing or in print, in the form of art, or through any media of their choice subject only to such limits as are prescribed by law, strictly necessary and demonstrably justified in a democratic society for the protection of individuals from imminent physical harm or to prevent incitement to racial hatred, and for the protection of the rights and freedoms of others as laid down in this Bill.
2. Everyone shall have the right of access to official information held by public authorities subject only to such limits as are prescribed by law, strictly necessary and demonstrably justified in a democratic society, for:
    (a) the protection of the rights and freedoms of others as laid down in this Bill.
    (b) the protection of public safety to the extent that is strictly necessary in exceptional circumstances. Nothing in this clause shall prohibit access to public information which it is in the public interest to acquire.

3. This Article shall not prevent the state from requiring the licensing of broadcasting, television or cinema enterprises.

Sources
Clause 1 is ICCPR, Article 19(2) which is similar to ECHR, Article 10(1), but adds the right to 'seek' information. The limitations attached to this Article are again much narrower than in Article 19(3) of the Covenant or 10(2) of the Convention. The inclusion of 'incitement to racial hatred' is in line with the 1986 Public Order Act and is similar to Article 20(2) of the Covenant. The inclusion of 'protection against imminent physical harm' is similar to, although tighter than, the 'clear and present danger' test used by the American courts to limit the First Amendment's right to freedom of speech.

Clause 2 provides a right to freedom of information as a separate right to freedom of expression subject to specific limitations. It is based on Liberty's policy which is in line with the position taken by the Liberal Democrat and Labour Parties and, of course, the Freedom of Information Campaign.

Clause 3 regarding licensing is the final sentence of ECHR, Article 10(1) and basically allows the current licensing system to operate without falling foul of this Bill.

Article 11 – *The right to organise and demonstrate*

1. Everyone has the right to freedom of peaceful assembly and to freedom of association with others, including the right to form and join trade unions for the protection of their interests. No restrictions shall be placed on the exercise of these rights other than the right to freedom of assembly and only provided that such restrictions are prescribed by law and are strictly necessary and demonstrably justified in a democratic society for the protection of individuals from imminent physical harm.

2. All workers and employees shall enjoy adequate protection against acts of anti-union discrimination in respect of their employment. Such protection shall apply more particularly in respect of acts calculated to:
   (a) make the employment of workers subject to the condition that they shall not join a trade union or shall relinquish trade union membership;
   (b) cause the dismissal of or otherwise prejudice a worker by reason of union membership.

3. All workers and employees have the right to democratically-agreed collective action in cases of conflict of interests, including the right to strike.

Sources
Clause 1 is ECHR, Article 11(1) with the addition of one limitation on the right to assembly, drawn from Articles 9 and 10.

Clause 2 is an abridged version of Article 1 of the International Labour

Organisation (ILO) Convention on the Right to Organise and Collective Bargaining, one of the ILO Charters which the European Court has stated should be referred to in interpreting the meaning and scope of Article 11 of the Convention.

Clause 3 is based on the European Social Charter, the complementary charter to the Convention covering social and economic rights signed by the Council of Europe in 1961. We have excluded the qualification that the right to strike should be subject to obligations arising out of collective agreements previously entered into, but have added a rider to the effect that the legally enforceable right to strike is dependent on the decision to strike being democratically determined.

Article 12 – *The right of all to marry and divorce*

1. Everyone of marriageable age shall have the right to marry the spouse of their choice without discrimination on any grounds. No marriage shall be entered into without the full consent of the intending spouses. Everyone who is married shall also have the right to divorce, subject only to such proceedings as are necessary to guarantee the protection of any children of the marriage, and to ensure an equitable disposition of any property jointly held by the parties to the marriage.
2. Everyone of marriageable age shall have the right to found a family.

Sources

Clause 1 combines parts of the ECHR, Article 12 with ICCPR, Article 23(3). We have altered 'men and women' to 'everyone' and added a clause prohibiting discrimination on any grounds to encompass gay men, lesbian women and transsexuals. We have added the right to divorce (along the lines of CAJ's draft Bill of Rights for Northern Ireland), as the Commission has ruled that this is not covered by the terms of the European Convention (1783/63). The only limitation placed on this Article is the reference from the Convention to 'marriageable age' and current safeguards concerning children's welfare and property rights on divorce in line with Article 5, Protocol 7 of the ECHR (not ratified by the UK).

Clause 2 is also from the ECHR, Article 12. We have extracted the right to found a family as a separate clause to clearly differentiate it from the right to marry.

Article 13 – *The rights of children*

1. Every child shall have the right without discrimination on any ground to such measures of protection on the part of the family, society and the state as are required by children's status as a minor. Children's rights as well as needs must be taken into account and their rights under this Bill shall apply in full subject only to such limits which are prescribed by law, strictly necessary

and demonstrably justified in a democratic society for their right to protection under this Article.

2. The child shall be protected from all forms of neglect, cruelty and exploitation whilst paying due regard to the rights of the child as laid down in this Bill.

3. The law shall recognise equal rights for children born out of wedlock and those born in wedlock.

4. Every child born in the UK is entitled to UK citizenship and nationality.

Sources

Clause 1 is ICCPR, Article 24(1) (the areas in which discrimination is prohibited are covered by Article 14), plus an additional sentence in line with Liberty policy and advice received from the Children's Legal Centre, to indicate that children have rights as well as needs.

Clause 2 is an abridged version of Article 9 of the 1989 United Nations Convention on the Rights of the Child. The UK has not ratified this instrument and has indicated that, when it does so, it will enter reservations on a number of issues. An additional phrase on rights is included for the same purpose in Clause 1.

Clause 3 is from the American Convention on Human Rights, Article 17(5). There is no reference in the Convention or Covenant to equal treatment for children born in and out of wedlock, although the European Commission has interpreted the right to family life under Article 8 in a way which is consistent with this clause.

Clause 4 is equivalent to the 14th Amendment to the US Constitution. It is in line with Article 24(3) of ICCPR and Article 7 of the UN Convention on the Rights of the Child that 'the child shall be entitled from birth to a name and nationality'.

Article 14 – *The right to freedom from discrimination*

1. The equal protection of the law and the enjoyment of rights, whether referred to in this Bill of Rights or not, shall be secured without discrimination on any ground such as gender, race, colour, language, religion, political or other opinion, ethnic, national or social origin, nationality or citizenship, mental or physical disability or illness, sexual orientation, gender identity, age, marital, economic or other status.

2. All persons belonging to ethnic, religious, linguistic or national minorities shall not be denied the right, in community with other members of their group, to use their own language and manifest their own culture or religion subject to the limitations in Article 9(2).

3. This article shall not preclude any law, programme or activity that has as its objective the amelioration of conditions of individuals or groups disadvantaged on any of the grounds listed in this Article.

Neither shall it preclude any differential services or entitlements based on special needs or genuine occupational qualifications.

4. Any conduct which is threatening, abusive and insulting and which is intended or which is likely, having regard to all the circumstances, to stir up racial hatred is in breach of this Bill.

Sources

Clause 1 is drawn from ICCPR, Article 26, with the addition of the following categories: ethnic origin, nationality or citizenship, mental or physical disability or illness, sexual orientation, gender identity, age and marital status. We have substituted 'economic status' for property. These additions reflect commonly recognised grounds for protection against discrimination in modern Britain.

We have not used Article 14 of the ECHR because although this covers similar grounds to the Covenant, it only gives protection against discrimination in relation to the rights and freedoms set out in the Convention itself (which is the equivalent of Article 1 of this Bill). We have added an explicit rider to Clause 1 to the effect that it applies to all rights whether referred to in this Bill or not. Freedom from discrimination is expressed as an absolute right in this Article, as in its equivalents in the Convention and Covenant.

Clause 2 is an edited version of ICCPR, Article 27, with the addition of the word 'national' in recognition of the different nations which make up the UK (see Article 22). The manifestation of religion or culture is subject to the same limitation as in Article 9(2) which touches similar grounds. There is no equivalent in the European Convention, but the 1990 Hong Kong Bill of Rights has included the equivalent Article from the Covenant.

Clause 3 is drawn from two sources. The first sentence is from the Canadian Charter of Rights and Freedoms, Article 15(2), adapted to tie in with this Article. The second sentence is based on the relevant sections of the 1975 Sex Discrimination and 1976 Race Relations Acts. The effect of this Clause is to ensure that positive action strategies are not in breach of this Bill of Rights.

Clause 4 is from the incitement to racial hatred provision of the 1986 Public Order Act. It is similar to ICCPR, Article 20(2) (also adopted by the Hong Kong Bill of Rights), but is more tightly worded.

Article 15 – *The right to a human rights education*

Everyone has the right to an education which prepares them to participate fully in society and the democratic process, to understand and respect human rights, including the rights in this Bill, and to respect diversity and minority rights.

Source

This Article is based on the principle outlined in the Universal Declaration of Human Rights, Article 26(2), updated using modern terminology and to include reference to participation in a democratic society.

Article 16 – *The right to democratic participation*

1. The will of the people shall be the basis of the authority of government. This shall be expressed in the following ways: every adult British citizen and every adult settled or ordinarily resident in the UK shall have the right and opportunity to:
   (a) take part in the conduct of public affairs both directly and through freely chosen representatives;
   (b) vote and stand for election at periodic elections which shall be by universal and equal suffrage and shall be held by secret ballot guaranteeing the free expression of the will of the electorate; have access, on general terms of equality, to public service;
   (c) have access, on general terms of equality, to public service. Nothing in this clause can be construed as limiting any rights to democratic participation to which any group not specifically mentioned in this Article is currently entitled.
2. The right to vote in any election shall not be denied or abridged for any reason.

Sources

Clause 1, sub-clauses (a) to (c) is based on ICCPR, Article 25, clauses (a) to (c). The preamble is based on the Universal Declaration of Human Rights, Article 21(3). The First Protocol of the ECHR, Article 3 (signed and ratified by the UK) only covers the issue of free elections whilst this Article and the Covenant include the right to stand for election and be involved generally in public service. The groups affected relate to categories under immigration law and are defined in Article 23. The rider at the end of this clause is aimed at protecting Commonwealth citizens who are entitled to vote if they are present in the UK even if they are not resident or settled here.

Clause 2 is based on the 24th Amendment to the US Constitution except that the latter prohibits curtailment of the right to vote on the grounds of non-payment of taxes only, whereas this version is broader in scope.

Article 17 – *The right to freedom of movement*

1. Everyone within the UK shall have the right to liberty of movement and freedom to choose their residence within that territory.
2. Everyone shall be free to leave the UK and no one who is settled in the UK shall thereby forfeit the right to return, regardless of length of absence.
3. Every British national shall be entitled to enter the territory of the UK and to a valid passport.
4. No restrictions shall be placed on the exercise of the rights in this Article other than the limitations to liberty and those concerning security of person in Article 5(1). The rights set out in Article 17(1) may also be subject to such limits as are prescribed by law, strictly necessary and demonstrably justified in a democratic soci-

ety for the protection of individuals from imminent physical harm.

Sources

Clauses 1 and 2 are based on the ECHR, Protocol 4, Article 2(1) and (2) (not ratified by the UK) which is the same as ICCPR Article 12(1) and (2). We have omitted the qualifications on the right to freedom of movement contained in the Convention and Covenant, but have set down what we consider to be the appropriate civil libertarian limitations on this right in Clause 4. An additional phrase at the end of Clause 2, which secures the right of return for people settled in the UK (see Article 23 for the definition of 'settled'), was proposed by JCWI whom we consulted on this issue.

Clause 3 is drawn from ECHR Protocol 4, Article 3(2) (which is similar to ICCPR Article 12(4). The reference to a valid passport is from *We, The People*, the model constitution prepared by the Liberal Democratic Party in 1990. To our knowledge there is no equivalent right to a passport in any international or regional human rights instrument.

Clause 4 is the same model limitation clause as used to limit the right to freedom of assembly under Article 11 (with the additional reference to the limitations on freedom of movement anyway contained in Article 5).

Article 18 – *The right to natural justice concerning deportation laws and procedures*

1. No British national or any individual settled in the UK shall be deported from the UK.
2. No one in the UK may be deported or removed until a decision is reached in accordance with the law and the principles of due process set out in Articles 5 and 6. Anyone subject to a deportation order or threatened with removal as an illegal entrant must, before the deportation or removal, be allowed to appeal. They must be allowed to submit reasons against their deportation or removal and to have their case reviewed by, and be represented for the purpose before, an independent and impartial court or tribunal established by law.
3. It shall be the general rule that persons subject to a deportation order or threatened with removal shall not be detained in custody but may be subject to guarantees to appear before a court or tribunal.
4. Collective expulsion of aliens is prohibited.

Sources

Clause 1 is based on ECHR Protocol 4, Article 3(1) (not ratified by the UK), which confines the right not to be 'expelled' to nationals. Clause 1 is broadened to include people who have settled status (see Article 23 for the definition of 'settled')

Clause 2 is based on the principles contained in ECHR, Protocol 7, Article 1 (not signed or ratified by the UK), although our formulation excludes national security or public order as reasons for denying the right to fair deportation procedures. (A similar Article in the Covenant (13) allows deportations to take place without an appeal 'where compelling reasons of national security otherwise require'.)

Clause 2 is worded to comply with the standards of natural justice guaranteed in Articles 5 and 6 and to clarify that appeals must take place prior to deportations or removals. The addition of the word 'removal' indicates that illegal entrants – people who allegedly enter the country illegally – are included in this Article as well as people subject to deportation orders such as 'overstayers' or foreign nationals convicted of a crime or considered 'not conducive to the public good'.

Clause 3 is based on Article 5(3) granting anyone threatened with deportation or removal the same entitlement to bail as if they had been charged with a criminal offence.

Clause 4 is ECHR Protocol 14, Article 4 (not ratified by the UK). It completely prohibits the repatriation of any group, a policy which some far right organisations in this country still support.

Article 19 – *The right to asylum*

1. Every person has the right to seek and be granted asylum in the UK in accordance with the law of the UK and international conventions if they are being pursued for political offences or have a well-founded fear of persecution for reasons of gender, race, colour, language, religion, political or other opinion, ethnic, national or social origin, nationality or citizenship, mental or physical disability or illness, sexual orientation or gender identity.
2. No penalties shall be imposed on any individual or body on account of the illegal entry or presence of refugees or asylum seekers who, coming from a territory where their life or freedom was threatened under the terms of Clause 1, seek to enter or are present in the territory without authorisation provided they present themselves without undue delay to the authorities and show good cause for their illegal entry or presence.
3. No refugee or asylum seeker shall be deported or removed to the frontiers of any territories where their life or freedom would be threatened on account of any of the grounds in Clause 1. No deportations or removals shall take place other than according to the procedures set out in Article 18 (2) which in all cases includes a right to appeal.

Sources

Clause 1 combines the terms of the American Convention on Human Rights, Article 22(7) with Article 1(2) from the 1951 Convention Relating to the Status of Refugees, commonly known as the Geneva Convention (updated by the 1967 Protocol to the Geneva Convention which extended its applicability to events anywhere in the world post 1951). The UK has ratified both the Geneva Convention and the Protocol (there is no right to seek or obtain asylum in either the European Convention or the Covenant). We have updated the grounds for obtaining refugee status in line with most of the antidiscrimination grounds of Article 14 to reflect modern concerns.

Clause 2 is an amended version of the Geneva Convention, Article 31(1). We have omitted reference to refugees coming 'directly' from the country of persecution to accommodate situations where their means of transport brings them to the UK via other countries. We have also added 'undue' before 'delay' to inhibit the imposition of arbitrary time limits.

Clause 3 is one of the most fundamental provisions of the Geneva Convention, Article 33(1), amended to reflect the areas covered by Clause 1. As in Clause 2, we have added 'asylum seekers' to ensure that the terms of this clause also apply to those who are seeking refugee status or have been given 'exceptional leave to remain' without full refugee status. We have also added a sentence to apply the same appeal procedures to asylum seekers as to others threatened with deportation or removal (see Article 18), all of whom would be entitled to hearings which conform to the principles of natural justice under Articles 5 and 6.

Article 20 – *The right not to be extradited without adequate safeguards*

1. No one shall be extradited from the UK to face criminal charges elsewhere unless the country requesting extradition has proved to a court that there is an arguable case that a serious criminal offence was committed by that person. Such persons shall be protected by the rights of due process provided for by Articles 5 and 6.
2. No one shall be extradited from the UK unless the offence alleged would be an offence under UK law.
3. No one shall be extradited from the UK if it appears to the court that:
   (a) the alleged offence is an offence under military law which is not also an offence under the general criminal law;
   (b) the request for the individual's return is in fact made for the purpose of prosecuting or punishing that person on account of gender, race, colour, language, religion, political or other opinion, ethnic, national or social origin, nationality or citizenship, mental or physical disability or illness, sexual orientation or sexual identity;
   (c) the individual might, if returned, be prejudiced during the course of the trial or punished, detained or face restrictions in personal liberty for any of the reasons in Article 20(3)(b).

Sources
Clause 1 is based on Liberty's policy. There is a European Convention on Extradition (1957) and a European Convention on Mutual Assistance in Criminal Matters, both of which the UK has recently ratified (1991). In fact the policies in Clauses 1 and 2 go beyond the provisions in either of these Conventions to broadly reflect the position in the UK prior to 1988.

Clauses 2 and 3 are broadly based on the Criminal Justice Act 1988.

Part II
Applicability and Definitions

Article 21

The rights in this Bill apply only to natural persons from the moment of their birth and the terms 'individual', 'everyone', or 'no one' shall be construed as having this meaning alone.

Article 22

Unless otherwise specified, every individual within the jurisdiction of the United Kingdom shall enjoy the fundamental rights and freedoms secured in this Bill against:

(a) any act or omission by the legislative, executive, judiciary or crown;

(b) any act or omission by any individual or body in the performance of any public function.

Article 23

In addition to the provisions in Articles 21 and 22, the following provisions shall have effect for the interpretation of this Bill.

The term 'slavery' under Article 4 refers to the condition of being wholly in the legal possession of another person, whilst the term 'servitude' covers debt-serfdom, being sold into marriage and sham adoptions. Whilst both these terms refer to the status of an individual, forced or compulsory labour characterise the type of work which is performed.

The term 'security of person' in Article 5 means protection against arbitrary arrest and detention.

The term 'civil rights and obligations' in Article 6 covers any question which a court or tribunal is empowered to determine, including any matter involving a dispute with government departments, local authorities and any other public body.

The term 'criminal charge' in Article 6 includes contempt of court and any matter which falls within the jurisdiction of a disciplinary body as a result of which a person found guilty may be deprived of liberty, or lose remission on a prison sentence.

The term 'public interest' in Articles 6 and 10 refers to official information which reveals the existence of crime, corruption, danger to the public, serious misconduct, abuse of authority or neglect in the performance of official duty.

The term 'public safety' in Articles 6, 8, and 10 means the ability of people to engage in ordinary social activity without danger of physical harm.

The term 'authority' in Article 8 refers to any constituted or unconstituted private or public body, organisation or company.

The term 'crime against humanity' in Article 7 derives from the 1945 Nuremburg trials at the end of the Second World War and the term 'genocide' is defined in the 1948 Convention on the Prevention and Punishment of the Crime of Genocide which has been ratified by the UK.

The term 'adult' in Articles 8 and 16 refers to any natural person of 18 years or more.

The 'right to assembly' in Article 11 refers to the right to demonstrate, march and hold public and private meetings, and the 'right of association' refers to the right to join any organisation without interference from the state.

The term 'marriageable age' in Article 12 refers to any natural person of 16 years or more.

The term 'child' in Article 13 refers to every natural person from the moment of their birth to the age of 18.

The term 'settled' in Articles 16, 17 and 18 refers to being resident in the UK without any restrictions on the period of stay (although still subject to immigration control).

The term 'ordinarily resident' in Article 16 refers to being in a particular country, voluntarily and for settled purposes, as part of the regular order of life for the time being, whether of short- or long-term duration.

The term 'serious criminal offence' in Article 20 refers to any offence for which the penalty involved is 12 months imprisonment or more.

CHAPTER TWO – PART THREE
REMEDIES AND ENFORCEMENT

Article 24

1. Everyone whose rights and freedoms as set forth in this Bill are being, have been or are about to be directly violated shall have an effective remedy before an independent and impartial tribunal or court. They shall be entitled to a declaration of their rights and to the appropriate remedy as follows:
   (a) in all cases reasonable financial compensation for breaches of the Bill;
   (b) an injunction restraining breaches of the rights and freedoms contained in this Bill;
   (c) an order to enforce the rights provided in this Bill;
   (d) an order quashing the decision of a public body, court or tribunal which has breached the provisions of this Bill.

2. Anyone who has been convicted of a crime where it has subsequently been shown there has been a miscarriage of justice shall have an enforceable right to financial compensation.
3. All such remedies will be available against the state, the Crown and any individual or body in the performance of any public function. Any group of persons whose individual rights under this Bill have been, are being, or are about to be directly violated shall be entitled to take action as a group or in cases where the court declares it to be in the interests of justice, be represented by a non-governmental or quasi-governmental non-profit-making organisation.

Article 25

If the validity of any Act of Parliament in relation to this Bill of Rights is challenged in the course of proceedings in a minor court or tribunal and there is an arguable case for proceeding on that issue, the court or tribunal shall refer the question to the High Court.

Article 26

1. Any acts, decisions or omissions by any of the individuals or bodies listed in Article 22, including the Crown, whether or not their powers are conferred by Act of Parliament, subordinate legislation passed or common law judgment made before or after this Bill of Rights has come into force, shall be subject to this Bill of Rights.
2. This Article shall not affect the legality of any acts, decisions or omissions prior to the coming into force of this Bill of Rights.

Article 27

Any Act of Parliament passed before this Bill of Rights has come into force and any subordinate legislation passed or common law judgment made before or after this Bill of Rights has come into force shall be so construed and applied as not to abrogate, abridge or infringe, whether directly or indirectly, any of the rights and freedoms in this Bill of Rights; and insofar as any such law or provision thereof is incapable of such construction or application, it shall cease to have effect.

Article 28

Any Act of Parliament passed after this Bill of Rights has come into force shall be so construed and applied as not to abrogate, abridge or infringe, whether directly or indirectly, any of the rights or freedoms in this Bill of Rights and any such Act shall be so construed and applied as not to repeal or amend any provision of this Bill of Rights. Insofar as any Act passed after this Bill of Rights has come into force is incapable of such a construction or application it shall not have effect except under the following circumstances:

(a) Where such an Act or provision thereof, or re-enactment of previous legislation, expressly declares within the legislation itself that it shall take effect in breach of the Bill of Rights.

(b) Where the Human Rights Scrutiny Committee, acting in accordance with its powers under Article 31, makes a declaration of rights on a two-thirds majority that an Act of Parliament or provision thereof is in accordance with the meaning, intention and spirit of this Bill of Rights and this has been confirmed by a resolution of a simple majority of both Houses of Parliament and this is expressly declared within the legislation itself. In such circumstances no court shall decline to apply an Act or provision thereof by reason only that it judges it to be inconsistent with any provision of this Bill of Rights. Nothing in this clause shall prejudice the right of the courts to express a view as to whether the said legislation or provision thereof is in breach of this Bill.

Article 29

An Act or a provision of an Act in respect of which an express declaration has been made under Article 28 shall operate as it would have but for this Bill of Rights except that in the case of declarations made under Article 28(a) the Act or provision shall cease to have effect five years after it comes into force (or any such earlier date as may be specified in the declaration) after which time the Act or provision will be deemed to have been repealed. The period in which any Act, or provision thereof, passed in accordance with the powers under Article 28(a) comes into force can be delayed by a simple majority of the second chamber of the legislature for up to five years.

Article 30

The powers of declaration under Article 28(a) and (b) do not apply to the following Articles: 1, 2, 3, 4(1), 7, 9(1), 14(1), 16 and any Act of Parliament, subordinate legislation or common law judgment or provision thereof passed before or after this Bill of Rights comes into force which is judged by the High Court to be incapable of a construction or application which upholds the rights in these Articles shall cease to have effect.

Article 31

A Human Rights Scrutiny Committee shall be elected by Members of the House of Commons as a Committee of the House of Commons on which no one political party shall predominate and no member of the executive shall sit. It shall have 15 members and a Chair. The Chair of the Committee shall be elected by the Committee members and shall have no voting rights. The Committee shall have the following functions:

(a) to scrutinise Acts of Parliament and provisions thereof for compliance with this Bill of Rights when requested to do so by a minister or after a resolution of one third of either House of

Parliament or by the Human Rights Commission in such circumstances where a ruling of the Supreme Court has declared an Act of Parliament or provision thereof, passed subsequent to this Bill of Rights coming into force, to be in breach or otherwise of this Bill.

(i) Should the Human Rights Scrutiny Committee, on giving due consideration to the advice of the Human Rights Commission, make a declaration of rights by a two-thirds majority to the effect that the said Act or provision thereof is in accordance with the meaning, intention and spirit of this Bill of Rights and this is confirmed by a resolution of a simple majority of both Houses of Parliament at the final reading of the Bill in question and is expressly declared within the legislation itself, no court shall decline to apply the Act or provision thereof by reason only that it judges it to be in breach of this Bill of Rights other than in relation to the Articles listed under Article 30.

(ii) Should the Human Rights Scrutiny Committee, on giving due consideration to the advice of the Human Rights Commission, declare by a two-thirds majority that the said legislation or provision thereof is in breach of the meaning, intention or spirit of this Bill of Rights an express declaration within the legislation itself under the powers conferred by Article 28(a) will be required to enable the legislation to proceed.

(iii) Should less than two-thirds of the Committee agree on a resolution in either of the circumstances in Article 31(a) subsections (i) and (ii), the legislation in question will proceed in the normal way and be subject to the ruling of the Courts under Article 28.

(b) to scrutinise any proposed amendments to the Bill of Rights and to express a view on whether such an amendment should be supported or otherwise, having given due consideration to the advice of the Human Rights Commission in this regard.

(c) to appoint the Commissioners and Chair of the Human Rights Commission;

(d) to receive the annual report of the Human Rights Commission, lay a copy of the report before both Houses of Parliament and cause the report to be published;

(e) to receive and advise Parliament on any other reports of the Human Rights Commission under Article 32(b) to (e).

Article 32

There shall be a body of Commissioners named the Human Rights Commission with the following functions:

(a) at its own discretion to request the Human Rights Scrutiny Committee to review Acts of Parliament or provisions thereof overturned by the courts and to express a view, which shall be announced in public, on all legislation or provisions thereof to be reviewed by the Human Rights Scrutiny Committee prior to the Committee exercising its powers of review under Article 31(a)(i) or (ii);

(b) at its own initiative or at the request of the executive, legislature, Supreme Court or Human Rights Scrutiny Committee to advise whether any current legislation or provisions thereof is consistent with or contrary to the Bill of Rights;

(c) at its own initiative or at the request of the executive, legislature or Human Rights Scrutiny Committee to advise whether any proposed legislation or provisions thereof is consistent with or contrary to the Bill of Rights, including any proposed amendments to the Bill of Rights itself;

(d) at its own initiative or at the request of the executive, legislature or Human Rights Scrutiny Committee to advise on any new legislation required to comply with this Bill of Rights and relevant regional or international human rights instruments ratified by the UK;

(e) to keep under review the Bill of Rights 1992 and advise the executive, legislature or Human Rights Scrutiny Committee where revisions are required to enhance human rights.

(f) to provide the Human Rights Scrutiny Committee with an annual report which shall include a general survey of human rights developments in the relevant period in so far as these relate to the rights and freedoms in this Bill of Rights.

(g) to directly assist individuals who are actual or prospective complainants under the Bill of Rights who apply to the Commission for assistance provided that the Commission considers one or more of the following apply:

    (i) the case raises a question of general principle;

    (ii) it is unreasonable, having regard to the complexity or cost of the case, to expect the applicant to deal with it unaided;

    (iii) the case has implications for a group or category of individuals.

(h) There shall be no less than 15 and no more than 25 commissioners appointed on a part or full time basis for a five-year term by an ad hoc Appointments Committee of three members of the Human Rights Scrutiny Committee. One of their number shall be appointed Chair by the Appointments Committee. The commissioners shall be drawn in equal proportion from the following three categories:

    (i) the legal profession, including legal academics, practising lawyers and judges;

    (ii) human rights non-government organisations;

    (iii) lay members of the community, reflecting in so far as is possible the categories laid down in Article 14, who have knowledge or experience of abuses of the rights and freedoms in this Bill of Rights. The Commissioners may appoint such officers as they think fit in furtherance of the aims of the Commission subject to the approval of the Civil Service as to numbers and remuneration.

Article 33

1. An amendment to this Bill of Rights shall only be made through an Act of Parliament following a resolution of a two-thirds majority of both Houses of Parliament on the final reading of the Bill in question having given due consideration to the advice of the Human Rights Scrutiny Committee. The coming into force of any such amendment may be delayed by a simple majority of the second chamber of the legislature for five years.
2. Repeal of this Bill of Rights can be made only by a resolution of a two-thirds majority of both Houses of Parliament on the final reading of the Bill in question having given due consideration to the advice of the Human Rights Scrutiny Committee, and the coming into force of such an Act will be delayed for five years.

Article 34

The fundamental rights and freedoms in this Bill of Rights are in addition to, and not in derogation from, any other fundamental rights and freedoms given to the individual by any statutory body or international or regional instrument ratified by the UK.

Article 35

1. Any court or tribunal which is called on to interpret or apply the Bill of Rights, and any body, including the Human Rights Scrutiny Committee and Commission, which is called on to assess the effect of the Bill on any other enactment shall pay due regard to the following:
   (a) the European Convention on Human Rights and Fundamental Freedoms, the International Covenant on Civil and Political Rights and any other international or regional treaty ratified by the UK concerning the rights and freedoms in this Bill;
   (b) reports and expressions of views on human rights by the European Commission of Human Rights, the Council of Europe and the United Nations Human Rights Committee;
   (c) judgments and advisory opinions of the European Court of Human Rights.

2. This Article shall not be construed as limiting or derogating from any rights or freedoms in this Bill which are not contained or not contained to the same degree in any of the aforementioned Instruments.

> *Liberty, A People's Charter* (Liberty's Bill of Rights: A Consultation Document), by Francesca Klug, 1991.

Other proposals by legal and political writers

51   DRAFT BILL OF RIGHTS 1969 (JOHN MACDONALD)

RB NOTE: The text of this proposal was first published as an appendix to the pamphlet Bill of Rights (1969) by John Macdonald (now QC). It subsequently formed the basis of the Bill of Rights (No. 2) Bill 1969 presented to the House of Commons by Emlyn Hooson.

A BILL TO

Declare the inalienable rights and liberties of the subject.

Be it enacted by the Queen's most Excellent Majesty, by and with the advice and consent of the Lords Spiritual and Temporal, and Commons, in this present Parliament assembled, and by the authority of the same, as follows:—

1. The laws of England, Wales, Northern Ireland and Scotland do and shall comprise and confer and secure on and to all the peoples of the United Kingdom within the respective jurisdictions of those laws, all those rights, liberties and privileges hereinafter set forth, and do and shall require of all persons within the said jurisdictions, in whatsoever capacities and offices they may act, to do and observe such things as may be necessary to give effect to the same.

2.—(1) Every person is entitled to the equal protection of the law.

(2) Obligations shall not be imposed and rights shall not be withheld or denied on the basis of race, religion, sex, national or social origin or condition, or adherence or non-adherence to any set of beliefs or principles.

(3) No person shall be denied access to any public place without reasonable cause.

3. No wilful injury shall be caused to any person and nothing harmful shall be practised upon him without his consent or, if he be for any reason unable to give that consent, without the consent of someone having the responsibility and care of him.

4.—(1) Every person is entitled to express his opinion on any thing or matter and no person shall incur any penalty or punishment on account of his opinions or his expression of them, subject only to the right of any person aggrieved thereby to seek relief at law for injury to reputation.

(2) No person shall be refused access to any of the public media or denied means of communication with the public solely on account of his opinions.

(3) No person who prints, publishes or otherwise disseminates the opinions of another or others shall incur any penalty or punishment for so doing, subject only to the right of any person aggrieved thereby to seek redress at law for injury to reputation.

5. Every person has the right freely to choose, profess and practise any religion, but not so as to cause harm to or endanger the well-being of any other person.

6. Every person has the right to associate with another or others for any lawful purpose and the right peacefully to assemble with others to petition the government for a redress of grievances or to propose or oppose any cause or matter or other thing but if in a public place, subject to the laws and rules from time to time in force concerning the conduct of public assemblies and the preservation of the peace.

7.—(1) No person shall be confined arbitrarily or without trial except that he be charged with an offence and be brought to trial as speedily as possible thereafter.

(2) No person shall deny liberty to another save by due process of law: Provided that nothing in this section shall prevent—
  (*a*) the lawful detention of persons of unsound mind;
  (*b*) the lawful detention of persons for the prevention of the spread of infectious diseases;
  (*c*) the lawful detention of minors by their parents or guardians or in furtherance of their education.

8. Subject to the law relating to prohibited degrees and bigamy no law shall prevent people of full age marrying and founding a family.

9. The education of children being a matter of concern to the community, the law shall provide minimum standards of education to which every child shall be entitled; subject thereto, no law shall restrict the right of a parent to provide education for his child in such a manner as the parent shall think fit.

10. Every person is entitled to protection from arbitrary interference in his personal, family or other private affairs.

11.—(1) No person shall be required to supply to any person information about his personal, family, financial or other private affairs, unless he be told the purpose for which such information is required and a written copy of the information as so supplied be given to him.

(2) Information acquired from or about a person shall not be used for any other purpose than that for which such information was supplied, unless the consent of the person or persons from whom and about whom it is given is first obtained.

12. No person shall be required as a condition of employment or continued employment, or otherwise, to work excessive hours or to do without reasonable rest and leisure time.

13.—(1) No citizen of the United Kingdom and Colonies shall be deprived of his citizenship except in accordance with a treaty which effectively confers the citizenship of some other state upon such citizen.

(2) Every citizen of the United Kingdom and Colonies shall be entitled to a valid passport.

(3) Entry to the United Kingdom shall not be denied without reasonable cause to any person.

(4) Entry to and residence in the United Kingdom and Colonies shall not be denied to any citizen of the United Kingdom and Colonies or to any dependant of any such citizen.

(5) No person who is lawfully at liberty shall be prevented from leaving the United Kingdom.

(6) Every person resident in the United Kingdom may travel in and reside in any part of the United Kingdom, save for any restrictions which may be prescribed by law for reasons of national security or public health.

14. Every person of full age and capacity shall be entitled to register as an elector in the district in which he normally resides. No elector shall be denied the right to vote by secret ballot in the district in which he is registered in any parliamentary or municipal election, provided that no person shall vote more than once in any election.

15. Every contract of employment shall entitle the employee to a just reward for his labour.

16.—(1) No law shall prevent any person of full age from working or restrict his right freely to choose his profession and place of work.

(2) No person shall be compelled to work or to do any particular work except—

(*a*) service reasonably required in the national interest, provided that no person shall be compelled to perform military service if such service is against his conscience;

(*b*) in case of an emergency or calamity threatening the life and well being of the community;

(*c*) in connection with a sentence of imprisonment or other sentence passed by a court of law upon a person convicted of a criminal offence.

17.—(1) No person shall be refused membership of a trades union without reasonable cause.

(2) No person shall as a condition of employment or continued employment or otherwise be compelled to join or shall be prevented from joining a trades union.

18.—(1) Every person is entitled to own property, and is entitled to protection from arbitrary interference with his property.

(2) No person shall be deprived of his property except by due process of law and in the case of compulsory acquisition against full, fair and prompt compensation.

19.—(1) There shall be no excessive or cruel or unusual punishments.

(2) The opinions and beliefs of an accused person not connected with the offence with which he is charged shall not be regarded in determining the sentence to be passed on him unless pleaded in mitigation.

20.—(1) A person charged with a criminal offence shall be presumed innocent of the charge until proved guilty according to law.

(2) No person shall be compelled to give or provide evidence in any proceedings in which he himself stands accused of any matter; nor, save as the law otherwise expressly provides, shall a wife be compelled to give or provide evidence in any proceedings in which her husband is accused, nor a husband in any proceedings in which his wife is accused.

(3) No person who has been tried and acquitted or convicted of any offence may again be tried for that offence.

(4) Every person detained for any reason whatsoever shall be entitled to legal advice and assistance of his own choosing and shall be entitled to the immediate access of his legal adviser under conditions of privacy.

21. No law shall impose retrospective liabilities or obligations upon any person.

22. A person who is a party to any proceedings of whatever nature wherein some matter is in dispute between that person, whether alone or with others, and any other person or persons is entitled to be given by the court or tribunal or other agency determining the matter without undue delay its decision and its reasons for arriving at such decision, and such reasons shall form part of the record.

23. The jurisdiction of the courts to inquire into any question of law is fundamental to the rights of every person and shall not be restricted or abridged.

24.—(1) It is hereby declared that the Crown is subject to the provisions of this Act in every respect as though it were a private citizen, and in any action brought against the Crown under the Act an injunction may be awarded against the Crown.

(2) Wherever anything is done or is sought to be done by the Crown on the grounds that it is in the national interest that such thing should be done which but for such allegation it would not be lawful for the Crown to do the courts shall have jurisdiction to inquire into the matter and if of the opinion that such thing cannot be said to be in the national interest may declare accordingly and the Crown shall be bound thereby.

25.—(1) No enactment or law or executive order or regulation or bye-law or rule of administration or any other rule or order made by any authority or by any person whatsoever shall in any wise abrogate or abridge, or shall operate or take effect so as to abrogate or abridge, the rights, liberties and privileges conferred by this Act or any of them; and in so far as any such enactment, law, order, regulation, bye-law or rule as aforesaid shall purport or operate or take effect so as to abrogate or abridge the same it shall be void and shall not be enforced to that end.

(2) The presumption that an Act of Parliament, the provisions of which are inconsistent with an earlier Act, intends to repeal that earlier Act to the extent of the inconsistency shall not apply to any Act passed after the commencement of this Act in so far as its provisions are inconsistent with this Act, but this Act may only be repealed or amended or otherwise affected by express provision to that effect contained in a subsequent Act.

26. The high court, and in appropriate cases the county court, shall have jurisdiction to grant such relief as may be required to give effect to the provisions of this Act.

27. This Act may be cited as the Bill of Rights 1969.

HC [1968–9] 205.

---

52   DRAFT BILL OF RIGHTS 1977 (WALLINGTON AND McBRIDE)

An Act to declare and protect certain fundamental rights and freedoms; to establish a Constitutional Court to determine questions connected with this

Act, and to provide for the reference of such questions to the Court; to ensure that existing law is in conformity with the fundamental rights and freedoms mentioned in this Act, and that future Acts of Parliament do not inadvertently abrogate, abridge or infringe any of the said rights or freedoms; and for purposes connected with these purposes.

Be it enacted by the Queen's most Excellent Majesty, by and with the consent of the Lords Spiritual and Temporal, and Commons, in this present Parliament assembled, and by the authority of the same, as follows:—

Part I: General

Title

1   This Act may be cited as the United Kingdom Bill of Rights, 1977.

Extent

2(1) Except where otherwise stated, this Act applies throughout the United Kingdom.

(2) Her Majesty may by Order in Council apply this Act to the Isle of Man or to any of the Channel Islands, and an Order under this subsection may contain such amendments or additional provisions as may appear necessary to Her Majesty to give effect to the intent of the Act.

Commencement

3   This Act comes into force on 1st January 1978.

Application to crown

4   This Act binds the Crown.

Part II: Incorporation of Bill of Rights

Enactment of European Convention

5(1) The provisions of Schedule 1 to this Act, being provisions of the European Convention for the Protection of Human Rights and Fundamental Freedoms, and of the First and Fourth Protocols to the Convention, are hereby enacted and incorporated as part of the law of the United Kingdom, and shall, as applied by Sections 18, 19, 20 and 21, be given effect to and enforced accordingly.

(2) The provisions of Schedule 1 and of Sections 18, 19, 20 and 21 are

referred to in the following provisions of this Act as the Bill of Rights.

Remedies for breach of Bill of Rights

6(1) The infringement of any provision of the Bill of Rights does not constitute a criminal offence simply because of this Act.

(2) Any person who proves to the Court that an act or omission has unlawfully infringed or is unlawfully infringing any of his rights or freedoms under the Bill of Rights, or that a threatened act or omission would if perpetrated constitute such an infringement, shall be entitled to whichever of the following remedies is appropriate to the case:

(a) in any case to a declaration of his rights under the Bill of Rights;

(b) in the case of an intentional act or omission, to reasonable compensation from the perpetrator or other person responsible (including in an appropriate case compensation for injury to his feelings);

(c) in an appropriate case, to an order restraining the perpetrator or other person responsible from continuing to infringe, or committing further infringements of, his rights or freedom, or in the case of a threatened act or omission, from perpetrating any such act or omission.

(3) Subsection (2) does not apply in the case of any act or omission of a court or authorised by a court, but without prejudice to the remedies mentioned in Section 16.

(4) Proceedings under this section shall be brought within three years of the date when the act or omission first came to the notice of the party initiating the proceedings, or within such shorter period as may be prescribed by rules of court in cases where the remedy sought is not limited to compensation.

(5) Nothing in this Section shall prejudice any remedy or relief which might be granted by a court in any case apart from the provisions of this Section: provided that no person shall by virtue of this Section be compensated twice for the same loss.

(6) In this Section 'the Court' means the Constitutional Court established by Section 10, or the High Court, or in Scotland the Court of Session.

Effect on existing law

7   All existing laws shall be so construed and applied as not to abrogate, abridge or infringe, or to require, authorise or permit the abrogation, abridgement or infringement of, any of the rights and freedoms mentioned in the Bill of Rights; and insofar as any such law is incapable of such construction or application, it shall cease to have effect.

Effect on statutory powers

8   Any authority, power or duty conferred or imposed on any person or body by or under any enactment shall have effect subject to this Act, and accordingly shall not authorise the abrogation, abridgement or infringement of any of the rights or freedoms mentioned in the Bill of Rights.

Effect on future law

9(1) Any Act passed after this Act shall be so construed and applied as not to abrogate, abridge or infringe, or to require, authorise or permit any abrogation, abridgement or infringement of, any of the rights or freedoms mentioned in the Bill of Rights; and any such Act shall be so construed and applied as not to repeal or amend, or permit the repeal or amendment of, any provision of this Act other than those set out in subsection (4).

(2) Insofar as any Act passed after this Act, or any part of such an Act, is incapable of such construction or application as may be required by subsection (1), it shall not have effect.

(3) Subsections (1) and (2) shall not apply to any Act or part of an Act as to which it is expressly declared in an Act of Parliament that it shall have effect notwithstanding this Act.

(4) The provisions of this Act referred to in subsection (1) are as follows: Sections 6(4) and (6), 10(2) (3) and (4), 12, 13, 14, 15, 16 and 17, and Schedule 2.

PART III: THE CONSTITUTIONAL COURT

Establishment of Constitutional Court

10(1) There shall be a Court, to be known as the Constitutional Court.

(2) The Constitutional Court shall be a superior court of record with jurisdiction throughout the United Kingdom.

(3) The decisions of the Constitutional Court shall have the same status in law as decisions of the House of Lords in its judicial capacity.

(4) Schedule 2 shall have effect to make provision for the composition and functioning of the Court and ancillary matters concerning its financing, staffing and jurisdiction.

Judges of Constitutional Court

11(1) The Constitutional Court shall consist of nine judges.

(2) Her Majesty may appoint judges to the Constitutional Court by Order in Council on the joint recommendation of the Prime Minister and the Lord Chancellor.

(3) No such appointment shall take effect unless it is approved by the House of Commons by a two thirds majority of those present and voting.

(4) Six of the judges shall be selected from persons qualified to hold high judicial office, and three, to be known as 'lay judges' shall be chosen from persons, not necessarily legally qualified, who have knowledge and experience in the field of human rights.

(5) Judges shall be appointed until the retiring age which is prescribed at the time of their appointment, and shall not be removed from office during their period of office except

    (a)   by unanimous resolution of the other judges for incapacity or neglect of duty, or

    (b)   by resolution of both Houses of Parliament on grounds of misconduct.

(6) The emoluments of the judges shall not be reduced during their tenure of office.

References to Constitutional Court

12(1) If in any proceedings before any court or tribunal constituted by statute, a question arises concerning the interpretation, application or effect of this Act, the court or tribunal may on the application of any party to the proceedings or on its own initiative with the consent of the parties, state a case for reference to the Constitutional Court on the question or questions concerned.

(2) The Constitutional Court shall not be required to determine, nor shall it be empowered to question, any matter of fact in a case referred to it under subsection (1).

(3) For the purposes of subsection (2) any question as to the meaning or effect of any provision of this Act in the context of any facts shall be treated as a matter of law.

(4) The Crown shall be entitled to be joined as a party to any proceedings referred to the Constitutional Court.

(5) The determination of the Constitutional Court on any question referred to it shall be final.

Appeals to Constitutional Court

13(1) Any party to a case, and the Crown, may appeal to the Constitutional Court against the decision of any court listed in subsection (3), on any question concerning the interpretation, application or effect of this Act.

(2) Appeal shall be with the leave of the court appealed from or with the leave of the Constitutional Court.

(3) The courts referred to in subsection (1) are as follows:

    (a)   for England and Wales, the Court of Appeal, or a Divisional Court of the High Court sitting in an appellate capacity;

    (b)   for Scotland, the Inner House of the Court of Session, or the High Court of Justiciary sitting in an appellate capacity;

(c)   for Northern Ireland, the Court of Appeal, or a Divisional Court of the High Court sitting in an appellate capacity;

(d)   for Great Britain, the Employment Appeal Tribunal; and

(e)   for the United Kingdom, the Courts-Martial Appeal Court.

Original jurisdiction of the Constitutional Court

14(1) Any person may apply to the Constitutional Court for leave to bring proceedings for a determination of the validity of any enactment.

(2) The Constitutional Court shall give leave to bring proceedings where it appears to the Court that there are sufficient grounds for bringing the proceedings and for believing that the enactment in question may be wholly or partially invalid or may have ceased to have effect by virtue of Section 7, 8 or 9, and where the applicant appears to the Court to have a sufficient interest in the proceedings.

(3) The Crown shall be joined as a party to any action for which leave has been granted under this Section.

(4) If on hearing the case on its merits the Constitutional Court is satisfied that the enactment, or part thereof, is wholly or partially invalid or has ceased to have effect by virtue of Sections 7, 8 or 9, the Court shall make a declaration to that effect.

(5) This Section does not prejudice the right of any defendant in criminal proceedings to contend that an enactment under which he is charged with an offence is wholly or partly invalid in consequence of this Act; or of any party to any proceedings before a court or tribunal established by statute to contend that any enactment which directly affects the outcome of the proceedings is wholly or partly invalid in consequence of this Act; or of the court or tribunal before which the matter is raised (if it is not referred to the Constitutional Court under Section 12) to determine that matter.

Prospective overruling

15 It is hereby declared that the Constitutional Court may determine that a statute or other enactment is wholly or partly invalid, or is to be construed or applied in a particular way, or that a previous decision of itself or another Court is to be overruled, with effect from the date on which the determination is announced (but without prejudice to the outcome of the case in which the determination is made).

PART IV: INCIDENTAL PROVISIONS

Ancillary relief

16(1) Where a court determines that a statute or other enactment is wholly or partly invalid, or is to be construed or applied in a particular way, and as a result determines that a party to the proceedings is not guilty of an offence of which he was charged, the court shall award compensation to that party for any period during which he was detained in custody because of the charge, and any other loss he has suffered as a result of the proceedings, including any injury to his feelings.

(2) Where a court determines that a trial of any person on a criminal charge did not comply with the requirements of the Bill of Rights, and as a result that person's conviction of the offence charged is set aside, the court shall award compensation in respect of the same matters as are mentioned in subsection (1).

(3) Any person who has been convicted of an offence under any provision of an enactment or constituted under any rule of law may, in a case where subsection (4) applies, make an application to the Court of Appeal (or in respect of a conviction before a court in Scotland, to the High Court of Justiciary) to have his conviction set aside and to recover compensation for any period during which he was detained in custody because of the charge and for any other loss he has suffered as a result of the proceedings. including any injury to his feelings.

(4) This subsection applies where the enactment or rule of law under which the offence was constituted has subsequently been held by a competent court not to have had effect at the time of the commission of the alleged offence, or to have had effect so as not to have applied to the circumstances of the alleged offence at the time of its commission.

(5) In this section:

    (a) 'offence' has the same meaning as is given to 'criminal offence' by section 20(5);

    (b) 'court' includes any body competent to try a person charged with an offence;

    (c) 'competent court' means the Constitutional Court, and any other court from which there is a right of appeal to the Constitutional Court, in a case where the right of appeal has not been exercised, or leave to appeal has been refused, or an appeal has been abandoned.

Rules of court

17(1) Rules of court (including rules for the procedure of any statutory tribunal) shall provide:

(a) for the notification by the court or tribunal to the appropriate officer of the Crown of any case to which the Crown is not a party, in which a determination is made on any matter connected with the interpretation, application or effect of the Bill of Rights;

(b) in any such case, for the Crown to be permitted to apply to be joined as a party to the case, and to be allowed to exercise any right of appeal which could be exercised by the prosecutor in a criminal case, or either party in a civil case; and

(c) such other matters as may be necessary to give effect to Sections 12, 13 and 16, and Article 13 of Part I of Schedule I; and existing powers to make rules of court shall be taken to include powers to make such rules as may be necessary to give effect to this subsection.

(2) Rules of the Constitutional Court made under Schedule 2 shall include provision for the Court to give leave to any person or organisation to intervene in any case before it, by way of the presentation of written submissions, or as amicus curiae, as the Court may determine.

PART V: THE BILL OF RIGHTS

Interpretation

18(1) A court or tribunal which is called on to interpret or apply the Bill of Rights, or determine the effect of the Bill on any other enactment or rule of law, or on the facts of any case, shall have regard to any Report of the European Commission of Human Rights, which appears to the court or tribunal to be relevant to the matter before it.

(2) Decisions of the European Court of Human Rights on any question of the interpretation of any provision of the European Convention for the Protection of Human Rights and Fundamental Freedoms or of its Protocols, which is incorporated by this Act into United Kingdom Law, or the effect of any such provision of the Convention or any of its Protocols on United Kingdom Law, shall have the same status in the United Kingdom as decisions of the Constitutional Court, but subject to the provisions of Sections 19, 20 and 21.

Burden of proof

19(1) It shall be for the party alleging an abrogation, abridgment or infringement of any of the rights or freedoms mentioned in the Bill of Rights to prove the same.

(2) Where any question arises whether any abrogation, abridgement or infringement of any of the rights or freedoms of any person as set out in Schedule 1 is or would be justified in terms of Articles 2(2), 5(1), 6(1), 8(2), 9(2), 10(2) or 11(2) of Part I, or Article 1 of Part II, or Article 2(3) or (4) of Part III of the Schedule, it shall be for the court (and not the Crown) to determine whether, and the party

asserting the justification to prove that, the abrogation, abridgement or infringement in question is or would be so justified.

Application of Bill of Rights

20(1) The following provisions of this Section shall have effect for the application and interpretation of Schedule 1, and as appropriate, of this Section.

(2) The word 'everyone' includes legal as well as natural persons wherever the context so admits; and 'no one' shall be interpreted accordingly.

(3) For the purposes of Article 4(3)(b) of Part I, the United Kingdom shall be taken to be a country where conscientious objectors are recognised.

(4) In Article 6(1) of Part I, the term 'civil rights and obligations' includes any question which a court or tribunal constituted by statute is empowered to determine, including any matter in dispute with the Crown or a public authority which is so determinable.

(5) In Article 6(2) and (3) of Part I, the term 'criminal offence' includes contempt of court, and any matter cognisable by a disciplinary body in respect of which a person found guilty may be sentenced to a deprivation of his liberty or a loss of remission of a sentence of imprisonment.

(6) It is hereby declared that Article 8(2) of Part I is not to be taken to diminish or prejudice any right under Article 8(1) as against a person or body which is not a public authority.

(7) Everyone who unjustifiably discriminates against any person on the ground of religion shall be taken to have violated that person's right to freedom of religion as set out in Article 9(1) of Part I.

(8) The powers expressed by Article 16 of Part I to be exercisable by the High Contracting Parties shall be exercisable only by Act of Parliament.

(9) The general principles of international law referred to in Article 1 of Part II shall be taken to include the payment of reasonable compensation for the expropriation of private property, whether owned by aliens or nationals.

(10) The principle affirmed in the second sentence of Article 2 of Part II shall have effect only so far as is compatible with the provision of efficient instruction and training, and the avoidance of unreasonable public expenditure.

(11) For the purposes of the application to the United Kingdom of Article 3 of Part III, 'national' means a citizen of the United Kingdom and Colonies as defined in the British Nationality Acts 1948 to 1965; and the definition of national herein contained may be amended, notwithstanding Section 9(2), by any future Act which is declared to apply to this Act, provided that the amendment does not deprive any person then in being of his nationality or of the benefit of Article 3 of Part III.

(12) Article 3 of Part III shall be taken to require that no person be deprived of his nationality as defined in subsection (11) arbitrarily or without due process of law.

(13) The right to an effective remedy provided by Article 13 of Part I shall be taken to include the right of a party to legal proceedings, whether civil or criminal, to object to the admission of any evidence that was obtained by means of or as a result of an infringement of his rights under the Bill of Rights.

Reservation for other rights

21 The enumeration in the Bill of Rights of certain rights shall not be construed to deny or disparage others retained by the people.

Peter Wallington and Jeremy McBride, *Civil Liberties and a Bill of Rights*, 1976, pp. 112–23.

---

53   DRAFT BILL OF RIGHTS 1980 (JOSEPH JACONELLI)

A Bill To

Declare certain fundamental rights and freedoms, to provide that they may be abrogated only by a special parliamentary procedure, and to limit accordingly the sovereignty of Parliament.

Be it enacted by the Queen's most Excellent Majesty, by and with the advice and consent of the Lords Spiritual and Temporal, and Commons, in this present Parliament assembled, and by the authority of the same, as follows:

Part I

1. Subject to the limitations contained in Part II of this Act, every person within the jurisdiction of the United Kingdom shall enjoy the fundamental rights and freedoms secured in this Part as against persons or bodies exercising governmental or public powers.

2. (1) Every person shall have the right to freedom of speech, subject to limitations either strictly necessary in the public interest or reasonably desirable in the legitimate interests of other persons.
    (2) Every person shall have the right to peaceful assembly and association.

3. (1) Every person shall have the right to personal freedom, subject to limitations either strictly necessary in the public interest or reasonably desirable in the legitimate interests of other persons.
    (2) Every person shall have the right to respect for his home and family life, subject to limitations strictly necessary in the public interest.

4. No public official shall have excessively wide powers of search, whether of the person, his goods, or his home.

5. No person shall incur any penal liability in respect of any act or omission which did not bear such liability at the time of such act or omission.

6. Only cogent evidence, fairly obtained according to the circumstances of the case, may be used against any person in the determination of his liabilities and obligations.

7. Property shall not be taken for public purposes except on payment of just compensation.

8. The provisions of this Part shall not be deemed to exhaust the fundamental rights and freedoms guaranteed to the individual.

9. (1) The fundamental rights and freedoms enumerated in this Part are in addition to, and not in derogation of, any other fundamental rights and freedoms specifically guaranteed to the individual by any statutory body appointed for that purpose.

   (2) Without prejudice to the preceding subsection, no law shall prevail against the provisions of this Part by reason only of the general nature of this Part and the specific nature of such other law.

10. No provision of this Part shall be so construed or applied as to restrict the freedom of the individual to an extent greater than at the date of entry into force of this Act.

11. The provisions of this Part shall be known as the Bill of Rights 1980.

Part II

12. (1) Every law shall be so construed as not to abrogate or infringe, whether directly or indirectly, the fundamental rights and freedoms guaranteed in Part I of this Act.

   (2) If a law cannot be construed so as not to abrogate or infringe the said fundamental rights and freedoms, then

   (a) any law in existence before the entry into force of this Act shall, in so far as it contravenes the said fundamental rights and freedoms, be repealed; and

   (b) any law purporting to be brought into existence after the entry into force of this Act shall, in so far as it contravenes the said fundamental rights and freedoms, be void.

13. This Act may not be repealed or suspended, whether wholly or in part, except by an Act of Parliament of the United Kingdom which shall expressly declare that it shall take effect notwithstanding the Bill of Rights 1980.

14. This Act shall apply notwithstanding any privileges of Parliament, save that statutes concerned only with the levying and spending of central government funds shall not be called into question in any court.

15. (1) This Act shall not extend to Northern Ireland except to the

extent and in the manner prescribed in subsections (2) and (3) of this section.

(2) Her Majesty may by Order in Council extend the application of the Bill of Rights 1980 to the acts of any authority or assembly subsequently established for the government of any region of the United Kingdom.

(3) No Order shall be made by Her Majesty in Council by virtue of the preceding subsection unless that Order has first been approved with respect to the several regional authorities or assemblies by resolutions of each House of Parliament.

16. The Crown may be joined as a party to any action in which the compatibility of a law with the Bill of Rights 1980 is in issue.

17. (1) Where a party to an action in any court or tribunal wishes to raise an issue of the compatibility between a law and the provisions of the Bill of Rights 1980 and the decisions of such court or tribunal are not subject to appeal under existing enactments to

    (a)   the Court of Appeal in England and Wales, or

    (b)   the High Court of Justiciary or the Inner House of the Court of Session, or

    (c)   the Court of Appeal of Northern Ireland (where appropriate), an appeal shall lie, by virtue of this section, to such courts and thence to the House of Lords.

(2) No issue of compatibility between any law and the Bill of Rights 1980 may be raised, whether by way of pleading or oral argument, save in the courts listed in the preceding subsection or in a court of equivalent status.

(3) Rules of court shall provide for all such purposes rendered necessary for the implementation of this section.

18. This Act shall come into force on a day to be appointed by the Secretary of State, save that such day shall not precede the promulgation of the rules of court required by the preceding section.

Joseph Jaconelli, *Enacting a Bill of Rights; The Legal Problems*, 1980, pp. 290–3.

---

54   COMMONWEALTH OF BRITAIN BILL 1991 (TONY BENN)

Whereas the constitution of the United Kingdom of Great Britain and Northern Ireland has evolved, over the centuries, from its feudal origins, without ever having been systematically examined in terms of its effectiveness in providing democracy or justice for its citizens ...

Whereas the citizens of the United Kingdom have no legally enforceable human, political, social, legal or economic rights, nor any safeguards against the denial of such rights; and

Whereas it is now urgent that the United Kingdom adopts a new constitution to remedy these and other defects;

Be it therefore enacted, by the Queen's most Excellent Majesty, by and with the advice and consent of the Lords Spiritual and Temporal, and Commons, in this present Parliament assembled, and by the authority of the same, as follows:—

THE COMMONWEALTH OF BRITAIN

1. Britain shall be a democratic, secular, federal Commonwealth, comprising the Nations of England, Scotland and Wales, in association with such islands as have historically been linked to the United Kingdom ...

2.—(1) The Commonwealth shall be dedicated to the maintenance of the welfare of all its citizens, in whom all sovereign power shall be vested, to be exercised by them, and on their behalf, by the representatives whom they shall elect.

(2) Schedule 1 to this Act shall have effect for the purposes of providing for and entrenching certain basic and fundamental human rights.

3.—(1) It shall be the duty of the President, the Government and the Courts to use their best endeavours to secure and safeguard these rights.

(2) The House of Commons shall appoint a Human Rights Commissioner, responsible to Parliament ('the Commissioner'), who shall be responsible for monitoring the observance of these rights.

(3) Any person who believes that he or she is being denied his or her rights may petition the Commonwealth Parliament or ask the Human Rights Commissioner to investigate such a complaint, and the Commissioner may examine the claim and submit a report upon it; any such report shall be published, and the House of Commons shall decide upon it within twelve months of publication.

4. The High Court established under section 24 below may undertake a judicial review of any administrative act of the Executive, on application by any person complaining of a denial of one or more of the rights set out in Schedule 1 to this Act.

SCHEDULE 1: THE CHAPTER OF RIGHTS

1. All citizens of Britain shall be entitled to enjoy, and to campaign for, universal democratic and enforceable rights, both individual and collective, enshrined in law, adhered to in practice and respected by society, as a precondition of self-government and the achievement of full political, social and economic emancipation within a civilized society:

2. Every citizen shall have the following political rights:
— to freedom of speech;
— to freedom of assembly and of association for the purpose of expressing an opinion, without interference from the State;
— to organize for common political, social or economic ends;
— to practise, or not to practise, any or all religions;
— to vote in all elections, participate in all electoral processes and institutions, and to contest all elections;
— to privacy and the protection of personal information and correspondence from surveillance or interference;
— to information about public, political, social or economic affairs;
— to freedom of movement, unhindered by arbitrary interference, and to be given asylum from political social or economic oppression; and
— to conscientious objection to service in the armed forces.

3. Every citizen shall have the following legal rights:
— to personal freedom from arbitrary arrest, detention or harassment;
— to a fair and impartial hearing by a jury of the citizen's peers if accused of any unlawful activity, and to equal treatment before the law and equal access to legal representation;
— to be presumed innocent until proved guilty, to be informed of all charges laid and the evidence in support of them, and the right to silence in court;
— to freedom from torture or cruel and degrading treatment, and from capital punishment;
— to legal advice and services, free at the point of use; and
— to equal treatment before the law, and in the community, without discrimination, and regardless of race, sex or sexual preference, colour, religious or political conviction or disability.

4. Every citizen shall have the following social rights;
— to adequate and warm housing and comfortable living conditions;
— to rest, recreation and leisure, to a limitation of working hours and to holidays;
— to enjoy access to literature, music, the arts and cultural activities;
— to good health care and preventive medicine, free at the moment of need;
— to lifelong and free educational provision;
— to dignity and care in retirement;
— in the case of women, to control of their own fertility and reproduction;
— to free and equal access to child care;
— to free, effective and equitable means of transportation;
— to a healthy, sustainable, accessible and attractive environment and to clean water and air;
— to media free from governmental or commercial domination; and
— to full access to personal information held by any public authority, subject only to a restriction order signed by a Minister and reported to Parliament.

5. Every citizen shall have the following economic rights:

— to useful work at a fair wage that provides an income sufficient to maintain a decent standard of living;

— to belong to a trade union and to withdraw labour in pursuit of an industrial dispute;

— to participate in all decisions, including those relating to health and safety, affecting the workplace and to information, representation and expression of opinion for all employed persons;

— to full and equal access to all state or social benefits at a level sufficient to meet basic needs; and

— to freedom from taxation in excess of an ability to pay.

HC [1990–1] 161.

(B)

A HUMAN RIGHTS COMMISSION AND PARLIAMENTARY REFORM

RB NOTE: There are several different kinds of UK Commission on Human Rights, with a variety of possible functions, which might be created to help promote human rights and civil liberties in the UK. A regional body of this nature, the Northern Ireland Human Rights Commission, has recently been created by the Northern Ireland Act 1998 (replacing the earlier Standing Advisory Commission on Human Rights) [152]. Similarly, there are a number of different functions that a Parliamentary Committee on Human Rights could perform. The following documents indicate what some of the central options involve. See also the human rights commissions provided for in the South African Bill of Rights [48] and Liberty's Bill of Rights proposal [50].

---

55 A COMMISSION OF HUMAN RIGHTS TO EXAMINE
COMPLAINTS ALLEGING A HUMAN RIGHTS
VIOLATION (SAMUEL SILKIN), 1971

Protection of Human Rights Bill

A BILL TO

Provide for the appointment and functions of a Commission of Human Rights to promote the greater protection and observance of human rights and fundamental freedoms and to provide the means of obtaining an effective remedy in respect of the infringement thereof; and for purposes connected therewith.

Be it enacted by the Queen's most Excellent Majesty, by and with the advice and consent of the Lords Spiritual and Temporal, and Commons, in this present Parliament assembled, and by the authority of the same, as follows:—

Part I: The Commission of Human Rights for the United Kingdom

1.—(1) For the purpose of protecting human rights in the United Kingdom in accordance with the following provisions of this Act there shall be appointed a Commission, to be known as the Commission of Human Rights for the United Kingdom.

(2) Her Majesty may by Letters Patent from time to time appoint a person to be chairman of the Commission and other persons, not being at any time more than four in number, to be members of the Commission.

(3) The chairman and members of the Commission shall be known as the Human Rights Commissioners.

(4) A Commissioner shall, subject to subsection (5) of this section, hold office during good behaviour.

(5) A Commissioner may be relieved of his office by Her Majesty at his own request or may be removed from office by Her Majesty in consequence of Addresses from both Houses of Parliament and shall in any case vacate office on completing the year of service in which he attains the age of sixty-five years.

(6) A Commissioner shall not be a member of the House of Commons or of the Senate or House of Commons of Northern Ireland, and accordingly—
   (*a*) in Part III of Schedule I to the House of Commons Disqualification Act 1957 there shall be inserted at the appropriate point in alphabetical order the entry 'The chairman and members of the Commission of Human Rights for the United Kingdom', and
   (*b*) the like amendment shall be made in the Part substituted for the said Part III by Schedule 3 to that Act in its application to the Senate and House of Commons of Northern Ireland.

(7) The chairman of the Commission shall by virtue of his office be a member of the Council on Tribunals, and of the Scottish Committee of that Council, in addition to the persons appointed or designated as such under the Tribunals and Inquiries Act 1958.

(8) Save as Her Majesty may provide by Order in Council a Commissioner, whilst holding office as such, shall not hold any other public office or appointment and shall not engage in any gainful employment or occupation, whether in the United Kingdom or elsewhere.

2.—(1) Subject to subsection (2) of this section, there shall be paid to the chairman of the Commission a salary at the rate of £14,000 a year and to each member of the Commission a salary at the rate of £11,500 a year.

(2) The House of Commons may from time to time by resolution increase

the rate of the salaries payable under this section and any such resolution may take effect from the date on which it is passed or such other date as may be specified therein.

(3) The salary payable to a Commissioner shall be abated by the amount of any salary payable to him in respect of any other public office or appointment held by him in the United Kingdom or elsewhere at the same time as holding office as Commissioner.

(4) The provisions of Schedule I to the Parliamentary Commissioner Act 1967, shall have effect with respect to the pensions and other benefits to be paid to or in respect of persons who have held office as Commissioners as if the said Schedule I were the Schedule to this Act and as if references therein to 'the Commissioner' were references to a Commissioner under this Act.

(5) The salary payable to a Commissioner shall be abated by the amount of any pension payable to him in respect of any public office in the United Kingdom or elsewhere to which he had previously been appointed or elected or which may be held by him at the same time as holding office as Commissioner, but any such abatement shall be disregarded in computing that salary for the purposes of the Schedule referred to in subsection (4) of this section.

(6) Any salary, pension or other benefit payable by virtue of this section shall be charged on and issued out of the Consolidated Fund.

3.—(1) The chairman of the Commission shall appoint such officers of the Commission as he may determine with the approval of the Minister for the Civil Service as to numbers and conditions of service.

(2) Any function of the Commission under this Act may be performed by any officer of the Commission authorised for that purpose by the rules of the Commission.

(3) The expenses of the Commission under this Act, to such amount as may be sanctioned by the Treasury, shall be defrayed out of moneys provided by Parliament.

Part II: The protection of human rights

4. Any reference in this Act to an Article of the European Convention or to any provisions thereof or rights or principles contained therein shall be construed as a reference to the said Article, provisions, rights or principles—

(*a*) as at the material time amended, added to or varied by any Protocol to the European Convention or other instrument to which the United Kingdom is at the material time a party; and

(*b*) as at the material time qualified by any relevant reservation made by or on behalf of the United Kingdom and at the material time in force.

5.—(1) For the purposes of this Act the expression 'human rights' means, subject to the provisions of subsection (2) of this section, the rights contained in Section I of the European Convention.

(2) Her Majesty may by Order in Council from time to time amend the provisions of subsection (1) of this section, but not so as to derogate from the rights therein referred to so long as the European Convention or any material Protocol thereto shall remain in force and the United Kingdom shall remain a party thereto.

(3) For the purposes of this Act, 'violation of human rights' means any action which in the opinion of the Commission is at the material time and in the material circumstances inconsistent with human rights.

(4) For the avoidance of doubt it is declared that each of the following may in appropriate circumstances consist of or involve a violation of human rights, that is to say—

    (*a*) the provisions of any statute or the absence of legislation on any subject;

    (*b*) the nature of prerogative rights or powers;

    (*c*) the provisions of statutory or other delegated rights, powers or duties or the absence thereof;

    (*d*) the decisions, practices or procedures of any court exercising judicial functions or of any tribunal exercising judicial, quasi-judicial or administrative functions;

    (*e*) any exercise of statutory or other powers by a Minister, officer or member of a Government department or of a public or local authority or by any other person whatsoever.

6.—(1) Any person who would by virtue of Article 25 of the European Convention be entitled to address to the Secretary-General of the Council of Europe a petition claiming to be the victim of a violation by the United Kingdom of the rights set forth in the European Convention, may in the like circumstances address to the Commission a petition alleging a violation of human rights.

(2) For the purposes of this Act, 'petition' means a petition addressed to the Commission as in the last foregoing sub-section provided, and 'petitioner' shall be construed accordingly.

(3) The rules of the Commission shall provide that any petition shall be made in writing and may be made in formal or in informal language.

7.—(1) The Commission shall deal with petitions received by it in accordance with the following provisions of this Act.

(2) In dealing with any petition the Commission may act through any number of Commissioners not being less than three:

Provided that the rules of the Commission may make provision for enabling any question of the admissibility of a petition or any procedural question arising out of a petition to be determined by less than three Commissioners.

8.—(1) Subject to the following provisions of this Act, the Commission shall make and publish rules for the manner in which its powers shall be exercised and for governing its procedures, and may from time to time rescind, amend or add to such rules.

(2) Any rules which by virtue of the foregoing sub-section are from time to time in force shall be known and are in this Act referred to as 'the rules of the Commission'.

9.—(1) Upon receiving any petition the Commission shall first determine whether the petition is admissible and unless it so determines shall reject it.

(2) No petition shall be considered admissible which is delivered to the Commission more than twelve months from the day on which the petitioner first had notice of the matters alleged in the petition or of the decision of any court or tribunal relating thereto (whichever is the later), unless the Commission considers that there are special circumstances justifying an extension of the said period.

(3) Subject to the provisions of the last preceding subsection a petition may be made in respect of matters which arose or which shall have arisen before the commencement of this Act.

(4) Subject to the provisions of the last two preceding subsections the Commission shall make such rules regulating the admissibility of petitions as shall, so far as may be considered practicable and desirable, apply thereto the principles contained in Articles 26 and 27 of the European Convention and provisions like to those contained in subsection (2) of section 5 of the Parliamentary Commissioner Act 1967.

10.—(1) Where the Commission determines a petition to be admissible, it shall, subject to the provisions of subsection (2) of this section, investigate the matters contained therein and such other matters as it may consider relevant thereto and shall conclude whether or not any such matters consist of or involve a violation of human rights.

(2) The Commission shall, so far as the rules of the Commission provide, afford an opportunity to give evidence and to submit oral and written representations to—
   (*a*) the petitioner; and
   (*b*) any Minister, officer or member of a Government department or of a public or local authority, or any other person whomsoever who is alleged to have committed or to be involved in the commission of a violation of human rights or who may prima facie appear to the Commission to have committed or to be involved in the commission of a violation of human rights.

11.—(1) Without prejudice to any other provisions of this Act, the relevant provisions of the Parliamentary Commissioner Act 1967 shall apply to petitions, determinations and investigations under this Act as they apply to complaints and investigations under that Act and the powers and duties of the Commission shall be construed accordingly.

(2) The rules of the Commission shall contain provision for enabling it to perform any of its functions in private but save as may therein be provided it shall hear evidence and oral representations in public and it may publish written representations in such manner as the rules of the Commission may provide.

(3) The Commission shall in such manner as the rules of the Commission may provide publish its determinations and its conclusions and its reasons therefore.

12.—(1) If after conducting an investigation under this Act the Commission concludes that any matter investigated by it amounts to or involves a violation of human rights and that in consequence thereof injustice has been done or may be done to any person if steps are not taken to remedy such violation or to compensate such person or both, it may, if it thinks fit, lay before each House of Parliament a special report upon the case.

(2) The Commission shall annually lay before each House of Parliament a general report upon the performance of its functions under this Act and may from time to time lay before each House of Parliament such other reports with respect to those functions as it thinks fit and shall in particular report any conclusion which it may have reached that any matter investigated by it amounts to or involves a violation of human rights.

13. For the purposes of the law of defamation all proceedings of and in connection with the Commission and all reports of the proceedings thereof shall enjoy the same protection as if the Commission were a court exercising judicial functions.

14. The determinations and conclusions of the Commission shall not be open to challenge in any court of law and no proceedings shall lie against the Commission or against any Commissioner or officer of the Commission in respect of the exercise of, or the failure to exercise, any of the powers, duties or functions referred to in this Act:

Provided that no determination or conclusion of the Commission shall operate to prevent any person from exercising any right which he may enjoy by virtue of the application to the United Kingdom of Article 25 of the European Convention.

15.—(1) In this Act the following expressions have the meanings hereby respectively assigned to them, that is to say—

'action' includes failure to act and other expressions connoting action shall be construed accordingly;

'The Commission' means the Commission of Human Rights for the United Kingdom;

'the Commissioners' mean the Human Rights Commissioners;

'the European Convention' means the Convention for the Protection of Human Rights and Fundamental Freedoms which was done at Rome on the fourth day of November, 1970;

'human rights' and 'violation of human rights' have the meanings respectively assigned thereto in section 5 of this Act;

'officer' includes employee;

'person' includes organisation and group of persons, including, in particular, any group of persons having a common interest or concern in the subject matter of a petition;

'petition' and 'petitioner' have the meanings respectively assigned thereto in subsection (2) of section 6 of this Act;

'the rules of the Commission' has the meaning assigned thereto in section 8 of this Act;

'tribunal' includes the person constituting a tribunal consisting of one person.

(2) For the purposes of this Act, 'the relevant provisions of the Parliamentary Commissioner Act 1967' are:—

(*a*) subsections (2) and (4) of section 6;

(*b*) subsections (3) and (4) of section 7;

(*c*) section 8;

(*d*) section 9;

(*e*) subsections (1) and (2) of section 11;

(*f*) so far as required to interpret the foregoing enactments, subsection (1) of section 12.

(3) References in this Act to any enactment are references to that enactment as amended or extended by or under any other enactment.

16. This Act shall extend to Northern Ireland if and so far as an Order made by Her Majesty in Council may provide.

17. No Order shall be made by Her Majesty in Council by virtue of subsection (2) of section 5 or by virtue of section 16 or by virtue of subsection (4) of section 18 of this Act, unless the same has first been approved by resolutions of each House of Parliament.

18.—(1) This Act may be cited as the Protection of Human Rights Act 1971.

(2) Parts I and III of this Act shall come into force on such date as Her Majesty may by Order in Council appoint.

(3) Part II of this Act shall come into force six months after the commencement of this Act.

(4) This Act shall cease to have effect to such extent as may be determined by an Order made by Her Majesty in Council:

Provided that no such Order shall be made so long as the European Convention, or any provision thereof or Protocol thereto, shall continue to have effect and the United Kingdom shall continue to be a party thereto and shall not have derogated from its obligations thereunder in accordance with Article 15 thereof.

HC [1970–1] 52.

---

56 A HUMAN RIGHTS COMMISSION TO MONITOR AND PROMOTE HUMAN RIGHTS (GRAHAM ALLEN), 1994

7.—(1) There shall be established a body corporate to be known as the Human Rights Commission (in this Act referred to as 'the Commission').

(2) The Commission shall have the general function of monitoring the workings of this Act and promoting the fundamental rights and freedoms that it contains.

(3) Without prejudice to the generality of subsection (2) above, the Commission may—

(a) make submissions either in writing or orally in any proceedings in any court or tribunal if, in the opinion of the Commission, such submissions are likely to promote the fundamental rights and freedoms contained in this Act;

(b) initiate proceedings in its own name before any court or tribunal for any breach of the rights and freedoms contained in this Act or to promote those fundamental rights and freedoms and for these purposes it shall have sufficient interest or standing for any such proceedings and, in Scotland, title and interest to sue in any such proceedings;

(c) conduct a formal investigation for any purpose connected with the carrying out of any of its functions;

(d) issue codes of practice containing such practical guidance as the Commission thinks fit to promote the fundamental rights and freedoms contained in this Act;

(e) with the approval of the Secretary of State and the consent of the Treasury give financial or other assistance to any local or national organisation appearing to the Commission to be concerned with the promotion of the fundamental rights and freedoms contained in this Act;

(f) examine all Bills presented to and statutory instruments laid before either House of Parliament for their compliance with the fundamental rights and freedoms contained in this Act and publish a report on its findings;

(g) undertake or assist (financially or otherwise) the undertaking by other persons of research and educational activities relevant to its functions; and

(h) provide educational or other facilities or services relevant to its functions, for which it may make such reasonable charges as it from time to time determines.

(4) A copy of each report published under subsection (3)(f) above shall be laid before each House of Parliament.

(5) Schedule 4 shall have effect in relation to the Commission ...

Schedule 4: The Human Rights Commission

PART I: APPOINTMENT AND ADMINISTRATION

Appointment of the Commission

1. The Commission shall consist of no fewer than 15 and no more than 24 members appointed on a part or full-time basis by the Lord Chancellor and the Lord Advocate after consulting the Home Affairs Committee and the Scottish Affairs Committee of the House of Commons and the Lord Chancellor, after consultation with the Lord Advocate, shall appoint one of the full-time members to be chair after consulting the Home Affairs Committee and the Scottish Affairs Committee of the House of Commons.

2. The Commission members shall be drawn in equal numbers from the following categories—
 (a) the legal profession, including practising lawyers and other persons knowledgable in the law;
 (b) non-governmental organisations concerned with human rights;
 (c) members of the community, reflecting so far as possible those groups or individuals who have knowledge of or experience of abuses of fundamental rights and freedoms.

Tenure of members

3. Subject to paragraphs 4 and 5 any member of the Commission shall hold and vacate office in accordance with the terms of his or her appointment, but a person shall not be appointed a member of the Commission for a period of more than 5 years.

4.—(1) The chair or a member may resign office by giving notice in writing to the Lord Chancellor or the Lord Advocate, and if the chair ceases to be a member he or she shall cease to be chair.

(2) A person who ceases to be the chair or a member shall be eligible for reappointment.

5. The Lord Chancellor or the Lord Advocate may terminate the appointment of a member of the Commission if satisfied that—

    (a) he or she is unable to carry out his or her duties by reason of physical or mental illness;

    (b) he or she has been absent from meetings of the Commission for a period longer than six consecutive months without permission of the Commission; or

    (c) he or she is otherwise unable or unfit to discharge the functions of a member of the Commission.

Remuneration of members

6.—(1) The Commission may—

    (a) pay to its members such remuneration; and

    (b) make provision for the payment of such pensions, allowances or gratuities to or in respect of its members,

as the Lord Chancellor may, with the approval of the Treasury, determine.

(2) Where a person ceases to be a member of the Commission otherwise than on the expiry of his or her term of office, and it appears to the Lord Chancellor that there are special circumstances which make it right for that person to receive compensation, the Lord Chancellor may, with the consent of the Treasury, direct the Commission to make that person a payment of such amount as the Lord Chancellor may, with the consent of the Treasury, determine.

Staff

7.—(1) The Commission shall appoint a person to be Director of the Commission who shall be responsible to the Commission for the exercise of its functions.

(2) The Commission may appoint such other employees as it thinks fit.

(3) Appointments under this paragraph may be made on such terms and conditions as the Commission, with the approval of the Lord Chancellor and the Lord Advocate and consent of the Treasury, may determine.

8.—(1) The Commission shall make, in respect of such of its employees as, with the approval of the Lord Chancellor and the Lord Advocate and the consent of the Treasury, it may determine, such arrangements for providing pensions, allowances or gratuities, including pensions, allowances or gratuities by way of compensation for loss of employment, as it may determine.

(2) Arrangements under sub-paragraph (1) above may include the establishment and administration, by the Commission or otherwise, of one or more pension schemes.

Proceedings

9.—(1) The Commission may regulate its own proceedings.

(2) The Commission may make such arrangements as it considers appropriate for the discharge of its functions, including the delegation of specified functions, and shall make such arrangements for the delegation of functions to committees and persons.

(3) Committees may be appointed and may be dissolved by the Commission and may include, or consist entirely of, persons who are not members of the Commission.

(4) A committee shall act in accordance with such directions as the Commission may from time to time give, and the Commission may provide for anything done by a committee to have effect as if it had been done by the Commission.

10. The Commission may pay to the members of any committee such fees and allowances as the Lord Chancellor may, with the consent of the Treasury, determine.

Annual and other reports

11.—(1) As soon as practicable after the end of each calendar year the Commission shall make to the Lord Chancellor and the Lord Advocate a report on their activities during the year (an 'annual report').

(2) Each annual report shall include a general survey of developments, during the period to which it relates, in respect of matters falling within the scope of the Commission's functions.

(3) The Commission may also publish other reports as it thinks fit.

(4) The Lord Chancellor and the Lord Advocate shall lay a copy of every annual report before each House of Parliament, and cause the report to be published.

PART II: ARRANGEMENTS FOR FINANCIAL ASSISTANCE IN LEGAL PROCEEDINGS

12. Where, in relation to proceedings or prospective proceedings under this Act, an individual who alleges that his or her fundamental rights and freedoms under this Act have been infringed, applies for assistance, the Commission shall consider the application and may grant it if it thinks fit to do so—

    (a) on the ground that the case raises a question of principle; or

    (b) on the ground that it is unreasonable, having regard to the complexity of the case, or to the applicant's position in relation to any other party or potential party to the proceedings, or to any other matter, to expect the applicant to deal with the case unaided; or

(c) by reason of any other special consideration.

13. Assistance by the Commission under this Schedule may include—
   (a) giving advice;
   (b) procuring or attempting to procure the settlement of any matter in dispute;
   (c) arranging for the giving of advice or assistance by a solicitor or counsel;
   (d) arranging for representation by any person, including all such assistance as is usually given by a solicitor or counsel, in the steps preliminary or incidental to any proceedings, or in arriving at or giving effect to a compromise to avoid or bring to an end any proceedings;
   (e) any other form of assistance which the Commission may reasonably consider is appropriate in all the circumstances.

14.—(1) Where under paragraph 12 an application for assistance under this Schedule is made in writing, the Commission shall, within the period of two months beginning when the application is received—
   (a) consider the application after making such enquiries as it sees fit;
   (b) decide whether or not to grant it; and
   (c) inform the applicant of its decision, stating whether or not assistance under this Schedule is to be provided by the Commission and, if so, what form it will take.

(2) Where the applicant's fundamental rights and freedoms are likely to be prejudiced during the period of two months referred to above the Commission shall make a decision as soon as reasonably practicable.

15. The recovery of expenses incurred by the Commission in providing the applicant with assistance under this Schedule (as taxed or assessed in such manner as may be prescribed by rules or regulations) shall constitute a first charge for the benefit of the Commission—
   (a) on any costs or expenses which (whether by virtue of a judgment or order of a court or tribunal or an agreement or otherwise) are payable to the applicant by any other person in respect to the matter in connection with which the assistance is given; and
   (b) so far as it relates to any costs or expenses, on his or her rights under any compromise or settlement arrived at in connection with that matter to avoid or to bring to an end any proceedings.

16. The charge referred to in paragraph 15 is subject to any charge under the Legal Aid Act 1988, any charge or obligation for payment in priority to other debts under the Legal Aid (Scotland) Act 1986, or any charge under Article 12 of the Legal Aid, Advice and Assistance (Northern Ireland)

Order 1981 and is subject to any provision in either of those Acts for payment of any sum to the Legal Aid Board, the Scottish Legal Aid Board or the Law Society of Northern Ireland.

PART III: FORMAL INVESTIGATIONS

17. The Commission may, with the approval of the Lord Chancellor and the Lord Advocate, appoint, on a full-time or part-time basis, one or more individuals as additional Commissioners for the purposes of a formal investigation.

18. The Commission may nominate one or more Commissioners, with or without one or more additional Commissioners, to conduct a formal investigation on their behalf, and may delegate any of their functions in relation to the investigation to the person so nominated.

Terms of reference

19. The Commission shall not embark on a formal investigation unless the requirements of this Part of this Schedule have been complied with.

20. Terms of reference for any formal investigation shall be drawn up by the Commission.

21. It shall be the duty of the Commission to give general notice of the holding of formal investigations unless the terms of reference confine it to activities of persons named in them, but in such a case the Commission shall in the prescribed manner give those persons notice of the holding of the said investigation.

22. Where the terms of reference of a formal investigation confine it to activities of persons named in them and the Commission in the course of it propose to investigate any act made unlawful by this Act which it believes that a person so named may have done, the Commission shall inform that person of its belief and of its proposal to investigate the act in question.

Power to obtain information

23.—(1) For the purposes of a formal investigation the Commission by a notice in the prescribed form served on him or her in the prescribed manner—

   (a) may require any person to furnish such written information as may be described in the notice, and may specify the time at which, and the manner and form in which, the information is to be furnished;

   (b) may require any person to attend at such time and place as is specified in the notice and give oral information about, and produce all documents in his or her possession or control relating to, any matter specified in the notice.

(2) A notice under sub-paragraph (1) above shall not require a person—

(a) to give information, or produce any documents, which he or she could not be compelled to given in evidence, or produce, in civil proceedings before the High Court or the Court of Session; or

(b) to attend any place unless the necessary expenses of his or her journey to and from that place are paid or tendered to him or her.

(3) If a person fails to comply with a notice served on him or her under sub-paragraph (1) above or the Commission have reasonable cause to believe that he or she intends not to comply with it, the Commission may apply to the County Court or, in Scotland, a Sheriff Court for an Order requiring him or her to comply with it or with such directions for the like purpose as may be contained in the Order.

(4) Section 55 of the County Courts Act 1984 (penalty for neglecting witness summons) shall apply to failure without reasonable excuse to comply with an order of a county court under sub-paragraph (3) above as it applies in the cases provided in the said section 55 and paragraph 73 of Schedule 1 to the Sheriff Courts (Scotland) Act 1907 (Power of sheriff to grant second diligence for compelling the attendance of witnesses or havers) shall apply to an order of a Sheriff Court under sub-paragraph (3) above as it applies in proceedings in the Sheriff Court.

(5) A person commits an offence if he or she—

(i) wilfully alters, suppresses, conceals or destroys a document which he or she has been required by a notice or order under this Schedule to produce; or

(ii) in complying with such a notice or order, knowingly or recklessly makes any statement that is false in a material particular,

and shall be liable on summary conviction to a fine not exceeding level 5 on the standard scale.

(6) Proceedings for an offence under sub-paragraph (5) above may (without prejudice to any jurisdiction exercisable apart from this sub-paragraph) be instituted—

(i) against any person at any place at which he or she has an office or other place of business; or

(ii) against an individual at any place where he or she resides, or at which he or she is for the time being.

24.—(1) If in the light of any of its findings in a formal investigation it appears to the Commission necessary or expedient, whether during the course of their investigation or after its conclusion—

(a) to make to any person, with a view to promoting the fundamental rights and freedoms contained in this Act, recommendations for changes in his or her policies or procedures, or as to any other matters; or

(b) to make to the Lord Chancellor or the Lord Advocate any recommendations, whether for changes in the law or otherwise, the Commission shall make those recommendations accordingly.

(2) The Commission shall make a report of its findings in any formal investigations conducted by it and shall publish that report.

25.—(1) No information given to the Commission by any person ('the informant') in connection with a formal investigation shall be disclosed by the Commission, or by any person who is or has been a Commissioner, additional Commissioner or employee of the Commission, except—

(a) on the order of any court; or

(b) with the informant's consent; or

(c) in the form of summary or other general statement published by the Commission which does not identify the informant or any other person to whom the information relates; or

(d) in a report published by the Commission; or

(e) to the Commissioners, additional Commissioners, or, so far as may be necessary for the proper performance of the functions of the Commission, to other persons; or

(f) for the purpose of any civil proceedings under this Act to which the Commission are a party, or any criminal proceedings.

(2) Any person who discloses information in contravention of sub-paragraph (1) above commits an offence and shall be liable on summary conviction to a fine not exceeding level 5 on the standard scale.

(3) In preparing any report for publication or for inspection the Commission shall exclude, so far as is consistent with their duties and the object of the report, any matter which relates to the private affairs of any individual or the business interests of any person where the publication of that matter might, in the opinion of the Commission, prejudicially affect that individual or person.

Extract from Human Rights Bill 1994, HC [1993–4] 30, see Doc. 39D.

---

57   THE OPTIONS FOR A HUMAN RIGHTS COMMISSION (CONSTITUTION UNIT) 1996

The case for establishing a Human Rights Commission in the UK alongside an incorporated ECHR is sometimes regarded as a 'given'. It is important, however, to determine whether a Human Rights Commission is necessary (or simply desirable) alongside the incorporation of the ECHR. It might be questioned whether a Human Rights Commission is necessary at this first stage of reform, particularly if some form of parliamentary committee, with a remit to conduct investigations, were established to monitor and review compliance with the ECHR and other rights instruments; and if the courts provided a longstop of judicial enforcement.

However, if incorporation takes place without the establishment of a Human Rights Commission, its impact is likely to be diluted. A Human Rights Commission would play a key role in nurturing a 'culture' of human rights and creating the idea of collective enforcement of rights, necessary not only for the effective observance of the human rights standards in the ECHR but also those provided for in other human rights instruments not judicially protected. A Human Rights Commission could also play an important role in giving practical effect to the formal guarantees provided for by the ECHR by promoting effective enforcement of the law and effective access to the courts. If resources are not made available to improve access to justice – and one means of achieving this would be through a Human Rights Commission – incorporation of the Convention could make individual victims worse off (requiring as it would the exhaustion of all domestic remedies before recourse could be had to Strasbourg).

Moreover, there would be a range of functions that a parliamentary committee could not carry out, but which might well be regarded as desirable, or essential: for example the provision of public information services – reactive and proactive (posters, information lines, etc.), the funding of research, and the provision of financial or other assistance in taking test cases. IPPR's forthcoming report, *Scrutiny and Accountability: Democratic Compliance with Human Rights Standards*, argues that: '... it is without question a Government responsibility to ensure the adequate recognition of these [human rights] standards, yet it is the Government against whom those standards are set and against whom the instruments are intended to provide a remedy. Therefore in order to achieve an objective review of the implementation of those standards in the UK, it cannot realistically be carried out by the Government and an independent body is needed.'

A Parliamentary Committee on human rights operating without a Human Rights Commission in parallel might also give the impression that human rights were the preserve and responsibility of experts in the House of Lords or on the Commons backbenches, rather than belonging to a wider community. Finally, if incorporation of the ECHR is intended as a first step towards a domestic bill of rights, as both the Labour Party and the Liberal Democrats propose, then a Human Rights Commission could also have a critical role to play in providing a focus for the process of public education and consultation in developing that bill of rights.

Functions and powers

It is usually assumed that a Human Rights Commission would have powers and functions parallel to those of the EOC and CRE. SACHR, for example, has recommended 'the creation of a Commission for Human Rights, with analogous functions and powers to those of the Equal Opportunities Commission and Commission for Racial Equality, in acting in the public interest to promote the protection of human rights'. Both these bodies are specifically empowered to undertake or assist (financially or otherwise) in research and educational activities pursuant to their particular anti-discrimination objectives; to conduct formal investigations 'for any purpose connected with the carrying out of [these] duties'; have power to compel production of persons and papers; and can bring cases on behalf of individuals in cases which raise a matter or principle or where an applicant could not reasonably be expected to take the case unaided. They also have power to investigate discriminatory practices on their own initiative and the power to issue 'non-discrimination notices' to deal with unlawful discrimination (such notices require cessation of the identified practices and are enforceable in the courts by way of injunction). Where appropriate, both bodies have also issued non-statutory codes of practice.

However, a far wider range of possible functions for a Human Rights Commission can be identified:

- taking test cases (initiating proceedings in its own name as well as assisting individuals).
- having powers to intervene in human rights cases as an *amicus curiae*.
- providing public education services and resources.
- conducting and commissioning research and issuing codes of practice
- initiating and conducting formal investigations into issues of specific concern.
- carrying out inquiries into current practices.
- having powers, or an obligation, to scrutinise legislation to assess for conformity with the ECHR – in addition to scrutiny undertaken by Parliament and by the Civil Service – possibly as an adviser to a dedicated Parliamentary Committee on human rights or in order to submit evidence to a special standing committee on a particular bill.
- being a source of independent advice to Parliament on human rights matters more generally – for example by offering expert views on actual and potential uses of the right of derogation.
- making recommendations to the Government about changes in existing law or practice which would facilitate the better protection of human rights.
- being involved in the reporting process under UN treaties.

It is clear that attempting to cover all of these fronts is both impossible and undesirable. In any case, some of the functions that might be assigned to a Human Rights Commission are already fulfilled – in whole or in part – by other bodies. A Human Rights Commission must complement and not subsume functions already carried out by others (for example, the powers of the Ombudsman to recommend changes in administrative practices to the Government need not be transferred to a Human Rights Commission). Equally, the identification of functions and powers must be realistic within the resources available, a point reinforced by the example of the Australian Human Rights and Equal Opportunities Commission, whose determinative powers have so swamped its resources that it has little left [to enable it] to attend to other more general duties. At a practical level, the early identification of key functions would also determine the support structures necessary for the organisation to operate effectively.

In the UK, some commentators regard the provision of financial support for prospective litigants as the principal argument for a Human Rights Commission, and thus its key function. It is argued that, by their nature, human rights instruments require judicial interpretation to give them full effect – unlike the tradition of domestic legislation, which is to specify to the highest degree the exact application of the statutory provisions and to support this with Codes of Practice and other guidance. This argument was recently advanced by Lord Lester: 'we will need a well-chosen well-run Human Rights Commission, bringing well-chosen, well-argued test cases before the courts.'

Others, however, believe that the key function of a Commission should be to facilitate the creation of a proactive 'rights culture' through public education, on the basis that the key objective of incorporation must be for human rights instruments to be understood and enforced by all those bodies exercising public powers; and by those who need to exercise the rights provided. The promotion of human rights standards might include practical schemes such as exchange of staff between the Human Rights Commission and Whitehall departments. Others argue that its core role should be to conduct strategic investigations and inquiries. Both public education and investigatory functions might be regarded as preferable to litigation as the primary means of promoting human rights. It could be argued, for example, that litigation should not be regarded as a mark of success – it is costly, slow and certainly not user-friendly – and that other more economical means of promoting human rights standards should be pursued. In the short term, public education about both the ECHR and other rights instruments would also be particularly important to ensure an informed public debate around the development of a domestic bill of rights, as proposed by both main opposition parties.

Of course, there is no need to define only one core function for a Human Rights Commission. Different functions can complement one another if managed in a strategic way. For example, litigation can play an important role in public education – one high profile case covered by the media can be worth several poster campaigns. Certainly, a number of NGOs active in the human rights field successfully combine a litigating role with a broader public education and campaigning remit. There is also no reason why the primary responsibilities of the Commission should not change over time. In the years immediately following incorporation, and during which a domestic bill of rights may be under development, the most important functions are likely to be public education (in order to ensure public awareness of the ECHR and human rights more generally, in order to ensure an informed debate about the 'next steps') and litigation, in order to highlight and give effect to the rights provided by the ECHR.

Operational framework

A Human Rights Commission must perform a difficult balancing act. It would rightly be judged by the extent to which it 'causes trouble', as it must challenge the status quo if it is to have a purpose at all. Thus the body should certainly not be dependent on Government, but it must have influence. This balancing act will inevitably create tensions and the structural and other arrangements must be designed to cope with this. The example of the existing rights agencies shows that this is not always easy. For example, a Human Rights Commission could be used to promote a higher profile for the reporting procedures linked to UN treaties, but both the EOC and CRE have shied away from such actions in their specialist fields for fear it would prove too adversarial to the Government (their funders).

A basic issue for a a Human Rights Commission would be how much freedom it should have. It would certainly need to be statutorily independent, to maintain a sharp cutting edge. The Northern Ireland SACHR model of a purely advisory and non-executive body cannot be regarded as particularly successful in influencing Government actions, given its long-standing and unheeded call for incorporation of the ECHR. Although it is an official body (acting in an independent capacity), SACHR has no sway over Government, nor even any automatic right to consultation. One means of strengthening the clout of the Commission would be to establish a direct link to a Parliamentary Select Committee. The question of independence is also linked to the question of where accountability should lie (some check on, and answerability for, its activities would be necessary if public funds are allocated and statutory powers are exercised). To ensure the body's independence, direct accountability of a Commission should ideally be to Parliament, rather than to a Government Department. There would also need to be accountability of a different kind to the various constituencies it serves (including the wider public), perhaps through a requirement to produce a public account of its actions.

One model for establishing the independence of a UK Human Rights Commission, with accountability to Parliament, would be to emulate the 'partnership' relationship between the National Audit Office and the Public Accounts Committee. The Comptroller and Auditor General is appointed on the recommendation of, and reports to, Parliament. But in practice only the Public Accounts Committee follows up reports (this was formally the case until a couple of years ago, but other select committees are now allowed to consider NAO reports in consultation with the Public Accounts Committee). The NAO's workplan is designed in consultation with the Public Accounts Committee, but the NAO has the last word. Unofficially, the NAO also briefs the Committee with questions for its hearings with Government Departments, and contributes to the drafting of its reports. Another similar model is provided by the relationship between the Parliamentary Ombudsman and the Select Committee on the Parliamentary Commissioner for Administration. Alternatively, a more arm's length model might be preferred in which distinctive but complementary roles for the Commission and a Parliamentary Committee on Human Rights are designated. The political impact of both the Committee and the Human Rights Commission is likely to be more effective with a 'partnership' style relationship, for two reasons. First, the relationship between the official bodies and the Committees which they serve can be mutually supportive; second, a knowledge that office-holders are linked to Parliament formally gives them additional clout.

A Human Rights Commission is not likely to represent a significant burden on the Exchequer, if the running costs of the EOC and CRE are any guide. The central government grant-in-aid to the EOC in 1995–96 was £6.43m, including the costs of employing nearly 180 staff. The equivalent figures for the CRE are: £16m grant-in-aid in 1995–96 and an average of 246 staff during the year. However, these are the costs of relatively long-standing organisations, with a wide range of responsibilities. A Human Rights Commission need not operate on such a large scale initially.

A further issue is the question of what controls would be imposed on how the money should be spent. If the same arrangements were adopted for a Human Rights Commission as for the existing rights agencies, a grant-in-aid from Parliament would be paid through the relevant Secretary of State, and the Accounting Officer would be the Permanent Secretary of the Department (although the Commission would itself have an additional Accounting Officer). The responsibility of the parent Department would be to ensure good systems of control and strategic and business planning, but it would be important to guard against departmental officials trying to second guess activities (and expecting to be consulted on business plans) and produce funds accordingly, squeezing out activities that the Department was unenthusiastic about. An alternative would be to adopt the same arrangements as for the NAO, which derives its funds through Parliament, not direct from the Treasury. The same arrangement has recently been proposed for the Ombudsman's Office.

A final consideration is whether a Human Rights Commission should fall within the jurisdiction of both the Comptroller and Auditor General and the Ombudsman. The EOC and CRE are within their jurisdiction, and have both been the subject of complaints to the Ombudsman about the way they have conducted formal investigations. It would be possible to limit the jurisdiction of the two officers of the House of Commons to a limited number of specific functions of the Commission, but such a distinction would be both difficult to make work in practice and undesirable in principle.

Relationship with existing statutory rights agencies
A key question of implementation is whether a Human Rights Commission should be a free-standing body or should merge with the CRE, EOC, the National Disability Council, the Fair Employment Commission and other similar bodies, which might conceivably be regarded as having overlapping responsibilities especially in the fields of discrimination. If the Human Rights Commission co-existed with the other bodies, it would need to defer to the specialist bodies in regard to problems within their jurisdiction.

For economic reasons, amalgamation may be preferred. This would also have the effect of reducing the number of quangos in existence, rather than adding to the total – which might be a political concern. Amalgamation would also make it easier to deal with issues that involved multiple discrimination and those 'grey' areas of discrimination in respect of which it is currently not clear whether they fall within the remit of the existing bodies e.g. discrimination on the grounds of sexuality as against gender; and religious discrimination. It should avoid the risk of duplication and the difficulties of determining boundaries between agencies.

However, some of the communities affected by such an amalgamation might well fear that their interests would be marginalised and specialist knowledge lost, or that a 'hierarchy of discrimination' would be created. Moreover, there is no guarantee that administrative amalgamation would produce any greater coherence of the approach to multiple discrimination. It is also worth noting that discrimination represents only a small part of the ECHR's subject matter (and claims of discrimination under the ECHR may only be invoked on the back of another substantive claim). But perhaps the main objection to such a move would be the disruption this would create; the mature views of the existing bodies would be most needed at a time of change, and any immediate change might damage people's access to justice. The argument can run both ways: either separate bodies reflect the relative importance of specific areas of concern, or the failure to regard a particular set of concerns as falling under the umbrella of human rights marginalises their importance

Ultimately, the decision must rest on the fact that the issues which any new Human Rights Commission would tackle are likely to be many and various. The existing agencies already have wide-ranging remits, and face a constant challenge to make choices and to be strategic in their allocation of resources. If a Human Rights Commission in the short to medium term were to be given the responsibilities of the EOC, CRE, FEC and NDC in addition to responsibility for human rights instruments (including but not necessarily limited to the ECHR), it would be a task of huge proportions. There would undoubtedly be great expectations of any new body and politically, there might be advantage in a Human Rights Commission proving its worth with limited terms of reference before any amalgamation is considered.

Effective arrangements would need to be put in place for co-ordination and co-operation between the bodies. One answer may be to have the Chairs of the various bodies represented ex officio on the Human Rights Commission. This is the approach already adopted in Northern Ireland, where the advisory body of SACHR includes the Chair of the Fair Employment Commission and the Ombudsman ex officio; and the Chairs of both the EOC and the Disability Action Group have been appointed as a matter of course, although not ex officio. Day to day co-ordination would obviously rely on the creation of official level working arrangements which would be needed in any case to shadow the group of Chairs. This sort of arrangement may in fact assist in the better operation of existing arrangements by providing a forum for co-ordination that does not currently exist.

Over time, however, there may be advantage in considering amalgamation if a significant degree of overlap becomes apparent. However, any possible amalgamation of the rights agencies would need to be the result of a comprehensive review of mechanisms for fulfilling the necessary responsibilities. Such a review would need to involve the existing rights agencies (to lock in the key players on delivery), and take place after the establishment of the Human Rights Commission, possibly as part of a wider review of anti-discrimination and equalities legislation.

Equally, the relationship between a Human Rights Commission and the various Ombudsmen would need to be considered, especially in respect of those areas of work where overlap could arise (in particular, dealing with complaints of maladministration that raise human rights issues and the promotion of good practice within government and the public service more generally).

A further question is the need for separate Human Rights Commissions for any devolved territories; and the arrangements for co-ordination between them. Whether or not a Human Rights Commission were to be established, it would also be necessary to consider the role post-incorporation of the Northern Ireland Standing Advisory Commission on Human Rights itself, whose responsibilities are: 'Advising the Secretary of State on the adequacy and effectiveness of the law for the time being in force in preventing discrimination on the grounds of religious belief or political opinion and in providing redress for persons aggrieved by discrimination on either ground.' It would appear incongruous to abolish SACHR at the same time as incorporating the ECHR, but equally inconsistent to allow for the continuation of this body, without establishing sister organisations covering England, Wales and Scotland.

Selection and appointment of Commissioners

This report has so far assumed that a Human Rights Commission would, in terms of its membership, be modelled on the multi-member boards of the EOC, CRE, Boundary Commissions and so on. An alternative that might be considered would be to create a single post of Commissioner, similar to the Ombudsmen and utility regulators. The choice would depend on the range of functions designated to the body. A predominantly administrative and regulatory role could well be fulfilled by a single Commissioner supported by appropriate staff. However, a Human Rights Commission is likely to have a more proactive role and will need to establish public credibility if it is successfully to promote human rights throughout the community. For these reasons, a multi-member Commission, which enables a range of interests to be represented among the membership, is likely to be more appropriate.

As to size, both the CRE and EOC consist of between 8 and 15 individuals; and it is likely that arrangements for appointment to the Human Rights Commission would follow the same pattern – with the addition, as suggested above, of the Chairs of the parallel rights agencies *ex officio*. The National Disability Council has 17 members, its larger size reflecting the desire to include a range of 'consumer representatives' – disabled people, carers, employers and service providers. Taking this further, Liberty has suggested that a Human Rights Commission should be a larger body – of between 15 and 24 members 'drawn in equal numbers from the following categories:- (a) the legal profession, including practising lawyers and other persons knowledgeable in the law; (b) non-governmental organisations concerned with human rights; (c) members of the community, reflecting so far as possible those groups or individuals who have knowledge of or experience of abuses of fundamental rights and freedoms'. Bearing in mind that one method of exercising Government control over independent bodies is through the appointments made to their boards, this discretion might usefully be limited by the statute categorising where members of the Commission should be drawn from, as Liberty suggest. The categories would, however, need to be widely drawn so as not to become redundant with the passage of time and to allow for the evolution of the membership. It might be preferable to impose a statutory duty to consult relevant bodies, before making appointments, rather than defining the categories in advance; this might be formalised into an arrangement whereby Ministers made at least some appointments from a slate of candidates provided by outside bodies.

Appointments to a Human Rights Commission would almost certainly be by the Crown on the recommendation of the Minister in charge of the department with policy responsibility for domestic human rights issues – currently the Home Office. Responsibility might alternatively fall to the Lord Chancellor. The selection process would be subject to the guidance produced by the Commissioner for Public Appointments, and any other arrangements instituted by the Government of the day – for example, both the Labour Party and the Liberal Democrats have proposed that specialist Select Committees should have a role in the appointment of key members of NDPBs (perhaps, in this case, the Chair and any Vice Chairs). An alternative would be for the Chair of the Human Rights Commission to be appointed by the Crown on the recommendation of Parliament in the same way as the Comptroller and Auditor General (and as proposed by the Select Committee on the PCA for the Ombudsman). This would clearly be dependent on the lines of accountability devised for the body; and it would be cumbersome for all members of the Commission to be appointed in this way.

Members might be appointed on a full-time professional basis or on a part-time voluntary basis, as with the EOC and CRE. Alternatively a hybrid model with both executive and non-executive board members might be considered. modus operandi of the organisation would be significantly influenced by the choice between a professional full-time board and a voluntary part-time board. The decision would necessarily depend on the core functions of the Commission (for example, for a largely advisory body like the NDC, its credibility is dependent on its members' links with outside interests). However, it should not necessarily be assumed that the model provided by the existing rights agencies is necessarily preferable; and it must also be recognised that finding members of voluntary unpaid boards is not always easy. There might well be advantage in appointing a mix of executive and non-executive board members.

Constitution Unit, *Human Rights Legislation*, 1996, pp. 69–73, 79–86.

---

58   THE POSSIBLE FUNCTIONS OF A HUMAN RIGHTS COMMISSION (INSTITUTE FOR PUBLIC POLICY RESEARCH), 1997

The role of a Human Rights Commission is to strengthen the promotion and protection of human rights throughout the country. Depending on the extent of its mandate it may monitor, advise, educate, investigate, mediate, adjudicate complaints, conduct inquiries and initiate litigation. In 1993, the UN agreed a set of principles for the establishment of Human Rights Commissions, the 'Paris Principles', followed by detailed guidelines in 1995. There is, however, intended to be no single model for such bodies. Existing Commissions range from large organisations with an extensive complaints machinery (eg Australia) to an advisory committee located within the Prime Minister's office (France).

Within the UK there are a number of bodies which bear some responsibility for protecting aspects of human rights, most notably those responsible for promoting equality, the Ombudsmen and the courts. But there are significant gaps in the existing provision, identified in this paper, which a Human Rights Commission could fill.

For some, the need to promote a culture of rights and responsibilities may be seen as the key role of the new body: to promote good practice in public bodies and awareness of human rights principles among the public at large. For others, the need to strengthen the role of Parliament in scrutinising government proposals, or to advise individuals how to achieve redress, may be of paramount concern. Others still may judge the Commission's key role to be the strategic enforcement of the ECHR by initiating legal proceedings, backing test cases or providing expert opinion to the court as 'amicus'. The possible roles of the Commission, the specific functions it could perform, and the powers it would need, are suggested below.

Those advocating the creation of a Human Rights Commission face tight constraints on public resources. The proposal must therefore be well argued, its public benefit fully demonstrated and the proposed structure designed to achieve maximum effect. The resource constraint has also led us to identify the minimum functions which would be necessary, with additional functions which could be added; and to consider the viability of using private finance for aspects of the Commission's work.

The UK ... lacks any systematic promotion, monitoring or enforcement of human rights. There is no body which monitors the extent to which UK law, policy and its administration conform to the international human rights standards to which the UK is committed; nor to assess the impact of proposed legislative and policy changes. Government legal advisers currently fulfil this role to a limited extent but do not have the resources nor the mandate to scrutinise the policy of each Whitehall department, local authorities and public bodies and advise on the changes necessary to bring practice into line with international standards.

Thus there is no body which effectively advises the Department for Education and Employment on the implications of Article 12 of the UN Convention on the Rights of the Child (requiring States to ensure that children are consulted and able to participate in decisions which affect them), nor the Home Office on the implications of the UN's 'Beijing Rules' (1987) for the administration of juvenile justice.

The responsible authorities may choose to bring their policy and practice into line, particularly if the Minister is sympathetic; but there is no independent body to advise, to encourage and to make Parliament and the public aware of the issues involved. The advice which civil service lawyers give to Ministers on conformity of proposals to international standards is largely limited to the ECHR because of the risk of challenge at the European Court of Human Rights. The focus is negative – how to avoid a legal challenge – not positive, how to ensure full compliance with obligations. Moreover, this legal advice remains confidential. Members of Parliament have no equivalent source of advice on, for instance, the extent to which it is legitimate for CCTV to infringe privacy in order to prevent or detect crime, whether new public order legislation imposes legitimate restrictions on freedom of assembly or whether statutory controls on telephone tapping provide adequate 'respect for private life'.

Secondly, there is no organisation to advise public and private bodies how to ensure that they find the right balance between protecting human rights and other policy objectives. The discrimination Commissions fulfil this important role in relation to the areas of discrimination which fall within their mandate, for instance advising employers how to achieve equality of opportunity for women. There is no body to advise similarly on what constitutes a 'fair hearing' or the avoidance of age discrimination, or whether a woman, under the right 'to found a family' should be able to use her dead husband's sperm without his consent.

Thirdly, there is no body to promote human rights education and awareness. Many feel that the principal benefit of incorporating the ECHR into UK domestic law will not be what happens in the courts but the impact it could have on public attitudes, engendering a culture of mutual rights and responsibilities. In the absence of a Human Rights Commission there would be no body to promote this change.

For many human rights there is, moreover, no independent means of investigation and enforcement available. After incorporation of the ECHR the rights it contains will be enforceable in our domestic courts but the extent to which protection is available in practice will depend on the remedies the Government chooses to provide (eg whether there is compensation) and on the availability of legal aid. There will be no specific legislative protection for many of the rights in the ECHR such as discrimination on grounds of religion (in Britain) or age, or for privacy, the right to found a family, freedom of information (until legislation is enacted) or free speech.

The public bodies which do, in effect, have some responsibility for enforcing human rights standards perform an extremely important role. Nevertheless there are significant limits to their remit and powers. Some of them are unable to investigate individual complaints and, where they do have such powers, the statutory jurisdiction may be limited (for example, to investigating maladministration causing injustice). Sometimes the body's terms of reference can be changed without reference to Parliament. Most of the bodies lack the ability or power to initiate wider independent inquiries. Sometimes the bodies' constitutional status may limit their scope for operating truly independently.

No public body is responsible for the strategic enforcement of human rights law. Thus no organisation exists which is capable of bringing or backing 'test cases' in order to clarify or reform human rights law.

In summary, this analysis suggests the need for a new body which is able to fill the gaps in protection which we have identified. It also prompts other questions. A new Human Rights Commission would replace SACHR in Northern Ireland; but what should its relationship be with the discrimination Commissions? Should some of them be merged into the new body?

ADVICE, EDUCATION AND PUBLIC PROMOTION

A key role of the Commission will be the advice it provides to Parliament, public and private bodies and to members of the public. Its emphasis could be on providing information and encouragement, promoting awareness and good practice. It should have a level of expertise which ensures that its opinion carries weight. Its advice will enable Parliament to question effectively the extent to which legislative proposals conform to the ECHR and to the UK's other international obligations, helping to ensure that new legislation does not lead to complaints and unnecessary litigation.

Individuals with a possible complaint under human rights law – particularly under the ECHR – will need advice on how to obtain redress. The Commission will have little credibility with the public if it is unable to provide this.

Public authorities and private organisations require guidance on how their practices can be made to match human rights standards, such as on privacy or equality. To meet this demand for advice, the Commission will have to undertake or commission research. Where an area of practice is causing particular concern, an inquiry may be needed.

The advice, education and promotion functions of the Commission could therefore be:

to promote public awareness
and understanding of human rights principles and their relationship to the rights and responsibilities of citizenship; eg advising the education authorities on the promotion of human rights principles within schools and colleges; use of conferences, training and the media to guide public debate on the balance to be struck between the achievement of human rights and other social objectives.

to preview legislative and policy proposals and advise Parliament and the Government
on their conformity to international human rights standards. The Commission's opinion could be appended to the notes on each Bill which are given to MPs. The Commission would thus enhance the scrutiny of draft legislation and help to ensure that it was not later subject to challenge in the courts. The Government could be required to submit its draft proposals to the Commission. It might also be required to state its reasons for ignoring advice that a particular provision would breach human rights standards.

to advise Parliament and the Government on the adequacy of existing arrangements
for the protection of human rights. The Commission could thus monitor and advise on the adequacy of the means of enforcing the incorporated ECHR, or on the division of responsibilities between the discrimination Commissions, or on the remit of the Prisons Ombudsman. It could monitor the operation of the safeguards for suspects in custody, the failure to provide reasons for refusing applications for Citizenship, or the basis of decisions to detain asylum seekers, and advise accordingly.

to advise public and private bodies
how they might comply with the European Convention and wider human rights standards, e.g. advising health authorities on the protection of privacy, local authorities on young people's access to their personal files or employers on removing age discrimination. Similarly, it might advise on the adequacy of safeguards for young people in care, on the implications of any proposed legislation to curb press intrusion into private life, or of proposed European Community directives and inter-governmental agreements (unless falling clearly within the remit of an existing body such as the Data Protection Registrar).

to advise those who believe that their human rights have been infringed
how they can seek to obtain redress. We envisage here a referral service – telling individuals where to seek assistance. We consider below the Commission's potential role in assisting individuals by investigating individual complaints or backing test cases.

to hold inquiries, conduct or commission research and publish findings
will be necessary functions if the body is to be able to provide authoritative advice as well as pursue its enforcement function (below). To this end the Commission may need the power to call for the production of documents and to summon witnesses.

ENFORCEMENT

How the Commission pursues or encourages the enforcement of human rights, particularly an incorporated ECHR, could be crucial to its effectiveness and credibility. Two broad approaches can be seen when examining the experience of the domestic discrimination Commissions and Human Rights Commissions elsewhere in the world. The first concentrates the resources, efforts and planning of the Commission on strategic enforcement of the law. Such an approach would rely on a careful analysis of the weakness or deficiencies of existing law and a planned pursuit of litigation to reform, extend or clarify legislation and policy. The second approach offers individual citizens a general complaints investigation body, receiving and considering individual grievances and seeking to obtain redress through mediation and, sometimes, adjudication of their claim.

Public interest enforcement

It can be argued that it is essential that the Commission undertake the former, a public interest enforcement role. The creation of an agency with specialist legal expertise and an interest in pursuing test cases would offer a cost-effective use of limited public resources and help to ensure that the aim of incorporating the ECHR is achieved by encouraging its rational and constructive development within UK law. Without a Commission able to contribute to the enforcement of the Convention, law will be developed by judges in a random way, depending on a lottery of individual cases. Significant public expenditure – in court time and legal aid – may then be wasted on unnecessary litigation. A Commission able to act in the public interest and accountable for doing so would help to prevent this occurring.

The Commission would need to be able to use the law in three distinct ways. First, it should have the power to give assistance to anyone pursuing a claim that their human rights have been infringed. Such assistance is given to complainants by the discrimination Commissions and enables them to support important test cases in the courts. Without it, individuals may not start proceedings or their lawyers may lack essential expertise needed to succeed in them. Many of the landmark judgments in sex equality law have been achieved by such a strategic selection and support of test cases. Such assistance would only be provided where there is an important point of general principle at stake.

Secondly, the Commission should have the power to initiate legal proceedings in its own name, permitting it to seek judicial review, for example, or to commence a class action on behalf of a number of people affected by a breach of human rights.

Thirdly, the Commission should be able to offer its expert opinion as an 'amicus', advising the court as a neutral party in proceedings brought by others. SACHR has acted in this way in a number of cases before the European Court of Human Rights.

Investigating individual complaints

Should the Commission be responsible for investigating individual complaints? It could investigate the complaint itself and seek to mediate between the complainant and the body against whom the complaint is made. Its role could extend further to an adjudication function, providing an alternative to the courts. In order to carry out even a limited investigation role, the Commission might need the power to enter premises where reasonably necessary, to call for the production of documents, and to summon witnesses.

Dealing with complaints in this way could:

- ensure that the Commission keeps in touch with public concerns and new issues as they arise
- enable it to speak with additional authority and expertise
- provide a cheaper (and perhaps quicker) means of obtaining redress than the judicial system.

Against this, there are also strong arguments:

- investigating complaints from the public would vastly increase the cost of the Commission because of the staff numbers needed to cope effectively with the likely demand.
- the complaints role could thus distort the priorities and resource allocation of the Commission, given high demand from the public and the need to meet reasonable standards of speed and thoroughness in dealing with such work. The Commission could become associated with a 'culture of complaints'. This has been the experience of the Australian Human Rights Commission. Its ability to carry out its advice function is judged to have been hampered in recent years by the overwhelming increase in its complaints handling duties.
- until the ECHR has been incorporated and its effectiveness monitored, it will not be clear whether the courts are able to provide adequate redress or whether additional means of enforcement are necessary. Nor, in relation to adjudicating complaints, will there be any domestic case law on which the Commission could base its judgments.
- the advisory service provided by the Commission would enable it to monitor the kinds of issues causing concern, albeit to a lesser extent than if it investigated complaints itself.
- some of the human rights bodies abroad are extremely influential without having any complaints investigation function, notably the Danish Center for Human Rights.

Our initial view is that the Commission should not be given a general complaints investigation function. Such a role could be added when it is clear how the existing means of individual enforcement under the ECHR are working. As a possible alternative, the feasibility of adding human rights complaints to the jurisdiction of the Local Ombudsmen and Parliamentary Commissioners for Administration could be considered.

Consulting the public

To fulfil its advisory functions the Commission would want to keep itself informed about changing public attitudes on human rights issues. There is also, however, a particular consultation exercise for which it could take responsibility – on the content of a future UK Bill of Rights. The public and interested parties will, over time, need to take a view on the adequacy of the ECHR and the potential for a more effective instrument, encompassing a wider set of rights and changing the permitted exceptions to those rights.

The expertise which the Commission will have in promoting public debate on human rights issues would make it ideally suited to this role, rather than the exercise being organised by a Government Department. The function is an important and complementary one but not essential to the Commission's viability.

International role

It would be desirable for the Commission to be able to participate at an international level in decisions on human rights standards and their enforcement. The UN urges each national Commission to cooperate in this way and the expertise which the body could share with, and learn from, its counterparts abroad would enhance its effectiveness and credibility at home. There would be no difficulty in the Commission attending such fora in an expert capacity, expressing opinions which might differ from those of Government representatives. Existing bodies such as the Data Protection Registrar have regularly been in this position and found that the differing roles of the Government and expert body are understood and respected. While such an international role is not essential, it is inexpensive and marginal in terms of staff resources; hence we include it within the recommended core functions listed below.

In summary, we suggest that the Commission's tasks could be divided into the following core functions and additional non-essential functions.

SUMMARY OF RECOMMENDED FUNCTIONS

Core functions

- to promote public awareness and acceptance of human rights principles
- to preview legislative and policy proposals and advise Parliament and the Government on their conformity to the ECHR and international standards
- to advise Parliament and the Government on the adequacy of existing arrangements for the protection of human rights and on the conformity of current policies and practices
- to advise public and private bodies how they might comply with human rights standards
- to advise those who believe that their human rights have been infringed

- to assist a complainant to seek redress through the courts by providing legal assistance or resources where there is an important point of principle at stake
- to conduct inquiries and research and to publish findings
- to initiate court proceedings to challenge legislation or policy which it believes infringes human rights standards
- to appear as amicus (expert opinion) in court proceedings
- to participate in international human rights policy-making

Non-essential functions

- to investigate general individual complaints and, where appropriate, mediate between the individual and the body against whom the complaint is made
- to adjudicate upon complaints as an alternative to their adjudication by the courts
- to conduct the consultation exercise on a future UK Bill of Rights

The Commission's constitution

How should the Commission be constituted and what should be its legal status? The chosen structure of the body will determine the extent of its independence and its accountability, its capacity to raise income and its ability to determine how that income should be spent. The UN guidelines state that the body should:

> be granted a separate and distinct legal personality of a nature which will permit it to exercise independent decision-making power. Independent legal status should be of a level sufficient to permit an institution to perform its functions without interference or obstruction from any branch of government or any public or private entity.

The necessary degree of independence and accountability could be provided by constituting the body as a corporation sole (with a single Commissioner) or corporation aggregate (with Commissioners), incorporated by Royal Charter or statute. Many public bodies are established in this way. The Commission should be made accountable to Parliament, having a duty to report annually and when requested, in practice reporting to a proposed Human Rights Select Committee. The Commission itself should come within the jurisdiction of the Parliamentary Commissioner for Administration. . .

IPPR (Sarah Spencer and Ian Bynoe), *A Human Rights Commission* (consultation paper), 1997. The ideas expressed in this paper were later developed and published in *A Human Rights Commission: The Options for Britain and Northern Ireland*, 1998.

---

59 THE OPTIONS FOR PARLIAMENTARY HUMAN
RIGHTS SCRUTINY PROCEDURES (ROBERT
BLACKBURN), 1998

A good case for establishing a parliamentary committee of human rights already existed before 1998.[1] But with the enactment of the Human Rights Act, bringing nearer the prospect of a homegrown constitutional Bill of Rights in the longer term, there are now even stronger grounds for setting up new parliamentary scrutiny procedures focused specifically upon human rights matters.

The parliamentary functions to be created

There are a number of different types of function that one or more parliamentary committees on human rights might take responsibility for. These might be usefully categorized as being:

(1) pre-legislative scrutiny;
(2) monitoring the operation of the Human Rights Act;
(3) international human rights treaty affairs; and
(4) advisory reports and ad hoc inquiries.

These functions and the work they would entail will now be considered in turn.

Pre-legislative Scrutiny

The most important function for any new procedures will be the scrutiny of legislative proposals for their compliance with the articles and jurisprudence of the European Convention on Human Rights. This is likely to be regarded as the highest priority for implementation, and will also be the most significant factor shaping the overall parliamentary scheme which emerges with respect to its new human rights work generally.

The work involved will be in the nature of a technical exercise, comparing and predicting the compatibility of the law proposed with the prospect of litigation under the European Convention on Human Rights, both in our domestic courts and before the European Court of Human Rights at

---

1 For earlier discussions of a human rights committee, see David Kinley, *The European Convention on Human Rights: Compliance without Incorporation* (Aldershot: Dartmouth, 1993); and Michael Ryle, 'Pre-legislative Scrutiny: A Prophylactic Approach to Protection of Human Rights', *Public Law*, 1994, p.192.

Strasbourg. The type of scrutiny would not extend into the merits of whether the legislation in question was desirable or not in itself, upon which diverse interpretations and ideological points of view might be adopted. Only the two chambers of Parliament as a whole, assisted in the normal way through their existing committees, would be equipped to conduct policy debates and decision-making of that kind.

Several significantly different forms and processes of legislation will have to be accommodated by whatever committee scheme of parliamentary scrutiny is devised.

Government Bills

First, there will be government primary legislation to consider for compliance with human rights standards, which consists of about 40 public bills each year.

Private Members Bills and Private Bills

Private Members Bills and Private Bills will need to be scrutinized separately, as the internal government audit procedures and the published ministerial human rights impact statement accompanying government bills, as required under section 19 of the Human Rights Act, will not apply to these types of legislation.

Statutory instruments

Third, there will be the very large quantity of secondary legislation to examine, which consists of at least 1,500 statutory instruments every year.

Remedial Orders under the Human Rights Act

Of special importance will be the special new category of Remedial Orders which may be enacted under sections 10 to 12 of the Human Rights Act as a fast-track legislative process when the government wishes to respond swiftly to a declaration of incompatibility in our domestic courts or an adverse ruling in the European Court of Human Rights.

European law-making

Finally, some consideration of human rights implications might be thought necessary with regard to European law-making. Any scrutiny arrangements thought necessary, however, will be of a very different nature to the scrutiny of domestic legislation, since the Westminster Parliament's role with respect to European legislation is limited to the expression of an opinion on Commission proposals in advance of the meeting of the Council of Ministers which is the body that decides to adopt the legislation or not.

Precisely what would be involved in carrying out the functions relating to these particular types of legislation is considered further below, together with a discussion of related procedural matters.

MONITORING THE OPERATION OF THE HUMAN RIGHTS ACT

Labour's 1996 consultation paper *Bringing Rights Home* proposed that a new parliamentary committee on human rights 'would have a continuing responsibility to monitor the operation of the Human Rights Act'.[2] The scope of a continuing function of this kind is less than clear, and could be drawn very widely. Such a function would include periodic general reviews of the Act, gauging the cumulative impact of incorporation of the European Convention on Human Rights upon the substance of British domestic law as well as upon the administration of the courts and litigation before the Court of Human Rights at Strasbourg. The committee might consider it worthwhile to initiate separate special inquiries into aspects of particular importance or significance to the working of the Act, such as the courts' use of its powers under section 4 to make 'declarations of incompatibility' between statutory provisions and human rights, and questions of citizens' access to justice in the enforcement of their human rights. The committee would no doubt seek to identify areas for improvement, where the Act was perceived by members as working less effectively than it might, and bring forward recommendations for action.

There is also the question whether some form of parliamentary examination is necessary or desirable into the question of compatibility between the ECHR and all *pre-existing* measures of parliamentary legislation enacted prior to the Human Rights Act 1998. This would be a major function of its own, which otherwise would fall to the usual law reform bodies to perform, notably the Law Commission. Without some extra-judicial examination of this large subject, future complaints of human rights violation founded on pre-1998 laws will still need to be resolved through the normal, costly process of litigation.

INTERNATIONAL HUMAN RIGHTS TREATY AFFAIRS

Parliamentary scrutiny of governmental decision-making in the field of international human rights treaties would have two points of focus. The first would be to scrutinize whether the present obligations of the UK government under the terms of the international instruments to which it was a party were being properly carried out to the satisfaction of the Westminister Parliament. This would have a wider remit than simply the European Convention on Human Rights (a treaty enactment of members belonging to the Council of Europe) and most certainly include the International Covenant on Civil and Political Rights and the International Covenant on Economic, Social and Cultural Rights (both being treaty enactments of the United Nations). One issue of recent controversy has been the failure of the

2 At p.12.

UK government to consult Parliament prior to carrying out its reporting obligations to the United Nations Human Rights Committee as required under the terms of the ICCPR.[3] Similar reporting obligations are owed under a number of other international agreements to which the UK is a member, such as the International Labour Organisation and the Committee on the Elimination of Discrimination against Women. Any new human rights scrutiny procedures, therefore, might be expected to involve these draft Reports being submitted to Parliament for debate, preceded by the examination and preparation of a report by a specialist committee on the subject.

An important second task for scrutiny procedures of treaty matters raises more fundamental issues governing the relationship between the Executive and Parliament. To what extent should Parliament be consulted, and possibly control, the treaty-making powers in general which the government possesses under the royal prerogative?[4] For the purpose of this paper which is concerned only with international human rights agreements, it is sufficient illustration to mention that in 1950 when the UK government agreed and ratified the European Convention on Human Rights itself, no parliamentary approval was sought or required, and no consultation or debate on the subject ever took place. This was similarly the case when the UK government ratified the ICCPR in 1976. More recently, Protocol 11 to the ECHR, reforming litigation procedures at Strasbourg and creating an enlarged Court of Human Rights, was ratified by the UK government in 1995 without any parliamentary scrutiny at all. There is now widespread agreement that Parliament should be involved in the process of human rights treaty-making and amendment, and any new scrutiny arrangements that emerge as a result are likely to involve a specialist committee for the purpose. Amendments to the articles of the European Convention on Human Rights will assume even greater significance after 1998, following our incorporation of the Convention under the terms of the Human Rights Act.

ENQUIRIES AND ADVISORY REPORTS

The Labour government's white paper *Rights Brought Home* in October 1997 said that 'the new Committee might conduct enquiries on a range of human rights issues relating to the Convention, and produce reports so as to assist the Government and Parliament in deciding what action to take'. The following month, when presenting the Human Rights Bill to the House of Lords for second reading debate, the Lord Chancellor Lord Irvine further stated that,[5]

3 See Lord Lester, 'Taking Human Rights Seriously', Ch. 4 in Robert Blackburn and James Busuttil (eds) *Human Rights for the 21st Century*, 1997.
4 The Labour Party proposed the power to ratify treaties should be transferred to Parliament in its policy statement *A New Agenda for Democracy: Labour's Proposals for Constitutional Reform*, 1993, p. 33.
5 HL Deb., 3 November 1997, col. 1234.

It would be a natural focus for the increased interest in human rights issues which Parliament will inevitably take when we have brought rights home. It could, for example, not only keep the protection of human rights under review, but could also be in the forefront of public education and consultation on human rights. It could receive written submissions and hold public hearings at a number of locations across the country. It could be in the van [sic] of the promotion of a human rights culture across the country.

As elaborated upon here by the Lord Chancellor, such a function would be unprecedented in Westminster terms. The public workload involved would be potentially vast, and the notion of a Westminster select committee travelling around the country holding public hearings seems rather unreal. These political utterances may be explicable in terms of the government trying to combat any disappointment that it failed to include the creation of a Human Rights Commission in its white paper and Human Rights Bill. For it is widely believed that a Human Rights Commission should indeed be established to facilitate the working of the Human Rights Act and that among its most important functions would be the promotion of greater public awareness and education about human rights matters, undertaking inquires into subjects of special concern, and constituting an expert independent advisory body for subjects referred to it by government and parliamentary bodies.[6]

Nonetheless, with or without a Human Rights Commission, there would be advantages to including enquiries and advisory reports on human rights affairs within the terms of reference of a suitable parliamentary body. To some extent this would overlap with the work of the House of Commons Home Affairs Committee, particularly as (post-Human Rights Act) it is likely to adopt the human rights principles of the ECHR as a de facto set of principles by which to interpret aspects of its work and the criteria to be applied to government administration and policy, not only in relation to the Home Office but also the responsibilities covered by the Lord Chancellor's department. But the new committee entrusted with this wide-ranging role could be relied upon to proceed by way of complementing rather than duplicating other existing forms of parliamentary enquiry, and to undertake enquiries where it felt that other forms of parliamentary attention to some issues of human rights importance did not exist or else had failed.

The committee structure on human rights affairs

Precisely how any or all of these new human rights functions might be carried out raises many practical issues, including questions of workload, compatibility of diverse forms of scrutiny or enquiry, and the pooling

---

6 See Standing Order 151, (1997) HC 400; and generally J.A.G. Griffith and Michael Ryle, *Parliament: Practice, Functions and Procedures*, 1989, pp. 444–5.

together of expertise for particular types of task. Whatever new form of human rights committee structure is adopted will have to take into account the organization of other existing forms of parliamentary scrutiny.

THREE OPTIONS TO CONSIDER

There are a number of ways in which the new human rights committee functions might be structured, most of which would work satisfactorily for immediate purposes. Three general approaches might be identified as follows.

Option One

The new human rights functions could be allocated among already existing parliamentary committees. This would be particularly feasible if, at least initially, the innovation concentrated on pre-legislative scrutiny for compliance with the ECHR.

The two principal contenders for taking on these new legislative responsibilities would be the Joint Committee on Statutory Instruments and the House of Lords Select Committee on Delegated Powers and Deregulation. Between them, these two bodies already sift through secondary and primary legislation respectively, and their terms of reference could be extended to include questions of human rights compliance. The enlarged workload for these committees would almost certainly involve the creation of one or more sub-committees to either or both of them. Additionally, with respect to special category of remedial orders under the Human Rights Act 1998, responsibility for detailed scrutiny and report to the two Houses could be passed to the present committees that deal with deregulation orders under the Deregulation and Contracting Out Act 1994, namely the Select Committee on Delegated Powers and Deregulation in the House of Lords and the Deregulation Committee in the House of Commons.

The non-legislative functions mooted in Labour's policy documents could be allocated to the relevant departmentally related Select Committees in the House of Commons. Thus responsibility for monitoring the operation of the Act and undertaking enquries and advisory reports might be undertaken by the Home Affairs Committee (having existing responsibility for administration and policy with respect to constitutional and judicial affairs), and scrutiny of international affairs could be taken on by the Foreign Affairs Committee or a new sub-committee specially created for the purpose.

Option Two

A second, more ambitious option would be to conduct a wider reorganization of pre-legislative select committees, integrating human rights into whatever new scheme of arrangements is adopted.

The two main existing bodies affected would, again, be the Joint Committee on Statutory Instruments and the House of Lords Select Committee on Delegated Powers and Deregulation. The most likely rationale for any such reorganization would be a streamlining of the special pre-legislative scrutiny processes, distinguishing between primary and secondary legislation.

So, for example, (i) the Committee on Delegated Powers and Deregulation might be wound up (and so too the Deregulation Committee in the House of Commons), (ii) a new joint committee on primary legislation created, to deal with human rights and delegated powers, and (iii) the existing Joint Committee on Statutory Instruments could have its terms of reference extended to include human rights and deregulation orders. The resulting two new joint committees would each need to establish a sub-committee structure to cope with their large overall workload.

Non-legislative human rights functions could be allocated either as in option one, or alternatively a new joint committee on human rights, or separate committees in each House, might possibly be created for general monitoring and advisory purposes at home and with respect to international treaties.

Option Three

A more straightforward approach would be simply to establish a new Select Committee on Human Rights to discharge most or all of the functions currently being proposed by Labour.

This could be in the form of (a) a single joint committee of both Houses, (b) two committees established in the Commons and Lords respectively, or (c) some structure combining both joint and independent elements for the purposes of carrying out functions of a different nature. Thus if each House contributed eleven members to a joint committee, they could deliberate jointly for the purposes of reporting on technical matters (notably in offering expert advice on legislative compliance with the jurisprudence of the ECHR) and meet separately on matters of a political or policy-orientated nature (such as in offering opinions on the merits of government policy at home or internationally).

EVALUATION

In order to evaluate these three different options, one needs to consider the existing work of the Joint Committee on Statutory Instruments and of the House of Lords Select Committee on Delegated Powers and Deregulation. This is because, first, they are the principal pre-legislative committees already existing at Westminster, and also, second, they have some analagous procedures which will be of relevance to whatever scheme of parliamentary committee on human rights which is eventually adopted. Also requiring consideration is whether any foreign legislatures have lessons for the structure and working of a British parliamentary committee on human rights.

The Joint Committee on Statutory Instruments

This parliamentary committee comprises seven members from each House, selected by their own respective Committees of Selection, with the chair being taken by an opposition MP. The Committee is empowered by each House to consider all statutory instruments (SIs) and draft SIs which are required to be presented to Parliament (as well as some which are not).

The committee does not consider the merits of a SI per se; rather, its job is to check that the issue and drafting of the SI has conformed to certain procedures or principles. In other words, its scrutiny process is essentially a technical process, not a policy-orientated one. There are specific grounds in the committee's terms of reference by which it may decide to draw an instrument to the special attention of Parliament.[16] These include, for example, 'unusual or unexpected' uses of a ministerial power, where the SI is beyond the scope originally envisaged in the Act conferring the power to make order, where the effect of the SI is unclear, or where it has public revenue implications. Formally the committee lacks the power to send for persons, papers and records, but in practice it liaises closely with the government department responsible for preparing the SI. Before reporting to each House, the committee invites the department to given an explanation on the matter of concern. As a joint committee, it was created in 1972 in substitution for two earlier separate committees, one in each House, which according to Erskine May it was felt had 'produced defects and anomalies in overall parliamentary control'.[7]

In the context of the proposal for new human rights scrutiny arrangements, therefore, it would be easy in theory to extend the grounds upon which this committee reviews all statutory instruments laid before Parliament to include reviewing such secondary legislation for compatibility with the articles and jurisprudence of the European Convention on Human Rights. This would undoubtedly add a major burden to the work of the committee, but this might be supported by the appointment of an additional legal adviser to the committee who was expert in human rights law. Another possibility is that the committee establishes its own special sub-committee on human rights. The Joint Committee on Statutory Instruments already possesses the power to appoint its own sub-committees, and this would allow it to recruit other suitably qualified MPs and peers who do not sit on the parent committee to be involved in the work. Certainly, if a distinction is to be drawn in scrutiny arrangements between primary and secondary legislation, then prima facie it would seem to make every sense to involve the Joint Committee on Statutory Instruments.

House of Lords Select Committee on Delegated Powers and Deregulation

A second existing committee which should be considered as a possible recipient of some human rights scrutiny function is the Delegated Powers

7 Erskine May, *Parliamentary Practice*, 1989, p. 551.

Scrutiny Committee in the House of Lords. This body was set up by peers in 1992–3 in direct response to growing unease about a significant recent increase in use being made of delegated legislation by the government.[8]

The committee's terms of reference are 'to report whether the provisions of any Bill inappropriately delegate legislative power; or whether they subject the exercise of legislative power to an inappropriate degree of Parliamentary scrutiny'.[9] It also has functions with respect to the scrutiny of deregulation orders, with some lessons for human rights scrutiny procedures, which are discussed separately below. It is the responsibility of the committee to consider all bills presented to the House of Lords and, where an enabling clause is found, to undertake an examination of the proposal and report on its desirability and drafting. The Lords have proceeded to select for this high-profile committee eight widely respected parliamentarians, some with senior political or legal experience (currently, for example, Lords Merlyn-Rees, Dahrendorf and its chairman Lord Alexander of Weedon). Although it has been in existence for only five years, the committee has already acquired considerable influence and is generally regarded as one of the most successful parliamentary innovations of the last two decades. Its views and recommendations are virtually always raised in the House and accepted by the government ministers concerned, leading to proposed amendments being carried. One significant example of its influence was in the case of the Education Bill in 1993–4, which as originally drafted allowed the Education Secretary to prescribe in the future by way of delegation legislation the kinds of activity upon which student unions could spent the financial support they received from the state. This enabling clause was withdrawn altogether, following a report of the committee that, 'The House may regard as inappropriate the delegation of legislative power to interfere with the freedom of association of students'.[10]

Significantly it was a question of human rights therefore that particularly served to sway the opinion of the committee that the proposed statutory provision was 'inappropriate'. The quasi-constitutional purpose of the Delegated Powers Scrutiny Committee is clearly recognized in the Second Chamber and by the committee itself. One of its earliest reports commenced with the words, 'Democracy is not only about the election of politicians; it is about setting limtis to their powers'.[11] As a parliamentary body that already sifts through all primary legislative proposals, therefore, and one which already conducts lines of inquiry bearing some semblance to that of a

8 See the remarks of Lord Ripon who first put forward the proposal for this committee, HL Deb., 14 February 1990, Col. 1407f.

9 First Report of the Select Committee on the Procedure of the House, 1992–3, HL 11; HL Deb., 10 November 1992, col. 91. See also C. Himsworth, 'The Delegated Powers Scrutiny Committee', *Public Law*, 1995, 34.

10 12th Report of the Select Committee on the Scrutiny of Delegated Powers, 1993–4, HL 90, para. 13.

11 Ibid., para.1.

constitutional watchdog, the Delegated Powers Scrutiny Committee – or some modified committee replacing it – would be well placed to assume terms of reference with respect to pre-legislative scrutiny on grounds of compatibility with the ECHR...

Conclusions and prospects for the form of the committee(s)

The precise form of committee structure for carrying out the new human rights scrutiny functions could operate effectively in a number of different ways for immediate purposes. There are some practical considerations to take into account, however, before assessing the likely or best way in which to construct the new committee or committees. The end result is less likely to be determined by abstract logic than a mixture of the personal preferences of the government ministers involved, the degree of respect paid to existing traditions, a desire to minimize administrative inconvenience and financial cost, and the effectiveness with which the Cabinet harmonizes its constitutional and parliamentary reform programme generally.

The initiation of new parliamentary procedures addressed at human rights could be incremental. In other words, the development of human rights scrutiny procedures at Westminster could be introduced as a building-block exercise. Parliamentary institutions in the UK tend to prefer a process of experiment and evolution before setting up for themselves any permanent major innovation. There is no necessity for all these human rights scrutiny functions to be introduced at Westminster simultaneously straightaway. The most immediate function to be addressed is that of pre-legislative scrutiny. Once such work had been seen to be carried out successfully, further functions with respect to reviewing the operation of the Human Rights Act, carrying out enquires and advisory reports, and examining international and treaty obligations could be added. However, it should be borne in mind that any ad hoc approach which failed to consider how the overall pattern of parliamentary scrutiny might best be developed in the future (and in the context of other actual or planned reforms) could end up as obstructionist to later developments...

The core work of the new human rights scrutiny procedures will almost certainly be undertaken by a joint committee of both Houses, at least initially. This will be so simply because the Labour leadership appears to have attached itself to the idea. Joint committees, which in the past have been relatively rare creatures at Westminster, seem set to become a mechanism favoured by the new Labour administration. Since May 1997 the usual joint committees on statutory instruments and consolidation bills have been established, as well as the new ad hoc joint committee on parliamentary privilege, and another joint committee has been proposed by Labour as the means for examining long-term reform of the House of Lords.[12] Although a reformed Second Chamber is likely to take on an elevated role with respect

---

12 The proposal was included both in Labour's 1997 general election manifesto and in the preceding Labour–Liberal Democrat Joint Consultative Committee Report on Constitutional Reform, 1997.

to human rights in the longer term,[13] for the time being MPs are unlikely to want to abrogate their involvement in a parliamentary development widely perceived as being of major significance. Furthermore, an added advantage of MPs' participation in the scrutiny process, even if of a less independent and expert character than that of peers selected for the task, will help foster the Commons' application of human rights principles to be applied in their work generally. In terms of establishing the new scrutiny procedures, the Commons' shared ownership of the committee will undoubtedly add to the strength, public profile and credibility generally of the procedures themselves.

There are some practical advantages in a joint committee too. One is that a joint committee is able to provide one single source of authoritative advice, for example on whether proposed legislation does or does not comply with the jurisprudence of the ECHR. Conflicting expert advice from committees in each House would give rise to great confusion and loss of confidence among the ranks of ordinary MPs and peers. It was for these reasons that in 1973 the two earlier committees on statutory instruments which had existed separately in the Commons and Lords were merged into the present single joint committee. Another working advantage is that a joint committee on legislation can commence its work at an early stage, regardless of the House in which a bill or draft order is first introduced. If, for example, the House of Lords Delegated Powers Scrutiny Committee was enlarged and given responsibility for ensuring compatibility of domestic legislation with the ECHR, most measures would pass through all their stages in the House of Commons before being subjected to its expert examination and report.

The human rights committee(s) at work

Pre-legislative Procedures

The most problematic issue in constructing the operation of the new scrutiny arrangements will be the effectiveness with which the new committees are permitted to examine legislative proposals and report on them to Parliament prior to final approval and enactment. However, in fact, many of the existing procedures and practices now operating with respect to the existing Delegated Powers Scrutiny Committee and the Joint Committee on Statutory Instruments can be adapted for use by the parliamentary committee (or committees) on human rights in their scrutiny of primary and secondary legislative proposals.

The committee with responsibility for primary legislation would need to examine all bills and report to both Houses on matters of significance for

---

13 See the author's discussion of House of Lords reform in Robert Blackburn and Raymond Plant (eds), *Constitutional Reform: The Labour Government's Constitutional Reform Agenda*, 1999, Ch. 1.

compliance with the terms of the ECHR. The practice of the existing Delegated Powers Scrutiny Committee is that its legal advisor sifts through all bills as they are presented to the House and a preliminary note is prepared on those measures to which s/he believes the committee's attention should be drawn. That committee then aims to conduct and complete its enquiry, usually between the second reading and committee stages of the bill concerned, so that its report can instruct peers as it scrutinized the legislation clause by clause in the House. Before its report is prepared, the committee commonly contacts the government department concerned and offers an opportunity for the government to present its explanation or views on any matter of concern to the committee. These practices could also suitably be adopted in the committee work of the new human rights scrutiny arrangements.

With respect to government bills, this scrutiny by the human rights committee would not be a mandatory part of the primary legislative process as such; rather, the committee should determine for itself which measures it should enquire into and report upon. Different considerations arise, however, with respect to private members bills and private bills which, as already mentioned, will have been presented to Parliament without the benefit of the government's own internal human rights scrutiny process and without any consequential accompanying human rights impact assessment statement. Analogous to government bills, it might come to be regarded as good practice for MPs to include some statement about human rights in the explanatory memorandum of the bill, though without recourse to expert human rights law advice this is unlikely to be regarded as adequate. There is a case, therefore, for the proposed new committee to become a necessary part of the legislative process under standing orders of each House, to the effect that all private members bills and private bills must, as a mandatory requirement after receiving a second reading, be examined for human rights implications and reported on by the human rights committee before proceeding further to the next stage of a standing committee.

With regard to the future scrutiny of normal SIs for human rights compliance, there is no reason for departing from the general present pattern of proceedings followed by the existing Committee on Statutory Instruments. The usual process could continue of, first, the committee's legal advisor sifting through all SIs and draft SIs in order to draw the attention of the committee to any significant matters; second, the committee examining the issues raised and conducting an exchange of information or views with the government department concerned; and third, preparing a report for both Houses. One procedural matter might be strengthened, however. Currently, it is a rule in the House of Lords, but not the Commons, that no debate should be held on an affirmative SI unless the Joint Committee on Statutory Instruments has reported on it.[14] With the enlarged powers of the new proposed committee on secondary legislation, a similar rule should apply to the House of Commons.

14 Standing Order 70, HL (1994) 15.

The question was raised earlier in this article whether European law-making should be made subject to any special procedures operating at Westminster. Since the Westminster Parliament is not the legislative body in question and its role is limited to advising the UK minister and issuing reports prior to external decision-making by the European Commission and Council of Ministers, the grounds for extending parliamentary scrutiny procedures in this respect are less pertinent than with respect to the other forms of legislation already considered. Furthermore, the existing Commons' Committee on European Legislation and Lords' Committee and Sub-Committees on the European Communities are already adequately equipped to take on board express human rights factors in their work, particularly Sub-Committee E of the Lords' Committee which deals with questions of law and institutions. Any problems picked up in proposed European directives or other measures with respect to human rights compliance could be reported upon to the House, and where necessary taken further by the UK minister or human rights committee(s) given responsibility for international human rights purposes.

Special Procedures with respect to Remedial Orders under the Human Rights Act

Parliamentary scrutiny procedures with regard to remedial orders to be enacted under the Human Rights Act raise special factors for consideration. One distinctive feature of the Human Rights Act is to provide a fast-track procedure under section 10 for changing legislation in response to a 'declaration of incompatibility' by the UK courts or to an adverse ruling in the European Court of Human Rights. This fast-track procedure will be desirable when speedy action is necessary to redress some individual or minority grievance of a serious nature, though in some cases the existing prerogative powers at the disposal of the Home Secretary may be sufficient to provide an immediate remedy.

It is important to emphasize as a preliminary observation that this fast-track legislative procedure should be regarded by ministers and parliamentarians as an exception to the normal process by which rectification of UK law for compliance with the Convention is made. It should not become simply a more administratively convenient and less time-consuming way of changing human rights law. The government should normally take positive action in response to adverse judicial rulings either at home or in Strasbourg by presenting a Bill to Parliament in the usual way, being subject to established parliamentary scrutiny arrangements.

The fast-track procedures in the Act provide for a draft statutory instrument (a 'remedial order') to be laid before Parliament 60 days prior to an affirmative resolution being voted upon in each House to bring the measure into effect. This single-stage of parliamentary approval is therefore substantially less extensive than the various stages and length of time devoted to government Bills. Yet the nature and importance of the legislation involved may be substantial in terms of our constitutional law and human rights. Furthermore, the Act contains a 'Henry VIII' clause under which it is possible for these orders to amend or repeal primary Acts of Parliament where the minister considers it appropriate.[15]

The architects of whatever new scrutiny arrangements are put in place will not need reminding that human rights law is concerned with striking an appropriate balance between conflicting individual rights or between particular rights and the national interest. This sometimes in practice involves the imposition of restrictions and the 'levelling-down' of individual rights. Emergency or urgent legislation in the past has not infrequently been concerned specifically with implementing such restrictions upon individual rights. It is therefore particularly important that parliamentary scrutiny procedures are effective in safeguarding against rushed legislation which may have wider implications for human rights beyond the different kinds of 'urgency' which might exist. If – as is the intention of the Human Rights Act – the courts are to refer matters of human rights violation to Parliament for legislative action, then the two Houses must have adequate procedures which provide for their in-depth consideration of the matter.

The way which the House of Lords Delegated Powers Scrutiny Committee and the House of Commons Deregulation Committee presently conduct their business with respect to the scrutiny of deregulation orders has some relevance to future parliamentary committee work in examining human rights remedial orders. This is particularly with regard to how special procedures can be evolved which *guarantee* that an effective scrutiny process has in fact been conducted prior to the enactment taking place. In 1994 the Deregulation and Contracting Out Act was passed which empowers ministers to make orders by way of statutory instrument amending or repealing any enactment which imposes unnecessary burdens on businesses or individuals in their commercial activities. An 'enactment' for this purpose was defined to include not only subordinate legislation but also Acts of Parliament. In other words, the 1994 Act contained a wide-ranging 'Henry VIII' clause, similar to the power to make remedial orders under the Human Rights Act, allowing statutory instruments to vary primary legislation. As a result, on the grounds that this power in the 1994 Act was contrary to normal constitutional wisdom, special consultation and scrutiny procedures were included in the Act over and above the normal process whereby an Order or draft Order is laid before each House for approval by means of a single resolution (as distinct from the various readings and stages through which primary legislation must pass).

Under the procedures contained in the 1994 Act with respect to deregulation orders, four mandatory stages are involved in the parliamentary process of scrutiny. These comprise (i) consultation with interested parties, (ii) preparation of explanatory memoranda, (iii) an extended period for parliamentary consideration, and (iv) an obligation to take any report of the

15 Schedule 2, para. 1(2)(a).

Lords' Delegated Powers Scrutiny Committee and/or Commons' Deregulation Committee into account before a draft order is presented for approval in each House. Section 3 of the 1994 Act specifies the process of consultation to be followed by the minister before presenting his draft order to Parliament, including that he 'consult such organisations as appear to him to be representative of interests substantially affected by his proposals'. The same section also specifies that when he presents the document containing his proposals to Parliament, he must accompany it with details relating to seven specified matters, including the rationale behind the proposal, its financial implications, and the nature of the representations he has received. Section 4 then lays down a period of 60 days in which Parliament has time in which to examine and scrutinise the minister's proposal. Finally, section 4 provides that 'the Minister concerned shall have regard to any representations made during the period for Parliamentary consideration and, in particular, to any resolution or report of, or of any committee of, either House of Parliament with regard to the document'. During the parliamentary passage of the Human Rights Bill, pressure from human rights groups and parliamentarians managed to secure some highly desirable amendments to the original form of the government's Bill, which was assisted by the precedent of how deregulation orders are dealt with.[16] Thus under Schedule 2 of the final version of the Bill, as enacted, there are now procedures for receiving representations, for explanatory memoranda accompanying draft orders, and for extended periods of time up to 120 days in which parliamentary scrutiny is to be conducted (rather than the 40 days which normally applies to statutory instruments).

However, the Human Rights Act still fails to institutionalize any committee into its procedures for scrutinising remedial orders. Accordingly, when the new committee arrangements on human rights are established, some amendments to the Act will be needed, and also some changes in the Standing Orders of both Houses. With respect to scrutiny of deregulation orders, Standing Orders of both Houses serve to strengthen a 'scrutiny reserve' over deregulation orders. Thus in the House of Commons, SO 141 requires the Deregulation Committee to report on every draft order not more than fifteen sitting days after the draft order was laid before the House, and where the Committee recommends that a draft order should not be approved, SO 18 provides that no motion to approve the draft order shall

16 An earlier draft of this paper was circulated to MPs and ministers prior to the House of Commons Committee Stage of the Human Rights Bill, and it formed the basis for representations by Liberty, Justice, Institute for Public Policy Research, Charter 88 and the Human Rights Incorporation Project on the need to substantially extend the remedial order procedure offered in the original Bill and to set up a human rights committee. Subsequently virtually all of the scrutiny procedures proposed in that earlier paper (dealing with e.g. the consultation process, explanatory statements and extended periods for consideration) were accepted, stopping short of creating a human rights committee simultaneously with enactment of the Bill. For the form of the original Bill see Doc. 40B.

be made unless the House has previously resolved to disagree with the Committee's report. In the House of Lords, SO 70 prohibits any resolution to affirm a draft deregulation orders until the Delegated Powers Scrutiny Committee has laid its report before the House, and SO 38 provides that any motion relating a report from the committee will be given precedence in the day's order paper over a motion to approve the draft order. Similar procedures to those which apply in the case of deregulation orders should be followed with respect to remedial orders enacted under the terms of the Human Rights Act. The new Standing Orders will need to ensure that the pre-legislative human rights committee has completed its work and presented a report to both Houses before the remedial order in question is debated and approved.

COMPOSITION AND POWERS OF THE COMMITTEE(S)

Less complex procedures to be settled will include matters of membership, support staff and the powers of the committee(s) to take evidence and appoint sub-committees. The importance of the legal adviser to any committee dealing with subject-matter of this nature cannot be over-emphasized. His or her role as a competent and reliable expert in human rights jurisprudence will be essential to the authoritative working of the committee(s), and the existing method of public appointment should be reviewed to see if any more professional or proactive procedures are desirable in order to ensure the recruitment of persons of first-rate ability for the job. Though the authorities in each House will handle personnel matters, the committee(s) in question should possess the power to remove, replace and appoint whomsoever they wish to work for them. The new committee(s) should be given the power to appoint sub-committees (as currently possessed by both the House of Lords Delegated Powers Scrutiny Committee and Joint Committee on Statutory Instruments), and in conducting enquiries it or they should be vested through Standing Orders with the power to send for persons, papers and records (currently possessed by the Delegated Powers Scrutiny Committee but not the Statutory Instruments Committee).

Some common characteristics of joint committees are worth citing if, as seems probable, this form of scrutiny does become the basis for some or all of the new human rights arrangements. Joint committees are composed of two groups, MPs and peers, each selected from the House from which they are drawn. A joint committee is in the nature of an inter-House conference, with each group being empowered to act according to the order and authority of their own House. One House cannot enlarge the powers of the joint committee unilaterally; to do so requires the agreement of both Houses. Depending on how the work of the committee is allocated, each of the two groups might meet independently, in advance of joint meetings or separately altogether for some purposes, and each group will possess its own clerk and have a de facto chairman distinct from the joint committee chairperson.

Parliamentary implementation and a Bill of Rights

The implementation of the new committee(s) on human rights should take into account the desirability of harmonizing arrangements with Labour's reform programme generally, both in its immediate and future objectives. So, for example, the long-term objective of both the Labour Party and the Liberal Democrats of a homegrown Bill of Rights should be born in mind. In *A New Agenda for Democracy: Labour's Proposals for Constitutional Reform*, Labour publicly backed the development of a Bill of Rights once incorporation of the ECHR had taken place and been seen to operate effectively: 'The incorporation of the European Convention on Human Rights is a necessary first step, but it is not a substitute for our own written Bill of Rights.' A Bill of Rights of this kind would carry major implications for Parliament, particularly since it is likely to involve some qualified form of entrenchment for the document in order to protect its articles from erosion by later ordinary statutes. Such entrenchment, in turn, would almost certainly mean that special legislative procedures and scrutiny arrangements would be desirable for the amendment or emergency derogation from its provisions. Whatever committee arrangements are put in place now should point in the direction of those which can be adapted for the purposes of a UK Bill of Rights.

The future role of a reformed House of Lords is another closely associated factor. The forthcoming changes to the Lords promised by the Labour government can only properly proceed upon the basis of some new statement or re-definition of the future work and functions of the reformed Second Chamber which are most likely to involve some elevated role with respect to constitutional and human rights affairs.[17] This, therefore, makes it all the more important that the House of Lords plays an essential role in whatever scrutiny arrangements are now put in place. In this context, it is worth observing how the memorandum cited above, co-authored by Lord Irvine, stressed that the Second Chamber should perform an essential role in any new human rights scrutiny procedures, as follows: 'We agree that it would be desirable for the House of Commons to devise procedures of its own or to join with our House in undertaking the work. However, it seems to us to be work which is, in any event, well suited to the interests and concerns of the House of Lords and to its constitutional role.'[18]

Edited extract from Robert Blackburn, 'A Parliamentary Committee on Human Rights', in Robert Blackburn and Raymond Plant (eds), *Constitutional Reform: The Labour Government's Constitutional Reform Agenda*, Longman, 1999.

17 Supra, note 13.
18 At para. 9.

CHAPTER 6

SOVEREIGNTY, THE JUDICIARY AND A BILL OF RIGHTS

(A)

THE JUDICIARY AS GUARDIANS OF FUNDAMENTAL RIGHTS

---

60   SIR WILLIAM WADE QC REJECTS THE
ARGUMENT THAT A BILL OF RIGHTS WOULD
POLITICIZE THE JUDICIARY, 1980

'POLITICISING THE JUDICIARY'

Whenever there is discussion of any extension of judicial review the objection is raised that it will bring the judges into politics. We must, it is said, at all costs avoid a politicised judiciary. I have never found it easy to give weight to this argument in its context, which is now usually that of a Bill of Rights. For as with policy, so with politics. The judges are already immersed in it, and have no hope of getting out of it. Books, articles and letters in the newspapers analyse their education and social backgrounds, accuse them of political prejudice, call their neutrality a pretence, and insinuate bias because, in selected instances, plaintiffs with bad cases lose them. The judges in the *Tameside* and *Laker* cases are said to have been motivated not by the need to control arbitrariness but by their aversion to certain political policies (Griffith, *The Politics of the Judiciary*, 3rd ed., p. 232). The fact that all this is accompanied by much misrepresentation is neither here nor there. The reality is that the judges are under a barrage of political fire. They are constantly having to decide cases which involve politics as well as law, some of which I have criticised myself – but in none of which would I accuse any one of bias or insincerity. That, again, is neither here nor there. The simple fact is that, like every one else, judges live in a world in which brickbats of all kinds are flying in all directions.

Yet among the judges themselves the fear of politicisation is strong. Lord Denning, not normally to be found among the timorous souls, said in a speech in the House of Lords that if judges were given power to overthrow Acts of Parliament they would become politicised, their appointments would be based on political grounds, and their reputation would suffer accordingly. He added:

One has only to see, in the great Constitutions of the United States of America and of India, the conflicts which arise from time to time between the judges and the legislature. I hope we shall not have such conflicts in this country.

This was one of Lord Denning's reasons for opposing the enactment of the European Convention in the form of a British Bill of Rights. In a later debate on the same subject the same anxiety induced Lord Diplock and Lord Morris of Borth-y-Gest to oppose it likewise. But other eminent judges think differently, and in the same debate Lord Hailsham made an effective reply, saying:

> We are seriously asked to believe that something awful is going to happen to us if we follow the example of nearly every country in the world.

Then, instancing some of the more sensational judicial exploits, he said of the opposing judges:

> They are under the curious illusion that the judges are not already in politics. Lord Diplock, as one of the authors of the *Anisminic* decision, practically abolished an Act of Parliament about the Foreign Compensation Commission. What about Gouriet? ... What about the Laker dispute? How about the Tameside education dispute? What about the decision invalidating Mr. Roy Jenkins' policy on wireless licences? How about the various decisions of this House and the Court of Appeal on the Race Relations Act? And what about their recent decisions on the trade union legislation? ... If they [the judges] assume jurisdiction they are in politics; if they decline jurisdiction they are in politics. All they can hope to be is impartial ...

This is a graphic and rhetorical version of the point which I made prosaically at the beginning of this lecture, when I stressed the wide range of alternative policies between which judges have to choose. If their primary object was to keep out of politics, they would have had to surrender to the executive in all the cases mentioned by Lord Hailsham and in many others. They would be confined to the literal interpretation of Acts of Parliament purporting to give ministers unfettered discretion, and the development of administrative law would be impossible. The law would be back in the shameful position in which it languished 30 years ago.

And why, to take up Lord Denning's point, should judges be horrified at the prospect of having to judge the constitutionality of Acts of Parliament, if they should be called upon to do so under a new Bill of Rights or a new constitutional settlement as advocated by Lord Scarman and Lord Hailsham? This is a primary function of the judiciary in any country which has a proper constitution. By a proper constitution I mean one in which no one organ has unlimited power and in which there is legal machinery to prevent violation. The Lords of Appeal, when they sit in the Privy Council, are very familiar with this activity in interpreting the constitutions of countries of the Commonwealth, and I do not think that any one has complained that it has politicised them. If the abortive Scotland Act 1978 had not been rejected in the referendum, they would have had to sit in judgment on the validity of Acts of the Scottish Assembly, quite probably in situations where different parties were in power in England and Scotland and political tension was high. If they could face this with equanimity, they could equally well face the responsibilities of a constitutional court as suggested by Lord Scarman. One of the reasons why there is so much dissatisfaction with the constitution, and why there is so much discussion of the need for a Bill of Rights, is that its primary proposition, the sovereignty of Parliament, assigns a subservient part to the judiciary. It is like a game without an umpire. Consequently the judiciary do not make the contribution to public affairs which in other countries is expected of them and is taken for granted.

It is understandable that judges may prefer the quiet life of subordination and non-involvement. But there are dangers in that which to my mind are graver than those which they fear as potential constitutional guardians. They are driven, as we have seen, to devious reasoning of the *Anisminic* type in order to evade statutory injustice. They must invent imaginary restrictions and read them freely into Acts of Parliament if they are to develop a satisfactory administrative law. Although in the present period they are doing this successfully, it involves just the same conflict between judiciary and legislature as Lord Denning wishes to avoid. In fact no judge has done more than he to accept the challenge and to dramatise the issues. Bearing in mind the relapses of the past, and the judicial voltes-face which have been needed to rectify them, one may well feel that we need a constitution which indicates in black and white the part that the judges are expected to play. When their position is left unspecified, and they veer from one extreme of policy to another, they are more likely to be accused of political bias than if they are given a proper constitutional status.

We have already an abundance of politically controversial legislation, and I doubt if any Bill of Rights would produce more attacks on the judges than the legislation on industrial relations has done already. They have been the target for abusive remarks by cabinet ministers in and out of Parliament, and many who might have known better, lawyers particularly, have joined in an unseemly clamour at the slightest opportunity, not hesitating to make charges of judicial partiality. I know that, as we are often reminded, Mr. Churchill did the same in 1911, but as every one of my age remembers, his accusations were not always fair. The extremist critics of the judges do not, I think, allow for the unenviable tasks which they have been given by Parliament. If certain organisations or individuals are given a statutory right to commit torts and other wrongs, which others are not allowed to commit, the judges have to decide where the limits of these immunities lie, often with nothing to guide them but imprecise phrases of elastic meaning, such as 'in contemplation and furtherance of a trade dispute'. Then, in borderline cases, they have to choose between rival interpretations. It is surely to be expected that immunities from the general law will not be interpreted in the widest possible sense, but will be kept within bounds, subject always to a fair reading of the Act. Otherwise if I may use Lord Scarman's words, 'there will arise a real risk of forces of great power in our society escaping from the rule of law altogether'. It is surely right that the judicial instinct should be to minimise that disaster. My purpose now, however, is not to join in the political fray, but to illustrate how deeply the judges are embroiled in it willy nilly. All that they can do is to grow thicker skins, in a sadly deteriorating climate. To expect them to change their spots is neither practicable nor right.

The judges must now be utterly weary of the endless discussion of their supposed prejudices, accompanied as it is by the dreary racket of political axe-grinding. It is made a matter of reproach that they are people of good education, that they are middle class, that they have had success in their profession – nothing is too absurd for those who seem to resent the one real safeguard that our distorted constitution still offers. Under all this buffeting they will, we may be sure, stand firm. And when the buffeting is shown to be in vain it will, we must hope, abate.

H. W. R. Wade, *Constitutional Fundamentals*, 1981, pp. 95–100

---

61 J. A. G. GRIFFITH'S THESIS THAT UK JUDGES ARE INSTITUTIONALLY CONSERVATIVE AND ILLIBERAL, 1981

My thesis is that judges in the United Kingdom cannot be politically neutral because they are placed in positions where they are required to make political choices which are sometimes presented to them, and often presented by them, as determinations of where the public interest lies; that their interpretation of what is in the public interest and therefore politically desirable is determined by the kind of people they are and the position they hold in our society; that this position is a part of established authority and so is necessarily conservative and illiberal. From all this flows that view of the public interest which is shown in judicial attitudes such as tenderness towards private property and dislike of trade unions, strong adherence to the maintenance of order, distaste for minority opinions, demonstrations and protests, indifference to the promotion of better race relations, support of governmental secrecy, concern for the preservation of the moral and social behaviour to which it is accustomed, and the rest.

J. A. G. Griffith, *The Politics of the Judiciary*, 2nd edn, 1981, p. 230.

---

62 PAUL SIEGHART ON THE FUNDAMENTAL IMPORTANCE OF AN INDEPENDENT JUDICIARY TO THE PROTECTION OF HUMAN RIGHTS, 1985

Now the most powerful entity in any community, and therefore the greatest potential violator of human rights, is the state itself, through its public authorities, and its officials and agents. What the ... state is therefore obliged to do is to create – if it does not already have it – a system which will provide remedies for its inhabitants *even against itself*. It must therefore now have laws which protect the rights and freedoms concerned, a law which enables individuals to obtain remedies for any violations, and a system which will ensure, in law and in fact, that those remedies will be enforced – even against the state itself ...

All this necessarily brings in what is often called the Rule of Law: the principle of legality which requires that there should be laws which lay down what the state may or may not do, and by which one can test whether any power which it claims, or any particular exercise of such a power, is legitimate; and a system of courts, *independent of every other institution of the state, including the legislature and the executive*, which interprets and applies those laws. The total independence of the judiciary from everyone else is central to the entire concept of the Rule of Law, for the whole point about a law is that it must be upheld impartially, and that no one must therefore be a judge in a cause in which he has any personal interest, or if he is open to illegitimate pressures behind the scenes from the friends of either of the parties – especially if one of them is the state, or one of its public authorities. No less important is an independent legal profession which has nothing to fear from appearing against the state on behalf of unpopular clients. Sir Thomas Erskine expressed this in resounding language as long ago as 1792, when he was answering a scurrilous campaign against him for accepting the brief for the defence of Tom Paine, who was being prosecuted for publishing a tract called *The Rights of Man*:

'From the moment that any advocate can be permitted to say that he will or will not stand between the Crown and the subject arraigned in the court where he daily sits to practise, from that moment the liberties of England are at an end.'

And for so long as either judges or lawyers are subject to pressures from the state, the Rule of Law cannot prevail.

Paul Sieghart, *The Lawful Rights of Mankind*, 1985, pp. 88–9.

---

63   LAW PROFESSORS KEITH EWING AND CONOR GEARTY SAY A BILL OF RIGHTS WOULD CREATE A JURISTOCRACY, 1991

A Bill of Rights would run counter to democratic instincts. The reason for this is that it empowers the courts to strike down legislation passed by Parliament. The effect would thus be to transfer the ultimate power in the community to the judges who by operating the Bill of Rights could dictate what the people through their political representatives could or could not do on any particular question. It is always to be kept in mind that a Bill of Rights has to be interpreted before it can be applied in any particular case.

Its terms are rarely if ever clear and in any situation it may reasonably be capable of more than one meaning. If we [turn] to the question of abortion, the judge who is anti abortion is likely to interpret the right to life widely to include the foetus, and thereby strike down abortion legislation as violating the Bill of Rights. On the other hand the judge who supports a woman's right to choose is likely to interpret the right to life narrowly to exclude the foetus and thereby uphold the legislation. The judges must decide which meaning they prefer, and their choice may be no more rational and no less informed by bile and prejudice than that of the people in the queue at the nearest bus-stop . . .

There are . . . objections to the transfer of political power to the judges. In the first place it is properly assumed that a fundamental requirement of a democracy is that every adult person should be entitled to participate in the system of government. But a Bill of Rights would seriously undermine this basic principle by creating a framework in which the ultimate power would be located in a small privileged elite. Participation would be closed to a handful of lawyers rather than be open to the community as a whole. But not only would the right to participate in the decision making process be the preserve of an exclusive club, the power to influence the way in which these decisions are made would also be confined to a small section of the population. Access to law requires money and power. Those who would be best able to play this game would be those with lashings of both. Corporations, for example, would be empowered to intervene through the legal process to disrupt decisions taken in the political arena, from which they are naturally denied any direct representation.

Secondly, the transfer of political power to the judges would undermine the principle that those who exercise political power should be representative of the community they serve. This principle is usually taken to refer to a process whereby the members of a community choose from amongst their number someone who will represent them in government. Judges are not chosen in this way (and we are not advocating that they should be) but are appointed by the executive, a process which would become even more politically sensitive if we were to adopt a Bill of Rights. But even if we use the idea of representativeness in a weaker sense as meaning that decision makers should broadly reflect the make-up of the communities over which they exercise power, we find that the judges are not representative of the different interests in the community. Above all the judges in this country are distinguished by their homogeneity not only in terms of their social background, but in terms also of their age, race and sex. If we look at our top court, the House of Lords, we find that its members are all men, that they are all white, that the youngest was born in 1926, that all but one were educated at either Oxford or Cambridge. Returning to the question of abortion, it is simply bizarre to suggest that the final authority to decide what will and what will not be permitted should be vested in a group from which at the present time women are completely excluded.

Thirdly, the introduction of a Bill of Rights would violate the principle that those who wield political power should be accountable to the community on whose behalf they purport to act when they exercise this power. That is to say, the community must have the opportunity to assess the work of its rule makers and if it so chooses replace them with others of their choice. Yet, apart from being exclusive and elitist, the judges are accountable to no one. Indeed the senior judges for all practical purposes cannot be removed from office until death or retirement ... The judges would operate as a kind of juristocracy, a body with extraordinary power without any political responsibility. That is no way to constrain what ought to be a vibrant and healthy democracy.

Keith Ewing and Conor Gearty, *Democracy or a Bill of Rights*, 1991, pp. 4–6.

---

64 LAW PROFESSOR DAWN OLIVER CRITICIZES THE CRITICS OF THE UK JUDICIARY, 1991

One of the arguments commonly advanced against a Bill of Rights is that the judiciary cannot be trusted to administer it in an acceptable way: 'The harsh reality is that we need to be protected by Parliament from the courts, as much as we need to be protected from the abuse of executive power' (Keith Ewing and Conor Gearty, *Freedom under Thatcher*, 1990, p. 270). This objection comes principally from the political left. Professor J. A. G. Griffith is mistrustful of the judges' attitude to a Bill of Rights, in particular when they have to decide whether the public interest in, for example, national security, outweighs the interests of the individual. Griffith prefers these decisions to be in the hands of politicians rather than of judges:

> [An] advantage in treating what others call rights as political claims is that their acceptance or rejection will be in the hands of politicians rather than judges and the advantage of *that* is not that politicians are more likely to come up with the right answer but that ... they are so much more vulnerable than judges and can be dismissed or at least made to suffer in their reputation. [I am] very strongly of the opinion that, in the United Kingdom, political decisions should be taken by politicians (*Public Law*, 1985, p. 582).

Here issues of the interrelationships of constitutional reform arise. The implication that existing political checks make politicians vulnerable in any real sense save in quite exceptional circumstances is unconvincing. It might be otherwise if the electoral system operated differently, or if government were less centralized, or if backbenchers could find a way of exerting more influence over ministers. But, it is suggested, experience of the willingness of politicians in central and local government to interfere with civil and political rights leaves little ground for complacency about their political vulnerability. And even if Parliament (and local government) were reformed and made more publicly and politically accountable, aggrieved citizens could not be sure of receiving redress or a fair hearing of their complaints if they were denied access to the courts on the grounds that politicians were better qualified to deal with their grievances ...

Reservations about giving the judges the power to deal with what would often be highly controversial and party political issues are also expressed on the political right on the grounds that this activity would expose the judges to political pressure and might ultimately politicize them in the sense of bringing political considerations into the process of appointing judges. But this has not been the experience in Canada whose Charter was adopted in 1982, and there is no evidence that the credibility of the Canadian Supreme Court will be undermined by the new duties of interpretation that the Charter has placed upon it. And a reformed system for the appointment of judges could preclude political considerations. [*RB NOTE: see Docs 68, 71, 72*]

The difficulties experienced by the judiciary under our present system in weighing up the competing claims to individual liberty on the one hand and the needs of national security, law and order and collective interests on the other, and the fact that they do not have a good track record in upholding civil and political rights in some fields of the law do not strengthen the argument that a court-enforced Bill of Rights is needed. But it is suggested that these difficulties do not imply that the British judiciary is inherently incapable of administering a Bill of Rights in the spirit in which it is drafted. It reflects rather an aspect of the British constitutional system that has attracted growing criticism in the last 20 years or so, namely the lack of a sense of direction or of any order of priority for these often competing values (a similar lack of any real sense of direction and priorities may be found in politics). The directionless consensus in the politics of the 1960s and 1970s is mirrored by the directionless development or 'ethical aimlessness' of the common law in constitutional matters. By way of example, Lord Diplock in the GCHQ case spoke of 'accepted moral values' and suggested that the courts could strike down actions which were in breach of these, but there is no document setting out what these values are and no consensus in the courts on this matter. As we have seen, the Court of Appeal and the House of Lords have recently in the *Brind* case (*Brind* v. *Secretary of State for the Home Department* [1991] 1 All ER 720) rejected an argument that the ECHR sets out these values and the courts are entitled to take it into account in dealing with wide discretionary powers granted to government. If a set of priorities for the resolution of competing values were introduced into the legal system in a Bill of Rights, there is no reason to assume that the judges could not operate it in the spirit in which it was enacted.

The system also suffers from a scarcely developed legal concept of proportionality, a concept that is important in the jurisprudence of the European Convention, and in the administrative law of the European Community, and of France and Germany. Broadly, it requires that if state activity interferes with the rights and expectations of individuals and other bodies, then the interference should be proportionate to the public benefit being promoted, and should not be excessive or inappropriate. English public law has little to say on this subject and, in recent cases of judicial review, the courts have expressed hostility to proportionality as a separate ground for review, preferring to treat it as a form of irrationality or 'Wednesbury unreasonableness'.

The courts in the UK are quite unable to develop criteria, operating on a case-by-case basis without a Constitution or a Bill of Rights or a developed doctrine of proportionality, for deciding when, for example, the value given to freedom of expression and freedom of association should outweigh the value attached to national security if they come into conflict. In the 'Spy-catcher' (*Attorney General* v. *Guardian Newspapers Ltd* (No. 2) [1988] 3 WLR 776) and GCHQ (*Council of Civil Service Unions* v. *Minister for the Civil Service* [1985] AC 374) cases, where exactly this issue arose, the judges were divided on where the balance should be struck and for the most part did not resolve it by reference to fundamental principles.

It is not surprising that differences of view emerge in these cases. The outcomes of the GCHQ case (the ban on trade unions was upheld) and of the Spycatcher case (the injunction was discharged principally because it was too late: the lifelong duty of confidentiality that a civil servant owes to the Crown was upheld), suggest that judges do tend to put the public interest, as defined by the government, before civil liberties.

It is in the lack of guidance about constitutional values and how they should be weighed against one another if they conflict that the judges in the UK differ from those of the USA, Canada and other countries with Constitutions and Bills of Rights. A Bill of Rights would require a court dealing with this type of issue to be satisfied by evidence and argument rather than by assertion or assumption that public interests should prevail over civil liberties. The burden would be on the state to justify its inter-vention, not on individuals to prove their rights. A Bill modelled on the ECHR would define the public interest arguments that were relevant (i.e. depending on the Article, necessity in a democratic society, in the interests of national security, territorial integrity, public safety, prevention of dis-order or crime, protection of health or morals, protection of the rights and freedoms of others and so on) and exclude irrelevant considerations when the balancing of civil liberties and public interests takes place ...

There is indeed a possibility that judges will be in a position to give effect to their own political preferences when dealing with Bill of Rights cases. This could amount to the exercise of power being unchecked. But this line of argument is flawed in a number of respects. In evaluating the point, we have to take into account the extent to which the sort of power judges would be reviewing under a Bill of Rights is at present subject to legal or political checks. Those who object to a Bill of Rights often focus on the power of judges to override an Act of Parliament. Other countries with written Constitutions and Bills of Rights have learned to live with this possibility; indeed, to take pride in it. But in practice, most decisions and actions that interfere with civil and political rights are not expressly authorized by Parliament but are taken by officials, local authorities and the police. At present, the political checks against abuses of power by these bodies are feeble and often ineffective and so, it is suggested, additional legal checks are needed.

Secondly, a problem of judicial power already exists under the present system. The position would in practice be improved rather than exacerbated if the ECHR or a Bill combining the ECHR and the IC were incorporated into English law, with guidelines for its interpretation that set out the rationales for civil and political rights. This would enable judges to avoid making party political decisions in line with their own preferences, since they would be applying the provisions and provisos of a Bill of Rights to a problem instead of having to resort to their own ill-assorted predispositions and judicial precedents, as is currently the position. Judicial training could also serve to prevent the judiciary from misunderstanding their functions in relation to a Bill of Rights.

Thirdly, the accusation that, unlike politicians, the courts exercise unchecked power, is an exaggeration of the position. In practice, politicians and administrators do exercise considerable unchecked power. Unlike most administrators, ministers and local councillors, judges operate in public in open court; they give reasoned judgments and they are subject to appeal and to public comment and criticism. They are in effect subject to a considerable degree of public and legal accountability. These, though not perfect, are real checks on their power.

Fourthly, judges would very rapidly learn to recognize their own prejudices and take care not to allow their preferences to influence them when applying a Bill of Rights. Many of the political views of judges, as of most individuals, are unarticulated and unconscious, but the bench would with experience come to recognize that some of their political assumptions were controversial and not self-evidently correct, and would therefore have to rationalize them or suppress them.

The terms of the Bill of Rights would provide the criteria by which the judges were to weigh up the arguments, and this in itself would reduce the scope for political preferences to influence the outcome. If necessary, procedures could be established to enable the social and political implications of a case to be investigated. In the USA, this is achieved through the use of the 'Brandeis brief', enabling views other than those of the parties to the case to be put. In this country, there have been proposals for a Director of Civil Proceedings who could perform this role, having an independent constitutional status comparable to that of the Director of Public Prosecutions. And finally, it is suggested, even the aberrant judgment influenced by irrelevant considerations, but delivered in open court after argument by the parties is preferable to unchallengeable actions, often taken in secret, by state or private institutions in breach of the provisions of the ECHR and of the rationales of civil and political rights, which is the present position.

In summary, the fear of judicial bias and politicization is exaggerated and outweighed by the considerable benefit to the quality of public administration and the rights of individuals that would flow from a Bill of Rights. As William Brennan, senior justice of the US Supreme Court put it, 'Whatever the danger of a politicised bench, it hardly seems sufficient to justify scrapping incorporation altogether.'

A Bill of Rights would enhance the legal accountability of government and guarantee the civil and political rights of citizenship. But the adoption of a Bill of Rights should be put in context in the constitution. Some commentators have assumed that supporters of a Bill of Rights regard it as a 'panacea of all our problems' and regard the idea as 'glib' (Ewing and Gearty, ibid, p. 275). This is unfair to the case. While some commentators have advocated a Bill of Rights and nothing else, most see it as part of a programme of constitutional reform that would include some or all of the following: public rights of access to official information, proportional representation, decentralization, reform of the second chamber ... But even if a Bill of Rights were adopted without any other reforms, it would not be simply a 'cosmetic change' (Ewing and Gearty); it would alter the ethos of public administration and public expectations, it would reinforce the status of citizenship and the processes for holding government legally and publicly accountable.

Dawn Oliver, *Government in the United Kingdom*, 1991, pp. 161–7.

---

65 THE SOCIAL COMPOSITION OF THE UK JUDICIARY, 1995

SUCCESS RATES OF FEMALE APPLICANTS FOR APPOINTMENT AS QUEEN'S COUNSEL

	1992	*1993*	*1994*
Applications:			
Men	435 (92%)	496 (92%)	450 (91%)
Women	37 (8%)	43 (8%)	42 (9%)
Total	472	539	492
Appointments:			
Men	64 (91%)	68 (88%)	63 (89%)
Women	6 (9%)	9 (12%)	8 (11%)
Total	70	77	71
Percentage of applicants who were successful:			
Men	15%	14%	14%
Women	16%	21%	19%
All applicants	15%	14%	14%

WOMEN IN THE JUDICIARY

	1 December 1992			1 December 1993			1 December 1994			1 December 1995		
	Total	Men	Women	Total	Men	Women	Total	Men	Women	Total	Men	Women
Lords of Appeal in Ordinary	10	10	0	10	10	0	10	10	0	12	12	—
Lord Justices of Appeal	27	26 96.3%	1 3.7%	29	28 96.5%	1 3.5%	29	28 96.5%	1 3.5%	32	31 96.9%	1 3.1%
High Court Judges	83	79 95.2%	4 4.8%	94	88 93.6%	6 6.4%	95	89 93.7%	6 6.3%	96	89 92.7%	7 7.3%
Circuit Judges	484	460 95%	24 5%	499	472 94.6%	27 5.4%	514	485 94.3%	29 5.7%	517	488 94.4%	29 5.6%
Recorders	779	741 95.1%	38 4.9%	826	786 95.1%	40 4.9%	866	825 95.3%	41 4.7%	891	837 93.9%	54 6.1%
Assistant Recorders	483	433 89.6%	50 10.4%	419	364 86.9%	55 13.1%	391	330 84.4%	61 15.6%	354	302 85.3%	52 14.7%
District Judges	258	241 93.4%	17 6.6%	282	260 92.2%	22 7.8%	301	272 90.4%	29 9.6%	322	289 89.8%	33 10.3%
Total	2,124	1,990 93.7%	134 6.3%	2,159	2,008 93.0%	151 7.0%	2,206	2,039 92.4%	167 7.6%	2,224	2,048 92.1%	176 7.9%

HOLDERS OF JUDICIAL OFFICE OF ETHNIC MINORITY ORIGIN

	1st December 1992				1st December 1994				1st December 1995			
	Black	Asian	Other Non-White	Percentage of Total	Black	Asian	Other Non-White	Percentage of Total	Black	Asian	Other Non-White	Percentage of Total
High Court Judges	0	0	0	0	0	0	0	0	0	0	0	0
Circuit Judges	0	2	0	0.6	0	3	1	0.8	0	3	2	1
Recorders	3	3	2	1.0	4	5	2	1.3	5	3	4	1.3
Assistant Recorders	4	4	0	1.6	6	3	1	2.5	5	3	1	2.5
District Judges	0	0	0	0	0	1	0	0.3	0	5	1	0.6
Total	7	9	3	0.9	10	12	4	1.2	10	10	8	1.3

EDUCATIONAL BACKGROUND OF THE JUDICIARY

Lords of Appeal	*10*	
Oxbridge	8	80.00%
Other	2	20.00%
College	0	
None	0	
Total	10	100.00%
Heads of Divisions	*4*	
Oxbridge	3	75.00%
Other	1	25.00%
College	0	
None	0	
Total	4	100.00%
Lords Justices of Appeal	*29*	
Oxbridge	23	79.31%
Other	5	17.24%
College	0	
None	1	3.45%
Total	29	100.00%
High Court Judges	*95*	
Oxbridge	77	81.05%
Other	15	15.79%
College	0	
None	3	3.16%
Total	95	100.00%
Circuit Judges	*514*	
Oxbridge	264	51.40%
Other	173	33.60%
College	41	8.00%
None	36	7.00%
Total	514	100.00%
District Judges	*301*	
Oxbridge	37	12.29%
Other	155	51.50%
College	63	20.93%
None	46	15.28%
Total	301	100.00%

AGE OF JUDGES IN ENGLAND AND WALES

	Average Age	*No in Post*
Heads of Divisions	63.0	4

Lords of Appeal in Ordinary	66.5	10
Lords Justices of Appeal	63.0	29
High Court Judges	57.6	95
Circuit Judges	57.8	499
Recorders	52.0	813
Assistant Recorders	45.7	432
Stipendiary Magistrates	53.1	78
Industrial Tribunal Chairmen	56.4	73
VAT Tribunal Chairmen	60.3	4
Social Security Appeal Tribunal Chairmen	50.3	33

NUMBERS OF SOLICITORS AND BARRISTERS HOLDING, JUDICIAL OFFICE IN ENGLAND AND WALES

The following table shows the total number of office-holders in post in the indicated categories as at 1 December 1995 and the number of barristers and solicitors and men and women in each category.

		Barristers	*Solicitors*	*Total*
Lords of Appeal in Ordinary	Men	12[1]	—	12
	Women	—	—	—
	Total	12	—	12
Heads of Divisions[2]	Men	4	—	4
	Women	—	—	—
	Total	4	—	4
Lords Justices of Appeal	Men	31	—	31
	Women	1	—	1
	Total	32	—	32
High Court Judges	Men	88	1	89
	Women	7	—	7
	Total	95	1	96
Circuit Judges	Men	420	68	488
	Women	25	4	29
	Total	445	72	517
Recorders	Men	760	77	837
	Women	52	2	54
	Total	812	79	891
Assistant Recorders	Men	248	54	302
	Women	39	13	52
	Total	287	67	354
District Judges	Men	0	289	289
	Women	1	32	33
	Total	1	321	322
Deputy District Judges	Men	13	610	623
	Women	9	89	98
	Total	22	699	721

Metropolitan Stipendiary	Men	18	25	43
Magistrates	Women	6	3	9
	Total	24	28	52
Provincial Stipendiary Magistrates	Men	8	28	36
	Women	3	1	4
	Total	11	29	40

[1] Including two members of the Faculty of Advocates.
[2] Excluding the Lord Chancellor.

Source: Report of the Home Affairs Committee on Judicial
Appointments Procedures [1995–96], 52-II. pp. 156, 160–3, 167

---

66   THE LORD CHANCELLOR'S DEPARTMENT PROCEDURES FOR JUDICIAL APPOINTMENTS, 1995

THE PRINCIPLES OF JUDICIAL APPOINTMENT

2.3.1 Three guiding principles underpin the Lord Chancellor's policies:
  (a) appointment is on merit;
  (b) candidates for full-time office should normally have served in a
      part-time capacity before being considered for appointment; and
  (c) significant weight is attached to the independent views of the
      judiciary and members of the legal profession in considering
      candidates for judicial appointment.
These guiding principles are described more fully in the following paragraphs.

Appointment on merit

   2.3.2 It is the cardinal principle of the Lord Chancellor's approach that
appointments are made on merit. Subject to the statutory requirements in
relation to eligibility, the Lord Chancellor appoints or recommends for
appointment to each judicial post the candidate who appears to him to be
best qualified to fill it without regard to ethnic origin, gender, marital status,
sexual orientation, political affiliation, religion, or (subject to the physical
requirements of the office) disability. He seeks to appoint candidates of the
highest integrity and judicial quality, looking in particular for the good
judgment once described by Lord Devlin as the first quality of a good judge.
In respect of appointments to the Circuit and District Benches, the Lord
Chancellor published in July 1994 a statement of explicit criteria. These
are:
   (a) an appropriate level of legal knowledge and experience and
       professional achievement;

    (b) intellectual and analytical ability;

    (c) sound judgment;

    (d) decisiveness;

    (e) the ability to communicate effectively with all types of court user; and

    (f) the ability to command the respect of court users and maintain the authority of the court.

In addition, he requires that candidates will demonstrate the following personal qualities:

    (a) integrity;

    (b) fairness;

    (c) an understanding of people and society;

    (d) sound temperament;

    (e) courtesy and humanity; and

    (f) a commitment to public service and to the proper and efficient administration of justice.

Full definitions of these criteria are contained in the application material for the offices of Circuit Judge and District Judge which accompanies this evidence.

2.3.3 The Lord Chancellor has no plans to reconstitute the professional judiciary to reflect the composition of society as a whole. It is not the function of the judiciary to reflect particular sections of the community, as it is of the democratically elected legislature. The judges' role is to administer justice in accordance with the laws of England and Wales. This requires above all professional legal knowledge and competence. Any litigant or defendant will usually appear before a single judge and it is of paramount importance that the judge is fully qualified for the office he or she holds, and is able to discharge his or her functions to the highest standards. Social or other considerations are not relevant for this purpose; the Lord Chancellor accordingly seeks to appoint or recommend for appointment those he assesses to be the best candidates available and willing to serve at the time.

2.3.4 This is not to say that the Lord Chancellor does not appreciate the value of the judiciary more closely reflecting the make-up of society as a whole. Other things being equal, that should tend over time to result from ensuring the fullest possible equality of opportunity for persons in all sections of society who wish to enter the legal profession and who aspire to sit judicially. This implies equality of opportunity at all levels of the educational system and the legal profession as well as in the appointments system itself. The Lord Chancellor appreciates the value of this in terms of the confidence of members of groups who are, or who are perceived (or perceive themselves) to be, disadvantaged that the justice system itself does not discriminate unfairly against them. The Lord Chancellor does, there-fore, encourage greater numbers of women and ethnic minority practitioners to apply to become judges, consistently with the principle that he should appoint, or recommend for appointment, those who are the best qualified individuals available and willing to serve.

Views of the judiciary and of the profession

The Lord Chancellor believes that serving judges and members of the legal profession are particularly well placed to assist him with their views on the extent to which a candidate has demonstrated that he or she has the necessary experience and other qualities required for judicial appointment, and that it is in the public interest that such assessments should be available to him before an individual is approved to exercise judicial functions and to take on the arduous public responsibility which this involves. This emphasis on consultation with the judiciary and the legal profession incorporates a valuable element of peer appraisal in a demanding professional environment and helps to sustain confidence and mutual respect between the Bench and the practising profession.

2.3.10 It is therefore a central feature of the appointments system that views and opinions about the suitability for office of applicants and those who sit part-time are periodically collected in an organised, systematic and structured manner from both the full-time judiciary (who are in a uniquely favourable position to weigh the strengths and weaknesses of the barristers and solicitors who appear before them), and from senior members of the practising profession. The way this is done is carefully designed to ensure that as wide as possible a range of views is collected on those concerned, supplementing (in the case of those applying for part-time judicial office) specific enquiries made of those nominated by the individual candidate as having knowledge of their work.

2.3.11 In respect of the High Court, regular meetings are held by senior officials with Supreme Court Judges and Law Lords, and also the Chairman of the Bar, who are asked to give their views on the aptitude and suitability for appointment of potential candidates with whose work they are sufficiently familiar. The Lord Chancellor personally consults the four Heads of Division, together with the Senior Presiding Judge, whenever an appointment falls to be made, before tendering his advice to The Queen.

2.3.12. Appointments to the House of Lords and Court of Appeal are made by The Queen on the advice of the Prime Minister, but the Lord Chancellor's opinion is generally sought. Here also, the views of the Lords of Appeal in Ordinary and (in respect of appointments to the Court of Appeal) of Lords Justices on the relative merits of potential candidates are regularly sought. These then form the basis for the Lord Chancellor's discussions with the Law Lords together with the Lord Chief Justice and Master of the Rolls (in respect of appointments to the House of Lords) and the Heads of Divisions (in respect of appointments to the Court of Appeal). Consultations also take place on a regular basis with the Heads of Divisions and Presiding Judges about those to be authorised to sit as deputy High Court judges in the Chancery, Queen's Bench or Family Divisions under section 9 of the Supreme Court Act 1981. It is a strength of the system that a body of authoritative opinion on a candidate for office will be available not only from the time at which a particular appointment is under consideration, but comprehensively in respect of the whole of the individual's professional career.

2.3.13. A review of potential candidates for appointment to the Circuit Bench, and as Recorders and Assistant Recorders, is conducted on each of the six circuits every year. Presiding Judges, Family Division Liaison Judges and judges at each main Centre are asked their views of the suitability of:

    (a) Recorders for full-time appointment to the Circuit Bench;

    (b) Assistant Recorders for appointment to Recorderships; and

    (c) Applicants for appointment as Assistant Recorders.

2.3.14 In order to ensure the views of the practising profession are given appropriate weight in this process, Leaders of the relevant Circuit Bar are included in the review and, since 1993, in support of the Lord Chancellor's desire to broaden the range of comment on solicitor applicants in particular, the process has been supplemented by consultation on each circuit with members of the Council of The Law Society, who have established local consultation arrangements on each circuit for this purpose.

2.3.15 These procedures are designed to ensure that as wide a range of views on candidates as possible from those with knowledge of their qualities is available to the Lord Chancellor when considering each appointment. They are the subject of regular review and enhancement, and the Lord Chancellor is always eager to receive suggestions for ways of widening and deepening the consultation process.

2.3.16 The cumulative results of these consultations, building as they do on the perceptions of many different individuals over a number of years, allow the Lord Chancellor to assemble a clear, multi-faceted and generally reliable picture of each candidate's abilities and limitations, and their suitability to hold judicial office. By the time that a person is being considered for full-time office, he or she will already have been considered as a candidate for part-time office on at least one occasion if not more ...

2.5   DEVELOPMENTS

The development of the Lord Chancellor's proposals

2.5.1 In July 1993, the Lord Chancellor announced that he intended to introduce a progressive programme of developments to judicial appointments procedures. In announcing these changes, the Lord Chancellor expressed his continued confidence in appointments made under the existing procedures, which he said had served the public well and were too little appreciated by their critics. He made clear that he had no doubts about the quality of the appointments which the existing procedures had produced, but said that there was room for development in the light of changing circumstances.

2.5.2. The programme of developments announced by the Lord Chancellor is designed to build on the strengths of present arrangements to make the appointments system as efficient, fair and open as possible, while maintaining that degree of confidentiality necessarily required. The programme consists of:—

    (a) measures to improve arrangements for forecasting and planning the numbers and the expertise of the judges required at the various levels;

(b) the progressive introduction of specific competitions for judicial vacancies;

(c) the preparation of more specific descriptions of the work of the judicial posts to be filled and of the qualities required;

(d) the progressive introduction of open advertisements for judicial vacancies below the level of the High Court Bench;

(e) further measures to encourage applications from women and black and Asian practitioners;

(f) a review of application forms and a more structured basis for consultations with the judiciary and the profession; and

(g) exploration of the scope for involving suitable lay people in the selection process.

Consultations with the judiciary and the profession

2.5.16 The Lord Chancellor is committed to the continuation of the system of consultations described [above] and envisages that increasingly the assessments will be collected with regard to the published criteria for appointment.

The interview

2.5.17 Selected applicants in the open competitions are interviewed by a three-member panel consisting of a member of the judiciary, one of the Lord Chancellor's senior officials, and, for the first time, a lay person. The role of the lay interviewer is to play a full part in the assessment and to exercise his or her personal judgment in assessing the extent to which candidates possess the qualities required of a judge and to bring to this process something of the perspective of the lay court-user and of the wider public.

2.5.18 For the first competitions, the lay interviewers have been selected from among the Chairmen and Members of the Lord Chancellor's Advisory Committees on Justices of the Peace, who will bring to their role both expertise in interviewing and a knowledge of the judicial system ... In nominating these individuals the Lord Chancellor has sought to ensure that the group as a whole reflects a balance in respect of gender and ethnic origin, between Justices of the Peace and non-Justices of the Peace and between people with experience in the public service and the private sector.

2.5.19 The Lord Chancellor believes that the group chosen provides an impressive array of talents, backgrounds and experience. The membership of his Advisory Committees is considered by the Lord Chancellor to be an excellent source of lay interviewers, but in future years, as the competitions develop and extend to other offices, he will consider whether lay interviewers may be sought from other sources.

2.5.20 After the interview, the Chairman will complete an assessment form representing the panel's collective assessment of the candidate which will constitute the panel's advice to the Lord Chancellor.

Decisions

2.5.21 The assessments of the interview panel will be an important part of the information available to the Lord Chancellor in deciding whom to appoint (or whom to recommend to The Queen for appointment, as appropriate) together with the application form, the comments collected from the judiciary and senior members of the profession in the regular consultations, and any comments which the Presiding Judges of the appropriate circuits may wish to offer. The responsibility for selection will remain the Lord Chancellor's alone.

2.5.22 Applicants whom the Lord Chancellor is minded to appoint (or to recommend to The Queen for appointment, as appropriate) will – as now – be invited to discuss with the Circuit Administrator the practical arrangements in respect of sittings. In the event that the Lord Chancellor concludes that he is unable immediately to recommend appointment, he may indicate that the applicant may be approached later if an unforeseen vacancy arises.

2.5.23 After the Lord Chancellor's decisions are notified to individual applicants, senior members of the Judicial Appointments Group staff will be available to discuss with unsuccessful applicants their position, whether invited to interview or not.

2.6 Equal Opportunities

Appointment on merit and equality of opportunity

2.6.1 As stated in paragraphs 2.3.2–2.3.4 above, the Lord Chancellor appoints or recommends for appointment to each judicial post the candidate who appears to him to be best qualified irrespective of ethnic origin, gender, marital status, sexual orientation, political affiliation, religion or (subject to the physical requirements of the office) disability. He takes decisions in the light of the merits of each candidate, their suitability for the office in question and the relative strengths of other candidates.

2.6.2 The Lord Chancellor is fully committed to the principle of equality of opportunity for all suitably-qualified aspirants to judicial office. He has taken steps to encourage applications from women and practitioners of minority ethnic origin, and to ensure that all who apply for judicial office are considered fairly. The Lord Chancellor will not positively discriminate in favour of any groups since he considers this would be wrong, but he is prepared to take affirmative action to ensure that all applicants or potential applicants are given appropriate encouragement and treated fairly on their merits. The Lord Chancellor's general approach to equal opportunity issues is that, as far as possible, with due allowance for the special role and position of judges, and for the absence of any conventional 'line-management' responsibility for the legal profession, appointment practices should be fully consistent with appropriate current principles in the general field of appointment.

2.6.3 The Lord Chancellor's equal opportunities initiatives are described in more detail from paragraph 2.6.18 below. He has made it clear that he considers it would be wrong to set quotas for the number of women or minority ethnic origin members of the judiciary, as that would be inconsistent with the principle of appointment on merit and could call into question the credibility and suitability of those appointed and could involve a lowering of standards.

2.6.4 Given the statutory qualifications for appointment and the nature of the knowledge and skills required for judicial office, appointments must in practice be restricted to individuals of particular professional standing. The number of women and minority ethnic origin members of the judiciary is substantially a reflection of the numbers of that seniority and experience in the legal profession. As more women and practitioners of minority ethnic origin progress through the profession, it is to be expected that the numbers from those groups within the judiciary will increase. The Lord Chancellor has no control over the racial or gender composition of the profession, but he has welcomed the steps being taken by the Bar Council and The Law Society to develop equal opportunities policies. Because full-time judges will normally serve for some 15 to 20 years, the rate of 'turn-over' is limited and the composition of the full-time judiciary at any time must largely reflect appointments made in the past. The scope for instant change in the overall composition of the judiciary does not therefore exist.

2.6.5 It is encouraging to note that the number of women and members of the judiciary of minority ethnic origin is showing a steady, albeit gradual, increase and the Lord Chancellor continues to monitor progress in this area.

Women in the judiciary

2.6.6 The table [RB NOTE: above, see Doc. 65] shows the number of women at the main levels of the judiciary. From this it will be seen that the most significant increases are at the lower levels, reflecting the gradual changes that are taking place within the legal profession. In particular, the number of female Assistant Recorders – one of the main entry levels to the judiciary – has increased by 22 per cent between 1992 and 1994 and at 1 December 1994 women comprised 15.6 per cent of all Assistant Recorders. There can be no doubt that the number of women in the judiciary will continue to increase and the gender mix of the judiciary can be expected to look very different from the current position in, say, 10 to 15 years' time.

Ethnic origin

2.6.7 The ethnic origin of applicants for judicial appointment was not recorded prior to the autumn of 1991 and therefore the available information may not be complete. The table [RB NOTE: above, see Doc. 65] shows, as far as it has been possible to ascertain, the number of members of certain categories of the judiciary who are known or believed to be of ethnic minority origin [since 1992]. Consideration is currently being given to how the data held on the ethnic origin of applicants and office-holders may be improved.

Disability

2.6.8 The Lord Chancellor opposes any form of discrimination on the grounds of disability. He does, however, require that the individual, whether disabled or not, must be able fully to carry out the functions of the office in question.

2.6.9 The Lord Chancellor recognises that disability comes in many forms and in widely varying degrees of seriousness and therefore each individual must be considered on his or her merits in the light of their particular circumstances; he strives to avoid making assumptions about the abilities of a disabled person except in the light of detailed information about the individual. He also recognises that changes in available technology can affect the range of responsibilities a disabled person can carry. The Lord Chancellor will be concerned to know what the individual is able to do and whether they are able to meet the physical and mental requirements of the job. It is of paramount importance, in the public interest and that of those who appear before him or her, that any member of the judiciary is able to participate fully in the proceedings before him or her but the requirements may vary from one post to another. For example, the requirements of a Chancery Master are different from those of the Circuit Judge who sits predominantly in the Crown Court. In the case of the Circuit Judge, satisfactory sight and hearing, with technological assistance if required, are generally necessary for the performance of the functions involved. Where a disabled person applies for a particular judicial post, their abilities must accordingly be considered in the context of the requirements of the post.

Age

2.6.10 Specific age requirements in relation to each tier of the judiciary differ, but there exist for each level lower and upper age limits for appointment. The table [*RB NOTE: above, see Doc. 65*] shows the average age of High Court Judges, Circuit Judges, Recorders and Assistant Recorders ...

2.6.11 The statutory criteria for appointment require appreciable experience as a practitioner and the Lord Chancellor considers that it is important to preserve the level of experience, of both the law and life in general, and the maturity of judgement which are brought to the Bench and does not therefore favour a reduction in current age limits. As it is, in exceptional cases Assistant Recordership appointments are made to people from the age of 36 or 37. The ages below which full-time appointments are not normally made also reflect the principle that before appointment to full-time office candidates must first serve in an appropriate part-time capacity long enough to establish their competence and suitability.

2.6.12 In the case of appointments to the initial part-time levels of the judiciary, the Lord Chancellor must bear in mind that, in determining the upper age limits for appointment to these levels, part-timers are the source for full-time appointments in the future. As it will take a number of years for an individual to achieve the potential progression to full-time appointment, assuming that they are otherwise suitable and interested, the upper age limits to the part-time levels must be fixed accordingly.

2.6.13 Some people start a career in the law later than is the norm or take a break to bring up a family. In these circumstances the Lord Chancellor applies the upper age limits flexibly where the candidate is otherwise suitable for appointment.

2.6.14 The Judicial Pensions and Retirement Act 1993, which is expected to come into operation during 1995, provides for a reduced and standard compulsory age of retirement for judicial posts and encourages movement from one post to another by removing some of the limitations on pension benefits which have previously operated in this respect. The Act provides for a normal compulsory retirement age of 70, for both full-time and part-time judicial post holders, subject to a power of extension (not applicable to the High Court Bench and above) on a year by year basis, where this is in the public interest, up to but not beyond the age of 75.

2.6.15 The age at which judges are required to retire must influence the age at which appointments are made. Given that full-time judges are appointed from around the age of 45 onwards, i.e. what might normally be considered to be 'mid-career' in other walks of life, a number of years in office would seem to be appropriate in order to secure a return on the investment made by the public in the cost of judicial appointments and to enable judges to be considered for promotion to the higher levels where appropriate.

Sexual orientation

2.6.16 The Lord Chancellor has made it clear that an individual's homosexuality does not disqualify him or her from appointments. The advertisement for the new style Circuit Judge and District Judge competitions made this more widely apparent, but the Lord Chancellor had for some time operated a policy whereby homosexuality was not of itself a bar to appointment. In their personal lives, of course, as in their professional lives, all members of the judiciary, whatever their sexual orientation, are expected to conduct themselves at all times in a manner which will maintain public confidence in the judiciary.

Educational and social background

2.6.17 As mentioned above, the Lord Chancellor includes the 'understanding of people and society' among the qualities which are specifically sought at Circuit and District Judge levels. But in considering candidates for appointment to judicial office, he does not base his decisions on where candidates were educated, nor does he pay regard to their social background, however defined. Whatever their own social background, almost all candidates in the course of lengthy experience in legal practice will have become familiar with social conditions and behaviour in many and diverse situations. The table [*RB NOTE: above, see Doc. 65*] shows the university background of the judiciary.

Equal opportunity measures

2.6.18 In a Parliamentary Answer given on 23 May 1994, the Lord Chancellor outlined his approach to equality of opportunity in judicial appointments for women and ethnic minority practitioners and the particular measures he has taken in this area. He has arranged for an official within the Judicial Appointments Group of his Department to advise on policies in this field and to liaise with others on equal opportunity issues in relation to judicial appointments. In implementing the Lord Chancellor's policies in relation to equal opportunities, constructive relationships have been established with the General Council of the Bar and The Law Society and with groups representing women and ethnic minority practitioners.

2.6.19 The Lord Chancellor continues to encourage applications from suitably qualified women and ethnic minority practitioners. He personally takes opportunities to encourage applications, for example, in speeches, and wrote in June 1994 to all Heads of Chambers, Presidents of Local Law Societies, female judges and ethnic minority judges seeking their assistance in encouraging suitably qualified women and practitioners of minority ethnic origin to apply for judicial appointment.

2.6.20 Events for women lawyers were held in July at the Bar Council's offices in London and in November at The Law Society to provide information about part-time judicial appointments to women. Further events are planned, the next being scheduled for the early spring of 1995 for both barristers and solicitors outside London. The Lord Chancellor is very encouraged by the positive reaction to these events.

2.6.21 Discussions are to be held with the Bar Council and The Law Society about arranging similar events for lawyers of minority ethnic origin.

2.6.22 From time to time the Judicial Appointments Group undertakes specific reviews of female and ethnic minority candidates to ensure that no suitable female or ethnic minority candidates are overlooked.

2.6.23 When considering appointments to particular posts, the Lord Chancellor has instructed that, wherever possible, women and ethnic minority candidates are included for consideration and, where appropriate, are among those short-listed.

2.6.24 Some prospective or current applicants for judicial appointments have little or no direct experience of the jurisdiction in which they might be required to sit. For example, a civil-only practitioner who has applied or wishes to apply to sit as an Assistant Recorder will almost certainly be required, if appointed, to sit in the Crown Court. In such circumstances arrangements can be made for the applicant or prospective applicant to 'sit-in' with an experienced Circuit Judge so that they may gain an insight into the requirements of the post. These opportunities for familiarisation are of benefit in appropriate circumstances to a range of candidates and may provide encouragement to those who might be hesitating about applying.

2.6.25 The Lord Chancellor takes due account of the domestic commitments and circumstances of individuals wherever possible when making appointments to particular geographical locations. In some cases appointments are deferred until such time as a vacancy in the appropriate location becomes available, or applicants are specifically informed when vacancies in a particular area are likely to arise where they have previously registered an interest in that location.

Fairness of the procedures

2.6.26 In 1992 the Lord Chancellor part funded, with the Bar Council, a research project undertaken by TMS Consultants into the treatment of women at the Bar and in the judiciary. The report was published in November 1992 and was entitled 'Without Prejudice?'. The report recommended, inter alia, a revision of the selection criteria for the judiciary and a review of the selection methods. Although the report was not entirely sympathetic to the particular relationships involved between the Lord Chancellor and the legal profession, the Lord Chancellor has given due consideration to its recommendations.

2.6.27 The new selection criteria for appointment to the Circuit Bench and District Bench have been clearly defined and relate to the experience, skills and personal qualities required to carry out the functions of the post. Each candidate will be assessed against each of the criteria and interviewers will not ask questions that are irrelevant to the criteria and will avoid questions which imply stereotypical assumptions about particular groups.

2.6.28 Further developments in relation to the criteria and selection methods for other judicial appointments will require the same approach, recognising the need to ensure that selection methods do not have an adverse impact on women or ethnic minority practitioners, or any other group.

Report of the Home Affairs Committee on Judicial Appointments Procedures (Memorandum by the Lord Chancellor's Department) [1995–96] 52–II, p. 129f.

RB NOTE: Further statements on present practice are to be found in Judicial Appointments: The Lord Chancellor's Policies and Procedures, *1990 (Central Office of Information).*

---

67   THE LAW SOCIETY PRESENTS THE CASE FOR A JUDICIAL APPOINTMENTS COMMISSION, 1995

Our system of judicial appointments has so far avoided the growing politicisation of public appointments which has taken place in recent years. The heavy reliance on the views of the serving judiciary itself acts as some safeguard against politicisation, although as we have argued it may be less beneficial in other ways.

This freedom from party political taint depends upon the integrity of successive Lord Chancellors and of the civil servants who operate the system. There is no institutional safeguard against bias. In the Society's view, it would be unwise to assume that the judicial appointments system will always remain immune from the pressures affecting other areas of public life. It would be preferable to establish arrangements which are more justifiable in principle, and which insulate the system from political influence.

We favour the establishment of a broad-based Judicial Appointments Commission to oversee the system of appointments. The Lord Chancellor has in the past resisted that proposal on the grounds that his personal responsibility to Parliament for each judicial appointment is beneficial, and that his responsibility would be lost if a Judicial Appointments Commission were created. We do not think that is in practice an overwhelming objection. There is little or no practical reality to the Lord Chancellor's present accountability to Parliament for individual judicial appointments. By the time it becomes evident that an individual appointment was misguided, it is likely that the Lord Chancellor who appointed the judge in question will no longer be in office. It seems unlikely therefore that much would be lost if the Lord Chancellor's personal responsibility for appointments was reduced or removed.

A Judicial Appointments Commission might operate either as an advisory or as an executive body. As an advisory body, it would be responsible for advising on the methods of selection which should be used for judicial appointments, including the criteria to be applied, and would report on the way in which the appointments system was operated from year to year, including reporting to Parliament on such matters as whether inadequate salaries impeded appointment of candidates of the requisite calibre. As an executive body, a Judicial Appointments Commission would take over the functions currently exercised by the Lord Chancellor's officials in obtaining and assessing references about applicants; conducting interviews and (under our proposals) operating the modern selection procedure we recommend. The commission could either provide the advice on which the Lord Chancellor exercised his functions of appointing or recommending for appointment, or could make the appointments and recommendations itself. We would prefer the Judicial Appointments Commission to have an executive rather than an advisory remit, but we have no preference as to whether the Commission should advise the Lord Chancellor on recommendations, or make the recommendations itself.

The main advantages of a Judicial Appointments Commission are that it would:
- distance the responsibility for individual appointments from Ministerial control;
- assist in formalising the procedures and criteria by which candidates are appointed; and,

- enable the appointment system to develop as necessary to reflect good recruitment practice;
- assist in achieving public confidence in the objectivity and even-handedness of the appointment process.

The establishment of a Judicial Appointments Commission would also enable better arrangements to be made for dealing with complaints about individual members of the judiciary. At present, the Lord Chancellor has power to dismiss a Circuit Judge for incapacity or misbehaviour, but it has proved very difficult to operate that procedure in the past. It is also difficult to deal with complaints for which less draconian action is required. It is occasionally made known that the Lord Chancellor has expressed displeasure to a judge about a particular matter, but it is not clear what status any such rebukes have. The Lord Chancellor is not managerially responsible for individual judges, and it is not suggested he should be. Nor are presiding judges in a position to deal with complaints about judicial behaviour. We believe that one function for a Judicial Appointments Commission should be to establish and operate proper complaints procedures, along the lines of those already applying to the two practising branches of the legal profession.

We therefore suggest that the Judicial Appointments Commission should have the following responsibilities:

- to appoint (or to recommend candidates for appointment) to all full-time and part-time judicial posts;
- to keep under review the procedures by which candidates are selected;
- to establish and develop appropriate criteria for appointments, building on the work already done by the Lord Chancellor;
- to ensure in particular that these procedures and criteria do not indirectly discriminate against solicitors or against women or ethnic minority candidates, and to consider how applications from such candidates could be encouraged;
- to oversee all judicial training,
- to establish and operate arrangements for dealing with complaints about members of the judiciary.

The composition of such a Commission will be important and there is unlikely to be a uniquely correct solution to be found. It is important that the Commission should command the confidence both of the legal profession and of the public at large. We suggest, therefore, that there should be four principal groups on the Commission, none of which should be in a dominant position: serving members of the judiciary; legal academics and members of the two branches of the legal profession; lay persons with particular expertise in recruitment and training methods at senior level; and lay persons representing the community as a whole. Appointments to the Commission should be made by the Lord Chancellor, after appropriate consultation, but some form of cross-party Parliamentary endorsement should be required in order to reduce the risk of party political considerations influencing appointments.

The judicial appointments system was designed at a time when almost all those who were eligible for appointment were barristers. Despite a number of improvements in recent years, the system is not a satisfactory means of identifying the best candidates among a much wider field, in which solicitors as well as barristers are eligible, and in which many potential candidates do not regularly practise as advocates.

We believe the proposals in this report would substantially improve the appointments system, building on the progress which has been made in recent years. Implementing these proposals would help ensure that all those eligible have an equal chance of appointment, based on merit rather than professional background. Our proposals would also improve the institutional structure within which the system operates. A Judicial Appointments Commission would ensure that appointments remain free from political bias. The Commission could also develop satisfactory means for dealing with complaints about members of the judiciary, and ensure that the appointments system was kept under regular review to ensure that it conformed to best modern practice.

Report of the Home Affairs Committee on Judicial Appointments Procedures (Memorandum by the Law Society) [1995–6] 52–II, pp. 236–8.

---

68   J. A. G. GRIFFITH PROPOSES A CAREER JUDICIARY AND A CONSTITUTIONAL COURT, 1995

The principal defects in the present system for the appointment of judges are these:
1. The system is secretive, being based on private consultations, the contents of which are not disclosed to candidates and so not open to question or challenge.
2. The category of those consulted is limited and closed.
3. Those consulted are almost all themselves judges, making the system self-perpetuating and self-justificatory. In effect, judges decide who shall, and who shall not, be judges, without the need to satisfy any external, objectively ascertainable, criteria, or to account to any other body.
4. The category of candidates is closed, being limited to 'members of the Bar of high standing who have been in practice for perhaps twenty or thirty years and hold the rank of Queen's Counsel. Those appointed are in the forefront of their profession and outstanding in their field: they will have enjoyed a substantial and successful practice and high professional regard, often in a specialist area of law'. Solicitors may qualify in exceptional cases.

This system has operated in the past, and operates at present, so as to produce, in the High Court and above, a group of persons, exercising the judicial function, who are drawn almost exclusively from a small section of the wealthy professional upper middle class. Their class origin is well known, often commented on, and indicated clearly by their educational background. Of the group at present, 80 per cent educated privately at public schools; and 80 per cent attended the universities of Oxford or Cambridge in the late 1940s and early 1950s when entry was largely restricted to the well-to-do. Over the post-war years these figures have varied very little.

The senior judges (High Court and above) represent a ruling class élite, chosen from a group of candidates far more limited in category than that of any comparable professional group in this country. To consider for appointment only those who fall within the category [referred to above] excludes, from the ranks of the senior judiciary, younger practitioners of great ability and ensures that the average age of senior judges remains at or over 60 years. No other profession relies so much on persons of such age. The Lord Chancellor sees the problem as one of identity.

The Lord Chancellor's Department's Memorandum [*RB NOTE: see Doc. 66*] states:

> The Lord Chancellor has no plans to reconstitute the professional judiciary to reflect the composition of society as a whole. It is not the function of the judiciary to reflect particular sections of the community (para 2.3.3).

But no one suggests judges should do either. To 'reflect' either the whole or the parts of the whole community is manifestly impossible. (The Memorandum shows its own confusion by suggesting that reflection of 'particular sections' is the function of the House of Commons which it is not and never has been.)

The Memorandum continues:

> This is not to say that the Lord Chancellor does not appreciate the value of the judiciary more closely reflecting the make-up of society as a whole. Other things being equal, that should tend over time to result from ensuring the fullest possible equality of opportunity for persons in all sections of society who wish to enter the legal profession and who aspire to sit judicially. This implies equality of opportunity at all levels of the educational system and the legal profession as well as in the appointments system itself.

These are weasel words indeed, from which almost all meaning has been extracted. After the cop-out clichés of 'other things being equal' and 'over time', the under-represented are bluntly told they must wait until equality of opportunity at all levels of the educational system is achieved. In the meantime the Lord Chancellor is happy to continue with a system based on educational privilege of an extreme kind.

But the problem is not one of identity. I believe that members of the public when driven, almost always against their wish, to litigation, want to be judged by professional people to whom they can relate, in physical conditions which are not strange, under procedures which are not artificial, and in language which is intelligible. Too often they do not meet these conditions. So they lack confidence in the system. And they are not impressed by reports in the press about failures to remedy miscarriages of justice, about the absurdity of the Spycatcher litigation, about GCHQ, about incomprehensible sentencing, or about judges being reprimanded.

The single most important reform is to introduce onto the bench a new generation of younger, better trained, more broadly qualified men and women. What follows suggests how this might be done. The result of its adoption would be to move towards a new structure for the judiciary. I trace the career of the future judge whom, to admit ambiguity, I call Evelyn.

1. At the age of 22 years, Evelyn graduates in law at a university in the United Kingdom, (ideally after a four-year course, one year having been spent at a university in France, Germany or Italy).

2. Three years later, Evelyn qualifies as a solicitor or barrister.

3. For the next five years, Evelyn is in private practice. Now Evelyn decides to seek a career as a judge.

4. At the age of 30 years, Evelyn sits a highly competitive examination (written, oral, interviews) for a place at the Judicial College.

5. For the next three years, Evelyn takes a wide range of full-time courses, specialising in the second and third year on the area of law he has chosen and in which he will pursue his judicial career.

6. At the age of 33 years, Evelyn passes out of the Judicial College.

7. For the next three years, Evelyn serves apprenticeship as a judge, alongside experienced judges, in his specialist area.

8. At the age of 36 years, Evelyn is appointed as a Circuit Judge (or other judicial office).

9. After four years, Evelyn is entitled to apply for promotion to the High Court.

Note. This is the only track to the High Court, there being no direct appointment from practice to the bench at that or any higher level.

THE CASE FOR A CONSTITUTIONAL COURT

Since nearly all High Court judges are appointed when they are between about 45 and 57 it is likely that they will have shed such political enthusiasms as they may have had when young and have formed firm views about how the country should be run. (Sir Frederick Lawton, former Lord Justice, *Solicitors' Journal*, 2 November 1990.)

... the deeper question, whether good judicial decisions are them-selves fuelled by ideals which are not normally neutral, but which represent ethical principles about how the state should be run, and in that sense may be said to be political principles ... The substantive principles of judicial review are judge-made, owing neither their content nor their authority as law to the legislature ... They constitute eithical ideals as to the virtuous conduct of the state's affairs. (Sir John Laws, Justice of the High Court, 'Law and Democracy' in *Public Law*, Spring 1995.)

Background

This discussion takes place at a peculiarly critical time. At the end of the 1980s the reputation of the senior judiciary (the Supreme Court and the Law Lords) was at its lowest point this century. For most of the first 15 years after 1945, in the potentially controversial sphere of public law (with which alone I am concerned in this paper), the judges were quiescent, not mixing it with the politicians. The change began when Lord Reid succeeded as senior Law Lord in 1962. He was, in the best sense of the words, a politically conscious judge who had been an active Conservative MP for 15 years, a Law Officer, and then a frontbench spokesman on a full range of issues. He became a Law Lord in 1948. Between 1959 and 1962, six Law Lords retired and Lord Denning moved to the Court of Appeal as Master of the Rolls. Reid's influence for the next ten years was dominant.

In seven major decisions in the 1960s, the Law Lords reversed the Court of Appeal or its Scottish equivalent. In five of these, the decision curtailed the powers of Government or other public body: *Ridge* v. *Baldwin* (1963), *Burmah Oil* v. *Lord Advocate* (1965), *Padfield* v. *Minister of Agriculture Fisheries and Food* (1968), *Conway* v. *Rimmer* (1968), *Anisminic Ltd.* v. *Foreign Compensation Commission* (1969). The other two decisions curtailed the powers of trade unions: *Rookes* v. *Barnard* (1964), *Stratford* v. *Lindley* (1965).

The 1970s followed the same general trend of increased judicial intervention. The senior Law Lords were Wilberforce and Diplock. Neither was a civil libertarian. The thalidomide litigation (*A–G.* v. *Times Newspapers* (1974) was Reid's last important case but not his most distinguished. The decade was mostly famous for the way the courts handled industrial relations. The story of the National Industrial Relations Court (1971–74) under Sir John Donaldson needs no re-telling. Politics apart, the judicial system was set a task for which it was unsuited. After the débâcle of *Heaton's Transport* v. *TGWU* (1972) when the Law Lords sprang the dockers from prison, and Denning in *Secretary of State for Employment* v. *Aslef* (No. 2) 1972 found a way round *Padfield* when trade unions appeared to be able to benefit from that decision, the attitude of the Court of Appeal towards Labour legislation from 1974 to 1979 was so antagonistic that the Law Lords had to restrain Denning.

The 1980s

The decline in the reputation of members of the senior judiciary was mainly the result of their response to three issues: cases concerned with freedom of expression and of association; miscarriages of justice; and the reform of the legal profession. During this decade judges were under public scrutiny more continuously than at any other time during this century.

Freedom of expression and of association
Over the years the judiciary have defined and re-defined the limits of these

freedoms. The presence or absence of a written constitution or of a Bill of Rights, while it shapes this process, does not otherwise greatly affect its outcome which depends on a wide range of changing economic, political and social events.

Two factors may have caused the large number of conflicts in the courts involving the media during the 1980s: the style of government and the growth of investigative journalism. In some cases Law Officers were clearly being driven by the insistence of Ministers, including the Prime Minister. In other cases, newspaper editors and television producers responded readily to information they received from unorthodox sources. But the decisions in the courts were those of the judges and often aroused resentment and, occasionally, ridicule. In 1980 the Law Lords in *British Steel Corporation* v. *Granada Television* upheld the Court of Appeal and required the respondents to disclose the name of the BSC employee who had supplied them with confidential documents used in a televised interview with the chairman of the corporation. Lord Salmon, dissenting, said: 'There are no circumstances in this case which have ever before deprived or ever should deprive the press of its immunity against revealing its sources of information.'

This decision was followed in *Secretary of State for Defence* v. *Guardian Newspapers* (1984) where the copy of a 'secret' Ministerial document was delivered anonymously to the editor of the *Guardian* newspaper. The document concerned parliamentary and public statements to be made on 1 November 1983 about, and contemporaneously with, the delivery of Cruise Missiles from the USA to Greenham Common air base. A majority of Law Lords upheld the decision of the Court of Appeal requiring the newspaper to deliver the copy to the Department. This was despite the provisions of section 10 of the Contempt of Court Act 1981 which protected newspapers from disclosure unless this was shown to be necessary in the interests of national security (amongst other things).

In 1985 and 1986, articles appeared in *The Times* and *The Independent* written by a financial journalist concerning two references to the Monopolies and Mergers Commission. Inspectors investigating insider dealings required the journalist to answer questions about the nature and sources of his information. His refusal to do so resulted in a fine of £20,000, a decision upheld by the Law Lords: *Re an Inquiry* (1988).

Section 10 of the Contempt of Court Act 1981 was further weakened by the Law Lords' decision in *X Ltd* v. *Morgan Grampian (Publishers) Ltd.* (1990) (an application is presently before the European Court of Human Rights, supported by a majority of the Commission). The journalist in this case was found guilty of contempt for refusing to disclose his source and threatened with imprisonment. In the event he was fined £5,000 with costs believed to exceed £100,000. Disclosure in the 'interests of justice' under section 10 was held to extend to include 'interests in the administration of justice'.

A cognate case was *Home Office* v. *Harman* (1981) by the Court of Appeal and a majority of Law Lords where a solicitor was found to be in contempt of court for showing a journalist documents which had been made public in court. On their basis the journalist wrote an article criticising the

Home Office for what he called 'internal bureaucratic intrigue'. Subsequently the European Commission of Human Rights accepted a complaint against the Government and a settlement was reached.

Similarly a majority in the Court of Appeal upheld the granting of an injunction restraining Thames Television from showing a film about the Primodos drug used in pregnancy testing. Shaw LJ said 'The law of England was indeed, as Blackstone declared, a law of liberty; but the freedoms it recognised did not include a licence for the mercenary betrayal of business confidences': *Schering Chemicals* v. *Falkman Ltd.* (1982). Lord Denning MR dissented on the ground that such prior restraints were not justified.

The general attitude of the courts was further shown in the strong criticisms made by senior members of the judiciary, especially Lord Lane CJ, of the BBC programmes *Rough Justice* and *Out of Court.*

But the overwhelming litigation was that surrounding Peter Wright's memoirs, *Spycatcher.* In September 1985, the Attorney General began proceedings in the Supreme Court of New South Wales, seeking to restrain publication of the book for breach of confidentiality. In July 1986, in the United Kingdom, the Attorney was granted injunctions, upheld by the Court of Appeal under Sir John Donaldson MR, preventing the *Guardian* and the *Observer* from publishing articles deriving directly or indirectly from Wright. In April 1987 they were joined by *The Independent* and in July 1987 by the *Sunday Times*.

By this time, the book was available in the United Kingdom, having been published in the USA. So the *Guardian* and the *Observer* in July 1987 sought the discharge of the injunctions against them. But, in crucial judgments, the Court of Appeal and, by a majority, the Law Lords continued the injunctions. In Lord Templeman's opinion, the continuance of the injuctions was fully consistent with the European Convention of Human Rights. This was when the reputation of the senior judiciary reached its lowest point, the absurdity of preventing newspaper publication in these circumstances being manifest.

Eventually the High Court, the Court of Appeal and, in October 1988, the Law Lords accepted that the injunctions must be discharged. But the damage had been done. As Sir Nicolas Browne-Wilkinson VAC had said on 22 July 1987 when supporting applications to discharge the injunctions (in which he was overruled):

> It is frequently said that the law is an ass. I, of course, do not agree. But there is a limit to what can be achieved by orders of the court. If the courts were to make orders manifestly incapable of achieving their avowed purpose, such as to prevent the dissemination of information which is already disseminated, the law would to my mind indeed be an ass.

A recent decision in this line of cases interfering with the freedom of expression was the upholding by the courts of the media ban on broadcasting any matter which included words spoken by a person representing or purporting to represent organisations in Northern Ireland. These included

Sinn Fein and the Ulster Defence Association, neither being a proscribed organisation.

Sinn Fein at this time was represented by one elected MP at Westminster and was supported by about 11 per cent of votes cast in local elections, with dozens of local councillors. The ban was imposed by the Government on 19 October 1988 in notices to the BBC under the Licence and Agreement and to the IBA under section 29(3) of the Broadcasting Act 1981. These provisions empowered the Secretary of State to require the broadcasting authorities to refrain from broadcasting specified matters.

Seven journalists sought to have the ban set aside on the grounds that the ban was contrary to Article 10 of the European Convention of Human Rights, disproportionate to the mischief at which it was aimed, perverse in that no reasonable Secretary of State properly directing himself could have made it, and that the statute and licence did not empower him to give such directives which prevented or hindered the broadcasting authorities from fulfilling their duties to preserve due impartiality: *ex parte Brind* (1991). The Law Lords rejected these arguments and held that the Secretary of State had not exceeded the limits of his discretion nor acted unreasonably.

A second fundamental freedom is that of association and membership of a trade union or other such body. Here the outstanding decision was that of the Law Lords upholding the Government's ban in December 1983 on trade union membership of civil servants at the Government Communications Headquarters (GCHQ): *Council of Civil Service Unions* v. *Minister for the Civil Service* (1985). The Prime Minister's decision was taken without consultation with the union. The question before the courts was whether the failure to consult invalidated the decision to ban. Before the Court of Appeal, the Government claimed that consultation might have endangered national security and supported this by an affidavit sworn by Sir Robert Armstrong as Secretary of the Cabinet and Head of the Home Civil Service. The crucial passage was in a paragraph 16:

> To have entered such consultations would have served to bring out the vulnerability of areas of operation to those who had shown themselves ready to organise disruption, and consultation with individual members of staff at GCHQ would have been impossible without involving the national unions.

The Law Lords accepted this claim without further investigation although its substance was strongly denied by the trade unions. In this, as in other cases, the courts refused to question the validity of the Government's defence of 'national security'.

Miscarriages of justice

This group of cases requires little elaboration. Nothing contributed more to the decline in the reputation of the senior judiciary than their failures to respond to allegations of wrongful convictions.

The Guildford Four were convicted of murder in September 1975 and in 1977 were refused leave to appeal after the Balcombe Street arrests of IRA members who claimed responsibility. The new evidence gave rise 'to no lurking doubts whatever' in the minds of the Court of Appeal. The Maguire Seven were convicted of unlawfully handling nitroglycerine in 1976. They also were refused leave to appeal in 1977, no member of the Court seeing any reason for disturbing any of the convictions on the basis that they were unsafe or unsatisfactory.

Doubts about the rightness of the convictions of these eleven persons persisted and in August 1987 the Avon and Somerset police were appointed to undertake an inquiry. Documents were found at Guildford which led to the conclusion of police fabrication and on 19 October 1989 the convictions of the Four were quashed. In June 1990 the Director of Public Prosecutions accepted that the convictions of the Maguire Seven were unsafe and unsatisfactory and could not be upheld.

On 21 November 1975 six men were convicted of the murder of twenty-one persons in a bomb attack at public houses in Birmingham. In March 1976 applications for leave to appeal were refused. When in 1980 the Court of Appeal accepted an application by the police to strike out civil proceedings brought by the Birmingham Six, Lord Denning MR said:

> Just consider the course of events if this action is allowed to proceed to trial. If the six men fail, it will mean that much time and money will have been expended by many people to no good purpose. If the six men win, it will mean that the police were guilty of perjury, that they were guilty of violence and threats, that the confessions were involuntary and were improperly admitted in evidence and that the convictions were erroneous. That would mean the Home Secretary would either have to recommend they be pardoned or he would have to remit the case to the Court of Appeal. This is such an appalling vista that every sensible person in the land would say: It cannot be right these actions should go any further.

In November 1981 the Law Lords upheld Lord Denning's judgment.

In 1987 the Devon and Cornwall police carried out an inquiry and subsequently the case was referred to the Court of Appeal. Lord Lane CJ, Lords Justices Stephen Brown and O'Connor reported in January 1988: 'The longer the hearing has gone on the more convinced this Court has become that the verdict of the jury was correct. We have no doubt that these convictions were both safe and satisfactory.' In August 1990, following the abandonment of the convictions of the Guildford Four and a further police investigation, the case was referred again to the Court of Appeal. On 14 March 1991 the Court set free the Birmingham Six.

Neither the conduct of the trial courts nor the evidence there adduced is here in issue. What matters are the misjudgments of the Court of Appeal in refusing leave to appeal and on referrals. On these the record was corrected only after continuous and persistent pressure from the Great and the Good, determined members of both Houses of Parliament, investigative journalists, and other campaigners.

The work and organisation of the legal profession

This was the title of the principal policy paper put forward by the Lord Chancellor in January 1989 (Cm 570). Two others concerned Contingency Fees (Cm 571) and Conveyancing by Authorised Practitioners (Cm 572). The response from the senior judiciary was extraordinary and verged on the hysterical.

Lord Lane CJ referred to the first papers as 'one of the most sinister documents ever to emanate from Government'. Lord Donaldson MR said he had 'absolutely no disagreement' with Lord Lane over the main issues. Lord Scarman criticised the papers as being 'ill-considered', 'superficial' in their reasoning, and 'flawed' in their logic. Lord Ackner spoke of the proposals as involving 'at the very least a substantial risk of the destruction of the Bar', of 'the myopic application of dogma'. The former Lord Chancellor, Lord Hailsham, was reported as saying that the Government was 'thinking with its bottom and sitting on its head'.

In a debate in the House of Lords on 7 April 1989, Lord Lane spoke of oppression not standing 'on the doorstep with a toothbrush moustache and swastika armband' but creeping up step by step until all of a sudden the unfortunate citizen realised that freedom had gone. Lord Donaldson spoke of an 'unmitigated disaster', Lord Bridge of a 'deep sense of unease' felt by the great majority of the judiciary and of 'hasty and ill-considered legislation'. Lords Goff, Griffiths, Ackner and Oliver spoke in like terms. Much of this was repeated by Lords Ackner and Donaldson during the Lords' debate on the Courts and Legal Services Bill which implemented, in a modified form, Lord Mackay's proposals.

The extremity of the language and the vehemence in which it was couched seemed to suggest that the senior judiciary were not to be trusted with a calm consideration of where the public interest lay on matters affecting the legal profession and the administration of justice.

Future developments

The European Convention on Human Rights

The campaign for the incorporation of this Convention into UK domestic law has now attracted the support of many members of the senior judiciary. Whatever may be said of the substantive merits and demerits of this proposal there is no doubt that incorporation would greatly increase the political influence of the courts and lead to further judicialisation of the political process or, according to one's view, politicisation of the judicial process.

In recent debates in the House of Lords (the Third Reading was on 1 May 1995) Lord Lester's Human Rights Bill advocated incorporation and was supported by Lord Taylor CJ, Lord Woolf, Lord Browne-Wilkinson, Lord Lloyd and Lord Slynn. The Lord Chief Justice said he also spoke with the strong support of Sir Thomas Bingham MR. Other judges of lower rank have expressed their support for incorporation. The Labour and Liberal Democratic parties have both endorsed incorporation.

Incorporation can take several forms but may increase the political involvement of the judiciary in three ways.

The first can be exemplified by Article 2 of the Convention. This provides: 'Everyone's life shall be protected by law'. Hitherto abortion and euthanasia have been matters for discussion and decision in Parliament. Under this Article, they will be transferred to the courts. In the USA, as is well known, this has involved Presidential nominees for the Supreme Court in much controversy.

Secondly, if incorporation is to be properly entrenched it must empower the courts to declare Acts of Parliament invalid. This is the consequence favoured, as we shall see, by at least one Law Lord. Other forms of incorporation stop short of this. Nevertheless they are bound to give rise to much political argument in the courts.

Thirdly, the provisions of several Articles of the Convention empower the courts to rule whether or not a particular restriction on a conferred 'right' is legal, and to do so on political grounds. Thus Article 10 provides: 'Everyone has the right to freedom of expression'. It continues:

> The exercise of these freedoms, since it carries with it duties and responsibilities, may be subject to such formalities, conditions, restrictions or penalties as are prescribed by law and are necessary in a democratic society, in the interests of national security, territorial integrity or public safety, for the prevention of disorder or crime, for the protection of health or morals, for the protection of the reputation or rights of others, for preventing the disclosure of information received in confidence, or for maintaining the authority and impartiality of the judiciary.

This, in some respects, actually weakens the rights of the individual under the common law by the imprecision of categories such as 'protection of health or morals'. But, more importantly, it vests in the courts the power to decide what restrictions etc. are 'necessary in a democratic society'. It is difficult to imagine any judgment more political and more comprehensive than that.

I am not here concerned with the arguments for or against incorporation, only to establish that incorporation seems likely to be enacted within the first session of a Parliament under a Labour or Liberal-Labour administration, and that this will result in a substantial transfer of political power to the senior judiciary.

The new jurisprudence

During the last few years, judges have actively extended their powers by the development of judicial review and other procedures. This has been spoken of largely as a reaction to the activities of over-zealous or careless Ministers and no doubt this is part of the story. But the other part is the greater willingness of the courts to extend their jurisdiction. It is easy to applaud the decision in *M* v. *Home Office* (1993) where the Law Lords held the Home Secretary to be guilty of contempt of court (albeit only in his official capacity, not personally) for disregarding an order of the court requiring an asylum seeker to be returned to the UK; and in *ex parte Hickey* (1994) requiring the Home Secretary to disclose fresh information he receives following inquiries on a petition to refer a conviction to the Court of Appeal. But the critical lines that separate executive power from judicial power were shown dramatically in *ex parte Fire Brigades Union and others* (1995). By a majority of 3 to 2, the Law Lords held that the Home Secretary could not ignore a statutory provision enabling him to bring into force a statutory scheme for payment of compensation to victims of crime, while proposing a different non-statutory scheme of his own.

For the minority Lord Keith said: 'The fact that the decision is of a political and administrative character means that any interference by a court of law would be a most improper intrusion into a field which lies peculiarly within the province of Parliament.' He was joined by Lord Mustill who said that some of the argument addressed to their Lordships 'would have the court push to the very boundaries of the distinction between court and Parliament established in, and recognised ever since the Bill of Rights 1689. 300 years have passed since then, and the political and social landscape has changed beyond recognition. But the boundaries remain; they are of crucial significance to our private and public lives; and the courts should I believe make sure that they are not overstepped.'

These recent cases may be seen as a continuation of the general trends of the 1980s. But there is another aspect. It seems there is a concerted drive by some members of the senior judiciary to extend their powers into new fields from which hitherto they have been excluded by the conventional laws of the constitution. I have already quoted as a headpiece to this paper the reference by Mr Justice Laws to the political principles which lie behind judicial decisions. With this proposition I have no quarrel. It is clear that judges often must have regard to their view of where the public interest lies and that, in a broad sense, must be a political decision shaped by their own personalities and experiences. It is less clear how far they should allow their own political philosophy – 'how the state should be run' – to influence their judgment. Sir John then hugely magnifies his claim of judicial supremacy by calling into existence a 'higher-order law' which could not be abrogated by Parliament. In his formulation it is the Constitution that is sovereign, not Parliament, and judges are the Constitution's custodians. We should recognise, says Sir John 'the moral force of the basis on which control of public power is effected by the unelected judges'. This is reminiscent of the old story of Labouchere saying that he did not object to Gladstone's always having the ace of trumps up his sleeve but only to his pretence that God put it there.

Sir John makes it clear how far his doctrine of judicial supremacy may go. First he considers Article 9 of the Bill of Rights protecting the freedom of speech and debates or proceedings in Parliament from being impeached or questioned in any court or place out of Parliament. This he calls 'a statute like any other' and so subject to judicial interpretation. To be specific, he says he is 'not convinced' that an MP who, motivated by actual personal malice, defames, in the course of debate, an individual outside Parliament, 'should not' be subject to 'the ordinary law of defamation' presumably in the ordinary courts 'out of Parliament'. He adds: 'Article 9 could *readily* be construed conformably with such a state of affairs' (my emphasis).

In the same issue of *Public Law* (Spring 1995) as Sir John Laws's article, Lord Woolf writes on 'Droit Public – English Style' and he is prepared to take the final step:

> I myself would consider there were advantages in making it clear that ultimately there are even limits on the supremacy of Parliament which it is the courts' inalienable responsibility to identify and uphold.

He concludes that this is necessary 'to enable the rule of law to be preserved'.

Over the years, judges have from time to time claimed this pre-eminence which today seems to be couched in the strongest terms. Those who take this view see themselves as occupying a position above Parliament as guardians of some ultimate political principles which they enshrine. In these days of 'sleaze' and Lord Nolan's committee such a claim may be popular. But it is dangerous in the extreme and the record of the courts in recent times does not begin to justify acceptance of such a position. In a democracy, 'how the state should be run' must be determined by the Queen in Parliament, not by judges however eminent.

SUMMARY AND CONCLUSIONS

My argument is that the influence of the senior judiciary has increased, is increasing, and ought to be diminished. At this point in our long island history, this is an unpopular view and might be thought more applicable to the early years of the Stuarts or the late years of Queen Victoria. The present Government is unpopular (which is usual) and ill-advised (which is not). But its shortcomings are providing a springboard for judicial activism of a dangerous kind. This is not, however, a situation that has suddenly arisen, nor is it one that will quickly disappear. Apart from the present discontents, it emerges from the relationships between the three principal institutions of our Constitution, and in particular from a newfound vitality among the judges which, in a modest way, began to show itself in the early 1960s. Why that happened at that time (apart from the influence of Lord Reid) it is perhaps too early to say.

This activism has led the senior judiciary into areas of decision-making where their particular expertise is limited, and where their judgment is open to criticism. The examples I have given from the 1980s, their restrictions on freedom of expression and of association, their failure to detect and remedy gross miscarriages of justice, and their intemperate and ill-judged reaction to the proposals put before them by Lord Mackay seem to me to support this conclusion. Other examples could be given.

Furthermore, the scope for greater judicial activity will be greatly increased if the European Convention on Human Rights is incorporated into UK domestic law.

And there is evidence to suggest that some members of the senior judiciary positively favour an extension of their jurisdiction which would result in setting themselves up as the final arbiters of the Constitution with powers to overrule Parliament and to intervene in its proceedings contrary to the Bill of Rights.

This situation is not remediable by merely procedural changes to the method of appointing judges. I suggest that it requires structural and institutional reform and the appointment of new non-legal members to the highest court.

A CONSTITUTIONAL COURT

Whatever procedural changes may be suggested in the appointment of judges, such as a Judicial Commission, a Minister of Justice responsible to the House of Commons, or a wider recruitment to all levels of the bench from amongst legal practitioners, in my view something extra is needed to deal properly with the mix of legal, political and social problems presented by public law cases. For this purpose I propose the creation of a Constitutional Court composed in part of judges and in part of persons from outside the legal profession.

Such a Court could take many forms. What follows is one model, in the barest outline.

1. *Jurisdiction.* This would include (1) all judicial review cases, (2) all referrals in cases of alleged miscarriages of justice (to investigate which the Court would need special powers), (3) all cases involving contempt of court or breaches of confidentiality where the public interest was involved and (4) all cases brought under the European Convention on Human Rights if incorporated in UK domestic law.
2. *Membership.* This would consist of panels of (1) 10 judges appointed by the same person or body entrusted with the appointment of judges generally and (2) 10 councillors (or some other such title) appointed by the Queen, on the nomination of the Prime Minister.

Appointments to the Court of judges and councillors would be for five years, not renewable. One judge and one councillor would be designated Joint President.

The panel of judges would be drawn from senior judges already in office who would continue to be available to hear cases in their own courts.

The panel of councillors would be drawn from those having experience in the conduct of public affairs or in business, trade unions, the media, the voluntary sector, or the professions. Excluded from nomination would be practising members of the legal profession, MPs and peers, those holding offices of profit under the Crown, and the employees of local authorities. The appointments would be part-time.

3. *Sittings.* Cases would, ordinarily, be heard by three judges and three councillors. Exceptionally, plenary sessions would consist of five judges and five councillors.

Sitting members would be chosen by their respective Joint Presidents (who might also sit as one of the members).

4. *Access.* Leave to appeal to the Constitutional Court from either

the court of first instance or the Court of Appeal would be granted only by the Constitutional Court who would need to be satisfied that a matter of sufficient public interest was involved. Leapfrogging from the court of first instance to the Constitutional Court would be common.

    5. *Presentation.* Written submission of argument would be the practice, followed by a short hearing. *Amicus* and Brandeis briefs would be encouraged. If the Court split 3–3 or 5–5, the appeal would be lost.

Report of the Home Affairs Select Committee on Judicial Appointments Procedures (Memorandum by J.A.G. Griffith) [1995–6] 52–II, pp. 260–7.

---

69   THE JUDGES' COUNCIL DEFENDS THE STATUS QUO, 1995

4. As our legal system is presently structured, the requirements placed upon those who are to be appointed as our most senior judges are essentially threefold. First, they must be men or women of complete integrity and impartiality: no Judge of the Supreme Court of England and Wales has ever been required to vacate office for corruption or impropriety. Secondly, they must have the highest level of legal ability: no case of importance can be judged by anybody less than the most able in the field if justice is to be done, and the system must ensure that sufficient judges are available at each tier to hear cases at each level of complexity and gravity. Thirdly, they must conclusively have demonstrated their impartiality, integrity and outstanding expertise, almost always by daily practice in the courts of justice, in the full face of the public and mass media, for a sufficient period to merit the trust the public places in them by virtue of their appointment.

5. These are the core qualities which are required for all appointees to the Supreme Court Bench. Within each Division there are specialist requirements, which narrow the field of candidates for any particular vacancy.

6. Under the system for recommending candidates to the Queen, which has been followed by successive Prime Ministers and Lord Chancellors over many years (with the continuous support and co-operation of successive Heads of Division), the necessary mix of intellectual, practical and personal qualities has been judged over the course of an individual's professional career on the basis of attributable, but confidential, judgments of their professional ability, independence, and effectiveness as advocates. There are a number of elements to this process of continuous assessment, including:

    (a) *Court Experience*
        The skills and experience of the trial advocate in our system are

fundamental. They do not merely (or even) consist in putting forward his or her client's case come what may. On the contrary, successful advocates must develop and exhibit the ability, founded upon sound judgment, to evaluate the strengths and weaknesses of their opponent's case as thoroughly as their own. In addition, the administration of justice in England and Wales depends upon lawyers who appear before the court owing their paramount duty to the interests of justice, and not advancing arguments or evidence which are improper, mendacious or corrupt. The ability, over a period of years, to observe the imperative boundary between the two (in the face of obvious temptations to the contrary) is of paramount importance to maintaining the impartiality of the Bench upon which everything else depends.

(b) *Balance*

Even in jurisdictions which share our heritage of the common law, many have a fragmented profession in which advocates habitually appear either for the prosecution or for the defence; for the drug company or for the trade union; for the individual or for the State. The system in England and Wales, however, places a premium on professional experience which is characterised by variety of client. This is the best guarantee we have that judges will not be 'prosecution' (or 'defence') minded: that unconscious bias cannot creep into the objective determinations which society demands of those in high judicial office.

(c) *Part-Time Service*

Another unique feature of our system is the prior use of senior practitioners as part-time judges. This occurs in a wide variety of courts: in criminal cases as Recorders (and Assistant Recorders); and in civil litigation as Deputy High Court Judges. This ensures that each and every appointee to tenured office is properly able to exercise the considerable responsibilities this entails.

Exceptionally, lawyers who do not have advocacy experience may be appointed to the Bench if they have nevertheless performed with particular distinction in other fields (including service in other judicial offices).

7. The system therefore operates in two stages. First, a practitioner must apply (or be invited to apply) to serve as a part-time judge. Secondly, the choice is made from within this field as to who is best fitted and able to exercise full-time judicial office.

8. At both stages, the opinions of serving judges provide the most solid base available upon which to found appointments. At the first stage, judges see and hear most of the potential candidates before them, day in, day out, from a position in which they are uniquely well placed to assess their professional competence and personal qualities, and to compare them with competitors in the field. At each court centre, the Resident Judge (i.e. the Circuit Judge who superintends judicial business at the court) collects comments from his or her fellow judges on the practitioners who appear before them. These are passed on to the Presiding Judges (i.e. the High Court Judges in charge of judicial business on that circuit), who supplement

them with consultations with the local Bar and Law Society, before passing them to the Lord Chancellor.

9. At the second stage, these evaluations are supplemented by observations of the candidates fulfilling their own judicial role, together with the published adjudications of the appellate courts whenever a particular decision of a part-timer is challenged by way of appeal (a discipline to which all judges are, of course, potentially subject in respect of most of the decisions they take). By using these assessments in the way it does, the system offers a comprehensive record of a candidate's competence across all the range of qualities required over many years, on the strength of which concrete assessments may be made any number of times. Very few recruitment systems in use in the private sector are able to offer anything approaching this degree of assurance.

10. It is worth emphasising that no questions of race, gender, social class, educational background, political affiliation, religion or other irrelevant considerations operate at any stage. It is, however, hard to see how there could be a place for 'affirmative action' involving the appointment of anyone other than the candidate most fitted for office at these levels: plaintiffs in major lawsuits concerning (for example) alleged negligence arising from a complex medical operation can no more be expected to entrust the determination of their rights after the event to someone who is not the best in their field than entrust their bodies to a doctor who was not sufficiently expert in the first place.

11. There is a comparative dimension here also. In the fields of patents and copyrights, and in the commercial and shipping cases, litigants (both here and abroad) have considerable choice as to the country in which they wish any dispute (should such arise) to be adjudicated. In both areas the UK courts are internationally pre-eminent, and make an important contribution to the invisible earnings which lawyers earn for the UK economy. These totalled £425m in 1992. Cases in both courts regularly involve parties neither of whom is resident or registered in the UK, and involve transactions in which there is no UK element. Cases are justiciable in these courts purely because the parties themselves have agreed they should be (with all the benefits to the UK economy this entails). This provides the clearest possible evidence that, in fields in which there is genuine competition between the UK and other countries, the quality of the determinations reached by English and Welsh judges is recognised as having a clear edge over everything else available.

12. No system for appointments to human institutions is infallible, and none of the Heads of Division would claim that the present system is perfect. The present Lord Chancellor has, with the Heads' of Divisions approval, instituted a number of important changes to the system with the aim of allowing it to evolve in line with the changing demands modern society makes of it. These are set out in the Lord Chancellor's own evidence, which the Heads of Division have seen, and which they endorse. More revolutionary changes have been suggested in some quarters, the principal of which (together with their main drawbacks) are summarised [below]. But, in this probably more than in any other area of the constitution,

revolutionary or dramatic change must provide not only clear and deliverable benefits, but also safeguards for the strengths of the status quo. The senior judiciary have increasingly provided the ultimate bulwark for the rights of the individual in the face of what some have characterised as an ever more powerful State. This responsibility requires that the judges must above all continue to be incorruptible, impartial and expert.

SUGGESTIONS FOR CHANGE

Four principal suggestions have been made for reforming current procedures for judicial appointments.

An elected judiciary

In many States in the USA, judges are elected by the populace (subject, obviously, to requirements for the candidates to possess the necessary legal qualifications to discharge the responsibilities of the offices they seek). Arguments have been advanced from time to time that such arrangements should be introduced into the UK in order to ensure the process of law is more responsive to public opinion.

The introduction of such a system in the UK would of course represent a fundamental break with our heritage, which has hitherto sought actively to insulate judicial officers from any form of political pressure for fear of undermining the objectivity of their decisions. Judicial officers who were elected for a finite but renewable term might be tempted to decide cases according to their perception of public opinion rather than as justice demanded. In modern society, in which the media play a strong part in shaping public opinion, elections for judges would call into question their independence from those whose views were given prominence at election time.

A career judiciary

Most other countries in the EU have a career judiciary recruited (and promoted) much in the way we recruit (and promote) members of our armed and civil services. It has been argued that the introduction of such a system here would lead to a younger and more expert judiciary.

In addressing this suggestion, it is necessary to bear in mind the profound differences which exist between the legal systems of countries whose law is derived from the Napoleonic Code (which have a career judiciary) and those which stem from the common law (which do not). Under the Napoleonic system (which does not, in general, use juries) judges in criminal cases combine adjudication with investigative functions, and apply legal rules which are derived from broad statements of principle on the basis of mainly written submissions, and the main focus of the process is considerably less court based than under the common law. Judges in these systems are recruited as postgraduates and follow a career entirely within the professional judiciary. These systems are in use in most of Continental Europe.

Common law systems, on the other hand, operate a court-based, adversarial system of trial, in which evidence is tested by oral cross-examination, and in which the law is derived from detailed statutes and previously decided cases. Judges in these systems (which are in use throughout most of the Commonwealth, and in the USA) are recruited from the ranks of the most senior practitioners while they are at the peak of their careers.

There is therefore limited scope to combine elements piecemeal from the two, since they rest upon profoundly different historical bases. It is not, however, true that career judges are necessarily more 'expert', merely that their experience is exclusively judicial rather than mixed between practice as a trial advocate and as a judge. It is true that the average age of judges in career systems is somewhat lower than in common law systems, but this has the necessary consequence that judges in the lower courts are very much younger than anyone the UK public currently expects to encounter in an adjudicative role.

Lay judges

Another suggestion (and one which has historical precedents in the UK system) is for professional judges to sit alongside lay members. This used to be the system at trials heard at Quarter Sessions (which were abolished by the Courts Act 1970) where judges (both full- and part-time) sat with magistrates, and it continues to be used in appeals on matters of fact to the Crown Court from magistrates' courts. It also has a place in the Employment Appeal Tribunal (which hears appeals from Industrial Tribunals) where professional judges sit with two lay members: one from an employers' organisation and one from a Trade Union. There is also provision for judges in the High Court to be assisted by expert assessors, a facility which is regularly used in the Patents and Admiralty Courts.

In the field of criminal law, of course, lay people have always been the principal arbiters of fact in England and Wales: the lay magistrates in the magistrates' courts and the jury in the Crown Court. Most issues of fact are conclusively determined at the trial stage by lay people; the issues raised upon appeal are those purely of law, or of the way in which legal rules should be applied to particular factual situations. The only area in which a lay element might be added is sentencing, but it is hard to see what this would actually achieve in practice. Sentencing maxima are nearly all set down in legislation: the function of the courts is to ensure consistency of treatment according to the iniquity of offence and offender in the light of the framework Parliament has provided. Adjustments to individual sentences (whether by application by the defendant or the prosecution) are effected by the appeal process.

On the civil side, by contrast, juries are retained only for malicious prosecution and libel (where their use is a source of considerable criticism from time to time). The reason this has happened is because the issues of fact which are raised in civil cases are apt to be arcane and complex. Similar considerations have led some to question the continued use of lay juries in (criminal) fraud trials.

Judicial appointments commission

A fourth suggestion is that appointments should continue to be made from the ranks of the most experienced and able practising lawyers, but that the process of recommendation (whether to the Queen, the Prime Minister or the Lord Chancellor) should be placed in the hands of an independent Commission, comprising judges, senior members of the profession, and lay members.

Various arguments have been advanced in favour of such a approach. The involvement of an independent body would, it is said, allay fears (however misplaced) that the current system is open to political interference. The participation of lay members might, in the opinion of some, serve to provide reassurance to a wider public that no improper criteria were allowed to impinge on the process of appointment. A particular point which has ben made is that greater openness in the system would allow candidates to ensure that personal information used in the process was accurate and up to date.

Each of these arguments is misguided. The creation of an 'Independent' Commission would introduce politics into the process rather than exclude them. Someone would have to appoint the Appointments Commission. The process of appointment to that body would inevitably involve a degree of compromise between the main parties. Furthermore, appointments by the Commission itself would be likely to be subjected to political scrutiny: the American experience with Senate Confirmation hearings should serve as a warning in this regard.

It is true that the presence of some lay element such as has been introduced for those stepping onto the judicial ladder might provide reassurance to the public. But to hand over appointments to a Commission risks politicisation and the involvement of extraneous or irrelevant criteria in a process which, at these senior levels, must focus exclusively upon legal expertise and judicial qualities. The requirement for openness in the information before the Commission would destroy the current system which, through its accumulation of the results of confidential consultations over many years, provides a uniquely solid base upon which to found appointment decisions. Persons consulted without the protection of confidentiality would be unlikely to express full and frank views. Unless the views collected are full and frank they would provide poor guidance to those making these important appointments.

Report of the Home Affairs Select Committee on Judicial Appointments Procedures (Memorandum by the Judges' Council), [1995–6] 52–II, pp. 219–20, 223–4.

---

70   LORD TAYLOR, FORMER LORD CHIEF JUSTICE, SAYS JUDGES NEED BE NO MORE REPRESENTATIVE OF THE PUBLIC THAN A BRAIN SURGEON, 1995

RB NOTE: In an interview with the Sunday Telegraph *published on 19 March 1995, Lord Taylor said:*

I do not think the judiciary should be representative of the public any more than a brain surgeon should be representative of the public. You want someone to do the job ... There is a danger political correctness will cause people to promote changes that are not beneficial ... When you appoint a judge you appoint the best candidate for the job ... You can only have one judge in any one case. If it's a man, it's a man, and I hope he will try the case fairly. If only a woman can hear rape cases, what about the interests of the defendants? ... So what if you're a bright chap from Eton or a comprehensive? The critics of our system seem to ignore that even though you have been to Eton, and Cambridge, and are a member of the Inner Temple – and there are cloisters in all these places – that you have been day by day immersing yourself in the problems of people in all strata of society. If you don't choose judges from the ranks of lawyers, where are you going to find the judges? ...

RB NOTE: Later that year, he was interviewed by members of the House of Commons Home Affairs Committee on the subject of judicial appointments.

Mr Mullin

268. If soundings are such a reasonable system, why is the outcome so predictable?

   (*Lord Taylor of Gosforth*) I assume you mean from that, predictably not satisfactory?

   269. I am not commenting on that. It is just that according to the memorandum we have received from the Lord Chancellor's Department, which has a table attached to it: 80 per cent of the Lords of Appeal are Oxbridge educated; 70 to 75 per cent of the Heads of Division are Oxbridge educated; 80 per cent of the Lord Justices of Appeal and 81 per cent of High Court Judges are Oxbridge educated. Then we had somebody else who submitted evidence. In a survey of 641 judges it found that of the House of Lords, 91 per cent were public school educated; in the Courts of Appeal, 77 per cent were public school educated; of the High Court, 80 per cent; and of all those surveyed nearly 80 per cent. That is what I mean by predictable.

   (*Lord Taylor of Gosforth*) I see. You have made it clear now. If what you are suggesting is that when the judges get together, or recommendations are made, or the Lord Chancellor makes his choice he says, 'Did this chap go to Oxford or Cambridge? Well, we can't have him if he didn't,' that is nonsense. If what you are suggesting is – if I may take one of two approaches to this – that there is some kind of stigma to having been to Oxford and Cambridge, I totally reject that too. I think that the Lord Chancellor does precisely what he says which is, he seeks to appoint those who, on all the information he has, are most suitable for the job. If it so happens that a large number of them have been to Oxford or Cambridge I would not be surprised by that because, by and large, one would want one's judges to be university educated. Not all of them are. There have been some notable ones.

270. But there are other universities.

(*Lord Taylor of Gosforth*) I am coming to that and certainly there are now judges – more judges than there used to be – coming from other universities because there are more universities now.

271. With respect, sir, at the top end of the judicial system there has been no change whatever. Indeed, the trend is marginally in the other direction; that is to say, more public schools and more Oxbridge.

(*Lord Taylor of Gosforth*) I cannot go through the judges. Lord Woolf went to London University and I do not think he is rated poorly on that account. I do not think he had any difficulty getting appointed. The fact is that those who are wanting to succeed and to go into professions very often aim at going to Oxford or Cambridge because, rightly or wrongly, they think those are the best places to go. They may be wrong about that. There are very good law faculties at other universities now. By the same token Oxford and Cambridge are anxious to have the best. So it would not be all that surprising to find that those who are found, at the end of the day, after 25 years in practice to be the best candidates, have been to one or other of those universities or some other university.

272. But it is not only which university they have been to, although that is an interesting feature of the figure.

(*Lord Taylor of Gosforth*) Schools, as well.

273. Yes, it is schools as well; but they are also white, male and usually upper middle-class, overwhelmingly.

(*Lord Taylor of Gosforth*) Of course, those who are judges now have been on the ladder, as it were, as I said before, for something like 25 years. I think I am right in saying that there is a much greater, a much wider catchment area of candidates, both to the universities and into the profession now, than there was. For example, even if you take Oxford and Cambridge, those who go to Oxford and Cambridge now are far more likely to come from state schools than 25 years ago. So you may find that somebody came from a comprehensive school and St John's College, Oxford. I do not know whether that would satisfy you. At least it would be one element coming from a non-upper elitist background. I think, if I may say so, this is a totally wrong approach to testing whether the present system is effective or not. The proof of the pudding is in the eating. Do we, by and large, have good judges? Do we, at the moment, have people who ought to be judges but who are not becoming judges because they have not been to Oxbridge or a public school? I am afraid that put in that way, which is the right way to put it, your statistics may—

274. They are the Lord Chancellor's statistics.

(*Lord Taylor of Gosforth*) The statistics you have quoted may be interesting but I do not think they are an indictment of the system.

275. John Griffith who, as you may know, has made a study in this area, says in his evidence to the Committee that the senior judges (by which he means High Court and above) and these are his words, not mine: 'The ruling class elite, chosen from a group of candidates far more limited in category than that of any comparable profession or group in this country.'

(*Lord Taylor of Gosforth*) He has, for years, had a particular angle on this. He wrote a book called *The Politics of the Judiciary* in which he sought to pursue that theme. I think more recently, frankly, he has taken a better view on the judiciary. In fact, I heard him on the television doing so.

276. His evidence is dated 30 May.

(*Lord Taylor of Gosforth*) As far as the quality of judges are concerned he was highly complimentary, particularly in the context of judges being prepared to stand up to Government, for example. So any suggestion that these are people who are, as it were, from establishment backgrounds and are therefore appointed because they will uphold the establishment, needs to be tested against the track record recently. When I say 'recently' I am thinking about the last ten years or so of the judges' role in judicial review, where time and again they have acted against the establishment. Indeed, there are those now who say that judges are doing it too much, so you really cannot have it both ways, by saying, 'Here are establishment judges who are far too establishment,' and then also saying, 'But they have no business to be overruling Ministers and so on, that is a matter for the Executive.'

277. So you do not accept that there is any weight in the allegation that the present system of judicial appointments results in a too narrow spectrum of people being appointed to senior judicial office?

(*Lord Taylor of Gosforth*) I certainly do not in terms of education. But I do not want to leave aside any of the issues you have raised. You also mentioned gender and you have also mentioned ethnic minorities. It may be that you know what I am going to say but it is true. The reason why there are so few women at the moment is because of the background of the last 25 years. When those who were entering the profession and who would be the judges being appointed now, when women were entering the profession in those days, there were far fewer of them; there were far fewer of them who stayed on; they tended to leave as soon as they were going to have children or get married. The idea of the professional woman, who manages to win through with children and with a working husband and so on, which is now very much the common form – I do not know how they do it but still it is very much common form – that simply did not exist then. What is to be looked at now are the numbers which are actually both entering the solicitors' branch of the profession and the Bar from the women's side, and the answer is that there are far more now than there ever were then; and, as time goes on, when they have matured in the job as a lawyer, then they will get appointed. I know it is not a very proud boast but we have doubled the number of women in the High Court. That means it has gone up from three to six. That is small beer but it is the trend.

278. I think everyone would acknowledge the factors which you have just mentioned, but it does seem remarkable to someone who is not a lawyer that only one woman has ever got in the top 30 or so judges, and she turned out to be the daughter of a High Court judge and the sister of the Lord Chancellor. Do you think any woman who has not got those qualifications could have made it?

(*Lord Taylor of Gosforth*) Absolutely.

279. Why has not one then?

(*Lord Taylor of Gosforth*) That particular judge actually came from being a Registrar in the Family Division. That was the route by which she got on to the Bench, and when she got on the Bench she turned out to be extremely good and was appointed higher on merit. Good heavens, let us not take that away from her. One of the reasons why we are very much against increasing the number of women on the Bench simply in order to be able to say, 'Look we have more women on the Bench,' is that we do not want to practise reverse discrimination, because it is unfair to the women who get there on merit. Your saying that the one woman who has made it to the top was because her brother was the Lord Chancellor is very offensive.

280. I do not say that at all. I am perfectly prepared for the possibility that she has one of the finest legal minds in the country. I just note she is the only one ever.

(*Lord Taylor of Gosforth*) I promise there will be more and they will not all be the sisters of the Lord Chancellor!

Ms Anderson

281. Just a very brief comment, Judge Taylor, on what you have said. You said you did not agree with – you called it reverse discrimination – I would prefer to call it positive action. If you found that in 20 years' time, when there were many more women in the profession and in the pool from which you draw the judiciary, that there still appeared too small a number of women coming through, compared to the proportion of that pool in which they performed, would you then reconsider your attitude towards positive action?

(*Lord Taylor of Gosforth*) I think if we get to the stage where the number of men and women who are available is equal – if you can imagine that situation, being exactly equal – and you found that women were not getting appointed as much as men, then you would be worried about something going wrong. All I am saying is that I do not think the shortage of women at the moment really proves that case, for the reasons I have already given. I did not go on to say, but exactly the same applies to members of ethnic minorities too. They have the greatest difficulty in trying to get a start at the Bar. Very often they are trying to pull themselves by their own bootlaces because they did not find it easy, in those days, to get into chambers which were structured with senior, middle and junior people. They started with chambers of their own and there was no silk and senior juniors from whom the work was going to drop down, so they had to pull themselves up. But now I think it is different and in their case, as well as with the women, there are more. To answer your specific question, I would never be in favour of reverse discrimination in the sense of saying, 'This man is the best chap for the job but this woman is not too far behind. Because there are not enough women we will appoint her.' I do not think that is right. If you can imagine a hypothetical situation in which you had two candidates who were absolutely level pegging, then I can see that there would a case for saying, 'Why not appoint the woman?'

Mr Greenway

285. Do you believe it would be wiser to isolate the appointment of judges from the influence of the Executive?

(*Lord Taylor of Gosforth*) Obviously the appointment of judges should not be affected by Executive considerations. That is axiomatic. But I do not believe it is. The only way in which it could be said it is, is that the Lord Chancellor has this extraordinary number of hats that he wears. That is a unique feature of our constitution. I do not think it exists anywhere else. It has worked. Like a number of English institutions, they may defy common sense but somehow they work. I believe that the Lord Chancellor, when it comes to appointments – and I am intimately connected with this – has absolutely no political motivation at all. It would be invidious to mention names but when you look at some of the judges who have been appointed in the very last few years, you can see that there have been those appointed who clearly could not be described as being of the same political colour as the Executive in power at the moment. But then to come on to your question which is, ought we not to isolate it, I do not see how you can wholly isolate [it] because if you were talking about having some appointments commission, somebody has got to appoint the commission. The Government of the day, the Lord Chancellor, the Prime Minister, whoever it may be, must be the person, one would have thought, or the body, who appoints the commission that is going to do the appointing. So you have got room for a political element – or an accusation, at any rate, of a political element – whether valid or not. Then you go on from this to say, 'Who would be on this commission?' Obviously you would have to have a balanced commission. As soon as you start talking about a balanced commission you have got political considerations. If you are going to have him, you have got to have somebody from the other party. You have got to have a women. You have got to have someone from an ethnic minority. Before you know where you are, the commission that is either going to be doing the advising or appointing is going to consist of people who are either actually going to be fighting the corner that they represent or, at any rate, are going to be open to the accusation that this is what they are doing. So I am not sure the public is going to feel any more reassured by a commission of that kind which admits of politicisation, both when it is appointed and when it is appointing, and whether it is any better than having the Lord Chancellor taking the widest consultations that he does at the moment and producing – as I say, I think the proof of the pudding is in the eating – a judiciary which does not kow-tow to the Executive at all . . .

I think in the end, however far you put it back, the Executive has to have a hand in the appointment of the judiciary even if it is only in appointing the appointers. I am not sure you do any better by doing it that way than we do at the moment. I would like to stress one point, if I may. Much is made at the moment about the extent to which the judiciary via judicial review is prepared to over-turn Ministerial decisions or Government decisions. We are very careful not to go too far. I can think of a number of cases, I do not want to bore you with them, but if you think of the challenge to Maastricht by Rees-Mogg, if you think of the challenge I heard to the Anglo-Irish Agreement, if you think about the case we had the other day where it was suggested the Government was making improper use of a statute brought into existence in 1939 for the emergency, we have said, 'This is a matter for Parliament' and we do stand off. What we do not stand off from is where some Minister or some civil servant has exceeded his powers. I believe that is what the judiciary is there to oversee. That is one of the main functions of the judiciary, to protect the citizen against abuse of power.

> Report of the Home Affairs Committee on Judicial Appointments
> Procedures [1995–6] 52–II, pp. 36–9.

---

71   LABOUR PARTY POLICY DOCUMENTS ON JUDICIAL REFORM, 1993–5

FROM *A NEW AGENDA FOR DEMOCRACY* (1993)

It is hard to think of a more important issue than the selection of those who are to judge over their fellow citizens. Judges must not only be expert lawyers, but must also be men and women of integrity who are able to do justice in the extremely demanding circumstances of contested trials. They must also be people who are independent of government, and are not influenced by any kind of social or political pressure.

Those standards have not been assisted by the present secretive methods of selection and the restricted range of people from amongst whom judges are chosen. Labour is committed to establishing a proper Ministry of Justice. But even allowing for this, the system will remain fundamentally wrong. As public expectations of the judiciary increase, so does the public need to be reassured about the selection, and the training, of its judges. In particular there has been profound public concern about sentencing and the apparent insensitivity of some judges when dealing with offences of rape and violence. The independence of the judiciary must, of course, be sacrosanct. But that is no reason to continue with a patently anachronistic method of appointment or a failure to provide proper training and support for them.

A Judicial Appointments and Training Commission will be established to advise over the whole field.

One of the commission's first tasks will be to produce proposals for a more rational career pattern for judges, which will enable those who are suitable for judicial work to enter it earlier in their careers and to do the job more professionally. Elements in that policy would be:

- A wider field of choice, to ensure that all of the most able people are considered. Solicitors and academic lawyers, as well as practising barristers, will be encouraged to put themselves forward. And, more generally, qualified candidates will be expected to express interest in appointment and not await private invitation by government.

- A significant proportion of judges, including High Court judges, to be appointed at a significantly earlier age than at present. That would not exclude selection later. But for the majority it would enable the proper development of judicial careers. And it would make earlier use on the bench of the talents of women and of members of ethnic minorities, who are woefully under-represented amongst the older lawyers from whom judges are now chosen.

- Judges will usually start their careers in the crown and county courts. The new county courts, with their enhanced range of work, will be important tribunals in which it will be a challenging task for many judges to spend the whole of their career. And those who go on to the High Court will benefit from first acquiring full-time experience of judicial work.

- Judges will retire at an age closer to the retirement age of the rest of the working population. The retiring age would be initially 65, with discretion (to be exercised on the recommendation of the commission) to give limited extensions in special cases if requested.

The commission will have a special responsibility for judicial training. Training for judges was once regarded as unnecessary, or even as constitutionally improper. That absurd view is now exploded, with the recognition that litigants deserve to have their cases heard by a person who has a proper grounding in what may be new and complex issues, and sufficient understanding and experience of every aspect of his job. Proper training for judges does not in any way threaten their independence, but makes them more effective in their task of applying the law according to its rules.

The commission will be responsible for monitoring the careers of existing and aspirant judges, and for openly discussing with them their performance and the judicial work for which they are suitable. This will in no way affect judicial independence in decision making. The commission will seek a wide range of information and opinion on the aptitudes and abilities of candidates and of existing judges, and will in every case present a reasoned report. The commission will become a major source of information. A small part of this information may have to be obtained in confidence but, subject to that, all those seeking judicial appointments will be given full advice as to their prospects, the reasons for decisions made about them, and advice about any further training or experience that they are thought to need.

For the commission, this will be extremely challenging and important work. It will be necessary to have a blend of full-time and part-time appointments, and also a range of legal and other expertise. The chair and two vice-chairs will be full-time appointments. The chair will be a senior legal figure, and the vice-chairs lay persons of similar status. Other members, who will serve part-time but on the basis of a substantial commitment to the commission's work, will be drawn from a wide range within and outside the law, including members with extensive experience of professional training and education. The commission as a whole will consider general issues of policy, review difficult or important cases and formulate guidelines to be operated by its staff.

The commission will make a formal annual report. The commissioner's work can be scrutinised by a new Departmental Select Committee on Legal Affairs. This is a long overdue reform in the House of Commons in any event, but is given added justification with the establishment of the commission. We will also seek to broaden the representative nature of the magistrates' bench so that it reflects fully the diverse nature of our society and its people.

FROM ACCESS TO JUSTICE (1995)

Judicial Appointments and Training Commission

The system for selecting and training those who preside as judges in civil and criminal cases must command public confidence. Winning this confidence is crucial to giving the public a real sense that justice is accessible through the courts. We are committed to the development of a more rational training and career structure for the judiciary together with a more open and objective selection process that can better identify and harnesses judicial talent from sources other than the bar, to include solicitors and academics.

The current system is widely perceived as being defective in several respects. We seek to remedy this by the creation of a Judicial Appointments and Training Commission, which will take over work currently carried out by the Lord Chancellor's Department and the Judicial Studies Board. This body will be independent of the Lord Chancellor's Department and answerable solely to the Lord Chancellor, whom it will advise on all aspects of judicial appointments and training. Commission Members will be appointed from amongst suitably qualified lawyers, academics and lay people with relevant experience. The Commission will have oversight of the advertisement of all judicial posts and of selection procedures and responsibility for the training functions currently performed by the Judicial Studies Board.

We are committed to maintaining the highest judicial standards and to ensuring that judges are appointed purely on merit. We are anxious to ensure that the judicial selection process is open, fair and accessible to all.

Special efforts should be made by the Commission to develop a strong equal opportunities policy and to encourage members of all those groups currently under-represented in the ranks of the judiciary to apply for appointment.

The widest possible consultation on the suitability of candidates will continue, but the secretive aspects of judicial appointment will give way to a new principle of openness. In so far as confidentiality permits, candidates will have the opportunity to comment in detail on the substance of any objections made to their appointment.

We believe that this reformed system will ensure that the calibre of the judiciary is enhanced, because all the most able candidates will be encouraged to apply and fairly considered for appointment.

Judicial training

The Judicial Appointments and Training Commission will conduct a review of judicial training which is the key to enhancing the accountability, the sensitivity and the effectiveness of the judiciary without jeopardising their independence.

A more coherent and systematic approach to judicial training is required, with closer links to academic research and teaching facilities.

Judicial monitoring

The development of a more rational career pattern for judges, a greater emphasis on effective judicial training and a need to strengthen public confidence in the accountability of the judiciary make it all the more imperative that judicial performance appraisal, as recommended by the Royal Commission on Criminal Justice, be introduced without further delay. This appraisal will be carried out under the supervision of the Judicial Appointments and Training Commission and by senior members of the judiciary.

The Commission will also be responsible for producing a comprehensive code of practice for the judiciary and for monitoring judicial discipline, though judges of High Court level and above will still only be able to be removed from office by address to both Houses of Parliament.

Complaints about judicial conduct

Court users sometimes have cause to complain about the way a judge has behaved, notwithstanding the legal merits or demerits of their case. The current mechanisms within the Lord Chancellor's Department for investigating such complaints are woefully inadequate, and serve to undermine confidence in the judiciary.

The Commission will have an important role to play in ensuring that such complaints are taken seriously and properly investigated, and that appropriate action is taken.

---

72   THE HOUSE OF COMMONS HOME AFFAIRS
COMMITTEE'S RECOMMENDATIONS ON JUDICIAL
APPOINTMENTS, 1996

PROFESSIONAL JUDICIARY

What do we need in our judiciary?

1.   We accept that to require judges to be representative of sections
     of the community would be inappropriate. Nevertheless, the
     make-up of the judiciary has an effect upon the public's percep-
     tion of, and confidence in, the criminal justice system: whilst
     public respect for the justice system is sustained primarily by
     sound adjudication and sentencing, genuine understanding by
     judges of the concerns of ordinary people must enhance their
     standing in the public eye.
2.   We see sound legal learning, independence of mind, an ability to
     handle the court, maturity, and integrity as key attributes for any
     professional judge.

The current system of appointment

3.   We believe that the detailed criteria published for a number of
     judicial offices offer a sound basis for an assessment of applicants.
     We recommend that an indication should be given of the need for
     maturity in judicial office.
4.   We commend the Lord Chancellor for his programme for reform
     of judicial appointments procedures.
5.   We welcome the establishment of 70 as the normal statutory
     retirement age for the vast majority of judges, at the same time as
     welcoming the trend towards younger judges.

Scope for reform of the current system

6.   The Committee welcomes that, with the advent of interviews with
     candidates for certain judicial offices, the system of appointment is
     becoming less reliant upon opinion which cannot be guaranteed to
     be objective. The Committee sees this shift as healthy. We are,
     however, satisfied that there is value in gathering opinions of
     serving judges and of practitioners, although we believe that there
     may be some scope for improvement in the methods by which
     comments are collated.
7.   We believe that the material presently submitted to members of
     the judiciary and to members of the professions in advance of
     meetings with Lord Chancellor's Department staff offers an
     acceptable basis upon which constructive comment may be
     recorded.

8. We consider that the letter sent to persons nominated by applicants for Assistant Recordership could not currently be described as structured, and could usefully be expanded to give some indication to the recipient of the kind of information which would be valuable in coming to decisions on appointment.

9. We believe that any system of consultations should only take account of recorded and attributable comment. We recommend that judges and practitioners who are to be consulted by Lord Chancellor's Department officials should make a written record of the content and source of comments which are made or reported to them. We recommend that, at face-to-face meetings with consultees, Lord Chancellor's Department officials should make a note of the content and source of those comments used by consultees to support their assessments.

10. We welcome the publication of a list of persons consulted on applicants for Assistant Recordership, and we acknowledge that the field for consultation has, in this respect, widened considerably.

11. We recommend that, in any application material for judicial office, a clear indication should be given of the field from which consultations are taken.

12. We recommend that the Lord Chancellor's Department should consider widening the field still further for consultations regarding appointment to each judicial office. We recommend that the Lord Chancellor's Department should consider taking consultations from senior Silks and from leaders of specialist Bar and Solicitors' Associations where it is not already the practice to do so.

13. We favour an increase in administrative back-up [for the consultation process]. We recommend that the Lord Chancellor's Department should study how administrative assistance might best be offered to those who collate opinions. We recommend that further administrative back-up be provided to allow regular meetings with all judges on the South-Eastern Circuit.

14. We encourage the Department, particularly in view of the current expansion of the legal professions, to explore all practicable means of assessing the work and performance of potential applicants for judicial office.

15. We welcome the move towards time-limited competitions; we believe that this will allow candidates to be better informed on the progress of their applications. We believe that there is no need to adopt the Bar Council's proposal for a fast track in dealing with applications from exceptionally strong candidates.

16. [In circumstances when the private life of a candidate for judicial appointment might cause embarrassment to the Lord Chancellor, or might bring the judiciary into disrepute,] it may be appropriate for the Lord Chancellor's Department to record information on sexual orientation, whether gathered from an application form or through the consultations procedure; we agree, however, with the

current policy that a candidate's homosexuality, in itself, should not preclude him or her from appointment.

17. We consider that, although the proportion of women in the judiciary is small (particularly amongst the higher echelons), positive discrimination and a system of quotas are not the ways forward.

18. We believe that there is now less cause for women to feel diffident in applying for judicial appointment; what is needed is to generate more applications from women, who should be encouraged to consider judicial appointment from an early stage in their careers.

19. We welcome the Lord Chancellor's initiatives to encourage ethnic minority practitioners to apply for judicial office.

20. We agree with the Lord Chancellor that ethnic minority practitioners might enhance their prospects, both within the profession and for judicial appointment, by joining general practices or chambers, enabling them to build a track record in a variety of different fields.

21. We believe that the experience gained by those who practise in the courts offers the best grounding in court practice and procedure.

22. We believe that an assessment of an applicant's ability in handling legal principles with clarity and authority should carry significant weight in selection procedures. We also believe that a judge who has appeared regularly as an advocate is well placed to detach the merits of an argument from the skill with which it is presented.

23. We welcome the steps taken by the Lord Chancellor to reassure those practitioners who lack a sound knowledge of court practice and procedure that they may be considered for appointment as Assistant Recorder.

24. We are concerned that the policy of appointing as Circuit Judges only those who have served for at least two years as a Recorder may be too rigid.

25. We do not doubt that, in the past, civil practitioners with considerable judicial potential may have been dissuaded from applying for Assistant Recordership by a perception that a comprehensive knowledge of the criminal law was required from applicants.

26. We acknowledge that efforts have been made to reassure practitioners with largely civil expertise that they may be considered for appointment as Assistant Recorder.

27. We recommend that the Lord Chancellor's Department should examine whether a longer period of training in handling criminal cases might be made available to newly-appointed Assistant Recorders who request it.

28. We recommend that newly-appointed Assistant Recorders with

civil expertise should, if they request it, be authorised whenever possible to sit initially in the County Court.

29. We are confident that decisions on judicial appointment are not guided by information on where candidates were educated.

30. We are not persuaded that the role of the executive [in judicial appointment] is necessarily unsatisfactory, and we do not see this as a reason for change in the procedures. We have some qualms about the role of the Prime Minister in appointment to the senior judiciary; in particular, we do not see how he or she might be better informed than the Lord Chancellor to make recommendations to the Queen. We therefore question whether the Prime Minister should play any part in appointing judges.

Possible reforms to current procedures

31. We have not been persuaded that the quality of appointees would necessarily improve if a Judicial Appointments Commission were to be established. We believe that the value of a consultations network might be diminished if a Judicial Appointments Commission were to play a part in selecting judges.

32. A Judicial Appointments Commission would not be our preferred means of achieving reform.

33. We reject any move to a career judiciary, not because it is necessarily a faulty system, but because it would impose large-scale change for no clear gain.

34. We consider that the difficulties [in using advertisement and competition to fill vacancies on the High Court Bench] outweigh the benefits in transparency that might result, and we do not recommend that this course be followed.

35. We recommend that [job descriptions and selection criteria for all senior judicial offices should] be formulated without delay.

36. We do not see the field for appointment to the judiciary as comparable to the field for appointment to the higher Civil Service, who are drawn from all disciplines and who may have little work history. We do not therefore see the need for applying to aspiring judges the extended assessment process undertaken by selection boards for recruitment to the higher levels of the Civil Service.

37. We consider part-time service to be of value to all parties.

38. We are not convinced that five years' service part-time as Assistant Recorder and as Recorder, before being considered for appointment to the full-time office of Circuit Judge, is excessive. However, we accept that to serve occasional weeks over several years may be unnecessarily disruptive, and we therefore recommend that the Lord Chancellor's Department should do as much as possible to allow part-time service to be sat in concentrated blocks. We recommend that the Lord Chancellor's Department should state in application material for part-time judicial offices

that there is scope for adjusting the periods of judicial service to suit the preferences of the practitioner.

39. We agree that judges should not all be specialists, but we believe that there are strong arguments for having larger numbers of specialists on the Circuit Bench. We agree with the Chancery Bar Association that it is an inefficient use of resources to allocate members of the judiciary to fields in which they are inexperienced and less well equipped to operate efficiently. We note that a number of Circuit Judges are appointed to hear exclusively civil cases; for such appointments, we endorse Lord Woolf's proposal that Masters and District Judges should be eligible for appointment to the Circuit Bench without first having had to sit in crime as a Recorder; we believe, however, that Circuit Judges who sit in criminal cases should have experience in sitting as a Recorder. We would also, in principle, encourage the Lord Chancellor to consider whether some Tribunal Chairmen might be considered for direct appointment to the Circuit Bench.

40. We are not persuaded by arguments that academic lawyers without court experience should be appointed to judicial office.

41. We welcome the Lord Chancellor's flexible approach to the application of upper age-limits, where they are not statutory. We see no reason for the Lord Chancellor to change his policy in this area.

42. We do not recommend that it should be made easier to qualify for the full pension by raising the current retirement age for judges. Nor do we recommend that the Lord Chancellor alter his guidelines for lower age limits for part-time judicial appointment. We are satisfied that current arrangements for judicial pensions allow a healthy sum to be paid even if the full qualifying period is not served.

43. We are attracted to the suggestion that practitioners move more freely from practice to the Bench and *vice versa*. We believe that it would meet the objections of those who are deterred from applying for a judicial office by the pension arrangements. We are not convinced that many years' unbroken judicial service are essential in order to perform well in the most senior judicial offices in this country; an active and varied legal career may provide an excellent background for senior judicial appointment.

44. We have confidence in the integrity of the Bench, and we are not convinced that judges need be barred by convention from returning to practice. We recommend that the Lord Chancellor actively consider the possibility of introducing fixed-term contracts for full-time judicial offices. This would answer some of the objections made to the present system, and could provide a solution to problems of recruitment that may arise.

Report of the Home Affairs Committee on Judicial Appointments Procedures [1995–6], pp. lxxvi–lxxix.

THE ENTRENCHMENT OF A CONSTITUTIONAL BILL OF RIGHTS IN THE UK

> ### 73 OWEN HOOD PHILLIPS ON THE NEED FOR A WRITTEN UK CONSTITUTION AND HOW IT MIGHT BE ENTRENCHED, 1970

NEED FOR A WRITTEN CONSTITUTION

Constitution at the mercy of party majority in the Commons

The British Constitution is found to be largely at the mercy of a small, temporary party majority in the House of Commons. We have seen that this situation has arisen as a result of unplanned historical development. Why has it been allowed to remain? Because it has suited the leaders of both sides in the political 'game', giving inordinate power to the Prime Minister of the day, which will be inherited by the Leader of the Opposition in due course, while the general public are apathetic or unaware.

[My previous writing] dealing with the Constitution generally, the Government, Parliament and both its Houses, the Courts, and individual liberties – has led to the conclusion that a written Constitution with judicial review is desirable for this country. We have seen that there are no legal limits to what Parliament can do by ordinary legislation, that the Government virtually controls the activities of Parliament, that the maximum duration of a Parliament is too long, that the existence of a (reformed) Second Chamber with some power of rejection or delay is essential, that important areas of law and practice are uncertain, that the 'Parliament Act 1949' is of doubtful force, that too much power is concentrated in the hands of the Prime Minister, that the dissolution of Parliament needs to be regulated, that the law relating to judicial tenure should be improved, and that there is a call for a new Bill of Rights. In our system, or lack of system, all exists on sufferance, depending on the legislative supremacy of Parliament. There are permanent, or at least abiding, principles of constitutional government in the national interest as against the sectional interest of a temporary and perhaps small party majority; but the former can only be secured against the latter by limiting the power of Parliament, which in effect means placing restrictions on the Government of the day.

Purpose of enacting a constitution

– would be partly to clarify the principles, but mainly to entrench the most important provisions against repeal or amendment except by some specially prescribed procedure. At present it is possible for constitutional changes to be brought about by a majority of one in the elected Chamber. A Government elected with a small majority may not be truly representative of the people after its first year of office. The strength of party discipline means that the Government controls the Legislature. Restrictions on the Legislature would therefore in practice be restrictions on the Government. In the recent proposals of the Canadian Government for a new written Constitution it was argued that the mechanism for ensuring democratic government should be the subject of constitutional guarantees, and that the institutions of government and individual rights are fundamental to the whole Constitution.

The function of a written Constitution, then, would be to entrench the main institutions of government, the relations among themselves and between them and the private citizen. Foremost among these provisions – apart from matters on which there has been no conflict since 1688, such as the Monarchy and succession to the throne, and taxation – would be the following:—

National rights of England, Scotland, Northern Ireland and Wales as members of the Union.

Regional rights, if there is a further measure of devolution.

The status of the Channel Islands and the Isle of Man.

The Second Chamber, its composition and numbers, and its powers in relation to legislation. Disputes between the two Houses might be settled differently according to whether the matter was general Government policy, such as economic policy, or Fundamental Rights.

Provisions relating to Parliamentary government, in particular, the reduction in the maximum life of Parliament to four (or perhaps three) years; annual meeting of Parliament; and Electoral laws, including Boundary Commissions.

[European Union] membership and obligations.

Formulation of certain constitutional conventions, to protect the Queen as ultimate guardian of the Constitution as far as possible from involvement in politics, and to reduce the power of the Prime Minister. Such formulations would include the choice of Prime Minister, and the dissolution of Parliament, when and by whom advised.

The appointment, tenure and independence of the Judiciary – a reformed judicial tenure, substituting the advice of the Judicial Committee of the Privy Council for an address from both Houses in the removal of Judges, and perhaps establishing a Judicial Services Commission.

A new Bill of Rights, preserving notably *habeas corpus* and the free expression of opinion, and taking account of the European Convention.

Emergency powers and their limits; entrenchment to prevent government by decree or the establishment of extreme one-party rule.

The Constitution would be declared to be the supreme law of the land. Jurisdiction in constitutional questions (judicial review) would be conferred on the superior Courts, with appeal to the Judicial Committee of the Privy Council or a Special Constitutional Court.

Procedure for constitutional amendment, e.g. a two-thirds majority in each House for a Bill describing itself as a Constitutional Amendment Bill.

A written Constitution in itself would not clear up uncertainties in the law; indeed, a cynic might argue that it would increase them; but the exercise of drafting one would provide a unique opportunity for a wide and thorough overhaul of both the laws and the conventions. Further, its enactment – even apart from entrenchment sanctioned by judicial review – would fit in with our current phase of codifying various branches of English law, in particular, the proposal for a Criminal Code.

Arguments against a written constitution with judicial review

The general arguments used by lawyers against the adoption by this country of a written Constitution with judicial review are that it would lead to rigidity, that it would increase the volume of litigation, and that interpretation of the Constitution would involve the Courts in the decision of political questions. Rigidity, however, is a matter of degree, depending on the method prescribed for constitutional amendment. It need not be excessive, nor need the enactment of a Constitution prevent the growth of new conventions. In a unitary State or Union it is unlikely that there would be a great increase in litigation. Nor is it likely that many of the questions of construction that came before the Courts would be policy questions. The main objection hitherto has arisen from the innate conservatism of the common lawyer, his attachment to judge-made law and his dislike of statute law. He is not accustomed to a category of cases called 'constitutional'.

With regard to constitutional conventions there are legitimate queries. Are some of the conventions sufficiently definite to be capable of formulation in a statute? Are there some conventions that it would be undesirable to crystallise in statutory form? Are the Courts a suitable forum for adjudicating upon the proper observance of conventions? It is undoubtedly difficult to formulate conventions, though in a number of the newer Commonwealth Constitutions it has been attempted. They have incorporated the most important conventions relating to the exercise of governmental powers, either specifically or by reference to the British practice. The kind of problem that may arise is illustrated by the case of *Adegbenro* v. *Akintola* (1963). Under the 1960 Constitution of the Western Region of Nigeria the Governor had power to dismiss the Premier if it appeared to him that the Premier no longer commanded the support of a majority of members of the House of Assembly. The Governor dismissed the Premier, Chief Akintola, on the strength of a letter signed by a majority of members of the House, and appointed Adegbenro in his place. A political emergency arose during which the matter was taken to the Courts. The majority of the Federal Supreme Court of Nigeria, following what they understood to be the constitutional convention in Britain, held that the dismissal of Chief Akintola was invalid, as the Governor's power to dismiss the Premier was exercisable only when the House of Assembly itself had formally signified its lack of confidence in him. This decision was reversed on appeal by the

Judicial Committee of the Privy Council, who came to the conclusion that the Governor was entitled to obtain his information as to whether the Premier had lost the confidence of the House from any apparently reliable source. A somewhat similar case arose in Sarawak in 1966 with the opposite result, when the High Court of Malaysia in Borneo held that the Governor of Sarawak (if he had power to dismiss his Chief Minister) could dismiss him only following the unfavourable vote of the Legislature, and that a letter of no confidence was insufficient. In each country a constitutional amendment later nullified the judicial decision.

Factors to be taken into consideration are that the making of declarations by the Court is discretionary; that the Courts are reluctant to make decisions that will be ineffective; and that matters of this kind, such as whether a Prime Minister ought to resign or whether the Head of State may dismiss him, are usually decided by political methods and procedures, depending ultimately on public opinion. Lord Radcliffe, in the Privy Council case cited, referred to the lack of judicially discoverable and manageable standards for resolving such disputes, and thought that Courts were hardly suitable bodies to answer such questions.

We would not propose the formulation of constitutional conventions except as part of the exercise of enacting the Constitution as a whole, although the conventions relating to the exercise of the powers of the Governor-General of New Zealand did have to be formulated without enacting the rest of that country's Constitution as it appeared that his Letters-Patent needed to be redrafted. On the other hand, if we find it desirable on other grounds to enact a Constitution we could not leave out the Executive altogether, while to incorporate the laws relating to the Executive without referring to the conventions would be equally impracticable. Mr. Trudeau thinks that in the new Canadian Constitution conventions should be formulated in a general way, and his draft includes outline provisions relating to the government and covering the Head of State, the Executive, the Privy Council, the Prime Minister, the Cabinet, and the Ministers. The solution to this problem may be to provide that such existing conventions as are enacted shall not be justiciable. We have some rules that are expressly non-justiciable, for example, the functions of the Speaker under the Parliament Acts. It has been held by the Court of Appeal of New Zealand in *Simpson* v. *Attorney-General* (1955) that the Governor-General's statutory obligation to issue writs for a general election is not justiciable. Although the Courts may find in such cases that the exercise of statutory discretions is impliedly not justiciable, it would be preferable in the Executive part of the proposed Constitution to specify any particular provisions that are to be non-justiciable.

Rights of the individual

The first problem in framing a declaration of rights is that of selection. Most of the 'rights' of the individual that would be contained in a declaration of rights would be liberties, involving restrictions on the Legislature and enforceable against members of the Executive, such as personal liberty, freedom of speech, association, assembly and worship. In some instances, for example, non-discrimination, there might be redress against private persons. Some, such as the franchise, would be political in the strict sense. This and a few others would be available to citizens only: most would be available to all persons lawfully present in this country. The inclusion of general duties of the State or Government to provide welfare benefits, education, health services and so on, is not suggested. Such economic or social rights find a place in some Constitutions as 'Directive Principles of State (or Social) Policy', and are expressly declared to be not judicially enforceable. They are rather ideals or guides to Legislatures and Governments, and at most might have some slight effect on the construction of ambiguous statutes.

The next major problem is that of drafting. One has to consider in each case both the proposition and the exceptions. Should the language be general like the American Bill of Rights, or should it be detailed, specifying the various limitations and exceptions like the Fundamental Rights in the Indian or Nigerian Constitution? On the one hand, the First Amendment to the United States Constitution provides simply that 'Congress shall make no law ... abridging the freedom of speech or of the press', an impossibly general statement that has caused endless difficulty for the Supreme Court. On the other hand, section 24 of the Federal Constitution of Nigeria (1960) read as follows: '(1) Every person shall be entitled to freedom of expression, including freedom to hold opinions and to receive and impart ideas and information without interference. (2) Nothing in this section shall invalidate any law that is reasonably justifiable in a democratic society – (*a*) in the interest of defence, public safety, public order, public morality or public health; (*b*) for the purpose of protecting the rights, reputations and freedom of other persons, preventing the disclosure of information received in confidence, maintaining the authority and independence of the courts or regulating telephony, wireless broadcasting, television, or the exhibition of cinematograph films; or (*c*) imposing restrictions upon persons holding office under the Crown, members of the armed forces of the Crown or members of a police force.' Expressions like 'reasonably justifiable' and 'democratic society' would provide many pitfalls for judges faced with the task of construing them; but prominence would rightly be given to 'protecting the rights, reputations and freedom of other persons' at a time of increasing licence on the part of the press, and growing intolerance on the part of noisy minorities who try to break up meetings held by speakers with whose opinions (if they listen to them) they do not agree.

Critics of a Bill of Rights raise the question, what would be the effect on existing legislation? The exceptions, they argue, might nullify the propositions. The Constitution would have to state, if that is the intention, that the declaration of Rights was not to have retrospective effect, though it would raise presumptions of interpretation. But if no change in the existing law is intended, why go through the trials and tribulations of drafting a Bill of Rights? As far as criminal or civil liability is concerned, the principle would remain that people may do what they like unless forbidden by law. Some changes might be made in the existing law, such as the recognition or extension of the right of privacy. What would be the effect of a declaration of the invalidity of a subsequent statute on those who have *bona fide* acted under it? There would be uncertainty and much litigation, it is said, and the Courts would be required to decide policy questions. These questions reveal fears that in this country might well prove unfounded. The answer may lie partly in the device of prospective overruling, which is discussed later.

Can Parliament bind itself?

'If an Act of Parliament had a clause in it that it should never be repealed', said Chief Justice Herbert in the celebrated case of *Godden* v. *Hales* (1686), 'yet without question, the same power that made it may repeal it.' The proposition that Parliament cannot bind itself or its successors appears to some people to express a paradox. If there is something Parliament cannot do, they ask, how can we speak of its legislative supremacy? But the paradox is verbal only. If the proposition is put in the form, 'Parliament is not bound by its predecessors', the difficulty vanishes. There is no judicial authority for the power of *express* repeal or amendment: it is so well established that it has not been raised in the Courts. If Parliament intends to repeal or amend a previous statute it usually does so expressly; but through oversight this may not be done, in which case the Courts will try to reconcile the two statutes as far as they reasonably can. Otherwise, a later Act or section supersedes an earlier Act or section with which it is inconsistent; in other words, it impliedly repeals or amends the earlier. So in *Ellen Street Estates Ltd.* v. *Minister of Health* (1934), where there was a discrepancy in the methods of assessing compensation prescribed by the Acquisition of Land (Assessment of Compensation) Act 1919 and the Housing Acts 1925 and 1930, the Court of Appeal held that the Housing Acts impliedly repealed the Act of 1919 in so far as they were inconsistent. 'If in a subsequent Act', said Lord Justice Maugham, 'Parliament chooses to make it plain that the earlier statute is being to some extent repealed, effect must be given to that intention just because it is the will of the Legislature.'

Special considerations may apply ... where the earlier Act is part of an arrangement of an international character, such as the Statute of Westminster, Independence Acts and perhaps the Act of Union with Scotland, though even there it is likely that British Courts would regard themselves as bound by the later Act, regardless of any political or international repercussions.

The advocacy by the Constitutional Society of New Zealand of a written and entrenched Constitution for that country, including a Bill of Rights, has not so far been successful. Meanwhile the New Zealand Legislature, suffering perhaps from a guilty conscience in having abolished the Second Chamber in 1950 and been unable to devise a substitute, included in the revised Electoral Act of 1956 a section (s. 189) stating that certain provisions relating to such matters as the life of Parliament (consisting now only of the House of Representatives and the Governor-General), the franchise and secret ballot, should not be repealed or amended except by a majority of 75 per cent of all the members of the House or by a simple majority of votes at

706 ENTRENCHMENT OF A BILL OF RIGHTS

a referendum. Section 189 was not itself one of the provisions requiring this special procedure for repeal or amendment. There are three views as to the effect of a provision such as this. The first is that it is binding on the Legislature as providing a new definition of 'Parliament' for this particular purpose: this is an adoption of the 'manner and form' argument discussed below. The second view is that the special amending procedure could be evaded, but that it would have to be done in two stages: the New Zealand Parliament could (and would need to) repeal section 189 first, and then it could proceed to amend the reserved provisions. This seems to be rather a pointless technical distinction, as the two things could be done in two consecutive sections of the same statute. The third view, which we think is the correct one, is that section 189 constitutes merely a moral sanction, albeit a strong moral sanction amounting to a constitutional convention. The reason why the Legislature did not try to 'entrench' section 189 itself is that it appreciated that a double pseudo-entrenchment would be no stronger than a single pseudo-entrenchment, and so *ad infinitum*. As Bacon said in his *Maxims of the Law:* 'Acts which are in their nature revocable, cannot by strength of words be fixed or perpetuated'.

Jurists tell us that there must be some 'rules of recognition' (Hart) or 'rules of competence' (Alf Ross) by which we may know what Parliament is and what is an Act of Parliament. From this some constitutional writers draw the conclusion that Parliament can bind itself as to the *manner and form* of legislation, and that therefore if it prescribed a special procedure for the alteration of particular laws, such as electoral laws or fundamental rights, the Courts would not uphold amendments to such laws unless they were made by the special procedure laid down. They follow the late Sir Ivor Jennings in citing the case of *Attorney-General for New South Wales* v. *Trethowan* (1932), in which the Judicial Committee of the Privy Council held that the New South Wales Legislature had no power by a statute passed in 1930 (after a change of Government) to abolish the Second Chamber without a referendum, because that Legislature had passed an Act in 1929 providing that the abolition of the Second Chamber would require approval at a referendum. But the reason for that decision was that the State of New South Wales was subject to the Colonial Laws Validity Act 1865, which declared that a representative colonial Legislature had wide powers of lawmaking so long as its laws did not conflict with statutes of the United Kingdom Parliament applying thereto, and provided that its laws were passed 'in such manner and form as may from time to time be required' by any law (including a Colonial law) for the time being in force in the territory. Clearly the decision was based on the fact that the New South Wales Legislature was a *subordinate* legislature, bound by the 'higher law' laid down by the United Kingdom Parliament. The analogy from a subordinate to an autonomous Legislature is false.

Then they cite the famous 'Cape Coloured Voters case' (*Harris* v. *Minister of the Interior*, or *Harris* v. *Dönges*, 1952), in which the Appellate Division of the Supreme Court of South Africa rightly held invalid a statute passed by the South African Parliament purporting to place the Cape coloured voters on a separate electoral roll, because it had not been passed in accordance with the special procedure (a two-thirds majority in both Houses sitting together) prescribed for this kind of constitutional amendment by section 152 of the South Africa Act 1909. Now the South Africa Act was the Constitution of South Africa, which created the South African Parliament itself. But because it happened for historical reasons to be an Act of the United Kingdom Parliament and South Africa had since the Statute of Westminster 1931 been recognised as an independent sovereign State, there was a good deal of confusion between State sovereignty and the 'sovereignty' of Parliament, although it was pointed out that Congress is limited by the American Constitution but no one would deny that the United States is a sovereign State. Partly to avoid the supposed difficulty of ascribing limits to a 'sovereign' Parliament, an ingenious formula propounded by Professor D. V. Cowen was adopted, which involved a quibble with the word 'Parliament'. Although for general purposes the bicameral 'Parliament' of South Africa was sovereign, the 'Parliament' for the purpose of amending section 152 of the South Africa Act was a two-thirds majority of a unicameral body. *Dicta* were thrown out to the effect that a similar line of reasoning might be applied to the United Kingdom Parliament, which could thus bind itself. Again, the *Harris* case is a false analogy, for the South African Parliament was bound by a higher law, namely, the South African Constitution.

The same applies to two recent appeals in the Privy Council from Ceylon. In *Bribery Commissioner* v. *Ranasinghe* (1965) it was held that the Bribery Tribunal by which the respondent had been convicted was not lawfully appointed; and in *Liyanage* v. *R.* (1967) it was held that a court of three Judges (without a jury) nominated for the particular case, by which the accused were convicted of offences arising out of an abortive *coup d'état*, was not lawfully appointed. In both cases the reason for the decision was that the statute under which the tribunal or Court was set up involved a constitutional amendment requiring a special legislative procedure which had not been complied with. Ceylon is an independent sovereign State by virtue of the Ceylon Independence Act 1947, but its Legislature is bound by a higher law, the Constitution of Ceylon, which is contained in an Order in Council of 1946.

One cannot be dogmatic on this matter, but the view put forward here is that a legislature cannot bind itself, whether as to subject-matter or the manner and form of legislation, unless it is authorised (directed or empowered) to do so by some 'higher law', that is, by some prior law *not laid down by itself.* Our test is the probable attitude of the Courts. Suppose Parliament passed an Act this year providing that the voting age should not be raised except with the approval of a majority of 75 per cent in the House of Commons. It is submitted that if Parliament passed another Act next year raising the voting age and approved by a bare majority in the House of Commons, British Courts would not hold the second Act void. As Lord Pearce said in *Bribery Commissioner* v. *Ranasinghe*, lawmaking powers in all countries with written Constitutions must be exercised in accordance with the terms of the Constitution from which the power is derived. His Lordship added that any analogy to the unwritten British Constitution 'must be very indirect, and provides no helpful guidance'. The reason why the New South Wales Legislature in *Trethowan's* case had to follow the procedure of a referendum prescribed by its own previous statute, was that it was directed to do so by the Colonial Laws Validity Act 1865 ('in such manner and form as may from time to time be required by any Act of Parliament, Letters Patent, Order in Council, or *Colonial Law* for the time being in force in the said Colony').

If there must be some rule logically prior to Parliament by which an act can be recognised as an Act of Parliament, this identifies Parliament: it does not limit its powers. Since the early middle ages (except during the revolutionary Commonwealth period in the seventeenth century) 'Parliament' has meant the Sovereign, the Lords and Commons in Parliament assembled. An Act assented to by the Queen by and with the consent of the Lords and Commons in Parliament assembled could abolish the monarchy or the House of Lords. P1 would not have bound itself as to the laws it can pass: it would have been replaced by P2. But to say that the prescription of some special legislative procedure for certain Bills is to alter the meaning of 'Parliament' for those purposes is a play upon words.

It would probably not be effective to try to *prevent* the passing of a Bill that infringed an enactment corresponding to the Canadian Bill of Rights or section 189 of the New Zealand Electoral Act. The case of *Harper* v. *Home Secretary* (1955), where an injunction was refused to restrain the Home Secretary from presenting a draft Order (approved by both Houses) relating to electoral boundaries to Her Majesty in Council, is an illustration of the unwillingness of the British Courts in our present system to interfere with the Parliamentary process, apart from the fact that by the Crown Proceedings Act no injunction (as distinct from a declaration of private rights) may be issued against a Minister in his official capacity.

How a new British Constitution might be entrenched

The solution is to bring into being a 'New' Parliament which would owe its existence to a Constitution *not enacted by itself*, from which it would derive both its powers and its limitations. When the possibility of Great Britain and Ireland forming a federation with a rigid Constitution was discussed in the 1880s, Bryce expressed the opinion that Parliament could extinguish itself and a new Federal Legislature could be established following this *breach of continuity*. Then the new Constitution could only be altered in accordance with its own terms. Dicey thought Parliament could *transfer* its powers to another Legislature, but it seems that the *extinction* of the existing or 'Old' Parliament and the creation of a new Parliament would be the more effective method. A Constitution limiting the powers of the 'New' Parliament, in the manner suggested earlier in this chapter, would be adopted by the 'Old' Parliament, and then submitted for adoption by the people in a referendum. The Old (unlimited) Parliament would be abolished, and it would be superseded by the New (limited) Parliament.

Alternatively, it might be preferable for Parliament first to transfer its powers to a *Constituent Assembly*, and at the same time to abolish itself. The

Constituent Assembly would then draft a Constitution creating a Parliament with limited powers. Again, the New Parliament would have only such powers as the Constitution gave it. That raises the question of how the Constituent Assembly would be appointed. In some countries the existing Legislature has functioned as a Constituent Assembly, but we can hardly envisage the present Parliament acting in this capacity until the composition of the House of Lords has been reformed. It is probable that a specially appointed Constituent Assembly, if one could be devised, would be the most influential.

The statute adopting the Constitution, or setting up the Constituent Assembly, as well as the Constitution itself, would require the Judges (existing as well as future) to take an oath of loyalty to the new Constitution.

We have suggested that the new Constitution should be submitted for adoption by the people at a referendum. This is because the establishment of a new Constitution is the most solemn and fundamental of all constitutional acts: its approval at a referendum, by putting the new Constitution in a special category, would confer on it the highest possible prestige. [We have also] expressed objections to the general or frequent use of the referendum as a constitutional process, and we do not suggest that this 'unEnglish' device should be employed for subsequent constitutional amendments. Our proposal is for an initial or fundamental referendum only.

Constitutional amendment

The argument from inflexibility would be largely met, first, by ensuring that all provisions of the Constitution would be amendable in one way or another, and, secondly, by providing that entrenchment need not be total. There would be no parts of the Constitution like the basic articles of the Cyprus Constitution or (according to the recent *Golak Nath case*) the fundamental rights in the Indian Constitution, that could not be amended at all. Some special procedure for amendment would be required for such parts as the Monarchy, the Unions with Scotland and Northern Ireland, the Islands, the Regions, the Second Chamber, the life and frequency of Parliament, the franchise, the Boundary Commissions, judicial tenure, fundamental rights, emergency powers, judicial review of legislation, and the procedure for constitutional amendment itself. Parts that need not be entrenched, but could be amended by the ordinary legislative procedure, could include details such as the number of seats in the House of Commons, and non-justiciable provisions covering what are now conventions.

An Amendment Bill should be so specified, for this draws the attention of members of Parliament and the public to its significance. The Lord Chancellor or Minister of Justice would be required to examine all Bills with reference to their compatibility with the Constitution and to report. In difficult cases an advisory opinion could be sought from the Judicial Committee of the Privy Council under the Judicial Committee Act 1833, which provides that the Crown may refer any question of law to the Committee for an advisory opinion. The opinion of the Judicial Committee may already be required on the validity of legislation of the Northern Ireland Parliament under the Government of Ireland Act 1920. This procedure would not be appropriate, however, if the Judicial Committee were to be given jurisdiction to decide cases arising out of the interpretation of the Constitution.

A referendum, we have already suggested, would not be desirable as part of the process of constitutional amendment. It is difficult to frame a complex technical question in a way suitable to be answered 'yes' or 'no' by large numbers of people who have not the necessary background and have not followed all the previous discussions. A joint sitting of the two Houses is a doubtful device, at least until we know what sort of Second Chamber we shall have and how its members will be chosen. The most satisfactory method for amending the entrenched clauses would therefore appear to be a Constitution Amendment Bill passed by a special majority of (say) two-thirds in each House. It would be necessary to state whether this was to be a two-thirds majority of members present and voting, or two-thirds of all the members of each House.

Judicial review of legislation

Judicial review is the traditional method of testing the validity of legislation in the United States and Commonwealth countries. A body of judicial precedents of constitutional interpretation is then gradually built up. Certain provisions could, as we have said, be expressly made non-justiciable, such as those relating to the Sovereign's exercise of the prerogative, the functions of the Speaker in the House, and existing conventions relating to the Cabinet system. It would not be necessary for the judges themselves to invent, as the American Supreme Court has done, a loosely defined class of 'political questions' which are not suitable for judicial decision.

The objection that difficulty would be created where acts have been *bona fide* performed under legislation later declared void by the Courts might be met, at least in some cases, by the doctrine of 'prospective invalidation' or (where a precedent of interpretation is being reversed) 'prospective overruling'. This means that the Court could declare, in cases where it thought there were compelling reasons for doing so, that the statute concerned would be invalid in future, but without prejudice to things *bona fide* done in reliance on it down to the time of the judgment. This device has been occasionally used by the American Supreme Court during the last forty years. Thus, previous cases having decided that the conviction of a person on the strength of evidence seized by the police in a manner contrary to the Constitution was void, the question arose in *Linkletter* v. *Walker* (1965) whether all prisoners convicted on evidence unlawfully obtained ought to be released and retried. The Supreme Court held that this drastic action was not necessary, but that the Court could deliver judgment with prospective effect. Again, in *Golak Nath* v. *State of Punjab* (1967) the Indian Supreme Court holding (probably wrongly) that the Indian Parliament had no power to amend any of the fundamental rights declared in the Constitution, even by the special amending process, overruled previous decisions of its own over a number of years upholding several amendments to the fundamental rights: but having regard to the history of the amendments (relating to such matters as agrarian reform), their impact on the social and economic affairs of the country and the chaotic situation that might be brought about by the sudden withdrawal of the constitutional amendments at that stage, the Court, borrowing the idea from its American counterpart, confined the operation of the decision to the future. On the other hand, the doctrine of 'prospective' overruling or invalidation has met with criticism from both American and Indian lawyers as being a repudiation of the principle that the function of judicial review is to declare unconstitutional laws to be *void*; that Courts which invalidate laws for the future are acting as legislators altering the law, although the Constitution is supposed to be supreme.

Ultimate appellate jurisdiction would be conferred by the new Constitution on some Court in any cases in which a constitutional issue is raised. Some countries have special Constitutional Courts with exclusive jurisdiction in constitutional cases, but it would be preferable for us to integrate this jurisdiction with the general jurisdiction of the superior Courts. Constitutional questions could then be dealt with in the normal course of litigation, and in relation to other legal questions that are usually involved in such cases. The House of Lords in its judicial capacity, being technically part of the Legislature, would not be an appropriate appellate Court for this purpose. This points to the Judicial Committee of the Privy Council as the most suitable choice. It already hears appeals from some Courts and tribunals in this country as well as from Courts overseas, and the judicial strength of these two bodies is much the same. It could hardly be objected that the Judicial Committee is in form a committee of the Executive.

The choice of the Judicial Committee would also fit in with the prospect that, as a result of a radical reform of the Second Chamber, the Judicial Committee might become the ultimate court of appeal for *all* kinds of cases, an idea that has been mooted from time to time during the last hundred years.

Moral and educational value of a written constitution

Finally, there is the moral and educational value of introducing a written Constitution enunciating in a systematic and inspiring way a set of principles by which people may be guided, and embodying the concepts of legality, stability and permanent values. It is not valid to compare the United Kingdom with other countries that have written Constitutions entrenching fundamental rights and judicial review, and to point to the present political chaos in some of these countries and the plethora of judicial precedents in the United States. There are political and social factors at work in some of the new Commonwealth countries that fortunately do not obtain here, while the American judicial experience is largely due to the manner in which the American Federal Constitution was originally drafted at a time when judicial review seems not to have been intended, and also to the exceptional difficulty of amending that Constitution. In view of the law-abiding tradition and political maturity of this country on the one hand, and the relative flexibility of our proposed new Constitution on the other, the only valid comparison is between the present lack of system in this country and the situation it is hoped would obtain if we had a written Constitution of the kind suggested. In other words, the comparison is between the United Kingdom before and after.

It may be that the leading politicians of the two main parties would at first be hesitant to adopt such a basic and comprehensive reform. The essence of the British constitutional system has been described as two alternating and self-perpetuating oligarchies with supporting retinues, who are capable of collusion when it suits them. Many lawyers would be sceptical, having a romantic attachment to 'judge-made' law and a prejudice against legislation. The initiative for such an ambitious but worthwhile project is therefore likely to depend for its support on the formation of a sufficiently strong body of informed public opinion.

Owen Hood Phillips, *Reform of the Constitution*, 1970, pp. 144–62.

---

74 A SPECIALIST ADVISER TO THE HOUSE OF LORDS SAYS THE PRINCIPLE OF PARLIAMENTARY SOVEREIGNTY IS A BAR TO ENTRENCHMENT, 1977

THE QUESTION OF ENTRENCHMENT

1. This paper is concerned with whether the provisions of a Bill of Rights in the United Kingdom could in any way be entrenched. 'Entrenched' is here used in a wide sense, to indicate a Bill so framed as to restrict the freedom of Parliament to override its provisions in a future Act. This question is examined in relation to the constitution as it now stands. It is not concerned with how a Bill of Rights might be entrenched under a new constitution. The conclusion is that under our existing constitution there is no way in which the provisions of a Bill of Rights could effectively be entrenched, though some legal writers have urged a contrary view.

2. The central feature of the modern British constitution is the sovereignty of Parliament. 'Sovereignty' has in this sense been used by writers on the United Kingdom constitution to denote the special characteristics of the United Kingdom Parliament whereby not only does Parliament have an unfettered power to make laws but there is no power residing in any other authority in the United Kingdom – in particular in the courts – to set aside those laws. It is important to distinguish 'sovereignty' in this sense from the expression 'a sovereign legislature' when used to describe a Parliament or other legislature that is not subordinate to any other legislature. There are sovereign legislatures in this sense all over the world but few other legislatures enjoy such unfettered law-making powers, and such freedom from control by the courts, as the United Kingdom Parliament. It is desirable to bear in mind these two senses in which the word 'sovereign' is used when

considering the question of entrenchment. A failure to draw the distinction has sometimes caused confusion.

3. Perhaps the most celebrated exposition of Parliamentary sovereignty as a principle of our constitution is that to be found in Chapter 1 of Dicey's Law of the Constitution: 'The principle of Parliamentary sovereignty means neither more nor less than this, that Parliament ... has, under the English constitution, the right to make or unmake any law whatever; and further, that no person or body is recognised by the Law of England as having a right to override or set aside the legislation of Parliament'. Perhaps the salient proposition here, from the point of view of entrenchment, is that Parliament can unmake any law. This is also expressed in the principle that Parliament cannot bind its successors. Also of the highest importance, however, is the principle expressed in the concluding part of the foregoing quotation, which can be expressed in the proposition that Acts of Parliament in the United Kingdom are not subject to judicial review.

4. An Act embodying a Bill of Rights would, as a matter of law, be as vulnerable to these principles as any other Act. Accordingly, nothing contained in such an Act could prevent its being amended or repealed by a subsequent Act. On this there is universal agreement. More than one writer on the subject of a Bill of Rights has nevertheless suggested that a Bill of Rights could at least protect itself against implied amendment or repeal by a future Act. This school of thought is exemplified by Clause 3 of the Bill presented by Lord Wade that has given rise to the present Select Committee. That Clause (Clause 1 of the Bill having provided for the European Convention on Human Rights to have the force of Law in the United Kingdom) provides as follows: 'In case of conflict between any enactment subsequent to the passing of this Act and the provisions of the said Convention and Protocols, the said Convention and Protocols shall prevail unless subsequent enactment shall explicitly state otherwise'. [*RB NOTE: See Alan Beith's 1975 Bill set out at Doc. 39A for this form of drafting. Lord Wade, in his later Bills on the subject, modified the wording of the clause: see Doc. 39A.*]

5. Thus, let it be assumed, for example, that after the enactment of a Bill of Rights in similar terms to Lord Wade's Bill an Act were passed by Parliament reintroducing corporal punishment for certain kinds of offence. It seems possible that any provision for this purpose would be regarded by the Courts as inconsistent with Article 3 of the European Convention ('No-one shall be subject to torture or inhuman or degrading treatment or punishment'). Accordingly, assuming that the latter Act did not expressly purport to repeal or amend the Bill of Rights, or to have effect notwithstanding anything in it, a United Kingdom court would be able, if Clause 3 of the Bill of Rights were given effect according to its terms, to hold that the provision for corporal punishment in the later Act (if the court regarded it as contrary to Article 3 of the Convention) was of no effect.

6. It will be seen that if a provision like Clause 3 (referred to in what follows as 'a Clause 3-type provision') were given full effect by the courts it would in practice provide an important degree of entrenchment. For it may be supposed (and it is certainly so argued by those who favour a Bill of

Rights) that if a Bill of Rights were enacted Governments would not lightly introduce Bills that expressly overrode it. On the other hand Acts that were ultimately proved to be inconsistent with a prior Bill of Rights, without expressly purporting to override it, might easily be passed. This is because, by their nature, the provisions of Bills of Rights are couched in such broad terms that the interpretation that will be put upon them by the courts cannot be confidently predicted.

7. In truth, however, a Clause 3-type provision could not, according to what may be called the orthodox view of Parliamentary sovereignty, have any effect. An Act can no more protect itself from implied derogation by a future Act than it can protect itself from express derogation. The principle that Parliament cannot bind its successors requires that the latest Act must always prevail. If that conflicts with an earlier Act, whether expressly or otherwise, the earlier Act has to yield. Thus, in the example posited above, the courts would have to give effect to the provision for corporal punishment in the later Act and could only do so by treating that as overriding any provision inconsistent with it in the prior Bill of Rights, including the provision stating that the Convention should prevail over later Acts unless they expressly provided otherwise.

8. All this follows from the nature of Parliamentary sovereignty in the United Kingdom, as that doctrine has been traditionally understood. Some modern writers have, however, questioned whether that principle is as absolute as has traditionally been supposed. No-one has seriously questioned the general proposition that there is no means whereby an Act of Parliament can protect itself absolutely against amendment or repeal by a subsequent Act. Some writers have, however, put forward the view that although Parliament cannot bind itself as to the substance of future Acts it may be able to bind itself as to their 'manner and form'. Some protagonists of this school of thought have in particular argued that a Clause 3-type provision, since it purports to bind Parliament only as to the form of future Acts derogating from a Bill of Rights, would, or at any rate might, be given effect by the courts. More will be said about this argument later, on the question of binding as to manner. Suffice it to say here that so far as form is concerned there are no United Kingdom cases that support the argument but, on the contrary, there are two cases where it was rejected, namely: *Vauxhall Estates* v. *Liverpool Corporation* [1932] 1KB.733 and *Ellen Street Estates* v. *Minister of Health* [1934] 1KB 590.

9. Both these cases turned on the effect of section 7(1) of the Acquisition of Land (Assessment of Compensation) Act 1919. That Act laid down general rules for the assessment of compensation for the compulsory acquisition of land by public authorities and section 7(1) provided as follows: 'The provisions of the Act or order by which the land is authorised to be acquired ... shall in relation to the matters dealt with in this Act have effect subject to this Act, and so far as inconsistent with this Act those provisions shall cease to have effect or shall not have effect ...'. In each case the question at issue was the effect of section 7(1) of the 1919 Act on section 46 of the Housing Act 1925. The latter section laid down a basis for the assessment of compensation, for land compulsorily acquired under certain

provisions of the 1925 Act, that was different in some respects from that prescribed by the 1919 Act. In both cases it was held that even on the assumption that section 7(1) of the 1919 Act purported to apply to future as well as past Acts the 1925 Act must prevail. What makes these decisions particularly pertinent to the argument as form in general and to a Clause 3-type provision in particular is that it was argued by counsel in both cases that the effect of section 7(1) of the 1919 Act was that, although a future Act which expressly overrode the 1919 Act would have to prevail over it, a future Act that did not purport expressly to override the 1919 Act would have to yield to the 1919 Act so far as inconsistent with it. In other words, the argument was that what is contained expressly in a Clause 3-type provision was implicit in section 7(1) of the 1919 Act. The argument was dealt with as follows by Humphreys J. in the *Vauxhall* case: 'He [counsel] says that these words mean that at no subsequent time shall it be competent for Parliament to alter the law as there laid down, except in one or other of two ways. He admits very frankly that it would be open to Parliament at any time to repeal [section 7(1) of the 1919 Act] by express enactment, and he admits that it would be open to Parliament at any subsequent time to amend that subsection by express enactment. He says, however, that the ordinary rule of construction which lays down that where two inconsistent provisions are found in two Acts of Parliament, the one passed subsequently to the other, the latter provision shall prevail and shall be deemed impliedly to repeal the earlier provision, cannot apply to this subsection because of its special terms. For my part I fail to follow that argument. If it is once admitted that Parliament, in spite of those words of the subsection, has power by a later Act expressly to repeal or expressly to amend the provisions of the subsection and to introduce provisions inconsistent with them, I am unable to understand why Parliament should not have power impliedly to repeal or impliedly to amend these provisions by the mere enactment of provisions completely inconsistent with them.'

10. Even more to the point perhaps is a passage in the judgment of Maughan L.J. when dealing with the same argument in the Court of Appeal in the *Ellen Street* case: 'I am quite unable to accept that view. The legislature cannot, according to our constitution, bind itself as to the form of subsequent legislation, and it is impossible for Parliament to enact that in a subsequent statute dealing with the same subject-matter there can be no implied repeal. If in a subsequent Act Parliament chooses to make it plain that the earlier statute is being to some extent repealed, effect must be given to that intention just because it is the will of the legislature.'

11. These judgments in these cases accordingly provide strong authority for saying that the United Kingdom courts would regard a clause 3-type provision as ineffective. Before leaving this aspect of the matter, however, there may be noticed a novel suggestion put forward by Wallington and McBride in their book 'Civil Liberties and a Bill of Rights', at page 86. They advocate a Bill of Rights with a clause 3-type provision and they deal as follows with the objection that such a clause could not be effective: 'But here the legal purist would again object that this is binding Parliament as to how it can legislate and that the judges will not accept it. One would hope that

judges would be sufficiently receptive to such a clear hint as this, and not stand dogmatically on tradition, but this could not be guaranteed in advance. To meet the point, the Lord Chancellor could, at the time the Bill of Rights came into force, persuade the judges of the House of Lords to issue a practice statement that they would accept that legislation not containing the 'notwithstanding' clause would be disallowed insofar as it conflicted with the Bill of Rights. This was done in 1966 when the House of Lords judges announced that they would no longer be absolutely bound by their previous decisions. Since the House of Lords is the final court of appeal its practice in such matters is the final arbiter of what the law is. If our proposal ... to set up a Constitutional Court is accepted, that Court, rather than the House of Lords, could as the final authority on the effect of the Bill of Rights make such an announcement.'

12. It is difficult to attach much weight to this suggestion. The idea that the House of Lords (or any other Court) would seek to introduce a fundamental change into the British Constitution by the issue of a practice note is hardly sustainable. The 1966 practice note referred to by the authors is really no precedent for an operation of the kind they envisage.

13. A final point is worth making in connection with Clause 3-type provisions, namely, that they are not to be confused with a mere rule of interpretation whereby the courts would, so far as possible, seek to construe subsequent Acts in such a way as not to conflict with a prior Bill of Rights. That is quite a different matter. Such a rule could be included in a Bill of Rights, but it would be no more than declaratory of the existing common law rule. In practice, where one Act is intended to override an earlier one it is usual to make express provision to that effect. Unless an Act expressly amends or repeals an earlier Act (or is expressly stated to have effect notwithstanding the provisions of the earlier Act) the courts will always try to give a meaning to the later Act that does not conflict with the earlier. No doubt the disposition to apply this rule would be particularly strong where the earlier Act was in the nature of a Bill of Rights. Nevertheless, this rule *is* only one of interpretation. It does not save the earlier Act where the later Act is clear. It may be added that in practice, where a Bill of Rights is concerned, it is much more likely to be the Bill of Rights that is ambiguous than the later Act. This is because – a point made earlier – it is in the nature of Bills of Rights to be couched in very broad and general terms.

14. Attention must now be turned to the other possible way of seeking to entrench a Bill of Rights. This consists of laying down, in such a Bill, a special (and more stringent) procedure for the enactment of any subsequent Act containing provisions inconsistent with the Bill. For example, it might be provided that any Act containing provisions inconsistent with the Bill of Rights would have to be passed in the House of Commons by a majority of not less than two-thirds of the members. A purported entrenchment of this kind, however, again comes up against the principle that Parliament cannot bind its successors. If Parliament passed an inconsistent later Act in the usual way (ie by simple majority) the courts could be expected, following this principle, to treat the later Act as overriding the Bill of Rights and, in particular, as overriding by implication the earlier provision for a two-thirds

majority in the House of Commons. There is no way round this unless one accepts the validity of the 'manner and form' argument mentioned earlier. The relevant point here is 'manner' since the type of provision now under discussion is one that lays down the manner in which an Act is to be passed if it is to override the Bill of Rights. The basis of the argument is that although any Act can undo what has been done by an earlier Act, the courts have first to be satisfied that the later Act is in fact an Act. An Act requires (apart from the procedure under the Parliament Acts 1911 and 1949) the consent of Queen, Lords and Commons. If one element is missing there is no Act (a point on which there is general agreement). From this the argument proceeds to the proposition that, in the example posited above, if there is less than a two-thirds majority in the Commons for the later Act there is no true consent by the Commons and therefore no Act. Another form of the argument has it that for this particular purpose 'Parliament' consists of Queen, Lords and not less than two-thirds of the Commons and, accordingly, if the later Act is passed by less than two-thirds of the Commons it has not been passed by Parliament and again, therefore, there is no Act.

15. The passages from the judgments in the *Vauxhall* and *Ellen Street* cases quoted above, although they dealt with a requirement as to form rather than manner, can be regarded as inimical to this argument. In any event, whatever view one takes of the argument as a means of surmounting the rule that Parliament cannot bind its successors it has also to face the rule that the courts will not enquire how an Act reached the Statute Book. The most often quoted statement of this rule is probably that of Lord Campbell in *Wauchope* v. *Edinburgh and Dalkeith Railway Company*, a decision of the House of Lords on a Scottish appeal in 1842: 'All that a court of justice can do is to look at the Parliamentary Roll: if from that it should appear that a Bill has passed both Houses and received royal assent no court of justice can enquire into the mode in which it was introduced in Parliament nor into what was done previous to its introduction or what passed in Parliament in its progress through its various stages in both Houses.' The rule was reaffirmed by the House of Lords as recently as 1974 in *Pickin* v. *British Railways Board* [1974] 1 AUER 609.

16. No argument in favour of the effectiveness of a procedural entrenching provision can be reconciled with this rule unless it can be said that the rule does not apply to procedural requirements laid down by Act of Parliament as opposed to those laid down by the Standing Orders of the two Houses. That point has certainly never been in issue in any case concerning an Act of the United Kingdom Parliament. There has been no opportunity for it to arise because no such Act has ever purported to lay down a restrictive procedural requirement for future Acts. Any argument, however, that the distinction between a statutory requirement and a requirement of the Standing Orders of either House is crucial in this regard comes up against yet another rule in the line of cases governing the relations between Parliament and the courts in the United Kingdom. That is the rule that neither House is subject to the control of the courts in the application of

Acts relating to the House's own proceedings. The leading case is *Bradlaugh* v. *Gossett* (1884) 12QBD 271. In that case the Court of Queen's Bench refused to declare void an order made by the House of Commons preventing Charles Bradlaugh from taking the Oath, even though he had been elected a member of the House. The plaintiff's contention was that this was contrary to the Parliamentary Oaths Act 1866. The Court refused to consider the question whether the House of Commons had rightly applied the provisions of that Act. The following celebrated passage appears in the judgment of Stephen J. in that case: 'If they misunderstand [the law], or (I apologise for the supposition) wilfully disregard it, they resemble mistaken or unjust judges; but in either case there is in my judgment no appeal from their decision.'

17. The writers who favour the manner and form argument rely entirely, so far as supporting authority is concerned on a number of Commonwealth cases. For example, in *Attorney General for New South Wales* v. *Trethowan* [1932] AC 526 the Judicial Committee of the Privy Council upheld the grant of injunctions restraining the presentation to the Governor General for Royal Assent of a Bill passed by the New South Wales Legislature for abolishing the Second Chamber, because there had been no compliance with an earlier Act of that Legislature that such an abolition should not be effected without a referendum. That case was, however, decided on the basis of section 5 of the Colonial Laws Validity Act 1865. Under that provision every representative Colonial legislature was given power to make laws respecting its constitution, powers and procedure 'provided that such laws shall have been passed in such manner and form as may from time to time be required by any Act of Parliament, Letters Patent, Order in Council or Colonial Law for the time being in force in the said Colony'. The case cannot be regarded as authority for the effectiveness of a procedural requirement laid down by the United Kingdom Parliament as respects later United Kingdom Acts. The New South Wales legislature derived its powers to legislate from the Colonial Laws Validity Act and was clearly bound, in exercising the power, to follow the 'manner and form' rule laid down by section 5 of that Act.

18. Similar considerations probably apply to the famous South African case of *Harris* v. *Minister of the Interior* [1952] (2) S.A.L.R. (A.D.) 428, which is also relied upon by the manner and form protagonists. That case concerned the validity of the Separate Representation of Voters Act 1951, an Act passed by the South African Parliament which purported to put the Cape coloured voters on to a separate electoral roll. The Act was passed in the ordinary way but this procedure was contrary to the provisions of the South Africa Act 1909, the United Kingdom Act which established the South African constitution. Under sections 35 and 152 of that Act an amendment of the Cape franchise was required to be effected under a procedure which required a two-thirds majority of both Houses sitting together. The Appellate Division of the Supreme Court of South Africa held that the Separate Representation of Voters Act was invalid by reason of its failure to comply with the special procedural requirements of the South Africa Act 1909. They held that those provisions of the 1909 Act were

still binding on the South African Parliament, notwithstanding that in the meantime there had been passed the Status of the Union Act 1934, a South African Act which re-enacted in South Africa the Statute of Westminster 1931 and declared that 'the Parliament of the Union shall be the sovereign legislative power in and over the Union'. The fact that the South African Parliament was, at the material time, a 'sovereign Parliament' has been treated by some writers as making the *Harris* case a particularly persuasive authority for the view that the same principle would be applied in the United Kingdom to a manner and form provision contained in a United Kingdom Act relating to later United Kingdom Acts. The *Harris* case is, however, explicable on the ground that the South African Parliament had been created by, and derived its power to legislate from, the South Africa Act 1909, and was accordingly bound by the procedural requirements laid down by the entrenched provisions of that Act, so long as those provisions remained unrepealed.

19. The distinction for present purposes between legislatures that owe their very power to legislate to a legislative Act, and the United Kingdom Parliament, which does not, seems to be crucial. That certainly seems to have been the view of the Judicial Committee of the Privy Council in *Bribery Commissioner* v. *Ranasinghe* [1965] A.C. 172, another case relied on by the manner and form school of thought. That case concerned section 29 of the Ceylon (Constitution) Order in Council 1946. Subsection (1) of that section provided that the Parliament of Ceylon should, subject to the provisions of the Order, have power to make laws for the peace, order and good government of Ceylon. Subsection (4) provided that in the exercise of the powers under the section the Ceylon Parliament could amend or repeal any provisions of the 1946 Order itself (ie the Ceylon Constitution) but this was coupled with a proviso that no Bill amending or repealing the Order should be presented for Royal Assent unless it had endorsed on it a Certificate of the Speaker to the effect that not less than two-thirds of the House of Representatives had voted in favour of the Bill. A later Act of the Ceylon Parliament, the Bribery Amendment Act 1958, contained a provision that was held to conflict with a provision of the 1946 Order, but the Bill for the 1958 Act contained no Speaker's Certificate showing the requisite two-thirds majority of the House of Representatives. It was argued for the Ceylon Government that the Ceylon Parliament, being a sovereign Parliament (which was not in dispute) was not fettered by section 29(4) of the 1946 Order and could override it by implication in a subsequent Act. The Privy Council held that section 29(4) was binding on the Ceylon Parliament. They accordingly held that the 1958 Act was void so far as it conflicted with the 1946 Order. The decision turned entirely, however, on the fact that as the Ceylon Parliament derived its power to legislate from the 1946 Order it must be bound by any procedural restrictions contained in that Order. The headnote to the Report correctly summarises the decision: 'A legislature has no power to ignore the conditions of law-making that are imposed by the instrument which itself regulates its power to make law.'

20. The judgment of the Privy Council in this case expressly referred to *Attorney-General of New South Wales* v. *Trethowan* and *Harris* v. *Minister*

of the Interior (the cases dealt with above) and treated them as decisions based on this principle. It is also of interest to observe that one strand of the argument on behalf of the Ceylon Government was based on the United Kingdom cases also noticed above in which the courts have refused to look behind an Act to the parliamentary proceedings which produced it. In rejecting that strand of the argument the Privy Council again expressly drew a distinction between the position in the United Kingdom and the case where a procedural requirement is contained in the written instrument that actually confers the law-making powers. On this they said (p.195): 'The English authorities have taken a narrow view of the courts' power to look behind an authentic copy of the Act. But in the Constitution of the United Kingdom there is no governing instrument which prescribes the law-making powers and the forms which are essential to those powers.'

21. Thus, the Commonwealth cases do not seem to provide support for the argument that a Bill of Rights could in some degree be entrenched. It remains only, so far as the cases are concerned, to consider the Scottish authorities. Any such consideration has to start by bearing in mind that the United Kingdom Parliament owes its existence first to the Union between England and Scotland in 1707 and secondly to the Union between Great Britain and Ireland in 1800. The Irish element does not appear to have given rise to any special case law and this paper need concern itself only with the Scottish element.

22. The Scottish case that has provoked discussion is *MacCormick* v. *The Lord Advocate* (1953) S.C.396 in which two Scottish subjects sought an order declaring that the use of the numeral 'II' in the title of Her Majesty Queen Elizabeth II contravened Article 1 of the Treaty of Union (Queen Elizabeth I having been Queen only of England). The petitioners argued that so far as the Royal Titles Act 1953 authorised the use of the numeral 'II' it was of no effect because Article 1 of the Treaty of Union was a fundamental condition of the Union and could not be abrogated by an Act of the United Kingdom Parliament. The action failed. In the Outer House, the Lord Ordinary, Lord Guthrie, held that the adoption of the numeral 'II' was not contrary to Article 1 of the Union. He also expressly rejected the argument that the absolute sovereignty of Parliament did not apply to Scotland, and in particular the argument that Parliament could not derogate from the Treaty of Union. On appeal to the Inner House the Lord Ordinary's decision to reject the petition was upheld on a variety of grounds which did not call for a decision on the question of Parliamentary sovereignty. Nevertheless, the Lord President, Lord Cooper, uttered certain dicta questioning the absoluteness of Parliamentary sovereignty so far as concerned Scotland and the fundamental conditions of the Union: 'The principle of the unlimited Sovereignty of Parliament is a distinctively English principle which has no counterpart in Scottish constitutional law ... Considering that the Union legislation extinguished the Parliaments of Scotland and England and replaced them by a new Parliament, I have difficulty in seeing why it should have been supposed that the new Parliament of Great Britain must inherit all the peculiar characteristics of the English Parliament but none of the Scottish Parliament ...'. The Lord

President then indicated that there were certain provisions of the Treaty of Union and associated legislation that constituted fundamental conditions of the Union which the United Kingdom Parliament was not free to abrogate.

23. The force of these dicta was a good deal tempered by Lord Cooper's qualification later in the judgment that, even if there were provisions of the Union constituting 'fundamental law' which Parliament was not free to alter, any contrary provision would still (subject to certain matters on which he reserved his opinion, including the provisions relating to the Court of Session itself) not be justiciable in the English or Scottish courts. In any event, the dicta have no bearing on the question of entrenching a possible Bill of Rights. Not only do they do no more than suggest that, so far as Scotland (but not England) is concerned, there may be certain fundamental provisions of the Act of Union that Parliament is not competent to alter. They are positively hostile to any argument that the courts would be competent to strike down an Act conflicting with a prior Bill of Rights containing a purported entrenching provision. They have, moreover, no bearing on the manner and form argument. The Act of Union did not confer on the Parliament of Great Britain its law-making powers, much less contain any provision as respects the manner or form of Acts of that Parliament. The United Kingdom Parliament derives its power to legislate from the common law, as did the English and Scottish Parliaments.

24. In this connection dicta in the later Scottish case of *Gibson* v. *Lord Advocate* (1975) S.L.T.R. 134 are of interest. In that case certain Scottish fishermen challenged the validity of the EEC Fishery Regulations which provide for equal access to the waters of all Member States. It was argued that so far as section 2(1) of the European Communities Act 1972 purported to give effect to these regulations as part of the law of Scotland it was of no effect, as being contrary to Article XVIII of the Treaty of Union. That Article provided that all existing laws in force in England and Scotland should be alterable by the Parliament of Great Britain 'But that no alteration be made in laws which concern private right except for evident utility of the subjects within Scotland'. The action was dismissed by Lord Keith (Outer House) on the ground that the rights of access by Scottish subjects to Scottish waters were public rather than private rights. He did, however, have something to say about the constitutional question. Referring to the dicta of Lord Cooper in the MacCormick case he said: 'Like Lord Cooper, I prefer to reserve my opinion on what the question would be if the United Kingdom Parliament passed an Act purporting to abolish the Court of Session or the Church of Scotland or to substitute English law for the whole body of Scots private law. I am, however, of the opinion that the question whether a particular Act of the United Kingdom Parliament altering a particular aspect of Scottish private law is or is not 'for the evident utility' of the subjects within Scotland is not a justiciable issue in this court.' Later he said: 'In justice to the argument presented to me on behalf of the pursuer, I should mention that I was referred to a number of reported decisions on constitutional matters by courts in Australia, and South Africa, and by the Judicial Committee of the Privy Council. These cases were, however,

concerned with situations where the constitutional arrangements of the countries concerned laid down specific procedures for certain legislative acts, and they do not, in my view, have any bearing on the issues in the present case.'

25. These dicta of Lord Keith emphasise that the Scottish cases in no way support the proposition that it would be possible to entrench a Bill of Rights. They conclude this paper's review of the matter of entrenchment so far as the judicial authorities are concerned. It remains only to consider briefly whether certain modern instances where Acts of Parliament have in fact purported to tie Parliament's hands for the future have any bearing on the matter. On the one hand there is the Statute of Westminster 1931 and the various post-war Acts granting independence to Commonwealth countries, and on the other there is the European Communities Act 1972.

26. The Statute of Westminster 1931 provided for the legislative independence of the old United Kingdom Dominions. Section 4 provides that no Act of Parliament of the United Kingdom passed after the commencement of that Act should extend to a Dominion unless it is expressly declared in the subsequent Act that the Dominion has requested and consented to its enactment. This is certainly a purported attempt to bind future Parliaments and similar provision is to be found in the various Acts that have since been passed for granting independence to various countries in the British Commonwealth. Section 4 provoked the celebrated dictum of the Lord Chancellor, Lord Sankey, in *British Coal Corporation* v. *The King* [1935] A.C.500: 'It is doubtless true that the power of the Imperial Parliament to pass on its own initiative any legislation that it thought fit extending to Canada remains unimpaired. Indeed, the Imperial Parliament could, as a matter of abstract law, repeal or disregard section 4 of the Statute. But that is theory and has no relation to realities.' That dictum is at once an assertion of the full rigour of Parliamentary sovereignty as a matter of law and its denial as a matter of practice. Even if, however, section 4 of the Statute of Westminster could be regarded as effective even in 'abstract law' as well as in reality it bears no true relevance to any attempt to entrench a Bill of Rights. The same is true of the various post-war Independence Acts. The grant of legislative independence to Dominions and Colonies overseas is a matter of the transfer of legislative power from the United Kingdom Parliament to another authority in respect of defined territories. That is quite a different matter from Parliament's purporting to fetter itself for the future as to the exercise of its legislative powers in the United Kingdom.

27. Finally, there is the European Communities Act 1972. Section 2(1) of that Act gives the force of law in the United Kingdom to the directly applicable provisions of Community law. Section 2(4) then provides, *inter alia*, that 'any enactment passed or to be passed, other than one contained in this Part of this Act shall be construed and have effect subject to the foregoing provisions of this section'. This is certainly a purported entrenching provision of the widest kind since 'the foregoing provisions' of section 2 include section 2(1). It is not simply a question of laying down the manner or form of future Acts affecting directly applicable Community law. Section 2(4) purports to secure that any Act of Parliament, even a future Act, must

always yield to such law. A number of points have, however, to be made about this provision.

28. The European Communities Act had, as a matter of political necessity, at least to seek on its face to do all it could to give overriding effect to directly applicable Community law. The European Treaties, as interpreted by the European Court, required this and the Act was passed in order to enable the United Kingdom to ratify the Treaties. The mere presence of section 2(4) in the European Communities Act is, however, no evidence that it is in fact effective as an entrenching provision. That has yet to be pronounced upon by the United Kingdom courts. It seems more than likely that if a United Kingdom court were faced with an irreconcilable conflict between an Act of Parliament and an earlier provision of directly applicable Community law the court would apply the ordinary principle of Parliamentary supremacy and give effect to the Act of Parliament, notwithstanding section 2(4). Any argument that section 2(4) is effective to make later Acts yield even to earlier Community law would presumably have to proceed on the footing that the passing of the European Communities Act, coupled with our accession to the Communities, has involved a transfer of Parliament's sovereign power, as respects legislation on Community matters, from Parliament to the Communities. This is indeed the view of Community membership taken by the European Court in the cases in which it has laid down the doctrine of the supremacy of directly applicable Community law. That, however, would make the European Communities Act analagous, for present purposes, to the Statute of Westminster and the various Independence Acts. On any footing the European Communities Act provides no precedent for suggesting that Parliament could effectively entrench a Bill of Rights. [*RB NOTE: Later judicial developments have effectively upheld the entrenchment provision in the 1972 Act: see Doc. 77.*]

SUMMARY

The foregoing may be summarised as follows:
(1) The principle of Parliamentary sovereignty as traditionally understood in the United Kingdom is a bar to the effectiveness of any purported form of entrenchment that a Bill of Rights might adopt.
(2) Although it is universally accepted that this principle precludes any device whereby an Act can be made immune altogether to amendment or repeal by a future Act, some modern writers have argued that an Act can bind future Acts in the matter of manner or form of enactment. If this argument were right, some degree of entrenchment of a Bill of Rights would be possible either (a) by means of a provision protecting the Bill against implied amendment or repeal, or (b) by means of a requirement laying down for any future Act derogating from the Bill some procedure going beyond the ordinary requirement of a simple majority in each House of Parliament.

(3) The judgments in more than one line of English cases, however, are hostile to the argument mentioned in (2) above.

(4) The Commonwealth cases in which a requirement for a special procedure laid down for future Acts has been held to be binding are all cases in which the Parliament in question derived its power to legislate from a written instrument which itself laid down, or authorised, the requirement. They are no authority for the proposition that a manner or form requirement as respects Acts of the United Kingdom Parliament would be held binding by the courts of the United Kingdom.

(5) Dicta in a recent Scottish case suggest that there may, as regards Scotland, be some limitation on the power of Parliament to override certain fundamental matters which the Acts of Union purport to protect for the future. Whether or not, however, these dicta are right they have no bearing on the question whether it would be possible to entrench a Bill of Rights.

(6) Neither the Statute of Westminster 1931 and the various post-war independence Acts, nor the European Communities Act 1972, whatever their effect on future Acts may be, provide any precedent for suggesting that a Bill of Rights could effectively be entrenched.

Report of the House of Lords Select Committee on a Bill of Rights (Memorandum by D. Rippengal) [1976–7] 81, 1–10.

---

75   LORD HAILSHAM, FORMER LORD CHANCELLOR, CALLS FOR AN ENTRENCHED BILL OF RIGHTS AS PART OF A NEW CONSTITUTION FOR THE UK, 1978

I am sure that Britain needs a new constitution. I am sure that it should be of the 'written' or 'controlled' variety, and that it should therefore contain entrenched clauses if it is at all possible to bring this about. The object of such a constitution should be to institutionalize the theory of limited government ...

The full benefit of entrenched clauses would only be attainable if the powers of Parliament could, by some means, be limited for the future by providing that constitutional change could only take place by a special procedure, involving some action by a process external to Parliament sanctioning the change. One such means would be a confirmatory referendum. But I would welcome such a course. I wish to put an end to the elective dictatorship. I wish to make it impossible for governments ever again to defy the will of the electorate as they have been doing in recent years by misusing, as I would claim, the unlimited powers of Parliament and insisting on overriding the House of Lords either by the use, actual or threatened, of the Parliament Acts or rejecting particular amendments.

From this point of view a Bill of Rights would be a blessing. A constitution of this type would, of course, not be unalterable. There would be procedures for amendment, probably involving a referendum, which could not be interfered with by the courts. There would also be political checks and balances additional to the limitations imposed by law, partly consisting in the installation of subordinate assemblies, and partly by the creation of an effective second chamber. But in this armoury of weapons against elective dictatorship, a Bill of Rights, embodying and entrenching the European Convention might well have a valuable, even if subordinate, part to play.

Lord Hailsham, *The Dilemma of Democracy*, 1978, pp. 226, 174.

---

76   SIR WILLIAM WADE QC ON HOW A UK BILL OF RIGHTS COULD BE ENTRENCHED, 1980

I am firmly on ... the side of the majority of the House of Lords who have called for the incorporation into our law of the European Convention on Human Rights. What I will attempt is to supply the missing legal link between the wish and the fulfilment. For none of the distinguished lawyers who have advocated entrenched Bills of Rights – and they include Lord Hailsham, Lord Salmon and Lord Scarman – have explained how entrenchment could be made to work consistently with the dogma of parliamentary sovereignty. I approach this now as a purely technical problem of legislation: how can our legislative machinery be made to deliver these particular goods? In any normal situation there is no need for any such question, since Parliament is omnipotent. But the one inherent limit on its omnipotence, which is the consequence of that omnipotence itself, is that the Parliament of today cannot fetter the Parliament of tomorrow with any sort of permanent restraint, so that entrenched provisions are impossible.

That, at any rate, appears to be the view of the legal establishment. It was accepted by the Select Committee of the House of Lords which in 1978 reported on the possibility of enacting a Bill of Rights incorporating the European Convention. The Committee employed a specialist adviser to guide them on this question, and he advised them, in a very lucid paper, that the judicial authorities led to the clear conclusion that there was no way in which a Bill of Rights could be made immune from amendment or repeal by a subsequent Act. Entrenched provisions, such as clauses alterable only by two-thirds majorities, or after approval in a referendum could not therefore be legally effective in the United Kingdom. A footnote informs us that Lord Diplock, Lord Scarman and Lord Wilberforce were in general agreement with this conclusion. This weighty consensus was qualified only by a reservation on the part of Lord Hailsham, but the Committee observe that that reservation was based more on hope that the specialist adviser's view might prove wrong than on any confident expectation that it would.

Lord Hailsham had himself categorically adopted the establishment view in the debates of 1972 on the European Communities Act. That Act, as we all know, has attempted to entrench the law of the European Communities in the most absolute way possible, providing that the European law is to prevail over 'any enactment passed or to be passed, other than one contained in this part of this Act'. So Parliament has ordained that every future Act of Parliament as well as every past Act, is to give way in case of conflict. There is nothing here about two-thirds majorities or approval by referendum. Parliament has attempted to bind its successors unconditionally. Yet the same ministers who were piloting the Bill through Parliament maintained that Parliament's ultimate sovereignty remained intact for the simple reason that it was indestructible by legislation. They used this proposition to resist an opposition amendment to the effect that the supremacy of Parliament should remain unaffected. This was unnecessary, they argued, because Parliament is bound to remain supreme anyway and no restriction on its powers, or on the manner of their exercise, is constitutionally possible. Sir Geoffrey Howe in the House of Commons and Lord Hailsham in the House of Lords quoted from an article of mine, my solitary contribution to the arguments over sovereignty, published many years ago. The clue which led to it was perhaps its mention by Lord Denning M.R. in the case in which Mr. Raymond Blackburn unsuccessfully contested the constitutionality of this country's joining the European Communities. I had said

> If no statute can establish the rule that the courts obey Acts of Parliament, similarly no statute can alter or abolish that rule. The rule is above and beyond the reach of statute ... because it is itself the source of the authority of statute. This puts it into a class by itself as a rule of common law, and the apparent paradox that it is unalterable by Parliament turns out to be a truism ... Legislation owes its authority to the rule: the rule does not owe its authority to legislation.

This was merely one way of expressing two obvious facts. The first is that in every legal system there must be a basic rule or rules for identifying a valid piece of legislation, whether we call it the grundnorm, like Kelsen, or the ultimate legal principle, like Salmond, or the rule of recognition, like Professor Hart. The second obvious fact is that this grundnorm, or whatever we call it, lies in the keeping of the judges and it is for them to say what they will recognise as effective legislation. For this one purpose Parliament's powers of giving orders to the judges are ineffective. It is futile for Parliament to command the judges not to recognise the validity of future Acts of Parliament which conflict with a Bill of Rights, or with European Community law, if the judges habitually accept that later Acts prevail over earlier Acts and are determined to go on doing so. In this one fundamental matter it is the judges who are sovereign.

That, in very condensed form, is the theory which underlies the view of the legal establishment. In my humble opinion that view is unquestionably sound. There is an abundance of judicial authority for it and a total dearth of authority against it. But nevertheless I hope to persuade you that it need not prevent the effective entrenchment of a Bill of Rights or of anything else that we may wish to establish as fundamental law ...

My own suggestion will seem, I fear, very simple and obvious. But I believe it to be the one to which logic inexorably leads. All that need be done in order to entrench any sort of fundamental law is to secure its recognition in the judicial oath of office. The only trouble at present is that the existing form of oath gives no assurance of obedience to statutes binding later Parliaments. But there is every assurance that if the judges undertake upon their oath to act in some particular way they will do so. If we should wish to adopt a new form of constitution, therefore, all that need be done is to put the judges under oath to enforce it. An Act of Parliament could be passed to discharge them from their former oaths, if that were thought necessary, and to require them to be resworn in the new terms. All the familiar problems of sovereignty then disappear: a fresh start has been made the doctrine that no Parliament can bind its successors becomes ancient history; and the new fundamental law is secured by a judiciary sworn to uphold it.

If critics should object that this would be a mere piece of manipulation and a subversive tampering with the status of the judges, I would meet them head on by denying the validity of the objection. It is only because we are so habituated to having no constitution at all that our minds can move in such grooves. There is no need to assume that there is only one kind of judge and only one form of oath. In fact, it is the most natural and normal procedure to relate the judicial oath specifically to any new fundamental law that is to be established. Article VI of the Constitution of the United States provides that judicial as well as executive officers both of the United States and of the States shall be bound by oath or affirmation to support the Constitution. In the Constitution of India a variety of oaths for judges, ministers, and members of Parliament are set out in the Third Schedule, and all are required to swear fidelity to the Constitution and the judges must swear to uphold it. There are similar requirements in the Constitution of Malaysia. But throughout history oaths have been used to secure revolutionary changes, such as the Reformation in the time of Henry VIII and the Revolution in the time of William III. William III, when he accepted the crown at the Revolution, took security for his legal position as sovereign by appointing new judges who swore allegiance to him personally, just as today the judges of the Supreme Court of Judicature take the oath of allegiance and the judicial oath in the forms prescribed by the Promissory Oaths Act 1868, which name the reigning sovereign. The one thing that our rudimentary constitution guarantees in this way is the personality of the sovereign. If we want to guarantee something else, such as a Bill of Rights or some particular entrenched clauses, all we have to do is extend the same security to them.

This is, as it appears to me, the one and only way in which we can take command of our constitution without having to wait for some sort of political revolution, which is most unlikely to arrive just when we want it, and without having to contrive some artificial legal discontinuity. Professor Hood Phillips, in his book on the Reform of the Constitution, suggests that

Parliament would have to abdicate or transfer its powers, with or without the intervention of a constituent assembly. But merely by a change in the judicial oath a new judicial attitude can be created, and that is all that is needed. Fundamentally the question simply is, what will the judges recognise as a valid Act of Parliament? If they solemnly undertake to recognise a new grundnorm and to refuse validity to Acts of Parliament which conflict with a Bill of Rights or other entrenched clauses, that is the best possible assurance that the entrenchment will work. Always in the end we come back to the ultimate legal reality: an Act of Parliament is valid only if the judges say it is, and only they can say what the rules for its validity are.

The logic could be pressed further by including in the judicial oath an undertaking to pay no attention to future legislation affecting the oath unless passed by (say) two-thirds majorities in Parliament. It could be pressed further still if the undertaking were to pay no attention to any such legislation of any kind. All that that would mean, however, would be that whole benches of new judges would have to be found to replace the old ones, just as at William III's accession, if and when the time for the second revolution arrived. Cheering as this prospect might be to the Bar, it is not a situation which one would wish to provoke. I mention it only because, theoretically at least, it seems to represent the ultimate in possible entrenchment. There is little merit in the ultimate, since in the end political forces, if they are strong enough, can always overcome legal restraints, and a system which will not bend will break. All that I am concerned to point out is that the supposed impossibility of any sort of entrenchment in our existing constitutional system is imaginary.

H. W. R. Wade, Constitutional Fundamentals, 1980, 30–3, 47–9.

---

77   THE LAW LORDS CONFIRM THE VALIDITY OF AN ENTRENCHMENT PROVISION IN THE EUROPEAN COMMUNITIES ACT 1972: THE *FACTORTAME* CASE, 1991

THE EUROPEAN COMMUNITIES ACT 1972

2.—(1) All such rights, powers, liabilities, obligations and restrictions from time to time created or arising by or under the Treaties, and all such remedies and procedures from time to time provided for by or under the Treaties, as in accordance with the Treaties are without further enactment to be given legal effect or used in the United Kingdom shall be recognised and available in law, and be enforced, allowed and followed accordingly ...

(4) ... any enactment passed or to be passed ... shall be construed and have effect subject to the foregoing provisions of this section ...

3.—(1) For the purposes of all legal proceedings any question as to the meaning or effect of any of the Treaties, or as to the validity, meaning or effect of any Community instrument, shall be treated as a question of law (and, if not referred to the European Court, be for determination as such in accordance with the principles laid down by and any relevant decision of the European Court).

THE FACTORTAME CASE 1991

Lord Bridge of Harwich. My Lords, when this appeal first came before the House in 1989 (see *Factortame Ltd* v *Secretary of State for Transport* [1989] 2 All ER 692, [1990] 2 AC 85) your Lordships held that, as a matter of English law, the courts had no jurisdiction to grant interim relief in terms which would involve either overturning an English statute in advance of any decision by the Court of Justice of the European Communities that the statute infringed Community law or granting an injunction against the Crown. It then became necessary to seek a preliminary ruling from the Court of Justice as to whether Community law itself invested us with such jurisdiction ...

In June 1990 we received the judgment of the Court of Justice replying to the questions we had posed and affirming that we had jurisdiction, in the circumstances postulated, to grant interim relief for the protection of directly enforceable rights under Community law and that no limitation on our jurisdiction imposed by any rule of national law could stand as the sole obstacle to preclude the grant of such relief. In the light of this judgment we were able to conclude the hearing of the appeal in July and unanimously decided that relief should be granted in terms of the orders which the House then made, indicating that we would give our reasons for the decision later.

Some public comments on the decision of the Court of Justice, affirming the jurisdiction of the courts of member states to override national legislation if necessary to enable interim relief to be granted in protection of rights under Community law, have suggested that this was a novel and dangerous invasion by a Community institution of the sovereignty of the United Kingdom Parliament. But such comments are based on a misconception. If the supremacy within the European Community of Community law over the national law of member states was not always inherent in the EEC Treaty it was certainly well established in the jurisprudence of the Court of Justice long before the United Kingdom joined the Community. Thus, whatever limitation of its sovereignty Parliament accepted when it enacted the European Communities Act 1972 was entirely voluntary. Under the terms of the 1972 Act it has always been clear that it was the duty of a United Kingdom court, when delivering final judgment, to override any rule of national law found to be in conflict with any directly enforceable rule of Community law. Similarly, when decisions of the Court of Justice have exposed areas of United Kingdom statute law which failed to implement Council directives, Parliament has always loyally accepted the obligation to make appropriate and prompt amendments. Thus there is nothing in any way novel in according supremacy to rules of Community law in those areas to which they apply, and to insist that, in the protection of rights under Community law, national courts must not be inhibited by rules of national law from granting interim relief in appropriate cases is no more than a logical recognition of that supremacy.

Factortame Ltd. v. *Secretary of State for Transport (No 2)* [1991] 1 All ER
107–8.

---

78 THE WRITTEN CONSTITUTION BILL, 1992

A BILL TO

Provide for the drawing up of a written constitution for the United Kingdom; for its consideration by the people and Parliament of the United Kingdom; and for connected purposes.

Be it enacted by the Queen's most Excellent Majesty, by and with the advice and consent of the Lords Spiritual and Temporal, and Commons, in this present Parliament assembled, and by the authority of the same, as follows:—

1.—(1) Within three months of the passing of this Act, the Speaker of the House of Commons shall convene a Speaker's Conference to consider the matter of a written constitution for the United Kingdom, to draw up a draft of such a constitution ('the draft constitution'), and to consider such related matters as the Conference shall think fit.

(2) There shall be eleven members of the Conference, of whom one shall be the Speaker of the House of Commons as Chairman.

(3) The Speaker of the House of Commons shall appoint the members of the Conference after consulting with such persons and bodies as he considers to be appropriate, and shall make such further appointments as may be required.

(4) The Conference shall have power to make such rules for the conduct of its business as are required.

(5) The Conference shall have power to appoint such staff as it considers necessary for the conduct of its business.

(6) The provisions of the Tribunals of Inquiry (Evidence) Act 1921 shall apply to the Conference.

2. In drawing up the draft constitution, the Conference shall make provision for—

    (a) the separation of constitutional powers as between the Executive and the Legislature;

    (b) the protection of individual and collective rights;

    (c) the entrenchment of the Constitution as eventually approved ('the Constitution');

    (d) methods of amendment of the Constitution;

    (e) the relationship between the provisions of the draft constitution and the legal and judicial systems of the United Kingdom; and

    (f) any other matters the Conference may think fit.

3.—(1) Not later than twelve months after the passing of this Act the Speaker of the House of Commons shall lay before each House of Parliament, and cause to be published, the draft constitution drawn up by the Conference, together with any report by the Conference on the discharge of its duties under this Act.

(2) The draft constitution shall be drawn up in the form of a Bill, and shall contain a provision that its commencement shall be dependent on approval by referendum under section 4(6) below.

(3) (a) The Conference may make such interim reports on the discharge of its duties under this Act as it sees fit.

    (b) Any such interim report shall be laid before each House of Parliament and published as provided for in subsection (1) above.

(4) The Conference shall continue in being after the draft constitution has been laid before each House of Parliament.

4.—(1) Not later than two months after the draft constitution has been laid before each House of Parliament, the Prime Minister shall present to the House of Commons a Bill embodying the draft constitution, the text of which shall be the same in all respects as that approved by the Conference.

(2) Immediately upon the passing of the Bill embodying the draft constitution, the Prime Minister shall make arrangements for the holding of a referendum to consider the draft constitution ('the referendum').

(3) The referendum shall be held within three months of the passing of the Bill.

(4) The administrative arrangements for the referendum and the requirements for the qualification of voters shall, so far as is practicable, follow those for a General Election.

(5) The Conference may give such advice as may be required in connection with the holding of the referendum.

(6) Approval or rejection of the draft constitution shall be by a simple majority of those voting in the referendum.

(7) Any matters of doubt or dispute in the conduct of the referendum shall be decided by the Conference, the decision of which shall be final, and in respect of which no proceedings shall lie.

5. If approved by the referendum, the Constitution shall enter into force twenty-one days after polling day in the referendum.

6. There shall be paid out of money provided by Parliament—
   (a) any expenses incurred under this Act by a Minister of the Crown or by the Conference; and
   (b) any increase attributable to this Act in the sums payable out of such money under any other Act.

7. This Act may be cited as the Written Constitution Act 1992.

Graham Allen, HC [1991–2] 38.

---

79   A PROPOSAL FOR THE DEMOCRATIC ENTRENCHMENT OF A UK BILL OF RIGHTS, 1993

RB NOTE: The following passage explains the form of entrenchment suggested as part of Liberty's proposal for a British Bill of Rights: see Doc. 50.

Protagonists and opponents alike tend to argue that a bill of rights *necessarily* involves the judges in having the *final* say on which Acts of Parliament do or do not comply with its terms. In practice, however, there are a number of possible approaches to enforcement. In New Zealand, for example, the attorney-general is the guardian of the 1990 Bill of Rights. Whilst this model stands accused of not being an entrenched bill at all, the 1982 Canadian Charter of Rights is entrenched and justiciable and yet allows Parliament (or a provincial legislature) expressly to override court decisions by passing acts 'notwithstanding' the provisions of the Charter. A similar opt-out clause was proposed by the Liberal Democrats in their 1990 draft constitution 'We, the People'. Others have suggested the use of a weaker device by which subsequent legislation would be interpreted consistently with a bill of rights *if at all possible* ...

There are two reasons why the issue of judicial entrenchment has attracted such attention. First, any bill of rights worthy of its name must be entrenched by one mechanism or another; that is, it must be a superior act to which all other legislation is supposed to conform and it must be difficult or impossible to amend or repeal. In a system like ours with no written constitution this is a departure from the doctrine of parliamentary sovereignty. According to this doctrine, the courts must give effect to an Act of Parliament whatever it says, and if Parliament changes its mind by a later act, the courts will give effect to that, as the most recent expression of the sovereign will. Of course British accession to the European Community (EC) has already dented this principle, with the judges giving priority to EC law where it proves inconsistent with domestic legislation.

Second, and just as important, a bill of rights is different from all other pieces of legislation in that it is a set of broad principles – some of which collide with each other – which are open to wide interpretation. Liberty's draft bill calls on the courts to pay due regard to the decisions and reports of international and regional human rights bodies in their rulings. However, none of the standard principles of statutory interpretation commonly employed by judges under the current British system – all of which rely on a degree of precision and detail in the act to be interpreted – can provide much guidance in the case of an open-textured bill of rights.

The combination of these two factors means that the body charged with entrenching the bill of rights effectively determines the law on civil and political rights ...

When drawing up its draft bill of rights – 'The People's Charter', published in October 1991 – Liberty examined several different models of entrenchment. The approach Liberty adopted can best be summarized as judicial enforcement and democratic entrenchment. Based on the European Convention on Human Rights but broader in its scope, Liberty's draft bill is judicially enforced in the sense that individuals would be able to seek remedies for infringements of their rights through the courts. It is democratically entrenched in the sense that elected representatives would, in most cases, have the final say in determining which acts stand or fall under the bill of rights, provided special parliamentary procedures are invoked. At the same time the bill of rights could only be directly amended or repealed with the support of two-thirds of both Houses of Parliament. Rights legislation would still be determined through the democratic process but all laws – and the actions and decisions of public officials – would be subject to the bill of rights.

A version of the Canadian legislative override – referred to as a 'health warning' – is included in Liberty's model along with the stipulation that such acts have a maximum five-year lifespan. (In a proposal borrowed from the Labour Party's policy review, a reformed second chamber would have the power, should it choose to use it, to delay the coming into force for five years of any such 'health warning' legislation.) The Canadian legislative override has hardly ever been used. This is not surprising, given the political fallout and attendant publicity likely to befall any legislature that passes an act which carries an express acknowledgement – like a health warning on a cigarette pack – that it breaches the bill of rights.

The legislative override is in fact best viewed as an alternative to the derogation procedure in the European Convention on Human Rights (inserted at the behest of British government lawyers). The drawback to derogation is that it involves a tacit acceptance that human rights can be flouted during wars or public emergencies, precisely the circumstances which spurred the evolution of international or regional human rights instruments, like the Convention, in the first place. The legislative override, on the other hand, does not involve getting sanction – and hence legitimacy – for a breach of the bill of rights from the courts.

Given that it is effectively a form of derogation, it is easy to see why politicians are so unwilling to use the device of legislative override in the conflict of rights situations described above. Presumably neither the women's movement, nor their backers in the Canadian Parliament, wanted to reintroduce the 'rape shield' provision by acknowledging that it did not conform with the Charter of Rights. As a result the provision fell.

Liberty has proposed a novel mechanism to address such a scenario. Suppose a new act was introduced to curb election expenditure by political parties at a national level. Under Liberty's proposals, should a newly created supreme court overturn such legislation as a breach of the right to freedom of expression – which is similar to what happened in Canada and the United States – this decision could, within a specified time limit, be referred by the courts, the government or a majority in Parliament to a special select committee called the Human Rights Scrutiny Committee (HRSC). (It must be emphasized that this would not apply where the courts outlawed subordinate legislation or administrative acts.) This committee would obviously not have any powers in itself but its decisions could affect subsequent parliamentary procedure.

There are, then, three possible outcomes. If two-thirds of the HRSC took the view that the hypothetical Election Expenditure Act was within the 'meaning, intention and spirit' of the bill of rights, Parliament could, by a resolution of both houses, attach a 'declaration of rights' to the legislation protecting it from further judicial (but not parliamentary) repeal. With such a formula the Canadian Parliament could have rescued its 'rape shield' and 'absolute liability' laws should it have wished to.

If, on the other hand, the Scrutiny Committee could not muster the requisite two-thirds majority then the court ruling would stand and the act would fall. If, finally, two-thirds of the HRSC considered that the act breached the bill of rights, it could only be re-enacted with a 'health warning' attached to it, and it would fall five years later.

Just as the European Convention sets aside certain articles which cannot be derogated from, so Liberty has proposed a distinction between those articles or clauses which involve a conflict of rights or are open to a wide variety of interpretations (the majority) and those which are much more clear cut and explicit. At the time of writing these include freedom of conscience, the right to be free from torture or slavery, and the right to vote and participate in public affairs. In these cases, judicial entrenchment would apply. (Following Liberty's consultation process, further Articles could well be added to this list when Liberty drafts its final bill.)

The composition and situation of the HRSC are vital if the committee is not to suffer from the executive domination which befalls the usual operation of the legislature under the British constitution. On the assumption that the bill of rights is introduced as part of a wider constitutional settlement, the HRSC would be based in a reformed second chamber which would be elected on a proportional basis. The chair would either be elected by the committee or would automatically be occupied by the largest opposition party (as per the Public Accounts Committee). The HRSC would be consulted on legislation prior to enactment, but its decisions could only affect parliamentary procedure along the lines described above following a court ruling on an Act of Parliament.

In all of its decisions this committee would be advised by a human rights commission, an appointed body composed of lawyers (academics and practitioners), human rights non-governmental organizations, and lay individuals with knowledge and/or experience of human rights abuse. In advising the HRSC, the commission would be required to draw upon international human rights jurisprudence. Its advice would be public and published, acting as a counter to any pressures placed on HRSC members by the whips.

Recourse to the European Commission of Human Rights would still be available in the unlikely event that the HRSC flouted the bill of rights for political ends. Judicial review would likewise be possible if HRSC decisions appeared to weaken rights rather than operate within the 'meaning, intention and spirit' of the bill.

Francesca Klug, 'The Role of a Bill of Rights in a Democratic Constitution', Ch. 6 in A. Barnett (ed.), *Debating the Constitution*, 1993.

---

80 THE INSTITUTE FOR PUBLIC POLICY RESEARCH ARGUES THAT THE NEED FOR ENTRENCHMENT OF HUMAN RIGHTS IMPLIES A CONSTITUTIONAL DOCUMENT, 1993

It is the belief that restraints on the Executive and on the centralisation of power must be given constitutional rather than political force that has become the common theme of reformers. The need for the entrenchment of rights both for individuals and for devolved governments implies a constitutional document ...

Particular reforms may be important and interesting. But the essential question is whether the time has come not to change the historical constitution incrementally as has been done in the past, but to change the basis of the Constitution. That is, to change from a single fundamental principle, the supremacy of Parliament, which is founded in custom and usage as recognised by the courts, to a fundamental law which is prior to, independent of and the source of authority for the system of government. A codification of existing practice and convention might be convenient, but it would not be enough. It is the peculiarity of our Constitution not that it is not codified, but that the laws which make it up, whether statute, common or case law, have no special status. Parliament can make and unmake them as it chooses; a million British subjects can be deprived of their rights of abode by the same means as an alteration of the speed limit. Essential features of the Constitution have no basis in law at all ...

The much vaunted flexibility of the Constitution suits nobody so much as an Executive which has inherited a reservoir of prerogative powers and enjoys a dominant position in relation to the legislature and all other public authorities. In the past these features of the Constitution, like the party system which exploits them, have been justified on the grounds that they help to provide firm and effective government. There is no doubt that single-party government has advantages of cohesion, speed of response and clear locus of responsibility. It is less clear that it performs any better than other systems in the promotion of effective and acceptable public policies. There may be some truth in the view that there would be less concern about the Constitution if the policies of successive British governments had been more successful. But there remains a constitutional case for reform: that the protection of individual rights, the decentralisation of power within the United Kingdom and the United Kingdom's role in the development of the European Community would all be more readily and more satisfactorily addressed within an explicitly constitutional framework.

IPPR, *A Written Constitution for the United Kingdom*, 1993, 7–8.

---

81   RODNEY BRAZIER AND STANLEY DE SMITH ON HOW PARLIAMENT MIGHT REDEFINE ITS PROCEDURE FOR ENACTING AMENDMENTS OF A BILL OF RIGHTS, 1995

Parliament is capable of redefining itself for particular purposes. It did so by the Parliament Acts, which provided a simpler, optional procedure for legislation on most topics.[1] It could make the procedure simpler still by abolishing the House of Lords. What if it were to lay down a more cumbersome procedure for legislating and prescribe it as the only procedure to be followed? Suppose, for example, that Parliament were to pass a Bill of Rights Act proclaiming the rights of the citizen, and which stated that no bill to vary that Act was to be presented for the royal assent unless it had first obtained the support of a majority of the voters at a referendum, or had been passed at its final reading with the support of two-thirds of the full membership of the House of Commons; and that no bill to amend or repeal

---

1 Professor H. W. R. Wade regards measures passed under this procedure as a special form of delegated legislation: see [1955] *Camb. L.J.* 172 and *Constitutional Fundamentals* (1980), pp. 27–8. I respectfully prefer Dr Geoffrey Marshall's view (*Parliamentary Sovereignty and the Commonwealth* (1957), pp. 42–6) that such legislation is primary and not delegated. Professor Hood Phillips (*Constitutional and Administrative Law* (7th edn, 1987 by Hood Phillips and Paul Jackson), p. 91) goes so far as to characterize legislation passed with a Regent's assent 'as a kind of delegated legislation', and on this ground would justify a judicial decision to the effect that an 'Act' assented to by a Regent in contravention of s. 4(2) of the 1937 Act was invalid. He has also suggested (*Reform of the Constitution* (1970), pp. 18–19, 91–2) that the Parliament Act 1949 is a nullity because the 'delegate' created in 1911 enlarged its own limited powers in passing it.

that Act was to be presented for the royal assent unless that same procedure had been followed.[2] Could Parliament nevertheless amend or repeal the Act by ordinary legislative procedure?[3]

1   It is not enough to incant the phrase: 'A sovereign Parliament cannot bind its own future action.'[4] One of the questions to be asked is: 'What is meant by 'Parliament'?' Another – essentially the same question expressed in a different way – is whether there cannot be new mandatory legal rules as to the manner and form of law-making which Parliament must observe if its enactments are to be recognized as authentic. The much-quoted dictum that

2 Unless this last entrenching provision was present – it is absent from section 1 of the Northern Ireland Constitution Act 1973, as it was from section 1(2) of the Ireland Act 1949 – it could easily be argued that the Act imposing the special requirement could itself be amended or repealed by ordinary legislative procedure.

3 Among the main contributions are those by Cowen (1952) 15 *Mod. L. Rev.* 282, (1953) 16 *Mod. L. Rev.* 273; Beinart [1954] *Butterworth's South African Law Rev.* 135; Geoffrey Marshall, *Parliamentary Sovereignty and the Commonwealth* (1957) and *Constitutional Theory* (1971), ch. 3; R. F. V. Heuston, *Essays in Constitutional Law* (2nd edn, 1964), ch. 4; J. D. B. Mitchell, *Constitutional Law* (2nd edn, 1968), ch. 4; Gray (1953) 10 *U. of Toronto L.J.* 54; Friedmann (1950) 24 *Australian L.J.* 103; O. Hood Phillips, op. cit., ch. 4; Harry Calvert, *Constitutional Law in Northern Ireland* (1968), ch. 1.

4 In this context the implications of *Att.-Gen. for N.S.W.* v. *Trethowan* (1931) 44 C.L.R. 394; [1932] A.C. 526 are often misunderstood by students. Under the constitution of New South Wales as amended by local legislation passed in 1929, a bill to abolish the upper House could not be presented for the royal assent unless it had first been approved by the electorate at a referendum, and a like requirement extended to any bill to amend or repeal this procedure. Following a change of government in 1931, bills were passed by both Houses of the New South Wales Parliament to remove the referendum rule and to abolish the upper House; neither bill was submitted to a referendum. Injunctions were obtained to restrain submission of the bills for the royal assent. This may have been an inappropriate remedy (see *Hughes and Vale Pty Ltd* v. *Gair* (1954) 90 C.L.R. 203 at 204–5), but the decision on the point of substantive law was clearly correct. Confusion has been caused by the fact that New South Wales had a non-sovereign legislature; and section 5 of the Colonial Laws Validity Act 1865, which applied to New South Wales, provided that a 'colonial' legislature could make laws relating to its constitution, powers and procedure 'in such manner and form as may ... be required' by existing law. The applicability of section 5 furnished one reason for holding the improper procedure to be unlawful; the decision should have been the same, however, even if New South Wales had had a 'sovereign' legislature: see cases cited in notes 119 and 120, below. There is a common but wholly unfounded misconception that *because* New South Wales had a non-sovereign legislature and was held to be competent to 'bind its own future action', *it therefore follows* that a sovereign legislature like the United Kingdom Parliament is incompetent to do so.

'Parliament cannot bind itself as to the form of subsequent legislation' carries us nowhere, for it was uttered merely to rebut the
optimistic argument that Parliament had protected an ordinary
enactment against implied repeal.[5] Another question, as we have
already seen, is the extent to which the courts have jurisdiction to
determine whether 'Parliament' has acted in conformity with the
law behind Parliament.

2 Modern decisions in constitutional cases arising in South Africa[6]
and Ceylon[7] show that a sovereign (i.e. omnicompetent) Parliament must function in the manner prescribed by existing law in
order validly to express its legislative will. In each of the cases the
constitution had laid down a special procedure (a two-thirds'
majority of the two Houses in joint session, or a two-thirds'
majority in the lower House, at final reading) to be followed for
the enactment of legislation on certain important matters. In each
of them the courts held that where bills dealing with these 'entrenched' matters had been passed by *ordinary* legislative majorities
and had been duly assented to and printed, they could not be
accepted as authentic Acts of Parliament. There was to be read
into the constitution a necessary implication that 'Parliament'
bore different meanings for different purposes.

3 These decisions, extremely interesting though they are as illustrations of basic principle, are of doubtful persuasive authority when
we try to answer our hypothetical problem set in a British constitutional context. In the first place, in each of them the wording

---

5 cf. *R.* v. *Drybones* [1970] S.C.R. 282 (Can.) for the position of an extraordinary
enactment (the Canadian Bill of Rights 1960) which the majority of the Supreme
Court held would prevail over inconsistent legislation not expressed to be made
'notwithstanding' the Bill of Rights.

6 *Harris* v. *Dönges* [1952] 1 T.L.R. 1245, *sub nom. Harris* v. *Minister of the Interior*
1952 (2) S.A. 428 (two-thirds' majority of both Houses of the South African
Parliament required by the South Africa Act 1909 for removal of Cape coloured
voters from the common voters' roll; held, a measure passed by both Houses sitting
separately by simple majorities was not an authentic Act of Parliament, although it
had been assented to); see also *Minister of the Interior* v. *Harris* 1952 (4) S.A. 769
(an 'Act' constituting the two Houses as the 'High Court of Parliament' with power
to override the previous decision by a simple majority, also held to be a nullity).
See, however, *Collins* v. *Minister of the Interior* 1957 (1) S.A. 552, where the desired
result was achieved by a sufficiently circuitous route. For the literature on this series
of legal battles, see Geoffrey Marshall, *Parliamentary Sovereignty and the Commonwealth* (1957).

7 *Bribery Commissioner* v. *Ranasinghe* [1965] A.C. 172 (royal assent did not cure
failure to obtain a two-thirds' majority in the lower House for a measure inconsistent with the constitution). See further *R. (O'Brien)* v. *Military Governor, N.D.U.
Internment Camp* [1924] I.R. 32 (failure to submit a bill to a referendum held fatal
to the validity of an ostensibly authentic Act; see Heuston, op. cit., pp. 11–14).

of a Speaker's certificate on the face of the Act or bill in question (or the absence of such a certificate) indicated that the specially prescribed procedure had not in fact been followed. Although the decisions suggest that the courts can look at the original of the bill as presented for assent (and are not confined to the bare text of the published Act), they do not offer clear guidance on the proper limits of a court's scope of inquiry if there is no requirement of a Speaker's certificate, or if a Speaker's certificate or the words of enactment are notoriously false or are alleged to be false. As far as British courts are concerned, these questions remain open. In the second place, none of them deals with the legal effects of *self-imposed* procedural requirements by the Parliaments of those countries; the requirements had been imposed by the constitutional instruments from which the Parliaments derived their authority to make law.

4 None the less, there is no *logical* reason why the United Kingdom Parliament should be incompetent so to redefine itself (or redefine the procedure for enacting legislation on any given matter) as to preclude Parliament *as ordinarily constituted* from passing a law on a matter. (There are, of course, doubts as to the jurisdiction or willingness of the courts to intervene.) If Parliament can make it easier to legislate, as by passing the Parliament Acts or abolishing the House of Lords, it can also make it harder to legislate.[8]

5 Hence a two-thirds' majority rule might be analysed either as a redefinition of the meaning of 'Parliament' or a prescription of essential procedural conditions before Parliament could speak with an authentic voice; a rule imposing a duty to hold a referendum could quite persuasively be analysed as the addition of a fourth element to 'Parliament', in much the same way as the Parliament Act procedure can be analysed as involving the conditional subtraction of one of the three elements from Parliament.

6 Such an analysis can be attacked on the ground that once it is conceded that Parliament can make legislation on any topic more difficult, one must then concede that it can make legislation impossible. If it can lay down a two-thirds' majority rule it can lay down a nine-tenths' majority rule, and a similar rule for the majority to be obtained at a referendum. In this way it could, by imposing requirements as to the manner of legislating, in practice bind itself not to change the substantive content of future legislation, and this would be contrary to both established principle and

8 The Parliament Acts analogy has been characterized as fallacious because the Acts only created an additional and permissive means of legislating, so that no question of limitation arises. See Colin Munro, *Studies in Constitutional Law* (1987), pp. 106–7.

public policy; a legislative vacuum must not be created; consequently the courts ought not to recognize the legal efficacy of *any* such restrictive rule. The only ways of answering this point are that there exist *political* safeguards against the adoption of such restrictive rules, just as there are political safeguards against the enactment of preposterous laws by ordinary legislative procedure; and that a court could draw a common-sense line between binding rules regulating the manner of legislating and ineffectual rules which if accepted as binding would, in substance, stop Parliament from legislating at all.[9] One must, however, recognize the distinct possibility that a court might decide not to engage in such a delicate exercise.

S. de Smith and R. Brazier, *Constitutional and Administrative Law*, 7th edn, 95–9.

---

82 THE ROLE AND POWERS OF A RECONSTITUTED SECOND CHAMBER WITH RESPECT TO A BILL OF RIGHTS, 1997

The Legal Status and Priority of the Bill of Rights

Under the system of reform I envisage, the general constitutional status of the Bill of Rights would be declared to be one of legal priority over all past or future parliamentary enactments. However, the Bill of Rights would provide a procedure whereby its legal primacy could be overridden by any Act of Parliament which was passed in a particular form and through a special legislative process. If the government and both Houses of Parliament wished a statute to take effect regardless of the Bill of Rights (including to effect an amendment to the Bill of Rights, or in order to reverse a recent judicial interpretation of the Bill of Rights) a clause would have to be inserted within the body of the Bill designating itself a Constitutional Act. The meaning of a Constitutional Act would need to be defined in the Bill of Rights, and might be 'any public Bill which affects any article of the Bill of Rights and contains a clause whereby it is designated a Constitutional Act'. The courts would be directed, by the relevant article in the legislation establishing the legal status of the Bill of Rights, to recognise and enforce the provisions of any such statute in priority to any pre-existing rule of law to the contrary, including any article, or previous judicial interpretation thereof, contained within the Bill of Rights itself.

Thus far, the degree of judicial entrenchment would be similar in effect, though not in form, to the 1990 Institute for Public Policy Research proposal

---

9 See Friedmann (1950) 24 *Australian L.J.* at 105–6.

[see Doc. 49]. So too, the qualification of full entrenchment by way of designation as a Constitutional Act would be similar in effect, though not in form, to the insertion of a 'notwithstanding clause' under the 1982 Canadian Charter of Rights and Freedoms. The reason for the particular form adopted is to provide for an appropriate mechanism whereby a reformed House of Lords might be given a special power and function with respect to the Bill of Rights.

LEGISLATIVE PROCEDURE FOR AMENDING OR OVERRULING THE BILL OF RIGHTS

In the parliamentary passage of any Constitutional Act, the reformed House of Lords would be vested with an equivalent legislative authority to that of the House of Commons. The requirement for the approval of a Constitutional Act by the second chamber would be absolute, equivalent to a legislative veto. This would be in contrast to the normal power of the House of Lords under the Parliament Acts 1911–49, whereby it can presently only delay public legislation for a period of one year. So, under the terms of the newly-established Bill of Rights, any public legislation which sought legal priority for itself as a Constitutional Act would require the House of Lords' formal agreement, and such agreement could not be overriden after a year's delay by the government choosing to utilise the Parliament Act procedure whereby a statute may be enacted on the authority of the Commons and Sovereign alone (as the government has chosen to do several times this century, always over measures of a constitutional or human rights nature, most recently in 1991).

To implement this arrangement in law, all that is necessary is a short amendment to the 1911 Parliament Act providing for the exclusion of Constitutional Acts, as defined, from the operation of its provisions. What might appear to some people as a novel power being conferred upon the House of Lords would not in fact be inconsistent with parliamentary traditions and is not without precedent. Another similar exception to the Parliament Act already exists, namely Bills 'to extend the maximum duration of Parliament beyond five years' over which the House of Lords has always possessed a power of legislative veto.

The report of the future commission which is set up to make recommendations on a Bill of Rights, together with the government White Paper preceeding the legislation to introduce the Bill of Rights, should explain the new responsibilities of the House of Lords which justify the power of veto. It would be the function of the House, in chamber and committee, to scrutinise draft Constitutional Acts to ensure they are not unwarranted infringements of the existing articles of the Bill of Rights. The second chamber would have the task of co-operating with the House of Commons to rectify any judicial rulings which had become out-dated or had proved democratically unacceptable or for any other reason unworkable. The House of Lords would represent the principal constitutional forum for the approval of modernising amendments, and emergency derogations.

The Need for a Reconstituted Second Chamber

As will be widely appreciated, the capacity of the House of Lords to perform these functions with respect to the Bill of Rights depends upon the reconstitution of its membership. A strengthened second chamber of Parliament is only feasible, indeed tolerable, if at the same time it becomes composed of representatives who are selected in a democratically acceptable manner.

Such a development has become practical politics in the 1990s. The Labour Party, and Liberal Democrats, are already pledged to recompose the House of Lords. The Conservative Party has been conducting inquiries of its own into reform. A 1995 report [*Second Chamber* by Lord Carnarvon *et al.*] by a group of Conservative peers concluded that,

> The challenge is to find a rational basis for a Second Chamber which would allow the continuance of the best features of the present House ... Our institutions have been distinguished both by their stability and by their capacity to change. Both qualities have their roots in wide public acceptance. Wide public debate is the path to that acceptance. What sort of Second Chamber – in what sort of constitution – do we believe will serve our nation best as we enter the next century? That is the question.

[Meanwhile the Labour Party have] prominently committed themselves, as a first step towards a reconstituted second chamber, to abolish the right of hereditary peers to sit and vote in the House. Giving the John Smith Memorial Lecture 1996, the Labour leader Tony Blair clearly indicated the way of reform ahead.

> The case for reform is simple and obvious. It is in principle wrong and absurd that people should wield power on the basis of birth, not merit or election ... There are no conceivable grounds for maintaining this system ... We have always favoured an elected second chamber but some, like my colleague Lord Richard [leader of the Labour peers in the Lords] have suggested that if there was a move to an elected second chamber, provision for people of a particularly distinguished position or record could be made. We are master of our own rules and procedure ...

This highly symbolic reform will immediately raise the credibility of the second chamber and facilitate its potential to play an invigorated role within the constitutional process. Some incremental system for replenishing the House with newly-elected members to sit alongside the remaining life peers is likely already be under consideration within a Labour Cabinet and at the Home Office. My preference, eventually, would be for a second chamber comprising around 240 members, with each member serving a six year tenure of office, and one-third of the membership standing for re-election on a biennial cycle.

There is no reason why the commission on a Bill of Rights should not include within its deliberations the questions of the powers and composition of the House of Lords. To the contrary, the commission should be encouraged to adopt a wide-ranging review of all the implications of a Bill of Rights, and to examine thoroughly any consequential issues to be decided upon. One of the principal difficulties of British constitutional development in modern times has been the marked tendency of our rulers to prescribe piecemeal changes for individual institutions without treating the constitution as the organic, interconnected whole.

FUNCTIONS APPROPRIATE TO A SECOND CHAMBER

Currently a working description of the principal business conducted by the House of Lords may be classified as follows: (1) the consideration of legislative proposals, especially the revision of government Bills passed by the House of Commons; (2) the consideration of statutory instruments; (3) the discussion and scrutiny of government policy and administration, by way of questions and debates; (4) debates on matters of public importance; (5) the scrutiny of particular areas of administration or legislation by way of Select Committee, including the Select Committee on the European Communities; and (6) the appellate jurisdiction of the House, as final court of appeal within the judicial system (although this is performed quite separately from the chamber). I am suggesting that an extended task be added to the legislative work of a reformed House of Lords, being (7) the consideration and scrutiny of legislation affecting the Bill of Rights.

Though no coherent consensus of principle about the purpose of the House of Lords has emerged over the past 85 years since the Liberal government's abrupt temporary expediency of curtailing its powers in 1911, in reaction to the Lords' rejection of the 1909 budget of the then Chancellor of the Exchequer David Lloyd George, yet the House of Lords, in common with second chambers of most modern Parliaments in the world, has always been widely perceived as possessing some elevated authority with respect to Bills affecting constitutional affairs and civil liberties. It was a distinctive function still identified in the years following the Parliament Act, most notably in the Conference on the Reform of the Second Chamber [Cd. 9038], whose valuable report in 1918 was unfortunately overshadowed that year by the Representation of the People Act, bringing in women's suffrage and universal voting, and by the government's initiatives in reconstructing the national economy after cessation of the First World War. Throughout the period since, numerous, though certainly not all, political and other reports have recognised and prescribed some special constitutional role for a newly-composed House of Lords, recently including published works by the former Conservative party chairman and Lord Chancellor Lord Hailsham, and official policies of the Liberal Democrats. In 1989 it was a function forming part of the Labour Party's Charter of Rights proposals for a series of human rights Acts of Parliament, conferring upon the House of Lords an extended legislative power over future measures designed to amend or repeal them in any way.

If political support was forthcoming for strengthened powers to be given to a reformed House of Lords, it is worth reflecting on the fact that the functions of the second chamber might be enlarged generally within the field of human rights. As part of the ordinary legislative process, a new Select Committee could be established within the House's existing sphere of competence to review and report on all Bills for compliance with the United Kingdom's international human rights treaty obligations (notably under the United Nations International Covenant and the Council of Europe's Convention on Human Rights). Additionally, the House of Lords, whether through the same Select Committee or another constituted specifically for the purpose, might become responsible for reviewing the operation of the British government's reporting obligations to the Human Rights Committee under the International Covenant or to other specialised human rights monitoring bodies (such as the Committee on the Elimination of Discrimination against Women, the International Labour Organisation Committee of Experts, and the Committee on the Elimination of Racial Discrimination).

In this connection, it is interesting to observe that there is already a precedent in the House of Lords for a Select Committee performing a scrutiny function with respect to legislation of a particular kind – as would be required in the case of monitoring Bills for compliance with international human rights codes. This is the House of Lords Select Committee on the Scrutiny of Delegated Powers, which is concerned with the appropriateness or otherwise of proposals in Bills to delegate legislative powers. Since the Committee's establishment in 1994, every Bill is now subjected by it to scrutiny to establish whether there is a delegation of legislative power in it. If there is, an examination is carried out and reported on to the House. The recommendations made by the Committee have proved very influential, with virtually all matters of concern raised by the Committee being accepted by ministers and reflected in amendments made to the Bill under scrutiny.

Robert Blackburn, 'A Bill of Rights for the 21st Century', Ch. 2 in Robert Blackburn and James Busuttil (eds), *Human Rights for the 21st Century*, 1997.

CHAPTER 7

POLITICAL OPINION ON A BILL OF RIGHTS

(A)
THE HOUSE OF LORDS

RB NOTE: Remarkably few debates have ever taken place at Westminster on the question of a homegrown British Bill of Rights. The 1977–8 House of Lords select committee inquiry (Doc. 83) is the only in-depth examination into the matter conducted by Parliament.

However, the subject of a Bill of Rights or factors relevant to it have regularly been raised either during debates on the state of civil liberties generally or when the separate proposal to incorporate the European Convention on Human Rights into UK law has been discussed since the mid-1970s. Furthermore, arguments and issues raised by parliamentarians in the past over the proposal to incorporate the European Convention have regularly been of a broadly similar nature to those adopted by the same persons or viewpoints towards the desirability or otherwise of a homegrown Bill of Rights – not surprisingly, since both measures raise questions of positive rights, the redress of human rights grievances, and the relationship between Parliament and the judiciary.

Similar to parliamentary proceedings, the attitudes and policy developments expressed within the three main political parties down to 1998 have often interconnected (and occasionally blurred the distinction between) incorporation of the European Convention and a home-grown British Bill of Rights.

For these reasons, and also so as to trace the history behind the Human Rights Act 1998, extracts from relevant parliamentary debates and party policy statements are included in the documents contained within sections A, B and C below.

For parliamentary debates taking place during passage of the Human Rights Act, see Doc. 40 (especially section D) which has been compiled to deal comprehensively with all key documentation affecting statutory incorporation of the European Convention in 1997–8. For the Labour–Liberal Democrats concord on constitutional reform matters in the present Parliament, see Docs 149 and 150.

---

83   REPORT OF THE HOUSE OF LORDS SELECT COMMITTEE ON A BILL OF RIGHTS, 1978

5. The Committee were required to consider two questions: first, whether a Bill of Rights was desirable, and, second, if a Bill was thought desirable,

what form it should take. The Committee have found it difficult in practice to make a sharp distinction between these two questions. They found that it was not feasible to consider the desirability of a Bill of Rights without having a broad idea of the likely contents of such a Bill; and much of the evidence on the question of desirability was found to be relevant to the form which a Bill of Rights might take.

6. Nevertheless, as the Committee's enquiry proceeded, they found that it was easier to reach agreement on the second question than on the first. They think it right to say straightaway that there was indeed unanimity that, if there was to be a Bill of Rights, it should be a Bill based on the European Convention on Human Rights. It proved impossible, however, to reach agreement on the question whether such a Bill was desirable. The reasons for these two conclusions are developed in some detail later in this Report. The Committee feel it is of great importance to emphasise that, although some of the members favour incorporation of the Convention into United Kingdom law and some oppose it, there was unanimity of view on the need to protect and advance human rights and unanimous recognition that both sides were wholly committed to the promotion of human rights.

7. Some of those who advocate a Bill of Rights see it as an element of a new constitutional settlement, involving a written constitution. The Committee however regarded their terms of reference as precluding them from considering a Bill of Rights in such a context; and considered that they were obliged to look at the arguments in the light of the existing constitutional arrangements – including the fact that we have a sovereign Parliament which may not bind its successors. The Committee made this clear to their witnesses. (It is right to add that some of those who have spoken in favour of a new constitutional settlement, notably Lord Hailsham and Lord Scarman, explained in their evidence that they were in favour of a Bill of Rights even on the assumption that there was no new constitutional settlement.)

8. The Committee took as their starting point the assumption that a Bill of Rights was a Bill incorporating into United Kingdom domestic law various rights of a fundamental nature for the protection of the individual. There are advocates of legislation for the protection of human rights who do not favour a Bill of that kind at all; they would prefer some sort of enactment which merely provided for machinery – for example, a Human Rights Commission for the United Kingdom – to keep the matter of human rights under review, to investigate and to make recommendations. But the Committee decided that it would be appropriate to consider, not that sort of Bill (what might be called a 'pure machinery' Bill), but rather a Bill of Rights in the primary sense of a Bill establishing rules of law, whether or not it also contained monitoring machinery.

9. There was an overwhelming body of evidence that, if there was to be a Bill of this kind, the only feasible way of proceeding was to rest on the European Convention on Human Rights.

10. Certainly, there was no lack of criticism of the Convention. It was pointed out that, even when it was drawn up, it represented only the minimum standards accepted by all the participating countries; that some of

the procedures in other countries which were permissible under the Convention fell below the relevant United Kingdom provisions for the protection of human rights; that it was now 30 years old; and that, although various Protocols had been added, it still fell short in some respects of the more modern United Nations Convenant on Civil and Political Rights. The Committee are themselves in no doubt that, in a good many respects, existing United Kingdom law can claim to do a good deal better than the minimum standards laid down in the Convention. Nevertheless they believe that to attempt to formulate *de novo* a set of fundamental rights which would command the necessary general assent would be a fruitless exercise. The Austrian experience is instructive. The Committee were informed that a Commission set up there in 1966 to draw up a new code of fundamental rights has encountered endless problems and has so far succeeded in producing a text in respect of only two rights, and even then only in the form of alternative drafts. Moreover, apart from the difficulty of getting agreement to its terms, we are signatories to the European Convention (unlike Canada, which introduced its own Bill of Rights in 1969) and if we produced for ourselves a new and different formulation of fundamental rights, we should then have to cope with two codes which would exist side-by-side. It is also relevant that, unlike the United Nations Convenant, the European Convention provides machinery for enforcement.

11. The United Kingdom signed the European Convention on Human Rights in November 1950. The Convention came into force in September 1953. All Member States of the Council of Europe have signed the Convention. All except Portugal have ratified it and she is likely to do so soon. The rights in the Convention have been extended by a First Protocol, which the United Kingdom has ratified subject to a reservation about education, and by a Fourth Protocol, about freedom of movement, which the United Kingdom has not ratified. Under the Convention, the Government of any Member State may charge any other Member State with a breach of its provisions. It is also open to any citizen of a State which has accepted the right of individual petition to take an allegation of a breach of the Convention to the European Commission of Human Rights, which carries with it the possibility of a subsequent recourse to the European Court of Human Rights ('the Court at Strasbourg'). In 1966, the United Kingdom accepted for five years both the rights of individual petition, and the jurisdiction of the Court. This acceptance was subsequently renewed, and again, in 1976, renewed for a further 5 years. Article 26 of the Convention provides that the Commission may deal with a petition only after the petitioner has exhausted whatever remedies he might have in his own country. In those countries which have incorporated the Convention into their domestic law, either expressly or by virtue of the requirement of their constitution that treaties when ratified automatically assume legal status within the country, this means that an individual may sue his Government in his national courts for an alleged breach of the Convention, and then apply, if dissatisfied with the result, to the Court at Strasbourg. Because under our constitution treaties are entered into by the Crown and do not by the mere process of ratification become part of our domestic law, the Convention does not have the force of

law in British courts. A British subject may therefore petition the Commission, and hope, if need be, to go to the Court at Strasbourg, if he is complaining of a breach of the Convention for which he can find no remedy in United Kingdom domestic law.

12. Although the Committee accepted the arguments put forward by so many of their witnesses that, if there was to be a Bill of Rights, it should be a Bill based on the European Convention, they also thought that some amendment would be needed to the Bill introduced by Lord Wade. Particular problems arise over clause 3. [*RB NOTE: For the context of the Bill referred to here, see Doc. 39A setting out Alan Beith's Bill of Rights Bill 1975 which is identical in form to the Bill introduced by Lord Wade as referred to here. Doc. 39B contains a later, different Bill presented by Lord Wade in 1981.*] These problems however also have an important bearing on the primary question whether it is desirable to have a Bill of Rights at all. This Report now turns, therefore, to that question, and returns to the form of the Bill thereafter.

The scope for a Bill of Rights

13. Whether a Bill of Rights is desirable depends on what it can achieve. Such a Bill could clearly override all existing laws, including Acts of Parliament, so far as inconsistent with its provisions. But could it in any way control the contents of Acts passed after the Bill of Rights? In other words, could it be entrenched – using that expression in a wide sense to indicate a Bill so framed as to restrict the freedom of Parliament to override its provisions in a later Act? The question of entrenchment is dealt with in a paper submitted at the Committee's request by their Specialist Adviser and the Committee accept his Conclusions [*RB NOTE: see Doc. 74*].

14. One thing is clear. That is that there is no way in which a Bill of Rights could be made immune altogether from amendment or repeal by a subsequent Act. That follows from the principle of the sovereignty of Parliament which is the central feature of our constitution. But is there any way in which it could at least be made more difficult for a subsequent Act to override a Bill of Rights? The usual way of entrenching provisions in countries with written constitutions is to require a special majority in the legislature, or in some cases a favourable vote in a referendum, for any Act amending or repealing, or otherwise overriding, the entrenched provision. The Committee think it is clear, however, that no such provision (*e.g.* a requirement for a two-thirds majority in the House of Commons for any Bill seeking to override a Bill of Rights) would be legally effective in the United Kingdom. The cases leading to this conclusion, which can probably all be said to turn on the principle of Parliamentary sovereignty, are dealt within the Committee's Specialist Adviser's paper on entrenchment.

15. The only other possibility is a provision such as is contained in clause 3 of Lord Wade's Bill. The main object of such a provision is to try to prevent a Bill of Rights being overridden inadvertently by a subsequent Act. Some sort of provision of this kind was advocated by most witnesses before the Committee who favoured a Bill of Rights, although they all

accepted that, at best, the efficacy of such a provision must be doubtful. Clause 3 of Lord Wade's provides as follows:

'In the case of conflict between any enactment subsequent to the passing of this Act and the passing of the said Convention and Protocols, the said Convention and Protocols shall prevail unless subsequent enactment shall explicitly state otherwise.'

It will be noted that such a provision purports to be more than a mere interpretation provision. It purports to secure that, unless a subsequent Act expressly amends or repeals the Bill of Rights, or is expressed to have effect notwithstanding the Bill of Rights, it will have to yield to the Bill of Rights so far as inconsistent with it. In other words, the clause proceeds on the assumption that, although a Bill of Rights could not protect itself against being expressly overridden by a later Act, it could protect itself from being overridden by implication by a later Act.

16. If such a clause were effective, it would, in the Committee's view, in practice provide an important degree of entrenchment. In this regard, the Committee do not accept the view that has been expressed that, if such a clause were included in a Bill of Rights, Governments would have no hesitation in including in future Acts the necessary express formula to ensure that the Act would override the Bill of Rights. They do not believe that in practice any Government would readily bring itself to take such a course. They think that, if a Bill of Rights were enacted, then, whatever form it took, there would in practice be the strongest political restraint against any acknowledged attempt to overturn it in a future Act. All the more would this be the case if, as the Committee have concluded that it should, such a Bill took the form of an Act giving domestic effect to the European Convention. For, in that event, an acknowledged attempt to overturn the Bill of Rights would amount to an announcement that the Government was proposing to put us in breach of our international obligations.

17. The Committee have, however, felt unable to accept the assumption on which a number of witnesses advocated a provision on the lines of clause 3 of Lord Wade's Bill, namely that a Bill of Rights could protect itself from being overriden by implication. It is contrary to the principle of Parliamentary sovereignty as it has hitherto been understood in the United Kingdom. Under that principle, Parliament cannot bind itself as to the future and a later Act must always prevail over an earlier one if it is inconsistent with it, whether the inconsistency is express or implied. The Committee are aware that some legal writers have advanced the view that the principle of Parliamentary sovereignty does not preclude Parliament from laying down a binding requirement as to the manner or form of subsequent Acts of a particular kind. This view is discussed in the Specialist Adviser's paper on entrenchment. If this view prevailed in the courts, a provision like clause 3 of Lord Wade's Bill would be efficacious in that it does no more than lay down the form in which a subsequent Act has to be framed if it is to override a Bill of Rights. The Committee are not, however, persuaded that the view is sound.

18. Some witnesses suggested that section 2(4) of the European Communities Act 1972 supported the proposition that a Bill of Rights could effectively control future Acts. They favoured a provision in similar terms in a United Kingdom Bill of Rights, although they did not see it as achieving anything more than clause 3 of Lord Wade's Bill was designed to achieve. The material part of section 2(4) of the European Communities Act provides as follows:

'any enactment, passed or to be passed, other than one contained in this part of this Act, shall be construed and have effect in accordance with the foregoing provisions of this section.'

There is no doubt that section 2(4) is intended to operate on later as well as earlier Acts ('passed or to be passed'). It does not seem to the Committee, however, that it provides any ground for thinking that the same provision in a Bill of Rights would have the effect of enabling such a Bill to override the provisions of a later Act. The fact that section 2(4) applies to Acts passed after the European Communities Act is not in itself inconsistent with the principle of Parliamentary sovereignty. The effect of section 2(4) is that all Acts have to be construed and have effect subject to 'the foregoing provisions' of section 2. This bears in particular on section 2(1) and 2(2) and most importantly on section 2(1). Section 2(1) gives direct effect in the United Kingdom to directly applicable Community law. Section 2(2) provides power to make regulations or Orders in Council giving effect to Community obligations (either by way of of supplementing directly applicable Community law or by way of implementing Community provisions which are not directly applicable within the Member States). The effect of section 2(1) is that all future Community instruments which are directly applicable (broadly speaking, Community regulations) will automatically become part of United Kingdom law. Such instruments must on any footing be allowed to override intervening United Kingdom Acts of Parliament, that is to say, Acts passed after the European Communities Act but before the relevant Community instrument. Section 2(4) achieves that. There is nothing inconsistent here with Parliamentary sovereignty. Similarly, section 2(4) allows the power in section 2(2) to be used to amend or repeal, in the light of later Community instruments, Acts passed after the European Communities Act.

19. It is true that our Community obligations require us to go even further. Decisions of the European Court have held that the European Treaties require the domestic Courts of the Member States to give effect to Community instruments in preference to inconsistent domestic legislation, even where the domestic legislation is later than the relevant Community instrument. Since that principle had become clear long before the United Kingdom acceded to the European Treaties, and since the European Communities Act was designed to enable the United Kingdom to ratify those Treaties, section 2(4) could be regarded as being designed to make a later United Kingdom Act give way to any Community instrument, even where the Act was later than the relevant instrument. That would indeed be contrary to the principle of Parliamentary sovereignty. No cases as yet,

however, have arisen in the United Kingdom courts in which the question whether section 2(4) could have that effect has been put to the test. Even if the United Kingdom courts ultimately hold that section 2(4) does indeed produce that result, it would not follow that a Bill of Rights could similarly control the contents of later Acts. If the Courts ever arrived at that conclusion with respect to section 2(4) of the European Communities Act, it might be on the ground that that Act, coupled with our accession to the Communities, had in fact produced a structural change in the United Kingdom constitution, given that we had become part of an international Community having its own legislative, executive and judicial organs. The same could not be said of a Bill of a kind falling within the Committee's remit.

20. The Committee also considered, in relation to clause 3 of Lord Wade's Bill, section 2 of the Canadian Bill of Rights. This section provides that:

'Every law of Canada shall, unless it is expressly declared by the Parliament of Canada that it shall operate notwithstanding the Canadian Bill of Rights, be so construed and applied as not to abrogate, breach or infringe any of the rights or freedoms herein recognised or declared ...'

It will be seen that this covers both earlier and later laws, and to that extent it covers ground covered by clause 2 as well as by clause 3 of Lord Wade's Bill. So far, however, as it bears on later laws it appears to have the same object as clause 3 of Lord Wade's Bill, namely, to secure that the Bill of Rights shall not be overridden by implication by a later Act. [*RB NOTE: The Canadian instrument referred to has now been superceded by the 1982 Charter of Rights and Freedoms: see Doc. 45, especially its section 33.*]

21. In considering section 2 of the Canadian Bill of Rights the Committee took into account the fact that, for historical reasons and because Canada has a federal system, the Canadian courts are used to reviewing the validity of Acts of Parliament. The scope for review may be limited, but this habit of judicial review does present a marked contrast to the United Kingdom, where the total absence of any power for the courts to review Acts of Parliament has been a cardinal feature of the principle of Parliamentary sovereignty. With this difference in the judicial climate between the two countries, even if section 2 of the Canadian Bill of Rights had proved effective in relation to later Acts it would not follow that the same result would be achieved by a similar provision in the United Kingdom.

22. The evidence before the Committee does not, however, suggest that section 2 has been successful in controlling later Acts. It was, it seems, only after a good deal of hesitation that the Canadian courts reached the conclusion that section 2 was effective to override even a provision in an Act passed before the Bill of Rights. This was ultimately settled (in the opinion of most lawyers) by the *Drybones* case, where the Supreme court held that the Bill of Rights rendered inoperative a provision of the Indian Act. The Supreme Court does not yet appear to have given a decision, however, in which a later Act has been made to yield to the Bill of Rights. Indeed, Professor Hood-Phillips pointed out in evidence that in the recent case of *R*

v. Miller and Cockrell [1977] 2 S.C.R. the opinion of the Supreme Court appeared to show that the Bill does not override later Acts. Professor Arthurs gave reasons, in evidence, for treating that particular decision with reserve, although at the same time he emphasised that the Canadian courts had been cautious (disappointingly so, in his opinion) in their treatment of the Bill of Rights. He suggested that the Canadian Bill 'does not at this time constitute a significant factor in the decision-making processes of the Supreme Court'. The Committee do not, therefore, think that the Canadian experience offers grounds for believing that a comparable provision in a United Kingdom Bill of Rights would be effective to achieve what is aimed for by clause 3 of Lord Wade's Bill.

23. It follows from the foregoing that the Committee conclude that the main scope for a Bill of Rights would be to operate on our existing law. Their view is that there is no way in which a Bill of Rights could protect itself from encroachment, whether express or implied, by later Acts. The most that such a Bill could do would be to include an interpretation provision which ensured that the Bill of Rights was always taken into account in the construction of later Acts and that, so far as a later Act could be construed in a way that was compatible with a Bill of Rights, such a construction would be preferred to one that was not.

24. As a next step from this conclusion, and the Committee's earlier conclusion that if the United Kingdom is to have a Bill of Rights at all it should take the form of a Bill to make the European Convention part of our domestic law, the Committee thought it desirable, in examining the scope for a Bill of Rights, to examine the extent to which the European Convention already plays a part in our domestic law. Subject to the special position of the Convention as respects the operation in the United Kingdom of directly applicable Community law, with which we deal below (paragraph 28), one proposition at least is clear, namely, that although we are parties to the Convention it is not part of our domestic law. Only by Act of Parliament could it be made part of our domestic law, and no such Act has been passed. We were able to ratify the Convention without passing such an Act because under our constitution it is the prerogative of the Crown to enter into Treaties on behalf of the United Kingdom.

25. Here perhaps a digression into the constitutional position would be useful. Where a Treaty would require a change in our domestic law, constitutional principle requires the Crown, before ratifying the Treaty, to obtain an Act of Parliament making the necessary change. This follows from the fact that although it is the Crown, and the Crown alone, that can ratify a Treaty, only Parliament can make a change in our domestic law. If the Crown ratified a Treaty requiring a change in our domestic law without first getting the necessary Act of Parliament, it would result in the United Kingdom's assuming an international obligation which we were not in a position to fulfil. From this, it must be inferred that United Kingdom ratification of the Convention proceeded upon two assumptions, namely: (i) that the Convention does not require adherent States to embody the Convention as such in their domestic law, but merely requires them to ensure that their domestic law in all respects measures up to the require-

ments of the Convention; and (ii) that, at the time of ratification, United Kingdom law did, in the view of the then Government, measure up in all respects to the Convention's requirements. The Foreign and Common- wealth Office, in evidence before the Committee, confirmed that the United Kingdom ratification of the Convention indeed proceeded upon these assumptions. The second of these assumptions is now a matter of only historical concern. (Whether United Kingdom law now conforms in all respects with the Convention is another matter and the Report will return to that question when considering the case for and against a Bill of Rights.) The validity of the first assumption, however, has twice been confirmed in judgments of the Strasbourg Court: the first time in the *Swedish Engine Driver's Union* case, judgment 6th February 1976, and the second time in the case brought by the Irish Government against the United Kingdom government in which judgment was given on 18th January this year. The Committee refer to these judgments because they dispose of an argument which has been advanced to them to the effect that the failure of the United Kingdom to embody the Convention in our domestic law is inconsistent with our obligations under the Convention.

26. The proposition that the European Convention is not part of our domestic law was confirmed by the Court of Appeal in 1976 in the case of *R v. Chief Immigration Officer, Heathrow Airport ex parte Salamat Bibi* [1976] 3 All ER 843. The Court there reaffirmed the constitutional principles enunciated above and, in holding that the Convention was not part of our domestic law, indicated that dicta of the court in certain earlier cases, suggesting that officials could take account of the Convention when admin- istering immigration rules, had gone too far. The Court also reaffirmed, however, that it was legitimate to refer to the Convention (as to any other Treaty we have ratified) for the purpose of resolving any ambiguity in a United Kingdom Act, so as, where possible, to adopt a construction compat- ible with the Convention.

27. This means that, even in the absence of legislation making the Convention part of our domestic law, the Convention does have some influence on the construction of Acts of Parliament. It is however a tenuous one. It comes into operation only if a Court first finds an ambiguity in an Act. This may be contrasted with the effect which would be produced by making the Convention part of our domestic law. In that case (a) earlier Acts could be made to yield entirely to the Convention and (b) even later Acts could be made subject to an interpretation provision which (although, as this Report has already indicated, it could not in the Committee's view override their clear meaning, express or implied) could at least ensure that a later Act would be construed subject to the Convention, without the Court first having to find an ambiguity in the later Act. Furthermore, there is a case for saying that even the tenuous influence the Convention does have on the construction of Acts of Parliament is confined to Acts passed since we ratified the Convention. With one exception, the cases in which there has been considered the question of using the Convention to resolve an ambi- guity have been concerned with Acts passed since we ratified the Convention and the judgments have not addressed themselves to the

question whether a distinction is to be drawn for this purpose between such Acts and Acts passed before we ratified. In principle, it is not easy to see how the Courts could justify invoking the terms of a Treaty for the purpose of construing Acts passing by Parliament before we ratified the Treaty. The justification for invoking the terms of a Treaty to construe an Act seems to be that Parliament must be taken to have been aware of our international obligations under the Treaty when it passed the Act and must be assumed not have to enacted something in breach of our Treaty obligations unless that is the unavoidable interpretation of the Act. This reasoning cannot apply to Acts passed before ratification, and as far as can be seen there is no case in which a United Kingdom court has looked at the terms of a Treaty for the purposes of resolving an ambiguity in an Act passed before ratification of the Treaty, except an Act passed to enable the Treaty in question to be implemented. The nearest the Courts have to an exception to this was in the dissenting judgment of Lord Justice Scarman, (as he then was) in the recent case of *Ahmed* v. *Inner London Education Authority* [1978] AII ER 574 in which he invoked the European Convention in connection with the construction of a provision in the Education Act 1944. The majority of the court did not follow him in this though they did not expressly disagree with that aspect of his judgment.

28. In short, the scope for recourse to the European Convention in construing Acts of Parliament is, as things stand, very limited and it is not clear whether it is permissible at all as respects Acts passed before we ratified the Convention. To the extent that recourse to the Convention is permissible at all, it may be said to represent a qualification – although a modest one – of the proposition that the Convention is not part of our domestic law. The only other qualification of this proposition concerns directly applicable Community law. The European Court at Luxembourg (that is, the Court of Justice of the European Communities) has held that fundamental human rights form an integral part of the general principles of law which that Court administers in interpreting the Treaties of the European Communities. Furthermore, the Court has treated the European Convention on Human Rights as one of the sources from which law for the protection of fundamental human rights can be deduced. The United Kingdom courts are under an obligation to follow the rulings of the European Court on the interpretation of Community law. Thus, so far as concerns the application of Community law in the United Kingdom, the European Convention is a source of law to which the United Kingdom courts are entitled, indeed obliged, to have regard.

29. This development may prove fruitful in the field within which it operates. The operation of Community law, important though it is, however, is too limited a field to make it a matter of central importance for the Committee's purposes. All the same, it prompted the Committee to consider whether the European Community might provide an avenue for the introduction of the European Convention into United Kingdom law, without the intervention of an Act of the United Kingdom Parliament. The Committee bore in mind in this regard the Joint Declaration made in 1977 by the European Parliament, Council and Commission pledging their

commitment to a respect for fundamental rights as recognised in the constitutions of the Member States of the European Community. The Committee considered whether the European Community might accede as a Community to the European Convention, thus giving the Convention the status of a Community Treaty for the purposes of section 1 of the European Communities Act, subject only to the necessity of an Order in Council under section 1(4). This would have the consequence that the material provisions of the Convention (which would undoubtedly be directly applicable) would flow into United Kingdom law for all purposes. The Committee are in no doubt however that this is not a possible course and can be discounted as a factor in measuring the desirability of a Bill of Rights.

30. To summarise the Committee's review of matters bearing on the scope for a Bill of Rights, they have concluded that the scope for any Bill of Rights within the present constitution would be confined largely to its impact on our existing law. To this they would add that in any country, whatever its constitution, the existence or absence of legislation in the nature of a Bill of Rights can in practice play only a relatively minor part in the protection of human rights. What is important, above all, is a country's political climate and traditions. This is, the Committee think, common ground among both those who favour and those who oppose a Bill of Rights, and they received no evidence that human rights are in practice better protected in countries which have a code of fundamental human rights embodied in their law than they are in the United Kingdom ...

31. These considerations have led the Committee to the view that, even if on balance a Bill of Rights were thought desirable, too much should not be expected of such a Bill. The Committee think that many of those advocating a Bill of Rights, including a number of witnesses before the Committee, pitch their case too high. Similar considerations equally suggest that the case against a Bill of Rights has also been exaggerated. It is from this standpoint that the Committee now set out what they see as the most important arguments on either side.

The arguments for and against

32. The Committee summarise in this paragraph the most important arguments (as they see it) put to them in favour of a Bill of Rights.

(a) The individual citizen might be better off, and could not be worse off, if the European Convention were made part of United Kingdom law, since in the event of conflict between the Convention and other provisions of United Kingdom law whichever was more favourable to the plaintiff would prevail.

(b) Embodying the Convention in our domestic law would provide the individual citizen with a positive and public declaration of the rights guaranteed him, thus complementing the United Kingdom's traditionally 'negative' definition of his common law rights. This would have special value at the present time for the many individuals and groups who tend to feel impotent in the face of the size and complexity of the public authorities which seem to dominate their lives.

(c) Although when the United Kingdom acceded to the Convention, and thus allowed the right of individual petition to the Court at Strasbourg, it was believed that our law had nothing to fear from any appeal to the Articles of the Convention, a number of doubts have emerged since that time. Experience has shown that there are a number of areas where the British subject must at present take the long road to Strasbourg as a court of first instance (as Golder) did, since the domestic law provides no remedy in the courts of the United Kingdom.

(d) The Commission and Court at Strasbourg were not established as a 'court of first instance', but rather as a 'court of appeal' to which the citizen can have recourse only when domestic procedures have been exhausted. Although there is no obligation on a Member State to incorporate the Convention, the Strasbourg Court has said that the intention of the drafters of the Convention that the rights set out should be directly secured to anyone within the jurisdiction of the contracting States finds a particularly faithful reflection in those instances where the Convention has been incorporated into domestic law. The United Kingdom is at present the only signatory which neither has a charter of fundamental human rights nor has incorporated the Convention into domestic law. So long as the Convention remains only an international treaty and forms no part of United Kingdom law, it suffers from the disadvantage of being both remote and expensive. Moreover the United Kingdom is exposed to unflattering world publicity. Our compliance with the Convention can already be tested judicially at Strasbourg. There is no reason to suppose that our own courts are not equally capable of determining these issues. Any uncertainty there may be about the impact of the Convention on our domestic law already exists and can be argued out at Strasbourg. Why not in the Strand?

(e) An Act incorporating the Convention would not be an alternative to the continued exercise by Parliament of its traditional sovereignty, but would complement other Acts by which Parliament may wish to make law affecting human rights, including any amendment of the law that Parliament thinks desirable in the light of a United Kingdom court decision. Meanwhile, however, the Convention, if embodied in our domestic law, would, in Lord Scarman's words, 'freshen up the principles of the common law' and when read with the common law would 'provide the judges with a revised body of legal principle upon which they could go on slowly developing the law, case by case, as they have been doing for centuries', without waiting until the opportunity for legislation occurred.

(f) Our membership of the European Economic Community reinforces the value of the European Convention on Human Rights and makes it the more desirable that United Kingdom citizens should become increasingly aware of the European dimension. It is therefore all the more important that our legal system and jurisprudence should be developed as part of the European Community and not in splendid isolation.

(g) The Act would constitute a framework of human rights guaranteed throughout the United Kingdom and this would have special value if Scottish and Welsh Assemblies are established with powers devolved from Westminster, to ensure the exercise of such powers (e.g. those respecting local government and education) by the Assemblies with due regard to the United Kingdom's international commitments under the Convention. Significance is attached to the unanimous recommendation of the Northern Ireland Standing Advisory Commission on Human Rights favouring the incorporation of the Convention into legislation applying to the whole of the United Kingdom. This the Northern Ireland Commission believed to be in the long-term interests of that province.

(h) The incorporating Act, though not limiting Parliamentary sovereignty, would nevertheless be a continuing reminder to legislators of the international commitment undertaken when the United Kingdom government ratified the Convention. Indeed, the Convention seems likely to have far more practical effect on legislators, administrators, the executive, the judiciary and individual citizens as well as legilsators if it ceases to be only an international treaty obligation and becomes an integral part of the United Kingdom law, guaranteeing the citizen specific minimum rights enforceable in the first instance in the United Kingdom courts.

33. The Committee now summarise in this paragraph the arguments against a Bill of Rights which seem to them to be the most important.

(i) Incorporation of the Convention would be to graft on to the existing law an Act of Parliament in a form totally at variance with any existing legislation and indeed incompatible with such legislation. Hitherto, it has been an accepted feature of our constitution that Parliament legislates in a specific form and that it is the role of the courts to interpret such legislation. Incorporation of the Convention would, for the first time, open up wide areas in which legislative policy on such matters as race relations, freedom of speech, freedom of the press, privacy, education and forms of punishment would be effectively handed over to the judiciary. All these are matters which our constitution has hitherto reposed in the hands of the legislature.

(ii) Nor is it right to say that the role the courts would have under a Bill of Rights would be no more than the kind of role they have always had under the common law. Under the common law the courts have developed legal principles slowly and empirically, from case to case. Under a Bill of Rights they would start with principles of the widest generality and would have a free hand to decide how those principles operated in the cases that came before them.

(iii) Parliament has on numerous occasions shown its readiness to intervene in new areas where fresh social problems have arisen, and it is better for Parliament to enact detailed legislation as it has done, for instance, on such matters as race relations and sex discrimination, rather than to look to the unelected judges to develop both the policy on such matters and the way in which it should be dealt with.

(iv) So far as possible, the law should be clear and certain, whereas if the European Convention, framed as it is in broad and general terms capable of a variety of interpretations, were to become part of our domestic law, it would introduce a substantial and wide-ranging element of uncertainty into our law. (The same would be true of a Bill not based on the European Convention because it is in the nature of any Bill of Rights to be framed in the same sort of way as the Convention.) Individuals and companies would no longer be able to obtain confident advice as to what their rights, powers, obligations and liabilities were. That in itself would be a price too high to pay for flexibility – and answers the point that the individual citizen could not on any footing be worse off with a Bill of Rights. The uncertainty thus brought into our law would itself afford opportunity for exploiting endless challenges in the courts or before any tribunal to the validity of the existing laws. No one would know where he stood until each question had been tested afresh, and the least that can be said is that there is the prospect of a very great extension of litigation in the courts.

To take only one example, the introduction of Article 10 of the European Convention into our domestic law would introduce serious doubts into such important areas of the law as those relating to defamation and contempt of court, and official secrets.

(v) It is fallacious to suggest, as some witnesses suggested, that to make the Convention part of our domestic law would simply to be give to our judges the same sort of role, in relation to the Convention, as is played by the judges in Strasbourg. There is a great difference between the Commission or the Court at Strasbourg from time to time measuring our domestic law against the yardstick of the Convention, and the United Kingdom courts applying the Convention as an instrument of our domestic law. As a set of principles of domestic law, the Convention would have a life of its own quite independent of its international existence. The Convention could then be invoked daily in our Courts and they would constantly have to give decisions on it without any guidance from the jurisprudence at Strasbourg (where the number of cases adjudicated is very limited). Moreover, our Courts would be free to give the Convention a wider effect than was required by such Strasbourg jurisprudence as was available. In doing so they would be acting quite consistently with our international obligations.

(vi) The present situation in the United Kingdom is in accord with the original philosophy of the European Convention. The Convention was intended to lay down minimum standards of human rights which it was assumed would be in accord with the spirit of all the legal systems of the signatories to the Convention. It was always contemplated, as in fact has proved to be the case, that from time to time there would be conflicts between the domestic laws of the signatory states and the Convention, and for this reason the Convention set up machinery by way of the European Commission and the European Court to deal with such cases. Such conflicts have inevitably arisen in all signatory states, whether or not the Convention is part of their domestic law. It is in accordance with the spirit of the Convention that, when it emerges that there is such a conflict in the case of the United Kingdom, this should be put right.

Where necessary this can be done by legislation, but often the deficiency will call for no more than a change of administrative regulation or instructions. But it is no more unflattering to this country than it is to any other signatory of the Convention if the kind of dispute contemplated by the drafters of the Convention from time to time goes to Strasbourg for argument; and it is not the case, as some of the witnesses assumed, that relatively more cases have gone to the Commission from the United Kingdom than from other countries.

(vii) Even on the most unfavourable view of the extent to which United Kingdom law at present falls short of the standards of the Convention, there are no more than a few marginal situations where the incorporation of a Bill of Rights might bestow a remedy where present law does not do so. They have mainly related to privacy and the conduct of the prison services. As to privacy, this has already been the subject of a thorough investigation by the Younger Committee, which made various suggestions for reform but came down against a general law of privacy. As to the conduct of the prison services, there has been one case so far, the *Golder* case, where a complaint has succeeded, and where the matter was dealt with by a change in the relevant regulations. The Committee are aware that there are several other cases now before the Commission but cannot properly comment on these.

(viii) There is no reason for supposing that the Government, and Parliament, are likely to proceed in ignorance of the country's international commitments; and indeed the Committee were given examples of proposals which had been modified by the Government in their preliminary stage to take account of our commitments under the European Convention. It is not realistic to fear that there is any risk of this country – whether at Westminster or in a devolved assembly – legislating in 'splendid isolation' and without regard to the treaty provisions by which we are bound. The effect of incorporating the Convention into United Kingdom law in the event of devolution to Scotland would be to introduce similar uncertainties into the operation of any legislation emanating from the Scottish Assembly to those injected into the law of the United Kingdom generally.

(ix) It is felt that adequate weight is not given in the Report of the Northern Ireland Standing Advisory Commission [see Doc. 126] to the arguments against incorporation from the point of view of its effect on the legal system as a whole; and that the argument that what is good for Northern Ireland must be good for the United Kingdom as a whole is unproven.

34. The two foregoing paragraphs briefly summarise the main arguments for and against a Bill of Rights which were reviewed by the Committee.

Much has been written in the various publications but the Committee hope that they have picked out those arguments which will seem to the House to be the most important. Which of the arguments have the greater force, as has already been indicated, is a question on which the Committee are irreconcilably divided. They can, however, offer certain conclusions on the second question – what form a Bill of Rights should take – and the Report now turns back to these.

The form a Bill of Rights should take

35. The primary conclusion here was indicated at the beginning of this Report, namely, that, if there is to be a Bill of Rights at all, it should take the form of a Bill giving effect in our domestic law to the European Convention. To that extent the Committee are in broad agreement with the form of Lord Wade's Bill. As already explained, however, the Committee think that it would require amendment, and they have considered some of the questions that arise in this regard.

36. There is first the question whether the whole of the European Convention, and its Protocols, should be included, as in Lord Wade's Bill. Only the first 18 Articles of the Convention, and parts of the Protocols, actually set out the rights to be protected. The rest of the Convention provides for the setting up and composition of the Commission on Human Rights and the Court of Human Rights, and for matters of procedure; and much of the material in the Protocols (including the whole of Protocols 2, 3 and 5) is concerned with matters of that kind. The Committee have therefore considered whether it would suffice for the Bill to incorporate only Articles 1–18 of the Convention and those Protocols which deal with substantive rights. They have concluded, however, that that would not be a satisfactory course. In the first place, even in Articles 1–18 of the Convention there are a number of provisions which would not appear to be self-executing – that is to say, they are not of such a nature as themselves to confer any rights. Precisely which provisions, however, fall into this category is not a question which can be answered definitely, and it would not be satisfactory for the Bill to seek to make a judgment on that matter. In the second place the Committee think that the Convention must be read as a whole because even provisions which do not confer rights as such may have a bearing on the true construction of those that do. That applies even to the Articles that follow Article 18. For example, the fact that Article 25 of the Convention allows petitions in Strasbourg to be directed only against Parties to the Convention might be thought to have a bearing on the question whether the rights in the Convention are enforceable only against public authorities and not against private individuals or corporations (a question considered further in paragraph 41 below). It was also put to the Committee in evidence that Article 60 might have an important bearing on the construction of substantive provisions of the Convention.

37. The Committee think, therefore, that the only safe course would be to include the whole of the Convention and its Protocols in the Bill. This is, however, subject to a qualification in respect of the First Protocol, which the

United Kingdom has ratified subject to a reservation about education, and the Fourth Protocol, which the United Kingdom has not ratified at all. The Bill would clearly have to secure that the Fourth Protocol did not become part of our domestic law and that the First Protocol became part of our domestic law subject to the reservations made on ratification. The Bill might however include provision – perhaps by conferring power to make an Order in Council for the purpose – whereby if we ratified the Fourth Protocol it could be brought within the scope of the Bill and if we relinquished our reservations to the First Protocol the corresponding effects could be reproduced in our domestic law. Such provision might also deal correspondingly with possible future Protocols. Without a provision of this kind, it would be necessary to have amending legislation every time our international position under the Convention and its Protocols was modified.

38. The Report next turns to clause 3 of Lord Wade's Bill, a matter to which the Committee have already devoted a good deal of attention. For the reasons already given, the Committee do not think that clause 3 is satisfactory. They are, however, in sympathy with the form of the Bill to the extent that it draws a distinction (in clauses 2 and 3 respectively) between the operation of the Bill in relation to enactments passed before the Bill and to enactments passed afterwards. They think this is right because it seems to them that if the Bill made the same provision with respect to both past and future enactments there would be at any rate some risk that the Courts would give it an unnecessarily restrictive construction in relation to past enactments. The assumption might be that as the Bill treated both classes of enactment alike it was intended to have the same effect on both; and as it could not have the effect (on the view the Committee have expressed) of overriding the clear meaning of later enactments, it might conceivably be construed as not being intended to override the clear meaning of earlier enactments. For this reason the Committee reject the suggestion made by more than one witness that the Bill should simply adopt the formula in the relevant part of section 2(4) of the European Communities Act:

> 'any enactment, passed or to be passed, ... shall be construed and have effect subject to the foregoing provisions of this section.'

The Committee have already considered that provision earlier in this Report and explained why they do not think that it provides a precedent for supposing that a Bill of Rights could override later enactments. They consider, however, that section 2(4) could usefully be drawn upon, provided that a distinction were made between earlier and later enactments. They suggest that (as foreshadowed in paragraph 23 above) in place of clauses 2 and 3 of Lord Wade's Bill, there might be a single provision in something of the following vein:

> 'All enactments passed before this Act shall be construed and have effect subject to this Act; and the same shall apply to any enactment passed after this Act unless it provides otherwise or does not admit of any construction compatible with this Act.'

39. The Committee next considered the question of remedies. In their

view, it would not be strictly necessary to include in the Bill any express provision with regard to remedies for a breach of its provisions. A Bill giving domestic effect to the European Convention would by no means be devoid of effect if it were silent on the question of remedies. Nevertheless, they consider that it would be desirable for the Bill to make express provision in this regard. As to what that provision should be, however, they do not offer any conclusion because it seems to them to be a matter that requires a far more wide-ranging examination than the Committee are equipped to undertake.

They do not see how the question of remedies for a breach of the Bill could satisfactorily be considered in isolation from the question of remedies available generally against the Crown and other public authorities. For instance, a number of witnesses have suggested that the Bill should provide a general right of damages in respect of breaches of its provisions. Although the Committee see merit in that suggestion, it provokes the question whether it would be appropriate to provide such a right in respect of any breach of the far-reaching provisions of a Bill of Rights, without reviewing the present position in administrative law under which, for example, the victim of maladministration is denied any right to damages.

40. Again, a number of witnesses suggested that the Bill should provide, *inter alia*, for the granting of injunctions against the Crown (as well as other public authorities) in respect of breaches of the provisions of the Bill. The present position, however, is that injunctions are not and never have been available against the Crown, though under section 21(1) of the Crown Proceedings Act 1947 (which precludes the granting of injunctions against the Crown) a declaration in lieu of an injunction is available. There are powerful reasons for the present rule. These reasons may not necessarily be conclusive – the Committee express no opinion as to that – but it seems clear that (a) any change in this respect would have serious constitutional implications and (b) it would not be easy to justify a provision which allowed the granting of injunctions against the Crown for breaches of a Bill of Rights while leaving the rule precluding the granting of injunctions against the Crown untouched in other respects.

41. Another matter considered by the Committee was whether the Bill should deal expressly with the question whether a remedy for breaches of its provisions was available against private individuals and corporations, as well as against public authorities. The question whether the European Convention can be invoked against private parties – known in West Germany as *Drittwirkung der Grundrechte* – has been the subject of much controversy among jurists. The Committee offer no opinion as to which school of thought will prevail. But it would appear that there is at least a possibility that the Convention bites on actions by private parties as well as public authorities. That being so, it seems to the Committee that a Bill of Rights ought to leave that possibility open. This the Bill could achieve by making no provision either way and leaving it to the interpretation of the Courts. The Committee recognise that this would leave a major area of uncertainty, and there could be no assurance that our courts would not, at any rate initially, decide the question in a sense contrary to that ultimately

established in Strasbourg. That, however, is a risk applicable to all aspects of the Convention. The only satisfactory alternative, in the Committee's view, would be for the Bill to provide expressly that its provisions *could* be invoked against private parties. A provision in that sense might ultimately prove to have gone further than the Convention requires, but that must always be legitimate.

42. Another difficult question is what, if anything, the Bill should provide with respect to decisions of the Commission and the Court at Strasbourg. Should the United Kingdom Courts be required, in construing the provisions of the Bill, to follow decisions of at any rate the Court at Strasbourg, as they are required by section 3(1) of the European Communities Act to follow decisions of the European Court at Luxembourg? Or should they be directed merely to have regard to such decisions? Or should the Bill say nothing on this question and leave it to the courts, in the light of the Convention, to determine what regard, if any, should be paid to decisions at Strasbourg?

43. On the view the Committee take as to the effect of a Bill of Rights on future Acts (namely, that it could not override the clear meaning of a future Act), they do not see how the jurisprudence at Strasbourg could be made binding on our Courts. Nor does the Convention so require. The Committee conclude that the effective choice is between on the one hand saying nothing and on the other hand including a provision whereby the courts are to have regard to the jurisprudence at Strasbourg, without making it binding on them. The Committee doubt whether the effect produced by the one course would be any different from that produced by the other. Even if the Bill were silent in this respect, given the jurisdiction conferred by the Convention on the Commission and the Court at Strasbourg (and given the Committee's earlier proposal that the Bill should embrace all the provisions of the Convention), it seems to the Committee that our Courts would be bound to conclude that they were entitled to, and indeed should, have regard to the jurisprudence at Strasbourg. The Committee accordingly express no strong preference but on balance think it would be salutory to include an express provision in the sense indicated above.

44. The Committee considered, finally, the question of derogation. Article 15 of the European Convention allows Governments to take measures derogating from the Convention (except from certain Articles specified in Article 14.2) 'In time of war or other public emergency threatening the life of the nation'. If the Convention were given domestic effect in a Bill of Rights the Committee do not think that it would be satisfactory to take derogation measures in reliance on Article 15 alone, because there is clearly a good deal of room for argument about whether any given situation falls within the words of the Article. It could hardly be left to the Courts to determine whether a situation was one of 'war or other public emergency threatening the life of the nation.' That is a matter which can only feasibly be left to the judgment of the Government. This seems to be recognised by Article 15.3, which requires no more than that a Government availing itself of the right of derogation should keep the Secretary General informed of

the measures it had taken and also inform him when the measures had ceased to operate.

45. The Committee's view is that the Bill should make express provision enabling the Government to make a definitive announcement of a state of war or other public emergency within the meaning of Article 15, and that this announcement should have conclusive effect for the purposes of the Convention in its domestic application. A Royal Proclamation might be the most appropriate way of proceeding for this purpose, by analogy with the procedure under the Emergency Powers Act 1920. The powers exercisable under that Act are dependent on the Proclamation of a state of emergency under section 1 of the Act. Any such provision in a Bill of Rights would have to seek to secure that the domestic position ran in harness with the necessary notifications to the Secretary General under Article 15.3 of the Convention.

Scrutinising machinery

46. The Committee considered whether any new machinery was desirable for ensuring that legislation conformed to the provisions of the Convention or, if the latter is incorporated in our domestic law, to a Bill of Rights. It was suggested that a Parliamentary Committee might be the appropriate means to this end, that is a Committee whose task it would be to scrutinise legislation either before it was introduced into Parliament or very soon thereafter. At present this responsibility falls on the Department which prepares the proposals, and the Committee were told that any Department which was in doubt about the effect of proposed legislation could obtain advice from the Foreign and Commonwealth Office or from the Law Officers. The Committee were told that care was taken to ensure that no Government proposals were laid before Parliament which might conflict with the international obligations of the United Kingdom.

47. The Committee were sceptical of the usefulness of a Parliamentary Committee. It did not seem likely that such a Committee would succeed in detecting a breach of the Convention in proposed legislation which had escaped notice at the various stages of preparation through which it would already have passed ...

Conclusions

53. The Committee are agreed in concluding that, if there is to be a Bill of Rights, it should be a Bill based on the European Convention; and that, in the event of such a Bill proceeding, there should be some changes in the Bill as introduced by Lord Wade last Session. Whether there should be a Bill at all is an issue on which the Committee are divided. Six members of the Committee (Lord Blake, Lady Gaitskell, Lord Jellicoe, Lord O'Hagan, Lord Redcliffe-Maud and Lord Wade) were in favour of a Bill; five members (Lord Allen of Abbeydale, Lord Boston of Faversham, Lord Foot, Lord Gordon-Walker and Lord Lloyd of Hampstead) took the opposite view. Although the Committee were thus unable to give an undivided answer to the first question put to them in their terms of reference, they nevertheless

hope that the arguments and considerations to which the Report draws attention will be of help to members of the House in formulating their own views.

HL [1977–8] 176, pp.20f.

---

84   DEBATE ON THE HUMAN RIGHTS AND FUNDAMENTAL FREEDOMS BILL, 1985

RB NOTE: For the text of the Bill, see Doc. 39.

Lord Broxbourne: My Lords, I beg to move that this Bill be now read a second time.

I do so fortuitously but perhaps appropriately on Human Rights Day. It would need somebody far more self-assured than I to address himself to the theme of human rights and fundamental freedom without a sense of diffidence and of my own personal inadequacy; conscious of the great difference, the contrast between the greatness of my theme and my own littleness; conscious too of the greatness of those who have made these things their concern over the ages.

These concepts have exercised the minds and fired the imagination of great men indeed. Rousseau said:

'Man is born free, and everywhere he is in chains.'

Jefferson defined the inalienable rights of man as,

'life, liberty and the pursuit of happiness'.

Two centuries later men are still seeking to strengthen these rights and freedoms, to proclaim their sanctity and guarantee their enjoyment. This Bill seeks to follow in that great tradition.

My speech today, like Caesar's Gaul, will be divided into three parts. First, I shall say something about the purpose and provenance of the Bill, then describe briefly its provisions and effect. Finally, I shall seek to deal with the doubts felt, criticisms expressed and misconceptions entertained in regard to the Bill.

The purpose of the Bill is I think clear from the Long Title and the Explanatory Memorandum. I shall expound further though not, I trust, wearisomely in the next part of my trilogy. The Bill has its roots deep in history. Human rights have long commanded the attention and engaged the aspirations of mankind. I mentioned two great protagonists, but this is not a case of *exclusio alterius*. There are many more whom I could pray in aid if time allowed. However, I say only this. This Bill is an attempt humbly but, I hope, faithfully to follow in the path set, and add to the edifice erected by, in the Tennysonian phrase,

'those simple great ones gone for ever and ever by.'

Coming to its more recent provenance, in a sense the Bill derives from the

European Convention on Human Rights, to which the United Kingdom adhered in 1952. That classic document was a manifestation of the aspirations for a better world which filled the minds and warmed the hearts of people in those years of hope and striving.

I should like to say a brief word about the previous considerations of these matters in your Lordships' House. When a Bill of Rights, which was introduced by Lord Wade, who is a highly respected figure and an old friend of mine from House of Commons' days was overtaken by Prorogation eight years ago, a select committee was set up to consider two questions: first, whether such a Bill was desirable; secondly, if so, what form it should take. On the first matter there was a division of opinion, six to five in favour; but on the second matter there was unanimity that if such a Bill were to be enacted, it should be based on the convention.

The committee was fortunate in the quality and authority of the evidence which it received. I should like to make particular mention of one witness, the noble and learned Lord, Lord Scarman, who testified to that committee on the desirability of such a measure and who has remained constant in his advocacy. Though this Bill stands in my name, in fact it is a joint effort. . . The noble and learned Lord is president of the Constitutional Reform Centre and I should like also to express my appreciation of the help given by that body and its eminent director Mr. Richard Holme. The noble and learned Lord, Lord Scarman, as a Lord of Appeal has no party political affiliation of course, while Mr. Holme is a leading Liberal and I received the Conservative Whip through 11 Parliaments in the House of Commons, as I receive it now in this House – which your Lordships may think says much for the forbearance and kindly disposition of the Conservative Whip's Office.

This non-party or perhaps all-party approach is reflected also in the House of Commons. Among those who support the concept are senior Conservatives and Privy Counsellors such as Geoffrey Rippon and Terence Higgins, who used to sit alongside me in the third Bench below the gangway in that House. Geoffrey Rippon started his professional life devilling for me, so your Lordships will readily appreciate the great quality and talent required to achieve so distinguished a career after so heavy an initial handicap. Of course there are many other supporters in the House of Commons: Mr. Maclennan, the respected Alliance Member, who in 1983 introduced a Bill, which was different perhaps from my Bill in emphasis but similar in purpose; Donald Anderson, who is a senior Labour Member; Sir Edward Gardner, who is the recently retired chairman of the Society of Conservative Lawyers; and many more. In summary, therefore, there is a broad basis of all-party support. . . Of course there are misconceptions and of course there are criticisms, arising perhaps in the main from the misconceptions. The main criticisms, I would think, are three. The definition of rights, it is said, is too generalised and at variance with our normal jurisprudential practice. The Bill, in the view of some critics, constitutes a threat to or a derogation from our constitutional doctrine of the sovereignty of Parliament. And some contend that the Bill would impose a European or continental pattern on our traditional practice and procedure. I can deal with these matters together, as they are interrelated.

Of course we in Parliament have a jealous regard for the sovereignty of Parliament. We, or at any rate the older among us, were brought up on Dicey, with his twin pillars of the constitution; but Dicey did not set up the sovereignty of Parliament as a lone pedestal. There were twin pillars, and the other was the rule of law. My submission to your Lordships is that this Bill strengthens the one without undermining the other and will thus be a valuable safeguard to our constitutional structure.

It would be surprising indeed if parliamentarians who put the European Communities Act on the statute book in 1972 were concerned at the alleged loss of sovereignty of Parliament in a projected human rights Act in 1985. It would surely be a classic case of straining at the gnat after swallowing the camel. After all, Article 189 of the Treaty of Rome says that the regulations of the Community are,

'binding in their entirety and directly applicable in the Member States'.

That is a real and substantial diminution of parliamentary sovereignty, to which by our adherence to the treaty we are committed in law and in good faith.

Here let me correct another misconception, if I may. The European Convention on Human Rights is not an instrument of the EC. It is the product of a different body, the Council of Europe; and its court at Strasbourg is not to be confused with the European Court of Justice at Luxembourg which exercises jurisdiction under the treaty.

I return then to the criticism that the approach is too generalised and imposes a European pattern on our procedures. The answer, I should think, is twofold. First, we are already bound to give effect to generalised rights by reason of their prescription in the Treaty of Rome; and these have the force of law in this country and must be applied by the courts. Secondly, we have to observe generalised rights in any event by reason of our adherence to the convention. The difference is that if this Bill becomes law, interpretation and adjudication will be a matter for British judges in British courts, instead of by the complex and cumbersome procedures of individual petition to the European Commission of Human Rights and thence, but only on the initiative of the commission, to a multinational court at Strasbourg. If jurisdiction is given to British courts as proposed in this Bill, the individual petition to Strasbourg will, I think, in time fall into desuetude. If not, individual petition is here to stay, as evidenced by the recent five-year renewal of the right by Her Majesty's Government.

Subject to further points that may arise in Committee, what I have said must in the interests of time suffice on these matters. Before concluding, however, may I briefly anticipate a thought that may be in the minds of some noble Lords? Is not the time and emphasis wrong, they may ask? At the present time should we not be concerned more with the enforcement of law than the enjoyment of rights? I take the point and I certainly subscribe to the importance of the enforcement of law and order, particularly in the climate of the present time. But there is no conflict; indeed, the reverse. The problems of rights and of law enforcement are not opposed; they are related and complementary.

Ten years ago in Luxembourg, on the threshold of the last quarter of the 20th century, I referred to the relationship between those two concepts at a time when I was chairman of what we called the Legal Affairs Committee of the European Parliament, which was our translation into English of its official title, *Président de la Commission Juridique.* I must say that for a little while I had to overcome a tendency to turn round to see who was being addressed or referred to under that sonorous and grandiloquent title.

At that time and in that town I used these words:

'I believe that the objective and analytical eye of history will identify two related problems in the last quarter of the twentieth century. They are, first, this problem of the rights of the citizen vis-à-vis the State, a problem necessarily aggravated by the increasing centralisation and bureaucracy, which contemporary economic and social practice seem increasingly to demand; and, secondly, the problem of the recognition of the duty and responsibility owed by the individual to society. These problems are related because the growth of State power and State activity provokes a resentment and a reaction which feed and foster revolts against authority and impatience with the restraints and obligations of the rule of law.

'The resulting manifestations'.

I concluded,

'are clear for all to see in the world today, including, alas, the countries of the Community. The ugly evidence is daily adduced in violence, aggression and in the invocation of force against the rule of law. Of course, the action which I am proposing in relation to the safeguarding of rights will not automatically solve the problem of irresponsibility and violence – and perhaps not even contribute directly to its solution. But, if I am right in my assessment of history's diagnosis and these problems are related, then indirectly at any rate progress in the field of rights can contribute powerfully to a restoration of the sense of responsibility and the acceptance of the rule of law.'

Can it be said that those words are less topical or less true now than then, 10 years ago? Are they not reinforced by the events of the intervening decade? What I said in Luxembourg in 1975 I say here at Westminster today; and on that I rest my case. In that faith, in that hope and in that conviction I commend this Bill to your Lordships and request its second reading at your hands.

Moved. That the Bill be now read a second time. – (*Lord Broxbourne.*)

Lord Scarman: My position is well known. I think that I have contributed in some measure to every debate there has been during the past seven or eight years in this House in which the possibility of enacting the European Convention on Human Rights has been discussed. I suppose that I should also declare an interest. I am, as some of your Lordships may know, a judge.

It will no doubt be said by some that, as a judge, I together with my colleagues on the Bench, should be getting too much power if the European convention should be enacted.

Perhaps I may say a word or two about that. If our judges are not to be trusted then they are not to be trusted with their present responsibility, which is the enforcement, application and development by judicial decision of the rule of law. That would be so whether or not the European Convention is enacted. If they are to be trusted – as I am sure the British public trusts them – then the European Convention on Human Rights once enacted will not add any new dimension to the responsibilities already daily undertaken by our judges in the field of judicial review of the exercise of executive powers by public authority. The argument based upon too much power to the courts can be immediately dismissed as one based not on reason but on a certain superficial distrust of the rule of law.

As I see it, the merit of this Bill can be expressed very shortly indeed. Its merit is that if enacted, under this Bill any individual person present within the jurisdiction of the United Kingdom will have immediate access – I emphasise the word 'immediate' – within the United Kingdom to a British court if he claims that a public authority has violated a right guaranteed to him by the European convention.

The Bill, by providing the aggrieved citizen with a remedy in a national court, will at the same time ensure that the United Kingdom meets its international obligations. ... There is great value to the individual in immediate access to a court. He may not have it now. He may have to wait until he can get to Strasbourg, where his case will be considered first by the European Commission and, at a later stage, if the European Commission publishes a report, by the European Court of Human Rights – a court, I would add, where the aggrieved citizen has himself no right to be heard. ... The point I am making is this. If one is so fortunate as to get a decision from the European Court of Human Rights in Strasbourg that process takes on average anything between four and six years. It will not surprise your Lordships to know that the first prisoner to test whether or not he had suffered a violation of a right guaranteed by the convention when he could not as a prisoner consult a solicitor eventually secured a declaration that his right had been infringed, some four years after he had been discharged from prison. No doubt that is a triumph morally but it is not very useful to the citizen after so much delay. ...

Quite apart from the positive advantages to aggrieved citizens in incorporating this convention into our law, if it were to become law it would immediately acquire a power to influence and to educate. Politicians, civil servants, Ministers and others concerned with the preparation of legislation would take account not only in the arcane chambers of Whitehall where these things are drafted but also in debate in the two Houses and in the national debate which often accompanies legislation as it passes through these two Houses. They would be astute to ensure that important detailed legislation ... complied with our international obligations under the European convention. All the time, the judges, who are now very experienced in the field of judicial review of the exercise of executive powers by public authorities, would be developing, explaining and applying this convention in a British context. . .

The Lord Bishop of Oxford: My Lords, my support for this Bill starts from the belief that among the ordinary people of this country there is quite a widespread fear that what are called in the Bill 'human rights and fundamental freedoms' are gradually being eroded. This fear may be thought irrational and yet I find it entirely natural, for we live in a century when not only have there been wars and tyrannies on a terrifying scale but when the complexity of administrative power has come more and more to dominate the daily life of the citizen.

It has become increasingly difficult for him to know where to turn for redress, or indeed to know where he stands. Less sure himself in many cases about right and wrong than he used to be, he sees this uncertainty reflected in a society of plural values. Although recourse to the law is, I suppose, more frequent than ever, he often fears that such recourse may be both expensive and slow, and may not in the end express those rather simple principles of morality to which he still feels himself attached.

Fortunately, this threatening process of erosion has not had it all its own way. From time to time there has been a counter-attack, and one of the most effective was the European Convention on Human Rights of 1950, born of the experiences of the war, and ratified first of all by this country which had played such a large part in framing it.

The language of the convention is simple; so simple that it can give occasion to some expert critics to say that is all too vague. But surely its simplicity is precisely the point. Here is language about human rights and freedoms that the ordinary person can be expected to understand, and which has proved itself able to cross a great many national frontiers and to find a response. That indeed is what has happened, as your Lordships are aware, both in democratic Europe and in the Commonwealth.

Who would have dared to prophesy in 1950 that British citizens would have thought of taking their grievances to a court in Strasbourg? Some of them would hardly have known whether Strasbourg was in Germany or in France, but yet today no state sends more individual petitions to the European court at Strasbourg than does the United Kingdom. Surely that is something of which the British Parliament and the British legal profession need to take serious note. This is why this Bill deserves to succeed where a number of earlier attempts to incorporate the convention into our law have failed.

I have the honour to be president of a modest ecumenical body called Christians for Europe, one of the organisations which supports a Bill of Rights. It is on both these counts that I wanted to take part in this debate. First, as a Christian, it may be argued that 'human rights' is not a phrase natural to Christianity, which speaks rather of duties and of laying aside selfish claims, and says that it is God's service which is perfect freedom. There is certainly more to human life and character than is to be found in the articles of this, or any other, convention.

Yet I would argue that a great deal which is in those articles derives from biblical teaching which has been common to the whole of Christendom and of course to Judaism as well. It springs from the belief that each person is of intrinsic value and dignity and deserves to be treated with the respect due to a child of God, so that no authority, whether of a dictator or of a bureaucracy, has the absolute right to treat that person as of little or no account.

It may be thought that traditionally in British society, as one branch of Christian civilisation, so to speak, such a principle was self-evident, but I believe that it would be either a very brave or a very complacent person who would claim that it is self-evident in our secularised society of today. I think that in modern terms we need a Bill of Rights not just as an adjunct to the law but also as some kind of protection against sin.

Then I should like to support the Bill as someone who values the European Community in a fairly wide sense of those words. I believe that the other democratic countries of Europe must find it rather strange that the United Kingdom, which was a pioneer in establishing the convention, should have taken so long to domesticate it on its own shores. They must surely wonder whether this is another manifestation of what they sometimes regard as our isolationism, and whether this is due to some false sense of superiority about the perfection of our own arrangements.

I say 'false' because when they look at the number of petitions which have come from this country to the court at Strasbourg, and the number of judgments given in favour of the petitioners, they could hardly believe that any claim to perfection on our part was true. The noble Lord, Lord Banks, has said all that is required on that subject.

It does not do much for the reputation of the United Kingdom if we are apparently unwilling to adopt quite explicitly for our own courts the principles to which we subscribed over 30 years ago and to be prepared to deal ourselves with any infringements of those same principles. We are, after all, supposed to have been the inventors of the idea of fair play, and fair play is something that is very much in need of defence in the world of today.

I hope I shall not be accused of some godless philosophy – bishops have to be rather careful nowadays – if I say that it is especially to the humble, powerless, and disadvantaged members of our nation that a Bill of Rights seems to be of value. In the past 10 years or so the European court has come to the assistance of the mentally handicapped, immigrants, and prisoners – to mention just three of the categories I have so described. But not every such person is likely to find the court in Strasbourg easy of access or to be represented with enough skill and perseverance to gain a hearing and to obtain redress. Surely the right place for them to look for these things is in the courts of their own country and to look for them on the basis of a charter of rights and freedoms which they themselves can understand and which they know to be honoured by their own representatives in Parliament. To enable this to happen is in one way quite simple in terms of this Bill, yet in another respect it seems to me a big and important step for British justice to take. I very much hope that the passing of this Bill will enable us to take it. . .

Lord Denning: My Lords, it has been my lot over the years to consider this proposal many times. I have been present at many of the debates on it in this House; I have written upon it; and I have heard cases in the courts in which people have raised this convention on human rights. I am afraid I do not think these clauses ought to be incorporated into our law, as part of our law. They are framed in the words of a treaty, vague and indefinite; and if they are brought before the courts of law those courts and, I am afraid, the European Court of Strasbourg, decide not by the words, as we do in our courts, but by the policy which they think underlies them.

This was strikingly illustrated when we had our debate about corporal punishment in schools. The court at Strasbourg decided, I think quite wrongly, on the words of a protocol, that it could only be done with the consent of the parents. Our English judge, Sir Vincent Evans, dissented, and I think quite rightly. They went on the policy that they thought the rule ought to be the same throughout Europe. When the matter came before your Lordships sitting legislatively, when the Government tried to put that decision into operation, I am glad to say your Lordships rejected it because the ultimate word on the law of England is Parliament, and not the European Court at Strasbourg.

Perhaps I may say this at once. When I read Clause 4 of this Bill, it offends all our constitutional principles. What it says is that any statute already made by both Houses can be examined by the courts of law, and the courts of law can say that that statute is invalid because it offends against the constitution. That is in regard to past Acts. In regard to future Acts, it says, again, that anyone can ask for a declaration in the courts of law to say that the Acts of this Parliament are invalid because they offend against the European Convention.

This is such a fundamental principle of our constitution that I remind your Lordships of what Lord Reid said in the latest case of *Pickin* v. *British Railways Board* reported in 1974 Appeal cases at page 782:

'The idea that a court is entitled to disregard a provision of an Act of Parliament on any ground must seem strange and startling to anyone with any knowledge of the history and law of our constitution.'

Then it goes on to say:

'In earlier times many learned writers seem to have believed that an Act of Parliament could be disregarded in so far as it was contrary to the law of God or to the law of nature or to natural justice, but since the supremacy of Parliament was finally demonstrated by the revolution of 1688 any such idea has become obsolete.'

I will not allow any contention here that that clause should ever appear in any statute, because it is really subordinating our Acts of Parliament to a determination by the courts on the ground that it is said that they are contrary to the conventions. So on that simple ground I oppose any interference with our constitution by directing the courts in that way. That is a fundamental constitutional point. . .

As I say, my objection is fundamental. It is that you are going to have a myriad of cases by a lot of crackpots, and they will have to be turned out sooner or later. ... The real truth is that this convention is not suitably phrased or suitably set out to be part of law or to set down legal principles to be interpreted in our courts. We can take them into account, as I have said, and apply them so far as we reasonably can. But do not make them part of an Act of Parliament. Therefore, I am against this Bill. ...

Lord Glenarthur: The Bill before us is one with profound constitutional implications. No one respects more than I the wisdom and experience of my noble friend Lord Broxbourne and that of his supporters who have aided him with this measure – or, indeed, my noble friend's success in picking this day of all days upon which to debate this subject. No one who has pride in the history and heritage of this country, which has traditionally acted as a champion of human rights, could fail to consider seriously the concept embodied in the Bill.

It is, however, the constitutional implications that cause the Government concern – concern that if the Bill should be enacted we may seriously damage the delicate machinery of parliamentary democracy built up over the centuries. The Government accept the principles on which the European Convention of Human Rights is founded. The United Kingdom played a major role in drafting these principles into the convention. The United Kingdom reaffirmed support for it. The present Government recently announced their intention of renewing for a further period of five years the United Kingdom's acceptance of the right of individual petition and acceptance of the compulsory jurisdiction of the European Court of Human Rights.

The Government's reservations about this Bill are not reservations, therefore, about conforming to the principles of human rights laid down in the convention ...

The reason for the Government's opposition to incorporation is not because of any desire to inhibit the pursuit of human rights. Indeed, it has nothing to do with human rights as such. Our concern is that incorporation could cause a shift in the balance of our democratic system. Our machinery of government does not depend on a written constitution. Our statutes are specific in nature and set out measures that the Government of the day decide are necessary for our democratic society. If society does not approve of the Government's actions, the Government will not be re-elected. ...

Were we to incorporate the provision of the European Convention in accordance with the provisions of this Bill, we should have taken a major step towards a written constitution and we should have on the statute book a series of non-specific provisions with no precise definition. For example, Article 8 requires that everyone has the right to respect for his private and family life, his home and his correspondence. Who then will have to decide what is necessary for our democratic society within that article? Not the elected Government, not Parliament, but the judiciary. With all respect to the learned members of the judiciary, and with all due deference to the noble and learned Lord, Lord Scarman, who foreshadowed a little of what I have to say, I must ask whether it is right that they should be required to take such decisions, many of which ... will be politically charged, and that they should take those decisions with no requirement to answer to Parliament or to society itself.

One has to ask whether this is a role that would be welcome to the judiciary. Judging by the remarks of the noble and learned Lord, Lord Denning, he at least did not seem to think that they would welcome it ...

Not only would there be this shift away from the determination of society's needs by its elected representatives to the determination of society's needs by a non-elected judiciary, but we should have the problems associated with the uncertain interpretation of the non-specific articles of the convention. If we were to enact the provisions of this Bill, could we be certain that the present statute book would not be open to challenge? If not, 'so be it' is a not unreasonable answer. But can we be sure that the present statute book and the laws we pass after incorporation will not be struck down a few years later as the interpretation of the articles of the convention evolves either in this country or at Strasbourg. And evolve it no doubt will. Who would have thought when the convention was drafted that our laws bearing upon homosexuality, corporal punishment in schools and marriage in prison would be found to be defective? ...

The Government's view is that we cannot readily predict what effect the enactment of this Bill would have on our constitutional heritage and what consequences would arise from the inevitable uncertainties which it would create. Were the Bill necessary to confer basic human rights on the individuals of our society, we should regard it differently. However, it is not necessary for this purpose and we consider the risks I have mentioned such that we should be taking a completely unjustifiable gamble were we to support the Bill. For those reasons, I have to tell your Lordships and my noble friend that the Government cannot support this measure.

Lord Broxbourne: My Lords, that, naturally, was a disappointing wind-up by my noble friend the Minister. . . . Perhaps he would like to seek a little advice from a colleague. I suggest that, away from the glare of these lights, he has a quiet word with the noble and learned Lord, Lord Hailsham, to see whether he can give him any guidance on this matter. . . . On a head count I think we just about win. I see the noble and learned Lord confirms this. However, in addition to that, it has been said that the lawyers are split. Well, lawyers never agree with each other, that is the nature of the calling. Thus it is no surprise that the lawyers split more or less 50–50. What is significant is that when one goes beyond them one finds unanimous support in both the voice of the Church and the citizen. That surely must be of some account in your Lordships' House. . .

On Question, Bill read a second time.

HL Deb., 10 December 1985, cols 155f.

85 DEBATE ON THE STATE OF CIVIL LIBERTIES UNDER THE THATCHER ADMINISTRATION, 1990

Lord Irvine of Lairg: My Lords:

'Thatcherism makes intellectual liberty just another commodity, to be enjoyed when there is no particular political or administrative price to be paid for it, but abandoned, with no evident grief, when the price begins to rise. That is not despotism. But it cheapens liberty and diminishes the nation.'

Those are not my words, though I agree with them. They are the words of the Professor of Jurisprudence at the University of Oxford, Professor Dworkin, in an important article at the end of 1988. His conclusion was that,

'liberty is ill in England'.

It is a theme to which he returned in a public lecture only last Thursday. His proposition was that the very concept of liberty,

'is being challenged and corroded by the Thatcher Government'.

True,

'the Government's challenge to freedom has nothing to do with ... despotism. It shows'—

he claimed—

'a more mundane but still corrupting insensitivity to liberty, a failure to grasp its force and place in modern democratic ideals'.

The argument is that the concept of liberty turns, first, on the sovereign idea that liberty of speech, conviction and information figure among fundamental human rights; and, secondly, on a set of working assumptions about how these rights must be protected – assumptions to be characterised as together forming the culture of liberty. So the basic argument is the high value that should be given to freedom of expression; that it should not be traded in the same way as one social good may be bartered against another; that government should ever bear the burden of proving to a high standard a real necessity to interfere with freedom of expression.

The weight of these charges could be assessed by reference to many freedoms – freedom of the press; of broadcasters; of assembly; academic freedom. But a sustained feature of this Administration has surely been their obsession with government secrecy and national security, to the prejudice of traditional freedoms. It is hard to think that in the GCHQ affair hostility to trade unions did not walk hand in hand with indifference to basic freedoms. Some industrial action at GCHQ caused the Government to announce that staff there could no longer be members of trade unions. They would be free to join only a staff association approved by the Government.

Their loss of freedom of association was to be bought off at £1,000 a head – subject to income tax! They had to accept or else; and ultimately be sacked if transfer elsewhere was impossible. The last sackings took place last year. . .

GCHQ, however, was only one step in a series where the Government have exaggerated state security to the prejudice of freedom. There has been a huge increase in prosecutions under the Official Secrets Act in the past decade. In 1983 Sarah Tisdall from the office of the Foreign Secretary delivered documents to the *Guardian* evidencing a government decision to delay a Statement to Parliament about the arrival of Cruise missiles in Greenham Common until after they had arrived. One object was to enable the Government to emphasise their position first, before the Opposition and the 'peace movement' could react. The courts ordered the *Guardian* to return the documents. As a result, Sarah Tisdall emerged as the suspect: she confessed, and was sentenced to imprisonment. Your Lordships' House, in its judicial capacity by a very narrow majority of three to two, held that national security had required the return of the documents. However, the distinct impression was left that the 'secret' tab on the documents was for reasons of parliamentary or political advantage, not genuine security interest.

Then there was the *Ponting* case in 1984. He had sent Mr. Tam Dalyell, MP, Ministry of Defence documents about parliamentary inquiries into the sinking of the 'General Belgrano'. At his trial he alleged that he had wanted to blow the whistle on how Parliament had been misled by Ministers and how Ministers had planned to mislead the Foreign Affairs Select Committee. This was an astonishing prosecution to bring under the Official Secrets Act and eventually the jury said 'no' to a prosecution it did not like by acquitting Mr. Ponting – astonishing because on day one it was conceded that his disclosure had caused no damage to national security, but only a breach of confidence. It was astonishing also because potential jurors were vetted by the Special Branch, although national security was not in issue. Ponting, of course, had no authority to reveal the documents to Mr. Dalyell. His defence was that he had revealed them because it was his duty in the interests of the state, under Section 2, to do so. The jury acquitted, despite a direction that 'duty' meant official duty and the 'interests of the state' meant the interests of the government of the day, which they do not.

Then in 1987 there was the bizarre Zircon affair. Your Lordships will recall that it concerned the withdrawal by the BBC of a film alleging that the Ministry of Defence had secretly launched a £500 million surveillance project unbeknown to Parliament, in breach of a clear undertaking that any defence projects exceeding £250 million would be disclosed to the Public Accounts Committee. Ineptitude followed – of a quite comic order. The offending journalist arranged for the film to be shown in the other place, in order to prove that there was no risk to national security. Incredibly, the Government went to the courts for an injunction. Obviously the courts refused – it was for Parliament to regulate its own affairs. Then the Speaker banned the film after the Attorney-General briefed him on the security implications.

The rest is history – the failed attempt to serve an injunction on the journalist; The *New Statesman* publishing the contents of the film; search warrants to search the offices of the *New Statesman*, followed by a search of the Scottish office of the BBC. So, this punitive action over, the problem went away, with injunctions lifted, the Speaker's ban withdrawn, the film transmitted by the BBC two years later, no prosecutions brought, and no damage at all to the national interest other than that the authorities had succeeded in making themselves look ridiculous.

But this was nothing alongside *Spycatcher*. Undoubtedly Wright was in breach of his obligation of confidence, but he had grave allegations to make affecting the public interest; that MI5 had attempted to destabilise a democratically elected government; had been implicated in an attempt to assassinate President Nasser; had been involved in the bugging and burglary of trade unions and political parties. I pass over the fiasco in Australia, the continued banning of the book in this country, long after publication in the United States and long after the information had become public knowledge throughout the world; and then the turning of the tide in the courts with the judge, who heard the trial at the end of 1987 for permanent injunctions against the press, declaring that the absolute protection that the Government were seeking for the security service,

'could not be achieved this side of the Iron Curtain'.

It became progressively bizarre to go on stubbornly trying to ban in this country what was freely available everywhere else, and here too with a modicum of effort.

In the aftermath of *Spycatcher* the staff counsellor for the security and intelligence services was invented. Members of the service could take their grievances to him. He has access to the Secretary to the Cabinet and reports annually to the Prime Minister, the Foreign Secretary and the Home Secretary. But the arrangement is all, in-house, within the Executive; the public can never know.

It is an offence under the Official Secrets Act 1989 to reveal any information about the activities of the security service. The opinion of the trial judge in the *Spycatcher* case that,

'the public was the proper recipient of information that MI5 was attempting to destroy public confidence in a democratically elected government',

was ignored. The counsellor has no duty to account to Parliament.

The Security Service Act 1989 puts MI5 on a statutory basis for the first time. However, its powers are so broad that it can do virtually anything. The service must not be used to further the interests of any political party, but there is no prohibition on acting contrary to the interests of a political party. The Government refused to accept an amendment borrowed from Canada which would have prevented surveillance of those engaged in lawful advocacy, protest or dissent.

It is the Home Secretary, not the courts, who may authorise warrants permitting literally any interference with property. It comes down to the fact that the Home Secretary is absolutely free to decide on the width of the legislation. True, there is to be a security service commissioner who reviews the grant of warrants by the Home Secretary. But he reviews them only after the event. He cannot order the Minister to cease what is improper. He reports annually to the Prime Minister, but any part of the report appearing to the Prime Minister to be prejudicial to the continued discharge of the functions of the service need not be laid before Parliament. . .

Then we had the Official Secrets Act of last year. The one thing that this measure is not is a liberalising measure. It provides no positive rights to information and no freedom of information. It fails to recognise the public interest to know of abuses by government of its powers. A narrow amendment was moved in your Lordships' House which would have allowed officials to reveal really serious misconduct involving crime, fraud or other gross impropriety. Even that could not be accepted. Under the common law, where breach of confidence is alleged, that is a defence. It is a defence that the public interest favours disclosure. But that defence is not available under the Act. As Mr. Edward Heath pointed out in another place, newspapers could be prosecuted for disclosing an Irangate in this country. Therefore there is no defence for a newspaper, whose source is a civil servant on a security or defence matter, which reveals that a Minister of the Crown has not told Parliament the truth, or has wilfully withheld it or been economical with it.

I do not accept that the categories of information protected under the Act represent a narrowing of the scope, in practice, of official secrets. An Act which was becoming substantially inoperable in practice has been replaced by one capable of being more repressive in practice. It is an offence for any member of the security service to disclose confidential information, even if it causes no harm. It is an offence for officials to leak information, however true, about unpreparedness in the military sphere, provided that the truth can be shown to be damaging. It would be an offence to reveal here information given in confidence by our Government to a foreign state where the information has been leaked by that state, and even if the information has had the widest currency abroad, provided that the truth could be shown to be damaging. We retain a system well fashioned to keep from the public view any information embarrassing to government, whether bureaucratic error or, worse, deception – laws which do not reflect the balance a modern democratic society requires between the public interest to receive, and the state interest to withold, information. . .

I shall not go on to multiply instances. I do not doubt that other noble Lords will do so in the course of this short debate. But I feel that I should not leave off opening this debate without at least touching upon a great issue which I imagine will be addressed by other noble Lords: has the time come for our country to incorporate into our law the European convention on Human Rights? The current position of my party is no, though it remains subject to debate. The Government's position is also no.

It was the 1951 Labour Government who were first among the members of the Council of Europe to ratify the convention. It was the Labour Government of 1966 who accepted the right of individual petition under the

European convention to complain to the European Commission of Human Rights of alleged violations of the rights and freedoms guaranteed by the convention.

Incorporation of the convention is no panacea for the decline in our civil liberties. The policy of my party is that we should have a freedom of information Act and that both M15 and M16 should be made subject to parliamentary supervision. However, the further issue is whether incorporation of the convention into our law would also advance civil liberty. The main argument against is that powers would be taken away from Parliament, where they belong, and given to the judiciary, where they do not belong. Your Lordships may think that there is one basic question: if civil liberties are worth protecting, is it sensible to rely upon Parliament alone to do the job?

The case for incorporation is that the protection of Parliament is not enough. The Executive dominate. Governments are characteristically elected on a minority of the votes cast in elections in which civil liberties issues rarely receive much attention. The Prime Minister dominates the Cabinet. The payroll vote becomes ever larger. This Administration have set a precedent for the use of three-line Whips, even on Private Members' Bills. Sheer lack of parliamentary time often makes proper scrutiny a mirage. It is difficult to believe that any of us are wholly satisfied with the parliamentary process as it operates today. Two to three years ago, the other place was given but three days to consider more than 1,000 amendments to the Education Reform Bill and the poll tax Bill – on average, 80 seconds per amendment. The poll tax was a classic case of legislating in haste and repenting at leisure.

I do not desire to detain your Lordships for too long. I well know the argument that the powers of the judiciary should not be enlarged at the expense of Parliament; that the judges are not the best equipped to decide those issues. But is it the final position of both major parties that we do not believe that our courts can help protect our citizens' rights under the European Convention; that we rely upon our Parliament alone, whoever is in power, and foreign judges only? . . .

Lord Alexander of Weedon: I do not believe that overall this country has at the present time a bad record in terms of human rights or civil liberties, or however one describes them. There are many areas in which this country has led the way. The evolution of parliamentary democracy, the safeguards that apply to procedures at trial and habeas corpus are obvious examples. I do not believe that the vitality of that trend in our national character is spent.

An obvious recent illustration to which the noble Lord, Lord Hutchinson of Lullington, drew attention was the immense development over the past 20 years of administrative law. An independent judiciary has resurrected, shaped and expanded the right of the courts to exercise some considerable fetter upon the actions of the Executive. We have seen that right across the board in cases affecting individual rights and involving rates, transport, social security, education and immigration, and in challenges to national security issues. Our administrative law has now become an important aspect of our freedom. Not for nothing, and in my view accurately, did the late Lord Diplock describe it as the greatest development in the law in his lifetime.

The impact of those developments has gone far wider than decided cases because the law as it has evolved and the concern as to how the courts will look at decisions must be taken into account by the Government in reaching many important decisions across the board. That legal development has restrained the power of both Labour and Conservative governments. In each case, governments of both political complexions have accepted the development of that restraint, at any rate publicly, without protest or demur. The checks and balances within our democracy have evolved and have been accepted. I see that as a tribute to both the judiciary and to successive governments, not least the present Administration.

However, as with so much of our historical development, that evolution has been pragmatic. We have declined to incorporate in our own law what has now become our most important and influential constitutional document. It is now almost 30 years since we became the first country to ratify the European convention. As noble Lords well know, in many countries ratification automatically incorporates a treaty into the domestic law of that country; but that is not so in our law. However, we have regarded the European convention sufficiently highly to include it as the basis of the constitution of some 24 former colonies when they gained independence. We have taken a different view of what is needed by former colonies than we take of our own needs. That no doubt reflects the remarkable pervasiveness of Professor Dicey's view that written constitutions were necessary for less fortunate peoples.

We have also accepted the right of individual petition to the European Commission of Human Rights at Strasbourg since 1966. We therefore acknowledge the importance of the convention. We accept its impact. We accept judicial decisions upon it, but we decline to take the ultimate step of making it part of our own law.

The decisions of the court at Strasbourg have already had a notable impact. That has not least been so in cases which affect the rights of prisoners – a minority who carry very few political votes. Cases from Strasbourg have improved the freedom of prisoners to correspond without restriction. They have enhanced the access of prisoners to legal advice. The European Court will shortly consider the case of Michael Thynne and will decide whether a failure to provide for the periodic review of an indefinite sentence, to see whether a personality disorder still subsists, is a breach of the convention. That argument highlights an important issue dealt with admirably in the report of the Select Committee on Murder and Life Imprisonment: what should be the procedure for reviewing the duration of an indefinite life sentence? It is important that that procedure should develop so as to ensure an independent review, conducted under fair procedures, with reasons given for decisions adverse to the prisoner.

In the area of prisoners' rights, we must also work increasingly towards emphasising that imprisonment involves deprivation of liberty but not human degradation and loss of other civil rights. In that regard – I very much hope that the Woolf Report on the Strangeways disturbances will prove an important and illuminating milestone – the European convention has proved that it has a role to play, and it has an important continuing role to play.

Why do we not then incorporate the convention? It may be because of a concern that it impinges upon the sovereignty of Parliament. It undoubtedly has the effect, unless it were enacted with the modification suggested by my noble and learned friend Lord Hailsham, that it would enable a court to declare legislation passed by Parliament in this country to be unlawful. However, although that sounds a startling proposition, perhaps we should reflect that we have in any event to some extent already accepted that principle. We accept that the court at Strasbourg can reach such decisions.

A few years ago I represented the present Government when they sought to defend legislation introduced under the previous government as being compatible with the convention. Both legislation which nationalised the shipbuilding and aircraft industries and legislation which provided for leasehold enfranchisement were involved. In each case, the applicants sought to challenge the legislation head on. The argument was heard by the European Court of Human Rights and in each case was determined in favour of the Government. However, if it had gone the other way, precedent suggests that the Government would have respected and implemented the decision of the court.

If we accept that legislation can be challenged under the convention before the Strasbourg court, would it not perhaps seem sensible that we should allow the issue to be considered by our own domestic courts? We can surely commit the issue to our judges. I do not believe that would politicise the judiciary. The fact that it has been involved in essential social questions in determining issues of judicial review has not for the most part led to anything other than enhanced respect for the wish and determination of the judiciary to uphold the individual against excesses of government power.

I do not want to suggest, perhaps especially in this Session, that incorporation of the convention is urgent. I certainly do not wish to suggest that it should be added to the burden of legislation in this current Session. It has in one sense become less urgent because of the willingness of the courts to interpret and shape our law in the light of the provisions of the convention.

However, there remain concerns that the sovereignty of Parliament alone is not a sufficient protection for all our citizens. There is a danger that, as I believe my noble and learned friend Lord Hailsham once described it, Parliament has increasingly become an elected dictatorship. Our society increasingly comprises minorities whose interests may not have enough widespread appeal or, to put in crudely, sufficient voting pull for them to be effectively protected in Parliament. The convention contains a framework within which our civil liberties and rights can be safeguarded. . .

Viscount Ullswater: My Lords, I am grateful to the noble Lord, Lord Irvine, for raising what has proved to be an interesting and stimulating topic in debate and for the thoughtful approach he brought to such a wide and complicated subject. There can be few matters as important and deserving of debate in your Lordships' House as this. I am grateful to other noble Lords who contributed and I hope to touch on most of the points raised in the time allowed.

It seems that the debate has turned on three main areas. First, we have the argument that basic freedoms have been diminished during this Government's term of office. Secondly, there is the question of the proper balance to be struck between the liberties of the individual on the one hand and the rights of others and the general public on the other. Thirdly, there is the issue of how civil liberties are protected under our present constitutional arrangements. These three areas are of course interlinked, but, with your Lordships' permission, I should like to look at each main area in turn.

Needless to say, I cannot accept the erosion of freedom hypothesis put forward by the noble Lord, Lord Irvine. I believe that his argument presents an altogether misguided picture of the true situation. Under this Government there have been a very real and worthwhile extension and enhancement of civil liberties. I hope I shall be able to persuade your Lordships that the Government's record bears close scrutiny and emerges with credit. As a Government we have set great store by the extension of economic freedoms because we believe that civic rights are much better extended under a prosperous economy. Our actions aimed at deregulation and the freeing of economic life have produced enormous benefits, increased productivity, lower taxes and more disposable income in real terms.

I believe strongly that reducing taxation gives the individual the freedom to spend his hard-earned money in the way he wants rather than the state saying where the money will go. Our guiding principle, therefore, is not materialism but a realisation that freedoms can only but be enhanced by increasing economic prosperity. Economic freedom is important. We have taken, for example, action against the closed shop; we have given trade union members the right to be balloted before any industrial action; and we took resolute action against secondary picketing. We on these benches view with utter dismay the fact that the Labour Party wants to relegalise secondary picketing.

There was precious little freedom under the last Labour Administration at factory gate strike meetings, and I am sure your Lordships will recall all too many an ugly scene involving intimidation by mass pickets. As your Lordships know, we are currently taking action in another place to end the practice of wildcat strikes, among other things. Where we think it right to give further protection to the public and indeed the ordinary employee, we will not hesitate to act.

We have taken action to give council tenants the right to buy – a measure which has since received grudging Labour Party support. Action which extends economic freedom has helped many ordinary citizens to do what would never otherwise have been possible. I shall give other examples. The Sex Discrimination Act and the Equal Pay Act are very important examples of the extension of individual liberty. We have put the Data Protection Act in place. We have given access to educational records and certain medical reports.

The Opposition are much concerned about police powers. But it was this Government who set out a new framework in the Police and Criminal Evidence Act which gave added safeguards for the citizen and for dealing with complaints against the police. We have given a statutory right to compensation for victims of violent crime, which is a measure that commands all your Lordships' support.

The noble Lord, Lord Irvine of Lairg, made much reference to the Official Secrets Act, quoting the cases of *Tisdall, Ponting* and others in some detail. ... As regards official secrets, the reform we introduced was radical and now only six types of official information are protected. In general, it is for the prosecution to prove that specific form of harm defined in the Act arose or was likely to arise from disclosure. It will also be for the prosecution to prove that the accused knew or had good reason to believe that harm would occur, except in the case of those treated under the Act as Crown servants. Under the 1989 Act the number of people prescribed as Crown servants has been greatly reduced, from an estimated 500,000 to an estimated 27,000.

We have made provision about the interception of communications, with the appointment of a commissioner, and for complaints to go to an independent tribunal. The security service has been put on a statutory footing, again with provision for the appointment of a commissioner and for complaints to go before an independent tribunal ...

Many more examples could be given. I think, however, that I have made my point. Our record is one of very positive achievement in extending and enhancing civil liberties. The noble Lord, Lord Mishcon, said that freedoms are counted by the vigilance we use to protect them. I agree with him and I believe that this Administration have been vigilant and protective.

I now turn to my second theme, the question of balance. The Government are fully committed to ensuring that the people of this country know their rights and that they are not infringed. That does not of course mean that those liberties can always be unqualified. That is because all governments have a duty to make a judgment of the rights of the individual as well as of society at large and of the conflict of rights between various groups in society. This is not always an easy task, but it is one which this Government have not sought to avoid.

I do not mind that IRA terrorists can travel less easily to and from Great Britain as a result of powers taken to prevent terrorism. Those powers are essential for the defence of ordinary law-abiding people, as, I am sorry to say, are other powers that the noble noble Lord, Lord Monkswell, and perhaps the Labour Party would like to see revoked.

Nor do I mind the curtailment of the liberty of a young man to carry a knife in his pocket; nor the fact that, should he appear in court, the burden of proving why he was carrying the knife now rests with him and not the prosecution. We are conscientious and meticulous in looking at issues of individual freedom. I must tell the noble Lord, Lord Monson, that where we decide to increase or diminish freedom we do not do so lightly or without clear evidence of need. Where the protection of the public has needed limited and well-defined reinforcement, we have provided it and will continue to do so ...

I turn now to my third theme, how civil liberties are protected under our present constitutional arrangements. We heard the suggestion from the noble Lords, Lord Irvine of Lairg, Lord Hutchinson of Lullington and Lord Mishcon, that civil rights would be better protected if civil liberties were enshrined in a Bill of Rights. Civil rights are already protected in our legal systems and by statute and are in far more precise terms than, for example, in the European convention, which most proponents of a Bill of Rights would like to incorporate in our domestic law.

Incorporating the European convention would mean that the courts rather than Parliament would determine society's needs. That is no reflection on the impartiality of the judiciary. Rather, it is a re-affirmation that it is for Parliament in the exercise of its sovereignty to decide. We do not doubt the ability of the judges, but we believe that requiring them to undertake such tasks would propel them into the political arena. One has only to look to the United States to see that the two most important criteria for appointment to the Supreme Court are the candidate's social views and his or her political opinions. There is no evidence that the general public favours either a written constitution or a new Bill of Rights. The Government therefore believe that until consensus as to such a need emerges, the present adequate safeguards should remain. . .

HL Deb., 23 May 1990, cols. 904f.

---

86   DEBATE ON THE CASE FOR INCORPORATION OF THE EUROPEAN CONVENTION ON HUMAN RIGHTS INTO UK LAW AS A BILL OF RIGHTS, 1990

Lord Holme of Cheltenham: My Lords, the Motion calls for attention to be paid to the case for the incorporation of the European Convention on Human Rights into British law as a Bill of Rights. It is worth saying that in moving this Motion I feel both some pride and some embarrassment. The pride I feel is that I am a Member of the party which has kept the torch alight for this specific issue in this House over many years. I refer to the consistent activities of Lord Wade. Donald Wade brought before your Lordships' House, on no fewer than three occasions, Motions for a Bill of Rights. He was a staunch supporter of this cause and would have been pleased to see how wide is the interest and support that now exists in this country for the proposition that I bring before the House today.

I am also very glad to be able to speak in this Chamber on this subject because in 1985, the last occasion on which your Lordships debated it, a Bill was brought forward by the noble Lord, Lord Broxbourne, with the active involvement of the noble and learned Lord, Lord Scarman, and I was able from outside the House, as chairman of the Constitutional Reform Centre and chairman of the rights campaign, to work with them closely on that Bill.

Any embarrassment that I feel is, first, because I am not a lawyer. I am a new Member of the House, which can be remedied by time, but I am not a lawyer and at my time of life I do not expect to be a lawyer. This is a subject which attracts lawyers, as can be seen from the noble Lords who intend to speak today. However, I do not believe that, in the end, the issues concerning a Bill of Rights in this country should be monopolised by lawyers. It is a subject on which lay voices should be heard and I am glad that I have this opportunity to be the voice of a layman.

The embarrassment I really feel is on behalf of this country. We are now the only country in the Council of Europe that does not have either a Bill of Rights or a written constitution. I am sure that we shall be told later in the debate that that is our glory, but I do not believe that it is. It is a great weakness of this country that we are the only country that is not prepared to delimit and demarcate the powers of the state, that we are the only country which is not prepared to have the rights of its citizens as a rock on which good government and genuine democracy are founded.

Some people may say that democracy and the demands of democracy are met by the election of Parliament, the House of Commons, and that that is both necessary and a sufficient condition for human rights and freedoms to be reflected. I do not take that view. First, Parliament has been elected by a minority of the electorate. Incidentally, how noteworthy it is that the German election has produced a fair result, conducted on a proportional representation system, in which the government will be based on a majority of the citizens of the Federal Republic.

However, even if we had a genuine majority government in this country, instead of alternating minority governments, we would have to pay heed to the wise words of John Stuart Mill that the rights of minorities are not always respected by the majority, that there are minorities and individuals who need permanent and enduring protection. It is in that spirit that I bring forward the Motion this afternoon.

Although I am pleased as a Member on these Benches to have this opportunity to introduce the Motion, it is worth emphasising that this has not been, either in the country or in this House, primarily a partisan issue. The cross-party support on the occasion of the Broxbourne Bill and the cross-party support shown when that Bill was revived in the other place by Sir Edward Gardner the following year demonstrates that there is interest and support across the party spectrum.

Even more recently than that we have seen interesting expressions of support by the Institute of Economic Affairs, a Right-wing think-tank, for the prospect of incorporating the European Convention on Human Rights, and next week the Institute for Public Policy Research, a think-tank linked with the Labour Party for producing policies for the Left in Britain, is to publish a paper called *A British Bill of Rights*. That institute is presided over by the noble Baroness, Lady Blackstone – she is not in the Chamber at the moment – and I am delighted, having been sent an advance copy of the paper, to be able to congratulate her on it and express the hope that the institute will have a benign effect on the formation of Labour Party policy on this important subject. Therefore, there is interest across the political spectrum.

In 1985 we drew particular encouragement from the support of the then Lord Chancellor, recently retired, the noble and learned Lord, Lord Hailsham, who I am glad to see is here this afternoon.

Many people would go further than the Motion. Many would say, as the noble and learned Lord, Lord Scarman, said in his Hamlyn lectures, that there should be a written constitution in this country with entrenched rights. My own party holds that view. However, the Motion has much more modest aims. It proposes simply to take the European convention and make it part of British law so that British citizens in British courts may have access to the rights for which at present they have to travel a long, expensive and weary road to Strasbourg. The Motion proposes to domesticate and bring into our domestic laws those rights which at present can only be obtained in Strasbourg. It does not have the profound constitutional implications in terms of the sovereignty of Parliament that a written constitution or a fully entrenched Bill of Rights would have. ... In 1978 your Lordships' House established a Select Committee which recommended by an extremely narrow majority – one – the incorporation of the European convention as a British Bill of Rights. We are now 12 years further on and nothing has happened. I wish very briefly to recapitulate the arguments for bringing the convention into our domestic courts. First, I have in a sense already mentioned ease of access and the closeness to remedy. Secondly, there should be in a European convention an openness of texture which would make it possible for future generations gradually to develop and interpret rights in the way that they are in other democracies such as the United States, and be responsive to the changing needs of society. Thirdly and crucially, the convention is to check the exercise of improperly administered power by the Executive and the state.

For most of the time we live in a country in which the intention of government of all kinds, including government agencies and local government, is honourable and administration is fair. But that is not always the case. To paraphrase Lord Acton, power is delightful; absolute power is absolutely delightful. The noble and learned Lord, Lord Hailsham, has said that too easily in this country we find ourselves with a system which is more properly characterised as an elective dictatorship where there are not limits on the exercise of executive power of the kind that other democracies take for granted.

Finally, I suggest that in many ways the most compelling argument for incorporation of the European convention is that it would have an effect on the democratic system as a whole and on the values by which we conduct our public affairs. Bills framed with a Bill of Rights in mind would be Bills more properly framed. Greater care would be taken by civil servants in the execution of their duties and they would be sensitive to the need not to encroach on the position of the citizen. . .

Lord Hutchinson of Lullington: My Lords, with this debate, as your Lordships will have already seen, the Chamber is following a well-trodden path. We have had two Bills and the report of the Select Committee chaired by the noble Lord, Lord Allen. If I may say so, we have never had the case put better than it has been by my noble friend Lord Holme.

I should like to place the matter in the context of recent events. When the Prime Minister stood on the steps at No. 10, he said that he wished to see a Britain at ease with itself. That was a most significant statement. It signalled (did it not?) an end to the strident divisiveness of recent years and foresaw a society which, being at ease with itself, is one surely in which the individual feels truly free, and where restraints on freedom are willingly accepted; where those who abuse civil rights are clearly identifiable and accountable. Furthermore, it is a society where information is readily available upon which to bring such abuses to book, and where a citizen's vote will to his knowledge count in the election of his representatives.

The debate points the way therefore for Mr. Major if he means what he says. Today the citizen wants to know what are his civil and political rights; where they are to be found; and how his children are to learn what they are. He wants to know how he can assert those rights, and so he needs access to the law which alone can offer him protection against abuse. We see around us today a profoundly dissatisfied society where people are confused as to what are their rights and where access to law is made less possible year by year.

No matter in what area one works, or in what activity one participates, the ordinary person is frustrated and at odds with the Government. Thatcherism has been obsessed with the concept of authority; with the centralisation of power; and with the paternalism of 'we know best-ism'. In every Bill that reaches the House, we find clauses removing power from the individual and vesting it in Ministers and civil servants. That culminated in the legal services Green Paper in which the noble and learned Lord the Lord Chancellor blatantly aimed to bring the administration of the law itself under the will of the Executive. The noble and learned Lord was finally forced by the House to abandon that aim. . .

In our complex world of information technology, freedom of the individual can no longer be defined negatively as it was in more leisurely and insular days in this country. 'You can do or say anything which is not prohibited by law' is a wholly unworkable and inadequate principle, I suggest, in the face of the torrent of rules and regulations which now govern the behaviour of the citizen. People must now know where they stand. They seek assurance that officials – the police, immigration officers, civil servants, local government officers, politicians; yes, even prison personnel – should be clearly accountable for the power which they wield. Surely it is a sign of political immaturity to continue to cling to the myth of the protection of the absolute power of the elected Chamber to which my noble friend referred, the myth of undiluted parliamentary sovereignty, at the expense of individual justice.

The power race at present is: first past the post, minority rule, an all-powerful executive with a massively powerful Prime Minister, a weakened and undemocratic second Chamber and a denigrated and frustrated local government. That is where we stand today.

The convention sets out – brilliantly, I suggest – the individual rights to which every citizen is entitled in a democracy. That is only his civil and political rights. It provides machinery by which an individual may secure those rights; machinery which is undoubtedly cumbersome and elaborate, but no wonder when it embraces the first unique stride forward under the umbrella of the Council of Europe towards a true international community of civilised states and of course a route which was envisaged as a last resort. Why should our citizens alone compared with those of our powerful neighbours have no first resort to this basic justice in their own country? Why should they have to embark on the long, five-year trek to Strasbourg, supported by lawyers who largely take no fee?

These questions should be put to the noble and learned Lord the Lord Chancellor. With the greatest respect to the noble Lord who is to reply to the debate, it is the noble and learned Lord, with his authoritative voice, who is responsible for the judiciary. He has been, I regret, conspicuously reticent on matters of human rights, unlike one of his illustrious predecessors – the noble and learned Lord, Lord Hailsham – who we are happy to see in his place this afternoon.

Perhaps the noble Lord was in communication with his noble and learned friend before this debate. I wonder whether he has asked him why a prisoner should have to go to Strasbourg to establish his right to see a lawyer or stop wrongful interference with his correspondence if he is in one of Her Majesty's prisons. Why should a mental patient have to go to Strasbourg in regard to his illegal detention? Why should a newspaper have to go there about an article truly inconvenient to the Government and suppressed? Why should a suspect subjected to inhuman treatment have to do so? Why should a prisoner who is subject to inhuman and degrading treatment have to go there? Why should a homosexual who is subject to discriminatory treatment have to do so? Why should a foreign husband banned from joining his wife in this country have to go there? Why should a juvenile subjected to degrading punishment have to do so? Why should a long-term prisoner kept incarcerated for years on the say-so of a junior Minister have to go there?

I ask the noble Lord also: why should at least 20 other of our fellow citizens have been forced successfully to seek justice in serious matters of principle in Strasbourg rather than here in London? Why has all that been necessary? Why have at least 80 laws and regulations been either repealed or amended as a result of these long journeys to Strasbourg? No doubt the noble Lord will give his answer in due course.

Do the Government believe that our judges alone in Europe are not to be trusted to interpret and uphold the provisions of the convention? Faced with the ever-increasing misuse of power by public bodies and in the absence of incorporation the judges have adapted the common law by a process of judicial review of administrative actions. So on a very limited front they have upheld their historic role of standing between the state and the citizen. For years, in the Judicial Committee of the Privy Council, the judges have been interpreting bills of rights incorporated in Commonwealth constitutions, modelled in almost every case on the European convention itself.

If it is not the unfitness of the judiciary, is it in reality the fear of any independent curb upon executive power? That is a fear so clearly evidenced by Whitehall's distaste for the doctrine of judicial review. Hitherto the Labour Party has wrapped up its reluctance with the populist cry of judicial prejudice and conservatism. However, the views expressed recently by the noble Baroness, Lady Blackstone, and the noble Lord, Lord Irvine of Lairg – I am happy to see the noble Lord in his place – give one hope that the noble Lord, Lord Mishcon, may have seen the light himself and will tell us later in the debate of his party's conversion to the policies of Charter 88 and the Institute for Public Policy Research.

Only on these Benches has the clear principle been consistently spelt out and advanced that, ultimately, protection of human rights and freedoms can only be guaranteed by a tribunal which is wholly independent of the Executive and is free to interpret and to apply the law set out in the convention.

Therefore in the end I am not embarrassed to say that that must be a matter for the lawyers. It is the independence, the training and the selection of the judges which will ensure the effectiveness of such a tribunal and the achievement of a Britain which is truly at ease with itself. . .

HL Deb., 5 December 1990, cols. 185f.

87 DEBATE ON THE HUMAN RIGHTS BILLS, 1994–6

RB NOTE: Lord (Anthony) Lester QC presented two Human Rights Bills between 1994–96, both of which sought to incorporate the ECHR into UK law. The texts of the two Bills are set out earlier in this book: Doc. 39E contains the Human Rights Bill 1994, Doc. 39F the Human Rights Bill 1996.

(A) ON THE HUMAN RIGHTS BILL 1994

Lord Lester of Herne Hill: The purpose of the Bill is to incorporate the rights declared by the European Convention on Human Rights and by the First Protocol to the Convention into the law of the land. The Bill authorises British courts to provide speedy and effective remedies to the victims of breaches by the public authorities of the United Kingdom. It gives practical effect to the European principle of subsidiarity and to the domestic remedies rule. That is what was intended by the makers of the convention. It requires judgments to be made locally by our own courts before recourse may be had internationally to the hugely overburdened European Commission on Human Rights and European Court of Human Rights. . .

The convention is the jewel in the crown of the Council of Europe. It

792 THE HOUSE OF LORDS

reflects universal human rights and freedoms, as well as duties and responsibilities. It owes much to British legal drafting and much to the philosophy and values of British thinkers of the past three centuries – ideas and values bequeathed to us by Edward Coke, John Locke, John Milton, William Blackstone, Tom Paine and John Stuart Mill as part of our precious heritage. The convention's makers also drew upon the English common law tradition, including the ancient writ of habeas corpus, and the great British constitutional charters which are our birthright: the Great Charter (the Magna Carta), the Petition of Rights, the English Bill of Rights, the Scottish Claim of Right and the Act of Settlement.

The convention has been ratified by 30 European states. By this summer all but two of the 30 states – the United Kingdom and Ireland – will have incorporated convention rights directly into their national legal systems. Sweden has done so recently and Norway is doing so. All other contracting states, including Ireland, also have constitutional Bills of Rights defining state power and protecting the individual citizen against the tyranny of majorities and the misuse of government power by public officials.

Even though it is not part of our law, the convention is well known in this country as an important means of protecting civil rights and liberties against the misuse of the powers of public authorities of the state. That is because of the many well-publicised and significant cases in which the United Kingdom has been found by the European Commission and Court of Human Rights to have breached the convention. In the absence of effective domestic remedies, there have been more findings of serious and significant breaches of the convention by the UK than by any other contracting state.

The relevant convention provisions are contained in the first schedule to the Bill. I shall not attempt to summarise them. The UK was the first state to ratify the convention on 8th March 1951. The convention came into force on 3rd September 1953. Since January 1966, successive governments have permitted alleged victims to have recourse against the UK to the European Commission and Court of Human Rights.

The Cabinet papers which I have read show that in 1950 Lord Chancellor Jowitt regarded it as axiomatic that the Attlee Government would have to introduce a measure to incorporate the convention's rights into domestic law as a necessary consequence of ratification. However, for the past 44 years since ratification successive governments have refused to do so, compelling our fellow citizens to take the long and costly road to Strasbourg instead of obtaining speedy and effective redress from British courts. Successive governments have refused to have their considerable powers limited by law or judicially reviewed against the standards of the convention.

Again and again, the European Commission on Human Rights and the European Court of Human Rights have had to deal with UK cases because of the absence of effective British remedies. Britain's dirty linen has been washed slowly, expensively and inefficiently in Strasbourg, much of the fabric still stained afterwards or cleaned far too late to be of value to the customer. Meanwhile, British judges are unable sufficiently to help at home because they have no parliamentary mandate to do so. Failure to incorporate also means that we lack a coherent legislative framework to guide our courts when deciding cases involving human rights questions, where choices have to be made between competing human rights and between individual claims and the interests of the community as a whole.

In November 1968, in a lecture given to a Fabian Society audience, I first called for the incorporation of the convention into UK law so that the people of this country, like the citizens of the other states parties, could obtain speedy and effective remedies before our own courts. That was then regarded as rank heresy by many supporters of the Labour Party, just as it has remained an anathema to successive Conservative administrations.

In 1972, a Conservative Government persuaded Parliament, upon our joining the European Community, to incorporate Community law into UK law. As noble Lords know, Community law takes priority over inconsistent national legislation and is directly effective in our courts. Community law also confers rights on individuals which national courts must protect. Where Community law is directly effective, our courts are commanded by Section 2 of the European Communities Act 1972 to interpret all existing and future UK legislation in conformity with Community law, where necessary displacing national legislation to give effect to Community rights and duties.

The present Bill seeks to give similar effect to European Convention law as the 1972 Act gave to European Community law. Parliament retains its sovereign power to repeal or to amend the Bill; but, unless and until it does so in plain terms, British courts are directed to interpret existing and future legislation so as to comply with convention law, just as they now do in giving effect to Community law.

I shall revert briefly to the history. In June 1976 the then Home Secretary, my noble friend Lord Jenkins of Hillhead, published a discussion document on legislation on human rights, with particular reference to the European Convention, summarising and analysing the relevant issues fairly and in depth. Later that year, Lord Wade introduced the second of his Bill of Rights Bills. It was referred to a Select Committee chaired by the noble Lord, Lord Allen of Abbeydale. The Select Committee took evidence from many quarters. One of the most eminent Conservative supporters of the Bill was the noble and learned Lord, Lord Hailsham of Saint Marylebone, who stated that, as part of,

> 'a radical overhaul of our constitutional arrangements, a Bill of Rights entrenching the European Convention is a modest, but desirable, addition to the armament of liberty against populist or bureaucratic intrusion and oppression'.

I respectfully agree.

Meanwhile, in November 1977, the Standing Advisory Commission on Human Rights in Northern Ireland published a report, to which I was privileged to contribute as a special adviser, strongly recommending incorporation of the convention. That was also the view of the Northern Ireland Constitutional Convention, chaired by the noble and learned Lord, Lord Lowry, which reported in November 1975, and is the prevailing view among both traditions, Republican and Unionist, in Northern Ireland.

In May 1978, the Select Committee of this House reported that it was in favour of the Bill, although its chairman, the noble Lord, Lord Allen of Abbeydale, was in the dissenting minority. Lord Wade's Bill was duly passed by this House but was defeated in another place in December 1979. In November 1980 the indefatigable Lord Wade made a third attempt. Once more his Bill was passed by this House and once more it was defeated in another place. A yet further attempt was made almost nine years ago – the last attempt – when Lord Broxbourne, with the support of the noble and learned Lord, Lord Scarman, introduced a Human Rights and Fundamental Freedoms Bill which was passed by this House in April 1986 [*RB NOTE: see Doc. 39(C)*], but after receiving a Second Reading in another place, on the initiative of the distinguished Conservative Member of Parliament, Sir Edward Gardiner, QC, the Bill progressed no further.

In passing these Bills, this House has been in close harmony with the popular will and informed opinion. Independent polls show that incorporation has the support of most of our fellow citizens. The early judicial supporters of incorporation, led by the noble and learned Lord, Lord Scarman, included two former Lord Chancellors, Lord Gardiner and the noble and learned Lord, Lord Hailsham. They have been joined – I hope he will not mind my taking his name in advance or in vain – by the Lord Chief Justice, the noble and learned Lord, Lord Taylor of Gosforth, the Master of the Rolls, Sir Thomas Bingham, and several Law Lords. The Bar Council and the Law Society also now favour incorporation. So does Justice, under the distinguished chairmanship of the noble Lord, Lord Alexander of Weedon, and a former Home Secretary, Sir Leon Brittan.

The Liberal Party was the first political party to advocate incorporation. For some 40 years the Labour Party, as I have said, was implacably hostile. But there has been a sea-change in its attitude. It now makes common cause with Liberal Democrats in supporting incorporation. Indeed, all of the Opposition parties, including the Ulster Unionists, are now in favour of making the convention directly enforceable in our courts.

In the absence of incorporation, our courts have done their best to give effect to the convention. They have treated it as persuasive where the common law is uncertain or incomplete or where statute law is ambiguous. Whether sitting in the Judicial Committee of the Privy Council and interpreting the Bills of Rights of Commonwealth constitutions or interpreting and applying European Community law, our judges have shown themselves as well equipped, in my opinion, as any courts anywhere in the world to use convention law in a wise and enlightened way.

But unless and until Parliament gives them a clear legislative mandate, there are limits to what our courts can do. Crucially, they cannot provide effective redress in cases involving the misuse of public powers in breach of convention rights; and our exceptionally able judges cannot make a full and powerful British judicial contribution to the progressive development of European legal principles in the human rights field. So we unnecessarily add to the excessive burdens of the European Commission and Court of Human Rights and weaken the potential influence of our own legal system right across Europe.

Four years ago, in the *Brind* case [RB NOTE: *see Doc. 28*], which sought unsuccessfully to challenge the Government's ban on the direct broadcasting of statements made by Sinn Fein and its supporters, the Law Lords rejected the judicial incorporation of the convention to review the scope and operation of Ministers' powers. They decided that, if they were to interpret Ministers' very broad statutory powers – in that case to censor broadcasting – as being limited by or subject to the convention, they would be usurping the functions of Parliament by incorporating the convention through the back-door. So legislative incorporation is plainly necessary.

The Government have recently accepted – I refer to the *Official Report*. House of Lords for 7th December 1994, col. *WA 84* – that Ministers and civil servants must comply with the convention in discharging their public functions. But the Government have not accepted that Her Majesty's judges in discharging their public functions have a similar duty to comply with the convention – *Official Report*, House of Lords, 9th January 1995, col. *WA 1*. Unless and until Parliament makes the convention part of our law, the duties of public authorities under the convention are not legally enforceable. They give rise to no legal remedy in our courts. The present Bill is designed to fill that major and significant gap.

Another consequence of the failure to incorporate the convention is that there is no constitutional citizen's charter prescribing core rights, freedoms and duties for everyone within the jurisdiction of the UK on the basis of equal citizenship. This Bill prescribes a binding code to strengthen the unity of our somewhat disunited kingdom. It encourages national unity by prescribing core standards which a future Scottish Parliament, or Welsh Assembly, or Northern Irish governing body, or English regional or local authority, like central government departments, will have to respect.

The statutory code enshrining the convention encourages everyone, everywhere within the UK, to cherish the positive value of being a British citizen. The code also gives guidance to Ministers and civil servants, to Parliament and the courts, and to ordinary men, women and young people. In place of ethical aimlessness and excessive bureaucratic discretionary powers, it encourages a culture of ordered liberty under the rule of law.

I shall not detain the House with a detailed account of the Bill's provisions as they are described in the explanatory memorandum. However, I will, if I may, draw attention to a few salient points. Clause 1(1) makes section 1 of the convention and the first protocol part of the law of the United Kingdom and ensures that they will be given full legal effect. I have confined the Bill to incorporation of the convention, together with the protocols so far ratified by the UK, as there is a consensus in the three main political parties that the rights set out in the schedule to the Bill should continue to be enjoyed by everyone within our jurisdiction. I am well aware that there are additional rights in the International Covenant on Civil and Political Rights which the UK is also bound to implement effectively in domestic law. That is a matter which requires further consideration once the present Bill is enacted.

Clause 1(2) has the effect of abrogating any existing rule of law in so far as it is inconsistent with the convention. Clause 1(3) prevents any Act of

Parliament or statutory instrument from being enforced or from being relied upon in any way in any legal proceedings to the extent that it is inconsistent with convention law. It is similar in its legal effect to Section 2(4) of the European Communities Act 1972, in that it requires our courts to interpret and apply existing and future legislation in accordance with European law. However, although Parliament cannot effectively legislate in contravention of Community law, that is not the case with the provisions being incorporated into this Bill. If it is enacted, it will remain open to a future Parliament to alter the position by clear and explicit amending legislation. In the absence of such legislation – which might risk being declared by the European Court to breach the convention – the task of our courts under Clause 1(3) would be to eliminate any mismatch between our statute law and European convention law.

Clause 1(4) provides that judicial interpretation of the convention shall follow the precedents set by the European court. Our courts will not have to start from a completely fresh standpoint in construing the convention and determining the extent of its rights and obligations but will follow Strasbourg case law.

Like Lord Broxbourne's Bill, Clause 4 creates a right of action as breach of statutory duty for violation of the incorporated convention rights in the performance of public functions. It does not create a direct right of action against persons acting in a private capacity, because that is not the object of the convention. The Bill creates what is in essence a constitutional tort. However, the incorporated convention would, as at present, continue to influence our courts' interpretation of private law as well as of public law; for example, the contours of defamation law or the protection of personal privacy.

In other common law jurisdictions, including Canada, India, the United States and Ireland, it is well established that compensation is payable for some breaches of constitutionally guaranteed human rights and freedoms. The Judicial Committee of the Privy Council has held that the same is true of breaches of Commonwealth and Caribbean constitutions.

As with any other statutory duty, the circumstances in which a breach gives rise to a claim for compensation will have to be determined on a case-by-case basis. The cases in which compensation is recoverable for breach of the convention are mainly well recognised categories of our existing law: cases not only of misfeasance in public office, but also trespasses by public officers involving assault and battery, false arrest, false imprisonment, malicious prosecution and wrongful interferences with the right to property. All those wrongs are actionable in our own courts now.

There may be other cases in which our courts will fashion appropriate remedies for the constitutional tort of breaching the convention, depending upon the nature and circumstances of the particular breach. They will have to do so, not least because of the need to secure effective domestic remedies in accordance with Article 13 of the convention.

The noble and learned Lord, Lord Woolf, who unfortunately cannot be present tonight but who has, I believe, authorised the noble and learned Lord, Lord Taylor of Gosforth, to explain his position, has kindly informed me of his doubts about the particular terms in which Clause 4 is drafted. I well understand his concerns about its potentially broad reach. I suggest that that is a matter which will merit careful scrutiny during the Committee stage so as to ensure that our courts are able to give effective domestic remedies, including compensation where appropriate, for breaches of convention rights.

Neither the European Convention nor the Bill is a panacea. As the eminent judge, Learned Hand, reminded his fellow Americans a half century ago:

> 'Liberty lies in the hearts of men and women; when it dies there, no constitution, no law, no court can save it. While it lies there, it needs no constitution, no law, no court to save it'.

But a constitutional guarantee surely acts as a rallying point and a bulwark for all who cherish freedom. It strengthens the sinews of democracy and promotes good governance. It provides orderly legal redress for infringements of civil rights and liberties, and it contributes to public education in winning hearts and minds. The power of government needs to be matched by the power of the law if the individual is to be secure. The law of the British constitution should encourage the spirit of liberty, and our courts should give redress where basic civil rights and freedoms are infringed. For those reasons, I commend the Bill to your Lordships.

Lord Taylor of Gosforth: My Lords, I shall not detain the House long. The Bill before us is short, and I venture to suggest that our speeches should reflect that. Nevertheless, it is of great importance. My noble friend, Lord Lester, has already outlined the main arguments in favour of the Bill, and I should like to endorse the points he has made. I should add that, although I cannot comment for the judiciary as a whole, I can assure the House that what follows has the strong support of the Master of the Rolls, Sir Thomas Bingham, and of my noble and learned friend, Lord Woolf, who, as has been mentioned, regrets that he is unable to be present during the debate.

We have a proud tradition of freedom in this country, a freedom which has largely derived from the strength and vigour of the common law. But, strong as that tradition is, I do not think that we may safely rely on it for all purposes in the modern world. Nor have successive Governments thought so.

We ratified the European Convention that forms the schedule to the Bill as long ago as 1950. We have allowed our citizens to enforce their rights under it through the European Court of Human Rights since 1966. The convention is therefore as much a feature of our constitution as life peerages or the holding of a referendum.

We are bound to give effect to decisions of the European court, and if our law does not accord with it we are bound by treaty to change our law. Despite our tradition of freedom, there have been many instances in which our law has had to be changed. One field in which that has occurred a number of times concerns the rights of prisoners, and especially the procedures regarding life prisoners.

It is not helpful to debate our record of compliance with the convention or to compare it with that of other signatories. The question is: why should any of those litigants who have exercised their right of petition in order to enforce their fundamental human rights have been compelled to go all the way to Strasbourg – distant not only in space but more importantly in time – to obtain a remedy which could have been granted by a domestic court in the United Kingdom?

The answer usually put forward in response is that to allow United Kingdom courts to apply the convention directly would involve the judiciary in political issues from which they are supposedly sheltered at present and would displace the supremacy of Parliament. I do not believe that those arguments withstand serious scrutiny.

Judges have, with the growth of judicial review, been increasingly required to consider issues having a political dimension. For example – and it is only one example – they have had to review the conduct of Ministers. They have on occasion struck down decisions of Ministers. That has not led to any collapse of confidence in the political impartiality or independence of the judges. Rather the reverse.

As to the supremacy of Parliament, in the field of European Community Law the *Factortame* case is an example of our own judges having to give an EC directive precedence over an Act of Parliament, the very thing which opponents of the Bill say would make the constitutional roof fall in.

In fact it is not the proposed change but the present situation which is worrying from a constitutional viewpoint. At present, the aggrieved citizen is advised that his or her fundamental rights under the convention have been infringed. He or she cannot obtain any immediate remedy but must pursue a hopeless application through all the United Kingdom courts, including your Lordships' House. At the end of this procedure, the case can be argued in Strasbourg (with all the delay which that involves). The European Court eventually decides that the Government are in breach of their obligations, with the attendant criticism and embarrassment to which I have already referred. Finally, many years after the actions complained of, the law has to be altered by Parliament. Is that any way to offer protection for freedoms which have existed under our constitution for nigh on half a century? All it does is to put off what the Government see as the evil day when we have to come into line with our treaty obligations. As I have said before, and I repeat it, it is as though when we signed the treaty we were saying, 'God, make us good, but not yet'. . .

The Lord Bishop of Southwark: The rights of the individual and the responsibility of nation states to maintain those rights are matters to which the Christian community is deeply committed. I therefore welcome the possibility that the European Convention for the Protection of Human Rights and Fundamental Freedoms should be incorporated into the domestic legal system of this nation.

Whereas we hear much said about the encroachment of European legislation and bureaucracy upon our lives, what we are talking about in this instance is something completely different. Our Government played a key role in drafting the convention that we now consider. For 40 years we have adhered to it. Countless numbers of ordinary people have over those years sought redress through its provisions for situations in which they have been the victims of injustice. In short, we have benefited as a nation from that convention.

Yet to this present time those remedies have had to be sought outside the United Kingdom. To incorporate the European convention into British law would make the entire process more transparent and much quicker. It would not undermine rights or freedoms, but would enhance them. That theme was touched upon by the most reverend Primate the Archbishop of Canterbury in the speech which he made to the Council of Europe in 1993. In recognising the importance of the convention and expressing his admiration for its achievements, he concluded by saying:

'The arguments for incorporation of the Convention into British law grow more pressing'.

In the two years that have passed since he made that speech, the pressure has not grown less.

There is also a dimension to this in which I have a more personal interest. There would be real additional advantages to the incorporation of the convention with respect to the future of Northern Ireland. As part of the domestic legislation of the Province, it would provide additional safeguards for the people so that justice is both done and seen to be done in that particularly difficult context. The incorporation of the European convention into domestic legislation in both Britain and Ireland was, as we heard, urged in the 1988 report, *Human Rights and Responsibilities in Britain and Ireland*, a project for which the most reverend Primate the Archbishop of York served as president, and the noble Lord, Lord Lester, and the current President of the Republic of Ireland, Mary Robinson, served as consultants.

We are already bound by the provisions of this convention. We already have the opportunity to have recourse to the remedies for which it provides. What we should be supporting here is the opportunity to make the citizens of this nation more aware of their rights and providing them with more speedy and accessible opportunities to right wrongs. Though I cannot claim any expertise in the legal and constitutional issues that are necessarily bound up in our consideration of the legislation before us, I believe that fundamentally we have nothing to fear from the proposal but much to gain...

Lord Browne-Wilkinson: My Lords, I join the noble and learned Lord the Lord Chief Justice and the right reverend Prelate the Bishop of Southwark in welcoming the presentation of the Bill. My noble and learned friends Lord Lester and the Lord Chief Justice have illustrated the extraordinary anomalies from which we now suffer. We have a treaty obligation, under Article 13 of which this country and this Government are bound to afford to everyone whose rights and freedoms are set forth in the Convention and which are violated, an effective remedy before a national authority. I do not know, but at first reading it appears that the failure to incorporate and provide an effective remedy before the national authority of the member state – in this case the United Kingdom – is itself in conflict with the treaty obligation. However that may be, this country has an honourable record in complying with decisions of the European Court of Human Rights. Retro-spectively it complies.

One asks oneself: how did we get to a position where this country – which ... prides itself on its freedoms going back over the centuries, it being in the forefront of democratic freedom; its principles of freedom being the very basis on which much of the convention was based in drafting; being one of the progenitors of the convention itself – is found more often to be in breach of that convention than any other member state? It is an astonishing position. I am tempted to call it an *Alice in Wonderland* position. We are in breach of the international obligation. All our governments for the past 40 years have accepted this obligation. They have accepted the duty to observe these human rights; and yet we do not allow our own courts to do that very thing themselves. That must be a major reason why we are so constantly and so publicly disgraced – I am afraid I use the word 'disgraced' with delibera-tion. That this country with its history should be found so repeatedly in breach of its international obligations to provide freedoms is very shock-ing.

The objection ... always comes down at the end of the day to sovereignty – the supremacy of Parliament. I am not one to disregard that factor. I do not share it, but I believe it is a very real consideration, and that to confer on the court the right to strike down the statute – which is effectively what this Bill will propose – is a very major constitutional step indeed. I fully recognise that different views can be held about it. I just hope that the Bill does not die the death in any form on that ground alone.

I hope not to be too technical – this looks too much like a lawyer's party anyway. The main reasons why this country has been held in breach of the convention is not that Parliament has specifically enacted any measure which is in breach of the convention. It is not because, save on one or two occasions, the common law of this country has been found to be in breach. It is for the very reason that ... our traditional English freedoms are freedoms, not rights; and like any other common law freedoms they are subject to abridgement and curtailment by Act of Parliament. That is where we have been found to be at fault – not in our general institutions but by the operation of Acts of Parliament. It is not in the substantive provisions of the Acts which this House and the other place have passed that we have been found wanting. We have been found wanting by accident.

It is an essential feature of any legislation in the modern state that it is bound to confer discretionary powers on the Executive to operate the powers that are conferred by Parliament. Ministers are given power to make such regulations as they may think fit to achieve this result or that. It is the operation under those powers that has given rise to most of our infringe-ments. . .

I believe that if people walking through the Lobbies in this place or in the other House were asked, as they voted on the usual Act which contains 123 discretionary powers conferred on the Minister to make regulations and do all the other things: 'Have you voted to allow the Minister to infringe the European Convention on Human Rights?', they would say, 'Of course not. We have given powers to act in accordance with law and in accordance with what this country has undertaken to do'. I only suggest this. But I hope that this Bill does not disappear, because it seeks, in typically wholehearted fashion, to go the whole way and enable the courts to strike down legislation completely. I hope that if, as seems possible, a 'whole hog' Bill is not attractive to a majority in the other place (if not here), consideration will be given by everybody concerned to putting right a ludicrous Mad Hatter's tea party position – and in this way: simply by providing in this Bill that the courts shall, to the extent possible, construe the Acts of Parliament so as to take effect on the basis that they are not intended to confer powers designed to infringe the convention. That is what the Nordic countries have done for many, many years and they have complied. That is what everybody else who has not had incorporated rights has done, and they have complied. . .

I have on occasion had to reach conclusions in cases which I knew to be contrary to the convention because I was not able to do otherwise. Why cannot we enable our courts to administer what the European Court of Human Rights does many months, many years, many hundreds of thousands of pounds later? Why should the courts here not give effect to what is undoubtedly the implied intention of Parliament, stopping short if necessary of declaring invalid any Act of Parliament? That brings about a position of true constitutional reform. I am, I am afraid, at much greater length saying what the noble and learned Lord the Lord Chief Justice said in about three words; namely, what about the New Zealand approach? That approach does not override Parliament's right to say, 'We are going to contravene the convention'. The courts are simply being allowed to apply legislation in accordance with what I believe most people would understand to be everybody's intention; namely, not to breach the convention.

Finally, and very shortly, I make one further comment in the hope that it can be considered in Committee. I am anxious about matters of this kind coming up all over the judicial system. A point taken that legislation, or executive powers, are contrary to the European Convention could as well arise in the Puddletown magistrates' court as in the High Court. If any power of challenge of this kind is to take place, considerable care has to be given to where and when that matter shall be adjudicated. Much of the trouble that has occurred in Canada, whose Bill was far more sweeping than anything that was proposed here, has arisen from the fact that it arises in multifarious jurisdictions. But that is a matter for the Committee. I commend this Bill and hope that it produces a fruitful result, putting an end to the absurdity that currently exists. . .

Lord Williams of Mostyn: My Lords, on behalf of the Labour Party I give the Bill the warmest welcome in principle, subject of course to detailed scrutiny in Committee, as was mentioned by noble and learned Lords who spoke earlier.

If the Bill becomes part of our law, it will be a constitutional advance of great importance, on several bases. The first is a basis of deep principle – namely, that an individual's human rights are precisely that: attributes capable of being enforced by legal mechanisms which are not the mere bare consequence of state, governmental or sovereign donation. The right should have these characteristics: clarity, simplicity, ease of enforceability. The incorporation of the convention fulfils those criteria.

Secondly, – and this will be of increasing importance in the next few years – the full incorporation of the convention into domestic law will improve the quality of domestic legislation. It will improve the quality of judicial interpretation and performance. I profoundly agree … about the specific importance of the Bill in the context of Northern Ireland. On that point I have encountered no dissent from any part of the political spectrum.

Thirdly, the Bill will reduce the number of dismal occasions when the United Kingdom Government are found to be in breach of their obligations under the convention. It will allow those who are wrongly treated a more efficient, prompt and less expensive method of obtaining redress. The true analysis … leads one to this conclusion: that is an exercise of sovereignty, not a derogation from it. It is too well known to need further specification that the record of the United Kingdom Government in this field has been lamentable. They have been at the bottom of every single league table on every possible occasion.

What will incorporation mean in practice in terms of legislation? I hope that it would have made us in this House a good deal more careful and critical in the scrutiny that we gave to the Criminal Justice and Public Order Act 1994. For example, Section 81 allows a constable to stop and search any vehicle, driver or passenger and any pedestrian, and to make:

> 'any search he thinks fit whether or not he has any grounds for suspecting that the vehicle or person is carrying articles',

of a certain type.

That draconian power went through this House, I regret to say, late at night when there was very little attendance. There was virtually no dissent. The criminal offence is absolute. There is no defence of reasonable excuse. When this Bill becomes law it will be interesting to see how that power is capable of co-existence with Article 5(1) (c). Can the right to peaceable assembly and demonstration be wholly reconciled with Section 68 and the subsequent sections of that same Act?

I turn to Article 6, which states:

> 'In the determination of his civil rights and obligations or of any criminal charge against him everyone is entitled to a fair and public hearing within a reasonable time',

and I emphasise those last words. I endorse the frequent and recent criticisms of delay and expense – those Siamese twins – made by the noble and learned Lords, Lord Taylor of Gosforth and Lord Woolf, on many public occasions. I particularly question whether the situation of a dismissed employee, whose only capital is his labour, having to wait in excess of two-and-a-half years for a concluded hearing at an industrial tribunal, can be said to fulfil our obligation. If we do not incorporate the convention, what redress is there for such people? I do not regard that as an elitist proposition.

Article 8 states:

'Everyone has the right to respect for his private and family life'.

Where is the common law there? It is notorious that our law recognises no right to privacy as such. The common law is dumb. It is not effective. There is a right to confidentiality in limited cases – employment, commercial relationships, and matrimonial matters. The individual, however mean, lowly and insignificant, has no shield from the common law when his privacy is grossly interfered with and abused. If this Bill becomes law, the present Government would have to stop agonising and come to a conclusion about their final decided view on a distinct right of privacy, giving access to injunctive relief and damages.

Article 10 on freedom of expression has already been of great consequential effect, not least in the speeches in the Judicial Committee of this House in *Bookbinder* v. *Derbyshire*, where an encouragingly fresh view was taken about what proper restrictions on free press comment ought to be in this country. I echo, if I may, the tributes paid to the noble and learned Lord, Lord Scarman. I am sorry that he has not been present tonight, since he has been a lighthouse and a beacon to so many lawyers, students and practitioners over so many years.

We cannot simply say, 'We do it better than foreigners', because experience sometimes demonstrates the contrary. As a country, a society, a parliamentary democracy and a legal system, we should be able to be sufficiently confident in our own virtues to recognise that an established framework can be a benefit. If we know that the convention is part of our domestic law, we are able to frame our judicial conclusions, legislation and general approach to individual human rights in a different way.

There is no cause for this country to be faint-hearted. We have plenty of historic traditions which have life only if they develop. The questions that I have put forward have been quite limited because, as always, I am obedient to the commands of the Lords Chief Justice and I intend to be brief. These are just a few matters which will arise if the Bill becomes law. It will improve the quality of political life in this country. It will transform people's attitudes to rights and responsibilities. It will provide a useful corrective for an Executive – I do not restrict that remark to the present Government – which has had insufficient control over the past 35 years. The control which has been offered has been substantially provided by the judiciary and not by what has been an over-acquiescent Parliament.

I recognise that those preliminary considerations are few. There are many others that we shall have to deal with on future occasions. I think the fact of their existence demonstrates the value of the Bill, in respect of whose introduction I believe the noble Lord, Lord Lester, deserves our full gratitude.

Baroness Blatch: My Lords, the preservation and development of the rights and freedoms of the individual are central to effective and legitimate constitutional arrangements. This evening's debate has demonstrated the proper seriousness with which your Lordships address these matters, and the quality of this debate is testimony to that. I welcome this opportunity to set out the Government's policy on a Bill which raises issues of great importance.

It may be helpful for me at the outset to summarise the Government's position. It is in three parts. First, we consider that our present arrangements, both in principle and in practice, provide properly and effectively throughout the United Kingdom for the securing of rights and freedoms, including but not exclusively, those in the European Convention on Human Rights. Secondly, the claimed advantages of incorporating the Convention into our domestic law are, in our assessment, few and arguable. Thirdly, and by contrast, we believe that the disadvantages of incorporation would be considerable and fundamental. Notably, incorporation would strike at the constitutional principle of parliamentary supremacy. The areas of public policy covered by the general principles set out in the convention have traditionally, and rightly, been the province of Parliament rather than the courts.

Turning then to the principle of our present arrangements, the Government do not consider that it is properly the role of our legislature to purport to confer rights and freedoms, such as those in the European Convention, which are in fact already enjoyed by all members of society. It is central to our position, which is the same position as that taken by successive governments before us, that the rights and freedoms recognised in international instruments to which the United Kingdom is party, including those in the ECHR, are inherent in the United Kingdom's legal systems, and are protected by them and by Parliament, unless removed or restricted by statute.

Baroness Williams of Crosby: My Lords, I apologise to the noble Baroness for interrupting and I shall not do so again. If it is true that all the rights and liberties of individuals are adequately protected under the present British arrangements, why have so many cases which have gone to Strasbourg been decided against the views of the British courts?

Baroness Blatch: My Lords, I shall deal with cases that go to Strasbourg in a moment. What is afforded is that all the national laws of the country, together with the rights backed by the European Convention, exist and are available to all our citizens. What we are talking about and what the debate has been about – and it is interesting to me, after listening to all the contributions – is not whether the citizens enjoy the protection, it is about the mechanisms, the efficiency and effectiveness of using the system. I shall say to the House that I think that in terms of the mechanisms and with all the protections of the ECHR, the arrangements that we have in place and the protection of our national law, the citizens of this country are not in any way disadvantaged ...

It is entirely consistent with this position that the Government attach great importance to the convention and take most seriously the United Kingdom's obligations under it. As we have been reminded earlier in this debate, the United Kingdom played a leading role in drafting the convention. Created very much with the horrors of the defeated war time regimes in mind, it was intended to give binding effect to the guarantee of various rights in the United Nations Declaration of Human Rights which had been adopted in December 1948. We were among the first states to ratify the convention, as long ago as 1951; and, again, we were among the first major countries to subscribe, nearly 30 years ago, to the right of individual petition to the European Commission of Human Rights, and to accept the compulsory jurisdiction of the European Court of Human Rights.

Our present arrangements already provide for our commitments under the convention to be taken into proper account in our governmental, legislative and judicial systems. Our obligations under the convention are systematically and carefully taken into account by Ministers and officials in the formulation and application of government policy, and in the preparation of draft legislation.

As regards the courts, judgments of this House have made it clear that the United Kingdom's international human rights obligations are part of the legal context in which the judges consider themselves to operate. For example, the judgment in the case of *Salomon* v. *the Commissioners of Customs and Excise*, stated – if I may be permitted to quote from it:

> 'There is a prima facie presumption that Parliament does not intend to act in breach of international law, including therein specific treaty obligations; and if one of the meanings which can reasonably be ascribed to the legislation is consonant with the treaty obligations and another or others are not, the meaning which is consonant is to be preferred.'

Another test of the seriousness and importance which the Government attach to the convention is our record in remedying breaches of the convention where these occur. If I may, I shall address the contention that incorporation might further minimise such breaches more fully later in my remarks. Perhaps it may suffice for the moment for me to say that, in our view, non-incorporation is not the reason why the United Kingdom is from time to time found to be in breach of the convention. Instead, the answer to that lies partly in the broad and general provisions of the convention itself – which are inevitably subject to different and changing interpretations – and partly in the inevitability of flaws in any human contrivance. . .

If and where the United Kingdom is found to be in breach of the convention by the European Court of Human Rights and the Committee of Ministers of the Council of Europe, effective arrangements are in place for remedying the matter. Any necessary changes in the law or administrative practice are made as soon as possible. The United Kingdom's record in this respect is second to none: of the 89 cases that are currently on the books of the Council of Ministers as awaiting substantive resolution under Article 54, only three arise from the United Kingdom, of which two relate to judgments given as recently as October 1994.

I come now to the second element in the Government's position; that is, our assessment of arguments made for incorporation. We have to ask in what respects, if any, incorporation would enhance the enjoyment in the United Kingdom of the rights and freedoms provided for in the convention. Any answer to this must entail a degree of speculation. But one objective test is to compare the United Kingdom's performance with that of other states party to the convention which have incorporated it into their domestic law. Information is available on which to compare both the extent to which, in the first place, states are found in breach of the convention; and the extent to which, in the second place, when such breaches are found, the necessary remedial action is taken by the countries concerned. By both these measures, the United Kingdom's record is good, and better than that of many countries which have incorporated the convention into their domestic law.

I noted that the noble and learned Lord, Lord Taylor, rather chided me on the possibility that I might introduce comparative figures. But I do not believe that we can dismiss this matter lightly. This debate has centered very much on speed, effectiveness, efficiency and justice for those at the receiving end. Such comparisons are very important.

We repeatedly hear claims (and we have heard them again in this debate) that the United Kingdom has a poor record before the convention institutions. In fact, such claims are ill-founded. In considering the figures for findings of violation, account should be taken both of the relative population size of states which are party to the convention and the date of acceptance of the right of individual petition. In the case of the United Kingdom, that was many years earlier than numerous other countries, including France, Italy, Portugal and Switzerland. Taking these factors into account, the United Kingdom is well down the so-called 'league table' for breaches of the convention. We are 15th overall, below many countries which have incorporated the convention into their domestic law, including Switzerland, Italy, Austria, Belgium, the Netherlands, Portugal, France and Finland.

Comparative information on practice in taking action to remedy breaches of the convention tells a similar story. I noted earlier that the United Kingdom has an excellent record in this regard. Information provided by the European Commission of Human Rights shows that the majority of cases in which remedial action is outstanding arise from Italy, France, Belgium, Greece and the Netherlands. What all these countries have in common is that they have incorporated the convention.

Comparative information also casts doubt on the contention that non-incorporation places citizens at a real disadvantage in seeking to remedy possible breaches of the convention. It is far from certain that being able to litigate the convention in our courts would lead to a reduction in the number of cases, or to more rapid disposal and resolution of cases overall.

Although alleged violations of the convention may be considered in the domestic courts of countries where it forms a part of the law, what happens is that a large number of those cases still find their way to the European Commission and Court of Human Rights, where they must be examined afresh. For example, in 1994 62 allegations of violation were referred to the Austrian Government; 723 allegations to the Turkish Government; 118 allegations to the French Government, and 356 allegations to the Italian Government. Those are all countries which have already incorporated the ECHR. During the same period 46 such allegations – only 46 – were referred to the United Kingdom. That would suggest that incorporation is hardly a way of reducing or speeding up the handling of cases.

Finally, as regards perceived merits, the delay in securing a decision or judgment under the convention, to which advocates of incorporation also sometimes refer, affects all applicants, irrespective of whether the countries concerned have or have not incorporated the convention. These delays are a matter of concern and one on which we, with other states party to the convention, have acted. Over recent years the United Kingdom has consistently played a leading role in the discussions in the Council of Europe which have resulted in various reforms of the ECHR procedures aimed at the speedier conduct of business. That work culminated most recently in Protocol 11 to the convention which provides, among other things for the present, part-time Commission and Court to be replaced by a single permanent court. The United Kingdom signed Protocol 11 as soon as it was available for signature. That was last May. We ratified the protocol last month, making us the fourth of the 33 states party to the convention to do so.

I come now to the disadvantages of incorporation which, as I indicated, the Government find serious and conclusive. As I have already said – and I make no apology for repeating – incorporation would strike at the long-held principle of parliamentary sovereignty which lies at the heart of our system of parliamentary democracy. The areas of public policy covered by the general principles set out in the convention have traditionally, and rightly, been the province of Parliament rather than the courts. Under our constitutional arrangements, it is for Parliament to enact detailed legislation on matters affecting the rights and liberties of the individual and to decide where the often difficult balance between competing public and individual interests is to be struck. In doing so, of course, it must have regard to the United Kingdom's obligations under the convention, as indeed it must in respect of all the United Kingdom's international obligations. Nevertheless, the final decision on such matters remains with Parliament. In our view they should continue to remain with Parliament.

That is a vital merit of our present arrangements. They provide that, if and when change is needed, often in areas of keen social and public interest, it is our democratically elected and accountable Parliament which decides how and when any such changes should be made. Among other things, that helps to ensure that change carries public support and understanding.

By contrast, to incorporate the convention into domestic law would transfer that final responsibility to the judiciary. United Kingdom judges would have to decide whether provisions approved in detail by Parliament, and clear in their meaning, offended against the general principles of the convention and, if so, whether effectively the courts should strike down that legislation. The question here is whether it is desirable or appropriate for these matters to rest with judges who are not directly accountable to the people rather than with democratically elected Members of Parliament. The Government's view is that the judges are not the right and appropriate people to be left with that power.

The Government also consider that incorporation would entail serious practical problems. In particular, incorporation would, in our view, have an adverse impact on the work of our courts. We could reasonably expect that, in innumerable challenges to action by public authorities, the convention would be invoked. Each complaint reaching the courts would have to be tried by reference to the principles of the convention but without the benefit of the initial screening process carried out by the Commission which currently sifts out as unfounded a very large number of cases – in excess of 80 per cent.

Further, if incorporation took the form the noble Lord's Bill proposes, the potential for allegations of 'breach of statutory duty' – a key provision in the Bill – would be enormous: every time someone disagreed with, say, a decision by an immigration officer or social worker, proceedings for breach of statutory duty under the Bill could be instituted. These various factors could lead to a great deal of complicated and time-consuming litigation in the courts, with an inevitable effect on the conduct of other court business and without any real and corresponding improvement to human rights in practice.

The noble Lord, Lord Lester, in a very eloquent introduction to the Bill which I enjoyed, said that the courts can already strike down provisions of United Kingdom primary legislation if they conflict with European Community law. I accept that the European Court of Justice and our domestic courts can suspend the operation of UK primary legislation where it conflicts with European Community law. There is no disagreement with us there. Such cases have, however, been very rare indeed. The nature of the international obligations which the UK assumed on joining the European Community on the one hand, and by ratifying the European Convention on Human Rights on the other, are nevertheless different. Our obligations under European Community law tend to be narrow and well defined while those under the ECHR are broad and general in nature. In joining the European Community, the United Kingdom was obliged to accept that Community law could have the effect of suspending any national law with which it conflicted. We could not have joined without accepting that. In the case of the ECHR, however, we are under no such obligation.

The convention recognises that contracting states have a choice as to whether or not to incorporate the convention in domestic law and as to how best to implement the Court decisions. If the European Court of Human Rights decides that our law does not satisfy the requirements of the convention in a particular case, it is for Parliament to decide how our domestic law should be amended. Until it is amended, it remains in force.

I submit that it is a far more satisfactory state of affairs than that proposed under Clause 1(3) of the Bill, which would give every judge and every magistrate in the country power to decide not to enforce the law of the land if he or she, by their own judgment, formed the view that any person would thereby be deprived of any of the rights and freedoms set out in the convention. That really would represent a shift of power from the sovereignty of Parliament to the judiciary.

The noble and learned Lord, Lord Taylor, mentioned that the extension of judicial review had weakened the case against incorporation. With great respect to the noble and learned Lord, that disregards the fundamental difference between judicial review and incorporation. In considering applications for judicial review, for example, the court is not concerned with the merits of a particular decision or a particular policy. It is concerned only to ensure that the appropriate procedures were followed in reaching that decision and that the decision was within the powers given by Parliament to the public body concerned. Incorporation, as proposed in the Bill, would require the courts to address the merits of decisions made by Parliament on matters of public policy and set down in detailed legislation. It would require the courts to adopt a much wider role very different from their current function in cases of judicial review ...

It has been my aim to indicate why we consider that incorporation is not necessary to secure the rights and freedoms protected under the European Convention on Human Rights in our country. Claims that incorporation would enhance enjoyment of those rights and freedoms are arguable and are certainly not supported by the comparative performance of countries which have incorporated the convention. There are substantial objections to incorporation both of principle and practice. The fact is that whether or not the convention has been incorporated into the domestic law of a country bears no relationship to how well that country affords legal protection for its people.

The drawbacks of incorporation are not minor matters but involve major changes to existing constitutional arrangements which have developed in this country over many hundreds of years. The Government remain unconvinced that the Bill would mark an advance in the protection of human rights in the United Kingdom sufficient to justify such a major departure from our current constitutional arrangements. Over a very long time the United Kingdom has developed a careful network of arrangements to ensure good government and fairness, including parliamentary sovereignty and full participation of both our Houses, ministerial accountability and judicial review.

To elevate the convention to the status of the primary source of good government and fairness would run the risk of upsetting the balance of arrangements for doubtful advantage, if any. This is a Private Member's Bill and the Government, therefore, would not propose to vote against it. However, the Government consider that incorporation is undesirable and unnecessary both in principle and in practice and for those reasons would not be able to support this Bill.

HL Deb, 25 January 1995, cols. 1136f.

(B) ON THE HUMAN RIGHTS BILL 1996

Lord Lester of Herne Hill: ... Successive Conservative governments over the past 18 years have refused to introduce a citizen's charter of constitutional rights and freedoms, and unfortunately I have no reason to suppose that the Minister will be any more sympathetic to my new Bill than the

Government were to the many previous attempts by noble Lords of Conservative and other political persuasions in this House, including, for example, the noble Lord, Lord Broxbourne.

However, I dare to hope that a new government soon to be elected, with the right honourable Tony Blair as Prime Minister, will speedily introduce, and that the next Parliament will speedily enact, a measure to make the convention a part of our fundamental law, as an important first step towards the making of a modern British Bill of Rights. I am delighted to see the noble and learned Lord, Lord Archer of Sandwell, in his place and I look forward to hearing what he will say about that from the Labour Front Bench.

This debate gives the House an opportunity – almost on the eve of a general election crucially important to those of us in the Opposition parties who seek to renew our democratic system of government – to discuss for the first time a measure modelled on the New Zealand Bill of Rights Act 1990. Previous versions, both mine and others, have been modelled more upon the European Communities Act and the Canadian Charter of Rights. I have chosen the New Zealand model because of the powerfully persuasive advice given during the debates two years ago, notably from the Cross-Benches, by some of our most senior and eminent judges. I believe the present version to have the best prospect of winning widespread cross-party, Cross-Bench and senior judicial approval, without challenging the English doctrine of parliamentary sovereignty and without significantly diluting the practical value of incorporation. . .

Unlike the previous version, the present Bill does not require or empower the courts to strike down provisions of Acts of Parliament which are plainly in conflict with the human rights and fundamental freedoms guaranteed by the convention. Instead, Clause 1(4), like Section 6 of the New Zealand Act, provides that, whenever an enactment can be given a meaning that is consistent with convention rights, that meaning shall be preferred to any other meaning.

I have taken another leaf out of the New Zealand statute book. Clause 3 requires Ministers, when introducing Bills into Parliament, to explain why a provision is, or appears to be, inconsistent with convention rights. This will enable Parliament to be properly informed so that it can act effectively as constitutional watchdog in enacting and scrutinising primary legislation. It will also mean that, in the absence of a Minister's notification, the courts will be able safely to assume that Parliament did not intend to repeal or amend convention rights by implication. In other words, by this device both Parliament and the judiciary will be much better informed and individual rights and freedoms will be protected against any implied repeal. In practice it will achieve what the noble and learned Lord, Lord Taylor of Gosforth, suggested during the Second Reading debate two years ago – namely, that Parliament could expressly but not impliedly override the provisions of the convention if an exceptional need arose.

I can think of few cases, during the past 30 years since the United Kingdom accepted the jurisdiction of the European Court of Human Rights in individual cases, in which a breach of the convention has been found to have occurred because of a patently inconsistent provision in an Act of Parliament. Breaches have usually arisen either from the exercise of administrative discretion under broad statutory powers – for example, in preventing prisoners from corresponding with Members of Parliament – or from the manner in which the courts develop the common law – for example, by giving too little weight to freedom of speech in the *Thalidomide* or *Harman* or, if the noble and learned Lord, Lord Donaldson, will forgive me, the *Spycatcher* cases.

I would hope and expect that the circumstances in which a government wished to introduce primary legislation inconsistent with convention rights would be rare, and that the requirement of having to make the position clear to Parliament would deter Ministers from doing so. However, as I have explained, the Bill does not attempt to fetter the rights of a future Parliament to legislate inconsistently with the convention, provided that the Government's intentions have been expressly made clear. In such exceptional cases – and only in such exceptional cases – the remedy for a breach of the convention by Parliament would, as at present, be by recourse to the European Court of Human Rights.

That means that European Convention law would to that extent have a weaker status in UK domestic law than does directly effective European Community law. I will be criticised by purists for having sold the past in that respect. I accept that that is not strictly logical as a matter of principle, especially as there are already cases in which our courts may be required by the European Communities Act 1972 to set aside provisions in Acts of Parliament which are inconsistent with Community law read with convention law. [*RB NOTE: On this point see Doc. 77.*] However, I do not believe that the effective legal protection given by the Bill will be seriously eroded by this pragmatic concession to political expediency.

If the courts were to interpret the present measure loosely, or if Parliament were habitually to enact legislation with the express intention of breaching convention rights, it would be necessary to legislate more strongly, so as to place our courts in the same position as courts in other Commonwealth countries when interpreting their written constitutional guarantees of human rights. However, I have confidence in the willingness and ability of our judiciary to make legislation of this kind effective. I pay tribute to the enlightened way in which the judiciary have done their best, in the absence of incorporating legislation, to give full faith and credit to the convention when interpreting and applying our written and unwritten laws. I would hope that Ministers, of whatever political colour, would feel greatly inhibited from having to certify to Parliament that proposed legislation would violate the minimum standards of the European human rights code.

Clause 1(2) of the Bill requires the courts to interpret the common law in accordance with convention rights. They already do so, most notably perhaps in the *Derbyshire County Council* case, where the Court of Appeal held that it would unnecessarily interfere with the right to free expression if government bodies were permitted to sue for libel on their governing reputation without proof of bad faith or special damage. The House of

Lords went further, holding that the common law matched the guarantee of free expression in Article 10 of the convention. [*RB NOTE: See also Docs 28 and 32 on the domestic status of the ECHR at the time of this debate.*]

The Bill will enable everyone to rely upon convention rights though the ordinary courts and tribunals. Clause 1(3) makes clear that it will apply to acts done by or for Ministers and to any person or body performing a public function, as distinct from persons acting in a private capacity.

Unlike my previous version, the Bill does not seek to create a general right to damages for breach of statutory duty. Clause 2 gives the courts the power to fashion remedies flexibly according to the justice of the case, including, where appropriate, the remedy of compensation.

Where a breach of the convention involves tortious conduct, the courts will be able to award common law damages. There will be cases where public officers and bodies, acting under cover of law, will breach the convention in circumstances amounting to a government tort, an extension of the existing tort of misfeasance in public office. Suppose, for example, that the police were to misuse statutory powers to carry out electronic surveillance of a newspaper or its lawyers' offices in connection with possible breaches of official secrecy or criminal contempt laws by the newspaper or a disloyal 'whistle-blower' civil servant. If such an abuse of power were to occur, for example, in circumstances which were for an improper purpose or were, knowingly, in breach of the convention right to respect for personal privacy, or of the right to free expression, then the courts would be able to award damages. Derogations from the convention in time of war or public emergency will be required by Clause 5 to be clearly framed and expressly authorised by Parliament.

Clause 5 also enables the Secretary of State to amend Schedule 1 to include provisions of other convention protocols which may be ratified. There are several additional protocols which have been ratified by many other major member countries of the Council of Europe but which the present Government have refused to ratify. If I may say so, I have better hopes of a future government.

One very important matter is excluded from the Bill because of its nature as a Private Member's Bill; namely, provision to secure effective access to justice. Once the convention is incorporated into UK law, anyone complaining of a breach of the convention will be required to exhaust all available domestic remedies all the way to the Appellate Committee of this House. I believe it is essential that there should be adequate and well targeted provision for legal advice and assistance in such cases. That would help citizens advice bureaux, local law centres and specialised public interest groups to bring test cases. I would hope and expect that a government Bill, as distinct from a Private Member's Bill, to incorporate the convention would create a human rights commissioner or commission to provide such advice and assistance and be able itself to bring proceedings, whether by judicial review or by representative proceedings on behalf of a number of people with a sufficient legal interest. That already happens with the two equal opportunities commissions and the Commission for Racial Equality. Quite small sums are spent in that way under their budgets, never in my experience more than a couple of hundred thousand pounds a year, for example, in the case of the EOC for Great Britain.

Indeed, I would hope and expect the next government to give effect to the very important recommendation made by the noble and learned Lord, Lord Woolf, in the final report *Access to Justice*, that, where proceedings are brought in the public interests, the courts should have a discretion not only to order that each side should bear its own costs but that the taxed costs of the applicant should be paid out of public funds. If that strikes someone as novel, a similar proposal was made by Lord Evershed's committee in 1953 (Cmd Paper 8878).

I submit that almost half a century after the United Kingdom became the first country to ratify the convention and 30 years after the United Kingdom accepted the jurisdiction of the European Court of Human Rights, the time is over-ripe to domesticate what are or should be British civil rights and liberties and to bring them home to British courts in a way that ensures effective access to justice. I beg to move. . .

Lord Woolf: Until fairly recently many judges, including myself, were sceptical as to the need for a Bill of this sort. The common law has served us well in the past and we doubted whether it could not equally serve this country in the future without being bolstered by domestic legislation which implemented the European Convention on Human Rights as part of our domestic law.

However, the judiciary have had no alternative but to increase our knowledge of the workings of the European Convention because even though the convention is not part of our domestic law it still can and does contribute to our decisions in a great variety of cases. As an advocate the noble Lord, Lord Lester, has been pre-eminent in educating the judiciary concerning the Bill and has persisted in that education notwithstanding the fact that not infrequently his education was received with barely concealed reluctance. Benefiting as I have from that education, I have no hesitation in supporting this Bill.

I do so for two reasons. The first is that we do now need a Bill of Rights which is part of our domestic law. The second reason I do so is that this particular Bill is the right Bill.

I do not need to rehearse all the reasons why we need a Bill, but perhaps I may emphasise two, which have already been mentioned by the noble Lord, Lord Lester. They are pragmatic reasons which are none the worse for that. The first is that it cannot be correct that our citizens should have to go to Europe to receive a remedy which they cannot receive from our domestic courts.

The second reason is that I believe we are losing a real opportunity to influence the European human rights jurisprudence as a result of our judiciary not being able to give judgments as to what should be the legal effect of the convention which I am sure would have a beneficial effect on the views expressed by both the Commission and the European Court of Human Rights in Strasbourg. I know that decisions of our highest court which directly deal with the effect of the convention would be extremely influential on the interpretation of the convention by the court at Strasbourg.

I turn to why in my judgment this is the right form of human rights Bill. It is the least intrusive form of what can be regarded as a constitutional innovation as far as this jurisdiction is concerned. Most importantly, insofar as it affects our constitutional balance, the influence is the minimum. It does not interfere with the sovereignty of Parliament. Parliament, if it makes it clear that that is what it intends to do, can override the provision of the Bill. That does not diminish the importance of the Bill since it avoids what happens at present which is that, unintentionally, Parliament contravenes human rights from time to time. It requires attention to be paid by Parliament to the nature of the provisions which it is bringing into law and to consider the implications which they have for human rights.

Secondly, it does not provide for the award of damages for contravention of the rights contained in the Bill. This is important because it is the tradition in this country, so far as the control of public bodies is concerned, that the courts are not primarily concerned with the enforcement of personal rights but the enforcement of public duties. That is why in the ordinary way one does not get damages as a remedy on an application for judicial review.

I attach great importance to the approach that we have to the enforcement of public duties rather than private rights. I regard that as being a healthy state of affairs. I do not myself want to move the emphasis in that area from public duty to private rights. That is one of the reasons why I commend this Bill. I regard it as very important that public bodies should do what Parliament required them to do, but I consider it unhealthy and unattractive that that should result in damages being awarded for alleged breaches of private rights. It is much better that we should continue with our discretionary use of our prerogative remedies when in the majority of situations there is no need for an award of any form of compensation, although I recognise that if this Bill becomes law there will be a minority of situations where compensation will be appropriate.

Finally, perhaps I may say a word about the dangers to the judiciary of their being sucked into politics in consequence of a Bill such as this becoming part of our domestic law. I am conscious of those dangers, but I would not regard that as a reason for not supporting this Bill. Unhappily, the reality is that today, because of the sort of issues that come before our courts, irrespective of the introduction of this type of Bill, the judiciary are continually having to reach highly sensitive decisions and, insofar as they can be unwillingly sucked into the political arena, that is happening anyway. As I have already said, even without this Bill the courts are required to have regard to the European Convention with increasing frequency for the purpose of construing legislation.

In addition, the most senior judges, exercising their jurisdiction in the Privy Council, regularly have to construe and apply Bills of Rights in Commonwealth jurisdictions where the Privy Council is still the final court of appeal. We have no difficulty in doing that. It will be no more difficult for us to deal with a United Kingdom Bill of Rights than it is to deal with the very similar Bills in Caribbean jurisdictions and in Hong Kong and New Zealand. The benefits of this Bill far outweigh its disadvantages. A Bill of a similar nature works in New Zealand. I am sure that this Bill would work in this jurisdiction. . .

Lord Archer of Sandwell: I hope that your Lordships will forgive me if I take a moment to analyse what we are and are not doing when we seek to attach some legal or constitutional significance to human rights – or, if I may reformulate that, when we attach to a principle the label 'human right'.

The normal way to make decisions in a democratic political community is to empower electors to choose their representatives after hearing a political debate about their proposals, and the will of the majority prevails. Of course, we recognise that a majority may be unfair, prejudiced or muddled, but the right to take a decision must include the right to take a wrong decision. In that respect I have the misfortune to differ from the noble Lord, Lord Holme; I do not believe that there is much historical evidence that a minority – be it an oligarchy, an intellectual elite or a group of platonic philosophers – is likely to be more fair or successful than the majority. . .

To declare that a principle is a human right is to withdraw it from that process; it is to say that it is so self-evident or that it commands so wide a consensus that it should be accepted without subjecting it to a political debate – or at least to place limitations on the methods of challenging it. I stand squarely with the noble Lord, Lord Lester, in that I believe that there are principles in respect of which that is desirable. I hope that I do not need to argue my record of support for both an international and a domestic machinery for the protection of human rights.

However, . . . we should exercise some care as to the legal and constitutional significance which we give to human rights . . .

If the noble Lord, Lord Lester, had sought to entrench the rights set out in the European Convention so as to render them immune from the decisions of Parliament I would have hesitated for two reasons. The first is because it would have represented an attempt by us in our generation to impose our culture and our views on subsequent generations. Indeed, some other countries have done that, but I would hesitate. The second is that it is often the most vulnerable groups which are most likely to have occasion to challenge the received wisdom of the past. . .

I believe that in a representative democracy it is that which we should seek to achieve. What is proposed in the Bill is parliamentary machinery which will alert legislators when they are in danger of passing legislation in contravention of the European Convention. Surely we may assume that they will not wish lightly to place the United Kingdom in breach of its international obligations. That, as I understand it, is largely what New Zealand has done.

I venture to develop that theme. It may be a matter of how this House and the other place arrange their consideration of business rather than an issue requiring statutory provision. I would like to see a Select Committee in each House, or even a joint committee, consider legislation which falls within Clause 3. Your Lordships have a Delegated Powers and Deregulation Committee on which I am privileged to serve. One of its functions is to scrutinise potential legislation to see what powers it is conferring on Ministers to effect subordinate legislation. The scrutiny of legislation for its conformity with our obligations under the convention seems to me worthy of consideration.

Therefore, I am in the fortunate position of being able, from this Bench, to welcome on behalf of my party proposals which I would in any event have welcomed enthusiastically on my own behalf. I would not necessarily wish to include in that the proposal which the noble Lord made in his speech, although, as he pointed out, it is not included in the Bill, for a human rights commissioner. That implies no lack of enthusiasm by my party for enforcing human rights, but simply that it may have implications for the very commissions which the noble Lord mentioned; namely, the Equal Opportunities Commissions for Great Britain and Northern Ireland, the Commission for Racial Equality, the National Disability Council and the Fair Employment Commission for Northern Ireland. That raises questions which may require consultation and careful thought. I say no more than that at this stage but I think it right to put down a marker.

Subject to that, on these Benches we support the proposals. Of course, even if we opposed them, it would be quite wrong to deny a Second Reading to a Private Member's Bill. But that is not the position here. It would be good if the noble Baroness were able to announce that the consensus included the present Government. Her body language has just indicated what I already suspected. I do not believe that she is as indifferent to human rights at that might indicate but, like all others, she has a brief. For those of us whose concern for human rights goes back for many years, our patience too may be rewarded. . . .

HL Deb, 5 February 1997, cols. 1727f.

(B)

THE HOUSE OF COMMONS

---

88   DEBATE ON A UK BILL OF RIGHTS, 1975

Mr. James Kilfedder: I beg to move,

> That this House urges HM Government to recommend the setting up of a Royal Commission to investigate and report upon the subject of a Bill of Rights extending to the whole of the United Kingdom.

I do not believe that this nation can refrain any longer from taking the historic and significant step of placing the liberties of its citizens in the safe keeping of a Bill of Rights. I am not advocating a change for the sake of change. Far from it. The common law is supposed to protect the rights of the individual. But those rights are being steadily eroded. Often the ordinary individual does not know that those rights have diminished over the years.

The facts of life in this country today are that the Government have infiltrated, sometimes with dire consequences, into every home of the land and affected the lives of every citizen for good or ill. A great mass of legislation emanates from Parliament every year. The rush of legislation is such that procedural devices such as guillotine motions have been used to force through controversial legislation without proper examination, discussion and amendment. Principal legislation is now subject to the same kind of criticism which we have always levelled against delegated legislation. The great bulk of administrative decisions derive from legislation that has never even been debated in this House.

We have seen an extension of the power and influence of an unbridled bureaucracy which could never have been conceived 20 or 30 years ago – even in wartime conditions. At every turn our lives are circumscribed by the edicts of administrators. I am not referring only to the Civil Service, although we live nowadays in what is probably the most highly centralised State in the world. Permanent officials in local government and on statutory bodies of all kinds wield an immense power over our daily lives. This is not unique to the public sector. It applies to the private sector as well.

The experience of large national and multinational industrial concerns shows that the growth of the arrogant bureaucratic mentality is by no means confined to Government agencies. Central Government domination over all aspects of the decision-making process in the public and private sectors is firmly established, to the detriment of the ordinary citizen.

Under local government reorganisation, the size of local government areas was increased and, in the search for greater efficiency, local councils have been left with less effective autonomy than they had before. The result is that permanent staff in local government and statutory boards paralleled the Whitehall bureaucracy at countless mini-Whitehalls throughout Great Britain. Most of these changes have been brought about by economic and social forces and no doubt were regarded as inevitable, indeed necessary. Although we have, thank goodness, greater security of employment and greater assurance of a reasonable standard of living, they have been achieved at considerable cost in freedom.

The response of Parliament to these great changes in the fabric of our society has been to protect the people from exploitation and hardship. Every liberty must be balanced. We should not like to see restored the liberty of people to suffer, as they suffered decades ago, from malnutrition and hardship. Provision has been made, for instance, for equal pay, for equality between the sexes and for industrial legislation on hours and safety at work. In Northern Ireland people have the right of direct access to a Commissioner for Complaints when they feel aggrieved by the action of a local authority or other public body, though there are some limitations, unfortunately, even to this protection ...

I am convinced of the need in this country for a Bill of Rights. Discussion of this question has been hampered by the technical point about how to entrench fundamental law in an unwritten constitution. I hold no brief for the solutions which have been suggested by various people over the years, but my personal inclination is to look at the Canadian Bill of Rights. However, that is better left for close examination by a Royal Commission, for which I have asked in the motion. The aim should be to protect the Bill of Rights from subsequent repeal. Therefore, some form of entrenchment would have to be devised. . .

Mr. Edward du Cann: It is a matter of fact that individual freedom in this country is being steadily eroded, as surely indeed as water wears away a stone. Of course, we do not live in chains. It is true that we can speak and write as we please provided that we are not blasphemous, obscene or seditious, although many of us think that the bounds of what is allowable are being stretched a little too far in all these regards today. True, there is no imprisonment except for a clear breach of the law. True, there are no secret police. True, we enjoy a degree of personal freedom which is rarely found outside the British Commonwealth or the United States. Yet there is, as the hon. Gentleman indicated, a widespread unease and a growing concern about the impact of modern life upon the individual . . .

For many years I have supported the proposal to introduce a new Bill of Rights in this country, a 'Little Man's Magna Carta' as it has sometimes been called. I am more than ever convinced that it is essential. . .

The old doctrine of parliamentary sovereignty is open to criticism both for what Parliament itself does, is inclined to do, or is able to do, and for what Parliament does not do. It is a fact that the unfettered legislative authority possessed by Parliament in these days – 'elected dictatorship' I have heard it called – has become a source of anxiety to many thinking people.

As every schoolboy knows, we do not have a written constitution. In these circumstances, it must be right to examine whether we need an alternative entrenchment of individual rights in the modern context of which I have been speaking. Were we to have a Bill of Rights, it would certainly provide a first line of defence for the protection of human freedom.

In 1689, again as every schoolboy will, I hope, remember, especially those in the West Country, the tyrant was the Crown. Now perhaps it is Parliament itself, innocently, I agree, but inevitably. Every new law, every new Order in Council, whittles away freedom a little.

How many laws as a matter of fact do we now deal with in these days? I will weary the House with some statistics. The average number of Acts of Parliament over the past 10 years has been 52 a year. We must take a long period to establish an average because of the incidence of General Elections, as all hon. Members know. This year, in my opinion wrongly and unnecessarily, we shall deal with 70. The number of pages of public general Acts has averaged 1,400 a year over the 30 years from 1943. In 1973 the number was 2,200, an increase of more than 50 per cent.

Every day it becomes more difficult for the citizen to know what he may or may not do. *Ignorantia juris non excusat* was the maxim that we were all taught in years gone by. I am not sure that that maxim is any longer a fair statement. I know that my local chief constable in Somerset, a most excellent, competent and devoted public servant, incessantly complains to me as his local Member of Parliament how difficult it is for his constables to be taught precisely what the law is.

Aggregated, the number of subjects we shall discuss on the Floor of the House this week comes to 19. That is an obvious sign of pressure in five days. If we aggregate the work that we are doing in the course of a year, or the course of a week, it will be seen that it is very formidable, and that is the obvious picture that is disclosed.

But if to that we add subordinate legislation – why it is called 'subordinate' I do not know, because much of it is primary – we have 2,000 instruments a year, 1,000 of them of general application. But in 1974 there were 2,200 instruments, about half of them of general application. That means that there were 6,000 new pages of legislation additional to the 2,200 pages of Acts of Parliament of which I have already spoken.

Then there is the European legislation, again surely primary. If you go to the Vote Office, Mr. Deputy Speaker, as I am sure you do, and ask for the latest report of the Select Committee that the House has established to look into European legislation, you will find that that for 17th June, the latest to be published, was the 24th such report made to Parliament about matters that that Committee says should have the careful consideration of the House most of which have not.

Yet, as my hon. Friend said, in this Chamber we deal with no more than a fraction of the total of our work. That is not surprising, because there is more pressure on Members of Parliament and a shortage of time.

In addition to the work on the Floor of the House, there is the Committee work to do. I wonder how many right hon. and hon. Members are aware that we have already had 265 sittings of Standing Committees this Session to 1st July. I do not know whether that is a record, but I know that the number of Standing Committees currently sitting is a record. To that number must be added the Standing Committees on regional affairs, the two on statutory instruments, the Northern Ireland Grand Committee and so on. The total is assuredly a record.

There is also a record number of Select Committees, no fewer than 14 sitting at present, and they have 19 sub-committees. The latest to divide itself amoeba-like is the Select Committee on the wealth tax, and the reason for its division hon. Members may think particularly sinister.

Then there are the party committees. The Conservative Party will have some 20 committee meetings this week. According to the whip, there are six meetings of all-party groups this week, and there is the CPA and the British Group of the IPU.

It is a formidable catalogue of activity. It is important to record it. The public outside the House has little comprehension of what is involved in its membership. Ordinarily that might not matter, but the public relies on two particular sentries of its interest and for the defence of its rights. It relies on the Press and perhaps on broadcasting and television, the 'media' as they are called. They no longer have the full facility for doing the work that is necessary. Indeed, one could fill a whole newspaper or a whole broadcasting day on any day with a week's casebook of any individual Member of Parliament ...

In fact, we are no longer the watch-dogs that once we were and that the public trust us to be. Indeed, we cannot perform that rôle. Legislation is now produced in such quantities and the work load of Members of Parliament is so heavy that detailed inspection is a physical impossibility. I wish it were not so, but I say plainly that it is. For that reason I am sure that Members of Parliament need the weapon of a Bill of Rights to enable them to fulfil the responsibility that the public expect us to discharge. If we were to have such a Bill we should have a fine net available for our use.

A Bill of Rights would not override parliamentary sovereignty because Parliament could amend or repeal it. In parenthesis, I would say that Parliamentary sovereignty is not only a legal fact but a political matter. I believe that it would be politically very difficult, if not impossible, for Parliament drastically to cancel or amend such an Act if the Bill became an Act. The whole nation would be alert to what was proposed. Surely that is the chief safeguard that we require. I suggest that we sleep today while freedom is reduced insidiously and inexorably, and that our crime in this House is carelessness.

I should like to see a modern Bill of Rights to supplement Magna Carta, the Petition of Rights and the 1689 Bill of Rights, to which I have already referred, those old cornerstones of the constitution. Just as the 1689 Bill formed the basis of a new contract between the Monarch and Parliament, since when the power of the Crown has waned in proportion to the increase in the powers of the executive, so a new Bill of Rights would form the basis of a new contract between Parliament and the individual.

Such a Bill would seek to enhance the principle of parliamentary sovereignty in that it could stipulate that all future legislation should be submitted to an authority – for example, the Solicitor-General, the Ombudsman or a judicial committee, whatever one might think appropriate – to ensure its consistency with the Bill of Rights. Any inconsistency would then be reported to Parliament, and we would then accept or reject the recommendations of the designated authority. In either case attention would be drawn to the matter.

Whether or not such a Bill of Rights is the right approach, above all it seems that we need fresh clarity of thought on the subject of authority, its rights, its obligations and its limits. We also need such thought on individual freedom, its meanings and its true extent. It must be a matter of the greatest concern to Parliament that we re-establish a clear and generally acceptable body of doctrine on the fundamental issue of the relationship between the individual and the State. We need a new contract between Parliament and the individual, howsoever it is written.

The question is how we are to proceed. It seems essential that there is the agreement of all the parties in the House. If we had a Bill that was too weak it would merely restate the obvious. If we had a Bill that was overly strong it would inevitably be unacceptable to some. Let us be plain: no party has a monopoly of caring for the individual, whatever some of us – and especially some Labour hon. Members – may pretend. Nor does any party have a monopoly of the defence of freedom. This is the business of us all. I hope that out of this discussion – again, I congratulate my hon. Friend the

Member for Down, North for initiating this debate – will come agreement that the matter should be inquired into fully by a Select Committee, or howsoever else, and that consideration should be given to whether existing safeguards are adequate for the protection of human rights in the United Kingdom. Recommendations should then be made in that regard. . . .

Mr. J. Enoch Powell: There are from time to time in politics 'South Sea Bubbles'. In such instances projects of an undefined character, projects of which the details are to be revealed later as the South Sea promoters said, become the subject of unthinking and infectious enthusiasm, until the demand for them becomes almost irresistible before the content has been considered.

I think that there is some little danger of a Bill of Rights project becoming a kind of political South Sea Bubble. There is a sure way in which such bubbles can be pricked, and that is by debate in the House. Whatever defects we may have in this Chamber, a football is never quite the same as it was at the beginning when it has been kicked around here for three or four hours. . .

It is my proposition that a Bill of Rights in that sense – and I believe it is the significant sense – is incompatible with our constitution. If the word 'constitution' be too vague and cloudy, I say that a Bill of Rights is incompatible with the responsibility of Government through this House to the electorate, the thing we call parliamentary democracy. . .

Mr. Jonathan Aitken: Whatever part of the United Kingdom we come from, we can all agree, I am sure, that the background to this debate is that we are living in an age when the sheer speed, pressure and complexity of modern life may cause even our most fundamental freedoms to be eroded all too easily, and often without much notice being taken of the erosion process. My right hon. Friend the Member for Taunton (Mr. du Cann) struck the right note when he gave figures showing the sheer volume of legislation with which we are being inundated. As a new Member of the House, I sometimes shiver when I realise how, during the 16 months I have been here, more than 2,000 pages of legislation have been added to the statute book and over 7,000 pages of statutory orders and regulations have been published. The idea that any one Member of Parliament, or even groups of Members, could adequately fulfil our watchdog function when we are swamped by such a volume of legislation is in itself a telling argument in favour of the Bill of Rights recommendations which we are discussing.

In the interests of brevity, I shall concentrate on one basic right, the right to freedom of speech and freedom of expression. Lest any hon. Members think that I am being a little fanciful in even suggesting that such a basic right should be included in a Bill of Rights, I refer them to the Bill of Human Rights of the Commonwealth of Australia, Section 11(2) of which provides that in Australia

'Everyone shall have the right to freedom of expression, including freedom to seek, receive and impart information and ideas of all kinds, regardless of frontiers, either orally, in writing or in print, in the form of art or in any other media of his choice'.

There are then certain exceptions defined in the statute, which, of course, cover such matters as national security and the invasion of privacy.

If we had such legislation as a similar Bill of Rights in our country, one would have to admit that there are already certain restrictions on freedom of expression through our law of libel, the Official Secrets Act and the law of contempt of court, and perhaps some of those laws could profitably be redrafted in the light of a Bill of Rights. . .

Mr. Leon Brittan: I welcome this debate and the fact that it is to inform rather than to force us to reach a conclusion. I have not reached a conclusion, though I recognise that the basic case etched out in favour of the Bill is a formidable one. The tendency of Governments of both parties to erode the liberties of the subject and of the corporations, which have the right to exist in this country, has been illustrated fully in this debate. It would be very difficult to look back objectively at the last 20 years and say that there has not been an erosion of liberty in this way.

However, a word of caution is needed because there is a tacit assumption that almost any injustice or wrong that hon. Members can call to mind would be rectified, remedied or prevented by a Bill of Rights. It is by no means certain that all the matters mentioned in the debate so far would be covered by such a Bill at all. A number of the matters mentioned amount to maladministration and would be covered by the efforts of the Ombudsman rather than a Bill of Rights and some of the matters have been of such detail that it is almost inconceivable that a Bill would cover them.

There has also been the assumption that we are all fully agreed on what the rights of the subject are or should be and that the only point of controversy is how they should be enforced and protected. If anybody has to work out what the Bill should contain, he will find that the apparent unanimity will disappear like gossamer. There is real controversy as to what should be in the Bill.

One thing is clear beyond peradventure – it would be an appalling mistake to attempt to introduce a Bill until its contents and the method of enforcement have received the widest possible degree of agreement and consent in this House and the country. To attempt to introduce a Bill which itself became a football of controversy of party political or other kinds would be a remedy worse than any conceivable disease.

It is not difficult to see how controversy could arise in the consideration of subjects to be included in the Bill. The most obvious subject – one which would perhaps distinguish this side of the House from the Government side – is the whole question of property rights. Many a Bill of Rights would regard it as essential and axiomatic that a prominent provision should be the protection of the right of property. Yet many Labour Members would be less enthusiastic in their support for the rights of property. They are entitled to that view, and they can argue it here and in the country.

Until we reach agreement on the content of a Bill, it would be hazardous indeed to embark on the adventure of trying to create one. Even if we do reach agreement – and this will be much more difficult than is sometimes thought – the question of enforcement and entrenchment remains. There have been a number of suggestions as to how this should be done, ranging in efficacy from the very weakest of measures to the very strongest. The further one goes to entrench and enforce a Bill of Rights, the further one goes to disrupt the present constitutional arrangements, which for good or ill, operate in the country.

The weakest of suggestions is that Parliament should be allowed to pass legislation that infringes a Bill of Rights only if it does so knowing that it is passing such legislation – in other words, if it has included in an Act an express proviso that it was being passed despite the fact that it conflicted with the Bill of Rights. The theory is that Parliament would at least have to put its mind to the question of whether it wished to pass legislation which conflicted with the Bill of Rights. Under that course, it would not take long for Governments to insert as a normal formula – and by common parlance for it to be accepted as such – a meaningless piece of mumbo-jumbo to the effect that the measure conflicted with the Bill of Rights. That is a protection that would be illusory and all the more damaging for being so.

One of the alternative methods involves Committees within Parliament which would have to decide whether legislation came within certain categories and whether it would require a certain majority to be passed or repealed. This is a more attractive proportion. It would give the parliamentary Committee entrusted with the task the most tremendous power. . .

The true Bill of Rights, as the right hon. Member for Down, South (Mr. Powell) said, is one which enables the courts to say that a particular piece of legislation will not be given the force of law because it conflicts with the Bill of Rights. It involves necessarily a system of judicial review, and the right hon. Gentleman is absolutely right in pointing out that any system of judicial review is fundamentally in conflict with our present constitutional arrangements and involves a major disturbance and alteration to the whole system of Government. That is not, of course, in any way conclusive, because one cannot regard something as being axiomatically right merely because it has been the way of government over a period of time. At a time when our rights and liberties are being threatened I do not believe that a system of judicial review should be regarded as an absolute bar to a Bill of Rights merely because it is a fundamental innovation.

It would be an innovation which had great consequences for our constitutional arrangements, and it would give to the law courts a power which in the past they neither had nor sought. Until now the law courts have been concerned either with the determination of factual issues between individuals or at least the interpretation of statutes by comparatively narrow points of construction, but to give them the power of enforcing a Bill of Rights would not only give them a greater power than they have had up to now but would involve them in a consideration of issues which hitherto they have not had to consider in the same sort of way.

The only alternative would be to make a Bill of Rights so detailed in form that it would be inflexible and require a kind of frequent revision which would be inappropriate in such a fundamental Bill. The essence, for example, of the American Bill of Rights and Constitution, which have stood the test of time, is that they are phrased in a general form and their meaning is valid according to the deliberations of the Supreme Court over the years. In the early nineteenth century in the case of *Marbury* v *Madison*, the Great Chief Justice of the United States Marshal, when called upon to decide a question relating to the United States Constitution, adjured the court to remember that it was the constitution that it was interpreting. In other words, the principles of interpreting a Bill of Rights or a constitution must be very different from those of interpreting a mere statute, and if that is so it means that the courts would be considering basic questions and not just the interstices of legislation which have been left open by Parliament in its wisdom or folly.

If the courts are to consider major social questions in this way one must ask, without disrespect to the judiciary, whether its members are qualified to do so, leaving aside any question of the democratic implications of requiring them to do so. They have carried out a very different rôle over the centuries, and, therefore, I would suggest that they are not at present necessarily qualified to do so. They have not equipped themselves with the form of legal consideration that the United States Supreme Court has always had because they are not as diverse in their origin and background as the members of that court. That court has always had among its number people who are experienced in government in a variety of forms, often in the legislature and sometimes in the executive. Our law courts do not consist of such people. They consist almost exclusively of people who have practised in the law, and there are very few exceptions. If they have practised in the law they have mostly studied the law. Legal studies in this country, although much improved in their quality, do not constitute the form of liberal wide-ranging education that the United States law schools, which are graduate institutions, impart.

It may seem a far cry from a consideration of a Bill of Rights to be talking about legal education, but it is fundamental to the question. If we are to impose a power of this kind on a repository other than Parliament, representative in a sense, if not in a democratic sense, of the long-term wishes of the people, we have to be sure what we are doing, to whom we are giving that power and how it is to be exercised. Great and unbounded as my admiration is for the judiciary carrying out its present rôles, I believe it would be extremely chary of undertaking such a new rôle.

These are my doubts and reservations about a proposal which has considerable attractions. So great are the attractions that, in spite of the reservations I have felt bound to put before the House, I warmly support the idea of this concept being given further consideration at greater length in a more leisurely, authoritative way than can be done in a brief debate of this kind. I also express my support for the idea that the matter should be considered further, if not by a Select Committee, then by a Royal Commission, and if not by a Royal Commission, by some other body which is calculated not only to reflect the knowledge of history and law required to reach conclusions on these matters but to add adequate weight to the differing political views which cannot be divorced from this matter. These views have to be reconciled if we are ever to create a Bill of Rights which is more than a snare and delusion ...

The Under-Secretary of State for the Home Department (Dr. Shirley

Summerskill): Views may differ about the best way of safeguarding individual rights, but, as this debate has shown, there can be no doubt about our agreement on the importance which we all attach to protecting these rights.

Mr. Lane: It is curious that we have had no contributions in the debate from any of the Under-Secretary's hon. Friends. Is there any reason for this? It is very disappointing.

Dr. Summerskill: I refer the hon. Gentleman to the words of his right hon. Friend the Member for Taunton (Mr. du Cann), who said that no party has a monopoly of concern for the freedom of the individual. Happily, this is not a party issue, and I hope that the hon. Gentleman will not try to make it into one.

Mr. Aitken: There seems to be a monopoly of lack of concern on the Government benches.

Dr. Summerskill: As hon. Members will recall, when answering a Question on 21st April from the hon. and learned Gentleman the Member for Wimbledon (Sir M. Havers), my right hon. Friend the Home Secretary said that, while in his view the time was not ripe for a Royal Commission to examine the need for a Bill of Rights, he would welcome further public discussion of the issue in general. It is, therefore, useful and important that we have been able to hear the views of hon. Members and the arguments about the relative merits of a Royal Commission or Select Committee on this subject, or the undesirability of either.

This is indeed a subject on which there is a wide spectrum of opinion, not only whether a Bill of Rights is desirable but also about the form it might take, and the rights which it should seek to protect. This has been illustrated by the range of views expressed today. Different advocates attach different importance to different rights. But I think it would be fair to say that their common intention is to give statutory force to the laws and customs on which the rights and liberties of the nation are founded: to reflect Parliament's respect for its constitutional authority; and to ensure the protection of fundamental human rights and freedoms.

Those who favour a Bill of Rights often cite, in support of their arguments, examples of the Bill of Rights found in other countries. Indeed, some examples have been quoted this afternoon. It is sometimes pointed out that this country, while rejecting a Bill of Rights for itself, has none the less in the past conferred on newly enfranchised Commonwealth countries a constitution which includes some such declaration of fundamental human rights. However, such provisions have to be seen in their general social and constitutional context, and, outside that context, comparisons with them have limited value – and may even be misleading.

Many of the countries which have Bills of Rights are countries which, unlike ours, have written constitutions. In some cases, these constitutions were created at a major turning point in the country's history in response to some radical change, such as revolution or the achievement of independence. What may have been appropriate for them is not necessarily equally suitable for our own very different system, which has evolved gradually – and for the most part peacefully – over so many years. And I am sure that none of us would make the mistake of thinking that, because we have no Bill of Rights, individual freedoms have been less fully protected here than in many of those countries which have. Conversely, those countries which have a Bill of Rights do not necessarily protect individual freedom more successfully than we do. It has to be admitted, I think, that there is room for more than one view about the effectiveness of some of these instruments in protecting the liberties which they declare. A Bill of Rights is not a fail-safe answer to all the problems which arise in the protection of individual liberties. Much more important is the respect which a society has, at root, for such freedoms and the importance which it is prepared to attach to them. That is the greatest safeguard not only for those individual liberties but for our whole democratic system.

But, having said that, I would not like the House to think that the Government – or I personally – are committed against a Bill of Rights. If I have said that we must recognise that such instruments are no panacea, we ought also to recognise that they do have attractions. These have been set out very clearly today by the hon. Member for Down, North and others who have spoken in support of his motion – and I have a good deal of sympathy with much of what they have said, especially the view that in a democracy adequate protection of human rights is an article of faith shared by all. But previous parliamentary efforts to introduce a Bill of Rights into our constitution have not succeeded. Let us consider, therefore, the strength of the arguments against such an innovation.

In the first place, we must consider how much any such Bill would be likely to circumscribe the sovereignty of the Queen in Parliament, which has always been regarded by most people – although it was questioned by the hon. Members for Cambridge (Mr. Lane) and Dundee, East (Mr. Wilson) – as the prime safeguard of the liberties of the subject. Obviously, the precise effect of any Bill of Rights in this respect would depend on the nature of its detailed provisions, but if the rights were to be truly entrenched and binding on our successors that could be done only at some sacrifice to the supreme authority of the Queen in Parliament. This would indeed be a momentous step, and it is one which we should not contemplate without the most thorough study of all its implications.

Secondly, if such a Bill were merely to catalogue rights without any corresponding statement of duties, it would evade the central problem of social organisation, which is to maintain a proper balance between freedom and order, and to reconcile the freedom of the individual with the obligations of the citizen. No right can be absolute. Freedom of speech, freedom of assembly, procession and demonstration – to which we would all certainly subscribe in principle – nevertheless have to be subject to some restriction, since there are circumstances in which their unrestrained exercise could lead, however unintentionally, to disturbance or disorder. Similarly, liberty and the security of the person must be circumscribed by the need to provide for the arrest, trial and punishment of those who break the law.

The balance between freedom and restraint is delicate and needs constantly to be redressed according to the circumstances of the time and of particular situations. Setting the balance is one of the tasks of a political system. The tensions created commonly have a political expression, and over the years they have commonly been resolved by political action, resulting in legislation designed to delimit the boundaries where rights and claims conflict.

Mr. Beith: Does the hon. Lady recall the occasions on which those tensions have led to the placing on the statute book of legislation which, in retrospect, many of us would have wished not to be there but which proves exceedingly difficult to repeal because Governments find it convenient to retain it even when the urgency of purpose does not dictate it? I have in mind parts of the Official Secrets Act and the Incitement to Disaffection Act which were passed under considerable tension. One wonders whether they should have been passed in their present form.

Dr. Summerskill: The hon. Gentleman is speaking for himself. Those Acts must have received the majority support of the House. If an Act is repealed, that also requires the majority support of the House. The hon. Gentleman has illustrated what I have been saying, namely, that there is a fine line to be drawn between individual freedoms and the restraints which are necessary in any society.

Whatever constitutional alternative were devised would have to allow reasonable latitude for adjustments and change. Two possible models have been suggested for a Bill of Rights. One would contain a detailed statement of the nature and extent of the rights to be protected. This would give rise to obvious difficulties for, quite apart from the initial problems in defining the rights, the provisions of the Bill would inevitably need adjustment in the light of changes in society's standards and attitudes; yet a measure which invited frequent amendment would be a mere shadow of what a true Bill of Rights might be expected to be.

On the other hand, the alternative model – a statement of rights expressed in general terms, with detailed interpretation and application of its provisions left to the courts – would give rise to different problems. True, it would have the advantage of flexibility, in that interpretations and applications could alter over time as society evolved, and public opinion as to what constituted acceptable activities changed. But the generality of its provisions would inevitably lead to uncertainty.

A system of case law takes a long time to build up and so, for a considerable period after the introduction of any Bill of Rights drafted in such broad terms, it would be impossible to predict with any certainty what was likely to be judged as an encroachment upon fundamental rights. The task of interpreting such a Bill would also place a heavy burden on our judges, as was pointed out this afternoon, and involve them in controversial political matters which have traditionally been regarded in this country as the proper sphere of a democratically elected Parliament. There would, therefore, be a significant shift in the relationship between the legislature and the judiciary, the effects of which it would be difficult to predict with any assurance. As the hon. Member for Cleveland and Whitby (Mr. Brittan) pointed out, the judiciary would also be asked to consider basic social questions, which is not its usual rôle.

Finally, it is impossible to be certain how far a catalogue of rights drafted in loose and general terms would be found to overlap or run parallel with existing legislation. The undesirable result would be that some matters would be dealt with in two statutes which would be open to conflicting interpretations. In such circumstances, if a Bill of Rights did not become a dead letter, its application would be likely to lead to an increasingly complex body of case law, which would defeat a prime object of the exercise – the provision of swift redress for those whose rights have been infringed.

I have dealt at some length with the various arguments which have in the past been employed against a Bill of Rights because they seem to me to have considerable strength. But, as I have said, the British constitution is one which evolves over time, and we have, therefore, to recognise that the balance of advantage with regard to any proposal for constitutional innovation may also change. That is why, while giving due weight to the arguments which I have listed, we should never – now or at any time in the future – regard them as being final or definitive. We should always be prepared to reassess them in the light of changing circumstances.

I am sure that the House will hardly need reminding of the recent developments which have had, or may prove to have, significant implications for the system of government in this country. The hon. Member for Barkston Ash (Mr. Alison) mentioned them and rightly stressed their importance. We have joined the EEC, and the arguments about the effects of accession on our constitution were fully rehearsed before the recent referendum. The referendum itself was a major constitutional innovation. The European Convention on Human Rights, of which we are signatories, and the interpretations placed upon that Convention by the European Commission or European Court, appear likely to make an increasing impact upon practices in this country, as in others, with what consequences we cannot yet know.

Referring to the European Convention on Human Rights, I should like to take up a point which was made by the hon. Member for Down, North and the right hon. Member for Taunton about the number of United Kingdom petitions to Strasbourg. Comparisons between the experiences of States under the European Convention on Human Rights are difficult as the periods for which States have accepted the right of individual petition are so varied. The number of United Kingdom petitions declared admissible – that is, worthy of deeper examination by the European Commission of Human Rights – was greater in the period for which figures are available than those of other States which are also subject to the petitions procedure. However, the number is not large. The United Kingdom figure for 1966 to 1973 was 43. A number of those were concerned with immigration and raised the same points. If those cases are treated as one, the United Kingdom figure is not out of keeping with those of other countries.

The fourth change or development which we are witnessing, and perhaps potentially the most significant of all, is the progress which we are making towards a degree of devolution for the various parts of the United Kingdom. But it is far too early to say what the full implications of all those several developments will be. As their full effects become apparent, the Government will welcome further public discussion about this important issue.

Meanwhile, wherever this discussion may lead, it would be wrong to suppose that the absence of a Bill of Rights in any way bars the path towards the enlargement of the true freedom of the individual and the enrichment of opportunity.

Many examples cited by hon. Members this afternoon alleged the infringement of human rights. For many of them there is nothing to stop Parliament from taking action where necessary. We have established legislation to create a parliamentary commissioner, a local government commissioner, a health service commissioner; the laws against racial discrimination and to enforce equal pay; and the current Bill to give equal opportunities to men and women. All those amply demonstrate the powers which Parliament already has. The Government will continue to protect the basic rights and liberties of the citizen and to ensure that they are effectively safeguarded.

The Government Departments concerned will also continue to make a careful study of all the implications of a Bill of Rights, and we hope that the public debate which has started will continue.

Mr. Kilfedder: I am extremely sad that the hon. Lady was not able to respond to the feeling of the House and to offer the hope that there would be a discussion on a Bill of Rights either by a Select Committee or, as I suggested in the motion, by a Royal Commission. I am surprised that the Government were not able to make a reasonable offer, bearing in mind that the Attorney-General, the Solicitor-General, and the former Lord Chancellor, Lord Gardiner, have at different times proposed a Bill of Rights. It seems strange that the Government should not be willing or able to offer something definite.

I do not wish to divide the House on this motion as I believe that a Bill of Rights should not be a political football. I hope that the debate will at least mean that there will be greater pressure for a Bill of Rights and that an opportunity will occur again for a full-length discussion on the subject.

HC Deb., 7 July 1975, cols, 32f.

89 DEBATE ON THE BILL OF RIGHTS BILL, 1981

RB NOTE: For the text of the Bill, see Doc. 39A.

Mr. A. J. Beith: I beg to move, That the [Bill of Rights] Bill be now read a Second time. . .

Why do we need special provision to protect human rights and fundamental freedoms? There is now a widespread body of opinion that some measure of protection is needed. In our system it is proving rather too easy for transient majorities to abrogate rights without effective challenge. One of the tendencies of our electoral system – curiously, it is no less notable in local government elections than in parliamentary elections – is to produce very large swings in representation, even when there are quite small changes in the voting of the electorate. The effect of that in this place is often to create majorities that carry through measures that may abrogate human rights without challenge.

Often these reductions in our rights and freedoms are not the result of some conscious attempt by Governments to narrow the scope of individual freedom. There is often a compelling reason for taking some action. There is often some reason or excuse which leads Governments to take steps that, perhaps because they become permanent or because they are wider than they need be, begin to infringe upon individual rights.

In 1911 the Official Secrets Act was passed in order to deal with a pressing problem and a gap in the law. It was very wide in its scope, and it has lasted far longer than it should have done. It was said at the time that it would be temporary in character, but its provisions are so wide and far-reaching that our courts are unable to operate them, even in the sense in which they were originally intended, so that they cry out for reform. They ought to have been and ought now to be challenged on the basis of some definition of fundamental rights.

Our protection of terrorism legislation, introduced with support in all parts of the House as a necessary temporary expedient, has become fearfully long-term and permanent. It is renewed and renewed without modification or amendment, although we have the opportunity to consider amendments. The Government who introduced the legislation and the parties that supported it did so because of a pressing cause, but there was no mechanism to test that, perhaps at a later stage, against fundamental rights and freedoms.

Sometimes Governments narrow or infringe upon human rights because they believe that they are properly responding to what they think are majority opinions. In areas such as immigration law and nationality law there are great pressures on Governments, which make them wish to respond in particular ways without being subject to any real test or challenge of the relationship of such things to fundamental freedoms.

Mr. John Ryman: Before the hon. Gentleman leaves the point about legislation that is properly brought in, for very good reasons, on a temporary basis, will he bear in mind the legislation under the taxes and management measures in the late eighteenth and early nineteenth centuries, which introduced income tax as a temporary measure?

Mr. Beith: I shall bear that point in mind. The hon. Member has displayed a knowledge of legislation that goes beyond mine. Only the other day I was looking at tax legislation and retrospective tax legislation. I noticed that in 1968 we managed to enact a piece of retrospective tax legislation without any debate in this Chamber, under timetable proceedings. That shows that, as a result of various pressures, legislation can slip through this place. Such legislation should be open to challenge.

I have tried to list the various reasons why Governments narrow or infringe human rights, or are open to that charge. There is another example. The Government sometimes act in what they believe to be the interests of legitimate and important groups in society. However, they do so at the expense of individuals. For example, the legislation that protects the closed shop limits the rights of individuals. In the course of this Parliament there have been some improvements in that legislation, but not enough. Individuals still have legitimate grievances as a result of that legislation.

The Solicitor-General knows that I have taxed and pressed him time and again on the curious position in which he finds himself in Strasbourg, when he has to deal with complaints as a result of that legislation. I would prefer to see him dealing with those complaints in the first instance in our courts. We welcome his presence and very much appreciate why the Attorney-General is engaged on other important but not very happy duties.

Mr. Clement Freud: Is my hon. Friend aware that one great cause of misery is that applications for nationality are made to the Government and are sometimes refused without any reasons being given? Would not this legislation put an end to that concern and injustice?

Mr. Beith: I agree that the right to a fair hearing and the need for proper handling of administration decisions need an objective measure against which it would be possible to test, in a judicial way, a Government's activities. Our system lacks such a measure. At one time, when the State's intervention in the life of an individual was far less, we were content to rest on written assumptions. Circumstances have changed dramatically. Regardless of which party is in power, the State's role has grown so much that the unwritten assumptions have proved inadequate and have not protected us in such circumstances.

There is a pressing need to look at the threats created by new technology, which make existing safeguards inadequate. I refer, for example, to telephone tapping, bugging, and eavesdropping on private conversations. Not all threats come from Governments; they also come from private individuals and outside organisations. In the past few days we have witnessed the invasion of the privacy of our own Royal Family by money-grubbing freelance journalists who will use any device and opportunity to eavesdrop and to intrude on the privacy of individuals. The Royal Family and its legal advisers have rightly moved swiftly.

The ordinary private citizen finds it difficult when his privacy is threatened by the Government or by other bodies.

Mr. David Alton: That is an interesting point. Does my hon. Friend agree that when we discussed the British Telecommunications Bill we missed a great opportunity, because the Government refused to accept the amendment moved by the hon. Member for Hendon, North (Mr. Gorst)? The hon. Gentleman attempted to introduce legislation that would prevent the unwarranted use of telephone-tapping techniques, which undoubtedly infringe civil liberties. Will not the Bill give us an opportunity to ensure that legitimate telephone calls are not listened to by anyone who wishes to pry into the conversations?

Mr. Beith: I agree with my hon. Friend. Again, we are discussing something that cuts across party lines, because it deals with fundamental civil liberties, for which there is no objective test or protection. We could seek to write our own Bill of Rights and to produce a British domestic Bill of Rights to deal with such matters. However, I do not advance that cause today. It would prove a difficult undertaking. It would be difficult to achieve in a short space of time the consensus necessary to get such a Bill on to the statute book. In immediate terms, there is a more practical way of dealing with the issue, and it should be followed. It is the way that my noble Friend Lord Wade has set out.

We have already given assent to a Bill of Rights and to a declaration of fundamental rights and freedoms. We are a signatory to the European Convention of Human Rights. Indeed, Britain signed in 1950. The convention is a product of the Council of Europe and not part of the machinery of the EEC. Lest anyone objects to our membership of the EEC – I do not – and thinks that this subject is not for him, I must make it clear that the convention is part of the apparatus of the 21-member Council of Europe. Among the European countries there is the broadest possible basis of agreement on human rights and other issues.

The convention came into existence long before the EEC and is a precursor of it. It still enjoys the support and ratification of many countries that are not members of the EEC. Its provisions cover many of the areas involved in fundamental rights and freedoms. For example, they cover the right to life, freedom from torture or inhuman or degrading treatment, freedom from slavery or forced labour, the right to liberty and a fair trial, the right to respect for family life, home and correspondence, freedom of thought and religion and freedom of expression and association, and the right to marry and to found a family.

All those basic rights, and developments of them, are to be found within that important European convention. All hon. Members could point to ways in which they would like to modify, alter, improve or even detract from that convention. However, the important point is that it enjoys widespread support and the ratification and endorsement of successive British Governments, as well as those of all other nations of Europe.

Although we have not failed to endorse the convention or to accept its principles, we have failed to incorporate it into our law. This Bill seeks to make that move. The Government are under an obligation to ensure that the provisions of the European convention are carried out in Britain. However, the courts have no power to consider them or enforce them. The Government are left with the job of waiting for the European Commission of Human Rights, or eventually the Council of Ministers, to determine whether an infringement has taken place, and are then given the task of bringing British law into conformity. . .

The Government's alternative has been to suggest on a number of occasions that the appropriate response is all-party. talks. That is an unusual burst of consensus politics by the Government, and I suppose that I must welcome that desire to secure agreement from all parties before we proceed. That is not new. In November 1979 the Lord Chancellor suggested that. That was confirmed by the Prime Minister in a letter to me in December 1979. We suggested that we were willing to accept such all-party talks.

On 6 May 1980 – just a year ago – the Prime Minister wrote to me. She said:

'We wish, as you say, to discuss a possible Bill of Rights with other parties. We said in our Manifesto that this was a subject which we would wish to discuss with all parties.

However, I can see no prospect of all-party talks about a Bill of Rights until the current talks on Scotland and Northern Ireland have been concluded. We shall approach the parties as soon as possible after that.'

As far as I know, the talks on Scotland and Northern Ireland have ended inconclusively. Further talks will take place, as we shall discuss Northern Ireland for many years, but the Bill of Rights cannot wait until we arrive at a solution to that intractable problem, quickly as I should like to see such a solution.

The discussions to which the Prime Minister referred are long over, yet we have not proceeded to all-party talks. We continue to pursue this matter in the present Session. I welcome the suggestion from the Front Bench on 10 April that all-party talks were still in the Government's mind. The Minister of State, Home Office – the hon. Member for Aylesbury (Mr. Raison) – answered that debate and said:

'We believe that important proposals for constitutional change of the type involved in any Bill of Rights should proceed as far as possible by agreement between the political parties. The Government have it in mind to initiate talks at a suitable time.' – [*Official Report.* 10 April 1981; Vol. 2, c. 1264.]

When would be a suitable time? The Government were all too busy with Scotland and Northern Ireland before, but perhaps now is a suitable time.

I wrote to the Prime Minister taking up the sensible offer and suggested that now was a suitable time. A day or two ago I received the reply:

'As Tim Raison said in the debate on 10 April to which you refer, we believe that important proposals for constitutional change of the type involved in any Bill of Rights should proceed as far as possible by agreement between the political parties. I am not yet ready to announce any timetable for a Government initiative in the shape of an approach to the other political parties, but I shall consider what may be appropriate in the light of relevant developments and the Government's other priorities.'

That choice phrase deserves repetition:

'I shall consider what may be appropriate in the light of relevant developments and the Government's other priorities.'

That is not the decisive Prime Minister that we have come to know. It is the Government stalling again and again on the sensible proposition that if the Government are not happy to proceed with the Bill at this stage we should have talks.

We cannot go on like that with Bills passing through every stage in another place, brought to this House and debated after determined hon. Members have struggled to create the opportunity for debate, only to have the Prime Minister and the rest of the Government Front Bench saying that they will consider whether an opportunity will arise, that there are other priorities, and all the other Civil Service stalling language that comes from the handbook on stalling phrases and words of which every Government Department must have a copy.

The House is entitled to better than that. At almost one stroke we could make some valuable achievements if we proceeded with the Bill. We could underline the commitment that we have already made to the principles of human rights in the European convention. We could give the citizen easier, cheaper and quicker means of enforcing those rights. We could entrust that enforcement to our judiciary, with its roots in the British tradition of civil liberty. We could avoid British citizens constantly arraigning their Government in Strasbourg.

I want to see progress on this matter. The Government have prevaricated for too long. There is broad enough agreement that at least we should go to talks quickly. I should like my Bill to be given detailed scrutiny very soon.

Mr. Geoffrey Rippon: Defence of the individual against arbitrary government and the abuse of power is one of the historic functions of Parliament. Today there is a growing concern that private rights hitherto regarded as fundamental to the liberty of the individual in a free society have in recent years been progressively eroded. There are those who in these circumstances have argued for a new written constitution, possibly with entrenched provisions that a bare majority of Parliament could not overthrow. But, whatever attractions that proposition may have, there is general agreement that the drafting of a new constitutional settlement of that kind, particularly with entrenched provisions, would present formidable difficulties.

As I understand it, the Conservative Party manifesto deals with that issue in the promise to discuss such a possible Bill of Rights with all parties. But I emphasise that that is not the issue in this Bill, which has the clear but limited purpose of giving effect in our domestic law to international treaty obligations to which we, with all the other signatory member States of the Council of Europe, are already committed. The House will know that the signing of a treaty is an exercise of the prerogative power of the Crown. A treaty can only be accepted or rejected by Parliament. It cannot be amended. We discussed that issue in the context of the European Communities Act 1972. Parliament is and must be entitled to make only such changes in our domestic law as are required to give effect to the terms of the treaty.

When we acceded to the European Convention on Human Rights in 1953, it was believed that our law had nothing to fear from any appeal to the articles of the convention. Unfortunately, experience since then has shown that there are a wide number of areas – the hon. Member for Berwick-upon-Tweed described some of them – where the British subject must take the long and expensive road to Strasbourg as a court of first instance, since our domestic law provides no remedy in our courts.

The United Kingdom is currently the only signatory which neither has a charter of fundamental human rights nor has incorporated the convention into domestic law. It is expressly required by article 13 of the convention, however, that there should be a right to go before a national tribunal before the ultimate appeal to the Strasbourg court. As long as the convention remains only a treaty and forms no part of our domestic law, our citizens alone have recourse only to this remote and expensive remedy in Strasbourg. Our judges cannot look directly at the convention when they have a human rights problem to resolve ...

If the Bill is passed, three things will happen. The first is that the European Convention on Human Rights will be enforceable in the courts of the United Kingdom. The second is that the convention will prevail over previous enactments. The third is that the convention will prevail over subsequent enactments unless stated to the contrary. This brings me to the point that I think worries my hon. Friend and a number of others.

There is no question of abrogating the ultimate sovereignty of Parliament or the ultimate responsibility of Parliament for ensuring human rights. I should like to examine what happens if the court in Strasbourg upholds the British Government and holds that there was no breach of the convention in the three rail cases and that there is no obligation under the convention to ensure that people have a right not to join a trade union. Following upon what the Prime Minister said yesterday, to the effect that the right not to join was as fundamental as the right to join, we can introduce and should introduce our own legislation in the House. We do not have to create a situation in which the only way we can deal with matters is by legislation when, if we rely on the convention and enforce it, a matter can be dealt with under due process of existing law.

There are those who say that Parliament can legislate for itself and should do so in respect of all these matters. If it desires to do so, well and good. They also say that the European convention is not sufficiently precise. In my view, those arguments are not adequate in themselves. We have, for example, the Sex Discrimination Act of about 75 pages, and the Race Relations Acts – three of them in the past 10 years – which are 80 pages long.

I agree with the present Lord Chancellor, who said:

'I would prefer a single sentence which said that people of all races should be treated alike and for the judges to view those cases as they arise'. –[*Official Report, House of Lords*, 29 November 1978; Vol. 396, c. 1386.]

Article 14 of the convention provides:

'The enjoyment of the rights and freedoms set forth in this Convention should be secured without discrimination on any ground such as sex, race, colour, language, religion, political or other opinion, national or social opinion, association with a national minority, property, birth, or other status'.

That is clear enough. We might have done without all that other legislation if we had allowed our courts to defend what we all accepted by signing the treaty as a fundamental human right.

But an Act incorporating the convention is not an alternative to the continued exercise by Parliament of its traditional sovereignty. It simply complements other Acts which Parliament may wish to pass affecting human rights. If the convention does not go far enough in protecting individual rights, we should, if necessary, supplement the convention.

The Bill provides our individual citizens with a positive and public declaration of the rights guaranteed them by treaty. There is, of course, no way in which this or any other Bill of Rights can be made altogether immune from amendment or repeal by a subsequent Act. The incorporating Bill, although it does not limit parliamentary sovereignty, would nevertheless be a continuing reminder to legislators of the international commitments that we undertook when we ratified the convention.

We pride ourselves in this country on our adherence to the concept of the rule of law, but we do not often study it carefully or consider what we mean. As Alexander Hamilton observed,

'It is one thing to be subordinate to the laws and another to be dependent on the legislative body'.

Our trouble today, as the late Lord Radcliffe said in his Reith lectures about 'The Problem of Power' as long ago as 1951, is that with what is practically single-chamber Government, with the Executive and the legislature combined,

'the security of what used to be called constitutional rights is a very frail thing'.

The great victories of the past to secure the rights of the subject were won by Parliament acting against the Crown, the Executive. Now, the Executive and the law-making power are, to all intents and purposes, the same. They are in the hands of the Government of the day. The old safeguards are not applying as they used to do.

Mr. Percy Grieve: Would it not be true to say that there are few countries, if any, where the Government and the Prime Minister dispose of greater power than here, where they dispose of not only the legislative powers, if they command a majority in the House of Commons, but the executive power of the Crown?

Mr. Rippon: We are, as the Lord Chancellor eloquently described it, an elective dictatorship, and a great responsibility falls upon the Members of this House who are not part of the payroll vote to ensure that the rights and liberties of the subject are adequately defended where necessary. We must remember that many of the so-called freedoms of which we talk today are not freedoms in the former sense of the right of the individual to be protected against the power of the State. It is rather the reverse. They tend to be claims of the individual to be dependent on the State and on society, such as the freedom from want and the so-called right to work. We must consider today how to protect the more traditional rights and freedoms of the very kind that are embodied in the European convention against the increasing encroachment of the State.

It is no secret that the Lord Chancellor is in favour of the Bill. He has said so over and over again. When it was debated in the other place on 8 November 1979, when he was admittedly discouraging about its possible progress in this House, at any rate in the last Session, which he said was over-full with legislation, he said:

'I shall vote for it on Second Reading – except that I do not think that a vote will be taken – and I shall give it as fair a wind as I can'. – [*Official Report, House of Lords*, 8 November, 1979; Vol. 402, c. 1,069.]

I trust that the Solicitor-General will range himself firmly on the side of the Lord Chancellor and say that it is the Government's intention to give the Bill as fair a wind as they can. Of course, the Lord Chancellor cannot give the Bill a fair wind here, but the Government can and should, and I hope that we shall be given that assurance today.

If the view is taken that a Private Member's Bill is unsuitable, because it involves great issues and the implementation of a treaty commitment, the Government themselves should undertake to provide the necessary time. It is possibly the most important issue that faces Parliament now. Budgets and Finance Bills occupy much of the time of the House, but whether they are good, bad or indifferent they are not likely to change the course of history. However, if we fail to bring our minds to bear on the sort of issue raised in this Bill, we shall be betraying the historic role of Parliament.

Mr. Stanbrook: My right hon. and learned Friend knows that at present our courts are pretty full. There are waiting lists and litigants, both civil and criminal, often have to wait a long time before their cases come before the courts. Does he think that giving our citizens the right to claim that they have some basic human rights guaranteed them by the European Convention on Human Rights in our own domestic courts will reduce or increase the waiting lists?

Mr. Rippon: That is the most appalling argument that I have heard in all the debates that have taken place on this subject. The idea that our courts would not have time to consider the thalidomide case, the Joanna Harris case, the three British Rail cases or an allegation about expropriation of property is truly horrifying. I do not imagine that matters of that kind would normally be taken in magistrates' courts. To say that we cannot do it because our courts are already overloaded is pathetic.

We cannot claim that the Bill will solve all the problems that arise from the abuse of power in a modern State, but in the armoury of weapons against the elective dictatorship, of which the Lord Chancellor spoke, this Bill would be of valuable – even if subordinate – assistance in securing the human rights of our people in accordance with our international obligations. . .

Mr. Nicholas Lyell: I should like to say something about what we should be doing in constitutional reform. Some have supported the Bill as a successor to Magna Carta or the great Bill of Rights of 1689. I may have misunderstood Lord Scarman, but I thought that – to my surprise – he put it in that category. Those who have said that documents of that nature in themselves provide for liberty deceive themselves. It was not the paper of

Magna Carta and it was not the parchment of the Bill of Rights of 1689 that provided the liberties therein set out. It was the reality of power in the country at the time – the power of the barons in the early thirteenth century and the power of the aristocracy and landed gentry, and to some extent the growing merchant classes, in the late seventeenth century – that underlay them.

If we are to provide the constitutional anchor which we require, we must legislate to provide it. We must provide it in the other place. The proper way forward is to leave the House of Commons as it stands, as the predominant legislative body, with a first-past-the-post system of election. However, we should provide as a constitutional anchor a House of Lords which is wholly or substantially elected on a basis of proportional representation. Subject to the same conventions which we enjoy today and which we allow to apply, and leaving executive government firmly in the hands, and under the control of, the House of Commons, we would provide a constitutional anchor by the full reflection of the whole spectrum of opinion in the House of Lords, backed by the natural authority which today can come only through the elective process.

Mr. Stanbrook: Can I believe my ears? Is my hon. Friend saying that 700 years of history has brought him to a conclusion which is completely at variance with the constitutional position today, in that this Chamber is democratically elected to express the will of the public? Is he saying that the House of Lords should take over that role?

Mr. Lyell: I suspect that history, whether over 700 years or a shorter period, is not my hon. Friend's strong point. If one considers the elective power of the Chamber, 700 years saw little of it. It is comparatively recent. Universal suffrage probably scarcely spans his lifetime.

It is a great strength that we are elected to this Chamber. However, as the Lord Chancellor has made wholly clear, there are dangers of an elected dictatorship. I do not wish my remarks to be considered as any sort of wets' charter because I believe in the strong leadership which we have seen from the Government. However, I do not believe that that strong leadership, for which the country has voted and for which I am confident it will vote when it next has the opportunity, is in any way diminished by the fact that the country also has an opportunity to express its broader views through its elected representatives in another place.

In the context of this debate I have developed that argument far enough. It is important to deal with it when we discuss such a major constitutional measure because I would hate it to be thought that a 'Bill of Rights' of this nature would be a satisfactory, fundamental safeguard which could let us move away from those even more important aspects to which I have referred.

Mr. Beith: I entirely agree with the hon. Gentleman in the proposition that the Bill of Rights can do only part of the job of safeguarding liberties. I and my hon. Friends and many other people outside our party would regard electoral reform and an electoral system which did not allow electoral dictatorship when there was no majority behind the Government as another essential element. I make that point to underline that we cannot be thought to suppose that the Bill of Rights, important though it is, can be the sole safeguard.

Mr. Lyell: I am grateful to the hon. Member for Berwick-upon-Tweed (Mr. Beith), and I know that he goes further in his views on electoral reform than I do – if bringing proportional representation into this place can be regarded as going further, as most people appear to think. I do not fear it, but I do not think that it would be to the long-term benefit of our constitution. I have expressed my own views on that, and I am happy to feel that I am a disciple in this matter of the Lord Chancellor.

The Bill has some considerable strengths in providing a defence against any encroachment on individual liberties. It seeks to introduce into our domestic law what at the moment is simply a treaty obligation. The benefits which come from that have already been described by right hon. and hon. Members.

It would be of enormous benefit if our judges had an opportunity carefully to consider – from the High Court of first instance through the Court of Appeal to the House of Lords – the issues which at the moment are thrown, ill-digested and wholly unconsidered by our judiciary, before the Strasbourg court. It would be beneficial to individuals to have an opportunity to bring matters of this kind simply and much more swiftly before our courts. There is no doubt that it might provide us with real benefits in areas such as the closed shop and nationalisation without compensation. But it is in some ways a very far-reaching measure whose effect upon our domestic law needs to be studied with immense care.

I have not yet read the report of the Select Committee of the other place, and I have not yet had an opportunity to look at the evidence that was put before it. However, from what I have read of the debates in the other place, it seems to me that to a great extent even the noble and learned lords who brought their brilliant minds to bear on this matter dealt with it in a fairly broad brush way. I have a good deal of sympathy with some of the caveats put forward by Lord Elwyn-Jones in the recent debates and by those in the other place a year ago.

It is one of the fascinating features of this debate that the radicals on the topic sit on the Government and the Cross-Benches and that, on the whole, the conservatives sit on the Opposition Benches.

Mr. Beith: The Labour Party.

Mr. Lyell: On the Labour Benches. I am grateful to the hon. Gentleman. . .

The Solicitor-General (Sir Ian Percival): I hope that it is for the convenience of the House if I intervene now. I speak in three capacities – first, on behalf of the Government. Secondly, I have the liberty to indicate personal views, as did my noble and learned Friend the Lord Chancellor in another place. Thirdly, I have the honour to be one of the Law Officers of the Crown. I have had practical experience of how the European Convention on Human Rights works. I hope to make some contribution to the debate in that rather special capacity. For a long time, Law Officers have regarded it as one of the most important traditions of their office that they should have a general interest in the protection of the liberty of the subject. . .

The Government are committed in the Conservative manifesto to discuss with all parties a possible Bill of Rights. That remains their wish. It is easy to pour scorn on that wish, but there have been references in the debate to the impossibility of making an entrenchment in our law. I think that we all accept that a Bill of Rights in the sense in which many of us understand it – namely, a schedule of rights which no one can be denied – cannot be made permanent in the United Kingdom.

The hon. and learned Member for Bradford, West (Mr. Lyons) referred to one of Lord Salmon's speeches in another place and his desire to see a 'statute of liberty'. That is why he cast doubt on the usefulness of what is now proposed. To a large extent it is a delusion because it would not afford the citizen anything like the rights that would be afforded by an entrenched position.

The hon. Member for Berwick-upon-Tweed said that it is far too easy for transient majorities to abrogate rights. I agree with him. It would not be made any more difficult for them to do so by the Bill. The Canadian experience is a good example. If a Government are legislating and they do not wish to be encumbered by a Bill of Rights, they may include the provision 'notwithstanding anything contained in such and such a Bill'. Let us consider the advantages but let us not assume advantages that are not there.

Mr. Michael Grylls: My right hon. and learned Friend is right technically, but a totalitarian Government would be flushed out if they felt it necessary to put such a provision into a measure that they put before the House. It would be a horrific admission of acting against human rights if the Government of the day had to incorporate such a provision. I should prefer a Government to have to do that openly.

The Solicitor-General: My hon. Friend is over-simplifying. I should like a real Bill of Rights to contain the right to have private education guaranteed for ever. I should like private choice in other areas to be guaranteed for ever. However, if the Opposition were to form a Government they would without hesitation reverse provisions of that sort. They would feel no shame in doing so. They would consider it their duty to do so. My hon. Friend's observation applies only to milk and water rights. Of course, either side of the House would be happy to change any provision with more meat in it if it had the chance to do so.

I beg hon. Members to accept what I am saying in the spirit in which it is offered. Let us not delude ourselves into thinking that we would be getting such a great deal by introducing such a Bill by getting rid of many major things that so many of us would dearly like to see disappear.

The hon. Member for Berwick-upon-Tweed said that we want these provisions to be straightforward, understandable and clear to the British people. That is almost like saying that the way in which a shuttle craft leaves the earth should be straightforward, clear and understandable to the British people. However much we may wish to have straightforwardness and clearness in certain matters it is not always possible to achieve it.

I stress the need for all party talks. Only to the extent that matters are agreed does my hon. Friend's proposition have any force. With an agreed programme, if anyone departs from it that enables the other party, which wants to adhere to it, to point out that it was agreed and should not be changed.

Mr. Beith: Is there any impediment whatsoever to the institution of those all-party talks?

The Solicitor-General: I am not trying to avoid anything; I am trying to get on. But dealing with that question is not my brief. It will not help if the hon. Gentleman takes that attitude. I hope he will not, because I want to get on to matters that may help in the argument. The hon. Gentleman knows, as I know, that such questions are arranged through the usual channels. I know of nothing to stop him or any other party pressing the appropriate people in the Government to get on with it.

There are two reasons why the talks are essential. I have mentioned one – the fact that the greater the measure of agreement, the more the proposition to which my hon. Friend referred holds force. The other is that we get the matter right. I want to say something that I hope will contribute to that. I have particular advice to offer, because in the past two years I have had something to do with the operation.

First, I should like to pay another tribute, this time to the part played in these debates by my noble and learned Friend the Lord Chancellor, who has spoken and written on many occasions, with his usual elegance of language and eloquence of argument, without hesitation or qualification, in favour of a Bill along these lines. It is unlikely that I shall be able to disguise the fact that although my objective is identical with my noble and learned Friend's, I see greater difficulties than he does.

All hon. Members are agreed that the rights and freedoms of the individual should be guaranteed. But that is almost the limit of the agreement, because there are as many views about what those rights are as there are individuals. There is a broad division between political parties, between those in politics who, when they talk about the right of the individual, are talking about the collective right of individuals to band together to protect their common rights, and those who believe in the rights of the individual against the various combinations.

We all share the same objectives, although we may all have different views once we get down to detail, when we try to itemise the ways in which that objective should be achieved. We must be careful not to fall into the syllogistic error of saying that because we all want to do something and the Bill is something, we must do it.

Many arguments have been advanced both ways. I had intended to try to summarise them, but I shall simply refer hon. Members to the speech of my noble and learned Friend the Lord Advocate in the most recent debate in another place, when he briefly summarised the main pros and cons. I prefer to go in to more detail on particular points.

There are those who say that the individual must surely be better off with a Bill of Rights. I say that we must examine the position closely and ask ourselves whether in fact he would be better off, to what extent, and what the price paid would be, not by the Government – I am not concerned about that – but by individuals, for such improvements as result.

We should not undersell our position. We are always trying to improve the position, but a large proportion of the world would be glad to have the protection afforded by our common law. It is a philosophy as much as a system of law. It is a philosophy that says 'We, the courts, are trying to do what is fair.' It leads the courts to say that their principal task is to protect the weak from the strong – the strong can look after themselves. It is a philosophy that says nobody should be liable to somebody else except on the basis of contract or tort. When we are thinking of prospective plaintiffs, we can be generous and we can think that we should give liability on a wider basis. When we are thinking of ourselves as defendents, we are glad that the philosophy of the common law is that we shall not be found liable to pay something to someone else unless it arises out of a contract or tort.

We start with all those advantages. Some say that if we had a statement of rights the individual would know better where he stands. Others say that he would be sorely confused. If the construction of the convention were as clear as a bell and everyone could understand it, the individual would have a positive and clear declaration of his rights. If in fact it is far from clear, there is some force in the argument that one is merely adding confusion to confusion.

All the arguments can be easily overstated. I shall try not to overstate them either way. I shall remind the House of what the Select Committee said in paragraph 30 of its report:

> 'in any country, whatever its constitution, the existence or absence of legislation in the nature of a Bill of Rights can in practice play only a relatively minor part in the protection of human rights.'

As everyone has professed to admire what was said by the Committee, let them hear this proposition as well:

> 'What is important above all, is a country's political climate and traditions. This is, the Committee think, common ground among both those who favour and those who oppose a Bill of Rights, and they received no evidence that human rights are in practice better protected in countries which have a code of fundamental rights embodied in their law than they are in the United Kingdom.'

I shall refer to some practical points. Some might say that they are points of law – of course they are. However, in my book, the law has no purpose at all save in its practical application, in how it works, how it affects people's rights and how it enables them to do this, that or the other. Those are essentially practical matters.

The Lord Chancellor places great importance on the point that one of the reasons for doing what is proposed is that the construction of statutes in this country is so confused and confusing. It is said that if we were to have the Bill, the courts would have a clear guide to construction. Of course, the Lord Chancellor is right. There are cases in which the courts have to struggle to put a meaning on the statute, but that is nothing to do with the rules of construction. That is because we happen to have passed legislation which is without a clear meaning; it is incomprehensible. This is extremely relevant when we are discussing safeguarding the liberty of the subject. The two factors which individually and collectively have impinged upon the liberty of the subject as much as anything in the past 20 years are the volume of legislation, which is oppressive in itself, and the quality of it, which is further oppressive.

We do not want to look for the solution to all those problems in a Bill such as this. The solution to those problems entails much greater self-denial and not, as some people say, greater expertise by the draftsman though of course, some drafting can be improved. We must recognise that it happens because either someone is legislating in a hurry and has not thought it through properly so that the draftsman does not get the proper instructions, or that we change it and get it wrong as it is going through the House.

Mr. Nicholas Baker: Some of us who came into this House relatively recently are still expecting the promised day of very much less legislation. Although I am not of the view that the Bill is the right approach to this matter, I think that the subject of human rights is extremely important and that it would be a much more profitable and suitable subject for an extended debate on the very matters mentioned by my right hon. and learned Friend about which rights should be protected. Perhaps my right hon. and learned Friend can give us some guarantee of time.

The Solicitor-General: I cannot give any guarantee. I am expressing opinions fairly freely. They are not new. I have expressed the same opinions year in and year out. We need to look at the fundamentals. We need to look at what is happening that is oppressive and try to put it right.

My hon. Friend the Member for Dorset, North (Mr. Baker) complained about the volume of legislation. Although I have been here a good deal longer than he has, I have shared the view expressed by my hon. Friend without interval all through my time here. When will the promised day come when there is less legislation?

This again is a practical matter. If we do not do what we have committed ourselves to do, we are accused of having failed to fulfil our pledges. If we fulfil them, there is more legislation in our programme than we want to see. We have to hold the balance.

I hope that I have said enough and said it freely enough to show where my sympathies lie in this respect. I speak for every member of the Government in saying that we recognise that the quantity of legislation should be reduced and that the quality of it should be improved. If we achieved both objectives, we would do more to assist the liberty of the subject than anything else that I can think of. . .

HC Deb. 8 May 1981, cols 419f.

90   DEBATE ON CIVIL LIBERTIES, 1985

Mr. Richard Ottaway: I beg to move, that this House strongly endorses the need to protect the essential rights and liberties of the individual citizen, while recognising the vital need to preserve order and stability in our society. . .

Individual liberties are enshrined in the unwritten common law and statutes as interpreted by the courts of England. It is becoming more and more apparent that the common law, on its own, is not a comprehensive safeguard of individual rights and liberties. The growing evidence of this is the increasing number of cases that are found to be admissible by the European Court and the many cases in which the United Kingdom is found to be in breach of the convention compared with other countries.

There have been tremendous developments in English law in recent years. We have seen especially the development of the process of judicial review, which examines the rights of the individual when confronted with authority. From time to time, common law needs assistance from statute law. The Sex Discrimination Act 1975 and the Race Relations Acts 1976 are two examples. Without these Acts, the common law would be entirely inadequate to deal with the issues to which they are directed. It was necessary to adjust the balance by introducing legislation.

Britain desperately needs a Bill of Rights. I support the call for the European convention on human rights to be incorporated into our legal system. It is not a perfect statement of rights, as it was drafted about 35 years ago. It is ironic that it lacks any express reference to the freedom of passage and the right to work, although such rights can be construed from it. However, it would be politically impossible to achieve consensus on anything other than the European convention. Accordingly, if there is to be any prospect of the incorporation of a Bill of Rights into our legislation it must be the European convention.

We have shown a marked reluctance to incorporate a Bill of Rights. After all, it took 15 years to establish the right of the individual to petition to the European Court. Despite a number of attempts to have the convention incorporated into our legal system, little progress has been made.

It is especially ironic that as the 'wind of change' swept across Africa, one by one the Commonwealth countries, as they gained their independence, adopted the European convention on the advice of United Kingdom Governments. It began with Nigeria in 1958, and the convention, as incorporated into the Nigerian constitution, became the model for the 'fundamental rights' which are to be found in the great majority of independent Commonwealth countries. In this way, the convention has been transplanted by Westminster legislation into the national laws of more countries and territories than are party to it.

There are many good reasons for the incorporation of the convention. As I have demonstrated, there is a substantial body of very learned opinion which believes that the common law has developed as far as it can go and has been found to be lacking on many occasions, the remedy having to be found in the European Court. The court has played an important role in developing and protecting human rights in Britain, from a prisoner's right of access to a lawyer to enabling *The Sunday Times* to publish its report on behalf of the disabled children in the Thalidomide tragedy. In this Session alone, two Bills have been introduced as a direct result of decisions of the European Court. These are the new regulations on telephone tapping and the new restrictions on corporal punishment in schools.

As the convention is not incorporated into our law, one practical effect is that a judgment of the European Court cannot be referred to by British judges or relied upon in their interpretation of statutes and civil liberties. This deprives the judges of the power and responsibility of protecting civil rights. If the convention were incorporated into our legislation, a body of case law would be built up to which judges could refer, and those with a grievance could obtain a remedy from the High Court without undue difficulty ...

The introduction of a statutory Bill of Rights to Britain will almost certainly stop civil liberties from becoming a political football. A classic example is the reference to the European Court of the GCHQ decision, which is clouded in political controversy. Another example is the three British Rail employees, Young, James and Webster, who established at the European Court the right not to join a trade union, a case which is still not recognised by the NCCL ...

A Bill of Rights would be a pillar in our midst with which the young would grow up. The establishment of the right would no longer be the subject of a political argument and sectarianism would be removed from our society. The rights of the individual are paramount and they will receive support from all quarters of the House. The current debate over collective and individual rights is most disturbing and a fundamental advance in individual rights and liberties would be the incorporation of a Bill of Rights into our legislation. That would go a long way towards ensuring that the rights of the individual do not become subservient to collective rights.

I recommend the motion and urge hon. Members to support it. . .

Mr. Alex Carlile: Not only the hon. Gentleman, but – I hope that he will forgive me for this – some of his as yet even more distinguished colleagues have expressed similar views in the past. In a celebrated Dimbleby lecture, the present Lord Chancellor expressed the opinion that the Houses of Parliament were no longer able to provide satisfactory or adequate safeguards for the fundamental liberties of the individual. As all right hon. and hon. Members know, the simple reason for that is that our work in the House is too great in volume and too complex in detail for hon. Members to be able to look day-by-day at breaches of possibly important and, indeed, fundamental civil rights, which may have occurred as a result of unfortunate excesses by the police, local authorities, the Civil Service or other public bodies.

That view had been expressed before by many others. Not least, it had been said in strong terms in a pamphlet, published by the Conservative Political Centre, by the present Secretary of State for Education and

Science. He had come to similar conclusions over 10 years ago on the same basis – that Parliament could no longer safeguard the liberties of the individual. The Liberal party and my hon. Friends in the Social Democratic party have long expressed similar views. Indeed, Lord Wade has a distinguished record of propounding that view, as have my hon. Friends the Members for Caithness and Sutherland and for Berwick-upon-Tweed (Mr. Beith). The roll of honour goes across party lines on to the more independent Benches. That most distinguished of judges and constitutional lawyers, Lord Scarman, has expressed a similar view on many occasions.

The problem is that the only remedy that is realistically available at present to the citizen who feels that his fundamental liberties have been interfered with is an application for judicial review. The procedure has improved in recent months, so that it is now easier to apply for judicial review and quicker to have an application heard. However, the procedure is expensive and risky, and it involves going to the High Court. Many of those who have been wronged are people who may find the prospect of applying to the High Court for judicial review somewhat intimidating. It is right to say that the judges have been pushing out the boundaries of judicial review. Because of the liberal judicial interpretation that has extended the range of circumstances in which judicial review can be applied for, it has become more possible for the citizen to obtain redress. However, it is a lengthy, expensive and intimidating procedure. . .

Another important reason for a Bill of Rights is that we are living in such a complicated society – much more complicated even than that of the late 1940s, when the convention was drafted – so that it is much more difficult for the citizen to know what his fundamental rights are. Indeed, I suspect that each of us from time to time is approached in his constituency surgery by someone who says, 'But it is my right.' Whether one be an expert constitutional lawyer or not, one cannot answer yes or no, because we have little understanding of what those 'It is my right' rights are. It is important to define them as far as possible.

Mr. Lyell: This is a most fascinating subject. Before we charge too rapidly in the direction of incorporation, is it not right to remember, as the hon. and learned Gentleman said, that the European convention has many faults, many wishy-washy aspects and obscurities, and that we have no opportunity now, or even if we incorporated it, to change it?

Mr. Carlile: The debate could develop into an interesting colloquy between myself and the hon. and learned Gentleman, but I have already spoken at length and I do not want that to happen.

At the moment we have no Bill of Rights worth the name. We need one, and the European convention provides a good basis from which our Bill of Rights could be drafted.

I congratulate the hon. Member for Nottingham, North, whom I criticised a few moments ago, on his luck in obtaining this debate and his good sense in choosing the subject of the debate. I hope that most of the rest of the debate will concentrate upon the constructive rather than the destructive parts of his speech.

Mr. Edward Leigh: The more time I spend in politics, the less certain I become about what other politicians tell me is certain. Usually there is an element of truth in what both sides say. But, no matter, because most of the great evils perpetrated in history have been caused by convinced adherents of a specific ideology or 'ism'. Those of us travelling hopefully on the road towards an elusive truth are usually driving too slowly and have our eyes too closely on the road to kill anyone.

For me, the only certainty in politics is that just as the individual can only find his individual salvation from within himself, so the principal aim of political organisation and thought must be to enable the individual to have the fullest freedom of action and expression consistent with equal freedom for others.

For those of us who support the Western liberal tradition of the supremacy of the individual, those beliefs conjure up more dilemmas than they provide answers. The question was first posed by J. S. Mill in 'On Liberty', when he wrote:

'The liberty of the individual must be thus far limited. He must not make himself a nuisance to other people.'

The classic dilemma is the right of the individual to speak out. That must include the right to criticise individuals and the right of other individuals to be given redress to protect their good names and reputations.

It is not surprising, therefore, that the doctrine of civil liberty, like that of democracy, is at once the most universally accepted doctrine and, in most countries, the most abused. Thus, the Soviet constitution has one of the most ringing acclamations of civil liberties, while we in this country have no Bill of Rights. I know, however, in which country my civil liberties are better protected.

As Burke said:

'Abstract liberty, like other mere abstractions, is not to be found.'

I find it useful to consider the analogy of the large house full of tenants, when addressing that dilemma. I should defend to the death the right of any of my fellow tenants to criticise me or the management of the house. I believe, however, that I have the right to stop, if necessary by force, one of my fellow inmates from wielding a pick-axe at the foundations of the house and bringing the whole lot tumbling down.

Let me illustrate my analogy with reference to the Campaign for Nuclear Disarmament. If our home is ringed with enemies armed to the teeth whose one aim is to destroy the pleasant liberal, democratic regime pertaining in the house, does one of my fellow tenants have the right to stand up and say that we should unbolt the door? Most decidely, yes. That is the right of free speech, however miguided. That is his civil liberty. It is a different matter if he insists on passing a message to the enemy outside, telling him how to unbolt the door. That is what CND is doing by telling the world where our cruise missiles are being deployed. Does the minority tenant have the right to demonstrate in the corridors of our house against the wishes of the majority? Most decidedly, yes. It is his civil liberty to demonstrate. Does he also have the right deliberately to sabotage the work of our house by sitting in the corridor and preventing the rest of us from moving about? That is different. It is denying the majority of us our civil liberties, and that is what CND means by civil disobedience. The British people agree.

In a recent Gallup poll commissioned by the Coalition for Peace Through Security, whose results have previously been unpublished, 52 per cent. of those who had an opinion approved of the monitoring by the security services of political organisations such as CND which have adopted civil disobedience in pursuit of their aims. . .

An even larger majority – 62 per cent. – supported the monitoring of trade union activists who are members of the Communist party. Why do the British people take that clear view? They recognise that those people are less interested in free speech than in bringing the whole house of freedom tumbling down.

The delicate plant of our civil liberties can flourish only if we respect the will of the majority. The alternative is the law of the jungle, the law of 'might is right', and the immediate degradation and ultimate destruction of all our civil liberties. . .

Mr. Andrew F. Bennett: It is questionable whether we ought to embrace such a Bill. Are there absolute, fundamental rights? All of us believe that there are fundamental rights, but when one examines them more carefully one finds that almost all of them have to be qualified. The right to work appears to be a fundamental right which we ought to embrace, yet in practice we do not embrace it because there are between 3 million and 4 million people in this country who are unemployed.

There also appears to be a fundamental right of free speech. However, I do not imagine that any Conservative Member would grant me the right, late at night, to knock at all the doors in the street in which I live and insist upon haranguing the people who live in those houses. That is a right which to a certain extent is limited. One also thinks that there is a right to breathe pure air, yet people also have the right to drive motor vehicles, which, to a certain extent, pollute the air.

When, therefore, one examines the question, one finds that many of the rights which we take for granted have to be modified to a certain extent, that for most rights there are corresponding responsibilities and that it becomes increasingly difficult to define those rights. Anybody who is to be tried ought to have the right to a trial in public, yet it is generally accepted that for certain offences against the state the trial ought to take place in camera. Although there is the right to an open trial, there is also the right to screen a juvenile from the publicity of an open trial. Therefore, a balance has to be struck between rights on the one hand and responsibilities on the other.

This causes problems over a Bill of Rights. If a Bill of Rights could be written in simple language, was absolute and self-enforcing, I should be enthusiastic about the introduction of such a Bill, but a Bill of Rights would not be self-enforcing. In almost every case it would have to be interpreted and implemented by somebody. One of the weaknesses of a Bill of Rights lies in its enforcement. It would have to be interpreted, and power would have to be handed over to the judiciary to interpret the Bill.

The hon. and learned Member for Montgomery (Mr. Carlile) pointed out that if a Bill of Rights or the European convention on human rights were enshrined in our legislation it could be implemented by the lowest courts of the land, but in practice there would be appeals to higher and yet higher courts. Ultimately, the implementation of a Bill of Rights would very much depend upon the views of High Court Judges, who are not elected.

Mr. Alex Carlile: I am puzzled by the approach of the hon. Member for Denton and Reddish (Mr. Bennett). He seems to be calling into question the whole concept of the rule of law. Issues are interpreted by judges every day. Who else is to interpret the laws that are made in this House? I would ask the hon. Gentleman what is wrong about adopting the ordinary circumstances of the rule of law? Let the judiciary interpret, and let us rely upon the political impartiality of the judiciary.

Mr. Bennett: The problem with a Bill of Rights is that in some way it is absolute. There are many examples of the way in which judges have interpreted the law. If Parliament does not like their interpretations, the law is changed. If there were a Bill of Rights which was continually being altered by Parliament because it did not like the interpretation that judges were placing upon it, I do not believe that it would hold any attraction. The attraction of a Bill of Rights is that it is absolute, but even if it were absolute it would be subject to the interpretation of judges.

If one considers the enforcement of the constitution of the United States, one finds that it has been the willingness of judges continually to adapt and modify their interpretations that has allowed the constitution to work. Before we grow too enthusiastic about a Bill of Rights, I suggest that we ought to realise that if we enshrined such a Bill absolutely in law we should be handing over parliamentary powers to the judiciary. I am not particularly happy about the economic, class and sex backgrounds of hon. Members, but I would certainly argue that this House is more representative of the whole country than are our High Court judges. . .

Mr. Clive Soley: As I have said on several occasions, the democratic and civil rights of the people of Britain have been seriously eroded in recent years, and particularly under this Government. That is the case that I shall advance again today.

I would be the first to concede that that erosion has been going on for many years. There are several reasons for it, not least the effect on this country of the political problems in Northern Ireland. We should address ourselves to that, but that is not the subject of today's debate. The United Kingdom has seen a terrifying erosion of civil rights and that is why we have such an appalling record before the European Court of Human Rights in Strasbourg. More than any other country, we have been brought to book by that court. As a Member of Parliament and a British citizen who is proud of our democracy, I am ashamed of that. I should like to think that Conservative Members were ashamed of it too, but I do not think that they are, or ever will be.

The Government are making a fundamental mistake in assuming that order can be imposed at a time of social and economic distress. I remind the Conservative party that social and economic distress, and in particular mass unemployment and hyper-inflation, lead to calls for authoritarian leaders.

Dictatorship lies at the end of that road. In the past week or so we have heard talks on the second world war. I remember, with respect, the comment by the President of West Germany. He said that the German people must take responsibility for what happened during the Hitler years. There is much in that, but all of us must take responsibility, because all of us are responsible in a way for what happened in Germany before 1933. When hon. Members consider the hyper-inflation in Germany then, the mass unemployment, the feeling of national disgrace and the fact that the Germans could not cope because of the burdens put on them from afar, they must bear in mind that we ploughed the fields in which Hitler so ably sowed his seeds. When we forget that, we forget what we are doing here.

More than anything else, my objection to this Government is that they have tried to impose order in numerous situations where that cannot be done...

We should always beware of the call for order. Order is one of the most dangerous concepts out, unless it is qualified with the need for law and for civil rights. If people argue for order alone, they are arguing for the Hitlerite example of order. That is what Conservative Members forget so easily. Sadly, the failure of the motion – I agree with the hon. and learned Member for Montgomery (Mr. Carlile) that the latter half of the speech of the hon. Member for Nottingham, North (Mr. Ottaway) was constructive – is that it is assumed that we can have stability in the face of economic distress. That is impossible, as can be seen in Poland, South Africa and – I hate to say it – in Northern Ireland. We should have learned from that lesson. Ultimately, one cannot go on imposing order without a severe risk to the democracy that one is trying to defend...

The concept of equality is important to Socialists because we know that civil rights are conditioned by social and economic circumstances. A person earning a high income has more real civil rights than a person who is unemployed or on low income. That is probably why the constituent of the hon. Member for South Hams (Mr. Steen) was lectured so terribly on the bus to the seaside.

The hon. and learned Member for Montgomery (Mr. Carlile) wanted to know the Labour party's position on a Bill of Rights. It is similar to the opinion expressed by my hon. Friend the Member for Denton and Reddish (Mr. Bennett). I recognise the strength of argument for a Bill of Rights and a written constitution, but the issue is complex. The Liberal view is to go for a European state in which a written constitution and a Bill of Rights applies. If one picked on part of what is, in effect, a written constitution, and put it into a constitution under which Parliament is seen as sovereign, difficulties would arise.

As my hon. Friend the Member for Denton and Reddish said so powerfully, one of the significant differences between Britain and other western European powers and America is that entry to the judiciary is restricted to the higher socio-economic groups. That is because grants are not given to train a person through to being a judge.

Mr. Alex Carlile: What about magistrates?

Mr. Soley: The hon. and learned Member for Montgomery is supposed to be a lawyer, although from his interruptions I should not have thought so. Magistrates do not preside at Strasbourg, nor are they likely to. The point is that entry into the higher ranks of the judiciary in Britain is restricted. The way to change that is to give grants for study to all people who want to go all the way to the top ranks. Until we achieve that the higher levels of the judiciary will be seen not only to be against, but not to understand the problems of many people whose cases go before them. That is why I should not want to pick up one part of a written constitution and incorporate it into our constitution. . .

HC Deb., 13 May 1985, cols. 44f.

---

91   DEBATE ON THE HUMAN RIGHTS BILL, 1987

RB NOTE: *The text of the Bill was similar in form to the Human Rights and Fundamental Freedoms Bill 1985, see Doc. 39C.*

Sir Edward Gardner: I beg to move, That the [Human Rights] Bill be now read a Second time. . .

Today is an important day for the future of British law. That is because at the moment, our law contains a gaping gap. Anyone who wants to rely on the convention to protect his human rights cannot come before a British court. That is because the court would say it could not look at the convention and the rights that are contained in it. It would say that the European convention on human rights is a treaty and, therefore, not part of British law, and that it could not take notice of it. If the Bill becomes law, every one of us will have the right to go to any court in the land and, subject to the Bill's stringent provisions, be able to say, 'I want to rely on my rights as contained in the convention, which is now part of English law.'

The rights that the Bill refers to are the rights in the European convention on human rights. That sounds a grand and, to some perhaps, off-putting title, but they are the rights which belong to each one of us. They are not the rights of an egotistical idealist or rights which give a licence to betray state secrets or to breach security; they are rights which we all recognise are fundamental to our lives. They are rights which shape society and guarantee our freedoms and to which, as Edmund Burke said of religion, nothing is so fatal as indifference. They are the rights to life, liberty, free trial, freedom of expression, privacy, freedom of association and the right to be protected from degrading punishment whether in the school or by the state.

I submit that there are rights, with or without the convention, to which we have looked throughout the centuries. The House should consider a way in which, without impediment, British people can take advantage of those rights.

The European convention on human rights was signed and ratified by the 21 countries of the Council of Europe. The rights were drafted by two English lawyers. One was a skilled parliamentary draughtsman and the other was Sir David Maxwell Fyfe, who later became Lord Chancellor Kilmuir. The House should look at the language of the articles in the convention. It is the language mainly of the English common law. It is language which echoes right down the corridors of history. It goes deep into our history and as far back as Magna Carta.

If anybody suggests that these are foreign laws which are foreign to our minds and spirits. I suggest that he has not read the convention's articles. In 1951, with the support of Churchill and Macmillan for the Conservatives. Lord Layton for the Liberals and Ungoed-Thomas for the Labour party, which was in government, Britain ratified the convention. We were the first country to ratify it. In those days, we saw it as I hope we see it today – as a supreme instrument to guarantee our rights. We thought it so important that, in 1953, the Government decided to extend what they believed to be the benefits of the rights in the convention to 97 million people who lived in Commonwealth territories for which we had some responsibility.

I am sure that the House agrees that, in 1951, when the Government ratified the convention, it was assumed – it must have been – that the rights in it were covered by the law in Britain. I am perfectly sure that it was not the intention of the Government or the Opposition to create two conflicting jurisdictions. We still hear – no doubt we shall hear it today – a reflection of the view that there are two conflicting jurisdictions. I hope that I anticipate wrongly, but I anticipate that hon. and possibly right hon. Members will say that we do not need the convention and the rights in it because it is all covered by English law and, if such law does not exist, we can deal with matters bit by bit. They argue that, when a problem comes up, we can introduce legislation piecemeal to deal with it. That view has gone on since the treaty was ratified. Since then, it has been demonstrated time and again in Strasbourg how wrong we are to suppose that our law in its present state covers all the needs demanded by the articles in the convention. It does not at all. . .

Mr. David Steel: When I was a student of constitutional law at Edinburgh university I was brought up on the classic doctrines of Dicey and the supremacy of Parliament. In my 20 years in the House I have come to recognise that the need for the Bill arises precisely because many of us feel that Parliament on its own can no longer adequately protect our citizens. The increase in the executive arm of Government and in the number of areas of Government activity, under Governments of all parties, and the increasing complexity and speed of modern life have meant that the individual is in need of greater protection, but is afforded less.

Our courts have had no set of guiding principles on individual liberties which is why so many of us have long campaigned for a Bill of Rights. As a result there has been a steep rise in the number of applications for judicial review from 533 in 1981 to 1,169 in 1985. As hon. Members we find ourselves unable to remedy a large number of wrongs. Despite the advent of the ombudsman, justice for the individual is still often frustrated.

The sheer scope of Government activity and the bureaucracy and technology that support it have increased exponentially over the past century since Dicey was writing his learned works. Inevitably, the individual is at an increasing disadvantage in the massive system of social management and ultimately of control, which is inherent in the world of computer files, satellite surveillance and telephone tapping.

It is a stange anomaly that British citizens must take the road to Strasbourg at great expense to seek redress for the abuse of rights which the Government have a treaty obligation to protect. The fact that more have done so and more have had their cases upheld than people from other signatory countries has been a proper embarrassment to successive Governments.

A good reason for incorporating the convention into law is so that we can start doing our own dirty laundry in Britain rather than send it abroad. Virtually every other signatory to the convention deals with human rights cases in its courts and we shall only be catching up with them if we approve the Bill today.

It is bad for the United Kingdom's reputation, for its citizens, administrators and judges alike that the freedoms guaranteed by the convention cannot be invoked directly before the courts of England and Scotland. Since 1965 when the right of individual petition was introduced in Britain, petitions have flowed to Strasbourg. About 800 provisional files are opened on cases from the United Kingdom every year. No other state sends as many cases as that to Strasbourg. No other state has had so many cases declared admissible by the Commission, or lost so many cases before the court.

The rights that have been upheld by the Commission have always been fundamental and often far-reaching. Few rights in a democracy are more fundamental than the right of a free press, yet, as the hon. and learned Gentleman has said, the European convention had to require English law to lift the muzzle that it had placed on *The Sunday Times* in the thalidomide campaign. It is thanks also to the European convention that prisoners in the United Kingdom are no longer fettered in what they may write to their Member of Parliament. It was the European convention which established an even more fundamental right: a prisoner's right of access to a lawyer in connection with prison discipline. Therefore, inch by painful inch the European Court has often pushed a reluctant British Government to conform to the convention. I side with the hon. and learned Gentleman rather than with the former Solicitor-General in agreeing that the existence of cases at Strasbourg has often pushed our Government towards legislation. . .

Sir Ian Percival: I wish to express some doubt about what we are doing . . . The biggest danger to democracy is that the expectations of most of our people are far higher than any Government can ever deliver with the result that almost everybody is almost always disappointed with the performance of every Government. This is an extremely serious development. The biggest danger of this Bill is that too many people could expect far too much to flow from it.

I am all for ensuring that our people enjoy the rights enshrined in the convention, but we must never forget that the remedy in most cases lies in our own hands. That must not be underestimated. The biggest danger of infringement of these rights, for example, lies in the hands of the House. In my view, the most oppressive development of recent years has been the quantity and the quality of the legislation that has emerged from the House. The remedy for that lies in our own hands, and our hands alone.

We should not underestimate what protection we already enjoy. How fortunate we are – we have been free men and women for centuries, not because of the 'one man, one vote' principle or because of the convention, but because we have established the rule of law. Under the rule of law, an independent judiciary has built up a body of law, the philosophy of which is to protect the weak from the strong. The strong can protect themselves. The strongest of all is the state. Our laws protect individuals, particularly the weak, against any kind of wrong. There must be an element of wrong. We tend sometimes to say that we shall give this, that and the other right, but sometimes we must think about the people against whom we are giving a right. The common law has held the balance between different contenders. Let us not forget that. . .

Mr. Austin Mitchell: We have two purposes in the House and Parliament. The first is to provide for the well-being of our people, to enlarge the nation and to increase their joy, as it is put in Isaiah. The second is to protect and advance their rights and freedoms. For both those purposes we have always used the power of Parliament, which these days means the power of the party majority, and thus the power of the Executive. We should ask, before we rush to reject the Bill as an infringement of the power of Parliament, whether that power has served the people well. We have had the strongest Executive but the slowest rate of economic growth and development. We are now one of the comparatively declining industrial powers, so a strong Executive has not served us well there.

When it comes to the rights and freedom of people, the strong Executive has become one of the most serious restrictions. This very week, as if the Government have carefully stage-managed the events to provide support for the Bill, what has been going on in BBC Scotland has shown that point.

The power of the Executive and of Parliament is a particular problem for us in the Labour party, and I address my remarks to my hon. Friend the Member for Newcastle upon Tyne. East (Mr. Brown) on the Front Bench. I would not want the Labour party to praise with faint damns. We can leave churlishness to the Government, to whom it comes naturally, and not take their position on this Bill, which is of great importance to the Labour party as well as to the rest of the House. In the Labour party we are traditionally suspicious of a Bill of Rights and of judges and courts – in many cases with good reason. We rely on Parliament as the engine or instrument of Social-ism and on the power that the mandate confers to carry through a programme as the lever of Socialism.

We have to ask now how well, in the past decade, those two instruments have served us to advance the cause of improving the lot of the people. They have in fact become engines for reversing so much of what we have achieved over the previous decades. I am clear that rights, properly defined as they are in a European convention – although less adequately defined than I would like them to be – would provide the basis for the resistance to the rearguard action carried out by the Government, undermining the rights and position of the people. They are a base for resisting the reaction that has gone on over the past few years.

We should also consider the role of rights in Socialism. In the past weeks, two books have been published, one by my right hon. Friend the Member for Birmingham. Sparkbrook (Mr. Hattersley), and a good book on Socialism and freedom by my hon. Friend the Member for Dagenham (Mr. Gould). They have both emphasised the undoubted truth that Socialism is about freedom. It must be about freedom, because economic advance gives people the power to fulfil their freedom, and a base from which they can grasp freedom. In the abstract, freedom is no use. The power and the means are needed to fulfil it. The advance of the economic well-being of the people is the advance of their freedom.

Freedom implies the opportunity to exercise rights, as well as the concession of them. Traditionally, we have looked to the state for that means of advance. We have seen it as Socialism by prescription, handed down by Government through the state. We have to ask whether, at the level of advance and well-being that our people have reached, as our pluralistic society develops, even if it is in slow motion here – we are behind the rest of the world, but we are becoming more a diverse and pluralistic society – prescription is any longer the sole and adequate weapon to advance the cause of the people. As people are making conscious and deliberate choices as consumers in a consumer society, we have to ask whether those choices can be compartmentalised and whether we should not enlarge their choices in the political arena, in administration and in justice.

Should we not look to Socialism to advance not only by prescription but by empowering the people, giving them rights and the ability to stand on their own two feet and pursue their causes in the way that they want and to make deliberate choices? That is now a major engine of advance to which we should look, through the concession of rights and the advancement of the people, to provide for the future and rights, to advance their cause, to give them information – information is power – to have Government brought closer to them by the process of decentralisation and to have Government more open to influence by them. In short, we progress by empowering the people because that is what our people want. There is a widespread desire for rights and for the strength that those rights will bring. They will give people the ability to stand on their feet and face the world. That is why it is so important that we get back to full employment. There is no greater power to help somebody face the world than the power that comes from having a job and to be able to tell one's boss to get knotted if one wants to move on to another job and to provide for one's family. We must enlarge that and bring it into the political arena. We need as a party to accept rights – not churlishly to quibble and deny them or find arguments against giving them, but to embrace the act of giving them.

I was born with one supreme advantage; I am not a lawyer. However, the Bill takes a major step on the road for rights. Even though I am not a lawyer I could write a better convention. Indeed, it is important to note that the New Zealand Labour party is now in the process of introducing a Bill of

Rights and drafting its own convention of rights that will update so many of the provisions of the European convention. It will give the people rights of trade union membership, rights in housing and all sorts of areas that are important.

It would be possible to write a better convention, but the advance proposed in the Bill is immediate, practicable, in our grasp and necessary. It is necessary because people are forced into the folly of pursuing cases to Strasbourg with an inordinate delay and expense. It can take up to eight years for a case to get through that procedure and five years is probably the minimum. It can cost about £70,000, for which only a pathetically inadequate sum of legal aid is available. Why should be people be forced to that expense when they could pursue those rights through our own courts, with our own judges, and when they can use our legal system rather than having to go all the way to Strasbourg?

It would help the image of Britain if those rights were brought into our law, because fewer cases would be ruled admissible by the court, to the humiliation of this country. We have been ruled against in twice as many cases as any other country in Europe. That is a national humiliation. We would not face that if we could pursue rights in our own courts in our own way. That is a major practical argument.

It is important to say that this measure is popular. The hon. and learned Member for Fylde quoted the opinion polls to shows the strength of support. That may well be but the 2:1 majority who said that the they wanted the Bill, 71 per cent of whom said that it would give them more faith in our system, did not know every dot and comma of the European convention, just as I do not. However, they have a yearning and a desire for rights. We see that in our constituencies. People want to be able to stand on their own feet and pursue their own rights. That is what they were expressing. This Bill satisfies that need. The list of organisations supporting the Bill such as the British Council of Churches, the Civil and Public Services Association, the Consumers Association, Justice, MIND, the National Council for Civil Liberties and the National Council for Voluntary Organisations should give us an indication of the support for the strengthening of rights that it will confer.

It will not be a new dawn of liberty, but it will strengthen the citizen against the Executive. The citizen will be given the right to complain and to pursue his rights and the Executive will have at the very least, to answer and put up a case for what they are doing and not to act on their abstract will and power. That is a major advance.

The Bill advances the cause of liberty in another way. It introduces an element of pluralism into our system which is necessary, given the overseeing power of the Executive in Britain. It is the dominant feature of our system of Government. It is all very well for the right hon. and learned Member for Southport to say that we should rely on the power of Parliament. The power of Parliament is a party majority, not, the power of independent judgment by independent-minded Members. It is a steamroller driven by the Executive. The Executive in Britain is all powerful. An element of pluralism is a check on that.

The words of Neal Ascherson in *The Observer* on Sunday sum up so many of my feelings about the Bill. He said that the convention

'is absolutely alien to the practices and theory of the British State and, if it survived, would begin to subvert, split and topple them one after another. And that is why – on balance – I am for it.'

So am I, for the same reason. The Bill will introduce an element of pluralism and choice. It is another opinion by which people have to be influenced. Incorporating the convention into our legislation will educate the judges. That is vital. I can think of no higher purpose than that. It is a tragedy that we cannot advance and strengthen rights in Britain because we do not trust the judges to enforce them. That is one of the problems for the Labour party.

Professor Griffith in his book on the politics of judiciary sees the judges, rightly, as hopelessly unfit to stand between the citizen and the state. In the view [of] Professor Griffith and myself they are insitinctively Conservative, respect property, have establishment attitudes and are grovellingly servile to the Executive. All that is true. We have to change that. How do we change it? We change it by educating them and by including another element in the system to which they have to pay attention. We have to introduce the rights which the convention will confer on the people. The judges must then listen to that and not follow their own instincts as they often do. They will have to listen to the rulings and prescriptions of the convention. That is an important process of education that we have to accept in our system. . .

Mr. Geoffrey Rippon: There has been a great clamour, especially on Opposition Benches, about human rights and civil liberties. That has not happened suddenly. Right hon. and hon. Members on both sides of the House – especially in opposition – I emphasise that – have made ringing speeches about individual freedoms in the face of the growing power of the Executive, to which the hon. Gentleman so rightly referred. I hope that all his right hon. and hon. Friends who made those ringing speeches about human rights and civil liberties will be here today to support the Bill instead of being at a coffee morning or a wine and cheese party in their con- stituencies.

This is a matter of concern particularly to right hon. and hon. Members when in opposition because I recall my right hon. Friend the Member for Leeds. North-East (Sir K. Joseph) saying that it was the actions of the right hon. Member for Blaenau Gwent (Mr. Foot) that had made him decide that we had to have a Bill of Rights. He said of the right hon. Member for Blaenau Gwent that he was a Brutus in opposition but Caesarian in office. Indeed, at that time, one did not hear very much from the right hon. Member for Blaenau Gwent or the right hon. Member for Chesterfield (Mr. Benn) about the importance of freedom of information. I have no doubt that when they were members of the defence and overseas policy committee sometimes they did not even talk about those matters to their colleagues in the Cabinet, much less their party.

The truth is that all Governments, of whatever persuasion, have a tendency to be authoritarian, and future Governments may be even more so. That is why it is important today that right hon. and hon. Members should demonstrate that their fine words and speeches are not merely 'sound and fury, signifying nothing'.

I emphasise to the hon. Member for Great Grimsby that this is not to say that the Bill would be of any help or encouragement to those who seek to act contrary to the interests of national security. It would, however, give everyone the opportunity to pursue his legitimate rights before the European Court, such as the right to respect for his private and family life, his home, his correspondence and his freedom of expression ...

Today we have the opportunity to recognise that the great victories of the past, including of course the Bill of Rights of 1688, were won by Parliament acting against the Crown, the Executive. Of course now, the Executive and the law-making power are predominantly in the hands of the Government of the day. I remember Harold Macmillan once saying to a group of junior Ministers, 'Remember, we are the Queen's men.'

The purpose of Government, whether it is Government from the Conservative Benches or from the Labour Benches, is to get their programme through. They have to deal with Parliament. Anyone who believes that in these days a Parliament rises time and time again to exercise its authority against the Lobby fodder or the payroll vote, is living in a world of total illusion and everyone in this House and outside knows that. We can no longer take for granted that human rights and civil liberties in this country need no more protection than is provided by parliamentary vigilance. The stream of citizens that have headed for Strasbourg to seek remedies over the years testifies to that.

Our trouble today, which was identified by the late Lord Radcliffe, in his Reith lectures on 'The Problem of Power' in 1951 – and I suggest that he was at least as good an authority on these matters as Lord McCluskey – is that at a time when the Executive and the legislature are combined:

> 'the Security of what used to be called constitutional rights is a very frail thing.'

The Bill, if it does not do everything, will help sustain such rights ...

Mr. Fred Silvester: The European Convention seems to be the basis on which a number of hon. Members have argued in favour of the Bill. The Bill incorporates the European convention as the Bill of Rights that would apply in the United Kingdom. The justification for that is slim. The convention has never been debated in the House or voted on. In 1950, it was debated on a take-note motion before it was completed, and no vote was taken. The House then went on to discuss the meat content of sausages. Since then, the matter has not come before the House at all.

The Royal prerogative and the Ponsonby rules, which apply to treaties, ensure that there is no need for the matter to be raised in the House. My right hon. and learned Friend the Member for Hexham (Mr. Rippon) said that we were the first to ratify the convention. Of course we were. In every other country, the parliament had to discuss the matter and vote on it. Here we simply do it on the nod.

We are asked to support the Bill because we are bound by a convention which Parliament has never discussed or accepted. It seems that the options which my hon. and learned Friend the Member for Fylde presented to us were that we could accept the Bill, which would enable us not to go to Strasbourg, or to renege on the convention. There is another way, which I hope in due course a Government will have the courage to pursue. It is to cease to adhere to articles 25 and 46.

Article 25 permits individual petition to Strasbourg and article 46 makes compulsory the jurisdiction of the court. They were added by the then Prime Minister, Harold Wilson, in 1966. Before then, British Governments of all complexions felt that the convention served a useful purpose but that there was no requirement for it to be adopted internally as part of our domestic law or to give citizens a right to appeal to Strasbourg. That seems right. A wrong decision was made in 1966. That decision also has not been referred to the House. Due to the assiduity of my right hon. Friend the Member for Worthing (Mr. Higgins), it was raised on the Floor of the House during Question Time but, since then, at two, three or five-yearly intervals, the matter has been dealt with by written answer.

This massive change in the British constitution – it is the largest since the war – has been done entirely by Executive order. I feel no moral or legal obligation to support the Bill on the grounds that it stops the journey to Strasbourg. There are other and more soundly based means of doing that.

The 1966 decision submitted Parliament to the jurisdiction of a panel of overseas judges. The Bill proposes that we should submit Parliament to a panel of English judges. That is somewhat more satisfactory, but it is not a sufficient argument. We must judge this matter entirely on the merits of the Bill and put the Strasbourg argument to one side. We have to face the fact that we have permitted the situation to develop without any debate or vote. I still cannot understand how the Commons, which huffs and puffs at the slightest prospect of constitutional change, has allowed this to go through with no voice and no vote. That has done Parliament no honour ...

Why are we so motivated towards this legislation? I remember that in 1976 the Lord Chancellor produced a booklet on elective dictatorship. In my view that phrase did us great harm, because this country is not an elective dictatorship, and will not become one while Parliament is elected. In that pamphlet, the Lord Chancellor encapsulated the fear of several of my hon. Friends. He stated that Parliament had not abused its powers, but that it might. However, he could produce no evidence that things were falling down about our ears and that our freedoms were being removed.

He was fixed on the question of parliamentary sovereignty and was concerned about the way in which this House works. God knows, we all know how ineffective it is in many ways. However, he was fixed on that issue and felt that he should do something about it. I remind the House that his solution was a written constitution, of which a Bill of Rights was only a part.

It is a curious argument to say that we should adopt a radical change in our constitution on the hypothesis that evil may come, but without any evidence that it has. The elective dictatorship could only come about if all the existing institutions that preserve our freedoms suddenly collapsed about us. However, I see no evidence of that. Where is the evidence that the press is to be silenced, that business is to be supine, that Parliament is to become subservient, or that the electorate will be permanently fooled? Why are we suddenly plunged into the position of feeling that in panic we must change our constitution because of an evil that is not yet with us? ...

Mr. Andrew F. Bennett: We have not fully explored the many problems that a Bill of Rights raises. I have three major objections. The Bill will encourage the House to abdicate its rights and duties further than it has done in recent years. We have not spent long enough exploring the fact that in many areas rights are not absolute – the convention itself sets out boldly most of the rights, but follows them up with qualifications and in many areas one individual's so-called right imposes a restriction on another individual. Finally if we enforce an Act of Rights, as it will become, through the courts, we must have a major reform of our courts.

Although we claim that everybody has equal access to the courts, in practice that is not the case. The courts are easily available to the rich, the articulate and those who can find their way around society, but for many people they are not easily accessible. So long as the courts enforce such an Act and the present system of legal expenses and so on remains, we shall confer rights only on a certain group, not on the whole of society.

To return to the question of the House relinquishing powers, it is ironic that we are discussing a Bill of Rights when recently the House has had many opportunities to enforce particular rights in detail and in practice. It was unfortunate that, in the last Parliament, the Freedom of Information Bill failed to attract 100 supporters to ensure that the debate could continue. I should have thought that it would have been far better for the House to assert itself and pass that legislation. This Parliament has passed data protection legislation that, in my view, is virtually worthless. It does not enforce individual rights of privacy. Of course, we imposed the Police and Criminal Evidence Act 1983 which, again, has considerable shortcomings.

If we were all that concerned about rights, would it not have been better for us to assert ourselves and insist, as a House of Commons, that those rights be enshrined in legislation, rather than leave it almost to the very end of the Parliament to say that we must come along with a blanket measure – a Bill of Rights – that may put right some of the omissions and errors? The House will be tempted to say, 'We have an Act of Rights, so we do not need to concern ourselves with particular bits of legislation.' It will be only too easy for us to pass Bills that give greater powers to the police or to the Executive. We can always say that the Act of Rights will step in. Hon. Members will be less diligent – they have not been all that good up till now – in asserting rights when they deal with individual pieces of legislation. It would be far better for us to act in the spirit of the European convention, but insist that we put it into our own detailed legislation.

If we give up our powers, we shall hand them to judges. I am amazed at the number of people who have such great confidence in judges, particularly in view of the sentences imposed this week in the rape case. The judges certainly demonstrated that they are not particularly attuned to the population at large. The more we hand over to judges the duty to take political decisions – in many cases it is a matter of balancing one right against another – the more we shall insist that judges become politically accountable. My hon. Friend the Member for Great Grimsby (Mr. Mitchell) welcomed such a move because it will educate judges. I do not think that judges will welcome the fact that they will have more and more to make political judgments. I certainly would not welcome asking them to make political judgments. They are appointees, not people who must face the problem of getting re-elected if they make wrong decisions. I am sure that few people would support an elected judiciary.

Mr. Alex Carlile: Will the hon. Gentleman tell the House what is political about having to decide whether someone is subjected to torture or inhuman or degrading treatment? What is political about having to decide whether a person has liberty or security? What is political about deciding whether a person's right to life is protected by law? Indeed, what is political about asking judges to decide these fundamental individuals freedoms?

Mr. Bennett: I disagree with the hon. and learned Gentleman. One cannot define these matters as fundamental. The hon. and learned Gentleman picked out only one or two.

Mr. Carlile: The hon. Gentleman should read the Bill.

Mr. Bennett: I have looked at it. The hon. and learned Gentleman should read it. The right to life is mentioned, but we qualify it by giving the state the right to take it away in certain circumstances. It is an absolute, it is there, yet we qualify it. All the way through, there is continual qualification. Different opinions have been voiced in the cases that have been argued in the House, particularly the principle of the closed shop. In the end, it is a political judgment. It is not an absolute right that we can define.

The more we draw judges into political matters, the more we shall create problems for them in terms of the general public's attitude to and respect for the judiciary. Most judges do not want to be political arbiters ...

The advantage of the House is that we legislate in detail on, for example, freedom of information, police or criminal evidence. The more we leave it to a general declaration, the more it becomes a matter of the judgment of the courts. Instead of the certainty that will avoid enthusiasm for going to the courts, there is doubt. I understand that lawyers love doubt because it keeps them in business, but it is not in the best interests of the general public. They want detailed legislation that gives them certainty. The House would be better employed in making decisions giving them certainty than in giving broad sweeping statements that will depend upon judges making choices of how they interpret the law.

Mr. Alex Carlile: The hon. Gentleman is the distinguished Chairman of the Joint Committee on Statutory Instruments. Does he not agree that statutory instruments, produced at least under the jurisdiction of the House, show that we are incapable of producing legislation that people understand? Is he really saying that the statutory instruments that pass through his hands on the subject of, say, social security, have any chance of being understood by the ordinary man in the street? Does he not agree with my right hon. Friend the Member for Tweeddale, Ettrick and Lauderdale (Mr. Steel) that the increase in the number of cases going for judicial review is clear evidence of the fact that we need a Bill of Rights?

Mr. Bennett: I do not see that a Bill of Rights gives clarity. We can say, 'Let us have no legislation and leave it to the judges to make choices.' I agree that in some sectors we are not making the law clear, and that we should be spending more time making that law clear, but it is important that we should be doing it rather than leaving it to people to go to court. Large numbers of people do not have the resources to do that. None of those involved in the judgments on social security in the past two or three years have been able to go to the courts to obtain a remedy. They have had to rely almost entirely on particular campaigning groups to finance the challenges they have made. We should be putting much more emphasis on getting certainty into our own legislation, rather than relying on the courts to enforce it.

Although we can all illustrate the many instances where statutory instruments are obscure and difficult to follow, considering the total volume of legislation produced in this country, the number of cases where there has been a judicial review and where the law is not clear and certain are more limited.

I argue strongly that if one wants to impose a Bill of Rights, one has to guarantee that anyone who wants to bring a case to court using the powers that they would claim in the Bill, must have free legal aid to help them to bring that case. There must not be the legal aid committees which make choices as to who can bring a case. I accept that that may be an expensive process, but I believe firmly that, if one is going to introduce a Bill of Rights, everyone must have equal access to the courts to enforce it.

I find it annoying when I go to a Minister to make representations on behalf of my constituents, only to be told, 'There is nothing that I can do about that, because it is up to the courts or a tribunal to provide a remedy.' It is annoying when I have a detailed and difficult case involving my constituents and I want to refer it to the ombudsman and he says. 'Your constituent has a theoretical remedy by taking it through the courts or to a tribunal. I cannot investigate.' There is a danger that the Bill of Rights may well become an excuse for people to say that certain matters should not be resolved in the House but that the individual involved should take it outside and pursue it through the courts. . .

The Solicitor-General (Sir Patrick Mayhew): Not for the first time, my hon. and learned friend the Member for Fylde (Sir E. Gardner) has rendered the House a signal service. His Bill gives rise to discussion of absorbing interest, one might say it is of perennial interest. He addressed himself to his Bill in a speech which was, if I may cite the words of the right hon. Gentleman the Leader of the Liberal party, lucid, charming and witty. I respectfully join in the grateful congratulations that have been showered upon him on his speech. My hon. and learned Friend and I are old personal and political friends and we are united in our objective of securing as best we may by law the underpinning of liberty. That can equally be described as the securing of fundamental freedoms and we are not divided in any way on that objective.

I am afraid that the House will not be surprised if I begin my argument with a platitude. The judiciary must be seen to be impartial. More especially, as far as practicable it must be kept free from political controversy. We must take great care not to propel judges into the political arena. However, that is what we would do if we asked them to take policy decisions of a nature that we ought properly to take ourselves and which under our present constitution we do take. We would increase that danger if we required or permitted them to alter or even reverse decisions taken by Parliament. For a long time I have felt that herein lies the key to the general issue that we are debating. Above all, it is the factor that shapes the Government's attitude to the Bill and which leads me to be unable, for reasons that I hope to develop, to commend the Bill to the House. I hope to show why that is my view and perhaps I will be forgiven for taking a little time to do that.

My hon. and learned Friend's speech did not deal with that aspect as thoroughly as I had hoped it would. Of course he did not overlook it. At the heart of the argument is that applying the convention calls for some highly political judgments. That point is often missed, but that is perfectly understandable because we focus, as no doubt do 70 per cent, of our fellow citizens, about whom we have heard, upon the general rights that are declared by the convention on human rights to belong to everyone. These are the right to respect for one's family, one's private life, and one's home and correspondence under article 8, the right to freedom of thought, conscience and religion and the right to freedom of peaceful assembly and so on.

These rights are noble declarations. To adopt the words of my hon. and learned Friend, the theme is one of grandeur. I hope that we shall never lose the ardour for enshrining and ensuring across all national frontiers the enjoyment of human rights that arose so soon after the end of the last war following revulsion from totalitarian regimes.

I strongly agree ... that the debate is not about whether we are for or against the European convention on human rights, although people may take a stance on it. The issue does not turn on that. Much less notice is taken of the qualifications and restrictions to these generally expressed and noble rights, but they also are to be found in the convention in articles 8, 9, 10 and 11.

I shall take just one example from article 8 which by way of qualification, speaks of the interests of national security, the interests of public safety, the interests of the economic well-being of the country, the prevention of disorder or crime, the protection of health or morals and the protection of the rights and freedoms of others. The Bill would require our judges to make their own assessments of these matters.

Article 8 says that any one of those matters can justify a public authority interfering with the exercise of the right. It provides that there should be no interference by a public authority with the exercise of the right of a home, or a person's private life

'except such as is in accordance with the law and is necessary in a democratic society in the interests of national security, public safety or the economic well-being of the country, for the prevention of disorder or crime, for the protection of health or morals, or for the protection of the rights and freedoms of others.'

Mr. Ottaway: Those are the very words which are to be found in section 10 of the Contempt of Court Act 1981. Why is it permissible to allow judges to interpret that section but not article 8?

The Solicitor-General: It is very dangerous to invite judges to apply their own assessment on what are essentially political matters. It is not that I do not trust the judges, for I trust them implicitly. It is not that I do not think that judges are able for, as has been said, they are the most able to be found in the world. It is that I fear what would happen to the public reputation for political impartiality of judges if that jurisdiction were extended to them and if that burden were imposed on them on so wide a scale.

Mr. Robert Maclennan: Will the Solicitor-General please address himself to the question asked by the hon. Member for Nottingham, North (Mr. Ottaway)? Is he not asserting that the Contempt of Court Act 1981 gives judges just the types of political power that we are talking about? If it was acceptable to the Government to do that then, why is the hon. and learned Gentleman baulking now?

The Solicitor-General: As I have said, I think it is very dangerous. To have done it once does not diminish the danger of doing it on a wide scale. That is quite a simple question, which I thought I had answered.

Mr. Robert Jackson: What reason do we have to believe that a Turkish or Icelandic judge sitting in Strasbourg is better qualified to make the type of judgment which the convention requires in a case arising out of the United Kingdom?

The Solicitor-General: He is no better qualified: I entirely agree with that extremely interesting remark. The consequences of the court at Strasbourg exercising jurisdiction are very different under present arrangements from the consequences which would follow if the convention were incorporated in our domestic law. . .

The point of the issue is made best by article 1 of the first protocol:

'No one shall be deprived of his possessions except in the public interest'.

I do not think that the House would be satisfied if it were dealing with an ordinary Bill with provisions that gave, on a matter of such importance to liberty, as little guidance to a judge as that. My hon. and learned Friend the Member for Fylde (Sir E. Gardner) said that the language was the language of 'celestial clarity'. I yield to no one in my admiration for the Bill's draftsmen. Celestial clarity there may be, but celestial certainty in its outcome there most certainly is not.

Of course I recognise that, under clause 6,

'judicial notice shall be taken ... of all published judgments of the European Court of Human Rights'.

Without doubt, in some of these areas, detailed interpretations have already been made. But judgments in that court tend to be closely applied to the facts of an individual case, and in many areas there has been no detailed interpretation at all. But, in any event, I understood it to be an argument for the Bill that there is an advantage in having British rather than Strasbourg decisions. I do not think that we can possibly escape the conclusion that, if we pass the Bill, we shall be thrusting the judges far into the arena of political controversy. Until now, it is generally Parliament that has addressed itself to these issues. That is what we have been elected to do. We may not get it right – or perhaps we do get it right – with the benefit of hindsight, but the law that we make on these very issues is law that has seemed to the majority of us at the time to have been a good idea.

Our constitutional history rather strongly shows that over the centuries the British people have preferred that these matters should be decided by people whom they can elect and sack rather than people immune from either process – wiser, less opportunist or even less venal than such people might well be considered to be. So it is that Parliament has passed Acts such as those of which we have been reminded today – the Interception of Communications Act 1985, the Public Order Act 1986, the Abortion Act 1967 and the Police and Criminal Evidence Act 1984. Each has represented the balance between conflicting interests that has seemed right to the majority of us in Parliament at the time. We have gone through the process of lobbying by special interest groups and the laboriously contested Standing Committee stages. But at the end of it, with royal assent, we have said to our fellow citizens, 'There you are. You must conform to that.' We have said to the judges. 'There you are. You have to apply that.' The judges have got on with it and applied the legislation judicially. That separation of functions is, I believe, generally thought to be beneficial ...

I am sorry that the hon. Member for Great Grimsby (Mr. Mitchell) is no longer in the Chamber, because I should have liked to have another go at him. He said that judges have an attitude of grovelling servility to the Executive. That does not stand up for a moment in the light of the fact that it is the judiciary, rather than Parliament, which has developed the jurisdiction of the judicial review of the exercise of discretionary power by any executive body, including the Government. That has been a very welcome development and also an immensely potent contribution to the rule of law. However, one cannot go on from that to the proposition that has been advanced that, somehow or other, the number of applications for judicial review shows how much we need to incorporate the convention on human rights – *Interruption.* That is what I understand to be the case.

It is said that, if judges can be trusted with judicial review, they can be trusted with the application of the convention on human rights. That is quite a separate matter because judges never review the merits of an administrative decision. They are wise enough to recognise that the merits of such a decision are a matter for a Minister who is responsible to this House. The judges review the method by which that decision has been taken. The criteria that they apply boil down to one word – 'fairness'. Is the decision unlawful? Has a legitimate expectation been disappointed so that an aggrieved person is deprived of what he reasonably expected would occur, or would be offered, in the way of procedure? Is the procedure improper?

Has there been an irrational, whimsical or capricious decision? It all boils down to whether the decision-making process has been fair. That has nothing to do with giving judges jurisdiction over an administrative function, choosing that which is necessary in the interests of national security.

My great fear is that, if we were to pass the Bill, the judges' reputation for political impartiality would seriously decline, with grievously damaging results, not through the fault of the judges, but because of the essentially political tasks with which we would burden them. . .

Mr. Robert Maclennan: Although the Solicitor-General in the course of his remarks spoke about this proposal as the subject of perennial debate, it is fair to say that the debate has not taken place on the Floor of this House perennially. This has been a subject for academic debate and comment perhaps by judges and politicians but not, alas, for this Chamber. There is a great opportunity today for the House to consider and pronounce upon these issues. . .

I have served in Parliament for 20 years, and I wish that I could say that Parliament can remedy grievances in the way in which the hon. Gentleman so idealistically described. Alas, the position is different. We must recognise – this bears upon the insularity of the Solicitor-General's approach – that our experience in the delivery of remedies for grievances is almost unique in that we do not have a Bill of Rights to which our citizens can turn for redress.

New Zealand and Israel are the only other countries to have held out against the introduction of a Bill of Rights. [*RB NOTE: In 1990, New Zealand did adopt a Bill of Rights; see Doc. 46.*] Many years ago, the House legislated to ensure that Canada should enjoy the benefits of a Bill of Rights, and there have been several cases since then. When giving independence to our former colonies, we almost invariably tried to give them the benefit of such a Bill. The only country to which we have denied the privilege is Britain. What is so unique about Britain that it stands apart from the tide of history in this matter and is so complacently content that its citizens are protected by the procedures which grew up in the 19th century, in an age when Governments had relatively limited responsibility?

The Solicitor-General invoked only one argument – the impact of such a Bill on the judiciary and the public perception of it. But I welcome his assertion, on behalf of the Government, that the rights guaranteed by the convention are rights which the Government wish to be retained, and that they accept that the right of individual petition to Strasbourg should be renewed. Other hon. Members pitch their opposition against the convention itself, but that was not the argument deployed by the Solicitor-General. He made it plain that our citizens should enjoy the rights guaranteed by the convention, but he also made it plain that, to obtain those rights, they must go through the tortuous, circuitous and expensive route of the Commission and court in Strasbourg.

The Solicitor-General was careful to say, I think rightly, that British judges are competent to consider issues that involve applying general constitutional provisions and general principles of law such as those enshrined in the European convention. He could scarcely have denied it, as the Judicial Committee of the Privy Council has adjudicated on precisely such matters. Indeed, I appeared before the Judicial Committee in a case where the definition of 'cruel and unusual punishment' had to be considered. Such matters have been in the jurisdiction of our judges for many years, and it is not difficult for them to apply those principles.

Had there been any doubt about judges' competence in that area – one can insulate their experience of acting as a court of appeal from foreign jurisdictions – that doubt has been removed by the development of the jurisprudence of British courts since we joined the European Community. European Community legislation is frequently cast in the civilian tradition that incorporates broad principles into the law and requires judges to make the sort of judgments that they are making at present without difficulty, greatly assisted by the jurisprudence of the European court. The jurisprudence of the European Court of Human Rights will be of assistance when, as they should, these matters come before our courts.

It is imperative that we give our citizens the greater benefit of enjoying judgments on these broad issues by our own judiciary rather than entrust them to a foreign court when that is not necessary.

It has been argued that there is still a right of appeal to Strasbourg. That is true, but I think that the Solicitor-General would agree that if a matter is settled in a higher court in Britain on an interpretation of the European convention, it is extremely unlikely that the judgment will be taken from our courts and placed in the European sphere, save in the most exceptional circumstances. The cost of doing that is great and involves much time and uncertainty. Most citizens who avail, themselves of the right to go to British courts will be satisfied by the domestic jurisdiction.

The Solicitor-General spoke about a threat that judges would be politicised. What is that threat? Surely he is not suggesting that our judges are not involved in politics. They take decisions of great political sensitivity and many cases, such as the Ponting and Tisdall cases, have great political resonance. In considering the wide range of issues which come before them for judicial review, it is impossible for judges to avoid taking a stance that may be of great political importance and politically highly controversial. As the Solicitor-General rightly said, judges have been developing this jurisdiction and have not feared to develop their roles in this way. They have not felt that they were becoming politicised. Why should we fear that they would be politicised when they do not fear it?

The Solicitor-General quoted Lord Diplock. He might also have quoted a number of equally senior judges who take a very different view from that of Lord Diplock. The movement of judicial opinion is towards recognising that it is the judicial role of judges to interpret the will of Parliament expressed in statute, and to do it against the background of the broad principles that Parliament has espoused for generations.

The Bill is long overdue and has had powerful support in the debate. It was supported in principle by the Lord Chancellor in a debate in another place when the noble Lord Wade introduced his Bill. The principle of this Bill has the support of many hon. Members, One of its most notable supporters is the right hon. Member for Barnsley, Central (Mr. Mason). As a result of his experience in Northern Ireland, he recognises that the entrenchment of the protection of human rights by a Bill of Rights in that troubled province of the United Kingdom could make a powerful contribution to restoring harmony and trust to that part of our realm. I happily commend the Bill to the House...

HC Deb., 6 February 1987, cols. 1223f.

92   DEBATE ON CONSTITUTIONAL REFORM, 1991

Mr. Archy Kirkwood: I wish to call attention to the case for constitutional reform and I beg to move, that this House, noting the results of the recent MORI opinion poll on the State of the Nation, calls on Her Majesty's Government to introduce measures designed to effect an extensive modernisation of the United Kingdom's democratic institutions and constitutional provisions ...

People have strange perceptions of the whole process of government. They may not have a perfect grasp of all the subleties of our unwritten constitution and they may not fully understand the relationship between the judiciary, the Executive and the legislature; they may also have many false expectations of what can be politically achieved and what is realistically possible. For example, people regularly tell me in the same breath that they are in favour of strong government and united parties, and that they believe that Members of Parliament should exercise their individual consciences in the Division Lobbies. Those, surely, are mutually exclusive objectives.

There is one issue, however, on which people are sufficiently wise and sufficiently tutored to decide: the question whether our system of government serves their needs. The current public feeling is that government is not working. We must, of course, ensure that proper respect is paid to our democratic institutions, which must be assiduously fostered and defended. None the less, a great deal of nonsensical cant and mystique surrounds much of our constitutional baggage and I feel that that should now be discarded.

Is it not more than a little strange that we have no permanent, open and accessible machinery to allow constant review of our constitutional arrangements? Can any hon. Member recall when we last engaged in a debate on constitutional reform, apart from Consolidated Fund debates in the middle of the night? The most recent such debate, as far as I know, took place in 1968, when the former Liberal leader Mr. Jeremy Thorpe – then Member of Parliament for Devon, North – introduced a debate on the Kilbrandon report when the House was dealing with the Gracious Speech.

That is a long time for which to leave such a subject undiscussed. Is it not more than ever necessary for effective checks and balances to be applied and constantly reviewed at a time when our country is experiencing exponential rates of change in social and economic matters? Statutory provision now regulates every aspect of our private lives from the cradle to the grave; information technology threatens to make slaves of us all.

Our ramshackle, amateurish, muddle-through mentality is now holding the United Kingdom back. Our system of government is shot through with administrative myths and political fictions, and is no longer adequate to carry out its task. The lack of a clearly defined, modern framework for our constitution is now one of the most urgent problems that face the country. I feel that hon. Members, representing as they do so many disparate constituencies, have a duty to respond clearly to the need for change.

I freely acknowledge that the body politic has been wrestling with the task of modernising our system of government for the past three decades. Much ingenuity and considerable energy have been expended, but, according to any test, the extent to which lasting results have been produced does not measure up to the effort deployed. Little real progress has been made, as a brief review of recent reforms will show. It is, in fact, a disappointing and depressing saga. . .

Successive Governments have been obsessively introspective. They have concentrated their efforts at reform on themselves, in the form of the Executive branch of government. Changes were often made on account of the siege mentality of the last Labour Government. The Executive started to do things, the motivation for which was to try to make things easier for themselves and to dig themselves out of holes. That is managerialism running absolutely riot. It led directly to ludicrous levels of state secrecy – to the Clive Ponting affair, Cathy Massiter, Peter Wright, GCHQ and the whole debate that surrounded the replacement of the Official Secrets Act. It also led to an increasingly political and politicised civil service. That led to all sorts of problems that we are now reading about – Westland and the unattributable briefings of Bernard Ingham. In addition, it led to the browbeating of the broadcasters – the 'Death on the Rock' fiasco, the Zircon case and all these other incidents and issues that caused a great deal of concern for those of use outside government who could see what was happening.

In all three areas of our policy – the judiciary, the legislature and the Executive – we need to throw open the doors and windows of Whitehall, Westminster and the courts and let light and air into the innermost recesses of the processes of government. The proper ordering of our polity requires not just recasting the activities of the Executive but renewing the roles of both the legislature and the judicial branches of government. Modernisation, properly conceived and executed, is not just about efficiency, narrowly defined. It is about democracy in the very widest and most generous sense. Equally, and just as important, it is about contriving a framework where the one can operate effectively in relation to the other. We need to renew the context in which the requirements of the Government machine can be accommodated alongside the needs and rights of and the ability to serve and protect individuals and communities.

In the recent past, discussion and practice have focused almost exclusively on management techniques rather than on constitutional remedies. Against all the innovations undertaken in the name of improved efficiency, I can think – other hon. Members may be able to assist me here – of only two offsetting reforms of a truly democratic and constitutional nature: the appointment of ombudsmen to cover various aspects of public policy and the modifications and improvements to the Select Committee procedures of the House. Welcome as both those modest steps are, they are modest indeed in comparison with what is required.

One of the major drawbacks and the main reason for the very limited success of recent reforms of the Executive branch of government is that they were imposed from the top down. Objections and criticisms were rejected, on the basis that they were no more than dinner table talk at the soirees of the chattering classes. The debate, such as it was, about the inadequacies of the Government system and the shortcomings of the constitution was seen as being conducted between two elites – the Government Front Bench and readers of *The Guardian*. The mass of voters were said not to be in any way interested in any of these questions. That perception is now shown to be wholly wrong. The general public are fully aware of the parlous state of the machinery of government and of the inadequacies of constitutional provision. They hold strong and consistent views about how they should be redressed. The reason for the public's apparent silence on these great matters of state is simply that in the past they had never been asked.

A recent MORI poll – a substantial piece of work that is bed-time reading for hon. Members – was commissioned by the Joseph Rowntree reform trust, of which I am a director [*RB NOTE: For opinion polling on a Bill of Rights see Doc. 149*]. I therefore declare an interest, although the office of trustee has no financial reward. It carried out a national survey of public opinion on the state of the nation. It was the first time that such extensive soundings had been taken on the subject, and the results showed a widespread and profound desire for democratic constitutional reform.

A clear majority would like to see improvements in the system of government. Three quarters think that a freedom of information Act is needed. Seven in 10 think that we need a Bill of Rights. Six in 10 think, not surprisingly given the Thatcher legacy, that the Government are too centralised. Three quarters favour greater use of referendums for major decisions, and more think that a petition of 1 million signatures should trigger a referendum. That is a plea for more consideration and participation if ever I heard one.

There is considerable popular support for electoral change. Eight in 10 think that national campaign spending should be limited. On a topical note, perhaps, the Prime Minister might like to be aware that more than half the electorate support fixed-term Parliaments – amen to that. Half the voters favour electoral reform, and the momentum for a change to a system of fair voting is gathering speed at such a rate that it is reluctantly engaging the attention of the Labour party.

The House may be interested to know that 59 per cent think that Parliament works well, and 16 per cent disagree. That might be a direct result of the positive impact of television. When the same question was asked in 1979, only 54 per cent, thought well of the workings of the House, while 39 per cent thought that it worked badly. Significantly – this correlates closely the feeling of overcentralised government – 50 per cent, think that Parliament has insufficient control over the Government. Only 23 per cent disagreed with that proposition. Forty per cent favour an elected second Chamber to replace the House of Lords, while only 29 per cent disagree, and 54 per cent believe that the Government can change citizens' right too easily, while 22 per cent disagree. Thirty eight per cent think that citizens' rights are less well protected in Britain than in the rest of the European Community, and 24 per cent disagree.

There is strong and growing support among Scots for a devolved assembly. In September 1989, 44 per cent of Scots favoured that reform, but now 51 per cent do so. More generally in Britain, six out of 10 favoured a devolved assembly for Britain.

The motion is clearly timely. The MORI poll revealed general disquiet among the public about the state of the nation, especially about the functioning of government and the need to review our constitutional safeguards. It is equally clear that, in many instances, those who campaign for improvement – many organisations democratically campaign for change – speak for a majority constituency of our fellow citizens. . .

Sooner or later, the Government, of whatever colour, and the House, whatever its composition, will have to apply themselves to a systematic review of the constitutional framework of the United Kingdom. Liberal Democrats will continue to press for such a review and robustly to argue our party political agenda to establish the need for change. I hope that the debate will allow the House to express a view. I have deliberately avoided a partisan, party-political approach. I hope that we shall be able to test opinion in the House. I remind hon. Members of the adage coined by George Bernard Shaw on the need to get one's jacket off and fight for what one believes in. He said that people have

> 'to be careful to get what they like, or they might have to like what they get.'

Mr. Tony Benn: I strongly welcome the debate. It is the first time in the 40 years in which I have been here that there has been a day devoted to constitutional reform as a whole.

. . . There is the question of people's rights. We have no rights in Britain. We are subjects, not citizens – I shall come back to that matter when I refer to the Crown – and there is an argument for a Bill of Rights. Women are grossly under-represented in this place. The 300 Group, which thinks that half the House of Commons should be made up of women, has a case. I am not personally in favour of what is called positive discrimination, but I am in favour of equality of representation, which is quite a different principle. I have no doubt that you, Madam Deputy Speaker, will move to higher things and that you, along with Edith Cresson, the new Prime Minister of France, will help to redress the balance.

I have always believed in the case for home rule for Scotland. We are talking about the old Keir Hardie principle. Freedom of information, devolution, local democracy, civil liberties, relations between Parliament and the Common Market are all massive questions which must be discussed.

The hon. Member for Roxburgh and Berwickshire had it right when he tabled his wide motion. People are interested in constitutional reform because they want this place to serve them. Very few people have an O-level or an A-level in government, but they know that, if they want something done and this place will not do it, something is wrong. I always think of this place as a steam engine. It needs some steam to move, but if there is lots of steam and the engine is defective all that happens is a great release of hot air; the engine stays where it is, which means that our mechanism is defective. I think that people are beginning to realise that ...

It is impossible to discuss the constitution without discussing the Crown, because, as I said earlier, we are subjects and not citizens and we have no rights whatever. I shall come to the implications of that in a moment. The thing about a royal or monarchical system of government is that all power comes from the top, and that makes it more difficult for pressure to come from below. I always attend royal occasions, because one learns so much from the speeches made from the throne. We tell the public that we are a democracy. In this place, we are cautious: we say that we are a parliamentary democracy. When the Queen addresses us, however, she says that we are a constitutional monarchy. There is all the difference in the world between the three. . .

It is not possible to discuss the matter without considering the Crown. I am perhaps one of the few people who, as a lifelong republican, has no ill-will towards the royal family. . . After all, the Queen did not choose the job, although I suppose she could have given it up. However, the crown is a totally insupportable basis for a constitution. . .

I am of the opinion that we should adhere to the sovereignty of the people. On 1 May 1649 – an early May day – John Lilburne, Richard Overton and William Walwyn produced

'The Agreement of the People'

and this is the basis upon which we should restructure our method of government. They wrote:

'We, the free People of England,'—

and this was before the Act of Union—

'to whom God hath given hearts, means and opportunity to effect the same, do with submission to his wisdom, in his name, and desiring the equity thereof may be to his praise and glory; Agree to ascertain our Government to abolish all arbitrary Power, and to set bounds and limits both to our Supreme, and all Subordinate Authority, and remove all known Grievances. And accordingly do declare and publish to all the world, that we are agreed as followeth,

That the Supreme Authority of England and the Territories therewith incorporate, shall be and reside henceforth in a Representative of the people consisting of four hundred persons, but no more; in the choice of whom (according to natural right) all men of the age of one and twenty years and upwards (not being servants, or receiving alms, or having served the King ...) shall have their voices.'

Mr. Alistair Darling: I congratulate the hon. Member for Roxburgh and Berwickshire (Mr. Kirkwood) on instigating the debate. We do not discuss constitutional matters as often as we should. It is an opportune moment to discuss constitutional arrangements, because Britain stands at a crossroads. In 1992, with the completion of the single market, we will see further and substantial steps towards the integration of decision making in Europe. The constitution of the United Kingdom is in a poor shape to meet that challenge and needs drastic overhaul. It is not capable of providing a check and balance against Westminster, let alone Brussels. . .

Constitutional change will be part of the next general election campaign. The economy, health and education will dominate that campaign, but the need to protect individual rights and to decentralise power from Whitehall to the regions and nations will be important. They will once again show the philosophical difference between the Conservative and Labour parties. I welcome the contribution of my right hon. Friend the Member for Chesterfield (Mr. Benn) who raised a number of interesting matters to which I have no doubt that we shall return on more than one occasion.

We propose to give real power and choice to the citizens of this country. Under the Conservative Government, the United Kingdom has become one of the most centralised of the large countries in the European Community. Over the past 12 years, local government has been taken over by central Government; Ministers have acquired more power and under the Education Reform Act 1988 the Secretary of State took up on himself 200 more powers. From hospitals to housing; from schools to social services. Whitehall and Tory Ministers say that they know best. On civil liberties, we must not forget that the Government organised a midnight raid on the BBC in Glasgow to recover tapes of programmes that they did not like. In 1987, the Government impounded copies of *Pravda* at Heathrow so that British people should not know what every Soviet citizen knew – what was in the book 'Spycatcher'.

We shall introduce legislation that will, for the first time, set out clear and specific rights and remedies available to every British citizen. Our charter of rights, published in January this year, has set out our programe. We shall provide for a Freedom of Information Act, which is long overdue. We shall provide laws to protect privacy and to strengthen the data protection provisions, including the implementing of substantial parts of the Calcutt report. We shall put the security service on a proper footing, making it answerable to a Select Committee of the House. We shall legislate to promote equality of opportunity. They are specific rights. I have yet to be persuaded about a Bill of Rights. I have no objection in principle to such a Bill, but it is important to avoid room for judicial manoeuvre. This Parliament – or the regional or national parliaments – should be able to spell out specific rights so that citizens are left in no doubt about where they stand. These rights are essential and long overdue in the United Kingdom, but they will be even more necessary in the Europe without frontiers.

Mr. James Sillars: Would those rights be justiciable?

Mr. Darling: There is nothing in the land that would not be justiciable. For example, under the Freedom of Information Act the system that we envisage is that a request for information would have to be answered within 30 days. In the event of the commissioner saying that the information was not to be released, that would be justiciable.

I think that the point that brought the hon. Member for Glasgow, Govan (Mr. Sillars) to his feet was that under a Bill of Rights, which would tend to contain general assertions, the room for judicial manoeuvre would be considerably greater than if there were tightly-drawn legislation, which reduced the scope for a judge to decide that no matter what Parliament thought that it had decided, something else was intended.

Mr. James Wallace: Does the hon. Gentleman agree that if the Labour party were to come to power and legislate for citizens' rights, a succeeding Conservative Government, who were elected on the basis of 40 or 42 per cent of the electorate and had absolute power, could legislate away those rights as easily as the Labour party could legislate for them?

Mr. Darling: I shall deal with that point a little later. The hon. Member knows that in our proposals to reform the second Chamber, we propose to give it the power to delay – no more than delay – any attempt to tear up what we regard as fundamental rights, such as the Freedom of Information Act. The supremacy of Parliament means that no Parliament can bind its successors. The best that we can do under the present constitutional arrangements is to make it more difficult and especially to force a Government to fight a general election on the proposal to tear up what I regard as fundamental rights.

I was referring to Europe because it is the driving force that will force us to amend our constitutional arrangements, and there is one especially striking example. After 1992, EC citizens will be able to move around Europe with their families, and frontiers will largely disappear. However, individuals will be subject to internal controls, certainly on continental Europe where they will be stopped and asked to account for themselves at various stages. Immigration authorities and police will have access to a common information system. Without data protection legislation and freedom of information legislation extending across Europe, citizens will be at a disadvantage against the bureaucracy that will be set up. Therefore, it is essential not only that we set out citizens' rights in the United Kingdom, but that the Government should argue in Europe that the same rights should be available to all EC citizens no matter where they happen to be in Europe at any time. . .

It is essential that rights are protected across Europe. The charter of rights that we have proposed for the United Kingdom will always be incomplete unless it is accepted that those rights are available in Europe. I said that a Freedom of Information Act and stronger data protection provisions are needed. It is interesting that the data protection provisions directive promulgated by the EC, which would go some way – although not as far as I should like – to improve the situation across Europe, is, I understand, to be blocked by the Government. That is indicative of precisely what is wrong with the Government – they will not accept that individual rights are very much on the political agenda in Britain and that people's concerns must be met.

It is also interesting that although we have heard much about the social charter and the promotion of employment rights in Europe, there is little legislation to outlaw racial discrimination. For all the criticisms that I and others in my party make of the Government on that subject, it must be said that Britain has a far better record than many other European countries on legislation to protect individuals against racial discrimination. It is essential that when Europe deals with the rights and remedies available to its citizens, especially when there is increased freedom of movement for some, but not for all those living in the EC, we must strengthen legislation to outlaw discrimination no matter where it occurs.

Mr. John Bowis: Does the hon. Gentleman recall that at the time of the Notting Hill riots, it was not written changes in the constitution or changes in the law which put a stop to them, but firm action in the courts? The great danger of having a written constitution is that the courts will be so tied down in the details and niceties of the law that they would not be able to extend the law as they are now able to do by setting precedents.

Mr. Darling: I was not advocating a written constitution and I do not want to go into that subject unless the hon. Gentleman wants me to do so. I agree that one of the problems of a written constitution is that it provides a field day for lawyers, and I speak as a lawyer. Although it is tempting profession- ally to advocate something that would keep me in living for the rest of my working life, as a politician I think that there are severe drawbacks to setting up a written constitution.

Race relations legislation is justiciable. It can be extended and inter- preted. I do not follow the argument of the hon. Member for Battersea (Mr. Bowis) that had there been race relations legislation that affected not only Britain but Europe generally, it would have made a difference to what happened in Notting Hill. It is important to stress that although there is legislation in Britain that outlaws discrimination – and which needs to be strengthened – such legislation does not exist in other European countries. It is essential that it should exist in other European countries.

The hon. Member for Battersea will know that after 1992, there will be substantial freedom of movement for all European Community citizens. However, about 15 million people living in Europe are not citizens, although they have the right to live in the country in which they are settled. They will be subject to stops and checks. There is a risk that unless there is protective legislation, those people will be subject to racial harassment of the type that we have seen in France with people from north Africa, in Germany with the Turks and in Brussels only this week, when unfortunate incidents took place. I suspect that they took place partly because of a lack of protective legislation.

Mr. Bowis: I do not suggest that one should not have protective legisla- tion. I said that such constitutional considerations should not be so tightly circumscribed that the courts are unable to be flexible. Courts can often solve problems far more quickly than waiting for laws to be changed.

Mr. Darling: I come back to my earlier point, which is the thrust behind the proposal that we intend to introduce. Such legislation should be fairly tightly drawn because it is important that Parliament's intention is set out clearly in legislation. It will always be open to people to go to court to seek a different interpretation. I should not like there to be a very general statement. A judge could perhaps make the law better. However, as we have seen in employment legislation, judges have taken the view that they cannot see why rights should have been afforded. No matter what Parliament may have thought it was doing, judges would ensure that those rights would be restricted. . .

The Parliamentary Under-Secretary of State for the Home Department (Mr. Peter Lloyd): . . . Answers on a complex matter such as a Bill of Rights are determined by the question asked. In one case, a Bill of Rights apparently had the support of nearly three quarters of the respondents. However, it is impossible to have a meaningful Bill of Rights without requiring judges to make decisions that are essentially political. I wonder what the answer from those respondents would have been if they had been asked whether they favoured removing some political decisions from the elected House of Commons and giving them to non-elected judges and whether they thought that judges should be brought into party political controversy.

Mr. Tony Banks: A way around that problem is to have a supreme court and to have judges elected. I see no reason why the spread of democracy should not go as far as the bench, as it does in this place as well.

Mr. Lloyd: I agree that the subject is arguable. As soon as one begins to look at it, one realises that it ramifies into a series of other decisions, such as those that the hon. Member for Roxburgh and Berwickshire mentioned. People were not asked whether they wanted an elected High Court. Perhaps they would have agreed with the hon. Gentleman – perhaps they would not – but that was not part of the question that was posed to them.

Mr. John Butterfill: Does my hon. Friend agree that the fact that we are a signatory to the European convention on human rights and therefore subject to decisions of the European Court of Human Rights already creates a problem which has been identified by the hon. Member for Newham North-West (Mr. Banks)? We have non-elected judges – they are not even non-elected British judges; they are non-elected foreign judges who make political decisions for us.

Mr. Lloyd: We decided on another constitutional change to adhere to that convention and we accepted the final jurisdiction of the court in those questions. It is debatable whether it was right to do so. I believe that it was, and I believe that it provides an added protection. I suspect that my hon. Friend's opinion is entirely different from that of 99 per cent. of the respondents who answered that survey. They did not know that we adhered to that convention and that it was possible finally to take a case to that court.

Mr. Robert Maclennan: On the point about political elements in judicial decisions, what distinction enables the Minister to conclude that it is acceptable for foreign judges to determine matters of human rights in this country, but not British judges? Every constitution that this country pre- pared for other countries that gained independence within the Commonwealth made provision for Bills of Rights which apparently have been acceptable in those countries and have not been repealed. Why does the Minister think that it was right for this country to do to others what it was not prepared to do here?

Mr. Lloyd: The experience of many countries to which we have given independence has shown that Bills of Rights are not worth the paper that they are written on. No doubt, the reason we sought to give them was that countries without our traditions and our unwritten constitution needed something. From experience I believe that it was second best. Other countries do things in their own ways and according to their own traditions. The hon. Gentleman's point would be good if Bills of Rights had acted to any benefit to those countries to which we gave independence. On the whole, they did not, and the hon. Gentleman should acknowledge that. . .

Mr. Butterfill: I, too, think that we are indebted to the hon. Member for Roxburgh and Berwickshire (Mr. Kirkwood) for moving this important motion. I was interested to see that it was inspired by a MORI poll. To the extent that this debate may have cast some more light on the issues referred to in that poll and to the extent that people may be better informed if they listen to the debate – indeed, hon. Members may be better informed having listened to each other – the hon. Gentleman will have done us all a service. His enthusiasm for some of the reforms proposed in the MORI poll are misplaced, and I shall say briefly why.

The hon. Gentleman advocates a Bill of Rights. The right hon. Member for Chesterfield (Mr. Benn) talked about a written constitution. That would be profoundly mistaken. If we look at the history of democracy in this country, we see that after the supremacy of Parliament, which was established by Cromwell, we have made an enormous transition from what amounted to a feudal monarchy to a modern democracy with universal suffrage and that we have gone through huge social and economic changes without wars or civil commotion of any significant degree. We have made those transitions relatively smoothly because we do not have a written constitution and we have the flexibility that is inherent in our present system. In other countries where that flexibility does not prevail, there has been much greater upheaval as a result of such social changes. In many cases, that may stem from the fact that the country has a written constitution which is relatively inflexible.

Where our country is subject to some form of written constitution, problems have arisen, which were mentioned in the debate. We are signatories to the European convention on human rights, which is written. It sets out in a detailed treaty certain rights for individuals who live in the countries that are signatories to it. The problem is that decisions that are often of a political nature are taken by judges. In the case of human rights, the judges are not resident in the United Kingdom. Their decisions may not reflect the customs, practices and wishes of people in the United Kingdom. That is profoundly unsatisfactory.

The European Court of Human Rights ruled that corporal punishment was against the convention. Whether or not the House of Commons wished to restore corporal punishment, it could not do so because of the decision of three foreign judges who are not accountable to the British public.

The court has also said that if we voted to restore capital punishment – to which I am opposed – it would consider that it had a right to rule on the matter. If we established a written constitution we would tie ourselves unnecessarily and undesirably to a written, inflexible framework which could override the democratic wishes of our citizens. . .

Mr. Maclennan: In his last sentence, the hon. Member for Gravesham (Mr. Arnold) sought to write off the complaints of those who are concerned about our constitutional arrangements as the background noise of the chattering classes.

An article in *The Economist* on 11 May, which thankfully is no longer edited by Walter Bagehot, said:

'It is absurd to write off such complaints as the background noise of the chattering classes.'

I agree. He characterised the British constitution by saying:

'It ain't broke, but like much of British industry in the 1970s its proper place is in a museum. It does not need to be fixed; it needs to be replaced.'

If public opinion about our constitutional arrangements is changing – I have no doubt but that it is – it is not because of the theoretical attractiveness of models of proportional representation, which have advantages and disadvantages, but because the public recognise that the system of Government under which the country has operated is not delivering the goods. Measured by international yardsticks or against public expectations and hopes, successive Governments have fallen far short in delivering what a political system is expected to deliver.

The theoretical arguments about the structure of our constitution carry little weight with the sensible British public. What carries weight is their awareness that whereas Britain was once the most prosperous in Europe, our rating in the international league has declined steadily in the past two decades. They have seen the poor environment of our inner cities, the inadequate provision of services in rural communities, our education shortcomings and, compared with other countries, our failure to take people on to further and higher education. They have seen many brilliant scientists and inventors failing to translate their ideas into industrial pre-eminence. They have seen successive Governments committing themselves to curb the expansion of crime, but have noticed that crime is rising and now live in greater fear for their personal security.

Although we have a long-established legal system, in which many people have taken pride, there have been some spectacular failures and miscarriages of justice, which called into question the adequacy of our arrangements. The public have recognised that the legal system is inaccessible, except to the rich and very poor, who enjoy legal aid. They recognise that throughout the country provision for the arts and the environment is, at best, patchy. They recognise the extent of monopolist abuse. Above all, they recognise that for 20 years Conservative and Labour Governments have set themselves the twin targets of increasing employment and reducing inflation but that, compared with countries operating under other constitutional systems, they have failed. The British public are increasingly convinced that it is not the dogmatisms, but the system that allows those dogmatisms to prevail against the good sense of the public, which is the explanation for the transparent failures of Governments in Britain.

Is it merely insularity and complacency that can lead to the conclusion that the Minister took 53 minutes of our debating time to expound? It is impossible to stand before the British public and laud the achievements of two decades of Labour and Conservative Governments. There have been two decades of missed opportunities, of late decision-making and of opportunities denied to the British people. I believe that the reason why the Minister chose to speak for 53 minutes in what has conventionally been regarded as a Back-Benchers' day was that he wanted to demonstrate one of the central weaknesses of our parliamentary democracy – the complete domination of the Chamber and of the legislature by the Executive...

The Minister is usually an extremely courteous man and I have exchanged views with him on many occasions. Indeed, I did so earlier today. However, I was incensed – justifiably so – by the way in which he twisted the debate and made it marginal and trivial when it is central and major. The reason why this country cannot get itself off its back is that we do not debate the issues raised by the right hon. Member for Chesterfield (Mr. Benn) in his powerful speech, much of which I agreed with.

Some commonsensical statements have been made in this debate by some of the less elevated members of the House. The right hon. Member for Brent, North (Sir R. Boyson) spoke simply and said that the system works so leave it alone. Do the British public believe that the system works? It is increasingly clear that they do not. They think that the way in which the Minister treated the subject today is a bit of a farce. They think it a farce that bloated and inflated claims are made for the success of the Government against all the evidence of failures.

It is clear that our constitutional arrangements are almost unique in the democratic world. In the past 40 years, different Governments applying widely differing theories within the same constitutional framework have failed to deliver not only what they tried to deliver, but certainly what the public expected.

What is most striking in our constitutional arrangements is not so much that they are not defined in a written constitution, singular though that is. What is unique is the almost unlimited Executive dominance over the nation's affairs. Governments with only minority support are able to treat the whole country as a test-bed for a temporarily fashionable economic nostrum or political theory. Our unitary constitutional system, without effective checks and balances, causes the country to lurch in a zig-zag fashion according to the will of the flock master in Downing Street. The people of Britain are not sheep to be corralled thus. Although it is imperfect, we live in a democracy. A halt is ultimately called to the wilder nonsenses of Governments such as the poll tax or Labour's utopian attempt to impose its so-called 'social contract' on the nation's unwilling employees in 1978–79.

Mr. Tony Banks: The hon. Gentleman was a member of the Labour party then.

Mr. Maclennan: I learned from that experience. The reversals of policy do not come in time to prevent hardship and great damage to the country's prospects. Our constitutional arrangements have not given us stability and direction. They have not given us constancy of purpose. An erratic course has been steered by successive Government's guided by dogmatism and doctrine.

What is most characteristically different about our constitutional arrangements is that we have the most centralised system of central Government in western Europe. Our system of government is even more centralised than that of France, where provincial government is being developed. Our system is more secretive than any other. The Minister told us today that he would like us to hear all that the Government thought that we should hear. It is precisely against such ministerial arrogance that constitutional safeguards need to be written in.

Our constitutional arrangements pay scant regard to the fundamental rights and freedoms of our citizens who are more frequently required to go to the court in Strasbourg to protect their rights than are the citizens of any other country in western Europe. It is true that other countries settle such matters domestically in accordance with the tenets of a fundamental law which gives people rights that can be protected in their own courts. They do not have to go to Strasbourg.

The matters to which I have referred are strange and our country is singularly different from the other democracies with which we are associated in the European Community. . .

HC Deb., 17 May 1991, cols. 538f.

(C)

THE POLICIES OF THE POLITICAL PARTIES

RB NOTE: Expressions of Liberal Democrat, Conservative and Labour party policy may also be gleaned from the various contributions of front-bench spokespersons in parliamentary debates on the subject, for which see Docs 83–92 above.

The Liberal Democrats

---

93 POLICY DOCUMENT FOR MODERNIZING BRITAIN'S DEMOCRACY, 1993

RB NOTE: The following policy on safeguarding basic rights involves an entrenched Bill of Rights forming part of a Written Constitution.

10 *Safeguarding Basic Rights*

10.0.1 A Bill of Rights is the cornerstone of a written constitution and it is central to our proposals for a new constitutional settlement. We must get rid of the doctrine of Parliamentary Sovereignty and start again.

10.0.2 The purpose of a Bill of Rights is to protect citizens against the abuse of power, to keep the political process open and contestable, and to make rights transparent. It is one of the checks and balances found in the constitutions of most modern democracies. It guarantees fundamental rights and freedoms, protecting minorities against the tyranny of elected majorities, and ordinary men and women against the misuse of administrative discretion and powers. It sets out the basic rights which citizens enjoy which cannot be taken away by Parliament.

10.0.3 The abuse of human rights is not just a United Kingdom problem. Liberal Democrats want to see the rights and fundamental freedoms which were adopted by the United Nations in the 1948 Universal Declaration of Human Rights enjoyed throughout the world. We believe that the political rights which we intend to include in the United Kingdom Bill of Rights would also form the basis of the new European citizenship. We make no apology, however, for concentrating first on the domestic situation, because the United Kingdom lags behind the rest of the democratic world.

10.1 *The Present Position*

10.1.1 The United Kingdom does not have a charter of fundamental rights and freedoms which can be enforced in our courts. The United Kingdom did sign the European Convention on Human Rights in 1950, but neither Labour nor Conservative governments have incorporated the convention into United Kingdom law. This means that citizens cannot enforce the European Convention in the British courts.

10.1.2 To make matters, worse individuals have to exhaust whatever other remedies they may have here, before they can apply to the European Commission and the European Court in Strasbourg. This may well take five to seven years. UK citizens should be able to look to UK judges in UK courts to safeguard their basic rights.

10.1.3 Since 1950, the European Court and the European Commission have played a very significant part in the development of human rights law.

It is real progress to have established an international court which (in contrast to the International Court of Justice) investigates and decides a significant number of disputes between individuals and states each year. The influence of the Court will continue to grow as the emerging democracies of Eastern Europe ratify the Convention; it may come to play an important role in the resolution of problems connected with ethnic minorities, but the expense and delay involved in taking a case to Strasbourg means that it is an unsatisfactory way of dealing with everyday problems.

10.1.4 Although the United Kingdom has not incorporated the convention into UK law, the list of British cases is long, controversial and far-reaching: inadequate safeguards for personal privacy against telephone tapping by the police; unfair discrimination against British wives of foreign husbands under the immigration rules; inhuman prison conditions in cases of solitary confinement and segregation; unjust restrictions upon prisoners' correspondence and visits; judicial birching in the Isle of Man; corporal punishment in Scottish schools; criminal sanctions against private homosexual conduct in Northern Ireland; ineffective judicial protection for detained mental patients and would-be immigrants; the dismissal of workers because of the oppressive operation of the closed shop; the nationalisation of aircraft and shipbuilding companies without adequate compensation; the denial of equal citizenship rights to British passport-holders from East Africa; the treatment of suspect terrorists in Northern Ireland; and the interference with free expression by the Law Lords in extending the common law offence of contempt of court.

10.1.5 Given this list, it is entirely understandable that successive governments should be opposed to the creation of speedy and effective remedies in the UK Courts for breaches of the Convention by public authorities. Governments prefer to remain judges in their own cause. Ministers, however, have been prepared to use the European Convention as a model for Commonwealth countries on independence and the former Dominions, which gained effective independence without Bills of Rights, have since come to embrace them, New Zealand being the latest of them to do so, in 1990. The UK has become increasingly isolated; Britain alone in the Commonwealth lacks an enforceable Bill of Rights.

10.1.6 Here support for a Bill of Rights has been gaining ground. The Liberal Party endorsed a Bill of Rights as long ago as 1951. A Bill to incorporate the European Convention into UK Law was introduced by Lord Wade in 1979, passed through all its stages in the House of Lords by a large majority but was rejected by Conservative and Labour members in the House of Commons. More recently the same idea has been put forward by Lord Scarman and is one of the main planks of the pressure group Charter 88. This year Lord Scarman has been joined by the new Lord Chief Justice and the new Master of the Rolls and incorporation of the European Convention has at last been endorsed by the leader of the Labour Party, John Smith, in his recent lecture to Charter 88.

10.1.7 The case against a Bill of Rights is threadbare. On its record, Parliament cannot be trusted to safeguard rights without an external check. The judiciary in adjudicating on a Bill of Rights is simply interpreting the constitution. Provided that the constitution is readily amendable, the courts can be overridden if they are widely perceived to have over-stepped the mark.

10.2 *Which Bill of Rights?*

10.2.1 In our Federal Green Paper 13, '*We The People ...*', we recommended the incorporation of the European Convention, and we set it out in full in our draft illustrative constitution.

10.2.2 The European Convention is, however, a very conservative document which gives very wide discretions to governments. The advantage of using the European Convention is that it has achieved very wide acceptance; the disadvantage is that the citizen needs more protection against government than the European Convention provides.

10.2.3 For example, the right of free expression in article 10 of the European Convention is qualified by the clause; '*The exercise of these freedoms, since it carries with it duties and responsibilities, may be subject to such formalities, conditions, restrictions or penalties as are prescribed by law and are necessary in a free society*'. We accept that, the stronger version in the United Nations International Covenant on Civil and Political Rights (The Covenant) is preferable.

10.2.4 We are impressed with the Bill of Rights in the written constitution published in 1991 by the Institute for Public Policy Research (IPPR) [*RB NOTE*: *The IPPR Bill of Rights in Doc. 49 above was subsequently included in a written constitution proposal* The Constitution of the UK *(1991; republished as* A Written Constitution for the UK, *Mansell, 1993)*.] The IPPR Bill draws on the European Convention and the Covenant, by both of which the United Kingdom is legally bound, but goes further than either in its definition and protection of rights. We would adopt the IPPR draft as the basic text of the Bill of Rights we wish to see in force in our eventual constitution.

10.2.5 The IPPR Constitution also has a section on social and economic rights but precludes the intervention of the courts in enforcing them. This reflects the view that, while the constitution should state the general principles on which public policy is to be conducted, it would not be appropriate for the courts to judge whether or not government or Parliament had provided, for example, an adequate level of income maintenance. While this question might be considered further by our proposed constituent assembly (see 12.0.2), it is our present view that the constitution should be as short as possible and should not seek to lay down the principles of state policy. We also think that it is best to leave environmental rights to specific legislation.

10.3 *The Role of the Judges*

10.3.1 Lord Denning's celebrated pronouncement 'We must trust someone – let it be the judges' is not a sentiment for which one would expect to find much support. Many judges are by training and temperament natural members of the establishment. To their credit this has not prevented judges in the Crown Office list trying cases involving central and local government, achieving a good record in keeping public authorities in check. One great advantage of introducing a Bill of Rights, however, is that it would clarify the role of the Judges in protecting human rights. At present there is no basic text to which they can refer. In the absence of statutes which cover problems coming before them, they have had to decide cases in the light of common law principles. This has given them far too much discretion.

10.3.2 Under a Bill of Rights their task would be clearly defined: it would be to ensure that Parliament does not exceed its power and encroach on the rights of citizens. Those who argue most fiercely that we do not need a Bill of Rights are those who do not wish to see further checks on executive power. If judges are given the task of enforcing a charter of fundamental rights, they would enforce it. Viewed from the position of the citizen this would do nothing but good. Given a chance British judges are well equipped to make a positive contribution to human rights law. For example, the Privy Council recently struck down provisions in Antigua law which sought to prevent the printing or distribution of any false statement likely to undermine public confidence. The Council found the legislation to be contrary to the right of freedom of expression guaranteed by the Antigua and Barbuda Constitution. Lord Bridge's words, 'in a free democratic society it is almost too obvious to need stating that those who hold office in government and who are responsible for public administration must always be open to criticism. Any attempt to stifle or fetter such criticism amounts to political censorship of the most insidious and objectionable kind' ring as clearly as any judgement of the United States Supreme Court.

10.4 *Introducing a Bill of Rights*

10.4.1 Liberal Democrats would adopt a Bill of Rights in two stages. The first stage would be to incorporate the European Convention on Human Rights into UK law. Our Constitutional Assembly would then draw up a Bill of Rights which would include the European Convention and the Covenant, and largely follow the IPPR Bill of Rights. It would:

- Give the rights and freedoms enshrined within the European Convention priority over all inconsistent statute and common law.
- Require courts in the UK to have regard to the published judgments of the European Court of Human Rights and the reports and decisions of the Commission of Human Rights.
- Make it clear that the Act applies to public authorities and all other bodies and persons for whose conduct the UK Government is responsible under the European Convention.
- Provide that a subsequent Act of Parliament would, in the absence of an express declaration to the contrary contained in it, be construed and applied so as not to infringe the rights and freedoms guaranteed by the Human Rights Act.
- Enable claims of breaches of the Bill of Rights to be decided by the ordinary courts and tribunals and provide that the legal costs of deter-

mining the effects of the provisions of the Bill of Rights be paid out of public funds unless there are special reasons to the contrary.

- Create a UK Commission of Human Rights empowered to assist complainants in bringing proceedings under the Bill of Rights, to bring proceedings to secure compliance with its provisions, systematically to review law and practice in the sphere of civil liberties and to recommend changes in the existing law and practice.

10.4.2 The second stage would be to require the Constituent Assembly (see 12.0.2), to consider any amendments which are needed in the Bill of Rights in the Human Rights Act. The Bill of Rights would then be included in the written constitution and would be entrenched when the referendum approving the constitution was passed and the written constitution of the United Kingdom took effect.

10.5 *Freedom of Information*

10.5.1 Liberal Democrats, and our predecessor parties, have argued and campaigned for twenty years and more against the obsessive secrecy of British government, and there is no need to repeat the arguments here. It is worth emphasising, however, that matters have, if anything, deteriorated since 1979. Secret government is the flipside of authoritarian government. The 1989 Official Secrets Act, although in a sense narrowing the scope of the criminal law in the protection of official secrets, has reinforced government's power to suppress information which it considers would be inconvenient in the public domain.

10.5.2 We believe that a democratic system can best function effectively when the public is fully informed. To ensure adequate participation of all in public life, it is necessary that the public should, subject to unavoidable exceptions and limitations, have access to information held by public authorities at all levels. As set out in *Partners for Freedom and Justice*, Liberal Democrats would pass a Freedom of Information Act to:

- Create a public right of access to government and other official information, covering documents which contain both factual information and policy advice;
- Create an individual right of access to information held by public authorities about that individual, and protect the information against misuse;
- Protect official information to the extent necessary in the public interest and to safeguard personal privacy;
- Establish procedures to achieve these purposes; and
- Greatly narrow the scope of the criminal law as set out in the 1989 Official Secrets Act, and introduce a public interest defence.

10.5.3 The Freedom of Information Act should confer a general right of access, except for a small number of narrowly-defined areas where it can be demonstrated that it is overwhelmingly in the public interest that confidentiality should be maintained – including, for example, cases where disclosure would seriously impair defence, security or international relations, hinder the solution of crime or impede law enforcement, allow an unfair advantage to competitors of a company or business concerned, or constitute an unwarranted invasion of an individual's privacy. Access to Cabinet papers would also be denied for a limited period of five or ten years. In general, however, the onus should be put on the authorities to justify secrecy, instead of on the public to justify access.

10.5.4 Complaints about refusal of access or unreasonable delay would be referred to an independent commissioner, with powers to carry out investigations and to make orders requiring access or to take other specified action, subject to appeal to an Information Tribunal, modelled on the Data Protection Tribunal. Both information-holder and the individual would be entitled to appeal to the Commissioner, and to appeal to the Tribunal against his or her decisions.

10.5.5 Only disclosure of information likely to put seriously at risk the nation's most fundamental interests or endanger the safety of the subject would be subject to the criminal law. The Act would contain a public interest defence; thus an individual charged with unauthorised disclosure would be able to offer a defence that the disclosure was justified because the information related to matters such as abuse of official status, crime, fraud, neglect of official duty or some other form of serious misconduct, or that the information was already publicly available either in the UK or abroad.

10.5.6 In a wider context, our objective would be to shatter the culture of secrecy which has grown up in Britain. We would seek to encourage transparency in business, in charities and in public services. We recognise the range and extent of this task but would seek to set an example through our action in federal government, as we have done by opening local government in recent years.

10.6 *Judicial Review*

10.6.1 'It ought to be unthinkable' said Lord Justice Nourse (in Jones v Swansea City Council [1990]) 'that our law should not require the highest standards of a public servant in the execution of his office.' This sentiment is one which all Liberal Democrats share, but if it is to become a reality it is necessary to widen the scope of our administrative law and to make better use of the Ombudsman. The new procedures for judicial review which were introduced in 1977 have undoubtedly led to a great increase in the number of administrative law cases decided by the courts, but the reforms have not all been in favour of the citizen.

10.6.2 A citizen who seeks judicial review has to obtain the leave of the Court to bring proceedings, which must be sought promptly and at least within three months. The application is usually decided on affidavit evidence alone and citizens have no right to cross examine the witnesses of the other side, or even to see the other side's documents (and the courts are very reluctant to allow them to do so). Furthermore, citizens cannot obtain injunctions against the Crown – i.e. against the government machine; all that the courts can do is to grant a 'declaration'. This determines the rights of the parties, which is fine at the end of the case because the government would comply with the declaration, but involves the practical difficulty that the Courts cannot make interim orders against the government to protect the citizen, pending a full hearing of the case. Furthermore, the Crown and ministers are not subject to the contempt jurisdiction of the courts. Another serious gap in our administrative law lies in the inability of citizens injured by the abuse of power to recover damages in the absence of malice or negligence, and the reluctance of the courts to examine the limits of government powers derived from the royal prerogative.

10.6.3 Above all, the grounds on which the Courts review a decision are uncertain and this makes it hard for administrators to know what is expected of them and it makes the settlement of cases difficult. We believe that the grounds of review should be codified. This should be done in an open ended way (as it has been in Australia) so that there continues to be scope for development. In codifying the grounds it is important to take account of European practice which increasingly affects our public law. The grounds should be:

- Illegality;
- Breach of the principle of equality and non-discrimination;
- Lack of proportionality;
- Breach of legitimate expectations and of the principle of legal certainty; and
- Procedural impropriety.

10.6.4 The giving of satisfactory reasons for a decision is the acid test of good administration. Sir Harry Woolf regards the introduction of a general requirement that reasons should be given as the single most beneficial improvement which could be made to English administrative law (see his 1989 Hamlyn Lectures, *Protection of the Public: A New Challenge*). We agree, and we would implement this reform immediately on taking office.

10.6.5 A serious anomaly in administrative law is the distinction between public and private law which governs the procedural route by which cases against public bodies can be brought to court. We believe this distinction should be abolished and instead claimants in respect of the exercise of public functions should be entitled to choose their procedure, but that there should be a prima facie limitation period within which such claims in respect of the exercise of public functions have to be brought, which can be extended by the courts as a matter of discretion, and depending on the remedy sought. For example, there is little reason to impose a short limitation period on actions for compensation, but there would often be good reasons for imposing strict time limits in cases where important public projects would be held up by litigation.

10.6.6 Finally, the law relating to public interest immunity, which came under public scrutiny in the Matrix-Churchill case, needs to be reformed. Governments should be under a duty to disclose information, save only where they are satisfied that a particular document ought not to be disclosed for public interest reasons. In such cases, the courts should have the last word.

10.6.7 The procedure where public interest immunity is claimed should also be clarified so that it is made clear that it is not part of the duty of the prosecution to defend such a claim. The body claiming the immunity should instruct an advocate on their own behalf to argue the case.

10.6.8 We would therefore amend the Crown Proceedings Act 1947 and The Supreme Courts Act 1981 so that:

- The grounds for judicial review are codified.
- The courts can grant injunctions and interim injunctions against the Crown.
- The procedural distinctions between public and private law are abolished and an applicant for judicial review does not need to obtain leave (the courts already have sufficient powers to strike out frivolous and improper applications).
- A person who is injured by unlawful government action is entitled to appropriate compensation. This would reflect the trend in the European Community (the Frankovich case).
- Time limits for ordinary actions apply – such that applications for injunctions and declarations would still have to be brought promptly, though not necessarily within six months, and that actions for compensation would have to brought within six years.
- Applicants for judicial review would be entitled to see the other side's documents and to cross examine witnesses where necessary.
- Judicial review would extend to prerogative powers.
- The Crown and ministers would be subject to the contempt jurisdiction of the courts. . . .

10.8 *The Ombudsman*

10.8.1 The Parliamentary Commissioner for Administration, or 'Ombudsman', has provided a source of redress for individual citizens. Liberal Democrats want to strengthen the Ombudsman's powers in a number of ways. The powers granted to the PCA by the 1967 Act are strictly limited; we would relax those limits, and empower the Ombudsman to investigate maladministration wherever it occurs. In particular we want to see the administration of the courts and the legal aid scheme brought within the jurisdiction of the Ombudsman.

10.8.2 We attach great importance to the accessibility of the Ombudsman. We would provide for direct access without the present requirement that the ombudsman be approached only through an MP. People should be able to lodge their complaints with their local citizens advice bureaux which would forward the complaint to the Ombudsman.

10.8.3 Liberal Democrats would establish a Commission for Public Administration, accountable to a select committee of the House of Commons as the Ombudsman should continue to be, and all the present Commissioners should operate under the auspices of that Commission and therefore be to a degree accountable to Parliament. This should help to enhance the authority of the Commissioners, a matter which is of particular importance in relation to local government where the commissioner does not have the support of a select committee which is so valuable to the PCA. The Commission should be free to organise itself in the manner which it believes to be most effective, subject to there being one point of access for all cases.

10.8.4 The Ombudsman should ensure that complainants have the opportunity to comment on the case put forward by the public authority under investigation before the Commissioner completes his report. We believe that the findings and recommendations of the Commissioners should be legally enforceable, subject to a right of appeal by an authority to the courts if it believes the Ombudsman has gone beyond its remit. However, we propose that in addition to the present power to recommend remedies, backed up by the publication of reports, in the case of the Commissioner for Local Administration, a fund should be established out of which the Commissioners should be empowered to make payments to those who have suffered injustice because of maladministration. Again, this would be in line with current developments in Community law which recognise a duty on the state in some circumstances to compensate the individual if he or she has suffered from the wrongful acts of organs of the state.

10.8.5 We also believe that the Commissioners should have the right to initiate investigations of particular complaints, or of particular areas of activity within a department or agency, and power to issue codes of practice and guidelines having advisory status.

10.8.6 The reforms set out in this chapter should establish a flexible and comprehensive system of administrative law in the United Kingdom; a crucial element in the protection of individual rights and liberties in the context of our written constitution.

11 Reforming the Judiciary

11.1 The Supreme Court

11.1.1 Article Three of the United States constitution provides that 'the judicial power of the United States shall be vested in one Supreme Court ... the Judges shall hold their offices during good behaviour, and shall at stated times, receive for their services compensation, which shall not be diminished during their continuance in office.' On the basis of this article, the Supreme Court in the United States has upheld the American constitution for upwards of 200 years.

11.1.2 A Supreme Court is an essential part of our proposed new constitutional settlement. The Supreme Court would be established by the written constitution. It would take the place of the Judicial Committee of the House of Lords in the United Kingdom legal system. It would have the following powers:
- To strike down legislation which is unconstitutional, and to curb the abuse of power by the executive.

- To resolve disputes between the Federal Parliament and National Parliaments and Regional Assemblies about their respective powers.
- To protect the rights of citizens guaranteed by the Bill of Rights, while respecting the jurisdiction of the European Court of Justice and the European Court of Human Rights.

11.1.3 The Supreme Court should consist of a president and not fewer than ten members, all required to take an oath to defend the constitution. Supreme court judges would be nominated by the Judicial Services Commission (see below), approved by resolution of the appropriate committee of the House of Commons and appointed by the Head of State. The first judges would be the existing Lords of Appeal should they agree to serve and take the oath. Supreme Court judges would only be able to be removed by resolutions of both the Houses of Commons and the Senate.

11.2 *Reforms of the Legal System*

11.2.1 A number of related reforms need to be considered. Liberal Democrats would establish a Ministry of Justice for England and Wales, bringing together the government's responsibilities for:
- Safeguarding the fundamental rights and liberties of the subjects.
- Keeping the law up-to-date and in a fit state.
- Making laws fair, workable and intelligible.
- The proper administration of justice between citizen and citizen, and between citizen and state.

11.2.2 At present in England and Wales these responsibilities are fragmented between the Lord Chancellor's Department, the Home Office and a host of other Departments – a highly unsatisfactory situation, as the Home Office also has law enforcement responsibilities which conflict with its 'justice' functions. We endorse the proposals for a Ministry of Justice published in Federal White Paper 2, *Partners for Freedom and Justice.*

11.2.3 We would establish a Judicial Services Commission to nominate all High Court Judges. The Commission would consist of a president, five judges (one from the Court of Sessions in Scotland, one from each division of the High Court in England and Wales, and one from Northern Ireland), four barristers or advocates of ten years call (on from Scotland, two from England and Wales and one from Northern Ireland), four solicitors (on the same basis) and four lay members. Members would be appointed by the Ministry of Justice and its counterparts in Scotland and Northern Ireland.

11.3 *Constitutional Amendment*

11.3.1 The written constitution, drawn up and adopted by at least two-thirds of the members of the House of Commons elected by proportional representation would derive its legitimacy from the citizens of the United Kingdom. Judges would be bound by oath to uphold the constitution; and so the tyranny of the elective dictatorship would have been laid finally to rest.

11.3.2 The written constitution would be amendable only by the consent of two-thirds of the members of both Houses of Parliament sitting separately. The reforms outlined in this paper would thus be entrenched. Amendment of its key provisions would also require a referendum.

12 *From Here to There*

12.0.1 In 'We the People' the Liberal Democrats proposed that the written constitution should be drawn up by a Constituent Assembly elected by proportional representation. This proposal received widespread support, particularly at the Charter 88 Convention in Manchester in November 1991.

12.0.2 We remain committed to a constituent assembly. The assembly should be elected by proportional representation; it should adopt the constitution by the affirmative vote of at least two thirds of its members; and the constitution it ratifies should be submitted to the people in a referendum. It would only come into force when it had been approved by a majority of those voting. In this way the new constitution will derive its authority directly from the people.

12.0.3 The Constituent Assembly should decide its own procedure. This means that it should be possible for it to complete its work within six months, and should be required to do so within two years.

12.1 *How Do We Get from Here to There?*

12.1.1 In the first session of the new Parliament Liberal Democrats would also bring forward bills to:
- Introduce PR for all elections to public office.
- Incorporate the European Convention on Human Rights into UK law.
- Establish a Scottish Parliament.
- Entrench rights to freedom of information.

These measures would, in due course, become part of the new constitution. It is likely that most of the other measures in this paper would also be introduced first by means of ordinary law, with the constituent assembly serving to revise, codify and supplement them.

12.1.2 We believe that a constituent assembly would have greater authority if the people elected to it are also elected as members of the House of Commons. The Constituent Assembly Bill would therefore propose that the members of the House of Commons returned in the (PR) election after its passage should also be elected to the assembly.

12.1.3 To stimulate debate and encourage this process we publish with this white paper an illustrative written constitution. The new settlement we propose would bring the United Kingdom into line with the Commonwealth and mainland Europe. It would not be a panacea for all our ills; but it will ensure that citizens have greater control over their lives and provide a proper framework for taking democratic decisions. It would for the first time, firmly embody and express our fundamental belief in the sovereignty of the people.

RB NOTE: *The Liberal Democrat policy document then attaches as an Annexe an 'Illustrative Written Constitution of the United Kingdom' prepared by John Macdonald QC, an extract from which is reproduced below. The document closely follows the earlier Bill of Rights proposal of the Institute for Public Policy Research: see Doc. 49.*

ILLUSTRATIVE WRITTEN CONSTITUTION
(extract)

1. *The basic law*

This Constitution is the basic law of the UK of Great Britain and Northern Ireland. It derives its validity from the people of the UK and defines the powers of Parliament, the executive and the judges. It guarantees/home rule to Scotland, Wales, Northern Ireland and the regions of England and establishes the independence of local government. This Constitution provides the framework through which alone the power of government may lawfully be exercised. It recognises and gives effect to the obligations assumed by the UK as a member of the Community of Nations and of the European Community.

2. *Citizens*

Everyone born or naturalised in the UK and the children of such persons and such other persons as Parliament may provide are citizens of the UK.

3. *The European Community*

1. The UK is a member of the European Community. This Constitution takes effect subject to Community Law which has full effect in the UK.

2. Any law, convention or practice that is inconsistent with this Constitution or Community Law is, to the extent of the inconsistency, of no force or effect.

4. *Right to life*

1. Everyone's right to life shall be protected by law.

2. No one shall be deprived of life intentionally.

3. Deprivation of life shall not be regarded as inflicted in contravention of this Article when it results from the use of force which is no more than absolutely necessary:
   a) in defence of any person against unlawful violence; or
   b) in action lawfully taken for the purpose of quelling a riot or insurrection.

4. No one shall be condemned to death or executed.

5. Nothing in this article shall prevent:
   a) the withdrawal of life support systems under proper medical procedures
   b) Parliament passing laws to provide for abortion

5. *Freedom from torture*

No one shall be subjected to torture or to cruel, inhuman or degrading treatment or punishment.

6. *Freedom from slavery and forced labour*

1. No one shall be held in slavery or servitude.

2. There shall be no forced or compulsory labour.

3. For the purpose of this Article, the expression 'forced or compulsory labour' does not include:

    a) any work required to be done in the ordinary course of detention according to Article 7 or during conditional release from such detention;

    b) any service of a military character or, in case of conscientious objectors, service exacted instead of compulsory military service;

    c) any service exacted in case of an emergency or calamity threatening the community;

    d) any work or service which forms part of normal civic obligations.

7. *Right to liberty and security*

1. Everyone has the right to liberty and security of person.

2. No one shall be deprived of their liberty except, on reasonable grounds and in accordance with fair procedures established by law, in the following cases:

    a) the detention of a person after conviction by a competent court;

    b) the arrest or detention of a person for noncompliance with the lawful order of a court or in order to secure the fulfilment of any obligation prescribed by law;

    c) the arrest or detention of a person effected for the purpose of bringing them before the competent legal authority on reasonable suspicion of having committed an offence or when it is reasonably considered necessary to prevent their committing an offence or fleeing after having done so;

    d) the detention of persons for the prevention of the spreading of infectious diseases constitution a serious threat to public health, or of persons suffering from mental disorder where necessary for the prevention of harm to themselves or others;

    e) the arrest or detention of a person to prevent their effecting an unauthorised entry into the UK or of a person against whom action is being taken with a view to deportation or extradition.

3. Anyone who is arrested shall, at the time of arrest, be informed in a language which they understand of the reasons for their arrest and shall be promptly informed of any charges against them.

4. Persons awaiting trial shall not, as a general rule be detained in custody.

5. Anyone arrested or detained on a criminal charge shall be brought promptly before a judge or other officer authorised by law to exercise judicial power and is entitled to trial within a reasonable time or to release pending trial.

6. Release may be subject to guarantees to appear for trial or at any other stage of the judicial proceedings.

7. Anyone who is deprived of liberty by arrest or detention is entitled to take proceedings before a court in order that the court decide without delay the lawfulness of the detention and may order a release if detention is not lawful.

8. Anyone who has been the victim of unlawful arrest or detention shall have an enforceable right to compensation.

9. All persons deprived of their liberty shall be treated with humanity and with respect for the inherent dignity of the human person.

10. Accused persons in detention shall, save in exceptional circumstances, be segregated from convicted persons and shall be subject to separate treatment appropriate to their status as persons who have not been convicted.

11. Accused juvenile persons in detention shall be separated from adults and brought as speedily as possible for adjudication.

12. Juvenile convicted persons shall be separated from adults and accorded treatment appropriate to their age and legal status.

13. No one shall be imprisoned merely on the ground of inability to fulfil a contractual obligation.

8. *Right to fair and public hearing*

1. Everyone is entitled to a fair and public hearing to determine any criminal charge brought against them and their civil rights, within a reasonable time by an independent and impartial tribunal established by law.

2. Judgment shall be pronounced publicly but the press and public may be excluded from all or any part of the trial to the extent strictly necessary in the opinion of the court:

    a) in the interests of national security in a democratic society;

    b) where the interests of juveniles or the protection of the private life of the parties so require; or

    c) where publicity would prejudice justice.

3. Everyone charged with a criminal offence is presumed innocent until proven guilty according to law.

4. Everyone charged with a criminal offence shall have the following minimum rights:

    a) to be informed promptly in a language which they understand and in detail of the nature and cause of the accusation against them;

    b) to have adequate time and facilities for the preparation of their defence:

    c) to defend themselves in person or through legal assistance of their own choosing or, if they have not sufficient means to pay for legal assistance, to be given it free when the interests of justice so require;

    d) to examine or have examined witnesses against them and to obtain the attendance and examination of witnesses on their behalf under the same conditions as witnesses against them;

    e) to have the free assistance of an interpreter if they cannot understand or speak the language used in court;

    f) not to be compelled to testify against themselves or to confess guilt.

5. When a person has by a final decision been convicted of a criminal offence, and has suffered punishment as a result of such conviction, and it is subsequently shown that there has been a miscarriage of justice, that person shall be compensated according to law.

6. Everyone convicted of a crime has the right to have their conviction and sentence reviewed by a higher tribunal according to law.

7. No one shall be liable to be tried or punished again for an offence for which they have already been finally convicted or acquitted according to the law and penal procedure.

9. *Retrospective offences prohibited*

1. No one shall be held guilty of any criminal offence on account of any act or omission which did not constitute a criminal offence under national or international law at the time when it was committed.

2. Nor shall a heavier penalty be imposed than the one that was applicable at the time the criminal offence was committed.

10. *Respect for privacy*

1. Everyone shall have the right to respect for their privacy.

2. There shall be no interference with the exercise of this right except such as is in accordance with the law and is necessary in a democratic society:

    a) in the interests of national security or public safety;

    b) for the prevention of disorder or crime; or

    c) for the protection of health; or

    d) for the protection of the rights/freedoms of others.

11. *Freedom of thought*

1. Everyone shall have the right to freedom of thought, conscience and religion.

2. This right shall include freedom to change one's religion or belief, and freedom, either alone or in community with others and in public or private, to manifest one's religion or belief in worship, teaching, practice and observance.

3. Freedom to manifest one's religion or belief shall be subject only to such limitations as are prescribed by law and are necessary in a democratic society:

    a) in the interests of public safety; or

    b) for the preservation of public order; or

    c) for the protection of health, or

    d) for the protection of the rights and freedoms of others.

4. No law shall be made establishing any religion or imposing any religious observance.

5. No religious test shall be required as a qualification for any office of public trust under any government in the UK.

12. *Right to education*

1. No person shall be denied the right to education.

2. In the exercise of their functions in relation to education and teaching, public authorities shall respect the right of parents to ensure education and

teaching in conformity with their own religious and philosophical convictions, so far as is compatible with the provision of efficient instruction and training.

13. *Freedom of expression*

1. Everyone shall have the right to hold opinions without interference.

2. Everyone shall have the right to freedom of expression.

3. This right shall include freedom to seek, receive and impart information and ideas of all kinds regardless of frontiers, either orally, in writing or in print, in the form of art, or through any other media of their choice.

4. The exercise of the right in 13.2 shall carry with it special duties and responsibilities. It may therefore be subject to certain restrictions, but only such as are provided by law and are necessary in a democratic society:

  a) for respect of the rights or reputations of others; or

  b) for the protection of national security or of public order or of public health.

  c) for the control of election expenditure.

5. A requirement by law that radio or television broadcasting, or cinema enterprises, must be licensed shall not be inconsistent with this Article.

14. *Freedom of assembly and association*

1. Everyone shall have the right to freedom of peaceful assembly.

2. Everyone shall have the right to freedom of association with others, including the right to form and to join trade unions, and the right not to join a trade union

3. No restriction shall be placed on the exercise of these rights other than such as are prescribed by law and are necessary in a democratic society:

  a) in the interests of national security, public safety or the preservation of public order; or

  b) for the protection of public health; or

  c) for the protection of the rights and freedoms of others.

4. This Article shall not prevent the imposition of restrictions prescribed by law and necessary in a democratic society on the exercise of the right in 14.2 by members of the Armed Forces or of the police or by persons charged with the administration of the state.

15. *Rights in respect of marriage*

1. Everyone of marriageable age shall have the right both to marry and to found a family.

2. No marriage shall be entered into without the free and full consent of the intending spouses.

3. Spouses shall have equality of rights and responsibilities as to marriage, during marriage, and at its dissolution.

4. In the case of dissolution, provision shall be made for the necessary protection of any children.

5. Every child shall have the right to appropriate protection by their family, society and public authorities.

16. *Right to enjoyment of possessions*

1. Every natural or legal person shall be entitled to the peaceful enjoyment of their possessions.

2. No one shall be deprived of their possessions except in the public interest and subject to the conditions provided for by law and to prompt, adequate and effective compensation.

3. This Article shall not in any way impair the right to enforce such laws as may be necessary to control the use of property in accordance with the general interest or to secure the payment of taxes or other contributions or penalties.

17. *Right to participate in public life and service*

Every adult citizen shall have the right and the opportunity, without unreasonable restrictions:

    a) to take part in the conduct of public affairs directly or through freely chosen representatives;

    b) to vote and to stand for election at periodic elections, which shall be by universal and equal suffrage and shall be held by secret ballot, guaranteeing the free expression of the will of the persons;

    c) to participate, on general terms of equality, in public service.

18. *Freedom of movement*

1. Everyone lawfully within the UK shall have the right of liberty of movement and freedom to choose their residence within the UK.

2. Everyone shall be free to leave the UK, and everyone holding UK citizenship is entitled to a passport.

3. No restrictions shall be placed on the exercise of the rights set out in this Article other than such as are in accordance with law and are necessary in a democratic society:

    a) in the interests of national security, public safety or the preservation of public order; or

    b) for the prevention of crime or under an order imposed by a court on conviction of crime; or

    c) for the protection of health; or

    d) for the protection of the rights/freedoms of others.

19. *Freedom from expulsion from UK*

1. No citizen of the UK shall be expelled from the UK or deprived of the right to enter the UK.

2. Other persons may be expelled from the UK only in pursuance of a decision reached in accordance with law.

3. Any such persons shall be allowed, prior to expulsion:

    a) to submit reasons against expulsion; and

    b) to have their cases reviewed by, and be represented for the purpose before, the competent authority or a person or persons especially designated by the competent authority.

4. This Article shall not prevent the extradition of persons, through established legal procedures, for the purpose of standing trial for a criminal

offence or serving a sentence lawfully imposed on them in another jurisdiction.

20. *Right of asylum*

1. Every person shall have the right to seek and be granted asylum in the
UK in accordance with the law of the UK and international conventions, if
they are being pursued for political offences.

2. In no case shall an alien be deported or returned to a country,
regardless of whether or not it is their country of origin, if in that country
their right to life or personal freedom is in danger of being violated because
of their race, nationality, religion, social status, or political opinions.

21. *Equality*

1. Everyone shall have the right to recognition as a person before the
law.

2. All persons shall be entitled without any discrimination to the equal
protection of the law.

3. The equal protection of the law and the enjoyment of the rights and
freedoms set out in this Bill of Rights shall be secured without discrimination on any ground such as sex, race, colour, language, religion, political or
other opinion, national or social origin, association with a national minority,
property, birth, sexual orientation, disability, age, or other status.

22. *Application of Bill of Rights*

The Bill of Rights shall apply to any act or omission by or on behalf of any
person or body in the performance of any public function, including an
omission by Government to take appropriate steps to secure compliance
with any provision of the Bill of Rights.

23. *Scope of exceptions*

Where the protection of any right or freedom by the Bill of Rights is
subject to any restriction or qualification, that restriction or qualification:

    a)   shall have no wider effect that is strictly necessary in the circum-
           stances; and

    b)   shall not be applied for any purpose other than that for which it
           has been prescribed.

24. *Interpretation*

The Bill of Rights:

    a)   is intended to give effect in the UK to the International Covenant
           on Civil and Political Rights and the European Convention for the
           Protection of Human Rights and Fundamental Freedoms which
           are hereby incorporated into UK law; and

    b)   shall be interpreted and applied accordingly, but without preju-
           dice to any rights and freedoms protected by the Bill of Rights
           which are more extensive than those protected by the Inter-
           national Covenant or the European Convention.

25. *Rights under other agreements*

Nothing in this Chapter shall be interpreted as limiting or derogating
from any of the human rights or fundamental freedoms which may be
enjoyed under any other agreement to which the UK is a party.

26. *Abuse of freedoms*

Nothing in the Bill of Rights shall be interpreted as implying for any group or person a right to engage in any activity or perform any act aimed at the destruction of any of the rights and freedoms set out therein.

27. *Remedies*

1. Without prejudice to any right to apply for judicial review, any person whose rights or freedoms protected by the Bill of Rights have been infringed or are threatened with infringement may bring civil proceedings for damages, an injunction or any other relief authorised by Rules of Court. If such person does not have sufficient means to pay for legal assistance that person shall be given it free where the interests of justice so require.

2. Act of Parliament shall provide for the appointment of a Human Rights Commission which shall have the power to institute proceedings and to assist individual complainants in legal proceedings in relation to the Bill of Rights...

Here We Stand: Liberal Democrat Policies for Modernising Britain's Democracy, 1993.

---

94   THE 1997 LIBERAL DEMOCRAT ELECTION MANIFESTO CALLS FOR THE ESTABLISHMENT OF A UK BILL OF RIGHTS, 1997

Our priorities are to:
* Restore trust between people and government, by ending secrecy and guaranteeing peoples' rights and freedoms.
* Renew Britain's democracy, by creating a fair voting system, reforming Parliament and setting higher standards for politicians' conduct.
* Give government back to the people, by decentralising power to the nations, regions and communities of the United Kingdom ...

We will:

Safeguard individual liberties, by establishing a Bill of Rights. As a first step, we will incorporate the European Convention on Human Rights into UK law so that it is enforceable by the courts in the UK. We will set up a Human Rights Commission to strengthen the protection of individual rights. We will create a Ministry for Justice responsible for protecting human rights and overseeing the administration of the legal system, the courts and legal aid. We oppose the introduction of Identity Cards.

Break open the excessive secrecy of government, by passing a Freedom of Information Act establishing a citizens right to know...

The Liberal Democrats Manifesto, 1997, p. 43.

The Conservative Party

---

95   THE CONSERVATIVE PARTY AT THE 1979
GENERAL ELECTION PROMISES TO CONVENE ALL-
PARTY TALKS ON A BILL OF RIGHTS, 1979

In recent years, Parliament has been weakened in two ways. First, outside groups have been allowed to usurp some of its democratic functions. Last winter the Government permitted strike committees and pickets to take on powers and responsibilities which should have been discharged by Parliament and the police. Second, the traditional role of our legislature has suffered badly from the growth of government over the last quarter of a century.

We will see that Parliament and no other body stands at the centre of the nation's life and decisions, and we will seek to make if effective in its job of controlling the Executive.

We sympathise with the approach of the all-party parliamentary committees which put forward proposals last year for improving the way the House of Commons legislates and scrutinises public spending and the work of government departments. We will give the new House of Commons an early chance of coming to a decision on these proposals.

The public has rightly grown anxious about many constitutional matters in the last few years – partly because our opponents have proposed major constitutional changes for party political advantage. Now Labour want not merely to abolish the House of Lords but to put nothing in its place. This would be a most dangerous step. A strong Second Chamber is necessary not only to revise legislation but also to guarantee our constitution and liberties.

It is not only the future of the Second Chamber which is at issue. We are committed to discussions about the future government of Scotland, and have put forward proposals for improved parliamentary control of administration in Wales. There are other important matters, such as a possible Bill of Rights, the use of referendums, and the relationship between Members of the European Parliament and Westminster, which we shall wish to discuss with all parties.

Conservative Party, Election Manifesto 1979, p. 21

96 THE CONSERVATIVE PARTY IN GOVERNMENT ANNOUNCES THAT THE TIME IS NOT RIPE FOR ALL-PARTY TALKS ON A BILL OF RIGHTS, 1985

PARLIAMENTARY QUESTION

Bill of Rights: Policy

Lord Hylton asked her Majesty's Government: When they will initiate constitutional discussions between all parties concerning a Bill of Rights for the United Kingdom, in accordance with undertaking given during the discussion of Lord Wade's Bill.

The Minister of State, Home Office (Lord Elton): The Government support the principles of the European Convention on Human Rights, to which they are a party. The question of incorporating such principles into United Kingdom law raises important constitutional issues which would need to be fully explored between the political parties. The Government do not judge that the present time is ripe for further initiatives on their part additional to those taken during the passage of the Bill to which the noble Lord refers; but they keep, and will continue to keep, closely in touch with public debate on this matter.

HC Deb., 12 March 1985, col. 159.

97 MARGARET THATCHER AS PRIME MINISTER TELLS THE HOUSE OF COMMONS SHE OPPOSES INCORPORATION OF THE EUROPEAN CONVENTION ON HUMAN RIGHTS, 1989

PARLIAMENTARY QUESTION

Human Rights

Mr. Graham Allen: To ask the Prime Minister if Her Majesty's Government will support the incorporation of the European Convention on Human Rights in the form outlined in the human Rights Bill which is set down for Second Reading on 7 July: and if she will make a statement.

The Prime Minister: No. We are committed to, and support, the principles of human rights in the European Convention on Human Rights but we believe that is is for Parliament rather than the judiciary to determine how these principles are best secured.

HC Deb., 6 July 1989, cols. WA251–2.

---

98   JOHN MAJOR AS PRIME MINISTER CONFIRMS THAT IT IS THE POLICY OF THE CONSERVATIVE GOVERNMENT NOT TO INCORPORATE THE EUROPEAN CONVENTION ON HUMAN RIGHTS, 1993

PARLIAMENTARY QUESTION

Human Rights

Mr. Solely: To ask the Prime Minister if he will make it his policy to incorporate article 10 of the European convention on human rights into British law.

The Prime Minister: No. Our policy remains not to incorporate the European convention on human rights into domestic law, since we believe that it is for Parliament, rather than the judiciary, to determine how the principles of human rights in the convention are best sourced.

HC Deb., 15 January 1993, col. WA822.

---

99   CHARLES WARDLE AS UNDER-SECRETARY OF STATE FOR THE HOME OFFICE GIVES THE CASE FOR THE CONSERVATIVE GOVERNMENT'S OPPOSITION TO A BILL OF RIGHTS, 1993

The Parliamentary Under-Secretary of State for the Home Department (Mr. Charles Wardle): Contrary to the impression given by critics of the present arrangements, this country's approach to rights and freedoms is more permissive than that found elsewhere. The possession of rights and freedoms is assumed. It is not dependent on their enshrinement in statute or through some other constitutional device. That means that only through specific action by Parliament – this relates to the point raised by the hon. Gentleman in his intervention – can those rights be curtailed.

There is an important and underlying principle here – that rights and freedoms are, in general, the property of individuals. They are not something to be bestowed by the state. We have heard criticisms that that approach to human rights in the United Kingdom is both ineffective and inappropriate to modern circumstances.

I do not believe that those who argue in that way have begun to show their case. Nor have they convinced me of the argument, which inevitably follows, that the only certain way of protecting the rights of our citizens is through some form of Bill of Rights, perhaps incorporating the European convention on human rights, as the hon. Gentleman suggested, and possibly entrenched in a written constitution as some have suggested.

I express it in that way because many of those proposing such a measure tend to be less than clear about the form that it will take. The Government do not believe that one can guarantee rights by the enactment of broad propositions. This is more a question of political culture, as can be seen by the prevalence of human rights abuses in certain parts of the world, which nevertheless can boast a Bill of Rights on the statute book ...

The political culture of the United Kingdom, with its strong system of law and parliamentary democracy, is soundly based. An essential part of that is an assumption and expectation on behalf of our citizens that certain rights and freedoms are theirs. Governments must seek to achieve a balance whereby the individual enjoys the optimum level of freedom.

Clearly it is necessary for the Government to strike a balance between the rights of the individual and of society at large and on the conflict of rights between various groups in society. However, given the nature of our society, to restrict the rights of our citizens is not an easy matter. Any Government seeking to do that would need to satisfy both public opinion and, beyond that, Parliament itself. I find it strange that those who argue for a Bill of Rights are so ready to dismiss the role of Parliament in this important area.

It is surely more consistent with our democratic traditions that decisions on crucial issues like this, which will affect the lives of many people, should be taken by those whom the people of this country have elected to represent them rather than placed in the hands of the judiciary, who after all are not elected.

I also find it surprising that it is suggested that a Bill of Rights would somehow be more sensitive to the changing needs of our people than Parliament would be in fulfilling its traditional role of enacting legislation in specific areas. A Bill of Rights, after all, can only embody the values of the time when it was drafted. The whole purpose of a Bill of Rights and its entrenchment into law, by whatever means, is to offer some permanent benchmark by which the actions of Government and the freedoms enjoyed by citizens can be judged.

However, public attitudes, and therefore the attitudes of society, are capable of change. We only have to consider how public opinion on a number of social and moral issues has developed over the past 50 years, 25 years, or, as some would say, the past decade. A Bill of Rights for the United Kingdom drafted 25 years ago would be most unlikely to reflect fully the aspirations and views of people today. However, any Bill of Rights that was subject to frequent amendment, if that were constitutionally possible, would surely defeat the object of the whole exercise.

The hon. Gentleman referred particularly to the possible incorporation of the European convention on human rights into domestic law. I shall deal with some of the points that he raised about that.

As the House knows, the Government are firm believers in and supporters of the European convention on human rights. The United Kingdom was closely associated with the convention at the outset, playing a major part in its drafting in 1950. We accepted the right of individual petition to the Commission in 1966 and agreed to be bound by the judgments of the court. We have been diligent in observing in the court's judgments, as even our most diehard critics would acknowledge ...

Judges have a vital role in the enforcement, application and development of the abstraction that we call the rule of law. It is the Government's firm view that imposing on the judges a duty to interpret the convention, or broad principles in a Bill of Rights, would add an unwelcome new dimension to their current role. That new role would be to decide broad issues of policy.

It is worth contemplating for a moment what that would mean in practice. A Bill of Rights would enable Parliament to pass a law, which could, the next day or next year, be struck down by a judge who, acting in good faith, took a different view according to his own perceptions of the public interest.

Not only would that undermine the sovereignty of Parliament – it would bring the judiciary into the political arena. The more we draw judges into political matters, the more we shall create problems for them in terms of the general public's attitude and respect for them. The point is not that our judges could not do the job – our fears are that such a job would damage their reputation and standing.

That is not to dismiss the important role that our judges can play in the protection of our citizens against the actions of Government. The hon. Member for Nottingham, North [Mr. Graham Allen] has drawn a picture of an Executive out of control, with no effective check on its actions. I have heard him talk about that before. The readiness of the citizens of the United Kingdom to seek judicial review of Government actions, and of the courts to entertain such applications, gives the lie to that argument.

This is an important safeguard against the unreasonable exercise of discretion by the Government. But what it does not do, which their interpretation of a Bill of Rights would do, is seek to challenge the merits of the broader policy issues.

I do not accept the proposition that these cases demonstrate that there has been some general erosion of human rights in this country. On the contrary, an objective examination of the record in recent years would show many areas in which rights have been extended. That has been achieved usually through Parliament, whose role the hon. Gentleman has lightly dismissed today. It is disappointing that there was no recognition of the role of Parliament in his speech, as he is such an active member of the House.

We can honestly claim to have a more open Government than ever before. That is the result of measures that have been initiated in recent years. The Data Protection Act 1984 provides a good example of how Parliament can legislate to afford rights in specific areas – in this case, access by individuals to information held about them on computers. Legislation has also been enacted in respect of information held by local authorities.

The Official Secrets Act 1988 cut back the information that is protected against disclosure by the criminal law. It replaced the previous casual provisions of section 2 of the Official Secrets Act 1911 with a narrowly targeted scheme that penalised only an unauthorised disclosure of official information which would give rise to a serious degree of harm to the interests of the country. More generally, the Government have demonstrated their commitment to open government, and have done more than any of their predecessors to open the processes of government to the scrutiny of Parliament.

There are other examples of Parliament acting to enhance the rights of individuals. The Police and Criminal Evidence Act 1984 was one such measure. Measures such as that – there are many more – are often ignored in any discussion on human rights in the United Kingdom. Yet, in terms of practical consequences, they have more direct relevance to the lives of our citizens than a list of broad principles set out in a Bill of Rights.

Parliament devotes much care and attention to measures of this kind. In doing so, it properly exercises its role, for which its Members were elected, of determining how to respond to the changing needs of society...

HC Deb., 27 May 1993, cols. 1029f.

---

100   EARL FERRERS AS HOME OFFICE MINISTER OF STATE SETS OUT THE CONSERVATIVE GOVERNMENT'S OPPOSITION TO A WRITTEN CONSTITUTION WITH ENTRENCHED INDIVIDUAL RIGHTS, 1992–4

PARLIAMENTARY DEBATE

Lord Kirkhill asked Her Majesty's Government: Whether they intend that Parliament should incorporate the provisions of the European Convention on Human Rights into the domestic law of the United Kingdom, and if not, why not.

Earl Ferrers: No, my Lords. The Government are fully committed to the principles of human rights but we consider that it should be Parliament rather than the judiciary which determines how human rights are best secured.

Lord Kirkhill: My Lords, I thank the noble Earl for that reply, which was predictable. It reflects the Government's long-standing view. Does the noble Earl agree that a person who has made his submission in the United Kingdom domestic court at considerable expense to himself and feels aggrieved can take his case to the Commission of the Court of Human Rights in Strasbourg where the judges are able to invoke the articles of the convention? Does he further agree that as a consequence that submission is frequently upheld and then, in the United Kingdom context, his submission is sustained? Will he accept, therefore, that on the one hand our judges have one hand tied behind their back and, on the other, the aggrieved person has too much difficulty in seeking justice?

Earl Ferrers: My Lords, the individual person can always seek justice. It may be difficult if one has to go to a European court or commission but it can be done. The view we take is that the incorporation of the convention would undermine our constitutional tradition. Parliament has supreme responsibility for enacting and changing our laws. Therefore, while we are in accord with the convention and have signed and ratified it, because Parliament is supreme we do not believe that it is right to put it into legislation.

Lord Hailsham of Saint Marylebone: My Lords, I accept completely what my noble friend says about the position of Parliament and the duties of the judiciary. Will he accept that it would save a great deal of time and money were British judges able to give effect to some of the provisions in the human rights convention? Would they not then be able to do it with a knowledge of British conditions?

Earl Ferrers: My Lords, that could well be the case but the fact is that Parliament makes the laws. If we were to put such a procedure into our laws we would end up with judges in the High Court determining whether or not matters which Parliament has decided are within the European legislation.

Lord Holme of Cheltenham: My Lords, is the Minister aware that at present British citizens who believe that their rights have been infringed can appeal to the European Court and the Commission? In that sense Parliament already acknowledges that human rights are protected by a court. The problem is that the court is in Strasbourg and it takes hundreds of thousands of pounds and many years for British subjects to have their rights redressed. Might not the rights of British subjects be more immediately and inexpensively redressed in British courts by British judges?

Earl Ferrers: My Lords, it is true that to go to the European Court takes a long time and is sometimes expensive. However, that is the route by which the European Convention is applied. It would be a difficult process to try to change that method and introduce it into our courts.

Lord Allen of Abbeydale: My Lords, this is a complicated subject which we have debated on a number of occasions. Is the Minister aware that some of us agree with his comments about remaining uneasy about the responsibilities which this would put on our judges, rather than on Parliament, to say what a new law is 'on the spot', as it were? Does the Minister agree that as a consequence there is a risk that, as in America, the social and political views of our judges might become matters of public interest?

Earl Ferrers: My Lords, I believe that the noble Lord is, not for the first time, 100 per cent right. If the judges have to determine matters of political substance, which is normally determined by Parliament, they could find themselves in an uneasy and uncomfortable position. . .

Parliamentary question

The Earl of Selkirk asked Her Majesty's Government:

Whether they propose to draw up a written constitution so that everyone will know their legal rights and obligations.

Earl Ferrers: No. Our present constitutional arrangements make effective provision for the individual's rights and obligations under the law. To attempt to codify or to replace those arrangements in a 'written' constitution, which would be subject to interpretation by a special court, would be neither desirable nor necessary.

HL Deb., 19 November 1992, cols. 714f; 12 April 1994, col. WA89.

---

101   THE CONSERVATIVE CHAIRMAN BRIAN
MAWHINNEY ATTACKS LABOUR'S PLANS FOR
CONSTITUTIONAL REFORM AND A BILL OF RIGHTS,
1996

There is wide agreement that our institutions have served this nation well for centuries. Yet no politician can hide from the fact that Parliament, the judiciary and increasingly the Monarchy are the target for more criticism today than for generations.

The rekindling of respect and admiration for these institutions is an urgent task, not just for those in public life but for the nation. But this mood of national questioning and cynicism has not led to any unanswerable case for fundamental change to the Constitution.

Our Constitution has evolved over the centuries in tune with the instincts of the British people. Whilst other countries – including many of our European neighbours – have seen their constitutions torn to shreds and replaced as the result of revolutions, unrest or war, our so-called unwritten constitution has given Britain stability.

Recognising the wisdom of Burke that 'a state without the means of some change is without the means of its conservation' Conservative opposition to radical constitutional reform is not an arcane attachment to the archaic. It is recognition that the experience of generations; the accumulation of wisdom and practice over centuries is a better and safer way of safeguarding liberty than the trendy theories and instant modern solutions of lawyers, academics or even, dare I say it, politicians.

Our constitution has continued to evolve as the nation has developed. Conservatives do not oppose constitutional change. Indeed Conservative governments have been responsible for some of the most far-reaching Constitutional reforms: from the extension of the franchise in 1867, to the completion of universal suffrage in 1928, and the introduction of life peerages in 1958. Since 1979 this Government has carried on the Conservative tradition of rolling Constitutional reform ...

Of course, there have been no dramatic statements or Declarations of Rights. No attempts to set in stone the wisdom of one age. That's never been the Conservative way.

Instead, we have kept to the successful Tory tradition of gradual reform.

Meeting the needs of an ever changing society. Working with the grain of British institutions which have served our nation well. . .

The British Constitution's strength is its flexibility. It embodies, in Philip Norton's words, the 'values and attitudes' of the British people.

There is no appetite across the nation for Labour's constitutional agenda. Radical change to Britain's constitution may be the all the rage at Islington dinner parties but it is not a subject of debate in shopping queues or during half time at any football match in the country. This is not to suggest that the Constitution is unimportant. As I will argue, it is vitally important. Because, at the next General Election, the British people are to be asked to vote for 'the most extensive package of constitutional change ever proposed'. Mr Blair's Labour Party promises a menu of constitutional reform which is more far reaching than anything ever suggested by a Party in pursuit of power. It is a programme of change so profound and, I believe, so threatening that it must remain at the heart of serious political debate between now and the general election . . .

What Labour propose amounts to nothing less than an attempt to foist an entirely new constitutional order on our people based on fashionable left-wing prejudices in defiance of the wisdom of the ages . . .

By the mid-1980s left-wing thinkers, so depressed by their failure to convince the electorate of their case (which our economic success had shattered), were arguing that government had become so powerful and so dominated by one Party that action had to be taken to entrench rights.

Labour's plans to impose a written constitution are just as ill thought through.

Labour is committed to both a United Kingdom Bill of Rights and the incorporation of the European Convention on Human Rights into UK law.

I ask simple questions.

- What would be in the British Bill of Rights?
- Who would define these rights?
- Why should the British people welcome a set of rights drafted by the long list of the politically correct and favoured minority groups which would lobby Labour?
- And if this Bill of Rights is to made part of our constitution, how is it to be made permanent?
- Would a future House of Commons with a different majority have the right to repeal or revise it – or not?
- And if not, what would give a transitory and rare Labour Government the entitlement to impose its views of rights on to further generations in perpetuity?

Perhaps this confusion explains why Mr Blair seems more keen to speak about Labour's plans to incorporate the European Convention. Although why Labour should be so keen to put something into our law which their own policy documents describe as 'inadequate and outdated' may be a matter for some speculation.

British citizens have had the right to petition the European Court of

Human Rights since 1966 and the Government is committed to implementing all the Court's judgements – even when, as recently with the Court's
decision on the 'Death on the Rock' case, they are unpalatable.

But incorporation into UK law would be a fundamental constitutional
change. The case against the codification of rights is profound. It is supremely
arrogant of one generation to assume that its views should wipe away the
wisdom of past generations and bind those unborn for decades to come. . .

Speech to Conservative Policy Centre, 7 February 1996.

---

102   LADY BLATCH AS CONSERVATIVE HOME OFFICE MINISTER OF STATE SAYS THE UK HAS NO NEED FOR A NEW BILL OF RIGHTS, 1996

Some noble Lords have argued that the freedom of the individual in this
country would be better protected if Britain had a written constitution and/
or a new Bill of Rights, setting out a list of fundamental rights. But as my
right honourable friend the Prime Minister reminded us recently, we
already have a living, breathing, working constitution, which already provides very effectively for the protection of the individual's rights and
freedoms and one which can also change with the spirit of the times.

The noble Lord, Lord Cocks of Hartcliffe, made a point most powerfully
when he asked rhetorically how many other countries would even recognise
a miscarriage of justice, let alone investigate one. He was rightly indignant
about those who do not value just how much protection of the individual
that there is in this country; and how right he is.

The noble Lord also reminded us that a written constitution is not
necessarily a guarantee of protection. Indeed, he used the analogy of the
Weimar Republic, which did have a written constitution and which, quite
specifically, included rights for religious freedom. Tell that to the Jews!
Frankly, that constitution was not worth the paper that it was written on. On
the noble Lord's other point about the Charity Commission and Charter 88.
I have no doubt that the commission will have noted what the noble Lord
had to say about the charter.

We have no need to immobilise our constitution in statutes, and we have
no need for a new Bill of Rights seeking to codify the rights and freedoms
enjoyed by people in this country. Most people would agree that human
rights are already very well safeguarded in the United Kingdom. Our rights
and freedoms are inherent in our legal systems, and are protected by them
and by Parliament, unless those protections are removed or restricted by
statute.

However, what such a Bill would do is to transfer responsibility for
determining matters affecting individual rights and freedoms from Parliament to the courts, eroding the principle of parliamentary sovereignty which
is fundamental to our constitution.

Some have suggested that the courts are already involved in such matters, that the boundary between policy-making and judicial interpretation has already been crossed, for example, through the use of judicial review. It is clearly right that the courts should hold Ministers to the proper use of their powers and should safeguard the procedural quality of decision-making. That is merely an example of our constitution working. But by the same token, it is of course ultimately up to Parliament to decide the laws and to create the framework within which judges and courts make their judgements.

It is too easy at times to take the safeguards and the protection that we enjoy for granted. We must not fall into the trap of doing so. We should be proud of those fundamental parts of our heritage and not seek to change them where there is neither a clear need nor an advantage in doing so. Some noble Lords have argued that, instead of a Bill of Rights, or as a first step towards one, the United Kingdom should incorporate the European Convention on Human Rights, or the International Covenant on Civil and Political Rights, into our domestic law. For the reasons I have already explained, the Government do not believe that seeking to codify individual rights and freedoms in our law, whether in the form of an incorporated treaty or a free-standing bill of rights, is either necessary or desirable.

Those who suggest that the United Kingdom's record on breaches of the ECHR is the worst in Europe are simply misinformed. The UK's record of compliance with the European Convention on Human Rights compares well with the record of any other country. Listening to the noble and learned Lord, Lord Bingham, I had to ask myself: what is the practical benefit of incorporation? On the contrary, incorporation would have required the Appellate Committee of the House of Lords to decide on yesterday's case in another way.

Perhaps I may give your Lordships some examples of the records of other countries as regards breaches of the ECHR: 27 allegations of violation respectively against the Portugese and Greek Governments were declared admissible by the Commission; 28 against the Austrian Government; 39 against the Government of the Netherlands; 57 against the Turkish Government; 148 against the French Government; and 453 against the Italian Government. Over the same period, only 24 allegations against the United Kingdom were declared admissible. [*RB NOTE: On further ECHR statistics see Doc. 33.*] Those figures hardly support the claim that incorporation reduces the number of cases going forward to Strasbourg. I agree with the powerful speech of my noble friend Lord Kingsland when he argued that incorporation is not necessary and, if it were suggested, it would only be futile.

I said earlier that we did not owe our constitution to political theories. It has been formed by the people of this country over the years. It is a lively, vibrant thing that embodies their values, their understandings, their respect for the individual and his freedom under the law. The changes which have taken place over the years have not been made for the sake of change or in the interests of particular institutions; they have been practical changes, driven by what people want and not what some people out there think they need. Over the centuries they have brought the government closer to the people. That is what we want. That is what we as a government have been concerned to do.

We have moved power away from central bureaucratic structures so that it is now closer to the people and to consumers. That has been done across the board in the fields of health, where hospital trusts now take decisions rather than the National Health Service; and in education where school governing bodies and not local government have the final say. It has also been done through the Citizen's Charter which has restored the individual's right to hold large, impersonal organisations to account; and, indeed, through a host of changes which have put consumers rather than providers in charge and have strengthened the independence of individuals. Contrary to the views of the noble Lord, Lord Williams of Mostyn, more individual choice has been opposed root and branch by noble Lords opposite.

In the words of my noble friend Lord Nickson, who spoke so well for the business community in Scotland, the Labour Party proposals would create doubt, disadvantage and disunity. They would do nothing for competitiveness, confidence and continuity. The process of evolutionary change is our great tradition and goes right back to the Magna Carta. It has given us a constitution with firm foundations which binds the people of this country to the institutions which serve them and uphold their freedom. We must not undermine this stability and strength by experimenting and tinkering to no good purpose, or worse, for some narrow political end to enhance the 'macho' image of the right honourable Member for Sedgefield.

At the end of the day any decision to change or not to change must be taken by Parliament. Parliament is the process through which the representatives of the people control the Executive. And, as I have said, it is Parliament which decides the laws on which judges and courts make their judgments. I believe passionately that the sovereignty of Parliament is fundamental to our constitution; that intricate complex of institutions and values which reflects our history as a nation and which values all the people of this country as individuals. . .

HL Deb., 3 July 1996, cols. 1566f.

---

103 LORD MACKAY AS CONSERVATIVE LORD CHANCELLOR SPEAKS AGAINST JUDICIAL SUPREMACISM AND ANY CHANGE IN THE CONSTITUTIONAL RELATIONSHIP BETWEEN PARLIAMENT AND THE JUDICIARY, 1996

In the United Kingdom, all power derives ultimately from the Crown. Parliament, in the tripartite form of Lords, Commons and the Monarch, is the supreme legislative authority. The powers of the Crown are also exercised by the judiciary, who apply the law to the cases which come before the courts, and by the executive, in the day-to-day business of government. Under our constitution there is a separation of the powers and responsibilities of these three organs, but this separation is by no means rigid. The legislative and judicial functions may take some rest in Parliamentary recesses and judicial vacations, although the amount of rest taken by the judiciary in the judicial vacations can certainly be overestimated. The day-to-day executive government of the country must nevertheless continue to operate around the clock and around the calendar, and in many cases cannot adequately do so unless allowed both to make rules and to decide disputes. When it does so, this may appear to some as an encroachment both on the legislative and on the judicial sphere. In practice, Parliament has found it necessary to delegate legislative powers to members of the executive, and to confer powers of adjudication on Ministers and other non-judicial agencies.

This kind of overlap is not only found in the legislative and adjudicative powers conferred on the executive. Under our Cabinet system of government the executive branch is recruited from, located within, and collectively responsible to Parliament. The same overlap with Parliament can be found within the judiciary – the most senior judges serve not only as judges but as legislators in Parliament, since they sit in the House of Lords. The office of Lord Chancellor overlaps all three strands of government by adding a Ministerial role to the judicial and legislative functions shared with the other judicial members of the House of Lords.

I believe these arrangements have tremendous advantages in practice. The presence of the most senior members of the judiciary in Parliament enables the legislative process to draw on a tremendous and unique concentration of legal expertise. The benefits of this are to be seen not just in relation to technical law, but in relation to the whole range of legislation that is put before Parliament.

The primary function of making the law rests with Parliament, and Parliament is the supreme law-making body. The Government can act only in accordance with the law, and the courts must apply and give effect to the law . . .

Once the Government has presented legislative proposals to Parliament and Parliament has enacted legislation, either as originally proposed or with such modifications as Parliament thinks fit to incorporate, then the courts will of course proceed to apply that legislation, consistently with the judicial oath and the legislative supremacy of Parliament.

Judicial independence should, however, be firmly distinguished from any hint of judicial supremacism. Just as the independence of the judiciary is fundamental to our constitutional arrangements, so is the idea that the judiciary is bound by an Act of Parliament. As I have said on other occasions, I am not convinced by arguments, although eloquently advanced, that there exists a higher order of law comprising basic or fundamental principles against which the judiciary may measure Acts of Parliament, and if necessary strike them down. . .

It is currently a matter of debate whether the European Convention should be incorporated into domestic law, and it is in this connection that I raise the question. As I have said, the judges presently approach their function on the basis of a collaborative approach with Parliament, employing techniques of adjudication which limit them to the individual case between specific litigants and generally keep them clear of the political arena in which policy issues are discussed. Thus they are selected for their ability to decide individual cases in accordance with the law, and their independence is assured.

Incorporation of the European Convention or a Bill of Rights as the yardstick by which Acts of Parliament are to be measured would inevitably draw judges into making decisions of a far more political nature, measuring policy against abstract principles with possible implications for the development of broad social and economic policy which is and has been accepted by the judiciary to be properly the preserve of Parliament. The question which would then be asked, and to which an answer could not be postponed indefinitely, is whether the introduction of such a political element into the judicial function would require a change in the criteria for appointment of judges, making the political stance of each candidate a matter of importance as much as his or her ability to decide cases on their individual facts and the law applicable to those facts. Following on from that is the question of how confidence in judicial independence and impartiality could be maintained, and whether their appointment should be subjected to political scrutiny of the sort recently seen in the United States. . .

The Convention in many places permits restriction of the rights protected so far as this is 'necessary in a democratic society'. If the Convention were to be incorporated into domestic law, which body should decide what is so necessary; the courts which are charged with the function of applying the law, or Parliament which is democratically elected? For these reasons, I do not agree that the Convention should be incorporated into our domestic law. The nature of these issues underlines once again the need to give close and careful consideration to the established principles on which our constitutional machinery operates before taking up the challenge of changing them.

Speech to the Citizenship Foundation, 'Parliament and the Judges: A Constitutional Challenge?', 8 July 1996.

---

104   THE CONSERVATIVE LEADER, JOHN MAJOR, DELIVERS A SPEECH ON THE CONSTITUTION OPPOSING REFORM AND A UK BILL OF RIGHTS, 1996

This evening I want to address a vital debate – the state of the British constitution. This debate is about the very nature of our nation. About the United Kingdom, and the constitutional fabric that underpin our freedoms and make us what we are.

The British constitution is complex and, in many ways, intangible. Too many people are put off by the word 'constitution', and make the mistake of thinking it a technical subject that only the experts can understand. Well I don't claim to be a constitutional expert. But I am a politician and a citizen, and it is from that practical experience that I want to address the issues. Because the constitution is not, to me, simply a matter of institutions – Parliament, the Crown, our legal system. At its heart I believe it's about individuals and individual freedom. How we influence and control the kind of nation we live in. The Constitution is shorthand for our rights and our democracy ... Tonight I want to [set] out my view of the constitution, its enduring strengths, and how it has adapted and must continue to adapt to serve the people of this country. And I shall cast a clear eye on some of the proposals for change that others have floated. Some are pointless. Others are damaging. But many are, in practical terms, irreversible.

We are fortunate. The British constitution is vibrant and robust. But it is not indestructible. People must realise that our Constitution is not a piece of architecture that one can re-engineer by knocking down a wall here or adding an extension there. It's a living, breathing Constitution. Its roots are ancient, but it has evolved. And it has been stable because it has popular support ... Our constitution isn't just dry institutions and legalistic relation-ships. It embodies a set of values, a legacy of understandings, that have developed year by year over the centuries – an understanding that is breathed in Parliament, referred every day in the media, taken for granted in the saloon bar arguments about the state of the Nation.

At its centre is something we are all instinctively proud of when pointed out to us, but – thankfully – rarely need to think about in our day to day lives. That is the fundamental freedom we each have as subjects of The Queen and citizens of the United Kingdom. And you only have to pause a moment and think how few countries can boast such freedom, for so long, with so little national strife and struggle, to realise what a precious gift that freedom is and how much we owe to the unseen, unsung constitutional backbone that binds together our British way of life.

A living constitution that changes with the times. Look at the history of this century and the changes there have been – not fundamental but significant nonetheless – in Parliament, our electoral system, the Civil Service, local administration, even the Monarchy and Church. Not change for change's sake. Not the result of some technocratic plan. Not to serve the interests of the institutions themselves. They have been changes to strengthen the links with the individual citizen who they are there to serve. That's the kind of constitutional change that I support. Practical change, not grand plans. And above all, change that is driven by what people want. Conservatives believe in giving the citizen the reins wherever possible ...

Protecting the freedom of the individual is an old principle, embodied in basic freedoms of speech and association. The principle of Habeas Corpus still lies at the heart of English common law today, although born before our language itself. But basic freedoms need to be constantly updated and applied to match the challenge of new technologies and social change. Where should the rights of the many give way to the rights of the few? When and how should a free and vigorous press be restrained from infringing the privacy of the individual? What are the right safeguards for people in their homes as information – and other things – flood down the superhighway? Some countries leave such questions to be decided by reference to a written constitution: we do so in the ordinary process of politics. I believe ours is the right way. Vigorous politics offers the best safeguard of individual freedoms. And in Britain it is our Parliament – the Parliament of the United Kingdom – that is, and should be, at the centre of that democratic, political process. That's why piecemeal reforms that threaten to erode the power and supremacy of Parliament are so dangerous.

I know that some people argue that the freedom of the individual would be better protected if Britain had a written constitution or a new bill of rights, setting out a list of fundamental rights. I don't agree. I simply don't believe that you could enshrine in a single piece of legislation the British conception of freedom. It's no exaggeration to say that we believe our individual freedom is absolute, unless restrained by law. It's a way of life. And we have no need for a bill of rights because we have freedom. Any attempt to define our freedoms by statute would diminish Parliament's historic role as the defender of individual freedoms.

Judges would become the guardians of a written constitution or bill of rights, and the supremacy of the elected representatives of the people in Parliament would – for the first time since the 17th Century – be eroded. Is that really the way we want to go? I think not. It is not as though the processes of judicial interpretation are infallible. In the United States, at different times, the Bill of Rights was held both to support and to outlaw slavery. More recently, Canada's 1982 Charter of Rights has been held to be inconsistent with earlier laws on Sunday Trading, drug trafficking, and abortion. It is no slur on our judicial system to say that such great issues should be decided by elected representatives, not judges and courts.

All of this is based, not on any formal separation of powers, but on a silent boundary: a boundary of mutual restraint. No-one has the power to make final pronouncements about that boundary. But collectively, as part of our living constitution, I believe we all know, understand and respect where that boundary lies. Some suggest that boundary is under pressure. That the greater use of judicial review means the Government is in conflict with the courts. I see nothing surprising in the increasing role of judicial review. I believe it is a function of the increasing complexity of administration, and the legislation which governs it. And it is clearly right that the courts should hold Ministers and departments to the proper use of their powers, and should safeguard the procedural quality of public decision-making. This is merely an example of our constitution working. But, by the same token, it is of course ultimately up to Parliament to decide the laws on which judges and courts make their judgements. In our constitution, Parliament is supreme, because the people are supreme. Parliament is the process through which the representatives of the people control the Executive. . .

Our constitutional fabric has been woven over the centuries. It's the product of hundreds of years of knowledge, experience and history. It's been stable, but not static. Along the way the key events stand out, spanning generations of our ancestors – the Magna Carta, the Bill of Rights, the Act of Union, the First and Second Reform Acts, step by step progress towards universal suffrage, Reform of the House of Lords, and the introduction of Life Peers. Each one a footprint in our nation's story, a step down the path towards today's modern constitution.

Out of this evolutionary change has grown one of the finest, strongest and most admired constitutions in the world. I'm all for practical change that would solve real problems or improve the way our constitution works. But pointless fiddling with our constitution wouldn't solve any problems. It would just create new ones. In the end, it would begin to unstitch our way of life. One group of politicians could unravel what generations of our predecessors have created. I don't make any apology for defending what works. I'm a Conservative and I reject change for change's sake.

Speech to the Centre for Policy Studies, 26 June 1996.

---

105   THE 1997 CONSERVATIVE ELECTION MANIFESTO STATES THERE IS NO CASE FOR A BILL OF RIGHTS AND THAT THE REFORM WOULD UNDERMINE THE DEMOCRATIC SUPREMACY OF THE HOUSE OF COMMONS

Alone in Europe, the history of the United Kingdom has been one of stability and security. We owe much of that to the strength and stability of our constitution – the institutions, laws and traditions that bind us together as a nation.

Our constitution has been stable, but not static. It has been woven over the centuries – the product of hundreds of years of knowledge, experience and history.

Radical changes that alter the whole character of our constitutional balance could unravel what generations of our predecessors have created. To preserve that stability in future – and the freedoms and rights of our citizens – we need to continue a process of evolution, not revolution.

Conservatives embrace evolutionary change that solves real problems and improves the way our constitution works. In recent years we have opened up government, devolved power and accountability, and introduced reforms to make parliament work more effectively. It is that evolutionary process that we are committed to continue . . .

We do not believe there is a case for more radical reform that would undermine the House of Commons. A new Bill of Rights, for example, would risk transferring power away from parliament to legal courts – undermining the democratic supremacy of parliament as representatives of the people. Whilst this may be a necessary check in other countries which depend upon more formalised written constitutions, we do not believe it is appropriate to the UK. . .

The Conservative Manifesto 1997, pp. 49–50

THE LABOUR PARTY

106   THE WILSON GOVERNMENT ISSUES A DISCUSSION DOCUMENT ON A STATUTORY CHARTER OF HUMAN RIGHTS, 1976

Foreword

The Labour Party series of Green Papers and Discussion Papers has played an important part in stimulating discussion and debate within the Labour Movement. As with the earlier papers of this kind, the present document does not represent a commitment on the part of the National Executive Committee to all of the detailed proposals put forward. But the National Executive Committee believes that these proposals merit detailed discussion within the Labour Movement; and it is hoped that affiliated organisations, individual members, and others, will come forward quickly with comments on this important discussion paper.

The proposals outlined here are the result of work by the Human Rights Sub-Committee, which reports direct to the N.E.C.'s Home Policy Committee. They concern an issue which is becoming increasingly important in this age of large scale organisation: the problem of fully safeguarding our basic human rights. The principal proposition here – that there is a need for a statutory Charter of Human Rights – was put forward by the Human Rights Sub-Committee only after giving close consideration to the various alternatives and the paper sets out the reasoning behind this choice.

Clearly, the introduction of such a Charter would represent an important constitutional change. I believe it is absolutely right, therefore, that the Party and the Movement should have the fullest opportunity to discuss in detail the implications of such a change – and I look forward to receiving comments from the widest possible range of opinion within the Labour Movement.

Ron Hayward,
General Secretary.
February 1976

Introduction

Some people believe that socialism involves a threat to the human rights and liberties of the individual. Nothing could be further from the truth. The Labour Party has a well-established and frequently illustrated tradition of fighting for and securing the rights and freedoms of the underprivileged the world over.

The October 1974 Election Manifesto states our position unambiguously:

> 'It is part of the very purpose of the Labour Party's existence to protect and extend the processes of democracy at all levels. It was a Labour Government which introduced the law which allows a citizen to sue Government itself; established the Parliamentary Commissioner, and legislated against racial discrimination and to enforce equal pay. Now we want to give a much bigger say to citizens in all their various capacities – as tenants, shoppers, patients, voters.'

Society has changed dramatically since the war. One of the most noticeable changes has been the growth in the number, size and power of large organisations in both the private and the public sectors, which increasingly affect our lives. In 'Labour's Programme 1973' we said:

> 'Many of the freedoms which we have so long taken for granted are now more likely to be threatened. Thus it is of growing importance that in our complex modern society the ordinary citizen has a system of 'watchdogs' to protect his rights and liberties against the abuse of power in the private as well as in the public sector ... Labour will establish the most effective possible machinery within our national system for ensuring that the fundamental rights and liberties of the citizen are not eroded'.

We saw a need to tip the scales away from public and private concentrations of power back in favour of the individual. Since that Programme was published, following local government and the health service reorganisation, the need has become even greater. In answer to this need and in carrying out the commitment to study the best method of protecting rights and liberties, the Human Rights Sub-Committee of the Labour Party, has come forward with a proposal to enact a *Charter of Human Rights*. The proposal is outlined and discussed in this pamphlet.

There has been some talk from Conservatives about the need for a Bill of Rights. But, because they have a different end in view, they make proposals which are fundamentally different from those outlined in this pamphlet. They unashamedly see a Bill of Rights as a way of curbing interventionist policies by this and future Labour Governments – of restricting public ownership, comprehensive education and so on. Consequently, they want a conservative Bill of Rights which would be biased in favour of traditional conservative values. Their proposal would, in short, stifle progressive change in a rapidly changing world.

The proposals outlined in this paper are quite different. We do not want to see massive extensions of state power at the expense of fundamental rights and freedoms, though we do want to see state intervention where this will give practical meaning to those rights and freedoms. Our aim is to promote and secure the rights of the ordinary man and woman, not to protect the rights of those who have gained so much at their expense. The Charter would not be entrenched against amendment by a future Parliament. It would not, therefore, challenge the basic principle of parliamentary sovereignty. It is designed, above all, to bring about a society more tolerant and respectful of the rights of all its citizens regardless of race, creed, sex, social status or the power of the purse.

To enact such a Charter would be an important step involving major constitutional change. That is why the National Executive Committee thought it right to give everyone in the Party an opportunity to consider and debate the advantages of the proposal.

1. *Why is better protection of human rights needed in Britain today?*

It is often said that Britain has as good a record as any in the protection of human rights. The Sub-Committee believe this to be true, but they do not regard this in itself as enough. The protection of human rights is not a form of international competition. The fact that we may be better provided than this or that foreign country is of less concern than whether we are doing as much as we should and whether any new forms of protection would assist us.

Thus, the introduction of the Ombudsman was opposed by some on the ground that the existing safeguards were adequate. Experience has shown, however, that this was a valuable innovation which is now being extended. Human rights have traditionally been protected by Parliament and the courts, with the press and other media and the general public providing support. Sometimes the remedy lies through legal action, either in the form of a test case to establish what the law is or, where the law is clear, to enforce it. Sometimes the remedy lies through legislation. Sometimes a letter to an MP or a complaint to the Ombudsman is enough to have the matter put right. But each of these methods has its shortcomings. Parliament, though theoretically able to tackle any problems, is, in practice, limited by many considerations especially shortage of time. There are always many more problems waiting for legislative action than there is time available.

The courts are limited by the state of the existing law. Where the law is unclear they have some room for making law by declaring or stating what it is, but if the law is clear the courts must adhere to it. Even when it is unclear, the room for manoeuvre is limited by the doctrine of binding precedent and by the conventions of judicial reasoning.

An MP can pose questions (both on and off the record), but if the Minister or his Department is unresponsive it is often difficult to get a complaint attended to.

The Ombudsman has a role limited broadly to maladministration. He cannot take up the cudgels for those whose remedy lies in the courts nor if the complaint can only be cured by reform of the law.

The citizen who believes he has a grievance may or may not succeed in getting a remedy, but no realistic observer of the process could pretend that the institutions now available to him make this easy. Moreover, human rights matters often affect individuals or groups who are not in the mainstream and who, accordingly, find it even more difficult to enlist the support of the powerful.

The purpose of a Charter of Human Rights would be to provide a new method for the citizen who believed himself to be the victim of injustice to seek a remedy. He could go to a court and claim to be aggrieved under this or that section of the Charter of Human Rights. The defendant, be he a Minister, chief constable or other public official, would have to justify his actions in public by argument capable of convincing an impartial tribunal. The court could not hide behind the traditional plea of government – that the time is not ripe or that action on the grievance, though from many points of view desirable, is for one or another reason, impolitic or inconvenient.

A Charter of Human Rights would therefore give power to the citizen by providing him with a new tool for having issues of public importance decided. The Human Rights Sub-Committee felt that a Charter of Human Rights was desirable not because Britain is or is about to be a country where human rights are grossly abused, but rather because the system is less sensitive and responsive than it should be to the grievances of individuals or groups in the community. It is time for the scales to be tipped back in favour of the ordinary man. A Charter of Human Rights could achieve this and provide a valuable new growth point in the system.

2. *Does Britain not already have what is needed in the form of the European Convention on Human Rights?*

It is true that the question of whether a Charter of Human Rights would be valuable has, in a sense, already been answered by Britain's adherence to the European Convention. This occurred long before our entry into the EEC. The Convention was first approved by the Council of Europe in 1950 and came into force in 1953, when ten countries had ratified it. The United Kingdom ratified the Convention in 1951 and since 1966 it has given individual complainants the right to take it before the Commission and ultimately the Human Rights Court in Strasburg.

In fact there have been significant numbers of cases brought against the United Kingdom. (In 1972 there were 294, in 1973 there were 105, and in 1974 there were 179.) As with the complaints brought against all countries, most are declared to be inadmissable. But in seven years 43 have been found to be admissible against Britain. These involved such matters as the refusal of admission to UK passport holders from East Africa, access of prisoners to lawyers, alleged torture in Northern Ireland and the law of contempt which prevented the *Sunday Times* from publishing its article about thalidomide. One case (access to a lawyer for a prisoner, Mr. Sydney Golder) reached the European Court which unanimously decided against the United Kingdom in February 1975.

The Convention protects a variety of rights – such as the right to life, the right not to be tortured or subjected to inhuman or degrading treatment or punishment; the right to liberty and security of person, the right to a fair and public hearing for the determination of civil rights or obligations or of a criminal charge; the right not to be punished under a retroactive criminal law, the right to respect for private and family life, home and correspondence; the right to freedom of thought, conscience and religion; the right to freedom of expression; the right to freedom of peaceful assembly and freedom of peaceful association with others, including the right to join trade unions; freedom from discrimination in the enjoyment of the rights and freedoms set out in the Convention.

The typical style of the Convention is to state the right to be protected in broad and general terms and then to qualify it by stating any necessary limitations. Thus the right to respect for private and family life, home and correspondence is qualified by such steps as are taken by a public authority which can be justified as being in accordance with law and as necessary in a democratic society in the interests of national security, public safety, the prevention of disorder or crime, the protection of health or morals or for the protection of the rights and freedom of others.

The interpretation of the Convention is entrusted in the first instance to the European Commission (of which the UK representative, Mr. James Fawcett, is the present President), and secondly to the judges of the European Court. If the Court gives a decision against one of the member countries, that country becomes obliged in international law to comply with the decision and, to the extent required by the decision, to adjust its own law to bring it into line with the law declared by the court.

Thus, when the Golder case was decided against the UK in February 1975, the Government came under an obligation to make such alteration in the Prison Rules as would give effect to the decision that Mr. Golder's rights under the Convention had been infringed by the Rule which prevented access to a lawyer, in some circumstances, save with the Secretary of State's consent. The Home Secretary, Mr. Roy Jenkins, announced shortly thereafter that he would comply with the decision and the Prison Rules were subsequently modified.

The existence of the European Convention does mean that people who believe themselves to be the victims of injustice, at the hands of public authorities or the law in this country, can seek a remedy in Strasburg. But the system has three disadvantages. First the process is extremely slow. The Golder case took no less than five years to the decision of the Court. Second, although the Commission does have a system of legal aid, it is very rudimentary and does not adequately cover the legal costs involved in preparing and arguing a case. This puts the system out of the reach of any who cannot afford to pay or who cannot find lawyers willing to act for reduced fees.

The third shortcoming of the system is that complaints are aired in the European forum before they have been properly examined internally. 'Dirty laundry' is washed abroad, harming our good name, which might be unnecessary if machinery for handling such matters existed locally.

This last difficulty would be met if the European Convention were incorporated into our law as a United Kingdom statute. The complainant would then go first to our own courts and would only go to Strasburg if our legal system did not give satisfaction. It would give the courts and Parliament the first opportunity to put matters right. By defusing grievances it would contribute to the well-ordering of society. By providing a remedy in the United Kingdom (as opposed to the European) courts it would improve the chances that the solution would be in line with the particular needs of this country.

3. *The Proposal*

The proposal put forward by the Human Rights Sub-Committee therefore is that the rights guaranteed by the European Convention on Human Rights be adopted in the form of a United Kingdom Act of Parliament. (The rights in question are contained in Articles 1 to 18, and the first two Protocols.) Britain is already subject to the Convention; its incorporation into our law would consolidate and strengthen the commitment to human rights implicit in our ratification of the Convention.

It is true that the Convention may not be in all respects a perfect instrument. Its drafting could, no doubt, be improved upon. Nevertheless, the existing draft has the great advantage that it has been accepted by both the Labour and Conservative Parties in Government. If it were decided that a Charter of Rights were desirable, but some new draft were thought preferable, it is inevitable that there would be a major problem of securing agreement as to its contents. This would involve considerable delay, postponing action for years whilst a Royal Commission or other similar body wrestled with the problem. But even more, it would probably be impossible to secure a sufficiently wide political consensus on any text that went significantly beyond the terms of the European Convention. Present agreement over a workable text would, therefore, be sacrificed for future disagreement over some other text.

In the view of the Sub-Committee, the benefits of broad political agreement over the text are likely to be much greater than the benefits obtainable from any speculative improvements in the drafting.

A Charter of Human Rights, to be a meaningful concept, should command the broad assent and respect of the community as a whole, including the main political parties. It would almost certainly be devalued if enactment were followed immediately by threats of repeal. This is not to say that it should be impossible to alter it – on the contrary, it should remain the subject of continual concern and re-examination – but rather that its initial adoption should, if at all possible, command general support.

The enactment of the European Convention in statutory form might secure such support; any attempt to produce an improved model would almost certainly have to go ahead without it. This, in practice, would gravely affect its long term authority and value.

4. *Would enactment of a statutory Charter or Bill of Rights not infringe the sovereignty of Parliament?*

The proposal accepted by, amongst others, Lord Hailsham and Sir Keith Joseph envisages a Bill of Rights entrenched in the constitution by a requirement that it be amended or repealed only by a stated majority, say two-thirds or three quarters of both Houses. This would indeed limit Parliament's freedom of action, especially now that small Parliamentary majorities are more common than in the past.

But the Human Rights Sub-Committee rejected this approach. It did not wish to see any reduction in a government's power to govern. Its proposal, therefore, is that the Charter of Human Rights be passed as an ordinary statute, the only difference being that it should provide that existing and future statutes should be interpreted so as to ensure conformity with the Charter unless there were express provision to the contrary. (This would avoid the danger of unintentional amendment or repeal.) Apart from this, governments (subject to the obvious political difficulties) would be free to introduce legislation to cancel or modify the effect of any court decision interpreting the Charter of Human Rights should the court find against the government. Parliament, therefore, would remain 'top dog'. Governments would normally tend to be slow to introduce such legislation – but this is only to say that a Bill of Rights, if it is meaningful at all, would have a certain special authority. In countries where human rights are disregarded, they serve little purpose other than to raise false expectations. But in countries which attempt to honour the rule of law, a Bill of Rights stands apart from ordinary legislation as something more fundamental. On the other hand, by providing that the Charter of Human Rights can technically be changed like any other statute, final power remains with the legislature.

5. *A Charter of Human Rights would have to be interpreted by the judges. Can they be trusted?*

There are many in the Labour Movement who distrust the judges – for being, variously, too conservative, too narrow-minded, too legalistic or too executive minded. Many people who hold these views have in mind, in particular, the record of the courts in their dealings with the trade unions. A Bill of Rights deals primarily with rights held by individuals in their personal rather than their collective capacity. The attitude of the courts towards the unions as such may, not therefore, be a fair test of the way in which the judges would interpret the Charter in respect of any individual complaint.

Nevertheless it cannot be taken for granted that British judges will work with a Charter or Rights in such a way as to advance rather than to retard the interests of the ordinary citizen.

Yet we believe that there are reasons for thinking that the experiment *would* be worth making. First, the question should be seen over a longer rather than a shorter time span – fifty years rather than the next five to ten. Over this period we would hope to introduce reforms to the legal system which would make judges more representative of and in tune with society. It seems improbable that over a long period of time any interest group in the community, whether of the Left or of the Right, would find itself consistently the loser (or the winner). If this proved wrong, a government would, sooner or later, abolish the Charter of Human Rights as a snare and a delusion. Second, Judges as a group present a far from uniform front. Although there have been judicial decisions that might be termed narrow, legalistic, executive-minded or conservative in approach, there have been others that were liberal and anti-establishment. Sometimes even the same judge may be 'progressive' and liberal on one issue and 'conservative' or legalistic on the next.

Third, a Charter of Rights would, almost certainly, push the judiciary in the direction of the more generous and open interpretation. A Bill of Rights manifestly does not invite a legalistic approach and the traditional tendency of English judges to emasculate broad powers in statutes would surely not prevail in this context.

Fourth the tendency in this direction would be promoted by the inevitable strengthening, through the Charter of Human Rights, of the human rights 'lobby'. At present this is to some extent a fringe group. A Human Rights Charter enacted into law would bring human rights matters into the centre of the stage. Such a fundamental document would be a vital part of every child's education. Interested lawyers, politicians, journalists and ordinary citizens would increase in number and political weight. The judges, over a period of time, would be 'educated' to a better appreciation of the human rights aspects of their decisions. If they were thought to be leaning too far in one or another direction this would tend to be reflected in critical comment in the press, the professional journals, in parliament and elsewhere.

The question is not whether a Charter of Human Rights would solve all problems in a satisfactory way – no machinery can hope to achieve this. There would continue to be many areas of dispute and controversy and many blemishes. The question rather is whether this device would on balance do more good than harm. Judged by this modest test, there would seem to be enough in the existing and likely future record of the judges to encourage the belief that they would not disgrace themselves.

6. *Would a Charter of Human Rights not be likely to favour the big battalions over the interests of the little man?*

This, to some extent, is a continuation of the argument that the judges cannot be trusted because of their traditional class and property bias. But there is a separate or further question as to whether bills of rights are, by their nature, conducive to the protection of the individual, or instead of the state and other public authorities. Everything here, of course, depends ultimately on the way in which the judges approached their task but, a Bill or Charter of Human Rights would tip the balance of power distinctly in favour of the individual. This is because the Charter is about individual basic rights. Of course the rights are qualified and require interpretation, but the bias of the Charter is in the direction of giving and preserving rights, not withholding them. The burden of proof is on the defendant, not on the person alleging violation of her rights. Thus, in the Golder case before the European Court, Mr. Golder succeeded because his right of correspondence with his lawyer was infringed and the Home Office could not persuade the court that such infringement was *necessary* in the interests of public safety or the prevention of disorder or crime.

7. *Even granted that a Charter of Human Rights would strengthen the position of individuals, would they not tend to be those with property or other interests to protect? Would it not help the 'haves' more than the 'have nots?'*

All the evidence, including the history of the US Bill of Rights, suggests that there is no reason to fear that a British equivalent would mainly serve to protect the strong against the weak. The US Bill of Rights, especially in the past forty years, has been a major weapon of disadvantaged groups, notably the blacks and defendants in criminal cases. At periods in its history the Supreme Court was conservative and a brake on 'progressive' policies but for more of its history, and especially in the recent past, it has insisted that even the weak were entitled to the rule of law.

The history of the US shows too the significance of a Bill of Rights where, for one or another reason, the political process is unresponsive to the needs of unpopular minorities. The idea that parliament is necessarily a more effective means of protecting the weak than the courts is too simplistic. In some contexts it may be the courts that are stronger and more effective. Human rights frequently concern the protection of the weak who are too easily swept aside or ignored by the legislative majority which may be influenced by crude political considerations of convenience or of narrow party interests. A court interpreting a Charter of Human Rights may find itself forced to deal with the issues more on the basis of principle and equality.

8. *Would incorporation of the European Convention not prevent a Government from passing legislation to nationalise or limit property rights through taxation?*

The United Kingdom is subject to the First Protocol to the Convention which guarantees the right to [the] peaceful enjoyment of one's possessions. But Article 1 states that no one should be deprived of his possessions '*except in the public interest* and subject to the conditions provided by law'. The article then states that these provisions shall not 'in any way impair the right of a state to enforce such laws as it seems necessary to control the use of property *in accordance with the general interest or to secure the payment of taxes or other contributions or penalties*'.

Provided that our courts were directed to have regard to Strasburg case law, it would appear that the qualifying clauses give ample safeguards for the kind of legislation that a Labour Government might wish to pass.

9. *Would implementation of the Convention prevent a Government from pressing ahead with legislation to abolish selection for state sector secondary schools?*

This fear is based on the provisions of Article 2 to the First Protocol of the Convention which says that in relation to education 'the State shall respect the right of parents to ensure education in conformity with their own religious and philosophical convictions'. Does this mean that parents could object, for instance, to legislation designed to abolish grammar schools in favour of comprehensive schools? All the relevant indications suggest not. First, the United Kingdom introduced a reservation to the Article stating that it was accepted only insofar as it was compatible with the provisions of efficient instruction and training and the avoidance of unreasonable public expenditure.

This reservation could also be incorporated into UK legislation and the switch to comprehensive schools might be justified on either ground. Second, case history suggests that comprehensive plans cannot be thwarted. In 1968 a case came before the European Court concerning the use in Belgian schools of the French language. A parent wished her child to be educated in Flemish, not French. Although not a directly comparable example, the Court's ruling is relevant: 'The Convention lays down no specific obligations concerning the extent of the means (of instruction) *and the manner of their organisation or subsidisation*' (our emphasis).

Finally, in the unlikely event that any United Kingdom judge ruled against comprehensive education, the Government would be able to reverse the decision by legislation.

10. *What would be the value of including the Charter of Human Rights in our programme?*

A Charter of Human Rights would be an indication of concern for the individual. There is a widespread feeling that in the increasingly complex conditions of modern society the individual is more and more the object of forces he cannot control. A Labour Government, with its tendency to prefer centralised and planning solutions to those of the free market is especially open to the charge that it regards the individual as subservient to the greater good of the community. Yet civil liberties are a traditional concern of the Labour Party and are wholly compatible with Socialism.

Incorporation of the European Convention of Human Rights into United Kingdom law could provide the Labour Government with a major initiative which would demonstrate its commitment to individual liberties without endangering its programme.

A Charter of Human Rights: A Discussion Document for the Labour Movement, 1976

107 LABOUR'S POLICY REVIEW ON INDIVIDUAL
RIGHTS FAILS TO INCLUDE A BILL OF RIGHTS BUT
PROPOSES TO EXTEND THE POWER OF THE SECOND
CHAMBER OVER HUMAN RIGHTS, 1989

A Modern Democracy: Report of the Policy Review Group on
Democracy for the Individual and the Community

Britain after ten years of Conservative government is less free and less fair. The Conservative government thinks that the only freedoms that matter are the ones you can buy. But real freedom means enabling everyone to make real choices. It means reducing the power of central government and enabling the people, the nations and the regions of Britain to make the decisions that affect them.

The true purpose of socialism is the creation of a genuinely free society in which a more equal distribution of power and wealth extends the rights and choices of the whole community. That society offers more than the chance to take better advantage of traditional liberties. It enables individuals – of every race and class – to take practical advantage of the opportunities which liberty provides. Those freedoms can only be protected and extended if the community cooperates to enhance the lives of the individuals of which it is composed.

Freedom in Britain is under threat – not least by the government itself which speaks constantly of liberty, but defines that condition in a way which is convenient to the ideology of new-conservatism. Liberty, to modern Tories, is the right of the rich and powerful to use their wealth and influence to exploit the poor and weak.

The government has defined freedom as liberation from public expenditure and collective obligation – a policy which often reduces the choices available to millions of men and women. In fact no government this century has been more authoritarian or concentrated more power in the hands of a central autocratic bureaucracy.

After the secrecy and oppression of a dozen years of Thatcherism, we shall open up our society and our institutions to the scrutiny and participation of all the people. We propose to put individual rights back into the centre of political debate.

Wider democracy: better government

Our proposals for the extension of freedom and the extension of liberty amount to a fundamental reform of the institutions which establish and entrench our individual and collective rights.

British citizens are denied fundamental rights which, in other democracies, are taken for granted as the basic liberties of a free society:
• The right of every individual to equal treatment, irrespective of race, sex, sexuality, creed or disability.

- The right to know how the government takes its decisions and the information on which those decisions are based.
- The right to privacy – from invasion by both public and private bodies and harassment by the media.
- The right to protection against the intrusive state operating through unaccountable security services.

Equal rights under the law has long been the principle on which our judicial system is based. But its effective application requires that there is equal access to the law throughout society.

We propose specific legislation to provide a massive extension of individual rights and to extend democracy in Great Britain. We intend to make a constitutional reform which can protect that legislation by ensuring that any government which seeks its repeal must obtain the consent of both Houses or else fight, and win, a further General Election. Since, within our system, there is no way in which an Act of Parliament can be 'entrenched', legislation remains on the Statute book for so long, but only as long as Parliament resists its repeal. We intend to create an Upper House of Parliament (to replace the present House of Lords) which will – because of its composition and constitutional functions – protect and preserve the rights which we incorporate in law.

A Bill of Rights – or one of the variants upon that constitutional proposal which is now being canvassed – would not provide the protection which we regard as necessary. Its purpose would be principally declaratory. For even if it were enshrined in an Act of Parliament other specific legislation would supercede it and it could be repealed by a government with no concern for individual liberty. A Bill of Rights would need constant and detailed interpretation by the courts, with no certainty that its general provisions would protect the most vulnerable members of the community. A more dependable and more permanent constitutional change is necessary.

Our programme for the extension and protection of individual rights is not dependent on our plans for constitutional reform. But, by creating the new second chamber, which is described in this paper, we will make it infinitely more difficult for some future authoritarian government to repeal our rights legislation.

A modern Parliament

Britain needs a modern constitution which decentralises decision-making and creates proper checks on central government. We propose an elected second chamber to replace the House of Lords, with particular responsibility for safeguarding human rights legislation. Streamlining the House of Commons will enable Members of Parliament to represent their constituents more effectively.

A new second chamber

A second chamber of Parliament based on inheritance and patronage is unacceptable in a modern democracy. For many years the Labour Party has been committed to the abolition of the House of Lords and the time has come to give precise and practical effect to that intention. We have considered whether democracy would best be served by the creation of a single chamber Parliament or by replacing the House of Lords with a new second chamber. We propose the abolition of the House of Lords and its replacement with an elected second chamber with a specific and precisely defined constitutional role.

In the decade ahead we must extend our democracy by passing out new powers to the nations and regions of Britain and establishing fundamental rights which cannot easily be overturned by authoritarian government. Parliament must scrutinise legislation with greater care than is now possible and ways must be found to ensure the proper examination of the increasing number of laws and regulations which emanate from the European Community. The new second chamber which we propose will play a substantial part in achieving all these essential objectives.

The form of election to the new second chamber will be a matter for further consideration, but, because of its nature, it may be appropriate to adopt a scheme different from that by which Members of Parliament are elected. We intend that members of the new second chamber should particularly reflect the interests and aspirations of the regions and nations of Britain. We do not, however, propose direct links between members of the national and regional assemblies and members of the upper house.

The new second chamber will not be a replica of the House of Commons. Ministers will not sit in the second chamber. Bills will not be introduced there. It will retain powers to delay legislation but for most bills its powers of delay will be restricted to only allow one opportunity for revision before final consideration by the House of Commons. To improve its efficiency as a revising chamber we propose that the second chamber develop a Standing Committees (including Special Standing Committees) system for the detailed scrutiny of bills and Special Select Committees for general examination of government policy.

The new second chamber will be an essential element in the protection and promotion of fundamental rights. For it will, in effect, entrench our fundamental rights legislation. In the British system of government there is only one way of preventing a government with a substantial majority and supine back-benchers from transforming Parliament into an elective dictatorship. That is the creation of at least one House of Parliament which, because of its composition and construction, will not automatically accept Cabinet directives.

We propose that the second chamber should be the instrument which prevents the swift repeal of legislation on fundamental rights by any authoritarian government which might, in the future, be elected. We propose therefore that the new second chamber should have new delaying powers over measures affecting fundamental rights. It will possess the power to delay repeal of legislation affecting fundamental rights for the whole life of a Parliament – thus providing an opportunity for the electorate to determine whether or not the government which proposes such measures should remain in office. The extra delaying power will apply to all items of legislation specifically designated as concerning fundamental rights and all legislation establishing the national and regional assemblies. The second chamber will also possess the absolute right of veto on any proposal to extend the life of Parliament beyond the constitutional maximum of five years.

The Judicial Committee of the present House of Lords will continue to function as the supreme court made up of senior judges appointed – not as now by a Cabinet Minister with clear political allegiance – but by an independent committee responsible to the Minister for Legal Administration.

Protecting our freedoms

British citizens are today denied fundamental rights which are taken for granted in other democracies. The right of every individual to equal treatment under fair laws; the right to privacy; and the right to know – these will be established through new laws, and protected by the new constitutional powers of our second chamber. . .

Meet the Challenge, Make the Change, Final Report of Labour's Policy Review for the 1990s, 1989, pp. 55–6.

> 108   THE LABOUR PARTY AT THE 1992 GENERAL ELECTION PROMISES A CHARTER OF RIGHTS MADE UP OF SPECIFIC ACTS OF PARLIAMENT REINFORCED BY A COMPLEMENTARY AND DEMOCRATICALLY ENFORCED BILL OF RIGHTS, 1992

It is time to modernise Britain's democracy. Central to Labour's purpose in government is our commitment to radical constitutional reform.

Our Charter of Rights, backed up by a complementary and democratically enforced bill of rights, will establish in law the specific rights of every citizen.

We will start in our first parliamentary session with a Freedom of Information Act which will open up government to the people. Exceptions will be tightly drawn . . .

We will remove unjustified restrictions on broadcasting and establish an urgent enquiry by the Monopolies and Mergers Commission into the concentration of media ownership. If the press fail to deal with abuses of individual privacy, we will implement the Calcutt Report's recommendations for statutory protection.

Individuals must be able to control personal information about themselves. We will strengthen Britain's Data Protection Act in line with European practice...

Stronger sex and race discrimination laws will ensure that organisations awarded government contracts take positive steps to promote equal treatment. We will introduce a new law dealing with discrimination on grounds of sexuality...

In order to safeguard the rights of people with disabilities, we will appoint a Minister for the Disabled and extend anti-discrimination laws to cover this group...

As well as strengthening the race discrimination laws and extending the powers of the Commission for Racial Equality, we will press for similar laws throughout the European Community. We will not tolerate the present level of racial harassment and attacks, and will ensure that more effective protection is given to vulnerable groups. Contract compliance laws will be the first step towards guaranteeing the black and Asian British their fair share of jobs.

We will introduce fair immigration and citizenship laws which restore the right to British citizenship for every child born in Britain. Our laws, which will not discriminate on grounds of sex or race, will respect the right to family life. A new Act will guarantee sanctuary to genuine refugees but prevent bogus applications for asylum.

We are determined to see that equally fair laws apply throughout the European Community and will oppose any attempt to remove voting rights from Commonwealth citizens in European elections...

We will fight terrorism by every lawful means, repealing the counterproductive Prevention of Terrorism Act and replacing it with a measure which is more effective and genuinely acceptable in a democratic society...

Further constitutional reforms will include those leading to the replacement of the House of Lords with a new elected Second Chamber which will have the power to delay, for the lifetime of a Parliament, change to designated legislation reducing individual or constitutional rights.

Labour Party election manifesto, 1992, p. 117.

---

109 LABOUR'S CHIEF SPOKESMAN IN THE HOUSE OF LORDS PRIOR TO THE 1992 ELECTION SAYS AN ELECTED LABOUR GOVERNMENT WILL INCORPORATE THE EUROPEAN CONVENTION ON HUMAN RIGHTS, 1992

As regards a Bill of Rights, as I have said on a previous occasion, we favour a Freedom of Information Act, . . . an individual's right to prohibit or restrict the collection of personal information, . . . the equal treatment of all citizens of this country irrespective of their sex or racial origin, . . . equal access to the law as well as equal treatment before the law. We would also introduce a Bill of Rights to incorporate the European Convention on Human Rights.

Lord Cledwyn, HL Deb., 11 March 1992, col. 1337.

---

110 JOHN SMITH AS LABOUR LEADER MAKES PUBLIC HIS STRONG SUPPORT FOR A NEW CONSTITUTION AND A BILL OF RIGHTS, 1992–3

Leadership election statements, 1992.

We know real freedom for the majority depends on economic efficiency and social justice. Democratic socialists have always rejected a narrow conception of freedom and have fought for the 'positive freedoms' of wide access to education, health care, housing and employment.

We must demonstrate that poverty, unemployment, low pay and low skills are not just barriers to individual opportunity, but that they undermine the capacity for wealth creation. This is our economic argument: a path to personal enrichment from the fruits of economic progress more widely shared.

But our idea needs to be strengthened with a political argument: a path to personal empowerment by encouraging responsibility and participation in a democracy in which power is more widely shared. It is a strategy for citizenship and community.

That is why I believe the time has come when Labour should commit itself to a Bill of Rights based on the European Convention of Human Rights. That is why we need a Freedom of Information Act, why government must be more pluralistic and more decentralised, and why we should fully explore electoral reform.

We need a new constitution for a new century. We must ensure government is brought closer to the people and communities it is elected to serve.

We must strengthen the rights of consumers and challenge the power of monopolies and big business. Labour must lead the challenge against the vested interests that control so much power and privilege. . .

We must modernise our system of government and our constitution so that it becomes pluralistic and decentralised and is underpinned by the specific recognition of individual rights. . .

We are alone among the major Western European nations in not laying down in legislation the basic rights of our citizens and in not giving them a direct means of asserting these through the courts. We should, in addition, introduce a Freedom of Information Act to break down the barriers of secrecy which surround Whitehall. In a modern society knowledge is not only power: it must be made more widely available to the community if meaningful democratic debate and decision is to take place.

I share the widespread desire in our Party to see the House of Lords replaced with an elected Second Chamber. It simply cannot be right for Britain to enter a new century with people participating in the passing of legislation who are only entitled to be present on a hereditary principle dating from the Middle Ages.

Speech on 'A Citizens' Democracy', 1993

I have no hesitation in saying there is an undeniable and pressing need for constitutional reform in this country. Undeniable because – as I hope to demonstrate – our structures and institutions are clearly failing properly to represent the people they were set in place to serve. And pressing because of the mounting sense of disenchantment and cynicism amongst the people of this country about our political system, a deeply disturbing trend that must be checked if we are to secure the future health of our democracy.

I am arguing for a new constitutional settlement, a new deal between the people and the state that puts the citizen centre stage. A deal that gives people new powers and a stronger voice in the affairs of the nation. And a deal that restores a sense of cohesion and vitality to our national life.

I want to see a fundamental shift in the balance of power between the citizen and the state – a shift away from an overpowering state to a citizen's democracy where people have rights and powers and where they are served by accountable and responsive government.

It used to be said that the subject of constitutional reform was of interest to no-one but the so-called chattering classes. Critics considered it a distraction from the bread and butter issues that matter to most voters. But in this atmosphere of decline and gloom, it is abundantly clear that people across the nation do care deeply about the way they are governed, and they feel angry and frustrated with a system that isn't working.

So our crumbling constitution can no longer be dismissed as a side-show. It is at the heart of what is wrong with our country. People care, and they want change ...

Are we going to limp into the twenty-first century on a constitution built for the nineteenth?. Are we going to face the demands of a new era dressed in a set of clothes that were tailored for our ancestors? Or are we going to shake off that which is cumbersome and archaic, and cut for ourselves a new cloth that fits today's needs and equips us for tomorrow's challenges?

It is time to bring our constitution up to date ...

The first step towards a citizens' democracy must be to create new structures of government that are more accountable, more responsive, and more relevant to our modern society.

The next step must be to strengthen people's individual rights. It is easy to forget that the role of government in our society ought to be instrumental and subordinate – subordinate, above all, to the democratic will. After all, its raison d'etre is to serve the people. And because of the enormous power of government in modern society, the people need greater safeguards against abuse of that power.

The Labour Party's concern for the rights of the citizen is long-standing and deep-rooted. It is worth reminding ourselves that it was the Attlee Government, in 1950, that put Britain amongst the first countries to sign the European Convention on Human Rights. And it was the Wilson Government in the 1960s and 1970s that passed pioneering Race Relations, Equal Pay and Sex Discrimination Acts.

But today, Britain is alone amongst major Western European nations in not laying down in law the basic rights of its people, and in not giving its people a direct means of asserting those rights through the country's courts.

The justification often offered is that in Britain the citizen is protected by the rights and freedoms established by the common law. But those rights and freedoms, important as they are, are incomplete, ill-defined and, perhaps most importantly of all, not immediately accessible to, or understood by, the ordinary citizen. And the extent and limits of those rights are controlled by the judges and not by Parliament.

This is a significant weakness. The task of judges is to interpret and apply the law, not to make it. Democracy demands that fundamental rules governing citizens' behaviour, and fundamental rights protecting citizens' freedoms, should be decided by Parliament and not by the judges. If we leave things as they are, we really are accepting that the final say will continue to be in the hands of people who, whatever their other merits may be, are unelected and therefore unqualified to be law-makers.

The quickest and simplest way of achieving democratic and legal recognition of a substantial package of human rights would be by incorporating into British law the European Convention on Human Rights.

At the moment, British citizens who seek the protection of the Convention must appeal to the Commission and Court in Strasbourg. That process is intolerably slow: three years at a minimum, sometimes as long as nine years. Only the most determined people, or those who are supported by pressure groups, are likely to stay the course. And whilst the process grinds on, the abuse of rights at home continues.

The failure directly to incorporate the Convention into British law has another unwelcome effect. Although the British government is subject to the requirements of the Convention, the present set-up makes the protection of basic rights appear difficult, remote, even foreign. It reinforces an atmosphere that suggests that basic rights are not that important, and that the government regards them as a nuisance rather than, as it should, as a primary obligation.

This view is reinforced in the courts. The judges will take note of the requirements of the Convention when interpreting legislation that is ambiguous or uncertain. But in the absence of Parliamentary instructions to the contrary, they have – perfectly properly in the light of the present rules – made it plain that if a law exists that affects human rights in a way that clearly breaches the Convention, it will be *that* law, and not the requirements of the Convention, that they will enforce.

The Convention is not a vague, untested or uncertain code, but a mature statement of rights which has been interpreted and applied over many years by an expert court in Strasbourg. To bring the Convention directly into British law would not be to introduce some new, foreign or alien being. Our law is already, and has been since 1950, ultimately subject to the requirements of the Convention. What is needed now is to make that protection real and accessible to our citizens, instead of a last resort available after years of struggle and litigation. Incorporation could be achieved fairly easily. Parliament should pass a Human Rights Act that incorporates the rules of the Convention directly into British law, and gives citizens the right to enforce those rules in the courts.

Although in technical terms a British Act of Parliament cannot be entrenched, effective protection of the Human Rights Act from undermining by the courts would be provided by a clause requiring that any other Act that intended to introduce laws inconsistent with the Convention must do so specifically and in express terms.

In a modern democracy, Parliament must decide what rights should apply, and should set them out in a manner that citizens can understand for themselves. Under these proposals, it would not be left to the discretion of the judges, or to archeological investigations by legal and constitutional experts, to decide what protections citizens do and do not have.

The rights we seek to protect are those of the individual against the state. The Human Rights Act would therefore provide that its protections could only be relied on by individuals, not by companies or organisations. We do not want to repeat here the confusion and injustice that has occurred in some other countries, where companies and commercial organisations have tried to resist social legislation controlling their activities by claiming that it infringes their 'human' rights.

And the Human Rights Act is not designed to alter existing legal relations between individuals, but to protect individuals from state power. So the bodies that would be subject to the Act would be state and state-related ones: national and local government, the police, and any organisation that exercises state power.

Subject to this, all government activity, and all the existing and future law, would be subject to the Human Rights legislation.

My own view is that the rights the legislation conferred should be asserted in the first instance through the ordinary courts, rather than by some system of special tribunals.

It is essential that regard for human rights pervades the work of all courts, and is recognised as an integral part of their work, for which courts bear direct responsibility; whether they are criminal courts dealing with claims of wrongful conviction or civil courts looking at government bans on free speech. That responsibility must be put on the regular courts, and the judges of those courts must be trained and be ready to respond to the challenge.

To assist the courts, and also to assist individuals in asserting their rights, there should be established an independent Human Rights Commission, along the lines of the Equal Opportunities Commission and Commission for Racial Equality that were established by Labour governments. The Commission would monitor the operation of the Human Rights Act; provide advice and support for those who wish to assert their rights; and where necessary itself institute cases to confirm or clarify particularly important issues. The Commission would thus act as a focus for human rights activities; and ensure that the protection of the public was not left to the accident of individual enthusiasm or willingness to pursue cases.

The next step towards building a citizen's democracy must be to make the law work more effectively on behalf of the people.

Because individual rights and social justice lie at the very heart of our programme of citizenship, I believe we need now to establish a new Ministry of Justice to be responsible for the administration of the law in its entirety. There is a clear need for such a Ministry, for a number of reasons.

At the moment, the issue of law reform is, at least in England and Wales, confusingly dispersed amongst government departments. The Lord Chancellor's Department keeps the civil law up to date, but criminal law is dealt with by the Home Office, and other departments like the DTI sometimes consider specific cases of their own. A single Ministry of Justice, giving direction and purpose to a proper programme for the reform, modernisation and constant up-dating of the law, would give a much-needed stimulus to this important but sorely neglected area ...

A new Ministry of Justice would undertake a distinct and specific responsibility for ensuring that all those working in the justice system observe high standards, and that the whole system is efficient, fair and just.

Our determination to strengthen individual rights will inevitably make new and heavy demands on our legal system. A necessary and important function of the Ministry of Justice would be to ensure the observation and promotion of human rights throughout the court and justice system.

Of course, it is no use whatever reforming the law and setting up new and better structures for the delivery of justice in our land if they remain out of the reach of the people.

For justice to have any real meaning, people must have access to the law.

The government's disgraceful plans to slash the Legal Aid budget have been rightly and angrily condemned by the whole legal profession as well as by many voluntary and consumer bodies ... The undermining of the Legal Aid system makes a mockery of any remaining pretence by the government that it believes in genuine individual rights. Restoring legal aid to a proper basis would do more for ordinary people and their rights than a dozen so-called Citizen's Charters stood end to end. This should never be viewed simply as a matter of public finance: access to the law must be seen as a vital constitutional right.

Far from cutting access to the law, we must improve it by developing a fully integrated network of advice centres and law centres across Britain, so that any citizen can walk in, seek advice, and know that justice is not simply an abstract concept but a real and practical force in this country. Unless we achieve that, all the laws and reforms in the world will be a waste of time.

If access to the law is essential for justice, so access to information is vital for democracy. A further important step toward achieving a citizens' democracy must be freedom of information.

Everyone should have the right to know what the Government knows and does on their behalf. And yet a culture of secrecy pervades our government. It is a culture that serves only to conceal mistakes, to protect decision-makers from challenge, to defend them from criticism, and to secure political advantage and control ...

1 March 1993, event hosted by Charter 88.

---

111   LABOUR'S CONSTITUTIONAL SPOKESMAN MAKES A STATEMENT TO THE HOUSE OF COMMONS ON HIS PARTY'S POLICY TO INCORPORATE THE EUROPEAN CONVENTION ON HUMAN RIGHTS AND CREATE A COMMISSION ON A BILL OF RIGHTS, 1993

Mr. Graham Allen: There is no magical bit of paper that can somehow defend our rights, and certainly a written Bill of Rights, although essential, is not a panacea. It can become meaningful only in a wider democracy, in which its values are accepted and practised by public authorities and private citizens. In order to build that sort of democratic practice in our country we need to take a long hard look at our democratic institutions and fundamentally reform them, and in some cases replace them, so that government at all levels can legitimately carry the stamp of democratic approval.

In essence, that means ending our long-unchallenged unitary system of government, in which all political power is decided in a winner-take-all general election, and establishing in our country for the first time a genuinely pluralist society in which many different centres of power are created, not dependent upon one another but each with its own electoral base and its own legitimacy, unafraid to challenge the monopoly of the over-powerful Executive in the United Kingdom.

That is the only long-term guarantee of our rights, ending the Executive's ability to control the Commons, to appoint the Lords, to select the judges, to instruct every local authority and to ignore Europe – centralised powers that would make a Stalin or even a Thatcher salivate.

Labour has crossed the great political watershed from unitarism – we no longer believe that we have the right to tell people what to do just because we are the good guys – to pluralism. There is a mature acceptance that people themselves should decide through democratic institutions what they want to do.

Since the election of my right hon. and learned Friend the Member for Monklands, East (Mr. Smith) as the leader of my party less than a year ago, Labour has committed itself to an impressive review of our democracy. We propose a Bill of Rights, scrutiny of prerogative powers, free-standing local government, elected regional authorities, a Scottish Parliament elected by the additional member system, an elected second Chamber under a proportional regional list system, a European Parliament elected on the same basis, and a thorough reform of the way in which this place works, in addition to a referendum on how we should elect Members to this the first Chamber.

Never again will an all-powerful Executive be able to control every facet of our political life. It is a frightening prospect for centralists everywhere, but an exciting one for democrats of all parties and at all representative levels of all parties. It is in that new context that the idea of human rights will find its home.

We are very complacent about our rights in this country. We like to think that abuses of rights take place elsewhere, but not in the United Kingdom. The reality is painfully different. It is almost so painful that we do not like to talk about it or even to admit that abuses exist. In a country with no clear list of rights, it is quite difficult to assess what rights have been abused. In a society that places emphasis on class and hierarchy, it is often the place one occupies rather than one's rights vis-à-vis other individuals that preoccupies many and colours their view of any abuse.

All that is now changing. Old certainties are breaking down, and old social structures and values have been dealt the death blow by Thatcherism, by the atomisation of society and by the exaltation of greed. A social and a spiritual vacuum has been created. We in this place need to put new values and new ideas into that vacuum. A central part of that will be to develop clearly understood and widely accepted rights and responsibilities for the modern British citizen.

Such ideas are not alien to this country, as many would have us believe. We were the first founding signatories of the European convention on human rights, a convention incorporated into the legal system of most of our fellow European nations. I am proud to say that it was a Labour Government who signed the convention in 1951 and it was the Labour Government of Harold Wilson who gave United Kingdom citizens the right of individual petition to the European Commission and the European Court of Human Rights in Strasbourg.

To the present Government's great shame, Britain as a country has since been found guilty of breaching the provisions of the treaty more often than any other member of the Council of Europe. Today, seven cases are proceeding against the Government in the European Court. One has been awaiting judgment for five years.

One of the major flaws of the European convention's being interpreted in

Strasbourg rather than the British courts is the time it takes for cases of human rights abuse in Britain to be heard. The time is currently five or six years, after a petitioner has exhausted all other means of redress under domestic law. Anthony Lester, a noted expert in administrative and constitutional law, has predicted that, in future, cases will take a minimum of 10 years to be heard, and perhaps as many as 15 if current trends continue.

The consequence of the long wait and the associated expense is that only those with the backing of large organisations or with substantial personal resources can make use of the only guarantee of rights available to the United Kingdom citizen. That amounts to the creation of a two-tier system of rights in this country. Yes, our rights are guaranteed, but only the select few can enforce them.

I make it plain to the House today that that is wholly unacceptable. An incoming Labour Government will incorporate the European convention on human rights into our law, so that cases can be dealt with speedily in the British courts ...

Labour believes that, if people have rights and freedoms as individuals – we certainly believe that people have those rights – there is no problem about writing them down. If an individual's right as a consumer can be expressed in a citizens charter, why cannot his or her rights as a citizen be expressed clearly in a Bill of Rights? All schoolchildren should carry in their pocket or purse a list of their rights as individuals. They should grow with those rights, and knowing those rights, so that they can become full citizens of our society.

The justification that is often offered by those opposed to incorporation is that, in Britain, every citizen is protected by rights and freedoms under the common law. But those rights and freedoms are ill defined and incomplete, and are not accessible to or understood by the average citizen. One needs a law degree to have even an inkling of the challenges that can be made, let alone of the detail of the rights. The extent of such rights is controlled by the judges and not by Parliament. That is unacceptable. The job of judges is to interpret and apply the law and not to make it.

Some claim that incorporation would create a political judiciary: it would not. Many judicial decisions made today could be viewed as political, but are made outside the framework of a statute explicitly defining people's rights. Far from politicising judges, the incorporation of the European convention on human rights and a subsequent British Bill of Rights would enable the judiciary to make decisions free from political pressure, thus guaranteeing its independence.

It is not as though our judges are incapable of deciding rights cases – indeed, many are themselves in favour of a Bill of Rights. The judiciary already makes decisions based on rights-oriented legislation, such as sex and race anti-discrimination laws, and there is no reason to suppose that it would be incapable of handling decisions once the European convention was incorporated.

If the Government are wary of granting judges the right to make decisions on basic rights, why do they not revoke the right of individual petition by a

British subject to the European Court of Human Rights, where European judges make decisions? Perhaps the Government lack confidence only in British judges.

To suggest that incorporation would destroy the political impartiality of the judiciary is to display a shameful lack of confidence in those to whom we entrust the administration of the law. That suggestion is certainly odd coming from a Government who once sought to style themselves the Government of law and order.

Labour has no such worries about incorporating the European convention on human rights, although we accept the need for changes in methods of judicial recruitment and appointment and for an improved continuing education programme for the judiciary. I hope that the Lord Chancellor's Department will take those comments to heart ...

Incorporation will take place speedily under the next Labour Government and will be just a beginning. We shall then need to examine – perhaps by means of an all-party commission – a home-grown British Bill of Rights. I suspect that that will have to be the subject of my next Adjournment debate, Mr. Deputy Speaker.

For the past 14 years, we have watched the Government ride roughshod over our rights. It is time that the balance was redressed. Our current constitutional system of checks and balances is in no way adequate for what is allegedly a modern democracy. We need to re-establish the fundamental pillar of democracy – the separation of powers. We need to consider once again the balance between the powers of the legislature, the Executive and the judiciary, and a Bill of Rights will be central to such a re-examination of political and democratic theory.

HC Deb., 27 May 1993, cols. 1024f

Mr. Graham Allen: It is a sad commentary on this place that our democracy and our constitution are rarely debated in the Chamber. The rights of our citizens should be the issue most keenly discussed and most urgently debated, yet it finds no room on our parliamentary agenda, which is given to us by the Executive who control the House. In many ways that is why Parliament has become increasingly irrelevant to finding the answers to our economic and social problems. Above all, it is the reason why reform of the House of Commons is so central to rebuilding democracy in our country.

Nowhere is that inadequacy more laughably illustrated than in the fact that an hon. Member must win a place in the weekly raffle for an Adjournment debate at odds of over 100:1 before using that precious opportunity to raise the issue of human rights. That such a matter is debated only due to a stroke of luck rather than as a deliberate duty of the House may explain why the House and its inmates are held in such low esteem and treated with such deserved contempt by the Government and people of this country.

Contrary to parliamentary mythology, people are interested in democracy. It is not only the chattering classes that talk about the failure of our political process. Everyone discusses the poll tax, pit closures, the state of our schools and hospitals and asks, 'Why?'. The simple truth is that command politics have not delivered. We need to try something different. Pluralism and a variety of independent and legitimate institutions and defensible human rights are a key part of that agenda.

It is essential that human rights are dealt with seriously and I have particular pleasure in initiating this debate on the day that Amnesty International launches a new worldwide campaign in protest at continuing political killings and disappearances. I am delighted to use this opportunity to extend my thanks and those of all who are concerned about human rights, to the work of Amnesty International. In the United Kingdom Parliament ringing tribute should also be put on record to Liberty, formerly the National Council for Civil Liberties, and for Charter 88, both of which have kept the candle of human rights alight in the recent darkest years of centralism ...

The 1993 Labour party conference endorsed as the policy of our party the most radical package of democratic reforms ever proposed. My right hon. and learned Friend the Leader of the Opposition summed it up when he said:

'We are proposing nothing less than a new constitution of citizenship for a new century. A new and modern conception of citizenship, which recognises the importance of the community acting together to advance individual freedom. A revitalised democracy which protects the fundamental rights of each and every citizen, regardless of race, colour, gender or creed. A system of government that is open, accountable and close to the people it is elected to serve.'

He went on to say:

'We in the Labour party – unlike any other party – see the vital link between rights in the workplace and rights at the ballot box. We need both, if we are to create a society of free and self-confident citizens.'

Labour's starting point for defining rights in the United Kingdom must begin with incorporating the European convention on human rights. At the moment, any person in the United Kingdom can take out a human rights case, but in Europe, not in our own country. Incorporation would allow the rights of British citizens to be directly protected in our British courts – rights to freedom of speech, freedom of assembly, the right of privacy and many others ...

A pressing need now exists to overhaul and modernise the structure of our democracy to break the stranglehold of the Executive and to end the winner-takes-all approach to politics. The political system in Britain is failing to protect individual rights, just as it is failing socially and economically. Free, confident and assertive individuals need open, democratic and accountable institutions to grow and flourish. We must create a new culture of rights that will give substance to the inalienable right of citizenship, ending for ever the debilitating culture of hierarchy, deference and class, which so holds back our country today.

The Labour party is committed to a major package of constitutional reforms: a Bill of Rights, reform of the royal prerogative, an elected second Chamber, independence for local government, a modernised judiciary, a Scottish Parliament, a Welsh assembly and the introduction of proportional representation to elect the European Parliament and the second Chamber. As a package, those measures are essential components in the safeguarding of individual rights and in the building of our democracy.

Sadly, the Government have a shameful record as the prime violators of the European convention on human rights. Since 1979, 29 landmark cases have been brought against the United Kingdom, more than against any other country in the European Community. The judgments did not involve marginal or trivial cases; they have invariably involved fundamental issues such as the ending of unfair press curbs in the United Kingdom, the ending of unjust restrictions on prisoners' access to lawyers, the ending of unacceptable restrictions on the husbands and wives of immigrants, the creating of effective judicial protection for mental patients and for prisoners serving life sentences and requirements for new controls on telephone tapping. The Government's record should concern all of us here, whether or not we are members of the Government.

I make a pledge as Labour's spokeman on the constitution: incorporating into British law of the citizen's rights found in the European convention will take place speedily under the next Labour Government and that will be only a beginning. We shall then examine, by means of an all-party commission, a home-grown British Bill of Rights to give effect to the equally important international covenant on civil and political rights.

HC Deb., 20 October 1993, cols. 364f.

> 112   THE LABOUR PARTY ADOPTS AS ITS OFFICIAL
> POLICY INCORPORATION OF THE EUROPEAN
> CONVENTION ON HUMAN RIGHTS AND THE
> ESTABLISHMENT OF AN ALL-PARTY COMMISSION TO
> DRAFT A NEW UK BILL OF RIGHTS, 1993

RB NOTE: This Policy Commission Report was presented as a National Executive Committee Statement by the 1993 Labour Conference where it was introduced by Tony Blair MP, then home affairs spokesperson for the party.

A New Agenda for Democracy: Labour's Proposals for Constitutional Reform

INTRODUCTION

The issue of 'the constitution' is not an academic one. It is one in which all people have a direct interest. It is about power; where it is located and how it is made accountable. Unusually in the UK, we have no written or formal constitution. It is a series of conventions and doctrines established through practice and tradition alongside a patchwork of legislation. This is not in itself of vital significance, except that it has meant we have never had to confront the task of putting our constitution into words and therefore concentrating the national mind on the hard decisions of the distribution of power. The result is a constitution urgently in need of radical change and modernisation. We set out here the basis of a new constitutional settlement, a modern notion of citizenship that establishes new rules to govern the bargain between the individual and society. We recognise the importance of the community acting collectively, but to advance individual freedom, not at the expense of it. Our aim is to create a revitalised democracy which protects the fundamental rights of the citizen from the abuse of power, which proposes the substantial devolution of central government authority, and which insists that the legitimacy of government rests on it being both open and accountable to the people it serves.

Today, the executive is immensely powerful. Parliament is easily over-whelmed. The ability of the ordinary citizen to challenge the executive is tightly limited. The UK has one of the most centralised systems of government in Europe. Under successive Conservative governments this process of centralisation has massively increased. Other institutions of government capable of exercising some restraining power over the centre – notably local government – have been hugely curtailed and undermined, often, unfortunately, as a result of deliberate policy. Unelected quangos, whose members are political appointees of government, now account for over £42 billion of public spending. We are a deeply secretive society, without even minimal legislation on freedom of information. The legal system – essential to any true implementation of the rule of law – is hopelessly out of date, dominated by vested interests and now seriously unravelling in the face of a massive restriction in legal aid.

In addition, the European Community now has a major impact on all our domestic institutions, including the executive. Its laws can have a direct effect and reach into almost all areas of national life. Yet the methods of holding to account decisions made in the European Community has not kept up with the pace and extent of change.

The result is that our democracy is profoundly flawed. If democracy is about content as well as form, the form of our constitution is imperfect and the content of our democracy even more seriously at fault. The case for change is clear.

It is also right that the Labour Party takes a leading role in making the case for change. The central belief of the Labour Party is that people do not live as isolated units but individuals within a society or community. Individual freedom to develop and prosper is held back by the absence of opportunity, particularly at work and in education – by the presence of powerful interests. The task of the Labour Party is to use the power of the community acting together to advance and liberate the individual.

The purpose of such action is not to give power to government but to give power to people. And it should not be merely through traditional forms of central government intervention that people are empowered. Government itself is a powerful interest that requires to be checked and controlled.

The failure of Conservative philosophy – even at its most elevated – is to believe that freedom is best secured through minimum intervention by government or community. The perception that has damaged the cause of socialism – often wrongly so far as democratic socialism is concerned – was that it put the interests of society or worse, the state, above those of the individual.

Precisely because we believe in using the power of the community, through government and in other ways, it is vital that we address the issue of its accountability. In particular, we should be seeking to re-shape the way government works. It is impossible to modernise Britain without modernising government.

We seek, therefore to retrieve the true ideological basis of democratic socialism – action by the community for the benefit of the individual – and set it to work for the modern age.

This requires, in turn, a new constitutional settlement for our country, one which establishes a just relationship between society and individual, one which above all, fundamentally redresses power in favour of the citizen from the state.

This new settlement should be effected in two ways: first it must grant individuals the rights needed to challenge arbitrary decisions and exercises of power that affect them, to guarantee equality of treatment without discrimination and the practical ability under the law to make these rights real. This is correct in itself but it also promotes much greater participation by people in the development of the country's democracy. The fairness of our society comes to be judged by the priority it gives to individual rights; and it encourages a more active idea of citizenship where rights are not simply a list of demands, but are accompanied by responsibilities as part of a contract between citizen and society.

Secondly, it should be based on the diversity of political institutions, each with their independence guaranteed, not on the belief that the government, once elected, should control – directly or indirectly – all other dependent political institutions. This means that the constitution should be subject to the necessary checks and balances, in order to hold the executive to proper account and to reflect the more pluralist, more decentralised, more devolved government which the people of our country want to see. The idea of a highly-centralised, paternalistic state handing out improvements to a dependent public belongs to a different age. We live in a society today whose culture, lifestyle and aspirations are much more diverse and varied than they ever have been. This must find an echo in our system of government.

This does not lessen our pride in past achievements. It is largely as a result of previous Labour governments that people have been able to achieve the greater material prosperity and quality of life that gives them the chance to take control of their own lives and shape their own future. These advances were not diminished through the existence of a strong community; on the contrary it was in part action by society as a whole that enabled individuals to gain that greater freedom. Such action, especially with millions in our country unemployed or in poverty and millions more blocked from reaching higher up the ladder of opportunity, is still vital. But the means of doing so and the terms of the bargain between individual and community will and should change constantly, with the changes in society itself.

So we put forward this programme of reform – which we believe is the most fundamental proposed by a major British political party – not simply as an itemised list of policies, but as part of a much bigger framework of ideas that define Labour's vision of the UK's future. Constitutional reform – alongside economic and social change – is one part of a different political agenda for our country. It is linked to the other parts. If the development of individual economic potential is essential both for personal and national economic success, then it can surely only benefit from a more active and developed notion of citizenship. And a more accountable public sector is likely also to produce more efficient public and social services.

We hope, too, that we can lay to rest the notion that this is just an issue for what are dismissively called 'the chattering classes'. It is real people who depend on local government services or suffer infringements through unreasonable executive action, or are held back through prejudice. It is to them that we must give the hope of change.

The following is a summary of our main proposals:

- support for a UK Bill of Rights;
- incorporation of the European Convention on Human Rights into UK law, with a provision that other laws are to be interpreted consistently with the Convention unless expressly provided;
- because it is recognised the Convention is inadequate and outdated, we propose an all-party commission be appointed to draft our own Bill of Rights and consider a more permanent form of entrenchment;
- a strengthening and modernising of anti-discrimination law to provide equal treatment of every citizen;
- employee and trade union rights;
- a Freedom of Information Act;
- reform of the Official Secrets legislation and proper scrutiny of the

security services; reform of the Royal Prerogative, with ratification by Parliament of both treaties and the declaration of war;
- a strengthened Data Protection Act;
- a recasting of the relationship between central and local government, with the Scottish Parliament, Welsh Assembly and regional councils in England replacing other tiers of administration, and the removal of capping restraints balanced by greater electoral accountability;
- reform of electoral law;
- reform of Parliament including the creation of an elected Second Chamber;
- reform of the judiciary and in particular a new system for the appointment of judges.

We do not claim this to be the final word on constitutional change. But it is a considerable start. We want it now to be the basis for the widest possible consultation in the Labour Party and beyond, involving those who are outside traditional party politics as well as colleagues in our own party. In this way we can prepare the ground for government and the creation of a modern democracy for the 21st century.

A BILL OF RIGHTS

The importance of human rights

The Labour Party's concern for the rights of the citizen is long-standing and deep-rooted. The party was founded to protect the oppressed and under-privileged against the powerful, whether the power of the state or the power of private organisations. Its traditions and attitudes make it proud to protect the rights and interests of individuals. That is why the Attlee government, in 1950, put the UK amongst the first countries to sign the European Convention on Human Rights. That is why the Wilson government in the 1960s and 1970s passed successive Race Relations Acts, and the Equal Pay and Sex Discrimination Acts.

However, in the last 13 years under the Tories, Britain has slipped behind the rest of Europe in the protection it gives to individual rights. The UK is virtually alone amongst major western European nations in not laying down in legislation the basic rights of its citizens, and in not giving those citizens a direct means of asserting those rights through the courts.

The European Convention on Human Rights

The quickest and simplest way of achieving democratic and legal recognition of a substantial package of human rights would be by incorporating into UK law the European Convention on Human Rights. That is now widely recognised, both within and outside the party, as a necessary and sensible step. Its implications, however, need to be carefully thought through.

The argument for incorporation

The essential effect of incorporating the convention as part of UK domestic law is that its protections can be relied on in the ordinary courts, and directly against the national government. At present, unlike the citizens of almost every other European country, citizens of the UK have no such rights. If they want to seek the protection of the convention, they must appeal to the Commission and Court in Strasbourg. That process is intolerably slow: three years at a minimum, and some have been known to take as long as nine years. Only the most determined people, or those who are supported by pressure groups, are likely to stay the course. And while the process grinds on, the abuse of rights at home continues.

The failure directly to incorporate the Convention into UK law has another unwelcome effect. Although, at the end of the day, the UK government is subject to the requirements of the Convention, the present set-up makes the protection of basic rights appear difficult and remote. It reinforces an atmosphere that suggests that basic rights are not of that much importance. and that the government regards them as a nuisance rather than, as it should, as a primary obligation. And that view is reinforced in the courts. The judges will take note of the requirements of the convention when interpreting legislation that is ambiguous or uncertain. But, in the absence of laws to the contrary, they have, perfectly properly, made it plain that, if a law exists that affects human rights in a way that clearly breaches the convention, it will be that law, and not the requirements of the convention, that they will enforce.

The convention is not a vague, untested or uncertain code, but a mature statement of rights that has been interpreted and applied over many years by an expert court in Strasbourg. Our government is already, and has been since 1950, ultimately subject to the requirements of the convention. What is needed now is to make that protection for our citizens a real one, and not something that is available only after years of effort and litigation.

The legislative steps: protecting the Human Rights Act from judicial attack

Incorporation could be achieved fairly easily. Parliament should pass a Human Rights Act that incorporates the rules of the convention directly into UK law, and gives citizens the right to enforce those rules in the courts.

It is often argued that in technical terms a British Act of Parliament cannot be 'entrenched'. We propose to protect the Human Rights Act from being undermined by either Parliament or the courts by a clause that requires that any other Act that is intended to introduce laws inconsistent with the convention must do so specifically and in express terms.

That arrangement will have a number of benefits. First, if a government genuinely thought, say in a time of national crisis, that it must curtail basic individual rights, it can still do so. But it will have to do so openly and expressly, as in a democracy ought always to be the practice.

Second, however, it will in practice be almost impossible for existing or subsequent law to be interpreted as being inconsistent with the convention. Judges applying the present rules of interpretation will know that Parliament had to hand a means of making clear that it was derogating from the convention but did not use it. It would therefore be unlawful for them to interpret legislation in a way that is intended to breach the convention unless the legislation states that in express terms.

Third, the Human Rights Act will be expressly stated to apply to, and override, all legislation existing at the time at which it is passed. If the government wishes to exempt any law from the provisions of the Human Rights Act it will have to say so expressly, using the procedure just described. Parliament will have the final decision in any case where legislation is brought into question as a result of the application of the European Convention; but it will have to make that decision openly and expressly. Here again, therefore, government will have to be entirely open about what it is trying to achieve, and will have to justify what it is doing both to Parliament and to the public. In a democracy, Parliament decides what rights should apply, and should set them out in a manner that citizens can understand for themselves. Under these proposals, it will not be left to the discretion of the judges, or to archaeological investigations by legal and constitutional experts, to decide what protections citizens do and do not have.

The scope of protection: the rights of individuals, not of corporations

The rights that we seek to protect are those of the individual against the state. The Human Rights Act will therefore provide that its protections can be relied on only by individuals, and not by companies or by organisations. We do not want to repeat here the confusion and injustice that has occurred in some other countries, where companies and commercial organisations have tried to resist social legislation controlling their activities by claiming that it infringes their 'human' rights. And the Human Rights Act is not designed to alter existing legal relations between individuals, but to protect individuals from state power. So the bodies that will be subject to the Human Rights Act will be state and state-related ones: national and local government; the police; and any organisation that exercises state power. Individuals will be able to use the Human Rights Act to try to force the government to legislate to protect them against abuse of human rights by private bodies or individuals, for example, in relation to the use of surveillance techniques by private bodies. Subject to this, all governmental activity, and all the existing and future law, will be subject to the Human Rights legislation.

The enforcement of human rights

The rights that the legislation confers will be asserted in the first instance through the ordinary courts: either by applications for judicial review, to assert or confirm the existence and operation of a right in a particular case, or by way of defence in an ordinary action, should a state body try to use against a citizen a law that is inconsistent with the Human Rights Act.

This use of the ordinary courts is important in two ways. First, a special series of human rights tribunals, which dealt simply with human rights issues, would be vulnerable to incessant disputes between them and the ordinary courts as to which body should be hearing a particular case or complaint. The result would be delay and confusion and benefit only the lawyers. Second, and even more important, it is essential that regard for human rights pervades the work of all courts, and is recognised as an integral part of their work, for which they bear direct responsibility: whether they are, for instance, criminal courts dealing with claims of wrongful conviction or civil courts looking at government bans on free speech. That responsibility must be put on the regular courts: and the judges of those courts must be trained and be ready to respond to the challenge.

There should, however, be two further safeguards. First, at the final appellate level, where points of fundamental or wide-ranging importance about human rights may have to be decided, the final court should have added to its judges three further lay members, drawn from a panel of people with knowledge and understanding of society and of human rights in the broad sense. That will ensure that principles are not laid down from too narrow a legal perspective. The lay members will be full members of the court, whose vote will rank equally with that of the judges. They will be appointed from a list to be drawn up, after wide consultation, by the Judicial Appointments Commission. Precedents for qualified laypersons being judges of a court already exist in the Employment Appeal Tribunal and the Restrictive Practices Court.

Second, to assist the courts, and also to assist individuals in asserting their rights, there should be established an independent Human Rights Commission, along the lines of the Equal Opportunities Commission and Commission for Racial Equality that were established by Labour governments. The commission would monitor the operation of the Human Rights Act, provide advice and support for those who wish to assert their rights and, where necessary, itself institute cases to confirm or clarify particularly important issues. The commission would thus act as a focus for human rights activities and ensure that the protection of the public was not left to the accident of individual enthusiasm or willingness to pursue cases.

Towards a UK Bill of Rights

The incorporation of the European Convention on Human Rights is a necessary first step, but it is not a substitute for our own written Bill of Rights. The European Convention is over 40 years old. It resulted from the excesses of Nazi Germany and was deliberately drawn with that in mind.

It does not cover freedom of information or data protection or the rights of disabled people and it is inadequate in its treatment of discrimination. It does not deal with economic or social rights.

In addition, some of the limitations in the convention relating to national security or disorder or the danger to morals go wider than we require in the UK. So there is a good case for drafting our own Bill of Rights. Its provisions would have to be carefully negotiated. There is also the immensely difficult issue of entrenchment. There are a range of different options that could be considered in more detail. There is the extreme form of entrenchment in the American system where judicial decisions can strike down any legislation and where judicial decisions are supreme, though this was not favoured by our commission. There is also the interesting idea put forward by Liberty of a hybrid system of democratic entrenchment which involves both the judiciary and Parliament in the enforcement process of a bill of rights. Another is the one that we are proposing for the European Convention, where Parliament retains the possibility of expressly opting out of the convention's provisions. Accompanying these forms of entrenchment are those constitutional arrangements where a special parliamentary majority, which is more than a mere majority, is required to alter the constitution or pass legislation inconsistent with it.

For these reasons the drafting of such a 'homegrown' Bill of Rights, together with its entrenchment, could not be done on a purely partisan basis. There would need to be a fairly wide consensus established in favour of its provisions for it to possess both credibility and durability. We therefore propose the establishment of an all-party commission that will be charged with drafting the Bill of Rights and considering a suitable method of entrenchment. This should report to Parliament within a specified and limited period of time. . .

Conclusion

The proposals in this statement constitute the most radical package of democratic reform ever presented to the British people by a major political party. Together they will open up our political system and make human rights and justice more readily available to all our citizens. We accept that this means that political action in future should be checked, negotiated and accountable – as it should be in a modern democracy. An open political system will be a catalyst for change – institutionalised, mediated and careful change no doubt – but change nevertheless.

The next Labour government will create a democracy which will no longer be confined by an over-powerful government, but where different institutions – each properly and legitimately established – can help to balance the executive power which has been so sorely abused in the eighties.

Having created clearly defined institutions and rights, the relationship which develops between those new features will be of great significance. There will undoubtedly be serious debate and even conflict between the different institutions – a reformed House of Commons will discomfort the executive; an elected Second chamber will want to spread its wings; individuals using the Bill of Rights will expose the government to much greater accountability and influence the future development of the judiciary; European decisions will have to be debated in greater detail; and local government will be rejuvenated. Above all, individuals will not only feel greater ownership of the political system and be more demanding of it, they will also be less tolerant of the abuse of power and better equipped to put it right.

Though these reforms do not mean a formal written constitution, in which each aspect of government and citizens' rights is set out, they are nonetheless a significant step in that direction. Each part will require legislation which is carefully formulated and consistent with the others. We leave open the question of whether at a later stage we make progress to formal codification.

For the immediate future, and certainly for the duration of the first Labour term, our task is to bring life to the various elements that will form the basis of a new constitutional settlement for Britain to create a democracy for the 21st century.

Labour Party, *A New Agenda for Democracy: Labour's Proposals for Constitutional Reform*, 1993.

RB NOTE: Lord Irvine, the Labour lord chancellor, reiterated the above policy document down to its section entitled 'The enforcement of human rights' almost verbatim in his article 'The Legal System and Law Reform under Labour' in David Bean (ed.), Law Reform for All, *1996. A few words were amended, for example in changing the passage on a Human Rights Commission from being that a Commission 'should' be established to that a Commission 'could' be.*

---

113   THE LABOUR PARTY CONFERENCE ENDORSES THE COMMITMENT TO A NEW UK BILL OF RIGHTS, 1994

Constitutional Reform

Composite 29 was moved by Sandra Parsons (Vale of Glamorgan CLP) and seconded by David Hurst (Bath CLP).

Conference calls for a commitment to a Bill of Rights to be included in Labour's manifesto as part of what John Smith called a new constitution for a new century which will include:

(1) the incorporation into UK law of the civil and political rights of the European Convention on Human Rights;

(2) a commission to deliver to Parliament within two years of establishment an implementable package of civil, political, economic and social rights for all;

(3) the reform of the judiciary;

(4) a Freedom of Information Act.

Carried

1994 Conference, *Record of Decisions.*

---

114 THE LABOUR LEADER, TONY BLAIR, GIVES HIS PERSONAL BACKING TO INCORPORATION OF THE EUROPEAN CONVENTION ON HUMAN RIGHTS AND AN ENTRENCHED UK BILL OF RIGHTS, 1994–6

Party Leadership Election Statement, 1994

Our political system is a conspiracy against reason: outdated, unfair and with the minimum of checks and balances. In the past 15 years, power has been concentrated in Whitehall, denied to the people of Britain, and handed over to Tory placemen. Our local authorities have been systematically stripped of power, unelected quangos have multiplied, and sleaze has become widespread.

In the cause of common citizenship – and as a source of the new support we must gain for victory in the general election – I want to see Labour reach out to the 10 million people who did not vote in 1992, and to the many more who rarely vote in local elections. Non-participation on such a scale is a symptom of social disintegration which threatens the health of our democracy. It denies people the means of their own emancipation. Just as we must open the doors of opportunity for work, training, childcare and housing, so we must campaign to reconnect the disenfranchised with the political process by showing how Labour makes the difference ... Parliamentary procedure is out of date and its style alienating. It must be reformed. We are the only democracy in the Western world to operate a hereditary principle. I support Labour's commitment to replacing the House of Lords with an elected Second Chamber and to entrenching clear rights for every citizen in a Bill of Rights for Britain. I fully support the party's commitment to a referendum on the issue of the electoral system for the Commons.

Tony Blair, *Change and National Renewal*, 1994.

Speech on the Constitution, 1996

There is a strong case for a code of citizens rights which guarantee the rights of individuals to basic freedoms and opportunites.

As a first step we should incorporate the European Convention of Human Rights. We have been signatories since 1951. It is quite separate from the

European Union or the European Court of Justice. People in this country have access to the protection and the guarantees of basic human rights that the Convention provides yet to gain access to those rights British citizens must appeal to the Commission and Court in Strasbourg. It is a long and expensive process and only the most diligent manage to stay the course.

I believe it makes sense to end the cumbersome practice of forcing people to go to Strasbourg to hold their government to account. By incorporating the Convention into British law the rights it guarantees would be available in courts in both Britain and Northern Ireland. This would make clear that the protection afforded by the Convention was not some foreign import but that it had been accepted by sucessive British Governments and that it should apply throughout the United Kingdom.

Some have said that this system takes power away from Parliament and places it in the hands of judges. In reality, since we are already signatories to the Convention, it means allowing British judges rather than European judges to pass judgement.

John Smith Memorial Lecture, 1996.

---

115   THE LABOUR LEADERSHIP'S DRAFT ELECTION MANIFESTO SUBMITTED TO ITS MEMBERS ON CITIZENS' BASIC RIGHTS, 1996

We should grant our citizens basic rights to fair treatment at the hands of government. There will be a Freedom of Information Act, opening up the unnecessary secretiveness of government.

We will allow people to sue directly in Britain for breaches of the European Convention on Human Rights – which is a Convention the UK signed in 1948 before the European Community was founded.

We will seek to end unjustifiable discrimination wherever it exists. For example, we support comprehensive, enforceable civil rights for disabled people against discrimination in society or at work, developed in partnership with all interested parties. We will also take measures to tackle age discrimination at work.

So we will create a political settlement in harmony with a modern civic society, one that decentralises power, opens up freedom, roots out injustice and gives good and effective government ...

Our proposals are not change for change's sake. They are long, long overdue reforms for the 21st century.

New Life for Britain, 1996, p. 31.

RB NOTE: The ballot of Labour Party members on the draft election manifesto resulted in a 95 per cent vote in favour.

---

116   THE LABOUR PARTY ISSUES A CONSULTATION
PAPER ON THE DETAILED FORM WHICH AN ACT OF
PARLIAMENT INCORPORATING THE EUROPEAN
CONVENTION ON HUMAN RIGHTS INTO UK LAW
SHOULD TAKE, 1996

Bringing Rights Home: Labour's plans to incorporate the European Convention on Human Rights into UK law

LEGISLATING ON INCORPORATION

Labour is committed to incorporating the ECHR into UK law through a new Act of Parliament. This will require five key issues to be decided:

1. the relationship of the ECHR to existing law,
2. derogation and reservations,
3. applicability,
4. eligibility to challenge, and
5. remedies.

Labour's approach to these issues is set out in this consultation paper so that we can obtain views before the details are settled.

1. *Relationship of the ECHR to existing law*

The ECHR is almost 50 years old, but it has to be interpreted as a living instrument, adapting to changing needs. Inevitably issues will arise over whether existing UK legislation is consistent with the Convention once it is incorporated into UK domestic law.

One approach would be to reconcile them both by combing through the existing body of UK law. This would be a massive, time-consuming task.

A simpler and more effective approach would be to allow case law to develop over time, and to point the way to any areas where Parliament might need to amend existing law. The courts would be required to construe all existing (as well as future) legislation, as far as is possible, consistently with the Convention.

2. *Derogations and Reservations*

Under Article 15 of the ECHR it is possible for Governments to derogate from their obligations under the Convention '*in time of war or other public emergency threatening the life of the nation*'.

Whilst it is important to guard against undermining the Convention through unnecessary or inappropriate derogations, future Governments cannot be prevented from acting in the national interest at times of genuine crisis.

Any future derogations at times of national crisis should be clearly framed and expressly authorised by Parliament. Their duration should be defined and subject to periodical parliamentary renewal. Incorporation of the ECHR would be subject to any necessary current UK derogations but these would be open to review in the light of changing circumstances.

Several protocols of the Convention have not been ratified by UK governments because of concerns about their compatibility with aspects of UK law. Some of these reservations are long standing. In government we would review carefully whether such concerns were still justified and decide whether or not changed circumstances meant that we could ratify these rights as the other major European countries have done.

3. *Applicability*

There are differences of view on whether the ECHR should be invoked directly against private individuals and corporations as well as public authorities.

The Standing Advisory Commission on Human Rights in Northern Ireland has recommended confining the scope of the Convention initially at least to public authorities.

The House of Lords select committee on incorporation of the ECHR thought that the possibility of actions against private individuals might be open under the Convention.

We take the view that the central purpose of the ECHR is to protect the individual against the misuse of power by the state. The Convention imposes obligations on states, not individuals, and it cannot be relied upon to bring a case against private persons.

For this reason we consider that it should apply only to public authorities – government departments, executive agencies, quangos, local authorities and other public services. An appropriate definition would be included in the new legislation and this might be framed in terms of bodies performing a public function. We would welcome views on this.

Individuals would in certain circumstances be able to use the new Act to seek to secure effective action by public authorities to protect them against abuse of human rights by private bodies or individuals. Nevertheless this new legislation is not intended to alter existing legal relationships between individuals.

4. *Eligibility to Challenge*

Complaints under the Convention can be brought to the European Court by '*a person, non-governmental organisation or group of individuals claiming to be the victim of a violation*' [Article 25].

Where applicants challenge the decisions of public authorities in UK judicial review proceedings, they must demonstrate that they have a '*sufficient interest in the matter to which the application relates.*' British courts have interpreted this requirement flexibly enough to allow challenges by public interest groups, trade unions, and statutory bodies such as the Equal Opportunities Commission. We believe this approach to be right for cases brought under the Act.

Those likely to be permitted to raise a challenge in national law under an incorporated ECHR would include:

- individuals and corporate bodies directly affected,
- individuals seeking to vindicate the broader public interest in constitutional government,
- pressure groups who believe that their cause may be prejudiced, and
- representative group interests who consider their collective interests are disadvantaged.

We would welcome views on this.

5. *Remedies*

The primary purpose of incorporating the ECHR is to enable individuals to use the UK courts to prevent and remedy the misuse of public power. Individuals already have access to judicial review as a means of obtaining redress for the misuse of power by public authorities. Existing powers and procedures of the courts in judicial review cases are capable of being used to include complaints about the infringement of Convention rights by public bodies.

The European Court of Human Rights may award compensation as '*just satisfaction*' to a party who has suffered a breach of the ECHR. In our view it would be wrong to impose a general liability on the state to pay damages to individuals or corporate bodies whose Convention rights have been infringed. Equally it would be wrong to rule out compensation in very serious and exceptional cases. We are therefore minded to leave the matter to be developed on a case by case basis by the British courts, taking proper account of the current practice of the European Court of Human Rights.

Northern Ireland

In Northern Ireland, as in Great Britain, the incorporation of the ECHR will be a valuable step in protecting basic human rights. Furthermore, there is widespread support for provisions in the Convention across both communities living there.

There is also the need to develop specific rights protections to deal with the unique problems of the divided community in Northern Ireland. There is currently considerable debate among the parties about the specific provisions that could be contained in a Northern Ireland bill of rights. We will continue to make suggestions and to consult widely with the parties in the talks on the development of a distinct package of rights as part of a new, agreed and balanced settlement for Northern Ireland.

Discussions with the Government of the Republic of Ireland will be needed with a view to reassuring both unionist and nationalist communities that their civil, cultural and religious rights will be protected now and into the future.

Parliamentary Sovereignty

A fundamental aspect of the British constitutional tradition is that of parliamentary sovereignty. This means that one Act of Parliament cannot bind a future Parliament, and that no other authority – including the courts – can set aside laws made by Parliament. A future Parliament can pass amending legislation.

This new Act would not alter Parliament's sovereignty. A future Parliament and government could, if it chose, withdraw from the Convention and its obligations, and end incorporation of the ECHR. The ECHR could not therefore be 'entrenched' in our UK constitutional arrangements.

In practice however, once incorporated, the Convention is likely to enjoy a high degree of permanence in UK law. Unilateral withdrawal by the UK is improbable and amendment of the Convention is subject to negotiation by all signatory governments.

The European Court of Human Rights would still retain the power to rule against legislation in breach of the Convention. There are no cases where a UK government has failed to act in response to an adverse Strasbourg ruling. We also intend to improve the parliamentary scrutiny of legislation to reduce the risk of breaches (see below).

There will always be special circumstances, for all signatories, relating to their own countries. That is why the ECHR allows for derogation and the European Court allows what they call a *'margin of appreciation'* to take account of different national traditions and jurisprudential approaches.

Taken with Parliament's right to pass exceptional legislation in times of national crisis these provide safeguards against excessively narrow interpretation of the Convention or unreasonable fettering of national sovereignty.

The Convention itself recognises that there may be special circumstances (eg combatting terrorism) in which governments may act contrary to what the ECHR requires. However, we would want to ensure that this was an explicit and open action related to particular circumstances. This could normally be ensured by the Bill stating that it was intended to apply whether or not its provisions were contrary to our Convention obligations.

Enforcement and Scrutiny

The new Act will allow British people to assert and enforce their rights under the ECHR through the ordinary UK courts and tribunals. They will be able to do this either by application for judicial review, or by way of defence in any action in which a public authority attempts to use a law which is inconsistent with the ECHR against a citizen.

By using the ordinary courts in this way citizens' rights will gain greater recognition as an integral part of the courts' work.

The UK government participated in the 1993 Vienna Conference on Human Rights and recognised in principle the benefit of an institution for the promotion and protection of human rights.

After the passage of the Act, it will be important to:

- provide advice and guidance for those who wish to assert their rights,
- institute or support individual or public interest cases based upon well-researched, well-founded evidence and arguments,
- conduct inquiries into particular issues or legal areas,
- monitor the operation of the Act,
- scrutinise new legislation, and
- ensure the conformity of EU law with human rights obligations under international treaties.

One way forward could be for the Act to establish a Human Rights Commission or Commissioner to take on some or all of the roles described, possibly in stages. However this would require careful consideration of the implications for the Equal Opportunities Commissions for Great Britain and for Northern Ireland, the Commission for Racial Equality, the National Disability Council and the Fair Employment Commission for Northern Ireland. We want to hear views on these arrangements before deciding what provision should be made.

In any event, Parliament and government departments will need to ensure they have adequate arrangements for scrutinising legislation to ensure conformity not only with the ECHR, but with other human rights obligations which UK governments have entered into by signing UN and other international treaties and conventions.

We consider it essential to distinguish the responsibility of the Executive to ensure that new legislation brought forwards does not breach human rights obligations, from Parliament's responsibility to scrutinise draft legislation for conformity with those obligations.

PARLIAMENT AND GOVERNMENT DEPARTMENTS

Departmental lawyers, parliamentary counsel and the Government's Law Officers are all expected to ensure that legislation presented to Parliament does not breach international treaty obligations such as the ECHR.

Despite this, legislation has been found to be in breach of the Convention.

We will review the present government machinery to see what improvements are necessary to prevent draft legislation being prepared that is in breach of human rights obligations.

We propose to ensure that departments and ministers are under an obligation to certify that they have, to the best of their ability, considered and concluded that proposed legislation does not breach the Convention. This would in no way reduce the obligation of Parliament itself to scrutinise proposed legislation to ensure that it conforms with the Convention. Where possible inconsistencies arose ministers would be obliged to notify the Lord Chancellor and the Speaker of the House of Commons, and explain the reasons for it (as is the case in New Zealand).

Parliament already has much machinery for giving detailed scrutiny to legislation (eg the standing committee system in the House of Commons, the Statutory Instruments select committee and the Joint Statutory Instruments committee).

However, none of these committees have a particular human rights focus. Parliament itself should play a leading role in protecting the rights which are at the heart of a parliamentary democracy.

- The passage of a new Act will provide an opportunity to strengthen parliamentary machinery on human rights.
- We also propose that a new Joint Committee on Human Rights of both Houses of Parliament should be established. This would have a continuing responsibility to monitor the operation of the new Act and other aspects of the UK's human rights obligations. It would have the powers of a select committee to compel witnesses to attend.
- Where new legislation was identified as having an impact on human rights issues it could be subject to scrutiny by the Joint Committee. The committee would be able to call on other bodies in discharging its responsibilities.
- More detailed work would need to be undertaken on how the Joint Committee would work in practice, should this proposal be adopted by Parliament.
- Under the incorporating Act some cases involving the ECHR will go to the final appellate level in the UK legal process – the House of Lords. In those cases, there will usually be points of fundamental or wide-ranging importance to be decided.
- Some have suggested that in these circumstances three further lay members should sit with the normal court of five Law Lords. These would form a panel of people with knowledge and understanding of society and human rights in the broadest sense. This would avoid principles being established from too narrow a legal perspective. These lay members would be full members of the Court whose vote would rank equally with the judges.
- We have yet to be convinced about the merits of this proposal and welcome views on this. We are unsympathetic to any idea of creating a special constitutional court.

Where, after due process UK legislation is ultimately found to be in breach of the ECHR under the Act, consideration will need to be given by the Government of the day and Parliament as to what action should be taken.

This seems likely to require new parliamentary machinery to consider judicial declarations of breach, particularly where major moral or political issues are involved. This could be by the proposed new Joint Committee.

CONCLUSION

The incorporation of the ECHR into UK law is an important part of Labour's programme for restoring trust in the way we are governed. This programme and why it is needed were described in more detail in our recent publication *New Politics, New Britain*.

We aim to change the relationship between the state and citizen, and to redress the dilution of individual rights by an over-centralising government that has taken place over the past two decades.

By increasing the stake which citizens have in society through a stronger constitutional framework of civil and political rights, we also encourage them to better fulfil their responsibilities. This is an essential part of our strategy to re-establish a balanced relationship between rights and responsibilities.

The new Act will improve awareness of human rights issues throughout our society. It is an important and worthwhile change in its own right. As experience of the new legislation develops it will nurture a culture of understanding of rights and responsibilities at all levels in our society and assist public discussion of what might be the character of any future UK Bill of Rights and Responsibilities.

Labour Party, *Bringing Rights Home*, consultation paper presented by Jack Straw MP, then Shadow Home Secretary, and Paul Boateng MP, then Shadow Minister for the Lord Chancellor's Department, 1996.

> ## 117   THE 1997 LABOUR ELECTION MANIFESTO STATES THAT CITIZENS SHOULD HAVE STATUTORY HUMAN RIGHTS ENFORCIBLE IN THE UK COURTS

Real Rights for Citizens

Citizens should have statutory rights to enforce their human rights in the UK courts. We will by statute incorporate the European Convention on Human Rights into UK law to bring these rights home and allow our people access to them in their national courts. The incorporation of the European Convention will establish a floor, not a ceiling, for human rights. Parliament will remain free to enhance these rights, for example by a Freedom of Information Act.

We will seek to end unjustifiable discrimination wherever it exists. For example, we support comprehensive, enforceable civil rights for disabled people against discrimination in society or at work, developed in partnership with all interested parties.

Labour will undertake a wide-ranging review both of the reform of the civil justice system and Legal Aid.

1997, p. 35.

CHAPTER 8

WRITINGS AND SPEECHES ON A BILL OF RIGHTS

118 J.S. MILL WARNS OF THE TYRANNY OF THE MAJORITY, 1859

Such phrases as 'self-government', and 'the power of the people over themselves', do not express the true state of the case. The 'people' who exercise the power are not always the same people with those over whom it is exercised; and the 'self-government' spoken of is not the government of each by himself, but of each by all the rest. The will of the people, moreover, practically means the will of the most numerous or the most active *part* of the people – the majority, or those who succeed in making themselves accepted as the majority; the people, consequently, *may* desire to oppress a part of their number, and precautions are as much needed against this as against any other abuse of power. The limitation, therefore, of the power of government over individuals loses none of its importance when the holders of power are regularly accountable to the community, that is, to the strongest party therein.

On Liberty, 1859 (Pelican ed. 1979, p. 62).

119 HAROLD LASKI ON THE POLITICAL VALUE OF A BILL OF RIGHTS, 1937

What, at the very outset, needs to be emphasised is that rights are not merely, or even greatly, a matter of the written record. Musty parchments will doubtless give them greater sanctity; they will not ensure their realisation ... It is always valuable to be able to attack the executive in terms of a law it has clearly offended; and the written enactment always serves to remind a people that it has had to fight for its rights. But, at least ultimately, only deliberate challenge will be successful in breaking the purpose of a government determined upon unlawful conduct. It is the proud spirit of citizens, less than the letter of the law, that is their most real safeguard.

A Grammar of Politics, 1925, pp. 103–4.

My own years of residence in the United States have convinced me that there is a real value in Bills of Rights which it is both easy, and mistaken, to under-estimate. Granted that the people are educated to the appreciation of their purpose, they serve to draw attention, as attention needs to be drawn, to the fact that vigilance is essential in the realm of what Cromwell called fundamentals. Bills of Rights are, quite undoubtedly, a check upon possible excess in the government of the day. They warn us that certain popular powers have had to be fought for, and may have to be fought for again. The solemnity they embody serves to set the people on their guard. It acts as a rallying-point in the state for all who care deeply for the ideals of freedom. I believe, for instance, that the existence of the First Amendment has drawn innumerable American citizens to defend freedom of speech who have no atom of sympathy with the purposes for which it is used. A Bill of Rights, so to say, canonizes the safeguards of freedom; and, thereby, it persuades men to worship at the altar who might not otherwise note its existence.

All this, I think, is true; but it does not for a moment imply that a Bill of Rights is an automatic guarantee of liberty. For the relationship of legislation to its substance has to be measured by the judiciary. Its members, after all, are human beings, likely, as the rest of us, to be swept off their feet by gusts of popular passion ...

The fact is that any Bill of Rights depends for its efficacy on the determination of the people that it shall be maintained. It is just as strong, and no more, as the popular will to freedom.

Liberty in the Modern State, 1937, p. 76.

> **120 A 1960s FABIAN PAMPHLET BY ANTHONY LESTER INITIATES THE DEBATE ON A UK BILL OF RIGHTS, 1968**

When democracy degenerates into populism it becomes a weapon of arbitrary power against individuals and minorities, the 'tyranny of the majority' about which John Stuart Mill gave his celebrated warning...

I realise, of course, that much social and economic legislation which we most cherish would have been regarded by Mill (at least when he wrote *On Liberty*) as a tyrannical invasion by Government, in the name of a majority, of the liberty of the individual. To that extent Mill's warning lacks force today; to that extent and no further; for democratic Socialists are especially vulnerable to the populist fallacy in an age of mass communications and opinion polls. Fortunately, political democracy has only occasionally been corrupted into the tyranny of the majority in modern Britain. But the danger is sufficient to justify serious consideration of possible safeguards.

It is also important at this time, when major reforms to our representative institutions appear to be imminent, to recognize a further limitation of the democratic process: it is certainly necessary that an institution of Government should be representative in the sense that its governors are freely elected by a majority of their citizens; and it is desirable that citizens should feel that they participate in the process of Government. But neither representation nor participation will prevent the abuse of power or secure redress to the citizen who is harmed by such abuse. The democratic method 'is that institutional arrangement for arriving at political decisions in which individuals acquire the power to decide by means of a competitive struggle for the people's vote' (J. A. Schumpeter). It decides who will govern, but it does not automatically guarantee that the governors will respect individual rights and interests ...

There is no reason why a Government which is accountable to the popular will, or expeditious in despatching its business, should inevitably also be fair to the individual citizen. . .

The safeguards of individual freedom have failed in Britain at the moment[s] when they were most needed. And they will fail again whenever it appears more prudent to our Parliamentarians to defer to than to resist powerful, popular prejudices. Mass media and the continual polling of public opinion have reinforced the pressures of social conformity and collective intolerance. During some future period of social tension the sacrifice by Parliament to populism might be the freedom of speech of an unpopular political group; perhaps instead an increase in violent crimes might stimulate widespread support for the removal of restraints on police powers, or a relaxation of the procedural guarantees for the fair trial of the accused, or more primitive punishments for the convicted. It is in such periods of crisis that Parliament is insufficiently protected from the people, and the people from Parliament ...

A Bill of Rights could make an important contribution to the protection of individual rights in Britain (including Northern Ireland) against abuse by the Legislature, the Executive, and Local Government. It would direct attention more insistently and systematically than at present to issues of principle involving the individual and the State. Those who would reject such a proposal out-of-hand might reflect that in few of the examples of abuse to which I have referred were the issues of principle widely under-stood at the time, and in no case could the abuse be challenged as a matter of right.

Parliament is, of course, capable of curing all these abuses by specific legislative reforms. To its credit, the present [Wilson] Government has a better record than its predecessors in increasing individual liberty, for example, by creating the Law Commission to promote law reform, by outlawing racial discrimination by Government and public bodies, by sup-porting the abolition of the Lord Chamberlain's functions of theatre censorship, by liberalising the grant of bail to persons accused of minor crimes, by introducing immigration appeals machinery and by permitting individuals to complain to the European Commission for Human Rights of alleged violations of the European Human Rights Convention by the British Government. But the process is slow and haphazard; it depends on a rare combination of liberalism, courage and political ingenuity in an individ-ual Minister; and, if it eventually produces reforming legislation, it does nothing for the citizen who has already suffered from past abuse; nor does it provide any safeguard against the consequences of a fit of legislative panic or folly on some future August afternoon.

A Bill of Rights would put a fence about the traditional liberties of the individual ... There is nothing uniquely socialist about proposals for restraining arbitrary or unfair State power and promoting individual justice; concern with these issues derives from a humanitarian tradition many centuries older than socialism, and indeed, there are some who described themselves as socialists, even in this country, who would regard such restraints as contrary to their fantasies of State power limited only by its mystical identity with the general will.

Their brand of authoritarianism is propagated by conservative enemies as essential to socialism. It is therefore important for democratic socialists to affirm their commitment to individual rights and liberties, without ambiguity.

Democratic socialism can contribute to the humanitarian tradition through the active use of State power to curb abuses of collective power and strengthen individual rights, and by defining those rights in socialist terms – not only the traditional right to freedom of speech, belief, assembly, personal liberty and due process of law, but also the right to civilized standards of employment, housing, and education, social security, privacy, and leisure.

Democracy and Individual Rights, Fabian Tract 390, 1969.

---

121   TOM SARGANT, FORMER SECRETARY OF JUSTICE, STRESSES THE NEED TO INSTIL HUMAN RIGHTS ETHICS WITHIN SOCIETY, 1968

However efficient the safeguards may be, the only real guarantee of human rights lies in the hearts and minds of those who are called upon to wield power at various levels and in various departments of life. In other words, human rights are a religious problem as well as a constitutional problem. We have to learn how to exercise power over each other and to be willing to submit not only to external disciplines but to standards and codes of behaviour which are as compelling as the external disciplines. This is what I mean by saying that the problem of human rights is basically a religious problem. For the right exercise of power involves some kind of training – the constant instilling of ethical concepts – and the recognition that any power that we are privileged to wield over our fellows does not come to us as of right – to do with it as we think fit – but as a sacred trusteeship for which we have to answer to a power higher than ourselves.

Speech in Bangalore, quoted in Sir N. Anderson, *Liberty, Law and Justice*, 1978, at p. 56.

122   LORD SCARMAN DRAWS NATIONAL ATTENTION TO THE ISSUE OF A UK BILL OF RIGHTS, 1974

When times are normal and fear is not stalking the land, English law sturdily protects the freedom of the individual and respects human personality. But when times are abnormally alive with fear and prejudice, the common law is at a disadvantage: it cannot resist the will, however frightened and prejudiced it may be, of Parliament … It is the helplessness of the law in face of the legislative sovereignty of Parliament which makes it difficult for the legal system to accommodate the concept of fundamental and inviolable human rights. Means therefore have to be found whereby (1) there is incorporated into English law a declaration of such rights, (2) these rights are protected against all encroachment, including the power of the state, even when that power is exerted by a representative legislative institution such as Parliament…

The legal system now ensures that the law of the land will itself meet the exacting standards of human rights declared by international instruments, to which the United Kingdom is a party, as inviolable. This calls for entrenched or fundamental laws protected by a Bill of Rights – a constitutional law which it is the duty of the courts to protect even against the power of Parliament. In other words, there must be a constitutional restraint placed upon the legislative power which is designed to protect the individual citizen from instant legislation, conceived in fear or prejudice and enacted in breach of human rights…

The common law system is part of our constitution: a new settlement is needed, which will retain its strengths, while eradicating its features of weakness and obsolescence. In times past the strength of the common law was its universality together with its origin in a customary law which owed nothing to the legislative activity of Parliament; indeed, it preceded it. This strength, when ranged alongside the power of Parliament, gave it victory over the King in the seventeenth century and led to the constitutional settlement of 1688–1689. But the true victor in that settlement was Parliament, whose sovereignty then began. Today, however, it is Parliament's sovereign power, more often than not exercised at the will of an executive sustained by an impregnable majority, that has brought about the modern imbalance in the legal system. The common law is no longer the strong, independent ally, but the servant of Parliament. This, perhaps, did not matter quite so much so long as the constitution of Parliament itself contained effective restraints upon the will of a bare majority in one House. The Parliament Act 1911 was, no doubt, a valuable democratic reform: but it did remove from our constitution an important check on legislative power and introduce an imbalance at its very centre – an imbalance which, if no redressing factor be found or devised, could well prove to be the precursor of further freedoms from restraint to be enjoyed by a bare majority in the Commons. I suggest that the less internal control Parliament is prepared to accept the greater the need for a constitutional settlement protecting entrenched provisions in the field of fundamental human rights, and the universality of the rule of law.

English Law – The New Dimension, Hamlyn Lectures, 1974, pp. 15, 20, 74–5.

---

123   THE SOCIETY OF CONSERVATIVE LAWYERS ADVOCATES A NEW ADMINISTRATIVE COURT AND STATUTORY INCORPORATION OF THE EUROPEAN CONVENTION OF HUMAN RIGHTS WITH OVERRIDING EFFECT, 1976

There is a widespread and growing concern that private rights, hitherto regarded as fundamental to the liberty of the individual in a free society, have in recent years been progressively eroded. Of this we have no doubt. That this concern is well founded we are equally in no doubt; nor do we doubt that the process of erosion is accelerating. It is from this concern that the growing desire for entrenchment of these fundamental rights in a new Bill of Rights arises. The basic question, therefore, is whether such a Bill can provide the requisite safeguards and if not, whether there is a more effective alternative ...

We believe that there is already a very wide-spread demand for greater protection of the citizen against abuse of bureaucratic power and – as a corollary – for greater control over administrative actions. We believe that the underlying concern is sufficiently deep to ensure such support for effective means of investigation and recompense that, once such machinery had been established, it would be extremely difficult for any government to undermine its efficacy.

In this context we include in the term bureaucracy not only civil servants and local government officials, but also the administrative staffs of government agencies (including that of the National Health Service) and the nationalised industries ...

Even at this late stage in the history of our administrative law we are entirely satisfied that the bringing together of all the various administrative jurisdictions of the higher courts into a single division of the High Court cannot fail of itself to bring simplification and greater coherence. That will not only be to the advantage of practitioners, but will enhance both public confidence in the ability of the courts to exercise effective control over administrative acts, and public respect for the rule of law. We believe this to be the pre-requisite to a more satisfactory state of affairs whether or not we ultimately embark upon a new Bill of Rights.

If anything, we regard the early establishment of an Administrative Court as even more essential if at some time in the future a Bill of Rights is to be adopted, for we think it of particular importance that the establishment of this court should precede the passing of such a Bill. We take this view because of the very great importance which we attach to any such Bill being seen to be effective from the outset. We are convinced that the existence of a court already operating in this specialised field could make a vital contribution to the achievement of this important objective.

We also propose that the European Convention of Human Rights should be given statutory force as overriding domestic law where the two codes conflict.

In making this recommendation, however, we envisage the statutory recognition of administrative law as a specific branch of our law as in a sense a parallel to the gradual development of equity in the seventeenth and eighteenth centuries. In other words, we would hope to see the judges of the Administrative Court positively seeking to develop a coherent body of law to protect the fundamental rights of the citizen in recognition of the increasing power and pervasiveness of the State. Just as equity – at its best – sought to give equitable relief where none was provided by an over-rigid common law, so we would hope that the Administrative Court would seek to give equitable relief where the operation of the administrative machine results in oppression.

Another Bill of Rights?, 1976, pp. 8, 15, 18.

---

124 LORD HAILSHAM ATTACKS THE UK POLITICAL SYSTEM AS AN ELECTIVE DICTATORSHIP AND CALLS FOR A NEW CONSTITUTION WITH AN ENTRENCHED BILL OF RIGHTS, 1976

I think the time has come to take stock and to recognise how far this nation, supposedly dedicated to freedom under law, has moved towards a totalitarianism which can only be altered by a systematic and radical overhaul of our constitution ...

The sovereignty of Parliament has increasingly become, in practice, the sovereignty of the Commons, and the sovereignty of the Commons has increasingly become the sovereignty of the government, which, in addition to its influence in Parliament, controls the party whips, the party machine and the civil service. This means that what has always been an elective dictatorship in theory, but one in which the component parts operated in practice to control one another, has become a machine in which one of those parts has come to exercise a predominant influence over the rest. ...

The revolt against elective dictatorship has taken the form of demands for a Bill of Rights, electoral reform, or, less often, the reform of the Second Chamber. The case for each of these is that it has become urgently necessary in the interest of liberty and the rule of law either to curb the legal powers of Parliament, or to recreate a system of checks and balances within it.

The advocates of a Bill of Rights are for limiting the powers [of Parliament]. They argue, correctly, that every other civilised nation has imposed some limits upon its legislature, and has laws which make changes in the Constitution either difficult or impossible. In such cases the judges, or some special constitutional Court, can strike down legislation which exceeds the bounds. But how can these limitations be made effective? Under our present arrangements, Parliament could always take away what it has given, by amending or repealing the Bill. To this the advocates of the Bill always reply that Governments would be restrained by public opinion from doing that sort of thing. I am afraid that I regard that view as extremely naïve. I fully accept that a Bill of Rights might, in some cases, prevent interference with individual rights by some oversight in an ill-drafted Act of Parliament. But I do not accept that a party government of either colour would hesitate for a moment, with its main programme bills, to insert when it wished to do so, the necessary exempting words: 'Notwithstanding anything in the Bill of Rights or any other rule of law or statute to the contrary'. I could almost compose the Ministerial speech, of course of the most soothing and conciliatory kind, which would accompany such a section. Surely if it is to be worth the paper it is written on, a Bill of Rights must be part of a written constitution in which the powers of the legislature are limited and subject to review by the courts. Otherwise it will prove to be a pure exercise in public relations. . .

I have reached the conclusion that our constitution is wearing out. Its central defects are gradually coming to outweigh its merits, and its central defects consist in the absolute powers we confer on our sovereign body, and the concentration of those powers in an executive government formed out of one party which may not fairly represent the popular will. . .

I envisage nothing less than a written constitution for the United Kingdom, and by that I mean one which limits the powers of Parliament and provides a means of enforcing these limitations either by political or legal means. . .

I would myself visualise a Parliament divided into two Chambers, each elected. The one, the Commons, would, as now, determine the political colour of the executive Government and retain control of finance. Preferably, in my view, it would be elected as now by single member constituencies. The other, you might call it a senate, but I would prefer the old name, would, like the Senate of the United States, be elected to represent whole regions, and unlike that Senate, would be chosen by some system of proportional representation.

The powers of Parliament, so formed, would be limited both by law, and a system of checks and balances. Regions would have devolved assemblies, and the respective spheres of influence of these and of Parliament would be defined by law and policed by the ordinary Courts. There would be a Bill of Rights, equally entrenched, containing as a minimum the rights defined by the European convention to which we are already parties, and which can already be enforced against us by an international body. Thus, Scotland, Wales and Northern Ireland would all obtain self-government in certain fields within the framework of a federal constitution of which the regions of

England would also be separate and equal parts. The interests of regions, minorities and individuals would be safeguarded by law, by the provision of a proportionately elected second Chamber, and by the separate regional assemblies. What we should have achieved is a recognisable version of the Westminster model modified so as to remove its disadvantages, as has already been done in Canada and Australia.

The creation of such a constitution would clearly be a matter of years rather than months and you may well ask how it could be done. Quite obviously, so long as we are content to muddle along in the good old British way, it cannot be done. But my own hunch is that circumstances, in the not too distant future, will force our hand and then we shall not be able to go on muddling along in the good old British way. If and when such a moment arrives, and, if possible, before then, here is my suggestion as to the stages by which we could hope to arrive at our destination. . .

My object is continuity and evolution, not change for its own sake. But my conviction remains that the best way of achieving continuity is by a thorough reconstruction of the fabric of our historic mansion. It is no longer wind or weather proof. Nor are its foundations still secure.

Elective Dictatorship, The Richard Dimbleby Lecture 1976, pp. 1, 8, 12, 14–15, 17.

---

125   A COBDEN TRUST STUDY BY PROFESSORS PETER WALLINGTON AND JEREMY McBRIDE SEES A BILL OF RIGHTS AS HELPING FILL THE GAPS IN SOCIETY'S AND THE GOVERNMENT'S CAPACITY FOR TOLERANCE, 1976

The main argument for a Bill of Rights rests on an assessment of the present state of civil liberties in Britain. Although in practice we enjoy a remarkable level of tolerance (at least by the standards of other countries) of individual behaviour, there are serious gaps, and the tolerance itself is fragile. Respect for individual liberties often seems to stop short at members of unpopular minority groups, and hostility and prejudice over immigration have fostered a climate where it is difficult, even if the effort is made, to ensure that elementary considerations of humanity extend to the procedures for deciding applications to enter the country. Tolerance is also fragile because it is not always protected by law. Civil liberties frequently have a precarious legal status in that they exist only so long as the law happens not to trample on them, and they have no autonomous legal muscle to assert against whatever other, and more authoritarian, pressures may happen to intervene . . . So long as there is a reasonable level of tolerance of diversity, individualism and dissent, the absence of legal safeguards may not be important. But when tolerance weakens in practice, the legal protection is not always there to fall back on. A Bill of Rights would set the minimum standards, and give the individual the legal backing to hold his corner in times of stress.

Just as freedom may be legally fragile, so too it is socially vulnerable. It is a truism that it is easy to accept dissent and unorthodoxy when the underlying fabric of society is reasonably homogeneous, and people are reasonably satisfied with standards of living. It takes more courage when the tensions are greater, and diversity, disagreement or even the wrong coloured skin comes to be seen as threatening. Every extra worker in the dole queue is a threat to liberty; so is every homeless family, every well publicised incident that can be presented as undermining the national economy, and every act of political terrorism ...

It is not only the U.K. Parliament that needs to be considered here. If the Government's proposals for devolution are duly enacted, there would be, in the eyes of many, a much greater danger that the Socttish Assembly would fall into the hands of an extreme group of one kind or another, and would be far more likely to yield to the temptation to override the liberties of opposing or minority groups. This view is presented as an argument for a Bill of Rights to be written into the devolution arrangements to limit the powers of the Assembly ... So the first argument is that a Bill of Rights would impose impartial standards, upheld by the judges, to fill the gaps in society's or the Government's capacity for tolerance. ...

To those who believe that the pressure towards a more authoritarian climate is apparent in the United Kingdom, even a relatively low standard of safeguards may be valuable as a potential check on the downward slide, and perhaps even in the longer term an instrument to reverse the slide. This point apart, however, the important question is not just the fact of minimum standards but what those minimum standards are. The extent to which liberty is guaranteed by a Bill of Rights may be less in some areas than the extent to which it is now protected by law, or respected in fact. In such cases the Bill's value would be as a fall-back; it would have no immediate impact, and might encourage a rather cynical response. In other areas the impact might be more immediate. So much depends on the content of the Bill – both its general tenor and the actual provisions in each field.

The other main advantage of a Bill of Rights which spells out the extent to which everyone is entitled to certain fundamental rights is its educative potential. It is a source of information and understanding about the concept of freedom, and a gathering together in accessible form of the major rights each individual has. Although most people in this country may claim to know their rights, relatively few actually do, and there is little emphasis within the educational system on the concept of liberty, the duties that one person's liberty imposes on others, or the machinery for the protection of liberty. In the U.S., by contrast, civil liberties are widely taught and studied, and there is probably much greater understanding of the rights protected by the Constitution than there is of equivalent legal rules here. Education, and public appreciation and awareness, can be a great asset to the fight for liberty.

Civil Liberties and a Bill of Rights, 1976, pp. 22–5.

---

126   THE STANDING ADVISORY COMMISSION ON
HUMAN RIGHTS IN NORTHERN IRELAND REPORTS
ON THE NEED FOR BETTER PROTECTION BY LAW OF
INDIVIDUAL RIGHTS AND FREEDOMS, 1977

The general arguments were correctly identified in our Discussion Paper as follows:

● 'On the one hand it may be argued that:

(1) It is complacent to assume that there is no need for new legal safeguards in Northern Ireland or indeed elsewhere in the United Kingdom. The existing legislative and common law safeguards against abuse of power are less comprehensive and effective than in many advanced democratic countries. For example:

   (*a*) there are inadequate constitutional guarantees against the abuse of power by the government or Parliament;

   (*b*) there is no modern and coherent system of administrative law enabling the citizen to obtain prompt, speedy and adequate legal redress for the misuse of administrative powers by public authorities;

   (*c*) there are important gaps in our legal system where basic rights and freedoms (*e.g.* in relation to freedom of expression conscience and association, respect for privacy and family life, or the right to a fair and public hearing in the determination of civil rights or criminal charges) are not adequately guaranteed;

   (*d*) the need for greater protection is especially important in relation to the increased powers and responsibilities of regional and local government and private institutions whose activities affect the basic rights and freedoms of the citizen; and

   (*e*) the absence of a Bill of Rights enforceable by the courts against the misuse of public powers may have contributed to the present situation in Northern Ireland.

(2) A Bill of Rights would remove certain fundamental values out of the reach of temporary political majorities, governments and officials and into the realm of legal principles by the courts. This would not be undemocratic because the exercise of political power in a, democracy should not be beyond criticism or restraint.

(3) A Bill of Rights would be especially important in the context of the devolution of the present powers of Central Government in maintaining a national framework of law and order, and guaranteeing the basic rights of citizens throughout United Kingdom.

(4) A Bill of Rights would encourage a more actively and socially responsive judicial role in protecting basic rights and freedoms; it would alter the method of judicial law-making, so as to enable the courts to recognise the fundamental importance of certain values and the relationship between them.

(5) The European Convention contains a minimum Bill of Rights for Council of Europe countries and is also being used as a source of guidance about common standards within the European Community in relation to human rights questions arising under the EEC Treaty. The enactment of a Bill of Rights in this country would enable the United Kingdom to be manifestly in conformity with its international obligations and would also enable the citizen to obtain redress from United Kingdom courts without needing, except in the last resort, to have recourse to the European Commission in Strasbourg.

(6) A Bill of Rights would not necessarily hamper strong, effective and democratic government because it could recognise that interference with certain rights would be justifiable if they were necessary in a democratic society, for example, in the interests of national security, public safety or the economic well-being of the country, for the prevention of disorder or crime, for the protection of health or morals, or for the protection of the rights and freedoms of others.

(7) The generality of a Bill of Rights makes it possible for the interpretation of such a document to evolve in accordance with changing social values and needs. This process of giving fresh meaning to basic human rights – and the obligations which flow from them – from generation to generation is valuable for its own sake, as a means of educating public opinion, and as a rallying point in the State for all who care deeply for the ideals of freedom.

(8) A Bill of Rights would not be a substitute for more specific statutory safeguards against specific abuses (*e.g.* anti-discrimination legislation or the Parliamentary Commissioner for Administration). It would supplement and strengthen those safeguards where they were incomplete.

(9) Although it would be difficult and perhaps divisive to envisage introducing a wholly new and comprehensive Bill of Rights except as part of a widely supported major constitutional settlement, this does not rule out more limited guarantees (*e.g.* on the lines of the European Convention); nor would such limited guarantees involve fettering the ultimate sovereignty of Parliament.

- On the other hand it may be argued that:

(1) Because of the general nature of Bills of Rights and the increased powers of judicial law-making which they require, the scope and effect of such documents is uncertain and unpredictable.

(2) A Bill of Rights would create expectations which could not be satisfied in practice. It would be regarded as a panacea for all grievances whereas its real value (if any) would be only a limited one. It would be least effective when it was most needed: *i.e.* to protect fundamental rights and freedoms against powerful currents of intolerance, passion, usurpation and tyranny.

(3) A Bill of Rights might be interpreted by the courts in a manner which would hamper strong, effective or progressive government, and the role of the courts would result in important public issues being discussed and resolved in legal or constitutional terms rather than in moral or political terms. It would risk compromising the necessary independence and imparti-

ality of the judiciary by requiring the judges to work in a more political arena.

(4) Most Bill of Rights stem from a constitutional settlement following revolution, rebellion, liberation or the peaceful attainment of independence. It would be difficult and perhaps divisive to seek to obtain a sufficient degree of political consensus about the nature and scope of a Bill of Rights in present circumstances.

(5) Human Rights are at least as well protected in the United Kingdom as in countries which have Bills of Rights since they are adequately safeguarded by traditional methods, *i.e.* legislative measures to deal with specific problems, combined with the unwritten but effective constitutional conventions; the sense of responsibility and fair dealing in legislators and administrators; the influence of a free press and the force of public opinion; the independence of the judiciary in upholding the rule of law; and free and secret elections.

(6) The United Kingdom differs from many advanced democratic countries in lacking (a) a written constitution, (b) a system of public law, and (c) a codified legal system. A Bill of Rights involves features of all three of these distinctive characteristics of other legal systems. It would therefore represent a fundamental departure from the existing legal tradition.

(7) A Bill of Rights which did not (i) contain a modern definition of the rights and freedoms relevant to the particular circumstances obtaining whether in the United Kingdom in general or in Northern Ireland in particular, (ii) have priority over other laws, (iii) create legally enforceable rights and (iv) apply to violations of human rights by private individuals and organisations as well as by public authorities would not satisfy some prominent supporters of such a measure. On the other hand a Bill of Rights which did have these characteristics would be unlikely to obtain widespread public support.

(8) A Bill of Rights would create wasteful duplication in relation to existing statutory safeguards for human rights and would generate unnecessary litigation.

(9) In Northern Ireland existing safeguards (*e.g.* Part III of the Northern Ireland Constitution Act 1973) have not in practice tended to be relied upon by those alleging that their human rights have been infringed. There is no evidence that this situation would be altered by the introduction of a Bill of Rights'.

6.05 None of the arguments which we have summarised on each side of the question is 'right' or 'wrong'. Some of the arguments on each side are controversial, but there are important points in all of them. However, the unanimous conclusion which we have reached in answer to our first question is that the legal protection of human rights in Northern Ireland should be increased and that one of the ways in which this should be done is by the enactment of an enforceable Bill of Rights. We believe that the most appropriate way of doing this would be to incorporate the European Convention into the domestic legal system of the United Kingdom.

6.06 We would summarise our main reasons for answering the first question in this way by referring to:

(a) the value of ensuring express compliance with the international obligations imposed by the European Convention which are designed to secure to everyone within the United Kingdom the rights and freedoms guaranteed by the Convention and to provide effective remedies for violations of those rights and freedoms by public authorities;

(b) the value of giving explicit and positive recognition in our constitutional and legal system to respect for basic human rights and freedoms;

(c) the need for effective legal safeguards against the misuse of power by public authorities;

(d) the necessity in a genuinely democratic society to ensure that government respect the rights and freedoms of minorities;

(e) the importance of legislating expressly for comprehensive and effective guarantees of human rights which are applicable to the United Kingdom as a whole so that the basic rights of the individual do not depend upon the particular part of the United Kingdom in which the individual was born or lives;

(f) the importance of having general principles or criteria to assist legislators and administrators, as well as judges, in matters concerning human rights;

(g) the need to encourage legislators, administrators and judges to be more systematically and consciously concerned with fundamental values when they perform their public functions (as part of the necessary process of adaptation to the legislative, administrative and judicial techniques of the other member countries of the European Community and of the Council of Europe);

(h) the advantages of a more actively and socially responsive judicial role in settling constitutional disputes and in protecting basic rights and freedoms;

(i) the need to remove the uncertainties about the present status and effect of the European Convention in the law of the United Kingdom;

(j) the benefits of a Bill of Rights as a source of public education about the values of a democratic society.

6.07 The present state of opinion, ... demonstrates wide agreement, both in Northern Ireland and among political groups and independent experts in Great Britain, in favour of modelling a Bill of Rights upon the European Convention rather than attempting to introduce a Bill of Rights which stands free from the Convention. We share this view. We doubt whether a sufficient degree of consensus could be obtained (whether in Northern Ireland alone or in the United Kingdom as a whole) as to the scope and effect of a free-standing Bill of Rights, especially if, as some have argued, such a change were to be made in advance of a new constitutional settlement involving entrenched rights and legal restraints on Parliamentary sovereignty, judicially enforced.

6.08 In our view, some of the arguments against any enforceable Bill of Rights (which we have summarised in paragraph 6.04) would have more force in relation to the introduction of a new free-standing Bill of Rights which was constitutionally entrenched. However, their force would be greatly diminished if the proposal were confined to the incorporation of the European Convention into our legal system. In particular, we consider that:

(1) although incorporation would introduce some uncertainty into our legal system, it would also clarify the present uncertain status of the Convention and provide our courts with the benefit of the guidance of the case law of the Convention organs;

(2) in view of the modest nature of the process of incorporation, it would be unlikely to be widely misconstrued as a panacea for grievances; on the other hand, because more effective domestic remedies would be available, the risks of violations of human rights might be reduced;

(3) anxiety about the manner in which our courts might interpret the Convention would be allayed by the fact that the courts would be obliged to have regard to the Strasbourg case law and that appeals would lie to the Convention organs;

(4) there would be no need to obtain a political consensus about the nature and scope of a Bill of Rights modelled on the Convention itself; the rights and obligations are already defined in the Convention itself; incorporation would create no new rights or obligations but would only give greater effect to existing rights and obligations;

(5) the Convention contains only the minimum international standards of human rights; its incorporation would therefore be no substitute for but rather a reinforcement of our traditional methods (*i.e.* legislative measures to deal with specific problems, combined with the unwritten but effective constitutional conventions; the sense of responsibility and fair dealing in legislators and administrators; the influence of a free press and the force of public opinion; the independence of the judiciary in upholding the rule of law; and free and secret elections);

(6) the incorporation of the Convention would be consistent with the implications of our membership of the European Community;

(7) although incorporation of the Convention would not satisfy some supporters of a Bill of Rights the modest nature of the exercise would make it more widely acceptable (*e.g.*, because it would not create new sources of legal liability for trade unions and other non-governmental organisations nor fetter the sovereignty of Parliament);

(8) incorporation of the Convention would not affect existing statutory safeguards for human rights but would supplement them; the normal risk as to costs and the inherent powers of the courts would discourage unnecessary litigation under the Convention;

(9) there have already been many applications from individuals in

Northern Ireland complaining to the European Commission of violations of the Convention; if the Convention were incorporated there would be more effective domestic remedies which would have to be exhausted before recourse to Strasbourg; given adequate legal assistance and enforcement machinery, it is therefore likely that greater use would be made of the Convention than has been the case as regards existing legal safeguards.

6.09 In view of the prominence which has been given to this matter during the public debate about the Bill of Rights issue, we should emphasise that, in our view, the incorporation of the European Convention into our law would not require a new constitutional settlement, entrenching the Convention rights and freedoms against the possibility of change by Parliament and thereby fettering the sovereignty of Parliament. We note that the other States parties to the Convention have not found it necessary to give such overriding priority to the Convention when making its provisions part of their domestic law. In our view, it would be sufficient to give the same priority to the Convention under our law as has been given to Community law ... The fact that the Convention would remain binding in international law upon future United Kingdom Governments would no doubt in practice inhibit Parliament from exercising its sovereignty in a manner which would violate the Convention; but we do not consider that a major constitutional departure should be undertaken by seeking to deprive Parliament of the power to act in breach of international law if it were minded to do so. Nor, in our view, would it be necessary to seek to entrench the Convention against the possibility of change by Parliament in order to persuade our courts to give sufficient priority and importance to the Convention in their work. Provided that the incorporating statute were to contain sufficient guidance (similar to that contained in the European Communities Act 1972 in relation to Community law) we believe that our courts would give proper weight to the Convention and to the evolving body of case law on the international plane. The Convention, like any Bill of Rights, would be no substitute for the vital role of democratic institutions in protecting human rights. Parliament must necessarily remain at the centre of our constitutional arrangements for redressing grievances by making specific changes in the law and calling the responsible bodies to account. However, there are clear limits to the reliance which can be placed on the operation of the democratic process in individual cases. Human rights cannot always be protected by the parliamentary process and unfortunately cases may occur of the misuse of power by central or devolved government or other public authorities.

6.10 The second question – whether any changes should be confined to Northern Ireland alone or should apply to the United Kingdom as a whole – was referred to in Part III of our Discussion Paper, where we gave the following brief summary of the arguments on each side:

'On the one hand it may be argued in favour of a measure limited to Northern Ireland that:

(1) Northern Ireland has special problems which call for special solutions, including special kinds of rights and exceptions. It

would not be practicable to devise a United Kingdom measure capable of being applied to present circumstances to Northern Ireland.

(2) By well-established custom and convention both before and since Direct Rule the Westminster Parliament has not normally applied human rights legislation (on such matters as race relations, equal pay and sex discrimination) directly to Northern Ireland. A Northern Ireland Bill of Rights would therefore be in accordance with past practice.

(3) Whereas there appears to be widespread support in Northern Ireland for a Bill of Rights, support seems at present to be less widespread at this stage in the rest of the United Kingdom.

(4) To await the introduction of a United Kingdom Bill would involve unnecessary delay for Northern Ireland.

On the other hand it may be argued in favour of a United Kingdom measure that:

(1) It would be impracticable to introduce a Bill of Rights exclusively in Northern Ireland where fundamental rights and freedoms have been under the greatest strain and where it would be difficult, if not impossible, at this stage to obtain a sufficient degree of consensus about the nature and scope of the rights guaranteed and the means by which they would be enforced.

(2) The majority of political opinion in Northern Ireland appears to favour a United Kingdom measure using the European Convention as a guide for a Bill of Rights.

(3) It is extremely unusual to introduce constitutional guarantees of fundamental rights in only one part of a country's territory. It would be especially unusual to incorporate the European Convention into only part of the legal system of a contracting State.

(4) A measure for the whole of the United Kingdom would underline the common character of the rights of all its citizens; on the other hand, an exclusively Northern Ireland measure would lack the moral and legal force of wider measures applied to the United Kingdom and compatible with the international obligations applicable to the member countries of the European Community and the Council of Europe.'

6.11 We have no doubt that the measure incorporating the European Convention into domestic law should apply to the United Kingdom as a whole rather than to Northern Ireland alone ...

The Protection of Human Rights by Law in Northern Ireland. Cmnd. 7009, 1977.

127   THE BRITISH INSTITUTE OF HUMAN RIGHTS PUTS THE CASE FOR A BILL OF RIGHTS BASED ON THE PRINCIPLES OF THE EUROPEAN CONVENTION ON HUMAN RIGHTS, 1977

MEMORANDUM SUBMITTED BY THE BRITISH INSTITUTE OF
HUMAN RIGHTS TO THE SELECT COMMITTEE OF THE HOUSE OF
LORDS ON A BILL OF RIGHTS

Introduction

The British Institute of Human Rights is a charitable body whose objects include public education and research in the field of human rights. The annex to this memorandum contains a list of the present officers and Governors. This memorandum has been prepared at the Institute's request by a working group consisting of The Rt. Hon. Sir Leslie Scarman, O.B.E.; Mr James Fawcett, Chairman of the Institute and President of the European Commission of Human Rights; Mr Anthony Lester, Q.C., formerly Special Adviser to the Home Secretary; Mr Anthony McNulty, C.B.E., Director of the Institute and formerly Secretary of the European Commission of Human Rights; and Mr Paul Sieghart, a Governor of the Institute.

On 3 February 1977 the House of Lords ordered that Lord Wade's Bill of Rights Bill should be read a second time but that the Bill should not proceed further until a Select Committee had reported on the question whether a Bill of Rights would be desirable and, if so, what form it should take. The Select Committee was accordingly appointed to report on these important questions. The object of Lord Wade's Bill is to incorporate into the domestic law of the United Kingdom the 'human rights and fundamental freedoms' which are guaranteed by the European Convention on Human Rights and those of its Protocols by which the United Kingdom is bound ('the Convention').

The Select Committee will presumably therefore wish to concentrate on examining the implications of the Convention if it were to become part of the law of the United Kingdom and be administered by our courts. In our view, there are compelling reasons for focussing the inquiry upon the Convention in preference to other international instruments, or to a free-standing Bill of Rights specially drafted for this country. We would summarise these reasons as follows:

(i)   the Convention has been in force for almost a quarter of a century and contains standards of human rights which have been freely accepted by all member States of the Council of Europe;

(ii)   the United Kingdom, in common with all the other Contracting States, has a clear obligation under international law to ensure that its domestic law conforms with the Convention, and to provide effective remedies in this country to everyone whose Convention rights and freedoms have been violated;

(iii)   individual complainants have a right of access to the institutions set up by the Convention (a right which is not available against this country under any other international instrument);

(iv)   there is a considerable body of existing case law on the interpretation and application of the Convention by the European Commission of Human Rights and the European Court of Human Rights;

(v)   the majority of the States parties to the Convention have already incorporated its rights and freedoms into their domestic laws, and case law is also being established on a national level in those States;

(vi)   the proposal to incorporate the Convention into United Kingdom law raises in a specific, limited and developed form the demand for an enforceable Bill of Rights, and an examination of this proposal illustrates the general issues involved with greater clarity than vaguer proposals;

(vii)   the great majority of those who support the introduction of an enforceable Bill of Rights in this country base their proposals upon the incorporation of the Convention into United Kingdom law;

(viii)   important legislation of this kind depends for its success upon the existence of a sufficient degree of political consensus about its desirability; the present state of opinion among the main political parties and other bodies and individuals in this country indicates that such a consensus would now be much more likely to be obtained for the incorporation of the Convention than for more radical and far-reaching constitutional proposals;

(ix)   in view of the novelty of an enforceable Bill of Rights for the United Kingdom, the existence of a considerable body of case law on the Convention would provide guidance to Parliament, the Executive and the Judiciary as to proper methods of interpreting and applying the provisions of a Bill of Rights in the form of the Convention;

(x)   to the extent that there was dissatisfaction with the interpretation and application of the Convention in the United Kingdom, aggrieved individuals would remain able to seek redress from the institutions established by the Convention;

(xi)   to the extent that the scope of the Convention is incomplete (in particular in comparison with the scope of the International Covenant on Civil and Political Rights) there are moves within the Council of Europe to bring the Convention into line with the International Covenant on Civil and Political Rights and so remove sources of potential conflict created by the coexistence of the two instruments;

(xii)   the valuable Discussion Document on Legislation on Human Rights which was published by the Government in June 1976 concentrated in detail upon the possible incorporation of the Convention.

It was for these reasons that the British Institute of Human Rights convened a symposium of experts from this country, North America and Europe in June 1976 to explore some of the issues and problems relating to the incorporation of the Convention into United Kingdom law. The report of the proceedings of that symposium has already been submitted to the Select Committee and should be regarded, together with the present memorandum, as constituting the Institute's written evidence. The central conclusion which was reached in that report was that incorporation of the Convention would be feasible if it was thought desirable.

The remainder of this memorandum has been prepared in response to the three questions asked by the Select Committee in their Special Report, to which we now turn.

Question (1): In what respects is the United Kingdom at present thought to be defective in the protection of human rights?

The purpose of this question appears to be to identify specific gaps in the existing protection of human rights afforded by law and practice in this country. It would no doubt be possible to a limited extent, to identify such gaps by measuring existing protection against the yardstick of the Convention. In a sense a gap is exposed whenever a complaint is made against the United Kingdom to the European Commission of Human Rights for which there is no effective domestic remedy under United Kingdom law. For example, there were no effective domestic remedies for the following complaints of violations of the Convention:

   (a) the allegation that the exclusion of citizens of the United Kingdom and Colonies of Asian descent seeking entry to this country from East Africa was based on their colour or ethnic origins and was therefore inherently degrading in violation of Article 3, in violation of the right to respect of family life guaranteed by Article 8, and discriminatory contrary to Article 14 of the Convention;

   (b) the allegation that the granting of an injunction to restrain the *Sunday Times* newspaper from publishing articles about the Thalidomide controversy in contempt of court was in violation of freedom of expression under Article 11;

   (c) the allegation that the denial to a prisoner of access to a lawyer was in violation of his right to respect for correspondence under Article 8 and of his right of access to the courts in determination of his civil rights under Article 6;

   (d) the allegation that judicial birching in the Isle of Man constituted degrading punishment contrary to Article 3.

It would also be possible to identify other gaps in existing protection which have not so far been the subject of complaint to the European Commission of Human Rights. The example often cited is the absence of a general right of privacy matching the right conferred by Article 8 of the Convention.

However, in our view, it would be misconceived to attempt to draw up a catalogue of specific gaps in the existing protection of human rights in this country for the purpose of determining whether an enforceable Bill of Rights would be desirable and, if so, what form it should take. In theory, if such gaps were identified, they could be filled by appropriate legislative or administrative changes without the need to incorporate the Convention into our legal system. But the case for incorporating the Convention does not depend upon the recital of a catalogue of specific gaps: the real gap is wider and more profound.

The United Kingdom is alone amongst the nineteen member States of the Council of Europe, and different from the United States and many Commonwealth countries, in having no enforceable Bill of Rights protecting fundamental human rights and freedoms against violation by public authorities. We are also in a minority within the Council of Europe in not permitting individuals to complain to our domestic courts of violations of the Convention. Unlike most member States of the Council of Europe, we also lack a coherent system of administrative law applied by specialised tribunals or courts, with its own appropriate remedies. But, above all, we lack any kind of model, or framework, in our legal system to tell us what 'human rights and fundamental freedoms' actually are. Where opinions differ about them, one must look at a State Treaty, not at one of our own statutes, to resolve the dispute.

The protection of human rights in the U.K. by Parliament, the Executive and the courts has been a justifiable source of national pride. But the absence of an enforceable Bill of Rights weakens the effectiveness of that protection. What are called 'human rights' are those rights and freedoms which are today generally regarded as fundamental to a genuinely democratic society. The Council of Europe took the first steps of defining certain of those basic political and civil rights and freedoms, because the countries of free Europe determined that they were worthy of special priority and protection. But within our present constitutional and legal system they have no special priority or protection; they are not even anywhere expressly stated, let alone defined. For example, the right to freedom of expression is nowhere declared to be a positive right, nor is explicitly declared to have a high value within our legal system. In the U.K., freedom of expression merely means that area of expression which is not restricted by the law of defamation, sedition, obscenity, official secrets, contempt of court, and so on. In short, our human rights and fundamental freedoms are negatively inferred, rather than positively declared and protected.

The protection of human rights in this country therefore: depends mainly upon the conscience and moral character of our legislators, administrators and judges, our press and broadcasting services, the state of public opinion, and the ability of the people periodically to change the government through free and secret elections. In practice, these will always remain the most important sources of protection, and without them no charter of rights has real meaning. But although they are necessary sources of protection, they are not sufficient especially in our increasingly complex, technological and bureaucratic society. The principal gap in our system is the absence of an enforceable Bill of Rights itself.

The Convention is important on the international plane; but in its present unincorporated state it counts for less within our legal system than the narrowest and most obscure statutory instrument. The rights and freedoms declared and recognised by the Convention have not been withdrawn from the vicissitudes of political controversy, to be enforced by an independent and impartial tribunal. It is therefore not surprising that the provisions of the Convention are treated with relatively little importance by legislators, administrators, judges, or ordinary members of the public.

It is rare, for example, for a legislative or administrative measure to be publicly scrutinised for its conformity with the rights and freedoms declared in the Convention. In the absence of Parliamentary guidance, the courts' references to the provisions of the Convention are uncertain and inconsistent. And the Convention is of only marginal importance as a source of public education about human rights.

The judges are in a peculiarly invidious position. Since human rights are not even listed or declared within our constitutional and legal system, the judiciary cannot fairly be criticised for failing to have sufficient regard to human rights when interpreting statutes or developing the common law. Their role in the field of human rights has traditionally been narrowly circumscribed, and most judges are so far unaccustomed to the judicial process which is commonplace in most other democratic societies where the courts seek to maintain a deliberate balance between different and competing rights and freedoms. Those judges who now venture into the human rights field unguided by a statutory compass risk criticism for inventing the relevant standards, values and priorities for themselves, and for thereby usurping their legislative functions.

In short, there is no charter of fundamental rights to influence our system of government with its values and to encourage our governors to be consciously and systematically concerned with the protection of human rights. The prevailing tendency is to regard Parliament as the exclusive protector of our rights and liberties. Unless Parliament has legislated in a particular field there is often a vacuum. And the judicial approach to statutory interpretation is textual and literal rather than based on general principles. There is heavy reliance on detailed and subordinate legislation, and on administrative discretion, and little reliance upon judicial review and constitutional evolution.

In our view, it is unhealthy for fundamental human rights to count for so little in a constitutional and legal sense, and for the protection of human rights to be unaided by the powerful statutory support which would be provided by the enactment of an enforceable Bill of Rights. The disadvantages of the absence of adequate statutory protection can be illustrated by a great variety of examples, general and particular. The tragic case of Northern Ireland is the most extreme example of the consequences of an excessive reliance upon the democratic process to protect human rights and freedoms. But the most typical examples arise from the careless delegation of administrative powers immune from legal challenge, and the inability of judges and administrators to obtain Parliamentary guidance about the relevance of human rights in performing their interpretative roles.

The absence of a statute incorporating the Convention has other adverse consequences. Victims of violations of the Convention are denied effective remedies in our courts and are compelled to seek recourse, if at all, to the European Commission of Human Rights at Strasbourg. The present unincorporated status of the Convention sometimes makes it extremely difficult for them to know whether there is an effective domestic remedy which must first be exhausted before applying to the Commission. The international machinery for the protection of human rights was intended to be the ultimate remedy, but in the case of the United Kingdom it has in many cases become a tribunal of first rather than last resort. Such a situation is neither fair to individual victims who are deprived of speedy and effective remedies in local courts, nor is it in the best interests of the United Kingdom Government which is compelled to defend its laws and practices on the international plane without benefit of any decision on the matter in dispute by its own courts. It also means that there is no contribution from the United Kingdom courts to the interpretation of the Convention by the European institutions.

Within the wider context of the Council of Europe, it is undesirable that the extent of the protection of the rights and freedoms of the Convention should vary so markedly from country to country. Moreover, the interpretation of the Convention by its institutions is evolutionary. The Convention is regarded as a living instrument whose scope and effect call for fresh elucidation according to changing values, needs and practices within Europe. This necessarily means that new decisions by the Convention institutions may reveal new gaps in the protection given to the Convention rights and freedoms in the United Kingdom. If the Convention were part of our legal system, there would be no hiatus when gaps were revealed. Our courts would have regard to the evolving case law of the Convention institutions. However, if the Convention continues to have no direct effect within our legal system, each new gap will have to be filled by legislative or administrative changes. Such a process is cumbersome and slow.

Question (2): In what respects is the enactment of a Bill of Rights thought to be a more satisfactory way of overcoming these defects than the piece-meal reform of the various areas of law concerned?

The enactment of a Bill of Rights and piece-meal reform should not be regarded as mutually exclusive alternatives; they are inter-dependent. None of the many countries which possesses an enforceable Bill of Rights regards such an instrument as a substitute for piece-meal reform. All such countries necessarily supplement the Bill of Rights with detailed legislative and administrative measures for the protection of human rights in particular fields. The guarantee of non-discrimination is accompanied by measures to combat particular types of discrimination; the guarantee of liberty and security of person is reinforced by laws defining the proper limits of judicial and police powers; the right to respect for family life is translated into family and matrimonial laws; and so on.

It is therefore no part of the case for an enforceable Bill of Rights that such a measure would diminish, still less replace, the central role of Parliament in creating new rights and remedies. A Bill of Rights would strengthen the legislative function by encouraging Parliament to be more consciously and systematically concerned with human rights, and by encouraging administrators and judges to have greater regard for human rights in performing their functions. The existence of a Bill of Rights would also provide broad guarantees in areas not covered by the existing statute law and common law. To the extent that Parliament were to intervene in areas covered by a Bill of Rights, to that extent the Bill of Rights could act as a framework only. But to the extent that gaps would remain in the scope of protection afforded by the existing legal system, those gaps would be filled by the Bill of Rights.

In the absence of an enforceable Bill of Rights, there are certain inherent disadvantages in an exclusive reliance upon piece-meal reform. Some of these have been referred to in response to question (i): the lack of sufficient definition of fundamental human rights and the consequences for the legislative, administrative and judicial functions, and for public education about human rights; the absence of effective domestic remedies for some violations of the Convention; the gaps likely to be created by the evolving case law of the Convention institutions; and the divergence between the protection given to individuals in the United Kingdom and in other member countries of the Council of Europe. None of these disadvantages could be satisfactorily avoided by an exclusive reliance upon piece-meal reform, even if Parliament and the Executive were ready, willing and able to remedy defects in the protection of human rights speedily and effectively.

There are further reasons why exclusive reliance upon piece-meal reform is unsatisfactory. The very fact that it is piece-meal means that the protection of human rights lacks an overall coherence within a properly defined Parliamentary framework. Moreover, although Parliament is able in theory to provide effective protection against future violations of human rights, it does not usually provide effective remedies for violations which occur before it has intervened. The victim of a violation of the Convention will normally obtain no redress from legislation passed to remove the possibility of further such violations in the future.

There are wider constitutional and political reasons why exclusive reliance upon piece-meal reform is unsatisfactory. They can be illustrated in the context of the devolution of legislative power to regional Assemblies. If the proposals contained in the Scotland and Wales Bill were enacted by Parliament, the new Scottish Assembly (like the former Parliament of Northern Ireland) would be empowered to enact legislation within any devolved field. But the United Kingdom Government would inevitably remain internationally responsible for violations of the Convention by the Scottish Assembly. For example, in the unlikely event that the Scottish Assembly were to introduce a form of judicial birching which was in violation of the protection against degrading punishment in Article 3 of the Convention, the United Kingdom Government would be under an international obligation to nullify the effect of the offending Scottish statute. In theory it could do so by promoting piece-meal reform overriding the Scottish legislation. But reliance upon executive or legislative action would be likely to provoke serious political friction between Scottish Assembly, and either Central Government or the Westminster Parliament. Central Government would therefore be faced with a painful dilemma. Non-interference would erode national standards of human rights and would place the United Kingdom in continuing breach of the Convention; on the other hand, legislative or administrative intervention to accomplish the necessary piece-meal reform would risk creating political conflict between Scotland and the United Kingdom.

Such a dilemma would be avoided if the Convention were incorporated into the law of the United Kingdom as a whole, so that its provisions were enforceable in our courts (including, of course, the Scottish courts). Any incompatibility between Scottish Assembly legislation and the rights and freedoms guaranteed by the Convention could then be resolved on the domestic plane (as it is now resolved on the international plane) by the judicial process. Like the courts of those countries which have already incorporated the Convention into their legal systems, our courts would be able to give direct effect to the judgments and decisions of the Convention institutions.

We would therefore emphasise the value of a Bill of Rights modelled upon the Convention in helping to create and preserve a *national* framework of standards of human rights. The dangers of exclusive reliance upon piece-meal reform by means of the political process are all too vividly illustrated, in the context of devolution, by the history of Northern Ireland since 1920.

Question (3): What steps might be taken to protect a Bill of Rights, if enacted, from the encroachments of future Parliaments?

The United Kingdom is bound in international law to secure to everyone within its jurisdiction the rights and freedoms defined in the Convention. Parliament of course retains its absolute sovereign right to enact any legislation, no matter how incompatible it might be with the international guarantees of human rights. But in practice the absolute sovereignty of Parliament is tempered by the realities of our membership of the international community, and of organisations such as the Council of Europe. If the European Court of Human Rights were to decide that a particular measure was incompatible with the Convention, it is highly improbable that any future Government or Parliament would deliberately decide to flout the judgment of the Court. To do so would be to risk not only international opprobrium but also our continued membership of the Council of Europe.

If a Bill of Rights were enacted to incorporate the Convention into United Kingdom law, the constraints of international law would in our view be a sufficient disincentive to deliberate encroachments by future Parliaments, and so make it unnecessary to seek to fetter the sovereign right of future Parliaments to violate the Convention if they should choose to do so. In any case, deliberate Parliamentary encroachment on a Bill of Rights, once enacted, would entail a nation-wide political debate.

It would only be possible to abridge the sovereignty of Parliament by means of a complete new constitutional settlement. No change of this kind would be required by incorporating the Convention; indeed, it is significant that no such change has been regarded as necessary by those member countries which have already incorporated the Convention into their domestic law. Different considerations would arise if a Bill of Rights were to be introduced in this country as part of a major constitutional resettlement defining in permanent and written form the respective competences of the different branches of government. However, the present proposal for a Bill of Rights incorporating the Convention is in no way dependent upon such wider constitutional changes, and should not be confused with them.

Although it would be unnecessary to seek to fetter Parliamentary sovereignty in the process of incorporating the Convention, it would be necessary to provide adequate statutory guidance as to the relationship which the Convention would have with our other laws, and as to the proper approach to the interpretation and application of its provisions. In particular, the incorporating statute would need to make clear (*a*) that in the absence of express statutory words to the contrary, all existing and future legislation should be interpreted and applied so as to be in conformity with the Convention, and (*b*) that our courts should have regard to the judgments and decisions of the European Court of Human Rights and the European Commission of Human Rights. In other words, the incorporating statute would give a similar effect to the Convention (as interpreted and applied by the Convention institutions) as Parliament has already given to European Community law by means of the European Communities Act 1972. This is the essential minimum in order to ensure that the rights and freedoms of the Convention would not be overlooked by Parliament, the Executive and the Judiciary, and that they would be interpreted and applied in accordance with the jurisprudence of the Convention institutions. It might also be desirable to include a provision similar to section 2(2) of the European Communities Act enabling the rights and freedoms contained in the Convention to be implemented in United Kingdom law by subordinate legislation.

From Report of the Select Committee on a Bill of Rights, HL [1977–8] 81,
pp. 117–23.

---

128   J. A. G. GRIFFITH'S VIEW THAT LAW IS NO SUBSTITUTE FOR THE POLITICAL CONTROL OF GOVERNMENT, 1978

The proposals for a written constitution, for a Bill of Rights, for a House of Lords with greater powers to restrain governmental legislation, for regional assemblies, for a supreme court to monitor all these proposals, are attempts to write laws so as to prevent Her Majesty's Government from exercising powers which hitherto that Government has exercised.

The fundamental political objection is this: that law is not and cannot be a substitute for politics. This is a hard truth, perhaps an unpleasant truth. For centuries political philosophers have sought that society in which government is by laws and not by men. It is an unattainable ideal. Written constitutions do not achieve it. Nor do Bills of Rights or any other devices. They merely pass political decisions out of the hands of politicians and into the hands of judges or other persons. To require a supreme court to make certain kinds of political decisions does not make those decisions any less political.

I believe firmly that political decisions should be taken by politicians. In a society like ours this means by people who are removable. It is an obvious corollary of this that the responsibility and accountability of our rulers should be real and not fictitious. And of course our existing institutions, especially the House of Commons, need strengthening. And we need to force governments out of secrecy and into the open. So also the freedom of the Press should be enlarged by the amendment of laws which restrict discussion. Governments are too easily able to act in an authoritarian manner. But the remedies are political. It is not by attempting to restrict the legal powers of government that we shall defeat authoritarianism. It is by insisting on open government.

That is why these present proposals by Lord Hailsham, Lord Scarman and others are not only mistaken but positively dangerous. They seem to indicate a way by which potential tyranny can be defeated by the intervention of the law and the invention of institutional devices. There is no such way. Only political control, politically exercised, can supply the remedy.

'The Political Constitution', *Modern Law Review*, 1979, p. 17.

129   LORD DENNING ON THE MISUSE OF POWER, 1980

In a civilised society there should be a system of checks and balances – to restrain the abuse of power. It is why in times past we stood firm against the oppression of King John, and set store by our Magna Carta. It is why we rebelled against the divine right of kings and enacted our Bill of Rights. It is why we resist today the conferring of absolute power on any person or body, or any section of the community. There is, as far as I know, only one restraint on which we can rely. It is the restraint afforded by the law . . .

The Judges for nearly 300 years now have been absolutely independent – not only of government and of ministers, but also of trade unions, of the press, and of the media. They will not be diverted from their duty by any extraneous influences; not by hope of reward nor by the fear of penalities; not by flattering praise nor by indignant reproach. It is the sure knowledge of this that gives the people their confidence in the Judges . . .

The longer I am in the law – and the more statutes I have to interpret – the more I think the Judges here ought to have a power of judicial review of legislation similar to that in the United States: whereby the Judges can set aside statutes which are contrary to our unwritten Constitution – in that they are repugnant to reason or to fundamentals ...

Every judge on his appointment discards all politics and all prejudices. You need have no fear. The Judges of England have always in the past – and always will – be vigilant in guarding our freedoms. Someone must be trusted. Let it be the Judges.

Lord Denning, *Misuse of Power*, 1980 Dimbleby Lecture, pp. 6, 12, 19.

> ### 130   JOSEPH JACONELLI ARGUES THAT THE HUMAN RIGHTS PRINCIPLES OF THE EUROPEAN CONVENTION ARE ILL-SUITED TO SERVE AS THE TEXT OF A UK BILL OF RIGHTS, 1980

It is submitted that ... the text of the European Convention is ill suited to serving as a Bill of Rights for the United Kingdom. It will be useful to list the objections one by one, since there is little common ground between most of them.

(1) Some of the rights guaranteed – for example, Article 4(1), 'No one shall be held in slavery or servitude', and Article 12, 'Men and women of marriageable age have the right to marry and to found a family, according to the national laws governing the exercise of this right' – seem very strange in a British social setting. At any rate, they would not seem to fall within the category of human rights which are most at risk in the United Kingdom of today.

(2) Article 12 suffers from the additional defect that it seems to impose no limit on the scope of any law which might be introduced to qualify the general right to marry. Much the same objection is made to some national constitutional provisions, for example Article 40(5) of the Irish Constitution 1937:

> The dwelling of every citizen is inviolable and shall not be forcibly entered save in accordance with law.

(3) The last objection could be subsumed under a general criticism, that many provisions of the Convention appear to mark no advance at all on the present state of English law. Article 5(2) gives the person who has been arrested the right to be informed promptly 'of the reasons for his arrest and of any charge against him'. What does that add to the general principles laid down in the leading case of *Christie* v. *Leachinsky* ([1947] A.C. 573)?

Again, we have seen how – contrary to the orthodox view of international law – the guarantes of parental rights in education and of free elections by secret ballot, etc., as assured by Articles 2 and 3 of the First Protocol, would amount to nothing in the absence of detailed supplementary measures. In which case, why not proceed directly to the enactment of such measures and omit the legally superfluous exhortation to action on the part of the legislature?

(4) According to Article 2(1),

Everyone's right to life shall be protected by law. No one shall be deprived of his life intentionally save in the execution of a sentence of a court following his conviction of a crime for which this penalty is provided by law.

The first sentence marks out no additional protection to that already afforded by our municipal law. The concluding words of the second sentence would seem to allow the infliction of the death penalty, consistently with the Convention, as punishment for any crime whatsoever. Quite apart from these specific objections, it is quite clear that Article 2(1) does not regard capital punishment as an abridgement of the right to life. This might be welcomed as tending to greater clarity. But a Bill of Rights which takes clear-cut decisions on the controversial issues of the day – in this case, capital punishment – is to be avoided as likely to alienate those members of the population who take the opposite point of view on the same issue.

(5) Of course few, if any, rights can be absolutely guaranteed; they must be subject to qualifications. However, the number and nature of the typical qualifications contained in the European Convention might well drain the guaranteed rights of nearly all their content. Consider, for example, Article 10(2) which qualifies the right to freedom of expression, and the interpretation which might be put by the English courts on such countervailing considerations as 'national security', 'public safety', the 'prevention of disorder or crime', the 'protection of health or morals', and 'the protection of the reputation or rights of others'.

(6) It is possible to envisage Article 8 posing considerable dangers to the freedom of the press. Paradoxically, Article 8 extends too far and yet not far enough. It does not provide a comprehensive protection of the right of privacy, yet it exposes the media to the possibility of actions for breach of statutory duty for invasion of this general right. Moreover, the defences provided in Article 8(2) fall well below the standards of clarity to be found in the Privacy Bills presented at various times to Parliament [The texts of these Bills are conveniently collected in Appendix F of the Younger Report on Privacy (Cmnd. 5012)]

(7) The European Convention was drawn up against the Western European background of legislative drafting, in a style which is much looser than that of the British parliamentary draftsman. Plunged into a British context, the Convention may well attract maxims of construction which presuppose the domestic statutes' standards of exactitude. For example, Article 7 places a general prohibition on retrospective criminal legislation. It would be easy to imagine an English court applying the principle, *expression unius exclusio alterius*, and thereby holding permissible retrospective legislation of any other kind.

(8) There is no equivalent in the European Convention to the Ninth Amendment to the U.S. Constitution:

The enumeration in the Constitution, of certain rights shall not be construed to deny or disparage others retained by the people.

This type of provision holds out a convenient avenue for the introduction into a Bill of Rights of new freedoms and rights. In *Griswold* v. *Connecticut* (381 U.S. 479 (1965)), the Ninth Amendment was used by three members of the U.S. Supreme Court in holding that there was a constitutionally protected right of privacy. Learned authority was cited for the proposition that the Ninth Amendment was introduced in order to prevent 'any perverse or ingenious misapplication' of the *expressio unius exclusio alterius* maxim.

To turn to the European Convention, one of two courses might seem advisable. In order to resist the temptation to treat the British statute as a comprehensive code of human rights, it should be made clear in the text of the Act that it aims at the domestic implementation of the European Convention *and nothing more*. Alternatively, some equivalent to the Ninth Amendment should be added to the statutory reproduction of the Convention. This short addition could well be justified in order to prevent any tendency to regard the European Convention/Bill of Rights as a maximum, rather than as a minimum, standard of protection of human rights.

(9) The First and Fourth Protocols apart, the substantive guarantees in the Convention end with Article 18 (the rest of the Convention being procedural in character). It is necessary, however, to emphasise the importance of Article 60:

Nothing in this Convention shall be construed as limiting or derogating from any of the human rights and fundamental freedoms which may be ensured under the laws of any High Contracting Party or under any other agreement to which it is a Party.

If this Article or an equivalent provision were omitted from the British statute, then Article 17 of the Convention might well impose greater restrictions than does present English law on the activities of extremist political groups. These groups might well recall the reliance placed on Article 17 by the Commission in rejecting the complaint of the dissolved German Communist Party (Application No. 250/57).

(10) Any British government intent on any extraordinary legislative programme might consider too restricting the circumstances in which it might derogate from the standards of the Bill of Rights – in 'time of war or other public emergency threatening the life of the nation' (Article 15(1)). Apart from the present circumstances in Northern Ireland, it seems that only a declaration of war would permit the removal of the restrictions of the Bill of Rights. . .

In both national and international publications, commentators have bemoaned the fact that the European Convention does not protect such-and-such a right of freedom. It would be pointless to produce a list of these suggested additions to the terms of the Convention. Any Bill of Rights will be vulnerable to such charges. In the above ten criticisms every attempt has been made to avoid that kind of objection. It has been our contention, rather, that these criticisms go to the very fabric of the Convention, and that the fabric cannot be repaired here or there without throwing the whole text of a British Bill of Rights into the melting-pot.

Enacting a Bill of Rights, 1980, pp. 277–81.

---

131   GEOFFREY RIPPON QC, THE CONSERVATIVE FORMER MINISTER WHO NEGOTIATED THE UK'S MEMBERSHIP OF THE EUROPEAN COMMUNITY IN 1972, PUBLICLY BACKS A BILL OF RIGHTS AND CALLS ON THE THATCHER GOVERNMENT TO HONOUR ITS UNDERTAKING TO HOLD ALL-PARTY TALKS, 1981

Letter to The Times

From Mr Geoffrey Rippon, QC, MP for Hexham (Conservative)
Sir, The time has come for Parliament to reassert its traditional function as the protector of the rights of individuals against the arbitrary acts of the Executive. Increasingly, we have exchanged the protection of the rule of law – the guarantee of individual rights under the law by independent courts – for a complex system of administrative law that is changed from day to day, and even retrospectively, by a Parliament that has become the passive tool of government.

We may increasingly envy the protection given to individual rights by the United States Supreme Court which can override unconstitutional executive action. This is why I welcomed the undertaking in the Conservative Party election manifesto that a Conservative Government would wish to discuss a possible Bill of Rights with all parties. No doubt the drafting of any form of written constitution, particularly one which seeks to entrench its provisions, raises formidable problems. There is, however, one step that can and should be taken immediately to restrain the abuse of power. Twice the Bill of Rights Bill, which is intended to render the provisions of the European Convention for the Protection of Human Rights enforceable in the courts of the United Kingdom, has been promoted in the House of Lords by the Liberal peer, Lord Wade, and carried through all its stages with support from members of all parties.

The Government should respond to the early-day motion signed by over 150 MPs and provide time at an early date for a second reading of this Bill in the House of Commons. All debates on it should take place with the same free vote that the Government advocated in the House of Lords. Such a Bill was recommended by a powerful committee of the Society of Conservative Lawyers in 1976 and approved by a majority in the report from the select committee of the House of Lords, to which it was referred.

On September 3, 1953, Sir Winston Churchill's last administration committed the United Kingdom Government under international law as a high contracting party to the European Convention of Human Rights. We have a treaty obligation to observe the terms of the convention, but that does not make the articles part of our law. Thus our judges cannot look at the convention directly when they have a human rights problem to resolve. In consequence, our citizens are increasingly being forced to seek remedies for what they regard as infringements of their rights by direct representation to the European Court in Strasbourg.

That court, as Lord Scarman has pointed out, is, in present circumstances, unfortunately deprived of 'the wisdom and experience of our judges and the traditions of English law' ...

The Government can hardly ignore the fact that the Lord Chancellor, Lord Hailsham, has long been an advocate of this measure which he has argued 'would prevent encroachment by Parliament upon individual liberties'. These encroachments, as he has observed, are not by any means so infrequent as might be supposed. In the armoury of weapons against what Lord Hailsham has eloquently described as 'elective dictatorship' a Bill of Rights embodying the European Convention would indeed have a valuable, even if subordinate, part to play.

Yours faithfully,
GEOFFREY RIPPON,
House of Commons.
March 24.

The Times, 30 March 1981.

---

132   LORD GIFFORD QC ARGUES FOR A BILL OF RIGHTS AS A FIRST STEP TOWARDS HUMAN RIGHTS REFORM, 1986

At present, even though Britain is a signatory to the European Convention, the British courts may ignore it. So a Bill of Rights needs to be enacted, obliging the courts to recognize and apply the Convention. There are precedents in history for the writing of positive rights into British law: Magna Carta in 1215, the Bill of Rights in 1688. Today, in the face of modern excesses of State power, another great declaration of the rights of the citizen is needed.

At the present time people only have the 'liberty' to do what is not prohibited by any law. Given the multiplicity of crimes, police powers and judge-made laws, this often means that they can do very little. For example, any gathering on the pavement is illegal, however little it inconveniences other pedestrians; for, as a judge put it recently in the case of a street entertainer, 'where stopping on the highway cannot properly be said to be ancillary or part and parcel of one's right to pass and re-pass along the highway, then the obstruction becomes unreasonable, and there is an obstruction contrary to the provisions of [the Highways Act].'

The passing of the Convention into British law would allow fundamental arguments about the ambit of human rights to be raised before judges and juries. In trials involving issues of free speech, such as Official Secrets Act cases, or free assembly, such as the miners' riot trials, the jury would be urged by the defence to accept that the State had violated the human rights of the accused. The 'common law' developed by the judges would be subordinated to the rights guaranteed by the Convention.

There is already a draft of a Bill of Rights before Parliament: the Human Rights and Fundamental Freedoms Bill [*RB NOTE: see Doc. 39C*], introduced in the House of Lords in December 1985, supported by peers of all parties, but denied Government backing. Under it, all previous laws and Acts of Parliament would need to be interpreted so as to conform with the Convention. Later Acts of Parliament would also be subject to the Convention unless Parliament specifically declared that the Convention would not apply.

Many socialists have argued against the incorporation of the Convention into British law, on the grounds that the judges would be sure to interpret it restrictively. To that there are two answers. First, as a matter of principle, it would be ridiculous to proclaim the value of an international statement of fundamental rights – which the Convention provides, even if incompletely – and yet refuse to make it part of one's own law. Second, the existence of such a statement in the law would certainly affect the way in which civil liberty issues were presented in the courts, and in time would affect the decisions of the judges themselves. It would be possible to present arguments about democratic principles, rather than about the meaning of legal rules. With growing awareness and debate by the public about their newly defined rights, the minds of the judges could be educated, and some at least of the arguments would be won by the individual against the State.

But enacting a Bill of Rights should be seen only as a first step. It is not a panacea for the evils of society. Many of the rights in the Convention are subject to exceptions which are expressed in broad terms. Article 8 is a typical example. After declaring that 'everyone has the right to respect for his private and family life, his home and his correspondence', it continues:

> There shall be no interference by a public authority with the exercise of this right except such as is in accordance with the law and is necessary in a democratic society in the interests of national security, public safety or the economic well-being of the country, for the prevention of disorder or crime, for the protection of health or morals, or for the protection of the rights and freedoms of others.

The rights of freedom of speech and freedom of association are qualified in similar language. One can easily foresee how many judges will interpret them.

Accordingly the commitment to human rights must go beyond the enactment of a Bill of Rights. Specific reforms will be needed as well before many of the rights can be universally enjoyed and enforced in reality.

For example, the right to respect for private life, quoted above from Article 8, is clearly not enjoyed by those young men between sixteen and twenty-one who wish to have homosexual relations. Everyone else in their age group can develop their sexuality in free relationships, if and when they chose to do so. But young gay men, if they wish to have sexual relations, must commit a crime. Their future should not have to depend on how judges or juries might interpret Article 8. The law should be specifically amended.

The right to freedom of expression, set out in Article 10, is denied, in an often outrageous way, to government employees who may be driven by their conscience to speak to the Press. Under section 2 of the Official Secrets Act they can be prosecuted and sentenced to two years' imprisonment, even if the leaked information has no security implications. For years governments have promised to repeal section 2 and replace it with a Freedom of Information Act. But the civil service delights in secrecy, and has prevented any change in the law.

As for the right of peaceful assembly, set out in Article 11, it may scarcely survive the Public Order Bill now going through Parliament. For if the police have powers to impose conditions about the size, location and duration of a demonstration, then there is no right to assemble, only a permission to assemble – if the police agree.

The judges, in their decisions during the miners' strike and in other picketing cases, have shown little inclination to restrict the discretionary powers of the police. Here again, specific legislation will be needed.

These are only examples of the problems to be tackled by a government which resolved that human rights must come first. The whole list of necessary reforms would require a book in itself. Not only laws must be changed, but administrative practices and procedures, especially in those departments of government where conservatism and prejudice are most pervasive. The secret service, the armed forces, the immigration service, the prison department, would all need particular attention.

Justice is not only the business of lawyers and courts. The whole of society must be vigilant to ensure that the human rights of all its members are protected by just laws, respected by the agencies of the State, and capable of being enforced by fair and impartial courts. We are far away from that ideal. The powers of those who want to perpetuate injustice are massive but they are not invincible. I have no doubt at all that if a government set its hand to the task of achieving justice, acting on the ideas and proposals in this book, the people of Britain would respond with enthusiasm. For the old promise of Magna Carta is still part of English law, and it needs again to be honoured: 'We will not deny or defer to anyone either justice or right.'

Where's the Justice?, 1986, pp. 115–19.

133   THE SCOTTISH JUDGE LORD McCLUSKEY IN HIS
REITH LECTURES SPEAKS AGAINST THE
ENACTMENT OF A BILL OF RIGHTS, 1986

The essential constitutional difference between our higher judicial system and that of the United States is that American judges are the guardians and interpreters of a written constitution. That constitution, containing the Bill of Rights, has long been regarded as a living source of philosophy and principle. It contains the text of a supreme law which provides the legal warrant for judges to make enduring social and political choices. By contrast, our judges, whatever the social or political implications of their lawmaking, are in no sense the final arbiters of such choices. Whatever law they create is at the immediate disposal of Parliament. The mistakes our judges make are not woven into the fabric of a supreme law beyond the reach of the legislature. The same applies to their achievements. Their finest works are, at least in theory, able to be swept away by a sovereign Parliament. This perception of the theoretical vulnerability both of the law's treasury of individual rights and of our essential constitutional machinery has led some to advocate a new constitutional settlement, designed and constructed to be proof against being dismantled by a temporary elected majority. A vital ingredient of such a settlement would be a statement of selected basic rights. If I am right in believing that such a change would make our judges perform tasks for which they are not equipped, and risk drawing them into the political arena in a way alien to the best traditions of the judiciary, we must before embarking upon it be satisfied that the change is reasonably necessary. As Murphy's law says: 'If a thing ain't broke, don't fix it.'. . .

A Bill of Rights embodies semi-permanent choices between the conflicting interests of citizens. And to present such choices as if they are the gratuitous enlargement of the human rights of all is to misuse language. Rights are not to be regarded as if they were roses without thorns. Any Bill of Rights which guarantees some rights and denies or conspicuously omits others – for example, economic or cultural rights – is entrenching one set of values at the expense of alternative sets of values. If those whose task it was to select the rights to be protected were to be situated behind a veil of ignorance, so that they did not know how the various alternatives would serve or hinder different interests; if, therefore, they had to choose on the basis of timeless principles acceptable to all right-thinking men; if they were clever enough to choose golden words to express those rights, words so pure and unambiguous that no man, no judge, who had to apply them to real life could possibly fail to ensure that the principles they encapsulated would be applied fairly and equally to all men in all circumstances, then no doubt they could fashion an honest charter of enduring freedoms that would do more than just buttress the interests and values of one class and one generation against the interests and values of their successors . . .

A Bill of Rights could serve certain interests and prejudice others. Thus a provision about a right to life would, depending upon how it was phrased by the draftsman and interpreted by the judges, favour one side or the other in the abortion argument. It could hardly avoid doing so. A right of freedom of association is bound to determine or to enable judges to determine, in some degree, and possibly totally, the arguments about the closed shop and collective bargaining. If rights are conferred upon but confined to human persons the results will be entirely different from those which would flow from the conferring of rights upon corporate or legal persons, such as limited companies or trade unions. The essential nature of rights is that they restrict the freedom of those who must respect them. A child's right not to be caned is a restriction upon a teacher's freedom to impose disciplinary sanctions. A worker's right not to join a trade union is a restriction upon the power of his fellow workers to present collectively a monolithic united front to the employer. A right to freedom of speech may be so large, so widely interpreted, that it interferes with the right of accused persons to a fair trial, because it permits the press to publish information which directly or more subtly prejudices the minds of potential jurors or judges. A right to choose freely how one's children are to be educated or one's illnesses are to be treated may confer advantages upon those who can afford to exercise their choice, but leave those who cannot afford to do so with meaningless paper rights. Indeed, the conferring of such rights in relation to education or health care might gravely prejudice the capacity of the community as a whole to allocate and distribute limited educational and health care resources in such a way as to benefit those in need or those who can benefit, rather than those who can pay. The point of offering such examples is not to indicate a preference for or against abortion, the closed shop, private medicine or public schools. The point is that these matters, and countless others, involve political choices. And their character does not alter because they are cast in the noble language of fundamental human rights. . .

In truth, statements of fundamental rights can seldom be enacted with precision. They are full of notions like 'due process' or 'respect for family life' or 'freedom to manifest one's religion'. And the rights are then qualified by equally elastic concepts, like 'reasonable', or 'necessary in a free society' or 'national security'. When rights are created in vague and imprecise terms, their content to be discovered by judges whose choices are not determined by familiar and well understood rules of law, no one really knows, till the courts have decided, what his rights are.

So, unless it can be shown that it is, on balance, necessary to enact a Bill of Rights to enable our citizens to achieve rights not available through the processes of democracy, unless it can be shown that we can agree on the content, and the precise expression, of particular rights, we should be slow to confer upon our judges an unreviewable power to evolve a miscellany of actual rights and restraints whose real content we cannot sensibly predict.

However inconvenient and untidy it is for our judges to have to stand aside and observe European judges, whether in Luxembourg or in Strasbourg, decide human rights and discrimination questions on the basis of materials not available to the domestic courts, that is not an argument for creating the great cloud of uncertainty that a domestic Bill of Rights would bring.

Law, Justice and Democracy, Reith Lectures 1986, 1987, pp. 41, 46–7, 50.

---

134   A CHRISTIAN PERSPECTIVE ON THE LEGAL PROTECTION OF HUMAN RIGHTS FROM A COMMISSION OF THE CHURCHES IN BRITAIN AND IRELAND, 1988

We believe that there would be substantial advantages, and no disadvantages which could not be overcome, for the United Kingdom to enact legislation to make the European Convention part of its ordinary domestic law, and for the Irish Republic to undertake parallel action to the same end.

The arguments ... to which we attach the greatest importance are that:

1. such a step would do much to harmonise the legal protection of human rights in all the parts of the two states and minimise differences between them in matters as fundamental as these
2. it would concentrate the minds of future policy-makers and legislators, and those who advise them, on the continuing need to observe the international obligations to their inhabitants which both states have assumed
3. it would help to remind the populations of both states about the scope and importance of the fundamental values which are shared by all of them and which are reflected in the concept of human rights
4. incorporation does not require anything as revolutionary as the creation of a written constitution for the United Kingdom, or any abridgement of the sovereignty of Parliament, not even to the extent that the European Communities Act 1972 has already done
5. if the ordinary domestic courts in each state were given jurisdiction to interpret and apply the European Convention as part of their own domestic law, taking account of the developing Strasbourg case-law, the inhabitants of both states would be able to obtain redress for any infringements of their human rights at home and would have to seek recourse to Strasbourg only in exceptional cases. . .

We regard this matter as one of the first importance for all the inhabitants of these islands, and especially for those who are members of minority communities, as well as for the governments of both states. We find it a matter for regret that a question as important but as modest as this has been allowed to drag on for so long without any perceptible progress. Clearly such legislation should not be enacted without a substantial degree of political consensus across party boundaries, and we would therefore urge those of the political parties in the two states which have not yet already done so to make every effort to achieve this by appropriate internal and external discussions, and thereafter to move with all due speed towards the enactment of this important legislation.

We observe that the proposal for incorporation has wide support in both communities in Northern Ireland, including the main political parties and the non-governmental organisations concerned with human rights, and in the Churches in Great Britain. [The Roman Catholic bishops of England and Wales supported the idea 'in principle' in November 1985, a majority of the Executive Committee of the British Council of Churches in January 1986.] A public opinion poll a few years ago showed three out of four Protestants in Northern Ireland and over 90 per cent of Catholics in favour of a bill of rights for Northern Ireland as soon as possible: the incorporation of the European Convention would provide citizens with such a bill of rights. . . The Standing Advisory Commission on Human Rights has repeatedly and unanimously advocated this, not as a gimmick for solving the problem of political violence in the Province, but as a measure which would enable aggrieved citizens to secure a more prompt and effective redress than is possible at present. All three options in the report of the New Ireland Forum referred to the need for a bill of rights (paras 5.2(6), 6.2, 7.2, and 8.5), and the Hillsborough Agreement stated that consideration would be given to 'the advantages and disadvantages of a Bill of Rights in some form in Northern Ireland' (Article 5(a)). . .

There may well be domestic civil rights and liberties for the protection of which there is a wide national consensus, but which are not reflected in the international treaties. If that is so, then there is of course no reason why these should not also be added to the national statute books.

S.D. Bailey (ed.), *Human Rights and Responsibilities in Britain and Ireland*, 1988, pp. 38–40, 43.

---

135   THE OXFORD LEGAL PHILOSOPHER RONALD DWORKIN BELIEVES A BILL OF RIGHTS IS NECESSARY TO HELP REDRESS THE DECLINE IN BRITAIN'S CULTURE OF LIBERTY, 1990

Great Britain was once a fortress for freedom. It claimed the great philosophers of liberty – Milton and Locke and Paine and Mill. Its legal tradition is irradiated with liberal ideas: that people accused of crime are presumed to be innocent, that no one owns another's conscience, that a man's home is his castle. But now Britain offers less formal legal protection to central freedoms than most of its neighbours in Europe. I do not mean that it has become a police state, of course. Citizens are free openly to criticise the government, and the government does not kidnap or torture or kill its opponents. But liberty is nevertheless under threat by a notable decline in the *culture* of liberty – the community's shared sense that individual privacy and dignity and freedom of speech and conscience are crucially important and that they are worth considerable sacrifices in official convenience or public expense to protect.

The erosion of liberty is not the doing of only one party or one government. Labour governments in the 1970s compromised the rights of immigrants, tried to stop publication of embarrassing political material, and tolerated an outrageous censorship and intimidation of journalists by the newspaper unions. But most of the worst examples of the attack on liberty have occurred in the last decade, and Margaret Thatcher and her government are more open in their indifference to liberty than their predecessors were ...

Britain stands alone in insisting that Parliament must have absolutely unlimited legal power to do anything it wishes.

British constitutional lawyers once bragged that a constitutional Bill of Rights was unnecessary because in Britain the people can trust the rulers they elect. But now a great many people – more than ever before – believe that this is no longer true, and that the time has come for Britain to join other democracies and put its Parliament under law. . . Would a charter of constitutional rights help to restore the British culture of liberty? Learned Hand, a great American constitutional judge, said that when the spirit of freedom dies in a people, no constitution or Supreme Court can bring it back to life. And it is true that many nations with formal constitutional guarantees, including some of the European nations that have made the European Convention of Human Rights part of their own law, fail fully to honour their constitutional rights in practice. But though a written constitution is certainly not a sufficient condition for liberty to thrive again in Britain, it may well be a necessary one.

A Bill of Rights for Britain, 1990, pp. 1–2, 14.

---

136   FERDINAND MOUNT ARGUES THAT NATIONAL SYSTEMS OF JUSTICE TODAY MUST BE CONSONANT WITH EXTERNAL AND INTERNATIONAL SYSTEMS, 1992

We have seen how English judges, so to speak, 'shadow' the provisions of the Convention – not relying on them to direct their judgments, but taking full account of them and trying as far as possible to establish a kind of consonance between the provisions of the Convention and the law of England.

Thereby the European Convention gains a growing authority and, with it, the findings of the European Court of Human Rights. Not merely are a growing assortment of litigants prepared to take their case to Strasbourg; the British government also finds itself unable to resist the findings of the Court, although Mrs Thatcher and several of her supporters never ceased to be darkly suspicious of it and to regard it as even less of 'a real court' than the European Court of Justice in Luxembourg. When Strasbourg issues a finding which reflects badly on English law or the British government, there is a dignified pause for reflection in London to demonstrate HMG's freedom of action; and then, a little shamefacedly and not without a good deal of grumbling behind the scenes, the finding is complied with. Thus, in a reluctant, informal way, not only the relevance of the Convention but its *superiority* is conceded. To hold fast to the nineteenth-century principles of non-intervention no longer seemed to be a politically stable option, even for the most robustly nationalist British administration since the war.

The consequences of this situation are clear. So long as the Convention is not actually part of our law but remains in this half-in, half-out position, a distant, shadowy but ineluctable authority, the majesty and authority of our own courts will continue to diminish. Judges will be looking, ever more nervously, over their shoulders at this alien code which must be referred to respectfully and accommodated as far as possible but cannot be robustly and openly interpreted, as it could be if it were part of our law.

It used to be said that the Convention could not be fitted in to English law because it was composed of high-sounding, typically Continental declarations of rights, and lacked the superb concreteness and specificity of English common law. Oakeshott wrote as far back as 1948: 'What went abroad as the concrete rights of the Englishman have returned home as the abstract Rights of Man, and they have returned to confound our politics and corrupt our minds.'

But how unbridgeable is this gap between the concrete, inductive Anglo-Saxon and the abstract, deductive Cartesian, between the specific negative prohibition and the general positive right? In practice, English judges seem to move readily enough between the two; a cumulative series of negative prohibitions may in time come to form the outline of a positive right, just as a series of judgments stemming from a positive general right may in time provide a list of specific unlawful actions *à l'anglaise*. Might not the differences and difficulties dwindle with the years, as the law fills out with case law and statute law? It may have been only in the early years of the European Convention's operation that it appeared so foreign, so hopelessly alien to our own conceptions of how the law protects our liberties.

In practice, as we have seen, English judges have turned out to be a good deal more agile than they pretended to be, and they now seem to cope tolerably well with the far more difficult challenge of achieving harmony with a code which is not law, although it is subscribed to by Her Majesty's Government.

The conclusion surely follows that English judges would find their work easier, rather than trickier, if the European Convention were incorporated into English Law. They could then begin to build up a body of case law which would translate these Continental declarations into usable specifics.

The familiar argument that incorporation would diminish the relative importance of English common law seems to me precisely the reverse of the truth. That relative importance is already being overshadowed by European institutions and European law of all types. Paradoxically, only by incorporating the European Convention do we rescue and revitalise the common law tradition – in much the same way as it has been rescued and revitalised in earlier centuries by the incorporation of other great charters into our law. Strasbourg becomes merely a higher court within our own legal system rather than, as at present, an *alternative* source of law which is also a higher one. If this line of argument sounds perverse, we have only to refer back to the rights of appeal from the Scottish High Courts to the House of Lords and from Commonwealth High Courts to the Judicial Committee of the Privy Council. These rights of appeal have not, I think, made those courts seem less Scottish or Australian to their citizens.

But we should not dodge the fact that, if we take the final step of incorporation (or even if we don't and leave the authority of the Convention increasingly to overshadow the authority of the common law), we are still taking a dramatic and memorable step.

Not merely are we acknowledging and signalling an end to the era of non-intervention; we are also retreating from the long-held principle that the administration of law is a strictly national business, indeed, is one of the defining characteristics of the nation. The Queen's writ is no longer to run exclusively unaided or unfortified by external and higher authority, and precisely on those matters which Dicey saw as the prime constituents of the rule of law – freedom of speech and assembly, habeas corpus, due process and so on. It is public opinion which has forced political parties and governments, step by step, to accept this dilution of their power, and public opinion driven, moreover, by nothing more organised than a general sense of what is fair and reasonable (the bodies campaigning for, say, British adherence to the European Convention have remained virtually unknown to the general public). On such matters, it seems, there is some difficulty in persuading public opinion that we are being 'bullied by Strasbourg' or that 'Europe has no right to be judging our domestic concerns'; on the contrary, justice is regarded as so precious that it seems quite reasonable, even to the nationalist tabloids, that people should go abroad in search of it; the quest, in fact, tends to be presented as rather romantic and certainly admirable.

'Constitutionalist' arguments that acceptance of outside intervention in our judicial process undermines our nationhood seem simply puzzling to many people. We are already familiar with international regulatory bodies which enjoy a variety of disciplinary powers, especially sporting bodies, such as the International Olympic Committee, FIFA and the International Cricket Conference. Whatever the substantial differences in law, the European Court of Human Rights would seem in many people's eyes merely one more extension of the right to appeal to higher authority.

A return to hermetically sealed national legal systems looks no longer plausible. By contrast, a revival of the plural, overlapping jurisdictions of the Middle Ages appears to be an accelerating trend – which makes it more rather than less important that national systems of justice should be internally coherent and externally consonant with other systems. To satisfy the unvarying requirements of justice – clarity, predictability, stability – we need, wherever possible, to aim for explicitness and entrenchment, the tools of constitutional recovery. This incoming tide cannot be mopped away; it can be converted into tidal energy for domestic use.

The British Constitution Now, 1992, pp. 230–3.

---

137   THE LAW LORD NICOLAS BROWNE-WILKINSON ON THE NEED TO RAISE JUDICIAL CONSCIOUSNESS OF THE IMPORTANCE OF FUNDAMENTAL RIGHTS, 1992

It has become so fashionable to urge constitutional reform by means of a Bill of Rights or by incorporating the ECHR in domestic law that attention has been diverted from the principles of our indigenous common law. Let me repeat what I have already said: the individual citizen in the United Kingdom is free to do what he or she wishes, unless there is some fetter imposed on that freedom by common law or by statute. It was those very freedoms enjoyed by us over the centuries which were principal sources of the E.C.H.R. itself. How can it be, then, that our own system of law is unable to protect those freedoms which in 1950 this country agreed to abide by in signing the E.C.H.R.? I suggest that the reason is primarily that Parliament has, either directly or (via statutory instruments) indirectly, conferred on the executive very wide powers expressed in general terms, and that the courts, in construing such legislation, have sometimes refused to adopt the same stringent approach as heretofore in defending individual freedoms.

We all know the rules of statutory construction which require penal and taxation provisions to be strictly construed so as to protect the physical liberty and property of the individual. The presumption against confiscatory legislation is equally well established. These are the areas of life in which, over the centuries, individual freedom has been under attack by the state. But although the presumption is well established in those cases, we seem on occasion to have lost sight of the fact that the rules applicable to penal, taxing and confiscatory legislation are only instances of a more general rule. *Maxwell on Statutes* states the following proposition: 'Statutes which encroach on the rights of the subject, whether as regards person or property, are subject to a strict construction in the same way as penal Acts.' (12th edn, 1969, p. 251.). . .

If it were to be held that general statutory powers were presumed not to interfere with human rights unless Parliament expressly or by necessary implication has so authorised, for most practical purposes the common law would provide protection to the individual at least equal to that provided by the ECHR The individual rights protected by the ECHR are for the most part not absolute rights: and many of them are subject to provisos which make them yield to the necessary requirements of good democratic government. In the same way, the courts of this country in construing Acts of Parliament, would not limit general powers so as to exclude interference with individual freedom to the extent that such interference was by necessary implication part of the intention of Parliament.

If such a strict approach to construction were adopted, there would remain the inability of the English courts to strike down an Act of Parliament which in express terms has unjustifiably interfered with individual freedom. But on how many occasions has Parliament in fact done this? I can only think of one or two instances where a statutory enactment has clearly been intended to achieve an impairment of human rights which would conflict with the provisions of the ECHR The main threat to our individual freedom comes not from intentional interference by Parliament, but from the creation of statutory powers expressed in general terms ...

For myself, unless there is some overwhelming policy reason, I would prefer to see the judges reassert their traditional concern to protect individual freedom against unjustified erosion. Even though the ECHR forms no part of our law, it contains a statement of fundamental human rights (accepted by this country) much wider than the freedoms of the person and of property which have, of late, become the only rights afforded special treatment by our courts. We must come to treat these wider freedoms on the same basis and afford to freedom of speech, for example, the same importance as we have afforded to freedom of the person.

There are great advantages in the pragmatic approach by which the courts in this country develop the law on a case by case basis rather than by deduction from principle. But in the field of human rights this approach has great dangers. In a substantial number of human rights cases, the individual alleging infringement of his rights will be unmeritorious or may hold views of which the court disapproves. In such cases, the lack of merits of the complainant may lead the court to erode his fundamental rights. Where the fundamental rights are of a kind deeply embedded in the judicial consciousness – freedom of the person or the sanctity of property rights – the courts have no difficulty in seeing that the importance of the general principle outweighs the demerits of the complainant in the instant case before it. What is required is to raise the judicial consciousness of the importance of the other fundamental rights so that in those cases too the courts will uphold those rights where 'the merits' of the particular case do not encourage such a conclusion. If the ECHR fulfils no other purpose, it has already served and will continue to serve this purpose by bringing home to the judicial mind that there are wider principles, more fundamental than the merits of the particular case, and that ultimately our freedom depends on defending those principles, come what may.

'The Infiltration of a Bill of Rights', *Public Law*, 1992, pp. 404–5, 408–10.

---

138   GEOFFREY ROBERTSON QC POINTS TO THE INADEQUACIES OF EXISTING UK LAW IN PROTECTING THE INDIVIDUAL, 1993

The absence of any written constitutional guarantees of liberty which would empower our courts to correct abuses of power by state agencies, an over-reliance on doctrines about the sovereignty of Parliament and the accountability of ministers, and the reluctance to guarantee to citizens enforceable legal rights have produced a society in which civil liberties are regarded as privileges granted at the discretion of the powerful rather than as rights capable of direct assertion by members of the public. There are gaps in the pieces of common and statute law, precisely because the politicians and judges responsible for producing the jigsaw have no clear idea of the ultimate picture. Amongst the main characteristics of the 'rule of law' in Britain can be included the following:

Discretionary Justice. We repose wide discretions in police and other officials in the hope that they will act fairly. These discretions are not controlled by the law, or by the courts, although they may be informed by 'guidelines' issued by the Home Office or the Attorney-General. 'Guidelines' cover such important matters as the use of informers and secret surveillance devices, the criteria for collection of information on law-abiding citizens, the operation of the security service, the handling of pickets and demonstrators, the censorship of films, the vetting of jurors, the use of CS gas and rubber bullets, and the treatment of immigrants. They do not have the force of law, and there is no sanction for disobedience. As one senior police officer said, when taxed with mounting secret operations in contravention of a Home Office circular, 'there is no reason to respect an obscure piece of paper'. There is no right of peaceful assembly guaranteed by British law – instead, we have a polite letter from the Home Office to chief constables, reminding them to bear such a 'right' in mind when exercising their powers under the 1986 Public Order Act to control meetings and processions. Even the Association of Chief Police Officers has taken to issuing its own secret guidelines, one of which advocates the striking of demonstrators 'in a controlled manner with batons about the arms and legs and torsos' in certain crowd-control situations. In this way, the rule of law is replaced by the rule of thumb, and occasionally the rule of fist.

Nominal Ministerial Control. Many basic decisions about civil liberties are made the responsibility of the Home Secretary rather than the courts. These include such important matters as the power to: issue warrants to tap telephones and burgle homes; detain suspects for up to seven days under the Prevention of Terrorism Act; refer doubtful convictions back to the Court of Appeal; exclude aliens on the ground that their presence is contrary to the national interest; decide how long 'life-sentence' prisoners will serve; grant asylum and carry out deportations. The notion that the Home Secretary makes all these decisions himself, with the care expected of a judge, after weighing the evidence, is the sheerest nonsense. For the most part, he has little time to do more than rubber-stamp the decisions advised by his officials. His 'accountability' to Parliament can be avoided by invoking the rule that no explanation is required where issues of national security are concerned, or because the case is *sub judice*: his decisions about individuals are rarely the subject of full parliamentary debate.

Pervasive Secrecy. Most decisions and many policies which affect civil liberties are made and even implemented in secret. The Official Secrets Act supplemented by the extended common law of confidentiality casts a blanket of secrecy over the operations of the public service. The Public Records Act ensures that work within Whitehall will not see the light of day for at least thirty years, and for much longer if there is any prospect of embarrassing civil servants who are still alive, or casting any light at all on security operations. Unjust practices develop for years unchecked by public outcry; jury vetting had been institutionalized for five years before it was accidentally uncovered, and 'virginity testing' of immigrant wives and X-raying of their children's bone structures went on for some time before these practices were publicized and prohibited. Even when questions were asked in Parliament – as they were about the trade in arms to Iraq – responses were carefully drafted so as to disguise the true picture. The Security Service Act shrouds every activity – lawful or otherwise – of the intelligence services. Freedom of information, now a routine characteristic of most comparable democracies, is firmly resisted.

Variable Local Practices. The extent to which you are allowed to enjoy a particular freedom may depend upon the part of the country in which you happen to reside. Police discretion means that the forty-three different chief constables have different policies on such basic matters as the use of summonses instead of warrants for arrest and imposition of blanket bans on marches under the Public Order Act. While John Alderson, as chief constable of Devon and Cornwall, shredded Special Branch intelligence on CND activists, Phillip Knights, Chief Constable of Birmingham, defended surreptitious surveillance of those who write letters in their local newspaper critical of nuclear weapons. The powers given to local councils over cinemas have led to marked inconsistencies, as controversial films are banned in some localities but not in others. Rates of conviction and sentencing patterns and legal-aid grants differ markedly from one magistrates' court to the next. There are remarkable variations in implementing duties to provide caravan sites for gypsies and facilities for the disabled; some local authorities purport to apply Section 28 by discriminating against homosexuals, while others ignore it.

Limited Powers of Judicial Review. The courts have a narrow role in examining the exercise of discretion by agents of the state. They will seldom upset a decision unless it can be shown to be so irrational that no reasonable official or tribunal could come to the same conclusion, or unless it has been made in 'bad faith' (i.e. corruptly or from some ulterior motive). Courts hardly ever find a police chief's operational decisions to be unreasonable, and are usually reluctant to question the logic of ministerial decisions in immigration cases. They can intervene if the minister has applied the wrong legal test, or acted unfairly by refusing to receive representations, but their 'supervisory role' is limited to ensuring that due process is observed. And when proprieties are not observed, the victim of abuse of power has no claim for compensation or damages. The courts are not permitted to apply directly the principles of the European Convention on Human Rights, or to require ministers to take them into account when making decisions which affect the liberty of the subject.

Sham Protections. Reliance is placed on certain institutions to protect citizens' rights or to check the oppressive use of power. Some of these are little more than confidence tricks. The Press Complaints Commission, for example, merely pretends to combat invasions of privacy by the press: its decisions are neither respected nor obeyed. The Police Complaints Authority has serious defects. Lay justices are meant to scrutinize police applications for search warrants, but rarely do more than rubber-stamp applications, and the Cleveland affair exposed them as unwilling to protect the rights of parents accused of abusing their children. Coroners' courts are expected to resolve the most serious disputes over deaths caused or contributed to by police action: their personnel and procedures are inadequate for uncovering truth or placing blame. The Commission for Racial Equality and the Equal Opportunities Commission lack the powers necessary to uncover and eradicate pervasive but hidden forms of discrimination. The independence of the BBC can be undermined by the Government's power of patronage, as it appoints its supporters both to the boards and to watchdog bodies like the BSC and BCC. The commissioners and tribunals appointed to monitor telephone tapping and MI5 lack the power to make proper investigations and to provide effective remedies.

Parliamentary Sloth. The theory of parliamentary sovereignty assumes that Governments and MPs will act to remedy defects in the laws affecting human rights. The Law Commission drafted a bill in 1979 to reform the law of breach of confidence: had it been enacted, much of the *Spycatcher* confusion would not have occurred. The Law Commission's reports on the need to reform the laws of treason, sedition, blasphemy and criminal libel have similarly been consigned either to the 'too hard' basket or to the waste basket. No action has been taken to implement the Younger Report on privacy, the Faulks Committee or the Neill committee recommendations for reforming the law of libel, the Wilson Committee Report on the Public Records Act, the Williams Committee Report on altering the law of obscenity or the Butler Committee's report urging changes in the law relating to mentally disordered offenders. Parliament has failed to establish, either as an independent body or as a committee of the House, any Human Rights Committee to warn of deficiencies in draft legislation or of laws which are in urgent need of reform. When its existing committees do venture into areas which relate to civil liberties, their performance is unimpressive: they lack investigative resources and skilled counsel, and tend to accept ministerial assurances. Thus the 'Supergun' committee, which held hearing on arms-related trade to Iraq in 1990, was unable to extract even a smattering of the true story which emerged at the Matrix Churchill trial and the ensuing Scott Inquiry.

Vulnerability to Emergency Legislation. Parliament's failure to imple-ment carefully considered recommendations for improving the standards of civil liberties contrasts starkly with its capacity to rush into action to cut down freedoms when Government convenience dictates or where public emotions have been whipped up on the strength of an isolated case. Emergency legislation is generally bad legislation, which has a habit of remaining on the statute books long after the so-called emergency has passed. The Official Secrets Act, the Prevention of Terrorism Act, the Commonwealth Immigration Act and the ban on Sinn Fein broadcasts are leading examples. Back-bench MPs obsessed with getting their names in newspapers in response to moral panics are a particular nuisance for civil liberties. In recent years they have erected a massive censorship apparatus to deal with a handful of 'video nasties', abolished the right to challenge jurors, passed the 'Surrogacy Arrangements Act' and inflicted 'Section 28' after one local council was alleged to have stocked a Danish sex-education book in one of its libraries. In these repressive exercises they have been incited and supported by the popular press, which frequently uses its own freedom to agitate against that of others, especially against the rights of prisoners and mental patients and unpopular minorities (such as blacks, immigrants and homosexuals) as well as against the freedom of speech of its competitors in television. The 1992 War Crimes Act, twice rejected by the House of Lords because of the necessarily unfair trials it envisages, is another example of how heightened emotions can produce laws which lead to injustice.

Lack of Awareness of Rights. There is a remarkable reluctance on the part of officialdom to acknowledge the existence of such rights as can be extracted from statutes and case law. This was epitomized in the parliamen-tary debates over whether a person 'invited' to a police-station interview should be told of his clear statutory entitlement to leave at will unless or until he is arrested. The Government resisted, on the ground that explaining this fundamental liberty to suspects 'would impose an enormous admin-istrative burden on the police'. The same reluctance was apparent throughout the debates on PACE. 'Rights' are too much trouble, and there is always the danger that, if they are publicized, they might be exercised. (For this reason, juries are never told of their 'right' to bring back a verdict according to their consciences.) This is an attitude frequently displayed by officials towards complainants, who are perceived as 'trouble-makers' rather than citizens to be assisted in obtaining their due. It is partly explained, of course, by the lack of any formal constitutional guarantee of basic freedoms. It is difficult to be aware, let alone be proud, of 'rights' which derive from obscure sources – convoluted legal cases and complicated statutes – and which require the assistance of lawyers to extract and to explain. It is, conversely, easy to dress up in the rhetoric of 'rights' initiatives like the 'Citizen's Charter', which encourage public servants to wear name badges and to answer telephones more promptly, but provide no enforce-able guarantees whatever that the answers provided by named bureaucrats will be consistent with fairness and justice.

Vulnerability to Cost-Cutting. One consequence of the lack of public appreciation of civil liberties is that politicians are unable to detect many votes in enhancing them at times of financial stringency. Cutbacks in the health service arouse a public outcry far more vehement than the drastic 1993 cut-backs in legal aid. Lay justices are cheaper than juries, so new penal statutes wherever possible exclude the right to elect for jury trial. Prisoners are treated inhumanely as a result of overcrowded prisons: the solution is to house them in squalid police cells (rather than to devote resources to bail hostels) and to experiment with privatization of prison and custodial services. The opposition to enacting freedom-of-information legislation is based on the expense of answering requests for information. Laws requiring caravan sites for gypsies and provision for the disabled are not enforced because of the expense that compliance would cause. The Asylum Act and Home Office directives are designed to cut costs by reducing the number of fugitives who may fairly claim asylum, irrespective of the strength of their case. The Home Office has for many years resisted demands for an independent tribunal to review doubtful convictions on the grounds that this would be too costly. The *value* of rights is rarely brought into account.

There is no single panacea which will cure all, or even most, of these unattractive features of British law relating to the liberty of the subject. Specific legislative reforms are required in almost every topic treated in this book, and may sooner or later receive piecemeal parliamentary attention. Changes in substantive law (such as the introduction of a Freedom of Information Act) are necessary, but not sufficient: attention must be paid to the procedures and remedies available to correct abuses of power. There is scope for considerable extension of administrative law, by providing the High Court with power to award compensation to victims of maladministration, to require that reasons be given for every decision – whether made by a minister or by a civil-service mandarin – which infringes the liberty of the subject, and in some cases to scrutinize those reasons for justice as well as for due process. But the deepest defects lie in systems and in attitudes, with their pervasive secrecy and their preference for pragmatism over principle. The Government's refusal to make the European Convention of Human Rights part of British law represents both a symptom of the disease and a rejection of the best hope for a cure.

There is a hypocritical aspect to the British Government's refusal to enact a Bill of Rights, namely that we are not prepared to adopt the standards we urge on others. In the days following the Tiananmen Square massacre in 1989, MPs at Westminster insisted that a Bill of Rights should immediately be introduced in Hong Kong, so that its courts could develop a 'human-rights culture' in the colony before its hand-over to the Chinese. As a result, Hong Kong judges (most of them British lawyers) have been developing human-rights law with the help of English Law Lords in the Privy Council, the colony's final court of appeal. The Chinese point out, accurately, that the United Kingdom by this arrangement seeks to impose upon them obligations to respect civil liberties more onerous than obtain in England. The double standard is flagrant, because Britain has bequeathed Bills of Rights to most of those former colonies which retain appeals to the Privy Council, where English Law Lords protect liberties with more force than is allowed them in England. In 1990, for example, the Privy Council struck down a criminal libel law passed by the Antiguan Government and used to prosecute a newspaper editor who exposed that Government's corruption. The Law Lords said that criminal libel was contrary to the guarantee of freedom of expression in the Antiguan Constitution – a decision they could not, sitting as English Law Lords, reach in respect of criminal libel law in England, because we have no similar constitutional guarantee.

Freedom, the Individual and the Law, 7th edn 1993, pp. 502–9.

---

139 THE INSTITUTE FOR PUBLIC POLICY RESEARCH ON A BILL OF RIGHTS AS PART OF THE RULES OF THE POLITICAL GAME WITHIN WHICH DEMOCRACY IS PLAYED, 1993

In our view certain individual rights are also part of the rules of the democratic game. Freedom of expression is one such right. It protects the right to speak one's mind, to persuade others; and it protects the right of others to hear a differing view. It allows individuals to obtain official information and to comment on the record of the government of the day. There is not much point in holding elections if censorship prevents the electors from making a critical judgment of the government. Freedom of speech is therefore part of democracy's structure and not just an optional extra. The fact that in some countries constitutional rights are widely abused and subverted is not an argument against constitutional rights. It is a warning that they require to be guarded jealously even when they are given a special status in law.

Speech-related freedoms are not the only rights fundamental to a democracy. In a democratic society every individual is entitled to equal respect. Everyone should have an equal say in the election of the government and everyone should be protected from arbitrary arrest, expropriation of property without compensation, from cruel and unusual punishment and so forth. Failure to provide such protection may expose individuals to intimidation, harassment, discrimination, degradation or punishment that is inconsistent with the respect democracy requires government to accord each of its citizens.

Some of these rights and freedoms are protected now by statute and by the criminal law. In the past this protection has been judged by governments to be sufficient, and the sophisticated have conforted themselves with the thought that liberty lies in the interstices of the Constitution. We do not regard these protections as adequate now, if they ever were. The abuses of civil liberties in Britain and Northern Ireland are well documented elsewhere, and the United Kingdom's record at the European Court of Human Rights demonstrates that our domestic law and practice do not adequately conform with our international human rights obligations.

It is often argued that it is the legislature's role to protect individual rights and freedoms and that legislation enacting specific rights is preferable to a generally worded Bill of Rights. This argument is mistaken on a number of grounds. First, a Bill of Rights is intended to be open textured so that it can be applied, without amendment, to new issues and problems as they arise. These cannot always be foreseen and may therefore not be covered by earlier legislation, however detailed. Someone whose rights have been infringed should not have to wait until new legislation catches up with changing circumstances. Secondly, a Bill of Rights cannot be dismissed as simply a statement of good intent on the part of the government, because it is enforceable in the courts. As such it acts in a real way to strengthen the position of the individual *vis-à-vis* the State, government and public authorities.

Thirdly, there are occasions on which the legislature is unwilling to protect rights; for example, when panicked by an emergency or motivated by prejudice. Two apt examples are some anti-terrorist and immigration legislation. In such cases, enforcement of a Bill of Rights by the courts holds Parliament to a paramount commitment to protect basic freedoms, and protects minorities against the tyranny of the majority.

A further argument against adopting a Bill of Rights is that it would be no substitute for a comprehensive programme of legislative reform such as the introduction of a Freedom of Information Act, strengthening of statutory equality laws, reform of immigration legislation and the strengthening of statutory rights for suspects. We agree that a Bill of Rights would be no substitute for such a programme and do not propose it as an alternative. Both kinds of change are needed: they are not mutually exclusive.

It is also agreed that the working of the European Convention is, in some respects, unacceptable, allowing wide exceptions to certain rights and excluding others altogether. Our proposal, incorporating provisions from the International Covenant on Civic and Political Rights as well as the European Convention on Human Rights, seeks to overcome this difficulty. It would not only secure compliance with our international obligations but extend the protection which they provide, where necessary. Article 21 will ensure, for the avoidance of doubt, that the exception clauses are interpreted strictly in favour of individuals and minorities, allowing restriction of their rights only in circumstances which make it 'strictly necessary'. The burden of proof will be on the public authority to establish that this is the case. In respect of most of the Articles, exceptions are also limited to those circumstances which make restrictions 'necessary in a democratic society' for particular, limited reasons.

A government Discussion Paper of June 1976 ('Legislation on Human Rights – with Particular Reference to the European Convention. A Discussion Document') [RB NOTE: *The document referred to is set out at length in Doc. 106 above*] identified the following four special consequences of a Bill of Rights which its advocates claim as advantages:

    a.   its provisions, being drafted in general terms, would be open to reinterpretation by future generations in accordance with their needs;

    b.   its special status could mean that it provided an effective and quasi-permanent check on oppressive action by future governments and indeed Parliaments;

    c.   it could be held to ensure conformity with current international obligations which themselves are framed in general and quasi-permanent terms;

    d.   it would help to provide a more systematic concern with fundamental values, and more informed public discussion about them; and would bring about corresponding changes in current methods of making, applying and interpreting the law as a whole.

Fifteen years later, these advantages are more obvious.

The fourth of these arguments, which applies equally to the Constitution as a whole, has received the least attention in the debate, yet it could prove to be highly significant. Recent government restrictions on civil rights and liberties have not been marked by widespread public protest. The public in general is more aware of the importance of maintaining law and order, or national security, than of protecting the sometimes competing requirements of, say, freedom of speech, personal privacy and confidentiality. The Bill of Rights would provide us with a statement of principles, a set of basic values on which there would be a general consensus of support across the political spectrum (even though there would be disagreements about their implementation in practice). Learning about these principles would become part of the school curriculum and adult education, encouraging pupils and students to debate the importance of protecting human rights and the difficulties which arise when they conflict. Such a development would encourage a more informed public, more sensitive to the implications of restricting civil liberties and of extending them.

No one should suppose that the Bill of Rights will give an easy solution to every difficult issue concerning individual rights and the proper extent of collective interests. There will still be many important issues involving aspects of conscience, morality and religious belief that cannot be resolved in a way that will attract unanimous support. The Bill of Rights is no substitute for political decisions taken by the electorate and by Parliament, but it should help to ensure that those decisions do not violate fundamental human rights and freedoms.

Effective protection of human rights requires effective access to justice. The present legal aid scheme enables the very poor to face the risks of expensive litigation, but the great majority of people are unable to do so. In order to ensure that the Bill of Rights is effective we have created a United Kingdom Human Rights Commission to bring proceedings in its own name, assist individual complainants in cases involving alleged breaches of the Bill of Rights, and investigate practices and procedures which appear to be incompatible with it. In our view, the inclusion in the Constitution of measures to improve access to justice in the field of public law, including the creation of a Human Rights Commission, is a necessary condition for an effective Bill of Rights.

Although it would be important to avoid detracting from the Commission's primary law enforcement role, it would also be able to act in an advisory capacity to Parliament in relation to pending legislation and other matters. Much unnecessary litigation could be avoided if Parliament established its own Human Rights Committee to scrutinise proposed domestic (and European) legislation and to examine the effect of existing legislation and policies in the context of the UK's international human rights obligations and its own Bill of Rights. The government's attention could be drawn systematically to the implications of its policies and proposals for individual rights and the necessary adjustments made to avoid later litigation.

The growing importance of European institutions in Britain's political and legal system gives added weight to the case for constitutional protection. The UK is now the only member of the Council of Europe with no written Constitution or enforceable Bill of Rights, our partners in Europe providing remedies for their citizens which are not available to UK citizens through the British courts. Moreover, the Westminster Parliament has accepted, through the Treaty of Rome and Single European Act 1986, the supremacy of European Community law. The British courts have become increasingly accustomed to interpreting domestic law in the light of EC law and, where necessary, overriding the domestic legislation. It is hardly defensible for Parliament to qualify its own sovereignty in commercial and employment matters while refusing to do so in matters such as human rights.

We believe that it is necessary to adopt an alternative constitutional idea, namely that democracy is not the same thing as majority rule and that, to make democracy a reality, fundamental individual rights and the basic structure and rules of government should have legal protection that even a properly elected Parliament cannot change by ordinary legislation. Constitutional government requires that these ground rules be part of the fundamental law, and that judges, who are not elected and who are therefore removed from the pressures of partisan politics, should be responsible for interpreting and enforcing them as they are for all other parts of the legal system.

A Written Constitution for the United Kingdom, 1993, pp. 10–14.

---

140   DAVID FELDMAN, AUTHOR OF A LEADING TEXT ON THE LAW RELATING TO CIVIL LIBERTIES IN THE UK, WRITES OF THE NEED FOR POLITICIANS TO BELIEVE IN INDIVIDUAL RIGHTS, 1993

Examination of the role of the European Court and the European Commission, and sidelong glances at the work of the US Supreme Court and judges elsewhere, show that the enactment of a justiciable and constitutionally entrenched Bill of Rights can be a powerful political and legal weapon in the hands of those who are in danger of having their rights systematically infringed or abrogated. Nevertheless, useful as it may be, such legislation has been seen to be an incomplete answer to the demands of individuals and groups. Bills of Rights are only as extensive as the rights which they identify and protect, and only as powerful as the politicians who draft them and are bound by them and the judges who enforce them wish them to be. Any failure of will on the part of any of these people will leave the citizens unprotected.

The entrenchment of a Bill of Rights, besides being only a partial answer, may not be strictly necessary. Entrenched or not, the values of a Bill of Rights must be imbibed, preferably at an early age, by everyone, and must exercise a practical as well as a symbolic influence over the work of politicians, judges, ombudsmen, and those responsible for internal complaints and review procedures in public agencies. There is evidence from abroad that, if judges have the appropriate determination, they can make something of very unpromising statutory material ...

Other people besides judges must take responsibility for protecting rights, whether under a Bill of Rights or without one. Special parliamentary procedures for scrutinizing legislation, and freedom of information legislation to open up government to the public gaze, will also be important elements in developing the system in a rights-conscious way. Legal approaches to achieving this are increasingly receiving attention, and this encourages the hope that the conditions for the political, as well as legal, protection of rights may be improving. Parliamentarians have a particularly heavy responsibility, because they carry the burden of scrutinizing legislation which, in our system, can so easily violate rights. But the ethos of rights must be accepted more generally. It must influence private or privatized bodies supplying goods and services to the public: gas and electricity supply companies, for example, control people's happiness and their abilities to achieve goals and advance plans at least as effectively as government departments or agencies.

In order to protect rights, politicians must think them important. This is true both of rights which would impose positive obligations on the state, as in the case of social and economic-equality-related rights, and of classical, liberal individualist rights to freedom from state interference. If the political will to respect rights is absent or in abeyance, the rights will not long flourish. This is no less true in democratic countries than others. Indeed, there is a particular danger that governments which are subject to electoral accountability will be too ready to restrict the rights of unpopular groups in order to be seen to be active in relation to some perceived problem which is exercising the electorate ...

The political will is particularly important where, as in the United Kingdom at present, there is no entrenched constitutional protection for rights. Although there are signs of a changing judicial attitude to rights, the English judicial approach has traditionally been one which gave relatively little weight to them, whether in domestic or international law. While this remains the case, the attitudes of politicians and administrators to the protection of rights assume prime importance. As a means of shaping those attitudes consistently with internationally accepted standards, recourse to the European Commission and Court of Human Rights, and other inter-national human rights agencies, is likely to be increasingly important: left to itself, the domestic political process is likely to tend towards devaluing rights and over-emphasizing order . . .

Ordinary citizens too must internalize the values of individual and group rights, because democracy can be reconciled with respect for rights only if the people who participate in political decision-making, however remotely, exercise their powers in the light of people's rights. For this, education is essential, and the state needs to facilitate it by making available the resources and opportunities for all students to receive a grounding in civil liberties and rights and their personal, constitutional, and political import-ance.' Rights which are essential to the democratic process are particularly in need of protection against erosion. . .

However, if liberties are to retain the support of politicians and others, and if rights are to be regarded as politically respectable and morally compelling values, those who claim them must exercise them responsibly. Claims to freedom lie ill in the mouths of those who refuse to formulate or comply with standards protecting people against abuse. To reject account-ability not only undermines the reputation of the people who abuse freedoms, but may also be held to justify curtailing the freedoms them-selves, with a consequential loss to all. This risk seems to be particularly acute in relation to press freedom. . . The desire to exercise freedom unaccompanied by the trammels of self-critical social responsibility is a tendency from which adults, as well as young children, have to be weaned. If those of us who enjoy freedom of the press do not appear to treat it seriously and responsibly, it should come as no surprise if politicians and others regard our actions as devaluing the freedom, and come to consider that it is legitimate to restrict it . . . The representatives of the press undermine the strength of their own case by indulging in a form of brinkmanship with government which makes it look as if they are prepared to put press freedom substantially at risk.

This is a topical example of a responsibility which attaches to all rights. Those who exercise rights enjoy them by the consent of others, and must be careful not to abuse their liberty by using the freedom in ways which deny others their rights or threaten the society by whose authority the rights are granted. Rights will inevitably sometimes conflict, and the bounds of each will have to be established by political or legal decision. At other times it may be permissible to flout other people's rights as part of a campaign of civil disobedience in order to achieve some greater social good. But in all such cases, a liberal citizen will respect freedom, and will permit its restric-tion or infringement only to achieve a goal which can be justified within a framework of liberal theory, and then only to the smallest extent necessary to achieve the goal.

Civil Liberties and Human Rights, 1993, pp. 910–13.

141   SIR JOHN LAWS ON THE IMPERATIVE OF A
HIGHER-ORDER LAW TO PROTECT FUNDAMENTAL
INDIVIDUAL RIGHTS AND FREEDOMS, 1995

The constitution must guarantee by positive law such rights as that of freedom of expression, since otherwise its credentials as a medium of honest rule are fatally undermined. But this requires for its achievement what I may call a higher-order law: a law which cannot be abrogated as other laws can, by the passage of a statute promoted by a government with the necessary majority in Parliament. Otherwise the right is not in the keeping of the constitution at all; it is not a guaranteed right; it exists, in point of law at least, only because the government chooses to let it exist, whereas in truth no such choice should be open to any government.

The democratic credentials of an elected government cannot justify its enjoyment of a right to abolish fundamental freedoms. If its power in the state is in the last resort absolute, such fundamental rights as free expression are only privileges; no less so if the absolute power rests in an elected body. The byword of every tyrant is 'My word is law'; a democratic assembly having sovereign power beyond the reach of curtailment or review may make just such an assertion, and its elective base cannot immunise it from playing the tyrant's role ...

A people's aspiration to democracy and the imperative of individual freedoms go hand in hand. Without democracy the government is by definition autocratic; though it may set just laws in place, and even elaborate a constitution providing for fundamental rights, there is no sanction for their preservation save revolution. While ... I do not think the notion of self-determination is the best model to vindicate the pressing moral claims of democracy so far as they concern the individual voter, nothing could be more elementary than that the power of government, to stay in office and make through Parliament compulsory laws for the obedience of the people, does and must depend utterly on the popular vote. But the sanction of the polling-booth is not merely a voice at the government's shoulder, a telling whisper that if it makes laws which do not more or less appeal to the public it will be thrown from office. It represents the legal and moral fact that the power of rule is bestowed at the people's choice; and it confers on the measures passed by government a crucial moral authority. Since in the last resort the government rules by consent, the source of public power is not the strong arm of the ruler, but the people themselves.

Even so, the fundamental sinews of the constitution, the cornerstones of democracy and of inalienable rights, ought not by law to be in the keeping of the government, because the only means by which these principles may be enshrined in the state is by their possessing a status which no government has the right to destroy ...

It is a condition of democracy's preservation that the power of a democratically elected government – or Parliament – be not absolute. The institution of free and regular elections, like fundamental individual rights, has to be vindicated by a higher-order law: very obviously, no government can tamper with it, if it is to avoid the mantle of tyranny; no government, therefore, must be allowed to do so. . .

The result of the constitutional settlement of the seventeenth century, whatever the logic of the matter, was to establish the supremacy of Parliament over the King; of the Legislature over the Executive. When the government was in the possession of the Monarch personally, the ideal of Parliamentary sovereignty amounted to a claim that the ultimate political power should rest in the hands of the people's elected representatives, not those of an unelected autocrat. But the function of Executive government has passed from the Sovereign to Her ministers, who are members of Parliament; and the very convention that requires command of a majority in the House of Commons as a condition of the right to rule has, in fact though not in name, given back the final power to the Crown, at least for most of the time; though it is exercised not by the Monarch but by others in Her name.

However the same convention means of course that the sovereign power in the state is effectively in the hands of an elected body. Those old battles have long ago been won. They have, however, been won at a certain cost, namely the suppression to a considerable degree of the power of Parliament as a body independent of the Executive. What has in crude terms happened since the seventeenth century is that there has been a trade-off between two ideals: one is the notion that Parliament should be sovereign; the other is that the Executive government should be democratically accountable. It has been done by clothing the Executive, previously autocratic and unaccountable, with the legitimacy of Parliament.

The power which is generally enjoyed by the Executive over the Legislature is so great that it loosens the ties between the people and their rulers. The benign force of democracy is diminished. While it rules, the Executive enjoys great autocratic power which is only indirectly vouchsafed by the elective process. But – and this is the emphasis of my position – even if Parliament enjoyed a true hegemony over the Executive, still its rule should not in the last resort be absolute: still a higher-order law would be needed for the entrenchment of constitutional rights and the protection of democracy itself.

We may now come full circle, and after this long discussion I can identify what seems to me to be the essence of the difference between judicial and elective power. The latter consists in the authority to make decisions of policy within the remit given by the electorate; this is a great power, with which neither the judges nor anyone else have any business to interfere. This is the place held by democracy in our constitution. It is the place of government. Within it, Parliament, even given its present unsatisfactory relationship with the Executive, is truly and totally supreme. It possesses what we may indeed call a political sovereignty. It is a sovereignty which cannot be objected to, save at the price of assaulting democracy itself. But it is not a constitutional sovereignty; it does not have the status of what earlier I called a sovereign text, of the kind found in states with written constitutions. Ultimate sovereignty rests, in every civilised constitution, not with those who wield governmental power, but in the conditions under which they are permitted to do so. The constitution, not the Parliament, is in this sense sovereign. In Britain these conditions should now be recognised as consisting in a framework of fundamental principles which include the imperative of democracy itself and those other rights, prime among them freedom of thought and expression, which cannot be denied save by a plea of guilty to totalitarianism.

'Law and Democracy', *Public Law*, 1995, pp. 84–5, 91–2.

---

142   THE LORD CHIEF JUSTICE, LORD BINGHAM, SPEAKS IN FAVOUR OF HUMAN RIGHTS LEGISLATION AND THE CONSTITUTIONAL ROLE OF UK JUDGES TO DEFEND CITIZENS' RIGHTS AND FREEDOMS, 1993–6

'The European Convention on Human Rights: Time to Incorporate'
(Denning Lecture, Bar Association for Commerce, Finance and
Industry), 1993

The elective dictatorship of the majority means that, by and large, the government of the day can get its way, even if its majority is small. If its programme or its practice involves some derogation from human rights Parliament cannot be relied on to correct this. Nor can the judges. If the derogation springs from a statute, they must faithfully apply the statute. If it is a result of administrative practice, there may well be no basis upon which they can interfere. There is no higher law, no frame of reference, to which they can properly appeal. None of this matters very much if human rights themselves are not thought to matter very much. But if the protection of its citizens' fundamental rights is genuinely seen as an important function of civil society, then it does matter. In saying this I do not suggest – and I must stress this – that the present government or any of its predecessors has acted with wilful or cynical disregard of fundamental human rights … What I do suggest is that a government intent on implementing a programme may overlook the human rights aspects of its policies and that, if a government of more sinister intent were to gain power, we should be defenceless. There would not, certainly, be much the judges could do about it. This would seem regrettable to those who, like me, would see the judges as properly playing an important part in this field.

Two factors give the question a special immediacy. The first of these is the parliamentary timetable. The pressure on parliamentary time is such that measures to remedy violations of human rights will not, in the ordinary way, find a place in the queue. They will not have featured in the party manifesto. They will not win elections. They command no political priority. If anyone doubts this, I would refer to the 38 reports of the Law Commission which currently await implementation. These reports, produced at quite considerable public expense, represent clear, well-argued and compelling proposals for improving the law; only two of the 38 have been specifically rejected by the government of the day; they gather dust not because their value is doubted but because there is inadequate parliamentary time to enact them. So anyone who sees Parliament as a reliable guardian of human rights in practice is, I suggest, guilty of wishful thinking.

The second factor which gives the question a special immediacy is of quite a different nature. It is the increasingly heterogeneous nature of our society and the increasingly assertive stance of minorities. The inhabitants of these islands have never, of course, sprung from a pure common stock: Jutes, Angles, Saxons, Vikings, Normans, Huguenots and Jewish refugees from various parts of Europe are among those who have over the centuries blended with the native Celt and the indigenous Gael. But it is probably true that post-war immigration, particularly from the Indian sub-continent and the West Indies, has made us a more heterogeneous people than we have ever been. And it is surely true that some of these more recent citizens have shown less willingness to be submerged in the prevailing British way of life, and more desire to preserve their own traditions of language, custom and religion, than most of their predecessors have been inclined to do. There is at the same time a general lessening of deference towards authority, a growing unwillingness to accept the say-so of the teacher, the local government officer or the man from the ministry. So it seems reasonable to predict a growing number of cases – not only involving the ethnic minorities, but very often involving some minority – in which prevailing practice, perhaps of very long standing, will be said to infringe the human rights of some smaller group or some individual. As it stands, our courts are not well-fitted to mediate in these situations.

Those who share my view that the situation is unsatisfactory may well ask whether it is nonetheless inevitable, one of those inescapable blemishes which must exist in an imperfect world. I would say not. In the European Convention an instrument lies ready to hand which, if not providing an ideal solution, nonetheless offers a clear improvement on the present position . . .

Since incorporation would seem, at first blush, to be a simple and obvious way not only of honouring the United Kingdom's international obligations but also of giving direct and relatively inexpensive protection to its citizens, one would suppose that very powerful reasons must exist for not taking this step. . .

Constitutional experts point out, first of all, that the unwritten British constitution, unlike virtually every written constitution, has no means of entrenching, that is of giving a higher or trump-like status, to a law of this kind. Therefore, it is said, what one sovereign Parliament enacts another sovereign Parliament may override: thus a government minded to undermine human rights could revoke the incorporation of the Convention and leave the citizen no better off than he is now, and perhaps worse. I would give this argument beta for ingenuity and gamma, or perhaps omega, for political nous. It is true that in theory any Act of Parliament may be repealed. Thus theoretically the legislation extending the vote to the adult population, or giving the vote to women, or allowing married women to own property in their own right, or forbidding cruel and unusual punishment, or safeguarding the independence of the judges, or providing for our adhesion to the European Community, could be revoked at the whim of a temporary parliamentary majority. But absent something approaching a revolution in our society such repeal would be unthinkable. Why? Because whatever their theoretical status constitutional measures of this kind are in practice regarded as enjoying a peculiar sanctity buttressed by overwhelming public support. If incorporated, the Convention would take its place at the head of this favoured list. There is a second reason why formal entrenchment is not necessary. Suppose the statute of incorporation were to provide that subject to any express abrogation or derogation in any later statute the rights specified in the Convention were to be fully recognised and enforced in the United Kingdom according to the tenor of the Convention. That would be good enough for the judges. They would give full effect to the Convention rights unless a later statute very explicitly and specifically told them not to. But the rights protected by the Convention are not stated in absolute terms: there are provisos to cover pressing considerations of national security and such like. Save in quite extraordinary circumstances one cannot imagine any government going to Parliament with a proposal that any human right guaranteed by the Convention be overridden. And even then (subject to any relevant derogation) the United Kingdom would in any event remain bound, in international law and also in honour, to comply with its Convention obligations. I find it hard to imagine a government going to Parliament with such a proposal. So while the argument on entrenchment has a superficial theoretical charm, it has in my opinion very little practical substance. There would be no question, as under Community law, of United Kingdom judges declaring United Kingdom statues to be invalid. Judges would either comply with the express will of Parliament by construing all legislation in a manner consistent with the Convention. Or, in the scarcely imaginable case of an express abrogation or derogation by Parliament, the judges would give effect to that provision also.

A second and quite different argument runs roughly along the following lines. Rulings on human rights, not least rulings on the lines of demarcation between one right and another, involve sensitive judgments important to individual citizens and to society as a whole. These are not judgments which unelected English (or perhaps British) judges are fitted to make, drawn as they are from a narrow, unrepresentative minority, the public-school and Oxbridge-educated, male, white, mostly protestant, mostly middle-class products of the Bar. They are judgments of an essentially political nature, properly to be made by democratically elected representatives of the people. I do not, unsurprisingly, agree with most of the criticisms which it is fashionable to direct at the composition of the modern judiciary, for reasons which could fill another lecture. Nor would I, again unsurprisingly, accept the charge sometimes made that protection of human rights cannot safely be entrusted to British judges: no one familiar with the development of the law in fields as divers as, for instance, the Rent Acts, the Factories Acts, labour law or judicial review could, I think, fairly accuse the judges of throwing their weight on the side of the big battalions against the small man or woman. But it is true that judgments on human rights do involve judgments about relations between the individual and the society of which the individual is part, and in that sense they can be described as political. If such questions are thought to be inappropriate for decision by judges, so be it. I do not agree, but I can understand the argument. What I simply do not understand is how it can be sensible to entrust the decision of these questions to an international panel of judges in Strasbourg – some of them drawn from societies markedly unlike our own – but not, in the first instance, to our own judges here. I am not suggesting that the final right of appeal to Strasbourg should be eliminated or in any way curtailed (which, indeed, is not something which most opponents of incorporation support). I am only suggesting that rights claimed under the Convention should, in the first place, be ruled upon by judges here before, if regrettably necessary, appeal is made to Strasbourg. The choice is not between judges and no judges; it is whether *all* matches in this field must be played away.

The proposition that judgments on questions of human rights are, in the sense indicated, political is relied on by opponents of incorporation to found a further argument. The argument is that if British judges were to rule on questions arising under the Convention they would ineluctably be drawn into political controversy with consequent damage to their reputation, constitutionally important as it is, for political neutrality. This argument, espoused by a number of senior and respected political figures, should not be lightly dismissed. But it should be examined. It cannot in my view withstand such examination for two main reasons. The first is that judges are already, on a regular and day by day basis, reviewing and often quashing decisions of ministers and government departments. They have been doing so on an increasing scale for 30 years. During that period ministers of both governing parties have fallen foul of court decisions, not once or twice but repeatedly. Some of these decisions have achieved great public notoriety. All judges are accustomed to making every effort to put aside their own personal viewpoints, and there is no reason to think that English judges are any less good at this than any others. Political controversy there has been, on occasion, a-plenty, but it has not by and large rubbed off on the judges. Why not? Because, I think, it is generally if not universally recognised that the judges have a job to do, which is not a political job, and their personal predilections have no more influence on their decisions than that of a boxing referee who is required to stop a fight. In a mature democracy like ours, this degree of understanding is not, surely, surprising, but it does in my view weaken this argument against incorporation. . .

I end on a downbeat note. It would be naïve to suppose that incorporation of the Convention would usher in the new Jerusalem. As on the morrow of a general election, however glamorous the promises of the campaign, the world would not at once feel very different. But the change would over time stifle the insidious and damaging belief that it is necessary to go abroad to obtain justice. It would restore this country to its former place as an international standard bearer of liberty and justice. It would help to reinvigorate the faith, which our eighteenth and nineteenth century forbears would not for an instant have doubted, that these were fields in which Britain was the world's teacher, not its pupil. And it would enable the judges more effectively to honour their ancient and sacred undertaking to do right to all manner of people after the laws and usages of this realm, without fear or favour, affection or ill will.

Law Quarterly Review, 1993, pp. 391–3, 395–8, 400.

Mansion House Dinner speech, 1996

[Y]ou may have noticed that there has in recent months been much discussion of the judges and their role in our society. Whatever other afflictions we have suffered, the neglect of the public has not been among them. There has been much misunderstanding.

Our position, I would suggest, is simple. We have no extra-territorial ambitions. We have our work cut out to do our own job without wishing to do anyone else's. But we will seek to honour our ancient promise to do right to all manner of people, according to the laws and usages of the realm, without fear or favour, affection or ill-will. We seek no other role and can conceive of none prouder.

The laws of the realm of course include, pre-eminently, statutes enacted by Parliament. To suggest that the judges are in any way equivocal in their deference to parliamentary sovereignty is preposterous. It is easy to pose speculative questions. Suppose Parliament were to enact the anti-semitic laws of the Third Reich, what would the judges do then? Questions such as this are a legitimate subject of debate. A learned profession cannot be expected to eschew speculation. But debates of this kind have as much to do with day-to-day judicial decision-making as the theological controversies of mediaeval schoolmen with running the Mothers' Union. In the future as in the past, the judges will do their best to give effect to the spirit and the letter of Parliamentary enactments. They will also, when need arises, contribute to the organic, incremental development of equity and the common law. So to declare is not to threaten judicial legislation, but to recognise the oldest, and in the eyes of international jurists perhaps the greatest, glory of our legal system.

Judicial review . . . is not a novel phenomenon, as the Latin names of the principal remedies bear witness. No constitutional democracy governed by the rule of law could function without it. Far from challenging the authority of Parliament, as is sometimes suggested, judicial review buttresses the authority of Parliament by ensuring that powers conferred by Parliament are used as Parliament intended. Nor does it involve any usurpation of ministerial authority. Judges are concerned with the lawfulness of administrative decisions, not their wisdom or advisability. It was after all a great judge, the late Lord Devlin, who reminded us that the British have no more wish to be governed by judges than they have to be judged by administrators.

Those who favour incorporation of the European Convention on Human Rights into our domestic law are sometimes accused of seeking to arrogate vast new areas of authority to the judges. There is room for more than one view on the merits of incorporation, but this accusation, I would suggest, cannot hold water. Breaches and alleged breaches of the Convention are already the subject of judicial decision – but only in Strasburg, not here. Incorporation would not subject to judicial decision anything not now the subject of judicial decision, but would give British judges the opportunity to rule before the court in Strasburg. Commentators who attach most importance to appreciation of conditions in this country, and who are most critical of decisions reached in Strasburg, might be expected to see merit in this reform ...

Crown, Legislature, Executive and Judiciary are not satellites in independent orbit but wheels on the same coach. Our constitution, I would suggest, works most effectively when relations between the different arms of the State are characterised by mutual respect and confidence – respect for the integrity and professional competence of the others, confidence that each will do its own job with skill, intelligence and dedication to the public interest.

This does not mean that there will be no tensions. It is the business of Parliament to hold the executive to account. That makes for tension. It is the business of judges to see that public powers are exercised lawfully. That can make for tension. A Minister whose decision is quashed is not gratified by the experience. Any judge who has ever been reversed – and that is almost all of us – will understand the feeling. These are constructive tensions. They show that the machine is working.

But we should not suppose that all tensions are constructive. In most of what we do, we (the judges) depend on the willingness of Parliament to recognise the needs of our system of justice, and vote additional resources when needed, and on officials at all levels to bear the administrative heat and burden of the day up and down the land.

'The Courts and the Constitution' (King's College London Public Lecture, 1996)

There are those – including a number of senior judges – who favour incorporation on the ground that human rights which the United Kingdom has bound itself by treaty to respect should in the first instance be safeguarded by our domestic courts here in the UK. Opponents of incorporation say that it would have the undesirable effect of drawing the judiciary into the political arena. Others again point out that the Convention is now 40 years old and argue that it is today an unsatisfactory statement of the rights which the law should protect. These are issues on which much can be, and has been, said. Most of the arguments are by now familiar, and it is perhaps unlikely that those who hold one view or the other will experience a sudden conversion.

The question I wish to pose tonight is not whether incorporation would be a good thing or a bad thing. Rather I wish to ask: would the constitutional

implication of incorporation be fundamental? Would it involve an important change in the functions of the judiciary or of the judiciary's relations
with the legislative or the executive? Would it undermine the sovereignty of
Parliament? My answers to all these questions are that it would not.

Those answers are given on what I take to be a readily acceptable
premise, that incorporation would be made effective by scheduling the
Convention to an Act of Parliament, which would require that effect should
be given to the Convention (subject to any relevant derogation) save insofar
as any later Act might expressly require otherwise. That Act would represent the will of Parliament. So long as it stood, unrepealed, the courts would
loyally give effect to it. There would be no question of striking down statutes
as incompatible with the Convention: if Parliament wished to depart from
the Convention, it would so provide; if it did not, the courts would strive to
interpret later statutes consistently with the Convention, as in cases of doubt
they already do.

This, as I understand, is what the Opposition propose. In his contribution
to 'Law Reform for All', recently published, Lord Irvine of Lairg QC,
Shadow Lord Chancellor, wrote:

> 'Incorporation could easily be achieved. Parliament should pass a
> Human Rights Act that incorporates the rules of the Convention
> directly into British law, and gives citizens the right to enforce those
> rules in their own courts.
>
> Although technically a British Act of Parliament cannot be 'entren-
> ched', effective protection of the Human Rights Act from
> undermining by the courts would be provided by a clause that requires
> that any other Act that is intended to introduce laws inconsistent with
> the Convention must do so specifically and in express terms.'

He went on:

> 'In a democracy, Parliament decides what rights should apply, and
> should set them out in a manner that citizens can understand for
> themselves. Under these proposals, it would not be left to the discre-
> tion of the judges, or to archaeological investigations by legal and
> constitutional experts, to decide what protections citizens do and do
> not have.'

I agree, only observing that the judges would still have to interpret the
provisions of the Convention, pay regard to previous authority and apply
the law as determined to the facts of the case. But there is nothing novel in
that. Nor is there anything which should alarm any informed student of our
constitution.

Constitutional arrangements, like motor cars, require periodic inspection
and overhaul, so that worn-out parts may be renewed and ill-fitting parts
adjusted. The fact that a constitution such as ours has been on the road for
a very long time makes this attention more necessary, not less. Many
commentators feel that we have of late allowed our constitutional arrangements to fall into disrepair, and talk of change is in the air. This is all to the
good. Nothing should be taken for granted. Nothing is incapable of

improvement. It is, however, important to distinguish between the law of the constitution as it is and speculation as to what the law of the constitution might be. At the heart of our constitution is the doctrine of Parliamentary sovereignty. Whatever political theorists, or even judges in their more speculative, off-duty, moments, may opine, that doctrine is not, as a matter of law, under threat. The courts do not question the legislative process and do their best to give full and fair effect to what Parliament enacts. Judicial review reinforces, and in no way undermines, the will of Parliament. Parliament for its part respects the function of the courts, for instance by curbing debate on issues which are awaiting judicial decision and restraining personal criticism of judges or questioning of their motives. This is part of a delicate but important constitutional balance. My plea this evening is not for an end to debate of constitutional issues, but for a more informed and enlightened approach to that debate.

---

143   JOHN WADHAM, DIRECTOR OF LIBERTY, ON WHY INCORPORATING THE EUROPEAN CONVENTION ON HUMAN RIGHTS INTO UK LAW IS NOT ENOUGH, 1996

Although incorporation is a necessary and essential first step, the inadequacy of the contents of the Convention means that in order to properly protect rights in this country we need to create the mechanisms to draft and implement our own domestic Bill of Rights.

Missing Rights

The Convention has a number of rights missing from its text which, I think, most people would now accept should be included.

(1) The Right to Know

There is no right to information from public bodies. The right to information from personal files held by local authorities and the right to access to medical files have already been set out in statute in this country (Access to Medical Reports Act 1988. Access to Health Records Act 1990 and Access to Personal Files Act 1987) and although their existence owes something to the Convention the cases in Strasbourg on freedom of information have only been successful as a corollary of other rights in the Convention, in particular, the right to privacy. The recent Code of Practice on Open Government has no force in law and provides a very inadequate basis for a right to know...

(2) The Rights of Immigrants, Asylum Seekers and Those Being Extradited

Under the Convention there is no duty on the State to provide rights of due process or to a fair trial in the extradition system or before deportation. The rights contained in Article 6 of the Convention – the right to a fair trial – do not apply because the deportee has no pre-existing civil right to remain in this country and the right to a fair trial only applies where there is such a pre-existing right. One obvious and important right for those at risk of deportation would be a duty on the State seeking extradition to demonstrate a *prima facie* case in court before extradition was ordered. Those extradited to other countries where they are likely to be far away from their friends and family and confronted by a foreign legal system conducted in a language they may not understand are at a considerable disadvantage and the State wishing to extradite them should, I suggest, only have the power to do so where the charge is serious, where there is sufficient evidence which, if proved, would be sufficient to convict them and where the trial system is patently fair.

The Convention also provides little assistance to those held in detention pending deportation or extradition because Article 5(1)(f) allows detention in such circumstances and there is apparently no limit to the length of detention nor any restriction on the merits of either the detention or the deportation. In fact the rights of 'aliens' are further and specifically restricted by Article 16 which states that the rights of freedom of expression and assembly and the anti-discrimination Article shall not 'be regarded as preventing the High Contracting Parties [the state] from imposing restrictions on the political activity of aliens'.

The only restrictions on removal from a country are those imposed by other Articles such as the right to family life or freedom from torture. Even in family life cases the Court has held that if the family life can take place in the country to which the person is being deported then there is no breach of that Article.

Of course, the Convention does not includes the right to enter a country either as a resident or as an asylum seeker. Furthermore there is also no right to due process or to a fair trial for those who believe that they have substantive rights to enter and remain in the country. Even the rules giving a right to asylum in the United Nations Convention are not referred to in the European Convention.

(3) Anti-discrimination provisions

The right to be free from discrimination contained in Article 14 is flawed because, being drafted many years ago, it only deals with discrimination based on membership of some groups and does not refer for instance to a person's sexual orientation or disability. It is also flawed because the freedom from discrimination provision only applies where, unlike for instance the United Nations International Covenant on Civil and Political Rights, another right of the Convention has been violated. This has led to the provision being treated inadequately by the Commission and Court in Strasbourg, with them often preferring only to give judgment on the breach of the substantive right and ignoring Article 14. This has left us with very little guidance on what Article 14 does mean but it is clear that at present it does not provided a proper basis to outlaw discrimination.

Thus Article 14 does not generally provide freedom from discrimination in jobs, services, or where a socio-economic right is at stake.

(4) Criminal justice

In the context of minimum standards within the criminal justice system the Convention does not contain any equivalent of Article 14(3)(g) of the International Covenant on Civil and Political Rights. That is, that in the determination of any criminal charge, a person shall not 'be compelled to testify against himself or to confess guilt.'

The United Nations Human Rights Committee when considering the extent that provisions of the Criminal Justice and Public Order Act 1994, which makes substantial inroads into the right of silence, complied with the requirements of Article 14 said:

> The Committee notes with concern that the provisions of the Criminal Justice and Public Order Act 1994 ... whereby inferences may be drawn from the silence of persons accused of crimes, violates various provisions in article 14 of the Covenant, despite the range of safe-guards built into the legislation and the rules enacted thereunder.

Finally, the right to trial by jury in serious criminal cases is not contained anywhere in the Convention.

(5) Detention

Although there are restrictions on the lawfulness of detention in the Convention no minimum conditions are set for conditions of detention outside those contained in Article 3 – the provision against torture, inhuman and degrading treatment or punishment. The conditions required to breach the rights contained in Article 3 would have to be particularly severe and this provision is not designed to deal with 'merely inadequate' conditions of detention. Also other positive rights for those incarcerated are missing, in particular the right of access to a lawyer and the right not to be held incommunicado.

(6) Privacy

The absence of any right of privacy in the United Kingdom means that for the purposes of Article 6, the right to a fair trial conducted by an independent court in any dispute concerning a *civil right*, does not exist in privacy cases. Thus the right to privacy is only protected to the extent of the provisions in Article 8 itself. This means that, for instance, a compulsory search of someone's home or the forcible taking of bodily samples by the police does not have to be authorized by an independent court-like body but merely has to be 'in accordance with the law'. Rights of due process in relation to privacy are not required by the Convention. This has meant that the domestic telephone tapping (Interception of Communications Act 1985) and security services tribunals (Security Services Act 1989 and Intelligent Services Act 1994) have been accepted by the Commission as providing sufficient protection. (See respectively *Esbester* v. *UK* (2 April 1993) No. 18601/91 and *Christie* v. *UK* (27 June 1994) No. 21482/93). This is despite the fact that there is no right to see any of the documents that the tribunal considers, no right to a hearing before the tribunal, no right for the tribunal to consider the actual merits of any surveillance and no right to challenge the decision of the tribunal in any court.

(7) Other rights

Also absent from the Convention are any specific rights for children.

Lastly it is important to realize that whilst some additional rights are contained in the protocols to the Convention most of these protocols have not been ratified by the United Kingdom and thus do not apply. Furthermore most of the attempts by parliamentarians to incorporate the Convention into domestic law have been restricted to incorporate only those rights which have been ratified, so that in addition to the rights of those about to be expelled from the country mentioned above other rights that are missing include: freedom from imprisonment for breach of contract, freedom of movement and residence, the right to appeal following conviction and the right of compensation for those wrongly convicted, the prohibition on double jeopardy in criminal cases and equality of rights between spouses.

Content of the Convention

Apart from wholesale omissions of important rights there are considerable gaps and limitations in the rights as provided by the Convention. I will choose some of the more important of these to illustrate the problems.

Whilst the right to life contained in Article 2 is protected by the condition that actions breaching the right need to be 'absolutely necessary' the limitations include allowing lethal force to be used

> (b) in order to effect a lawful arrest or to prevent the escape of a person lawfully detained;
> (c) in action lawfully taken for the purpose of quelling a riot or insurrection.

I do not think that it can be right to allow the State to kill merely to effect an arrest or to prevent escape or even in order to end a riot. Although it may be justified to kill in order to protect the lives of others where this is 'absolutely necessary'.

Article 5(1)(e) allows the

> detention of persons for the prevention of the spreading of infectious

diseases, of persons of unsound mind, alcoholics or drug addicts or vagrants.

Surely no one drafting a Bill of Rights today could include a right to imprison vagrants and alcoholics merely for what they are rather than for what they have done whatever differing views there may be of locking up those with infectious diseases?

The rights of privacy and the freedoms of religion, expression, and assembly are all subject to similar limitations in the Convention which are contained in the second part of the relevant Article:

> except such as in accordance with the law and is necessary in a democratic society in the interests of national security, public safety or the economic well-being of the country, for the prevention of disorder or crime, for the protection of health or morals, or for the protection of the rights and freedoms of others.

Whilst significant numbers of cases against the United Kingdom in Strasbourg have succeeded because the interference with the right was not 'in accordance with the law' or the interference was not proportionate – not 'necessary in a democratic society' – few have failed because the purported aim of the restriction was outside of the range provided for in the second part of the article. There is not space here to deal with all of the difficulties that the expression 'national security' creates for the courts but it is arguable that the expression is too vague to be contained in a Bill of Rights.

Similarly the expression public safety makes too wide an exception and Liberty has substituted 'imminent physical harm' in its Bill of Rights. Interestingly 'the economic well being of the country' features only as a limitation in Article 8, the right to privacy and not as a limitation for the freedoms of religion, expression, and assembly.

It is difficult to oppose the provision of a limitation based on the prevention of crime although Liberty's Bill of Rights avoids this altogether arguing that the 'protection of the rights and freedoms of others' is the only justifiable limitation that is necessary.

For similar reasons exceptions based on the prevention of disorder or the protection of health or morals are not only very vague but potentially unlimited in their effect and generally unacceptable as a limitation in themselves. As limitations on the rights of privacy and the freedoms of religion, expression, and assembly they are particularly problematic and, in my view, have no place in any Bill of Rights.

Article 12 of the Convention includes a right to marry and found a family but does not provide such a right for transsexuals. It also, of course, only allows men and women to marry and makes no provision for partnerships between lesbians or between gay men.

One can certainly conclude from this brief analysis of the Convention that it is an inadequate basis for a Bill of Rights.

'Why Incorporation of the European Convention on Human Rights is Not Enough', in R. Gordon & R. Wilmot-Smith (eds), *Human Rights in the United Kingdom*, 1996, pp. 25f.

144   FRANCESCA KLUG ON A BILL OF RIGHTS AS SECULAR ETHICS, 1996

Bills of Rights are the only vehicle human beings have so far devised to establish the fundamental rights and responsibilities of every individual and the balance between them. Backed up by specific legislation and court rulings, they translate abstract values into concrete proposals. Their survival is dependent on their moral authority far more than any special parliamentary majorities designed to protect them. To attract this weight they must reflect not only the aspirations of a particular society but also the timeless values which define any democracy. . .

In essence a Bill of Rights represents a vision of democracy in which content matters as much as form; in which the election of a government is not an open mandate to usher in any policy regardless of its effect on individual or minority rights; in which a vote every five years is not the only right to which all individuals – regardless of their citizenship – can lay claim; in which fundamental rights to security, free speech, information, privacy, family life, protest and association or freedom from discrimination, arbitrary surveillance and abuse of power are perceived as essential to achieve any meaningful participation in the political process; in which a common framework of democratic values sets the limits of acceptable behaviour in both the public and private sphere.

In [a] future Britain which had incorporated the European Convention and adopted a domestic Bill of Rights, there would for the first time be what amounted to a 'higher law' which would set the ethical framework of public policy.

Governments of all parties would frequently refer to the values in the Bill of Rights when explaining their actions or making new proposals. Ministers from the Prime Minister down would be asked to justify their policies in these terms during Parliamentary questions, through the media, or by their constituents ... MPs would see themselves as custodians of the Bill of Rights. The Bill would be introduced by Parliament and it would be Parliament which would take the lead in ensuring that human rights values infused all relevant debates and legislation. The courts would be expected to apply human rights values in their judgements; no longer would they have to defend themselves from the charge that applying instruments ratified by the UK government is a usurpation of their role.

Human rights standards and their interpretation by international bodies would form a part of education in schools and colleges. Every individual in the country would receive a copy of these basic standards – expressed in simple language as a Bill of Rights ... Over time familiarity with these human rights values would begin to inform debate on the fundamental dilemmas that all societies face. Should there be limits on the right to free speech when individuals are offended by what people say or only when they are harmed? Should the private lives of public figures receive the same protection or less than other individuals? Is it legitimate for communities to publish pictures of convicted paedophiles, or even suspected paedophiles, to protect children or would this hamper the opportunity for rehabilitation to which everyone should be entitled? Are sexual practices between consenting adults in private ever the concern of public policy? Can children be held responsible for crimes to the same degree as adults and if so at what age? Is it possible to both protect children from harm and accord them fundamental rights? Should divorce be made difficult to safeguard the welfare of children or is this fundamentally a private issue in which the state's role should be limited to facilitating arrangements for the dissolution of marriage? Should all family types be accorded the same legitimacy?

Human rights values as they have evolved over the last 50 years are relevant to all these questions and more. They have the capacity to set the parameters for most of the ethical debates of our age. It is not that these issues are not thoroughly aired currently; it is that we lack any common language or value system to do justice to them.

Reinventing Community: The Rights and Responsibilities Debate, 1996, pp. 17–18.

Constitutional reformers and advocates of a Bill of Rights for the United Kingdom claim that in contrast to virtually every other democracy there are no rights in this country – however old and however revered – which the government of the day cannot take away at will ... The following statement by Geoffrey Robertson QC typifies this concern:

> Rights and freedoms are in Britain at the mercy of Parliament which passes the statutes which give them and take them away. And Parliament is controlled, with rare exceptions, by the executive government ... A democracy that subordinates fundamental rights to the exigencies of executive government leaves them dilapidated, outdated and legally insecure.

Contrast that statement with the following. First, an opinion expressed by former lecturer and community activist Dick Atkinson for the think-tank Demos and second a statement by author and historian David Selbourne in his book *The Principle of Duty:*

> The pendulum has swung so far from subjective authority and obligation towards reason, authority and rights that their interdependence has been fractured and serious damage has been caused.
>
> The ethics and politics of dutiless right, demand-satisfaction and self-realisation through unimpeded freedom of action have been a costly moral failure in the corrupted liberal order.

Are these different perceptions of the state of rights and liberties in the United Kingdom merely a reflection of the opposing political perspectives of their authors? Or is it possible that they are not mutually exclusive viewpoints? That they point to a complex reality only partially expressed by most political commentators? Could the absence of constitutionally protected rights described by Robertson actually contribute to the malaise depicted by Atkinson and Selbourne? ...

The assertion that we have too many rights and not enough duties in the United Kingdom has been given intellectual backing by a group of (mainly) American philosophers cum political activists known as communitarians. Beginning as a theoretical response to what was perceived as the individualistic theory of justice advanced by John Rawls [in *A Theory of Justice*, 1977] and others in the 1970s, the social movement known as communitarianism is described by its founder Amitai Etzioni, as 'aiming at shoring up the moral, social and political environment' [*The Spirit of Community*, 1993].

Etzioni, a professor at George Washington University and a former White House adviser to President Clinton, advocates a four-point agenda:

> a moratorium on the minting of most, if not all, new rights; re-establishing the link between rights and responsibilities; recognising that some responsibilities do not entail rights and, most carefully, adjusting some rights to the changed circumstances.

Etzioni is not an opponent of rights. Far from it. His argument is that rights are becoming devalued by the elevating of personal desires into the language of rights.

> Once rights were very solomn moral/legal claims, ensconced in the constitution and treated with much reverence. We all lose if the publicity department of every special interest can claim that someone's rights are violated every time they don't get what want.

The 'core mission' for communitarians is to 'shore up morality' through the restoration of community – 'we find reinforcement for our moral inclinations and provide reinforcement to our fellow human beings through the community'.

Whilst this is not the place to delve into the details of communitarian philosophy, it is important to note that its influence in the UK is growing. When Etzioni visited Britain in March 1995 he was received by the leaders of the Labour and Liberal Democrat parties and cabinet ministers attended a dinner in his honour. Tickets for Etzioni's public lecture were sold out. His ideas have been spread here by pamphleteers and columnists. The principle ideas of communitarianism have also begun to creep into the literature on citizenship, particularly where active citizenship is advocated.

Most notable is the growing influence of communitarian values on new Labour. Leading members of the party are increasingly emphasizing the importance of individual citizens fulfilling their duties and responsibilities if the project of a revitalized society is to be achieved. In a lecture to a local community group in November 1995 Shadow Home Secretary, Jack Straw, asserted that if Britain is to become a society based on mutual responsibility:

> The most important change involves a change in attitude. We need to break out of the language of dutiless rights and begin insisting upon mutual responsibility. Rights and duty go hand in hand.

In their book *The Blair Revolution*, Peter Mandelson MP and Roger Liddle argue that this emphasis on responsibilities is one of the defining features of New Labour. 'Whereas the left appeared to argue for rights without responsibilities and that one was responsible for oneself alone, New Labour stresses the importance of mutual obligations.'

This claim is reflected in the new Clause Four of Labour's constitution – which defines the party's aims and values – with the statement that 'the rights we enjoy reflect the duties we owe' (and not, it should be noted, the other way round).

There can be little doubt that this emphasis on duties and responsibilities reflects a growing sense of unease about a society which appears to be increasingly fragmented. For many on the centre left this is blamed on the corrosive effect of the entry of market forces into virtually all areas of social as well as economic life with its emphasis on competition and individual achievement and its creation of winners and losers. For the centre right and an expanding section of the left it is the decline of the two-parent family which is the cause of this disintegration witnessed by the soaring divorce rate and an apparent explosion of juvenile crime (although there is some debate about whether this is largely due to a small number of youths committing an increasing number of crimes). Others blame the waning of religion and what is perceived to be an absence of moral values taught in schools.

The problem, however, in importing Etzioni's ideas lock, stock, and barrel is that they have developed in response to factors which are by no means identical to those which prevail in the United Kingdom. When he calls for a halt on creating new rights he is writing in the context of a society which has the oldest set of constitutionally entrenched rights in the world. When he laments that the only responsibility that is assumed in the American 'rights dialect' is to avoid harming others he is referring to the philosophy of the American Constitution. Although related, this is significantly different to the international human rights standards which developed since the Second World War ...

If the European Convention were incorporated into United Kingdom law, as both the Labour and Liberal Democrat parties have pledged, then the primary effect would be to provide international human rights standards with a constitutional protection they have never before received in the United Kingdom. According to most proposals under consideration, the rights and freedoms in the ECHR would amount to a 'higher law' which legislation and the policy and procedures of government and public officials would be bound by.

In this sense we would, for the first time, have fundamental rights in the United Kingdom; political parties could no longer simply barter our rights away in an unseemly Dutch auction whenever elections are drawing near. Whether it be the shackling of women political prisoners at hospital visits, executive control over the release dates of life prisoners, legislation which criminalizes many kinds of peaceful protest, or the sacking of gay and lesbian armed service personnel on the grounds of their sexuality, these decisions or policies would be subject to a clear and written code. Rather than political expediency or populist outcry (usually mediated through the tabloid press rather than any serious test of public opinion) a set of fundamental values, based on a clear moral philosophy, would be the driving force behind such policies.

To argue that this would usher in a further deluge of dutiless rights when what we need is more responsibilities is to miss the point entirely. By incorporating international human rights standards into our law we would simultaneously create a new set of responsibilities, some of which would take the form of legal requirements, others moral exhortations. Rights would be balanced not only against each other but against specific limitations which apply to most of the Articles in the Convention. Indeed many would argue that far from reinforcing liberty at all costs the limitations placed on rights under the Convention, such as the protection of national security or morals, are too numerous ...

It is presumably because other countries' experiences suggest that [the enactment of a Bill of Rights] has the potential to unite rather than divide – even if there are disputes and debates along the way – that the Labour party has expressed its commitment to following up incorporation of the European Convention with a domestic Bill of Rights. Jack Straw has described this as 'our great project to give the British people the rights and responsibilities upon which a properly functioning civil society is founded' (Speech to Labour Party Conference, 5 Oct. 1995).

The success of any future Bill of Rights should not be measured in terms of how many legal cases it generates. As with the race relations and sex discrimination legislation of the 1970s, it should influence the moral values of society as a whole; not merely regulate the actions of the State. If it were truly successful there should in fact be far fewer civil rights cases than currently. In this sense the goals which drive the demand for a Bill of Rights for the United Kingdom are consistent with the communitarian vision discussed earlier. Both assume that as far as civil society is concerned, widely shared values which involve an intricate balance between rights and responsibilities can be morally persuasive in themselves, without necessarily resorting to law.

'A Bill of Rights as Secular Ethics' in R. Gordon & R. Wilmot-Smith (eds), *Human Rights in the United Kingdom*, 1996, pp. 37f.

---

145   THE LORD CHANCELLOR LORD IRVINE ON THE FUTURE DEVELOPMENT OF HUMAN RIGHTS IN THE UK AFTER THE HUMAN RIGHTS ACT, 1998

A major change which the Act will bring flows from the shift to a rights based system. Under this system a citizen's right is asserted as a positive entitlement expressed in clear and principled terms. For example, under Article 5 of the Convention 'Everyone has the right to liberty and security of person'. Whilst there are reservations to that right, the reservations take effect as explicit exceptions and derogations which must be justified according to the terms of the Article. They represent exceptions which, in the public interest, are justified and reasonable. For example, the basic right in Article 5 is qualified by a list of the defined and circumscribed cases where a person may be deprived of his liberty. So, where a national authority wants to justify a detention, it will need to show how the facts fit into one of those defined categories and how it has met other requirements of the Convention; for example, the fair trial guarantees in Article 6.

This approach contrasts with the traditional common law approach to the protection of individual liberties. The common law treats liberty only as a 'negative' right ... what is left over when all the prohibitions have limited the area of lawful conduct. There are numerous examples of prohibitions either by the common law (for instance, the law of libel limiting the extent of free speech to prohibit defamatory statements or the law of nuisance limiting the activities in which a person may engage on his own land) or by statute (of which the examples are too obvious and numerous to merit illustration).

Dicey saw merit in this negative approach. He believed that the absence of writing lent the common law a flexibility to develop to meet changing conditions. But the approach has disadvantages which are greater. By proposing this law the Government has decisively demonstrated its view that the more serious threat to liberty is an absence of written guarantees of freedom. For the negative approach offers little protection against a creeping erosion of freedom by a legislature willing to countenance infringement of liberty or simply blind to the effect of an otherwise well intentioned piece of law. The Human Rights Bill is our bulwark against that danger. The traditional freedom of the individual under an unwritten constitution to do himself that which is not prohibited by law gives no protection from misuse of power by the State, nor any protection from acts or omissions by public bodies which harm individuals in a way that is incompatible with their human rights under the Convention.

What then are the practical implications of this change to a rights based system within the field of civil liberties? ...

Domestication of remedies

First, the Act will give to the courts the tools to uphold freedoms at the very time their infringement is threatened. Until now, the only remedy where a freedom guaranteed by the Convention is infringed and domestic law is deficient has been expensive and slow proceedings in Strasbourg. They could not even be commenced until after all the domestic avenues of complaint and appeal had been exhausted. The courts will now have the power to give effect to the Convention rights in the course of proceedings when they arise in this country and to grant relief against an unlawful act of a public authority (a necessarily widely drawn concept). The courts will not be able to strike down primary legislation. But they will be able to make a declaration of incompatibility where a piece of primary legislation conflicts with a Convention right. This will trigger the ability to use in Parliament a special fast-track procedure to bring the law into line with the Convention.

This innovative technique will provide the right balance between the judiciary and Parliament. Parliament is the democratically elected representative of the people and must remain sovereign. The judiciary will be able to exercise to the full the power to scrutinise legislation rigorously against the fundamental freedoms guaranteed by the Convention but without becoming politicised. The ultimate decision to amend legislation to bring it into line with the Convention, however, will rest with Parliament. The ultimate responsibility for compliance with the Convention must be Parliament's alone.

Prioritising rights

That point illustrates the second important effect of our new approach. If there are to be differences or departures from the principles of the Convention they should be conscious and reasoned departures, and not the product of rashness, muddle or ignorance. This will be guaranteed both by the powers given to the courts [and] by other provisions which will be enacted. In particular, Ministers and administrators will be obliged to do all their work keeping clearly and directly in mind its impact on human rights, as expressed in the Convention and in the jurisprudence which attaches to it. For, where any Bill is introduced in either House, the Minister of the Crown, in whose charge it is, will be required to make a written statement that, either, in his view, the provisions of the Bill are compatible with the Convention rights; or that he cannot make that statement but the Government nonetheless wishes the House to proceed with the Bill. In the latter case the Bill would inevitably be subject to close and critical scrutiny by Parliament. Human rights will not be a matter of fudge. The responsible Minister will have to ensure that the legislation does not infringe guaranteed freedoms, or be prepared to justify his decision openly and in the full glare of parliamentary and public opinion.

That will be particularly important whenever there come under consideration those articles of the Convention which lay down what I call principled rights, subject to possible limitation. I have in mind Articles 8–11, dealing with respect for private life, freedom of religion freedom of expression, and freedom of assembly and association. These articles confer those freedoms subject to possible limitations, such as, for instance in the case of Article 10 (freedom of expression)

> are prescribed by law and are necessary in a democratic society in the interests of national security, territorial integrity or public safety, for the prevention of disorder or crime, for the protection of health or morals, for the protection of the reputation or rights of others, for preventing the disclosure of information received in confidence, or for maintaining the authority and impartiality of the judiciary.

In such cases, administrators and legislators will have to think clearly about whether what they propose really is necessary in a democratic society and for what object it is necessary. Quite apart from the concentration on the Convention and its jurisprudence this will require, the process should produce better thought-out, clearer and more transparent administration.

The important requirements of transparency on Convention issues that will accompany the introduction of all future legislation will ensure that Parliament knows exactly what it is doing in a human rights context. I regard this improvement in both the efficiency and the openness of our legislative process as one of the main benefits produced by incorporation of the Convention.

Substantive rights

Thirdly, the Convention will enable the courts to reach results in cases which give full effect to the substantive rights guaranteed by the Convention. . . It is likely . . . that the position will in at least some cases be different from what it would have been under the pre-incorporation practice. The reason for this lies in the techniques to be followed once the Act is in force. Unlike the old Diceyan approach where the Court would go straight to what restriction had been imposed, the focus will first be on the positive right and then on the justifiability of the exception. Moreover, the Act will require the courts to read and give effect to the legislation in a way compatible with the Convention rights 'so far as it is possible to do so . . .' This, as the White Paper makes clear, goes far beyond the present rule. It will not be necessary to find an ambiguity. On the contrary the courts will be required to interpret legislation so as to uphold the Convention rights unless the legislation itself is so clearly incompatible with the Convention that it is impossible to do so. Moreover, it should be clear from the parliamentary history, and in particular the Ministerial statement of compatibility which will be required by the Act, that Parliament did not intend to cut across a Convention right. Ministerial statements of compatibility will inevitably be a strong spur to the courts to find means of construing statutes compatibly with the Convention.

Whilst this particular approach is innovative, there are some precedents which will assist the courts. In cases involving European Community law, decisions of our courts already show that interpretative techniques may be used to make the domestic legislation comply with the Community law, even where this requires straining the meaning of words or reading in words which are not there. . .

Guidance may also be found in the jurisprudence of the New Zealand courts. Under the New Zealand Bill of Rights Act 1990 a meaning consistent with the rights and freedoms contained in the Bill of Rights is to be given in preference to any other meaning 'wherever an enactment can be given [such] a meaning'. The existing New Zealand decisions seem to show that the only cases where the legislation will *not* be interpreted consistently with the protected rights is where a statutory provision contains a clear limitation of fundamental rights (See especially *R.* v. *Laugalis* (1993) 10 C.R.N.Z.) The difference from the approach until now applied by the English courts will be this: the Court will interpret as consistent with the

Convention not only those provisions which are ambiguous in the sense that the *language* used is capable of two different meanings, but also those provisions where there is *no* ambiguity in that sense, unless a *clear* limitation is expressed. In the latter category of case it will be 'possible' (to use the statutory language) to read the legislation in a conforming sense because there will be no clear indication that a limitation on the protected rights was intended so as to make it 'impossible' to read it as conforming.

Principled decision-making

The fourth point may be shortly stated but is of immense importance. The courts' decisions will be based on a more overtly principled, and perhaps moral, basis. The Court will look at the positive right. It will only accept an interference with that right where a justification, allowed under the Convention, is made out. The scrutiny will not be limited to seeing if the *words* of an exception can be satisfied. The Court will need to be satisfied that the *spirit* of this exception is made out. It will need to be satisfied that the interference with the protected right is justified in the public interests in a free democratic society. Moreover, the courts will in this area have to apply the Convention principle of proportionality. This means the Court will be looking *substantively* at that question. It will not be limited to a secondary review of the decision-making process but at the primary question of the merits of the decision itself.

In reaching its judgment, therefore, the Court will need to expand and explain its own view of whether the conduct is legitimate. It will produce in short a decision on the *morality* of the conduct and not simply its compliance with the bare letter of the law. . .

The emergence of a new approach

Any court or tribunal determining any question relating to a Convention right will be obliged to take into account the body of jurisprudence of the Court and Commission of Human Rights and of the Council of Ministers. This is obviously right; it gives British courts the benefit of 50 years careful analysis of the Convention rights and ensures British courts interpret the Convention consistently with Strasbourg. The British courts will therefore need to apply the same techniques of interpretation and decision-making as the Strasbourg bodies. I have already mentioned recourse to parliamentary materials such as *Hansard* – where we are now more closely in line with our continental colleagues. I will mention three more aspects. As I do so, it should be remembered that the courts which will be applying these techniques will be the ordinary courts of the land; we have not considered it right to create some special human rights court alongside the ordinary system; the Convention rights must pervade all law and all court systems. Our courts will therefore learn these techniques and inevitably will consider their utility in deciding other non-Convention cases.

First there is the approach to statutory construction. The tools of construction in use in mainland Europe are known to be different from those the English courts have traditionally used. I will refer to just one: the teleological approach, which is concerned with giving the instrument its presumed legislative intent. It is less concerned with the textual analysis usual to the common law tradition of interpretation. (The Court of Human Rights also adopts a dynamic approach which enables it to take account of changing social conditions.) It is a process of moulding the law to what the Court believes the law should be trying to achieve. It is undoubtedly the case that our own domestic approach to interpretation of statutes has become more purposive. . .

Yet as the courts, through familiarity with the Convention jurisprudence, become more exposed to methods of interpretation which pay more heed to the purpose, and less to whether the words were felicitously chosen to achieve that end, the balance is likely to swing more firmly yet in the direction of the purposive approach.

Secondly, there is the doctrine of proportionality [which] is applied by the European Court of Human Rights (see e.g. *Soering* v. *U.K.* (1989) Series A, Vol. 161). Its application is to ensure that a measure imposes no greater restriction upon a Convention right than is absolutely necessary to achieve its objectives. Although not identical to the principle as applied in Luxembourg, it shares the feature that it raises questions foreign to the traditional *Wednesbury* (*Associated Provincial Picture Houses* v. *Wednesbury Corporation* [1948] K.B. 223.) approach to judicial review. Under the *Wednesbury* doctrine an administrative decision will only be struck down if it is so bad that no reasonable decision-maker could have taken it.

Closely allied with the doctrine of proportionality is the concept of the margin of appreciation. The Court of Human Rights has developed this doctrine which permits national courts a discretion in the application of the requirements of the Convention to their own national conditions. This discretion is not absolute, since the Court of Human Rights reserves the power to review any act of a national authority or court; and the discretion is more likely to be recognised in the application of those articles of the Convention which expressly include generally stated conditions or exceptions, such as Articles 8–11, rather than in the area of obligations which in any civilised society should be absolute, such as the rights to life, freedom from torture and freedom from slavery and forced labour that are provided by Articles 2–4.

The margin of appreciation was first developed by the Court in a British case, *Handyside* v. *U.K.* ((1976), Series A, Vol. 24). It concerned whether a conviction for possessing an obscene article could be justified under Article 10(2) of the Convention as a limitation upon freedom of expression that was necessary for the 'protection of morals'. The court said:

> By reason of their direct and continuous contact with the vital forces of their countries, state authorities are in principle in a better position than the international judge to give an opinion on the exact content of those requirements [of morals] as well as on the 'necessity' of a 'restriction' or 'penalty' intended to meet them . . .

Although there is some encouragement in British decisions for the view that the margin of appreciation under the Convention is simply the *Wednesbury* test under another guise statements by the Court of Human Rights seem to draw a significant distinction. The Court of Human Rights has said in terms that its review is not limited to checking that the national authority 'exercised its discretion reasonably, carefully and in good faith'. It has to go further. It has to satisfy itself that the decision was based on an 'acceptable assessment of the relevant facts' and that the interference was no more than reasonably necessary to achieve the legitimate aim pursued.

That approach shows that there is a profound difference between the Convention margin of appreciation and the common law test of rationality. The latter would be satisfied by an exercise of discretion done 'reasonably, carefully and in good faith' although the passage I have cited indicates that the Court of Human Rights' review of action is not so restricted. In these cases a more rigorous scrutiny than traditional judicial review will be required. An illustration of the difference is to be found in the speech of Simon Brown L.J. in *R. v. Ministry of Defence, ex p. Smith* [1996] Q.B. 517 (the armed forces homosexual policy case):

> If the Convention for the Protection of Human Rights and Funda-mental Freedoms were part of our law and we were accordingly entitled to ask whether the policy answers a pressing social need and whether the restriction on human rights involved can be shown proportionate to its benefits, then clearly the primary judgment (sub-ject only to a limited 'margin of appreciation') would be for us and not for others; the constitutional balance would shift. But that is not the position. In exercising merely a secondary judgment, this court is bound, even though acting in a human rights context, to act with some reticence.

The question I pose is how long the courts will restrict their review to a narrow *Wednesbury* approach in non-Convention cases, if used to inquiring more deeply in Convention cases? . . .

British officials were closely involved in the drafting of the Convention. When our British courts make their own pronouncements on the Convention, their views will be studied in other Convention countries and in Strasbourg itself with great respect. I am sure that British judges' influence for the good of the Convention will be considerable. They will bring to the application of the Convention their great skills of analysis and inter-pretation. But they will also bring to it our proud British traditions of liberty.

The shift from form to substance

So there is room to predict some decisive and far reaching changes in future judicial decision making. The major shift may be away from a concern with form to a concern with substance. Let me summarise the reasons.

In the field of review by judges of administrative action, the courts' decisions to date have been largely based on something akin to the applica-tion of a set of rules. If the rules are broken, the conduct will be condemned.

But if the rules are obeyed, (the right factors are taken into account, no irrelevant factors taken into account, no misdirection of law and no out and out irrationality) the decision will be upheld, usually irrespective of the overall objective merits of the policy. In some cases much may turn – or at least appear to turn – on the form in which a decision is expressed rather than its substance. Does the decision as expressed show that the right reasons have been taken into account? Does it disclose potentially irrational reasoning? Might the court's view be different if the reasoning were expressed differently so as to avoid the court's *Wednesbury* scrutiny?

Now, in areas where the Convention applies, the Court will be less concerned whether there has been a failure in this sense but will inquire more closely into the merits of the decision to see for example that necessity justified the limitation of a positive right, and that it was no more of a limitation than was needed. There is a discernible shift which may be seen in essence as a shift from form to substance. If, as I have suggested, there is a spillover into other areas of law, then that shift from form to substance will become more marked.

This may be seen as a progression of an existing and now long standing trend. In modern times, the emphasis on identifying the true substance at issue has been seen in diverse areas: in tax where new techniques have developed to view the substance of a transaction overall rather than to be mesmerised by the form of an isolated step, or in the areas of statutory control of leases, where the Courts are astute to prevent form being used to obscure the reality of the underlying transaction. In what may seem at first blush a very different area, that of interpretation of contracts, recent decisions also emphasise the need to cast away the baggage of older years where literal and semantic analysis was allowed to override the real intent of the parties. In a very broad sense we can see here a similarity of approach: to get to the substance of the issue and not be distracted by the form.

These are trends already well developed but I believe they will gain impetus from incorporation of the Convention. In addition the courts will be making decisions founded more explicitly and frequently on considerations of morality and justifiability.

This Bill will therefore create a more explicitly moral approach to decisions and decision making; will promote both a culture where positive rights and liberties become the focus and concern of legislators, administrators and judges alike, and a culture in judicial decision making where there will be a greater concentration on substance rather than form.

From Lord Irvine of Lairg, 'The Development of Human Rights in Britain under an Incorporated Convention on Human Rights', JUSTICE/Tom Sargant Memorial Lecture, *Public Law* (1998) 224ff.

CHAPTER 9

IMPLEMENTATION OF A UK BILL OF RIGHTS

What is needed, I believe, is a permanent advisory Constitutional Commission with the status of a standing Royal Commission. In essence, it might have two tasks. One would be to consider and report on any constitutional provisions which, in its opinion, were in need of clarification or reformulation. For ease of reference, that might be labelled its declaratory role. The other task – its reforming role – would be to consider any aspect of the United Kingdom constitution referred to it by a Minister, and to report on whether and how it might be reformed. It must be stressed from the start that the government would have a large degree of control over the Commission's work through the requirement that the Commission could only exercise its reforming function following a ministerial reference. If the Commission were able to gain the confidence of the government, however, Ministers might feel encouraged to increase the number and scope of such references. If (as would be essential) such a Constitutional Commission were to have the support at least of the Conservative and Labour Parties, they would have to have a say in its composition. Discussions through the usual channels might produce agreement on membership. Politicians are among the principal actors in the constitution: it would be essential that the Commission had some politician members and perhaps senior back-benchers in the House of Commons would form the nucleus of the Commission. Equally, the Commission ought to include representatives of the law, industry, universities, and other walks of life. The chairman would have to be a respected and impartial public figure; all the Commissioners would have part-time appointments. The Commission should have access to official advice from government departments, and could seek other evidence; it would need adequate resources, certainly enough to enable it to pay for research. Public consultation ... would be very important, and it would be a welcome development if ... publishing draft proposals for comment were to be followed. Progress through expert committees ... would be an efficient way forward, especially because any other method of working would demand too great a commitment from part-time Commissioners. The Commission's final reports might be laid before Parliament and published as White Papers.

The declaratory role of the Constitutional Commission should not be too threatening to the main political parties, for it would be limited to consideration of existing rules and practices which are unclear or which would be better for being expressed authoritatively ...

If the Commission proved its worth in its declaratory work, and in carrying out any references which the government might ask it to undertake in the place of *ad hoc* inquiries, rather bolder references might follow ... the political parties might feel able to agree on references concerning fundamental constitutional reform for the United Kingdom, such as, for example, whether the electoral system is the most satisfactory that can be devised, or whether the rights of the citizen might be better protected by a new Bill of Rights of some kind, or whether the structure of government outside London might be recast, or whether any aspects of the royal prerogative might be reduced to statute and perhaps circumscribed. In a forum such as a Constitutional Commission protagonists and antagonists could argue their cases rationally, without the party-political rhetoric which frequently clouds such matters – deliberations worthy of the subjects might take place. . . .

A Constitutional Commission of this type would be a typically British answer to a very British problem. It would be non-statutory, all-party, and advisory. But beyond that it would be a single body which could act as a clearing-house for constitutional ideas, and, being permanent, it should establish a body of expertise which no succession of *ad hoc* mechanisms could possibly rival. Public opinion would be canvassed to an unprecedented extent. The creation of a Constitutional Commission would put in place a means of taking a planned look at the constitutional system. Naturally, such a Commission might be seen by the Conservative and Labour Parties as a challenge to their Panglossian view of the main features of the constitution. Any government which set up a Constitutional Commission would certainly want to proceed with caution; but perhaps the two main parties would be wise to give at least private consideration to the idea, because support for it (or something like it) might be the price demanded one day by a smaller party (or parties) for coalition, or a party pact, in the event of the return of a hung Parliament. It should be remembered that Mr Edward Heath as Prime Minister and Leader of the Conservative Party felt able to offer the Liberal Party a Speaker's Conference on proportional representation in February 1974 as part of his suggested coalition deal. Advance planning for a repeat of such an event might be prudent. Whatever might be the ultimate reason for the establishment of a Constitutional Commission, it might be used in the early days primarily as a replacement for the constitutional inquiries previously conducted by *ad hoc* bodies, and in furthering its declaratory role. The government which established such a Commission could take some reassurance from the fact that politicians would account for a significant part of its membership, and that Ministers would be in command of its reforming function. But the main political parties will have reservations about and raise objections to the principle of such a Commission; two of these objections need to be addressed now.

One (which would certainly be endorsed by the Treasury) is that a Constitutional Commission would require additional human and financial resources, not least to pay for research: by contrast, the existing system is cheap. There are two points to be made about that. A minor consideration is that the cost of the Commission would not be wholly additional public expenditure. Far fewer *ad hoc* constitutional inquiries would be needed, and the savings on them could, at least notionally, be set against the costs of the Commission. The much more important point is that the shaping of the best structure for the country's constitution is vital, and has as legitimate a claim on public spending as anything else. Why should the country's constitution, of all aspects of national life, be conducted on the cheap? All other areas of law can be calmly considered by authoritative and impartial bodies to ensure sensible development. Most aspects of English law have a Rolls-Royce service from the Law Commission, but the constitution usually has to falter before the government is reluctantly persuaded to despatch the equivalent of the Automobile Association to patch it up. This is completely unsatisfactory. Another objection from the two main political parties might be that the existence of such a Constitutional Commission would slow down the implementation of constitutional changes which they might wish to introduce. This can be explained through the following hypothesis. Suppose that such a Commission were in existence when the Labour Party next formed a government. It might then consider itself bound to refer its clutch of constitutional policies to the Commission for its consideration. There would then be a delay of many months before the Commission could report on them, and the Labour government might not be prepared to countenance such a delay. Now while things could happen in that fashion, there would be another way of proceeding. References made by the government to the Constitutional Commission would often be preceded by discussions through the usual channels; Labour, in opposition, could ask the Government to refer the principal constitutional issues raised in its policy review to the Commission. It might become an accepted practice that, the Commission's other commitments permitting, Opposition requests for references would be acquiesced in by the Government of the day – without, of course, any implication that the Government agreed in any way with the proposals so referred. After consideration, the Commission might approve some of those ideas and reject others. But its role would be *advisory*, and nothing would stop any party putting whatever it wished into its general election manifesto, or prevent it, once it became the government, from implementing its policies whether or not they had been reviewed by the Commission and regardless of any view expressed on them by the Commission.

Constitutional Reform, 1991, pp. 30–4.

---

147   A PROPOSAL FOR THE WORKING AND COMPOSITION OF A BILL OF RIGHTS COMMISSION, 1994

HUMAN RIGHTS BILL 1994

RB NOTE: For the full text of this Bill, apart from section 9 and schedule 5 below, see Doc. 39D.

THE UNITED KINGDOM BILL OF RIGHTS COMMISSION

9.—(1) There shall be a body corporate known as the United Kingdom Bill of Rights Commission (the Bill of Rights Commission), with the function of preparing a draft Bill of Rights relating to all civil, political, economic and social rights in the United Kingdom.

(2) The Bill of Rights Commission shall consist of twelve members appointed after public consultation by the Lord Chancellor and the Lord Advocate, one of whom shall be appointed Chair.

(3) It shall be the duty of the Lord Chancellor and the Lord Advocate to appoint the Bill of Rights Commission within a period of two months beginning with the date on which this Part of this Act comes into force.

(4) It shall be the duty of the Bill of Rights Commission to cause the draft Bill referred to in subsection (1) above to be delivered to the Lord Chancellor not later than two years after this Part of this Act comes into force.

(5) The Lord Chancellor shall lay before each House of Parliament copies of the draft Bill referred to in subsection (1) above within one month of its receipt.

(6) Schedule 5 makes further provision in relation to the Bill of Rights Commission ...

SCHEDULE 5

The United Kingdom Bill of Rights Commission

Membership

1. The Board shall consist of twelve members, appointed after public consultation by the Lord Chancellor and the Lord Advocate, of whom one shall be appointed to take the chair.

2.—(1) The Lord Chancellor and the Lord Advocate shall by regulation provide for the composition of the Board, which, subject to sub-paragraph (2) below, shall include among its members—
   (a) persons who hold or have held high judicial office, and
   (b) persons who have particular knowledge or expertise in relation to civil, political, economic or social rights.

(2) Regulations made under sub-paragraph (1) above shall prescribe a minimum number of women and a minimum number of members of ethnic minorities who shall be members of the Commission.

Tenure of office

3.—(1) A person appointed to be a member of the Commission shall hold and vacate office under the terms of the instrument by which that member is appointed.

(2) A member may at any time resign office by notice in writing to the Lord Chancellor or the Lord Advocate.

(3) The Lord Chancellor or the Lord Advocate may remove a person from office on the ground that—
- (a) that person has been absent from meetings of the Commission for a period longer than three consecutive months without the Commission's consent,
- (b) a bankruptcy order has been made against that person or that person's estate has been sequestrated or that person has made a composition or arrangement with, or granted a trust deed for, that person's creditors, or
- (c) that person is unable or unfit to discharge the functions of a member.

(4) If the person appointed to take the chair ceases to be a member, that person shall also cease to occupy the chair.

Staff

4.—(1) The Commission may appoint such staff as they determine with the Lord Chancellor's and Lord Advocate's approval as to numbers and terms and conditions of service.

(2) The Commission may in the application of funds provided by the Lord Chancellor and the Lord Advocate and with the Lord Chancellor's and the Lord Advocate's approval—
- (a) pay such remuneration, pensions, allowances or gratuities to or in respect of any persons who have been or are members of their staff as they may determine;
- (b) provide and maintain such schemes as they may determine (whether contributory or not) for the payment of pensions, allowances or gratuities, to or in respect of any such persons.

(3) The Lord Chancellor and the Lord Advocate shall not give an approval under this paragraph without the Treasury's consent.

Remuneration and allowances

5.—(1) There shall be paid out of funds provided by the Lord Chancellor or the Lord Advocate to the members of the Commission such remuneration, travelling and other allowances as the Lord Chancellor or the Lord Advocate may determine.

(2) Where the Lord Chancellor or the Lord Advocate so determine in the case of a former holder of the office of member of the Commission, the Commission shall—
- (a) pay to or in respect of that person such pension, allowances or gratuities, or
- (b) make such payments towards the provision of a pension, allowances or gratuities in respect of that person,

as the Lord Chancellor or the Lord Advocate may determine.

(3) A determination under this paragraph shall not have effect unless it has been approved by the Treasury.

Proceedings

6.—(1) Subject to the provisions of this Schedule and of section 9 above, the Commission may regulate their own procedure, except that the quorum for meetings of the Commission shall be five.

(2) The validity of any proceedings of the Commission shall not be affected by any vacancy among their members, or by any defect in the appointment of any person to the chair or as a member.

Application of seal and evidence

7. The application of the seal of the Commission shall be authenticated by the signature of any member of the Commission.

8. A document purporting to be duly executed under the seal of the Commission or to be signed on their behalf shall be received in evidence and, unless the contrary is proved, be taken to be so executed or signed.

Status of the commission

9. The Commission shall not be regarded as the servant or agent of the Crown or as enjoying any status, immunity or privilege of the Crown.

Parliamentary disqualification

10.—(1) In the House of Commons Disqualification Act 1975, in Part III of Schedule 1 (other disqualifying offices), the following entry shall be inserted at the appropriate place—
'Member of the United Kingdom Bill of Rights Commission.'

(2) The same entry shall be inserted at the appropriate place in Part III of Schedule 1 to the Northern Ireland Assembly Disqualification Act 1975.

HC [1993–4] 30.

---

148 THE CONSTITUTION UNIT REPORTS ON THE POLICY DEVELOPMENT MECHANISMS IN THE DRAWING UP OF A UK BILL OF RIGHTS, 1997

299. The Labour Party and the Liberal Democrats are committed to the development of domestic human rights charters that go beyond the terms of

the ECHR ... Most importantly, it is both unlikely and undesirable that any domestic bill or bills of rights could be formulated without some exercise in public consultation. This chapter looks at the process of policy development ... and consider[s] how the UK might tackle the task of developing a domestic bill of rights.

Terms of Reference and Timetable

300. The Labour Party has proposed 'an all-party commission that will be charged with drafting the bill of rights and considering a suitable method of entrenchment'; while the Liberal Democrats propose a two stage process: 'Our Constitutional Assembly would ... draw up a Bill of Rights which would include the European Convention and the Covenant, and largely follow the IPPR Bill of Rights ... The second stage would be to require the Constituent Assembly to consider any amendments which are needed to the Bill of Rights. The Bill of Rights would then be included in the written constitution and would be entrenched when the referendum approving the constitution was passed ...'

301. Whoever is charged with the task, the development of a domestic bill or bill of rights within the UK will require a clear definition of the starting point. This will depend in part on whether ... the development phase is part of a wider process of negotiation towards a new constitutional settlement – of which a bill of rights forms only a part – and which may therefore require the accommodation of political or partisan views as to the terms of reference. Equally, it will depend on whether there is strong political leadership from the Government of the day. However, as a domestic instrument of fundamental rights could not be framed in terms inconsistent with or in disregard of existing human rights obligations, whether incorporated into UK law or not, two starting points can immediately be suggested:

- the provisions of some or all of the UK's existing international obligations could be combined into one coherent document, which included the 'highest' degree of protection from the range of texts in each area of human rights: essentially a task for experts, not politicians.
- a more fundamental process of inquiry and policy development could be initiated, which would produce a set of rights which were not in contravention of existing obligations, but need not expressly include all their provisions and might add some new provisions that were entirely self-developed or drawn from human rights instruments not ratified by the UK ...

UK Experience

304. There is a strong expectation within the British tradition that constitutional reform should be based on broad public and cross-party consultation. This view is clearly held by both the Labour and Liberal Democrats in relation to the development of domestic bills of rights. However, attempts at resolving constitutional issues through consultation do not have a happy track record within the UK (some attempts, like the Conservative Party's

1979 manifesto pledge of all-party talks on a bill of rights, fail to reach even the starting gates). Protracted consultation is clearly not the most efficient or necessarily productive way of making and implementing policy. If there is the necessary political will and party unity can be assumed, or manufactured, there is every reason to regard the resources of Whitehall as the most efficient way of developing policy. But getting legislation on the statute book is not all. 'Efficiency' also includes making constitutional reforms endure beyond the lifetime of a particular Government: coherence and legitimacy are equally important. Those interested in embarking on constitutional reform in the UK this century have nearly always attempted to engage with other political parties and consult outside of political elites, even if these attempts are subsequently abandoned. This is likely to be particularly important where (as with a bill of rights) it is desirable that the legislation be regarded as, for all intents and purposes, not subject to repeal by a future Government.

305. The absence of any fixed procedure for constitutional amendment means that where a Government does not have definitive plans for reform or chooses to consult on its proposals before implementation, there is a range of vehicles that it might use. In this sense, the UK's unwritten constitution makes a degree of innovation more possible than in those countries where procedures for constitutional amendment are closely defined. In the UK, specific problems can have solutions designed to meet them: one example being the Nolan Committee on Standards in Public Life. This section considers some of the possible models available to a Government intent on developing policy in relation to constitutional issues.

Building Political Consensus

Cross-party talks

306. During the twentieth century there have been repeated attempts to secure consensus on constitutional measures through cross-party talks. These have been held under various titles and include both private talks at a Privy Councillor level and more public and formal inter-party talks ...

308. The option of inter-party talks will inevitably be raised in the context of future constitutional reform. It is obvious that, given the different constitutional views and political interests of the parties, it is never going to be easy to reach cross-party agreement on constitutional issues. Yet the success of such an approach requires the politics of consensus to prevail. If it does not, the consequential reforms are likely to be either piecemeal – introduced on the basis of whatever agreement was reached, not the comprehensive reforms originally intended – or rejected by the opposition parties. There is significant scope for tactical manoeuvering by opposition parties during the talks, or even for frustrating the very establishment of talks by non-participation. There is also a danger that the party leaders may not be representative of the party at large, and may not be willing or able to whip their backbenchers into line during subsequent parliamentary proceedings.

309. The process of inter-party talks therefore needs to engage back-benchers in the consultation process as far as is possible. Even if formal involvement is not practicable, there is value in keeping backbenchers up to date with the progress of discussions and the reasons for any apparent compromises made. Equally, debate and agreement within the Cabinet on the Government's own stance is a crucial pre-requisite to successful negotiations in any cross-party forum. Where talks break down, any decision to proceed with the measure should recognise that it can no longer expect support across the House and the bill should be framed accordingly. It is also important that those taking part in the negotiations are in a position within their own parties to ensure that the decisions reached are accepted. Otherwise, even where agreements are reached, they may not be sustained through the parliamentary passage of resulting legislation.

310. The keys to success are likely to be ensuring sufficiently high level political engagement whilst avoiding the danger of establishing an inward looking clique, immersed in the detail of the issues and unconcerned with the wider political ramifications (as happened in 1969 with the reform of the House of Lords). The principal advantages are that the concerns and preferences of the parties can be teased out in negotiations which enable suitable solutions to be developed at an early stage – especially if the talks are focused on principles rather than the detail. Moreover, if successful in reaching a conclusion, they should smooth the passage of legislation. This approach does not preclude the commissioning of research to assist in deliberations nor the publication of consultative papers (or the use of other consultative mechanisms e.g. polling) to discover public opinion.

Constituent assemblies and constitutional conventions

311. A constituent assembly is a body comprised of people elected for the purpose of drafting a constitution, although the term 'constitutional convention' has also been used to apply to what are essentially constituent assemblies, as with the United States Constitutional Convention in 1787 and the Northern Ireland Constitutional Convention of 1973. The term constitutional convention is used here to refer to a body made up of a combination of politicians, experts and the wider civic community – as, for example, in the case of the Scottish Constitutional Convention ...

313. The role, functions and timeframe of a constituent assembly are issues that require negotiation rather than imposition. Experience shows that the use of a constituent assembly can be time consuming and does not guarantee the acceptance or durability of any agreement reached. Ultimately, the device of a constituent assembly does not avoid the need to tackle party political differences and to maintain the momentum of reform through negotiation as well as consensus building. It may also prove inadequate to deal with a non-crisis situation, as 'the motive power of constituent assemblies will come from acting quickly, in periods of great public euphoria where natural law ideas are dominant – normally following on some great political or social revolution or similar upheaval, when there is little difficulty for the constitution-makers in perceiving the nature of the public mood and in translating it into technical legal form.'

314. Although it has no official status, the Scottish Constitutional Convention (SCC) launched in 1989 provides an example of how a constitutional convention could work. It is made up of representatives of the Scottish Labour Party, the Scottish Liberal Democrats and representatives of other parts of Scottish civic society: the trade unions, local government, churches, women's movement, ethnic minority groups and sections of the business and industrial community. The aim of the SCC was to develop a workable and realistic scheme for a Scottish Parliament. The SCC proceeded initially through working groups and prepared a draft scheme in 1990. Issues which were left outstanding, such as proposals on gender balance, electoral system and constitutional implications at a UK level, were referred to a Constitutional Commission which was established in 1993. The Commission was a much smaller body which took expert evidence on these technical issues and reported its findings back to the Convention for decision.

315. The Scottish Constitutional Convention has been successful in attracting support and achieving consensus in its decision making. In bringing together such a wide cross-section of people and engaging politicians in the process, the SCC has managed to be both educational and consultative and to combine technical advice with building political consensus. It represents a degree of cross party cooperation which is quite alien to national politics (although not so uncommon at local government level). Even so, three important limitations should be noted. First, the Scottish Conservatives and the SNP both refused to participate in the Convention thus limiting the authority of its recommendations. Second, although its recommendations have been endorsed by the leaders of both main opposition parties, the Labour Party's recent announcement that it would not introduce a Scottish Parliament unless approved by a referendum demonstrates the political weakness of a policy position developed by those other than national party leaders. Second, the consensus rule for decision-making meant that where no such consensus could be reached, the Convention has remained silent. Hence its proposals do not deal exhaustively with all the issues that are raised by the prospect of devolution, nor have their proposals yet faced the test of implementation.

Calling in the Experts

Royal Commissions

316. There is some appeal in setting up a small committee of experts to produce a draft bill of rights, not least because most of the legal intricacies and technicalities of drafting would be of little interest to most members of the public; whilst those parties with an interest could easily give evidence. The Human Rights Bill introduced by Graham Allen MP in 1994 [*RB NOTE: see Doc. 147*], for example, proposed the establishment of a Bill of Rights Commission, with the function of preparing a draft bill of rights relating to all civil, political, economic and social rights in the United Kingdom. The members of the Commission were to be appointed by the Lord Chancellor and Lord Advocate after public consultation, but within two months of

incorporation of the ECHR. They were to have a 'duty' to report within two years, and the Lord Chancellor was to be obliged to lay copies of the draft bill before both Houses of Parliament not later than one month afterwards.

317. There are no standard criteria for when it is appropriate or helpful to set up an expert commission, nor when it is appropriate for a Commission to be designated Royal. There has been one previous attempt to refer constitutional reform to a Royal Commission. In 1968, the Wilson Government set up the Royal Commission on the Constitution, chaired first by Lord Crowther and then by Lord Kilbrandon, in response to growing demands for decentralisation. The Commission was first decided on in 1968, started work in 1969 and reported in October 1973. Professor Vernon Bogdanor has argued, and the view is widely supported, that the Commission was established as the 'expedient of a harassed administration ... the demand for immediate concessions to meet the nationalist threat could be contained, and by the time the Kilbrandon Commission reported the SNP and Plaid Cymru might no longer be so credible politically, in which case its findings could be quietly pigeonholed.'

319. The principal advantage of a Royal Commission is that it is a public body which is expected to invite evidence from a wide range of bodies and individuals. In doing so a Royal Commission can raise and address new ideas and may also create a climate sympathetic to change. However, it is not overstating the case to say that there are more reasons why a Royal Commission might be inappropriate or ineffectual, particularly in considering the contents of a domestic bill of rights. First, Royal Commissions are famously regarded as an 'excuse for procrastination' and even setting one up would raise questions about a Government's commitment to reform. Second, Royal Commissions may produce findings which are not sufficiently policy oriented or which fail to reflect the realities of the political environment into which their recommendations are delivered. There is always a risk that the Government may not welcome the findings produced. The decision then is whether to accept the recommendations despite the Government's own reservations; or to disagree and face the political consequences. The decision to appoint a Royal Commission may therefore serve two unhelpful ends: keeping a contentious issue alive, and without resolution, for a period of years; whilst adversely affecting the reputation and authority of the Government because of public perceptions about the purposes to which Governments put Royal Commissions and their inherent utility.

320. Finally, and perhaps most critical, is the importance of engaging parliamentarians in negotiating a settlement of a constitutional issue, rather than collecting the views of external experts. The contents of a bill of rights will have to reflect political direction as well as the objective analysis which is ostensibly the input of the Royal Commission (quite apart from the fact that it is extremely difficult to identify a range of sufficiently expert, but nonpartisan, Commission members). A Royal Commission might well be able to conduct the sort of exercise that others have done in drawing together international best practice and producing a coherent text that also acknowledged any unique domestic issues identified during the course of

consultation. But to the extent that this sort of objective analysis is required to feed policy decisions, it can just as well be carried out by Departmental or commissioned researchers ...

Constitutional Commission

322. The term constitutional commission is used here to describe an independent, expert, standing body, such as the Law Commission ... It has been suggested by the Editors of the Political Quarterly that a constitutional commission could be established as part of the reform process, providing a new agency which cut across Whitehall boundaries and would be 'committed to the enterprise and has the expertise and authority to drive it along'; and by Dr Geoffrey Marshall and Lord Armstrong (the former Cabinet Secretary) that a constitutional committee composed of Privy Councillors could perform 'an advisory role and make recommendations on issues referred to it.'

323. Were such a Commission in place, it might be a natural home for deliberations on a domestic bill of rights. The advantages of such a constitutional commission would be its potential for ensuring that the reform programme as a whole was coherent and that the interaction of the various elements within it was fully thought through. It would be a means of removing thinking about, if not legislating on, constitutional questions from the political arena; would offer opportunities for ongoing public education in constitutional and citizenship matters (if the Secretariat were appropriately staffed) and could develop as an independent point of reference for ad hoc constitutional questions e.g. the wording of referendum questions ...

Public Consultation

324. There is clearly advantage in ensuring that fundamental rights are not only agreed between politicians, or experts, but also broadly reflect the views of the public at large. This has been the view taken in many other countries, where information exercises, invitations to submit evidence, and so on, have been a central part of the process. However, the classic Green and White Papers are increasingly outmoded, and official dissemination channels are not designed to attract widespread public interest. Public forums, advertising campaigns and more user-friendly and widely available documentation (see, for example, the distribution of the Northern Ireland Frameworks for the Future document) may be used to some effect in improving accessibility and encouraging public participation. The developing tools of electronic democracy may make effective consultation a more manageable and attractive prospect – communications technology may be used to engage citizens through 'electronic summits', on-line provision and exchange of information, and so on, as well as through more traditional 'passive' media such as the televising of the special Committee proceedings in Canada.

325. In respect of a bill of rights, however, there is a particular problem of public education that would need to precede any such debate. There is very

limited public understanding of the notions of 'civil and political rights' (perhaps in significant part because they are taken for granted); and far more enthusiasm for those rights which fall into the categories of social and economic rights ... Politically, therefore, there is a danger of public debate creating expectations that cannot be met because of financial constraints, and of undermining support for existing rights if the debate is mismanaged.

326. In some countries, referendums are required before changes to the constitution can be given effect, and many other countries have chosen to use referendums to settle constitutional issues. There is, however, no example of a referendum being used specifically to approve a bill of rights. In the UK, all three main parties either support, or have not ruled out a referendum on further European integration; and whichever party is in power, some form of referendum is likely to accompany any settlement in Northern Ireland. The Liberal Democrats have promised to extend powers to hold referendums to local and regional government and to introduce advisory citizens' initiative referendums. The Labour Party has promised referendums on electoral reform, the introduction of elected assemblies in the English regions, and on the creation of devolved assemblies for Scotland and Wales. Commenting on this range of planned referendums, Tony Blair has recently said: 'I don't believe in governing by referendum as a general principle, but these are all things that arise because of changes to the constitution.' To the extent that the development of a domestic bill of rights is a core constitutional issue, it must be for consideration whether a referendum might be an appropriate entrenchment mechanism. The judgment will be a political one and, given the UK's limited and not altogether happy experience of referendums, will inevitably be influenced by the experience of referendums held between now and then.

327. However, it would clearly be difficult to conduct a referendum on a new bill of rights unless it had first been exposed to some more in depth form of public consultation – 'yes' and 'no' options are unlikely to be sufficiently sophisticated to offer guidance on the acceptability of a set of fundamental rights. It would certainly be both difficult and absurd to conduct a pre-legislative referendum on the principle of a domestic bill of rights (as Labour proposed in respect of the devolved assemblies) once the ECHR was already incorporated and therefore the principle had been established. However, a referendum might be used as a practical (although not legally binding) entrenchment mechanism once the substance of a bill of rights had been considered by Parliament in the form of legislation – as with the devolution referendums in the 1970s; or a pre-legislative referendum could be held on the basis of a White Paper, including the text of the Bill proposed by the Government ...

International Experience

328. Elsewhere in the world, national bills of rights, and especially those developed over the last twenty years, have been the product of public consultation and inquiry. Even international human rights agreements,

traditionally the preserve of inter-governmental negotiation behind closed doors, have increasingly been influenced by lobbying from non-governmental organisations. The development of tools of mass communications means that there is little excuse for not engaging public interest effectively. Those developing bills of rights have also recognised the importance of avoiding Government dominance of the process (or at least the appearance of such): independent or cross-party bodies have been deployed to assist in the development process ...

329. It is never possible to try to extract any compelling wisdom from the experiences of other countries, not least because the specific political backdrop to any process of policy development and consultation will have significant influence. But some generalisations may be suggested:

- the development of a bill of rights will not come to fruition without (ideally) Government sponsorship at the outset and (certainly) Government support for a specific course of action. Most important is the personal commitment and authoritative leadership of a senior Government figure both during the development process and in 'selling' the outcome to Parliament.
- some sort of consultation process is useful, but must establish public credibility through its *modus operandi.*
- if recommendations are to be made by an independent body, the Government should set clear terms of reference, which offer a framework of principle. For example, the terms of reference could establish that the body is to consider only the possible contents of a bill of rights, not whether one is a good idea or not; and could offer an indication of the Government's own views on existing examples of bills of rights to provide a political steer, which the Commission can choose to adopt or not.
- it is possible to combine expert, public and parliamentary input to the policy development process ...

Conclusion

333. The process of defining a bill of rights will involve discussion not only of its contents but of the entrenchment and enforcement mechanisms. There are two distinct aspects to the development of a domestic bill of rights – the production of a skeleton bill, drawing on international standards; and the use of a consultative forum that engages the public and expert opinion. A commitment to the second stage should be included in either the legislation incorporating the ECHR or in a White Paper; and the consultation processes and timetable should be declared as soon as possible. A referendum might be used as an entrenchment mechanism for a new domestic bill of rights; alternatively the proposals might form part of a subsequent election platform. But ultimately, the successful adoption of a bill of rights will depend upon it having genuine political backing within the Government and deft political execution of the process of development.

334. In respect of contents as well as entrenchment and enforcement mechanisms, there is considerable international experience to draw on, not

only that of Canada. The various international rights instruments will undoubtedly be drawn upon for the substance of the text, but a clear decision will be needed at the outset – influencing the choice of consultative vehicle(s) – as to whether the exercise is to be limited to amalgamation of these texts. The issue of a domestic bill of rights is likely to bring to the fore ideological differences as to what new rights, especially social and economic rights, should be recognised. Such differences of opinion have largely disappeared in relation to the ECHR (e.g. on the question of trade union rights and the private ownership of property) because of the absence of any committed position in the Convention on these issues. As to the domestic enforcement machinery, the framework adopted for the ECHR will provide a starting point, but the extent to which it will prove appropriate for a domestic bill of rights will depend on two factors: the changing constitutional backdrop; and the reactions to the operation of the ECHR in practice. In addition, if social and economic rights are provided for, it will also be important to recognise that they give rise to rather different problems of justiciability and enforcement than civil and political rights. For these reasons, this report does not seek to examine the detailed process of adopting a domestic bill of rights.

335. However, a few concluding observations can be made. The recurring objections to the adoption of a bill of rights in the UK have been its possible impact on parliamentary sovereignty and the perceived risk of 'politicizing' the judiciary. These fears are likely to be greater in relation to a domestic bill of rights, newly created, as compared to the rights set out in a instrument to which the UK has been a signatory for nearly fifty years. They might be lessened if the ECHR had been seen to operate without threat to the constitutional fabric. This argues for considerable care to be given to the planning of this first stage of reform, with one eye to the impact of the initial arrangements on the subsequent debate. A further factor influencing change in the operating machinery would be the potential financial costs of the existing arrangements in relation to the ECHR and the likely implications of any new rights, especially if they went beyond those rights already covered by the UK's international human rights obligations. There are also likely to be fundamental disagreements across the political parties (and in the wider community) as to which rights should be included. There would therefore be every advantage in relying on the international human rights instruments that already bind the UK as the basis of a domestic bill of rights.

Constitution Unit, *Human Rights Legislation*, 1996, pp. 114f.

---

149   BRITISH PUBLIC OPINION'S SUPPORT FOR A DOMESTIC BILL OF RIGHTS, 1989–97

MORI

Q. To what extent do you agree or disagree with these statements? 'Britain needs a Bill of Rights to protect the liberty of the individual'

	1989	Mar 1991	Jan 1995	25–28 Apr 1997
	%	%	%	%
Strongly agree	24	25	35	28
Tend to agree	36	47	38	42
Neither agree nor disagree	30	12	9	12
Tend to disagree	6	9	8	9
Strongly disagree	2	2	2	2
Don't know	2	5	8	7
Agree	60	72	73	70
Disagree	8	11	10	11
Net agree	+52	+61	+63	+59

MORI interviewed a representative quota sample of 962 British adults aged 18+ at 86 ED-cluster sampling points across Great Britain. Interviews were conducted face-to-face, in home, on 25–28 April 1997 as part of MORI's regular CAPI Omnibus survey. The survey was conducted for *The Economist* and published on 2 May 1997.

---

150   THE PRE-1997 ELECTION LABOUR PARTY – LIBERAL DEMOCRATS JOINT AGREEMENT ON CONSTITUTIONAL REFORM AND HUMAN RIGHTS LEGISLATION, 1997

The establishment of the Joint Consultative Committee

1. In Summer 1996 Tony Blair and Paddy Ashdown asked Robin Cook and Robert Maclennan to explore the possibility of co-operation between the Labour and Liberal Democrat parties in relation to constitutional reform. Both parties had for some time been committed to a programme of constitutional change and shared a common view of the need to reform our democratic institutions and to renew the relationship between politics and the people. Following progress in the initial discussions the two parties

agreed in October 1996 to establish a Joint Consultative Committee with the following terms of reference:

2. 'To examine the current proposals of the Labour and Liberal Democrat Parties for constitutional reform: to consider whether there might be sufficient common ground to enable the parties to reach agreement on a legislative programme for constitutional reform; to consider means by which such a programme might best be implemented and to make recommendations.'

This is the report of the Joint Consultative Committee's work …

Foreword

4. The objectives of the British Constitution should be to secure a government that is democratic and a society that is open and free. Democratic Government should ensure that those who hold power in the name of the people are accountable to the collective wishes and interests of the people. Each individual citizen should have equal rights and responsibilities in an open society where the aim is to guarantee civil liberty, social cohesion and economic opportunity.

5. Democracy and freedom cannot be taken for granted. Every generation has a responsibility to ensure that these principles are given fresh meaning and defended against any tendency on the part of those in power to diminish their accountability to the people. There is today a pressing need to renew democracy in Britain.

6. There is too much power centralised in the hands of too few people and too little freedom for local communities to decide their own priorities.

7. Government holds more information than ever before, but the public still has no legal right to share information collected by their Government.

8. Parliament itself has probably not been held in lower esteem since the completion of the universal franchise. The passage of deeply unpopular and impractical measures such as the poll tax has raised doubts about both the accountability of MPs and the effectiveness of their scrutiny.

9. And Britain is alone in the Western world in allowing some people to take a seat in Parliament on the hereditary principle rather than by the democratic process.

10. Democracy cannot stay healthy if one party always stays in power. The defeat of the Conservative Government would in itself be an important demonstration that Government must be accountable to the people and cannot persistently ignore the wishes of the people.

11. However, a change of Government is not in itself sufficient. We believe we must also change our constitution in line with British traditions in order to renew democracy and to bring power closer to the people.

12. These objectives are not a minority concern. The accountability of power in our country determines how decisions are taken every day in ways which affect the lives of every citizen. The new system of local control of the NHS is only one of many recent examples of the manner in which public services have become more remote from local communities.

13. Nor is a modern and accountable constitution a more expensive constitution. On the contrary, we believe that local people often know better what will provide a more cost effective local use of public resources. A more open and devolved constitution will liberate talent, energy and initiative which at present does not find adequate outlet in our centralised state.

14. In the sections which follow we set out our priorities for reform. This programme represents a transfer of power to make political institutions more responsive to the people. It is a programme which offers Britain a constitution for the future, not the past. It will share power with the many, not preserve it in the hands of the few.

15. We have not attempted to spell out in detail the legislative programme for the next Parliament. The programme set out here will be implemented over a period of time. There are some agreed necessary priorities but it would be quite mistaken to suggest that measures of constitutional reform which are not to be implemented immediately, or in the first year of government, are somehow of lesser importance. A reform process must establish momentum and carry through a stage by stage programme of reform.

16. If this programme is enacted, Britain's democracy will have been transformed. We will enter the twenty first century a stronger, more democratic and more open society. It is a prize for which both our parties are determined to work.

Robin Cook   Robert Maclennan

Bringing rights home

17. The provision in UK law of a code of human rights is essential to guarantee an open society and a modern democracy. The United Kingdom has been a signatory to the European Convention of Human Rights since 1951. People in this country are offered the protection and the guarantees of basic human rights that the Convention provides yet to gain access to those rights, British citizens must appeal to the Commission and Court in Strasbourg.

18. Both parties agree that the rights and duties defined by the ECHR and its First Protocol should be incorporated by Act of Parliament into United Kingdom law. This Act would not affect the sovereign powers of Parliament.

19. When introducing Bills into Parliament, Ministers would be required to explain why any provision is, or appears to be, inconsistent with ECHR rights. This would strengthen Parliamentary scrutiny and aid the courts in interpreting Parliament's intentions in legislating.

20. The new Act would enable everyone to rely upon ECHR rights through the ordinary courts and tribunals.

21. A Joint Select Committee of both Houses of Parliament would monitor the operation of the new Act, scrutinise pending legislative meas-

ures in the light of ECHR rights, and advise Parliament about compliance with the UK's obligations under the international human rights codes to which it is party.

22. A Human Rights Commissioner or Commission, or similar public body, would provide advice and assistance to those seeking the protection of the rights enshrined in the Convention, and be itself able to bring proceedings to secure effective compliance with the ECHR, whether by judicial review or by representative proceedings on behalf of a number of people.

23. Incorporation of the ECHR would represent a very significant strengthening in practice of what amounts to the UK's fundamental law. The Convention, written in 1950, would need to be updated over time as a model for modern constitutional protection of basic human rights and responsibilities inherent in being a British citizen ...

Conclusion

86. The proposals set out in our report are presented as distinct measures yet they are closely related. Through them runs the common thread of empowering the people. To make this clear the new Government should make an early declaration setting out the principles behind its programme of constitutional reform and outlining the more open and modern democracy it seeks to create.

Report of the Joint Consultative Committee on Constitutional Reform, 1997, pp. 2, 4–6, 18.

RB NOTE: This concord reached between the Labour Party and Liberal Democrats in the above Joint Consultative Committee Report bodes well not only for implementing the measures of constitutional reform contained within the document within the lifetime of the Parliament commenced in May 1997, but for longer-term planning purposes including those affecting a constitutional Bill of Rights.

Significantly, paragraph 23 of the document refers to the fact that, insofar as statutory incorporation of the European Convention on Human Rights might be regarded as a first-stage form of Bill of Rights for the UK, it will 'need to be updated over time as a model for modern constitutional protection of basic human rights and responsibilities inherent in being a British citizen'. This refers to the desirability of our own indigenous Bill of Rights and is to be interpreted within the context of both political parties' long-term objective, included in Chapter 6 (see especially Docs 93 and 112), and regularly referred to in this book, in favour of the construction of a homegrown entrenched Bill of Rights for the UK.

Tony Blair's strong level of commitment as Labour Prime Minister to his government working closely with the Liberal Democrats over constitutional matters was evidenced by his creation in July 1997 of a special Cabinet Committee devoted to their collaboration (see Doc. 151 below).

That Labour's 418 MPs are now allied with 46 Liberal Democrats over constitutional affairs, a combined overall majority in the House of Commons of 269 MPs, indicates the great potential which now exists for planning further reform which builds upon the success of the Human Rights Act 1998, both in terms of policy initiation with respect to a home-grown Bill of Rights, and for the prospects of achieving the necessary degree of widespread political acceptance required before implementing a measure of such fundamental importance to the constitution.

---

151 THE PRIME MINISTER, TONY BLAIR, APPOINTS A
SPECIAL CABINET COMMITTEE FOR POLICY
COLLABORATION BETWEEN LABOUR AND THE
LIBERAL DEMOCRATS, 1997

Joint Consultative Committee with the Liberal Democrats

Composition
Prime Minister (Chairman)

Other Ministers and Liberal Democrat spokesmen are invited to attend as necessary.

Terms of reference
'To consider policy issues of joint interest to the Government and the Liberal Democrats'.

---

152 THE NEW NORTHERN IRELAND HUMAN RIGHTS
COMMISSION IS AUTHORIZED TO CONSULT AND
ADVISE THE GOVERNMENT ON A BILL OF RIGHTS
FOR NORTHERN IRELAND, 1998

The Good Friday Agreement

Rights, Safeguards and Equality of Opportunity: Human
Rights

1. The parties affirm their commitment to the mutual respect, the civil rights and the religious liberties of everyone in the community. Against the background of the recent history of communal conflict, the parties affirm in particular:
● the right of free political thought;

- the right to freedom and expression of religion;
- the right to pursue democratically national and political aspirations;
- the right to seek constitutional change by peaceful and legitimate means;
- the right to freely choose one's place of residence;
- the right to equal opportunity in all social and economic activity, regardless of class, creed, disability, gender or ethnicity;
- the right to freedom from sectarian harassment; and
- the right of women to full and equal political participation.

United Kingdom legislation

2. The British Government will complete incorporation into Northern Ireland law of the European Convention on Human Rights (ECHR), with direct access to the courts, and remedies for breach of the Convention, including power for the courts to overrule Assembly legislation on grounds of inconsistency.

3. Subject to the outcome of public consultation under way, the British Government intends, as a particular priority, to create a statutory obligation on public authorities in Northern Ireland to carry out all their functions with due regard to the need to promote equality of opportunity in relation to religion and political opinion; gender; race; disability; age; marital status; dependants; and sexual orientation. Public bodies would be required to draw up statutory schemes showing how they would implement this obligation. Such schemes would cover arrangements for policy appraisal, including an assessment of impact on relevant categories, public consultation, public access to information and services, monitoring and timetables.

4. The new Northern Ireland Human Rights Commission (see paragraph 5 below) will be invited to consult and to advise on the scope for defining, in Westminster legislation, rights supplementary to those in the European Convention on Human Rights, to reflect the particular circumstances of Northern Ireland, drawing as appropriate on international instruments and experience. These additional rights to reflect the principles of mutual respect for the identity and ethos of both communities and parity of esteem, and – taken together with the ECHR – to constitute a Bill of Rights for Northern Ireland. Among the issues for consideration by the Commission will be:

- the formulation of a general obligation on government and public bodies fully to respect, on the basis of equality of treatment, the identity and ethos of both communities in Northern Ireland; and
- a clear formulation of the rights not to be discriminated against and to equality of opportunity in both the public and private sectors.

New institutions in Northern Ireland

5. A new Northern Ireland Human Rights Commission, with membership from Northern Ireland reflecting the community balance, will be established by Westminster legislation, independent of Government, with an extended

and enhanced role beyond that currently exercised by the Standing Advisory Commission on Human Rights, to include keeping under review the adequacy and effectiveness of laws and practices, making recommendations to Government as necessary; providing information and promoting awareness of human rights; considering draft legislation referred to them by the new Assembly; and, in appropriate cases, bringing court proceedings or providing assistance to individuals doing so.

6. Subject to the outcome of public consultation currently under way, the British Government intends a new statutory Equality Commission to replace the Fair Employment Commission, the Equal Opportunities Commission (NI), the Commission for Racial Equality (NI) and the Disability Council. Such a unified Commission will advise on, validate and monitor the statutory obligation and will investigate complaints of default.

7. It would be open to a new Northern Ireland Assembly to consider bringing together its responsibilities for these matters into a dedicated Department of Equality.

8. These improvements will build on existing protections in Westminster legislation in respect of the judiciary, the system of justice and policing.

Comparable steps by the Irish Government

9. The Irish Government will also take steps to further strengthen the protection of human rights in its jurisdiction. The Government will, taking account of the work of the All-Party Oireachtas Committee on the Constitution and the Report of the Constitution Review Group, bring forward measures to strengthen and underpin the constitutional protection of human rights. These proposals will draw on the European Convention on Human Rights and other international legal instruments in the field of human rights and the question of the incorporation of the ECHR will be further examined in this context. The measures brought forward would ensure at least an equivalent level of protection of human rights as will pertain in Northern Ireland. In addition, the Irish Government will:

- establish a Human Rights Commission with a mandate and remit equivalent to that within Northern Ireland;
- proceed with arrangements as quickly as possible to ratify the Council of Europe Framework Convention on National Minorities (already ratified by the UK);
- implement enhanced employment equality legislation;
- introduce equal status legislation; and
- continue to take further active steps to demonstrate its respect for the different traditions in the island of Ireland.

A joint committee

10. It is envisaged that there would be a joint committee of representatives of the two Human Rights Commissions, North and South, as a forum for consideration of human rights issues in the island of Ireland. The joint committee will consider, among other matters, the possibility of establishing a charter, open to signature by all democratic political parties, reflecting and

endorsing agreed measures for the protection of the fundamental rights of everyone living in the island of Ireland.

Cm 3883, 1998.

Northern Ireland Act 1998

Human Rights and Equal Opportunities

68.—(1) There shall be a body corporate to be known as the Northern Ireland Human Rights Commission.

(2) The Commission shall consist of a Chief Commissioner and other Commissioners appointed by the Secretary of State.

(3) In making appointments under this section, the Secretary of State shall as far as practicable secure that the Commissioners, as a group, are representative of the community in Northern Ireland.

(4) Schedule 7 (which makes supplementary provision about the Commission) shall have effect.

69.—(1) The Commission shall keep under review the adequacy and effectiveness in Northern Ireland of law and practice relating to the protection of human rights.

(2) The Commission shall, before the end of the period of two years beginning with the commencement of this section, make to the Secretary of State such recommendations as it thinks fit for improving—
  (a) its effectiveness;
  (b) the adequacy and effectiveness of the functions conferred on it by this Part; and
  (c) the adequacy and effectiveness of the provisions of this Part relating to it.

(3) The Commission shall advise the Secretary of State and the Executive Committee of the Assembly of legislative and other measures which ought to be taken to protect human rights—
  (a) as soon as reasonably practicable after receipt of a general or specific request for advice; and
  (b) on such other occasions as the Commission thinks appropriate.

(4) The Commission shall advise the Assembly whether a Bill is compatible with human rights—
  (a) as soon as reasonably practicable after receipt of a request for advice; and
  (b) on such other occasions as the Commission thinks appropriate.

(5) The Commission may—
  (a) give assistance to individuals in accordance with section 70; and

(b) bring proceedings involving law or practice relating to the protection of human rights.

(6) The Commission shall promote understanding and awareness of the importance of human rights in Northern Ireland; and for this purpose it may undertake, commission or provide financial or other assistance for—
  (a) research; and
  (b) educational activities.

(7) The Secretary of State shall request the Commission to provide advice of the kind referred to in paragraph 4 of the Human Rights section of the Belfast Agreement.

(8) For the purpose of exercising its functions under this section the Commission may conduct such investigations as it considers necessary or expedient.

(9) The Commission may decide to publish its advice and the outcome of its research and investigations.

(10) The Commission shall do all that it can to ensure the establishment of the committee referred to in paragraph 10 of that section of that Agreement.

(11) In this section—
  (a) a reference to the Assembly includes a reference to a committee of the Assembly;
  (b) 'human rights' includes the Convention rights.

70.—(1) This section applies to—
  (a) proceedings involving law or practice relating to the protection of human rights which a person in Northern Ireland has commenced, or wishes to commence; or
  (b) proceedings in the course of which such a person relies, or wishes to rely, on such law or practice.

(2) Where the person applies to the Northern Ireland Human Rights Commission for assistance in relation to proceedings to which this section applies, the Commission may grant the application on any of the following grounds—
  (a) that the case raises a question of principle;
  (b) that it would be unreasonable to expect the person to deal with the case without assistance because of its complexity, or because of the person's position in relation to another person involved, or for some other reason,
  (c) that there are other special circumstances which make it appropriate for the Commission to provide assistance.

(3) Where the Commission grants an application under subsection (2) it may—
  (a) provide, or arrange for the provision of, legal advice;
  (b) arrange for the provision of legal representation;

(c) provide any other assistance which it thinks appropriate.

(4) Arrangements made by the Commission for the provision of assistance to a person may include provision for recovery of expenses from the person in certain circumstances.

Schedule 7: The Northern Ireland Human Rights Commission

Introductory

1. In this Schedule 'the Commission' means the Northern Ireland Human Rights Commission.

Commissioners' tenure

2.—(1) Subject to the provisions of this Schedule, a Commissioner shall hold office in accordance with the terms of his appointment.

(2) A Commissioner shall not be appointed—
   (a) in the case of the Chief Commissioner, for more than five years at a time; and
   (b) in any other case, for more than three years at a time.

(3) A person may resign as a Commissioner or as Chief Commissioner by notice in writing to the Secretary of State.

(4) The Secretary of State may dismiss a person from his office as Commissioner or Chief Commissioner if satisfied—
   (a) that he has without reasonable excuse failed to discharge his functions for a continuous period of three months beginning not earlier than six months before, the day of dismissal;
   (b) that he has been convicted of a criminal offence;
   (c) that a bankruptcy order has been made against him, or his estate has been sequestrated, or he has made a composition or arrangement with, or granted a trust deed for, his creditors; or
   (d) that he is unable or unfit to carry out his functions.

Commissioners' salary etc.

3.—(1) The Commission shall pay to or in respect of Commissioners—
   (a) remuneration;
   (b) allowances and fees; and
   (c) sums for the provision of pensions,

in accordance with directions of the Secretary of State.

(2) Where a person who by reference to any office or employment is a participant in a scheme under section 1 of the Superannuation Act 1972 becomes a Commissioner or the Chief Commissioner, the Minister for the Civil Service may, notwithstanding any provision made under sub-paragraph (1)(c), determine that the person's service as Commissioner or

Chief Commissioner shall be treated for the purposes of the scheme as service in that office or employment.

Staff

4.—(1) The Commission may employ staff subject to the approval of the Secretary of State as to numbers and as to remuneration and other terms and conditions of employment.

(2) Employment with the Commission shall be included among the kinds of employment to which a superannuation scheme under section 1 of the Superannuation Act 1972 can apply, and accordingly in Schedule 1 to that Act (in which those kinds of employment are listed) after 'Commission for Racial Equality' insert—

'Northern Ireland Human Rights Commission'.

(3) The Commission shall pay to the Minister for the Civil Service, at such times as he may direct, such sums as he may determine in respect of any increase attributable to sub-paragraph (2) in the sums payable out of money provided by Parliament under the Superannuation Act 1972.

Annual report

5.—(1) The Commission shall, as soon as reasonably practicable after the end of each year, make a report to the Secretary of State on the performance of its functions during the year.

(2)The Secretary of State shall lay a copy of the report before each House of Parliament . . .

Procedure

8.—(1) In determining its own procedure the Commission may, in partic- ular, make provision about—
    (a) the discharge of its functions by committees (which may include persons who are not Commissioners);
    (b) a quorum for meetings of the Commission or a committee . . .

Status

11. The Commission shall not be regarded as the servant or agent of the Crown or as enjoying any status, immunity or privilege of the Crown; and property of the Commission shall not be regarded as property of, or held on behalf of, the Crown.

1998, Doc. 47.

> # 153 THE MINISTERIAL COMMITTEE AND SUB-COMMITTEES OF THE CABINET APPOINTED BY PRIME MINISTER TONY BLAIR TO CONSIDER AND CO-ORDINATE POLICIES ON CONSTITUTIONAL REFORM, 1997–8

MINISTERIAL COMMITTEE ON CONSTITUTIONAL REFORM POLICY

Composition
Prime Minister (Chairman)
Deputy Prime Minister and Secretary of State for Environment, Transport and the Regions
Chancellor of the Exchequer
Secretary of State for Foreign and Commonwealth Affairs
Lord Chancellor
Secretary of State for the Home Department
Secretary of State for Scotland
President of the Council
Secretary of State for Northern Ireland
Secretary of State for Wales
Lord Privy Seal
Parliamentary Secretary, Treasury
Minister without Portfolio

Other Ministers may be invited to attend as necessary.

Terms of reference
'To consider strategic issues relating to the Government's constitutional reform policies.'

RB NOTE: Various Sub-Committees have been created by the Prime Minister, Tony Blair, to report to the above Committee on Constitutional Reform Policy. Two are documented below, one being a body concerned with incorporation of the European Convention on Human Rights, another being concerned with reform of the House of Lords. Other Ministerial Committees of relevance to future human rights reform include one on Legislation (dealing with issues of parliamentary procedure).

MINISTERIAL SUB-COMMITTEE ON INCORPORATION OF THE EUROPEAN CONVENTION ON HUMAN RIGHTS

Composition
Lord Chancellor (Chairman)
Deputy Prime Minister and Secretary of State for Environment, Transport and the Regions

Secretary of State for Foreign and Commonwealth Affairs
Secretary of State for the Home Department
Secretary of State for Education and Employment
Secretary of State for Scotland
Secretary of State for Defence
Secretary of State for Health
President of the Council
Secretary of State for Social Security
Secretary of State for Northern Ireland
Secretary of State for Wales
Lord Privy Seal
Chief Secretary, Treasury
Parliamentary Secretary, Treasury
Attorney General
Lord Advocate

Other Ministers are invited to attend for items in which they have a departmental interest.

Terms of reference
'To consider policy and other issues arising from the Government's decision to legislate for the incorporation of the ECHR in UK law and to promote and oversee progress of the relevant legislation through Parliament and its subsequent implementation, reporting as necessary to the Ministerial Committee on Constitutional Reform Policy.'

MINISTERIAL SUB-COMMITTEE ON HOUSE OF LORDS REFORM

Composition
Lord Chancellor (Chairman)
Home Secretary
President of the Council
Lord Privy Seal
Parliamentary Secretary, Treasury
Captain of the Gentleman at Arms
Minister without Portfolio
Other Ministers may be invited to attend as necessary.

Terms of reference
'To consider policy and other issues arising from the Government's plans for reform of the House of Lords and to make recommendations to the Ministerial Committee on Constitutional Reform Policy.'

SELECT BIBLIOGRAPHY

The bibliography is of selected works which are relevant to the proposal for a constitutional Bill of Rights for the United Kingdom. They are listed under the general headings of (1) Constitutional Reform and the Bill of Rights Debate, (2) Legal Works of Reference, (3) Comparative and International, and (4) Theoretical and Historical. There then follows a list of (5) Parliamentary Debates, comprising the principal occasions on which House of Commons and House of Lords has considered the question of a Bill of Rights or some subject of relevance to the reform.

(1) CONSTITUTIONAL REFORM AND THE BILL OF RIGHTS DEBATE

Allen, Graham, *Reinventing Democracy* (London: Features Unlimited, 1995).

Barnett, A., Ellis, C. and Hirst, P. (ed.), *Debating the Constitution: New Perspectives on Constitutional Reform* (Cambridge: Polity Press, 1993).

Bean, David (ed.), *Law Reform for All* (London: Blackstone Press, 1996).

Benn, Tony and Hood, Tony, *Common Sense: A New Constitution for Britain* (London: Random House, 1993).

Bingham, T. H., "The Courts and the Constitution", (1996) *King's College Law Journal* 12.

Bingham, T. H., "The European Convention on Human Rights: Time to Incorporate", (1993) *Law Quarterly Review* 390.

Black, Charles, "Is There Already a British Bill of Rights?", (1973) 89 *Law Quarterly Review* 173.

Blackburn, Robert, "Parliamentary Opinion on a New Bill of Rights", (1989) *Political Quarterly* 469.

Blackburn, Robert and Taylor, John (eds), *Human Rights for the 1990s* (London: Mansell, 1991).

Blackburn, Robert and Busuttil, James (eds), *Human Rights for the 21st Century* (London: Pinter, 1997).

Blackburn, Robert and Plant, Raymond (eds), *Constitutional Reform: The Labour Government's Constitutional Reform Agenda* (London: Longman, 1999).

Blair, Tony, *New Britain: My Vision of a Young Country* (London: Fourth Estate, 1996).

Brazier, Rodney, *Constitutional Reform* (Oxford University Press, 1991).

Brown, Gordon, "The Servant State: Towards a New Constitutional Settlement", (1992) 63 *Political Quarterly* 394.

Browne-Wilkinson, Lord, "The Infiltration of a Bill of Rights", (1992) *Public Law* 397.

Campbell, Colin (ed.), *Do We Need a Bill of Rights?* (London: Maurice Temple Smith, 1980).

Commission on Citizenship, *Report on Encouraging Citizenship* (London: HMSO, 1990).

Conservative Party, *The Campaign Guide 1997: A Comprehensive Survey of Conservative Policy* (London: Conservative Research Department, 1997).

Conservative Party, *You Can Only Be Sure with the Conservatives: The Conservative Manifesto 1997* (London: Conservative Central Office, 1997).

Constitution Unit, *Delivering Constitutional Reform* (London: Constitution Unit, 1995).

Constitution Unit, *Human Rights Legislation* (London: Constitution Unit, 1996).

Denning, Lord, *Misuse of Power* (London: BBC, 1980).

Denning, Lord, *What Next in the Law?* (London: Butterworths, 1982).

Donnelly, Katy, "Parliamentary Reform: Paving the Way for Constitutional Reform", (1997) *Parliamentary Affairs* 246.

Duncanson, Ian, "Balloonists, Bills of Rights and Dinosaurs", (1978) *Public Law* 391.

Dworkin, Ronald, *A Bill of Rights for Britain* (London: Chatto and Windus, 1990).

Ewing, K. D. and Gearty, C. A., *Democracy or a Bill of Rights* (London: Society of Labour Lawyers, 1991).

Ewing, K. D. and Gearty, C. A., *Freedom under Thatcher: Civil Liberties in Modern Britain* (Oxford University Press, 1990).

Ewing, K. D., Gearty, C. A. and Hepple, B. A. (eds), *Human Rights and Labour Law* (London: Mansell, 1994).

Fawcett, J. E. S., "A Bill of Rights for the United Kingdom?", (1976) 1 *Human Rights Review* 57.

Fazal, M. A., "Entrenched Rights and Parliamentary Sovereignty", (1974) *Public Law* 295.

Fenwick, Helen, "Protection for the European Convention on Human Rights as a British Bill of Rights", (1997) 21 *Statute Law Review* 12.

Finnie, W., Himsworth, C. and Walker, N. (eds), *Edinburgh Essays in Public Law* (Edinburgh University Press, 1991).

Gardner, J. P. (ed.), *Aspects of Incorporation of the European Convention on Human Rights into Domestic Law* (London: BIICL, 1993).

Gordon, R. and Wilmot-Smith, R. (eds), *Human Rights in the United Kingdom* (Oxford University Press, 1996).

Griffith, J. A. G., "The Political Constitution", (1979) 42 *Modern Law Review* 1.

Griffith, J. A. G., "Judicial Decision-Making in Public Law", (1985) *Public Law* 564.

Griffith, J. A. G., *The Politics of the Judiciary* (London: Fontana, 5th edn 1997).

Hailsham, Lord, *Elective Dictatorship* (London: BBC, 1976).

Hailsham, Lord, *The Dilemma of Democracy* (Glasgow: William Collins, 1978).

Hewitt, Patricia, *The Abuse of Power: Civil Liberties in the United Kingdom* (Oxford: Martin Robertson, 1982).

Holmes, R. and Elliot, M. (eds), 1688–1988: *Time for a New Constitution* (London: Macmillan, 1988).

Home Office discussion document, *Legislation on Human Rights* (London: Home Office, 1976).

Hood Phillips, O., *Reform of the Constitution* (London: Chatto and Windus, 1970).

Independent, The, Series of articles on incorporation of the European Human Rights Convention and a Bill of Rights (by Sarah Helm, Nicolas Browne-Wilkinson, Roy Hattersley, John Roberts, Anthony Lester, William Bennan, Anthony Barnett and Lord Scarman), 20 April to 9 June (1989).

Institute for Public Policy Research, *A British Bill of Rights* (London: IPPR, 2nd edn 1996).

Institute for Public Policy Research, *A Human Rights Commission for the United Kingdom: The Options* (London: IPPR, 1996).

Institute for Public Policy Research, *A Written Constitution for the United Kingdom* (London: Mansell, rev. edn 1993).

Irvine, Lord, "Judges and Decision-Makers", (1996) *Public Law* 59.

Jacobs, F. G., "Towards a United Kingdom Bill of Rights", (1984) 18 *University of Michigan Journal of Law Reform* 29.

Jaconelli, Joseph, *Enacting a Bill of Rights: The Legal Problems* (Oxford University Press, 1980).

Jaconelli, Joseph, "Incorporation of the European Human Rights Convention: Arguments and Misconceptions", (1988) 59 *Political Quarterly* 343.

Johnson, Nevil, *In Search of the Constitution* (London: Methuen, 1977).

Joseph, Sir Keith, *Freedom under the Law* (London: Conservative Political Centre, 1975).

Jowell, J. and Oliver, D. (eds), *The Changing Constitution* (Oxford University Press, 3rd edn 1994).

Kinley, David, *The European Convention on Human Rights: Compliance without Incorporation* (Aldershot: Dartmouth, 1993).

Klug, Francesca and Wadham, John, "The Democratic Entrenchment of a Bill of Rights: Liberty's Proposals", (1993) *Public Law* 579.

Klug, Francesca, *Reinventing Community: The Rights and Responsibilities Debate* (London: Charter 88, 1996).

Klug, Francesca, Starmer, K. and Weir, S., *The Three Pillars of Liberty: Political Rights and Freedoms in the United Kingdom* (London: Routledge, 1996).

Labour Party, *A Charter of Human Rights: Discussion Paper* (London: Labour Party, 1976).

Labour Party, *Meet the Challenge, Make the Change: Final Report of Labour's Policy Review for the 1990s* (London: Labour Party, 1989).

Labour Party, *A New Agenda for Democracy: Labour's Proposals for Constitutional Reform* (London: Labour Party, 1993).

Labour Party, *New Labour, New Life for Britain: Labour's Contract for a New Britain* (London: Labour Party, 1996).

Labour Party (Straw, J. and Boeteng, P.), *Bringing Rights Home: Consultation Paper on Labour's Plans to Incorporate the European Convention on Human Rights into UK Law* (London: Labour Party, 1996).

Labour Party, *New Labour Because Britain Deserves Better: The Labour Manifesto 1997*, (London: Labour Party, 1997).

Labour Party and Liberal Democrats, *Report of the Joint Consultative Committee on Constitutional Reform* (London: Labour Party/Liberal Democrats, 1997).

Lacey, Nicola, "Are Rights Best Left Unwritten?", (1989) 60 *Political Quarterly* 433.

Lester, Anthony, *Democracy and Individual Rights* (London: Fabian Tract 1968).

Lester, Anthony, "Fundamental Rights: The United Kingdom Isolated", (1984) *Public Law* 46.

Lester, Lord, "The Mouse that Roared: the Human Rights Bill 1995", (1995) *Public Law* 198.

Lester, Lord, "First Steps Towards a Constitutional Bill of Rights", (1997) *European Human Rights Law Review* 124.

Lewis, Norman (ed.), *Happy and Glorious: The Constitution in Transition* (Oxford University Press, 1990).

Liberal Democrats, *Here We Stand: Proposals for Modernising Britain's Democracy* (London: Liberal Democrats, 1993).

Liberal Democrats, *Make the Difference: The Liberal Democrat Manfesto 1997* (London: Liberal Democrats, 1997).

Liberty, *A People's Charter: Liberty's Bill of Rights* (London: Liberty, 1991).

Lloyd, Lord, "Do We Need a Bill of Rights?", (1976) 39 *Modern Law Review* 121.

Macdonald, John, *Bill of Rights* (London: Liberal Party, 1969).

Mann, F. A., "Britain's Bill of Rights", (1978) 94 *Law Quarterly Review* 512.

Marshall, Geoffrey, "Overriding a Bill of Rights", (1987) *Public Law* 9.

McCluskey, Lord, *Law, Justice and Democracy* (London: Sweet and Maxwell, 1987).

Milne, A. J., "Should We Have a Bill of Rights?", (1977) 40 *Modern Law Review* 389.

Mount, Ferdinand, *The British Constitution Now* (London: William Heinemann, 1992).

Northern Ireland Standing Advisory Commission on Human Rights, *The Protection of Human Rights by Law in Northern Ireland* (London: HMSO, Cmnd. 7009, 1977).

Norton, Philip, *The Constitution in Flux* (Oxford: Basil Blackwell, 1982).

Oliver, Dawn, *Government in the United Kingdom: The Search for Accountability, Effectiveness and Citizenship* (Buckingham: Open University Press, 1991).

Patten, John, *Political Culture, Conservatism and Rolling Constitutional Change* (London: Conservative Political Centre, 1991).

Political Quarterly, The, *Human Rights in the UK*, Special Issue (Oxford: Blackwell, vol. 68, no. 2, 1997).

Robertson G., *Freedom, the Individual and the Law* (London: Penguin, 7th edn 1993).

Royal Commission on the Constitution, Report of, (London: HMSO, Cmnd. 5460, 1973).

Ryle, Michael, "Pre-legislative Scrutiny: a Prophylactic Approach to the Protection of Human Rights", (1994) *Public Law* 192.

Scarman, Lord, *English Law – The New Dimension* (London: Stevens, 1974).

Scarman, Lord, *Why Britain Needs a Written Constitution* (London: Charter 88, The Fourth Sovereignty Lecture 1992).

Society for Conservative Lawyers, Committee of, *Another Bill of Rights?* (London: Conservative Political Centre, 1976).

Wade, H. W. R., *Constitutional Fundamentals* (London: Stevens, 1980).

Wadham, John, "Bringing Rights Home: Labour's Plans to Incorporate the European Convention on Human Rights into UK Law", (1997) *Public Law* 75.

Wallington, P. and McBride, J., *Civil Liberties and a Bill of Rights*, (London: Cobden Trust, 1976).

Zander, Michael, *A Bill of Rights?* (London: Sweet and Maxwell, 4th edn 1997).

(2) LEGAL WORKS OF REFERENCE

Bailey, S. H., Harris, D. J. and Jones, B. L. (eds), *Civil Liberties: Cases and Materials* (London: Butterworths, 4th edn 1995).

Blackburn, Robert (ed.), *Rights of Citizenship* (London: Mansell, 1993).

Craig, P. P., *Administrative Law* (London: Sweet and Maxwell, 3rd edn 1994).

De Smith, S. A. and Brazier, Rodney, *Constitutional and Administrative Law* (London: Penguin, 7th edn 1994).

De Smith, S. A., Woolf, H. and Jowell, J., *Judicial Review of Administrative Action* (London: Sweet and Maxwell, 5th edn 1995).

Dicey, A. V., *The Law of the Constitution* (London: Macmillan, 10th edn by E. C. S. Wade 1959).

Dickson, B. (ed.), *Civil Liberties in Northern Ireland* (Belfast: Committee on the Administration of Justice, 2nd edn 1993).

Feldman, D., *Civil Liberties and Human Rights in England and Wales* (Oxford University Press, 1993).

Griffith, J. A. G. and Ryle, Michael, *Parliament: Functions, Practice and Procedures* (London: Sweet and Maxwell, 1989).

Hadfield, B., *The Constitution of Northern Ireland* (Belfast: SLS Legal Publications, 1989).

Hunt, Murray, *Using Human Rights Law in English Courts* (Oxford: Hart Publishing, 1997).

Jennings, Sir Ivor, *The British Constitution* (Cambridge University Press, 5th edn 1966).

Jennings, Sir Ivor, *The Law and the Constitution* (London: Hodder and Stoughton, 5th edn 1959).

Lester, Lord, and Oliver, Dawn, *Constitutional Law and Human Rights* (London: Butterworth, Halsbury's Laws of England, 4th edn, vol. 8(2), 1996).

Loveland, Ian, *Constitutional Law: A Critical Introduction* (London: Butterworths, 1996).

McCrudden, C. and Chambers, G. (eds), *Individual Rights and the Law in Britain* (Oxford University Press, 1994).

McEldowney, John, *Public Law* (London: Sweet and Maxwell, 2nd edn 1997).

Miers, D. R. and Page, A. C., *Legislation* (London: Sweet and Maxwell, 2nd edn 1990).

O'Higgins, Paul (ed.), *Cases and Materials on Civil Liberties* (London: Sweet and Maxwell, 1980).

Palley, Claire, *The United Kingdom and Human Rights* (London: Stevens and Sons, 1991).

Stevens, I. N. and Yardley, D. C., *The Protection of Liberty* (Oxford: Basil Blackwell, 1982).

Stone, Richard, *Textbook on Civil Liberties* (London: Blackstone Press, 1994).

Wade and Bradley, *Constitutional and Administrative Law* (London: Longman, 8th edn by A. W. Bradley and K. D. Ewing 1997).

Wade, H. W. R., *Administrative Law* (Oxford University Press, 7th edn 1994).

Wadham, John (ed.), *Your Rights: The Liberty Guide* (London: Pluto Press, 5th edn 1994).

Wallington, Peter (ed.), *Civil Liberties 1984* (Oxford: Martin Robertson, 1984).

(3) COMPARATIVE AND INTERNATIONAL

Alexander, E. R., "The Canadian Charter of Rights and Freedoms in the Supreme Court in Canada", (1989) 105 *Law Quarterly Review* 561.

Alston, P. (ed.), *A Bill of Rights for Australia?* (Canberra: Human Rights and Equal Opportunity Commission and Centre for International and Public Law, 1994).

Beaudoin, C. and Ratuskny, E. (eds), *The Canadian Charter of Rights and*

Freedoms (Ontario: Carswell, 2nd edn 1989: includes bibliography at pages 843–921).

Beddard, Ralph, *Human Rights and Europe* (Cambridge: Grotius Publications, 3rd edn 1993).

Bell, John, *French Constitutional Law* (Oxford University Press, 1992).

Berger, Vincent (ed.), *Case Law of the European Court of Human Rights* (Dublin: Round Hall Press, 3 vols, 1989–95).

Blackburn, Robert and Polakiewicz, Jorg (eds), *The European Convention on Human Rights: The Impact of the European Convention on Human Rights on the Legal and Political Systems of Member States, 1950–2000* (London: Cassell–Council of Europe, forthcoming).

Blaustein, Albert and Glanz, Gisbert (eds), *Constitutions of the Countries of the World* (New York: Oceana, 1987).

Bradley, Anthony, "The Constitutional Protection of Human Rights in the Commonwealth", (1991) *Public Law* 477.

Brownlie, I. (ed.), *Basic Documents on Human Rights* (Oxford University Press, 3rd edn 1993).

Brownlie, I., *Principles of Public International Law* (Oxford University Press, 4th edn 1990).

Butler, D. and Ranney, A. (eds), *Referendums around the World* (Basingstake: Macmillan, 1994).

Casey, James, *Constitutional Law in Ireland* (London: Sweet and Maxwell, 2nd edn 1992).

Clapham, A., *Human Rights in the Private Sphere* (Oxford University Press, 1993).

Commonwealth Human Rights Initiative, *Put Our World to Rights: Towards a Commonwealth Human Rights Policy* (London: Commonwealth Human Rights Initiative, 1991).

Constitutional Commission, Australia, Report of Advisory Committee to, *Individual and Democratic Rights* (Canberra: Australian Government Publishing, 1987).

Craig, P. P., *Public Law and Democracy in the United Kingdom and the United States of America* (Oxford University Press, 1990).

Cygan, Adam, *The Role of the United Kingdom Parliament in the Legislative Process of the European Union* (London: Martinus Nijhoff, 1998).

De Merieux, Margaret, "Setting the Limits of Fundamental Rights and Freedoms in the Commonwealth Caribbean", (1987) 7 *Legal Studies* 39.

Dickson, B. and Connelly, A., *Human Rights and the European Convention* (London: Sweet and Maxwell, 1995).

Drzemczewski, A., *European Human Rights Convention in Domestic Law: A Comparative Study* (Oxford University Press, 1983).

Elkind, Jerome, "A New Look at Entrenchment [of the New Zealand Bill of Rights]", (1987) 50 *Modern Law Review* 158.

Fawcett, J., *The Application of the European Convention on Human Rights* (Oxford University Press, 1987).

Finer, S. E., *Comparative Government* (Harmondsworth: Penguin, 1970).

Finer, S. E., Bogdanor, V. and Rudden, B., *Comparing Constitutions* (Oxford University Press, 1995).

Finkelstein, Neil, "The Role of an Entrenched Charter of Rights [in Canada]", (1992) 3 *King's College Law Journal* 98.

Foster, Nigel, *German Legal System and Laws* (London: Blackstone Press, 2nd edn 1996).

Furmston, M. P., Kerridge, R. and Sufrin, B. E. (eds), *The Effect on English Domestic Law of Membership of the European Communities and of Ratification of the ECHR* (London: Martinus Nijhoff, 1983).

Gearty, C. A., "The European Court of Human Rights and the Protection of Civil Liberties: An Overview", (1995) 52 *Cambridge Law Journal* 89.

Gearty, C. A. (ed.), *European Civil Liberties and the European Convention on Human Rights: A Comparative Study* (The Hague: Martinus Nijhoff, 1997).

Ghandhi, P. R. (ed.), *International Human Rights Documents* (London: Blackstone Press, 1995).

Gomien, D., Harris D. and Zwaak, L., *Law and Practice of the European Convention on Human Rights and the European Social Charter* (Strasbourg: Council of Europe, 1996).

Harris, D. J., *The European Social Charter* (Charlottesville: University Press of Virginia, 1984).

Harris, D. J., O'Boyle, M. and Warbrick, C., *Law of the European Convention on Human Rights* (London: Butterworths, 1995).

Hartley, T. C., *The Foundations of European Community Law* (Oxford University Press, 3rd edn 1994).

Hogg, Peter W., *Constitutional Law of Canada* (Ontario: Carswell, 4th edn 1996).

Inter-Parliamentary Union, *Parliaments of the World* (Aldershot: Gower, 2nd edn 1986).

Jacobs, F. G., "Human Rights in Europe: New Dimensions", (1992) 3 *King's College Law Journal* 49.

Jacobs, F. G. and Roberts, S. (eds), *The Effect of Treaties in Domestic Law* (London: Sweet and Maxwell, 1987).

Jacobs, F. G. and White, R. C., *The European Convention on Human Rights* (Oxford University Press, 1996).

Janis, M., Kay, R. and Bradley, A., *European Human Rights Law: Text and Materials* (Oxford University Press, 1995).

Joseph, Philip, *Constitutional and Administrative Law in New Zealand* (Sydney: Law Book Company, 1993).

Kay, Richard, "Substance and Structure as Constitutional Protections: Centennial Comparisons [between English Bill of Rights 1689 and American Bill of Rights 1791], (1989) *Public Law* 428.

Kentridge, Sydney, "Bills of Rights – The South African Experiment", (1996) 112 *Law Quarterly Review* 237.

Kentridge, Sydney, "Parliamentary Supremacy and the Judiciary under a Bill of Rights: Some Lessons from the Commonwealth", (1997) *Public Law* 96.

Lumb, R. D. and Moens, G. A., *The Constitution of the Commonwealth of Australia: Annotated* (Sydney: Butterworth, 5th edn 1995).

Mandel, M., *The Charter of Rights and the Legalisation of Politics in Canada* (Toronto: Wall and Thompson, 1992).

Marston, G., "The United Kingdom's Part in the Preparation of the European Convention on Human Rights", (1993) 42 *International and Comparative Law Quarterly* 796.

McCullough, H. B., "Parliamentary Supremacy and a Constitutional Grid: the Canadian Charter of Rights", (1992) 41 *International and Comparative Law Quarterly* 751.

McGoldrick, D., *The Human Rights Committee: its Role in the Development of the International Covenant on Civil and Political Rights* (Oxford University Press, 1991).

Morris, Dennis, "Interpreting Hong Kong's Bill of Rights: Some Basic Queestions", (1994) 15 *Statute Law Review* 126.

Minister of Justice, New Zealand, *A Bill of Rights for New Zealand: A White Paper* (Wellington: Government Printer, 1985).

Peaslee, A. J. (ed.), *Constitutions of Nations: Vol 1 Africa* (The Hague: Nijhoff, rev. 3rd edn 1965).

Peaslee, A. J. (ed.), *Constitutions of Nations: Vol 2 Asia, Australia and Oceania* (Dordecht: M. Nijhoff, rev 4th edn 1985).

Penner, Ronald, "The Canadian Experience with the Charter of Rights: Are there Lessons for the United Kingdom?", (1996) *Public Law* 104.

Polakiewicz, J., "The Application of the European Convention on Human Rights in Domestic Law", (1997) *Human Rights Law Journal* 405.

Price, Nigel, "Constitutional Adjudication in the Privy Council and Reflections on the Bill of Rights Debate", (1986) 35 *International and Comparative Law Quarterly* 946.

Robertson, A. H., *The Council of Europe: Its Structure, Functions and Achievements* (London: Stevens, 2nd edn 1961).

Robertson, A. H. (ed.), *Human Rights in National and International Law* (Manchester University Press, 1968).

Robertson, A. H. and Merrills, J. G., *Human Rights in the World: An Introduction to the Study of the International Protection of Human Rights* (Manchester University Press, 3rd edn 1992).

Robertson, A. H. and Merrills, J. G., *Human Rights in Europe: A Study of the European Convention on Human Rights* (Manchester University Press: 3rd edn 1993).

Robinson, O. F., Fergus, T. D. and Gordon, W. M., *European Legal History* (London: Butterworths, 2nd edn 1994).

Schermers, H. G., *The Influence of the European Commission of Human Rights* (The Hague: T. M. C. Asser Instituut, 1992).

Sieghart, Paul, *The International Law of Human Rights* (Oxford University Press, 1983).

Sieghart, Paul, *The Lawful Rights of Mankind* (Oxford University Press, 1985).

Skordaki, Eleni, *Judicial Appointments: An International Review of Existing Models* (London: The Law Society, 1991).

Suksi, H., *Bringing in the People: A Comparison of Constitutional Forms and Practices of the Referendum* (London: Martinus Nihjoff, 1993).

Van Dijk, P. and Van Hoof, G. J. H., *Theory and Practice of the European Convention on Human Rights* (London: Kluwer, 2nd edn 1990).

Wacks, Raymond (ed.), *Human Rights in Hong Kong* (Oxford University Press, 1992).

Walker, Kristen, "Who's the Boss? The Judiciary, the Executive, the Parliament and the Protection of Human Rights [in Australia]", (1995) 25 *Western Australian Law Review* 238.

Wright, Skelly, "The Bill of Rights in Britain and America: A Not Quite Full Circle", (1981) 55 *Tulane Law Review* 291.

(4) THEORETICAL AND HISTORICAL

Atiyah, P., *Law and Modern Society* (Oxford University Press, 1983).

Bailey, S. D. (ed.), *Human Rights and Responsibilities: A Christian Perspective* (London: Macmillan, 1988).

Barker, Rodney, *Political Ideas in Modern Britain* (London: Methuen, 2nd edn 1997).

Birch, A. H., *Representative and Responsible Government: An Essay on the British Constitution* (London: George Allen and Unwin, 1964).

Craig, P. P., *Public Law and Democracy in the United Kingdom and the United States of America* (Oxford University Press, 1990).

Cranston, Maurice, *What are Human Rights?* (New York: Japlinger Publishing, 1973).

Denning, Sir Alfred (later Lord), *Freedom under the Law* (London: Stevens, 1949).

Dworkin, Ronald, *Taking Rights Seriously* (London: Duckworth, 1977).

Etzioni, Amitai, *The Spirit of Community* (New York: Crown Publishing, 1993).

Gearty, C. A. and Tomkins, A. (eds), *Understanding Human Rights* (London: Mansell, 1996).

Gough, J. W., *Fundamental Law in English Constitutional History* (Oxford University Press, 1955).

Hart, H. L. A., *Law, Liberty and Morality* (Oxford University Press, 1963).

Hayek, F. A., *Law, Liberty and Legislation* (London: Routledge and Kegan Paul, 3 vols. rev. edn 1982).

Held, David, *Models of Democracy* (Cambridge: Polity Press, 2nd edn 1996).

Hohfeld, W. N., *Fundamental Legal Conceptions as Applied in Judical Reasoning* (Yale University Press, 1923).

Holt, J. C., *Magna Carta* (Cambridge University Press, 2nd edn 1992).

Irvine, Lord, "Judges and Decision-Makers", (1996) *Public Law* 59.

Johnson, Nevil, *In Search of the Constitution* (London: Methuen, 1977).

Jones, G. W., "The British Bill of Rights", (1990) 43 *Parliamentary Affairs* 27.

Kennedy, Ian, "In the Public Interest – Says Who?", (1983) 33 *King's Counsel* 9.

Laski, Harold J., *A Grammar of Politics* (London: Unwin Brothers, 1925).

Laski, Harold J., *Liberty in the Modern State* (Harmondsworth: Penguin, 1937).

Laski, Harold J., *Parliamentary Government in England* (London: George Allen and Unwin, 1938).

Laws, Sir John, "Is the High Court the Guardian of Fundamental Constitutional Rights?", (1993) *Public Law* 59.

Laws, Sir John, "Law and Democracy", (1995) *Public Law* 72.

Laws, Sir John, "The Constitution: Morals and Rights", (1996) *Public Law* 622.

Loughlin, M., *Public Law and Political Theory* (Oxford: Clarendon Press, 1992).

Maitland, F. W., *The Constitutional History of England* (Cambridge University Press, 1908).

Marshall, Geoffrey, *Constitutional Theory* (Oxford University Press, 1971).

McEldowney, John, *Public Law* (London: Sweet and Maxwell, 2nd edn 1997).

Mill, J. S., *On Liberty* (1859, Harmondsworth: Penguin, 1979).

Paine, Thomas, *The Rights of Man* (1791, London: Penguin, 1985).

Rawls, John, *A Theory of Justice* (Oxford University Press, 1972).

Selbourne, David, *The Principle of Duty* (London: Sinclair Stevenson, 1994).

Taswell-Langmead, T. P., *English Constitutional History* (London: Sweet and Maxwell, 11th edn by T. F. T. Plucknett, 1960).

Tawney, R. H., *Equality* (London: George Allen and Unwin, 4th edn 1952).

Tawney, R. H., *The Acquisitive Society* (London: G. Bell and Sons, 1922).

Vallat, Sir Francis (ed.), *An Introduction to the Study of Human Rights* (London: Europa, 1971).

Vile, M. J. C., *Constitutionalism and the Separation of Powers* (Oxford University Press, 1967).

Wade, H. W. R., "The Basis of Legal Sovereignty", (1955) *Cambridge Law Journal* 172.

Wheare, K. C., *Modern Constitutions* (Oxford University Press, 2nd edn 1966).

(5) PARLIAMENTARY DEBATES

House of Lords Debate, Liberties of the Subject Bill (Viscount Samuel, 34, 1949–50), Second reading, 27 June 1950, Cols 1041–114.

House of Commons Debate, Motion condemning the ever increasing destruction of the liberties of the subject (Norman St. John Stevas), 1 December 1967, Cols 808–909.

House of Commons Debate, Motion to introduce Bill of Rights Bill (Viscount Lambton), 23 April 1969, Cols 474–82.

House of Lords Debate, Motion calling attention to the need for protection of human rights and fundamental freedoms and possible measures including enactment of a Bill of Rights (Lord Wade), 18 June 1969, Cols 1026–96.

House of Commons Debate, Motion to introduce Bill of Rights (No. 2) Bill (Emlyn Hooson, 205, 1968–9), 22 July 1969, Cols 1519–22.

House of Lords Debate, Bill of Right Bill (Earl of Arran, Bill of Rights Bill, 19, 1970–1), Second reading, 26 November 1970, Cols 243–319.

House of Commons Debate, Protection of Human Rights Bill (Samuel Silkin, 52, 1970–1), Second reading, 2 April 1971, Cols 1854–64.

House of Commons Debate, Adjournment debate on civil liberties (Paul Rose), 18 May 1971, Cols 847–58.

House of Commons Debate, Motion that the House reaffirms its commitment to extent civil liberties in the United Kingdom through a Bill of Rights (Robin Corbett), 29 November 1974, Cols 1059–72.

House of Commons Debate, Motion urging the government to recommend the setting up of a Royal Commission to investigate and report upon the subject of a Bill of Rights (James Kilfedder), 7 July 1975, Cols 32–87.

House of Commons Debate, Motion to introduce Bill of Rights Bill (Alan Beith, 214, 1974–5), 15 July 1975, Cols 1270–3.

House of Lords Debate, Bill of Rights Bill (Lord Wade, 92, 1975–6), Second reading, 25 March 1976, Cols 775–817.

House of Commons Debate, Motion that the House deplores the continuing erosion of personal liberty and freedom of choice (Ian Gow), 26 March 1976, Cols 769–856.

House of Lords Debate, Bill of Rights Bill (Lord Wade, 11, 1976–7), Second reading, 3 February 1977, Cols 973–1022.

House of Lords, Report of the Select Committee on a Bill of Rights, 81 (1976–7). House of Lords Debate on the Report, 29 November 1978, Cols 1301–98.

House of Lords Debate, Bill of Rights Bill (Lord Wade, 54, 1979–80), Second reading, 8 November 1979, Cols 999–1071; Committee and Report stages, 29 November 1979, Cols 287–311, 502–9; Third reading, 6 December 1979, Cols 911–15.

House of Lords Debate, Bill of Rights Bill (Lord Wade, 4, 1980–1), Second reading, 4 December 1980, Cols 533–61; Committee stage, 14 January 1981, Cols. 152–5; Report, 27 January 1981, Col. 689; Third reading, 13 February 1981, Cols 1102–6. Sent to the House of Commons, Second Reading, 8 May 1981, Cols 419–57.

House of Commons Debate, European Human Rights Convention Bill (Robert Maclennan, 73, 1983–4), Motion for leave to introduce Bill, 13 December 1983, Cols 860–2.

House of Commons Debate, Motion on the need to protect the essential rights and liberties of the individual citizen whilst recognizing the need to preserve order and stability in society (Richard Ottaway), 13 May 1985, Cols 44–73.

House of Lords Debate, Human Rights and Fundamental Freedoms Bill (Lord Broxbourne, 21, 1985–6), Second reading, 10 December 1985, Cols 156–96; Committee stage, 20 March 1986, Cols 1087–116; Report stage, 9 April 1986, Cols 267–78; Third reading, 30 April 1986, Cols 334–42.

House of Commons Debate, Human Rights Bill (Sir Edward Gardner, 19, 1986–7), Second reading debate, 6 February 1987, Cols 1223–89.

House of Commons Debate, Opposition day debate on civil liberties and a Bill of Rights (Robert Maclennan), 19 June 1989, Cols 76–117.

House of Lords Debate, Motion to call attention to appropriate powers and constitution of a second chamber within the British Constitution (Lord Simon), 25 April 1990, Cols 606–37.

House of Lords Debate, Motion (Lord Irvine) to call attention to the state of civil liberties, 23 May 1990, Cols 904–35.

House of Lords Debate, Motion calling attention to the case for incorporation of the European Convention on Human Rights into UK law as a Bill of Rights (Lord Holme), 5 December 1990, Cols 185–214.

House of Commons Debate, Motion calling attention to the case for constitutional reform (Archy Kirkwood), 17 May 1991, Cols 538–610.

House of Commons Debate, Protection of Fundamental Rights and Freedoms Bill (Robert Maclennan, 76, 1991–2), Motion for leave to introduce Bill, 12 February 1992, Cols 991–3, 979–81.

House of Lords Debate, Motion calling attention to the case for constitutional reform (Lord Jenkins), 11 March 1992, Cols 1331–72.

House of Lords Debate, Motion to take note of report of European Communities Committee on Human Rights Re-Examined (Baroness Elles), 26 November 1992, Cols 1087–118.

House of Commons Debate, Adjournment debate on a Bill of Rights (Graham Allen), 27 May 1993, Cols 1024–34.

House of Commons Debate, Adjournment debate on incorporation of the European Convention on Human Rights and a Bill of Rights (Graham Allen), 20 October 1993, Cols 364–70.

House of Lords Debate, Motion calling attention to the constitutional role of the House of Lords (Lord Simon), 13 April 1994, Cols 1541–75.

House of Commons Debates, Adjournment debate on the International Covenant for Civil and Political Rights (Graham Allen), 21 June 1994, Cols 188–216.

House of Lords Debate, Human Rights Bill (Lord Lester, 5, 1994–5), Second reading, 25 January 1995, Cols 1136–74; Committee stage, 15 February 1995, Cols 762–84; Report stage, 29 March 1995, Cols 1692–702; Third reading, 1 May 1995, Cols 1271–85.

House of Lords Debate, Motion to take note of the United Kingdom's existing constitutional settlement and of the implications of proposals for change (Lord Mackay), (first day) 3 July 1996, Cols 1449–570; (second day) 4 July 1996, Cols 1581–690.

House of Lords Debate, Human Rights Bill (Lord Lester, 11, 1996–7), Second Reading debate, 5 February 1997, Cols 1725–58.

House of Commons Debate, Adjournment debate on the Constitution (John Major), 20 February 1997, Cols 1055–150.

House of Commons Debate, Queens Speech debate (third day) on the Constitution (Donald Dewar), 16 May 1997, Cols 275–351.

House of Lords Debate, Queens Speech debate (third day) on the Constitution (Lord Irvine), 19 May 1997, Cols 145–254.

The Human Rights Act

The parliamentary stages through which the Human Rights Act 1998 (cap. 42) passed before receiving the royal assent on 9 November 1998 are as follows:

House of Lords (Bills numbers 38, 51, 70, 157): 1st reading 23 October 1997; 2nd reading 3 November 1997; Committee 18, 24 and 27 November 1997; Report 19 and 29 January 1998; 3rd reading 5 February 1998; Commons amendments 29 October 1998.

House of Commons (Bill number 119, 219): 1st reading 6 February 1998; 2nd reading 16 February 1998; Committee 20 May, 3, 17 and 24 June and 2 July 1998; PM 1 June 1998; PM (no. 2) 17 June 1998; PM (no. 3) 21 October 1998; Report 21 October 1998; 3rd reading 21 October 1998.

(PM = a formal programme motion was carried)

INDEX